China's Provincial Statistics 1949–1989

China's Provincial Statistics 1949–1989

EDITED BY

Hsueh Tien-tung
Li Qiang
Liu Shucheng

Routledge
Taylor & Francis Group
LONDON AND NEW YORK

First published 1993 by Westview Press, Inc.

Published 2018 by Routledge
52 Vanderbilt Avenue, New York, NY 10017
2 Park Square, Milton Park, Abingdon, Oxon OX14 4RN

Routledge is an imprint of the Taylor & Francis Group, an informa business

A CIP catalog record for this book is available from the Library Congress.
ISBN 13: 978-0-367-01176-5 (hbk)
ISBN 13: 978-0-367-16163-7 (pbk)

Contents

Preface

In this volume, we have recorded systematically and comprehensively the regional economic and social development data for the People's Republic of China (PRC) for the past forty years. It covers the statistics on various aspects of the thirty provinces, autonomous regions and municipalities (directly under the Central Government).

As a matter of record, the statistics are the product of our project entitled "China's Regional Economic Development" sponsored by the University and Polytechnic Grants Committee (UPGC) of Hong Kong Government. The project has been jointly organized by the China's Reform and Development Programme, Hong Kong Institute of Asia-Pacific Studies at The Chinese University of Hong Kong (CUHK) in cooperation with the Institute of Quantitative and Technical Economics, Chinese Academy of Social Sciences, and the Department of Statistics on National Economic Balances, State Statistical Bureau (SSB), the People's Republic of China. The major outcomes of the project, in addition to the statistics, will be another forthcoming volume entitled *China's Regional Economic Development, 1949–1989*.

It is common knowledge that China's national statistical system has moved a step forward since the implementation of economic opening and reform policy in 1979. It is now a matter of consensus that the establishment of China's national economic statistical system should not only be adapted to the actual needs of national economic management, regional economic development and the rejuvenated national economic activities, but also be comparable to the statistics of other economies in the rest of the world. It is exactly in this spirit that the SSB of the PRC has made its best effort to undertake the project of extending the original MPS (system of material product balances) into the SNA (system of national accounts) as suggested by the United Nations and as already adopted by most member countries.

To complete the task, on the basis of the original statistical data, the SSB has paid great attention to possible adjustments and transformations between these two systems, MPS and SNA, so that a more comprehensive and comparable national economic statistical system can be set up. It is hoped that, under such a consistent framework, the development process of national economic activities from production, distribution, circulation to utilization can be more accurately traced. The system embraces not only the calibre of economic variables and the scope of their accounting and reckoning in the MPS, such as total product of society, gross output value of agriculture, national income consisting of five major material product sectors; but also contains the specification of economic variables and their coverages in the SNA, such as gross domestic product with components of primary, secondary and tertiary sectors, consumption, investment and so on.

The new consolidated system has been jointly worked out by the various Departments of SSB for several years. It is expected that some preliminary findings will make their appearance in the near future. Following the same line of attack, in the *Statistics*, we have presented more than 100 economic and social variables under 15 categories, namely, national output and income, investment, consumption, public finance and banking, labor force, population, agriculture, industry, transport, domestic trade, foreign trade, prices, education, social factors, and natural environment.

It is imperative for us to point out two important facts about the variables in the *Statistics*. First, as the specification of the variables is concerned, each substantive element has kept its consistent connotation. Thus in redelimiting the boundary line of some provinces, the necessary adjustment of the variables in question was done correspondingly. In 1988, when Hainan was separated from Guangdong province to become an independent province, the data for various variables of Guangdong province were adjusted accordingly by excluding Hainan's portions. In 1979, Hu Lun Bei Er Meng (league), Zhao Wu Da Meng and Zhe Li Mu Meng were parted respectively from Heilongjiang province, Liaoning province, and Jilin province to be incorporated into the jurisdiction of Inner Mongolia. Therefore, the data for various variables of these four provinces were accordingly revised.

Secondly, as the general sources of data are concerned, the Balance Office of Statistical Bureau of each province, autonomous region and municipality has to submit local national income and the relevant data to the Department of Statistics on National Economic Balances, SSB on a regular basis. Thus the Department is able to furnish the major part of data for the *Statistics* in addition to recent publications of other relevant data collected for the volume. These publications are *Striving and Advancing Forty Years*, *Statistical Yearbooks*, *Yearbooks of Social and Economic Statistics*, and *Annual Reports of National Income Statistics* by each province, autonomous region and municipality, and *Compilation of Provinces, Autonomous Regions and Municipalities' Historical Statistical Data (1949–1989)* by the Department of Synthesis, SSB, 1990.

I would like to use this occasion to add these few words. This research programme is dedicated to tackling systematically the fundamental issues and the relevant statistics of the Chinese economy in a consistent framework by means of modern economic theory. It is hoped that the work launched and the findings obtained will be beneficial to students of the China field all over the world.

Last but not least, on behalf of the project participants, I would like to express our gratitude to UPGC and CUHK for their financial support making the research possible, to Ms. Alison Auch of Westview Press, Dr. Maurice Brosseau, Ms. Po-san Wan, Mr. Kam-wah Mok and Ms. Mei-lin Kwan of the Institute for their kind help with the editorial work. Nevertheless, they have nothing to do with any remaining mistakes, for which the editors are solely responsible.

Hsueh Tien-tung
Programme director
China's Reform and Development Programme
Hong Kong Institute of Asia-Pacific Studies
The Chinese University of Hong Kong

Provinces

Name of Provinces	*Abbreviations*	*Name of Provinces*	*Abbreviations*
1. Beijing	BJ	16. Henan	HEN
2. Tianjin	TJ	17. Hubei	HUB
3. Hebei	HEB	18. Hunan	HUN
4. Shanxi	SAX	19. Guangdong	GD
5. Inner Mongolia	IM	20. Guangxi	GX
6. Liaoning	LN	21. Hainan	HN
7. Jilin	JL	22. Sichuan	SC
8. Heilongjiang	HLJ	23. Guizhou	GZ
9. Shanghai	SH	24. Yunnan	YN
10. Jiangsu	JS	25. Tibet	TB
11. Zhejiang	ZJ	26. Shaanxi	SHX
12. Anhui	AH	27. Gansu	GS
13. Fujian	FJ	28. Qinghai	QH
14. Jiangxi	JX	29. Ningxia	NX
15. Shandong	SD	30. Xinjiang	XJ

Categories of Variables

1.	National Output and Income	Y	8.	Industry	IN
2.	Investment	I	9.	Transport	TR
3.	Consumption	C	10.	Domestic Trade	DT
4.	Public Finance and Banking	FB	11.	Foreign Trade	FT
5.	Labor Force	L	12.	Prices	PR
6.	Population	PO	13.	Education	ED
7.	Agriculture	A	14.	Social Factors	SF
			15.	Natural Environment	NE

Lists of Variables

1. National Output and Income (Y)

v1a: Total Product of Society (at current prices, Renminbi (Rmb) 100 million)
- v1a1: Agriculture
- v1a2: Industry
- v1a3: Construction
- v1a4: Transport, post and telecommunications
- v1a5: Domestic trade

v1b: Total Product of Society (at comparable prices, preceding year = 100)
- v1b1: Agriculture
- v1b2: Industry
- v1b3: Construction
- v1b4: Transport, post and telecommunications
- v1b5: Domestic trade

v1c: Material Consumption (Rmb 100 million)

v1d: National Income (at current prices, Rmb 100 million)
- v1d1: Agriculture
- v1d2: Industry
- v1d3: Construction
- v1d4: Transport, post and telecommunications
- v1d5: Domestic trade

v1e: National Income (at comparable prices, preceding year = 100)
- v1e1: Agriculture
- v1e2: Industry
- v1e3: Construction
- v1e4: Transport, post and telecommunications
- v1e5: Domestic trade

v1f: Gross Domestic Product (Rmb 100 million)
- v1f1: Primary sector
- v1f2: Secondary sector
- v1f3: Tertiary sector

v1g: National Income Available (Rmb 100 million)

v1h: Per Capita Peasant Household Net Income (Rmb)

v1i: Total Wage Bill of Staff and Workers (Rmb 100 million)

v1j: Average Wage of Staff and Workers (Rmb)
- v1j1: State-owned units
- v1j2: Collective-owned units in cities and towns
- v1j3: Other ownership units

v1k: Labour Insurance and Welfare Funds of Staff and Workers (Rmb 100 million)

2. Investment (I)

v2a: Total Accumulation (Rmb 100 million)
- v2a1: Fixed assets

v2a2: Circulating assets

v2b: Total Investment in Fixed Assets (Rmb 100 million)

v2c: Total Investment in Fixed Assets by State-owned Units (Rmb 100 million)
- v2c1: Industry—basic construction investment
- v2c2: Commerce—basic construction investment in commerce, catering services and material supply sectors

v2d: Fixed Assets of State-owned Independent Accounting Industrial Enterprises (Rmb 100 million)
- v2d1: Original value
- v2d2: Net value

v2e: Average Yearly Balance of the Quota Circulating Fund of State-owned Independent Accounting Industrial Enterprises (Rmb 100 million)

3. Consumption (C)

v3a: Total Consumption (Rmb 100 million)

v3b: Residents' Consumption (Rmb 100 million)
- v3b1: Rural residents
- v3b2: Non-rural residents

v3c: Public Consumption (Rmb 100 million)

v3d: Consumption Level of Residents (Rmb)
- v3d1: Rural residents
- v3d2: Non-rural residents

v3e: Per Capita Living Expenses of Cities' and Towns' Residents (Rmb)
- v3e1: Food
- v3e2: Clothing
- v3e3: Housing
- v3e4: Fuels

v3f: Per Capita Living Expenses of Rural Residents (Rmb)
- v3f1: Food
- v3f2: Clothing
- v3f3: Housing
- v3f4: Fuels

4. Public Finance and Banking (FB)

v4a: Public Revenues and Expenditures of Local Governments (Rmb 100 million)
- v4a1: Public revenues of local governments
  - v4a1a: revenues from enterprises
  - v4a1b: industrial and commercial tax
  - v4a1c: agricultural tax
  - v4a1d: other revenues
- v4a2: Public expenditures of local governments
  - v4a2a: economic construction—basic construction appropriations
  - v4a2b: society and culture—cultural, educational, scientific and public health funds
  - v4a2c: administrative expenditures
  - v4a2d: other expenditures

v4b: Balance of Savings Deposits by Urban and Rural Residents (year-end figures, Rmb 100 million)

v4b1: Urban area (cities and towns)
v4b2: Rural peasant households
v4b3: Rural area

v4c: Profits and Taxes of State-owned Independent Accounting Industrial Enterprises
v4c1: Total profits and taxes (Rmb 100 million)
v4c2: Profit and tax—invested funds ratio (%)

5. Labor Force(L)

v5a: Total Employed Labor Force of Society (year-end figures, 10 thousand people)
v5a1: Staff and workers of state-owned units
v5a2: Staff and workers of collective-owned units in cities and towns
v5a3: Self-employed laborers in cities and towns
v5a4: Laborers in rural area

v5b: Labor Force of Society (year-end figures, 10 thousand people)
v5b1: Primary sector
v5b2: Secondary sector
v5b3: Tertiary sector

v5c: Labor Force in Industrial Sector (year-end figures, 10 thousand people)
v5c1: State-owned Units

v5d: Labor Force in Agricultural Sector (year-end figures, 10 thousand people)

6. Population (PO)

v6a: Total Population (year-end figures, 10 thousand people)
v6a1: Urban
v6a2: Rural

v6b: Birth Rate (%)

v6c: Mortality Rate (%)

v6d: Population and Composition (year-end figures, 10 thousand people)
v6d1: Non-peasants
v6d2: Peasants
v6d3: Male
v6d4: Female
v6d5: In the largest city
v6d6: In the second largest city

7. Agriculture (A)

v7a: Total Power of Farm Machinery (100 million kilowatt)

v7b: Tractor-ploughed Area (10 thousand mu)

v7c: Irrigated Area (10 thousand mu)

v7d: Total Sown Area (10 thousand mu)

v7e: Disaster Area Caused by Natural Calamities (10 thousand mu)

v7f: Chemical Fertilizers Applied in Agriculture (10 thousand tons)

v7g: Electricity Consumed in Rural Areas (100 million kilowatt/hour (kWh))

v7h: Gross Output Value of Agriculture (Rmb 100 million)
v7h1: Farming
v7h2: Forestry
v7h3: Animal husbandry
v7h4: Fishery
v7h5: Sideline production

v7i: Number of Draught Animals (year-end figures, 10 thousand head)

8. Industry (IN)

v8a: Gross Output Value of Industry by Forms of Ownership (Rmb 100 million)
- v8a1: State ownership
- v8a2: Collective ownership
- v8a3: Others

v8b: Gross Output Value of State-owned Independent Accounting Industrial Enterprises (Rmb 100 million)

- v8c1: Gross output value of heavy industry (Rmb 100 million)
- v8c2: Gross output value of light industry (Rmb 100 million)

v8d: Net Output Value of Heavy Industry (Rmb 100 million)

v8f: Output of Major Industrial Products
- v8f1: Steel (10 thousand tons)
- v8f2: Coal (10 thousand tons)
- v8f3: Crude oil (10 thousand tons)
- v8f4: Electricity (100 million kWh)
- v8f5: Cement (10 thousand tons)

v8g: Number of Industrial Enterprises (unit)
- v8g1: State-owned independent accounting industrial enterprises (unit)

9. Transport (TR)

v9a: Passenger Traffic Turnover Volume (100 million person-km)
- v9a1: Railways (100 million person-km)
- v9a2: Highways (100 million person-km)
- v9a3: Waterways (100 million person-km)

v9b: Freight Traffic Turnover Volume (100 million ton-km)
- v9b1: Railways
- v9b2: Highways
- v9b3: Waterways

v9c: Business Revenue by Post and Telecommunications (Rmb 10 thousand)

10. Domestic Trade (DT)

v10a: Total Value of Commodities Retail Sales of Society (Rmb 100 million)
- v10a1: Consumer goods

v10b: Total Value of Commodities Retail Sales of Society by Forms of Ownership (Rmb 100 million)
- v10b1: State ownership
- v10b2: Supply and marketing cooperative
- v10b3: other collective ownership
- v10b4: Joint ownership
- v10b5: Self-employed
- v10b6: Sales by peasants to non-rural residents

v10d: Total Value of Procured Farm and Sideline Products of Society (Rmb 100 million)

11. Foreign Trade (FT)

v11a: Composition of Exports (US$100 million)
- v11a1: Agricultural and sideline products
- v11a2: Light industry products
- v11a3: Heavy industry products

v11b: Total Imports and Exports (US$100 million)
- v11b1: Total exports
- v11b2: Total imports

v11c: Total Value of Foreign Capital through Signed Contracts or Agreements (US$100 million)

v11d: Total Value of Foreign Capital Utilized (US$100 million)

12. Prices (PR)

v12a: General Retail Price Index (preceding year = 100)

v12b: General Index of Cost of Living for Staff and Workers (preceding year = 100)

v12c: General Index of Procurement Prices for Farm and Sideline Products (preceding year = 100)

13. Education (ED)

v13a: Percentage Share of Educational Expenditure in Local Public Expenditures (%)

v13b: Enrollment Rate of Primary-school Age Children (%)

v13c: Student Enrollment in All Levels of Schools (10 thousand people)
- v13c1: Institutions of higher learning
- v13c2: Secondary schools
- v13c3: Primary schools

v13d: University Graduates (10 thousand people)

14. Social Factors (SF)

v14a: Hospital Beds (bed)

v14b: Technical Personnel in the Medical Field (10 thousand people)

v14c: Newspapers, Magazines and Books Published (100 million copies)

15. Natural Environment (NE)

v15a: Total Cultivated Area (10 thousand mu)

v15b: Total Forest Area (10 thousand mu)

v15c: Annual River Flow (100 million cubic metres)

v15d: Hydropower Resources (10 thousand kilowatt)

v15e: Coal Reserves (100 million tons)

v15f: Iron Ore Reserves (100 million tons)

PART ONE

The Provincial Statistics

1

Beijing

1. Beijing

1–1

Year	v1a	v1a1	v1a2	v1a3	v1a4	v1a5	v1b	v1b1	v1b2	v1b3	v1b4	v1b5	v1c	v1d	v1d1
1949															
1950	7.10												3.86	3.24	
1951	12.62												7.26	5.36	
1952	14.84	2.54	9.07	1.10	0.60	1.52	116.7	113.9	120.2	106.2	149.4	103.7	8.59	6.24	1.74
1953	23.02	2.72	12.96	3.76	0.95	2.63	155.0	106.8	142.9	341.2	156.2	161.5	13.38	9.63	2.13
1954	27.14	2.48	14.95	5.59	0.96	3.15	118.1	91.2	115.4	148.9	100.7	117.6	16.57	10.57	1.93
1955	28.92	2.83	16.63	5.16	1.14	3.17	106.2	114.0	111.2	92.3	119.1	99.6	16.98	11.94	2.20
1956	34.41	2.90	20.03	5.57	1.87	4.04	128.8	102.6	137.9	108.0	173.1	127.2	20.71	13.70	2.25
1957	35.71	3.03	22.00	5.77	1.27	3.65	105.0	113.8	109.8	103.5	68.9	89.7	21.42	14.29	2.07
1958	61.11	4.90	42.78	7.53	1.59	4.31	181.2	130.0	214.8	130.0	130.1	118.6	36.75	24.38	3.33
1959	88.72	5.01	63.33	11.72	2.42	6.23	149.8	103.2	152.7	155.7	155.4	145.9	55.40	33.32	3.35
1960	111.75	4.91	85.87	11.23	3.46	6.28	125.0	95.4	132.9	95.8	143.9	101.1	70.37	41.38	3.37
1961	70.45	4.76	53.17	5.11	2.41	5.00	59.9	95.3	59.0	45.5	69.4	74.4	43.40	27.05	3.50
1962	56.62	5.15	41.87	4.06	1.94	3.60	77.8	109.3	76.3	79.5	80.2	69.5	34.72	21.90	3.67
1963	60.01	5.52	44.47	4.53	1.94	3.55	104.1	106.1	103.8	111.7	100.0	97.7	36.54	23.48	3.90
1964	67.01	6.23	49.40	5.65	2.20	3.52	113.0	108.7	113.2	124.7	112.1	99.2	40.37	26.64	4.48
1965	75.46	7.05	55.90	6.73	2.23	3.55	118.3	116.7	119.8	119.1	101.7	106.2	45.39	30.07	5.05
1966	87.76	7.08	69.01	5.85	2.17	3.65	115.0	99.0	120.9	86.8	97.2	102.9	54.18	33.58	4.85
1967	75.80	7.31	58.22	4.58	2.04	3.64	90.8	103.3	90.4	78.3	94.1	99.9	47.17	28.62	5.09
1968	79.37	7.49	61.39	4.60	2.11	3.78	104.6	98.6	105.4	100.6	103.2	104.2	50.77	28.60	5.18
1969	108.32	6.89	87.51	5.85	2.52	5.55	138.3	92.0	142.5	127.1	119.9	146.3	70.04	38.28	4.24
1970	119.74	8.20	97.14	6.77	2.98	4.65	129.1	117.1	133.1	115.6	118.6	84.7	71.83	47.91	5.56
1971	122.17	8.48	99.32	6.10	3.09	5.18	119.1	101.7	122.0	90.1	104.1	111.1	75.95	46.22	5.65
1972	128.54	8.07	105.28	6.23	3.45	5.50	105.3	96.2	106.0	102.1	110.8	106.1	76.80	51.74	5.09
1973	140.39	9.21	113.09	8.01	3.73	6.34	108.9	111.5	107.4	128.7	106.5	115.3	84.16	56.23	5.75
1974	154.05	9.99	123.29	9.99	4.05	6.72	109.7	108.4	109.0	124.7	109.3	105.9	92.31	61.75	5.95
1975	170.74	10.57	133.79	12.66	5.73	7.99	110.7	106.0	108.5	126.7	142.9	119.1	100.40	70.35	6.27
1976	174.96	10.36	141.21	9.72	5.77	7.90	102.5	97.3	105.3	76.8	100.8	99.1	102.94	72.03	6.03
1977	188.26	9.82	149.27	13.60	6.63	8.95	109.3	94.1	108.0	139.9	112.6	113.3	110.97	77.29	5.78
1978	216.98	11.52	169.97	17.92	7.70	9.86	115.0	112.2	114.0	131.4	118.9	109.5	128.85	88.13	5.95
1979	241.16	12.40	189.61	20.33	8.31	10.51	110.8	100.1	111.5	113.4	107.8	104.7	144.11	97.04	6.13
1980	275.88	14.35	213.37	26.07	8.53	13.56	110.5	101.3	110.2	114.9	101.4	122.9	165.44	110.44	7.44
1981	285.22	14.96	218.96	27.38	9.37	14.55	101.8	99.3	101.2	103.7	109.1	105.8	173.01	112.21	8.19
1982	302.62	16.80	230.84	30.33	10.24	14.42	106.7	108.3	106.1	109.2	110.2	107.9	184.82	117.80	9.93
1983	344.61	19.61	256.81	40.69	10.86	16.64	113.3	114.5	112.4	133.2	92.0	101.9	209.31	135.30	12.56
1984	397.13	22.15	292.36	50.06	12.77	19.79	114.9	111.2	113.8	124.7	109.2	116.7	239.79	157.35	14.55
1985	482.16	25.94	338.69	66.64	18.43	32.47	113.6	106.3	110.3	119.8	148.8	138.2	287.67	194.49	17.40
1986	525.94	28.14	371.24	70.28	22.46	33.82	105.5	100.4	106.1	100.6	133.3	97.6	319.93	206.01	18.67
1987	625.88	34.42	434.63	80.38	30.40	42.05	113.2	109.6	112.8	110.2	132.6	114.4	389.59	236.29	23.81
1988	818.16	52.50	571.57	101.11	34.37	58.66	119.7	114.8	122.5	112.3	108.1	114.3	516.43	301.73	36.50
1989	972.15	60.35	700.90	118.20	38.00	54.70	105.8	110.6	107.2	106.0	109.1	78.8	635.35	336.80	37.80

1. Beijing

1–2

Year	v1d2	v1d3	v1d4	v1d5	v1e	v1e1	v1e2	v1e3	v1e4	v1e5	v1f	v1f1	v1f2	v1f3	v1g
1949															
1950															
1951															
1952	2.47	0.35	0.45	1.23	115.0	111.3	120.6	104.3	142.3	107.1	7.9	1.7	3.1	3.1	9.60
1953	3.71	0.99	0.61	2.19	152.3	122.4	150.3	281.3	128.7	166.4					16.15
1954	4.17	1.42	0.62	2.42	109.3	90.6	112.5	143.2	98.9	108.5					19.84
1955	4.60	1.44	0.73	2.96	112.8	114.0	110.3	101.7	121.9	121.1					17.90
1956	5.46	1.69	0.90	3.41	121.4	101.9	135.8	116.9	127.2	114.8					24.15
1957	6.77	1.77	0.78	2.91	106.9	100.1	124.0	104.6	93.2	84.7					22.96
1958	14.10	2.44	0.95	3.57	176.7	129.6	229.8	138.0	125.1	123.2					29.46
1959	20.39	2.84	1.30	5.44	141.7	101.7	149.5	116.7	139.1	153.6					40.49
1960	27.22	2.75	2.61	5.43	123.5	97.9	130.8	96.8	203.4	100.3					44.51
1961	16.32	1.36	1.65	4.21	61.5	102.3	57.1	49.5	62.9	72.5					27.30
1962	13.10	1.29	1.16	2.68	78.3	105.8	77.8	94.3	70.0	61.5					17.69
1963	14.36	1.41	1.05	2.75	105.5	105.3	107.2	110.1	90.1	101.6					20.26
1964	16.30	1.73	1.27	2.86	114.3	110.4	115.6	122.1	121.0	104.1					25.25
1965	18.92	2.03	1.30	2.77	118.5	116.5	122.8	117.7	102.6	102.1	39.8	5.0	23.5	11.3	29.99
1966	22.86	1.77	1.22	2.88	111.0	94.5	118.3	87.2	94.6	104.0					32.75
1967	18.25	1.38	1.09	2.81	88.3	105.1	85.6	78.1	87.9	97.7					28.41
1968	17.83	1.37	1.11	3.10	99.2	98.0	97.7	99.1	102.7	110.8					27.70
1969	26.46	1.72	1.29	4.57	137.9	81.8	148.4	125.2	118.1	146.8					32.11
1970	34.80	1.92	1.77	3.86	144.8	130.2	157.7	111.7	128.9	85.2					30.02
1971	32.61	1.76	1.83	4.37	110.5	101.1	111.8	91.9	109.6	113.0					35.33
1972	38.18	1.84	1.95	4.68	112.7	91.2	117.1	104.4	104.5	106.8					35.42
1973	40.48	2.40	2.14	5.45	108.1	110.5	106.0	130.4	108.3	116.7					50.04
1974	44.74	3.00	2.42	5.64	109.9	103.3	110.5	124.9	113.5	103.3					49.96
1975	50.00	3.95	3.62	6.50	113.8	105.5	116.8	131.8	150.4	115.5					48.37
1976	53.00	3.31	3.51	6.18	102.5	95.6	105.7	83.7	97.0	95.3					41.67
1977	56.02	4.31	4.10	7.08	108.8	95.5	108.0	130.3	113.5	114.6					52.82
1978	63.90	5.72	4.54	8.03	114.1	98.3	114.2	132.5	114.5	112.6	108.8	5.6	77.4	25.8	65.55
1979	70.74	6.81	4.86	8.51	109.7	95.6	110.6	119.1	107.1	104.1	120.1	5.2	85.2	29.8	77.16
1980	79.44	7.96	5.03	10.57	110.4	107.9	110.0	113.8	100.8	118.4	139.1	6.1	95.8	37.2	90.12
1981	78.65	8.55	5.47	11.36	100.2	106.6	98.4	106.1	107.2	105.9	139.2	6.6	92.5	40.0	93.21
1982	81.98	9.46	5.96	10.47	105.6	117.6	103.9	110.6	109.9	104.3	154.9	7.8	102.4	44.8	92.10
1983	90.87	12.65	6.25	12.98	112.9	124.6	111.7	133.6	92.7	105.4	183.1	8.1	117.4	57.6	116.02
1984	105.50	15.46	7.12	14.72	116.0	114.7	116.3	120.8	112.9	111.2	216.6	7.7	137.8	71.1	148.30
1985	122.11	21.82	8.46	24.70	114.7	106.0	110.5	127.7	112.7	141.3	257.1	17.8	153.7	85.6	212.16
1986	128.43	23.05	9.92	25.94	101.6	99.3	101.0	99.2	133.3	98.4	284.9	19.1	165.8	100.0	227.91
1987	143.52	26.43	11.43	31.09	108.2	114.2	107.1	106.8	112.5	110.3	326.8	24.3	182.6	119.9	279.02
1988	178.94	30.28	11.33	44.68	111.6	112.4	112.3	107.6	95.1	117.9	410.2	37.1	221.3	151.9	339.56
1989	204.90	37.70	11.70	44.70	102.5	99.8	104.5	112.6	101.5	84.4	455.8	38.5	252.2	165.2	385.60

1. Beijing

1–3

Year	v1h	v1i	v1j	v1j1	v1j2	v1j3	v1k	v2a	v2a1	v2a2	v2b	v2c	v2c1	v2c2	v2d1
1949											0.01				
1950											0.30				
1951											0.90				
1952		3.12	544	553		428		1.8	0.8	1.0	0.99				
1953		4.47	637	634				6.2	5.1	1.1	4.57				
1954		4.80	609	675				9.0	7.8	1.2	7.27				
1955		5.19	642	706				6.7	7.4	-0.7	6.38				
1956	136.15	6.72	760	757				10.1	10.8	-0.7	8.90				
1957	135.79	7.63	748	764		569		10.6	6.8	3.8	7.47				
1958	125.03	8.24	637	705	867			16.3	11.3	5.0	12.13				
1959	110.30	10.67	655	673	518			24.1	16.9	7.2	17.86				
1960	76.60	11.68	648	680	404			24.7	17.5	7.2	16.82				
1961	109.00	11.18	642	689	395			8.5	8.3	0.2	6.80				
1962	175.92	10.37	666	723	413			-0.7	2.9	-3.6	2.81				
1963	150.45	10.42	697	754	439			2.7	5.4	-2.7	3.72				
1964	141.75	11.10	716	767	444			7.0	7.7	-0.7	5.57				
1965		11.48	703	752	447			9.2	7.9	1.3	7.92				
1966		11.08	677	741	427			11.6	8.6	3.0	5.83				
1967		10.94	683	727	424			8.5	6.0	2.5	3.84				
1968		10.81	678	724	423			8.3	5.6	2.7	3.76				
1969		10.75	673	729	423			12.6	8.4	4.2	6.93				
1970		10.24	631	686	469			11.3	6.8	4.5	8.71				
1971		10.84	629	665	478			16.1	9.4	6.7	7.72				
1972		12.15	645	676	487			15.0	9.3	5.7	7.56				
1973		12.88	642	680	478			26.4	13.8	12.6	10.32				
1974		13.47	640	684	459			26.2	18.1	8.1	13.85				
1975	143.89	14.49	640	681	463			21.6	16.0	5.6	18.70				90.52
1976	148.61	15.23	620	664	449			14.2	10.0	4.2	13.46				103.86
1977	162.01	15.92	616	659	455			21.0	13.5	7.5	17.21				113.23
1978	224.80	18.65	673	703	471		2.57	27.5	20.7	6.8	22.58				121.17
1979	225.00	22.40	742	778	556		3.07	31.5	23.8	7.7	26.53	23.27	7.35	1.17	126.24
1980	308.14	26.92	848	889	635		4.33	36.6	28.6	8.0	33.17	26.15	9.03	1.50	136.69
1981	361.44	28.27	837	880	685		5.23	28.1	23.6	9.3	31.42	30.16	5.74	1.78	147.45
1982	430.20	30.49	863	896	715		5.84	32.9	25.3	2.8	34.47	32.92	6.97	2.36	158.19
1983	519.48	33.78	931	964	785		7.66	40.7	35.0	5.7	38.55	40.36	6.68	3.70	169.36
1984	664.17	40.35	1086	1127	946		9.35	59.0	49.0	10.0	52.20	53.31	8.73	3.23	181.27
1985	775.08	50.72	1343	1367	1231		11.49	108.5	70.5	38.0	77.77	73.59	12.37	2.42	205.14
1986	823.06	57.97	1488	1530	1287		13.95	113.1	86.5	26.6	94.54	89.06	11.23	1.63	228.10
1987	916.38	66.74	1670	1712	1449		17.04	143.9	105.2	38.7	121.39	115.83	13.87	5.21	260.46
1988	1062.61	81.23	2000	2048	1738	5463	24.33	176.6	124.4	52.2	138.66	133.24	17.57	3.28	294.90
1989	1230.56	96.32	2312	2366	1992		33.87	206.5	109.8	96.7	146.24	116.30	12.83	3.20	329.42

1. Beijing

1–4

Year	v2d2	v2e	v3a	v3b	v3b1	v3b2	v3c	v3d	v3d1	v3d2	v3e	v3e1	v3e2	v3e3	v3e4
1949															
1950															
1951															
1952			7.8	6.6	1.7	4.9	1.2	141	64	239					
1953			9.9	8.7	1.6	7.1	1.2	179	63	315					
1954			10.8	9.2	1.6	7.6	1.6	177	62	297					
1955			11.2	10.0	1.8	8.2	1.2	182	65	295	205.4	118.4	20.7	9.6	10.7
1956			14.1	12.4	1.8	10.6	1.7	214	64	352	214.3	125.6	35.0	4.3	6.2
1957			12.3	10.9	2.2	8.7	1.4	179	77	266	238.6	133.4	27.1	8.6	9.2
1958			13.1	11.6	2.3	9.3	1.5	186	82	270	218.6	124.6	15.2	8.6	8.2
1959			16.4	13.1	2.1	11.0	3.3	199	76	290	229.1	133.8	30.4	7.7	8.0
1960			19.8	14.8	2.2	12.6	5.0	208	79	292	240.2	139.6	29.6	7.9	9.1
1961			18.8	15.1	3.6	11.5	3.7	208	128	259	233.8	131.4	21.2	9.3	9.4
1962			18.4	15.3	3.1	12.2	3.1	213	105	289	221.4	128.1	19.9	8.2	9.4
1963			17.6	13.5	2.7	10.8	4.1	184	87	254	232.5	136.5	24.6	7.1	8.8
1964			18.2	13.9	2.7	11.2	4.3	184	85	256	243.3	141.9	28.7	7.7	8.6
1965			20.8	17.1	3.9	13.2	3.7	222	120	294	246.7	138.5	30.8	8.9	7.9
1966			21.1	17.2	4.1	13.1	3.9	222	122	298					
1967			19.9	16.9	4.1	12.8	3.0	217	120	292					
1968			19.4	17.0	4.2	12.8	2.4	216	122	291					
1969			19.5	17.2	4.4	12.8	2.3	223	123	310					
1970			18.7	16.4	4.5	11.9	2.4	213	123	295					
1971			19.2	16.5	4.5	12.0	2.7	212	122	294					
1972			20.4	17.3	4.2	13.1	3.1	219	113	313					
1973			23.7	19.7	4.8	14.9	4.0	246	128	351					
1974			23.8	19.5	5.2	14.3	4.3	235	136	334					
1975	60.70		26.7	21.4	5.1	16.2	5.4	261	134	374					
1976	70.49		27.5	22.4	4.8	17.6	5.1	271	127	395					
1977	75.99		31.8	25.6	5.8	19.8	6.2	307	150	440					
1978	80.42		38.0	29.3	7.2	22.1	8.7	347	186	483	359.9	211.2	50.4	8.4	9.6
1979	81.47	43.13	45.7	34.8	8.4	26.4	10.9	403	224	542	408.7	236.7	58.5	8.6	11.1
1980	87.68	47.21	53.5	45.3	10.3	32.3	10.9	484	274	642	490.4	270.9	74.8	7.7	10.3
1981	93.77	49.12	65.1	48.5	11.7	34.1	16.7	513	313	660	511.4	295.1	77.7	8.1	10.2
1982	99.09	50.82	59.2	45.8	13.3	35.1	13.4	533	349	666	534.8	317.6	75.6	9.1	9.6
1983	105.21	51.77	75.3	54.6	16.4	38.2	20.7	589	424	707	574.1	337.7	82.9	9.7	9.6
1984	110.70	55.16	89.3	65.6	20.8	44.8	23.7	699	538	811	666.8	379.1	101.9	10.3	9.4
1985	127.24	64.55	103.7	79.4	24.1	55.3	24.3	835	622	981	923.3	466.9	138.4	11.1	12.3
1986	141.60	78.23	114.8	87.4	25.2	62.2	27.4	907	653	1076	1067.4	543.4	143.0	11.0	12.3
1987	165.24	88.65	135.1	101.6	28.3	73.3	33.5	1038	734	1236	1147.6	605.0	161.4	11.1	12.3
1988	188.24	102.21	162.9	124.2	36.0	88.2	38.8	1249	928	1454	1455.6	743.4	224.3	11.8	12.4
1989	210.85	130.25	179.1	130.2	48.9	85.2	48.9	1284	1150	1368	1520.4	841.3			

1. Beijing

1–5

Year	v3f	v3f1	v3f2	v3f3	v3f4	v4a1	v4a1a	v4a1b	v4a1c	v4a1d	v4a2	v4a2a	v4a2b	v4a2c	v4a2d
1949						0.2386	0.0002	0.14	0.08	0.0192	0.2195	0.0005	0.0699	0.1084	0.0407
1950						0.6570	0.0014			0.0440	0.4621	0.0005	0.1103	0.1464	0.2049
1951						1.4037	0.0438			0.0968	0.6330	0.2575	0.1645	0.1726	0.0384
1952						2.0903	0.1707			0.1495	1.0143	0.4230	0.2874	0.2081	0.0957
1953						3.6581	0.2754			0.1089	1.6786	0.9923	0.3448	0.2439	0.0976
1954						3.9770	0.5242			0.1241	1.8568	0.9498	0.3781	0.2845	0.2444
1955						4.0635	0.7299			0.1284	2.0843	1.2207	0.4102	0.2888	0.1646
1956	150.6	57.8	32.8	17.5	7.8	5.8120	0.9790			0.3418	2.8666	1.6029	0.5752	0.3547	0.3338
1957	120.8	61.5	14.4	3.5	7.2	6.3996	1.0189	4.91	0.15	0.3251	2.2201	1.0290	0.6309	0.3367	0.2236
1958	108.5	58.5	13.4	4.7	7.1	11.4652	5.7646			0.3066	7.3693	5.8440	0.8661	0.3237	0.3355
1959	100.4	58.1	14.2	5.7	9.4	15.3836	9.2586			0.0558	7.1549	4.2042	0.9572	0.4757	1.5173
1960	60.3	35.6	13.1	1.3	3.5	20.2032	12.7400			0.1355	8.6047	5.0455	1.0634	0.4841	2.0117
1961	94.3	47.8	12.5	7.7	12.5	13.1995	7.8047			0.0944	3.2709	0.9631	0.8394	0.4569	1.0115
1962	158.2	78.8	16.5		12.9	9.0874	4.3905			0.0621	2.5495	0.5196	0.8549	0.3412	0.8338
1963	138.5	72.9	18.6		10.3	10.1117	4.7707			0.0781	3.7779	1.0150	0.9438	0.3886	1.4305
1964	130.3	76.5	16.0		10.3	10.6195	5.1163			0.0721	4.0790	1.2091	1.1496	0.4127	1.3076
1965						10.9818	5.2970	5.48	0.15	0.0567	4.3812	1.3771	1.2114	0.4017	1.3910
1966						12.0850	6.2260			0.0636	5.2586	1.2106	1.1686	0.3830	2.4964
1967						9.8962	4.6651			0.0527	3.4757	0.6648	1.1762	0.3606	1.2741
1968						9.8904	4.8360			0.0837	2.4838	0.4388	1.0682	0.3647	0.6121
1969						15.6439	8.3450			0.0627	4.0861	1.5884	1.0835	0.3099	1.1043
1970						21.6204	12.9039			0.0749	6.6101	2.2566	1.2805	0.2984	2.7746
1971						26.8536	16.5829			0.0621	6.3181	1.7062	1.4754	0.4244	2.7121
1972						31.5182	20.6452			0.0674	6.8825	1.8113	1.6687	0.5044	2.8981
1973						30.8733	18.9849			0.0604	9.1425	3.4115	1.9734	0.5202	3.2374
1974						36.1245	23.1475			0.0497	14.1544	7.1152	2.0853	0.5751	4.3788
1975	135.4	79.7	16.5	1.9	6.5	39.3493	25.0397			0.0714	16.0309	8.1972	2.1794	0.6013	5.0530
1976	141.3	75.4	17.6	4.0	10.7	37.7863	23.1487			0.0440	16.2014	7.9220	2.2183	0.6180	5.4431
1977	144.3	76.6	17.3	5.0	10.0	42.7676	26.4690			0.1487	15.9700	7.3069	2.3164	0.6473	5.6994
1978	185.4	116.7	21.6	0.2	10.6	50.4559	32.1454	18.08	0.18	0.0563	20.3779	10.8874	2.4318	0.7436	6.3151
1979	204.7	130.7	26.9		8.4	47.7517	28.3731			-0.0327	20.0564	10.0732	2.9443	0.8736	6.1653
1980	256.8	138.5	33.8	26.5	8.6	51.2890	29.9913	21.04	0.18	0.0771	14.8710	5.6479	3.2154	0.9836	5.0241
1981	307.2	159.3	38.2	45.7	8.5	49.1214	26.6142			0.0416	14.8462	5.9478	3.6477	1.0719	4.1788
1982	345.5	180.2	42.4	52.2	10.0	47.2504	22.7041			0.1478	16.8003	6.4448	4.1670	1.1437	5.0448
1983	384.4	193.2	48.8	64.7	12.2	39.8441	13.2661			0.1239	19.6054	6.4682	4.6260	1.3799	7.1313
1984	435.0	222.2	47.9	67.5	14.1	45.6226	13.7756	17.98	0.19	0.3528	27.1539	10.0605	5.5341	1.8875	9.6718
1985	510.0	239.9	53.6	88.2	18.3	52.4369	7.6183	31.28	0.26	0.4189	32.9859	10.8258	6.8419	1.5868	13.7314
1986	645.3	292.2	60.8	139.8	20.3	60.3390	9.5581			0.9639	44.2724	11.2202	8.2013	1.9761	22.8748
1987	705.5	340.9	69.1	133.7	23.0	63.6150	7.5301			0.9270	49.6734	10.4679	9.2138	1.7619	28.2298
1988	883.3	407.9	82.1	171.4	24.2	68.1093	-2.7493	66.74	0.53	3.5846	52.9340	10.5280	11.4593	1.1614	29.7853
1989	976.2	481.8	82.7	151.3	26.4	71.0499	-11.7468			3.5040	59.5088	11.6617	13.1329	1.2584	33.4558

1. Beijing

Year	v4b	v4b1	v4b2	v4b3	v4c1	v4c2	v5a	v5a1	v5a2	v5a3	v5a4	v5b1	v5b2	v5b3	v5c
1949		0.0065					153	12		11	110				10.68
1950	0.1691						167	16		11	117				
1951	0.3029						183	26		14	117				
1952	0.5818						203	37		16	125				
1953	0.8428						220	51		19	123				
1954	1.1714						226	55		22	124				
1955	1.3309						223	61		20	122				
1956	1.7355						237	75		20	121				
1957	2.0597	2.0116	0.0481				231	92		13	110				34.38
1958	2.2952						274	128	23	15	108				
1959	2.7292						280	142	33	4	101				
1960	3.0747						281	156	29	5	91				
1961	2.6945						267	139	24	4	100				
1962	2.4577						268	126	22	4	116				
1963	2.7134						281	128	23	12	118	120	71	90	
1964	3.3819						293	135	24	12	122				
1965	3.9214	3.8007	0.1207				299	141	26	9	123				60.66
1966	4.0341						298	135	25	8	130				
1967	4.1698						300	136	24	8	132				
1968	4.2260						309	136	23	8	142				
1969	3.9552						320	139	22	8	151				
1970	4.0747						328	142	22	8	156				
1971	4.5113						345	151	30	7	157				
1972	5.2313						356	162	34	7	154				
1973	5.8409						372	169	37	7	159				
1974	6.4923						380	176	39	6	159	135	127	118	
1975	7.1486				35.19	36.5	396	191	46	1	158	127	147	122	
1976	7.5722				34.52	31.4	414	203	51	1	159	129	160	125	
1977	8.2100				38.48	32.4	425	208	55	2	160	127	166	132	
1978	9.3280	8.8991	0.4289		43.51	34.9	444	241	51		162	126	178	140	128.18
1979	11.0694				48.05	37.8	474	254	58		162	122	195	157	
1980	14.3922	13.3310	1.0612		52.10	37.9	484	269	57		158	124	210	150	139.56
1981	17.3900				52.10	36.3	512	283	61	1	167	127	224	161	
1982	21.7665	19.1882	2.5783		52.15	34.8	535	293	67	1	174	128	232	175	
1983	29.8114	25.1065	4.7049		54.51	34.7	552	303	68	2	178	126	241	185	
1984	38.8172	31.9908	6.6725		58.96	35.3	556	302	72	2	179	111	248	197	
1985	51.6954	42.2447	9.4507		67.79	35.3	567	308	73	1	174	101	260	206	
1986	68.5787				67.69	30.8	573	325	71	3	172	86	255	232	
1987	92.9769				73.24	28.8	580	332	71	3	172	92	264	224	
1988	111.6444	90.5519	21.0925		88.25	30.4	584	336	70	4	170	88	268	228	147.40
1989	161.9000	133.6000	28.3000		88.86	26.0	610	343	68	6	170	91	266	237	

1. Beijing

1–7

Year	v5c1	v5d	v6a	v6a1	v6a2	v6b	v6c	v6d1	v6d2	v6d3	v6d4	v6d5	v6d6
1949		0.12	203.1			19.40	11.90	164.9	38.2	114.5	88.6	203.10	
1950			204.3	176.0	253.9	36.30	14.57	161.6	42.7	115.3	89.0		
1951			222.0	195.5	254.7	36.89	15.25	182.1	39.9	128.4	93.6		
1952			248.8	212.9	264.1	34.44	10.89	194.3	54.5	143.0	105.8	251.90	
1953			276.6	236.4	266.0	37.26	10.46	224.5	52.1	158.6	118.0		
1954			310.4	274.2	266.0	40.87	8.63	257.5	52.9	176.6	133.8		
1955			320.1	283.8	272.1	40.07	9.47	267.1	53.0	177.9	142.2		
1956			383.2	317.8	280.4	40.02	7.73	299.3	83.9	207.8	175.4		
1957		0.93	401.1	341.2	277.9	42.10	8.19	320.5	80.6	213.6	187.5	401.15	
1958			631.8	350.2	281.6	37.02	8.08	350.2	281.6	329.8	302.0	552.28	
1959			684.1	407.4	276.7	30.70	9.66	407.4	276.7	364.0	320.1		
1960			732.1	455.6	276.5	33.03	9.14	455.6	276.5	388.6	343.5		
1961			721.0	433.8	287.2	25.70	10.80	433.8	287.2	376.2	344.8	456.09	
1962			723.6	420.6	303.0	35.92	8.77	420.6	303.0	372.6	351.6	448.62	
1963			747.4	433.1	314.3	43.41	8.11	433.1	314.3	384.6	362.8	461.96	
1964			765.0	442.6	322.4	30.40	8.27	442.6	322.4	393.4	371.6	471.18	
1965		6.83	775.9	447.8	328.1	22.95	6.75	447.8	328.1	400.2	375.7	476.00	
1966			770.1	433.7	336.4	19.41	7.24	433.7	336.4	397.5	372.6		
1967			782.0	439.3	342.7	18.16	5.07	439.3	342.7	403.4	378.6		
1968			781.7	430.7	351.0	23.75	6.75	430.7	351.0	402.0	379.7		
1969			767.6	405.9	361.7	22.36	7.39	405.9	361.7	393.1	374.5		
1970			771.2	403.1	368.1	20.68	6.34	403.1	368.1	394.0	377.2	439.09	
1971			782.5	410.9	371.6	18.82	6.40	410.9	371.6	400.0	382.5		
1972			792.7	421.6	371.1	17.81	6.74	421.6	371.1	404.0	388.7		
1973			805.8	426.4	379.4	15.70	6.12	426.4	379.4	411.3	394.5		
1974			814.0	433.0	381.0	11.61	6.22	433.0	381.0	415.4	398.6		
1975			822.3	442.7	379.6	9.93	6.54	442.7	379.6	419.6	402.7	471.32	
1976			828.5	447.0	381.5	9.06	6.53	447.0	381.5	422.4	406.1		
1977			838.1	452.8	385.3	10.23	6.21	452.8	385.3	426.6	411.5		
1978		6.61	849.7	467.0	382.7	12.93	6.12	467.0	382.7	432.1	417.6	492.60	
1979			870.6	495.2	375.4	13.67	5.92	495.2	375.4	441.2	437.3		
1980		6.30	885.7	510.4	375.3	15.56	6.30	510.4	375.3	448.4	437.3	530.74	
1981			900.8	522.6	378.2	16.93	6.02	522.6	378.2	456.6	444.2		
1982			917.8	534.0	383.8	20.04	5.68	534.0	383.8	465.5	452.3		
1983			933.2	547.1	386.1	15.63	5.49	547.0	386.1	474.7	458.5		
1984	107.80		945.2	558.1	387.1	14.05	5.46	558.1	387.1	481.2	464.0		
1985	110.22		957.9	572.5	385.4	12.44	5.51	572.5	385.4	488.0	469.9	586.03	
1986	112.22		971.0	586.8	384.4	13.41	5.34	586.8	384.4	495.5	475.5	596.44	
1987	112.73		988.0	601.0	387.0	17.29	5.40	601.0	387.0	504.1	483.9	670.46	
1988	112.71	7.80	1001.2	614.2	387.0	14.40	5.54	614.2	387.0	510.4	490.8	679.37	
1989	118.10		1021.1	630.6	390.5	12.84	5.63	630.6	390.5	520.3	500.8	692.05	

1. Beijing

1–8

Year	v7a	v7b	v7c	v7d	v7e	v7f	v7g	v7h	v7h1	v7h2	v7h3	v7h4	v7h5	v7i	v8a
1949						1.04									1.85
1950			24.3	912			0.0015								3.87
1951			29.6	930			0.0034								7.55
1952			37.3	990			0.0051	2.54							9.07
1953		1.5	35.6	1014			0.0040	2.72							12.96
1954		4.5	35.9	1008			0.0030	2.48							14.95
1955		13.5	36.4	1019			0.0045	2.83							16.63
1956		19.5	54.0	1025			0.0111	2.89							20.03
1957	0.22	66.0	58.2	1011		1.26	0.0316	3.03	2.33	0.02	0.33	0.35	0.003	25.20	22.00
1958		109.5	142.9	912			0.1406	4.90	3.31	0.33	1.13	0.13	0.003	22.60	42.78
1959		135.0	206.0	861			0.2473	5.01	3.27	0.21	0.59	0.93	0.010	21.90	63.33
1960	1.00	310.5	222.9	863			0.2813	4.91	3.01	0.17	0.56	1.16	0.010	18.80	85.87
1961		312.0	151.5	864			0.4938	4.76	3.15	0.06	0.42	1.06	0.080	18.10	53.17
1962	1.48	267.0	161.6	864			0.5252	5.15	3.54	0.06	0.64	0.91	0.005	18.90	41.87
1963		250.5	241.9	842			1.0732	5.52	3.65	0.07	0.82	0.98	0.005	19.90	44.47
1964		225.0	310.3	886			1.0429	6.23	6.96	0.12	1.05	1.08	0.006	20.30	49.40
1965	2.41	313.5	368.2	878		1.31	1.6627	7.04	4.68	0.12	1.14	1.09	0.007	21.70	55.90
1966	2.79	256.5	377.4	1021			1.9349	7.08	4.57	0.11	1.23	1.15	0.007	21.80	69.01
1967	3.06	240.0	371.0	948			1.8906	7.31	4.64	0.12	1.24	1.30	0.007	22.00	58.22
1968	3.32	343.5	383.4	910			2.3029	7.49	4.66	0.07	1.08	1.66	0.010	22.40	61.39
1969	3.80	282.0	393.0	935			1.9406	6.89	4.25	0.08	1.05	1.50	0.007	22.60	87.51
1970	4.24	325.5	417.1	941			1.9682	8.20	5.84	0.14	1.26	0.95	0.010	23.30	97.14
1971	5.39	360.0	424.9	972			2.4875	8.48	6.03	0.16	1.61	0.67	0.010	23.50	99.32
1972	6.65	382.5	413.7	957			3.1697	8.07	5.37	0.20	2.09	0.39	0.020	23.20	105.28
1973	8.34	418.5	433.0	985			3.0460	9.21	6.61	0.22	2.01	0.35	0.020	22.90	113.09
1974	10.17	448.5	462.1	1011			3.6798	9.99	7.39	0.25	1.98	0.35	0.020	22.50	123.29
1975	12.44	475.5	487.8	1051			4.9664	10.57	7.81	0.19	2.20	0.35	0.020	22.13	133.78
1976	14.37	460.5	495.8	1058			5.1264	10.36	7.72	0.18	2.09	0.35	0.020	21.84	141.21
1977	16.61	483.0	505.6	1048			5.1447	9.82	7.04	0.21	2.19	0.35	0.020	21.99	149.27
1978	18.93	483.0	512.6	1036		1.61	5.8802	11.64	8.64	0.25	2.38	0.35	0.020	21.53	169.97
1979	21.23	478.5	511.3	1016			6.3123	12.35	8.54	0.21	3.22	0.35	0.030	20.45	189.61
1980	23.47	475.5	510.5	986		1.54	7.6754	14.31	9.44	0.54	3.83	0.45	0.050	19.33	213.37
1981	24.48	480.0	511.9	966			9.1842	14.92	9.68	0.69	4.02	0.48	0.050	19.22	218.96
1982	24.21	483.0	509.0	963			9.6960	16.76	10.85	0.70	4.65	0.51	0.050	18.18	230.84
1983	26.19	478.5	514.9	957			10.4608	19.60	12.15	0.81	5.89	0.64	0.110	18.13	256.81
1984	29.11	474.0	514.0	950			11.9287	22.15	13.51	0.86	6.66	0.91	0.210	17.64	292.36
1985	32.02	460.5	507.6	927			12.6830	25.94	15.25	0.77	8.53	0.95	0.440	16.57	338.69
1986	34.55	454.5	505.9	907			14.6717	28.14	16.31	0.80	9.39	0.95	0.690	17.30	371.24
1987	38.84	451.5	507.0	897			15.9450	34.42	19.12	0.80	12.24	1.22	1.040	17.50	434.63
1988	39.97	448.5	507.3	893		1.43	16.3986	52.50	30.15	0.86	18.58	1.23	1.680	16.90	571.57
1989	42.39	450.7	507.7	884			19.0000	60.35	32.88	0.70	23.22	1.34	2.210	16.60	700.90

1. Beijing

1–9

Year	v8a1	v8a2	v8a3	v8b	v8c1	v8c2	v8d	v8f1	v8f2	v8f3	v8f4	v8f5	v8g
1949	1.26	0.14	0.45		0.74	1.11		0.0	111.4		1.5	3.5	
1950	2.64	0.29	0.93		1.55	2.32		0.1	80.6		2.0	11.1	23461
1951	5.15	0.57	1.82		3.02	4.53		0.1	174.1		2.3	13.1	29839
1952	6.19	0.69	2.19		3.46	5.61		0.2	222.0		2.8	20.4	34386
1953	8.85	0.15	3.96		5.17	7.79		0.4	187.7		3.5	26.7	38632
1954	10.21	1.14	3.60		6.13	8.82		0.4	178.4		3.9	29.1	39595
1955	11.36	1.26	4.01		7.00	9.63		0.6	197.1		4.4	35.0	32036
1956	13.68	1.52	4.83		8.61	11.42		1.3	184.5		5.7	41.6	3574
1957	15.02	1.67	5.30		9.88	12.11		2.8	256.8		7.0	44.6	4234
1958	36.45	6.33			21.90	20.88		12.0	459.5		10.5	50.3	2084
1959	53.96	9.37			32.71	30.62		38.0	673.8		20.6	58.4	2890
1960	73.16	12.71			49.28	36.58		62.1	839.4		30.6	70.2	2238
1961	45.30	7.87			28.55	24.62		33.1	781.4		28.7	53.8	2207
1962	35.70	6.19			19.77	22.10		10.6	652.9		26.3	51.0	2049
1963	37.88	6.58			21.67	22.79		10.4	632.9		27.5	57.2	2039
1964	42.09	7.31			25.09	24.31		16.3	568.6		32.3	74.7	1715
1965	47.63	8.27			30.66	25.24		35.6	529.0		38.2	88.9	1790
1966	58.80	10.20			39.72	29.30		63.5	534.3		44.1	99.9	1842
1967	49.60	8.62			30.83	27.39		49.0	428.4		41.8	60.0	1841
1968	52.31	9.09			32.39	29.00		32.8	471.8		43.2	61.9	1792
1969	74.56	12.95			50.60	36.91		72.5	532.1	28.5	52.3	110.7	1740
1970	82.55	14.34			63.70	33.43		110.2	624.9	254.5	61.1	121.7	1819
1971	84.08	14.61			70.23	29.09		134.3	680.1	344.1	67.8	131.4	1931
1972	87.79	16.48			68.45	36.83		148.9	691.8	373.5	72.3	127.6	2059
1973	94.26	17.69			71.59	41.50		161.0	706.3	372.8	75.2	130.1	2167
1974	102.72	19.28			77.75	45.54		161.8	736.9	424.3	83.2	136.6	2255
1975	111.44	20.91			83.99	49.81	41.10	165.8	749.0	443.3	90.4	153.0	3739
1976	117.24	22.00			87.71	53.50		163.0	747.5	512.1	92.7	165.2	3877
1977	123.87	23.24		122.13	93.34	55.93	46.41	151.2	780.3	566.6	100.1	165.2	4036
1978	140.93	26.45		139.71	108.03	61.94	52.50	191.0	818.7	600.7	99.1	191.5	4225
1979	157.03	29.47		154.36	113.57	76.04	57.45	196.5	811.1	586.5	104.3	196.9	3746
1980	176.05	33.04		169.43	120.96	92.41	63.82	200.9	791.0	591.1	106.5	217.4	3733
1981	180.12	33.80		171.61	113.34	105.62	62.73	190.3	788.7	533.5	99.3	225.7	3778
1982	173.48	46.45	4.49	179.42	122.64	108.20	64.43	200.4	811.3	533.5	100.3	249.1	3867
1983	190.44	50.99	4.93	191.87	136.63	120.19	68.21	214.1	840.5	563.8	102.9	270.8	4011
1984	214.02	57.31	5.54	211.73	158.30	134.06	76.88	241.7	884.3	589.4	103.9	291.6	4291
1985	261.81	70.11	6.77	239.41	204.87	133.82	86.09	267.7	944.3	591.1	103.7	318.5	4458
1986	286.97	76.85	7.42	260.18	196.71	174.53	91.27	303.6	917.2	619.0	104.3	310.5	5461
1987	335.97	89.97	8.69	297.09	228.72	205.92	100.90	335.5	899.8	640.2	105.7	319.6	5746
1988	441.82	118.31	11.43	369.54	284.60	286.97	120.02	369.0	906.0	645.0	111.1	334.0	5932
1989	541.81	145.09	14.02	435.29	337.40	363.50	134.40	386.0	1016.6	651.9	119.4	345.9	6175

1. Beijing

1–10

Year	v8g1	v9a	v9a1	v9a2	v9a3	v9b	v9b1	v9b2	v9b3	v9c	v10a	v10a1	v10b1	v10b2	v10b3
1949										769	2.82	2.77	0.33		0.14
1950		0.20				0.25				877	4.59	4.52			
1951		0.37				0.51				1157	8.17	8.07			
1952		0.51				1.06				1255	8.73	8.60	2.31		1.46
1953		0.79				1.70				1471	13.71	13.50			
1954		0.79				1.58				1641	13.61	13.36			
1955		0.87				1.56				1826	12.99	12.75			
1956		1.04				1.51				2179	17.41	17.06			
1957		1.23				1.49				2334	17.12	16.80	7.89		3.84
1958		1.15				2.50				2630	18.52	17.82			
1959		1.72				4.72				3462	22.22	21.46			
1960		1.67				6.36				4063	25.35	24.21			
1961		2.51				4.13				3741	21.24	20.29			
1962		1.59				2.95				3480	18.81	17.90	16.23		2.54
1963		1.56				2.48				3489	18.29	17.39			
1964		1.66				2.71				3705	19.05	18.17			
1965		1.84				2.62				3860	19.66	18.54	15.76		3.91
1966		2.56				2.56				4065	21.29	20.04			
1967		2.93				2.43				3822	20.79	19.73			
1968		3.16				2.62				3496	20.02	18.96			
1969		3.22				3.55				3689	22.18	20.72			
1970		3.29				4.11				3832	21.89	20.22	17.43		4.46
1971		3.58				4.29				3864	24.05	22.05			
1972		3.77				5.02				4290	26.10	23.71			
1973		3.57				5.12				4552	29.51	26.85			
1974		3.82				5.40				4901	33.18	30.17			
1975	899	4.54				5.58				5399	36.04	32.74	29.57		6.47
1976	910	4.16				5.75				7652	37.78	34.20	31.42		6.36
1977	923	5.36				6.12				8328	40.38	37.12	34.25		6.12
1978	974	5.94				6.74				9051	44.17	40.64	37.15		7.01
1979	981	6.40				7.31				9987	52.20	48.58	44.14		7.94
1980	985	7.37				7.35				11404	61.32	57.68	49.06		11.83
1981	983	8.19				7.49				12782	68.82	64.85	48.74		19.17
1982	1001	9.01				8.40				13987	73.31	68.14	51.06		21.20
1983	1008	10.37				9.24				15724	83.57	77.80	55.98		26.09
1984	1007	11.39				9.61				18357	101.66	95.20	67.69		32.10
1985	1040	10.92				9.99				22413	127.90	121.67	78.33		44.90
1986	1104	11.91				10.43				25348	146.46	139.36	84.52		50.95
1987	1163	13.37				10.45				29282	176.59	168.96	97.06		64.49
1988	1199	14.16				10.73				35472	234.30	223.01	129.46		84.51
1989	1212	10.53				10.80				45050	266.73	251.72	143.75		92.24

1. Beijing

1–11

Year	v10b4	v10b5	v10b6	v10d	v11a1	v11a2	v11a3	v11b	v11b1	v11b2	v11c	v11d	v12a	v12b	v12c
1949	0.01	2.34		0.35											
1950				0.46		0.0242		0.0242	0.0242	0.0000					
1951				0.58				0.0125	0.0125	0.0000			114.2	116.2	
1952	0.06	4.89		0.85				0.0063	0.0063	0.0000			104.1	104.1	
1953				1.16				0.0101	0.0101	0.0000			110.0	109.7	
1954				1.20				0.0088	0.0088	0.0000			101.8	102.9	
1955				1.20				0.0093	0.0093	0.0000			100.8	100.7	
1956				1.16				0.0168	0.0168	0.0000			100.3	100.1	
1957	5.13	0.27		1.45		0.0227		0.0227	0.0227	0.0000			100.8	100.7	
1958				1.64				0.1300	0.1300	0.0000			99.5	98.8	
1959				1.99				0.2495	0.2495	0.0000			99.7	99.5	
1960				1.90				0.2553	0.2553	0.0000			99.6	99.6	102.0
1961				1.59				0.4657	0.4657	0.0000			103.6	103.6	109.9
1962		0.03		2.03				0.4413	0.4413	0.0000			104.3	104.6	104.5
1963				2.20				0.4568	0.4568	0.0000			100.4	100.2	96.4
1964				2.50				0.5082	0.5082	0.0000			98.8	98.8	99.5
1965				2.83	0.0296	0.4260	0.0384	0.4940	0.4940	0.0000			94.5	94.9	96.2
1966				2.70				0.5294	0.5294	0.0000			99.8	99.6	100.7
1967				2.74				0.4390	0.4390	0.0000			100.0	100.0	99.9
1968				2.79				0.4858	0.4858	0.0000			99.5	99.9	99.6
1969				2.68				0.6081	0.6081	0.0000			100.4	100.3	100.0
1970				2.97				0.6532	0.6532	0.0000			98.8	98.9	100.0
1971				3.14				0.7491	0.7491	0.0000			100.2	100.2	101.9
1972				3.23				0.9532	0.9532	0.0000			100.2	100.2	101.9
1973				3.77				1.4851	1.4851	0.0000			100.3	100.2	101.1
1974				3.94				1.6017	1.5693	0.0324			99.9	99.9	100.7
1975				4.47				1.9139	1.7965	0.1174			100.0	100.0	101.6
1976				4.44				2.0667	1.9565	0.1102			99.7	99.7	98.8
1977				4.24				2.4385	2.3162	0.1223			99.9	99.9	99.8
1978				4.98				2.9751	2.8524	0.1227			100.6	100.6	103.9
1979			0.12	5.88	0.2056	2.3138	0.3330	4.5036	4.1757	0.3279			101.8	101.8	109.5
1980		0.01	0.42	6.58				6.6280	5.9277	0.7003			106.7	106.0	105.5
1981	0.20	0.05	0.66	8.11	0.1856	4.3485	1.3936	7.0091	6.3230	0.6861			101.4	101.3	109.4
1982	0.17	0.13	0.75	8.99	0.2759	4.6916	1.3555	6.8921	6.1339	0.7582			102.0	100.8	101.9
1983	0.14	0.50	0.86	10.56	0.2735	4.4599	1.4005	6.9621	5.9009	1.0612			100.6	100.5	101.8
1984	0.20	0.76	0.89	10.09	0.3770	4.1655	1.3584	7.6303	6.2632	1.3671	1.3826		102.1	102.2	102.3
1985	0.31	1.55	2.76	14.24	0.4279	4.6544	1.1459	9.7360	6.2075	3.5285	4.0788		118.6	117.6	117.6
1986	0.44	4.28	6.27	19.06	0.5333	4.5163	1.1579	10.8492	7.2485	3.6007	5.5888	1.7725	106.7	106.8	108.1
1987	0.58	6.21	8.24	22.46	0.5086	6.0900	2.2226	11.9575	8.8236	3.1339	6.6515	6.1944	108.7	108.6	116.1
1988	0.63	8.92	10.81	31.27	0.5603	7.1972	2.2425	12.9717	10.0275	2.9442	1.8533	4.7704	121.9	120.4	123.2
1989	2.57	15.47	12.71	37.15				16.4911	11.6157	4.8754	1.4252	4.7704	118.5	117.2	106.8

1. Beijing 1–12

Year	v13a	v13b	v13c1	v13c2	v13c3	v13d	v14a	v14b	v14c	v15a	v15b	v15c	v15d	v15e	v15f
1949															
1950			1.6940		34.8681					831					
1951		74.12	2.0028		43.3723					847					
1952		82.99	3.0620		57.8655	0.3306	4534	10000		912					
1953		83.90	3.7287		58.4126	0.8071				895					
1954		85.12	4.6702		60.4440	0.8424				885					
1955		90.75	5.7430		63.5769	0.8141				873					
1956		95.21	7.6700		69.8675	0.7411				859					
1957		85.00	7.9650		72.8793	0.1625				799					
1958		88.68	9.7786		82.0821	1.1255				739					
1959		93.15	11.2960		91.6155	1.3244				669					
1960		94.97	15.1152		102.6607	2.0264				652					
1961		90.38	12.7062		103.8262	0.1429				656					
1962		86.62	12.8688		105.0227	1.8600				667					
1963		86.82	12.1826		111.4424	2.6175				670					
1964		89.61	11.5569		122.7738	2.8922				671					
1965		93.76	11.1435		132.0808	2.9617	21211	39000		670					
1966			11.1157		122.6648					667					
1967			11.1157		134.0881					667					
1968			4.3906		130.9872	6.7251				665					
1969			1.3094		129.9915	1.3030				666					
1970			0.8808		135.8517	1.1421				661					
1971			1.3952		140.5647	0.1314				661					
1972			2.2356		141.8390	0.2317				661					
1973		97.66	3.3462		131.7062	0.4133				658					
1974		97.83	4.1614		112.1941	0.5669				656					
1975		99.03	4.4475		102.1621	1.2847				654					
1976		98.99	4.6016		89.1953	1.4066				651					
1977		99.09	4.0846		91.4855	1.6906				648					
1978	7.2	98.98	6.4661		93.7336	1.0881	26432	66000		644					
1979	8.8	98.45	7.2931		96.8723	0.8585				640					
1980	13.0	98.68	8.3032		95.1763	0.8233	28495	75000		639					
1981	14.5	98.89	9.8103		90.0350	0.2289	29783			637					
1982	14.1	98.93	9.3878		85.4516	2.5753	30940			636					
1983	13.5	99.06	9.0894		83.8078	3.1009	32242			634					
1984	11.0	99.28	10.2962		76.3204	2.0110	34602			633					
1985	11.7	99.09	12.2791		73.3605	2.1442	38180	91000		631					
1986	10.0	99.49	12.9646		74.9101	2.6954				628					
1987	9.6	99.46	13.5974		77.7982	3.4605				627					
1988	11.4	99.50	14.5134		85.0577	3.3066	48711	105000		624					
1989		99.71	14.1600		93.5000	3.5600	51877	108000	6.0253	622					

Notes

1. National Output and Income (Y)

v1a: (A); (E), p.68
v1a1: (E), p.68
v1a2: (E), p.68
v1a3: (E), p.68
v1a4: (E), p.68
v1a5: (E), p.68

v1b: (A)
v1b1: (A)
v1b2: (A)
v1b3: (A)
v1b4: (A)
v1b5: (A)

v1c: v1a – v1d

v1d: (A); (E), p.65
v1d1: (E), p.65
v1d2: (E), p.65
v1d3: (E), p.65
v1d4: (E), p.65
v1d5: (E), p.65

v1e: (A)
v1e1: (A)
v1e2: (A)
v1e3: (A)
v1e4: (A)
v1e5: (A)

v1f: (B), p.28; (E), p.64
v1f1: (B), p.28; (E), p.64
v1f2: (B), p.28; (E), p.64
v1f3: (B), p.28; (E), p.64

v1g: (E), p.67

v1h: (A); (E), p.89

v1i: (E), p.88

v1j: (E), p.88
v1j1: (E), p.88
v1j2: (E), p.88
v1j3: (B), p.148—various kind of joint ownership and sino-foreign joint ventures

v1k: (E), p.88

2. Investment (I)

v2a: (E), p.67
v2a1: (A); (D), p.101
v2a2: (A); (D), p.101

v2b: (A)

v2c: (E), p.79
v2c1: (E), p.81
v2c2: (E), p.81

v2d:
v2d1: (E), p.78
v2d2: (E), p.78

v2e: (E), p.78

3. Consumption (C)

v3a: (E), p.67

v3b: (E), p.67
v3b1: (A); (D), p.99
v3b2: (A); (D), p.99

v3c: (E), p.67

v3d: (E), p.87
v3d1: (E), p.87
v3d2: (E), p.87

v3e: (A); (E), p.89
v3e1: (A); (E), p.89
v3e2: (A)
v3e3: (A)
v3e4: (A)

v3f: (A); (E), p.89
- v3f1: (A); (E), p.89
- v3f2: (A)
- v3f3: (A)
- v3f4: (A)

4. Public Finance and Banking (FB)

v4a:
- v4a1: (E), p.85
  - v4a1a: (E), p.85
  - v4a1b: (B), p.34
  - v4a1c: (B), p.34
  - v4a1d: (B), p.34; v4a1d': v4a1 – v4a1a – v4a1b (v4a1b': total tax revenues, which come from (E), p.85)
- v4a2: (E), p.85
  - v4a2a: (E), p.85
  - v4a2b: (E), p.85
  - v4a2c: (E), p.85
  - v4a2d: v4a2 – v4a2a – v4a2b – v4a2c

v4b:
- v4b1: (A); (B), p.142
- v4b2: (A)—peasant's saving; (B), p.142
- v4b3: NA

v4c:
- v4c1: (E), p.78
- v4c2: (E), p.78

5. Labor Force (L)

v5a: (A); (E), p.63
- v5a1: (E), p.63
- v5a2: (E), p.63
- v5a3: (E), p.63
- v5a4: (E), p.63—excluding rural people working outside

v5b:
- v5b1: (E), p.63
- v5b2: (E), p.63
- v5b3: (E), p.63

v5c: (B), p.24
- v5c1: (C), 1985, p.374; 1986, p.462; 1987, p.576; 1989, p.465; 1990, p.214

v5d: (B), p.24

6. Population (PO)

v6a: (E), p.62—data from public security department
- v6a1: (A)
- v6a2: (A)

v6b: (E), p.62—data collected by sample survey

v6c: (E), p.62—(ditto)

v6d:
- v6d1: (E), p.62—data from public security department
- v6d2: (E), p.62—(ditto)
- v6d3: (E), p.62—(ditto)
- v6d4: (E), p.62—(ditto)
- v6d5: (A)
- v6d6: NA

7. Agriculture (A)

v7a: (A); (E), p.74

v7b: (A); (E), p.74

v7c: (A); (E), p.74

v7d: (A); (E), p.74

v7e: NA

v7f: (A), reckoned pure amount, unit: ton

v7g: (A); (E), p.74

v7h: (E), p.68
- v7h1: (A); (E), p.71
- v7h2: (A); (E), p.71

v7h3: (A); (E), p.71
v7h4: (A); (E), p.71
v7h5: (A); (E), p.71

v7i: (E), p.73

8. Industry (IN)

v8a: (A)
v8a1: (A)
v8a2: (A)
v8a3: (A)

v8b: (E), p.78

v8c1: (A)
v8c2: (A)

v8d: (E), p.78
v8f1: (E), p.77
v8f2: (E), p.77
v8f3: (A)
v8f4: (E), p.77
v8f5: (E), p.77

v8g: (A), including the enterprises at *xiang* level and the above only (the same for the rest)
v8g1: (E), p.78

9. Transport (TR)

v9a: (E), p.79—figures in transport system, excluding urban traffic volume
v9a1: NA
v9a2: NA
v9a3: NA

v9b: (E), p.79—figure in transport system
v9b1: NA
v9b2: NA
v9b3: NA

v9c: (E), p.79

10. Domestic Trade (DT)

v10a: (E), p.82
v10a1: (E), p.82

v10b:
v10b1: (E), p.82
v10b2: NA
v10b3: (E), p.82—collective ownership, including supply and marketing cooperative and other collectives
v10b4: (E), p.82
v10b5: (E), p.82
v10b6: (E), p.82

v10d: (E), p.83—calculated on calendar year basis

11. Foreign Trade (FT)

v11a:
v11a1: (C), 1989, p.419—agricultural (including sideline and local) products
v11a2: (C), 1989, p.419—light industrial products
v11a3: (C), 1989, p.419—heavy industrial products

v11b: (E), p.84
v11b1: (E), p.84
v11b2: v11b – v11b1

v11c: (E), p.84

v11d: (E), p.84

12. Prices (PR)

v12a: (E), p.86

v12b: (E), p.86

v12c: (E), p.86

13. Education (ED)

v13a: (A)

v13b: (A); (E), p.89

v13c:
- v13c1: (A); (E), p.89
- v13c2: NA
- v13c3: (A); (E), p.89

v13d: (A)—data from the item of higher learning institutions in which the students graduated by various levels of school in Beijing for past 40 years were indicated

14. Social Factors (SF)

v14a: (E), p.89

v14b: (E), p.89

v14c: (A)

15. Natural Environment (NE)

v15a: (A); (E), p.74

v15b: NA

v15c: NA

v15d: NA

v15e: NA

v15f: NA

Sources of Data

(A) Data supplied by the Department of Statistics on National Economic Balances (DSNEB), State Statistical Bureau (SSB), the People's Republic of China (PRC).
(B) Statistical Bureau of Beijing Municipality ed. *Striving and Advancing Beijing—Economic and Social Development Statistics for Beijing's Past Forty Years*, Beijing: China's Statistical Publishing House (CSPH), 1989.
(C) ________ ed. *Yearbook of Beijing's Social and Economic Data*, Beijing: CSPH, various issues
(D) DSNEB, SSB, ed. *Compilation of National Income Statistical Data 1949–1985*, Beijing: CSPH, 1987.
(E) The Department of Synthesis, SSB, ed. *Compilation of Provinces, Autonomous Regions and Municipalities' Historical Statistical Data (1949–1989)*, Beijing: CSPH, 1990.

2

Tianjin

2. Tianjin

2–1

Year	v1a	v1a1	v1a2	v1a3	v1a4	v1a5	v1b	v1b1	v1b2	v1b3	v1b4	v1b5	v1c	v1d	v1d1
1949	10.56	1.39	7.29	0.19	0.47	1.22							6.93	3.63	0.94
1950	16.81	1.83	11.60	0.61	0.66	2.11	159.5	131.5	160.2	314.1	142.2	173.9	9.98	6.83	1.22
1951	24.32	2.43	17.32	0.86	0.75	2.96	138.7	134.1	143.5	140.9	113.2	129.9	13.84	10.48	1.62
1952	27.37	2.73	19.71	0.66	0.76	3.51	112.2	110.9	115.6	76.9	102.2	109.7	15.87	11.50	1.80
1953	37.31	2.47	26.21	1.32	1.01	6.30	135.1	92.1	133.7	206.9	139.1	165.3	20.55	16.76	1.69
1954	39.80	2.38	29.43	1.83	1.15	5.01	105.4	97.1	112.5	142.3	115.4	78.2	23.74	16.06	1.69
1955	39.39	3.00	30.09	1.00	1.16	4.14	100.8	125.6	104.9	55.9	102.1	82.6	23.33	16.06	2.25
1956	46.49	3.02	35.68	1.21	1.39	5.19	122.2	102.0	125.2	108.2	122.7	125.6	27.31	19.18	2.16
1957	53.32	3.23	40.44	1.68	1.66	6.31	112.0	105.1	109.2	164.1	126.1	119.3	30.32	23.00	2.40
1958	76.67	2.94	61.94	3.34	2.04	6.41	139.6	92.9	149.6	198.1	124.0	102.9	45.28	31.39	2.17
1959	101.54	3.39	85.15	3.85	2.62	6.53	128.9	115.7	134.8	107.6	128.0	101.8	61.98	39.56	2.63
1960	113.67	3.17	96.04	4.84	3.22	6.40	111.6	93.9	113.1	123.2	123.8	96.8	73.14	40.53	2.46
1961	64.14	2.95	51.54	1.66	2.18	5.81	53.4	91.7	49.6	33.9	67.6	82.5	38.61	25.53	2.35
1962	56.40	2.77	45.39	1.05	2.06	5.13	89.3	94.9	90.2	65.7	93.3	85.0	35.48	20.92	1.95
1963	61.21	2.98	48.95	1.72	1.91	5.65	108.6	103.1	108.1	166.3	92.8	109.5	37.12	24.09	2.10
1964	68.92	3.11	55.20	2.46	2.09	6.06	114.8	105.0	115.5	141.6	109.1	109.4	40.80	28.12	2.12
1965	81.79	4.82	66.35	1.63	2.50	6.49	122.0	155.0	123.2	69.9	119.6	112.6	47.79	34.00	3.64
1966	95.70	3.98	80.42	2.54	2.32	6.44	113.3	82.0	117.7	157.3	93.0	100.2	59.27	36.43	2.47
1967	82.50	4.59	68.27	1.60	2.00	6.04	87.3	113.6	85.6	62.8	87.1	94.1	52.22	30.28	3.19
1968	83.53	4.49	39.13	1.83	2.04	6.04	107.7	98.0	109.4	114.5	103.2	100.0	52.80	30.73	3.28
1969	103.92	3.99	88.47	2.54	2.57	6.35	125.1	88.9	130.0	139.2	125.6	104.5	64.78	39.14	3.03
1970	120.41	5.20	102.77	2.73	3.07	6.64	114.4	130.2	114.1	107.6	120.1	106.6	73.30	47.11	3.72
1971	130.79	5.42	111.57	3.51	3.74	6.55	110.0	102.8	110.5	126.4	121.7	98.7	79.53	51.26	3.81
1972	132.41	4.44	112.24	4.64	4.02	7.07	104.1	80.8	104.4	130.3	107.7	107.9	80.23	52.18	3.36
1973	147.33	4.43	123.50	6.20	4.83	8.37	111.9	105.8	110.6	131.1	120.0	117.8	91.59	55.74	3.81
1974	162.37	5.51	134.55	8.04	4.99	9.28	110.2	121.9	108.9	126.7	103.3	111.2	99.60	62.77	4.68
1975	175.62	5.39	145.57	10.57	5.15	8.94	108.2	98.7	108.4	128.9	103.3	96.4	110.49	65.13	4.25
1976	162.12	5.21	135.60	6.77	5.99	8.55	92.8	96.5	93.9	63.1	116.3	95.6	102.95	59.17	3.86
1977	167.56	4.23	138.12	9.06	6.69	9.46	103.3	81.8	102.1	131.8	111.6	110.5	106.04	61.52	3.36
1978	198.18	6.72	157.90	13.51	8.02	12.03	118.1	123.0	114.3	162.7	119.9	125.9	123.45	74.73	5.14
1979	224.06	8.88	175.52	17.08	9.38	13.20	110.8	116.8	109.6	118.9	117.1	108.5	139.43	84.63	6.23
1980	247.97	9.25	195.94	17.64	11.31	13.83	109.7	104.9	111.4	97.1	120.5	99.3	154.87	93.10	5.20
1981	259.59	9.34	205.87	18.45	11.93	15.00	105.4	89.9	106.6	98.3	105.5	106.9	163.59	96.00	4.37
1982	284.69	12.56	218.41	26.06	12.76	14.90	108.3	120.9	106.4	135.1	107.0	98.8	183.66	101.03	6.92
1983	311.48	12.67	235.33	29.43	15.26	18.79	109.7	101.3	108.5	109.5	119.6	125.5	203.11	108.37	7.20
1984	346.05	16.69	259.10	32.08	16.86	21.32	111.2	120.5	111.7	102.2	110.5	111.5	224.37	121.68	10.69
1985	426.82	20.44	319.47	37.53	20.74	28.64	115.5	119.4	115.7	105.8	123.0	118.1	275.91	150.91	12.07
1986	473.45	26.92	344.73	42.46	26.03	33.31	106.8	111.4	106.2	105.7	111.2	108.4	307.50	165.95	16.77
1987	552.91	32.93	405.49	46.81	27.76	39.92	110.4	111.7	111.4	102.1	103.6	112.1	367.25	185.66	19.33
1988	707.15	44.49	521.10	53.40	34.02	54.14	116.2	109.0	118.7	100.1	105.2	115.2	486.06	221.09	25.03
1989	828.38	51.82	634.24	58.57	37.42	46.33	107.5	114.0	109.1	97.9	98.8	97.9	593.97	234.41	28.48

2. Tianjin

Year	v1d2	v1d3	v1d4	v1d5	v1e	v1e1	v1e2	v1e3	v1e4	v1e5	v1f	v1f1	v1f2	v1f3	v1g
1949	1.34	0.05	0.33	0.97											
1950	3.29	0.17	0.48	1.67											
1951	5.70	0.25	0.55	2.36											
1952	6.09	0.19	0.57	2.85	108.80	109.40	108.50	78.50	103.30	111.90					7.90
1953	8.23	0.32	0.81	5.71	143.10	95.20	135.90	174.20	147.50	184.60					11.84
1954	8.69	0.43	0.88	4.37	94.30	100.20	105.90	138.20	111.30	75.20					13.24
1955	9.13	0.28	0.87	3.53	101.70	133.80	107.60	65.90	100.50	80.70					10.06
1956	11.05	0.31	1.03	4.63	122.10	97.20	127.90	97.40	121.40	131.60					9.08
1957	13.16	0.43	1.26	5.75	117.20	109.50	114.80	166.00	128.20	121.90					15.18
1958	21.58	0.88	1.45	5.31	131.40	92.40	160.10	202.70	116.40	93.70					19.18
1959	28.65	1.04	1.85	5.39	123.00	120.50	130.20	111.30	126.90	101.60					28.26
1960	29.16	1.21	2.26	5.44	102.20	93.70	102.10	113.70	123.60	99.50					23.58
1961	16.18	0.59	1.50	4.91	60.60	94.20	51.30	48.20	66.10	82.10					13.89
1962	13.81	0.40	1.41	3.35	82.30	84.00	87.40	69.90	92.40	65.80					11.47
1963	15.55	0.56	1.33	4.55	114.70	103.50	112.90	142.60	95.00	134.80					12.55
1964	19.25	0.81	1.45	4.49	117.80	101.70	126.60	143.70	108.50	100.70					16.78
1965	22.47	0.62	1.67	5.60	124.90	171.30	118.40	80.50	115.30	131.20					20.74
1966	26.31	0.69	1.74	5.22	103.70	67.60	115.10	111.70	104.10	94.10					22.81
1967	20.07	0.63	1.49	4.90	85.40	126.80	77.00	92.30	86.40	94.10					21.73
1968	20.43	0.60	1.53	4.89	106.40	103.00	109.70	94.60	104.50	100.00					21.48
1969	28.51	0.64	1.81	5.15	126.70	92.20	141.80	106.50	117.70	104.50					22.52
1970	35.24	0.71	2.28	5.16	119.00	122.10	121.60	110.60	126.40	102.30					24.98
1971	38.39	1.18	2.56	5.32	109.90	100.90	110.80	165.60	112.40	102.90					29.18
1972	38.81	1.57	2.69	5.75	104.00	86.50	104.70	130.30	105.00	108.20					30.42
1973	40.32	1.81	3.09	6.71	107.70	117.60	104.50	112.90	115.00	116.10					35.89
1974	45.20	2.34	3.25	7.30	112.50	120.30	112.00	127.20	105.10	109.30					42.26
1975	48.15	2.57	3.14	7.02	103.50	91.40	106.60	107.30	97.60	96.10					40.95
1976	43.45	1.70	3.22	6.94	91.30	90.70	91.00	65.20	101.50	98.90					39.14
1977	44.72	2.16	3.60	7.68	103.70	86.40	103.10	125.00	112.00	110.40					43.11
1978	52.86	3.23	4.09	9.41	120.50	125.20	118.30	164.10	113.40	121.50	82.65	5.03	57.53	20.09	49.39
1979	59.48	3.83	4.83	10.26	110.60	109.40	110.70	111.00	118.20	107.70	93.00	6.54	64.76	21.70	59.74
1980	66.25	4.90	5.73	11.02	109.00	83.50	111.30	120.50	118.60	101.90	103.52	6.53	72.43	24.56	64.34
1981	68.23	5.04	6.15	12.21	103.70	83.80	104.50	96.50	107.20	109.10	107.96	5.18	76.77	26.01	59.05
1982	68.58	7.09	6.24	12.20	103.80	132.40	100.90	134.60	101.60	99.40	114.10	7.00	79.59	27.51	69.49
1983	72.12	7.75	6.95	14.35	107.40	104.70	105.80	106.10	111.20	117.10	123.40	7.60	84.11	31.69	80.61
1984	79.65	8.47	7.62	15.25	111.90	124.40	113.50	102.50	109.80	104.30	147.47	11.13	95.97	40.37	90.89
1985	98.06	10.04	9.95	20.79	116.00	117.50	113.90	120.20	130.40	119.90	175.71	12.95	114.23	48.53	139.90
1986	104.16	11.01	11.95	22.06	105.06	115.60	104.50	111.28	106.64	98.91	194.67	16.51	122.49	55.67	159.32
1987	116.05	12.55	12.73	25.00	107.16	104.60	107.90	108.52	103.40	106.01	220.00	19.65	136.96	63.41	162.99
1988	138.59	14.08	14.27	29.12	105.53	104.40	108.30	98.51	96.75	99.02	259.64	26.21	159.58	73.85	227.78
1989	150.82	14.35	16.21	24.55	101.48	111.35	99.02	90.92	101.90	117.01	283.34	29.85	175.88	77.61	226.92

2. Tianjin

2–3

Year	v1h	v1i	v1j	v1j1	v1j2	v1j3	v1k	v2a	v2a1	v2a2	v2b	v2c	v2c1	v2c2	v2d1
1949															2.54
1950															3.87
1951															5.42
1952		2.56		573				0.97	0.70	0.27					5.90
1953		3.08		619				3.37	1.31	2.06					6.55
1954		3.41		645				5.03	1.72	3.31					7.31
1955		3.56		658				2.00	1.06	0.94					8.22
1956		4.36		717				-0.14	1.89	-2.03					9.30
1957		5.05		749				5.50	1.86	3.64					10.60
1958		6.02		689				8.28	5.26	3.02					13.08
1959		7.08		647				15.15	5.74	9.41					6.48
1960		7.80		672				8.93	6.43	2.50					21.22
1961		7.56		655				-0.56	1.48	-2.04					22.88
1962		7.11		685				-0.98	0.46	-1.44					24.84
1963		6.86		730				-1.22	1.15	-2.37					24.64
1964		7.20		763				2.52	1.98	0.54					25.91
1965		8.48	714	745	569			5.77	1.37	4.40					28.32
1966		8.29	690	718	565			6.78	1.76	5.02					32.47
1967		8.28	683	714	549			4.97	-0.13	5.10					26.02
1968		8.31	672	699	554			4.65	0.17	4.48					27.56
1969		8.39	661	685	556			4.63	1.54	3.09					34.33
1970		8.58	652	673	564			7.39	4.07	3.32					38.62
1971		9.05	631	663	508			11.45	4.56	6.89					45.03
1972		9.81	634	675	483			11.54	5.65	5.89					47.05
1973		9.98	629	669	490			15.58	9.07	6.51					53.14
1974		10.27	633	674	496			20.13	12.61	7.52					59.31
1975		10.66	618	663	481			17.21	12.41	4.80					65.62
1976		11.26	600	652	453			13.89	9.69	4.20					64.80
1977		11.81	596	644	464			15.75	11.39	4.36					68.84
1978	153	14.00	640	690	478			19.54	11.69	7.85		19.33	10.31	0.54	79.47
1979	178	16.34	732	781	565			26.04	16.68	9.36	23.55	23.55	11.18	0.76	86.83
1980	278	19.32	820	865	667		3.77	25.99	15.89	10.10	22.13	22.13	9.71	0.92	94.64
1981	298	19.93	805	845	674		4.64	16.28	16.22	0.06	23.72	23.72	6.45	1.37	103.83
1982	326	21.03	820	865	672		5.47	23.53	21.08	2.45	30.05	30.04	5.05	1.22	108.52
1983	412	22.90	868	916	721		6.12	29.21	25.54	3.67	33.47	33.47	5.35	1.11	115.06
1984	505	28.99	1071	1132	900		7.45	32.01	32.38	-0.37	37.89	37.90	7.55	1.31	136.56
1985	565	31.81	1165	1223	995	1272	9.24	70.27	49.22	21.05	54.16	54.16	11.41	1.42	159.35
1986	635	38.22	1380	1455	1149	1588	11.76	79.82	54.61	25.21	61.03	61.03	12.34	0.77	174.95
1987	749	42.86	1535	1622	1256	1786	14.07	70.40	59.33	11.07	61.32	61.32	15.65	1.38	196.14
1988	891	51.91	1859	1972	1475		19.34	112.20	66.77	45.43	66.11	66.11	19.84	1.20	223.16
1989	1020	64.00	2262	2274	1691		22.29	94.89	53.12	41.78	85.27	68.40	25.04	1.13	258.69

2. Tianjin

2–4

Year	v2d2	v2e	v3a	v3b	v3b1	v3b2	v3c	v3d	v3d1	v3d2	v3e	v3e1	v3e2	v3e3	v3e4
1949	1.81														
1950	2.58	0.26									145.20	92.28	7.44	3.24	15.36
1951	3.46	0.98									159.00	97.92	8.40	3.36	15.60
1952	3.58	1.97	6.93	6.09	1.20	4.89	0.84	142	58	222	176.16	105.00	9.60	3.36	16.08
1953	3.98	2.21	8.47	7.19	1.14	6.05	1.28	161	53	258	192.00	118.08	14.16	3.48	13.92
1954	4.45	2.53	8.21	7.15	1.13	6.02	1.06	153	52	239	196.80	121.92	15.48	3.60	13.32
1955	5.02	2.97	8.06	7.08	1.46	5.62	0.98	148	66	217	211.20	132.96	18.36	3.60	12.84
1956	6.06	4.07	9.22	7.98	1.43	6.55	1.24	162	63	246	199.20	123.84	16.20	3.72	12.96
1957	6.51	4.39	9.68	8.64	1.51	7.13	1.04	168	65	251	216.36	137.88	21.12	3.84	10.68
1958	8.46	6.44	10.90	9.49	1.65	7.84	1.41	177	71	259	217.08	138.00	21.00	4.08	10.68
1959	11.24	9.59	13.11	11.69	2.04	9.65	1.42	211	87	302	227.28	145.08	22.08	4.32	11.16
1960	15.35	14.56	14.65	13.26	2.30	10.96	1.39	232	97	327	235.44	143.04	27.24	4.56	9.36
1961	16.30	12.51	14.45	13.12	2.35	10.77	1.33	226	98	317	249.60	155.40	22.08	4.80	13.20
1962	17.45	11.09	12.45	11.03	1.92	9.11	1.42	188	76	272	237.84	144.24	21.12	5.04	12.84
1963	17.29	10.66	13.77	12.25	2.15	10.10	1.52	203	81	298	223.56	132.72	21.84	5.28	12.00
1964	18.04	10.74	14.26	12.64	2.21	10.43	1.62	204	81	301	228.24	136.20	23.04	5.52	11.40
1965	19.52	10.88	14.97	13.23	2.68	10.55	1.74	210	96	302	234.00	141.12	25.80	5.88	9.96
1966	22.16	13.65	16.03	14.48	2.74	11.74	1.55	228	95	338	232.80	132.84	30.00	5.88	12.36
1967	17.32	11.76	16.76	15.51	3.37	12.14	1.25	242	114	351	237.60	139.20	33.48	5.88	9.84
1968	18.03	13.71	16.83	15.74	3.48	12.26	1.09	242	115	353	239.28	140.76	33.84	5.88	9.96
1969	21.99	18.86	17.89	16.52	3.88	12.64	1.37	255	125	375	241.80	133.56	39.96	5.88	13.08
1970	24.46	23.31	17.59	16.12	4.44	11.68	1.47	250	137	365	254.76	144.60	39.60	5.88	12.48
1971	28.72	26.24	17.73	16.30	4.64	11.66	1.43	249	138	368	267.00	151.20	41.88	5.88	13.32
1972	29.85	26.17	18.88	17.35	4.43	12.92	1.53	261	130	398	279.36	163.20	35.76	6.00	13.20
1973	33.53	28.29	20.31	18.53	4.83	13.70	1.78	274	140	413	280.80	165.00	42.72	6.00	13.68
1974	37.29	30.08	22.13	20.14	5.56	14.58	1.99	295	159	437	286.80	170.52	46.08	6.00	10.08
1975	41.00	31.41	23.74	21.55	5.95	15.60	2.19	312	169	461	295.20	170.16	50.16	6.00	7.80
1976	39.97	30.77	25.25	22.65	6.11	16.54	2.60	322	171	478	307.20	177.36	49.92	6.00	9.12
1977	41.95	32.74	27.36	24.28	6.24	18.04	3.08	345	174	521	322.80	181.56	54.12	6.00	9.72
1978	47.87	38.24	29.85	26.19	6.73	19.46	3.68	368	187	553	344.88	200.40	53.52	6.00	9.60
1979	53.37	36.83	33.70	29.59	7.86	21.73	4.11	405	218	585	385.20	219.60	64.08	6.00	9.72
1980	58.87	37.06	38.35	34.21	9.37	24.84	4.14	460	262	644	474.72	260.76	86.04	6.00	11.04
1981	64.62	39.18	42.81	36.40	10.28	26.12	6.41	483	288	660	485.88	271.08	84.84	7.08	11.28
1982	66.51	41.68	45.96	39.46	12.08	27.38	6.50	515	334	677	496.56	290.28	79.68	8.16	11.04
1983	70.25	43.72	51.40	43.68	13.39	30.29	7.72	560	367	731	520.80	318.48	79.56	8.76	10.44
1984	87.68	49.26	58.88	49.14	16.30	32.84	9.74	622	445	776	599.64	365.40	91.32	9.24	11.64
1985	102.07	51.58	69.63	58.37	18.45	39.92	11.26	729	510	911	770.64	418.92	117.84	9.96	13.68
1986	111.83	61.81	79.50	66.05	20.04	46.01	13.45	816	552	1030	949.08	517.56	135.48	11.52	12.36
1987	126.57	69.58	92.59	74.40	22.07	52.33	18.19	907	596	1163	1071.12	577.92	154.92	12.24	10.32
1988	144.22	76.64	115.58	94.53	28.16	66.37	21.03	1135	753	1446	1278.84	665.76	192.96	12.00	9.96
1989	160.37	93.85	132.03	106.27	31.39	74.88	25.76	1258	840	1589	1291.00	756.00			

2. Tianjin

2–5

Year	v3f	v3f1	v3f2	v3f3	v3f4	v4a1	v4a1a	v4a1b	v4a1c	v4a1d	v4a2	v4a2a	v4a2b	v4a2c	v4a2d
1949	49.00	42.20	3.50	1.00	1.80	0.44		0.21			0.18		0.04	0.11	
1950	67.60	60.30	3.70	1.00	1.90	1.91					0.44	0.02	0.11	0.14	0.17
1951	74.30	65.30	4.20	1.20	2.10	3.24	0.26			0.09	0.73	0.24	0.12	0.17	0.20
1952	76.10	66.50	5.00	1.30	2.10	3.88	0.33	2.35		0.19	1.08	0.55	0.15	0.15	0.23
1953	84.20	72.90	5.90	1.30	2.10	5.82	0.43			0.16	1.19	0.50	0.24	0.20	0.25
1954	92.07	79.81	6.79	1.48	2.20	5.87	0.78			0.17	1.25	0.51	0.26	0.20	0.28
1955	78.20	65.50	6.00	1.50	2.30	6.10	1.06			0.19	1.40	0.48	0.26	0.21	0.45
1956	69.50	57.60	5.00	1.60	2.00	6.68	1.04			0.15	1.54	0.56	0.36	0.26	0.36
1957	83.70	71.47	5.07	0.98	1.96	7.99	1.57	5.19		0.13	1.63	0.66	0.42	0.24	0.31
1958	66.30	54.10	5.20	1.20	2.10	16.31	8.06			0.07	4.64	3.59	0.47	0.23	0.35
1959	87.40	73.30	5.70	1.50	2.70	22.38	12.82			0.07	7.20	3.53	0.87	0.48	2.32
1960	87.40	73.10	5.70	1.60	2.80	22.43	12.88			0.07	8.00	4.23	1.07	0.50	2.20
1961	72.40	57.90	5.70	1.90	2.70	11.88	6.45			0.10	2.65	0.49	0.68	0.38	1.10
1962	61.00	46.20	5.10	2.30	3.00	9.77	4.41			0.11	2.49	0.60	0.73	0.31	0.85
1963	82.90	65.50	6.30	2.90	3.50	10.06	4.67			0.09	3.27	0.74	0.65	0.25	1.63
1964	78.80	58.20	7.50	3.70	4.20	12.82	6.71			0.07	3.46	1.05	0.75	0.26	1.40
1965	70.60	42.90	10.60	5.30	5.80	13.33	7.25	4.93		0.08	3.50	0.81	0.68	0.29	1.72
1966	108.00	79.10	11.00	5.80	6.90	15.91	9.30			0.04	3.25	0.75	0.69	0.25	1.56
1967	134.00	106.50	10.50	6.20	6.10	12.64	5.66			0.03	2.62	0.48	0.71	0.24	1.19
1968	110.80	79.60	12.50	6.50	6.70	12.75	5.34			0.05	2.25	0.50	0.65	0.24	0.86
1969	81.70	50.10	13.10	6.80	7.10	19.52	10.08			0.05	3.82	1.42	0.69	0.34	1.37
1970	130.30	95.70	14.50	7.10	7.40	28.02	14.68			0.07	6.40	3.76	0.81	0.31	1.52
1971	144.90	106.50	16.10	7.80	7.90	32.35	18.79			0.06	6.63	3.38	0.89	0.43	1.93
1972	122.90	84.00	17.20	8.10	8.00	31.22	17.97			0.10	7.56	3.98	0.99	0.40	2.19
1973	125.80	83.20	18.90	9.20	8.50	34.67	20.34			0.07	8.13	3.84	1.19	0.42	2.68
1974	127.70	82.30	19.10	11.10	8.90	36.98	21.08			0.07	9.70	4.21	1.40	0.54	3.55
1975	124.10	77.50	19.20	12.20	9.10	39.17	22.01			0.05	10.61	4.74	1.43	0.54	3.90
1976	94.00	44.70	19.90	14.10	10.00	33.30	17.37			0.04	11.09	4.72	1.47	0.54	4.36
1977	113.90	58.80	21.00	16.00	12.00	33.27	16.75			0.04	13.40	6.19	1.51	0.56	5.13
1978	131.75	79.32	19.52	8.40	6.02	39.25	19.47	14.32		1.41	14.51	6.00	1.76	0.59	6.16
1979	135.17	87.37	19.04	6.15	5.81	37.64	17.36			1.06	15.10	6.83	2.06	0.66	5.65
1980	208.37	118.63	31.39	16.46	14.06	40.94	19.22	17.34		1.04	14.67	4.58	2.39	0.67	7.03
1981	249.17	126.42	37.49	41.44	10.07	40.20	17.98			0.18	14.44	4.96	2.63	0.67	6.18
1982	266.65	135.20	36.40	44.16	10.47	38.71	16.72			-0.96	21.38	11.06	2.97	0.84	6.51
1983	336.49	164.05	42.39	60.39	12.86	38.74	13.39			0.86	20.49	9.97	3.36	0.97	6.19
1984	371.79	183.22	40.61	72.30	14.14	40.46	11.27			1.23	18.79	7.94	3.82	1.24	5.79
1985	426.10	201.99	48.53	71.11	18.49	48.21	10.27	26.50		2.56	26.97	11.27	4.83	1.22	9.65
1986	480.32	235.49	50.55	97.23	17.91	54.50	12.27	29.67		2.83	34.85	7.39	6.09	1.42	19.95
1987	538.89	267.65	51.19	112.31	18.66	55.87	11.01	31.42		2.62	31.16	5.20	6.15	1.55	18.26
1988	713.86	326.87	72.66	154.53	21.05	44.48	-6.67			5.29	34.67	4.42	7.47	1.27	21.51
1989	781.37	369.54	65.98	161.11	20.94	46.49	-12.48			8.26	39.26	4.89	8.75	1.52	24.10

2. Tianjin

2–6

Year	v4b	v4b1	v4b2	v4b3	v4c1	v4c2	v5a	v5a1	v5a2	v5a3	v5a4	v5b1	v5b2	v5b3	v5c
1949	0.0053				0.16		135	27	1	18	83				
1950	0.1022				0.90	31.7	137	34	1	19	84				
1951	0.2988				1.64	36.9	151	44	1	21	85				
1952	0.4968				3.16	56.9	160	44	1	20	89				
1953	0.6740				3.77	60.9	159	48	2	20	89				
1954	0.7525				4.41	63.2	165	51	3	22	89				
1955	0.7849				4.96	62.1	169	51	4	22	92				
1956	0.8833				6.39	63.1	181	64	13	6	98				
1957	1.0450				7.93	72.8	187	68	18	6	95				
1958	1.3022				17.33	116.3	209	106	7	3	93				
1959	1.6491				21.81	104.7	209	113	10	1	85				
1960	1.5628				21.97	73.5	222	119	16	1	86				
1961	1.0688				9.93	34.5	212	111	11	1	89				
1962	0.9296				8.36	29.3	204	97	9	2	96				
1963	1.0552				10.02	35.8	205	93	15	1	96				
1964	1.3790				12.96	45.0	221	96	21		104				
1965	1.5672				15.19	50.0	228	99	22		107				
1966	1.6143				18.59	51.9	227	97	23		107				
1967	1.6349				13.12	45.1	237	100	23		114				
1968	1.6270				13.21	41.6	241	102	23		116				
1969	1.4589				19.59	48.0	250	104	24		122				
1970	1.5921				24.52	51.3	270	110	26		134				
1971	1.8398				26.41	48.1	277	118	33		126				
1972	2.1684				26.07	46.5	288	125	34		129				
1973	2.3310				26.80	43.4	294	124	36		134				
1974	2.6096				28.81	42.8	296	126	38		132				
1975	2.8816				30.64	42.3	329	134	47		147				
1976	3.0457				27.41	38.7	344	145	50		149				
1977	3.4648				26.99	36.1	352	149	55		148				
1978	4.0218				33.31	37.3	356	157	49		149				
1979	5.7718				35.75	39.6	375	172	52		150				
1980	7.9625				38.16	39.9	388	181	55	1	151				
1981	9.7023				41.40	39.9	407	188	60	1	158				
1982	12.4989				39.77	36.8	421	199	62	2	158				
1983	16.6733				40.69	35.7	436	201	67	2	166				
1984	22.1940				44.36	32.4	448	201	72	3	171				
1985	29.3771	23.7691	7.0250		53.54	35.5	456	205	70	5	175				
1986	40.5171	32.4803	9.5811		52.29	30.6	467	210	68	4	182				
1987	54.9453	43.8135	10.6140		55.63	28.4	471	212	67	5	184				
1988	62.6454				55.12	25.0	465	214	64	5	179				
1989	89.4000	72.2000	17.2000		46.15	18.2	460	217	63	5	171				

2. Tianjin

2–7

Year	v5c1	v5d	v6a	v6a1	v6a2	v6b	v6c	v6d1	v6d2	v6d3	v6d4	v6d5	v6d6
1949			403	195.84	206.70	19.11	10.19	196	207	213	190	243.15	
1950			407	199.70	207.44	34.63	11.99	200	207	213	194		
1951			424	215.51	208.69	34.90	12.52	215	209	225	199		
1952			439	225.41	213.81	32.76	10.74	225	214	233	206	274.35	
1953			462	243.01	219.20	34.56	10.18	243	219	245	217		
1954			478	260.63	217.00	37.25	9.26	261	217	252	226		
1955			487	258.79	228.00	37.12	9.85	259	228	254	233		
1956			507	273.73	233.17	34.39	8.79	274	233	262	245		
1957			530	294.27	236.00	37.28	9.35	294	236	273	257	302.40	
1958			548	310.62	237.00	34.56	8.66	311	237	283	265	311.61	
1959			568	328.95	238.57	28.49	9.88	329	239	295	273		
1960			584	341.34	242.19	27.38	10.34	342	242	302	282		
1961			584	337.01	247.22	20.42	9.89	337	247	299	285	403.36	
1962			596	333.12	262.51	33.68	7.36	333	263	303	293	406.78	
1963			615	342.73	272.60	40.61	7.30	343	272	315	300	421.39	
1964			630	349.64	279.88	28.72	7.79	350	280	323	307	430.68	
1965			638	350.19	287.61	24.33	6.17	350	288	326	312	434.71	
1966			641	344.36	296.49	21.02	6.91	344	297	327	314		
1967			650	347.35	303.00	18.05	5.93	347	303	332	318		
1968			655	344.94	310.09	23.16	6.28	345	310	333	322		
1969			651	329.53	321.22	21.24	6.51	330	321	330	321		
1970			653	313.27	340.00	22.10	6.25	313	340	331	322	423.04	
1971			663	319.90	343.50	19.67	5.90	320	343	336	327		
1972			675	328.99	345.66	19.06	6.51	329	346	342	333		
1973			683	332.76	350.55	16.48	5.82	333	350	347	336		
1974			692	335.59	356.88	13.99	6.22	335	357	352	340		
1975			703	344.02	358.83	13.89	6.59	344	359	358	345	453.33	
1976			707	345.53	360.96	12.79	10.03	346	361	360	347		
1977			713	347.19	365.68	13.18	6.36	347	366	363	350		
1978			724	358.45	365.82	15.47	6.26	358	366	368	356	469.53	
1979			739	380.57	358.85	14.57	5.94	380	359	375	364		
1980			749	392.62	356.29	13.30	6.05	393	356	380	369	492.44	
1981			760	400.75	359.00	17.90	5.99	401	359	385	375		
1982			775	410.70	364.21	20.07	5.64	411	364	393	382		
1983			785	419.00	365.72	17.16	5.41	419	366	398	387		
1984			796	437.09	359.00	15.69	5.44	437	359	404	392		
1985			805	445.69	359.11	13.98	5.80	446	359	409	396	535.78	
1986			815	447.05	367.92	15.02	5.72	447	368	415	400	543.78	
1987			829	454.68	374.05	17.07	6.08	455	374	422	407	552.22	
1988			839	467.38	371.83	15.92	5.65	467	372	427	412	562.17	
1989			856	476.00	385.00	15.48	6.47	476	376	433	419	569.77	

2. Tianjin

2–8

Year	v7a	v7b	v7c	v7d	v7e	v7f	v7g	v7h	v7h1	v7h2	v7h3	v7h4	v7h5	v7i	v8a
1949			72.3	833.80	484.7	0.01	0.04	1.39	0.99	0.05	0.10	0.06	0.19	12.84	7.29
1950			74.9	852.40		0.23	0.05	1.83	1.37	0.04	0.12	0.09	0.21	12.63	11.60
1951			81.0	891.20		0.26	0.08	2.43	1.91	0.06	0.13	0.13	0.21	13.17	17.32
1952			102.9	1017.60	65.6	0.36	0.08	2.73	2.21	0.04	0.14	0.12	0.22	15.00	19.71
1953		0.5	109.5	980.20		0.57	0.07	2.48	1.86	0.09	0.15	0.12	0.26	16.16	26.21
1954		1.9	114.8	969.50		0.80	0.07	2.38	1.67	0.05	0.16	0.19	0.31	17.24	29.43
1955		5.8	122.1	939.90		1.30	0.08	3.00	2.25	0.07	0.17	0.20	0.30	16.23	30.09
1956		31.4	178.9	941.10		1.47	0.15	3.01	2.24	0.07	0.17	0.25	0.29	15.96	35.68
1957		74.4	214.9	915.60	71.2	1.96	0.22	3.23	2.54	0.09	0.17	0.18	0.26	15.62	40.44
1958		119.9	270.4	890.30		2.55	0.24	2.94	2.13	0.12	0.17	0.21	0.31	13.72	61.94
1959		109.0	281.3	829.40		2.27	0.36	3.40	2.45	0.12	0.18	0.27	0.38	13.33	85.15
1960		135.8	297.9	805.40		2.72	0.69	3.17	2.21	0.10	0.17	0.29	0.40	10.89	96.04
1961		184.2	231.9	817.30		2.36	0.99	2.95	2.20	0.08	0.19	0.24	0.25	10.77	51.54
1962		192.6	255.8	824.70	273.0	2.49	1.29	2.78	2.08	0.10	0.17	0.24	0.19	11.02	45.39
1963		152.3	259.6	826.40		3.42	1.21	2.98	2.42	0.05	0.22	0.15	0.15	11.41	48.95
1964		160.6	299.1	813.30		3.81	1.55	3.11	2.32	0.07	0.18	0.17	0.38	11.58	55.20
1965		305.0	329.7	911.90	73.7	5.32	1.67	4.82	3.90	0.09	0.36	0.24	0.23	12.50	66.35
1966		275.1	312.1	999.90		6.27	1.94	3.98	3.03	0.12	0.30	0.13	0.40	14.11	80.42
1967		249.6	307.9	992.70		7.31	1.85	4.59	3.57	0.10	0.35	0.11	0.46	14.77	68.27
1968		259.8	353.5	954.90		8.56	2.10	4.49	3.47	0.09	0.34	0.14	0.46	15.30	69.13
1969		249.8	336.5	1000.90		11.72	2.81	3.99	2.98	0.09	0.27	0.14	0.51	15.58	88.47
1970		317.0	391.0	1005.60	66.5	12.05	2.98	5.20	4.06	0.11	0.42	0.13	0.48	16.50	102.77
1971		364.3	416.9	979.70		13.54	3.45	5.41	3.79	0.07	0.85	0.11	0.59	17.43	111.57
1972		305.2	416.6	958.10		12.32	3.68	4.44	2.73	0.05	0.68	0.14	0.84	17.72	112.24
1973		366.3	432.8	1031.70		15.26	3.41	4.43	3.30	0.05	0.62	0.15	0.31	18.37	123.50
1974		466.4	474.6	1062.20		13.81	3.37	5.52	4.50	0.06	0.64	0.16	0.15	19.03	134.55
1975		521.0	512.1	1072.50	81.6	12.18	3.73	5.39	4.27	0.05	0.83	0.20	0.04	19.91	145.57
1976		558.6	512.8	1077.70		16.20	4.04	5.21	4.04	0.04	0.91	0.19	0.03	19.65	125.60
1977		581.3	520.3	1056.90		18.14	5.21	4.23	3.26	0.04	0.71	0.19	0.04	19.41	138.12
1978	17.7	602.0	556.3	1050.70		29.03	5.31	6.72	5.25	0.04	1.05	0.22	0.15	19.03	157.90
1979		606.3	571.4	1032.03		32.86	6.11	8.88	6.91	0.04	1.48	0.26	0.19	18.77	175.52
1980	22.0	585.8	568.9	1003.50	115.7	27.62	6.73	9.25	6.83	0.05	1.63	0.33	0.42	17.90	195.94
1981		578.4	569.3	955.54		26.27	6.74	8.34	5.71	0.05	1.95	0.23	0.40	16.74	205.87
1982		570.4	556.1	914.89	107.0	26.53	6.88	12.56	9.05	0.11	1.90	0.37	1.12	16.31	218.41
1983		503.6	548.7	911.47	227.0	28.77	8.20	12.68	8.57	0.16	2.47	0.47	1.01	17.40	235.33
1984		510.7	541.4	935.16	233.0	25.56	9.68	16.68	11.42	0.25	3.70	0.56	0.75	19.06	239.10
1985	33.1	480.4	524.2	894.24	123.3	27.12	10.31	20.44	12.75	0.27	5.10	1.25	1.06	20.20	319.47
1986		532.7	510.9	873.20	96.3	27.56	11.29	26.93	17.14	0.31	5.67	2.14	1.65	21.27	344.73
1987		567.9	511.3	860.40	127.2	28.04	11.58	32.93	20.24	0.37	7.22	2.87	2.23	22.56	405.49
1988	41.8	592.9	513.9	864.75	214.4	34.18	13.21	44.11	26.47	0.34	10.09	4.29	2.92	22.81	521.10
1989	42.9	595.5	513.3	859.50	16.0	40.00	15.43	51.82	31.45	0.33	12.83	3.26	3.95	24.60	635.22

2. Tianjin

2–9

Year	v8a1	v8a2	v8a3	v8b	v8c1	v8c2	v8d	v8f1	v8f2	v8f3	v8f4	v8f5	v8g
1949	2.88	0.11	4.30	2.67	0.91	6.39	0.49	0.57			2.63		4708
1950	5.00	0.18	6.41	4.88	1.61	9.99	1.39	1.62			2.98		6358
1951	7.43	0.23	9.66	7.47	2.52	14.79	2.46	4.36			3.60		9190
1952	10.79	0.40	8.52	10.61	3.34	16.36	3.27	6.98			3.92		8100
1953	13.21	0.60	12.40	12.99	5.59	20.61	4.07	8.75			4.52		8459
1954	18.22	0.94	10.27	18.85	3.36	23.07	5.54	9.65			5.50		8918
1955	21.26	1.21	7.62	21.66	6.78	23.31	6.54	13.47			5.86		7250
1956	32.05	3.51	0.12	31.97	9.23	26.46	9.88	18.71			6.91		2710
1957	35.78	4.43	0.22	33.75	11.43	29.00	10.97	21.29			7.40		2507
1958	60.99	0.75	0.20	60.94	24.43	37.50	21.21	23.12			9.08	0.31	2376
1959	82.28	2.71	0.16	82.00	34.76	50.39	27.55	26.38			10.57	1.90	2169
1960	89.56	6.38	0.09	87.35	44.27	51.76	26.46	40.10			11.38	7.21	2213
1961	47.54	3.91	0.09	47.41	20.52	31.02	14.84	21.70		0.03	2.83	3.47	1968
1962	41.41	3.89	0.09	40.50	16.27	29.12	12.27	15.33		0.01	8.68	1.59	2018
1963	44.09	4.74	0.11	44.55	18.32	30.62	14.12	17.47			8.91	1.42	1976
1964	49.58	5.60	0.03	50.00	21.83	33.38	17.40	27.20			9.86	5.09	1881
1965	59.79	6.53	0.03	58.77	27.27	39.08	19.63	36.87		1.34	11.52	9.63	1969
1966	72.36	8.04	0.02	72.31	34.88	45.53	23.64	45.72		11.47	12.65	12.30	2214
1967	60.23	8.04		60.51	27.82	40.45	17.73	32.16		17.67	13.03	11.20	2308
1968	61.10	8.03		61.14	28.86	40.27	17.98	33.70		36.34	13.10	10.00	2284
1969	77.98	10.49		77.70	38.15	50.32	24.94	38.47		49.67	18.44	14.70	2220
1970	89.73	13.04		84.53	47.94	54.83	28.91	48.62		101.93	21.09	21.70	2806
1971	96.23	15.34	0.01	95.76	56.45	55.13	32.84	66.55		170.24	28.23	23.90	3216
1972	93.75	18.49		95.37	54.69	57.55	32.81	79.66		220.05	29.27	25.97	3249
1973	102.33	21.17	-0.01	103.67	60.95	62.55	33.59	87.85		320.18	31.66	24.77	3463
1974	110.21	24.34		111.29	66.57	67.98	37.06	86.73		400.21	37.26	28.08	3641
1975	118.54	27.03	-0.01	116.92	71.10	74.46	38.23	96.69		456.02	44.99	29.11	3764
1976	109.29	26.31	-10.00	110.32	65.51	70.09	34.86	71.41		370.91	47.45	26.04	3718
1977	109.92	28.20		119.39	67.54	70.58	38.08	77.76		325.67	47.28	33.33	3906
1978	127.49	30.41	0.01	127.15	76.42	81.48	42.09	101.75		316.90	51.68	47.34	3981
1979	141.43	34.07	0.02	138.14	85.79	89.72	46.14	109.53		307.30	52.56	56.52	4001
1980	156.11	39.44	0.39	153.00	89.94	106.00	50.71	124.94		307.41	63.20	62.55	4171
1981	161.96	42.84	1.06	158.52	83.95	121.91	52.48	125.15		303.84	72.96	75.71	4333
1982	170.49	46.46	1.45	166.06	94.54	123.87	51.70	124.56		302.24	75.01	81.80	4411
1983	182.47	50.90	1.96	177.15	107.50	121.83	52.94	133.86		310.41	77.34	82.68	4422
1984	195.34	60.50	-16.74	193.29	120.74	138.36	58.91	132.50		320.81	79.57	90.52	4649
1985	230.34	83.89	5.23	229.92	155.25	164.22	70.85	111.93		374.63	80.65	105.11	5278
1986	243.52	92.77	8.44	244.84	169.89	174.84	73.05	150.32		413.33	78.38	112.41	5831
1987	273.06	119.98	12.45	275.27	199.98	205.51	79.44	162.96		453.01	81.09	120.19	5852
1988	320.06	179.73	21.31	330.74	253.62	267.48	89.60	156.44		462.79	91.07	129.37	6154
1989	386.40	219.13	29.69	373.78	298.96	336.26	92.95	151.57		470.43	96.60	127.84	6495

2. Tianjin

2–10

Year	v8g1	v9a	v9a1	v9a2	v9a3	v9b	v9b1	v9b2	v9b3	v9c	v10a	v10a1	v10b1	v10b2	v10b3
1949	106			0.14				0.47		762					
1950	166			0.11				0.62		863	4.46	4.37			
1951	229			0.18				0.73		1043	6.73	6.62			
1952	181			0.19				0.70		894	7.38	7.19			
1953	211			0.24				1.12	0.14	970	9.49	9.28			
1954	250			0.36				1.08	0.23	878	9.10	8.85			
1955	219			0.38				1.18	0.24	823	8.72	8.46			
1956	258			0.52				1.18	0.26	953	10.22	9.86			
1957	252			0.59				1.57	0.24	935	10.87	10.55			
1958	1424			0.86				2.56	0.24	1154	12.49	11.85			
1959	1222			0.84				3.38	0.23	1429	14.22	13.47			
1960	1137			0.91				4.42	0.39	1557	15.30	14.48			
1961	980			0.71				2.56	0.28	1528	14.41	13.71			
1962	902			0.83				2.40	0.26	1436	12.93	12.31			
1963	853			0.86				2.11	0.28	1482	12.68	12.05			
1964	877			0.92				2.22	0.39	1523	13.15	12.51			
1965	973			1.01				2.33	0.35	1621	13.08	12.32			
1966	999			0.99				2.47	0.28	1617	13.32	12.42			
1967	1018			0.99				2.42	0.15	1536	13.98	13.19			
1968	1026			1.02				2.81	0.11	1487	13.89	13.01			
1969	1043			1.29				3.37	0.17	1598	15.35	14.30			
1970	1145			1.10				4.02	0.26	1660	15.93	14.57			
1971	1201			1.18				4.34	0.26	1660	16.50	15.10			
1972	1219			1.41				4.79	0.24	1751	17.88	16.27			
1973	1208			1.40				5.27	0.25	1889	19.42	17.55			
1974	1202			1.62				5.71	0.27	2275	21.16	19.14			
1975	1194			1.85				5.90	0.27	2385	23.60	21.18	16.83		
1976	1202			1.81				6.06	0.22	2565	25.13	22.41	17.83		
1977	1209			2.13				7.29	0.27	2651	26.36	23.62	18.68		
1978	1224			2.43				8.42	0.32	2710	28.30	25.10	20.51	6.59	1.19
1979	1179			2.65				13.79	0.31	2901	32.12	29.08	23.48		
1980	1062	33.17	30.28	2.89		161.11	143.27	17.70	0.14	3163	37.50	34.64	26.13	7.48	3.36
1981	1049	36.84	33.63	3.21		165.14	143.87	21.17	0.10	3441	41.02	38.04	27.42	7.88	4.84
1982	1049	38.93	35.45	3.48		173.91	149.18	24.61	0.12	3642	43.02	39.76	29.19	6.26	6.43
1983	1040	43.52	39.51	4.01		187.35	160.59	26.60	0.16	3890	48.18	44.63	31.42	6.83	7.52
1984	1004	50.65	46.15	4.50		198.73	169.24	29.26	0.23	4478	56.62	52.17	36.52	7.41	9.45
1985	1059	56.90	52.34	4.56		223.86	189.98	33.80	0.08	5290	68.95	64.12	40.26	10.75	11.02
1986	1041	60.25	55.58	4.67		238.03	203.84	34.15	0.04	6158	87.19	81.39	43.80	11.35	17.66
1987	1083	64.08	59.60	4.48		257.38	222.13	35.23	0.02	7244	102.53	95.57	50.31	11.98	20.97
1988	1083	71.69	67.45	4.24		273.92	229.99	43.91	0.02	10061	129.93	121.28	60.59		
1989	1091	65.43	62.14	3.29		277.27	234.98	46.40	0.03	12635	144.53	134.30	62.56	14.53	30.57

2. Tianjin

Year	v10b4	v10b5	v10b6	v10d	v11a1	v11a2	v11a3	v11b	v11b1	v11b2	v11c	v11d	v12a	v12b	v12c
1949															
1950															
1951													114.6	114.5	
1952													101.8	101.6	
1953													108.5	107.8	
1954													101.8	101.7	
1955													100.1	100.0	
1956													99.8	99.8	
1957													101.8	101.8	
1958													98.6	98.9	
1959													100.0	99.9	
1960													101.3	101.3	
1961													112.3	111.5	
1962													100.1	100.2	
1963													97.0	97.4	
1964								3.0682	3.0231	0.0451			95.1	95.3	
1965								3.5351	3.4118	0.1233			96.4	96.5	
1966								3.9368	3.7247	0.2121			99.3	99.2	
1967								3.5891	3.2949	0.2942			99.4	99.4	
1968								3.4874	3.2992	0.1882			99.9	99.9	
1969								3.4008	3.2248	0.1760			100.6	100.6	
1970								3.5845	3.1892	0.3953			99.1	99.1	
1971								4.1700	3.7296	0.4404			99.9	99.8	
1972								4.9365	4.5192	0.4173			100.0	100.0	
1973								7.6544	7.0584	0.5960			100.4	100.4	
1974								8.6022	7.7581	0.8441			99.7	99.7	
1975		0.01	0.03					8.8638	7.7195	1.1443			100.1	100.1	
1976			0.01					8.0082	6.8830	1.1252			100.0	100.0	100.7
1977			0.04					7.8369	6.9143	0.9226			100.3	100.3	100.0
1978			0.01	3.13				9.8838	8.6474	1.2364			100.0	100.0	102.6
1979			0.17	4.08				13.8321	12.2081	1.6240			101.1	101.0	122.5
1980		0.03	0.50	4.77				18.2700	15.4222	2.8478			105.5	105.1	105.4
1981		0.16	0.72	5.32				16.8330	15.3670	1.4660			101.5	101.3	105.7
1982		0.42	0.72	5.64				15.3729	14.2411	1.1318			100.5	100.5	97.7
1983		1.35	1.06	6.54				15.7817	14.2734	1.5083			100.5	100.5	104.4
1984		1.99	1.25	8.29				14.6749	12.3365	2.3384			101.8	101.8	101.1
1985		4.89	2.07	12.17				14.8924	11.5274	3.3650	1.5618	0.6059	113.9	113.1	115.4
1986		11.73	2.64	16.13				16.6405	12.5494	4.0911	2.9612	1.5328	107.2	106.8	116.5
1987	0.24	15.86	3.42	18.38				20.1281	15.1712	4.9569	1.0283	2.8984	106.9	106.8	108.5
1988	0.72	21.62	4.69	25.85				22.7846	16.8268	5.9578	3.0976	3.4401	117.7	116.9	119.2
1989	0.89	28.70	7.28	27.73				22.1421	16.8200	5.3200	2.4517	1.6800	115.1	114.7	108.7

2. Tianjin

2–12

Year	v13a	v13b	v13c1	v13c2	v13c3	v13d	v14a	v14b	v14c	v15a	v15b	v15c	v15d	v15e	v15f
1949	29.4			2.9534	28.8323		2155	5227		791	3.03				
1950				2.8535	32.3449		2481	5994		805					
1951				3.9764	41.1159		2840	6756		834					
1952	10.0		1.0000	5.7510	50.6436		3751	8481	0.49	839	6.23				
1953				7.6149	51.2636		4316	9386	0.40	850					
1954				10.1704	54.1759		5148	10547	0.42	853					
1955				12.6566	56.1189		5481	12019	0.46	835					
1956				15.3982	61.3896		7790	13142	0.78	812					
1957	18.6			17.3052	65.0677		8568	15124	0.72	817	16.62				
1958				18.0355	72.6509		12323	15966	1.17	762					
1959				18.6798	80.3510		12003	17910	1.44	690					
1960				18.5879	83.5015		12150	20289	1.45	672					
1961				17.6000	84.3233		12037	22039	0.90	655					
1962	20.0			18.2505	85.0231		12927	23858	0.94	682	20.85				
1963				19.9799	90.1412		13719	24714	1.01	697					
1964				25.2771	104.2894		13671	25929	1.01	706					
1965	12.0		3.0000	32.1219	113.1800		14417	26393	1.24	726	15.08				
1966				32.0411	112.4046		14480	24156	1.43	750					
1967				30.4866	111.4492		14557	26055	1.34	769					
1968				34.9081	115.4851		12681	26996	1.61	772					
1969				35.2342	117.0808		11928	23666	1.56	775					
1970	9.2			36.4491	111.6877		11615	23591	1.27	772	21.54				
1971				40.3750	114.1709		12183	25546	1.76	755					
1972				51.7881	111.4162		12634	26839	1.66	747					
1973				59.6405	103.6640		14188	30211	1.62	739					
1974			1.4159	65.6139	99.8505	0.0947	15034	31367	1.84	732					
1975	8.6			76.3445	91.8403		17733	33734	2.17	728	35.08				
1976	8.4		1.7054	82.6570	83.1677	0.3878	18316	35325	1.86	724					
1977	7.2		1.6320	84.1032	79.5820	0.5614	18303	37837	2.18	714					
1978	7.1	97.2	2.3235	81.3074	78.6752	0.5782	18974	40653	2.05	704					
1979	8.0		2.8197	69.5540	80.1476	0.0165	19937	46099	2.28	703					
1980	9.4	96.8	3.0238	57.1224	78.9213	0.5345	20911	50662	2.88	696	40.26				
1981	10.2	98.2	3.6975	48.3709	75.6339	0.0618	21987	54535	4.23	694					
1982	7.8	99.0	3.4622	45.0011	72.7890	1.0274	23332	56152	5.13	692					
1983	9.0	99.0	3.4000	41.7574	72.1875	1.2307	24351	58645	5.18	688					
1984	11.0	99.4	3.9597	40.7887	73.6939	0.7096	25611	59405	7.48	681					
1985	9.9	99.3	4.5328	43.2879	73.2696	0.9137	27402	60412	8.47	671	54.31				
1986	9.8	99.8	4.8442	45.2023	73.0579	1.0630	29218	62897	7.76	662	55.31				
1987	10.8	99.7	5.0657	45.8612	73.3180	1.2493	30786	63067	8.36	658	57.77				
1988	12.0	99.6	5.3071	44.3180	75.7081	1.3374	33245	63924	6.70	650	60.88				
1989		99.7	5.2800	37.5800	81.1000	1.4400	32000	66000	5.19	648					

Notes

1. National Output and Income (Y)

v1a: (E), p.96
  v1a1: (E), p.96
  v1a2: (E), p.96
  v1a3: (E), p.96
  v1a4: (E), p.96
  v1a5: (E), p.96

v1b: (A); (D), p.106
  v1b1: (A); (D), p.106
  v1b2: (A); (D), p.106
  v1b3: (A); (D), p.106
  v1b4: (A); (D), p.106
  v1b5: (A); (D), p.106

v1c: v1a – v1d

v1d: (E), p.93
  v1d1: (E), p.93
  v1d2: (E), p.93
  v1d3: (E), p.93
  v1d4: (E), p.93
  v1d5: (E), p.93

v1e: (A); (D), p.109
  v1e1: (A); (D), p.109
  v1e2: (A); (D), p.109
  v1e3: (A); (D), p.109
  v1e4: (A); (D), p.109
  v1e5: (A); (D), p.109

v1f: (E), p.92
  v1f1: (E), p.92
  v1f2: (E), p.92
  v1f3: (E), p.92

v1g: v2a + v3a

v1h: (E), p.121

v1i: (A); (E), p.120

v1j: (A); (E), p.120
  v1j1: (E), p.120
  v1j2: (E), p.120
  v1j3: (C), 1988, p.245—various kinds of jointly-owned units

v1k: (E), p.120

2. Investment (I)

v2a: (E), p.95
  v2a1: (A); (D), p.114
  v2a2: (A); (D), p.114

v2b: (A)

v2c: (E), p.111
  v2c1: (E), p.112
  v2c2: (E), p.112

v2d:
  v2d1: (E), p.109
  v2d2: (E), p.109

v2e: (E), p.109

3. Consumption (C)

v3a: (E), p.95

v3b: (E), p.95
  v3b1: (A); (D), p.110
  v3b2: (A); (D), p.110

v3c: (E), p.95

v3d: (E), p.119
  v3d1: (E), p.119
  v3d2: (E), p.119

v3e: (A); (E), p.121
  v3e1: (A); (E), p.121
  v3e2: (A)
  v3e3: (A)
  v3e4: (A)

v3f: (A); (E), p.121

v3f1: (A); (E), p.121
v3f2: (A)
v3f3: (A)
v3f4: (A)

4. Public Finance and Banking (FB)

v4a:
v4a1: (E), p.117—local government budgetary revenue
v4a1a: (E), p.117—local government budgetary revenue
v4a1b: (C), 1986, p.672; 1988, p.237
v4a1c: NA
v4a1d: v4a1 – v4a1a – v4a1b' (v4a1b':total tax revenues which come from (E), p.117)
v4a2: (E), p.117—local government budgetary expenditure
v4a2a: (E), p.117—(ditto)
v4a2b: (E), p.117—(ditto)
v4a2c: (E), p.117—(ditto)
v4a2d: v4a2 – v4a2a – v4a2b – v4a2c

v4b: (A)
v4b1: (C), 1988, p.238
v4b2: (A); (C), 1988, p.238
v4b3: NA

v4c:
v4c1: (E), p.109
v4c2: (E), p.109

5. Labor Force (L)

v5a: (E), p.91—capitalists were not included as the labor input in 1949 and 1952, therefore the summation of single items would not be equal to labor force of the society
v5a1: (E), p.91
v5a2: (E), p.91
v5a3: (E), p.91
v5a4: (E), p.91

v5b:
v5b1: NA
v5b2: NA
v5b3: NA

v5c: NA
v5c1: NA

v5d: NA

6. Population (PO)

v6a: (E), p.90—data from public security department
v6a1: (A)
v6a2: (A)

v6b: (A); (E), p.90—data of 1987, 1988 are acquired from sample surveys from 1% of the population

v6c: (A); (E), p.90—(ditto)

v6d:
v6d1: (E), p.90—data from public security department
v6d2: (E), p.90—(ditto)
v6d3: (E), p.90—(ditto)
v6d4: (E), p.90—(ditto)
v6d5: (A)
v6d6: NA

7. Agriculture (A)

v7a: (E), p.103

v7b: (A); (E), p.103

v7c: (A); (E), p.103

v7d: (A); (E), p.103

v7e: (A)

v7f: (A); (E), p.103

v7g: (A); (E), p.103

v7h: (E), p.98
v7h1: (E), p.98
v7h2: (E), p.98
v7h3: (E), p.98
v7h4: (E), p.98
v7h5: (E), p.98

v7i: (E), p.102

8. Industry (IN)

v8a: (E), p.104
v8a1: (E), p.104
v8a2: (E), p.104
v8a3: v8a – v8a1 – v8a2

v8b: (E), p.109

v8c1: (A); (E), p.96
v8c2: (A(; (E), p.96

v8d: (E), p.109

v8f:
v8f1: (E), p.108
v8f2: NA
v8f3: (E), p.108
v8f4: (E), p.108
v8f5: (E), p.108

v8g: (A)
v8g1: (E), p.109—figures of 1979 and before are numbers of all industrial enterprises

9. Transport (TR)

v9a: (E), p.110—excluding urban traffic volume
v9a1: (E), p.110—including central and local railways
v9a2: (E), p.110
v9a3: NA

v9b: (E), p.110
v9b1: (E), p.110—including central and local railway
v9b2: (E), p.110
v9b3: (E), p.110—excluding distant ocean and coastal freight volume

v9c: (E), p.110

10. Domestic Trade (DT)

v10a: (E), p.113
v10a1: (E), p.113

v10b:
v10b1: (E), p.113
v10b2: (A); (C), 1988, p.208, p.668
v10b3: (A); (C), 1986, p.668; 1988, p.208; (E), p.113—the number of supply and marketing cooperative is included in 1975–1989. The figures are: 6.73, 7.20, 7.64, 7.78, 8.47, 10.84, 12.72, 12.69, 14.35, 16.86, 21.73, 29.02, 32.70, 42.31, 45.10 for the respective year
v10b4: (E), p.113
v10b5: (E), p.113
v10b6: (E), p.113

v10d: (E), p.115—calculated on calendar year basis, amount of the society

11. Foreign Trade (FT)

v11a:
v11a1: NA
v11a2: NA
v11a3: NA

v11b: (E), p.116—data from foreign trade department
v11b1: (E), p.116—(ditto)
v11b2: v11b – v11b1

v11c: (E), p.116

v11d: (A); (E), p.116

12. Prices (PR)

v12a: (E), p.118

v12b: (E), p.118

v12c: (E), p.118

13. Education (ED)

v13a: (A)

v13b: (A); (E), p.121

v13c:
- v13c1: (A); (E), p.121
- v13c2: (A); (E), p.121—technical, technician, agricultural and vocational, and ordinary secondary schools
- v13c3: (A); (E), p.121

v13d: (A)

14. Social Factors (SF)

v14a: (A); (E), p.121

v14b: (A); (E), p.121—doctors, nurses, pharmacists, laboratory specialists and others

v14c: (A)

15. Natural Environment (NE)

v15a: (A); (E), p.103

v15b: (A)

v15c: NA

v15d: NA

v15e: NA

v15f: NA

Sources of Data

(A) Data supplied by the DSNEB, SSB, the PRC, and Statistical Bureau of Tianjin Municipality ed. *Tianjin Forty Years*, Beijing: CSPH, 1989.
(C) Statistical Bureau of Tianjin Municipality ed. *Statistical Yearbook of Tianjin*, Beijing: CSPH, various issues.
(D) Same as (D) in Beijing's sources of data.
(E) Same as (E) in Beijing's sources of data.

3

Hebei

3. Hebei

3–1

Year	v1a	v1a1	v1a2	v1a3	v1a4	v1a5	v1b	v1b1	v1b2	v1b3	v1b4	v1b5	v1c	v1d	v1d1
1949	31.80	20.31	6.59	0.16	1.22	3.52							10.58	21.22	15.36
1950	39.66	25.03	8.97	0.51	1.22	3.93							13.60	26.06	18.82
1951	44.91	26.09	11.78	0.95	1.54	4.55							16.19	28.72	19.76
1952	56.60	29.70	16.56	2.25	2.25	5.84							20.77	35.83	22.79
1953	61.26	29.07	18.17	3.36	2.70	7.96	105.0	91.1	110.7	154.5	125.6	130.1	23.67	37.59	21.81
1954	67.39	30.44	22.04	3.24	3.09	8.58	110.1	103.1	123.3	98.9	116.1	105.4	27.29	40.10	23.11
1955	72.75	34.39	22.96	3.40	3.21	8.79	108.9	113.0	105.9	106.9	105.6	102.7	29.21	43.54	25.75
1956	74.18	30.77	24.48	5.77	3.60	9.56	103.8	88.4	113.2	152.7	114.9	108.7	30.08	44.10	23.09
1957	75.72	30.77	25.86	5.23	4.19	9.67	110.5	118.6	107.4	106.6	122.7	98.9	29.44	46.28	24.32
1958	98.21	33.15	39.63	8.95	6.30	10.18	129.2	104.6	154.2	170.3	152.0	105.2	41.90	56.29	25.86
1959	125.65	31.99	63.84	10.41	8.45	10.96	126.6	94.8	160.2	109.0	133.7	107.6	59.98	65.67	25.10
1960	134.02	28.50	74.73	10.99	9.15	10.65	106.2	84.4	117.9	103.2	109.0	96.7	69.03	64.99	21.88
1961	92.54	31.28	42.09	3.99	5.31	9.87	62.2	86.7	53.7	35.8	57.9	81.5	43.98	48.56	22.72
1962	81.14	31.26	33.42	3.33	4.86	8.27	86.7	101.5	76.6	86.5	90.3	97.7	38.02	43.12	22.73
1963	77.41	26.22	33.49	4.36	5.17	8.17	96.8	84.9	100.7	133.1	106.4	106.7	37.74	39.67	18.85
1964	92.61	34.14	39.10	5.41	5.64	8.32	121.2	132.5	119.0	123.0	109.1	101.1	42.45	50.16	25.43
1965	118.50	45.49	49.38	6.34	7.37	9.92	128.1	124.3	130.7	123.2	130.7	100.0	54.15	64.35	34.48
1966	131.91	49.07	55.21	7.41	8.38	11.84	114.5	107.1	118.0	118.2	113.7	120.0	60.90	71.01	36.70
1967	128.52	48.93	53.76	7.03	7.07	11.73	96.9	99.6	98.5	94.9	85.4	100.4	59.40	69.12	36.67
1968	134.43	49.06	60.52	6.66	6.82	11.37	104.4	97.1	114.9	94.8	132.1	96.7	64.14	70.29	37.00
1969	159.54	53.63	73.64	11.21	8.14	12.92	123.7	108.0	126.0	168.3	87.9	114.8	77.98	81.56	40.31
1970	186.07	59.69	89.52	13.08	9.62	14.16	121.3	111.3	127.0	116.7	118.8	111.6	93.81	92.26	42.35
1971	197.30	57.86	98.64	15.70	10.52	14.58	105.9	105.7	111.8	118.1	109.4	102.9	102.08	95.22	40.20
1972	195.15	51.40	100.91	16.31	11.18	15.35	98.8	87.3	102.9	102.6	106.3	105.3	104.00	91.15	35.17
1973	217.26	59.67	111.79	16.91	11.83	17.06	111.3	115.2	111.4	101.6	105.8	111.1	117.64	99.62	39.51
1974	238.07	65.24	124.92	18.98	11.67	17.26	109.8	109.3	112.5	109.7	98.6	101.2	132.51	105.56	41.80
1975	270.12	72.73	146.61	22.06	12.15	16.57	114.3	103.1	118.9	114.0	104.1	105.8	154.92	115.20	46.42
1976	274.41	65.83	157.34	21.84	11.77	17.63	102.0	94.4	104.8	97.5	98.0	113.0	158.94	115.47	41.86
1977	314.72	67.19	185.13	28.08	14.95	19.37	114.5	92.2	118.6	126.6	125.6	96.6	182.06	132.66	43.61
1978	362.33	75.86	219.25	30.36	16.03	20.83	114.2	122.1	117.0	106.5	107.2	107.2	204.15	158.18	50.63
1979	398.94	91.10	228.34	39.87	17.84	21.79	107.0	106.9	101.7	128.3	111.4	122.2	223.70	175.24	59.11
1980	417.25	97.79	238.62	38.78	17.67	24.39	101.6	93.8	102.7	95.2	99.1	110.6	228.89	188.36	65.22
1981	419.33	100.23	236.77	38.41	17.25	26.67	100.3	103.8	99.7	96.1	97.6	108.3	229.86	189.47	69.12
1982	461.16	118.58	249.53	43.56	19.94	29.55	108.1	117.5	105.2	101.4	108.9	109.0	249.81	211.35	83.44
1983	518.82	139.22	276.68	45.42	22.02	35.48	111.8	117.2	110.5	99.7	105.4	122.0	280.21	238.61	99.71
1984	608.00	153.07	334.26	54.26	23.74	42.67	115.5	109.1	119.2	112.3	106.1	119.1	326.00	282.01	108.76
1985	751.30	167.33	435.82	69.82	26.11	52.22	114.5	103.3	119.8	115.2	109.2	113.8	410.40	340.87	117.50
1986	847.73	174.39	506.19	79.78	29.05	58.32	107.7	98.5	111.7	104.3	109.4	106.2	472.03	375.70	120.30
1987	1032.20	200.66	640.85	88.78	35.13	67.48	113.2	104.5	117.9	99.7	119.6	106.8	583.77	448.43	135.01
1988	1354.93	256.90	841.12	121.16	41.60	94.15	111.8	107.8	119.5	117.8	113.2	117.7	796.61	558.32	164.83
1989	1596.99	306.99	1026.09	117.42	46.97	99.52	105.4	103.1	108.8	84.4	105.9	94.3	947.29	649.70	194.96

3. Hebei

3–2

Year	v1d2	v1d3	v1d4	v1d5	v1e	v1e1	v1e2	v1e3	v1e4	v1e5	v1f	v1f1	v1f2	v1f3	v1g
1949	2.22	0.06	0.77	2.81											
1950	3.09	0.19	0.90	3.06											
1951	3.92	0.33	1.14	3.57											
1952	6.15	0.74	1.64	4.51											31.59
1953	6.58	1.02	1.93	6.25	99.4	88.6	105.4	141.5	121.8	132.9					35.13
1954	7.30	1.06	2.13	6.50	107.0	103.8	118.4	108.6	113.2	101.8					38.36
1955	8.02	1.07	2.19	6.51	109.7	112.0	113.5	99.4	102.6	100.1					42.25
1956	9.36	1.87	2.48	7.30	103.3	88.9	127.7	164.6	118.4	110.9					44.81
1957	9.97	1.75	2.85	7.39	106.5	112.2	98.1	105.8	116.9	99.2					49.26
1958	15.21	2.87	4.31	8.04	120.5	102.9	153.3	164.2	154.0	109.5					65.88
1959	22.99	3.29	5.70	8.59	114.5	95.0	150.4	103.2	131.5	106.1					68.41
1960	25.76	3.08	6.06	8.21	97.7	82.0	112.9	91.2	106.3	95.0					71.92
1961	13.90	1.12	3.43	7.39	63.9	80.9	51.5	37.7	57.2	78.1					57.16
1962	11.00	0.93	3.01	5.45	89.5	101.9	76.2	81.5	92.7	91.1					36.91
1963	11.37	1.27	3.24	4.94	94.1	84.1	104.6	137.9	107.8	103.7					49.50
1964	14.15	1.76	3.54	5.28	126.3	136.2	123.9	140.1	109.3	104.1					52.72
1965	16.51	1.99	4.65	6.72	126.2	127.0	124.2	118.0	131.1	102.2					58.43
1966	18.16	2.37	5.42	8.36	112.9	105.9	114.9	119.2	116.8	120.1					58.35
1967	17.20	2.21	4.38	8.66	96.3	100.0	95.8	93.0	82.3	104.0					64.49
1968	19.03	2.07	4.20	7.99	99.9	97.5	113.1	93.7	95.8	92.4					65.99
1969	23.63	3.25	5.04	9.33	121.1	108.2	128.9	157.3	119.8	118.1					72.99
1970	29.76	3.92	5.98	10.25	117.1	102.8	131.5	117.7	119.8	110.6					83.23
1971	33.47	4.66	6.57	10.32	102.4	92.8	113.0	116.3	109.9	100.7					91.78
1972	33.82	4.73	7.01	10.42	95.8	86.6	101.4	104.9	106.6	101.0					88.38
1973	36.69	4.99	7.43	11.00	109.1	111.7	109.5	102.1	106.1	105.6					95.33
1974	40.35	5.70	7.18	10.53	105.8	105.7	110.0	112.1	96.6	95.7					102.86
1975	45.85	6.51	7.52	8.90	110.9	110.4	115.2	112.1	104.8	84.5					112.16
1976	51.06	6.33	7.04	9.18	100.6	89.1	111.8	96.0	93.6	116.6					111.04
1977	62.91	8.14	8.22	9.78	113.7	104.6	124.0	126.9	116.9	85.2					118.62
1978	78.05	9.41	8.42	11.67	117.6	112.1	123.3	113.6	102.4	118.3	183.06	52.20	92.37	38.49	134.82
1979	84.70	12.36	8.88	10.19	106.5	101.1	107.0	128.6	105.5	112.0	203.22	61.12	101.76	40.34	148.74
1980	90.56	11.86	8.76	11.96	103.9	101.5	107.1	87.5	98.6	117.1	219.24	68.09	105.88	45.27	154.64
1981	87.09	11.05	8.94	13.27	101.2	104.5	96.0	90.7	102.2	109.9	222.54	71.03	103.15	48.36	158.49
1982	89.57	12.78	10.81	14.75	109.6	119.5	103.1	110.7	114.0	109.3	251.45	85.59	107.83	58.03	184.91
1983	95.11	13.23	11.97	18.59	111.9	118.0	106.1	99.0	105.3	128.2	283.21	102.10	114.89	66.22	213.07
1984	122.35	16.38	12.41	22.11	115.3	112.0	122.8	110.7	102.6	117.7	332.23	111.46	145.85	74.92	257.38
1985	161.28	20.29	14.24	27.56	113.3	102.1	122.0	118.7	113.7	115.5	396.75	120.34	184.26	92.15	328.32
1986	185.77	22.41	15.48	31.74	104.8	97.0	110.6	102.9	107.4	104.3	436.65	123.45	207.28	105.92	363.04
1987	230.55	24.64	19.02	39.21	110.2	101.9	115.2	97.5	120.8	114.7	521.92	137.66	255.97	128.29	425.48
1988	288.29	34.56	22.23	48.41	111.3	102.7	114.1	111.9	111.9	123.2	660.16	162.31	323.40	174.45	543.96
1989	336.74	35.20	23.53	59.27	103.4	101.9	106.7	86.7	105.7	96.4	767.26	196.35	374.92	195.99	615.94

3. Hebei

Year	v1h	v1i	v1j	v1j1	v1j2	v1j3	v1k	v2a	v2a1	v2a2	v2b	v2c	v2c1	v2c2	v2d1
1949		0.94	318	319	265										
1950		1.27	357	359	298							0.20			
1951		1.70	397	400	332							0.36			
1952		2.42	435	438	364			5.68	2.39	3.29		1.47			
1953		2.95	468	472	375			5.46	3.19	2.27		2.24			
1954	63	3.93	484	500	391			6.99	3.00	3.99		3.14			
1955	66	4.51	490	513	392			9.00	4.31	4.69		3.44			
1956	62	6.22	543	574	439			9.41	4.49	4.92		5.41			
1957	64	7.59	566	598	457			11.79	6.77	5.02		5.77			
1958		9.17	514	536	410			24.20	17.67	6.53		15.09			
1959		11.39	520	538	411			25.27	18.53	6.74		15.83			
1960		12.57	540	554	423			27,94	20.50	7.44		17.52			
1961		11.62	536	549	420			14.08	6.32	7.76		5.40			
1962	90	9.77	577	593	453			-4.49	1.58	-6.07		3.25			
1963	94	9.15	612	632	483			7.38	4.35	3.03		4.75			
1964	86	9.70	635	654	500			9.05	5.41	3.64		5.90			
1965	88	9.92	627	647	495			12.01	6.83	5.18		6.00			
1966	88	10.02	611	631	482			8.95	6.77	2.18		7.07			
1967		10.18	609	629	481			13.25	7.06	6.19		6.25			
1968		10.34	587	608	465			13.92	6.82	7.10		6.03			
1969		10.82	573	594	454			17.00	8.21	8.79		7.25			
1970		11.87	568	590	451			23.16	11.08	12.08		9.80			
1971		13.49	554	567	479			28.63	15.52	13.11		13.71			
1972		15.49	571	587	489			26.68	16.42	10.26		14.50			
1973		16.18	568	581	494			27.83	17.09	10.74		15.10			
1974		17.20	567	581	491			32.02	20.61	11.41		18.21			
1975		18.92	564	579	484			38.75	29.04	9.71		26.60			
1976		20.35	554	571	467			36.17	28.49	7.68		27.50			
1977	83	22.42	560	573	489			41.33	29.85	11.48		31.77			
1978	114	25.65	592	608	512		3.12	47.04	34.17	12.87		36.69	16.74	0.70	
1979	136	28.66	632	655	517		3.79	50.47	39.89	10.58		37.53	14.89	0.65	
1980	176	34.05	726	753	592		4.70	46.73	34.75	11.98		36.17	12.56	1.07	
1981	204	36.13	744	771	617		5.66	37.45	32.16	5.29	53.31	29.67	9.73	0.88	
1982	239	38.86	773	800	648		6.63	54.87	46.03	8.84	78.09	39.26	13.35	1.07	
1983	298	40.26	796	824	668		8.33	65.95	50.20	15.75	74.34	42.33	12.63	0.94	
1984	345	47.63	918	965	765		9.68	83.13	53.59	29.54	84.68	48.33	12.86	1.01	
1985	385	58.04	1075	1128	901		12.47	113.75	73.23	40.52	110.66	62.64	14.78	1.78	
1986	408	71.68	1268	1338	1035		15.63	118.02	82.86	35.16	131.30	76.28	19.10	1.97	313.38
1987	444	82.51	1394	1471	1139		18.96	128.22	89.26	38.96	152.01	86.36	29.84	2.38	351.11
1988	547	103.54	1688	1788	1351		26.04	175.73	128.51	47.22	210.85	111.35	39.83	2.79	408.03
1989	589	114.71	1821	1940	1421		31.16	214.22	99.82	114.40	214.29	101.25	36.72	1.72	486.14

3. Hebei

3–4

Year	v2d2	v2e	v3a	v3b	v3b1	v3b2	v3c	v3d	v3d1	v3d2	v3e	v3e1	v3e2	v3e3	v3e4
1949															
1950															
1951															
1952			25.91	24.97	21.16	3.81	0.94	77	71	155	138.00	89.11	18.03		8.13
1953			29.67	28.57	24.42	4.15	1.10	86	80	157					
1954			31.37	29.87	25.18	4.69	1.50	88	81	165					
1955			33.25	31.25	26.05	5.20	2.00	90	82	170					
1956			35.40	33.20	26.92	6.28	2.20	93	83	199					
1957			37.47	35.39	28.52	6.87	2.08	98	87	200	180.96	108.12	21.96		7.44
1958			41.68	39.48	30.72	8.76	2.20	107	93	220					
1959			43.14	40.74	30.36	10.38	2.40	108	92	225					
1960			43.98	41.48	30.03	11.45	2.50	110	91	236					
1961			43.08	40.98	30.43	10.55	2.10	108	91	238					
1962			41.40	39.85	31.07	8.78	1.55	104	90	238	192.60	115.08	16.20		11.04
1963			42.12	40.66	32.56	8.10	1.46	104	91	237					
1964			43.67	42.09	33.72	8.37	1.58	106	93	239					
1965			46.42	44.78	35.77	9.01	1.64	111	97	249	196.08	121.32	25.92		9.84
1966			49.40	47.30	37.68	9.62	2.10	114	100	262					
1967			51.24	48.42	38.47	9.95	2.82	115	100	268					
1968			52.07	48.92	38.87	10.05	3.15	114	99	269					
1969			55.99	52.12	41.76	10.36	3.87	119	104	278					
1970			60.07	55.94	45.42	10.52	4.13	124	110	280					
1971			63.15	59.06	47.73	11.33	4.09	129	114	290					
1972			61.70	57.27	44.73	12.54	4.43	122	105	296					
1973			67.50	62.86	48.69	14.17	4.64	132	113	310					
1974			70.84	65.93	50.58	15.35	4.91	136	116	325					
1975			73.41	68.47	51.95	16.52	4.94	140	118	340					
1976			74.87	69.60	52.25	17.35	5.27	141	118	337					
1977			77.29	71.36	53.06	18.30	5.93	144	119	355					
1978			87.78	80.66	59.64	21.02	7.12	160	133	390	275.28	158.64	42.24	2.64	6.96
1979			98.27	89.51	66.28	23.23	8.76	176	147	407	312.24	176.28	49.20	3.60	7.80
1980			107.91	98.46	71.74	26.72	9.45	192	158	444	365.40	204.96	59.76	3.60	10.80
1981			121.04	111.45	82.28	29.17	9.59	214	179	480	401.16	213.96	63.36	3.96	9.84
1982			130.04	118.66	87.36	31.30	11.38	224	188	467	401.04	225.72	59.88	5.04	10.44
1983			147.12	134.95	101.10	33.85	12.17	250	215	498	419.88	239.04	64.32	6.48	11.40
1984			174.25	157.86	118.97	38.89	16.39	289	251	547	475.80	263.40	74.16	9.12	12.00
1985			214.57	195.58	147.29	48.29	18.99	354	308	650	605.52	302.52	93.84	12.96	14.28
1986	205.06	76.01	245.02	221.99	164.68	57.31	23.03	397	342	744	717.72	360.60	108.72	22.32	14.04
1987	235.92	88.97	297.26	268.45	197.13	71.32	28.81	474	406	878	799.68	413.16	118.80	29.04	14.40
1988	277.86	102.06	368.23	335.15	240.80	94.34	33.09	583	489	1142	1118.76	520.18	167.54	40.56	15.92
1989	339.16	133.49	401.72	370.52	258.94	111.58	31.20	635	518	1331	1188.00	618.00			

3. Hebei

3–5

Year	v3f	v3f1	v3f2	v3f3	v3f4	v4a1	v4a1a	v4a1b	v4a1c	v4a1d	v4a2	v4a2a	v4a2b	v4a2c	v4a2d
1949															
1950						2.71	0.01	0.86	1.69	0.15	0.77		0.12	0.29	
1951						3.66	0.03	1.54	1.95	0.14	1.11		0.20	0.42	
1952						4.44	0.14	2.18	1.96	0.17	1.88	0.51	0.32	0.70	0.35
1953						5.25	0.39	2.90	1.75	0.22	2.95	0.69	0.98	0.70	0.59
1954	56.86	39.09	6.46	2.68	4.39	6.19	0.60	3.11	1.98	0.50	3.21	0.87	0.96	0.72	0.65
1955	60.10	41.17	7.22	2.70	3.95	6.45	0.71	3.21	2.11	0.42	3.25	0.86	0.95	0.77	0.67
1956	58.61	40.12	7.29	2.73	3.99	6.57	0.76	3.58	1.86	0.38	6.28	2.28	1.37	1.03	1.60
1957	58.08	37.71	7.69	2.65	4.32	6.69	0.69	3.85	1.70	0.45	5.07	1.66	1.31	0.91	1.18
1958						14.84	7.17	4.95	2.18	0.54	12.21	8.35	1.49	1.01	1.37
1959						21.02	9.67	6.28	2.29	2.78	13.25	7.40	1.74	1.17	2.94
1960						22.15	11.27	6.56	1.74	2.58	21.73	11.57	2.52	1.23	6.41
1961						15.16	6.35	4.67	0.86	3.28	11.04	1.79	1.82	1.31	6.12
1962	80.50	43.55	7.18	5.15	10.20	10.76	1.91	4.73	1.01	3.10	5.88	0.82	1.64	1.07	2.36
1963	89.83	53.95	8.41	5.23	10.00	8.18	1.70	4.54	0.75	1.19	9.05	1.87	1.71	1.16	4.31
1964	80.87	51.00	7.14	5.04	8.67	10.83	3.03	4.97	1.04	1.79	12.00	3.18	1.86	1.18	5.78
1965	76.50	51.70	7.90	3.60	6.10	12.38	4.19	5.33	1.09	1.76	9.65	2.63	1.90	1.18	3.94
1966	76.55	53.31	7.47	2.55	5.76	13.31	4.96	5.50	1.29	1.56	9.97	2.35	2.13	1.26	4.24
1967						10.76	4.20	5.17	1.29	0.10	8.30	2.69	2.15	1.22	2.24
1968						12.06	5.36	5.32	1.22	0.16	7.38	2.76	1.77	1.23	1.62
1969						14.93	6.74	6.66	1.37	0.16	9.75	4.01	1.67	1.66	2.41
1970						20.55	9.63	9.22	1.52	0.18	12.13	6.40	1.76	1.43	2.53
1971						23.14	11.82	9.76	1.39	0.18	14.34	6.73	2.34	1.69	3.58
1972						24.39	12.32	10.65	1.21	0.21	16.53	7.21	2.81	1.70	4.81
1973						25.83	12.19	11.89	1.40	0.35	17.62	6.55	3.16	1.60	6.31
1974						26.57	11.34	13.49	1.43	0.31	19.76	7.75	3.47	1.73	6.80
1975						30.37	12.78	15.83	1.39	0.38	20.92	7.95	3.60	1.73	7.64
1976						28.34	10.62	16.24	1.15	0.32	27.36	10.96	3.78	1.84	10.78
1977	69.26	45.90	10.17	2.02	5.32	32.69	12.63	18.34	1.18	0.54	31.52	12.42	4.03	2.01	13.06
1978	95.02	62.97	13.95	2.77	7.30	45.10	20.69	20.45	1.36	2.60	32.44	10.97	4.78	2.19	14.51
1979	116.43	69.76	17.14	10.14	8.38	42.87	18.86	20.42	1.33	2.26	34.22	12.18	5.37	2.49	14.18
1980	142.00	79.61	19.70	14.43	8.25	35.02	11.59	7.26	1.06	15.11	28.36	8.25	6.35	2.76	10.99
1981	164.66	85.93	23.48	19.41	8.66	34.10	10.29	20.74	1.29	1.78	23.29	2.68	6.60	2.66	11.35
1982	175.39	95.21	22.83	22.44	9.33	31.78	5.21	23.12	1.43	2.02	25.94	5.37	7.79	3.24	9.53
1983	224.65	120.23	28.97	31.79	10.99	36.39	-0.96	24.72	1.53	11.10	28.27	5.87	9.14	3.95	9.30
1984	243.21	127.05	29.03	34.58	13.11	39.11	6.19	28.89	1.58	2.45	35.86	6.73	10.35	5.25	13.53
1985	297.72	148.95	32.25	49.62	16.49	45.15	3.55	38.66	1.95	0.98	41.66	6.60	12.26	5.24	17.55
1986	333.04	161.57	35.29	60.70	19.09	51.17	5.09	42.94	1.85	1.29	53.82	5.67	14.62	6.69	26.84
1987	365.35	180.34	38.31	65.30	17.79	57.62	5.37	47.87	1.98	2.40	53.33	3.90	15.42	7.06	26.95
1988	445.68	209.23	44.84	80.98	22.24	64.78	0.52	55.77	3.02	5.48	67.52	4.26	19.72	7.50	36.04
1989	495.20	238.30	47.79	86.26	27.53	76.12	-1.71				77.30	3.51	21.79	8.57	43.43

3. Hebei

3–6

Year	v4b	v4b1	v4b2	v4b3	v4c1	v4c2	v5a	v5a1	v5a2	v5a3	v5a4	v5b1	v5b2	v5b3	v5c
1949								32	1	30.54					
1950	0.05	0.05						37	2	35.15					
1951	0.16	0.16						45	2	40.43					
1952	0.29	0.29					1377	58	3	45.25	1272				
1953	0.31	0.30	0.01					65	2	44.04					
1954	0.70	0.60	0.10	0.09				73	13	40.84					
1955	0.78	0.50	0.28	0.55				78	18	35.24					
1956	1.27	0.60	0.67	1.15				94	28	10.45					
1957	1.72	0.83	0.89	1.84			1521	104	31	3.14	1383				
1958	3.76	1.36	2.40	2.36				196	31	1.97					
1959	3.84	2.18	1.66	4.39				194	31	1.96					
1960	3.35	1.99	1.36	4.38				212	25	2.14					
1961	2.40	1.19	1.21	3.43				178	21	2.33					
1962	1.57	0.87	0.70	1.60				133	17	2.63					
1963	1.82	1.06	0.76	1.88				129	20	2.48					
1964	2.29	1.41	0.88	2.16				135	19	1.76					
1965	2.62	1.63	0.99	2.53			1614	140	22	1.32	1451				
1966	2.47	1.65	0.82	2.37				146	22	1.10					
1967	2.72	1.81	0.91	2.90				147	22	0.89					
1968	2.87	1.94	0.93	3.78				155	25	0.67					
1969	2.76	1.96	0.80	4.00				166	29	0.47					
1970	3.13	2.15	0.98	4.63				186	34	0.19					
1971	3.67	2.58	1.09	5.35				217	39	0.16					
1972	4.38	3.13	1.25	4.39				234	43	0.14					
1973	5.12	3.53	1.59	5.79				238	45	0.13					
1974	6.35	4.16	2.19	7.66				258	52	0.10					
1975	7.59	4.74	2.85	8.53				290	55	0.08					
1976	8.25	5.15	3.10	9.00				316	62	0.06					
1977	10.06	5.90	4.16	10.31				350	64	0.08					
1978	11.17	6.69	4.48	10.60			2109	370	75	0.07	1664	1621	293	195	217.05
1979	14.35	8.81	5.54	13.40			2142	387	80	0.14	1674	1614	316	211	220.88
1980	21.06	12.46	8.60	18.32			2183	394	83	1.34	1705	1637	321	224	225.13
1981	29.09	15.87	13.22	21.46			2264	409	88	2.55	1765	1700	325	239	233.36
1982	40.17	20.90	19.26	27.91			2347	422	91	3.05	1831	1742	346	259	239.89
1983	57.48	28.15	29.33	35.91			2489	415	92	4.53	1978	1835	352	302	238.74
1984	79.78	38.92	40.86	34.51			2534	405	125	8.23	1994	1763	426	345	248.29
1985	102.86	52.08	50.78	41.21			2555	424	130	10.54	1990	1603	557	395	256.80
1986	145.98	76.21	69.77	50.19	48.90		2626	445	135	10.91	2034	1602	607	417	269.63
1987	207.21	113.32	93.89	53.52	55.16		2726	466	143	13.07	2103	1615	653	457	282.10
1988	262.03	151.78	110.25	56.59	67.78		2808	482	147	20.15	2517	1660	690	458	293.05
1989	355.40	216.70	138.70		64.85		2928	488	148	14.00	2205	1739	674	445	

3. Hebei

3–7

Year	v5c1	v5d	v6a	v6a1	v6a2	v6b	v6c	v6d1	v6d2	v6d3	v6d4	v6d5	v6d6
1949			3086	263	2823	27.30	12.73	207	2879	1564	1522	343.0	173.4
1950			3147	273	2875	28.47	12.43	215	2932	1593	1554		
1951			3205	282	2923	28.71	12.29	234	2971	1620	1585		
1952			3272	319	2953	29.17	12.10	258	3014	1653	1619	365.0	181.5
1953			3343	343	3000	29.47	11.48	271	3072	1688	1655		
1954			3443	367	3076	32.63	12.10	298	3145	1743	1699		
1955			3529	387	3142	32.29	11.64	308	3221	1789	1740		
1956			3589	513	3076	29.29	11.34	323	3266	1821	1767		
1957			3670	568	3102	29.62	11.30	363	3307	1865	1805	413.9	191.7
1958			3732	567	3165	24.45	10.92	433	3299	1898	1834		
1959			3791	535	3257	23.09	12.29	490	3301	1933	1858		
1960			3779	433	3736	20.51	15.84	481	3298	1923	1856		
1961			3795	501	3294	15.13	13.63	406	3389	1922	1874		
1962			3884	475	3409	28.68	9.06	338	3546	1961	1922		
1963			3956	401	3555	38.61	11.20	345	3611	2018	1938		
1964			3997	458	3539	33.63	10.91	357	3640	2044	1953		
1965			4087	441	3646	32.92	8.74	367	3720	2084	2003	475.0	218.3
1966			4183	444	3739	29.22	8.69	368	3815	2133	2051		
1967			4254	449	3805	25.74	7.17	375	3879	2170	2084		
1968			4347	456	3891	26.86	6.52	373	3974	2217	2130		
1969			4445	465	3980	24.70	6.48	371	4074	2267	2178		
1970			4550	483	4067	26.73	6.49	381	4169	2320	2229		
1971			4640	498	4142	25.06	6.49	401	4239	2367	2273		
1972			4728	526	4202	25.27	7.22	446	4282	2416	2312		
1973			4804	529	4275	21.88	6.56	468	4336	2456	2348		
1974			4862	542	4320	18.19	6.80	476	4386	2487	2375		
1975			4913	559	4354	17.78	7.22	495	4418	2515	2399		
1976			4943	560	4383	18.44	11.39	505	4438	2534	2409		
1977			4998	574	4424	19.62	6.77	525	4473	2563	2435		
1978	166.05	23.96	5057	606	4451	20.88	6.49	553	4504	2595	2462	558.5	272.2
1979	167.47	23.86	5105	644	4461	19.86	6.36	589	4516	2620	2485		
1980	170.10	23.72	5168	671	4497	20.47	6.46	614	4554	2651	2517	573.1	276.2
1981	175.89	23.37	5256	701	4555	23.99	6.05	636	4620	2692	2565		
1982	181.38	21.77	5356	722	4634	19.35	5.94	668	4688	2742	2614		
1983	180.00	20.50	5420	841	4579	17.91	6.60	692	4728	2777	2643		
1984	180.57	20.20	5487	1511	3976	16.73	5.41	728	4759	2815	2673		
1985	187.97	20.70	5548	1748	3800	17.10	5.30	757	4791	2852	2696		
1986	196.81	20.92	5627	2013	3614	20.42	6.12	784	4843	2893	2734		
1987	206.23	22.08	5710	2102	3608	22.50	6.00	812	4898	2936	2774		
1988	213.93	22.08	5795	2298	3497	20.35	5.50	840	4955	2978	2817	633.8	317.0
1989			5881	2563	3318	20.19	5.44	871	5010	3021	2860		

3. Hebei

3–8

Year	v7a	v7b	v7c	v7d	v7e	v7f	v7g	v7h	v7h1	v7h2	v7h3	v7h4	v7h5	v7i	v8a
1949								20.31	16.13	0.26	1.76	0.21	1.95	250.68	6.59
1950		3.08	1158		655	0.73		25.03	20.43	0.33	2.04	0.25	1.98	268.49	8.97
1951		3.08	1238		721	0.87		26.09	21.36	0.37	2.20	0.27	1.89	288.62	11.78
1952		3.08	1419	13607	1433	2.28		29.70	24.71	0.44	2.28	0.29	1.98	308.30	16.56
1953		4.06	1467		2076	4.01	0.01	29.07	23.56	0.54	2.43	0.35	2.19	298.22	18.17
1954		10.62	1501		2975	6.41	0.03	30.44	24.58	0.59	2.46	0.42	2.39	305.77	22.04
1955		48.83	1509		1386	9.47	0.06	34.39	29.00	0.61	2.19	0.43	2.16	293.66	22.96
1956		298.70	1960		4026	12.12	0.08	30.77	24.57	0.82	2.55	0.42	2.41	293.65	24.48
1957		720.67	2269	14562	1089	14.47	0.11	30.77	25.40	0.70	2.43	0.33	1.91	280.87	25.86
1958		1067.11	2857		718	20.96	0.19	33.15	27.61	0.90	2.46	0.34	1.84	253.42	39.63
1959		1303.12	3001		1277	16.89	0.26	31.99	26.12	0.92	2.48	0.34	2.13	241.57	63.84
1960		1628.57	2765		2316	18.39	0.52	28.50	23.21	0.82	2.07	0.38	2.02	209.14	74.73
1961		2182.95	2168		2811	12.28	1.03	31.28	25.72	0.69	2.22	0.28	2.37	190.11	42.09
1962		1982.51	1928	12705	3067	13.00	1.92	31.26	25.52	0.55	2.55	0.24	2.40	194.45	33.42
1963		1969.09	1928		6016	15.73	2.90	26.22	20.05	0.45	2.78	0.33	2.61	197.81	33.49
1964		2352.86	1975		4128	15.79	3.72	34.14	27.20	0.82	3.39	0.35	2.38	203.14	39.10
1965		2646.47	2503	12928	2436	31.60	5.42	45.49	36.68	1.02	4.33	0.29	3.17	216.71	49.38
1966		2254.51	3353		1688	39.21	7.00	49.07	38.78	1.50	5.02	0.20	3.57	228.94	55.21
1967		1910.30	3273		1068	51.86	8.50	48.93	38.20	1.27	5.45	0.26	3.75	238.08	63.76
1968		1805.55	3460		1248	49.54	9.44	49.06	38.63	1.32	5.10	0.22	3.79	244.61	60.52
1969		2072.64	3604		828	80.75	10.91	53.63	42.71	1.65	4.60	0.21	4.46	245.15	73.64
1970		2227.53	3878		521	88.17	11.43	59.69	48.06	1.88	5.93	0.30	3.52	257.71	89.52
1971		2500.59	4482		1033	98.66	14.49	57.86	43.98	1.57	8.96	0.23	3.12	267.57	98.64
1972		2515.36	4200		3178	115.08	18.11	51.40	39.72	1.50	6.78	0.33	2.45	270.23	100.91
1973		2944.44	4561		921	169.23	15.92	59.67	48.18	1.77	6.74	0.33	2.61	273.86	111.79
1974		3648.65	4864		745	155.07	17.10	65.24	53.10	1.66	7.77	0.39	2.32	274.45	124.92
1975		4111.03	5306		1572	175.89	20.12	72.73	56.77	2.13	9.80	0.53	3.50	283.41	146.61
1976		4361.60	5355			191.75	20.48	65.83	50.84	2.15	9.04	0.46	3.34	273.96	157.34
1977		5582.43	5321		3204	219.86	20.91	67.19	49.36	2.25	9.68	0.59	5.31	276.55	185.13
1978	108.39	5794.92	5335	14056	1455	311.03	23.84	75.86	59.43	2.39	8.81	0.56	4.67	270.43	219.25
1979		5980.00	5506	13865		364.60	26.70	91.10	70.81	2.34	11.66	0.47	5.82	260.40	228.34
1980	125.47	5729.00	5433	13521		342.80	32.20	97.79	74.72	3.10	13.96	0.83	5.18	252.91	238.62
1981	128.73	4850.00	5322	13240		332.20	35.50	100.23	77.64	2.62	16.16	0.61	3.20	247.81	236.77
1982	135.50	4557.00	5342	12902	1342	397.60	35.40	118.58	92.40	3.72	17.82	0.75	3.89	277.78	249.53
1983	157.81	3976.00	5365	13011	2637	499.00	41.50	139.22	113.00	4.05	16.89	0.72	4.56	299.06	276.68
1984	182.98	3999.00	5377	13062	2181	525.10	41.10	153.07	121.67	5.07	20.56	0.94	4.83	320.75	334.26
1985	199.50	4188.00	5359	12972	1492	477.10	40.90	167.33	123.42	6.15	31.15	1.37	5.24	341.94	435.82
1986	222.23	4435.00	5331	13159	3863	511.04	57.58	174.39	125.25	5.82	33.28	2.86	7.18	362.84	506.20
1987	240.67	4917.00	5408	13035	4126	535.74	50.18	200.66	137.80	6.83	43.63	4.29	8.11	369.46	640.85
1988	256.27	5241.00	5448	13180	1815	575.70	53.32	256.90	161.93	7.85	69.82	7.26	10.04	380.22	841.12
1989	270.76	5575.40	5524	13147	188		60.49	306.99	193.43	8.75	79.83	7.55	17.43	382.43	1026.09

3. Hebei

3–9

Year	v8a1	v8a2	v8a3	v8b	v8c1	v8c2	v8d	v8f1	v8f2	v8f3	v8f4	v8f5	v8g
1949	1.01	0.75	4.83		4.82	1.77		0.37	495		2.60	10.20	6479
1950	1.92	1.19	5.86		6.88	2.09		1.39	671		2.94	19.77	6931
1951	3.06	1.96	6.76		9.17	2.61		3.68	908		3.55	29.90	7554
1952	6.57	3.23	6.76		11.74	4.82		6.61	997		4.22	31.98	7553
1953	8.76	2.41	7.00		12.52	5.65		9.29	937		4.85	44.08	6387
1954	11.25	3.45	7.34		15.27	6.77		15.41	1157		5.79	45.53	5688
1955	13.14	4.17	5.65		16.03	6.93		21.28	1277		6.55	44.22	2850
1956	14.46	5.92	4.10		16.57	7.91		24.78	1358		8.74	57.77	1060
1957	15.21	5.87	4.78		17.72	8.14		24.77	1520		9.76	60.65	1076
1958	30.97	5.08	3.58		23.49	16.14		36.91	2527		16.15	67.44	3708
1959	56.85	6.98	0.01		37.46	26.38		42.35	3608		23.35	89.26	7605
1960	65.37	9.35	0.01		41.68	33.05		69.81	4144		35.10	107.61	6697
1961	36.33	5.75	0.01		23.16	18.93		19.00	2964		29.36	29.84	6380
1962	28.34	5.05	0.03		21.04	12.38		13.15	2510		25.19	26.59	5611
1963	28.96	4.49	0.04		21.74	11.75		14.44	2323		26.69	45.01	4465
1964	34.30	4.78	0.02		26.44	12.66		20.53	2339		29.26	64.44	4294
1965	43.61	5.77			31.49	17.89		29.25	2492		35.91	82.20	4298
1966	47.80	7.41			34.25	20.96		41.44	2541		43.22	96.60	4422
1967	55.29	8.47			44.81	18.95		46.65	2318		42.95	75.09	4438
1968	52.96	7.56			39.46	21.06		49.17	2820		49.56	83.46	4194
1969	64.33	9.31			47.19	26.45		48.35	3082		55.92	121.84	4659
1970	76.95	12.57			56.58	32.94		62.53	3566		65.41	187.16	7997
1971	80.77	17.87			50.53	48.11		80.25	3874		74.48	228.12	8881
1972	82.24	18.67			48.53	52.38		88.51	3995		80.95	255.07	9611
1973	89.96	21.83			53.89	57.90		101.77	4254		87.33	255.62	10131
1974	99.11	25.81			60.14	64.78		97.87	4629		97.23	317.14	10453
1975	112.81	33.80			71.83	74.78		111.16	5198		112.95	363.82	11207
1976	117.29	40.05			74.07	83.27		67.38	4374	597.30	113.28	379.07	12246
1977	132.25	52.88			86.62	98.51		94.16	4517	1229.80	122.68	399.65	13227
1978	157.48	61.77			97.64	121.61		145.49	5742	1723.00	168.69	463.50	14154
1979	167.02	61.32			99.42	128.92		167.58	5841	1733.00	190.51	515.37	14720
1980	174.96	62.63	1.03		110.50	128.12		190.39	5353	1602.70	196.36	549.82	15238
1981	173.35	60.40	3.02		118.84	117.93		182.87	5235	1221.70	199.32	522.41	15215
1982	181.39	64.47	3.67		122.80	126.73		185.90	5351	1130.58	204.60	587.40	15554
1983	200.45	69.49	6.74		133.46	143.22		214.63	5555	1055.34	218.30	644.73	15482
1984	213.11	107.72	13.43		159.80	174.46		230.76	5629	1021.10	241.14	776.80	17940
1985	255.83	160.11	19.88		202.68	233.14		249.13	6008	1031.71	261.97	942.72	18254
1986	283.43	191.25	31.52		236.83	269.37		269.52	6284	1000.97	292.44	1106.27	21204
1987	341.23	247.89	51.73		301.86	338.99		286.84	6381	795.39	312.59	1229.79	21624
1988	423.35	338.32	79.45	407.53	408.39	432.73		308.74	6434	630.52	346.34	1426.97	21981
1989	516.74	407.89	101.45	498.37	495.27	530.82		351.17	6324	577.96	365.58	1402.20	21789

3. Hebei

3–10

Year	v8g1	v9a	v9a1	v9a2	v9a3	v9b	v9b1	v9b2	v9b3	v9c	v10a	v10a1	v10b1	v10b2	v10b3
1949		0.30	0.02	0.28		1.18	0.03	0.27	0.88		8.95	8.33			
1950		0.73	0.01	0.54	0.17	1.65		0.61	1.04		11.01	10.25			
1951		1.35	0.02	1.04	0.29	2.30		1.03	1.27		14.76	13.75			
1952		1.78	0.03	1.52	0.23	3.19	0.01	1.75	1.44		16.92	15.79			
1953		2.26	0.04	1.88	0.34	3.96	0.02	2.42	1.52		20.41	18.81			
1954		2.84	0.04	2.51	0.29	5.11	0.03	3.41	1.67		22.22	20.24			
1955		3.17	0.03	2.86	0.28	5.47	0.02	3.61	1.84		23.93	21.84			
1956		3.34	0.03	2.99	0.32	5.83	0.03	4.04	1.75		28.26	25.38			
1957		3.92	0.04	3.55	0.32	6.15	0.04	4.46	1.65		26.82	24.59			
1958		5.48	0.06	5.21	0.21	8.23	0.07	6.53	1.63		31.63	25.04			
1959		6.55	0.05	6.18	0.32	12.81	0.16	10.49	2.17		35.26	29.47			
1960		6.70	0.08	6.33	0.29	13.29	0.24	10.59	2.46		37.83	29.47			
1961		5.74	0.30	5.10	0.34	7.49	0.39	5.42	1.61		32.65	26.27			
1962		7.01	0.35	6.31	0.35	5.85	0.35	4.25	1.25		31.04	26.25			
1963		5.51	0.22	5.10	0.19	5.95	0.39	4.28	1.29		30.71	26.28			
1964		5.22	0.25	4.73	0.24	8.33	0.57	5.99	1.77		34.04	29.14			
1965		6.74	0.32	6.30	0.13	7.99	0.42	6.25	1.32		32.04	26.63			
1966		8.21	0.42	7.65	0.14	8.30	0.69	6.47	1.15		33.85	27.59			
1967		7.78	0.43	7.25	0.10	6.98	0.51	5.72	0.69		32.88	27.15			
1968		7.79	0.40	7.35	0.03	7.16	0.62	5.99	0.55		31.88	26.52			
1969		9.53	0.42	9.04	0.07	8.99	0.73	7.32	0.94		37.24	29.89			
1970		10.74	0.49	10.16	0.09	13.55	1.27	8.87	3.41		42.26	32.36			
1971		12.26	0.47	11.73	0.06	18.85	1.62	10.55	6.68		45.13	33.71			
1972		14.10	0.56	13.52	0.02	20.51	1.65	12.90	5.95		51.22	37.71			
1973		15.04	0.49	14.51	0.04	23.44	1.82	13.61	8.01		54.17	39.98			
1974		17.03	0.48	16.51	0.04	27.16	2.11	15.85	9.21		58.99	43.19			
1975		105.71	87.89	17.81	0.01	493.10	463.66	19.85	9.60		66.83	47.56			
1976		106.84	87.67	19.15	0.02	451.28	421.73	22.06	7.50		71.98	52.48			
1977		119.65	97.42	22.20	0.03	538.48	502.29	27.75	8.44		78.56	57.55			
1978		127.11	101.79	25.24	0.03	620.10	579.99	31.48	8.93	5904	83.68	60.34	44.22		38.83
1979		136.11	108.60	27.50	0.01	658.23	617.83	30.94	9.46	6198	93.44	69.15	48.02		44.25
1980		151.13	121.08	30.05		682.69	646.22	25.44	11.03	6420	103.93	81.21	51.32		49.68
1981		162.32	129.99	32.34		716.63	684.84	21.94	9.85	9313	111.82	90.20	54.35		51.24
1982		176.81	141.79	35.01		768.94	730.25	27.56	11.13	9459	121.11	96.49	55.81		53.74
1983		202.49	162.51	39.98		849.15	799.43	33.26	16.46	10045	138.05	108.41	65.43		56.64
1984		236.94	189.44	47.50		916.51	856.47	34.54	25.50	11075	173.96	139.11	77.94		65.99
1985	3381	278.39	226.84	51.55		1725.96	967.01	168.03	28.35	12618	204.45	169.69	84.30		76.39
1986	3498	302.28	246.33	55.95		1857.55	1068.38	155.87	35.27	13822	230.55	192.28	93.54		80.31
1987	3544	336.35	274.46	61.89		1401.86	1166.94	188.66	37.59	16165	271.32	223.44	108.43		94.57
1988		420.80	313.04	107.76		1479.72	1178.49	234.44	43.56	20233	355.12	290.56	144.80		121.21
1989	3625	397.00	286.00	111.00		1545.32	1254.00	252.40	45.69	23733	374.48	304.60	156.10		123.82

3. Hebei

3–11

Year	v10b4	v10b5	v10b6	v10d	v11a1	v11a2	v11a3	v11b	v11b1	v11b2	v11c	v11d	v12a	v12b	v12c
1949			0.50												
1950			0.60	3.80											
1951			0.85	6.11									113.0	115.3	117.2
1952			1.03	7.17									102.8	101.2	102.6
1953			0.99	7.74	0.6960		0.1036						102.4	100.0	108.1
1954			0.93	11.15	0.5778	0.0312	0.1191						103.7	103.6	103.1
1955			1.02	12.48	0.5920	0.0039	0.1619						100.8	100.7	96.0
1956			0.98	9.94	0.7128	0.1378	0.2629						99.7	100.0	99.4
1957			1.01	11.27	0.5955	0.2739	0.2700						101.3	101.2	102.1
1958			0.32	13.95	0.9710	0.3292	0.3686						99.0	98.8	101.5
1959			0.50	19.44	1.5255	0.2876	0.2856						99.6	100.2	100.9
1960			0.66	15.39	0.8152	0.7187	0.4235						104.4	104.5	102.2
1961			1.26	10.80	0.5460	1.2037	0.3539						104.8	105.7	141.4
1962			1.36	8.78	0.5549	0.4990	0.5216						100.4	100.1	92.2
1963			0.92	9.43	0.6689	0.4954	0.5479						92.6	88.8	97.0
1964			0.54	11.34	0.7178	0.7528	0.5613						96.1	94.1	98.5
1965			0.41	14.49	1.1535	1.2306	0.7643						97.1	96.5	98.2
1966			0.40	14.52	1.3375	1.2548	0.9755						100.1	100.1	103.0
1967			0.36	14.64	1.3905	1.3010	0.8206						99.9	100.3	100.0
1968			0.32	15.66	1.2978	1.5484	0.7579						99.9	100.1	100.0
1969			0.33	16.26	1.2648	1.2095	0.4644						99.6	99.9	100.0
1970			0.33	15.69	1.1711	1.3308	0.4558						99.6	99.7	99.7
1971			0.31	18.96	1.2677	1.5161	0.8961						99.3	100.3	100.7
1972			0.31	17.32	1.5784	2.0091	0.9295						99.4	100.1	101.3
1973			0.27	18.81	1.9799	2.8276	1.1094						99.6	100.2	100.1
1974			0.24	20.64	2.2778	3.1762	1.3256						99.9	100.0	100.0
1975			0.27	20.94	2.6768	3.2852	1.3189	0.7832	0.7832				100.0	100.0	100.6
1976			0.36	18.75	2.0240	3.9118	0.8755	1.4202	1.4093	0.0109			100.2	100.2	100.1
1977			0.47	19.33	2.0252	3.7564	0.8033	2.3848	2.2694	0.1154			100.1	100.5	100.0
1978		0.08	0.55	21.11	1.9773	4.3247	1.0147	2.9852	2.7636	0.2216			99.8	100.2	106.1
1979		0.17	0.98	28.48	2.2591	6.3291	1.5679	4.3567	4.1628	0.1939			101.4	101.7	123.0
1980		1.40	1.53	37.91	2.5567	8.2681	2.3656	6.2962	6.0880	0.2082			105.3	107.2	114.2
1981		4.07	2.16	40.44	2.8328	10.0497	3.0251	8.0483	7.6663	0.3820			102.1	103.2	99.4
1982	0.02	8.12	3.42	48.39	3.1415	11.9253	3.2811	8.6071	8.0988	0.5083			101.5	100.9	101.2
1983	0.02	15.10	3.86	69.90	4.1149	12.1937	3.0659	8.6880	8.1693	0.5187			101.4	102.0	107.9
1984	0.11	24.16	5.76	88.90	4.1169	12.1207	2.3475	8.3730	7.6047	0.7683	0.0904	0.0546	103.4	103.1	105.3
1985	0.11	33.65	10.00	87.60	4.5771	15.7493	2.2075	14.1609	12.9854	1.1755	0.4804	0.1424	106.8	108.9	112.2
1986	0.28	42.51	13.91	95.43	7.5497	21.6857	4.0788	11.3134	10.5312	0.7822	0.1751	0.1127	105.2	106.0	105.1
1987	0.38	52.47	15.47	98.22	9.9893	23.9582	5.0247	15.9574	14.8475	1.1099	0.4539	0.1033	108.3	108.2	107.5
1988	0.40	66.51	22.20	130.67	11.2768	28.6171	6.9574	17.7832	15.4626	2.3206	1.9962	0.1910	118.3	118.1	113.9
1989	0.18	70.37	24.01	143.87	10.6613			18.6733	16.3743	2.2990	0.9487	0.9291	118.4	115.9	119.0

3. Hebei

3–12

Year	v13a	v13b	v13c1	v13c2	v13c3	v13d	v14a	v14b	v14c	v15a	v15b	v15c	v15d	v15e	v15f
1949	9.75		0.18	3.78	226.56	0.01	2200	25100		10899					
1950	12.03		0.22	4.94	257.43	0.02				11035					
1951	12.67		0.23	7.08	306.38	0.05				11194					
1952	12.40		0.21	12.77	372.28	0.08	8000	52000	0.0735	11425	101				
1953	25.64		0.28	16.44	367.16	0.07				11468					
1954	24.02		0.35	21.17	369.57	0.06				11465					
1955	23.54		0.37	23.51	376.66	0.10				11390					
1956	18.06		0.67	35.21	409.00	0.11				11394					
1957	20.82		0.85	45.82	412.29	0.11	18500	109000	0.0738	11319	197				
1958	9.92		1.80	75.15	486.79	0.14				10898					
1959	10.32		2.54	82.25	512.70	0.14				10657					
1960	8.24		3.11	95.85	528.43	0.49				10507					
1961	11.96		3.28	58.97	456.42	0.54				10427					
1962	20.84		2.70	42.79	402.43	0.64	40300	69100	0.0400	10431	206				
1963	13.54		2.40	39.05	430.81	0.75				10423					
1964	10.99		2.36	47.28	573.03	0.61				10488					
1965	14.14		2.55	68.78	687.83	0.56	41300	73400	0.0859	10476	1678				
1966	15.64		2.62	68.83	662.05					10437					
1967	18.77		2.59	64.92	661.71					10403					
1968			0.98	83.09	628.26	1.61				10357					
1969	12.31		0.86	122.84	608.41	0.11				10324					
1970	9.83		0.55	162.87	627.89	0.86	47100	72100	0.4812	10274					
1971	11.06		0.55	231.71	652.56					10189					
1972	11.52		0.91	239.97	699.00	0.31				10087					
1973	11.59		1.43	228.60	729.07	0.01				10115					
1974	11.98		1.68	230.50	760.63	0.30				10099					
1975	11.70	97.7	1.71	274.72	768.73	0.64	72400	106300	2.1357	10078					
1976	9.23	98.0	1.85	352.70	753.37	0.56	74500	113800	1.2419	10043					
1977	8.48	97.4	2.42	407.34	728.69	0.52	82200	117500	1.6407	10029					
1978	9.56	96.7	2.90	389.98	746.32	0.71	89000	129600	3.4385	10013	4462				
1979	10.34	96.5	3.10	359.89	744.30	0.64	95000	144400	3.3385	9989	4188				
1980	15.27	97.0	4.15	334.03	734.57	0.23	95500	152300	3.8773	9972	4243			141.71	61.22
1981	19.29	96.9	4.50	290.42	720.30	0.07	97900	161900	5.4771	9968	4226				
1982	19.51	96.7	3.87	261.13	680.61	1.74	101800	172500	5.7976	9962	4329				
1983	20.46	97.0	4.19	253.50	634.10	1.20	107100	179800	6.0473	9955	4579				
1984	18.36	97.6	4.86	259.23	607.90	1.10	110200	186400	6.8201	9943	4783				
1985	22.34	97.7	5.82	266.31	601.30	1.20	120900	187400	7.0427	9905	4749			147.56	63.59
1986	21.88	98.2	6.51	269.15	601.39	1.42	124800	195200	7.6702	9888	4436		200	147.60	62.03
1987	23.40	98.7	6.92	266.13	608.44	1.85	133200	199700	9.4955	9864	4706		200	148.81	64.63
1988	23.94	98.7	7.30	248.46	639.98	2.08	138100	205500	10.2144	9851	4938		200	148.84	65.64
1989		98.9	7.51	218.27	677.10	2.12	124000	175000	7.8001	9841					

Notes

1. National Output and Income (Y)

v1a: (E), p.128
  v1a1: (E), p.128
  v1a2: (E), p.128
  v1a3: (E), p.128
  v1a4: (E), p.128
  v1a5: (E), p.128

v1b: (A); (D), p.119
  v1b1: (A); (D), p.119
  v1b2: (A); (D), p.119
  v1b3: (A); (D), p.119
  v1b4: (A); (D), p.119
  v1b5: (A); (D), p.119

v1c: v1a – v1d

v1d: (A); (E), p.125
  v1d1: (E), p.125
  v1d2: (E), p.125
  v1d3: (E), p.125
  v1d4: (E), p.125
  v1d5: (E), p.125

v1e: (A); (D), p.122
  v1e1: (A); (D), p.122
  v1e2: (A); (D), p.122
  v1e3: (A); (D), p.122
  v1e4: (A); (D), p.122
  v1e5: (A); (D), p.122

v1f: (E), p.124
  v1f1: (E), p.124
  v1f2: (E), p.124
  v1f3: (E), p.124

v1g: v2a + v3a

v1h: (A); (E), p.152

v1i: (E), p.151

v1j: (E), p.151
  v1j1: (E), p.151
  v1j2: (E), p.151
  v1j3: NA

v1k: (E), p.151

2. Investment (I)

v2a: (E), p.127
  v2a1: (A); (D), p.127
  v2a2: (A); (D), p.127

v2b: (A)

v2c: (A); (E), p.142
  v2c1: (E), p.143
  v2c2: (E), p.143

v2d:
  v2d1: (A)
  v2d2: (A)

v2e: (A)

3. Consumption (C)

v3a: (E), p.127

v3b: (E), p.127
  v3b1: (E), p.127
  v3b2: (E), p.127

v3c: (E), p.127

v3d: (E), p.150
  v3d1: (E), p.150
  v3d2: (E), p.150

v3e: (A)
  v3e1: (A); (E), p.152
  v3e2: (A)
  v3e3: (A)
  v3e4: (A)

v3f: (A); (E), p.152
  v3f1: (A)

v3f2: (A)
v3f3: (A)
v3f4: (A)

4. Public Finance and Banking (FB)

v4a:
v4a1: (E), p.148
v4a1a: (E), p.148
v4a1b: (B), p.392
v4a1c: (B), p.392
v4a1d: v4a1 – v4a1a – v4a1b – v4a1c
v4a2: (E), p.148
v4a2a: (E), p.148
v4a2b: (E), p.148
v4a2c: (E), p.148
v4a2d: v4a2 – v4a2a – v4a2b – v4a2c

v4b: (A)
v4b1: (A); (B), p.435
v4b2: (A); (B), p.435
v4b3: (B), p.394

v4c:
v4c1: (A)
v4c2: NA

5. Labor Force (L)

v5a: (E), p.123; (A)
v5a1: (E), p.123
v5a2: (E), p.123
v5a3: (E), p.123
v5a4: (E), p.123—excluding rural people working outside

v5b:
v5b1: (E), p.123
v5b2: (E), p.123
v5b3: (E), p.123

v5c: (B), p.424
v5c1: (B), p.425

v5d: (B), p.424—farming, forestry, animal husbandry, fishery and irrigation works

6. Population (PO)

v6a: (E), p.122—population in 1986–89 are estimated from sample surveys, while the rest from the estimates by public security department
v6a1: (E), p.122
v6a2: (E), p.122

v6b: (E), p.122—data of 1973–80 were based on information from the Third Population Census; since 1984 they have been based on sample surveys

v6c: (E), p.122—(ditto)

v6d:
v6d1: (E), p.122
v6d2: (E), p.122
v6d3: (E), p.122
v6d4: (E), p.122
v6d5: (B), p.447—Tangshan
v6d6: (B), p.454—Langfang

7. Agriculture (A)

v7a: (A); (E), p.135

v7b: (A); (E), p.135

v7c: (A); (E), p.135

v7d: (A)

v7e: (A)

v7f: (A)

v7g: (A); (E), p.135

v7h: (E), p.130
v7h1: (E), p.130
v7h2: (E), p.130
v7h3: (E), p.130

v7h4: (E), p.130
v7h5: (E), p.130

v7i: (E), p.134

8. Industry (IN)

v8a: (E), p.136
v8a1: (E), p.136
v8a2: (E), p.136
v8a3: v8a – v8a1 – v8a2

v8b: (A)

v8c1: (E), p.128
v8c2: (E), p.128

v8d: NA

v8f:
v8f1: (E), p.140
v8f2: (E), p.140
v8f3: (E), p.140
v8f4: (E), p.140
v8f5: (E), p.140

v8g: (A); (B), p.333
v8g1: (A)

9. Transport (TR)

v9a: (E), p.141—excluding urban traffic volume; 1974 and before were local figures, afterward figures are of the whole society
v9a1: (E), p.141—including central and local railways
v9a2: (E), p.141
v9a3: (E), p.141—excluding distant ocean and coastal passenger traffic

v9b: (E), p.141—1974 and before were local figures, afterward figures are of the whole society
v9b1: (A); (E), p.141—including central and local railways
v9b2: (A); (E), p.141
v9b3: (E), p.141—excluding distant ocean and coastal freight volume

v9c: (E), p.141—figures of 1981 and before are based on 1970's constant price, the rest are based on 1980's constant price

10. Domestic Trade (DT)

v10a: (E), p.144
v10a1: (E), p.144

v10b:
v10b1: (E), p.144
v10b2: NA
v10b3: (E), p.144—collective ownership
v10b4: (E), p.144
v10b5: (E), p.144
v10b6: (E), p.144

v10d: (E), p.146—calculated on calendar year basis. Figures of 1978 and before are the amount procured by state and collective commercial system, figures afterward by the whole society

11. Foreign Trade (FT)

v11a:
v11a1: (A); (B), p.386
v11a2: (B), p.386—textile and other products of light industry
v11a3: (B), p.386—industrial and mining products

v11b: (E), p.147
v11b1: (E), p.147
v11b2: v11b – v11b1

v11c: (E), p.147

v11d: (E), p.147

12. Prices (PR)

v12a: (E), p.149

v12b: (E), p.149

v12c: (E), p.149

13. Education (ED)

v13a: (A); (B), p.408

v13b: (A); (B), p.152

v13c:

- v13c1: (A); (E), p.152—general institutions of higher learning
- v13c2: (A); (E), p.152
- v13c3: (A); (E), p.152

v13d: (A); (B), p.403—general institutions of higher learning

14. Social Factors (SF)

v14a: (A); (E), p.152

v14b: (A)—medical technicians, other technicians, management people and other workers

v14c: (A)

15. Natural Environment (NE)

v15a: (A); (E), p.135

v15b: (A)

v15c: NA

v15d: (A)

v15e: (A)

v15f: (A)

Sources of Data

(A) Data supplied by the DSNEB, SSB, the PRC.

(B) Statistical Bureau of Hebei Province, People's Government General Office of Hebei province ed. *New Hebei's Forty Years 1949–1989*, Beijing: CSPH, 1989.

(D) Same as (D) in Beijing's sources of data.

(E) Same as (E) in Beijing's sources of data.

4

Shanxi

4. Shanxi

4–1

Year	v1a	v1a1	v1a2	v1a3	v1a4	v1a5	v1b	v1b1	v1b2	v1b3	v1b4	v1b5	v1c	v1d	v1d1
1949	10.83	8.27	2.03	0.01	0.05	0.47							3.56	7.27	6.15
1950	13.60	9.58	2.92	0.29	0.11	0.70							4.76	8.84	7.12
1951	16.37	10.60	3.87	0.53	0.25	1.12							5.96	10.41	7.89
1952	21.33	12.24	5.57	1.13	0.70	1.69	131.0	121.9	147.4	187.7	289.7	148.9	8.32	13.01	9.10
1953	26.06	14.42	7.00	1.58	0.68	2.38	112.2	105.7	123.8	140.3	94.4	144.5	10.25	15.81	10.72
1954	29.04	14.86	9.11	1.80	0.82	2.45	109.8	101.5	134.4	119.6	118.4	105.7	11.57	17.47	11.21
1955	31.27	15.19	10.53	1.93	1.25	2.37	101.3	91.1	120.9	108.6	149.1	97.1	12.19	19.08	11.72
1956	39.25	17.61	12.91	4.21	1.19	3.33	125.5	120.4	122.5	197.5	94.4	140.4	16.79	22.46	13.18
1957	42.16	15.41	14.84	6.60	1.45	3.86	109.3	92.3	115.4	184.9	115.2	117.9	19.30	22.86	11.18
1958	59.24	17.82	23.66	10.06	2.73	4.97	139.4	115.7	166.2	151.1	186.8	128.6	28.37	30.87	13.26
1959	78.27	17.65	39.80	12.28	2.93	5.61	120.2	99.2	145.3	114.5	107.9	113.1	40.97	37.30	12.03
1960	83.32	11.98	49.90	14.22	2.94	4.28	102.8	73.1	123.4	113.0	99.7	76.6	45.36	37.96	8.59
1961	53.32	14.39	27.81	4.61	2.24	4.27	65.7	102.4	56.0	32.0	76.6	113.8	28.19	25.13	10.04
1962	50.77	15.07	25.65	3.82	2.06	4.17	92.0	103.8	85.8	86.2	93.5	83.7	26.35	24.42	10.72
1963	54.16	15.82	28.17	3.98	2.19	4.00	108.5	110.7	110.9	105.5	106.0	88.9	28.73	25.43	11.15
1964	61.86	17.69	32.53	4.89	2.27	4.48	115.2	115.5	115.2	121.9	103.9	112.7	32.50	29.36	12.68
1965	72.92	17.35	42.34	5.82	2.62	4.79	120.7	104.2	133.7	125.4	114.5	127.5	39.37	33.55	12.30
1966	83.27	19.53	50.47	5.45	2.85	4.97	107.4	100.2	114.7	94.6	109.5	103.2	45.22	38.05	13.77
1967	73.29	19.94	43.01	3.48	2.27	4.59	88.4	107.8	80.3	63.8	78.4	92.0	38.52	34.77	13.88
1968	56.24	19.23	27.40	3.30	2.11	4.20	81.1	87.9	72.2	94.7	91.6	91.7	27.74	28.50	13.27
1969	72.36	21.68	39.49	3.98	2.54	4.67	123.9	112.6	137.9	120.9	121.9	109.7	36.92	35.44	15.17
1970	99.79	20.72	62.57	7.16	2.91	6.43	130.8	97.9	151.6	180.0	113.3	135.3	54.99	44.80	14.71
1971	107.30	24.58	62.81	10.03	3.17	6.71	111.2	106.9	110.6	137.8	107.2	104.3	59.06	48.24	17.62
1972	106.54	22.27	64.03	9.80	3.44	6.99	100.5	90.9	105.2	95.7	110.5	104.1	59.34	47.20	15.15
1973	115.95	26.11	70.55	9.41	3.72	6.16	108.7	116.8	109.9	94.9	108.0	88.1	65.16	50.79	18.09
1974	112.00	27.42	65.77	8.88	3.57	6.36	97.5	105.4	94.1	92.2	96.0	103.4	62.80	49.20	18.59
1975	125.16	29.96	76.17	8.90	3.38	6.75	110.6	109.2	115.3	98.4	94.7	96.2	71.61	53.55	20.10
1976	118.26	28.55	70.60	8.49	3.16	7.47	94.4	95.0	93.3	93.8	93.1	104.3	69.67	48.59	18.38
1977	141.41	28.97	89.44	10.51	3.90	8.59	119.0	102.0	125.7	122.0	123.6	130.4	85.09	56.32	18.31
1978	163.44	29.01	106.43	12.97	5.17	9.86	114.0	93.8	120.3	121.4	132.5	115.4	95.53	67.91	17.67
1979	192.64	36.76	120.71	16.45	6.43	12.29	115.3	113.5	107.7	123.8	124.5	106.6	107.26	85.38	22.35
1980	197.72	38.23	126.34	14.22	9.20	9.73	95.2	93.7	102.9	84.6	143.0	80.1	112.79	84.93	20.25
1981	214.64	46.02	128.87	18.73	9.85	11.17	103.3	103.5	99.8	127.8	107.1	108.9	120.47	94.17	30.64
1982	245.72	53.08	141.80	26.14	11.98	12.72	116.0	121.9	112.1	135.6	121.6	103.6	136.16	109.56	36.23
1983	280.52	53.81	166.34	32.11	13.40	14.86	112.5	101.9	115.4	117.5	111.8	112.2	156.79	123.73	36.69
1984	337.25	65.15	194.60	43.21	17.40	16.89	119.2	117.9	116.5	129.2	129.9	127.4	185.18	152.07	44.90
1985	404.54	62.92	238.09	60.58	22.31	20.64	114.7	92.3	116.1	138.2	128.2	112.1	232.32	172.22	42.66
1986	430.80	58.82	261.80	61.63	24.76	23.79	105.4	91.7	108.1	101.4	109.9		250.71	180.09	38.06
1987	486.77	61.42	304.29	69.63	23.34	28.09	107.7	97.2	111.5	109.3	85.7		297.70	189.07	37.63
1988	613.64	87.25	387.22	69.94	26.30	42.93	110.7	112.5	114.9	89.4	101.5		380.30	233.34	51.32
1989	732.06	104.94	487.65	65.03	30.02	44.41	105.9	107.4	111.2	83.0	102.3		453.07	278.99	66.91

4. Shanxi

4–2

Year	v1d2	v1d3	v1d4	v1d5	v1e	v1e1	v1e2	v1e3	v1e4	v1e5	v1f	v1f1	v1f2	v1f3	v1g
1949	0.73		0.02	0.37											
1950	1.02	0.10	0.04	0.56											
1951	1.35	0.19	0.10	0.88											
1952	1.90	0.40	0.28	1.33	127.8	122.0	146.8	203.9	289.8	148.9					12.23
1953	2.41	0.53	0.30	1.86	110.7	105.5	125.4	139.7	105.2	143.7					14.65
1954	3.52	0.53	0.37	1.84	108.7	103.1	151.0	104.7	123.3	102.2					16.62
1955	4.36	0.62	0.60	1.78	100.8	93.3	129.1	114.8	160.2	96.7					17.40
1956	4.89	1.44	0.56	2.40	119.5	116.7	112.5	218.3	89.2	134.8					23.16
1957	6.02	2.22	0.66	2.78	103.4	89.7	123.5	173.7	115.0	117.8					25.17
1958	9.62	3.18	1.30	3.51	134.0	118.6	166.1	145.0	195.2	126.0					33.11
1959	16.42	3.45	1.43	3.97	110.6	91.0	147.6	102.3	109.7	113.5					40.05
1960	20.41	4.32	1.44	3.21	99.1	76.9	122.4	121.8	100.6	81.0					37.97
1961	9.86	1.39	0.99	2.85	67.9	99.7	48.5	33.1	68.0	101.3					25.23
1962	8.88	1.25	0.93	2.64	94.3	105.7	84.1	87.8	97.0	79.4					20.22
1963	9.68	1.29	0.96	2.35	106.6	109.8	109.9	103.0	102.7	82.7					22.98
1964	11.41	1.60	0.99	2.68	117.3	117.5	117.7	125.5	102.6	114.5					24.15
1965	15.25	1.89	1.16	2.94	117.0	103.0	137.1	123.9	119.0	130.9					30.65
1966	18.32	1.98	1.41	2.58	105.2	99.6	115.8	105.1	120.7	87.3					31.77
1967	15.61	1.63	1.11	2.55	92.0	100.2	84.1	82.1	76.2	98.6					28.43
1968	10.28	1.68	1.00	2.27	85.0	92.7	70.8	102.6	90.7	89.2					27.26
1969	14.67	1.85	1.22	2.53	120.8	114.3	137.1	109.9	123.7	109.9					34.86
1970	23.04	2.22	1.44	3.39	120.4	99.3	150.6	117.3	116.1	131.8					37.35
1971	22.91	2.76	1.51	3.42	108.5	107.9	108.9	121.2	104.9	100.8					47.50
1972	22.94	4.14	1.61	3.37	98.7	86.2	103.2	149.5	106.4	101.7					49.68
1973	24.92	2.66	1.71	3.40	107.5	119.0	108.4	62.7	106.4	100.9					46.95
1974	23.08	2.44	1.70	3.39	97.2	103.1	93.4	89.7	99.2	100.3					51.22
1975	26.16	2.27	1.47	3.55	107.8	108.0	113.0	91.3	86.6	94.5					52.84
1976	24.01	1.50	1.35	3.34	90.5	91.9	92.3	65.4	91.9	88.8					49.83
1977	30.13	2.06	1.72	4.10	115.3	100.3	124.5	134.7	127.8	139.2					58.90
1978	39.44	3.11	2.33	5.36	118.9	93.5	133.2	148.8	134.9	131.3	87.99	18.20	51.47	18.32	63.25
1979	46.98	5.70	3.27	7.08	116.0	109.6	113.4	180.1	140.5	112.9	105.92	22.65	62.73	20.54	78.89
1980	51.45	4.95	2.82	5.45	96.1	84.9	107.5	79.0	86.2	77.9	107.68	20.63	63.51	23.53	82.24
1981	48.34	5.69	3.00	6.51	103.9	125.6	93.4	112.0	106.1	113.5	118.02	31.13	62.45	24.44	90.00
1982	53.76	7.75	4.49	7.34	118.3	123.6	114.0	131.8	149.9	102.5	136.64	37.33	70.25	29.06	105.03
1983	61.73	10.71	5.75	8.84	111.5	102.1	112.6	132.3	128.1	115.8	151.55	37.79	82.55	31.20	122.12
1984	75.74	12.89	8.28	10.27	121.6	120.1	120.3	115.5	143.9	130.1	191.86	46.25	103.12	42.49	147.29
1985	89.05	17.83	10.27	12.41	108.1	90.0	110.3	137.5	124.1	111.6	211.38	42.26	120.06	49.06	187.19
1986	96.98	18.61	12.02	14.42	104.1	90.5	107.1	104.5	110.7	120.1	224.67	37.90	128.25	58.52	198.28
1987	104.53	19.04	10.91	16.96	103.1	90.4	107.1	107.3	86.9	116.0	243.92	39.06	137.97	66.88	223.71
1988	125.36	20.23	11.95	24.48	107.7	115.8	108.9	89.9	101.9	107.9	297.24	48.54	163.29	85.41	266.13
1989	153.82	18.92	12.14	27.20	104.4	106.5	110.5	83.5	88.4	89.2	351.69	63.75	188.75	99.19	300.91

4. Shanxi

4–3

Year	v1h	v1i	v1j	v1j1	v1j2	v1j3	v1k	v2a	v2a1	v2a2	v2b	v2c	v2c1	v2c2	v2d1
1949	52.21	0.3274	159	161	126		0.0359								1.01
1950		0.5613	229	232	181		0.0576								
1951		0.9733	312	322	251		0.0961								
1952		1.5415	375	394	307		0.1485	2.20	1.54	0.66					3.28
1953		2.0364	450	452	325		0.2179	2.83	2.04	0.79					
1954	74.80	2.7134	455	483	377		0.3129	4.08	3.18	0.90					
1955	85.00	3.2783	501	512	399		0.4537	4.21	3.35	0.86					
1956	86.50	5.1319	543	598	466		0.7005	7.74	7.05	0.68					
1957	80.00	6.0468	608	625	488		0.7560	10.04	7.39	2.65					12.50
1958	76.51	7.0274	519	565	441		0.7730	15.35	14.54	0.81					
1959	67.55	8.7200	512	541	422		1.0165	21.14	15.20	5.94					
1960		9.5634	528	556	434		1.1732	18.40	16.90	1.50					
1961	100.05	8.7333	536	564	440		1.2294	6.16	5.77	0.39					
1962	94.40	7.2769	571	630	491		0.9613	1.40	3.26	-1.86					32.75
1963	86.40	7.3752	646	682	532		0.9529	3.79	4.04	-0.25					
1964	83.74	7.8377	662	694	541		0.9507	4.25	5.62	-1.37					
1965	91.83	8.0425	638	682	532		0.9599	10.24	6.92	3.32					39.86
1966	91.40	8.1556	616	659	514		0.8559	10.20	8.05	2.15					
1967	92.65	8.1368	615	641	500		0.8346	6.14	5.16	0.99					
1968	85.51	8.4014	611	640	499		0.8600	5.92	3.96	1.96					
1969	99.52	8.6342	579	633	494		0.8824	11.07	5.88	5.19					
1970	94.66	9.2890	588	631	492		0.9620	12.87	10.88	1.99					53.94
1971	103.06	10.5909	564	615	480		1.0644	20.56	14.43	6.13					59.28
1972	92.93	11.7334	604	634	495		1.1954	21.52	14.29	7.23					
1973	102.65	12.0065	617	637	518		1.2135	16.53	14.11	2.42					
1974	101.32	12.4675	629	643	539		1.2455	18.94	13.33	5.61					
1975	100.72	12.8565	622	643	507		1.2822	19.53	14.53	4.99					102.20
1976	88.52	13.3630	610	635	482		1.2420	15.68	13.50	2.18					110.21
1977	93.60	13.8436	611	636	489		1.4394	22.66	17.06	5.61					120.43
1978	101.61	16.6539	632	655	519		1.9890	25.41	18.92	6.48		19.47	10.31	0.51	131.57
1979	145.41	18.7194	672	712	528		2.1466	28.24	18.78	9.46		20.13	9.97	0.43	140.55
1980	155.78	21.9497	754	795	581		2.8919	24.72	19.27	5.45		22.51	10.97	0.55	153.47
1981	179.53	23.2787	761	802	593		3.3293	25.91	17.69	8.22	25.47	17.93	6.76	0.58	164.58
1982	227.18	25.1330	785	830	600		3.7351	34.14	24.39	9.75	34.55	25.17	10.14	1.10	184.41
1983	275.77	27.1215	827	868	649		4.5624	43.29	32.19	11.10	44.83	31.46	14.95	1.00	196.64
1984	338.78	35.5910	1024	1086	807	1000	5.6103	56.48	42.48	14.00	68.90	49.23	25.00	0.65	208.23
1985	358.32	40.9818	1122	1200	856	1606	7.0663	82.09	61.73	20.36	91.69	67.70	32.24	1.63	246.86
1986	344.98	49.8937	1299	1386	992	2670	8.3367	85.71	67.76	17.95	97.02	72.99	34.68	1.17	275.23
1987	376.87	56.9955	1427	1521	1097	3050	9.5599	98.25	71.27	26.98	106.24	90.03	31.81	1.32	310.29
1988	438.73	68.1929	1661	1786	1216	3672	12.6885	106.43	65.57	40.86	107.68	78.55	32.44	1.47	352.68
1989	513.87	79.5060	1902	2035	1402		16.5705	117.87	56.66	61.21	105.34	80.37	35.10	1.07	397.19

4. Shanxi

4–4

Year	v2d2	v2e	v3a	v3b	v3b1	v3b2	v3c	v3d	v3d1	v3d2	v3e	v3e1	v3e2	v3e3	v3e4
1949	0.61														
1950															
1951															
1952	2.07		10.03	9.85	8.03	1.82	0.18	71	66	119					
1953			11.82	11.54	8.82	2.72	0.28	81	71	154					
1954			12.54	12.23	8.83	3.39	0.31	84	70	177					
1955			13.19	12.85	9.01	3.84	0.34	86	71	178					
1956			15.42	14.94	10.06	4.88	0.48	97	78	198					
1957	9.97		15.13	14.55	9.04	5.51	0.58	92	69	206					
1958			17.76	17.03	10.49	6.54	0.73	105	78	229					
1959			18.91	17.80	9.89	7.91	1.11	107	73	257					
1960			19.57	18.35	8.96	9.40	1.22	108	66	277					
1961			19.07	17.84	9.67	8.17	1.23	104	70	241					
1962	26.89	6.65	18.82	17.96	10.30	7.66	0.86	103	70	288					
1963			19.19	18.22	11.04	7.18	0.97	103	72	293					
1964			19.90	18.83	11.86	6.97	1.07	104	76	272					
1965	30.96	5.32	20.41	19.29	12.27	7.02	1.12	104	77	260					
1966			21.57	20.66	13.24	7.41	0.91	109	82	265					
1967			22.29	21.64	13.90	7.73	0.65	111	84	260					
1968			21.35	20.86	13.60	7.27	0.48	105	81	240					
1969			23.79	23.13	15.53	7.59	0.66	113	90	246					
1970	38.11		24.48	23.70	15.72	7.98	0.78	113	88	250					
1971	43.81	13.99	26.94	25.82	17.09	8.73	1.12	120	94	259					
1972			28.16	26.92	16.45	10.48	1.24	122	89	298					
1973			30.42	28.91	18.01	10.90	1.51	128	95	299					
1974			32.28	30.35	19.20	11.15	1.93	132	100	299					
1975	75.98	26.11	33.31	31.04	19.63	11.41	2.27	133	100	298					
1976	81.94	27.74	34.15	32.07	19.75	12.32	2.08	135	99	315					
1977	88.96	29.21	36.24	33.95	20.59	13.36	2.29	141	103	335					
1978	97.62	30.49	37.84	35.23	20.84	14.40	2.61	144	103	343	275.4				
1979	99.03	32.78	50.65	45.19	27.72	17.47	5.46	184	138	399	304.8				
1980	106.78	33.47	57.52	51.97	30.54	21.43	5.55	209	150	465	356.6	194.8			
1981	115.46	33.84	64.08	58.59	35.11	23.48	5.50	232	172	488	373.2	196.8			
1982	126.10	36.87	70.89	64.21	40.02	24.19	6.68	251	194	495	389.9	209.6			
1983	131.07	38.40	78.83	70.71	44.09	26.62	8.12	274	212	525	393.5	216.1			
1984	139.61	41.23	90.81	80.37	49.86	30.51	10.44	308	240	577	433.3	230.8			
1985	168.26	48.63	105.10	93.25	54.50	38.80	11.85	354	261	713	533.4	262.2			
1986	185.57	55.71	112.57	98.74	56.82	41.75	13.84	374	271	774	634.8	303.4			
1987	211.42	62.86	125.46	109.73	60.66	49.07	15.73	411	287	873	707.5	347.2			
1988	233.14	72.52	159.70	139.85	75.86	63.99	19.85	516	356	1099	855.6	403.9			
1989	274.56	90.68	183.04	157.28	87.12	70.16	25.76	571	405	1169	993.5	479.7			

4. Shanxi

4–5

Year	v3f	v3f1	v3f2	v3f3	v3f4	v4a1	v4a1a	v4a1b	v4a1c	v4a1d	v4a2	v4a2a	v4a2b	v4a2c	v4a2d
1949						0.08		0.0345			0.08			0.05	
1950						0.67	0.0021	0.2421		-0.0021	0.39			0.13	
1951						1.32	0.1169	0.4930		0.0931	0.59			0.22	
1952						1.83	0.2953	0.7826		0.0547	1.09			0.36	
1953						2.35	0.2970	1.2091		0.1130	1.66			0.44	
1954	70.30	39.50	9.40	0.50	5.00	3.05	0.4823	1.5073		0.2077	2.07			0.50	
1955	77.10	43.65	9.30	0.20	5.60	3.15	0.5356	1.5699		0.1944	1.96			0.51	
1956	76.10	42.40	10.30	0.27	5.80	3.22	0.4891	1.7720		0.1809	3.02			0.66	
1957	76.60	42.80	9.20	0.10	6.10	3.52	0.5375	1.9780		0.2525	2.88			0.57	
1958	67.70	41.57	10.88	0.16	5.25	6.74	2.9822	2.7375		0.2378	6.88			0.60	
1959	67.50	37.27	11.99	0.51	7.90	9.38	5.0743	3.4228		0.0457	9.67			0.78	
1960						11.61	6.9757	3.8811		0.0943	13.08			0.84	
1961	86.59	50.06	9.83		10.86	6.88	3.3033	2.8334		0.0767	7.30			0.71	
1962	98.01	53.00	11.48	6.11	10.63	5.40	1.7787	2.9348		0.0813	3.64			0.58	
1963	85.19	51.45	9.13	3.85	7.71	6.22	2.5131	2.9354		0.0769	4.21			0.73	
1964	79.30	50.73	8.45	3.12	7.38	5.97	1.9472	3.1989		0.0928	4.95			0.78	
1965	85.01	55.38	11.49	1.66	6.54	6.86	2.5093	3.6184		0.1107	5.11			0.78	
1966	77.49	52.22	9.46	1.29	5.34	7.74	3.2243	3.7003		0.0557	6.74			0.77	
1967	82.54	54.17	9.81	1.03	6.14	6.17	2.1666	3.2523		0.0434	5.88			0.69	
1968	75.48	50.49	9.01	1.21	5.25	3.88	0.6493	2.5304		0.0207	4.84			0.68	
1969	90.42	59.48	10.65	1.63	6.53	5.08	1.1243	3.1286		0.0257	6.28			0.80	
1970	84.28	54.94	10.81	0.91	6.13	9.21	3.8886	4.5069		0.0514	9.42			0.86	
1971	92.46	57.26	13.60	1.21	6.52	12.68	6.8022	5.0120		0.0678	9.96			0.94	
1972	81.63	51.46	9.22	1.43	4.89	13.71	7.2470	5.7101		0.0530	11.47			1.03	
1973	90.24	56.21	11.53	1.54	5.14	14.73	7.6330	6.2638		0.0370	12.36			1.00	
1974	88.16	55.43	12.15	0.83	5.01	10.93	3.9534	6.1126		0.0366	15.33			1.03	
1975	86.35	55.21	11.23	1.63	4.22	12.39	4.5548	6.9855		0.0352	14.98	6.73	2.09	1.12	5.04
1976	72.14	47.21	9.87	2.10	5.32	9.74	2.1287	6.6980		0.0713	15.98	7.39	2.20	1.16	5.23
1977	84.28	56.32	11.32	1.45	4.89	13.23	4.2130	8.1239		0.0570	16.41	6.72	2.30	1.29	6.10
1978	90.64	61.02	13.02	0.50	5.42	19.64	8.4698	9.4709		0.9802	21.11	8.81	2.86	1.46	7.98
1979	118.31	72.95	18.04	4.14	5.76	20.29	8.8895	9.8876		0.6905	20.74	6.68	3.36	1.67	9.03
1980	134.38	80.48	20.81	9.20	6.18	20.96	9.3571	10.1562		0.7429	19.61	6.30	4.00	1.95	7.36
1981	147.78	85.86	23.88	12.15	5.55	19.70	7.6191	10.6609		0.7209	17.47	4.76	4.10	2.00	6.61
1982	167.66	104.78	25.11	9.89	6.46	20.27	6.4589	12.1428		0.8911	20.84	5.40	5.08	2.38	7.98
1983	203.35	117.42	27.92	19.46	7.65	24.15	8.4766	11.6213		1.1034	24.01	6.13	6.01	2.83	9.04
1984	224.33	130.42	29.63	21.58	9.34	27.18	8.1966	17.0331		1.0334	29.98	7.00	7.19	4.13	11.67
1985	272.74	148.13	39.88	28.72	8.95	24.99	1.8759	22.5666		-5.4759	35.55	9.22	8.17	4.09	14.07
1986	287.44	156.98	37.35	35.59	8.68	28.64	-0.0375	24.1584		-1.7325	41.17	7.43	9.86	5.05	18.83
1987	312.72	162.23	38.79	44.08	8.78	33.61	0.2648	28.8259		-2.2648	41.95	6.16	10.10	5.18	20.51
1988	354.25	188.69	46.35	38.58	10.72	39.04	-4.9400	33.8546		2.2400	43.49	4.16	12.16	4.94	22.23
1989	409.25	214.69	53.89	42.55	13.57	48.31	-6.2100			4.4400	50.85	3.77	14.12	6.07	26.89

4. Shanxi

4–6

Year	v4b	v4b1	v4b2	v4b3	v4c1	v4c2	v5a	v5a1	v5a2	v5a3	v5a4	v5b1	v5b2	v5b3	v5c
1949		0.0013			0.24	22.78	582.78	20.34	0.15	21.12	541.17	522.55			27.55
1950		0.0173					604.09	24.38	0.15	22.70	556.86	535.46			30.59
1951	0.0658	0.0528	0.0130				623.39	29.53	1.66	23.95	568.25	547.24			35.37
1952	0.1042	0.0335	0.0207		0.79	22.02	650.59	37.72	3.38	25.22	584.27	561.63			39.47
1953	0.2341	0.1285	0.1056				671.96	41.89	3.28	26.76	600.03	578.42			43.11
1954	0.3866	0.1975	0.1891				671.31	50.20	9.50	22.41	589.20	574.72			45.95
1955	0.4015	0.2740	0.1275				671.07	55.12	10.38	22.27	583.30	572.85			43.92
1956	0.6478	0.4639	0.1839				661.06	77.86	16.70	6.96	559.54	557.97			39.24
1957	0.9638	0.6144	0.3494		2.29	10.69	643.01	80.00	19.52	5.75	537.74	536.50			39.80
1958	1.2603	0.7403	0.5200				643.62	154.28	17.11	1.48	470.75	471.77			77.16
1959	2.3838	1.3253	1.0585				633.03	150.25	20.22	1.14	461.42	464.24			69.64
1960	2.0745	1.3234	0.7511				632.28	155.56	25.45	0.24	451.03	454.62			80.13
1961	2.0287	0.9271	1.1016				635.88	120.17	24.49	0.35	490.87	497.23			61.63
1962	1.3206	0.6472	0.6734		2.09	6.22	633.19	95.23	15.03	1.32	521.61	515.52			50.22
1963	1.3764	0.7268	0.6496				649.98	98.28	15.80	1.32	534.58	538.70			49.32
1964	1.6437	1.0024	0.6413				663.76	102.20	16.26	1.09	544.21	548.93			50.38
1965	1.9361	1.1725	0.7636		7.61	20.96	720.85	107.63	18.49	0.74	593.99	598.77			55.42
1966	1.8488	1.2237	0.6251				729.29	112.45	19.91	0.38	596.55	601.92			59.66
1967	1.8922	1.2933	0.5989				732.33	116.04	16.31		599.98	605.36			61.01
1968	2.2021	1.4610	0.7411				754.13	120.21	17.18		616.74	622.43			64.80
1969	2.2263	1.4743	0.7520				773.49	126.45	18.09		628.95	633.60			71.16
1970	2.4083	1.6045	0.8038		6.11	12.22	806.81	140.82	17.28		648.71	652.85			83.72
1971	2.7473	1.8682	0.8791				862.19	161.81	26.12		674.26	678.37			95.37
1972	3.1670	2.1815	0.9855				849.73	169.14	25.20		655.39	659.95			108.88
1973	3.7967	2.4811	1.3156				872.85	167.37	27.40		678.08	682.74			108.73
1974	4.3131	2.8530	1.4601				889.87	171.76	29.80		688.31	693.14			114.51
1975	4.8887	3.1813	1.7074		7.76	7.60	914.52	177.93	35.02	0.65	700.92	706.03			124.79
1976	5.3347	3.4277	1.9070				919.96	188.46	37.76	0.11	693.63	699.37			133.02
1977	6.3555	3.9173	2.4382				927.74	190.95	39.21	0.13	697.45	704.76			141.57
1978	7.2019	4.4282	2.7737		13.49	10.53	965.23	227.34	40.96	0.12	696.81	650.80	188.95	148.21	158.62
1979	8.8904	5.6002	3.2902		18.30	13.89	981.10	234.65	49.36	0.14	696.95	649.00			164.14
1980	12.8705	7.7374	5.1331		20.47	14.29	1002.64	246.24	52.74	1.08	702.58	656.53	249.18	141.67	170.30
1981	16.6949	9.4940	7.2009		21.27	14.25	1031.92	258.97	59.57	1.81	711.57	670.03			176.91
1982	21.9636	11.8453	10.1183		26.46	16.24	1062.36	263.53	62.86	2.67	733.30	689.11			188.42
1983	28.8045	15.3854	13.4191		26.93	15.89	1080.17	274.60	65.38	4.48	735.71	673.44	235.22	171.69	190.66
1984	40.5322	21.7649	18.7673		29.31	16.21	1116.69	277.64	79.86	5.68	753.24	638.07	344.45	212.87	202.10
1985	52.9220	29.6904	23.2316		26.69	12.31	1154.11	291.49	85.27	8.18	768.84	575.90	337.79	240.35	271.60
1986	70.4837	41.1933	29.2904		27.61	11.44	1189.46	304.44	88.98	11.50	783.97	579.38	358.53	251.55	288.02
1987	94.4179	57.3738	37.0441		32.35	11.79	1223.04	316.24	92.66	16.42	797.13	580.89	371.04	271.11	298.05
1988	124.4252	78.5850	45.8402		37.00	12.10	1257.06	327.11	94.12	19.10	815.98	592.06	381.85	283.15	309.61
1989	176.3000	113.0000	63.3000		35.75	9.79	1305.20	333.74	93.42	14.07	839.60		379.50	291.15	

4. Shanxi

4–7

Year	v5c1	v5d	v6a	v6a1	v6a2	v6b	v6c	v6d1	v6d2	v6d3	v6d4	v6d5	v6d6
1949		522.55	1280.86	102.58	1178.28	19.9	13.7	106.14	1174.72	676.16	604.70	42.39	39.55
1950		535.46	1311.57	107.97	1203.60	26.8	7.0	111.78	1199.78	691.26	620.31		
1951		547.24	1351.94	116.29	1235.64	30.4	12.8	123.15	1228.79	714.87	637.07		
1952		561.63	1395.20	130.90	1264.30	32.9	12.2	143.94	1251.26	737.68	657.52	61.83	44.22
1953		578.42	1426.78	150.37	1276.41	33.2	11.4	159.40	1267.38	754.68	672.10		
1954		574.72	1464.53	166.67	1297.85	36.9	14.7	180.86	1283.67	778.10	686.43		
1955		572.85	1580.70	182.85	1325.85	34.2	12.9	205.55	1303.15	807.93	706.97		
1956		557.97	1553.58	237.06	1316.52	29.9	11.6	240.83	1312.75	829.28	724.30		
1957		536.50	1586.74	251.78	1334.95	33.3	12.7	242.41	1344.32	846.63	740.11	109.04	62.12
1958		471.77	1621.07	295.22	1325.85	28.7	11.7	305.87	1315.20	862.76	758.32	120.31	65.15
1959		464.24	1666.57	317.73	1348.84	27.5	12.8	329.56	1337.01	890.18	776.28		
1960		454.62	1703.02	337.77	1365.25	27.3	14.2	326.03	1376.99	909.66	793.37		
1961		497.23	1710.04	319.15	1390.88	19.0	12.2	282.95	1427.09	906.20	803.84	122.93	72.70
1962		515.52	1745.33	287.89	1457.44	37.7	11.3	230.93	1514.40	921.73	823.60	111.08	70.43
1963		538.70	1790.11	277.47	1512.64	38.1	11.4	242.44	1547.68	946.74	843.37	116.60	74.21
1964		548.93	1824.37	293.39	1530.98	36.2	14.0	257.29	1567.08	965.03	859.34	121.44	45.89
1965		598.77	1871.56	307.39	1564.17	33.9	10.4	271.96	1599.61	9887.75	883.81	126.17	134.05
1966		601.92	1911.05	309.41	1601.64	30.0	10.3	273.99	1637.07	1008.91	902.14		
1967		605.36	1946.95	313.35	1633.61	28.7	8.4	282.46	1664.49	1030.11	916.84		
1968		622.43	1999.65	321.64	1678.01	31.5	8.3	284.98	1714.67	1054.38	945.28		
1969		633.60	2049.09	322.89	1826.19	30.6	7.7	290.13	1758.96	1080.79	968.30		
1970		652.85	2111.35	341.90	1769.45	31.1	8.2	311.00	1800.35	1111.69	999.66	134.05	62.04
1971		678.37	2164.40	385.58	1778.82	29.1	8.1	324.06	1840.34	1139.65	1024.75		
1972		659.95	2213.09	406.89	1806.19	29.5	8.6	342.46	1870.63	1167.16	1045.93		
1973		682.74	2257.26	418.32	1838.95	27.0	8.1	350.30	1906.96	1189.40	1067.87		
1974		693.14	2301.89	430.09	1871.81	25.9	7.7	356.85	1945.04	1212.19	1089.71		
1975		706.03	2340.03	438.49	1901.53	23.2	7.8	364.13	1975.89	1230.27	1109.76	148.74	75.31
1976		699.37	2373.05	448.42	1924.64	19.6	7.2	375.20	1997.85	1248.10	1124.95		
1977		704.76	2398.44	453.59	1944.86	17.5	7.1	380.81	2017.64	1260.01	1138.43		
1978		650.80	2423.60	464.79	1958.81	15.7	6.6	393.79	2029.81	1273.07	1150.53	155.65	79.95
1979		649.00	2447.20	484.67	1962.53	15.6	6.4	415.39	2031.80	1283.91	1163.29		
1980		656.53	2476.46	502.71	1973.75	17.0	6.5	439.81	2036.66	1299.32	1177.15	166.41	84.60
1981		670.03	2508.77	516.97	1991.79	20.3	6.5	459.11	2049.66	1311.24	1197.52		
1982		689.11	2546.00	541.43	2004.57	21.0	6.6	474.67	2071.33	1330.05	1215.95		
1983		673.44	2572.31	712.02	1860.28	17.3	6.6	489.06	2083.24	1346.38	1225.92		
1984		638.07	2600.35	1453.34	1147.01	16.5	6.0	511.69	2088.66	1363.36	1236.99		
1985		575.90	2626.51	1482.87	1143.64	17.3	6.4	527.49	2099.21	1378.75	1247.76	188.18	100.01
1986		579.38	2655.07	1211.68	1143.39	19.1	6.5	552.21	2102.86	1393.29	1261.78	192.86	102.03
1987		580.89	2690.81	1538.33	1152.48	20.1	6.5	572.26	2118.56	1411.16	1279.65	197.60	103.79
1988		592.06	2731.43	1572.88	1158.56	20.3	6.4	591.42	2140.01	1430.57	1300.86	186.14	106.50
1989			2774.41	1644.35	1130.06	20.2	6.3	608.52	2165.89	1453.67	1320.06	190.73	109.26

4. Shanxi

4–8

Year	v7a	v7b	v7c	v7d	v7e	v7f	v7g	v7h	v7h1	v7h2	v7h3	v7h4	v7h5	v7i	v8a
1949			379.09	6463.54				8.27	6.65	0.01	0.74		0.87	95.95	2.03
1950	0.002		441.01	6484.12		0.05		9.58	7.69	0.05	0.81		1.03	112.19	2.92
1951	0.002	1.10	513.35	6631.92		0.10		10.60	8.66	0.04	0.82		1.08	131.16	3.87
1952	0.004	1.20	609.37	7317.12		0.53		12.24	10.15	0.11	0.83		1.15	132.57	5.57
1953	0.005	1.80	637.18	7164.80		0.36	0.0002	14.42	12.06	0.09	1.04		1.23	139.60	7.00
1954	0.012	3.20	656.01	7412.91		0.61	0.0002	14.86	12.14	0.09	1.37	0.0001	1.26	143.04	9.11
1955	0.033	77.60	700.95	7280.69		1.19	0.0002	15.19	12.47	0.11	0.27	0.0002	1.34	167.08	10.53
1956	0.165	108.10	802.90	7528.97		4.05	0.0002	17.61	14.80	0.30	1.04	0.0002	1.47	168.11	12.91
1957	0.356	202.44	874.01	7329.01		5.72	0.0023	15.41	12.09	0.26	1.74	0.0005	1.32	157.75	14.84
1958	0.883	233.13	1073.46	6965.89		10.32	0.0200	17.82	14.85	0.39	1.55	0.0005	1.03	145.93	23.66
1959	1.233	443.50	1124.37	6645.29		14.74	0.0900	17.65	14.45	0.46	1.80	0.0034	0.94	139.73	39.80
1960	2.331	505.32	1128.20	7053.77		18.84	0.3900	11.98	10.10	0.14	0.88	0.0038	0.86	138.01	49.90
1961	2.795	686.00	961.54	6931.69		10.49	0.5900	14.39	12.51	0.20	1.02	0.0016	0.66	133.26	27.81
1962	2.929	698.00	965.05	6777.02		9.68	0.8200	15.07	12.28	0.23	1.20	0.0029	1.36	134.85	25.65
1963	2.924	901.73	1029.33	6844.96		14.87	1.0100	15.82	13.16	0.25	1.61	0.0046	0.79	139.10	28.17
1964	3.240	1045.64	1059.62	6848.49		11.86	1.2400	17.69	14.85	0.52	1.63	0.0064	0.68	143.39	32.53
1965	4.023	1284.17	1052.50	6714.47		24.85	1.8100	17.35	14.01	0.48	2.22	0.0070	0.63	147.44	42.34
1966	5.169	1208.49	1315.58	6900.72		27.09	2.4900	19.53	16.35	0.63	1.78	0.0049	0.76	152.32	50.47
1967	5.535	1074.53	1259.41	6640.59		20.47	2.6400	19.94	15.39	0.56	2.31	0.0038	1.68	156.03	43.01
1968	5.935	1128.20	1242.42	6467.24		15.45	2.8100	19.23	14.42	0.56	2.13	0.0038	2.12	157.05	27.40
1969	6.675	1155.61	1248.00	6360.25		22.38	3.0600	21.68	16.86	0.63	1.95	0.0038	2.23	155.15	39.49
1970	8.181	1332.11	1285.14	6488.36		44.52	3.6200	20.72	17.09	0.81	2.09	0.0039	0.73	155.67	62.57
1971	10.587	1582.97	1327.36	6366.64		51.48	4.7600	24.58	20.30	0.91	2.58	0.0047	0.79	158.94	62.81
1972	14.310	1691.83	1359.56	6334.14		58.61	5.8900	22.28	17.78	0.87	2.81	0.0049	0.82	165.88	64.03
1973	18.914	1913.67	1398.68	6481.63		66.73	7.2500	26.11	21.38	0.98	2.48	0.0054	1.26	160.89	70.55
1974	24.323	2067.50	1494.62	6369.28		72.17	7.4400	27.42	22.44	1.15	2.96	0.0030	0.87	162.43	65.77
1975	29.357	2190.53	1564.40	6483.04		85.66	9.3100	29.96	24.71	1.23	3.15	0.0029	0.87	162.38	76.17
1976	34.729	2442.44	1631.48	6425.70		93.98	9.2000	28.54	23.02	0.94	3.71	0.0027	0.87	160.65	70.60
1977	43.529	2803.69	1702.83	6523.86		107.77	9.8500	28.97	23.35	1.04	3.88	0.0031	0.69	159.20	89.44
1978	46.252	2905.48	1638.72	6583.87		175.36	12.2700	29.01	23.14	1.74	3.28	0.0066	0.84	161.02	106.43
1979	50.328	2749.03	1681.97	6444.96		156.06	13.1400	36.76	28.85	2.17	4.59	0.0062	1.14	159.13	120.71
1980	54.208	2666.64	1672.71	6399.90		142.90	13.5900	38.23	27.64	4.02	5.53	0.0082	1.03	162.35	126.34
1981	57.373	2210.10	1659.80	6217.32		104.43	14.0500	46.02	36.26	2.86	5.51	0.0081	1.38	168.93	128.87
1982	60.265	2266.95	1649.63	6161.28	1524	135.06	14.4300	53.08	41.01	3.58	6.48	0.0129	2.00	178.03	141.80
1983	67.669	2377.90	1651.34	6191.23	2610	148.35	13.1600	53.81	39.23	5.08	7.14	0.0134	2.35	188.61	166.34
1984	77.446	2787.43	1653.99	6247.28	2876	186.24	14.3000	65.15	46.94	6.82	9.05	0.0329	2.31	191.26	194.60
1985	82.214	2875.11	1618.65	5967.34	3200	164.03	15.1100	62.92	45.64	4.12	10.29	0.0663	2.80	195.61	238.09
1986	85.293	2815.75	1581.08	5928.06	2055	169.75	17.6600	58.82	42.24	3.62	10.23	0.1025	2.63	204.36	261.80
1987	89.516	2909.35	1516.29	5988.75	1860	177.91	20.4200	61.42	42.35	3.37	12.37	0.1402	3.19	201.23	304.29
1988	92.471	2923.25	1647.66	5998.94	660	192.62	21.3000	87.25	58.23	4.29	21.12	0.3328	3.28	204.28	387.22
1989	98.460	2987.33	1671.60	6007.44			24.4100	104.94	71.59	4.43	24.75	0.4300	3.74	209.85	487.65

4. Shanxi

4–9

Year	v8a1	v8a2	v8a3	v8b	v8c1	v8c2	v8d	v8f1	v8f2	v8f3	v8f4	v8f5	v8g
1949	1.39	0.64		1.12	0.89	1.14	0.50	1.22	267		0.44	1.44	2864
1950	2.16	0.76			1.34	1.58	0.75	4.27	380		0.54	4.48	3142
1951	2.99	0.88			2.04	1.83	1.05	5.62	603		0.69	6.42	3594
1952	4.55	1.02		3.62	3.21	2.36	1.55	9.20	994		1.53	9.69	3421
1953	6.60	1.38			4.05	2.95	1.98	12.58	906		1.94	11.65	4018
1954	7.63	1.48			5.37	3.74	2.89	16.45	1310		2.59	10.33	5732
1955	8.65	1.88			6.73	3.80	3.65	20.19	1696		3.47	17.66	5262
1956	10.81	2.10			8.93	3.98	4.14	25.31	1930		4.78	22.99	4728
1957	12.86	2.00		10.58	10.13	4.71	4.98	26.37	2368		5.72	51.41	4509
1958	21.48	2.18			18.37	5.29	8.56	42.00	3715		9.42	86.62	5016
1959	35.48	4.32			28.16	11.64	14.36	58.11	4355		14.85	109.47	7388
1960	43.97	5.93			37.88	12.02	17.58	74.95	4412		21.84	127.17	7141
1961	23.33	4.57			18.94	8.87	7.84	39.08	3258		18.69	38.41	5743
1962	21.89	3.76		16.42	17.80	7.85	7.21	23.64	3180		17.99	49.84	5244
1963	24.97	3.51			20.25	7.92	8.10	25.99	3466		18.70	52.04	3981
1964	28.67	3.86			23.31	9.22	9.55	29.44	3597		21.00	68.69	3791
1965	37.16	5.18		32.12	31.58	10.76	12.72	39.97	3927		25.70	86.44	3566
1966	43.94	6.53			34.27	16.20	15.29	48.36	4198		30.89	106.60	3390
1967	36.98	6.13			27.90	15.11	12.70	33.60	3386		29.84	81.84	3738
1968	21.84	5.56			15.77	11.63	7.51	22.62	3664		23.08	70.69	3765
1969	32.47	7.02			24.71	14.77	11.19	26.44	4465		30.70	98.34	3782
1970	52.66	9.90		45.37	41.75	20.82	18.23	52.12	5298		42.05	115.57	4880
1971	53.61	9.20			42.64	20.17	17.70	76.14	5487		49.83	131.38	4910
1972	52.29	11.74			43.57	20.46	17.50	93.61	5994		57.83	159.25	6093
1973	57.40	13.15			48.14	22.41	18.96	106.09	6398		66.22	166.01	6423
1974	51.05	14.72			43.04	22.73	16.62	59.14	6796		68.81	161.00	7115
1975	59.71	16.46		57.11	51.62	24.54	19.21	79.13	7542		77.85	180.16	7505
1976	52.95	17.65			45.80	24.80	16.81	47.32	7720		75.83	184.13	8429
1977	66.59	22.85			57.73	31.71	20.55	76.46	8754		88.29	221.66	9218
1978	99.19	7.24		77.93	70.34	36.09	27.61	119.99	9825		106.63	255.87	9381
1979	69.34	51.37		89.76	79.48	41.23	34.16	136.75	10893		114.10	269.48	9307
1980	93.49	32.94		93.08	80.78	45.56	38.17	149.38	12103		120.24	287.88	9533
1981	94.25	34.62		91.40	79.48	49.39	37.26	138.46	13255		124.57	270.80	9540
1982	104.18	37.56	0.05	107.13	90.72	51.09	41.17	150.04	14532		136.92	312.41	9637
1983	121.67	44.39	0.28	122.51	106.14	60.20	43.87	158.61	15918		151.27	362.37	9806
1984	131.59	62.63	0.38	133.96	122.64	71.96	50.05	176.33	18716		167.53	400.84	10977
1985	150.79	74.18	13.12	154.02	143.72	94.37	51.84	183.74	21418		184.59	458.68	11004
1986	162.05	84.01	14.96	167.09	157.70	104.10	54.37	190.20	22180		220.02	520.68	11513
1987	184.51	83.15	36.63	195.55	218.38	85.91	62.77	203.60	23164		263.42	542.42	11567
1988	225.26	129.06	32.89	243.69	275.63	111.58	76.22	216.05	24648		277.74	573.05	11792
1989	266.82	175.45	45.38	296.49	356.67	130.98	89.27	227.55	27501		303.13	633.75	11964

4. Shanxi

4–10

Year	v8g1	v9a	v9a1	v9a2	v9a3	v9b	v9b1	v9b2	v9b3	v9c	v10a	v10a1	v10b1	v10b2	v10b3
1949	200			0.08				0.06			1.68	1.66	0.08		0.05
1950				0.18				0.10			2.54	2.50	0.27		0.20
1951				0.29				0.24			4.01	3.91	0.56		0.51
1952	655			0.43				0.76			5.98	5.75	1.02		1.06
1953		7.54	6.74	0.80		14.83	13.82	1.01			7.71	7.52	1.26		2.10
1954		8.69	7.82	0.87		20.66	19.79	1.37			9.71	9.25	1.87		4.41
1955		9.39	8.15	1.24		25.25	23.63	1.62			10.24	9.58	2.94		4.42
1956		10.50	8.86	1.64		31.41	29.63	1.78			12.54	11.40	4.48		5.36
1957	1376	12.16	10.10	2.06		41.17	39.13	2.05		1382	12.90	11.96	4.64		4.88
1958		15.77	13.16	2.61		64.68	61.38	3.28	0.0190	1571	15.93	13.66	11.77		2.07
1959		17.87	14.45	3.42		81.50	76.73	4.74	0.0340	2137	19.27	16.60	16.14		2.39
1960		22.39	18.55	3.84		89.34	84.40	4.89	0.0470	2848	22.07	18.29	18.56		2.64
1961		28.04	24.62	3.41		65.46	63.16	2.28	0.0210	2563	17.56	14.94	14.58		4.94
1962	1186	27.51	23.65	3.86		55.11	53.41	1.70	0.0030	2132	16.74	14.65	8.24		7.49
1963		17.23	14.05	3.17		61.21	59.38	1.83	0.0030	2011	15.97	14.21	8.19		7.02
1964		16.09	13.01	3.08		38.10	65.86	2.24	0.0030	2189	16.31	14.47	8.74		6.97
1965	984	17.24	13.30	3.94		82.08	78.15	2.93	0.0040	2311	18.03	15.32	9.68		7.78
1966		18.67	13.98	4.68		94.64	91.40	3.23	0.0050	2373	18.92	15.95			
1967		21.92	17.24	4.67		72.28	69.13	3.15	0.0020	2170	18.98	16.46			
1968		23.66	19.11	4.55		64.98	63.20	2.78	0.0020	1915	17.89	15.62			
1969		25.20	20.67	4.53		75.25	71.95	3.30	0.0030	2384	20.16	17.44			
1970	1137	24.66	19.15	5.52		107.37	103.03	4.33	0.0090	2674	22.65	19.10			
1971		27.36	19.96	7.40		117.18	112.24	4.93	0.0140	3014	25.57	20.59			
1972		29.59	22.90	6.69		128.31	122.55	5.75	0.0070	3338	27.89	22.21			
1973		31.13	23.76	7.37		125.01	118.29	6.71	0.0090	3532	30.38	23.81			
1974		30.79	23.54	7.25		111.98	105.38	6.59	0.0070	3076	31.69	24.81			
1975	1902	31.43	13.78	7.60		134.59	127.46	7.11	0.0090	3596	34.35	26.52	32.64		1.32
1976		31.71	23.22	8.45		120.25	112.99	7.23	0.0080	3909	36.22	28.42	34.66		1.46
1977		34.18	24.13	10.01		151.03	145.18	9.43	0.0080	4080	39.76	30.71	38.29		1.46
1978	2146	38.79	27.10	11.64		189.64	178.48	11.15	0.0077	4258	42.22	32.38	40.65		1.45
1979	2178	43.15	30.98	12.12		204.24	189.65	14.57	0.0105	4525	45.53	35.75	43.45		1.64
1980	2159	49.82	35.64	14.15		225.38	209.65	15.71	0.0042	4970	51.73	42.66	48.07		2.54
1981	2154	53.72	37.88	15.81		237.01	219.51	17.47	0.0060	5082	56.51	48.76	49.96		4.39
1982	2260	59.57	41.04	18.51		257.41	233.77	23.61	0.0097	5214	61.34	52.50	52.12		6.32
1983	2265	68.10	46.39	21.69		280.39	251.74	28.62		5552	69.42	58.32	56.66		7.70
1984	2216	79.93	54.85	25.02		311.13	271.63	39.46		6032	84.59	70.58	44.54		30.82
1985	2212	93.26	62.14	31.04		361.01	308.69	52.29		6746	102.12	89.44	46.68		37.13
1986	2288	103.31	65.66	37.57		406.65	342.64	63.97		7107	112.10	99.24	50.61		40.41
1987	2365	113.95	68.44	45.42		447.16	373.66	74.94	0.0215	8109	128.43	113.57	57.13		44.88
1988	2408	131.97	77.19	54.35		506.30	414.99	91.17	0.0220	9788	163.15	144.57	73.17		53.26
1989	2452	135.00	77.94	59.62		543.78	440.59	103.00		11478	176.62	154.31	83.75		56.22

4. Shanxi

4–11

Year	v10b4	v10b5	v10b6	v10d	v11a1	v11a2	v11a3	v11b	v11b1	v11b2	v11c	v11d	v12a	v12b	v12c
1949		1.39	0.16	1.55											
1950		1.87	0.20	2.15											
1951	0.02	2.70	0.22	2.96									115.1	113.3	125.8
1952	0.02	3.65	0.23	3.56									104.7	105.6	103.2
1953	0.03	4.17	0.15	4.29									101.4	102.4	107.0
1954	0.28	3.00	0.15	4.68									103.5	103.4	103.9
1955	0.94	1.78	0.15	4.40									104.6	103.6	101.1
1956	2.32	0.14	0.24	4.55									101.0	99.6	101.3
1957	2.96	0.12	0.30	4.98					0.0145				101.9	101.4	102.6
1958	1.72	0.29	0.08	4.72					0.0641				98.4	98.3	102.0
1959		0.56	0.19	8.87					0.0822				100.5	100.5	100.7
1960		0.65	0.22	5.57					0.0958				103.9	102.7	101.4
1961		0.42	0.63	5.93					0.0707				115.7	115.6	112.4
1962		0.40	0.61	4.90					0.0889				100.4	100.5	107.5
1963		0.33	0.43	5.76					0.1232				87.9	87.7	92.1
1964		0.31	0.29	6.13					0.0891				93.7	92.7	96.9
1965		0.34	0.23	7.07					0.0806				97.5	97.6	99.0
1966				6.01					0.0895				97.9	97.8	101.8
1967				6.24					0.0965				98.9	98.9	100.0
1968				6.03					0.0405				100.0	99.8	99.8
1969				6.63					0.0480				99.6	99.9	100.6
1970				7.38					0.0581				99.5	99.3	100.4
1971				7.15					0.0328				99.6	99.8	101.7
1972				7.30					0.0257				99.8	100.2	101.9
1973				8.17					0.0284				100.3	100.4	100.8
1974				8.36					0.0226				99.8	99.9	100.8
1975		0.02	0.37	9.17					0.0211				99.9	99.8	101.0
1976		0.01	0.09	9.28					0.0162				100.1	100.1	100.9
1977		0.01		10.09					0.0567				100.1	99.9	99.8
1978		0.02	0.10	9.66					0.0731				100.0	100.0	104.0
1979		0.03	0.41	11.89					0.1328				100.5	101.0	122.5
1980		0.26	0.86	14.10					0.1513				103.5	105.5	105.7
1981		0.63	1.53	15.04					0.2852				102.3	103.1	102.6
1982		1.12	1.78	19.68					0.3307				102.2	102.3	104.5
1983	0.02	2.81	2.23	20.01				0.7852	0.2835	0.5017			101.2	101.5	101.6
1984	0.05	5.77	3.41	23.91				2.5068	1.6654	0.8414	72.1		103.0	103.0	106.4
1985	0.16	12.78	5.37	24.94				3.4043	2.2679	1.1364	85.0	217	107.6	109.1	106.5
1986	0.21	13.65	7.22	29.79				3.8851	3.0226	0.8625	160.4	630	105.3	106.4	107.5
1987	0.12	17.70	8.60	36.65				4.1680	3.4551	0.7129	235.5	723	107.5	108.5	108.8
1988	0.01	25.83	10.88	45.81				3.8215	3.2954	0.5261	1449.0	1449	121.0	122.1	128.8
1989	0.01	24.16	12.48	54.27				4.9184	4.0001	0.9183		1000	119.1	116.3	121.0

4. Shanxi

4–12

Year	v13a	v13b	v13c1	v13c2	v13c3	v13d	v14a	v14b	v14c	v15a	v15b	v15c	v15d	v15e	v15f
1949	10.20		0.0528	1.6941	101.53	0.0102				6235.44					
1950	6.65		0.0819	2.1349	116.08	0.0160				6384.68					
1951	7.17		0.1271	3.0636	136.90	0.0103			0.22	6492.38					
1952	14.72		0.1881	6.3225	160.81	0.0352	3679	12800	0.41	6934.69					
1953	24.32		0.2230	8.1648	171.76	0.0499			0.37	7017.79					
1954	18.86		0.3052	10.3835	167.85	0.0399			0.45	7031.85					
1955	20.68		0.4064	11.2096	169.90	0.0654			0.58	6972.92					
1956	16.44		0.6334	16.0158	190.62	0.0799			0.77	6834.42					
1957	19.05		0.7315	17.3695	190.81	0.0838			0.71	6812.64					
1958	9.13		1.4039	27.8635	231.04	0.1378			1.56	6205.88					
1959	8.06		1.4624	34.2473	247.92	0.1176			1.84	6165.90					
1960	7.46		1.8751	39.9239	272.78	0.1926			1.56	6197.21					
1961	11.93		1.8969	31.2750	273.16	0.3324			0.87	6192.98					
1962	20.63		1.5086	24.1183	248.47	0.4162			0.73	6203.89					
1963	17.25		1.4982	20.7946	240.62	0.3084			0.82	6251.65					
1964	15.36		1.3753	21.7779	274.27	0.3817			1.09	6273.25					
1965	15.25		1.4548	26.9447	305.49	0.4296	18497	48000	1.43	6230.05					
1966	12.96		1.0014	32.3261	299.34	0.1182				6140.13					
1967	14.44		1.0235	31.4399	304.17	0.0490				6076.23					
1968			0.6975	41.1142	306.84	0.3260				6009.10					
1969	11.85		0.3904	67.9645	313.09	0.3071				5951.41					
1970	7.98		0.4384	79.3410	330.80	0.3901				5831.44					
1971	9.28		0.0106	93.0218	353.10					5822.16					
1972	8.87		0.4129	104.8651	378.10					5854.16					
1973	9.00	97.70	0.7674	103.7422	382.42	0.0281				5870.00					
1974	7.78	98.11	1.0155	114.6003	392.29	0.1689				5870.68					
1975	8.49	98.45	1.1908	141.3237	385.59	0.2999			2.17	5882.69					
1976	8.28	98.70	1.2681	176.9690	374.87	0.4167			2.57	5876.06					
1977	8.39	98.35	1.4438	207.3300	365.86	0.4432			2.66	5881.59					
1978	7.88	98.30	2.0940	198.3689	377.36	0.4523	63293	76500	2.49	5885.11					
1979	9.40	98.40	2.5308	183.7024	383.32	0.3606			2.18	5885.61					
1980	12.58	98.56	3.3104	185.8012	384.16		69141	87800	2.85	5882.19					
1981	14.52	98.39	3.6975	165.4786	389.10	0.3909			2.94	5840.97					
1982	14.52	98.20	3.1733	155.7340	382.13	1.4172			3.42	5820.25					
1983	14.27	98.60	3.2858	148.0097	366.22	0.8672			5.00	5807.58					
1984	13.80	98.80	3.6338	156.5482	351.48	0.8482			6.57	5778.87					
1985	13.31	98.95	4.1946	163.9717	335.20	0.8499	82.76	109600	7.31	5641.63					
1986	13.98	99.00	4.6607	170.8095	319.19	0.9930			7.98	5597.69					
1987	14.21	99.20	4.9121	173.2697	305.39	1.2363			7.64	5579.03					
1988	16.79	99.00	4.9450	172.3428	298.09	1.7139	93538	122300	7.72	5559.94	2408.1		142.0	2423.9	34.8
1989			5.1200	157.4400	297.40	1.3800	95579	125300	6.66	5552.66					

Notes

1. National Output and Income (Y)

v1a: (E), p.159
v1a1: (E), p.159
v1a2: (E), p.159
v1a3: (E), p.159
v1a4: (E), p.159
v1a5: (E), p.159

v1b: (A); (D), p.132
v1b1: (A); (D), p.132
v1b2: (A); (D), p.132
v1b3: (A); (D), p.132
v1b4: (A); (D), p.132
v1b5: (A); (D), p.132

v1c: v1a – v1d

v1d: (E), p.156
v1d1: (E), p.156
v1d2: (E), p.156
v1d3: (E), p.156
v1d4: (E), p.156
v1d5: (E), p.156

v1e: (A); (D), p.136
v1e1: (A); (D), p.136
v1e2: (A); (D), p.136
v1e3: (A); (D), p.136
v1e4: (A); (D), p.136
v1e5: (A); (D), p.136

v1f: (E), p.155
v1f1: (E), p.155
v1f2: (E), p.155
v1f3: (E), p.155

v1g: v2a + v3a

v1h: (A); (E), p.183

v1i: (E), p.182—figures of 1985 and after include meat price subsidies

v1j: (E), p.182—(ditto)
v1j1: (E), p.182—(ditto)
v1j2: (E), p.182—data of 1949–72 are estimated by related information
v1j3: (B), p.II-310—jointly-owned units

v1k: (E), p.182

2. Investment (I)

v2a: (E), p.158
v2a1: (A); (D), p.141
v2a2: (A); (D), p.141

v2b: (A)

v2c: (E), p.173—including inter-regional investment
v2c1: (E), p.174
v2c2: (E), p.174

v2d:
v2d1: (E), p.171
v2d2: (E), p.171

v2e: (E), p.171

3. Consumption (C)

v3a: (E), p.158

v3b: (E), p.158
v3b1: (A); (E), p.137
v3b2: (A); (E), p.137

v3c: (E), p.158

v3d: (E), p.181
v3d1: (E), p.181
v3d2: (E), p.181

v3e: (E), p.183
v3e1: (E), p.183
v3e2: NA

v3e3: NA
v3e4: NA

v3f: (A); (E), p.183
v3f1: (A); (E), p.183
v3f2: (A)
v3f3: (A)
v3f4: (A)

4. Public Finance and Banking (FB)

v4a:
v4a1: (E), p.179
v4a1a: (E), p.179—including profit surrendered, subsidies for planned deficits, and contract revenues withdrawal in 1988, 1989
v4a1b: (B), p.II-228; v4a1b': (E), p.179—total tax revenues
v4a1c: NA
v4a1d: v4a1 – v4a1a – v4a1b'
v4a2: (E), p.179
v4a2a: (E), p.179
v4a2b: (E), p.179
v4a2c: (E), p.179
v4a2d: v4a2 – v4a2a – v4a2b – v4a2c

v4b: (A)
v4b1: (A); (B), p.II-318
v4b2: (A); (B), p.II-318—rural people's deposits
v4b3: NA

v4c:
v4c1: (E), p.171
v4c2: (E), p.171

5. Labor Force (L)

v5a: (A); (E), p.154
v5a1: (E), p.154
v5a2: (E), p.154
v5a3: (E), p.154
v5a4: (E), p.154—excluding rural people working outside

v5b:
v5b1: (E), p.154
v5b2: (E), p.154
v5b3: (E), p.154

v5c: (B), p.II-293—industrial labor force
v5c1: NA

v5d: (B), p.II-293

6. Population (PO)

v6a: (E), p.153—data from public security department
v6a1: (E), p.153—(ditto)
v6a2: (E), p.153—(ditto)

v6b: (E), p.153—(ditto)

v6c: (E), p.153—(ditto)

v6d:
v6d1: (E), p.153—(ditto)
v6d2: (E), p.153—(ditto)
v6d3: (E), p.153—(ditto)
v6d4: (E), p.153—(ditto)
v6d5: (A)—Taiyuan
v6d6: (A)—Datong

7. Agriculture (A)

v7a: (A); (E), p.166

v7b: (A); (E), p.166

v7c: (A); (E), p.166

v7d: (A); (E), p.166

v7e: (A)

v7f: (A); (E), p.166

v7g: (A); (B), p.II-128; (E), p.166

v7h: (E), p.161

v7h1: (E), p.161
v7h2: (E), p.161
v7h3: (E), p.161
v7h4: (A); (E), p.161
v7h5: (E), p.161

v7i: (E), p.165

8. Industry (IN)

v8a: (A)
v8a1: (A)
v8a2: (A)
v8a3: (A)

v8b: (E), p.171

v8c1: (E), p.159
v8c2: (E), p.159

v8d: (E), p.171—figures of 1986 and before include the part of non-independent accounting units

v8f:
v8f1: (E), p.170
v8f2: (E), p.170
v8f3: NA
v8f4: (E), p.170
v8f5: (E), p.170

v8g: (A)
v8g1: (E), p.171

9. Transport (TR)

v9a: (E), p.172—excluding urban traffic volume
v9a1: (E), p.172—including central and local railways
v9a2: (E), p.172
v9a3: NA

v9b: (E), p.172—figures of 1975 and afterward include civil air traffic volume
v9b1: (E), p.172—including central and local railways
v9b2: (E), p.172
v9b3: (A)—referring to wooden junk transport

v9c: (E), p.172—based on 1980's constant price

10. Domestic Trade (DT)

v10a: (E), p.175
v10a1: (E), p.175

v10b:
v10b1: (E), p.175
v10b2: NA
v10b3: (E), p.175—includes supply and marketing cooperative and other collectives
v10b4: (E), p.175
v10b5: (E), p.175
v10b6: (E), p.175

v10d: (E), p.177

11. Foreign Trade (FT)

v11a:
v11a1: NA
v11a2: NA
v11a3: NA

v11b: (E), p.178—data from foreign trade department
v11b1: (E), p.178—(ditto)
v11b2: v11b – v11b1

v11c: (A): US$ 10,000

v11d: (A): US$ 10,000

12. Prices (PR)

v12a: (E), p.180

v12b: (E), p.180

v12c: (E), p.180

13. Education (ED)

v13a: (A)

v13b: (A)

v13c:
- v13c1: (A); (E), p.183
- v13c2: (A)—technical and ordinary secondary schools
- v13c3: (A); (E), p.183

v13d: (A)—institutions of higher learning

14. Social Factors (SF)

v14a: (E), p.183

v14b: (E), p.183

v14c: (A)

15. Natural Environment (NE)

v15a: (A); (E), p.166

v15b: (A)

v15c: NA

v15d: (A)

v15e: (A)

v15f: (A)

Sources of Data

(A) Data supplied by the DSNEB, SSB, the PRC.
(B) Editorial Board for Shanxi Forty Years ed. *Shanxi Forty Years 1949–1989*, Beijing: CSPH, 1989.
(D) Same as (D) in Beijing's sources of data.
(E) Same as (E) in Beijing's sources of data.

5

Inner Mongolia

5. Inner Mongolia

5–1

Year	v1a	v1a1	v1a2	v1a3	v1a4	v1a5	v1b	v1b1	v1b2	v1b3	v1b4	v1b5	v1c	v1d	v1d1
1949															
1950															
1951															
1952	15.61	12.06	1.63	0.55	0.48	0.89							4.90	10.71	8.55
1953	20.31	14.35	2.55	1.20	0.70	1.51	115.2	106.0	152.0	216.9	146.0	169.9	6.55	13.76	10.23
1954	25.58	16.77	3.77	2.28	0.97	1.79	118.1	109.7	147.8	189.8	138.4	118.4	8.39	17.19	12.06
1955	24.83	15.60	4.41	2.03	1.03	1.76	96.8	94.0	117.5	89.3	106.9	98.4	9.89	14.94	9.91
1956	33.11	19.52	6.05	3.78	1.47	2.29	131.0	124.2	135.1	185.7	142.6	130.4	12.00	21.11	13.75
1957	24.39	11.18	6.33	3.04	1.17	2.67	89.0	84.1	110.7	80.4	79.2	116.7	9.37	15.02	8.32
1958	38.21	15.60	12.03	5.00	2.39	3.19	145.0	132.2	183.1	164.5	204.9	119.3	14.44	23.77	12.10
1959	51.77	18.14	18.78	7.25	3.75	3.85	127.0	111.4	156.0	145.0	156.8	120.7	21.27	30.50	14.21
1960	60.19	16.57	28.57	7.48	3.49	4.08	108.0	88.9	151.2	103.2	93.1	106.0	29.91	30.28	11.24
1961	41.02	17.04	15.93	2.94	2.09	3.02	66.3	86.0	51.6	39.3	60.0	74.0	20.30	20.72	10.79
1962	38.09	17.05	14.26	1.67	2.30	2.81	89.3	94.1	83.5	56.7	110.0	93.0	17.36	20.73	12.14
1963	49.32	17.43	21.26	4.88	2.63	3.12	128.8	111.7	147.1	292.7	114.1	111.2	24.94	24.38	12.04
1964	56.09	20.82	23.05	5.65	2.95	3.62	116.3	120.8	109.8	115.7	112.4	115.9	28.70	27.39	13.37
1965	59.60	19.39	26.79	6.23	3.17	4.02	104.5	91.0	124.9	110.1	107.4	111.1	29.92	29.68	14.48
1966	65.79	20.93	29.56	7.15	3.53	4.62	112.4	107.9	117.3	114.9	111.1	115.0	33.29	32.50	16.39
1967	54.03	21.46	20.28	5.87	2.81	3.61	86.0	102.6	69.6	82.0	79.7	78.1	27.96	26.07	13.07
1968	55.93	22.08	21.19	5.99	2.79	3.88	99.8	95.0	106.1	102.1	99.3	107.4	28.88	27.05	14.05
1969	55.11	19.95	22.32	6.11	2.76	3.97	98.4	90.4	109.1	102.0	99.0	102.5	28.32	26.79	13.93
1970	69.07	24.04	27.80	8.24	3.62	5.37	130.7	120.5	142.1	134.8	131.1	135.1	34.83	34.24	18.28
1971	73.75	23.67	31.09	9.14	3.90	5.95	107.5	98.4	115.9	110.9	107.7	110.9	34.87	38.88	20.19
1972	71.79	21.17	31.57	9.23	3.82	6.00	94.8	87.5	101.6	94.7	93.6	96.3	39.63	32.16	13.67
1973	82.14	27.72	32.67	10.60	4.26	6.89	115.2	130.2	103.5	114.8	111.5	114.8	45.81	36.33	15.35
1974	80.27	29.57	29.78	10.26	4.01	6.65	96.6	102.1	91.2	96.8	94.1	96.5	45.07	35.20	15.09
1975	91.56	30.83	36.89	11.78	4.47	7.59	112.8	102.5	123.9	114.8	111.5	114.1	51.63	39.93	17.13
1976	93.33	31.29	37.61	12.16	4.47	7.80	102.2	101.3	103.0	103.2	100.0	102.8	52.97	40.36	17.46
1977	98.39	28.43	44.08	12.98	4.63	8.27	104.5	90.9	116.6	106.7	103.6	106.0	56.10	42.29	17.85
1978	109.76	28.35	52.96	14.39	4.98	9.08	109.4	100.2	115.9	110.9	107.6	109.8	63.25	46.51	18.34
1979	119.06	31.58	57.40	15.40	5.21	9.47	105.7	105.7	105.6	107.0	104.6	104.3	68.83	50.23	19.92
1980	120.97	30.68	59.39	15.25	6.74	8.91	97.7	86.7	102.1	99.0	129.4	94.1	68.22	52.75	18.25
1981	129.83	39.42	61.76	13.23	6.32	9.10	103.5	119.8	100.3	86.8	93.8	102.1	69.41	60.42	27.34
1982	154.97	47.16	73.73	17.76	7.44	8.88	116.1	115.8	115.1	134.2	117.7	97.6	81.84	73.13	33.68
1983	175.32	52.43	81.53	21.14	10.19	10.03	109.6	107.2	109.6	109.7	125.3	108.0	94.70	80.62	35.92
1984	201.10	61.28	90.02	25.92	10.96	12.92	111.9	116.4	105.4	125.6	101.9	123.4	104.92	96.18	42.93
1985	252.53	73.20	109.19	35.36	13.89	17.14	116.6	111.7	115.8	124.3	126.9	122.3	134.18	118.35	51.98
1986	276.26	77.25	126.46	36.06	16.45	20.04	104.0	90.0	113.2	94.9	116.7	113.5	149.05	127.21	52.99
1987	316.84	87.77	150.84	37.26	17.50	23.49	107.2	104.1	112.5	95.6	101.8	108.6	172.85	143.99	59.81
1988	413.04	122.38	193.86	45.90	21.00	29.90	112.7	114.2	113.9	103.8	119.6	107.1	221.87	191.57	87.62
1989	479.08	128.32	243.13	47.84	27.81	31.98	106.4	99.5	112.6	94.2	119.7	92.3	268.56	210.52	87.25

5. Inner Mongolia

5–2

Year	v1d2	v1d3	v1d4	v1d5	v1e	v1e1	v1e2	v1e3	v1e4	v1e5	v1f	v1f1	v1f2	v1f3	v1g
1949															
1950															
1951															
1952	0.89	0.25	0.31	0.71											8.77
1953	1.40	0.47	0.43	1.23	116.7	106.4	153.2	188.5	140.6	174.3					10.47
1954	2.32	0.78	0.59	1.44	119.4	110.7	163.9	167.3	137.8	117.1					12.57
1955	2.39	0.62	0.60	1.42	87.7	83.0	103.8	79.3	101.6	98.0					11.23
1956	3.36	1.31	0.80	1.89	139.3	137.7	139.2	183.1	133.3	133.8					15.60
1957	3.18	0.88	0.50	2.14	91.2	88.9	100.0	77.3	61.9	113.1					16.46
1958	6.16	1.72	1.18	2.61	150.1	137.7	186.5	195.7	238.5	121.9					25.84
1959	8.80	2.32	1.98	3.19	123.9	112.5	143.1	135.0	166.9	122.0					33.41
1960	11.95	2.05	1.66	3.38	95.7	77.0	134.7	88.5	84.1	106.0					31.76
1961	5.31	0.90	1.10	2.62	62.9	80.2	41.2	43.7	66.1	77.6					20.57
1962	5.10	0.57	0.99	1.93	95.2	105.8	89.5	63.8	90.4	73.7					17.60
1963	7.39	1.36	1.14	2.45	121.9	108.3	142.7	238.3	114.4	126.7					19.48
1964	8.39	1.59	1.28	2.76	113.4	112.4	115.2	116.8	112.6	112.9					22.52
1965	8.59	1.79	1.73	3.09	109.4	105.8	110.1	112.6	135.1	111.8					25.92
1966	9.24	2.08	1.53	3.26	111.3	113.0	114.3	116.0	88.4	105.6					27.38
1967	7.46	1.73	1.21	2.60	80.6	79.9	81.8	83.0	79.4	79.8					23.78
1968	7.47	1.79	1.20	2.54	100.0	99.2	101.7	103.9	99.2	97.8					24.06
1969	7.33	1.85	1.19	2.49	100.0	99.2	101.7	103.2	99.2	97.7					24.41
1970	8.65	2.53	1.55	3.23	132.3	131.2	134.5	136.6	129.6	130.0					29.87
1971	11.09	2.85	1.67	3.08	109.1	110.4	110.5	112.8	108.0	95.3					33.13
1972	10.75	2.91	1.63	3.20	94.2	91.5	96.9	97.3	93.1	99.4					35.25
1973	12.67	3.39	1.82	3.10	112.7	111.7	117.9	116.5	111.7	96.9					39.28
1974	11.77	3.34	1.71	3.29	95.0	94.2	92.9	98.5	94.0	106.1					41.92
1975	13.72	3.98	1.90	3.20	112.5	111.6	116.5	119.2	111.1	97.3					46.14
1976	13.71	4.06	1.90	3.23	101.4	101.7	101.0	102.0	100.0	100.9					48.72
1977	14.65	4.55	1.96	3.28	104.4	102.3	106.3	112.1	103.2	101.5					54.03
1978	17.67	4.94	2.11	3.45	108.4	103.8	115.9	108.6	107.7	105.2	56.05	18.96	24.92	12.17	60.79
1979	19.30	5.28	2.18	3.55	104.6	102.9	106.5	106.9	103.3	102.9	61.58	21.03	27.11	13.44	66.06
1980	21.49	5.18	3.82	4.01	100.7	81.6	114.8	98.1	175.2	113.0	65.16	18.03	30.93	16.20	70.71
1981	22.50	4.30	2.83	3.45	108.7	140.4	96.4	83.0	74.1	86.0	73.46	27.14	30.40	15.92	78.01
1982	26.78	5.08	3.30	4.29	119.6	118.7	120.6	118.1	116.6	124.3	87.50	33.32	35.48	18.70	94.83
1983	29.18	6.36	4.19	4.97	106.9	104.0	107.3	115.4	116.1	110.7	98.09	35.90	39.88	22.31	104.29
1984	32.78	8.26	5.45	6.76	115.5	117.0	106.3	133.1	123.2	130.3	116.66	42.98	45.19	28.49	121.13
1985	39.27	10.50	7.01	9.59	114.1	112.8	109.7	115.8	126.9	130.7	144.30	53.54	54.18	36.58	147.68
1986	43.51	11.01	8.42	11.28	101.5	87.6	115.3	97.6	119.7	115.1	156.03	54.64	58.31	43.08	153.90
1987	50.49	11.21	8.51	13.97	106.3	105.9	108.3	99.9	95.8	114.0	177.43	62.21	66.58	48.64	173.02
1988	62.89	14.18	9.20	17.28	111.9	117.2	111.7	100.6	108.0	104.1	235.30	90.20	85.72	59.38	230.20
1989	77.44	14.52	11.66	19.65	102.7	94.5	110.9	98.4	118.3	98.1	257.16	89.08	98.96	69.12	263.30

5. Inner Mongolia

Year	v1h	v1i	v1j	v1j1	v1j2	v1j3	v1k	v2a	v2a1	v2a2	v2b	v2c	v2c1	v2c2	v2d1
1949															
1950															
1951															
1952			454	454				1.65	0.90	0.75					
1953				555				2.67	1.47	1.20					
1954				619				3.95	2.38	1.57					
1955				617				2.65	1.61	1.04					
1956				685				5.02	3.22	1.80					
1957			691	729				5.16	3.26	1.90					
1958				668				13.56	11.34	2.22					
1959				646				19.95	12.57	7.38					
1960				639				17.85	15.45	2.40					20.34
1961				624				6.42	3.69	2.73					21.24
1962			652	675				3.85	2.69	1.16					20.31
1963				746				5.72	4.00	1.72					21.27
1964				769				8.00	5.60	2.40					22.15
1965			728	751				10.40	7.33	3.07					25.26
1966				732				9.94	6.95	2.99					26.91
1967				719				4.73	3.30	1.43					
1968				715				5.47	3.94	1.53					
1969				726				5.68	3.98	1.70					
1970			648	671				9.25	6.85	2.40					
1971				671				10.42	7.61	2.81					45.59
1972				714				9.94	6.96	2.98					49.44
1973				696				11.18	7.94	3.24					53.71
1974				774				12.57	9.36	3.21					56.72
1975			667	707				13.50	9.99	3.51					60.13
1976				702				13.50	9.70	3.80					66.93
1977				702				15.74	11.98	3.76					70.94
1978	130		712	749	563			20.16	15.52	4.64		13.91	7.34	0.49	80.29
1979	156	16.9906	716	750	579		1.8712	22.13	16.60	5.53		14.55	6.39	0.68	87.07
1980	181	19.9329	796	839	635		2.0933	18.29	15.19	3.10		14.97	5.85	0.83	91.48
1981	228	21.0486	807	851	642		2.6247	18.27	15.00	3.27		12.18	4.36	0.49	99.10
1982	273	23.0005	826	869	669		3.1300	26.80	21.64	5.16	20.65	17.43	6.19	0.73	104.58
1983	294	24.7989	862	903	714		3.8312	31.75	25.83	5.92	28.76	24.16	11.55	0.52	113.21
1984	336	29.2786	986	1047	801		4.7441	33.24	28.28	4.96	40.48	29.28	14.11	0.68	122.67
1985	360	33.9494	1095	1169	872		5.5836	46.32	35.66	10.66	51.20	37.62	15.47	1.27	152.47
1986	340	40.5310	1239	1325	982		6.4608	43.43	30.78	12.65	49.51	37.00	11.63	0.84	168.45
1987	389	44.6335	1331	1410	1083		9.5796	50.19	35.67	14.52	54.05	39.05	13.53	1.00	185.69
1988	500	53.1584	1548	1641	1251		10.8242	79.13	41.03	38.10		49.23	18.40	0.85	210.02
1989	478	58.9385	1685	1779	1381		11.7902	92.87	48.07	44.80	55.69	52.92	28.49	0.80	245.53

5. Inner Mongolia

5–4

Year	v2d2	v2e	v3a	v3b	v3b1	v3b2	v3c	v3d	v3d1	v3d2	v3e	v3e1	v3e2	v3e3	v3e4
1949															
1950															
1951															
1952			7.12	6.55	5.16	1.39	0.57	93	83	158					
1953			7.80	7.23	5.54	1.69	0.57	98	87	152					
1954			8.62	7.86	5.73	2.13	0.76	101	90	165					
1955			8.58	7.89	5.49	2.40	0.69	98	83	172					
1956			10.58	9.71	6.56	3.15	0.87	112	93	192					
1957			11.30	10.44	6.96	3.48	0.86	114	94	195					
1958			12.28	11.38	7.22	4.16	0.90	118	94	213					
1959			13.46	12.66	7.32	5.34	0.80	124	94	216					
1960			13.91	13.40	6.97	6.43	0.51	119	88	191					
1961			14.15	13.84	7.45	6.39	0.31	118	91	178					
1962		3.96	13.75	13.40	8.06	5.34	0.35	115	94	175					
1963		3.98	13.76	13.40	8.07	5.33	0.36	112	90	168					
1964		3.52	14.52	13.82	8.68	5.14	0.70	111	92	179					
1965		3.01	15.52	14.51	8.70	5.81	1.01	113	91	179					
1966			17.44	16.38	9.54	6.84	1.06	124	97	197					
1967			19.05	17.90	10.31	7.59	1.15	131	102	208					
1968			18.59	17.51	9.79	7.72	1.08	125	94	204					
1969			18.73	17.60	8.88	8.72	1.13	121	83	218					
1970			20.62	19.53	10.04	9.49	1.09	131	93	223					
1971		14.46	22.71	21.15	10.37	10.78	1.56	138	91	249					
1972		16.09	25.31	23.38	10.52	12.86	1.93	147	91	279					
1973		14.96	28.10	26.16	12.58	13.58	1.94	159	107	282					
1974		15.16	29.35	27.07	13.29	13.78	2.28	160	108	286					
1975		15.54	32.64	29.30	14.37	14.93	3.34	169	115	297					
1976		16.81	35.22	31.69	15.41	16.28	3.53	179	121	318					
1977		17.30	38.29	33.88	16.39	17.49	4.41	188	128	330					
1978		19.13	40.63	35.75	16.72	19.03	4.88	196	129	347	268.77				
1979	66.22	21.55	43.93	38.61	18.11	20.50	5.32	207	139	363	350.64				
1980	67.96	23.33	52.42	47.15	23.83	23.32	5.27	249	180	409	353.04				
1981	71.31	23.59	59.74	52.38	26.96	25.42	7.36	273	201	443	377.85				
1982	73.03	24.35	68.03	61.12	33.75	27.37	6.91	315	246	478	397.12				
1983	78.18	25.47	72.54	64.65	35.62	29.03	7.89	327	259	490	411.38				
1984	84.79	27.74	87.89	73.71	40.24	33.47	14.18	368	289	557	448.98	236.29			
1985	109.87	31.15	101.36	84.48	45.34	39.14	16.88	417	325	634	594.82	271.75			
1986	122.28	36.71	110.47	90.34	45.21	45.13	19.75	442	320	728	680.04	328.63			
1987	134.53	41.91	122.83	100.94	49.94	51.00	21.89	487	349	812	711.85	353.86			
1988	153.13	49.47	151.07	126.30	64.34	61.96	24.77	602	449	935	843.86	394.14			
1989	180.03	65.31	170.43	144.27	74.70	69.57	26.16	679	518	1019	913.47	455.72	135.53	5.3	16.74

5. Inner Mongolia

Year	v3f	v3f1	v3f2	v3f3	v3f4	v4a1	v4a1a	v4a1b	v4a1c	v4a1d	v4a2	v4a2a	v4a2b	v4a2c	v4a2d
1949						0.07	0.02	0.01		0.01	0.08		0.0023	0.04	0.04
1950						0.53	0.16	0.19		0.02	0.46		0.0375	0.16	0.26
1951						0.54	0.13	0.23		0.12	0.60		0.1055	0.28	0.22
1952						1.33	0.50	0.37		0.18	1.03	0.25	0.1467	0.30	0.33
1953						0.87	0.23	0.45		0.14	1.40	0.49	0.2939	0.39	0.23
1954						1.85	0.53	0.77		0.08	1.80	0.62	0.3165	0.47	0.40
1955						2.11	0.63	0.85		0.06	1.75	0.57	0.2949	0.44	0.44
1956						2.76	0.93	1.18		0.05	2.90	1.32	0.4354	0.58	0.57
1957						3.14	0.94	1.25		0.04	2.68	0.98	0.5345	0.57	0.59
1958						4.28	1.71	1.52		0.04	6.44	1.42	0.6187	0.62	3.78
1959						7.03	3.92	1.92		0.18	9.94	6.01	0.7072	0.80	2.41
1960						8.99	5.29	2.47		0.29	12.22	6.45	1.0306	0.89	3.85
1961						4.95	2.42	1.65		0.20	5.65	1.16	0.8767	0.86	2.75
1962						3.36	0.78	1.80		0.14	3.76	0.74	0.8096	0.71	1.50
1963						3.83	0.97	1.99		0.14	4.00	0.90	0.8913	0.74	1.46
1964						4.32	1.25	2.02		0.10	4.97	1.28	1.0158	0.83	1.84
1965						4.60	1.31	2.26		0.10	5.18	1.87	1.0560	0.80	1.45
1966						4.85	1.61	2.17		0.07	5.92	2.02	1.0912	0.86	1.96
1967						4.02	0.91	2.03		0.04	4.79	1.67	1.0812	0.74	1.31
1968						3.89	0.75	2.05		0.07	4.15	1.36	0.9194	0.77	1.10
1969						2.77	0.15	2.02		0.05	6.17	2.36	0.9706	0.95	1.89
1970						4.41	0.61	2.74		0.06	7.86	3.51	1.1013	1.09	2.16
1971						3.65	-0.18	2.95		0.08	9.09	3.75	1.3650	1.25	2.73
1972						3.13	-0.58	3.11		0.07	9.80	3.70	1.7094	1.30	3.09
1973						3.41	-0.93	3.50		0.05	11.50	3.94	1.8509	1.28	4.42
1974						2.69	-1.61	3.43		0.07	12.48	4.85	1.9931	1.31	4.33
1975						2.74	-2.10	4.03		0.07	12.92	4.47	2.1228	1.40	4.92
1976						2.66	-2.57	4.31		0.06	13.83	4.31	2.3035	1.50	5.72
1977						2.93	-2.92	4.96		0.11	14.05	3.70	2.4444	1.62	6.29
1978						6.90	0.32	5.45		0.50	18.69	5.60	3.0439	1.72	8.33
1979						4.56	-2.07	5.46		0.25	21.04	6.11	3.4134	2.00	9.52
1980	158	102				4.13	-2.67	5.85		0.31	18.37	4.07	3.8017	2.26	8.24
1981	177	111				4.16	-3.26	6.25		0.31	16.35	2.08	4.1396	2.34	7.79
1982	203	128				5.18	-3.56	7.15		0.56	20.31	2.81	5.0282	2.90	9.57
1983	227	136				6.99	-2.52	7.84		0.53	22.83	3.55	5.7613	3.42	10.10
1984	246	154				8.46	-2.06	8.69		0.53	30.86	4.45	7.4432	4.90	14.07
1985	291	184				13.39	-1.97	10.47		2.30	36.22	5.68	8.3952	4.07	18.08
1986	307	186				16.02	0.04	14.59		0.46	43.90	7.29	9.8484	5.10	21.66
1987	349	209				19.43	-0.09	17.69		0.81	45.56	5.41	10.1132	5.10	24.94
1988	404	230				24.13	-0.98	21.41		2.23	51.01	5.02	12.3436	4.85	28.80
1989	448	245	43.34	43.26	23.49	28.67	-2.39			3.35	55.81	4.58	13.4500	5.23	32.55

5. Inner Mongolia

5–6

Year	v4b	v4b1	v4b2	v4b3	v4c1	v4c2	v5a	v5a1	v5a2	v5a3	v5a4	v5b1	v5b2	v5b3	v5c
1949								7.1			268.5				
1950								10.4			274.5				
1951								13.3			286.9				
1952		0.0344		0.0069			345.3	16.9		33.0	295.4	302.6	13.0	29.7	
1953								21.1			304.0				
1954								27.3			312.0				
1955								29.7			324.7				
1956								45.0			339.7				
1957		0.3769		0.2225			400.6	46.1	9.4	0.8	344.3	347.4	21.1	32.1	
1958								92.8			311.0				
1959								107.9			302.8				
1960								136.8			303.6				
1961								101.4			334.2				
1962		0.3708		0.2844			440.4	80.8	10.9	1.3	347.1	359.1	40.8	40.5	
1963							458.2	80.1	11.2	1.7	364.9				
1964							474.3	81.6	11.9	1.5	378.6				
1965		0.6196		0.3028			476.8	86.5	13.4	1.3	375.5	379.7	45.3	51.8	
1966								90.8			391.1				
1967								90.5			377.1				
1968								89.7			383.3				
1969								100.9			389.5				
1970		0.7844					524.4	110.9	13.9		399.6	405.2	63.6	55.6	
1971								123.0			415.2				
1972								135.5			408.9				
1973								135.8			413.1				
1974								137.6			419.9				
1975		1.7464					607.5	143.8	32.9	0.2	430.6	441.6	95.5	70.4	
1976								152.3			427.5				
1977								158.8			424.6				
1978	3.1	3.1453		1.1994			652.8	183.2	44.4	0.2	425.0	438.0	120.5	94.3	
1979	4.5	4.6582		1.7164	5.65	6.4	674.0	193.0	49.8	0.2	431.0				
1980	6.6	6.0032		2.8554	6.26	6.9	698.4	200.6	53.7	1.1	443.0	460.7	129.7	108.0	
1981	8.8	7.9918		4.3073	6.47	6.8	731.2	214.4	56.5	2.3	458.0	478.8	136.4	116.0	
1982	12.3	11.2596		5.1966	8.84	9.1	762.4	220.1	61.3	3.3	477.7	501.5	140.1	120.8	
1983	16.5	15.5599		6.2701	10.86	10.5	791.6	229.3	64.8	6.7	490.8	515.8	146.7	136.3	
1984	21.8	21.0077		7.7721	11.69	10.4	817.2	229.6	75.0	10.0	502.6	524.5	154.5	148.8	
1985	28.8	29.0738		9.7191	14.15	10.0	841.3	241.4	79.0	15.2	505.7	517.8	174.8	164.0	
1986	38.8	38.9691		18.1517	14.56	9.2	860.3	251.5	83.3	15.8	509.6	521.7	184.6	169.1	
1987	50.8				17.10	9.7	875.5	260.2	82.5	16.9	515.8	490.3	188.0	212.7	
1988					23.27	11.5	893.1	268.3	84.7	20.1	519.8	490.0	200.1	219.6	
1989	82.2	68.0000			24.32	9.9	910.3	271.0	86.0	18.1	523.1	491.3	199.1	219.9	

5. Inner Mongolia

5–7

Year	v5c1	v5d	v6a	v6a1	v6a2	v6b	v6c	v6d1	v6d2	v6d3	v6d4	v6d5	v6d6
1949			608	75	533					334	274	14.10	20.86
1950			660	83	577					363	297		
1951			687	88	599					379	308		
1952			716	92	624					394	322	15.54	23.35
1953			758	102	656					421	337		
1954			801	115	686	58.8	20.9			444	357		
1955			843	122	721	37.5	11.4			467	376		
1956			897	176	721	29.5	7.9			499	397		
1957			936	175	761	37.2	10.5			519	417	47.54	35.55
1958			986	217	769	28.4	7.9			546	440	64.79	37.14
1959			1063	328	735	30.8	11.0			594	469		
1960			1191	360	831	29.4	9.4			671	520		
1961			1163	319	844	22.1	8.8			640	523	97.26	47.30
1962			1172	277	895	38.2	9.0			639	533	72.60	43.92
1963			1215	281	934	41.3	8.5			661	555	71.31	45.36
1964			1254	249	1005	41.9	11.8			679	575	73.12	47.49
1965			1296	268	1028	40.0	9.3			700	596	77.56	50.04
1966			1330	273	1057	36.1	8.1			717	613		
1967			1371	283	1088	34.9	7.7			737	634		
1968			1411	291	1120	34.9	7.3			757	654		
1969			1460	302	1158	32.5	6.8			783	677		
1970			1491	321	1170	32.3	6.2			799	692	88.04	55.22
1971			1555	322	1233	29.7	5.6	377	1178	828	727		
1972			1603	343	1260	30.7	6.6	399	1204	850	753		
1973			1651	360	1291	28.3	5.7	409	1242	874	777		
1974			1705	359	1346	25.9	6.1	419	1286	902	803		
1975			1738	379	1359	23.3	6.1	432	1306	919	819	99.15	63.71
1976			1769	379	1390	20.1	5.5	442	1327	932	837		
1977			1798	389	1409	18.1	5.4	401	1347	947	851		
1978			1823	397	1426	18.5	5.2	462	1361	958	865	100.64	66.32
1979			1852	409	1443	18.1	4.9	480	1372	971	881		
1980			1876	433	1443	16.5	4.9	496	1381	981	895	102.29	69.88
1981			1903	445	1458	17.3	4.9	512	1391	995	908		
1982			1942	565	1377	21.2	5.7	527	1414	996	946		
1983			1970	574	1396	20.0	5.5	538	1432	1010	960		
1984			1993	847	1146	18.9	5.5	548	1445	1023	970		
1985			2016	874	1142	17.2	5.7	575	1441	1044	972	109.73	79.20
1986			2041	932	1109	19.1	5.9	589	1452	1058	983	111.87	80.95
1987			2066	1004	1062	19.7	6.1	610	1457	1062	1004	113.38	82.82
1988			2094	1034	1060	19.0	5.7	632	1462	1083	1011	116.10	113.38
1989			2122	1056	1066	19.3	5.8	651	1471	1102	1020	118.05	87.18

5. Inner Mongolia

5–8

Year	v7a	v7b	v7c	v7d	v7e	v7f	v7g	v7h	v7h1	v7h2	v7h3	v7h4	v7h5	v7i	v8a
1949		433.1													
1950		472.6													
1951		506.3													
1952		517.4	649.0	7424				12.06							1.63
1953		531.9						14.35							2.55
1954		531.6						16.77							3.77
1955		542.3						15.60							4.41
1956		569.9						19.52							6.05
1957		571.5	900.0	7919				11.18							6.33
1958		555.3						15.60							12.03
1959		539.3						18.14							18.78
1960		602.0						16.57							28.57
1961		609.7						17.04							15.93
1962		586.7	1144.0					17.05							14.26
1963		554.2						17.43							21.26
1964		561.4						20.82							23.05
1965		561.5	1740.1	7922		2.8	0.07	19.39							26.79
1966		548.0						20.93							29.56
1967		540.3						21.46							20.28
1968		531.2						22.08							21.19
1969		534.3						19.95							22.32
1970		545.0				4.7		24.04							27.80
1971		544.1	962.7					73.75							31.09
1972		542.7						71.79							31.57
1973		541.2						82.14							32.67
1974		537.7						29.57							29.78
1975		534.1	1086.0			7.0		30.83							36.89
1976		526.7						31.29							37.61
1977		525.1						28.43							44.08
1978		532.6	993.9	7236			3.94	28.35							52.96
1979		534.7	1772.6			4.7		31.58	20.57	1.08	7.68	0.07	2.18	180.35	57.40
1980	42.07	525.2	1656.1	7196		3.6	4.59	30.68	18.13	1.35	9.52	0.08	1.60	175.57	59.39
1981		518.6	1556.6			8.3		39.42	23.27	2.28	11.48	0.11	2.28	192.00	61.76
1982		510.9	1540.0			10.1		47.16						213.24	73.73
1983		506.5	1529.6			14.4		52.43	29.96	3.81	13.69	0.19	4.78	241.30	81.53
1984		500.6	1470.7			16.3		61.28	34.20	4.44	15.72	0.24	6.68	248.65	90.02
1985	47.27	493.0	1447.4	6824		19.9	6.39	73.20	40.12	4.83	21.40	0.40	6.45	258.13	112.94
1986		489.5	1508.5			21.7		77.25	40.28	4.37	23.99	0.54	8.07	261.22	126.46
1987		485.1	1556.7			23.9		87.74	45.06	3.63	29.02	0.65	9.38	251.72	150.84
1988	67.23	487.1	1680.4	6839			9.17	122.38	61.43	3.86	44.74	0.84	11.51	239.33	193.86
1989	72.84		1730.0	6864			9.88	126.72	63.98	4.00	45.33	1.04	12.37	246.84	241.72

5. Inner Mongolia

5–9

Year	v8a1	v8a2	v8a3	v8b	v8c1	v8c2	v8d	v8f1	v8f2	v8f3	v8f4	v8f5	v8g
1949									46		0.12		765
1950									52		0.13		
1951									66		0.15		
1952					0.57	1.06			75		0.15		1353
1953					1.04	1.51			85		0.29		
1954					1.66	2.11			108		0.38		
1955					1.86	2.55			140		0.49		
1956					2.67	3.38			172		0.73		
1957					2.79	3.54			217		0.92		2110
1958					6.35	5.68		1.0	588		1.99	0.03	
1959					11.07	7.71		6.0	900		4.63	2.03	
1960					18.69	9.88		30.0	1188		12.10	15.42	
1961					9.41	6.52		18.0	876		9.99	3.78	
1962					7.89	6.37		8.0	694		8.79	1.04	3614
1963					12.91	8.35		23.0	726		10.33	0.34	
1964					14.24	8.81		29.0	703		10.68	1.17	
1965					16.37	10.42		34.0	806		12.55	3.06	2490
1966					17.44	12.12		69.0	970		17.83	4.07	
1967					11.09	9.19		30.0	755		15.04	3.49	
1968					12.41	8.78		28.0	899		14.39	5.77	
1969					13.76	8.56		34.0	756		16.67	4.48	
1970					17.74	10.06		81.0	1215		22.01	11.14	3341
1971					19.53	11.56		70.0	1293		25.89	25.13	
1972					19.69	11.88		69.0	1389		26.04	44.52	
1973					19.39	13.28		44.0	1433		26.01	52.79	
1974					16.29	13.49		27.0	1398		25.11	39.31	
1975					21.80	15.09		49.0	1699		28.26	57.64	5373
1976					20.96	16.65		44.0	1761		30.13	57.53	
1977					24.83	19.25		59.0	1954		33.07	83.03	
1978					31.37	21.59		99.0	2194		37.78	91.91	7272
1979				41.97	35.25	22.15	13.21	121.0	2275		44.08	103.56	
1980				44.74	34.84	24.55	15.47	133.0	2211		49.05	109.85	7687
1981				47.95	33.55	28.21	16.77	132.0	2180		54.50	104.40	7401
1982	59.72	11.22	2.79	57.45	42.28	31.45	19.84	129.0	2382		58.40	124.43	7278
1983	67.07	12.17	2.29	64.79	47.47	34.06	21.87	134.0	2487		60.82	145.88	7203
1984	73.49	13.97	2.56	71.18	53.03	36.99	24.78	149.0	2740		69.55	151.40	7085
1985	90.87	18.28	3.79	87.83	65.16	44.03	28.87	170.0	3204		80.46	185.11	7563
1986	100.60	20.78	5.08	96.85	73.81	52.65	30.46	186.0	3292		111.24	207.97	7769
1987	119.43	24.58	6.83		86.74	64.10	35.47	216.0	3410		126.54	218.84	8122
1988	150.80	32.47	10.59	144.85	107.45	86.41	45.69	221.0	3734		138.47	239.62	8293
1989	186.81	46.71	8.19	179.77	136.42	105.31	54.76	242.1	4382		153.72	250.55	8500

5. Inner Mongolia

5–10

Year	v8g1	v9a	v9a1	v9a2	v9a3	v9b	v9b1	v9b2	v9b3	v9c	v10a	v10a1	v10b1	v10b2	v10b3
1949											1.09	0.99	0.14		0.08
1950											1.56	1.42	0.23		0.23
1951											2.24	2.03	0.52		0.32
1952				0.19				0.24			3.53	3.25	0.81		0.95
1953											4.64	4.25	1.17		1.66
1954											6.46	6.00	2.03		2.72
1955				0.87				1.73			6.56	6.07	2.63		2.61
1956				1.20				1.66			8.17	7.40	3.37		3.34
1957				1.52				2.06			8.63	8.00	3.73		3.67
1958				1.41				3.00			10.33	9.31	4.44		4.62
1959				1.83				5.98			12.99	11.68	5.85		5.86
1960				2.43				5.01			15.85	14.29	8.27		6.30
1961				1.97				2.82			12.53	11.11	5.85		6.21
1962			0.16	2.11				2.50			12.97	11.62	6.26		6.18
1963				2.13				2.16			12.70	11.71	6.82		5.50
1964				2.38				2.27			13.34	12.30	7.55		5.43
1965			0.09	2.97				2.87			14.25	12.89	8.39		5.47
1966				3.15				3.21			15.98	14.22	9.69		5.89
1967				3.01				3.09			17.44	15.49	10.21		6.83
1968				3.26				2.88			17.06	15.16	10.00		6.65
1969				3.33				3.15			17.18	15.12	10.07		6.70
1970			13.17	3.74			118.68	4.05			18.89	16.30	11.32		7.17
1971				4.04				4.62			20.27	17.35	11.79		8.08
1972				5.12				5.11			22.92	19.38	13.88		8.62
1973				5.60				5.33			25.63	21.47	15.99		9.20
1974				6.79				5.96			26.76	22.52	16.49		9.82
1975			17.08	7.22			158.61	6.75			29.70	24.72	18.77		10.48
1976				6.92				6.93			32.01	26.32	20.37		11.18
1977				8.19				8.63			34.74	28.56	22.35		11.94
1978		31.80	22.38	9.42		224.55	214.96	9.59			36.83	30.56	23.64		12.74
1979	1544	31.83	21.83	10.00		235.47	226.86	8.59			39.63	33.70	25.43		13.71
1980	1529	43.19	31.84	11.35		174.92	164.78	10.14		3249	44.31	38.31	26.77		16.25
1981	1507	45.70	34.33	11.22		254.93	246.55	8.38		4135	47.36	42.11	28.72		17.11
1982	1522	52.06	37.50	14.40		301.80	291.07	10.73		4736	52.12	45.80	29.71		20.04
1983	1510	61.28	43.92	17.36		348.94	335.57	13.37		5161	57.65	50.31	32.35		21.31
1984	1551	70.63	50.29	20.34		391.85	376.45	15.49		5592	68.29	58.98	36.67		23.64
1985	1707	82.52	58.34	23.86		442.51	424.30	18.20		6348	82.70	71.28	41.76		29.46
1986	1741	90.85	62.57	28.03		470.56	449.30	21.26		7128	92.65	79.75	46.27		32.47
1987	1801	100.92	65.55	33.78		492.65	469.12	23.51		7989	105.40	96.30	51.39		36.42
1988	1823	116.11	74.48	30.01		544.89	466.07	78.80		9474	130.50	118.90	63.29		44.96
1989	1878	108.00	68.00	39.54		584.20	511.80	77.60		10221	138.59	125.69	67.17		45.40

5. Inner Mongolia

5–11

Year	v10b4	v10b5	v10b6	v10d	v11a1	v11a2	v11a3	v11b	v11b1	v11b2	v11c	v11d	v12a	v12b	v12c
1949		0.81	0.07	0.44					0.0269						
1950		1.01	0.09	0.86					0.0265						
1951		1.26	0.14	1.20					0.1157				112.7	110.9	142.3
1952		1.57	0.19	1.82					0.1062				109.8	110.8	100.1
1953		1.62	0.19	2.37					0.2236				103.2	104.7	113.3
1954	0.43	1.16	0.12	4.11					0.2472				102.4	102.4	107.1
1955	0.43	0.76	0.12	3.43					0.2063				103.9	104.1	99.4
1956	1.19	0.12	0.16	3.42					0.1705				103.0	104.1	98.4
1957	0.93	0.13	0.17	3.88					0.1754				99.3	98.7	105.1
1958	1.02	0.08	0.17	4.22					0.1971				98.5	98.8	105.6
1959	1.00	0.09	0.19	5.86					0.3196				99.6	101.5	104.3
1960	1.00	0.08	0.20	5.30					0.2627				102.0	100.2	102.7
1961		0.10	0.38	4.06					0.0737				106.7	109.7	119.6
1962		0.13	0.41	4.29					0.0753				108.2	104.9	101.7
1963		0.14	0.24	4.68					0.0320				99.1	97.8	98.5
1964		0.13	0.22	5.59					0.0302				95.9	96.6	99.3
1965		0.14	0.25	5.37					0.0333				99.6	98.6	99.1
1966		0.14	0.27	6.19					0.0245				100.2	100.7	99.9
1967		0.11	0.29	6.19				0.0370	0.0231	0.0139			100.5	101.3	101.1
1968		0.09	0.32	5.50				0.0410	0.0139	0.0271			100.5	100.4	101.0
1969		0.07	0.33	5.08				0.0487	0.0266	0.0221			100.4	100.9	101.0
1970		0.05	0.36	5.90				0.0554	0.0158	0.0396			100.1	100.4	101.1
1971		0.04	0.37	5.79				0.0468	0.0220	0.0248			99.9	100.9	101.7
1972		0.03	0.39	5.57				0.0847	0.0429	0.0418			100.2	101.2	100.5
1973		0.03	0.41	7.23				0.0914	0.0334	0.0580			101.4	101.6	100.6
1974		0.02	0.43	8.11				0.0985	0.0386	0.0599			101.2	101.7	103.9
1975		0.02	0.43	8.86				0.0925	0.0394	0.0531			100.7	101.4	101.8
1976		0.01	0.44	9.09				0.1502	0.0982	0.0520			101.1	101.7	100.2
1977		0.01	0.45	9.12				0.1421	0.0988	0.0433			101.0	101.1	98.8
1978		0.01	0.45	9.01				0.1552	0.1026	0.0526			101.0	101.5	101.3
1979		0.01	0.48	10.09				0.2016	0.1263	0.0753			101.9	102.3	120.2
1980		0.11	1.17	12.95				0.4398	0.2663	0.1735			105.5	106.1	112.0
1981		0.26	1.26	15.75				0.6504	0.4884	0.1620			101.8	101.9	106.3
1982		0.77	1.60	18.05				0.8108	0.7211	0.0897			101.7	101.7	99.9
1983		2.13	1.84	20.78				0.9001	0.5710	0.3291			101.0	101.2	101.6
1984	0.01	5.15	2.82	21.87				1.0912	0.7895	0.3017			104.4	104.9	106.9
1985		7.13	4.36	29.21				1.8450	1.3710	0.4740			108.5	108.9	113.5
1986		8.78	5.13	32.80				2.3936	1.7104	0.6832	0.0426	0.0136	105.0	105.5	114.1
1987		11.57	6.02	38.72				3.0398	2.2654	0.7744	0.1697	0.0109	108.1	108.5	118.6
1988		14.96	7.27	54.61				3.7968	2.9393	0.8575			116.3	117.0	124.6
1989	0.27	17.56	8.19	55.09				4.3312	3.3630	0.9682		0.0400	115.9	114.2	105.1

5. Inner Mongolia

5–12

Year	v13a	v13b	v13c1	v13c2	v13c3	v13d	v14a	v14b	v14c	v15a	v15b	v15c	v15d	v15e	v15f
1949	1.02	35.5		0.93	35.33			7204	0.02						
1950	3.29														
1951	6.26														
1952	6.56	57.9	0.06	2.17	68.45		1274	10727	0.19	7761					
1953	12.75					0.02									
1954	10.56														
1955	10.83														
1956	9.00														
1957	12.46	56.9	0.25	8.33	87.34	0.03		18290	0.27	8572					
1958	6.16														
1959	4.17														
1960	4.96	85.5				0.10									
1961	9.45														
1962	13.46	73.9	1.14	13.22	130.96	0.22		30613	0.48						
1963	14.00														
1964	12.36														
1965	12.57	83.1	0.90	25.87	209.77		15820	33215	0.24	8422					
1966	11.86														
1967	14.84														
1968	14.69														
1969	9.43														
1970	8.10														
1971	9.01														
1972	10.47														
1973	9.55														
1974	9.40														
1975	9.57														
1976	9.75														
1977	10.16							55018							
1978	8.49		1.21	162.56	291.78		44174	59277	0.32	7989					
1979	9.41	94.3	1.57	156.06	293.42	0.14		65615	0.30						
1980	12.38	94.2	1.74	139.12	289.86	0.34	47271	70022	0.78	7878					
1981	15.04	92.6	2.06	121.41	284.02	0.23		77647	1.68						
1982	14.48	92.0	1.95	108.88	270.85	0.69		80450	1.76						
1983	14.15	92.4	2.15	106.47	260.69	0.51		82873	1.95						
1984	13.50	94.6	2.45	111.23	261.93	0.44		85185	2.09						
1985	13.37	96.8	3.12	115.68	254.90	0.62	50567	87130	3.06	7395					
1986	12.70	97.4	3.12	120.30	250.14	0.68		89257	2.67						
1987	13.25		3.12	120.98	243.16	0.93			2.86						
1988	14.03	97.3	3.30	117.39	237.45	1.00	55867	94000	2.80	7306	1664.6			1974.2	16
1989		97.5	3.31	112.71	235.20	0.91	56776	95000	2.63	7367					

Notes

1. National Output and Income (Y)

v1a: (E), p.190
- v1a1: (E), p.190
- v1a2: (E), p.190
- v1a3: (E), p.190
- v1a4: (E), p.190
- v1a5: (E), p.190

v1b: (A); (D), p.147
- v1b1: (A); (D), p.147
- v1b2: (A); (D), p.147
- v1b3: (A); (D), p.147
- v1b4: (A); (D), p.147
- v1b5: (A); (D), p.147

v1c: v1a – v1d

v1d: (E), p.187
- v1d1: (E), p.187
- v1d2: (E), p.187
- v1d3: (E), p.187
- v1d4: (E), p.187
- v1d5: (E), p.187

v1e: (A); (D), p.150
- v1e1: (A); (D), p.150
- v1e2: (A); (D), p.150
- v1e3: (A); (D), p.150
- v1e4: (A); (D), p.150
- v1e5: (A); (D), p.150

v1f: (E), p.186
- v1f1: (E), p.186
- v1f2: (E), p.186
- v1f3: (E), p.186

v1g: v2a + v3a

v1h: (E), p.212

v1i: (E), p.211

v1j: (E), p.211
- v1j1: (E), p.211
- v1j2: (E), p.211
- v1j3: NA

v1k: (E), p.211—insurance and welfare expenses of staff and workers in state-owned units

2. Investment (I)

v2a: (A)
- v2a1: (A)
- v2a2: (A)

v2b: (A)

v2c: (E), p.203
- v2c1: (E), p.204
- v2c2: (E), p.204

v2d:
- v2d1: (E), p.201
- v2d2: (E), p.201

v2e: (E), p.201

3. Consumption (C)

v3a: (E), p.189

v3b: (E), p.189
- v3b1: (A); (E), p.151
- v3b2: (A); (E), p.151

v3c: (E), p.189

v3d: (E), p.210
- v3d1: (E), p.210
- v3d2: (E), p.210

v3e: (E), p.212
- v3e1: (E), p.212
- v3e2: (A)
- v3e3: (A)
- v3e4: (A)

v3f: (E), p.212
  v3f1: (E), p.212
  v3f2: (A)
  v3f3: (A)
  v3f4: (A)

4. Public Finance and Banking (FB)

v4a:
  v4a1: (E), p.208
    v4a1a: (E), p.208
    v4a1b: (B), p.417–418
    v4a1c: NA
    v4a1d: v4a1 – v4a1a – v4a1b' (v4a1b': total tax revenues, which come from (E), p.208)
  v4a2: (E), p.208
    v4a2a: (E), p.208
    v4a2b: (E), p.208
    v4a2c: (E), p.208
    v4a2d: v4a2 – v4a2a – v4a2b – v4a2c

v4b: (A)
  v4b1: (C), 1987, p.124
  v4b2: NA
  v4b3: (C), 1987, p.124

v4c:
  v4c1: (E), p.201
  v4c2: (E), p.201

5. Labor Force (L)

v5a: (E), p.185
  v5a1: (E), p.185
  v5a2: (E), p.185
  v5a3: (E), p.185
  v5a4: (E), p.185

v5b:
  v5b1: (E), p.185
  v5b2: (E), p.185
  v5b3: (E), p.185

v5c: NA
  v5c1: NA

v5d: NA

6. Population (PO)

v6a: (E), p.184—population of 1982 and before are from public security department, afterward from the estimates based on sample surveys
  v6a1: (E), p.184—(ditto)
  v6a2: (E), p.184—(ditto)

v6b: (E), p.184—(ditto)

v6c: (E), p.184—(ditto)

v6d:
  v6d1: (E), p.184—(ditto)
  v6d2: (E), p.184—(ditto)
  v6d3: (E), p.184—(ditto)
  v6d4: (E), p.184—(ditto)
  v6d5: (A)—Baotou
  v6d6: (A)—Hohhot

7. Agriculture (A)

v7a: (E), p.196

v7b: (A); (E), p.196—10,000 hectares

v7c: (A); (E), p.196

v7d: (E)

v7e: NA

v7f: (A)—reckoned pure amount

v7g: (E), p.196

v7h: (E), p.190
  v7h1: (E), p.194
  v7h2: (E), p.194
  v7h3: (E), p.194
  v7h4: (E), p.194
  v7h5: (E), p.194

v7i: (E), p.195

8. Industry (IN)

v8a: (E), p.190
- v8a1: (E), p.198
- v8a2: (E), p.198
- v8a3: v8a – v8a1 – v8a2

v8b: (E), p.201
- v8c1: (E), p.190
- v8c2: (E), p.190

v8d: (E), p.201

v8f:
- v8f1: (E), p.199
- v8f2: (E), p.199
- v8f3: NA
- v8f4: (E), p.199
- v8f5: (E), p.199

v8g: (A); (B), p.325
- v8g1: (E), p.201

9. Transport (TR)

v9a: (E), p.202—excluding urban traffic volume
- v9a1: (E), p.202—including central and local railways
- v9a2: (E), p.202
- v9a3: NA

v9b: (E), p.202
- v9b1: (E), p.202—including central and local railways
- v9b2: (E), p.202
- v9b3: NA

v9c: (E), p.202

10. Domestic Trade (DT)

v10a: (E), p.205
- v10a1: (E), p.205

v10b:
- v10b1: (E), p.205
- v10b2: NA
- v10b3: (E), p.205—supply and marketing cooperative and other collectives
- v10b4: (E), p.205
- v10b5: (E), p.205
- v10b6: (E), p.205

v10d: (E), p.207—calculated on calendar year basis

11. Foreign Trade (FT)

v11a:
- v11a1: NA
- v11a2: NA
- v11a3: NA

v11b: (E), p.207—data from foreign trade department
- v11b1: (E), p.207—(ditto)
- v11b2: v11b – v11b1

v11c: (A)

v11d: (A)

12. Prices (PR)

v12a: (E), p.209

v12b: (E), p.209

v12c: (E), p.209

13. Education (ED)

v13a: (A)

v13b: (E), p.212; (F), p.241

v13c:
- v13c1: (A); (B), pp.438–439; (E), p.212
- v13c2: (A); (B), pp.438–439; (E), p.212—technical and ordinary secondary schools
- v13c3: (B), pp.438–439; (E), p.212

v13d: (A); (C), 1988, p.352; 1989, p.365; (F), p.202

14. Social Factors (SF)

v14a: (E), p.212

v14b: (A)

v14c: (A); (C), 1989, p.37; (F), p.349

15. Natural Environment (NE)

v15a: (A); (E), p.196

v15b: (A)—10,000 hectares

v15c: NA

v15d: NA

v15e: (A)

v15f: (A)

Sources of Data

(A) Data supplied by the DSNEB, SSB, the PRC.
(B) Statistical Bureau of Inner Mongolia Autonomous Region ed. *Striving and Advancing Inner Mongolia 1947–1989*, Beijing: CSPH, 1989.
(C) ________ ed. *Statistical Yearbook of Inner Mongolia, Beijing: CSPH, various issues.*
(D) Same as (D) in Beijing's sources of data.
(E) Same as (E) in Beijing's sources of data.
(F) Social Office of Statistical Bureau, Inner Mongolia Autonomous Region ed. *Inner Mongolia Social Statistics, 1947–86*, Beijing: CSPH, 1989.

6

Liaoning

6. Liaoning

6–1

Year	v1a	v1a1	v1a2	v1a3	v1a4	v1a5	v1b	v1b1	v1b2	v1b3	v1b4	v1b5	v1c	v1d	v1d1
1949		10.51													
1950		13.23					155.5	125.7	197.5	71.4	154.5	150.0			
1951		14.75					123.1	112.1	133.6	106.7	76.5	161.9			
1952	76.20	16.60	44.20	5.90	3.50	6.00	141.3	114.2	144.3	312.5	134.6	155.9	38.80	37.40	11.70
1953	99.10	16.90	57.80	9.60	5.00	9.80	129.3	100.6	129.6	170.0	145.7	169.8	50.60	48.50	12.00
1954	106.80	18.80	64.20	9.40	5.50	8.90	109.0	108.2	111.8	105.9	115.7	91.1	54.70	52.10	13.70
1955	108.30	19.40	67.80	7.70	6.10	7.30	102.7	101.6	109.5	85.6	86.4	81.7	54.40	53.90	14.20
1956	133.10	22.10	83.50	11.50	7.10	8.90	133.2	108.0	141.1	139.0	117.6	123.9	67.60	65.50	16.30
1957	142.00	21.20	94.40	10.40	6.70	9.30	107.4	94.1	115.6	81.3	83.3	91.6	70.60	71.40	15.40
1958	195.10	21.20	138.90	16.80	7.50	10.70	145.4	117.7	160.5	106.1	104.5	102.3	97.00	98.10	15.60
1959	258.70	24.60	198.60	14.20	10.50	10.80	124.7	109.4	129.7	107.7	108.6	102.2	132.60	126.70	17.80
1960	303.30	19.20	243.10	18.70	11.80	10.50	116.8	68.7	121.8	109.8	132.9	119.8	157.50	145.80	13.20
1961	151.90	19.60	107.90	6.80	8.70	8.90	47.7	87.5	43.2	77.2	96.0	81.7	87.00	64.90	14.00
1962	146.20	21.20	107.40	2.70	4.90	10.00	91.2	108.6	93.0	22.1	51.5	87.6	82.70	63.50	15.10
1963	160.20	21.80	117.90	4.60	5.20	10.70	112.5	116.4	111.7	133.3	106.0	114.1	94.40	65.80	15.90
1964	185.80	22.60	138.20	7.40	5.90	11.70	117.8	106.8	118.6	175.0	113.2	113.5	110.50	75.30	16.10
1965	223.00	26.50	170.50	6.70	7.20	12.10	122.5	112.2	125.1	110.2	125.0	110.9	132.20	90.80	19.40
1966	249.70	29.40	193.60	6.20	7.60	12.90	113.9	100.0	117.4	87.0	104.0	106.3	148.00	101.70	21.70
1967	190.60	29.30	137.90	4.80	5.90	12.70	77.9	100.9	73.9	91.7	88.5	98.3	108.40	82.20	21.70
1968	168.60	30.40	115.80	4.50	6.10	11.80	89.0	100.9	86.4	91.7	102.9	91.5	93.00	75.60	22.50
1969	244.50	30.00	186.10	6.90	9.60	11.90	151.5	95.8	165.3	145.5	149.3	100.0	142.70	101.80	21.40
1970	296.50	37.70	226.40	8.90	11.80	11.80	124.0	124.2	125.3	127.1	121.7	100.9	172.40	124.20	27.50
1971	328.10	35.50	252.50	14.20	13.30	12.60	111.3	92.6	112.3	154.1	112.4	107.4	192.50	135.60	25.60
1972	341.20	33.00	265.20	15.40	13.70	13.90	104.4	92.0	105.8	105.8	103.0	109.4	201.40	139.80	23.50
1973	376.00	40.30	289.30	16.50	14.50	15.40	110.7	121.4	109.9	104.1	105.8	111.5	218.80	157.20	30.40
1974	401.80	43.90	307.30	19.60	14.10	16.90	107.3	109.2	107.1	115.8	97.2	109.0	233.00	168.80	32.00
1975	430.90	48.30	325.50	23.60	14.90	18.60	107.5	108.4	106.8	117.0	105.7	110.1	249.00	181.90	34.90
1976	446.60	47.40	343.20	22.90	14.10	19.00	104.0	96.8	106.1	94.2	94.6	102.2	259.60	187.00	33.70
1977	437.20	46.60	337.00	19.30	14.60	19.70	98.7	99.8	99.0	88.0	103.7	103.7	251.00	186.20	33.33
1978	483.70	49.20	376.80	20.20	16.30	21.20	110.8	106.5	111.9	101.9	111.6	107.1	278.20	205.50	31.53
1979	529.30	59.80	396.00	33.80	18.30	21.40	107.7	103.4	106.2	163.0	111.7	100.5	309.80	219.50	39.08
1980	615.23	73.56	452.61	40.83	25.02	23.22	110.7	107.5	110.4	109.5	137.4	102.4	365.67	249.56	44.46
1981	635.28	78.60	461.06	46.00	22.60	27.00	101.1	102.1	100.2	112.5	90.4	114.7	385.84	249.42	48.64
1982	677.38	85.36	482.30	56.81	25.28	27.63	106.1	103.7	105.9	111.3	111.9	101.5	415.76	261.62	52.95
1983	749.61	106.53	527.71	59.90	27.15	31.32	109.7	121.1	109.0	100.2	107.1	111.5	451.76	298.00	71.27
1984	866.10	117.62	612.53	64.51	35.41	36.03	112.9	104.3	114.0	111.9	129.9	105.0	511.95	354.15	77.39
1985	1076.80	118.05	774.57	92.28	42.70	49.20	115.9	90.8	118.4	129.4	120.4	115.5	651.08	425.72	70.97
1986	1232.28	142.03	874.93	107.16	47.99	60.11	109.7	106.9	109.6	108.4	113.2	115.8	750.85	481.43	89.77
1987	1472.36	169.22	1044.00	130.60	53.95	74.59	112.4	105.2	113.1	110.6	112.4	116.8	905.97	566.39	108.19
1988	1861.40	227.39	1304.84	160.11	70.27	98.80	115.1	111.0	115.3	109.7	130.2	112.3	1166.92	694.48	140.06
1989	2122.75	222.82	1546.43	158.33	77.38	117.79	104.3	95.7	105.9	95.9	105.5	103.8	1351.80	770.95	139.51

6. Liaoning

6–2

Year	v1d2	v1d3	v1d4	v1d5	v1e	v1e1	v1e2	v1e3	v1e4	v1e5	v1f	v1f1	v1f2	v1f3	v1g
1949															
1950															
1951															
1952	16.50	1.70	2.40	5.10											37.00
1953	21.60	3.20	3.10	8.60	129.9	101.70	129.00	229.40	124.00	168.60					48.40
1954	24.50	3.20	3.40	7.30	109.7	109.80	117.20	128.20	109.70	83.70					49.60
1955	27.50	2.60	3.90	5.70	105.0	102.20	116.70	86.00	117.00	77.80					39.80
1956	32.90	4.20	4.80	7.30	128.6	108.80	135.00	148.80	125.00	132.10					47.10
1957	40.10	4.00	4.40	7.50	108.2	90.60	121.20	90.60	92.00	101.40					54.80
1958	62.00	6.20	5.40	8.90	147.6	116.70	158.30	212.80	120.50	120.00					72.90
1959	86.40	5.60	8.10	8.80	124.0	109.70	130.60	102.40	150.90	101.10					91.30
1960	108.20	7.10	8.70	8.60	111.1	63.30	120.00	124.70	110.00	97.80					101.60
1961	35.50	2.40	6.10	6.90	41.7	93.50	33.10	34.90	68.20	68.50					49.30
1962	35.70	1.00	3.50	8.20	89.4	108.00	93.70	18.90	60.00	104.90					37.80
1963	36.30	1.70	3.70	8.20	107.9	119.40	104.10	142.90	105.60	106.30					63.20
1964	43.40	2.80	4.10	8.90	117.1	104.70	121.00	190.00	110.50	113.20					68.30
1965	54.60	2.60	5.10	9.10	122.7	115.60	127.60	110.50	126.20	109.10					74.00
1966	62.50	2.40	5.40	9.70	112.5	101.30	118.30	85.70	103.80	107.10					67.30
1967	45.00	1.80	4.20	9.50	82.0	101.30	74.70	77.80	89.10	97.80					68.40
1968	38.20	1.70	4.30	8.90	99.6	100.60	100.80	85.70	102.00	92.00					67.70
1969	62.00	2.60	6.90	8.90	130.1	96.90	144.60	150.00	140.00	98.80					76.70
1970	76.10	3.40	8.40	8.80	124.5	125.60	126.30	127.80	130.00	100.00					87.90
1971	86.00	5.40	9.40	9.20	110.3	86.20	113.80	156.50	119.80	106.30					100.80
1972	91.10	5.90	9.60	9.70	103.3	90.90	106.00	107.70	102.10	104.30					94.90
1973	100.30	6.30	10.20	10.00	112.8	129.00	111.70	103.60	106.30	104.10					104.10
1974	107.90	7.50	9.90	11.50	107.8	104.90	108.40	115.50	97.10	113.90					115.50
1975	115.30	9.00	10.10	12.60	107.9	107.70	107.70	117.90	102.00	109.60					130.40
1976	122.70	8.70	9.50	12.40	103.1	95.80	107.10	93.70	94.10	98.40					140.30
1977	122.27	7.30	10.30	13.00	100.2	97.90	100.30	90.50	108.40	104.80					128.80
1978	142.87	7.70	10.80	12.60	110.7	96.80	116.90	92.50	104.90	96.90	223.20	32.40	161.90	28.90	149.00
1979	146.92	8.40	12.10	13.00	104.6	105.50	103.90	106.50	112.00	103.20	239.60	40.70	168.80	30.10	168.50
1980	168.40	10.21	13.72	12.77	108.5	104.60	110.30	109.10	113.20	92.30	266.22	46.05	182.65	37.52	182.36
1981	161.82	12.61	11.83	14.52	97.0	100.30	95.10	123.60	86.10	111.70	285.80	50.15	187.54	48.11	193.00
1982	165.88	16.47	12.59	13.73	103.9	104.30	103.80	113.60	106.50	94.40	301.90	54.67	189.23	57.90	202.42
1983	180.53	16.64	14.30	15.26	112.6	130.60	108.40	104.40	113.50	108.90	347.20	72.24	207.66	67.30	233.76
1984	220.71	19.37	19.67	17.01	115.8	102.50	120.10	110.70	136.60	102.70	415.60	80.40	254.20	81.00	301.03
1985	280.46	26.37	22.47	25.45	112.3	82.70	118.80	127.80	114.20	125.30	489.60	74.90	312.10	102.60	370.54
1986	302.86	30.94	24.83	33.03	107.9	112.34	105.49	109.57	111.30	123.01	558.53	92.53	340.80	125.14	433.19
1987	350.69	37.64	27.89	41.98	109.9	107.33	109.90	110.38	112.32	113.22	663.74	109.52	397.62	156.05	507.95
1988	417.43	48.31	32.27	56.41	110.4	107.66	109.01	114.85	115.70	122.82	814.03	141.75	472.54	199.74	647.78
1989	480.88	47.52	35.54	67.50	102.1	95.21	103.13	95.43	105.70	108.36	921.27	141.86	545.06	234.35	722.15

6. Liaoning

6–3

Year	v1h	v1i	v1j	v1j1	v1j2	v1j3	v1k	v2a	v2a1	v2a2	v2b	v2c	v2c1	v2c2	v2d1
1949												2.07			
1950												2.11			
1951												2.39			
1952				549				13.10	7.00	6.10		7.89			46.90
1953				631				17.90	8.80	9.10		11.70			52.97
1954				635				17.00	11.90	5.10		12.94			69.09
1955				644				7.60	8.30	-0.70		11.01			76.36
1956				731				9.70	9.10	0.60		15.29			86.25
1957	125.00			749				14.00	8.50	5.50		14.11			96.70
1958				709				30.40	22.40	8.00		22.19			110.58
1959				660				42.00	27.90	14.10		24.34			120.98
1960				646				48.20	32.30	15.90		24.81			134.66
1961				639				2.50	1.50	1.00		7.18			137.47
1962				699				-9.50	-0.60	-8.90		4.18			140.79
1963				745				14.40	8.10	6.30		5.90			142.91
1964				761				17.90	11.20	6.70		9.49			148.84
1965				750				21.60	12.40	9.20		7.30			155.19
1966				735				17.30	9.10	8.20		6.24			
1967				746				15.00	5.10	9.90		3.85			
1968				718				14.20	5.10	9.10		3.43			
1969				716				18.20	7.30	10.90		7.71			
1970				696				24.90	9.30	15.60		12.31			
1971				691				35.90	13.60	22.30		17.10			
1972		29.31	637	690	470			27.00	15.50	11.50		18.71			
1973		30.01	635	687	479			33.80	19.70	14.10		20.93			235.80
1974		30.85	633	683	487			40.20	22.00	18.20		22.98			254.62
1975	128.00	32.43	619	675	469			52.80	23.70	29.10		30.78			272.13
1976		33.88	610	667	472			53.90	21.50	32.40		31.89			291.29
1977		35.27	611	664	481			38.30	20.80	17.50		23.74			318.49
1978	185.20	39.89	637	687	489		6.95	54.20	25.50	28.70		25.32	19.27	0.78	339.63
1979		46.22	698	746	558			54.50	35.20	19.30		27.44	17.86	1.11	351.75
1980	273.02	56.72	779	833	640		11.58	47.72	33.84	13.88		46.12	19.93	1.94	382.10
1981		67.20	777	822	667		14.85	43.14	32.44	10.70	60.91	46.44	16.50	1.93	406.83
1982		71.80	784	829	675		16.87	44.71	39.87	4.84	70.76	55.61	16.59	2.63	429.13
1983		75.21	806	852	704		19.52	61.38	46.12	15.26	74.22	57.47	15.35	1.68	476.46
1984	477.44	81.89	925	989	807		24.05	97.64	62.65	34.97	96.68	73.26	19.19	1.86	503.86
1985	485.72	96.44	1064	1126	947		31.25	125.63	82.30	43.33	142.18	110.41	25.37	3.21	567.76
1986	533.20	115.82	1243	1334	1069		33.89	153.21	95.84	57.37	171.78	138.66	30.36	3.63	626.33
1987	599.25	131.63	1374	1477	1171		43.99	185.34	138.74	46.60	218.18	172.87	47.26	4.10	715.48
1988	699.58	166.64	1709	1854	1413		55.26	236.86	161.77	75.09	261.33	212.25	56.18	5.35	828.98
1989	740.22	195.65	1982	2155	1620		65.75	243.07	145.95	97.12	251.03	198.85	65.09	3.29	941.83

6. Liaoning

6–4

Year	v2d2	v2e	v3a	v3b	v3b1	v3b2	v3c	v3d	v3d1	v3d2	v3e	v3e1	v3e2	v3e3	v3e4
1949															
1950															
1951															
1952	31.67		23.90	21.80	10.60	11.20	2.10	114	72	248	179	106			
1953	34.91		30.50	27.60	11.90	15.70	2.90	139	81	299					
1954	47.37		32.60	29.50	13.00	16.50	3.10	141	90	253					
1955	51.65		32.20	29.10	13.70	15.40	3.10	133	93	214					
1956	59.53		37.40	33.90	15.00	18.90	3.50	150	99	255					
1957	67.41		40.80	37.00	15.10	21.90	3.80	157	99	268	213	120			
1958	77.84		42.50	38.70	16.80	21.90	3.80	160	111	242					
1959	86.83		49.30	44.40	18.10	26.30	4.90	179	123	268					
1960	97.02		53.40	47.30	16.20	31.10	6.10	187	115	276					
1961	97.32		46.80	42.10	13.20	28.90	4.70	166	93	260					
1962	97.70		47.30	43.30	17.30	26.00	4.00	171	113	259					
1963	96.58		48.80	45.40	22.00	23.40	3.40	175	135	242					
1964	99.74		50.40	46.00	23.30	22.70	4.40	171	136	232					
1965	103.07		52.40	48.00	23.10	24.90	4.40	173	130	249	216	127			
1966			50.00	46.20	26.30	19.90	3.80	163	144	197					
1967			53.40	48.50	23.50	25.00	4.90	168	128	235					
1968			53.50	48.90	25.10	23.80	4.60	165	133	225					
1969			58.50	53.40	26.90	26.50	5.10	177	132	270					
1970			63.00	57.80	31.90	25.90	5.20	188	151	274					
1971			64.90	59.20	30.50	28.70	5.70	190	141	304					
1972			67.90	61.90	30.80	31.10	6.00	196	142	318					
1973	144.71		70.30	63.70	30.10	33.60	6.60	199	138	333					
1974	155.50		75.30	66.80	31.10	35.70	8.50	206	140	349					
1975	166.67	90.87	77.60	68.20	31.10	37.10	9.40	209	139	362					
1976	178.60	98.02	86.40	75.50	35.60	39.90	10.90	229	157	388					
1977	196.50	99.81	90.50	80.30	38.50	41.80	10.20	241	167	408					
1978	209.21	104.65	94.80	84.90	40.20	44.70	9.90	252	173	425	337				
1979	209.40	107.49	114.00	102.40	46.40	56.00	11.60	299	202	500					
1980	227.41	108.77	134.63	120.73	52.40	68.23	13.90	343	232	545	426	242			
1981	243.24	107.66	149.86	135.56	58.38	77.18	14.30	380	260	586	455	249	79.56	6.36	8.76
1982	254.78	109.03	157.71	141.64	60.12	81.52	16.07	392	267	596	460	272	74.16	7.08	7.80
1983	290.19	116.43	172.38	155.05	66.67	88.38	17.33	423	296	625	487	290	84.61	7.50	7.34
1984	305.23	116.66	203.39	180.47	78.84	101.63	22.92	488	354	693	545	324	100.08	8.13	8.03
1985	348.63	133.31	244.91	216.33	88.95	127.38	28.58	581	405	833	655	367	122.90	7.90	10.48
1986	387.02	154.22	279.98	247.78	97.95	149.83	32.20	659	445	961	794	439	143.99	8.62	10.75
1987	451.84	173.21	322.61	286.23	110.27	175.96	36.38	752	496	1110	937	513	147.83	9.34	10.88
1988	535.78	195.15	410.92	362.74	128.14	234.60	48.18	941	575	1442	1203	606	192.28	10.08	11.45
1989	608.88	239.49	479.08	415.45	144.29	271.16	63.63	1065	644	1635	1276	693			

6. Liaoning

6–5

Year	v3f	v3f1	v3f2	v3f3	v3f4	v4a1	v4a1a	v4a1b	v4a1c	v4a1d	v4a2	v4a2a	v4a2b	v4a2c	v4a2d
1949															
1950															
1951															
1952						7.82	1.30	0.69		1.3	3.85	1.76	0.84	0.66	0.59
1953						10.31	1.14			1.9	3.98	1.64	1.24	0.73	0.37
1954						10.54	1.46	0.25		1.5	3.93	1.31	1.16	0.82	0.64
1955						10.79	1.93	0.21	0.16	1.3	3.32	0.83	1.09	0.80	0.60
1956						12.83	2.40		0.19	1.0	4.41	1.41	1.36	0.98	0.66
1957						15.63	3.53	0.15	0.18	1.5	4.06	1.17	1.35	0.94	0.60
1958						34.85	18.95			0.9	11.83	8.06	1.61	0.98	1.18
1959						42.77	23.45	15.23	1.28	2.9	14.50	6.84	1.94	1.35	4.37
1960						49.53	28.92	16.65	0.89	3.0	19.82	9.93	2.55	1.41	5.93
1961						20.58	8.23	8.82	0.79	2.8	9.89	1.99	2.17	1.38	4.35
1962						17.56	3.80	9.21	0.77	2.7	6.47	0.94	1.91	1.07	2.55
1963						18.92	5.40	10.15	0.82	2.6	8.32	1.69	1.99	1.14	3.50
1964						20.71	5.91	11.83	0.84	2.2	9.49	2.76	2.22	1.24	3.27
1965						23.38	6.92	12.95	0.76	2.9	9.66	2.59	2.30	1.21	3.56
1966						28.33	8.60	17.04	0.88	1.9	10.70	3.11	2.58	1.24	3.77
1967						20.05	4.33	13.21	0.88	1.7	9.37	2.83	2.65	1.17	2.72
1968						14.00	0.82	10.78	0.89	1.7	7.83	1.94	2.20	1.17	2.52
1969						30.26	9.48	16.53	0.99	3.3	12.53	4.45	2.45	1.05	4.58
1970						37.71	11.77	23.56	0.98	1.4	13.82	5.75	2.60	1.23	3.74
1971						70.91	36.88	29.12	1.00	4.0	16.45	6.15	2.96	1.57	5.77
1972						77.96	42.02	30.55	0.80	4.6	19.01	6.46	3.50	1.86	7.19
1973						80.52	50.05	25.19	1.08	4.2	19.87	6.89	3.75	1.66	7.57
1974						77.66	45.33	26.56	1.01	5.1	22.36	6.52	4.08	1.93	9.83
1975						76.89	41.63	28.47	0.98	5.8	26.69	8.94	4.29	1.98	11.48
1976						77.03	40.14	29.78	0.97	6.2	27.43	9.33	4.60	2.15	11.35
1977						75.41	37.67	30.45	0.98	6.3	26.75	7.69	4.71	2.24	12.11
1978	154.59	102	24.86	5.33	11.48	95.81	51.58	33.33	0.98	6.8	31.28	8.36	5.31	2.45	15.16
1979		113				87.27	44.96	34.49	0.96	1.8	34.55	7.21	5.59	2.64	19.11
1980	220.85	129	30.44	16.72	15.71	86.93	43.25	36.30	0.96	6.4	34.11	5.94	6.59	2.91	18.67
1981	253.60	139	35.87	25.16	16.44	79.47	35.20	40.27	0.96	3.0	26.65	3.38	6.93	2.77	13.57
1982		146				78.66	29.24	44.11	0.95	5.7	30.73	4.24	8.52	3.23	14.74
1983	301.64	163	37.79	40.71	19.70	67.88	14.61	47.68	1.05	4.5	34.17	4.83	10.33	3.89	15.12
1984	327.62	184	36.65	39.26	20.34	77.11	14.88	56.74	1.09	4.3	39.25	7.02	11.72	4.68	15.83
1985	390.61	207	44.07	53.26	27.76	85.24	7.78	74.80	0.85	1.7	56.91	12.42	14.04	4.97	25.48
1986	422.42	221	47.83	65.95	27.26	98.88	11.39	82.47	1.25	3.2	75.51	14.10	16.56	6.02	38.83
1987	449.34	237	50.98	66.69	26.27	108.00	9.19	90.98	1.84	6.0	80.37	10.67	16.93	6.31	46.46
1988	535.04	272	61.69	85.07	27.43	115.88	-1.65		2.56		95.18	9.44	20.80	9.51	55.43
1989	668.38	325	71.70	107.10	32.86	133.88	-11.70				114.29	9.02	24.86	7.79	72.62

6. Liaoning

6–6

Year	v4b	v4b1	v4b2	v4b3	v4c1	v4c2	v5a	v5a1	v5a2	v5a3	v5a4	v5b1	v5b2	v5b3	v5c
1949							619	52			521				
1950															
1951															
1952	0.17	0.16			10.07		707	134	54		520	507	114	86	95
1953	0.27	0.26	0.01		11.28		714	156	60		497	484	131	99	
1954	0.54	0.48	0.06		13.77		712	158	61		493	481	131	100	
1955	0.85	0.72	0.13		16.82		716	158	54		503	496	124	96	
1956	1.33	1.13	0.20		20.66		768	203	40		524	520	146	102	
1957	1.80	1.53	0.27		25.16		770	208	42		520	485	154	131	132
1958	2.20	2.01	0.19		42.86		913	315	42		556	437	301	175	
1959	3.67	2.92	0.75				814	313	46		455	370	263	181	
1960	3.83	3.41	0.42		62.47		905	362	81		462	380	295	230	
1961	2.44	1.84	0.60		19.28		854	299	68	3	484	474	217	163	
1962	1.72	1.26	0.46		19.78		819	248	50	7	514	518	174	127	
1963	1.94	1.49	0.45		26.03		816	245	53	7	511	518	171	127	
1964	3.12	2.17	0.95		33.47		818	254	58	6	500	503	182	133	
1965	3.09	2.48	0.61		42.28		847	261	64	4	517	511	182	154	
1966	3.24	2.60	0.65					272							
1967	3.49	2.71	0.77					276							
1968	3.60	2.89	0.70					283							
1969	3.21	2.61	0.60				967	295	54		618	611	207	149	
1970	3.34	2.74	0.60				1047	312	80		655				
1971	3.96	3.24	0.72				1114	341	107		666	622	287	205	
1972	4.79	3.96	0.83				1106	350	116		638	589	316	201	
1973	5.86	4.62	1.24				1115	352	120		641	599	320	196	
1974	6.80	5.37	1.43				1086	363	130		592	553	340	193	
1975	7.47	5.86	1.62		75.68	29.39	1125	378	157		589	542	376	207	
1976	8.11	6.39	1.72		75.72	27.37	1141	393	163		584	525	402	214	
1977	9.64	7.27	2.37		73.86	24.93	1181	404	168		595	571	412	198	
1978	11.97	8.79	3.19		83.90	26.73	1254	471	151		630	595	433	225	397
1979	16.74	12.02	4.72		86.54	27.31	1322	507	188	1	617	590	486	246	
1980	24.58	17.90	6.68		91.71	27.28	1442	541	222	5	664	597	565	280	516
1981	32.51	22.63	9.88		83.46	23.78	1505	579	236	7	673	611	594	300	
1982	41.60	28.99	12.61		81.64	22.44	1572	593	250	8	709	639	600	333	
1983	55.21	37.63	17.58		90.56	22.27	1639	593	275	12	742	670	619	350	
1984	73.59	50.33	23.26		105.73	25.06	1681	581	308	18	743	646	657	378	
1985	100.98	70.16	30.82		121.56	25.22	1769	601	308	25	799	634	726	408	616
1986	140.62	102.44	38.18		121.89	25.52	1799	620	317	26	799	640	735	424	
1987	196.01	144.84	51.17		128.71	20.59	1835	634	322	34	803	631	771	434	643
1988	256.52	198.13	58.39		140.51	19.22	1859	651	325	38	797	625	784	449	652
1989	339.00	270.60	68.30		128.48	15.14	1868	656	320	46	799	638	777	460	

6. Liaoning

6–7

Year	v5c1	v5d	v6a	v6a1	v6a2	v6b	v6c	v6d1	v6d2	v6d3	v6d4	v6d5	v6d6
1949			1831	443	1388					949	882	160.29	55.90
1950			1876	486	1390					973	903		
1951			1889	523	1365					979	910		
1952		507	1932	560	1372			452	1480	1003	929	195.30	73.80
1953			2039	668	1370			597	1442	1061	978		
1954			2153	768	1385	45	9	707	1446	1116	1036		
1955			2217	806	1411	39	9	730	1487	1145	1072		
1956			2307	862	1444	34	7	752	1554	1195	1112		
1957		485	2395	950	1445	42	9	884	1511	1239	1156	293.50	106.80
1958			2445	998	1447	39	9	927	1518	1263	1182	299.65	109.84
1959			2502	1097	1405	28	12	1065	1437	1303	1199		
1960			2560	1212	1348	32	12	1015	1545	1334	1225		
1961			2519	1129	1391	17	18	1032	1488	1303	1216	314.18	123.60
1962			2549	1078	1471	34	9	931	1618	1313	1236	306.97	121.39
1963			2653	1117	1536	49	8	970	1683	1364	1289	320.72	125.55
1964			2734	1133	1601	40	9	987	1747	1404	1330	330.69	128.62
1965			2808	1155	1654	36	7	1014	1795	1439	1369	338.09	129.51
1966			2870	1166	1704	29	6	1019	1851	1471	1399		
1967			2918	1155	1764	27	6	1021	1897	1494	1424		
1968			2982	1133	1849	29	6	997	1985	1523	1459		
1969			3045	1104	1941	28	5	963	2082	1560	1485		
1970			3084	1075	2009	27	5	927	2157	1579	1505	317.82	109.07
1971			3134	1097	2036	24	5	961	2173	1602	1532		
1972			3171	1128	2043	24	6	997	2174	1621	1550		
1973			3221	1159	2063	22	5	1023	2198	1646	1575		
1974			3257	1161	2096	18	6	1023	2234	1665	1592		
1975			3282	1179	2103	16	6	1030	2252	1679	1603	335.90	122.74
1976			3311	1177	2134	14	6	1025	2286	1694	1617		
1977			3345	1185	2160	15	6	1025	2319	1710	1634		
1978		595	3394	1242	2152	18	5	1077	2317	1735	1659	354.40	126.40
1979			3443	1361	2082	17	5	1165	2277	1756	1686		
1980		597	3487	1420	2067	14	5	1237	2250	1779	1708	382.60	141.50
1981			3535	1466	2069	17	5	1289	2246	1803	1732		
1982			3592	1509	2083	19	5	1340	2253	1832	1760		
1983			3629	1547	2083	13	5	1380	2249	1853	1776		
1984			3655	2001	1654	11	5	1447	2208	1867	1788		
1985		634	3686	2268	1418	12	5	1502	2184	1883	1803	420.10	162.90
1986			3726	2361	1365	15	5	1509	2217	1904	1822	428.50	168.20
1987		631	3777	2517	1260	17	5	1552	2225	1930	1847	436.80	227.60
1988		625	3826	2618	1208	15	5	1594	2232	1956	1870	444.10	232.90
1989			3876	2842	1034	15	6	1625	2251	1980	1896	450.22	236.85

6. Liaoning

6–8

Year	v7a	v7b	v7c	v7d	v7e	v7f	v7g	v7h	v7h1	v7h2	v7h3	v7h4	v7h5	v7i	v8a
1949				6958.0				10.51	6.76	0.08	1.03	0.24	2.41	137.50	
1950				7321.9				13.23	10.28	0.12	1.37	0.38	1.09		
1951				7301.6				14.75	11.66	0.13	1.47	0.41	1.06		
1952			152.6	7404.7		3.6		16.60	11.38	0.13	1.79	0.50	2.80	195.34	44.2
1953				7281.3				16.90	11.75	0.11	1.48	0.50	3.06	196.37	57.8
1954				7394.8				18.80	13.13	0.06	1.81	0.71	3.08	203.76	64.2
1955				7243.1				19.40	13.84	0.09	1.75	0.65	3.07	188.61	67.8
1956				7599.8				22.10	16.31	0.70	1.44	0.73	2.92	156.20	83.5
1957		157.5	540.2	7418.0		8.1		21.20	15.55	0.74	2.75	0.69	1.47	156.84	94.4
1958				7346.8				21.20	16.52	0.71	1.35	0.64	1.99	160.62	138.9
1959				7048.0				24.60	17.84	0.92	2.53	0.78	2.54	148.93	198.6
1960				7171.1				19.20	13.40	0.94	1.18	1.17	2.52	147.42	243.1
1961				6790.3				19.60	14.56	0.25	1.01	0.98	2.80	140.35	107.9
1962		696.4	301.0	6646.5		7.7		21.20	15.25	0.23	2.08	0.95	2.69	140.92	107.4
1963				6517.3				21.80	16.27	0.24	2.48	0.63	2.18	145.66	117.9
1964				6523.8				22.60	16.19	0.57	3.18	0.66	2.00	151.82	138.2
1965	4.20	1333.2	458.8	6553.3		13.0	3.3	26.50	19.46	0.67	3.31	0.65	2.40	157.22	170.5
1966				6360.1				29.40	21.42	0.77	3.70	0.82	2.68	166.80	193.6
1967				6299.3				29.30	20.84	0.78	4.14	0.75	2.79	172.36	137.9
1968				6298.3				30.40	22.08	0.82	3.93	0.74	2.83	181.62	115.8
1969				6309.6				30.00	22.04	0.70	3.56	0.94	2.76	193.19	186.1
1970		1887.0	945.5	6370.4		56.7		37.70	28.22	0.55	4.55	1.34	3.04	200.22	226.4
1971				6241.5				35.50	24.64	0.85	6.67	1.20	2.14	201.62	252.5
1972				6111.8				33.00	21.85	1.13	6.42	1.37	2.23	198.04	265.2
1973				6165.4				40.30	28.82	0.99	6.61	1.58	2.30	200.50	289.3
1974				6045.4				43.90	32.03	1.40	6.44	1.71	2.33	198.23	307.3
1975		2929.7	1106.5	6114.8		155.5		48.30	35.21	1.34	7.50	1.88	2.38	197.36	325.5
1976				6200.5				47.40	34.61	1.24	7.62	1.91	2.02	193.78	343.2
1977				6033.3				46.60	33.23	1.31	7.63	2.02	2.41	198.39	337.0
1978	52.00	3068.2	1280.0	6062.6		205.8	17.8	49.20	36.52	1.10	7.12	2.07	2.39	193.65	376.8
1979		2642.2	1205.4	5950.3		243.2		59.80	43.32	1.38	10.60	2.09	2.42	188.30	396.0
1980	56.80	3125.6	1139.5	5872.2		298.4	23.8	73.56	50.15	2.55	13.20	2.20	5.46	177.30	452.6
1981		2865.7	1077.4	5770.2		302.4		78.65	54.09	3.20	16.10	2.52	2.73	177.30	461.1
1982		2795.7	1084.7	5679.4	1181.0	302.3		85.36	56.44	3.37	18.89	3.10	3.55	183.50	482.3
1983		2658.1	1014.4	5607.9	607.5	307.4		106.54	74.12	3.53	19.50	3.39	6.00	197.40	527.7
1984		2781.8	1043.8	5606.4	1020.0	320.0		117.62	78.02	4.08	22.80	4.91	7.81	209.90	612.5
1985	83.00	2815.2	1085.9	5558.7	2130.0	273.4	29.3	118.05	65.68	4.24	31.26	7.97	8.90	216.40	774.6
1986		2917.5	1096.2	5495.5	1689.6	264.0		142.03	84.47	4.19	32.31	10.55	10.51	219.50	874.9
1987		3116.4	1153.4	5430.9	1275.0	265.2		169.22	96.10	4.86	39.58	16.42	12.26	254.60	1043.7
1988	102.40	3297.6	1144.3	5404.8	585.0	273.5	41.1	227.39	117.53	4.97	67.76	22.86	14.27	217.40	1304.8
1989	103.80	3288.2	1139.7	5391.7		281.6	41.8	222.82	109.87	4.77	69.83	22.83	15.52	217.30	1546.4

6. Liaoning

6–9

Year	v8a1	v8a2	v8a3	v8b	v8c1	v8c2	v8d	v8f1	v8f2	v8f3	v8f4	v8f5	v8g
1949								11.4	539.55	5.01	8.1	26.4	8816
1950								50.2	753.25	10.16	13.4	60.0	10762
1951								67.1	891.08	16.14	17.5	89.5	12216
1952	36.71	0.24	7.25		30.80	13.40		94.1	1176.63	23.43	17.3	112.8	10690
1953	47.39	0.17	9.82		40.60	17.20		115.4	1416.97	30.81	21.1	140.2	11258
1954	50.03	0.88	7.84		46.40	17.80		130.6	1743.56	38.76	23.0	169.5	9683
1955	60.39	0.99	5.93		50.60	17.20		155.6	2024.68	51.82	29.2	148.8	7281
1956	75.23	3.78	4.55		63.10	20.40		277.6	2168.46	54.08	44.8	225.7	4908
1957	84.36	4.27	4.74		71.60	22.80		338.2	2284.39	55.98	52.0	249.7	5629
1958	126.12	6.79	7.78		112.50	26.40		470.1	3834.41	73.83	70.4	303.6	2884
1959	176.60	12.78	9.23		158.20	40.40		677.6	4873.43	83.94	98.0	335.5	6992
1960	227.89	8.89	9.95		193.80	49.30		748.0	5060.69	80.07	112.6	332.1	6577
1961	100.98	11.20	4.54		28.90	25.00		364.4	3184.86	41.86	83.9	87.2	6718
1962	96.17	8.59	4.59		74.00	33.40		344.0	2279.80	45.28	82.0	104.6	7042
1963	104.92	7.94	3.62		91.20	26.70		377.7	2156.73	51.06	86.2	142.1	7047
1964	124.36	9.50	4.20		108.00	30.20		431.0	2125.16	51.84	92.1	221.3	7016
1965	163.17	11.42	0.57		124.30	46.20		511.3	2274.53	52.01	112.3	285.4	6791
1966	193.60	17.42			143.10	50.50		589.4	2847.10	51.44	127.0	336.2	4728
1967	128.90	10.25			94.70	43.20		346.8	2067.10	22.58	106.3	215.8	4731
1968	221.96	19.91			81.60	34.20		369.6	2310.70	13.22	98.1	205.7	4646
1969	170.28	15.66	0.67		131.20	54.80		548.3	3243.40	31.02	144.7	258.4	6419
1970	206.58	22.34			171.20	55.20		613.2	3959.63	38.60	164.2	357.9	7854
1971	228.62	24.30	1.82		191.90	60.60		669.6	3975.46	48.45	179.6	398.9	8712
1972	234.46	30.03	2.94		199.50	65.70		713.6	3913.92	77.92	195.9	411.8	8889
1973	255.73	33.16	4.18		217.50	71.80		741.7	3762.14	144.64	204.4	427.3	9997
1974	270.51	35.82	2.52		226.50	80.80		728.0	4010.50	250.95	221.0	436.3	10404
1975	273.88	49.93	7.36		238.60	86.90		692.2	3992.83	306.59	237.0	481.3	11222
1976	283.59	57.96	10.25		249.90	93.30	96.61	681.9	4065.60	275.40	247.3	493.5	12740
1977	264.80	58.80	13.40	264.84	246.00	91.00	95.56	692.0	3948.06	278.12	242.6	498.3	13451
1978	302.90	58.80	15.10	302.94	279.00	97.80	115.04	848.7	4298.35	381.25	278.0	551.9	13805
1979	325.80	62.80	7.40	325.77	289.10	106.90	119.70	886.6	4182.88	474.84	296.2	652.6	14455
1980	347.00	73.40	32.20	346.96	308.20	144.40	127.49	904.6	3732.62	533.12	299.0	726.7	15985
1981	342.70	72.20	46.20	342.66	289.30	171.70	117.68	872.9	3370.74	525.05	280.0	729.0	16753
1982	353.30	83.60	45.40	353.33	310.00	172.30	118.74	885.6	3608.46	555.03	297.1	812.6	17075
1983	388.40	95.60	43.70	388.37	345.90	181.90	129.03	927.2	3766.23	635.21	311.2	872.1	17539
1984	431.20	116.30	65.00	431.19	406.80	205.80	151.98	968.6	4300.37	783.01	323.9	939.1	19515
1985	520.40	154.90	99.30	520.45	544.90	229.70	187.89	1026.2	4595.02	922.21	353.0	1030.0	23385
1986	568.00	175.00	131.90	568.03	599.40	275.60	194.42	1084.0	4446.95	1020.99	347.7	1150.5	23891
1987	615.00	203.70	225.00	651.02	704.80	338.90	218.19	1130.4	4351.60	1146.10	384.4	1204.2	24506
1988	778.60	254.80	271.40	778.65	864.50	440.38	246.54	1207.6	4589.01	1267.20	413.6	1320.6	25030
1989	930.50	287.80	328.10	930.45	1036.90	509.60	276.60	1206.8	4980.45	1345.03	418.7	1239.5	25415

6. Liaoning

6–10

Year	v8g1	v9a	v9a1	v9a2	v9a3	v9b	v9b1	v9b2	v9b3	v9c	v10a	v10a1	v10b1	v10b2	v10b3
1949										1274	5.9	5.9	1.8		0.5
1950				0.32				0.23		1574	7.8	7.7	1.4		1.7
1951				0.63				1.19		2043	12.3	12.0	3.0		2.6
1952				1.42		142.73	140.40	2.20	0.13	2271	19.2	18.4	7.3		6.7
1953				1.39		194.33	191.10	3.07	0.16	2692	24.9	23.9	9.0		9.8
1954				1.67	0.02	236.18	233.10	2.93	0.15	2921	26.0	24.8	9.7		11.2
1955				1.96	0.04	247.00	244.60	2.18	0.22	1950	24.1	23.0	12.5		7.0
1956		68.81	65.80	2.96	0.05	286.08	283.30	1.99	0.79	3444	29.6	28.3	17.0		10.8
1957		74.95	71.50	3.40	0.05	304.09	300.70	2.38	1.01	3636	31.3	30.1	17.6		12.6
1958		79.19	74.70	4.44	0.05	395.61	390.30	3.44	1.87	4013	35.1	32.8	21.0		13.2
1959		95.94	90.70	5.14	0.10	508.95	501.10	5.64	2.21	5105	41.0	38.5	26.6		13.7
1960		128.040	123.5	4.44	0.10	544.56	535.10	7.01	2.45	6467	45.4	41.3	31.4		13.7
1961		166.55	162.40	4.02	0.13	371.65	366.60	3.59	1.46	5664	39.8	36.8	26.9		11.5
1962		149.10	143.90	5.03	0.17	340.01	366.00	2.71	1.30	4992	38.2	35.6	25.0		11.8
1963	1483	99.34	94.60	5.15	0.09	361.56	357.80	2.49	1.27	4770	37.3	34.9	23.8		12.4
1964	1507	90.08	84.80	5.19	0.09	411.26	407.00	2.91	1.35	4867	38.3	35.9	25.1		12.3
1965	1694	85.21	78.80	6.34	0.07	503.25	498.80	3.15	1.30	5003	38.7	36.0	25.8		12.2
1966		96.55	88.10	8.39	0.06	532.88	527.80	3.61	1.47	5150	41.5	38.1	27.9		14.0
1967		98.29	90.10	8.13	0.06	417.15	412.60	3.38	1.17	4933	43.1	39.2	27.9		14.9
1968		111.13	102.80	8.29	0.04	424.81	420.70	3.25	0.86	4869	40.3	36.8	27.4		12.6
1969		128.48	118.00	10.42	0.06	519.30	513.50	4.39	1.41	5164	45.7	41.1	29.3		16.2
1970		119.02	108.10	10.86	0.06	615.83	604.90	9.42	1.51	5468	45.6	39.8	27.5		17.8
1971		129.90	117.50	12.34	0.06	673.80	650.80	11.61	1.98	6339	48.9	42.8	29.1		19.4
1972		146.31	130.50	15.75	0.06	748.83	672.90	15.63	3.33	6849	54.9	47.4	32.6		21.1
1973	2257	152.96	137.20	15.69	0.07	812.52	705.30	17.11	3.14	7680	59.9	51.5	38.0		21.5
1974	2303	159.81	143.00	16.75	0.06	873.40	683.90	23.02	3.28	8092	65.6	55.3	40.5		24.8
1975	2515	165.63	147.70	17.88	0.05	948.83	697.00	26.58	3.35	8662	72.3	60.0	44.6		27.5
1976	2588	167.72	148.60	19.07	0.05	939.27	597.60	31.46	3.12	9229	77.3	64.8	48.0		29.0
1977	2709	188.04	167.10	20.86	0.08	1003.80	637.50	35.13	2.96	9422	80.8	68.1	49.7		30.5
1978	2712	193.80	169.70	23.97	0.08	1093.18	729.90	37.26	3.68	9580	85.3	72.0	53.0		31.5
1979	2755	171.99	145.40	25.60	0.10	1139.25	769.50	38.28	2.72	9939	98.3	84.9	61.5		34.9
1980	2813	188.01	157.10	28.80	0.12	1178.43	785.40	51.18	2.58	10576	120.1	105.4	69.9		45.3
1981	2799	200.06	166.00	31.40	0.13	1190.47	785.90	53.18	3.81	11209	137.0	121.0	71.5		57.3
1982	2817	206.60	168.00	35.30	0.15	1272.95	859.70	55.91	6.54	11776	145.5	127.9	74.5		60.0
1983	2841	227.23	185.30	39.30	0.16	962.27	705.80	60.47	10.32	12873	160.9	141.8	79.4		64.7
1984	2847	276.36	223.50	48.90	0.10	1058.43	758.50	93.25	13.58	14711	189.0	167.5	90.2		73.2
1985	3103	316.38	251.10	62.20	0.17	1156.12	825.70	109.21	15.18	17303	231.5	209.6	103.7		85.2
1986	3181	343.81	264.40	73.90	0.17	1200.81	859.40	106.17	16.30	18962	266.4	244.3	119.0		91.9
1987	3283	374.39	286.60	80.10	0.19	1262.91	883.30	129.86	38.29	21732	313.0	285.9	135.5		103.3
1988	3322	434.32	327.70	96.50	0.18	1339.08	903.80	178.23	35.94	26878	402.7	368.0	175.3		127.8
1989	3380	402.00	300.54	100.84	0.14	1173.50	947.70	186.41	39.40	34519	451.0	411.7	192.6		131.3

6. Liaoning

Year	v10b4	v10b5	v10b6	v10d	v11a1	v11a2	v11a3	v11b	v11b1	v11b2	v11c	v11d	v12a	v12b	v12c
1949		3.40	0.3												
1950		4.40	0.3	4.28											
1951		6.46	0.2	5.41									114.3	108.8	118.8
1952		4.93	0.2	6.60									105.3	103.7	107.0
1953		5.87	0.2	7.67	0.5187	0.1296	0.2912	0.9395	0.9395				103.7	103.6	113.4
1954		4.82	0.2	8.19	0.5779	0.1849	0.5157	1.2785	1.2785				102.3	100.5	102.4
1955		4.28	0.3	8.14	0.8958	0.1529	0.8320	1.8807	1.8807				100.8	100.4	99.2
1956		1.40	0.3	8.83	0.8366	0.1912	0.8330	1.8608	1.8608				99.5	97.2	102.1
1957		0.59	0.6	8.45	0.6975	0.2462	0.6607	1.6044	1.6044				103.2	103.4	106.0
1958		0.29	0.7	8.96	0.6880	0.4006	0.6720	1.7606	1.7606				98.0	97.8	102.2
1959		0.30	0.4	10.08	0.7538	0.4489	0.6650	1.8677	1.8677				100.5	100.7	103.0
1960		0.04	0.3	8.60	0.6381	0.3402	0.5615	1.5398	1.5398				102.0	102.7	103.7
1961		0.04	1.3	8.37	0.3492	0.3638	0.3841	1.1086	1.0971	0.0115			127.9	129.2	124.6
1962		0.28	1.2	8.62	0.2564	0.4015	0.5248	1.2068	1.1827	0.0241			103.0	102.3	103.5
1963		0.41	0.7	9.25	0.4677	0.4245	0.5885	1.4880	1.4807	0.0073			96.6	96.8	88.1
1964		0.48	0.4	10.10	0.8034	0.2878	0.6921	1.7934	1.7833	0.0101			95.1	96.2	96.3
1965		0.43	0.4	10.27	1.0493	0.2931	0.5849	1.9717	1.9263	0.0454			95.0	94.2	99.4
1966		0.13	0.3	10.85	1.1425	0.3169	0.7014	2.2407	2.1608	0.0799			99.2	98.8	106.7
1967		0.10	0.2	11.14	1.0005	0.2855	0.4376	1.7823	1.7236	0.0587			100.1	100.4	101.5
1968		0.09	0.2	12.03	1.0481	0.2578	0.3553	1.7156	1.6612	0.0544			100.6	99.6	99.2
1969			0.3	10.89	0.9621	0.3415	0.4111	1.7795	1.7147	0.0648			99.7	99.9	100.7
1970			0.3	13.54	0.8563	0.2932	0.4828	1.8100	1.6323	0.1777			98.5	98.4	98.3
1971			0.4	13.03	1.2259	0.3142	0.8889	2.5451	2.4290	0.1161			99.6	100.0	104.7
1972			0.4	11.71	1.1557	0.4421	1.1110	2.8049	2.7088	0.0961			100.8	100.9	99.3
1973			0.4	15.63	1.8077	0.8700	1.7024	4.5588	4.3801	0.1787			100.3	100.4	100.7
1974			0.3	16.36	2.2289	0.9421	5.8932	9.3048	9.0642	0.2406			100.0	100.2	101.2
1975		0.01	0.2	19.47	2.2807	1.0069	9.5425	13.2079	12.8301	0.3778			100.1	100.1	102.7
1976		0.01	0.3	18.07	1.6212	1.0878	8.1579	11.3248	10.8669	0.4579			100.0	100.0	107.7
1977		0.02	0.6	18.79	1.5259	1.1423	8.9964	11.9855	11.6646	0.3209			100.2	100.2	99.4
1978		0.02	0.8	21.82	2.4799	1.5928	11.1040	15.7888	15.1767	0.6121			100.3	100.3	100.9
1979		0.14	1.8	26.49	3.9443	2.1941	19.8944	26.7373	26.0328	0.7045	0.0113	0.0113	101.1	101.7	115.8
1980		1.32	3.6	32.11	3.4239	2.8689	33.5061	40.5427	39.7989	0.7438	0.0487	0.0457	105.9	104.4	108.6
1981	0.2	2.51	5.5	42.67	2.7852	3.1296	37.5092	44.2873	43.4198	0.8675	0.0138	0.0080	101.6	102.0	107.1
1982	0.2	4.32	6.5	42.56	2.4163	2.9212	37.6375	43.6789	42.9750	0.7039	0.2448	0.0750	101.2	101.4	98.7
1983	0.1	9.09	7.5	55.89	2.9745	3.5468	32.6597	39.9623	39.1810	0.7813	0.1458	0.0720	101.5	101.7	112.8
1984	0.1	16.15	9.4	53.94	4.6127	3.7202	41.5825	51.1516	49.9154	1.2362	0.6366	0.1523	103.6	103.6	97.4
1985	0.1	28.51	14.2	59.90	4.9943	3.1319	42.2955	53.8997	50.4217	3.4780	2.4213	0.4192	110.0	111.4	111.9
1986	0.2	38.24	17.1	75.32	4.1775	4.3690	22.2524	34.2875	30.7989	3.4886	4.3852	0.9003	106.0	107.0	107.7
1987	0.3	52.10	21.8	91.44	4.7062	5.8399	27.3339	42.4942	37.8800	4.6142	5.6494	5.5338	109.0	109.8	112.3
1988	0.5	70.70	28.4	114.79	5.9902	6.7874	25.9655	44.5015	38.7431	5.7584	13.2271	5.5011	119.3	119.6	114.9
1989	0.8	89.54	36.7	139.77				53.3384	44.4571	8.8813	8.4960	5.8900	118.4	117.2	116.5

6. Liaoning

6–12

Year	v13a	v13b	v13c1	v13c2	v13c3	v13d	v14a	v14b	v14c	v15a	v15b	v15c	v15d	v15e	v15f
1949															
1950			0.7791			0.1218									
1951			1.3442			0.2043									
1952			1.6319	23	297	0.1939	11275	30000	3.20						
1953			1.7666			0.3822			2.58						
1954		63.8	2.0988			0.3780			2.35						
1955		61.4	2.3039			0.4537			1.88						
1956		67.4	2.6399			0.6347			2.39						
1957		66.2	2.5902			0.5875			1.98	7159.1					
1958		78.9	4.1665			0.3784			4.22						
1959		75.5	5.2429			0.5504			3.94						
1960		83.7	6.7859			0.8715			4.23						
1961		72.4	6.1205			1.0098			1.87						
1962		71.4	5.1180			1.3211			1.70						
1963		73.8	4.2867			1.3752			2.20						
1964		79.9	3.9338			1.2078			2.74						
1965		88.3	4.0201	83	520	1.0584	53997	90000	3.30						
1966			3.7014			0.0049									
1967			3.7009												
1968			1.4795			2.2214									
1969	13.3		1.3168			0.1627									
1970						1.2548									
1971															
1972		93.4	0.5656						4.78						
1973	12.1	91.1	1.4734						5.13						
1974	11.6	94.5	2.5123			0.0155			5.50						
1975	10.2	96.4	3.1506			0.5735			5.78						
1976	10.6	96.4	3.7495			0.9631			6.13						
1977	11.2	95.5	3.9371			1.0590			5.79						
1978	10.5	94.4	5.0863	353	462	1.0497	105089	130000	6.15	5735.0					
1979	9.8	94.6	5.8042			0.4659			6.28	5679.9					
1980	11.8	95.1	6.2514	268	442	1.1068	109252	160000	7.08	5461.9					
1981	15.8	96.1	7.4885			0.2776			8.45	5563.8					
1982	16.2	96.7	6.0979			3.1121			9.37	5500.1					
1983	16.4	96.1	6.7218			1.6565			10.35	5481.4					
1984	15.7		7.9001			1.5612			13.30	5436.9					
1985	13.9	98.5	9.5161	194	422	1.7495	136429	190000	17.50	5382.8					
1986	12.3	99.5	10.7434			2.0583			13.30	5294.2					
1987	11.7	99.0	11.2652			2.9394			15.13	5237.7	5479				
1988	12.5	98.9	12.0510	206	408	3.1552	165331	210000	14.51	5217.7	5908	324.7	175	68.3	122.57
1989		99.0	12.2500	193	413	3.2700	169797	218000	11.36	5205.6					

Notes

1. National Output and Income (Y)

v1a: (E), p.219
- v1a1: (A); (E), p.219
- v1a2: (E), p.219
- v1a3: (E), p.219
- v1a4: (E), p.219
- v1a5: (E), p.219

v1b: (A); (B), p.312
- v1b1: (A); (B), p.312
- v1b2: (A); (B), p.312
- v1b3: (A); (B), p.312
- v1b4: (A); (B), p.312
- v1b5: (A); (B), p.312

v1c: v1a – v1d

v1d: (E), p.216
- v1d1: (E), p.216
- v1d2: (E), p.216
- v1d3: (E), p.216
- v1d4: (E), p.216
- v1d5: (E), p.216

v1e: (A); (B), p.318
- v1e1: (A); (B), p.318
- v1e2: (A); (B), p.318
- v1e3: (A); (B), p.318
- v1e4: (A); (B), p.318
- v1e5: (A); (B), p.318

v1f: (E), p.215—figure of 1989 includes major repairs fund
- v1f1: (E), p.215
- v1f2: (E), p.215
- v1f3: (E), p.215

v1g: v2a + v3a

v1h: (E), p.244

v1i: (E), p.243

v1j: (E), p.243
- v1j1: (E), p.243
- v1j2: (E), p.243
- v1j3: NA

v1k: (E), p.243

2. Investment (I)

v2a: (E), p.218
- v2a1: (A); (D), p.169
- v2a2: (A); (D), p.169

v2b: (A)

v2c: (A); (E), p.233
- v2c1: (E), p.234
- v2c2: (E), p.234

v2d:
- v2d1: (E), p.231
- v2d2: (E), p.231

v2e: (E), p.231

3. Consumption (C)

v3a: (E), p.218

v3b: (E), p.218
- v3b1: (A); (D), p.165
- v3b2: (A); (D), p.165

v3c: (E), p.218

v3d: (E), p.242
- v3d1: (E), p.242
- v3d2: (E), p.242

v3e: (E), p.244
- v3e1: (E), p.244
- v3e2: (A)
- v3e3: (A)
- v3e4: (A)

v3f: (A)

v3f1: (E), p.244
v3f2: (A)
v3f3: (A)
v3f4: (A)

4. Public Finance and Banking (FB)

v4a:
v4a1: (E), p.240
v4a1a: (E), p.240
v4a1b: (C), p.615
v4a1c: (C), p.615
v4a1d: v4a1 – v4a1a – v4a1b – v4a1c
v4a2: (E), p.240
v4a2a: (E), p.240
v4a2b: (E), p.240
v4a2c: (E), p.240
v4a2d: v4a2 – v4a2a – v4a2b – v4a2c

v4b: (A)
v4b1: (B), p.452
v4b2: (B), p.452
v4b3: NA

v4c:
v4c1: (E), p.231
v4c2: (E), p.231

5. Labor Force (L)

v5a: (E), p.214—including other labor force in the society, therefore the sum of the separate items (i.e. different economic modes) will not be equal to the sum total
v5a1: (E), p.214
v5a2: (E), p.214
v5a3: (E), p.214
v5a4: (E), p.214—excluding rural people working outside

v5b:
v5b1: (E), p.214
v5b2: (E), p.214
v5b3: (E), p.214

v5c: (A)
v5c1: NA

v5d: (A)

6. Population (PO)

v6a: (E), p.213—data from public security department
v6a1: (E), p.213—(ditto)
v6a2: (E), p.213—(ditto)

v6b: (E), p.213—(ditto)

v6c: (A); (E), p.213—(ditto)

v6d:
v6d1: (E), p.213—(ditto)
v6d2: (E), p.213—(ditto)
v6d3: (E), p.213—(ditto)
v6d4: (E), p.213—(ditto)
v6d5: (A)—Shenyang
v6d6: (A)—Dalian

7. Agriculture (A)

v7a: (E), p.226

v7b: (A); (E), p.226

v7c: (A); (E), p.226

v7d: (A); (E), p.226

v7e: (A)

v7f: (A); (E), p.226

v7g: (E), p.226

v7h: (E), p.221
v7h1: (E), p.221
v7h2: (E), p.221
v7h3: (E), p.221
v7h4: (E), p.221
v7h5: (E), p.221

v7i: (E), p.225

8. Industry (IN)

v8a: (A)
 v8a1: (A)
 v8a2: (A)
 v8a3: (A)

v8b: (E), p.231

 v8c1: (A)
 v8c2: (A)

v8d: (E), p.231

v8f:
 v8f1: (E), p.230
 v8f2: (E), p.230
 v8f3: (E), p.230
 v8f4: (E), p.230
 v8f5: (E), p.230

v8g: (A)
 v8g1: (E), p.231

9. Transport (TR)

v9a: (E), p.232—excluding urban traffic volume
 v9a1: (E), p.232—including central and local railways. Figures of 1978 and before are the sum of Shenyang and Jinzhou Bureax
 v9a2: (E), p.232
 v9a3: (E), p.232—excluding distant ocean and coastal passenger traffic

v9b: (E), p.232
 v9b1: (E), p.232—including central and local railways. Figures of 1978 and before are the sum of Shenyang and Jinzhou Bureax
 v9b2: (E), p.232
 v9b3: (E), p.232—excluding distant ocean and coastal freight volume

v9c: (E), p.232—based on constant price in each period

10. Domestic Trade (DT)

v10a: (E), p.235
 v10a1: (E), p.235

v10b:
 v10b1: (E), p.235
 v10b2: NA
 v10b3: (E), p.235—including supply and marketing cooperative and other collectives
 v10b4: (E), p.235
 v10b5: (E), p.235
 v10b6: (E), p.235

v10d: (E), p.237—calculated on calendar year basis

11. Foreign Trade (FT)

v11a:
 v11a1: (B), p.434
 v11a2: (B), p.434
 v11a3: (B), p.434

v11b: (E), p.238—data from foreign trade department
 v11b1: (E), p.238—(ditto)
 v11b2: (A)

v11c: (E), p.239

v11d: (E), p.239

12. Prices (PR)

v12a: (E), p.241

v12b: (E), p.241

v12c: (E), p.241

13. Education (ED)

v13a: (A)

v13b: (A); (E), p.244

v13c:
- v13c1: (A)
- v13c2: (E), p.244—technical and teachers training secondary schools
- v13c3: (E), p.244

v13d: (A)—general institutions of higher learning

14. Social Factors (SF)

v14a: (E), p.244

v14b: (A); (E), p.244

v14c: (A)

15. Natural Environment (NE)

v15a: (A); (E), p.226

v15b: (A)

v15c: (A)

v15d: (A)

v15e: (A)

v15f: (A)

Sources of Data

(A) Data supplied by the DSNEB, SSB, the PRC.
(B) Statistical Bureau of Liaoning Province ed. *Liaoning Striving and Advancing for Forty Years 1949–1989*, Beijing: CSPH, 1989.
(C) Editorial Board of Statistical Yearbook of Liaoning Economy ed. *Statistical Yearbook of Liaoning Economy*, Beijing: CSPH, 1989.
(D) Same as (D) in Beijing's sources of data.
(E) Same as (E) in Beijing's sources of data.

7

Jilin

7. Jilin

7–1

Year	v1a	v1a1	v1a2	v1a3	v1a4	v1a5	v1b	v1b1	v1b2	v1b3	v1b4	v1b5	v1c	v1d	v1d1
1949		8.12													
1950		9.65													
1951		9.52													
1952	27.22	12.42	10.48	1.32	1.30	1.70							12.01	15.21	9.01
1953	32.77	12.54	13.28	2.33	1.63	2.99	114.7	93.3	126.0	176.7	117.6	169.8	15.32	17.45	8.77
1954	35.44	12.40	15.11	3.13	1.85	2.95	107.2	97.5	112.1	139.8	115.7	97.4	17.20	18.25	8.92
1955	34.75	13.34	13.89	2.64	1.94	2.94	100.3	105.4	98.3	88.7	104.0	99.1	16.02	18.73	9.68
1956	40.05	13.43	16.92	4.22	2.10	3.37	115.5	92.8	126.7	167.4	109.2	114.8	18.40	21.65	10.35
1957	42.61	12.84	20.80	3.11	2.04	3.82	106.0	94.9	120.8	73.8	96.8	113.9	20.72	21.89	8.64
1958	55.79	12.38	30.88	5.97	2.56	4.00	137.4	118.3	146.1	196.7	125.4	100.6	28.49	27.30	9.12
1959	71.10	13.92	41.84	8.07	2.84	4.43	127.6	110.6	135.5	136.1	110.8	116.5	38.36	32.74	9.73
1960	88.25	12.89	57.33	9.01	3.63	5.39	121.3	83.0	135.8	109.6	127.8	119.0	51.18	37.07	8.10
1961	58.42	14.89	32.71	3.17	2.91	4.74	60.5	106.2	54.3	31.4	74.3	69.7	31.06	27.36	10.15
1962	54.89	14.24	30.06	2.88	3.09	4.62	92.1	95.7	90.2	86.8	103.8	91.5	28.41	26.48	9.73
1963	63.11	16.07	35.47	4.17	3.49	3.91	116.2	110.8	118.6	147.2	111.4	96.8	32.70	30.41	11.45
1964	71.95	16.93	40.31	6.38	3.45	4.88	114.0	104.2	113.1	156.7	100.7	128.1	39.72	32.23	11.49
1965	79.02	17.75	47.49	5.63	3.65	4.50	112.5	105.2	122.2	87.4	101.2	90.0	42.70	36.32	12.94
1966	90.75	22.67	53.95	4.94	4.36	4.83	117.8	109.7	124.5	87.0	117.5	107.2	50.71	40.04	15.94
1967	75.70	24.14	40.01	3.95	3.69	3.91	81.2	106.5	74.2	79.3	86.7	82.0	38.49	37.20	17.31
1968	65.39	23.23	31.76	3.47	3.36	3.57	87.0	96.2	82.8	87.2	91.6	91.4	30.21	35.17	16.82
1969	84.79	19.82	52.43	4.49	3.55	4.50	133.4	85.3	158.3	128.4	106.4	126.6	47.21	37.58	14.02
1970	106.69	26.86	63.47	6.01	5.08	5.27	126.9	135.5	121.1	151.1	161.2	129.6	58.51	48.18	18.37
1971	120.62	27.48	74.25	7.51	5.80	5.58	114.7	101.2	117.7	128.2	117.2	105.9	68.00	52.62	19.18
1972	124.68	26.06	78.96	7.53	5.85	6.28	102.5	91.5	106.9	92.4	101.0	112.5	77.35	47.33	15.24
1973	137.72	31.55	84.91	8.42	6.25	6.59	110.8	120.5	108.1	116.1	106.7	105.0	83.41	54.31	20.85
1974	144.77	37.44	84.90	8.96	6.41	7.06	102.9	108.1	100.5	106.4	102.6	101.7	89.19	55.58	21.68
1975	158.82	35.27	99.30	9.71	6.85	7.69	112.9	102.8	117.9	108.5	106.8	109.0	96.80	62.02	20.82
1976	157.75	31.17	103.39	8.73	6.87	7.59	99.8	87.4	104.7	89.8	100.4	98.7	100.86	56.89	16.48
1977	157.81	31.25	104.34	7.58	7.13	7.51	99.7	99.4	100.6	86.9	103.7	98.2	97.42	60.39	19.33
1978	180.84	37.78	112.87	13.21	8.20	8.78	114.7	119.2	109.3	179.8	115.1	113.2	109.77	71.07	23.46
1979	203.50	42.02	125.74	17.62	10.38	7.74	108.0	96.7	108.3	136.1	126.5	89.5	125.05	78.45	24.76
1980	219.89	47.47	134.67	17.10	11.42	9.23	105.3	104.0	105.8	97.8	110.0	113.9	134.82	85.07	26.51
1981	229.43	56.08	136.64	16.25	7.91	11.75	99.9	107.1	101.2	84.1	69.2	122.1	135.81	93.61	33.33
1982	251.69	60.58	148.75	21.62	9.15	11.59	108.2	105.8	107.4	129.8	115.6	95.8	150.13	101.56	38.33
1983	298.14	78.11	172.04	21.99	10.42	15.58	117.5	129.2	114.3	101.7	113.9	130.8	170.41	127.73	56.64
1984	356.35	89.99	208.84	27.86	12.00	18.66	115.0	110.5	116.0	123.8	113.8	115.1	209.06	147.28	60.11
1985	422.24	85.89	256.75	40.27	14.43	24.90	111.2	92.0	116.0	128.7	111.0	121.5	252.62	169.62	55.78
1986	473.59	98.43	282.48	44.32	18.41	29.95	107.5	104.4	107.4	102.8	127.3	114.3	283.78	189.81	62.93
1987	587.41	120.81	359.46	53.87	21.16	32.11	115.7	114.4	118.1	113.8	114.9	98.4	349.29	238.12	80.40
1988	725.78	140.91	454.25	62.68	23.74	44.20	113.9	105.4	118.2	101.1	112.2	114.2	432.57	293.21	91.24
1989	801.02	133.79	530.26	55.86	26.89	54.12	101.0	88.3	106.3	73.9	113.3	104.7	496.27	304.75	81.41

7. Jilin

7–2

Year	v1d2	v1d3	v1d4	v1d5	v1e	v1e1	v1e2	v1e3	v1e4	v1e5	v1f	v1f1	v1f2	v1f3	v1g
1949															
1950															
1951															
1952	3.86	0.31	0.73	1.30											14.47
1953	4.77	0.72	0.86	2.33	108.3	91.3	121.1	131.1	109.9	173.6					17.20
1954	5.41	0.94	0.98	2.00	103.8	100.6	112.0	135.3	116.2	84.5					19.62
1955	5.10	0.83	0.99	2.13	103.0	106.0	99.0	93.1	100.4	105.9					19.75
1956	6.08	1.39	1.20	2.63	114.9	98.5	131.3	171.7	122.1	123.9					22.51
1957	8.19	1.03	1.21	2.82	99.7	82.2	128.5	74.3	100.2	103.9					20.96
1958	12.02	1.69	1.47	3.00	129.9	117.4	147.4	166.1	121.6	102.1					23.94
1959	16.34	1.67	1.68	3.32	119.2	105.1	133.1	102.2	114.4	116.6					27.94
1960	20.38	2.17	2.19	4.23	110.2	76.2	123.5	126.2	130.8	124.4					28.76
1961	10.91	1.19	1.71	3.40	66.5	112.7	52.4	47.0	71.3	62.2					27.02
1962	10.54	1.25	1.80	3.16	96.1	96.7	95.3	104.4	104.2	89.7					24.36
1963	12.92	1.42	1.93	2.69	116.5	115.7	122.8	120.2	106.2	97.2					28.31
1964	14.82	1.61	1.83	2.48	105.2	100.7	111.0	111.8	95.9	94.4					30.32
1965	17.57	1.38	1.93	2.50	114.0	111.0	122.8	85.2	101.0	98.1					33.03
1966	18.04	1.17	2.30	2.59	109.1	105.5	112.5	83.5	119.8	105.6					35.11
1967	15.09	0.93	1.87	2.00	90.7	108.6	83.7	79.3	81.8	77.0					36.20
1968	14.07	0.75	1.70	1.83	96.1	97.1	97.2	79.7	91.6	91.3					36.19
1969	18.37	0.99	1.83	2.37	109.1	83.3	125.2	130.8	108.4	130.0					39.66
1970	23.25	1.13	2.50	2.93	129.9	131.0	126.6	124.6	157.5	137.1					45.40
1971	26.10	1.28	2.74	3.32	110.5	103.6	113.4	120.8	109.4	113.2					47.05
1972	25.42	1.41	2.76	2.50	88.7	76.2	97.3	108.8	101.0	75.3					48.63
1973	26.15	1.60	3.00	2.71	114.7	136.5	103.6	117.4	108.5	108.5					51.21
1974	26.60	1.75	2.96	2.59	101.7	101.7	102.2	109.9	98.7	95.3					54.28
1975	33.43	1.91	3.42	2.44	113.6	97.9	126.9	111.0	115.6	94.2					61.93
1976	32.48	1.92	3.31	2.70	92.1	79.1	97.9	100.1	96.8	110.7					62.64
1977	32.78	2.00	3.63	2.65	104.9	116.2	99.9	102.4	109.7	97.6					64.59
1978	36.75	2.52	4.18	4.16	118.1	119.7	113.9	132.1	115.1	155.9	81.98	23.99	42.96	15.04	76.08
1979	41.28	4.21	4.18	4.02	104.3	91.8	108.4	166.9	99.9	96.8	91.13	25.34	49.22	16.56	83.54
1980	45.41	4.49	4.57	4.09	104.9	98.5	108.4	103.8	109.4	96.1	98.61	27.24	52.24	19.13	89.36
1981	45.65	4.85	3.66	6.12	104.4	112.5	100.5	100.2	80.2	143.8	111.17	34.31	56.53	20.32	98.40
1982	47.79	5.79	4.39	5.26	107.3	115.2	103.2	116.5	119.8	83.5	121.66	38.40	60.35	22.91	109.37
1983	53.72	6.15	4.85	6.37	124.4	147.7	111.1	106.1	110.6	116.6	148.24	56.74	65.38	26.13	132.39
1984	66.92	7.78	5.63	6.84	112.1	104.5	119.0	123.6	114.4	104.3	171.17	60.04	80.46	30.68	159.71
1985	83.41	11.30	6.89	12.24	107.5	86.7	116.8	134.9	113.2	162.9	194.55	55.74	97.21	41.60	187.35
1986	90.24	12.34	9.39	14.91	106.6	103.1	105.9	99.4	136.0	115.8	217.87	63.35	104.30	49.22	208.61
1987	117.41	15.10	10.56	14.65	116.3	117.1	120.5	111.9	112.3	90.2	283.31	80.57	139.37	63.37	250.42
1988	148.29	17.77	11.90	24.01	113.0	102.5	118.6	97.6	112.7	136.0	347.83	92.59	173.58	81.66	301.97
1989	162.19	16.45	12.48	32.22	95.5	84.8	99.4	76.6	104.8	114.8	361.37	80.53	181.02	99.82	329.50

7. Jilin

7–3

Year	v1h	v1i	v1j	v1j1	v1j2	v1j3	v1k	v2a	v2a1	v2a2	v2b	v2c	v2c1	v2c2	v2d1
1949											0.23				
1950											0.62				
1951											0.71				
1952		2.15	480	480				3.12	1.08	2.04	1.86				9.21
1953		3.44	573	573				3.22	1.32	1.90	3.21				10.51
1954	77.48	3.72	588	588				5.44	2.20	3.24	5.39				12.45
1955	76.00	3.63	600	600				5.21	3.67	1.54	5.57				14.42
1956	86.32	4.62	671	671				5.99	5.94	0.05	6.47				19.99
1957	86.69	5.34	699	699				5.64	3.52	2.12	4.22				24.26
1958	92.99	5.96	647	647				7.75	5.46	2.29	8.37				29.08
1959		8.09	615	615				9.01	6.07	2.94	10.74				33.43
1960		9.48	611	611				8.73	7.88	0.85	11.07				35.84
1961	163.20	9.20	602	602				5.31	2.60	2.71	5.10				39.64
1962	193.08	8.36	661	661				2.27	2.43	-0.16	3.92				40.75
1963	157.23	8.56	721	721				5.19	3.05	2.14	5.21				42.22
1964	122.48	9.14	744	744				6.78	6.45	0.33	6.90				44.13
1965	138.33	9.09	740	740				8.07	5.75	2.32	6.79				40.93
1966		9.44	718	718				8.42	5.77	2.65	5.94				47.46
1967		9.15	685	685				8.82	5.78	3.04	4.35				49.74
1968		9.62	670	670				9.27	5.80	3.47	4.20				51.73
1969		10.21	744	744				9.78	5.82	3.96	6.44				55.12
1970		10.51	698	698				10.35	5.82	4.53	8.82				64.75
1971		11.82	677	677				11.45	6.61	4.84	11.62				67.86
1972		13.91	736	736				12.70	7.12	5.58	11.59				78.68
1973		14.94	668	690	553			13.62	7.67	5.95	13.39				86.11
1974	160.32	15.45	671	700	539			14.94	8.25	6.69	13.68				90.59
1975	146.52	16.32	657	690	534			18.72	9.30	9.42	15.44				96.54
1976	129.98	17.26	636	680	496			18.58	13.53	5.05	12.42				104.68
1977	161.83			680				17.08	9.79	7.29	11.73				112.57
1978	181.65	21.44	651	712	467			25.06	10.45	14.61	18.16	15.60	10.42	0.30	119.85
1979	222.57	23.46	700	753	539			21.58	14.44	7.14	19.54	17.21	10.05	0.52	128.40
1980	237.12	27.57	763	827	588		4.39	20.44	12.28	8.16	20.88	17.65	9.13	0.57	135.32
1981	293.34	29.83	776	840	611		5.11	21.90	14.86	7.04	20.98	17.05	5.57	0.39	146.46
1982	333.09	32.31	799	863	637		6.15	23.92	15.94	7.98	27.50	22.08	7.64	0.55	156.13
1983	440.40	34.06	823	881	680		6.75	32.14	22.88	9.26	30.30	21.99	7.90	0.51	167.73
1984	456.78	39.32	927	1008	751		8.22	43.41	27.17	16.24	42.10	25.50	7.96	0.72	189.40
1985	413.74	47.44	1081	1175	880		9.76	57.12	38.35	18.77	62.90	37.38	11.68	1.73	220.14
1986	456.70	55.68	1221	1333	974		11.76	61.61	38.18	23.43	64.40	42.12	12.08	1.51	245.08
1987	523.09	64.41	1366	1491	1088		16.21	83.52	48.29	35.23	78.50	53.96	17.81	1.65	285.02
1988	627.54	78.90	1630	1771	1311		21.91	94.49	52.74	41.75	94.50	67.80	21.61	2.79	320.66
1989	623.96	87.08	1755	1914	1388		24.40	101.44	34.91	66.53	80.31	58.13	16.75	1.60	365.06

7. Jilin

7–4

Year	v2d2	v2e	v3a	v3b	v3b1	v3b2	v3c	v3d	v3d1	v3d2	v3e	v3e1	v3e2	v3e3	v3e4
1949															
1950															
1951															
1952	6.87	1.13	11.35	11.08	7.07	4.01	0.27	103	85	163					
1953	7.79	1.83	13.98	13.70	8.05	5.65	0.28	120	98	177					
1954	9.26	2.04	14.18	13.90	7.96	5.94	0.28	119	95	183					
1955	10.86	2.00	14.54	14.25	8.20	6.06	0.29	119	96	176					
1956	15.57	3.19	16.52	16.14	9.42	6.72	0.38	131	107	191					
1957	19.12	3.60	15.32	14.97	7.52	7.45	0.35	120	86	197					
1958	22.58	4.21	16.19	15.76	7.61	8.15	0.43	123	87	203					
1959	25.91	7.40	18.93	18.46	8.11	10.35	0.47	139	92	233					
1960	28.27	9.09	20.03	19.46	7.31	12.15	0.57	134	79	229					
1961	30.70	12.02	21.71	21.31	8.41	12.90	0.40	142	89	234					
1962	30.28	10.86	22.09	21.72	9.41	12.31	0.37	145	98	232					
1963	30.96	7.04	23.12	22.69	10.53	12.16	0.43	148	106	227					
1964	31.86	6.72	23.54	22.98	10.38	12.60	0.56	147	101	236					
1965	29.75	5.76	24.96	24.49	11.84	12.65	0.47	150	111	223					
1966	34.17	6.88	26.69	26.13	12.66	13.46	0.56	156	111	248					
1967	36.11	8.46	27.38	26.70	13.55	13.15	0.68	155	116	237					
1968	36.21	10.35	26.92	26.10	13.25	12.85	0.82	148	111	226					
1969	38.03	13.78	29.88	28.89	14.53	14.36	0.99	160	117	252					
1970	50.04	18.38	35.05	33.85	16.59	17.26	1.20	183	130	300					
1971	46.78	19.25	35.60	34.33	16.48	17.85	1.27	180	125	304					
1972	54.95	22.19	35.93	34.51	15.68	18.84	1.42	176	116	310					
1973	59.51	23.67	37.59	36.21	16.34	19.87	1.38	181	118	318					
1974	62.52	26.62	39.34	37.75	16.79	20.96	1.59	185	119	331					
1975	65.45	27.22	43.21	41.23	19.07	22.16	1.98	199	134	344					
1976	72.34	30.10	44.06	42.00	19.43	22.57	2.06	200	134	349					
1977	75.16	31.60	47.51	45.35	21.33	24.02	2.16	213	145	367					
1978	77.90	33.20	51.02	48.99	23.44	25.54	2.03	227	158	382					
1979	84.57	35.28	61.96	57.62	28.27	29.35	4.34	263	192	412					
1980	86.02	37.08	68.92	64.37	30.48	33.89	4.55	290	205	463					
1981	92.57	38.08	76.50	71.60	34.84	36.76	4.90	320	234	487	347.91	198.06			
1982	97.86	41.19	85.45	80.31	38.85	41.45	5.14	355	261	535	366.85	212.20			
1983	105.98	39.80	100.25	92.47	48.09	44.38	7.78	405	323	561	397.01	228.02			
1984	122.68	42.73	116.30	106.45	54.44	52.01	9.85	464	367	642	424.99	244.21	64.37	5.84	11.59
1985	148.22	50.68	130.23	118.25	55.42	62.83	11.98	512	377	750	554.15	303.19	87.34	5.70	13.78
1986	164.40	61.55	147.00	132.55	59.42	73.13	14.45	570	407	845	661.92	355.44	110.04	5.88	16.32
1987	196.61	69.72	166.90	149.74	67.22	82.52	17.16	639	462	929	715.20	390.00	117.24	6.24	16.56
1988	221.52	80.38	207.48	184.97	79.65	105.32	22.50	782	549	1152	901.08	455.16	150.96	7.08	16.68
1989	253.30	104.43	228.06	202.83	86.27	116.56	25.23	847	593	1243	967.44	511.32			

7. Jilin

Year	v3f	v3f1	v3f2	v3f3	v3f4	v4a1	v4a1a	v4a1b	v4a1c	v4a1d	v4a2	v4a2a	v4a2b	v4a2c	v4a2d
1949															
1950															
1951															
1952						3.57	1.07	1.32	0.98	0.20	1.02	0.33	0.22	0.27	0.20
1953						4.70	1.61	2.07	0.93	0.09	1.59	0.36	0.53	0.37	0.32
1954	83.71	48.53	14.61	0.63	10.99	5.12	1.92	2.09	0.99	0.12	2.02	0.61	0.52	0.43	0.46
1955	70.62	44.26	11.96	0.26	7.24	5.04	1.96	1.90	1.05	0.12	1.79	0.57	0.53	0.44	0.25
1956	83.05	54.78	12.05	0.39	7.82	5.83	2.46	2.24	1.05	0.08	2.73	0.96	0.65	0.59	0.53
1957	84.33	53.15	10.29	1.27	12.58	6.85	3.35	2.57	0.86	0.06	2.62	0.69	0.75	0.55	0.63
1958	86.64	51.82	13.42	1.59	10.99	8.19	3.96	3.30	0.83	0.09	6.55	3.50	0.92	0.59	1.54
1959						11.51	6.09	4.26	1.10	0.06	8.50	3.82	1.23	0.81	2.65
1960						14.08	7.77	5.24	0.97	0.09	11.63	5.58	1.63	0.88	3.54
1961	114.50	63.80	12.00	3.90	16.20	6.90	2.66	3.43	0.71	0.10	6.03	1.84	1.39	0.85	1.95
1962	190.01	102.85	23.40	13.94	21.51	4.92	0.70	3.52	0.65	0.05	3.98	0.71	1.09	0.66	1.52
1963	148.39	82.92	19.72	7.54	19.09	6.00	1.57	3.67	0.70	0.07	5.20	1.12	1.20	0.72	2.17
1964	135.25	82.43	16.49	2.89	18.78	6.74	1.83	4.09	0.78	0.04	5.26	1.41	1.31	0.81	1.73
1965	122.61	74.79	15.58	3.31	18.58	7.26	1.51	4.92	0.77	0.06	5.34	1.72	1.36	0.76	1.51
1966						8.18	2.05	5.17	0.93	0.03	6.53	2.14	1.56	0.82	2.00
1967						5.36	0.57	3.81	0.94	0.04	5.75	1.86	1.62	0.74	1.54
1968						3.54	-0.66	3.33	0.85	0.02	4.97	1.40	1.36	0.82	1.39
1969						7.17	1.17	5.19	0.78	0.03	7.13	2.79	1.39	0.96	2.00
1970						10.31	2.43	6.68	1.17	0.03	9.65	4.68	1.45	0.78	2.74
1971						13.64	3.46	9.18	0.96	0.04	9.74	3.84	1.73	1.01	3.16
1972						14.42	4.24	9.47	0.68	0.04	10.94	4.44	1.93	1.08	3.48
1973						13.35	4.44	7.94	0.97	0.02	11.30	4.23	2.11	1.12	3.84
1974						12.20	2.96	8.26	0.97	0.02	12.18	4.32	2.33	1.03	4.49
1975						12.71	2.23	9.49	0.97	0.02	12.32	4.24	2.40	1.04	4.65
1976						12.34	1.38	10.06	0.88	0.03	12.54	4.11	2.54	1.08	4.80
1977						12.27	0.81	10.49	0.95	0.02	13.35	3.95	2.64	1.14	5.62
1978						16.41	3.68	10.90	0.97	0.87	16.35	5.54	3.02	1.25	6.54
1979	193.83	130.90	26.10	5.82	13.40	12.65	0.40	10.88	1.05	0.32	17.88	5.17	3.40	1.50	7.80
1980	216.25	140.07	27.61	12.59	12.12	14.39	1.30	11.53	1.05	0.51	17.32	3.13	4.32	1.70	8.18
1981	246.08	152.40	34.04	13.70	15.24	10.72	-2.24	11.46	0.98	0.53	15.87	2.21	4.94	1.76	6.96
1982	253.44	159.37	33.38	11.80	18.39	11.97	-2.17	12.61	0.88	0.65	17.30	2.25	5.72	2.06	7.28
1983	274.98	174.22	31.17	18.05	15.19	14.12	-1.83	14.17	1.01	0.77	19.41	3.02	6.51	2.44	7.45
1984	320.81	196.38	32.39	30.77	17.98	15.22	-2.75	16.21	1.07	0.70	23.34	3.41	7.56	3.09	9.27
1985	364.47	199.48	37.12	43.05	23.58	21.67	-2.16	22.18	1.11	0.53	34.50	4.90	9.15	2.99	17.46
1986	388.77	214.66	40.35	52.91	22.66	29.52	1.40	26.10	1.06	0.94	50.12	5.11	11.02	3.69	30.30
1987	441.60	239.54	43.72	56.97	22.50	37.52	3.21	30.26	1.71	2.29	53.23	3.66	11.25	4.22	34.11
1988	516.36	275.63	51.72	64.22	22.79	43.32	0.97	35.93	1.53	4.32	61.26	4.47	13.36	3.77	39.65
1989	562.78	313.59	54.29	66.20	19.93	49.40	-0.79			5.60	67.14	3.80	15.00	4.20	44.14

7. Jilin

7–6

Year	v4b	v4b1	v4b2	v4b3	v4c1	v4c2	v5a	v5a1	v5a2	v5a3	v5a4	v5b1	v5b2	v5b3	v5c
1949							263.89	23.38	15.35		225.16	223.7	18.8	21.4	
1950	0.0133	0.0133					270.37	30.08	15.88		224.41				
1951	0.0934	0.0934					280.51	39.48	15.40		225.63				
1952	0.0427	0.0424	0.0003		1.07	13.4	301.73	48.38	15.52		237.83	236.1	31.0	34.6	
1953	0.0798	0.0736	0.0062		1.74	18.1	321.39	59.68	17.38		244.33				
1954	0.1791	0.1448	0.0343		1.96	17.4	318.25	60.56	14.98		242.71				
1955	0.3599	0.2437	0.1162		1.92	14.9	321.56	57.38	14.67		249.51				
1956	0.5278	0.3951	0.1327		2.42	12.9	327.67	71.66	12.94		243.07				
1957	0.6107	0.4784	0.1323		3.71	16.3	327.22	74.41	18.84		233.97	231.1	43.8	52.3	
1958	1.0984	0.7155	0.3829		7.97	29.7	383.48	123.55	15.66		244.27				
1959	2.3144	0.9298	1.3846		10.02	30.1	384.58	135.33	12.33		236.92				
1960	2.9620	1.2082	1.7538		12.99	34.8	417.80	167.09	15.79		234.92				
1961	2.6863	0.8405	1.8458		3.66	8.6	407.59	147.18	23.30		237.11				
1962	1.3403	0.5428	0.7975		1.97	4.8	414.98	119.19	26.86		268.93	278.4	69.7	66.9	
1963	1.5762	0.6112	0.9650		6.80	17.9	433.95	120.56	27.78		285.61				
1964	1.9551	0.8742	1.0809		8.85	23.0	428.75	123.38	25.98		279.39				
1965	2.0896	1.0057	1.0839		8.02	22.6	437.79	124.50	27.75		285.54	293.1	73.3	71.4	
1966	2.8872	1.0415	1.8457		9.02	22.0	431.05	130.77	19.53		280.75				
1967	3.3393	1.1108	2.2285		8.20	18.4	455.96	132.19	19.98		303.79				
1968	3.6946	1.2157	2.4789		8.28	17.8	470.15	135.15	20.49		314.51				
1969	2.4050	1.0305	1.3745		9.37	18.1	484.00	139.67	20.67		323.66				
1970	3.7250	1.1080	2.6170		13.54	19.8	532.13	159.73	27.87		344.53	337.3	100.0	94.8	
1971	3.9092	1.3539	2.5553		14.21	21.5	568.25	183.74	31.97		352.54	344.1	118.1	106.1	
1972	3.1765	1.7096	1.4669		12.99	16.8	559.43	189.55	33.54		336.34	325.3	130.7	103.4	
1973	4.6288	2.0297	2.5991		15.77	19.0	562.10	184.81	37.77		339.52	325.6	133.9	102.6	
1974	5.8318	2.4780	3.3538		13.05	14.6	568.58	188.44	44.54		335.60	322.5	144.8	101.3	
1975	7.1710	2.7775	4.3935		16.43	17.7	590.51	196.41	60.37		333.73	326.1	160.8	103.6	
1976	5.9687	3.0958	2.8729		15.11	14.7	595.80	204.09	68.94		322.77	308.2	180.3	107.3	
1977	6.7274	3.5787	3.1487		13.99	13.1	620.54	211.33	88.03		321.18	307.7	200.0	112.8	
1978	8.4264	4.2742	4.1522		16.66	15.0	645.38	250.02	74.90		320.46	318.1	205.0	122.3	
1979	10.3416	5.6539	4.6877		18.28	15.3	671.29	257.50	91.09	0.81	321.89	318.4	216.3	136.6	
1980	12.2033	8.0413	4.1620		19.54	15.9	715.30	270.50	103.38	3.37	338.05	329.3	231.7	154.3	
1981	17.6949	10.5160	7.1789		17.14	13.1	754.52	282.81	113.67	5.57	352.47	349.8	242.0	162.7	
1982	21.5818	13.3414	8.2404		19.45	14.0	849.62	292.30	118.94	7.58	430.80	413.8	248.0	187.8	
1983	26.5568	17.1299	9.4269		24.25	16.6	847.50	296.87	125.01	10.60	415.02	410.8	256.9	179.8	
1984	29.4738	23.6614	5.8124		26.96	16.3	858.24	293.07	138.19	15.91	410.99	401.1	258.6	207.6	
1985	39.7998	32.2015	7.5983		33.81	17.0	920.89	304.43	144.91	21.37	450.01	421.9	286.2	222.1	
1986	55.4577	43.2068	12.2509		29.38	13.0	978.57	320.78	149.95	21.17	486.50	432.5	302.6	252.9	
1987	76.3534	63.1314	13.2220		40.38	15.2	1023.82	331.87	154.03	22.96	514.75	465.8	313.9	253.0	
1988	103.6174	87.8418	15.7756		51.34	17.0	1097.56	343.69	153.54	28.53	571.55	520.2	326.9	259.1	
1989	141.9000	118.1000	23.8000		51.91	14.5	1133.62	352.74	156.19	29.25	594.92	549.0	329.7	263.5	

7. Jilin

7–7

Year	v5c1	v5d	v6a	v6a1	v6a2	v6b	v6c	v6d1	v6d2	v6d3	v6d4	v6d5	v6d6
1949			1008.5	222.3	786.2	31.8	12.9	180.3	828.2	536.6	471.9	47.54	28.42
1950			1029.5	228.2	801.3	41.7	12.4	192.9	836.6	546.9	482.6		
1951			1039.8	235.5	804.3	40.6	11.8	215.4	824.4	550.5	489.3		
1952			1064.6	254.3	810.3	44.4	11.5	233.0	831.6	561.1	503.5	61.81	36.37
1953			1133.2	320.4	812.8	41.8	10.9	312.0	821.2	602.1	531.1		
1954			1164.7	338.7	826.0	48.4	10.4	327.7	837.0	614.7	550.0		
1955			1202.1	342.5	859.6	37.6	9.9	350.9	851.2	634.5	567.6		
1956			1224.5	360.4	864.1	32.6	7.5	318.6	905.9	641.7	582.8		
1957			1248.1	383.8	864.3	35.5	9.1	365.5	882.6	656.0	592.1	97.54	56.78
1958			1280.9	417.0	863.9	33.3	9.1	400.7	880.2	674.0	606.0	102.09	61.04
1959			1313.0	530.7	782.3	28.0	13.4	468.7	844.3	692.4	620.6		
1960			1397.1	604.7	792.4	32.5	10.1	549.2	847.9	740.7	656.4		
1961			1414.3	612.8	801.5	26.5	12.0	523.1	891.2	743.0	671.3	125.32	78.92
1962			1476.4	535.4	941.0	40.7	10.0	480.5	995.9	768.9	707.5	122.33	74.19
1963			1537.1	543.9	993.2	47.0	9.4	494.0	1043.1	800.7	736.4	126.71	76.92
1964			1595.1	564.3	1030.8	44.2	12.6	503.7	1091.4	831.3	763.8	130.71	79.47
1965			1639.1	578.7	1060.4	40.5	9.7	520.2	1118.9	850.1	789.0	132.66	80.67
1966			1679.3	589.1	1090.2	34.6	8.6	526.4	1152.9	869.4	809.9		
1967			1722.1	604.4	1117.7	37.6	9.2	542.2	1179.9	891.7	830.4		
1968			1766.3	619.1	1147.2	37.6	9.1	555.7	1210.6	910.4	855.9		
1969			1808.2	625.4	1182.8	31.6	6.6	542.6	1265.6	932.0	876.2		
1970			1860.4	629.4	1231.0	33.2	6.4	555.1	1305.3	959.0	901.4	125.08	78.52
1971			1915.2	647.7	1267.5	32.5	6.5	578.9	1336.3	983.8	931.4		
1972			1962.7	718.4	1244.3	31.4	7.5	596.5	1366.2	1008.3	954.4		
1973			2007.9	702.0	1305.9	26.1	6.2	611.5	1396.4	1032.1	975.8		
1974			2034.5	711.5	1323.0	20.7	6.7	614.7	1419.8	1045.5	989.0		
1975			2063.9	722.7	1341.2	19.6	6.7	620.5	1443.4	1060.5	1003.4	143.56	89.00
1976			2092.6	738.1	1354.5	18.6	6.2	632.6	1460.0	1075.1	1017.5		
1977			2117.9	747.8	1370.1	18.6	6.4	636.3	1481.6	1087.8	1030.1		
1978			2149.3	774.0	1375.3	20.0	6.1	659.5	1489.8	1102.3	1047.0	153.49	94.19
1979			2184.6	810.4	1374.2	19.4	5.5	701.2	1483.4	1119.0	1065.6		
1980			2210.7	853.8	1356.9	15.8	5.8	723.3	1487.4	1132.1	1078.6	164.31	101.82
1981			2230.9	871.7	1359.2	17.7	5.3	745.7	1485.2	1141.4	1089.5		
1982			2257.6	893.9	1363.7	16.8	5.8	763.7	1493.9	1155.1	1102.5		
1983			2269.5	877.8	1391.7	12.4	5.4	782.1	1487.4	1162.3	1107.2		
1984			2284.5	1256.1	1028.4	11.8	5.3	802.6	1481.9	1170.7	1113.8		
1985			2298.0	1421.8	876.2	11.9	5.3	837.0	1461.0	1177.4	1120.6	186.49	113.82
1986			2315.3	1470.7	844.6	13.7	5.4	857.0	1458.3	1186.4	1128.9	190.90	116.92
1987			2336.4	1597.7	738.7	15.3	5.4	883.5	1452.9	1196.9	1139.5	200.21	119.94
1988			2357.4	1728.6	628.8	14.1	5.2	908.7	1448.7	1208.3	1149.1	201.68	122.78
1989			2403.0	1778.3	617.1	19.4	6.4	930.8	1464.6	1228.2	1167.2	206.92	125.34

7. Jilin

7–8

Year	v7a	v7b	v7c	v7d	v7e	v7f	v7g	v7h	v7h1	v7h2	v7h3	v7h4	v7h5	v7i	v8a
1949			130.4					8.12	5.92	0.02	0.95	0.03	1.20	131.40	3.54
1950			147.2					9.65	7.01	0.02	1.13	0.04	1.45	140.50	5.87
1951			154.4					9.52	6.39	0.05	1.27	0.04	1.77	153.20	7.18
1952		17.7	173.0	6912				12.42	8.56	0.26	1.35	0.03	2.22	162.40	10.48
1953		18.0	164.0					12.54	8.63	0.07	1.37	0.06	2.41	163.00	13.28
1954		26.5	187.4					12.40	8.36	0.06	1.46	0.06	2.46	165.00	15.11
1955		38.1	210.0					13.34	8.83	0.08	1.31	0.07	3.05	141.70	13.89
1956		133.9	497.2					13.43	8.30	0.15	1.14	0.07	3.77	126.60	16.93
1957	0.27	133.5	553.5	6906				12.84	9.31	0.39	1.69	0.09	1.36	124.70	20.80
1958		169.6	740.4					12.37	9.02	0.83	1.36	0.11	1.05	128.50	30.88
1959		255.0	528.7					13.92	10.11	0.54	1.13	0.12	2.02	129.30	41.84
1960		276.0	386.4					12.89	8.47	0.37	1.19	0.18	2.68	132.00	57.33
1961		239.7	266.2					14.89	10.51	0.27	1.01	0.18	2.92	119.70	32.71
1962	1.17	206.7	231.4					14.24	9.67	0.26	1.45	0.13	2.73	128.60	30.05
1963	1.80	398.4	223.9				0.60	16.07	11.36	0.29	1.85	0.10	2.47		35.47
1964	2.15	693.4	252.2				0.80	16.93	11.58	0.36	2.25	0.10	2.64		40.31
1965	2.38	728.8	307.1	6526		7.57	0.95	17.75	12.02	0.55	2.24	0.12	2.82		47.49
1966		459.3	362.2			12.50	1.10	22.67	16.17	0.88	2.45	0.11	3.06		53.95
1967		584.0	379.8			17.00	1.30	24.14	17.38	0.82	2.82	0.10	3.02		40.01
1968		625.5	398.9			16.00	1.40	23.22	16.61	0.88	2.62	0.09	3.02		31.76
1969		586.1	425.5			23.10	1.90	19.82	13.36	0.97	2.46	0.08	2.95		52.43
1970	3.44	858.5	527.0			30.93	2.29	26.86	19.23	1.13	2.34	0.11	4.05		63.47
1971		1077.5	691.2			44.50	2.90	27.47	20.03	0.96	3.98	0.05	2.45		74.25
1972	8.23	865.6	509.8			42.90	3.90	26.05	18.63	1.04	3.23	0.05	3.10		78.95
1973	8.69	1357.2	594.7			48.50	4.30	31.54	23.66	0.82	3.88	0.09	3.09		84.91
1974	10.55	1068.2	717.2			63.50	5.10	37.44	27.93	0.94	4.38	0.11	4.08		84.90
1975	18.83	1816.5	820.7			60.60	6.43	35.27	27.51	1.09	4.48	0.11	2.08		99.31
1976	21.54	1255.0	900.6			66.10	7.60	31.17	23.91	1.03	4.30	0.09	1.84		103.39
1977	25.09	1706.8	913.8			57.90	7.90	31.24	23.72	1.12	4.37	0.09	1.94		104.34
1978	28.41	1991.1	897.9	6080		66.69	8.10	37.78	30.15	0.87	4.50	0.07	2.19		112.87
1979	30.31	2331.2	856.2		1007.0	91.30	8.80	42.01	32.48	1.13	5.67	0.08	2.65		125.74
1980	36.75	2120.8	1096.0	6086	1680.0	120.20	9.71	47.47	32.99	2.47	9.26	0.04	2.71		134.67
1981	39.58	2086.1	1117.4		1218.8	114.93	11.18	56.88	41.81	1.96	9.63	0.15	3.33	145.18	136.64
1982	39.61	1979.7	1100.3		1419.6	135.30	12.34	60.58	44.99	2.54	9.61	0.27	3.17	160.38	148.75
1983	41.77	1546.8	1074.1		648.5	152.24	12.40	78.11	62.29	2.10	9.95	0.31	3.46	180.77	172.04
1984	45.27	1546.9	1067.1		1172.0	180.53	12.42	88.99	69.03	3.55	11.94	0.39	4.08	189.94	208.84
1985	47.63	2079.5	1044.4	6096	2789.1	159.23	11.91	85.89	59.03	3.32	18.12	0.54	4.88	201.28	256.75
1986	52.85	2292.9	1076.2		2315.2	179.06	13.90	98.43	70.70	2.94	18.55	0.84	5.40	188.16	282.48
1987	53.49	2186.2	1129.3		2013.4	195.80	14.88	120.81	86.12	2.93	23.40	1.28	7.08	183.11	359.46
1988	55.26	2363.1	1161.8	6053	1050.0	190.67	15.83	140.91	100.03	2.84	29.47	2.17	6.40	186.29	454.24
1989	59.05	2432.6	1254.0	6032		201.20	16.20	133.79	86.61	3.46	36.23	2.56	4.93	193.60	530.26

7. Jilin

7–9

Year	v8a1	v8a2	v8a3	v8b	v8c1	v8c2	v8d	v8f1	v8f2	v8f3	v8f4	v8f5	v8g
1949	2.93	0.62			1.86	1.68			250.8	0.1	7.32		2561
1950	4.98	0.89			2.94	2.93			284.5	0.2	8.49		3042
1951	6.01	1.17			3.09	4.09			337.3	0.4	9.95		3707
1952	9.07	1.41		8.61	4.59	5.89	3.02		418.8	0.6	13.41		3542
1953	11.01	2.27		10.46	5.86	7.42	3.66		448.1	0.9	15.86		3385
1954	12.88	2.23		12.24	7.03	8.08	4.09		455.9	1.9	21.99		3472
1955	12.25	1.64		11.64	6.40	7.48	4.06		506.7	2.6	24.39		3348
1956	14.83	2.10		14.09	8.15	8.78	5.32		576.4	3.4	22.15		3033
1957	18.61	2.19		17.68	11.27	9.53	6.45	0.1	679.3	3.7	30.04		3093
1958	29.17	1.72		28.58	19.44	11.44	9.52	2.4	1001.0	4.3	33.74	0.5	4281
1959	39.47	2.36		37.50	26.76	15.08	12.64	3.7	1376.0	5.6	42.05	2.5	5470
1960	51.14	6.19		48.56	38.37	18.96	15.59	11.3	1508.0	6.1	63.81	7.8	5574
1961	29.00	3.71		27.55	19.23	13.48	8.19	2.9	1292.0	2.9	42.57	5.9	5107
1962	27.22	2.84		25.85	17.62	12.44	7.80	1.2	1052.0	3.1	44.34	6.6	4640
1963	32.70	2.77		31.07	21.81	13.66	10.60	1.1	1022.0	4.4	49.45	10.8	3733
1964	37.09	3.22		35.24	25.26	15.05	10.60	1.2	990.0	4.7	55.43	19.2	3509
1965	43.80	3.68		41.61	28.09	19.40	13.10	1.5	1028.0	5.4	58.20	25.6	3677
1966	50.01	3.94		47.51	32.12	21.83	14.28	3.3	1141.0	11.0	70.57	32.7	3027
1967	36.01	4.00		34.21	23.35	16.66	11.35	2.9	939.0	9.7	64.30	20.5	3419
1968	27.88	3.88		26.48	17.51	14.25	10.27	2.2	995.0	11.0	48.90	17.1	3526
1969	47.37	5.06	0.01	44.99	31.00	21.43	14.51	3.3	1159.0	23.0	65.89	28.6	3395
1970	56.97	6.50		54.12	39.12	24.35	18.93	8.7	1410.0	80.5	69.88	41.2	5303
1971	66.43	7.82		63.11	47.06	27.19	19.97	12.7	1528.0	112.5	85.58	63.1	5678
1972	70.06	8.89	-0.01	66.56	50.41	28.55	20.75	15.1	1543.0	126.4	94.57	75.9	5506
1973	74.08	10.84		70.37	53.49	31.42	22.78	16.1	1564.0	132.6	96.17	84.3	5634
1974	72.60	12.30		68.97	51.31	33.59	21.15	16.4	1606.0	119.7	89.47	97.4	5654
1975	81.91	17.40		77.82	59.98	39.32	25.19	17.2	1716.0	135.5	91.66	119.6	6510
1976	83.76	19.63		79.58	61.58	41.81	24.68	17.7	1794.0	162.5	89.85	125.8	7324
1977	84.19	20.15		78.25	61.31	43.03	22.30	16.7	1916.0	177.9	89.16	130.6	7796
1978	89.07	23.80	0.01	85.97	68.11	44.76	27.34	20.1	2060.0	185.1	93.24	138.3	9863
1979	99.21	26.54		96.38	79.29	46.65	20.35	24.0	2080.0	186.2	101.62	157.7	10213
1980	105.94	28.65	0.08	102.79	80.70	53.97	33.43	24.3	1807.0	176.4	111.83	179.4	10988
1981	107.03	29.45	0.16	103.20	77.93	58.71	33.19	21.0	1807.1	163.2	126.35	171.5	11083
1982	115.38	33.12	0.24	111.96	85.41	63.34	33.94	24.4	1893.2	170.0	115.22	203.2	11221
1983	133.25	38.39	0.40	126.04	102.03	70.01	37.22	29.1	1981.8	178.6	122.28	227.6	11452
1984	158.47	49.72	0.65	148.88	127.03	81.82	48.02	33.0	2136.7	191.4	131.68	256.7	12457
1985	191.38	58.54	6.83	184.10	159.27	97.48	58.23	37.9	2311.8	213.0	133.76	295.6	12927
1986	206.25	66.62	9.61	201.57	168.22	114.26	61.81	42.6	2133.0	237.0	162.96	339.2	13563
1987	258.05	84.92	16.49	252.65	214.56	144.90	80.55	39.6	2108.7	286.5	165.34	378.5	13586
1988	320.94	108.03	25.27	314.54	264.79	189.46	100.76	54.9	2227.9	315.1	165.83	421.1	13791
1989	370.05	126.51	33.80	361.34	306.85	223.51	102.63	65.2	2438.5	342.2	157.51	413.4	14115

7. Jilin

7–10

Year	v8g1	v9a	v9a1	v9a2	v9a3	v9b	v9b1	v9b2	v9b3	v9c	v10a	v10a1	v10b1	v10b2	v10b3
1949				0.18				0.02	0.10	475	2.07	2.01	0.35		0.45
1950				0.28				0.13	0.34	558	3.63	3.55	0.57		0.84
1951				0.42				0.33	0.21	712	5.32	5.18	1.09		1.35
1952		2.35	1.66	0.69	0.0006	4.34	3.56	0.70	0.08	770	7.67	7.38	2.02		3.25
1953				0.94				1.17	0.06	913	10.22	9.76	2.57		4.77
1954				1.09				1.25	0.11	966	11.09	10.48	3.06		5.55
1955				1.13	0.0100			0.99	0.10	1034	10.34	9.86	4.05		4.16
1956				1.31	0.0100			1.10	0.17	1089	12.13	11.45	5.65		4.15
1957		5.33	3.90	1.41	0.0216	7.71	6.42	1.12	0.17	1089	12.43	11.94	6.12		3.56
1958				1.69	0.0200			1.79	0.09	1361	14.33	12.95	7.36		4.29
1959				2.04	0.0200			3.44	0.18	1817	18.50	17.20	9.45		5.75
1960				2.02	0.0500			3.62	0.29	2376	21.71	19.71	12.11		6.32
1961				1.76	0.0400			1.94	0.19	2251	20.30	18.85	12.18		6.80
1962		15.50	13.18	2.27	0.0514	26.54	24.66	1.69	0.19	1969	20.17	18.93	11.91		7.46
1963				2.45	0.0300			1.37	0.13	1892	19.49	18.37	11.19		7.60
1964				2.75	0.0200			1.57	0.12	1991	19.73	18.64	11.67		7.55
1965		26.12	22.87	3.23	0.0200	34.28	32.41	1.76	0.11	2016	20.04	18.68	12.46		7.13
1966				4.09	0.0200			2.05	0.20	2306	21.31	19.49	13.31		7.55
1967				4.25	0.0200			1.96	0.15	2017	22.35	20.34	13.62		8.27
1968				4.37	0.0200			2.04	0.14	1909	21.76	19.75	13.06		8.22
1969				5.52	0.0200			2.74	0.16	2130	24.27	21.91	14.92		8.86
1970		45.92	39.85	6.04	0.0313	111.19	108.11	2.91	0.17	2501	25.75	22.59	15.96		9.14
1971				6.95	0.0300			3.35	0.24	2098	28.17	24.11	16.90		10.68
1972				8.02	0.0400			3.89	0.31	2275	31.18	27.02	19.18		11.35
1973				8.68	0.0400			4.44	0.31	2465	32.91	28.30	20.57		11.68
1974				9.74	0.0200			4.62	0.29	2620	35.13	30.13	21.68		12.79
1975		63.45	52.65	10.78	0.0219	171.08	165.31	5.41	0.36	3466	38.46	33.19	23.27		14.52
1976				11.04	0.0100			5.33	0.36	3490	40.67	34.80	24.88		15.25
1977				11.98	0.0200			6.45	0.50	3685	42.56	36.61	25.96		16.05
1978		78.02	65.14	12.86	0.0177	257.82	250.42	6.87	0.53	3853	43.76	37.90	26.74		16.33
1979	1890	81.81	68.12	13.66	0.0200					5690	51.68	45.06	31.09		19.26
1980	1857	84.29	69.46	14.80	0.0312	245.58	239.67	5.62	0.29	4055	60.25	52.83	34.26		23.54
1981	1839	91.69	75.55	16.11	0.0328	246.63	240.09	6.13	0.41	6057	67.55	59.26	35.30		27.93
1982	1843	99.47	80.85	18.59	0.0319	280.38	272.12	7.78	0.48	6293	76.25	67.02	37.17		32.01
1983	1858	109.31	88.57	20.71	0.0314	315.76	307.47	7.90	0.39	6779	85.92	75.54	38.82		35.07
1984	1886	123.92	98.17	25.72	0.0299	318.82	307.26	10.95	0.60	7517	104.60	91.40	46.06		41.49
1985	2172	134.64	106.71	27.91	0.0228	343.09	330.70	11.60	0.79	8886	124.09	112.00	51.05		46.63
1986	2158	151.13	112.09	39.01	0.0255	381.30	335.56	44.91	0.83	9503	142.00	127.81	59.03		50.78
1987	2196	167.53	122.59	44.91	0.0268	422.57	359.92	61.62	1.03	10540	162.84	145.50	67.24		58.55
1988	2255	187.53	139.76	47.94	0.0290	433.73	368.65	63.70	1.38	13539	202.04	180.81	82.53		68.81
1989	2332	176.49	129.68	46.75	0.0600	466.23	398.50	78.00	1.30	17046	222.66	198.30	89.54		69.77

7. Jilin

7–11

Year	v10b4	v10b5	v10b6	v10d	v11a1	v11a2	v11a3	v11b	v11b1	v11b2	v11c	v11d	v12a	v12b	v12c
1949		0.87	0.40												
1950	0.08	1.69	0.45												
1951	0.12	2.36	0.40										109.7		117.2
1952	0.09	1.96	0.35	4.18									110.8		113.3
1953	0.24	2.38	0.26	4.59									103.9	105.9	112.3
1954	0.29	1.95	0.23	4.65				0.1512	0.1512				102.5	103.5	103.5
1955	0.43	1.39	0.31	4.62				0.0770	0.0770				102.2	100.5	103.8
1956	1.86	0.19	0.28	4.16				0.0874	0.0874				99.0	98.0	101.6
1957	2.27	0.16	0.33	4.25	0.0749	0.0357		0.1106	0.1106				102.8	102.5	106.3
1958	2.33	0.11	0.24	6.59				0.1185	0.1185				99.8	98.7	108.8
1959	2.85	0.15	0.30	7.53				0.1619	0.1589	0.0030			99.5	99.6	103.4
1960	2.75	0.13	0.40	6.57				0.2094	0.2002	0.0092			108.1	108.6	103.2
1961		0.12	1.20	7.04				0.1376	0.1356	0.0020			112.6	113.4	124.2
1962		0.10	0.70	5.81		0.0524	0.0305	0.0849	0.0829	0.0020			103.4	103.1	99.9
1963		0.09	0.60	5.56				0.1169	0.1159	0.0010			99.0	98.9	95.5
1964		0.09	0.41	6.18				0.1416	0.1393	0.0023			98.3	98.4	98.5
1965		0.10	0.35	6.49	0.1156	0.0760	0.0972	0.3021	0.2888	0.0133			99.5	100.5	99.1
1966		0.11	0.34	7.52				0.1820	0.1639	0.0181			99.2	99.2	111.9
1967		0.10	0.36	8.16				0.0930	0.0738	0.0192			100.2	100.8	100.0
1968		0.11	0.37	6.39				0.0487	0.0361	0.0126			100.2	100.2	100.0
1969		0.09	0.40	6.20				0.0802	0.0414	0.0388			99.5	99.3	100.0
1970		0.08	0.57	9.31	0.0093			0.0495	0.0093	0.0402			99.4	99.2	100.0
1971		0.08	0.51	8.75				0.5653	0.5415	0.0238			99.9	100.3	101.7
1972		0.09	0.56	6.97				0.3862	0.3346	0.0516			100.0	100.3	103.1
1973		0.07	0.59	10.64				0.7290	0.6837	0.0453			100.2	100.3	101.4
1974		0.06	0.60	10.73				0.5653	0.4903	0.0750			100.0	100.1	101.7
1975		0.05	0.62	12.20	0.0315	0.0428	0.1143	0.2623	0.1886	0.0737			100.0	100.1	100.2
1976		0.05	0.49	9.88				0.3062	0.1857	0.1205			100.6	100.7	100.0
1977		0.04	0.51	10.58				0.2798	0.1803	0.0995			100.1	100.2	100.2
1978		0.03	0.66	11.68	0.1276	0.0824	0.0257	0.3704	0.2357	0.1347			100.2	100.1	104.1
1979		0.08	1.25	13.18				0.6067	0.4413	0.1654			101.2	101.7	117.5
1980		0.50	1.95	17.52	0.2187	0.2206	0.2231	1.1108	0.6625	0.4483	0.0081		106.3	105.6	109.4
1981		1.74	2.58	25.11	0.5074	0.4166	0.3656	1.7196	1.2896	0.4300	0.0106		101.7	101.6	110.0
1982		3.60	3.47	25.79	0.6102	0.4425	0.2680	1.7753	1.3207	0.4546	0.0765		103.0	104.2	100.5
1983	0.01	7.41	4.61	36.10	0.8059	0.6093	0.2509	2.1884	1.6661	0.5223	0.0674		102.6	104.5	102.9
1984		10.63	6.42	45.43	1.4974	0.6903	0.3095	3.4046	2.4972	0.9074	0.0669	0.0215	104.2	103.5	105.6
1985		17.44	8.97	42.82	3.4677	0.5295	0.2740	5.5072	4.2712	1.2360	0.2454	0.0488	109.7	110.3	106.0
1986	0.08	21.48	10.64	54.41	4.2126	0.6664	0.3725	7.1716	5.2515	1.9201	0.4317	0.2576	105.4	106.0	109.8
1987	0.18	23.72	13.15	73.14	2.9556	1.0616	0.6594	6.3946	4.6766	1.7180	0.7079	0.3933	107.5	107.6	108.0
1988	0.50	33.33	16.88	91.23	3.0820	1.1309	1.1085	7.0766	5.3214	1.7552	0.5590	0.5118	119.9	120.3	107.0
1989	0.81	43.11	19.43	102.13				9.4459	6.8447	2.6012	0.8099	0.7700	116.9	116.9	118.7

7. Jilin

7–12

Year	v13a	v13b	v13c1	v13c2	v13c3	v13d	v14a	v14b	v14c	v15a	v15b	v15c	v15d	v15e	v15f
1949		61.78	0.37	3.92	90.37	0.0317	2028	10056	0.12						
1950		73.28	0.37	4.75	109.43	0.0586	3153	11995	0.22						
1951		83.39	0.38	6.57	125.77	0.0525	3458	13279	0.34						
1952	17.50	77.12	0.67	11.27	119.09	0.0799	4096	17732	0.44	6993					
1953		64.58	0.81	13.88	143.38	0.0749	5736	22304	0.35						
1954		59.70	0.93	17.11	126.87	0.2635	5869	25440	0.35						
1955		56.87	1.18	17.35	115.29	0.1503	6337	25847	0.33						
1956		66.39	1.69	20.37	131.94	0.2914	7672	27916	0.89						
1957	21.10	69.90	1.82	21.46	142.15	0.2265	8554	31078	0.70	7084					
1958		86.00	2.86	37.81	179.59	0.2821	25863	30309	1.28						
1959		90.00	3.27	34.53	196.52	0.3412	21064	38244	1.58						
1960		89.00	3.91	37.92	235.60	0.6263	24307	48642	1.65						
1961		83.40	3.82	34.67	223.79	0.5739	22504	47983	0.90						
1962		82.62	3.49	34.29	230.17	0.6991	21261	45716	0.87	6544					
1963		79.04	3.21	35.13	229.28	0.7280	20823	46761	1.06		9061.5		457		
1964		83.90	2.87	43.30	269.08	0.8225	22374	48361	1.27						
1965	17.30	91.80	2.60	59.66	303.20	0.8349	23599	48404	1.03	6508					
1966			2.59	61.95	282.06	0.5687	27915	45446	1.40						
1967			1.57	63.30	295.95	0.4490	28469	46854	1.35						
1968			0.98	66.69	299.41	0.5899	29002	47620	1.98						
1969			0.46	66.34	309.55	0.5181	31224	47608	1.51						
1970	10.00		0.30	77.14	307.17	0.4558	39344	41507	0.36	6327					
1971			0.30	97.81	331.55		40217	46508	0.57						
1972			0.70	128.56	342.65	0.1631	43699	51473	0.69						
1973			1.18	130.66	344.49	0.1366	45325	56054	0.73						
1974			1.70	142.87	346.34	0.0193	47433	59054	0.96						
1975			2.21	164.82	346.92	0.2229	48716	61992	0.94	6151	9768.0		457		
1976			2.30	202.55	342.09	0.7266	51669	65637	0.81						
1977			2.35	213.35	335.90	0.8706	53384	68630	0.65					15.40	5.30
1978			2.99	209.10	342.97	0.6291	58051	73624	4.00	6076			457	21.60	5.50
1979	10.89	95.30	3.57	196.57	350.41	0.2681	59687	81890	2.37						
1980	14.95	96.50	3.80	189.29	355.29	0.7962	60682	85747	2.68	6066	9117.0		457	19.65	5.70
1981	18.92	96.50	4.65	173.86	349.30	0.1568	61921	94405	3.64	6083	9118.5	356.57		20.69	6.00
1982	19.81	96.50	4.14	165.15	330.98	1.6227	65099	96995	3.93	6074					
1983	19.63	97.00	4.54	156.39	306.12	1.3261	66653	99936	4.28	6090				19.99	6.35
1984	18.52	97.80	5.10	158.25	300.88	1.0613	69336	103548	4.87	6059				19.83	6.34
1985	19.20	97.70	5.95	158.47	299.81	1.2900	70750	105404	7.24	5999		356.57	457	20.30	6.30
1986	18.30	98.00	6.55	154.42	306.90	1.4374	74312	107879	5.64	5960	9347.0	627.00		20.10	6.30
1987	18.30	98.30	6.87	154.49	299.39	1.7854	77910	110410	6.81	5941		450.00		19.90	5.10
1988	19.40	98.50	7.29	152.32	291.02	1.7973	80421	113421	6.58	5927		287.10	457	19.80	5.03
1989			7.31	126.63	283.42	2.0300	82000	117000	4.79	5903					

Notes

1. National Output and Income (Y)

v1a: (E), p.250
v1a1: (A); (E), p.250
v1a2: (E), p.250
v1a3: (E), p.250
v1a4: (E), p.250
v1a5: (E), p.250

v1b: (A); (D), p.175
v1b1: (A); (D), p.175
v1b2: (A); (D), p.175
v1b3: (A); (D), p.175
v1b4: (A); (D), p.175
v1b5: (A); (D), p.175

v1c: v1a – v1d

v1d: (E), p.247
v1d1: (E), p.247
v1d2: (E), p.247
v1d3: (E), p.247
v1d4: (E), p.247
v1d5: (E), p.247

v1e: (A); (D), p.178
v1e1: (A); (D), p.178
v1e2: (A); (D), p.178
v1e3: (A); (D), p.178
v1e4: (A); (D), p.178
v1e5: (A); (D), p.178

v1f: (A)
v1f1: (A)
v1f2: (A)
v1f3: (A)

v1g: v2a + v3a

v1h: (B), p.345; (E), p.276

v1i: (E), p.275

v1j: (E), p.275
v1j1: (E), p.275
v1j2: (E), p.275—collective ownership
v1j3: NA

v1k: (E), p.275

2. Investment (I)

v2a: (E), p.249
v2a1: (A); (D), p.183
v2a2: (A); (D), p.183

v2b: (A)

v2c: (E), p.265
v2c1: (E), p.266
v2c2: (E), p.266

v2d:
v2d1: (E), p.263
v2d2: (E), p.263

v2e: (E), p.263

3. Consumption (C)

v3a: (E), p.249

v3b: (E), p.249
v3b1: (A); (D), p.179
v3b2: (A); (D), p.179

v3c: (E), p.249

v3d: (E), p.274
v3d1: (E), p.274
v3d2: (E), p.274

v3e: (E), p.276
v3e1: (E), p.276
v3e2: (A)
v3e3: (A)
v3e4: (A)

v3f: (A); (E), p.276
v3f1: (A); (E), p.276
v3f2: (A)
v3f3: (A)
v3f4: (A)

4. Public Finance and Banking (FB)

v4a:
v4a1: (E), p.272
v4a1a: (E), p.272
v4a1b: (B), p.320
v4a1c: (B), p.320
v4a1d: v4a1 – v4a1a – v4a1b' (v4a1b':total tax revenues which come from (E), p.272)
v4a2: (E), p.272
v4a2a: (E), p.272
v4a2b: (E), p.272
v4a2c: (E), p.272
v4a2d: v4a2 – v4a2a – v4a2b – v4a2c

v4b: (A)
v4b1: (B), p.324
v4b2: (B), p.324
v4b3: NA

v4c:
v4c1: (E), p.263
v4c2: (E), p.263

5. Labor Force (L)

v5a: (E), p.246
v5a1: (E), p.246
v5a2: (E), p.246
v5a3: (E), p.246
v5a4: (E), p.246

v5b:
v5b1: (E), p.246
v5b2: (E), p.246
v5b3: (E), p.246

v5c: NA
v5c1: NA

v5d: NA

6. Population (PO)

v6a: (E), p.245—data from public security department
v6a1: (E), p.245—(ditto)
v6a2: (E), p.245—(ditto)

v6b: (A); (E), p.245—(ditto)

v6c: (A); (E), p.245—(ditto)

v6d:
v6d1: (E), p.245—(ditto)
v6d2: (E), p.245—(ditto)
v6d3: (E), p.245—(ditto)
v6d4: (E), p.245—(ditto)
v6d5: (A)—Changchun
v6d6: (A)—Jilin

7. Agriculture (A)

v7a: (A); (E), p.257

v7b: (A); (E), p.257

v7c: (A); (E), p.257

v7d: (E), p.257

v7e: (A)

v7f: (A); (E), p.257

v7g: (A); (E), p.257

v7h: (E), p.252
v7h1: (E), p.252
v7h2: (E), p.252
v7h3: (E), p.252
v7h4: (E), p.252
v7h5: (E), p.252

v7i: (E), p.256

8. Industry (IN)

v8a: (E), p.258
- v8a1: (E), p.258
- v8a2: (E), p.258
- v8a3: v8a – v8a1 – v8a2

v8b: (E), p.263

- v8c1: (A); (E), p.250
- v8c2: (A); (E), p.250

v8d: (E), p.263

v8f:
- v8f1: (E), p.262
- v8f2: (E), p.262
- v8f3: (E), p.262
- v8f4: (E), p.262
- v8f5: (E), p.262

v8g: (A)
- v8g1: (E), p.263

9. Transport (TR)

v9a: (E), p.264—excluding urban traffic volume
- v9a1: (E), p.264—including central and local railways
- v9a2: (E), p.264
- v9a3: (E), p.264—excluding distant ocean and coastal passenger traffic

v9b: (E), p.264
- v9b1: (A); (E), p.264—including central and local railways
- v9b2: (A); (E), p.264
- v9b3: (E), p.264—excluding distant ocean and coastal freight volume

v9c: (E), p.264

10. Domestic Trade (DT)

v10a: (E), p.267
- v10a1: (E), p.267

v10b:
- v10b1: (E), p.267
- v10b2: NA
- v10b3: (E), p.267—including supply and marketing cooperative and other collectives
- v10b4: (E), p.267
- v10b5: (E), p.267
- v10b6: (E), p.267

v10d: (E), p.269—calculated on calendar year basis

11. Foreign Trade (FT)

v11a:
- v11a1: (B), p.316—farming products
- v11a2: (B), p.316
- v11a3: (B), p.316

v11b: (E), p.270
- v11b1: (E), p.270
- v11b2: (A)

v11c: (E), p.271

v11d: (A); (E), p.271

12. Prices (PR)

v12a: (E), p.273

v12b: (A); (E), p.273

v12c: (E), p.273

13. Education (ED)

v13a: (A)

v13b: (A)

v13c:
- v13c1: (A); (E), p.276

v13c2: (A)—technical and ordinary secondary schools
v13c3: (A); (E), p.276

v13d: (A)—institutions of higher learning

14. Social Factors (SF)

v14a: (E), p.276

v14b: (E), p.276

v14c: (A)

15. Natural Environment (NE)

v15a: (A); (E), p.257

v15b: (A)

v15c: (A)

v15d: (A)

v15e: (A)

v15f: (A)

Sources of Data

(A) Data supplied by the DSNEB, SSB, the PRC.
(B) Propaganda Department, Jilin Provincial Party Committee of Chinese Communist Party, and Statistical Bureau of Jilin province eds. *Striving and Advancing Forty Years 1949–1989, Jilin's Volume*, Beijing: CSPH, 1989.
(D) Same as (D) in Beijing's sources of data.
(E) Same as (E) in Beijing's sources of data.

8

Heilongjiang

8. Heilongjiang

8–1

Year	v1a	v1a1	v1a2	v1a3	v1a4	v1a5	v1b	v1b1	v1b2	v1b3	v1b4	v1b5	v1c	v1d	v1d1
1949	24.00	12.30	6.90	1.20	0.90	2.70							11.06	12.94	8.06
1950	32.60	12.90	10.40	2.50	2.20	4.60							15.00	17.60	8.25
1951	34.50	16.00	11.60	2.00	1.60	3.30							15.86	18.64	10.29
1952	41.81	16.37	17.88	2.42	1.78	3.36	122.60	115.80	149.60	121.20	113.30	103.10	18.72	23.09	11.88
1953	55.17	18.28	25.10	4.00	2.94	4.85	110.40	93.10	132.30	148.50	148.90	130.20	26.86	28.31	12.88
1954	60.79	20.25	28.23	4.60	2.92	4.79	105.50	103.20	109.00	111.50	95.30	99.20	28.34	32.45	14.96
1955	62.26	22.42	26.87	4.64	3.23	5.10	104.30	108.30	99.30	101.80	112.00	103.90	28.71	33.55	16.57
1956	70.50	24.42	31.33	5.31	3.59	5.85	109.90	96.20	127.80	116.70	113.20	116.40	33.94	36.56	17.91
1957	73.54	23.89	35.03	4.44	3.87	6.31	103.80	95.00	113.00	86.20	111.10	110.90	35.77	37.77	17.08
1958	108.25	22.95	61.81	10.93	5.20	7.36	153.80	132.60	174.50	265.70	144.50	126.00	52.34	55.91	18.17
1959	139.25	22.84	89.68	10.44	7.10	9.19	119.80	96.00	141.60	93.10	133.20	121.50	72.85	66.40	17.40
1960	155.77	17.91	107.33	13.71	8.41	8.41	105.50	76.80	117.50	128.90	116.40	91.20	84.10	71.67	11.57
1961	101.60	18.59	62.18	5.59	7.32	7.92	55.60	83.90	46.70	32.80	70.30	75.70	58.35	43.25	10.74
1962	90.16	22.35	49.69	4.32	6.78	7.02	94.60	102.60	91.80	91.00	97.80	75.10	46.58	43.58	14.49
1963	97.87	24.01	55.47	7.28	5.52	5.59	117.00	117.50	111.60	170.80	85.70	141.90	47.51	50.36	17.70
1964	116.51	23.42	69.91	9.01	6.41	7.79	114.50	112.80	118.70	112.40	112.90	99.50	60.06	56.45	16.44
1965	139.71	24.93	88.54	9.53	7.85	8.86	119.60	105.70	126.50	107.20	123.80	115.60	72.78	66.93	19.08
1966	170.86	32.36	108.35	11.65	8.23	10.27	123.50	131.30	122.40	124.20	106.50	117.60	90.82	80.04	22.77
1967	161.37	36.30	97.39	10.48	7.55	9.65	96.40	112.20	89.80	85.20	87.00	88.90	83.88	77.49	25.49
1968	154.85	34.94	93.62	10.07	7.25	8.97	96.30	96.40	96.00	96.30	95.90	93.50	80.27	74.58	24.58
1969	174.30	33.71	108.70	12.77	9.19	9.93	115.80	96.90	126.50	133.50	133.50	116.10	88.32	85.98	23.70
1970	207.11	34.97	136.84	14.64	10.03	10.63	117.00	111.00	122.40	115.10	110.00	107.90	111.84	95.27	24.55
1971	217.73	50.38	130.56	15.30	10.91	10.58	102.00	100.60	103.10	102.10	106.00	97.10	119.18	98.55	24.93
1972	214.65	42.99	137.07	14.24	10.34	10.01	98.00	85.50	105.00	93.80	95.70	95.50	117.72	96.93	26.35
1973	229.17	47.10	147.70	14.07	10.21	10.09	107.10	109.50	107.80	100.40	100.20	102.00	125.69	103.48	28.86
1974	246.31	51.03	158.33	15.11	10.91	10.93	107.40	108.70	107.10	107.20	107.00	108.20	135.24	111.07	31.26
1975	271.10	56.35	176.06	17.91	10.60	10.18	109.90	110.30	111.20	119.30	97.90	93.90	149.86	121.24	32.07
1976	272.00	48.30	186.60	14.92	10.73	11.45	100.50	87.00	106.00	87.40	106.10	118.00	149.31	122.69	31.76
1977	289.51	49.33	202.09	15.05	10.83	12.21	105.80	101.20	108.50	97.80	97.80	103.20	156.38	133.13	35.70
1978	317.23	60.90	212.14	20.71	12.44	11.04	112.10	120.60	108.60	138.30	101.90	92.50	165.76	151.47	37.35
1979	349.58	69.93	230.75	23.79	13.09	12.02	105.50	100.30	106.60	115.10	107.00	106.80	190.24	159.34	37.57
1980	387.25	85.61	244.17	27.73	16.15	13.59	107.50	108.80	105.50	116.50	116.20	107.60	199.76	187.49	51.87
1981	411.46	87.01	254.19	35.78	18.83	15.65	104.80	98.20	103.70	129.50	116.90	115.40	222.68	188.78	52.23
1982	449.78	94.34	273.77	45.41	20.80	15.46	107.30	104.60	106.90	122.50	106.90	93.10	244.79	204.99	59.71
1983	500.14	106.88	305.90	48.17	21.78	17.41	108.90	116.20	107.80	101.20	103.90	111.30	269.22	230.92	72.91
1984	554.88	121.54	336.55	56.22	22.27	18.30	109.00	109.40	110.10	111.70	101.50	100.50	290.04	264.84	83.16
1985	629.79	114.31	391.95	72.12	27.39	24.02	106.50	92.40	110.90	95.10	119.40	117.50	348.04	281.75	74.80
1986	740.86	137.18	468.58	76.45	29.43	29.22	108.70	113.40	107.90	162.10	116.20	152.80	409.70	331.16	90.21
1987	863.24	137.00	563.97	86.16	33.98	42.13	108.30	97.40	111.00	106.20	106.90	144.70	480.79	382.45	87.35
1988	1041.32	151.72	686.04	107.53	42.76	53.37	109.90	104.00	114.50	107.30	113.40	112.10	593.11	448.21	93.36
1989	1224.41	162.20	804.77	151.50	45.40	60.50	105.40	96.10	106.10	123.20	104.50	99.40	719.21	505.20	95.27

8. Heilongjiang

8–2

Year	v1d2	v1d3	v1d4	v1d5	v1e	v1e1	v1e2	v1e3	v1e4	v1e5	v1f	v1f1	v1f2	v1f3	v1g
1949	3.14	0.32	0.41	1.01											
1950	4.62	0.88	1.13	2.72											
1951	5.18	0.56	0.73	1.88											
1952	6.76	0.82	1.06	2.57	121.80	115.50	130.50	146.50	145.30	137.10					21.27
1953	9.05	1.37	1.52	3.49	110.70	98.40	134.70	165.80	110.60	128.90					29.39
1954	11.19	1.56	1.50	3.24	110.80	106.10	130.00	120.50	106.40	91.20					29.84
1955	9.95	1.51	1.67	3.85	105.60	111.00	92.10	100.60	110.20	117.10					28.44
1956	10.58	1.77	1.90	4.40	105.50	95.90	120.80	124.50	108.20	113.70					30.83
1957	12.54	1.49	2.09	4.57	107.50	106.60	115.40	84.10	111.60	100.60					38.35
1958	26.39	2.78	2.90	5.67	150.80	133.80	187.00	159.70	142.50	127.50					48.27
1959	34.25	3.14	4.89	6.74	111.40	93.20	126.60	109.70	164.40	116.00					56.27
1960	42.97	4.13	6.12	6.85	99.40	65.40	123.20	129.30	122.90	99.90					56.81
1961	21.62	1.57	4.18	5.15	51.60	74.80	40.80	30.80	54.90	60.70					41.29
1962	18.97	1.30	3.89	4.94	104.00	121.90	94.90	85.60	94.00	92.20					35.46
1963	23.12	2.57	2.85	4.12	123.90	132.50	122.60	227.10	84.80	93.50					45.82
1964	27.59	3.31	3.59	5.52	112.10	102.20	118.40	116.80	116.80	133.90					54.04
1965	34.94	3.50	3.84	5.57	118.10	116.00	126.60	105.30	106.40	100.90					56.69
1966	42.74	4.28	4.61	5.64	119.50	119.40	122.40	122.70	120.70	100.40					62.36
1967	38.44	3.85	4.23	5.48	99.80	111.90	89.90	89.90	98.80	97.40					67.86
1968	36.92	3.70	4.06	5.32	101.50	96.40	110.00	96.10	88.70	97.60					63.18
1969	46.85	4.69	5.15	5.59	105.50	96.40	110.70	126.80	127.20	105.20					65.19
1970	54.15	5.38	5.62	5.57	116.30	110.50	122.00	121.60	119.70	101.90					78.72
1971	56.42	5.62	6.11	5.47	102.00	101.70	103.10	103.30	103.90	100.40					83.78
1972	54.20	5.23	5.79	5.36	97.30	84.40	105.10	102.60	102.60	105.60					80.49
1973	58.44	5.17	5.72	5.29	106.90	109.50	107.80	98.80	98.80	98.30					93.82
1974	62.67	5.55	6.11	5.48	107.40	108.30	107.10	107.20	107.00	103.90					98.40
1975	69.60	6.58	7.06	5.93	109.20	110.30	111.00	100.20	100.10	100.20					106.33
1976	74.16	5.48	6.01	5.28	100.70	92.60	106.50	98.00	98.50	97.80					98.54
1977	80.53	5.53	6.07	5.30	108.80	112.40	107.70	100.90	100.80	100.70					107.68
1978	96.37	6.07	6.81	4.87	112.80	103.50	120.80	101.10	113.40	99.40	173.25	41.01	110.78	21.46	121.10
1979	103.40	7.33	6.95	4.09	101.60	86.50	110.50	98.50	112.80	82.30	183.78	44.27	116.57	22.94	129.57
1980	111.23	7.88	8.75	7.76	113.40	121.30	105.50	145.20	109.10	180.80	218.12	56.99	126.98	34.15	146.71
1981	108.86	9.83	8.92	8.94	99.90	100.10	97.00	124.50	101.60	114.70	222.50	57.78	129.68	35.04	158.37
1982	114.02	12.44	10.16	8.66	106.70	111.50	103.60	124.30	111.20	94.70	241.68	63.75	135.26	42.67	179.13
1983	121.73	14.03	11.39	10.86	108.80	122.90	103.60	106.20	109.00	88.10	273.31	78.93	143.12	51.26	206.10
1984	139.66	19.23	11.90	10.89	109.40	106.10	112.50	102.90	102.10	110.60	306.74	87.04	168.01	51.69	234.84
1985	156.67	21.83	14.27	14.18	104.90	100.50	103.80	107.40	120.70	130.30	332.96	77.20	192.61	64.53	271.38
1986	182.77	25.56	15.17	17.45	107.40	104.00	97.90	112.70	107.90	85.30	368.27	91.29	201.98	75.00	321.73
1987	219.44	28.56	18.92	28.18	107.10	94.50	124.20	107.72	118.32	153.30	432.34	89.36	248.52	94.46	371.29
1988	261.90	35.88	23.56	33.51	108.50	100.42	109.55	113.18	111.74	129.40	517.36	94.26	295.64	127.46	434.76
1989	301.76	47.68	24.51	35.80	103.80	94.41	105.25	118.44	102.65	112.24	585.62	93.86	345.51	146.25	499.72

8. Heilongjiang

8–3

Year	v1h	v1i	v1j	v1j1	v1j2	v1j3	v1k	v2a	v2a1	v2a2	v2b	v2c	v2c1	v2c2	v2d1
1949		0.84	252	253	197										
1950		1.20	286	288	225										
1951		2.10	372	374	291										
1952		3.66	508	509	397			5.48	2.76	2.72					12.36
1953		5.65	625	627	407			9.18	4.11	5.07					15.00
1954		6.14	629	630	544			8.75	5.64	3.11					20.21
1955		6.12	629	629	566			7.02	4.99	2.03					23.44
1956		8.37	699	704	633			5.89	8.63	-2.73					29.29
1957		10.55	725	745	573		1.54	12.27	8.41	3.86					35.47
1958		12.20	683	700	546		1.80	21.44	14.94	6.50					41.84
1959		18.10	644	662	516		2.06	25.26	18.62	6.64					50.14
1960		22.03	614	636	465		2.38	24.32	18.44	5.88					56.34
1961		19.60	604	619	570		2.02	6.79	5.79	1.00					57.02
1962		16.66	657	688	423		1.86	-0.47	1.33	-1.80					63.23
1963		17.35	727	756	494		2.11	9.18	5.53	3.65					66.40
1964		17.94	748	776	538		1.96	16.21	15.54	0.67					72.64
1965		18.46	742	770	566			15.44	15.27	0.17					76.24
1966		18.66	717	757	456			15.32	14.52	0.80					
1967		19.59	727	754	536			13.89	13.35	0.54					
1968		20.39	697	716	580			11.94	10.88	1.06					
1969		21.92	667	691	521			16.55	10.83	5.72					
1970		24.05	658	678	539			19.48	12.89	6.59					
1971		26.83	656	674	553			17.64	12.75	4.89					109.92
1972		28.47	655	685	471			18.51	14.03	4.48					117.47
1973		29.86	677	695	573			23.83	18.23	5.60					133.48
1974		30.42	679	718	483			26.14	19.93	6.21					141.68
1975		30.84	666	712	467		3.23	31.06	21.78	9.28					151.49
1976		31.89	656	712	439		3.19	23.58	15.99	7.59					164.05
1977		33.18	663	706	496		3.72	24.68	21.11	3.57					178.50
1978	171.65	39.07	721	763	555		4.04	35.75	21.41	14.34	26.99	25.53	13.25	0.81	193.93
1979	190.64	43.75	744	787	598		5.05	38.13	21.56	16.57		26.65	12.70	1.05	212.76
1980	208.14	49.59	821	880	638		6.56	34.85	24.85	10.00	38.52	37.90	15.90	1.23	235.53
1981	224.41	53.96	831	889	670		7.84	35.98	25.41	10.57	47.04	39.27	14.05	1.34	259.48
1982	254.83	58.22	855	912	703		9.27	49.47	34.30	15.17	62.90	53.48	18.68	1.83	288.50
1983	387.51	61.84	869	930	719		12.24	65.68	43.05	22.63	71.88	65.41	24.39	1.50	316.99
1984	431.74	70.18	967	1046	787		13.40	72.71	50.87	21.84	88.52	73.94	26.10	1.19	356.55
1985	397.84	82.52	1104	1190	906	833	17.49	86.89	60.57	26.32	111.79	89.18	28.65	1.93	398.13
1986	476.28	97.88	1279	1387	1024	1070	20.71	111.11	55.54	55.55	123.55	101.53	34.09	2.03	442.80
1987	474.46	106.03	1356	1454	1119	1215	24.29	125.67	82.43	43.24	140.31	115.54	41.22	2.28	502.83
1988	553.26	125.65	1578	1698	1269	1611	30.29	142.20	91.97	50.23	160.55	132.29	43.57	2.49	604.73
1989	535.19	141.40	1739	1878	1372		33.34	168.03	89.68	78.35	157.57	128.76	38.97	2.61	691.05

8. Heilongjiang

8–4

Year	v2d2	v2e	v3a	v3b	v3b1	v3b2	v3c	v3d	v3d1	v3d2	v3e	v3e1	v3e2	v3e3	v3e4
1949															
1950															
1951															
1952	8.72	4.03	15.79	15.04	8.66	6.38	0.75	137	126	226					
1953	10.23	5.34	20.21	19.03	10.39	8.64	1.18	170	148	267					
1954	14.92	6.63	21.09	19.79	11.46	8.33	1.30	166	152	224					
1955	17.78	6.38	21.42	20.05	11.84	8.21	1.37	161	145	209					
1956	22.36	5.55	24.94	23.37	13.29	10.08	1.57	168	151	229					
1957	27.31	7.02	26.08	24.49	12.23	12.26	1.59	178	150	234					
1958	33.59	13.87	26.83	26.45	14.76	11.69	0.38	172	147	245					
1959	40.43	17.96	31.01	30.58	15.99	14.58	0.43	183	147	263					
1960	44.51	21.52	32.49	31.87	14.12	17.75	0.62	174	122	274					
1961	44.86	21.16	34.50	34.02	15.34	18.68	0.48	142	138	258					
1962	48.38	16.46	35.93	35.49	14.27	21.22	0.44	149	149	239					
1963	50.88	14.58	36.64	36.20	15.88	20.32	0.44	187	134	272					
1964	53.57	13.25	37.83	32.88	11.63	21.25	4.95	164	93	279					
1965	55.94	11.48	41.25	34.85	13.54	21.31	6.40	167	104	269					
1966			47.04	40.20	18.31	21.89	6.84	186	136	267					
1967			53.97	46.31	23.46	22.85	7.66	208	167	276					
1968			51.24	43.34	20.02	23.32	7.90	188	137	276					
1969			48.64	41.54	16.74	24.80	7.10	173	110	285					
1970			59.24	51.18	23.97	27.21	8.06	206	152	300					
1971	73.87	35.81	66.14	57.05	27.06	29.99	9.09	221	166	316					
1972	85.10	38.87	61.98	53.69	20.94	32.75	8.29	200	125	326					
1973	93.77	41.04	69.99	60.19	25.49	34.70	9.80	217	147	333					
1974	98.53	43.13	72.26	61.41	36.06	35.35	10.85	215	144	336					
1975	104.17	45.23	75.27	63.14	27.20	35.94	12.13	215	145	340					
1976	111.64	50.31	74.96	63.12	27.15	40.97	11.84	211	115	384					
1977	127.46	50.94	83.00	70.79	27.17	43.62	12.21	232	138	405					
1978	132.88	53.89	85.35	77.58	29.33	48.25	7.77	250	146	441					
1979	142.72	59.85	91.44	82.61	32.23	50.38	8.83	262	160	444					
1980	154.21	61.96	111.86	101.09	42.25	58.84	10.76	317	210	500	361.01	204.75	63.89	4.19	15.41
1981	169.33	62.55	122.39	114.55	49.48	65.07	7.84	356	246	538	377.54	216.41	60.26	4.55	10.41
1982	186.01	70.34	129.66	121.00	53.07	67.93	8.66	371	263	548	404.86	236.28	63.59	4.79	11.20
1983	199.00	73.47	140.42	129.56	58.34	71.22	10.88	393	288	563	458.94	267.24	72.51	5.43	13.18
1984	204.21	78.74	162.13	148.06	62.60	85.46	14.07	446	310	659	504.54	286.60	93.30	5.49	13.68
1985	266.21	92.76	184.49	167.94	65.90	102.04	16.55	502	328	763	651.38	343.92	126.11	5.82	13.54
1986	292.79	110.50	210.62	190.18	74.27	115.91	20.44	564	370	849	726.26	373.68	138.24	5.64	15.84
1987	336.56	125.48	245.62	215.75	85.72	130.03	29.87	641	431	943	771.49	404.17	144.41	6.47	16.81
1988	416.26	141.26	292.56	253.19	99.21	153.98	39.37	748	503	1093	932.64	467.16	175.80	6.00	16.68
1989	481.55	177.35	331.69	285.92	102.89	183.03	45.77	836	519	1270	1004.40	518.04			

8. Heilongjiang

8–5

Year	v3f	v3f1	v3f2	v3f3	v3f4	v4a1	v4a1a	v4a1b	v4a1c	v4a1d	v4a2	v4a2a	v4a2b	v4a2c	v4a2d
1949															
1950															
1951															
1952						4.73	0.51	2.26		0.38	1.62	0.76	0.38	0.36	0.12
1953						5.65	0.49	3.51		0.24	2.34	1.00	0.68	0.47	0.19
1954						6.62	0.52	3.90		0.60	2.62	0.91	0.68	0.53	0.14
1955						6.45	0.90	3.79		0.35	2.52	0.92	0.69	0.52	0.39
1956						7.33	1.47	4.34		0.09	4.64	1.85	0.90	0.69	1.20
1957						8.21	1.50	4.66		0.68	4.28	1.41	0.86	0.64	1.37
1958						18.42	9.85	6.28		0.77	11.86	7.67	1.09	0.75	2.35
1959						21.51	11.37	8.20		0.32	12.25	5.80	1.30	1.05	4.10
1960						23.06	12.48	9.10		0.29	16.94	8.70	1.76	1.78	4.70
1961						9.30	2.86	5.28		0.14	6.68	1.36	1.50	3.55	0.27
1962						7.15	0.92	5.10		0.16	5.32	0.52	1.49	3.23	0.08
1963						8.12	1.21	5.62		0.10	7.15	1.75	1.59	2.40	1.41
1964						9.71	1.80	6.63		0.07	7.47	2.43	1.76	3.72	-0.44
1965						9.91	1.28	7.37		0.09	7.96	2.38	1.84	3.73	0.01
1966						12.54	3.12	7.76		0.08	8.56	2.54	2.06	4.15	-0.19
1967						10.92	2.41	6.80		0.09	7.86	2.79	1.88	1.01	2.18
1968						10.87	1.96	6.93		0.42	7.59	2.85	1.75	1.01	1.98
1969						12.38	2.79	8.11		0.08	12.78	5.32	1.62	1.07	4.77
1970						14.41	2.42	10.11		0.06	15.35	7.73	1.74	1.12	4.76
1971						40.31	24.32	14.46		0.03	14.44	5.59	2.18	1.37	5.30
1972						37.48	24.40	11.85		0.07	16.21	6.79	2.60	1.73	5.09
1973						37.63	23.86	12.23		0.04	19.73	8.20	2.79	1.69	7.05
1974						44.26	29.57	13.15		0.02	20.79	8.49	2.96	1.69	7.65
1975						50.56	34.20	14.86		0.03	20.28	7.25	3.06	1.72	8.25
1976						51.04	34.49	15.27		0.04	21.32	7.74	3.24	1.81	8.53
1977						52.49	34.51	16.62		0.04	21.27	7.28	3.37	1.81	8.81
1978	124.93	77.15	21.40	2.21	7.86	63.25	40.86	18.86	1.39	2.07	31.54	10.28	4.31	2.27	14.68
1979	146.70					54.07	33.12	18.48		0.90	28.29	7.16	4.45	2.26	14.42
1980	166.17	95.89	27.60	8.87	9.36	17.04	-4.18	19.05	1.62	0.55	25.76	4.83	5.38	2.71	12.84
1981	175.62	102.15				15.64	-6.72	20.56		0.43	25.87	3.81	5.96	2.91	13.19
1982	201.19	116.06	29.82	13.76	13.32	17.31	-8.37	23.74	1.19	-1.25	28.01	4.40	6.74	3.29	13.58
1983	219.53	120.75	31.58	15.81	11.60	21.56	-7.88	26.67	1.76	0.98	30.71	4.91	7.63	4.16	14.01
1984	238.58	127.38	29.93	21.08	20.03	26.74	-5.92	29.75	1.88	1.02	36.12	5.56	8.80	5.39	16.37
1985	306.63	176.77	32.04	27.61	24.71	37.42	-8.65	41.86	2.07	0.82	44.63	5.57	10.62	5.63	22.81
1986	338.30	190.77	37.15	29.91	24.12	43.36	-4.98	47.51	2.42	1.24	61.27	6.31	12.44	6.07	36.45
1987	361.04	199.25	38.98	33.49	26.55	53.76	-5.83	53.81	2.53	1.69	66.00	5.07	13.63	6.37	40.93
1988	424.13	235.49	47.22	36.13	29.98	62.58	-8.30	61.54	2.46	4.72	74.05	4.49	16.00	8.04	45.52
1989	481.96	265.05	51.20	50.00	34.72	72.32	-11.38			7.75	85.36	3.92	18.18	6.00	57.26

8. Heilongjiang

8–6

Year	v4b	v4b1	v4b2	v4b3	v4c1	v4c2	v5a	v5a1	v5a2	v5a3	v5a4	v5b1	v5b2	v5b3	v5c
1949							311.50	31.70	1.00	34.70	237.40				
1950							336.50	47.70	0.80	36.00	251.40				
1951							349.50	62.70	0.70	35.90	250.50				
1952	0.06	0.06			2.47	19.40	376.80	76.40	1.10	36.40	257.30	279.00	53.10	44.70	
1953	0.12	0.12	0.00		2.68	17.20	388.90	95.20	1.00	38.10	249.50	272.30	67.60	49.00	
1954	0.21	0.21	0.00		3.38	15.70	396.00	98.50	1.80	35.00	256.80	279.30	67.00	49.70	
1955	0.28	0.28	0.00		3.83	15.90	391.70	90.40	2.90	29.40	265.80	285.90	55.00	50.80	
1956	0.56	0.56	0.00		4.77	17.10	448.80	117.00	16.20	9.70	301.40	310.30	76.80	61.70	
1957	0.68	0.68	0.00		6.10	17.80	449.90	126.30	17.40	8.70	292.30	302.20	80.30	67.40	
1958	1.88	1.18	0.71		12.04	25.40	531.40	206.40	22.40	6.90	292.20	311.50	152.40	67.50	
1959	3.72	2.45	1.27		17.68	30.30	592.00	261.20	46.60	7.10	277.10	317.70	182.10	92.20	
1960	3.81	2.99	0.82		19.31	29.20	648.40	316.60	48.20	2.00	281.60	327.80	205.40	115.20	
1961	2.02	1.49	0.53		8.68	13.10	592.60	261.90	33.20	1.60	295.90	331.70	151.20	109.70	
1962	1.28	1.14	0.15		7.13	10.90	543.30	214.20	25.30	2.60	301.20	326.20	118.60	98.50	
1963	1.55	1.34	0.21		10.05	15.30	545.80	210.10	27.50	3.30	304.90	330.70	119.90	95.20	
1964	1.53	1.33	0.20		14.28	21.40	561.00	212.30	30.10	3.20	315.40	309.30	123.60	128.10	
1965	1.84	1.56	0.28		19.30	28.60	598.80	219.20	37.90	2.10	339.60	348.30	129.80	120.70	
1966	1.84	1.60	0.25				587.20	232.80	30.50	3.20	320.70	348.00	128.80	110.40	
1967	2.33	1.72	0.61				593.40	241.00	34.20	3.10	315.10	347.60	135.00	110.80	
1968	2.23	1.87	0.36				637.10	263.80	45.70	2.80	324.80	376.50	146.90	113.70	
1969	1.75	1.51	0.24				678.40	299.80	48.20	1.80	328.60	382.90	169.20	126.30	
1970	2.14	1.71	0.44				725.40	327.70	54.70	1.20	341.80	416.20	184.80	124.40	
1971	2.46	2.09	0.37		38.89	35.50	786.70	370.00	65.50	0.80	350.40	429.80	218.30	138.60	
1972	3.23	2.75	0.49		46.57	37.60	780.60	376.90	56.80	0.60	346.30	423.60	220.40	136.60	
1973	4.17	3.20	0.97		44.20	32.80	815.50	374.50	73.80	0.50	366.70	440.60	234.50	140.40	
1974	4.98	3.98	1.01		48.01	33.90	832.80	373.40	73.90	0.50	385.00	458.20	230.60	144.00	
1975	5.84	4.36	1.48		52.35	35.00	881.40	380.20	98.60	0.50	402.10	491.30	244.00	146.10	
1976	6.06	4.91	1.15		55.00	34.00	897.20	392.20	101.40	0.50	403.10	492.40	254.10	150.70	
1977	7.46	6.00	1.47		58.73	32.90	931.60	402.90	104.50	0.40	423.80	520.60	258.40	152.60	
1978	9.23	7.26	1.97		61.00	32.70	1000.60	460.10	117.10	0.50	422.90	530.00	294.50	176.10	
1979	12.15	9.48	2.67		61.24	30.20	1032.70	454.50	152.80	1.00	424.40	504.80	329.40	198.50	
1980	17.08	13.19	3.88		63.92	29.60	1073.30	467.70	162.20	4.90	438.50	507.40	347.80	218.10	
1981	25.86	19.89	5.96		59.51	25.70	1110.10	490.30	181.70	8.00	430.10	506.20	373.80	230.10	
1982	31.49	24.91	6.58		58.48	22.80	1126.00	500.90	191.40	8.10	425.60	501.50	388.20	236.30	
1983	40.03	32.48	7.55		65.34	23.90	1188.90	512.20	211.90	14.70	450.10	526.20	404.70	258.00	
1984	53.34	42.96	10.38		71.11	25.10	1240.80	513.40	228.30	22.30	476.60	536.40	421.50	282.90	
1985	70.13	57.38	12.75		62.10	17.30	1281.20	532.20	234.60	29.40	484.60	533.30	451.90	296.00	
1986	94.00	76.96	17.04		68.60	17.00	1310.50	555.10	239.30	31.50	483.90	535.50	474.50	300.50	
1987	127.07	105.05	22.01		78.62	17.00	1326.00	569.60	236.30	33.30	486.00	529.80	482.30	313.90	
1988	167.54	141.71	25.84		86.14	15.50	1351.40	588.00	235.60	44.20	482.60	522.90	496.20	332.30	
1989	231.40	199.90	31.50		66.59	10.10	1388.10	599.20	235.90	37.80	513.80	553.90	498.90	335.30	

8. Heilongjiang

8–7

Year	v5c1	v5d	v6a	v6a1	v6a2	v6b	v6c	v6d1	v6d2	v6d3	v6d4	v6d5	v6d6
1949			1011.90	265.80	746.10			252.00	759.90	550.10	461.80	78.51	24.77
1950			1037.00	273.40	763.60			256.10	780.90	560.80	476.20		
1951			1072.80	295.20	777.60			286.40	786.40	580.60	492.20		
1952			1110.50	319.80	790.70			308.70	801.80	599.50	511.00	93.90	29.81
1953			1189.70	378.90	810.80			391.40	798.30	646.40	543.30		
1954			1250.20	416.70	833.50	43.36	11.12	430.10	820.10	676.20	574.00		
1955			1321.20	433.80	887.40	40.46	11.33	462.60	858.80	714.20	607.00		
1956			1418.20	496.00	922.20	33.12	10.08	493.50	924.70	770.90	647.30		
1957			1478.50	545.10	933.40	36.59	10.45	573.70	904.80	796.80	681.70	155.24	66.79
1958			1563.70	587.10	976.60	33.01	9.17	456.60	1107.10	842.20	721.50	161.98	70.25
1959			1682.00	741.90	940.10	30.36	12.76	780.50	901.50	908.10	773.90		
1960			1807.10	877.60	929.50	32.57	10.57	869.20	937.90	973.40	833.70		
1961			1897.10	900.10	997.00	27.26	11.13	793.00	1104.10	1018.40	878.70	194.75	90.86
1962			1893.50	811.20	1082.30	33.46	8.62	728.30	1165.20	1001.80	891.70	182.27	85.40
1963			1972.00	796.00	1176.00	45.06	8.56	764.10	1207.90	1041.00	931.00	189.52	89.23
1964			2053.30	811.50	1241.80	42.47	11.47	759.60	1293.70	1078.70	974.60	196.20	92.49
1965			2133.90	805.60	1328.30	40.38	8.00	823.70	1310.20	1116.80	1017.10	201.00	94.70
1966			2188.60	822.20	1366.40	34.31	7.36	974.90	1213.70	1143.90	1044.70		
1967			2258.90	842.00	1416.90	32.51	6.01	968.80	1290.10	1179.60	1079.30		
1968			2343.40	867.20	1476.20	34.97	6.03	981.00	1362.40	1218.80	1124.60		
1969			2440.80	865.90	1574.90	29.13	5.94	891.10	1549.70	1264.70	1176.10		
1970			2522.60	907.30	1615.30	34.80	5.81	922.30	1600.30	1306.90	1215.70	200.04	94.70
1971			2627.20	936.70	1690.50	32.92	5.83	972.30	1654.90	1361.60	1265.60		
1972			2723.40	1007.30	1716.10	33.04	6.25	1030.10	1693.30	1409.70	1313.70		
1973			2818.60	1034.00	1784.60	30.56	5.60	1048.50	1770.10	1499.40	1359.20		
1974			2894.00	1059.10	1834.90	25.82	5.57	1049.50	1844.50	1496.60	1397.40		
1975			2958.10	1078.80	1879.30	21.93	5.43	1057.50	1900.60	1528.70	1429.40	212.35	107.69
1976			3019.40	1093.70	1925.70	18.58	4.94	1072.00	1947.40	1558.30	1461.10		
1977			3072.50	1118.20	1954.30	17.18	5.00	1082.40	1990.10	1585.30	1487.20		
1978			3129.60	1122.90	2006.70	16.84	4.68	1104.10	2025.50	1614.20	1515.40	217.68	111.21
1979			3168.70	1181.40	1987.30	15.40	4.33	1162.40	2006.30	1629.20	1539.50		
1980			3203.80	1232.70	1971.10	13.49	4.86	1192.30	2011.50	1642.40	1561.40	241.90	117.20
1981			3239.30	1275.30	1964.00	13.07	4.83	1227.80	2011.50	1660.30	1579.00		
1982			3281.10	1309.40	1971.70	15.52	4.88	1254.80	2026.30	1677.90	1603.20		
1983			3278.20	1416.90	1861.30	11.85	4.51	1275.10	2003.10	1677.80	1600.40		
1984			3295.40	1692.60	1602.80	11.07	4.48	1304.60	1990.80	1687.80	1607.60		
1985			3311.40	1928.80	1382.60	10.74	4.29	1336.10	1975.30	1695.30	1616.10	262.55	126.05
1986			3331.50	2038.00	1293.50	12.02	4.38	1358.90	1972.60	1706.20	1625.30	266.85	130.14
1987			3364.00	2145.20	1218.80	13.47	4.24	1391.70	1972.30	1722.30	1641.70	270.74	132.56
1988			3401.50	2331.50	1070.00	13.86	4.32	1426.30	1975.20	1741.40	1660.10	274.76	134.60
1989			3442.40	2358.40	1084.00	18.84	5.47	1455.90	1986.50	1762.00	1680.40	279.82	136.50

8. Heilongjiang

8–8

Year	v7a	v7b	v7c	v7d	v7e	v7f	v7g	v7h	v7h1	v7h2	v7h3	v7h4	v7h5	v7i	v8a
1949				8534				12.32	7.79		1.22	0.04	3.27	108.00	
1950				8926				12.91	8.88		1.26	0.04	2.73	132.00	
1951				9023				16.00	11.09		1.42	0.04	3.45	139.60	
1952		162.10		9615			0.07	16.37	11.81		1.53	0.03	3.00	152.80	17.88
1953				9534				18.28	12.65	0.03	1.55	0.07	3.98	156.10	25.10
1954				9716				20.25	14.15	0.01	1.77	0.07	4.24	149.80	28.23
1955				9892				22.24	15.76	0.14	1.86	0.07	4.41	146.30	26.87
1956				10721				24.42	16.18	0.45	1.99	0.10	5.70	139.90	31.33
1957		1264.50		10660		0.50	0.11	23.89	14.23	0.18	1.70	0.10	7.68	133.00	35.03
1958				10506				22.95	18.17	0.39	2.58	0.21	1.60	118.00	61.81
1959				10149				22.84	17.29	0.63	2.30	0.21	2.41	105.10	89.68
1960				10039				17.91	13.00	0.88	1.53	0.43	2.07	96.00	107.33
1961				9990				18.59	14.09	0.24	1.70	0.42	2.14	103.00	62.18
1962				9794		0.70	0.69	22.35	16.82	0.19	2.33	0.35	2.66	122.80	49.69
1963		2195.10		9962				24.01	17.81	0.30	2.85	0.32	2.73	129.20	55.47
1964				10186				23.42	17.34	0.43	3.12	0.23	2.30	133.40	69.91
1965		4111.00		10649		2.50	1.52	24.93	18.12	0.72	3.27	0.19	2.63	146.80	88.54
1966				10886				32.36	24.28	0.98	3.98	0.21	2.91	151.00	108.35
1967				11036				36.30	27.65	1.08	4.27	0.22	3.08	148.60	97.39
1968				10873				34.94	26.85	0.94	4.27	0.13	2.75	162.80	93.62
1969				11190				33.71	25.88	0.91	4.14	0.12	2.66	196.90	108.70
1970				11295				34.97	28.80	0.92	3.67	0.14	1.44	197.60	136.84
1971				11428				50.38	40.57	2.05	5.54	0.21	2.01	172.90	130.56
1972				11410				42.99	34.66	1.24	5.78	0.22	1.09	181.20	137.07
1973				11285				47.10	38.64	1.33	5.97	0.28	0.88	182.40	147.70
1974				11661				51.03	42.31	2.07	5.80	0.15	0.70	177.50	158.33
1975				11838				56.35	46.35	2.31	6.67	0.20	0.82	179.70	176.06
1976				12042				48.30	38.88	2.52	6.42	0.20	0.28	181.50	186.60
1977				12169				49.33	39.06	2.42	7.13	0.16	0.56	175.80	202.09
1978	51.98	8838.70	967.20	12419		17.50	13.37	60.90	50.20	2.62	7.14	0.14	0.80	170.90	212.14
1979	55.80	9023.80	907.50	12786			13.70	69.93	56.00	2.78	9.50	0.16	1.49	161.10	230.75
1980	70.91	9000.50	1005.70	13086		34.60	15.54	85.61	67.86	3.48	12.20	0.27	1.80	149.00	244.17
1981	76.07	8731.70	1047.40	13091			16.90	87.01	66.67	4.20	13.01	0.43	2.70	151.60	254.19
1982	81.45	9383.90	1010.40	12718	3064		15.30	94.34	68.01	5.91	16.82	0.46	3.14	156.20	273.77
1983	86.19	8437.80	946.50	12911	1009		15.00	106.88	81.32	6.80	14.76	0.67	3.33	179.40	305.90
1984	90.21	8784.50	935.40	12933	995		15.60	121.54	90.55	7.83	18.63	1.03	3.50	184.30	336.55
1985	96.01	7909.70	1019.30	12873	3030	42.10	14.40	114.31	80.61	7.01	21.43	1.23	4.03	195.10	391.95
1986	93.50	8202.20	1079.50	12695	1530		15.20	137.17	101.67	6.36	22.36	2.02	4.76	191.90	468.58
1987	109.50	7948.40	1149.40	12773	2220	54.40	15.90	137.00	99.75	6.69	22.82	2.54	5.20	183.30	563.89
1988	110.50	7911.10	1109.40	12349	3060	66.10	14.67	151.72	106.84	6.82	29.23	3.17	5.66	183.40	686.05
1989	116.30	8119.90	1166.20	12679			16.40	162.18	111.48	7.28	33.92	3.69	5.81	183.80	804.77

8. Heilongjiang

Year	v8a1	v8a2	v8a3	v8b	v8c1	v8c2	v8d	v8f1	v8f2	v8f3	v8f4	v8f5	v8g
1949				4.64	3.41	3.49		0.03	461.00		1.90	7.10	5227
1950				7.56	5.20	5.20		0.06	491.00		2.30	12.30	
1951				8.71	5.66	5.94		0.07	477.00		3.10	15.30	
1952	13.48	0.32	4.08	14.43	10.74	7.14		0.36	615.00		4.20	18.60	5769
1953	19.25	0.61	5.24	19.47	12.12	12.98		0.53	661.00		4.90	24.90	
1954	23.97	0.75	3.51	23.40	14.70	13.53		1.17	713.00		5.90	39.60	
1955	24.01	0.80	2.06	24.62	13.02	13.85		1.45	873.00		7.30	34.20	
1956	26.48	2.77	2.08	31.65	15.58	15.75		3.77	1101.00		9.50	54.40	
1957	29.25	3.34	2.44	34.62	24.69	10.34		12.07	1326.00		10.70	54.20	4256
1958	56.53	4.62	0.66	61.43	37.41	24.39		34.50	2126.00	0.30	16.60	68.60	
1959	83.40	6.28		84.54	59.65	30.03		52.57	3063.00	0.80	23.50	78.20	
1960	92.85	14.48		103.02	72.96	34.37		61.14	3078.00	98.50	30.00	78.60	
1961	54.48	7.70		45.35	38.19	23.99		19.49	2145.00	274.50	23.70	40.00	
1962	43.89	5.75	0.05	38.84	29.69	20.00		21.23	1915.00	355.50	23.40	46.30	6509
1963	50.32	5.09	0.06	42.45	34.45	21.02		21.70	1941.00	439.30	25.50	53.00	
1964	63.98	5.89	0.04	53.59	48.01	21.90		26.25	1985.00	625.10	28.20	61.00	
1965	81.26	7.28		68.01	60.70	27.84		32.33	2049.00	834.20	33.30	65.40	4971
1966	100.61	7.74		83.61	79.69	28.66		37.37	2147.00	1060.90	38.60	72.40	
1967	89.58	7.81		74.34	68.46	28.93		27.11	1584.00	1032.00	37.50	60.60	
1968	85.50	8.12		70.79	65.45	28.17		24.07	1868.00	1151.00	36.40	53.20	
1969	98.89	9.81		90.48	77.57	31.13		37.18	2265.00	1581.00	45.00	72.00	
1970	123.13	13.27	0.44	108.90	100.79	36.05		41.31	2630.00	2118.40	50.90	92.00	8914
1971	116.88	13.18	0.50	110.35	93.55	37.01		37.90	2515.00	2669.10	53.60	100.30	
1972	121.72	14.64	0.71	108.87	96.76	40.81		46.61	2401.00	3051.30	58.60	109.00	
1973	129.98	16.85	0.87	107.48	105.12	42.58		49.44	2485.00	3365.10	63.90	114.50	
1974	137.88	19.43	1.02	121.76	112.71	45.62		44.18	2656.00	4105.70	71.80	122.00	
1975	151.84	23.13	1.09	136.18	124.26	51.80		43.93	2933.00	4626.00	77.80	156.00	10483
1976	158.20	26.77	1.63	139.32	132.87	53.73		37.78	3137.00	5030.00	87.80	171.10	
1977	168.50	31.66	1.93	159.34	142.12	59.97	75.80	42.83	3160.00	5031.00	98.50	187.70	
1978	176.34	32.95	2.85	173.08	150.58	61.56	82.20	54.74	3710.00	5038.00	107.50	212.70	13521
1979	191.55	34.25	4.95	184.01	163.18	67.57	85.10	53.17	4197.00	5075.00	118.00	245.30	14015
1980	198.96	39.79	5.42	192.77	168.86	75.31	91.20	52.53	4245.00	5150.00	129.10	272.00	14889
1981	206.44	40.92	6.83	202.22	168.26	85.93	89.50	47.44	4174.00	5175.00	135.80	279.90	14839
1982	224.70	43.07	6.00	217.13	176.85	96.92	91.80	55.61	4569.00	5194.00	149.10	321.10	15297
1983	248.91	49.20	7.79	240.40	202.10	103.80	95.80	64.23	5047.00	5235.00	162.60	351.40	15500
1984	271.84	54.37	10.34	264.70	222.37	114.18	109.00	69.69	5716.00	5356.00	176.60	364.90	16169
1985	312.17	73.09	6.69	307.53	260.61	131.34	115.40	75.93	6246.00	5529.00	187.00	424.20	17624
1986	376.74	83.39	8.45	367.79	310.12	158.46	145.40	74.87	6572.00	5555.00	202.20	460.40	18180
1987	454.31	96.65	12.93	446.11	380.84	183.13	177.90	80.82	6821.00	5555.00	223.50	483.40	17620
1988	547.07	120.11	18.87	527.61	456.46	229.58	207.10	92.54	7172.00	5570.00	246.80	521.50	17790
1989	644.26	140.42	20.09	619.30	531.21	273.56	226.30	95.72	7616.47	5555.56	279.07	539.47	18013

8. Heilongjiang

8–10

Year	v8g1	v9a	v9a1	v9a2	v9a3	v9b	v9b1	v9b2	v9b3	v9c	v10a	v10a1	v10b1	v10b2	v10b3
1949	549									538.00	3.90	3.80			
1950	607									659.00	4.30	4.10			
1951	684									949.00	6.70	6.40			
1952	782	19.94	18.85	0.67	0.42	87.61	85.20	1.10	1.30	1105.00	11.60	10.90	3.80		4.20
1953	872	27.96	26.18	1.20	0.58	104.40	101.30	1.70	1.40	1271.00	15.30	14.40	5.00		5.00
1954	1019	28.17	25.95	1.64	0.58	114.30	110.40	1.70	2.20	1399.00	15.80	14.80	5.70		6.50
1955	977	22.69	20.25	1.72	0.72	125.50	120.70	1.90	2.90	1459.00	14.90	13.90	6.30		5.70
1956	1022	25.45	22.26	2.33	0.86	136.60	131.80	2.00	2.50	1805.00	19.00	17.70	9.60		6.00
1957	1151	28.04	24.72	2.41	0.91	156.30	151.10	2.50	2.70	1975.00	20.10	19.10	10.50		5.20
1958	2283	34.36	30.72	2.65	0.99	187.00	179.10	3.80	4.10	2525.00	25.10	22.10	21.20		
1959	1897	46.78	42.39	3.33	1.06	249.10	238.70	6.20	4.20	3566.00	31.80	28.50	31.00		0.30
1960	2457	62.82	57.83	3.65	1.34	279.40	266.30	8.30	4.80	5862.00	37.20	32.70	35.20		1.60
1961	1622	75.05	69.86	3.50	1.69	206.20	198.80	3.40	4.00	4890.00	32.40	30.20	29.30		1.10
1962	1570	67.02	61.91	3.70	1.41	183.60	177.10	2.50	4.00	3507.00	30.00	27.90	27.70		1.10
1963	1506	46.37	41.84	3.68	0.85	184.10	177.80	2.40	3.90	4148.00	29.10	27.50	26.60		0.90
1964	1459	41.00	36.00	4.21	0.79	205.90	198.70	2.90	4.30	4235.00	30.40	28.90	28.00		1.20
1965	1438	38.97	33.21	5.06	0.70	231.30	223.30	3.00	5.00	3610.00	31.10	29.20	28.40		1.30
1966	1515	42.62	37.63	7.03	0.69	241.90	233.10	3.40	5.40	3605.00	34.20	31.50	31.20		2.60
1967	1584	45.86	34.90	7.59	0.64	202.30	194.80	3.80	3.70	3512.00	37.50	34.60	34.40		2.70
1968	1580	50.66	42.77	7.30	0.59	210.90	203.50	3.60	3.80	3629.00	36.40	33.60	33.60		2.40
1969	1842	59.10	49.49	8.86	0.75	247.70	239.60	4.10	4.00	4294.00	41.50	37.90	38.70		2.30
1970	2150	57.68	47.29	9.76	0.63	278.70	268.90	4.90	4.90	5254.00	42.20	37.70	39.00		2.70
1971	2311	62.81	52.33	9.80	0.68	286.70	276.80	5.10	4.80	4825.00	44.50	40.00	41.70		2.40
1972	2334	67.40	56.04	10.59	0.77	277.80	267.50	5.40	4.70	5164.00	48.40	44.20	45.40		2.40
1973	2454	71.29	59.23	11.31	0.75	289.40	278.50	6.10	4.80	5329.00	52.10	46.70	48.90		2.70
1974	2481	72.41	59.84	11.95	0.62	288.90	278.30	6.60	4.00	5534.00	55.70	50.00	52.20		2.90
1975	2596	78.06	64.03	13.35	0.68	355.60	308.50	7.90	6.20	6765.00	60.90	54.20	57.30		2.90
1976	2694	77.72	62.32	14.74	0.66	365.60	307.10	9.00	6.20	7230.00	62.50	55.10	58.60		3.20
1977	2867	84.09	70.16	13.25	0.68	386.60	325.70	8.00	7.00	7542.00	66.90	59.20	62.90		3.20
1978	2921	90.78	72.22	17.53	0.72	441.10	376.90	11.10	7.80	7802.00	71.20	61.80	66.80		4.00
1979	2851	97.22	78.67	17.94	0.61	461.90	398.40	10.00	7.50	8214.00	81.00	70.40	74.80		5.30
1980	2861	102.62	83.47	18.35	0.59	486.30	419.20	12.20	8.00	8463.00	94.10	82.40	80.90		11.10
1981	2837	110.70	90.80	18.91	0.85	504.40	420.70	27.50	8.30	8637.00	105.50	93.60	86.10		15.80
1982	2882	119.71	97.15	21.79	0.59	524.30	455.20	12.40	8.50	8772.00	115.10	102.80	89.60		20.30
1983	2935	130.81	106.07	23.75	0.85	564.20	494.40	10.30	10.70	9356.00	124.10	111.70	92.20		22.60
1984	2933	146.38	118.24	27.17	0.79	581.40	509.40	9.70	11.60	9978.00	145.00	130.30	79.00		49.30
1985	3630	162.56	132.01	29.45	0.89	633.90	559.90	18.20	13.90	11193.00	172.60	156.70	87.10		57.40
1986	3572	176.46	140.14	35.39	0.72	697.70	598.10	34.30	13.80	12569.00	197.60	180.00	99.60		64.50
1987	3702	209.19	151.84	56.27	0.69	743.40	629.10	47.70	15.10	13707.00	236.40	214.20	114.70		72.40
1988	3346	227.89	174.00	52.85	0.65	758.30	639.40	51.10	15.80	18014.00	294.10	268.10	141.00		83.30
1989	3363	215.83	162.41	52.13	0.52	810.20	705.90	54.90	15.30	21508.80	332.87	302.50	157.42		91.10

8. Heilongjiang

8–11

Year	v10b4	v10b5	v10b6	v10d	v11a1	v11a2	v11a3	v11b	v11b1	v11b2	v11c	v11d	v12a	v12b	v12c
1949															
1950															
1951													110.00	111.50	116.60
1952	0.13	2.82	0.60	5.94									111.70	113.10	112.90
1953	0.31	3.47	0.45	6.88	0.58		0.03	0.61	0.61				105.50	106.00	120.90
1954	0.44	2.74	0.40	6.77				0.69	0.69				101.60	101.70	106.00
1955	0.63	1.81	0.45	7.23				0.71	0.71				101.30	101.00	99.60
1956	2.62	0.36	0.43	6.66				0.81	0.81				100.60	99.90	104.00
1957	3.60	0.32	0.55	8.20	0.60	0.08	0.09	0.77	0.77				102.80	101.90	103.80
1958	3.39	0.16	0.38	10.84				0.87	0.87				98.20	98.30	106.80
1959		0.19	0.31	14.34				1.04	1.04				100.00	100.00	103.90
1960		0.22	0.20	10.24				0.70	0.70				101.00	101.00	103.80
1961		0.44	1.65	8.98				0.22	0.22				122.00	123.70	127.80
1962		0.41	0.76	7.12	0.02	0.04	0.17	0.22	0.22				102.90	103.90	97.40
1963		1.05	0.52	7.71				0.22	0.22				92.10	99.60	95.60
1964		0.84	0.38	8.95				0.21	0.21				97.30	99.30	98.50
1965		0.99	0.41	10.22	0.05	0.02	0.15	0.22	0.22				98.90	99.70	98.50
1966			0.38	13.05				0.25	0.25				100.00	100.30	112.20
1967			0.41	18.21				0.20	0.20				100.90	100.00	100.00
1968			0.40	15.09				0.18	0.18				100.00	100.00	100.00
1969		0.01	0.45	11.16				0.13	0.13				100.00	100.00	100.00
1970		0.05	0.46	17.22	0.04	0.02	0.13	0.20	0.20				100.20	100.20	100.00
1971		0.06	0.48	12.76				0.30	0.30				99.80	99.90	104.40
1972		0.06	0.53	10.37				0.39	0.39				100.50	101.10	101.60
1973		0.06	0.57	15.46				0.44	0.44				100.40	100.30	100.60
1974		0.06	0.61	17.80				0.41	0.41				100.40	100.50	100.90
1975		0.04	0.66	20.36	0.11	0.04	0.51	0.66	0.66				100.10	100.10	99.90
1976		0.04	0.68	14.55				0.45	0.45				100.60	100.80	100.40
1977		0.04	0.72	16.11				0.41	0.41				100.50	100.80	100.00
1978		0.05	0.34	22.08	0.12	0.06	0.27	0.45	0.45				100.20	100.50	102.40
1979		0.10	0.82	27.33	0.17	0.08	0.50	0.74	0.74				101.80	102.50	130.60
1980		0.70	1.44	33.56	0.23	0.10	0.65	1.31	0.98	0.32			105.60	107.30	103.40
1981		1.56	2.07	34.20	0.44	0.32	0.57	1.60	1.34	0.26			102.10	102.10	121.30
1982		2.54	2.67	35.91	0.67	0.46	0.60	1.98	1.75	0.24			102.80	103.00	90.20
1983	0.01	5.54	3.73	45.84	1.27	0.76	0.70	3.23	2.73	0.50			102.20	102.50	104.70
1984	0.01	10.69	5.95	51.46	1.89	0.86	0.64	4.29	3.39	0.90	0.15	0.24	104.40	104.40	107.70
1985	0.02	18.73	9.36	56.05	2.65	0.85	0.63	5.10	4.13	0.97	0.53	0.10	111.70	111.90	104.70
1986	0.03	27.75	10.70	71.81	3.69	1.29	1.06	7.38	6.05	1.33	0.53	0.48	105.90	106.00	113.40
1987	0.07	36.62	12.63	79.89	4.52	1.92	1.54	8.99	7.98	1.01	1.16	0.63	106.60	109.70	105.00
1988	0.17	51.54	18.14	107.21	4.86	1.99	1.87	11.69	9.49	2.21	1.11	0.92	117.80	118.60	107.60
1989	0.17	65.93	18.30	124.00				13.41	10.27	3.14	1.30	1.05	114.00	114.60	115.10

8. Heilongjiang

8–12

Year	v13a	v13b	v13c1	v13c2	v13c3	v13d	v14a	v14b	v14c	v15a	v15b	v15c	v15d	v15e	v15f
1949					89.45	0.03	2800	5900		8547					
1950										9093					
1951										9227					
1952			0.92	9.50	125.06	0.15	5300	14300	0.66	9729					
1953		60.30							0.51	9815					
1954									0.43	9959					
1955									0.55	10178					
1956									0.71	11049					
1957		67.60	1.88		167.81	0.38	17500	39200	0.63	11255					
1958									1.45	11291					
1959									1.97	10830					
1960									2.40	10529					
1961									1.01	10393					
1962		74.60	3.56		275.99	0.51	37100	63100	1.01	10142					
1963									1.66	10182					
1964									2.25	10459					
1965		89.60	2.70	64.01	372.50	0.85	43900	65000	2.65	10956					
1966									2.49	11115					
1967									1.85	11235					
1968									1.51	10991					
1969									1.97	11358					
1970			0.03		387.66	0.78	61200	69500	1.77	11563					
1971		84.30							2.77	11671					
1972									3.04	11652					
1973									3.08	11856					
1974									2.11	11927					
1975		96.70	1.74		498.69	0.27	83900	102400	2.41	12062					
1976									2.35	12193					
1977									2.21	12308					
1978		95.10	3.32	264.37	495.81	0.61	91500	120700	2.57	12687					
1979		94.80	3.78		494.39	0.45	91900	126400	2.57	12995					
1980		94.50	4.36	255.99	500.26	0.78	93300	133500	2.86	13089					
1981		95.50	4.96		509.04	0.41	92600	140300	3.04	13133					
1982		96.30	4.31		503.37	1.88	91500	145700	4.99	13080					
1983		97.00	4.53		486.28	1.31	94600	150300	5.66	13127					
1984		97.70	5.32		479.35	1.09	95100	150500	7.05	13363					
1985		97.70	6.59	226.90	467.79	1.18	95400	151300	6.90	13396					
1986		98.40	7.36		454.50	1.48	97400	155000	7.16	13304					
1987		98.60	7.47		437.09	2.29	100100	161000	9.22	13288					
1988		99.90	7.89	226.65	417.54	2.04	105100	166000	8.91	13251		656.00	844.00	132.61	3.47
1989		98.90	7.92	214.97	406.40	2.32	108900	170400	9.65	13240					

Notes

1. National Output and Income (Y)

v1a: (E), p.283
  v1a1: (E), p.283
  v1a2: (E), p.283
  v1a3: (E), p.283
  v1a4: (E), p.283
  v1a5: (E), p.283

v1b: (A); (D), p.189
  v1b1: (A); (D), p.189
  v1b2: (A); (D), p.189
  v1b3: (A); (D), p.189
  v1b4: (A); (D), p.189
  v1b5: (A); (D), p.189

v1c: v1a – v1d

v1d: (E), p.280
  v1d1: (E), p.280
  v1d2: (E), p.280
  v1d3: (E), p.280
  v1d4: (E), p.280
  v1d5: (E), p.280

v1e: (A); (D), p.192
  v1e1: (A); (D), p.192
  v1e2: (A); (D), p.192
  v1e3: (A); (D), p.192
  v1e4: (A); (D), p.192
  v1e5: (A); (D), p.192

v1f: (E), p.279
  v1f1: (E), p.279
  v1f2: (E), p.279
  v1f3: (E), p.279

v1g: v2a + v3a

v1h: (A); (E), p.308

v1i: (A); (E), p.307—data of 1985–89 include meat price subsidies

v1j: (E), p.307—(ditto)
  v1j1: (E), p.307
  v1j2: (E), p.307
  v1j3: (A)

v1k: (E), p.307

2. Investment (I)

v2a: (E), p.382
  v2a1: (A); (D), p.197
  v2a2: (A); (D), p.197

v2b: (A)

v2c: (E), p.298
  v2c1: (E), p.299
  v2c2: (E), p.299

v2d:
  v2d1: (E), p.296
  v2d2: (E), p.296

v2e: (E), p.296

3. Consumption (C)

v3a: (E), p.282

v3b: (E), p.282
  v3b1: (A); (D), p.193
  v3b2: (A); (D), p.193

v3c: (E), p.282

v3d: (E), p.306
  v3d1: (E), p.306
  v3d2: (E), p.306

v3e: (A)
  v3e1: (A)
  v3e2: (A)
  v3e3: (A)
  v3e4: (A)

v3f: (A)

v3f1: (A)
v3f2: (A)
v3f3: (A)
v3f4: (A)

4. Public Finance and Banking (FB)

v4a:
v4a1: (E), p.304
v4a1a: (E), p.304
v4a1b: (B), p.280
v4a1c: (C), 1989, p.458—tax revenues from farming and animal husbandry
v4a1d: v4a1 – v4a1a – v4a1b' (v4a1b':total tax revenues which come from (E), p.304)
v4a2: (E), p.304
v4a2a: (E), p.304
v4a2b: (E), p.304
v4a2c: (E), p.304
v4a2d: v4a2 – v4a2a – v4a2b – v4a2c

v4b: (A)
v4b1: (B), p.289
v4b2: (B), p.289
v4b3: NA

v4c:
v4c1: (E), p.296
v4c2: (E), p.296

5. Labor Force (L)

v5a: (E), p.278
v5a1: (E), p.278
v5a2: (E), p.278
v5a3: (E), p.278
v5a4: (E), p.278—excluding rural people working outside

v5b:
v5b1: (E), p.278
v5b2: (E), p.278
v5b3: (E), p.278

v5c: NA
v5c1: NA

v5d: NA

6. Population (PO)

v6a: (E), p.277—data from public security department
v6a1: (E), p.277—(ditto)
v6a2: (E), p.277—(ditto)

v6b: (A); (E), p.277—(ditto)

v6c: (A); (E), p.277—(ditto)

v6d:
v6d1: (E), p.277—(ditto)
v6d2: (E), p.277—(ditto)
v6d3: (E), p.277—(ditto)
v6d4: (E), p.277—(ditto)
v6d5: (A)—Harbin
v6d6: (A)—Qiqihar

7. Agriculture (A)

v7a: (A); (E), p.290

v7b: (A); (E), p.290

v7c: (A); (E), p.290

v7d: (A); (E), p.290

v7e: (A)

v7f: (A)

v7g: (A); (E), p.290

v7h: (E), p.285
v7h1: (E), p.285
v7h2: (E), p.285
v7h3: (E), p.285
v7h4: (E), p.285
v7h5: (E), p.285

v7i: (E), p.289

8. Industry (IN)

v8a: (E), p.291
  v8a1: (E), p.291
  v8a2: (E), p.291
  v8a3: v8a – v8a1 – v8a2

v8b: (E), p.296

  v8c1: (E), p.283
  v8c2: (E), p.283

v8d: (E), p.296

v8f:
  v8f1: (E), p.295
  v8f2: (A); (E), p.295
  v8f3: (A); (E), p.295
  v8f4: (A); (E), p.295
  v8f5: (A); (E), p.295

v8g: (A)
  v8g1: (E), p.296

9. Transport (TR)

v9a: (E), p.297—excluding urban traffic volume
  v9a1: (E), p.297—including central and local railways
  v9a2: (E), p.297
  v9a3: (E), p.297—excluding distant ocean and coastal passenger traffic

v9b: (E), p.297
  v9b1: (E), p.297—including central and local railways
  v9b2: (E), p.297
  v9b3: (E), p.297—excluding distant ocean and coastal freight volume

v9c: (A); (E), p.297

10. Domestic Trade (DT)

v10a: (A); (E), p.300
  v10a1: (E), p.300

v10b:
  v10b1: (E), p.300
  v10b2: NA—figures of supply and marketing cooperative are included in collective ownership from 1952–57, included in state ownership from 1958–83, and then included in collective ownership after 1984
  v10b3: (E), p.300
  v10b4: (E), p.300
  v10b5: (E), p.300
  v10b6: (E), p.300

v10d: (E), p.302—calculated on calendar year basis

11. Foreign Trade (FT)

v11a:
  v11a1: (B), p.274
  v11a2: (B), p.274
  v11a3: (B), p.274

v11b: (E), p.303—data from foreign trade department
  v11b1: (E), p.303—(ditto)
  v11b2: v11b – v11b1

v11c: (E), p.303

v11d: (E), p.303

12. Prices (PR)

v12a: (E), p.305

v12b: (E), p.305

v12c: (E), p.305

13. Education (ED)

v13a: NA

v13b: (A); (E), p.308

v13c:
- v13c1: (A); (E), p.308
- v13c2: (E), p.308
- v13c3: (A); (E), p.308

v13d: (A); (C), 1990, p.588

14. Social Factors (SF)

v14a: (E), p.308

v14b: (E), p.308

v14c: (A); (C), 1990, p.569

15. Natural Environment (NE)

v15a: (A); (E), p.290

v15b: NA

v15c: (A)

v15d: (A)

v15e: (A)

v15f: (A)

Sources of Data

(A) Data supplied by the DSNEB, SSB, the PRC.

(B) Statistical Bureau of Heilongjiang Province ed. *Tremendous Changes in Heilongjiang's Forty Years 1949–1989*, Beijing: CSPH, 1989.

(C) ________ ed. *Yearbook of Heilongjiang Economic Statistics*, Beijing: CSPH.

(D) Same as (D) in Beijing's sources of data.

(E) Same as (E) in Beijing's sources of data.

9

Shanghai

9. Shanghai

9–1

Year	v1a	v1a1	v1a2	v1a3	v1a4	v1a5	v1b	v1b1	v1b2	v1b3	v1b4	v1b5	v1c	v1d	v1d1
1949															
1950															
1951															
1952	87.05	3.43	66.60	2.88	1.43	12.71							53.60	33.45	2.16
1953	119.99	3.70	91.50	5.26	1.87	17.66	137.2	109.7	136.9	195.9	131.5	134.0	71.91	48.08	2.49
1954	125.15	3.36	96.37	4.04	2.32	19.06	103.2	94.7	105.2	83.0	124.6	98.3	74.31	50.84	2.24
1955	120.23	3.79	91.42	5.40	2.09	17.53	96.4	120.9	97.1	84.5	88.9	91.1	70.79	49.44	2.69
1956	144.63	3.78	113.92	2.79	2.11	22.03	131.0	92.7	134.3	90.0	106.0	128.5	86.49	58.14	2.32
1957	150.83	4.13	118.82	4.26	2.16	21.46	104.2	97.8	104.9	158.3	102.7	91.1	87.25	63.58	2.63
1958	214.93	5.71	176.44	5.81	3.40	23.57	140.4	117.8	150.0	127.6	154.1	74.9	126.40	88.53	3.36
1959	298.04	6.61	254.68	7.34	5.13	24.28	141.5	105.1	145.1	138.5	159.8	97.0	178.27	119.77	4.07
1960	342.88	6.69	298.97	7.79	6.15	23.28	117.7	100.7	120.3	104.5	119.3	75.7	195.79	147.09	4.02
1961	221.36	6.73	187.43	3.41	4.60	19.19	64.2	96.3	61.2	44.8	66.6	174.1	131.00	90.36	4.21
1962	181.51	7.61	151.98	2.34	4.17	15.41	80.1	107.2	89.0	64.9	79.6	89.4	107.41	74.10	4.28
1963	199.05	7.66	168.91	2.83	4.44	15.21	111.1	104.0	112.9	118.3	109.9	92.6	117.92	81.13	4.31
1964	232.14	9.61	196.95	4.13	5.11	16.34	120.0	120.9	120.0	146.7	121.0	112.9	141.04	91.10	5.97
1965	267.77	10.61	230.77	3.92	5.16	17.31	120.1	114.4	123.8	97.1	106.0	103.3	164.49	103.28	6.19
1966	297.39	10.77	259.59	3.65	5.35	18.03	116.0	101.7	116.2	105.9	92.3	101.5	183.37	114.02	6.47
1967	261.67	11.09	226.88	2.43	4.59	16.68	91.0	98.9	90.3	66.3	109.5	106.7	162.24	99.43	6.85
1968	288.54	12.34	251.87	2.13	4.95	17.25	113.9	113.0	115.0	89.0	110.4	102.1	177.68	110.86	7.95
1969	324.24	12.54	284.42	2.94	5.11	19.23	115.9	103.5	117.3	135.3	109.4	96.7	194.62	129.62	7.55
1970	353.40	12.29	312.18	4.33	5.65	18.95	114.2	96.6	114.9	150.0	112.4	99.8	210.08	143.32	7.05
1971	378.19	12.71	336.52	3.85	6.07	19.04	109.0	102.1	109.6	88.7	113.7	102.1	227.64	150.55	7.17
1972	400.50	14.24	355.39	4.33	6.60	19.94	106.7	108.0	106.9	112.5	110.1	98.1	243.36	157.14	8.09
1973	431.91	13.89	383.33	5.37	7.36	21.96	108.7	96.4	109.0	124.4	115.3	98.9	262.94	168.97	8.52
1974	452.45	14.96	398.40	7.47	8.08	23.54	106.7	102.4	106.4	141.0	107.9	109.4	276.44	176.01	9.00
1975	478.55	14.17	420.37	10.26	9.46	24.29	106.0	92.3	105.5	138.6	113.2	109.9	293.05	185.50	7.76
1976	484.62	15.95	423.45	9.48	10.25	25.49	102.8	104.9	102.1	92.2	108.3	102.2	297.46	187.16	8.25
1977	521.67	14.72	458.40	7.60	13.88	27.07	106.5	85.4	108.7	79.8	111.4	103.9	313.74	207.93	7.36
1978	592.43	18.26	514.01	13.46	16.91	29.80	113.3	132.6	112.1	177.3	123.2	107.7	346.92	245.51	10.25
1979	645.62	20.41	556.30	17.31	18.91	32.69	109.6	101.4	108.6	120.1	109.7	107.3	383.05	262.57	10.76
1980	699.00	18.90	598.75	20.13	20.60	40.62	106.1	90.9	106.5	108.4	108.2	121.6	416.58	282.42	9.39
1981	729.24	20.33	620.12	24.04	22.00	42.75	104.5	108.6	103.7	118.6	103.5	112.5	438.30	290.94	9.65
1982	749.62	23.97	634.65	26.06	24.14	40.80	105.2	117.4	104.7	108.5	110.6	103.0	454.63	294.99	12.33
1983	785.11	22.68	663.53	27.57	25.91	45.42	106.6	93.6	107.0	105.4	103.7	109.0	481.62	303.49	12.43
1984	874.99	26.59	728.12	34.94	31.13	54.21	110.7	113.3	109.9	119.3	108.3	115.8	533.79	341.20	16.49
1985	1055.77	31.38	862.73	47.52	39.06	75.08	113.3	90.8	113.6	110.6	111.1	120.8	646.04	409.73	18.52
1986	1177.05	33.76	952.21	62.28	43.95	84.85	105.9	106.0	105.5	113.7	107.0	105.7	751.97	425.08	18.51
1987	1361.47	38.84	1073.84	101.47	53.13	94.19	107.0	102.3	106.8	114.4	113.5	104.5	887.86	473.61	21.28
1988	1657.87	53.07	1304.66	120.78	64.54	114.82	110.7	106.3	110.5	103.7	106.8	119.1	1091.66	566.21	27.08
1989	1886.60	60.63	1524.67	120.60	74.65	106.05	103.1	101.3	103.0	92.4	105.3	108.8	1299.76	586.84	30.76

9. Shanghai

9–2

Year	v1d2	v1d3	v1d4	v1d5	v1e	v1e1	v1e2	v1e3	v1e4	v1e5	v1f	v1f1	v1f2	v1f3	v1g
1949															
1950															
1951															
1952	17.98	1.00	0.97	11.34											28.37
1953	26.61	1.84	1.35	15.79	141.40	117.10	143.50	197.50	140.10	134.40					30.39
1954	28.04	1.28	1.73	17.55	103.50	94.10	107.00	75.40	127.10	101.10					30.03
1955	27.54	1.36	1.58	16.27	99.00	128.60	103.00	67.90	91.80	92.00					29.25
1956	33.49	0.82	1.45	20.06	123.10	80.00	127.90	102.00	94.60	126.40					25.67
1957	38.56	1.24	1.49	19.66	107.20	98.00	114.70	161.70	103.00	91.10					41.53
1958	61.77	1.70	2.16	19.54	133.90	108.80	161.60	104.00	140.10	67.60					51.49
1959	91.56	1.82	2.89	19.43	138.40	102.50	146.80	130.20	147.00	93.50					69.26
1960	119.70	1.84	3.07	18.46	127.80	96.50	135.40	100.70	102.40	75.00					65.23
1961	68.04	0.91	2.23	14.97	60.60	101.70	53.80	55.30	53.50	171.30					41.35
1962	56.02	0.73	1.87	11.20	71.90	101.60	69.90	65.40	53.30	83.00					25.64
1963	62.73	0.90	1.94	11.25	115.30	97.20	120.30	115.80	126.60	94.30					39.35
1964	68.82	1.14	2.36	12.81	117.90	138.50	116.20	124.20	148.30	117.70					45.94
1965	79.55	1.04	2.75	13.75	120.90	104.30	128.40	100.00	135.60	106.60					38.26
1966	88.85	0.95	3.05	14.70	115.90	110.90	113.50	95.20	128.20	104.30					56.99
1967	76.43	0.57	2.19	13.39	91.40	98.90	90.00	57.60	83.10	105.20					39.83
1968	86.18	0.44	2.48	13.81	112.70	123.80	113.90	81.20	115.70	101.80					54.66
1969	102.62	0.67	2.59	16.19	115.90	93.40	119.00	141.20	119.00	99.70					40.96
1970	116.79	0.90	2.92	15.66	112.50	91.70	114.70	147.70	114.50	97.90					49.41
1971	123.77	1.08	3.23	15.30	105.90	101.70	106.20	121.70	117.40	99.30					59.31
1972	128.14	1.06	3.59	16.26	103.20	104.20	103.30	98.00	112.60	99.60					70.29
1973	137.17	1.30	3.94	18.04	109.20	96.40	109.60	125.80	116.30	99.60					75.14
1974	141.77	1.80	4.12	19.32	109.00	102.40	111.60	146.50	103.00	109.30					81.21
1975	150.82	2.05	4.93	19.94	104.20	86.30	103.60	118.30	112.60	110.10					80.79
1976	151.85	1.79	5.24	20.03	101.80	106.10	100.30	87.30	107.90	98.30					72.34
1977	169.89	1.78	7.24	21.66	108.10	79.50	111.90	103.70	97.60	105.80					72.72
1978	197.97	3.39	8.69	25.21	115.30	127.00	115.60	190.40	122.40	113.90	272.81	11.00	211.05	50.76	94.08
1979	209.30	4.34	9.74	28.43	111.70	99.00	108.50	96.60	117.90	110.30	286.43	11.39	221.21	53.83	99.52
1980	222.43	4.85	10.67	35.08	105.40	99.70	106.30	98.90	113.60	120.80	311.89	10.10	236.10	65.69	127.85
1981	227.79	6.76	10.41	36.33	104.80	100.30	103.90	140.60	93.60	111.80	324.76	10.58	244.34	69.84	141.98
1982	231.24	8.00	10.33	33.09	104.60	126.00	104.10	110.80	111.20	99.00	337.07	13.31	249.32	74.44	156.67
1983	234.20	8.36	11.66	36.84	106.60	100.10	109.90	115.20	108.60	109.30	351.81	13.52	255.32	82.97	144.05
1984	256.10	10.32	13.64	44.65	113.20	121.60	111.90	112.50	107.80	118.30	390.85	17.26	275.37	98.22	187.38
1985	299.52	13.75	16.40	61.54	113.20	75.50	114.10	111.10	106.70	120.70	466.75	19.53	325.63	121.59	304.34
1986	305.53	15.61	19.63	65.80	103.50	98.90	103.47	106.89	108.80	103.01	490.83	19.69	336.02	135.12	360.70
1987	329.86	27.30	22.74	72.43	107.00	98.80	107.10	122.27	113.53	103.80	545.46	21.60	364.38	159.48	384.97
1988	393.13	32.37	27.43	86.20	110.80	104.50	109.52	109.85	106.20	120.00	648.30	27.36	433.05	187.89	525.16
1989	420.00	32.01	31.61	72.46	103.10	100.27	102.05	96.09	104.74	109.13	696.54	29.63	466.18	200.73	542.11

9. Shanghai

9–3

Year	v1h	v1i	v1j	v1j1	v1j2	v1j3	v1k	v2a	v2a1	v2a2	v2b	v2c	v2c1	v2c2	v2d1
1949											0.22				
1950											0.22	0.18			
1951											0.73	0.61			
1952				782				7.27	1.92	5.35	1.98	1.64			
1953				832				5.05	3.38	1.67	3.65	3.02			
1954				834				5.54	2.90	2.64	3.25	2.69			
1955				801				5.88	2.99	2.87	3.43	2.84			
1956				840				0.61	3.55	-2.94	3.76	3.11			
1957				859				14.38	4.09	10.29	5.20	4.33			
1958				848				22.75	10.57	12.18	11.32	11.01			
1959				814				37.99	14.57	23.42	15.61	14.87			
1960				787				33.11	15.83	17.28	17.65	16.66			
1961				798				9.47	4.98	4.49	7.21	6.68			
1962				821				-4.76	1.66	-6.42	3.82	3.40			
1963				840				9.20	2.95	6.25	5.32	4.69			
1964				849				13.58	4.83	8.75	7.22	6.32			
1965				835				4.76	4.99	-0.23	7.75	6.82			
1966				808				21.33	4.45	16.88	7.22	6.32			
1967				807				4.15	1.79	2.36	4.61	3.91			
1968				743				19.83	1.60	18.23	4.58	3.78			
1969				747				4.35	4.21	0.14	7.45	6.41			
1970		20.63	675	736	431			13.98	7.27	6.71	10.90	9.60			96.12
1971		21.14	672	738	425			22.04	8.08	13.96	11.36	10.01			103.23
1972		22.08	672	737	440			31.71	9.66	22.05	13.23	11.96			109.27
1973		22.37	664	729	433			33.19	12.31	20.88	16.24	14.73			117.20
1974		22.80	660	723	433			36.67	17.90	18.77	22.43	20.41			126.31
1975		23.49	641	699	432			33.13	27.65	5.48	32.53	29.46			135.67
1976		24.79	633	686	443			22.26	18.21	4.05	23.96	21.65			144.01
1977		24.97	623	673	441			22.09	11.20	10.89	18.00	15.24			155.14
1978	281	28.12	672	716	500			38.55	22.28	16.27	27.91	23.83	6.24	0.57	177.23
1979	360	32.74	784	834	590			32.63	28.07	4.56	35.58	32.08	12.55	1.05	183.87
1980	402	38.10	873	918	702			53.64	32.69	20.95	45.43	40.27	17.40	0.71	190.96
1981	444	39.59	870	910	727		12.41	62.23	20.65	21.58	54.60	45.00	22.08	0.82	202.73
1982	536	41.34	883	920	750		13.91	74.55	54.77	19.78	71.34	61.62	34.47	1.14	216.24
1983	563	42.91	897	935	763		15.70	53.94	56.59	-2.65	75.94	65.01	32.59	1.35	235.02
1984	785	53.71	1110	1160	938	1149	18.94	81.62	70.69	10.93	91.72	75.80	34.41	1.38	259.39
1985	806	65.48	1344	1395	1155	1556	23.86	164.83	92.40	72.43	118.56	95.92	31.61	1.96	301.61
1986	937	78.61	1593	1656	1347	1933	29.25	196.34	112.63	83.70	143.47	122.46	33.66	7.45	401.40
1987	1059	89.98	1797	1864	1527	2414	35.44	200.29	143.06	57.23	182.99	154.45	48.05	9.84	457.20
1988	1301	109.64	2181	2258	1855	2619	46.99	287.11	188.47	98.64	245.27	198.68	67.05	13.69	512.94
1989	1380	126.27	2512	2595	2163		54.26	275.99	156.53	119.46	244.19	178.81	70.13	12.67	569.17

9. Shanghai

9–4

Year	v2d2	v2e	v3a	v3b	v3b1	v3b2	v3c	v3d	v3d1	v3d2	v3e	v3e1	v3e2	v3e3	v3e4
1949															
1950															
1951															
1952			21.10	18.44			2.66	219	94	265					
1953			25.34	21.79			3.55	249	99	302					
1954			24.49	21.05			3.44	227	92	271					
1955			23.27	20.27			3.10	215	88	257					
1956			25.06	21.62			3.44	232	91	281					
1957			27.15	23.61			3.54	242	99	293					
1958			28.74	24.65			4.09	246	102	291					
1959			31.27	26.54			4.73	262	110	319					
1960			32.12	26.90			5.22	258	107	328					
1961			31.88	27.91			3.97	265	116	334					
1962			30.40	26.78			3.62	254	114	321					
1963			30.15	26.22			3.93	246	115	302					
1964			32.36	27.45			4.91	254	130	318					
1965			33.50	28.55			4.95	262	135	329					
1966			35.66	30.69			4.97	280	145	353					
1967			35.68	31.13			4.55	283	152	354					
1968			34.83	30.50			4.33	276	175	330					
1969			36.61	32.01			4.60	291	166	361					
1970	57.89	56.60	35.43	31.02			4.41	286	161	362					
1971	60.31	60.91	37.27	32.00			5.27	299	167	383					
1972	64.42	64.01	38.58	33.52			5.06	315	187	399					
1973	68.66	68.56	41.95	35.88			6.07	336	202	427					
1974	74.07	72.40	44.54	38.30			6.24	357	220	450					
1975	79.47	79.10	47.66	40.18			7.48	374	231	471					
1976	83.25	87.22	50.08	41.45			8.63	384	238	485					
1977	89.79	91.96	50.63	41.93			8.70	387	239	492					
1978	109.05	94.88	55.53	45.43			10.10	416	264	510					
1979	112.70	94.32	66.89	55.31			11.58	496	362	587					
1980	115.90	92.03	74.21	61.99			12.22	544	420	623	552.84	309.60	79.08	9.24	4.44
1981	121.04	93.33	79.75	67.91			11.84	588	500	643	584.52	331.80			
1982	129.69	93.86	82.12	69.54			12.58	593	514	643	575.64	338.52			
1983	146.10	96.86	90.11	75.57			14.54	636	586	667	615.24	360.48			
1984	162.84	105.69	105.76	87.42			18.34	729	682	757	726.00	410.04			
1985	191.90	129.28	139.51	116.31	37.55	78.76	23.20	961	850	1024	991.80	516.96	150.00	13.08	5.76
1986	281.51	160.76	164.36	135.74	41.58	94.16	28.62	1108	956	1192	1170.24	616.68	160.20	14.52	6.00
1987	325.10	183.56	184.68	150.59	46.19	104.40	34.09	1213	1079	1286	1282.08	698.28	182.88	15.72	7.68
1988	360.46	215.65	238.05	196.22	52.75	146.44	41.83	1562	1318	1682	1648.44	867.96	249.24	15.12	9.24
1989	395.66	264.45	266.12	233.11	59.86	173.25	33.01	1784	1398	1976	1812.00	1010.52	207.24	16.20	9.60

9. Shanghai

9–5

Year	v3f	v3f1	v3f2	v3f3	v3f4	v4a1	v4a1a	v4a1b	v4a1c	v4a1d	v4a2	v4a2a	v4a2b	v4a2c	v4a2d
1949						0.08				0.03	0.07				
1950						1.09	0.10			0.44	0.80				
1951						1.45	0.13			0.77	1.48	0.46	0.32	0.54	0.16
1952						2.55	0.28			1.73	2.10	0.91	0.43	0.54	0.22
1953						1.99	0.47			0.60	1.87	0.64	0.41	0.57	0.25
1954						2.72	0.72			0.87	2.34	0.75	0.49	0.66	0.44
1955						2.54	1.07			0.65	1.88	0.35	0.49	0.69	0.35
1956						3.06	1.64			0.66	2.41	0.54	0.76	0.72	0.39
1957						4.62	3.15			0.77	3.75	1.32	0.95	0.65	0.83
1958						13.94	12.34			0.97	12.40	9.15	1.21	0.60	1.44
1959						85.13	58.75			1.12	16.42	8.51	1.52	0.81	5.58
1960						101.26	73.83			1.33	19.25	10.20	2.11	0.79	6.15
1961						59.58	40.51			1.12	8.85	3.50	1.31	0.71	3.33
1962						44.37	27.01			0.99	3.87	1.44	1.18	0.54	0.71
1963						51.73	33.28			1.02	4.92	1.42	1.31	0.53	1.66
1964						57.88	37.09			1.20	6.77	2.64	1.54	0.58	2.01
1965						62.90	39.87			1.32	7.59	2.24	1.58	0.56	3.21
1966						70.83	48.60			1.37	7.24	2.10	1.86	0.57	2.71
1967						56.04	36.20			1.27	5.99	1.63	1.82	0.55	1.99
1968						62.43	40.98			1.31	4.83	1.50	1.52	0.51	1.30
1969						84.99	59.24			1.60	8.47	3.61	1.55	0.54	2.77
1970						99.91	69.12			1.65	12.88	5.80	1.77	0.63	4.68
1971						114.13	81.99			1.80	11.59	5.17	1.85	0.67	3.90
1972						121.15	87.24			1.94	11.20	4.64	2.18	0.71	3.67
1973						129.58	91.45			2.01	15.40	5.82	2.56	0.63	6.39
1974						132.75	92.13			2.10	22.06	9.90	2.70	0.67	8.79
1975						136.18	93.41			2.12	26.53	12.87	2.75	0.69	10.22
1976						133.23	89.48			2.19	21.87	9.29	2.81	0.69	9.08
1977						147.69	100.01			2.32	17.18	5.86	2.75	0.66	7.91
1978	192.52	116.96				169.22	115.30			2.41	26.01	11.75	3.06	0.83	10.37
1979	247.44	137.05				172.69	116.59			2.37	27.06	12.73	3.61	0.90	9.82
1980	322.92	166.82	34.83	70.21	11.55	174.73	114.39			2.75	19.18	6.16	4.23	1.14	7.65
1981	389.84	197.98				174.35	109.14			3.00	19.06	5.42	4.62	1.15	7.87
1982	444.29	220.83				167.99	99.55			3.44	20.68	4.96	5.19	1.24	9.29
1983	511.60	241.48				156.39	85.94			3.41	22.39	4.80	5.62	1.41	10.56
1984	619.04	286.69				163.96	84.45			2.61	30.32	7.97	6.43	1.73	14.19
1985	778.45	341.45	67.13	233.14	15.85	184.23	78.32			3.75	46.07	14.23	9.08	1.84	20.92
1986	895.76	405.94	74.14	261.55	19.17	179.46	65.76			5.04	59.08	14.19	10.87	2.08	31.94
1987	977.40	450.38	80.61	266.73	20.07	168.97	48.41			6.56	53.85	10.03	11.98	2.28	29.56
1988	1229.20	488.43	110.02	330.23	12.28	161.62	24.01			10.89	65.88	5.65	14.31	1.65	44.27
1989	1207.93	509.16	99.65	310.40	11.81	166.56	11.53			11.80	73.31	5.49	16.51	1.89	49.42

9. Shanghai

9–6

Year	v4b	v4b1	v4b2	v4b3	v4c1	v4c2	v5a	v5a1	v5a2	v5a3	v5a4	v5b1	v5b2	v5b3	v5c
1949	0.07	0.07													
1950	0.32	0.32													
1951	1.01	1.01													
1952	2.27	2.27					307.29	132.64	8.74	35.30	130.61	130.87	91.06	85.36	
1953	3.44	3.41	0.03				317.17	140.85	10.99	34.70	130.63				
1954	3.63	3.56	0.07				323.83	142.25	14.30	34.23	133.05				
1955	3.93	3.90	0.03				321.16	138.85	14.94	31.84	133.53				
1956	4.74	4.74					354.18	172.80	23.03	22.09	136.26				
1957	5.49	5.37	0.12				365.53	174.66	37.12	19.72	134.03	132.08	133.14	100.31	
1958	5.76	5.60	0.16				400.51	223.29	30.58	8.35	138.29				
1959	6.51	6.40	0.11				407.38	224.98	42.56	6.80	133.04				
1960	7.19	6.96	0.23				432.76	223.43	62.52	7.90	138.91				
1961	7.14	6.84	0.30				412.87	206.98	57.42	4.41	144.06				
1962	6.64	6.38	0.26				403.06	188.20	45.13	8.78	160.95	163.01	142.02	98.03	
1963	7.31	7.07	0.24				412.95	192.03	47.04	6.94	166.94				
1964	8.64	8.34	0.30				438.31	201.65	54.89	7.67	174.10				
1965	9.98	9.48	0.50				460.76	212.37	59.76	5.05	183.58	188.70	160.68	111.38	
1966	10.68	10.19	0.49				462.62	213.36	60.39	3.42	185.45				
1967	10.60	10.12	0.48				478.39	219.13	61.02	2.32	195.92				
1968	10.56	10.03	0.53				516.44	242.90	61.66	1.57	210.31				
1969	10.18	9.66	0.52				536.70	247.11	62.31	1.06	226.22				
1970	10.47	9.94	0.53		97.90	85.81	540.87	244.53	62.97	0.72	232.65	199.65	229.59	111.63	
1971	11.29	10.72	0.57		102.16	84.27	560.29	252.80	68.51	0.72	238.26	202.98	239.25	118.06	
1972	12.51	11.78	0.73		105.48	82.13	576.74	261.26	71.53	0.72	243.23	208.62	249.25	118.87	
1973	13.13	12.28	0.85		113.03	82.37	589.52	266.86	73.67	0.72	248.27	214.69	254.37	120.46	
1974	13.85	12.96	0.89		115.52	78.87	610.16	273.36	77.32	0.72	258.76	220.78	263.62	125.76	
1975	14.66	13.66	1.00		117.46	74.07	646.88	293.84	82.69	1.28	269.07	237.00	277.19	132.69	
1976	15.37	14.37	1.00		115.31	67.64	669.56	312.26	87.01	1.28	269.01	241.25	287.53	140.78	
1977	16.00	15.05	0.95		128.48	70.69	679.65	320.76	87.46	1.28	270.15	243.95	295.41	140.29	
1978	18.18	16.92	1.26		153.76	75.40	696.09	336.30	86.51	0.83	272.45	240.05	306.84	149.20	
1979	24.88	22.96	1.92		161.89	78.20	707.13	340.99	91.06	0.78	274.30	224.84	329.27	153.02	
1980	30.20	27.64	2.56		167.21	80.41	726.14	351.90	95.02	1.11	277.75	212.04	353.50	160.60	
1981	32.92	29.52	3.40		164.77	76.86	746.15	363.77	100.68	1.35	279.59	204.85	373.70	167.60	
1982	37.94	32.68	5.26		164.19	73.44	758.22	371.20	103.96	2.32	278.89	194.34	386.87	177.01	
1983	45.97	40.17	5.80		159.50	65.65	761.91	377.52	105.49	2.90	274.06	176.60	403.50	181.81	
1984	56.10	50.13	5.97		169.21	63.01	761.03	376.08	107.45	3.71	268.05	150.57	421.37	189.09	
1985	70.09	62.79	7.30		188.01	58.53	763.52	383.34	106.03	4.08	263.94	126.75	442.27	194.50	
1986	90.95	80.69	10.26		179.90	40.68	766.35	392.10	104.44	3.77	258.97	111.44	453.09	201.82	
1987	120.33	106.79	13.54		173.49	34.11	771.11	399.21	103.07	5.16	255.85	102.47	459.07	209.57	
1988	141.21	125.74	15.47		184.23	31.98	771.62	405.16	99.59	5.51	250.75	93.12	462.08	216.42	
1989	195.60	175.10	20.50		182.06	27.58	761.50	393.76	104.81	5.73	246.05	88.66	458.20	216.96	

9. Shanghai

9–7

Year	v5c1	v5d	v6a	v6a1	v6a2	v6b	v6c	v6d1	v6d2	v6d3	v6d4	v6d5	v6d6
1949			502.92	452.63	50.29			467.75	35.17	274.87	228.05	418.94	
1950			492.73	443.46	49.27	24.2	8.5	457.35	35.38	266.03	226.70		
1951			552.20	500.48	51.72	45.9	14.1	516.45	35.75	300.52	251.68		
1952			572.63	525.20	47.43	39.1	8.8	536.08	36.55	310.72	261.91	505.76	
1953			615.24	564.79	50.45	42.9	8.8	577.15	38.09	332.23	283.01		
1954			662.71	609.81	52.90	52.6	7.1	622.57	40.14	353.56	309.15		
1955			623.10	573.25	49.85	41.7	8.1	582.76	40.34	328.43	294.67		
1956			634.94	584.03	50.91	40.5	6.8	596.75	38.19	329.99	304.95		
1957			689.69	633.72	55.97	45.6	6.0	651.65	38.04	358.22	331.47	609.83	
1958			750.80	665.00	85.80	36.0	5.9	686.45	64.35	385.45	365.35	578.13	
1959			1028.39	692.27	336.12	27.8	6.9	702.98	325.41	519.48	508.91		
1960			1056.30	715.85	340.45	27.6	6.8	724.11	332.19	533.66	522.64		
1961			1058.99	714.07	344.92	22.4	7.7	722.97	336.02	528.94	530.05	641.21	
1962			1057.86	698.71	359.15	26.3	7.3	707.21	350.65	523.99	533.87	635.84	
1963			1073.64	698.93	374.71	30.3	7.0	710.15	363.49	532.82	540.82	639.00	
1964			1086.22	695.12	391.10	20.6	6.1	712.83	373.39	529.12	547.10	642.79	
1965			1093.79	697.69	396.10	17.0	5.7	716.04	377.75	543.15	550.64	643.07	
1966			1095.83	691.58	404.25	14.6	5.3	708.53	387.30	544.40	551.43		
1967			1105.72	695.65	410.07	12.5	5.1	722.07	383.65	550.83	554.89		
1968			1108.97	688.87	420.10	14.9	5.3	717.25	391.72	552.60	556.37		
1969			1093.99	662.06	431.93	14.8	4.7	694.20	399.79	542.65	551.34		
1970			1072.55	632.61	439.94	13.9	5.0	662.00	410.55	531.92	540.63	580.23	
1971			1066.82	623.89	442.93	12.2	5.2	645.10	421.72	528.08	538.74		
1972			1064.11	619.42	444.69	10.8	5.6	640.29	423.82	525.94	538.17		
1973			1070.01	618.13	451.88	10.2	5.5	636.70	433.31	529.76	540.25		
1974			1073.78	617.72	456.06	9.2	5.8	640.19	433.59	531.74	542.04		
1975			1076.72	613.60	463.12	9.4	6.0	638.37	438.35	533.10	543.62	557.05	
1976			1081.30	607.35	473.95	10.2	6.1	637.33	443.97	535.33	545.97		
1977			1086.47	602.66	483.81	10.8	6.5	632.41	454.06	537.68	548.79		
1978			1098.28	615.01	483.27	11.3	6.2	645.23	453.05	542.70	555.58	557.38	
1979			1132.14	654.41	477.73	12.3	6.1	687.38	444.76	560.40	571.74		
1980			1146.52	667.06	479.46	11.8	6.5	702.43	444.09	569.30	577.22	601.29	
1981			1162.84	680.70	482.14	16.8	6.5	715.08	447.76	578.76	584.08		
1982			1180.51	695.29	485.22	18.5	6.3	731.31	449.20	588.82	591.69		
1983			1194.01	711.24	482.77	15.4	6.9	745.86	448.15	596.67	597.34		
1984			1204.78	737.58	467.20	13.7	6.5	760.75	444.03	602.59	602.19		
1985			1216.69	749.72	466.97	12.7	6.7	776.37	440.32	609.70	606.99	698.30	
1986			1232.33	780.01	452.32	14.5	6.5	802.56	429.77	618.88	613.45	710.16	
1987			1249.51	798.86	450.65	15.3	6.7	822.31	427.20	628.78	620.73	721.77	
1988			1262.42	812.20	450.22	13.2	6.8	838.93	423.49	635.82	626.60	732.65	
1989			1276.00	858.70	417.75	12.5	6.6	855.84	420.61	643.51	632.94	777.79	

9. Shanghai

9–8

Year	v7a	v7b	v7c	v7d	v7e	v7f	v7g	v7h	v7h1	v7h2	v7h3	v7h4	v7h5	v7i	v8a
1949				996.37											
1950				1069.51		0.34									
1951				1104.54		0.49									
1952				1111.65		1.14		3.43	2.77	0.02	0.41	0.07	0.16		66.60
1953				1069.79		1.71		3.70	3.02	0.02	0.42	0.08	0.16		91.50
1954				1096.37		2.45		3.36	2.59	0.02	0.50	0.11	0.14		96.37
1955				1124.13		3.27		3.79	3.06	0.02	0.46	0.12	0.13		91.42
1956				1203.47		4.21		3.87	3.10	0.02	0.50	0.11	0.14		113.92
1957	0.12	4.5	47.3	1150.89		4.21		4.13	3.37	0.01	0.42	0.17	0.16		118.82
1958		6.0	69.2	1120.65		6.48		5.71	5.18	0.02	0.21	0.16	0.15		176.43
1959		16.0	136.5	1015.49		9.23		6.61	5.81	0.03	0.36	0.24	0.17		254.68
1960		42.5	246.6	1060.08		10.51		6.69	5.81	0.03	0.33	0.27	0.25	9.80	298.97
1961		41.4	321.2	1140.92		8.22		6.73	6.10	0.03	0.26	0.28	0.06	8.90	187.43
1962	1.15	42.6	366.6	1139.49		11.05		7.61	6.78	0.03	0.27	0.31	0.22	8.44	151.98
1963		46.6	393.1	1130.13		12.71		7.66	6.93	0.03	0.23	0.32	0.15	7.98	168.91
1964		67.7	411.6	1132.45		23.20		9.61	8.44	0.04	0.50	0.49	0.13	7.28	196.95
1965	1.44	95.5	425.5	1184.74		37.19	1.28	10.61	8.76	0.04	1.04	0.62	0.15	7.40	230.77
1966		110.5	426.9	1200.75		39.43	1.69	10.77	8.81	0.04	1.20	0.57	0.15	6.86	259.59
1967		132.1	454.4	1164.63		43.36	2.02	11.09	8.84	0.03	1.19	0.47	0.36	5.84	226.88
1968		173.8	474.5	1174.70		39.51	2.10	12.34	9.74	0.02	1.43	0.63	0.52	5.71	251.87
1969		276.2	483.4	1222.43		49.94	2.52	12.54	9.66	0.02	1.80	0.56	0.50	5.57	284.42
1970	5.00	386.0	495.6	1247.92		53.00	2.81	12.29	9.33	0.03	1.95	0.40	0.58	5.40	312.18
1971		413.5	513.6	1268.19		60.90	3.70	12.71	8.92	0.04	2.46	0.65	0.64	4.97	336.52
1972		415.0	525.6	1272.92		63.86	4.59	14.24	10.60	0.03	2.66	0.54	0.41	4.77	355.39
1973		481.8	531.3	1283.84		78.63	4.85	13.89	10.03	0.06	2.52	0.54	0.74	4.36	
1974		454.6	533.9	1209.09		71.55	5.70	14.96	11.45	0.06	2.16	0.52	0.77	4.08	398.40
1975	13.69	492.6	533.6	1293.39		75.73	6.45	14.17	9.70	0.07	3.03	0.74	0.63	3.90	420.37
1976		491.2	531.9	1275.17		74.94	7.33	15.95	11.24	0.08	3.35	0.57	0.71	3.62	423.45
1977		503.2	533.6	1274.93		65.92	7.67	14.72	10.57	0.06	3.24	0.58	0.27	3.27	458.40
1978	18.71	461.3	530.1	1242.88		87.43	8.93	18.26	13.49	0.06	3.67	0.86	0.18	3.13	514.01
1979	20.36	463.9	524.0	1237.12		102.25	10.82	20.41	15.10	0.04	4.22	0.90	0.15	3.06	556.30
1980	21.48	467.1	523.8	1163.97		103.56	12.23	18.90	11.40	0.06	6.27	0.97	0.20	2.78	598.75
1981	21.95	478.2	520.4	1137.77		102.42	13.65	20.33	11.91	0.21	6.38	1.23	0.60	2.61	620.12
1982	22.56	479.2	521.1	1138.58		100.10	15.04	23.97	13.80	0.23	7.81	1.56	0.57	2.46	634.65
1983	23.08	492.5	519.3	1145.70		95.37	16.60	22.68	12.59	0.20	7.80	1.29	0.80	2.23	663.53
1984	23.18	484.5	512.5	1103.96		89.50	18.48	26.59	16.41	0.21	8.06	1.40	0.51	1.94	728.12
1985	23.66	465.8	502.6	1044.10		72.42	21.87	31.38	15.63	0.21	12.25	2.82	0.47	1.58	862.73
1986	24.74	453.3	490.2	1018.54		85.36	25.63	33.76	16.83	0.24	12.75	3.45	0.49	1.43	952.21
1987	25.61	444.7	490.3	1005.35		91.70	28.58	38.84	17.69	0.34	15.48	4.79	0.54	1.27	1067.31
1988	26.77	434.1	485.3	971.88		90.80	30.78	53.07	22.47	0.45	22.18	7.43	0.54	1.11	1295.89
1989	27.71	444.3	480.7	954.40			30.43	60.63	25.54	0.39	26.41	7.87	0.42	1.04	1515.35

9. Shanghai

9–9

Year	v8a1	v8a2	v8a3	v8b	v8c1	v8c2	v8d	v8f1	v8f2	v8f3	v8f4	v8f5	v8g
1949								0.52			10.09	3.79	20307
1950								2.10			8.81	6.26	
1951								3.40			11.92	11.67	
1952	17.76	0.23	48.61					7.14			13.19	11.35	25878
1953	24.40	1.38	65.72					14.28		1.25	15.77	14.09	
1954	28.63	1.56	66.18					22.71		2.17	17.11	17.28	
1955	28.90	2.42	60.10					31.81		8.71	15.26	15.11	
1956	36.59	4.29	73.04					40.37		15.17	18.91	18.99	
1957	36.01	5.56	77.25					51.82		18.59	18.89	17.04	16316
1958	173.44	2.35	0.64					122.26		21.68	28.24	20.27	14240
1959	251.15	3.41	0.12					179.15		24.23	43.30	45.44	12205
1960	294.04	4.93						251.94		23.36	55.12	72.90	13488
1961	182.37	5.06						165.22		70.29	42.16	40.37	11447
1962	147.75	4.09	0.14					120.77		101.70	38.08	24.98	8809
1963	164.84	4.01	0.06					140.33		102.73	47.72	42.70	8522
1964	190.96	5.93	0.06					196.97		110.10	52.14	59.23	8343
1965	223.98	6.72	0.07		101.21	129.56		242.00		113.68	65.10	67.58	8189
1966	251.77	7.77	0.05		116.72	142.87		263.11		115.41	72.07	72.85	
1967	219.05	7.79	0.04		95.19	131.69		218.18		126.22	67.40	59.76	
1968	243.02	8.80	0.05		107.42	144.45		212.13		142.34	72.79	57.90	
1969	274.31	10.07	0.04		125.86	158.56		259.24		155.91	81.71	70.15	
1970	299.53	12.61	0.04	294.64	150.07	162.11	110.20	301.42		231.37	89.97	85.96	9834
1971	318.43	18.09		312.70	178.63	157.89	115.07	352.67		344.25	101.47	94.48	9307
1972	333.90	21.49		327.89	189.34	166.05	118.37	388.71		336.84	116.26	96.46	9327
1973				352.70	201.65	181.68	126.27	428.02		326.48	123.83	97.96	9069
1974	369.14	29.26		359.91	205.12	193.28	128.13	375.17		370.80	138.18	104.10	8867
1975	386.06	34.31		376.41	216.40	203.97	135.13	398.00		362.01	152.06	119.49	8743
1976	385.98	37.47		376.33	215.63	207.82	134.34	373.80		447.16	168.84	121.53	8798
1977	419.49	38.91		403.38	224.46	233.94	148.02	409.04		534.74	175.22	116.63	8572
1978	471.36	42.66		457.71	247.99	266.02	174.55	476.52		590.61	199.32	139.47	7962
1979	505.88	50.41	0.01	493.62	265.52	290.78	183.85	494.07		588.94	209.96	153.91	6770
1980	526.93	65.58	6.24	514.72	267.62	331.13	189.68	521.61		607.43	206.41	161.28	7149
1981	532.12	77.79	10.21	518.84	260.00	360.12	190.30	506.30		566.84	204.69	177.42	8017
1982	538.99	82.71	12.95	524.72	275.03	359.62	190.18	494.26		569.48	219.90	187.28	8368
1983	552.73	94.68	16.12	536.63	299.61	363.92	186.66	511.64		579.80	224.77	197.22	8562
1984	595.73	114.92	17.47	584.04	332.52	395.60	204.40	549.17		577.16	245.38	209.84	8764
1985	672.87	160.40	29.46	661.58	406.14	456.59	227.82	570.16		610.10	256.25	219.31	10656
1986	734.22	177.10	40.89	722.38	459.12	493.09	226.75	801.39		650.77	267.63	227.28	11029
1987	790.30	204.81	72.20	777.11	516.88	556.96	229.99	866.92		662.41	276.34	232.81	11812
1988	913.26	266.60	116.03	895.98	625.49	679.17	259.29	859.80			280.59	261.84	12431
1989	1049.38	317.21	148.77	1027.78	725.82	789.32	279.29	808.78			278.33	251.85	13277

9. Shanghai

9–10

Year	v8g1	v9a	v9a1	v9a2	v9a3	v9b	v9b1	v9b2	v9b3	v9c	v10a	v10a1	v10b1	v10b2	v10b3
1949					0.61				0.86	3205					
1950					1.28				1.24	3169	15.00	14.87			
1951					1.60			0.27	1.29	3312	21.74	21.54			
1952					1.51			0.66	1.28	3247	19.79	19.50			
1953					2.01			0.94	2.20	3651	25.92	25.56			
1954					2.20			0.95	2.44	3454	24.03	23.58			
1955					1.63			0.68	2.06	3284	22.21	21.64			
1956					1.75			1.08	2.16	3403	25.27	24.63			
1957					1.61			1.14	2.10	3509	26.22	25.61			
1958					1.44			1.90	2.07	3762	28.18	27.07			
1959					0.75			3.52	4.22	4151	31.36	29.89			
1960					0.88			4.95	6.16	4464	34.17	32.24			
1961					1.06			3.36	4.08	4334	31.02	29.43			
1962					0.94			2.64	3.47	4167	28.51	27.19			
1963					0.69			2.47	4.01	4091	27.03	25.82			
1964					0.75			2.23	4.58	4210	28.02	26.55			
1965					0.83			2.59	4.91	4331	29.15	27.13			
1966					0.94			2.90	5.04	4397	30.95	28.72			
1967					1.19			2.86	4.94	4450	32.93	30.78			
1968					1.24			3.11	5.26	4308	32.15	29.94			
1969					1.43			3.54	5.54	4585	35.40	32.57			
1970	2678		4.45		1.21			3.90	6.10	4730	34.55	31.85			
1971	2654		4.07		1.52			4.29	6.55	4713	36.14	32.91			
1972	2638		4.68		1.96			4.62	7.60	5023	39.94	36.15			
1973	2590		5.11		2.23			5.43	8.56	5434	44.16	39.79			
1974	2598		8.45		2.46			5.56	9.97	5721	48.52	44.06			
1975	2592		9.33		2.78		23.63	5.82	11.39	5984	52.80	47.71			
1976	2592		15.01		3.21		24.02	5.74	12.42	6384	55.80	49.98			
1977	2587		13.44		3.14			5.95	13.12	6546	54.92	49.28			
1978	2595		11.44	0.92	3.36		30.13	7.10	14.51	6979	60.81	54.10	41.51		19.11
1979	2566		13.04	1.03	3.41		31.48	7.69	15.72	8044	75.72	68.28	48.70		26.53
1980	2483		15.67	1.24	2.43		32.66	7.98	15.75	9016	88.16	80.43	56.33		30.72
1981	2449		17.17	1.37	2.25		32.11	8.34	16.27	9383	95.27	88.73	58.53		34.86
1982	2410		17.54	1.39	2.16		32.49	8.97	18.00	10005	97.33	89.80	59.08		36.32
1983	2426		18.89	2.48	2.51		32.82	9.54	18.62	11369	108.87	100.68	65.64		40.28
1984	2696		21.59	3.25	2.69		35.01	10.31	20.89	12911	132.38	123.72	78.23		49.84
1985	2702		24.30	4.32	3.05		36.62	11.07	22.50	15494	183.16	173.39	105.52		66.31
1986	2656		25.89	6.43	3.33		37.68	12.59	23.41	17355	208.27	196.84	115.17		77.06
1987	2660		28.93	8.08	3.44		38.14	12.14	23.94	20368	238.75	225.25	127.10		89.82
1988	2629		31.83	8.61	3.59		37.40	13.32	26.09	29050	313.49	295.83	166.94		116.20
1989	2673		29.92	8.24	3.69		39.48	12.72	24.65	36652	352.79	331.38	182.49		134.96

9. Shanghai

Year	v10b4	v10b5	v10b6	v10d	v11a1	v11a2	v11a3	v11b	v11b1	v11b2	v11c	v11d	v12a	v12b	v12c
1949								0.93	0.82	0.11					
1950			0.24					1.19	1.04	0.15					
1951			0.28					1.08	1.00	0.08					
1952			0.26		0.85	0.33	0.01	1.25	1.19	0.06					
1953			0.13		1.17	0.64	0.02	1.89	1.83	0.06			106.9	105.8	105.8
1954			0.08		1.74	0.97	0.03	3.17	2.74	0.43			101.8	101.9	98.6
1955			0.08		1.95	1.54	0.11	3.94	3.60	0.34			101.6	101.4	100.9
1956			0.08		2.31	2.31	0.15	4.98	4.77	0.21			100.8	100.4	103.0
1957			0.05		1.67	2.62	0.23	4.90	4.52	0.38			100.9	100.8	100.5
1958			0.07		2.81	3.14	0.34	6.95	6.29	0.66			100.0	100.0	102.6
1959			0.09		3.07	3.99	0.36	7.96	7.42	0.54			100.2	100.2	98.6
1960			0.10		1.79	3.76	0.65	6.73	6.20	0.53			100.4	100.4	102.3
1961			0.24		0.89	4.08	0.58	5.81	5.55	0.26			106.4	105.1	109.4
1962			0.37		1.00	3.82	0.72	5.79	5.54	0.25			99.1	99.4	99.8
1963			0.17		1.46	3.73	0.76	6.19	5.95	0.24			92.9	93.9	99.6
1964			0.09		1.89	3.65	0.98	6.89	6.52	0.37			97.4	97.8	99.6
1965			0.07		2.64	3.90	1.11	8.25	7.65	0.60			101.0	100.6	98.8
1966					3.03	4.33	1.38	9.12	8.74	0.38			96.4	96.9	103.2
1967					3.02	4.20	1.20	8.89	8.42	0.47			101.1	100.9	100.2
1968					3.18	4.31	1.00	8.83	8.49	0.34			99.9	99.9	99.3
1969					2.95	4.57	1.24	8.92	8.76	0.16			100.5	100.4	101.1
1970					3.13	4.43	1.11	9.13	8.67	0.46			99.5	99.6	99.4
1971					3.39	4.84	1.58	10.39	9.81	0.58			100.0	100.0	101.6
1972					4.17	7.60	1.53	13.93	13.30	0.63			99.9	99.9	100.4
1973					9.26	11.77	2.13	23.97	23.16	0.81			100.2	100.2	102.3
1974					10.16	11.35	2.88	25.37	24.39	0.98			99.8	99.8	99.7
1975					8.30	10.85	3.05	23.28	22.20	1.08			100.1	100.1	100.4
1976					5.99	11.15	2.64	21.03	19.78	1.25			99.8	99.4	98.9
1977					6.85	12.73	2.63	23.21	22.21	1.00			100.4	100.3	100.6
1978		0.19			9.02	16.36	3.55	30.26	28.93	1.33			100.5	100.5	102.4
1979		0.20	0.29	13.79	10.42	20.85	5.48	38.78	36.75	2.03			101.0	100.9	118.0
1980		0.24	0.87	14.05	11.28	23.25	8.13	45.06	42.66	2.40	0.34		106.5	105.9	105.4
1981	0.04	0.29	1.55	14.55	8.46	21.95	7.66	41.50	38.07	3.43	0.50		101.5	101.4	102.8
1982	0.03	0.32	1.58	17.14	8.63	20.37	7.05	38.93	36.05	2.88	0.86		100.3	100.3	99.8
1983	0.02	0.69	2.24	18.60	9.22	20.52	6.74	41.40	36.48	4.92	1.41		100.1	100.2	103.1
1984	0.02	1.70	2.59	19.67	9.23	20.76	5.88	44.00	35.87	8.13	4.69	0.42	102.2	102.2	103.9
1985	0.19	6.42	4.72	24.74	7.67	19.66	6.28	51.74	33.61	18.13	8.16	1.15	116.4	115.2	122.7
1986	0.67	8.47	6.90	30.07	7.15	22.56	6.11	52.04	35.82	16.22	6.24	2.61	106.7	106.3	90.4
1987	0.89	11.46	9.48	35.81	7.55	25.76	8.29	59.95	41.60	18.35	10.92	7.00	108.8	108.1	103.9
1988	1.71	14.56	14.08	45.35	7.52	28.50	10.03	72.45	46.05	26.40	10.55	13.22	121.3	120.1	121.4
1989	1.76	16.15	17.42	56.94				78.48	50.32	28.16	12.02	11.90	116.7	115.9	124.7

9. Shanghai

9–12

Year	v13a	v13b	v13c1	v13c2	v13c3	v13d	v14a	v14b	v14c	v15a	v15b	v15c	v15d	v15e	v15f
1949			2.02	10.45	48.17					562.50					
1950			2.29	11.35	58.11	0.44			2.27	570.51					
1951	10.8		2.21	12.92	72.78	0.38			4.00	579.00					
1952	9.6		2.23	18.90	91.17	0.58	13970	18800	3.78	580.95					
1953	12.4		2.34	20.80	88.50	0.69			4.54	581.72					
1954	12.4		2.74	25.00	95.04	0.57			4.74	580.06					
1955	16.9		3.01	27.91	100.41	0.71			4.96	582.98					
1956	22.4		3.99	35.90	114.37	0.63			7.18	580.50					
1957	21.9		3.87	39.09	124.48	0.69			6.08	573.76					
1958	7.1		4.58	46.28	155.13	0.66			7.91	559.36					
1959	6.0		5.59	44.62	162.91	0.48			6.27	545.33					
1960	8.3		6.34	49.73	179.16	0.99			5.01	543.51					
1961	11.2		6.36	48.93	178.80	1.05			3.65	542.08					
1962	23.0		5.86	51.03	175.94	1.27			3.85	544.47					
1963	18.3		5.36	55.86	183.88	1.45			4.66	545.76					
1964	14.9		5.29	66.42	199.17	1.17			5.58	546.47					
1965	14.1		5.20	72.63	207.92	1.21	31671	49000	6.72	551.50					
1966	18.6		5.27	54.86	202.60				7.99	551.46					
1967	22.2		4.80	52.98	199.72	0.46			8.83	550.50					
1968	23.1		2.86	57.52	192.44	1.90			6.96	550.97					
1969	14.3		2.18	77.30	169.86	0.68			5.29	549.17					
1970	12.0		0.38	71.60	164.59	2.12			6.73	547.23					
1971	13.6		0.35	76.58	155.73	0.04			7.73	548.75					
1972	13.0		0.81	103.81	163.52	0.03			8.79	548.75					
1973	10.5		1.68	125.32	152.33	0.06			7.95	547.11					
1974	8.6		2.51	115.11	138.23	0.26			10.17	548.96					
1975	7.0		3.13	111.81	123.93	0.48			9.98	547.05					
1976	9.1		3.36	113.26	104.83	1.00			9.69	543.15					
1977	11.1		3.56	122.91	84.06	1.23			9.41	544.72					
1978	7.8	99.3	5.66	101.81	87.06	1.03	46791	85000	10.80	540.19					
1979	9.1		6.74	90.80	88.00	0.04			12.63	533.64					
1980	15.1	99.2	7.67	71.68	85.47	1.18	49363	94100	15.39	531.08					
1981	17.0		9.11	58.83	83.22	0.36			18.32	529.09					
1982	16.3	99.5	8.39	61.69	78.88	2.66			23.31	527.48					
1983	16.7	99.8	7.87	60.53	79.82	2.91			25.29	524.90					
1984	13.2	99.9	8.99	60.93	83.48	1.84			28.10	518.63					
1985	12.6	99.9	10.79	63.50	84.18	1.93	53232	104200	27.95	509.36					
1986	11.3	99.8	11.77	64.82	86.56	2.39			26.63	499.55					
1987	13.2	99.9	12.25	64.50	89.35	3.09			29.84	496.30					
1988	12.4	99.9	12.82	61.21	98.39	3.06	58933	114600	28.37	490.79					
1989		99.9	12.61	52.94	107.10	3.25	60427	116500	21.00	486.02					

Notes

1. National Output and Income (Y)

v1a: (E), p.315
 v1a1: (E), p.315
 v1a2: (E), p.315—data of 1987–89 include output value of electricity established by raised funds
 v1a3: (E), p.315
 v1a4: (E), p.315
 v1a5: (E), p.315

v1b: (A)
 v1b1: (A)
 v1b2: (A)
 v1b3: (A)
 v1b4: (A)
 v1b5: (A)

v1c: v1a – v1d

v1d: (E), p.312
 v1d1: (E), p.312
 v1d2: (E), p.312
 v1d3: (E), p.312
 v1d4: (E), p.312
 v1d5: (E), p.312

v1e: (A); (D), p.205
 v1e1: (A)
 v1e2: (A)
 v1e3: (A)
 v1e4: (A)
 v1e5: (A)

v1f: (E), p.311
 v1f1: (E), p.311
 v1f2: (E), p.311
 v1f3: (E), p.311

v1g: v2a + v3a, excluding net national income outflow; (E), p.314—1988: 525.16

v1h: (A); (E), p.340

v1i: (A); (E), p.339—excluding meat price subsidies

v1j: (E), p.339—(ditto)
 v1j1: (E), p.339—(ditto)
 v1j2: (E), p.339—(ditto)
 v1j3: (B), p.453; (C), 1989, p.460–461

v1k: (E), p.339—figures of 1984 and before exclude various kinds of jointly-owned units

2. Investment (I)

v2a: (E), p.314
 v2a1: (A); (D), p.207
 v2a2: (A); (D), p.207

v2b: (A)

v2c: (A); (E), p.330
 v2c1: (E), p.331
 v2c2: (E), p.331

v2d:
 v2d1: (E), p.328
 v2d2: (E), p.328

v2e: (E), p.328

3. Consumption (C)

v3a: v3b + v3c; (E), p.314

v3b: (A); (D), p.206; (E), p.314—1988: 196.22
 v3b1: (A)
 v3b2: (A)

v3c: (A); (D), p.206; (E), p.314—1988: 41.03

v3d: (E), p.338
 v3d1: (E), p.338

v3d2: (E), p.338

v3e: (E), p.340
v3e1: (E), p.340
v3e2: (A)
v3e3: (A)
v3e4: (A)

v3f: (A); (E), p.340
v3f1: (A); (E), p.340
v3f2: (A)
v3f3: (A)
v3f4: (A)

4. Public Finance and Banking (FB)

v4a:
v4a1: (E), p.336
v4a1a: (E), p.336
v4a1b: NA
v4a1c: NA
v4a1d: v4a1 – v4a1a – v4a1b' (v4a1b':total tax revenues which come from (E), p.336)
v4a2: (E), p.336
v4a2a: (E), p.336
v4a2b: (E), p.336
v4a2c: (E), p.336
v4a2d: v4a2 – v4a2a – v4a2b – v4a2c

v4b: (A)
v4b1: (A); (C), 1989, p.488
v4b2: (C), 1989, p.488—rural savings
v4b3: NA

v4c:
v4c1: (E), p.328
v4c2: (E), p.328

5. Labor Force (L)

v5a: (A); (E), p.310—figures of 1980 and afterward include other labor force in the society
v5a1: (E), p.310
v5a2: (E), p.310
v5a3: (E), p.310
v5a4: (E), p.310

v5b:
v5b1: (E), p.310
v5b2: (E), p.310
v5b3: (E), p.310

v5c: NA
v5c1: NA

v5d: NA

6. Population (PO)

v6a: (E), p.309—year-end population are based on administrative region defined by Shanghai public security department. In 1958 ten counties were incorporated into Shanghai from Jiangsu province, which resulted in larger variation in population figures
v6a1: (E), p.309—(ditto)
v6a2: (E), p.309—(ditto)

v6b: (E), p.309—(ditto)

v6c: (E), p.309—(ditto)

v6d:
v6d1: (E), p.309—(ditto)
v6d2: (E), p.309—(ditto)
v6d3: (E), p.309—(ditto)
v6d4: (E), p.309—(ditto)
v6d5: (A)
v6d6: NA

7. Agriculture (A)

v7a: (A); (E), p.322

v7b: (A); (E), p.322

v7c: (A); (E), p.322

v7d: (A); (E), p.322

v7e: NA

v7f: (A)

v7g: (A); (E), p.322

v7h: (E), p.317
- v7h1: (A); (E), p.317
- v7h2: (E), p.317
- v7h3: (E), p.317
- v7h4: (A); (E), p.317
- v7h5: (E), p.317

v7i: (E), p.321

8. Industry (IN)

v8a: (E), p.323—data of 1987–89 include output value of electricity established by raised funds
- v8a1: (E), p.323
- v8a2: (E), p.323
- v8a3: v8a – v8a1 – v8a2

v8b: (E), p.328

- v8c1: (A); (E), p.315
- v8c2: (A); (E), p.315

v8d: (E), p.328

v8f:
- v8f1: (E), p.327
- v8f2: NA
- v8f3: (E), p.327—after processing
- v8f4: (E), p.327
- v8f5: (E), p.327

v8g: (A)
- v8g1: (E), p.328

9. Transport (TR)

v9a: NA
- v9a1: (E), p.329—excluding urban traffic volume, but including central and local railways
- v9a2: (E), p.329—data from transport department, excluding urban traffic volume
- v9a3: (E), p.329—excluding distant ocean and coastal passenger traffic

v9b: NA
- v9b1: (E), p.329—including central and local railways
- v9b2: (E), p.329—data from transport department
- v9b3: (E), p.329—excluding distant ocean and coastal freight volume

v9c: (E), p.329

10. Domestic Trade (DT)

v10a: (E), p.332
- v10a1: (E), p.332

v10b:
- v10b1: (E), p.332
- v10b2: NA
- v10b3: (E), p.332—including supply and marketing cooperative and other collectives
- v10b4: (E), p.332
- v10b5: (E), p.332
- v10b6: (E), p.332

v10d: (E), p.334—calculated on calendar year basis

11. Foreign Trade (FT)

v11a:
- v11a1: (C), 1989, p.351
- v11a2: (C), 1989, p.351—textile and other products of light industry
- v11a3: (C), 1989, p.351—heavy industrial products

v11b: (E), p.335
- v11b1: (E), p.335
- v11b2: v11b – v11b1

v11c: (E), p.334

v11d: (E), p.334

12. Prices (PR)

v12a: (E), p.337

v12b: (E), p.337

v12c: (E), p.337

13. Education (ED)

v13a: (A)

v13b: (A); (E), p.340

v13c:
- v13c1: (A); (E), p.340
- v13c2: (A); (E), p.340—technical, teachers training and ordinary secondary schools
- v13c3: (A); (E), p.340

v13d: (C), 1987, p.319; 1989, p.386—institutions of higher learning

14. Social Factors (SF)

v14a: (E), p.340

v14b: (E), p.340

v14c: (A); data of 1971 comes from (C), 1989, p.406–408

15. Natural Environment (NE)

v15a: (C), 1989, p.214; (E), p.322

v15b: NA

v15c: NA

v15d: NA

v15e: NA

v15f: NA

Sources of Data

(A) Data supplied by the DSNEB, SSB, the PRC.
(B) Statistical Bureau of Shanghai Municipality ed. *New Shanghai Forty Years*, Beijing: CSPH, 1989.
(C) ________ ed. *Statistical Yearbook of Shanghai*, Beijing: CSPH, various issues.
(D) Same as (D) in Beijing's sources of data.
(E) Same as (E) in Beijing's sources of data.

10

Jiangsu

10. Jiangsu

10–1

Year	v1a	v1a1	v1a2	v1a3	v1a4	v1a5	v1b	v1b1	v1b2	v1b3	v1b4	v1b5	v1c	v1d	v1d1
1949		22.59	15.89												
1950		24.27	19.00												
1951		27.37	22.55												
1952	65.64	31.87	25.53	1.66	1.00	5.58							30.01	35.63	23.46
1953	74.64	32.31	29.81	2.70	1.23	8.59	110.3	100.9	117.6	158.2	119.3	149.4	34.36	40.28	23.78
1954	76.80	32.45	31.66	3.15	1.51	8.03	102.2	100.7	107.5	115.8	121.6	92.9	36.63	40.17	23.61
1955	82.10	36.22	32.82	2.95	1.53	8.58	108.0	111.3	102.6	94.6	103.0	107.8	37.34	44.76	27.33
1956	86.73	33.60	38.60	2.83	1.72	9.98	103.0	93.4	125.1	93.5	109.6	113.4	40.37	46.36	25.49
1957	93.13	36.81	41.01	3.62	1.92	9.77	102.6	103.4	102.3	122.3	106.6	93.6	44.44	48.69	27.42
1958	134.88	38.74	75.22	7.44	3.81	9.67	119.3	101.7	159.2	169.3	163.5	81.5	76.76	58.12	26.30
1959	157.08	37.35	96.00	8.12	5.26	10.35	112.8	93.3	139.3	105.6	133.8	103.8	96.33	60.75	22.94
1960	161.45	36.76	100.32	10.34	5.41	8.62	101.5	92.1	109.6	125.8	101.3	82.2	95.15	66.30	22.23
1961	115.05	35.73	62.50	4.70	2.72	9.40	76.5	96.9	62.3	48.8	54.2	116.9	62.73	52.32	22.51
1962	107.61	40.15	53.36	3.02	2.62	8.46	90.9	101.1	82.9	62.4	93.5	87.5	57.75	49.86	26.08
1963	115.95	46.77	54.66	3.70	3.10	7.72	112.0	119.5	103.3	127.6	123.0	94.9	59.45	56.50	32.28
1964	141.11	56.62	68.17	4.36	3.50	8.46	120.2	118.5	126.4	116.2	111.3	108.2	70.79	70.32	39.41
1965	168.52	57.27	88.08	9.41	4.52	9.24	121.0	105.7	134.1	216.9	129.6	126.2	93.63	74.89	37.95
1966	197.87	66.08	104.19	10.86	5.23	11.51	118.4	116.5	122.7	117.4	117.9	110.0	109.44	88.43	44.05
1967	169.23	61.19	84.80	8.26	4.03	10.95	87.6	92.4	81.6	77.8	78.7	97.4	90.62	78.61	40.86
1968	174.35	65.38	85.48	7.80	4.22	11.47	102.9	103.4	103.0	94.4	104.7	104.6	93.12	81.23	43.60
1969	197.60	65.60	102.80	11.79	4.92	12.49	112.1	99.3	124.6	149.5	115.3	107.7	109.03	88.57	43.75
1970	240.04	71.33	135.47	14.18	5.70	13.36	121.5	107.7	137.8	120.2	115.8	106.9	136.32	103.72	47.44
1971	286.03	79.90	167.15	17.46	6.75	14.77	117.9	111.0	123.8	121.9	117.3	109.4	164.96	121.07	53.41
1972	309.07	83.24	183.38	18.80	7.50	16.15	107.3	102.7	110.4	106.9	110.3	108.6	179.78	129.29	55.84
1973	343.86	89.71	208.10	19.85	8.01	18.19	110.7	106.7	114.1	105.1	106.4	112.1	201.54	142.32	60.15
1974	342.53	89.88	205.39	21.61	7.65	18.00	100.1	100.2	99.3	109.5	96.0	99.5	200.96	141.57	60.67
1975	377.21	91.66	235.28	24.95	8.75	16.57	109.3	100.9	115.5	114.6	113.6	91.4	225.75	151.46	62.62
1976	402.36	100.71	247.59	23.60	11.00	19.46	108.2	103.9	110.3	95.9	127.4	119.1	248.49	153.87	57.10
1977	448.90	89.16	297.12	29.25	12.30	21.07	110.5	90.0	120.1	122.8	110.9	107.3	283.07	165.83	47.71
1978	521.15	105.87	337.65	41.34	13.90	22.39	117.2	121.5	113.8	142.7	114.0	107.3	312.87	208.28	63.00
1979	618.33	145.25	386.05	41.31	14.60	31.12	111.6	110.9	113.9	94.3	99.2	122.8	360.41	257.92	98.19
1980	703.46	138.45	467.82	47.89	14.93	34.37	113.1	94.5	120.9	115.2	101.5	110.4	430.57	272.89	86.90
1981	756.07	153.62	496.23	52.47	15.78	37.97	108.3	107.9	108.3	110.6	106.7	107.5	457.50	298.57	102.60
1982	833.31	188.11	528.85	58.65	18.07	39.63	109.2	114.9	107.7	110.8	113.5	102.0	498.31	335.00	128.42
1983	952.50	206.86	594.86	78.97	21.57	50.24	114.1	105.9	113.9	134.8	119.5	121.6	570.10	382.40	142.88
1984	1173.34	253.82	744.92	90.66	26.03	57.91	120.7	116.4	123.3	112.1	117.9	120.1	707.03	466.31	170.37
1985	1526.66	288.55	1019.26	120.85	30.73	67.27	125.7	103.1	133.4	127.1	112.7	112.4	948.20	578.46	188.72
1986	1834.95	332.66	1234.40	144.78	40.23	82.88	115.0	106.3	116.7	114.7	125.2	116.2	1170.96	663.99	218.13
1987	2316.64	380.25	1587.78	181.54	62.93	104.14	119.4	103.1	123.8	107.4	137.9	114.0	1527.45	789.19	241.79
1988	3075.21	497.95	2149.74	217.88	82.81	126.83	123.5	106.6	125.4	124.4	132.5	130.3	2105.99	969.22	305.47
1989	3458.66	522.26	2500.37	206.08	90.34	139.61	102.5	100.3	104.7	86.1	99.2	100.2	2403.14	1055.52	310.56

10. Jiangsu

10–2

Year	v1d2	v1d3	v1d4	v1d5	v1e	v1e1	v1e2	v1e3	v1e4	v1e5	v1f	v1f1	v1f2	v1f3	v1g
1949															
1950															
1951															
1952	6.86	0.64	0.75	3.92											33.63
1953	8.31	0.89	0.92	6.38	109.10	100.90	122.00	136.00	119.00	157.90					35.77
1954	8.89	0.95	1.14	5.58	99.30	99.50	108.40	105.80	122.40	86.90					35.82
1955	9.08	0.94	1.17	6.24	112.90	115.40	101.00	100.00	104.60	112.90					40.10
1956	11.28	1.16	1.31	7.12	100.60	93.90	132.20	120.30	108.70	111.30					41.31
1957	11.28	1.60	1.50	6.89	100.50	101.50	96.20	131.80	109.80	92.50					43.19
1958	19.04	2.48	2.97	7.33	101.70	92.60	146.50	128.10	162.80	87.70					55.24
1959	23.36	2.35	4.15	7.95	98.10	84.40	133.90	91.50	135.40	105.20					55.47
1960	31.20	2.64	3.30	6.93	102.40	90.70	140.10	110.90	78.40	86.00					62.04
1961	19.38	1.50	2.00	6.93	85.30	100.90	62.20	61.00	65.20	107.20					48.32
1962	14.08	1.21	1.65	6.84	93.40	104.20	70.50	78.30	80.50	96.00					44.47
1963	14.71	1.40	1.85	6.26	118.50	126.90	105.40	120.60	116.20	95.20					51.20
1964	20.41	1.39	2.22	6.89	121.40	119.50	140.60	98.00	118.40	108.70					64.01
1965	24.62	3.32	2.56	6.44	108.70	100.70	123.60	239.60	115.50	108.00					63.80
1966	29.12	3.78	3.01	8.47	117.70	115.80	123.60	116.00	120.00	116.20					74.75
1967	23.70	3.38	2.15	8.52	90.50	92.60	82.60	91.50	83.00	103.00					66.10
1968	23.90	3.02	2.19	8.52	102.30	103.40	102.90	89.20	101.70	99.80					71.25
1969	28.73	3.82	2.73	9.54	107.30	99.30	124.60	125.10	123.30	110.80					73.86
1970	37.87	4.95	3.20	10.26	116.30	107.90	137.70	129.60	117.20	107.50					88.69
1971	46.72	6.06	3.74	11.14	115.10	111.00	124.20	121.20	115.50	107.50					102.60
1972	51.25	6.13	4.10	11.97	105.70	103.00	110.40	100.50	109.00	106.70					108.76
1973	58.16	6.53	4.38	13.10	109.30	106.70	114.10	106.00	106.30	108.80					121.35
1974	57.41	6.85	4.04	12.60	99.80	100.70	99.30	105.40	92.60	96.80					121.33
1975	65.76	7.81	4.63	10.64	105.90	102.20	115.20	113.20	113.90	83.80					130.33
1976	70.95	7.67	4.70	13.45	100.10	86.10	113.30	99.60	102.80	128.20					139.37
1977	88.21	9.74	5.38	14.79	106.10	84.40	124.40	125.80	113.60	109.00					144.69
1978	109.67	13.11	6.07	16.43	127.90	146.80	117.80	135.90	113.90	112.10	249.24	68.71	131.09	49.44	179.23
1979	118.24	13.95	6.37	21.17	113.60	121.50	110.20	100.40	99.10	110.10	300.55	104.04	141.14	55.37	214.90
1980	141.74	15.18	7.18	21.89	104.90	84.80	123.20	108.10	111.80	103.00	321.80	94.24	167.41	60.15	230.35
1981	148.84	15.61	8.08	23.44	109.20	114.20	107.60	103.80	113.70	101.20	350.91	109.39	175.40	66.12	252.40
1982	156.10	16.19	9.28	25.01	109.70	118.20	105.30	102.80	113.80	103.70	392.53	135.15	183.72	73.66	286.78
1983	175.04	20.70	11.13	32.65	113.20	107.50	114.40	128.00	120.00	122.50	443.06	150.41	209.09	83.56	327.15
1984	219.08	27.37	13.57	35.92	119.50	115.20	121.60	129.20	119.00	118.60	523.77	179.00	250.39	94.38	408.48
1985	299.17	35.18	15.87	39.52	117.20	98.80	130.80	122.50	111.70	106.60	651.54	195.66	334.45	121.43	507.50
1986	339.15	38.44	19.78	48.40	109.90	106.20	111.40	104.60	119.20	114.20	751.99	224.26	376.32	151.41	595.00
1987	406.16	50.30	29.69	61.25	110.30	100.60	113.30	109.80	133.00	115.00	892.93	245.28	461.72	185.93	709.40
1988	498.15	56.88	40.08	68.64	114.30	102.50	115.90	119.70	135.40	128.20	1132.01	319.18	586.82	226.01	899.01
1989	572.21	53.45	42.07	77.23	100.40	97.30	103.30	85.50	95.50	102.40	1228.49	324.18	655.45	248.86	978.94

10. Jiangsu

10–3

Year	v1h	v1i	v1j	v1j1	v1j2	v1j3	v1k	v2a	v2a1	v2a2	v2b	v2c	v2c1	v2c2	v2d1
1949															
1950															
1951															
1952		3.48	421	421			0.01	5.70	2.23	3.47					
1953		4.05	455	455				6.52	4.69	1.83					
1954		4.08	469	469				5.95	1.61	4.34					
1955		4.37	474	474				8.36	2.39	5.97					
1956		6.21	513	513				8.70	4.00	4.70					
1957	83.7	7.07	531	531				8.71	4.86	3.85					
1958		7.92	476	476				14.30	7.94	6.36					
1959		9.62	459	459				18.43	10.78	7.65					
1960		10.08	471	471				19.94	16.01	3.93					
1961		9.75	477	477				7.72	6.91	0.81					
1962		8.99	515	515				3.68	5.13	-1.45					26.52
1963		8.61	564	564				8.74	5.66	3.08					26.52
1964		9.12	583	583				14.04	6.27	7.77					28.62
1965	113.9	9.27	565	565				15.20	6.15	9.05					30.74
1966		9.32	547	547				20.60	5.72	14.88					
1967		9.60	546	546				11.32	4.25	7.07					
1968								12.27	3.69	8.58					
1969								14.26	4.76	9.50					
1970		10.68		511				27.07	8.27	18.80					
1971		16.38	467	502	396		0.01	32.57	10.40	22.17					
1972		18.51	481	515	415		0.01	31.42	12.59	18.83					
1973		19.38	476	523	396			37.00	13.76	23.24					69.11
1974		20.22	495	543	416			36.24	11.85	24.39					75.56
1975		21.20	491	534	423			41.20	14.80	26.40					83.44
1976		22.50	483	531	414		1.84	42.32	17.13	25.19					91.95
1977		26.24	474	517	402		2.22	44.80	17.56	27.24					101.20
1978	155.0	29.05	513	563	432		2.82	62.07	24.49	37.58	21.75	20.70	11.28	0.63	113.90
1979	200.1	33.10	566	618	479		4.14	69.64	30.36	39.28	26.75	25.52	12.64	0.86	130.15
1980	217.9	41.63	667	721	578		7.12	72.90	34.75	38.15	34.73	31.65	15.42	1.86	145.54
1981	258.0	44.13	672	718	594		8.71	73.68	33.48	40.20	30.90	26.09	10.42	1.78	165.20
1982	309.0	48.14	703	748	626		9.86	77.60	40.22	37.38	43.01	35.58	11.31	1.69	185.58
1983	356.6	50.78	723	768	643		12.21	102.53	65.81	36.72	54.71	46.79	14.28	1.01	204.69
1984	447.9	67.28	931	1003	820		15.94	142.24	75.01	67.23	63.53	53.85	18.15	1.27	219.54
1985	492.6	86.17	1135	1211	1015		20.17	194.02	90.75	103.27	100.03	80.43	23.50	2.28	255.34
1986	561.3	105.56	1327	1430	1166		26.96	237.69	121.65	116.04	124.67	100.97	32.06	2.25	292.15
1987	626.5	121.26	1471	1581	1295		31.86	302.69	199.79	102.90	156.85	128.43	47.76	2.55	356.44
1988	796.8	152.53	1796	1936	1564		42.01	387.94	236.16	151.78	188.36	154.04	56.50	3.16	409.56
1989	875.7	165.38	1918	2082	1639		48.48	395.03	202.83	192.20	324.60	119.14	43.10	1.95	494.70

10. Jiangsu

10–4

Year	v2d2	v2e	v3a	v3b	v3b1	v3b2	v3c	v3d	v3d1	v3d2	v3e	v3e1	v3e2	v3e3	v3e4
1949															
1950															
1951											102.76	70.32	12.56	7.44	4.00
1952			27.93	27.36	22.14	5.22	0.57	74	70	96					
1953			29.25	28.60	22.64	5.96	0.65	76	70	107					
1954			29.87	29.16	23.19	5.97	0.71	76	70	107					
1955			31.74	30.74	24.56	6.18	1.00	78	73	108					
1956			32.61	31.21	23.82	7.39	1.40	77	71	110					
1957			34.48	33.00	25.60	7.40	1.48	80	75	101	219.84	125.52	22.20	7.80	11.52
1958			40.94	38.40	28.43	9.97	2.54	91	82	135					
1959			37.04	34.28	24.90	9.38	2.76	80	71	123					
1960			42.10	40.20	26.88	13.32	1.90	94	77	171					
1961			40.60	38.85	26.44	12.41	1.75	92	76	166					
1962	19.44	6.01	40.79	39.31	26.79	12.52	1.48	92	74	187	207.84	132.24	12.36	11.16	10.80
1963	19.44	6.01	42.46	41.15	29.05	12.13	1.31	94	78	189	199.68	124.32	15.12	9.60	10.92
1964	20.72	6.76	49.97	48.43	34.15	14.28	1.54	108	89	222	206.02	126.02	19.20	8.40	10.82
1965	22.53	8.83	48.60	46.96	32.43	14.53	1.64	103	83	224	206.74	122.24	23.26	8.14	10.87
1966			54.15	52.29	37.68	14.61	1.86	112	94	222					
1967			57.78	53.15	38.10	15.05	1.63	111	92	229					
1968			58.98	56.98	40.85	16.13	2.00	116	96	246					
1969			59.40	56.60	40.58	16.02	2.80	112	92	250					
1970			61.62	57.72	41.38	16.34	3.90	111	90	268					
1971			70.03	65.69	47.61	18.08	4.34	124	101	296					
1972			77.34	72.13	52.18	19.95	5.21	134	109	320					
1973	48.61	34.70	84.35	78.67	56.91	21.76	5.68	144	118	329					
1974	52.69	39.19	85.03	78.80	56.60	22.20	6.23	142	117	325					
1975	57.44	41.37	89.13	82.96	59.61	23.35	6.17	148	121	346					
1976	63.45	45.04	97.05	90.53	61.03	29.50	6.52	160	122	431					
1977	68.41	47.94	99.89	92.52	59.54	32.98	7.37	161	118	474					
1978	76.97	52.67	117.16	108.64	72.49	36.15	8.52	187	143	507	276.00	152.20	38.00	9.40	11.40
1979	84.90	56.68	145.26	134.85	91.58	43.27	10.41	230	180	557					
1980	95.77	60.39	157.45	146.05	100.13	45.92	11.40	247	197	547	434.88	239.64	77.04	9.96	11.40
1981	109.92	62.74	178.72	164.61	116.03	48.58	14.11	276	227	562	440.76	246.60	63.84	9.12	12.00
1982	124.14	66.32	209.18	192.26	140.66	51.60	16.92	318	273	577	452.28	263.40	64.32	9.36	13.92
1983	136.93	67.69	224.62	204.17	150.52	53.65	20.45	334	290	579	486.60	285.12	67.56	9.72	15.48
1984	145.76	71.07	266.24	244.32	180.50	63.82	21.92	397	347	669	577.50	324.90	94.10	10.00	17.00
1985	171.62	86.95	313.48	288.60	213.68	74.92	24.88	466	410	765	719.59	377.87	116.04	10.88	15.83
1986	200.42	106.16	357.31	328.13	234.49	93.64	29.18	526	454	869	866.43	443.52	130.92	12.05	16.85
1987	249.91	123.81	406.71	371.68	263.57	108.11	35.03	589	512	933	952.89	495.95	142.19	12.79	19.89
1988	286.72	147.42	524.86	473.91	334.14	139.77	50.95	741	647	1138	1238.68	629.24	184.24	13.74	21.30
1989	353.71	194.27	583.91	526.82	366.69	160.13	57.09	812	711	1206	1300.60	701.20			

10. Jiangsu

10–5

Year	v3f	v3f1	v3f2	v3f3	v3f4	v4a1	v4a1a	v4a1b	v4a1c	v4a1d	v4a2	v4a2a	v4a2b	v4a2c	v4a2d
1949															
1950						3.95	0.01			0.05	0.76				0.76
1951						5.32	0.06			0.12	0.98				0.98
1952						6.80	0.18	3.64		0.29	2.11				2.11
1953						7.78	0.25	4.56		0.35	2.50				2.50
1954						8.67	0.42	5.07		0.34	2.88				2.88
1955						8.47	0.50	4.80		0.23	2.89				2.89
1956						9.66	0.63	5.69		0.54	4.08				4.08
1957	83.2	59.5	6.3	0.9	7.5	10.10	1.00	5.72		0.54	4.80				4.80
1958						17.82	6.24	7.85		0.61	11.27				11.27
1959						24.94	12.28	8.20		0.13	14.36				14.36
1960						26.19	13.43	8.62		0.24	17.52	8.29	2.61	1.07	5.55
1961						17.45	7.59	6.33		0.18	8.66	1.87	2.06	1.02	3.71
1962						13.31	3.37	6.61		0.18	6.23	0.93	1.91	0.87	2.52
1963						13.70	4.39	6.56		0.20	6.63	1.14	1.80	0.88	2.81
1964						17.24	6.65	7.61		0.15	7.50	1.53	2.01	0.94	3.02
1965	102.7	68.3	10.5	4.1	9.2	19.40	7.39	8.90		0.22	7.98	1.86	2.09	0.97	3.06
1966						22.89	9.72	9.54		0.20	9.05	2.06	2.36	0.97	3.66
1967						17.02	5.56	8.28		0.08	7.93	2.24	2.30	0.87	2.52
1968						16.20	5.03	8.07		0.10	6.14	1.46	2.05	0.86	1.77
1969						21.75	7.76	10.48		0.14	8.58	3.20	2.09	0.87	2.42
1970						28.66	11.10	13.49		0.21	11.33	4.52	2.34	0.86	3.61
1971						34.12	14.38	15.84		0.24	12.51	4.86	2.62	1.01	4.02
1972						37.84	15.74	18.27		0.15	14.97	6.33	3.03	1.11	4.50
1973						42.22	18.67	20.34		0.13	16.31	6.07	3.35	1.20	5.69
1974						39.51	15.77	20.30		0.11	17.89	6.80	3.69	1.27	6.13
1975						43.41	17.03	22.80		0.12	17.70	5.99	3.88	1.38	6.45
1976						44.02	15.54	24.88		0.13	18.71	6.05	4.08	1.43	7.15
1977						51.65	19.34	28.79		0.11	19.96	6.31	4.32	1.61	7.72
1978	139.7	87.1	17.4	10.9	8.3	61.09	25.04	32.52		0.12	28.38	9.26	4.98	1.80	12.34
1979	169.2	101.4	20.6	18.0	9.7	59.28	20.89	34.89		0.06	32.06	11.51	5.64	2.02	12.89
1980	194.7	112.9	24.4	24.1	8.8	62.45	21.00	38.17		0.09	28.95	8.67	6.79	2.39	11.10
1981	225.5	128.2	25.8	33.1	9.5	63.04	18.25	41.58		0.15	23.79	3.29	7.53	2.48	10.49
1982	261.4	145.0	29.1	42.6	11.7	66.61	16.52	46.60		0.25	24.63	3.29	8.69	2.87	9.78
1983	322.2	178.2	33.7	54.7	15.8	73.07	18.29	51.03		0.21	32.29	5.33	10.62	3.68	12.66
1984	360.3	191.0	35.1	68.5	20.1	75.34	13.50	58.28		0.00	39.15	6.19	12.52	4.95	15.49
1985	415.6	216.5	37.4	81.4	19.7	87.81	7.28	75.97		0.21	50.53	7.22	14.70	4.88	23.73
1986	499.3	247.2	43.3	117.5	21.4	98.73	9.53	84.10		1.91	66.16	6.98	17.61	5.57	36.00
1987	578.9	278.3	40.8	144.2	29.3	107.17	10.07	91.23		2.14	68.00	5.91	18.10	5.99	38.00
1988	746.6	341.2	51.1	205.3	28.6	115.50	2.51	102.80		5.25	78.99	5.35	22.72	7.90	43.02
1989	804.0	402.7	60.7	184.9	21.9	124.01	-6.81			8.00	89.87	5.25	26.16	10.25	48.21

10. Jiangsu

10–6

Year	v4b	v4b1	v4b2	v4b3	v4c1	v4c2	v5a	v5a1	v5a2	v5a3	v5a4	v5b1	v5b2	v5b3	v5c
1949								48.20							
1950								55.56							
1951								66.77							
1952	0.58	0.58						84.08							
1953								89.66							
1954								87.62							
1955								95.74							
1956								129.75							
1957	1.84	1.46	0.38				1736.80	130.80							
1958								234.45							
1959								204.17							
1960								214.96							
1961								190.23							
1962	2.09	1.56	0.53		6.54	25.69		161.07	128.64						
1963					7.33	27.38		149.00							
1964					10.60	38.57		158.84							
1965	3.64	2.65	0.99		13.14		1909.37	168.52	129.48						
1966								172.64	129.86						
1967								178.63							
1968								179.62							
1969								191.49	110.14						
1970	4.04	2.87	1.17					219.34							
1971								250.83	116.88						
1972								258.51	146.81						
1973								253.21	151.05						
1974								258.47	159.37						
1975	7.76	5.30	2.46					270.39	183.08						
1976	8.46	5.72	2.74					284.10	201.79						
1977	9.66	6.44	3.22					357.88	212.02						
1978	12.40	7.59	4.81		39.18	30.22	2777.72	366.37	215.13	1.62	2194.60	1940.69	546.73	290.30	
1979	16.68	10.14	6.54		48.11	33.98	2762.34	373.92	229.91	1.70	2156.81	2012.38	489.02	260.94	
1980	23.72	13.86	9.86		52.22	33.44	2821.03	401.98	242.17	2.75	2174.13	1991.30	548.78	280.95	
1981	30.42	21.84	8.58		52.04	31.01	2910.58	425.72	249.10	5.07	2230.69	2022.91	584.04	303.63	
1982	40.59	28.79	11.80		57.27	30.07	2993.03	444.00	255.36	5.31	2288.36	2032.13	624.41	336.49	
1983	56.92	30.83	26.09		60.77	29.70	3056.53	455.78	257.75	7.28	2335.72	2046.50	653.08	356.95	
1984	74.75	41.51	33.24		67.23	31.01	3158.81	442.64	290.51	9.63	2409.13	1817.87	934.40	406.54	
1985	99.35	57.81	41.54		77.40	29.94	3262.97	468.80	305.39	11.86	2468.67	1743.36	1069.24	450.37	
1986	139.59	81.87	57.72		77.36	25.23	3350.02	487.91	318.73	11.69	2522.33	1683.95	1143.81	522.26	
1987	193.69	118.60	75.09		88.73	23.74	3429.69	506.68	326.72	14.53	2569.90	1659.30	1217.00	553.39	
1988	231.85	149.27	82.58		103.44	23.83	3502.65	527.52	331.40	16.13	2613.52	1661.18	1254.33	587.14	
1989	329.20	223.40	105.80		103.27	18.85	3650.50	525.24	324.73	19.09	2633.19	1712.20	1218.61	580.02	

10. Jiangsu

10–7

Year	v5c1	v5d	v6a	v6a1	v6a2	v6b	v6c	v6d1	v6d2	v6d3	v6d4	v6d5	v6d6
1949			3512	437	3075	34.72	16.45	521	2991	1779	1733	108.81	48.67
1950			3583	447	3136	35.68	15.11	528	3055	1814	1769		
1951			3656	457	3199	36.45	15.92	535	3121	1850	1806		
1952			3739	468	3271	35.68	15.68	551	3188	1892	1847	101.55	48.79
1953			3817	494	3323	35.68	13.62	560	3257	1928	1889		
1954			3892	510	3382	36.62	12.16	555	3337	1973	1919		
1955			3984	534	3450	32.21	11.76	563	3421	1999	1985		
1956			4089	543	3546	37.60	13.02	570	3519	2047	2042		
1957			4183	579	3604	34.38	10.26	621	3562	2087	2096	141.88	56.28
1958			4258	599	3659	24.83	9.40	701	3557	2123	2135	146.98	42.19
1959			4290	867	3423	20.92	14.55	761	3529	2147	2143		
1960			4246	876	3370	18.56	18.41	767	3479	2116	2130		
1961			4243	873	3370	18.84	13.35	698	3545	2110	2133	162.32	61.75
1962			4334	820	3514	33.27	10.36	644	3690	2155	2179	160.86	60.73
1963			4441	775	3666	37.68	9.04	643	3798	2215	2226	164.36	61.07
1964			4512	690	3822	34.70	10.13	643	3869	2268	2244	167.18	61.61
1965			4624	688	3936	36.91	9.48	655	3969	2320	2304	168.98	61.99
1966			4748	698	4050	34.89	8.05	664	4084	2383	2365		
1967			4862	689	4173	31.76	7.81	648	4214	2449	2413		
1968			4996	693	4303	33.33	7.65	662	4334	2520	2476		
1969			5119	668	4451	32.78	6.80	619	4500	2571	2548		
1970			5252	656	4596	30.68	6.85	601	4651	2635	2617	151.78	56.38
1971			5361	672	4689	26.37	7.38	619	4742	2693	2668		
1972			5434	695	4739	21.93	6.84	627	4807	2731	2703		
1973			5506	710	4796	18.69	6.52	696	4810	2773	2733		
1974			5566	727	4839	17.34	6.61	672	4894	2805	2761		
1975			5636	741	4895	17.86	6.46	677	4959	2843	2793	166.64	61.17
1976			5701	760	4941	16.56	6.48	693	5008	2879	2822		
1977			5765	771	4994	16.45	6.48	698	5067	2913	2852		
1978			5834	801	5033	15.63	6.09	728	5106	2950	2884	177.50	66.51
1979			5893	874	5019	14.63	5.85	825	5068	2981	2912		
1980			5938	902	5036	14.69	6.57	853	5085	3004	2934	203.29	76.49
1981			6010	928	5082	16.83	6.22	876	5134	3048	2962		
1982			6089	954	5135	16.43	5.75	913	5176	3094	2995		
1983			6135	1229	4906	11.97	5.95	939	5196	3122	3013		
1984			6171	1396	4775	10.42	5.90	969	5202	3143	3028		
1985			6213	1596	4617	10.84	5.87	1014	5199	3168	3045	224.98	84.27
1986			6270	2059	4211	13.20	5.80	1143	5127	3199	3071	228.89	86.08
1987			6348	2881	3467	15.42	5.79	1175	5173	3242	3106	239.07	87.80
1988			6438	3213	3225	16.03	5.89	1281	5157	3289	3149	243.36	89.86
1989			6536	3494	3042	20.38	6.54	1374	5162	3339	3197	246.90	91.32

10. Jiangsu

10–8

Year	v7a	v7b	v7c	v7d	v7e	v7f	v7g	v7h	v7h1	v7h2	v7h3	v7h4	v7h5	v7i	v8a
1949	0.45		1080.25			0.18	0.01	22.59	18.84		2.96	0.16	0.63	121.90	15.89
1950								24.27	19.68	0.02	3.76	0.54	0.27	126.00	19.00
1951								27.37	22.14	0.01	3.45	0.41	1.36	130.20	22.55
1952	0.56	2.78	1337.21	14120		0.87	0.02	31.87	25.84	0.03	4.94	0.70	0.36	131.10	25.53
1953								32.31	27.37	0.03	3.59	0.84	0.48	137.80	29.81
1954								32.45	26.61	0.03	4.19	1.07	0.55	151.20	31.66
1955								36.22	31.84	0.04	2.75	1.12	0.47	156.10	32.82
1956								33.60	27.63	0.07	4.20	1.14	0.56	155.00	38.60
1957	1.33	75.78	1709.51	14161		8.94	0.06	36.81	29.43	0.22	5.15	1.24	0.77	140.50	41.01
1958								38.74	32.54	0.35	3.18	1.84	0.85	131.60	75.22
1959								37.35	26.69	0.52	4.00	2.32	0.82	124.80	96.00
1960								36.76	30.95	0.51	2.06	2.17	1.07	115.50	100.32
1961								35.73	30.30	0.39	2.82	1.29	0.93	108.20	62.50
1962	6.61	305.00	2411.74			22.63	1.14	40.15	33.09	0.32	4.42	1.16	1.16	106.80	53.36
1963								46.77	38.30	0.37	5.10	1.36	1.64	102.70	54.66
1964								56.62	47.31	0.40	6.17	1.58	1.16	102.50	68.17
1965	8.26	559.09	2908.57	11747		68.03	2.50	57.27	45.88	0.63	8.19	1.37	1.20	104.70	88.08
1966								66.08	52.27	0.66	10.44	1.39	1.32	107.44	104.19
1967								61.19	50.97	0.61	7.28	1.41	0.92	114.46	84.80
1968								65.38	54.71	0.65	7.98	1.24	0.80	126.10	85.48
1969								65.60	53.81	0.65	8.99	1.25	0.90	124.98	102.80
1970	14.61	981.28	3485.56			116.87	7.25	71.33	56.21	0.85	11.70	1.64	0.93	121.08	135.47
1971								79.90	63.80	0.94	12.28	1.84	1.04	119.67	167.15
1972								83.24	64.94	1.25	14.40	1.58	1.07	116.70	183.38
1973								89.71	72.71	1.08	13.01	1.79	1.12	113.00	208.10
1974								89.88	72.52	1.08	13.21	1.89	1.18	112.24	205.39
1975	54.10	2925.77	4701.28			149.36	15.07	91.66	71.03	1.47	15.49	2.47	1.20	106.91	235.28
1976								100.71	81.68	1.31	14.80	2.01	0.91	103.52	247.59
1977								89.16	72.04	1.25	12.84	1.96	1.07	101.12	297.12
1978	85.52	3887.94	4905.42	13874		371.75	23.28	105.87	83.96	1.48	16.72	2.44	1.27	98.25	337.65
1979	99.86	4222.85	5054.29	12737		484.03	27.75	145.25	113.30	2.03	25.71	3.19	1.02	95.42	386.05
1980	111.31	4325.51	5119.47	13121		576.79	33.74	138.45	105.08	1.94	26.58	3.88	0.97	87.40	467.82
1981	120.42	4427.74	5183.50	12760		604.27	38.87	153.62	118.59	2.00	27.04	4.61	1.38	84.63	504.94
1982	131.30	4402.03	5213.85	12938		696.51	42.61	188.11	143.33	1.96	35.74	4.66	2.42	82.46	534.87
1983	143.04	4693.19	5243.20	12813	939	736.45	47.64	206.86	155.47	3.30	36.55	6.52	5.02	78.97	600.70
1984	155.81	4876.64	5394.49	12875	842	717.62	53.23	253.82	179.57	4.33	46.97	9.04	13.91	67.47	745.36
1985	167.51	4866.06	5381.89	12837	645	701.99	63.57	288.55	183.66	4.63	66.30	15.53	18.43	67.72	1036.67
1986	181.13	5078.46	5306.71	12771	1230	769.63	71.20	332.66	211.50	5.15	69.47	22.61	23.93	68.18	1235.38
1987	197.44	5162.60	5275.92	12751	870	812.55	85.23	380.25	228.11	6.02	87.45	28.38	30.29	63.04	1590.31
1988	210.09	5265.64	5245.97	12577	2790	866.68	94.76	497.95	274.26	7.29	139.98	39.97	36.45	65.77	2152.93
1989	221.24	5380.00	5296.85	12577			98.39	522.26	286.55	7.02	147.79	42.08	38.81	60.10	2507.42

10. Jiangsu

10–9

Year	v8a1	v8a2	v8a3	v8b	v8c1	v8c2	v8d	v8f1	v8f2	v8f3	v8f4	v8f5	v8g
1949	9.71	6.18			0.88	15.01		0.10	81.49		1.98	3.10	
1950	11.93	7.07			1.06	17.94		0.15	98.39		2.25	10.30	
1951	15.04	7.51			1.35	21.20		0.24	101.37		3.26	31.60	
1952	17.39	8.14			1.56	23.97		0.43	113.21		4.10	36.90	
1953	19.98	9.83			2.15	27.66		0.49	117.75		4.82	44.60	
1954	22.54	9.12			2.66	29.00		1.04	135.33		5.37	51.30	
1955	23.43	9.39			3.25	29.57		1.15	150.35		5.16	53.80	
1956	28.37	10.23			5.06	33.54		1.25	164.80		6.82	75.00	
1957	30.21	10.80			6.23	34.78	7.91	1.68	193.11		7.08	80.70	
1958	65.90	9.32			17.15	58.07	16.48	3.26	355.00	0.03	9.45	101.70	
1959	81.67	14.33			24.19	71.81	18.92	9.97	540.00	0.38	14.24	101.10	
1960	82.24	18.08			31.60	68.72	27.30	17.79	560.19	0.10	20.69	111.20	
1961	49.96	12.54			15.13	47.37	12.92	6.15	524.22	0.06	17.63	57.10	
1962	43.76	9.60			10.41	42.95	10.56	3.03	462.70	1.26	15.43	58.60	
1963	45.35	9.31			11.70	42.96	11.24	3.18	455.46		13.69	6.43	
1964	56.36	11.81			14.52	53.65		4.23	456.70		20.30	84.41	
1965	73.10	14.98			21.80	66.28		6.53	485.66		25.78	103.00	
1966	84.41	19.78			29.59	74.60		11.49	519.22		32.79	129.20	
1967	67.09	17.71			21.54	63.26		6.38	406.28		29.70	87.05	
1968	67.56	17.92			25.99	59.49		4.93	249.11		28.25	90.22	
1969	82.49	20.31			33.72	69.08		7.61	178.34		32.93	100.09	
1970	107.68	27.79			52.33	83.14		16.18	699.17		49.96	163.09	
1971	131.24	35.91			73.56	93.59		27.10	978.74		69.70	199.46	
1972	141.20	42.18			82.30	101.08		41.74	1093.50		75.72	220.40	
1973	156.63	51.47			93.21	114.89		51.41	1182.76		79.21	244.50	
1974	145.69	59.70			87.94	117.45		26.58	888.28		64.06	210.93	
1975	161.62	73.66			105.00	130.28		42.25	1143.75		81.80	274.16	
1976	169.03	78.56			112.62	134.97		40.58	1310.85	4.35	92.79	308.81	
1977	183.45	113.67		178.20	139.00	158.12	49.12	48.28	1408.44	12.69	104.41	367.39	
1978	207.52	130.13		203.52	160.71	176.94	58.98	54.51	1707.02	27.40	126.42	444.10	27257
1979	238.58	147.47		232.76	177.94	208.11	65.50	62.19	1725.73	30.54	147.00	520.42	32687
1980	268.11	195.96	3.75	260.63	199.85	267.97	71.93	68.17	1690.00	33.58	156.32	629.00	32687
1981	276.70	222.58	5.66	270.51	196.96	307.98	74.85	62.08	1736.90	32.89	169.90	666.42	33816
1982	297.64	229.48	7.75	287.87	217.33	317.54	77.57	62.50	1802.88	35.40	180.16	749.44	33867
1983	320.97	268.74	10.99	310.54	252.14	348.56	82.80	72.19	1915.87	40.00	184.89	863.00	
1984	350.35	381.36	13.65	339.28	312.36	433.00	96.13	84.95	2049.96	44.63	210.13	982.68	
1985	426.24	578.65	31.78	411.45	484.44	552.23	115.31	98.97	2193.85	55.81	234.48	1116.90	43269
1986	482.50	707.94	44.94	469.55	564.14	671.24	124.36	114.32	2173.82	60.11	263.75	1329.40	47248
1987	582.51	932.35	75.45	562.61	730.91	859.40	144.28	134.07	2235.08	65.80	301.16	1524.47	47252
1988	747.21	1278.61	127.11	707.18	1001.93	1151.00	173.38	152.35	2331.77	72.00	345.32	1660.97	
1989	877.21	1455.49	174.72	851.40	1168.88	1338.54	196.30	168.76	2446.05	83.29	366.38	1515.02	47351

10. Jiangsu

10–10

Year	v8g1	v9a	v9a1	v9a2	v9a3	v9b	v9b1	v9b2	v9b3	v9c	v10a	v10a1	v10b1	v10b2	v10b3
1949	9049			1.03	1.97			0.14	1.95	740.5	9.15	8.51	0.02		0.16
1950	9899			1.14	2.19			0.16	2.36	927.3	11.40	10.48	0.88		0.40
1951	10129			1.51	2.93			0.22	2.95	1185.8	16.49	15.04	1.38		1.38
1952	9661			1.54	2.91			0.29	6.41	1414.1	19.20	17.37	2.28		3.98
1953	9829			2.31	3.72			0.49	8.24	1712.8	23.73	21.40	3.07		6.61
1954	10008			2.30	3.41			0.60	9.99	1797.0	25.30	22.59	3.24		12.34
1955	7773			2.62	4.02			0.66	11.17	1836.1	26.63	23.57	4.99		10.37
1956	2426			4.06	4.64			0.87	13.79	2123.8	29.77	26.08	8.11		14.34
1957	2322			4.17	5.35			0.87	16.04	2302.3	29.18	26.77	9.74		12.57
1958	5868			8.13	8.02			1.57	23.74	1859.7	33.80	29.70	14.00		13.32
1959	4809			9.73	11.39			2.62	32.76	4185.0	38.85	33.30	13.40		19.25
1960	6131			10.98	11.89			2.97	35.04	5097.2	40.50	34.36	23.28		15.19
1961	3284			11.68	15.45			1.77	23.42	4817.8	35.66	31.12	20.05		12.80
1962	3018			11.71	16.77			1.67	21.34	4574.7	37.35	33.04	15.38		19.06
1963	2587			11.14	11.42			1.72	24.48	4470.2	34.97	30.85	14.87		17.94
1964	2003			11.73	9.63			1.98	30.42	4511.6	38.89	33.57	17.28		19.94
1965				12.53	5.77			2.39	32.85	4729.0	44.11	36.79	18.52		24.13
1966				14.76	6.48			2.86	34.25	4873.9	47.45	39.49	20.04		25.90
1967				14.12	7.03			2.53	30.47	4521.2	50.10	42.55	21.16		27.27
1968				14.57	7.11			2.28	31.69	4294.6	48.05	41.34	20.29		26.09
1969				15.58	8.13			2.54	35.58	4792.9	49.53	39.77	20.98		26.98
1970				18.12	7.23			3.39	40.86	5094.5	53.07	43.53	22.77		28.86
1971				21.43	7.05			4.60	44.53	5641.8	58.56	46.61	25.38		31.74
1972				25.08	7.63			5.48	52.22	6247.1	65.02	51.85	28.47		35.12
1973	2956	72.48	35.44	28.80	8.24	187.92	122.76	6.40	58.76	6764.3	70.86	56.09	31.26		38.03
1974	3008	76.65	36.99	31.26	8.40	166.26	98.94	6.46	60.86	7172.1	74.12	59.02	32.97		39.56
1975	3096	82.26	39.31	33.97	8.98	192.01	118.09	7.21	66.71	7663.4	81.51	65.35	36.53		43.21
1976	3159	80.41	34.71	36.67	9.03	204.15	125.23	7.95	70.97	8247.7	87.62	69.23	37.43		48.66
1977	3245	90.12	39.02	41.83	9.27	231.03	143.55	9.47	78.01	8766.7	91.46	72.90	40.04		50.00
1978	3321	105.29	46.35	49.93	9.01	283.85	172.72	11.24	87.97	9254.5	106.49	84.79	44.98		59.50
1979	3396	119.93	52.79	57.79	9.35	308.84	180.31	11.13	89.76	10050.2	127.69	99.16	52.36		71.79
1980	3377	140.15	61.60	68.25	10.30	382.77	186.31	11.45	93.56	11182.8	154.48	122.56	61.17		87.83
1981	3367	154.44	66.48	77.50	10.46	384.08	188.26	12.01	100.66	11886.7	167.84	134.79	65.15		95.54
1982	3401	170.84	70.72	89.89	10.23	414.44	198.92	15.30	113.43	12736.1	186.31	150.01	71.55		105.34
1983	3436	191.76	79.43	102.75	9.58	444.76	206.82	17.29	120.61	14158.8	207.48	169.12	78.21		113.47
1984	3329	225.09	94.22	121.56	9.31	490.22	222.73	18.48	135.95	16135.7	246.15	205.05	88.61		130.31
1985	3673	259.97	107.46	143.45	9.06	530.83	240.48	19.99	151.67	19688.5	307.68	262.57	102.11		158.54
1986	3683	279.06	117.59	153.40	8.07	571.27	260.85	21.31	161.31	22787.5	355.76	304.58	118.17		182.66
1987	3799	303.01	129.37	166.45	7.19	590.34	271.22	22.21	168.20	28053.9	422.01	360.74	136.79		214.64
1988	3753	324.80	146.99	170.90	6.91	614.59	279.31	24.46	172.78	35725.9	548.56	471.83	179.78		271.15
1989	3731	313.28	138.51	169.17	5.60	628.97	292.40	22.70	171.75	41158.5	597.32	509.56	197.82		280.13

10. Jiangsu

Year	v10b4	v10b5	v10b6	v10d	v11a1	v11a2	v11a3	v11b	v11b1	v11b2	v11c	v11d	v12a	v12b	v12c
1949		7.59	1.38												
1950		8.63	1.49	9.18											
1951	0.01	12.00	1.72	9.97											
1952	0.03	10.89	2.02	14.22											
1953	0.07	12.77	1.21	13.98											
1954	1.50	7.21	1.01	16.49											
1955	3.32	6.19	1.76	18.56											
1956	4.52	1.75	1.05	15.22											
1957	4.40	1.32	1.25	17.11											
1958	4.75	1.21	0.52	17.46											
1959	4.11	1.25	0.84	18.00											
1960		1.23	0.80	15.84											
1961		1.01	0.80	16.81											
1962		0.81	2.00	14.60											
1963		0.82	1.34	17.22											
1964		0.74	0.93	22.94											
1965		0.67	0.79	24.07											
1966		0.61	0.90	26.82											
1967		0.55	1.12	23.62											
1968		0.50	1.17	30.54											
1969		0.45	1.12	25.16											
1970		0.41	1.03	25.26											
1971		0.37	1.07	28.42											
1972		0.33	1.10	31.07											
1973		0.31	1.26	34.79											
1974		0.28	1.31	35.21					0.7689						
1975		0.25	1.52	37.57					1.6946						
1976		0.19	1.34	35.80					2.2765						
1977		0.18	1.24	32.39					2.7579						
1978		0.18	1.83	45.63				4.2749	4.1846	0.0903		1.3867			
1979		0.28	3.26	63.06				6.7675	6.1898	0.5777		1.3867	102.0	101.0	123.1
1980	0.08	0.58	4.82	70.18				9.4609	8.5401	0.9208		1.3867	104.8	105.7	102.4
1981	0.11	1.21	5.83	78.33	0.5785	8.2919	2.0981	11.9323	10.9685	0.9638		1.3867	101.1	101.1	102.7
1982	0.06	2.39	6.97	90.88	0.8341	8.7589	2.3606	12.7904	11.9536	0.8368		1.3867	101.1	100.9	102.6
1983	0.14	7.74	7.92	100.82	1.2407	10.1077	2.3758	14.5136	13.7242	0.7894		1.3867	100.8	100.5	102.1
1984	0.27	16.53	10.43	111.06	1.9343	10.9849	1.9512	16.3150	14.8704	1.4446		1.3867	103.5	104.1	104.2
1985	0.31	31.06	15.66	110.98	2.0576	10.7729	2.7546	18.5343	15.5851	2.9492	2.0218	0.9326	109.2	109.6	106.9
1986	0.42	34.73	19.78	133.25	2.0923	12.4281	2.6787	20.8166	17.1991	3.6175	2.2553	1.8250	106.5	106.4	106.1
1987	0.69	44.13	25.76	151.02	1.3364	16.6001	3.2500	27.0245	21.1860	5.8385	2.2684	2.1422	109.3	110.5	110.9
1988	1.19	62.38	34.06	186.41	1.6635	18.1976	3.6376	31.6498	23.4987	8.1511	7.2991	2.6476	121.7	122.6	126.0
1989	1.19	75.61	42.57	222.26				33.0674	24.4111	8.6563	4.8940	1.6100	118.0	116.0	115.8

10. Jiangsu

10–12

Year	v13a	v13b	v13c1	v13c2	v13c3	v13d	v14a	v14b	v14c	v15a	v15b	v15c	v15d	v15e	v15f
1949			0.72	10.84	135.30		4500			8285					
1950	16.81		0.82	12.06	168.40	0.14		6900		8401					
1951	18.96		0.93	14.53	220.40	0.14		11300		8573					
1952	27.90		1.13	27.47	335.20	0.17	8300	52400		8713					
1953	30.45		1.55	32.68	323.40	0.19	9800	57000		8833					
1954	28.78		1.91	34.88	338.30	0.28	10100	57400		8901					
1955	27.64		2.07	36.04	359.30	0.47	10600	67700		8902					
1956	20.76		2.58	47.07	416.70	0.43	12500	95600		8827					
1957	24.66		2.91	56.33	412.80	0.29	13200	92700		8738					
1958	12.17		4.49	65.57	565.70	0.57	39700	65200		7834					
1959	10.76		6.07	78.34	595.10	0.29	38600	72700		7630					
1960	10.45		7.03	94.28	630.00	1.02	43000	80300		7521					
1961	16.92		6.95	85.09	535.11	1.33	46300	82400		7497					
1962	21.87		5.25	67.61	448.30	1.58	37100	84700		7524					
1963	18.92		4.62	61.18	418.67	1.37	36900	83700		7513					
1964	14.66		4.15	65.34	570.78	1.31	37000	84500		7478					
1965	18.10	80.2	3.90	74.10	698.68	1.17	39800	85600		7421					
1966	18.53		4.05	91.51	587.68		47000	77500		7402					
1967	20.90		4.05	95.24	623.24		49900	78700		7363					
1968			2.55	107.82	640.49	1.50	55200	79500		7306					
1969	17.36		1.60	129.75	656.63	0.95	59300	79800		7276					
1970	13.90		0.11	148.82	664.18	1.60	68800	67800		7231					
1971	14.35		0.08	183.68	725.15	0.01	72800	72800		7177					
1972	13.50		1.01	217.27	781.50	0.05	76400	82000		7143					
1973	13.46		1.92	206.79	814.40	0.07	84000	91100		7107					
1974	13.67		2.79	213.67	888.28	0.21	89700	96000		7081					
1975	14.29		3.00	250.23	925.42	0.79	95700	107900		7058					
1976	14.09		3.74	352.58	911.81	0.36	98800	115400		7034					
1977	13.93		4.17	409.14	896.66	1.24	104300	132900		7009					
1978	10.81	96.7	6.05	389.69	868.90	1.51	110700	140000	4.52	6991					
1979	10.82		7.39	353.11	855.76	0.08	114000	145800		6976					
1980	14.89	97.0	8.41	326.60	836.90	1.07	116200	150400	5.04	6962					
1981	20.02		8.52	298.96	785.93	1.72	119600	162300	6.00	6956					
1982	22.20	96.5	7.20	289.20	736.71	3.34	120100	169300	6.52	6947					
1983	20.04	97.1	7.90	291.61	706.24	1.91	122500	172200	8.50	6945					
1984	19.35	98.4	9.57	292.18	690.56	1.81	125000	176800	9.69	6932					
1985	18.29	99.5	11.96	293.98	677.92	2.19	126500	182800	12.51	6906					
1986	16.12	99.6	13.27	295.02	670.65	2.76	130700	189000	11.76	6886					
1987	16.54	99.8	14.02	292.91	653.48	3.65	135900	191800	13.86	6870					
1988	17.90	99.8	14.77	285.75	641.89	3.94	140600	200500	14.46	6853	710	248.68	199		
1989		98.8	14.79	288.06	631.49	4.18	142200	202500	12.90	6844					

Notes

1. National Output and Income (Y)

v1a: (E), p.347
  v1a1: (E), p.347
  v1a2: (E), p.347
  v1a3: (E), p.347
  v1a4: (E), p.347
  v1a5: (E), p.347

v1b: (A); (D), p.213
  v1b1: (A); (D), p.213
  v1b2: (A); (D), p.213
  v1b3: (A); (D), p.213
  v1b4: (A); (D), p.213
  v1b5: (A); (D), p.213

v1c: v1a – v1d

v1d: (E), p.344
  v1d1: (E), p.344
  v1d2: (E), p.344
  v1d3: (E), p.344
  v1d4: (E), p.344
  v1d5: (E), p.344

v1e: (A); (D), p.215
  v1e1: (A); (D), p.215
  v1e2: (A); (D), p.215
  v1e3: (A); (D), p.215
  v1e4: (A); (D), p.215
  v1e5: (A); (D), p.215

v1f: (E), p.343
  v1f1: (E), p.343
  v1f2: (E), p.343
  v1f3: (E), p.343

v1g: v2a + v3a

v1h: (E), p.369

v1i: (E), p.371

v1j: (E), p.371
  v1j1: (E), p.371
  v1j2: (E), p.371
  v1j3: NA

v1k: (E), p.371—figures of 1975–79 include state-owned units only

2. Investment (I)

v2a: (E), p.346
  v2a1: (A); (B), p.25
  v2a2: (A); (B), p.25

v2b: (A)

v2c: (E), p.362
  v2c1: (E), p.363
  v2c2: (E), p.363

v2d:
  v2d1: (E), p.360
  v2d2: (E), p.360

v2e: (E), p.360

3. Consumption (C)

v3a: (E), p.346

v3b: (E), p.346
  v3b1: (A); (D), p.216
  v3b2: (A); (D), p.216

v3c: (E), p.346

v3d: (E), p.370
  v3d1: (E), p.370
  v3d2: (E), p.370

v3e: (A); (E), p.369
  v3e1: (A); (E), p.369
  v3e2: (A)
  v3e3: (A)
  v3e4: (A)

v3f: (A); (E), p.369

v3f1: (E), p.369
v3f2: (A)
v3f3: (A)
v3f4: (A)

4. Public Finance and Banking (FB)

v4a:
v4a1: (E), p.368
v4a1a: (E), p.368
v4a1b: (B), p.166
v4a1c: NA
v4a1d: v4a1 – v4a1a – v4a1b' (v4a1b':total tax revenues which come from (E), p.368)
v4a2: (E), p.368
v4a2a: (E), p.368
v4a2b: (E), p.368
v4a2c: (E), p.368
v4a2d: v4a2 – v4a2a – v4a2b – v4a2c

v4b: (A); (C), p.269
v4b1: (A); (C), p.269
v4b2: (A); (C), p.269—rural residents' savings deposits
v4b3: NA

v4c:
v4c1: (E), p.360
v4c2: (E), p.360

5. Labor Force (L)

v5a: (A); (E), p.342
v5a1: (E), p.342
v5a2: (E), p.342
v5a3: (E), p.342
v5a4: (E), p.342—excluding rural people working outside

v5b:
v5b1: (E), p.342
v5b2: (E), p.342
v5b3: (E), p.342

v5c: NA
v5c1: NA

v5d: NA

6. Population (PO)

v6a: (E), p.341—data from public security department
v6a1: (E), p.341—(ditto)
v6a2: (E), p.341—(ditto)

v6b: (A); (E), p.341—(ditto)

v6c: (A); (E), p.341—(ditto)

v6d:
v6d1: (E), p.341—(ditto)
v6d2: (E), p.341—(ditto)
v6d3: (E), p.341—(ditto)
v6d4: (E), p.341—(ditto)
v6d5: (A)—Nanjing
v6d6: (A)—Wuxi

7. Agriculture (A)

v7a: (A); (E), p.354

v7b: (A); (E), p.354

v7c: (A); (E), p.354

v7d: (A); (E), p.354

v7e: (A)

v7f: (A)

v7g: (A); (E), p.354

v7h: (E), p.349
v7h1: (E), p.349
v7h2: (E), p.349
v7h3: (E), p.349
v7h4: (E), p.349
v7h5: (E), p.349

v7i: (E), p.353

8. Industry (IN)

v8a: (E), p.355
  v8a1: (E), p.355
  v8a2: (E), p.355
  v8a3: v8a – v8a1 – v8a2

v8b: (E), p.360

  v8c1: (E), p.347
  v8c2: (E), p.347

v8d: (E), p.360

v8f:
  v8f1: (E), p.359
  v8f2: (E), p.359
  v8f3: (E), p.359
  v8f4: (E), p.359
  v8f5: (E), p.359

v8g: (A)
  v8g1: (E), p.360

9. Transport (TR)

v9a: (E), p.361—excluding urban traffic volume
  v9a1: (E), p.361—including central and local railways
  v9a2: (E), p.361
  v9a3: (E), p.361—excluding distant ocean and coastal passenger traffic

v9b: (E), p.361—excluding non-traffic system data
  v9b1: (E), p.361—including central and local railways
  v9b2: (E), p.361
  v9b3: (E), p.361—excluding distant ocean and coastal freight volume

v9c: (A); (E), p.361—based on 1980's constant price

10. Domestic Trade (DT)

v10a: (E), p.364
  v10a1: (E), p.364

v10b:
  v10b1: (E), p.364
  v10b2: NA
  v10b3: (E), p.364—including supply and marketing cooperative and other collectives
  v10b4: (E), p.364
  v10b5: (E), p.364
  v10b6: (E), p.364

v10d: (E), p.366—calculated on calendar year basis

11. Foreign Trade (FT)

v11a:
  v11a1: (C), p.283
  v11a2: (C), p.283
  v11a3: (C), p.283

v11b: (E), p.367
  v11b1: (E), p.367
  v11b2: v11b – v11b1

v11c: (E), p.367

v11d: (A); (E), p.367

12. Prices (PR)

v12a: (E), p.369

v12b: (E), p.369

v12c: (E), p.369

13. Education (ED)

v13a: (A)

v13b: (A); (E), p.372—1988: 99.1%

v13c:
- v13c1: (B), p.170; (E), p.372
- v13c2: (A); (B), p.171–172; (E), p.372—technical, ordinary and agricultural, vocational secondary schools
- v13c3: (B), p.173; (E), p.372

v13d: (A)—institutions of higher learning

14. Social Factors (SF)

v14a: (E), p.372

v14b: (E), p.372—medical technicians, other technicians, and other personnel

v14c: (A); (C), p.348

15. Natural Environment (NE)

v15a: (A); (E), p.354

v15b: (A)

v15c: (A)—10,000 cubic metres

v15d: (A)

v15e: NA

v15f: NA

Sources of Data

(A) Data supplied by the DSNEB, SSB, the PRC.
(B) Statistical Bureau of Jiangsu Province ed. *Jiangsu's Forty Years 1949–1989*, Beijing: CSPH, 1989.
(C) ________ ed *Statistical Yearbook of Jiangsu, 1989*, Beijing: CSPH, 1989.
(D) Same as (D) in Beijing's sources of data.
(E) Same as (E) in Beijing's sources of data.

11

Zhejiang

11. Zhejiang

11–1

Year	v1a	v1a1	v1a2	v1a3	v1a4	v1a5	v1b	v1b1	v1b2	v1b3	v1b4	v1b5	v1c	v1d	v1d1
1949	20.92	13.92	4.05	0.27	0.43	2.25							7.36	13.56	10.09
1950	24.61	15.91	5.13	0.59	0.72	2.26							8.86	15.75	11.59
1951	30.89	18.59	7.46	0.72	0.98	3.14							11.53	19.36	13.49
1952	35.57	21.77	8.24	1.06	1.25	3.24	113.6	114.1	112.7	145.7	126.6	101.6	13.04	22.53	16.04
1953	40.82	22.01	11.71	1.45	1.48	4.17	113.8	102.6	129.2	135.6	119.4	123.7	15.93	24.89	16.28
1954	43.30	23.44	12.97	1.36	1.50	4.03	106.6	107.8	109.2	99.4	105.4	95.8	17.17	26.13	17.48
1955	45.39	25.06	12.57	1.49	1.53	4.74	106.8	107.7	102.5	111.2	105.6	117.6	17.74	27.65	18.48
1956	51.67	25.78	16.35	2.29	1.59	5.66	113.2	102.5	123.2	157.2	117.4	119.2	21.42	30.25	18.57
1957	58.46	26.48	20.88	3.10	1.92	6.08	112.3	110.0	113.6	136.7	118.4	106.7	24.88	33.58	18.90
1958	80.78	26.09	38.25	6.93	2.81	6.72	139.5	97.8	189.6	222.6	146.9	105.6	40.72	40.06	17.84
1959	94.99	25.68	50.33	7.99	3.76	7.24	114.7	96.3	128.0	111.9	134.1	102.2	51.69	43.30	17.38
1960	96.57	23.03	54.33	8.26	4.40	6.55	102.6	86.7	112.1	100.0	117.9	85.2	53.76	42.81	15.51
1961	74.46	24.14	37.56	3.72	3.39	5.65	70.0	90.8	64.0	44.5	77.7	83.0	38.50	35.96	16.53
1962	74.84	29.07	33.62	2.80	2.89	6.46	94.2	112.2	85.4	72.2	85.8	108.4	36.19	38.65	19.76
1963	79.69	32.53	33.97	3.84	3.05	6.30	108.3	114.4	102.3	148.8	105.4	101.6	37.69	42.00	22.80
1964	89.03	35.04	39.08	4.41	3.41	7.08	114.6	110.8	115.9	122.4	112.4	122.0	42.18	46.84	24.30
1965	96.92	37.46	44.01	4.59	3.47	7.39	112.2	108.0	117.5	106.0	101.5	110.3	46.51	50.41	25.31
1966	106.67	40.26	50.52	4.42	3.68	7.79	108.7	103.1	114.8	95.1	106.2	106.5	53.77	52.90	27.30
1967	101.52	39.78	47.27	3.80	3.38	7.29	95.0	99.0	93.7	85.7	92.1	93.9	50.99	50.53	26.85
1968	98.67	40.65	44.91	3.65	3.10	6.36	96.5	101.4	95.1	95.4	91.8	87.2	49.98	48.69	27.85
1969	116.15	42.76	57.85	5.00	3.65	6.89	118.3	103.8	128.4	137.7	117.2	108.7	60.28	55.87	29.50
1970	129.19	45.36	66.66	5.93	4.15	7.09	111.7	105.0	115.6	119.2	113.6	103.9	67.42	61.77	31.53
1971	133.92	45.21	70.59	8.09	2.62	7.41	108.8	99.0	115.0	140.2	106.3	105.4	71.41	61.61	31.17
1972	150.30	54.23	76.78	8.72	2.77	7.80	110.8	115.2	109.1	106.3	105.8	105.6	75.18	75.12	38.77
1973	159.70	53.85	85.56	9.22	2.87	8.20	105.9	98.2	111.5	105.3	103.4	105.4	82.35	77.35	38.23
1974	150.72	56.38	73.54	9.90	2.54	8.36	94.6	102.8	87.5	107.6	88.3	102.0	74.17	76.55	41.03
1975	152.36	52.73	77.59	10.94	2.42	8.68	100.6	91.9	105.5	109.9	95.4	103.8	78.35	74.01	35.21
1976	158.65	52.98	82.07	12.32	2.42	8.86	104.5	101.1	105.8	113.0	100.3	102.0	82.63	76.02	38.55
1977	188.79	54.00	107.62	14.26	2.90	10.01	119.4	101.9	131.2	116.2	121.1	112.9	101.36	87.43	38.15
1978	232.79	65.71	132.11	19.76	3.98	11.23	122.5	119.4	122.7	136.5	136.5	112.1	124.76	108.03	45.94
1979	289.80	91.84	158.22	21.76	5.08	12.90	115.2	112.3	118.1	105.7	117.5	112.5	150.13	139.67	66.05
1980	344.17	92.67	201.61	28.74	6.04	15.11	120.1	97.9	129.0	133.7	120.4	108.4	185.83	158.34	62.86
1981	387.26	95.56	232.98	30.71	8.54	19.47	111.6	100.8	115.0	103.2	140.1	126.9	208.20	179.06	67.56
1982	440.14	118.04	251.52	33.96	10.92	25.70	111.9	116.5	108.3	110.3	124.7	130.9	235.26	204.88	83.04
1983	489.32	118.68	293.55	34.95	13.10	29.04	110.6	96.8	117.4	100.7	119.8	110.8	269.14	220.18	80.83
1984	627.26	147.49	382.60	43.10	18.57	35.50	125.7	116.5	130.0	115.9	140.4	118.4	350.56	276.70	102.18
1985	869.23	174.05	550.62	72.24	22.37	49.94	131.6	103.9	139.5	156.2	114.2	123.4	503.30	365.93	122.05
1986	1041.73	192.04	674.86	86.70	27.91	60.22	116.5	105.4	119.8	111.3	118.9	113.6	619.63	422.10	133.91
1987	1302.43	228.12	853.10	113.46	33.67	74.08	119.5	103.7	123.1	121.5	119.0	112.9	794.08	508.35	156.50
1988	1710.40	282.62	1141.03	143.47	42.01	101.27	119.7	102.3	124.4	106.7	118.1	114.1	1071.71	638.69	191.39
1989	1938.20	307.84	1333.87	142.67	45.06	108.76	104.1	101.7	106.9	88.4	91.0	92.4	1239.79	698.41	206.37

11. Zhejiang

11–2

Year	v1d2	v1d3	v1d4	v1d5	v1e	v1e1	v1e2	v1e3	v1e4	v1e5	v1f	v1f1	v1f2	v1f3	v1g
1949	1.05	0.14	0.30	1.98											13.50
1950	1.38	0.30	0.50	1.98											15.24
1951	2.09	0.37	0.69	2.72											18.04
1952	2.26	0.50	0.94	2.79											20.91
1953	3.20	0.58	1.11	3.72	109.6	101.9	128.3	114.3	112.7	128.0					22.89
1954	3.54	0.50	1.11	3.50	105.4	107.7	108.6	93.5	110.2	93.2					23.82
1955	3.22	0.58	1.14	4.23	108.7	107.4	103.1	116.4	105.9	121.0					25.35
1956	4.31	1.16	1.19	5.02	107.6	99.1	120.4	200.1	108.8	118.2					26.97
1957	6.36	1.43	1.44	5.45	112.1	107.6	123.8	128.9	128.4	108.1					30.22
1958	11.61	2.53	2.17	5.91	119.1	96.2	173.9	173.8	151.9	103.9					37.04
1959	14.09	2.66	2.65	6.52	106.3	95.4	121.3	101.6	122.5	104.4					39.97
1960	15.52	2.63	3.34	5.81	96.1	85.1	108.5	94.8	127.3	83.8					38.24
1961	11.07	1.23	2.28	4.85	77.6	93.3	70.0	42.0	68.7	80.2					30.74
1962	10.46	1.14	1.90	5.39	100.6	114.0	87.5	86.1	83.9	105.6					33.47
1963	10.62	1.44	2.01	5.13	111.0	118.5	103.5	135.4	105.3	99.1					36.32
1964	12.85	1.67	2.26	5.76	115.1	109.5	121.6	125.5	112.6	121.8					38.77
1965	14.94	1.81	2.32	6.03	100.8	105.0	121.2	114.3	102.6	110.8					41.79
1966	15.14	1.70	2.44	6.32	112.3	102.4	101.3	91.0	104.8	106.0					
1967	14.06	1.43	2.21	5.98	95.3	98.6	93.0	83.9	90.8	94.7					
1968	12.23	1.34	1.99	5.28	95.1	102.9	87.0	92.3	90.5	88.3					
1969	16.72	1.79	2.32	5.54	115.3	104.5	136.7	134.8	115.7	105.5					
1970	19.83	2.07	2.59	5.75	110.7	105.8	118.6	115.8	111.9	104.7					
1971	20.27	2.73	1.50	5.94	104.4	99.5	109.7	136.4	103.1	104.4					
1972	25.72	2.82	1.53	6.28	119.5	119.5	127.3	101.2	101.0	105.9					
1973	28.24	2.86	1.51	6.51	102.4	97.6	109.8	100.7	98.8	103.8					
1974	24.65	2.94	1.27	6.66	98.6	105.4	88.9	102.3	84.1	102.3					
1975	27.74	3.09	1.17	6.80	95.8	91.5	100.4	104.1	91.5	102.1					66.44
1976	26.11	3.65	1.16	6.55	103.1	101.6	105.5	118.9	100.0	96.4					69.24
1977	35.71	4.36	1.52	7.69	115.4	98.9	136.8	120.0	131.0	117.3					78.94
1978	45.08	6.42	2.09	8.50	122.8	118.9	126.0	146.5	136.9	110.4	122.54	47.09	53.52	21.93	99.58
1979	53.03	8.33	2.88	9.38	114.1	111.1	116.3	124.5	119.7	108.1	156.47	67.56	64.07	24.84	125.90
1980	70.71	10.16	3.26	11.35	116.5	96.9	134.0	123.5	117.7	112.0	178.45	64.60	84.07	29.78	146.73
1981	80.33	10.33	4.99	15.85	111.4	104.0	113.8	98.2	151.8	137.6	202.07	69.06	94.68	38.33	158.42
1982	84.71	10.90	6.53	19.70	112.2	118.0	105.5	105.2	127.5	123.2	229.33	84.88	98.44	46.01	185.96
1983	98.87	10.18	7.73	22.57	106.4	93.6	117.6	91.3	117.6	112.3	249.95	82.90	113.12	53.93	195.75
1984	123.97	12.61	10.87	27.07	122.3	119.4	112.5	116.5	139.6	116.2	312.77	104.70	141.48	66.59	255.61
1985	173.35	19.95	12.92	37.66	122.8	102.8	135.1	147.4	113.0	122.9	412.07	123.88	198.91	89.28	345.48
1986	203.95	23.80	15.67	44.77	112.0	103.7	116.2	110.6	115.9	112.3	477.81	136.29	230.89	110.63	412.41
1987	247.60	31.29	18.64	54.32	112.7	101.3	117.0	122.1	116.9	111.6	573.46	159.41	281.47	132.58	500.28
1988	311.50	38.45	22.74	74.61	111.8	98.4	117.1	103.6	115.6	115.1	715.42	195.58	348.04	171.80	636.97
1989	349.07	39.51	24.39	79.07	100.4	100.2	103.4	91.3	90.8	91.4	789.66	210.93	386.25	192.48	672.87

11. Zhejiang

11–3

Year	v1h	v1i	v1j	v1j1	v1j2	v1j3	v1k	v2a	v2a1	v2a2	v2b	v2c	v2c1	v2c2	v2d1
1949	47.00							0.59							1.04
1950								1.17				0.21			
1951								1.60				0.28			
1952								1.84	1.12	0.92		0.54			1.39
1953								2.41	1.16	1.25		0.61			1.65
1954	102.35							2.45	1.28	1.17		0.76			1.93
1955	96.09							2.12	1.23	0.89		0.79			2.16
1956	80.12							2.70	2.16	0.54		1.19			2.50
1957	86.82							5.11	2.71	2.40		1.75			2.88
1958								11.77	7.81	3.96		6.08			5.47
1959								14.50	9.05	5.45		7.13			7.82
1960								11.79	10.10	1.69		8.91			13.40
1961								3.65	4.34	-0.69		3.56			15.28
1962	142.27							2.80	3.35	-0.55		1.87			16.04
1963	134.15		505	573	408			4.77	3.63	1.14		2.24			17.23
1964	145.08							5.90	4.56	1.34		2.90			17.84
1965	133.42							7.11	4.85	2.26		2.82			19.47
1966								8.17	5.29	2.88		2.91			
1967								7.58	4.72	2.86		2.38			
1968								7.20	4.46	2.74		2.08			
1969								10.74	7.22	3.52		3.33			
1970								12.63	8.75	3.88		4.36			
1971								12.74	9.38	3.36		6.25			
1972								16.19	12.26	3.93		6.96			
1973		11.42	533	572	468			15.31	11.53	3.78		6.22			39.11
1974		11.67	537	583	464			15.37	11.70	3.67		5.53			36.42
1975		12.02	536	583	465			14.03	11.12	2.91		5.94			42.28
1976		12.80	523	579	447			13.89	12.95	0.94		6.11			45.20
1977		13.62	522	580	450			21.15	15.09	6.06		7.99			48.46
1978	165.00	16.19	544	597	470		1.64	30.05	20.63	19.42	23.23	12.27	5.40	0.34	53.33
1979		18.91	585	647	500		2.17	35.04	23.50	11.55	26.11	13.05	4.78	0.49	59.96
1980	219.21	24.23	701	772	604		4.40	45.73	29.69	16.04	33.25	15.99	4.98	1.02	67.42
1981	286.02	26.00	709	768	625		5.54	47.97	30.60	17.37	34.16	15.13	4.34	0.87	75.57
1982	346.01	27.32	740	783	671		6.22	60.13	40.06	20.07	41.72	20.74	6.35	1.01	85.38
1983	358.86	28.57	760	797	697		7.21	60.56	45.10	15.46	44.04	21.27	6.40	0.78	94.44
1984	446.37	35.72	913	976	828	937	9.29	91.49	55.74	35.75	64.89	27.28	7.25	1.12	104.91
1985	548.60	47.85	1159	1226	1071	1247	12.02	142.48	96.16	46.32	105.49	39.51	10.01	1.32	129.51
1986	609.31	58.01	1346	1442	1217	1455	15.55	169.10	105.47	63.63	127.39	50.83	11.44	1.62	148.39
1987	725.13	66.62	1493	1584	1365	1635	18.14	216.83	136.92	79.91	165.37	59.44	14.72	1.86	175.17
1988	902.36	85.40	1841	1961	1667	2014	25.28	265.21	156.26	108.45	204.16	69.72	19.58	2.43	199.74
1989	1010.72	94.46	2031	2158	1838		28.62	265.34	144.69	120.65	212.72	66.78	20.88	2.03	229.89

11. Zhejiang

11–4

Year	v2d2	v2e	v3a	v3b	v3b1	v3b2	v3c	v3d	v3d1	v3d2	v3e	v3e1	v3e2	v3e3	v3e4
1949	0.72		12.91	12.76			0.15	62	51	126					
1950			14.07	13.89			0.18	66	55	131					
1951			16.44	16.22			0.22	76	65	141					
1952	0.99	0.25	19.07	18.62	14.13	4.49	0.45	85	76	143					
1953	1.21	0.37	20.48	19.84	14.60	5.24	0.64	88	76	161					
1954	1.28	0.53	21.37	20.71	15.59	5.12	0.66	90	80	153					
1955	1.41	0.51	23.23	22.24	16.96	5.28	0.99	94	84	152					
1956	1.61	0.73	24.27	23.27	17.22	6.05	1.00	97	84	172					
1957	1.94	0.88	25.11	24.23	17.43	6.80	0.88	98	84	174	182.0	111.0	17.0	6.0	7.0
1958	4.45	1.92	25.27	24.07	16.47	7.60	1.20	95	78	180	168.4	104.9	15.0	5.4	7.0
1959	6.50	3.95	25.47	24.14	15.46	8.68	1.33	94	73	187					
1960	11.61	5.39	26.45	24.70	15.34	9.36	1.75	94	72	189					
1961	12.89	6.13	27.09	25.62	16.17	9.45	1.47	98	75	198	186.3	119.9	11.7	5.4	9.9
1962	13.45	4.36	30.67	29.29	20.02	9.27	1.38	110	91	205					
1963	14.30	3.87	31.55	30.20	21.90	8.30	1.35	110	95	190					
1964	14.57		32.87	31.72	23.09	8.63	1.15	112	97	192					
1965	15.89		34.68	33.50	24.56	8.94	1.18	115	100	194	188.0	115.8	20.9	5.9	7.1
1966															
1967															
1968															
1969															
1970															
1971															
1972															
1973	28.69														
1974	26.13														
1975	30.22	19.04	52.41	49.00	35.75	13.25	3.41	137	118	234					
1976	31.88		55.35	51.87	37.74	14.13	3.48	143	123	247					
1977	33.58	20.44	57.79	53.86	39.06	14.80	3.93	146	126	256					
1978	36.92	21.60	69.53	64.58	48.00	16.58	4.95	173	153	284					
1979	41.77	24.43	90.86	82.69	62.42	20.27	8.17	219	196	344					
1980	47.27	26.32	101.00	90.78	64.95	25.83	10.22	238	202	431	428.0				
1981	53.07	28.74	110.45	99.21	71.09	28.12	11.24	258	219	462	475.8	264.4	68.6	6.4	9.4
1982	59.90	32.58	125.83	114.13	84.47	29.66	11.70	293	258	480	470.9	270.0	60.2	7.3	9.1
1983	65.36	34.99	135.19	122.20	91.15	31.05	12.99	310	275	491	483.8	287.8	63.3	7.7	9.7
1984	73.53	35.72	164.12	145.22	107.87	37.35	18.90	365	324	574	561.8	316.0	81.0	8.3	10.0
1985	89.66	44.67	203.00	180.86	132.79	48.07	22.14	451	398	715	795.1	407.5	117.2	9.0	11.2
1986	107.14	55.42	243.31	218.10	158.57	59.53	25.21	539	472	861	968.9	492.1	134.4	9.5	11.5
1987	127.09	66.11	283.45	251.12	183.01	68.11	32.33	613	540	963	1100.5	570.1	138.3	10.0	13.6
1988	144.37	78.63	371.76	329.69	233.73	95.96	42.07	795	683	1330	1453.0	740.6	196.3	10.8	17.3
1989	164.19	105.58	407.53	360.41	255.90	104.51	47.12	860	741	1421	1555.9	851.1			

11. Zhejiang

11–5

Year	v3f	v3f1	v3f2	v3f3	v3f4	v4a1	v4a1a	v4a1b	v4a1c	v4a1d	v4a2	v4a2a	v4a2b	v4a2c	v4a2d
1949						0.45		0.07	0.36	0.02	0.05			0.02	0.03
1950						1.69		0.81	0.85	0.03	0.35	0.02	0.05	0.26	0.02
1951						2.86	0.15	1.50	1.11	0.10	0.75	0.27	0.08	0.31	0.09
1952						3.88	0.23	1.92	1.47	0.26	1.10	0.34	0.22	0.31	0.23
1953						4.10	0.31	2.47	1.15	0.17	1.42	0.28	0.58	0.40	0.16
1954	109.4	69.6	12.9	3.8	11.3	4.65	0.30	2.66	1.52	0.17	1.55	0.40	0.52	0.45	0.18
1955	91.0	57.9	10.7	3.1	9.4	4.83	0.37	2.60	1.75	0.11	1.57	0.30	0.49	0.52	0.26
1956	88.1	62.7	8.1	1.6	7.1	6.32	0.47	3.04	1.55	1.26	2.34	0.52	0.68	0.73	0.41
1957	94.7	66.3	8.3	1.5	7.6	6.52	0.83	3.56	1.84	0.29	2.58	0.66	0.77	0.68	0.47
1958						11.90	5.01	4.81	1.77	0.31	8.09	3.67	0.74	0.76	2.92
1959						15.64	8.33	5.11	1.76	0.44	8.89	4.38	0.88	0.89	2.74
1960						16.90	9.43	5.31	1.60	0.56	12.22	5.76	1.33	0.87	4.26
1961						10.75	5.32	3.91	1.16	0.36	6.52	1.54	1.14	0.83	3.01
1962	138.1	87.2	9.6	4.7	17.9	10.36	4.03	4.82	1.23	0.28	4.25	0.91	1.06	0.69	1.59
1963	125.7	80.6	10.9	3.9	13.0	11.01	4.17	5.22	1.35	0.27	4.52	1.05	1.11	0.68	1.68
1964	131.1	86.5	12.2	4.4	12.1	12.38	4.90	5.75	1.36	0.37	4.77	1.42	1.18	0.68	1.49
1965	133.4	87.6	14.5	4.3	11.2	13.20	5.81	5.70	1.31	0.38	4.92	1.62	1.20	0.68	1.42
1966						14.04	6.84	5.32	1.49	0.39	5.43	1.56	1.47	0.73	1.67
1967						10.91	4.52	4.80	1.24	0.35	4.48	1.27	1.47	0.67	1.07
1968						9.44	3.15	4.53	1.34	0.42	3.76	0.93	1.33	0.65	0.85
1969						12.48	4.98	5.52	1.50	0.48	5.59	2.16	1.37	0.79	1.27
1970						15.42	6.60	6.88	1.42	0.52	7.21	2.81	1.50	0.84	2.06
1971						15.94	6.37	7.73	1.38	0.46	7.96	3.10	1.73	0.96	2.17
1972						17.90	7.29	8.72	1.42	0.47	9.12	3.81	1.99	1.02	2.30
1973						20.18	8.24	10.08	1.42	0.44	9.53	3.31	2.26	1.02	2.94
1974						15.43	4.62	8.93	1.41	0.47	10.75	3.61	2.42	1.05	3.67
1975						13.37	2.46	9.04	1.43	0.44	9.98	3.10	2.53	1.06	3.29
1976						13.72	2.12	9.80	1.42	0.38	10.96	3.35	2.65	1.06	3.90
1977						19.64	5.28	12.49	1.48	0.39	12.24	3.71	2.77	1.17	4.59
1978	157.0	92.7	17.2	14.4	11.0	27.45	9.92	15.14	1.47	0.92	17.43	6.07	3.40	1.35	6.61
1979						25.87	7.16	16.58	1.51	0.62	17.74	5.26	3.83	1.45	7.20
1980	191.9	107.0	21.5	23.1	11.6	31.13	10.11	18.85	1.45	0.72	17.34	3.81	4.68	1.90	6.95
1981	266.5	144.8	30.4	38.0	11.8	34.34	10.32	21.64	1.53	0.85	17.12	2.80	5.14	2.05	7.13
1982	301.9	167.6	31.3	36.0	12.7	36.64	8.91	25.06	1.59	1.08	18.88	3.04	5.82	2.34	7.68
1983	325.9	179.6	34.0	43.6	13.9	41.79	10.03	28.78	1.75	1.23	21.94	3.56	6.80	2.76	8.82
1984	369.2	198.3	33.2	55.5	15.0	46.67	9.12	34.57	1.80	1.18	28.80	4.38	8.56	4.05	11.81
1985	473.8	243.3	42.0	77.2	21.2	58.25	7.64	47.36	2.25	1.00	37.40	4.77	10.58	4.19	17.86
1986	560.6	277.8	46.9	108.9	21.3	68.61	9.40	55.18	2.43	1.60	50.96	5.56	13.44	4.80	27.16
1987	659.4	320.4	46.2	146.5	21.1	76.36	9.30	62.65	2.39	5.02	51.24	4.28	14.01	5.19	27.76
1988	838.7	389.1	58.6	199.3	23.7	85.55	4.37	74.72	2.46	4.00	63.13	4.05	17.55	5.29	36.24
1989	927.0	444.8	60.9	215.2	23.0	98.21	2.05				74.77	3.87	20.37	6.25	44.28

11. Zhejiang

11–6

Year	v4b	v4b1	v4b2	v4b3	v4c1	v4c2	v5a	v5a1	v5a2	v5a3	v5a4	v5b1	v5b2	v5b3	v5c
1949							850.3	31.7				731.5	50.6	68.2	
1950								35.1							
1951								42.0							
1952	0.37	0.37			0.32	26.1	963.3	53.4	1.5			810.8	73.7	78.8	
1953					0.51	32.3		54.6							
1954					1.08	59.7		56.7							
1955					0.93	48.4	1042.5	57.9	15.8			891.4	72.8	78.3	
1956					1.18	50.4	1084.7	75.3	66.1			926.2	78.8	79.7	
1957	1.07	0.91	0.16		1.96	69.5	1096.5	76.3	68.5			939.2	79.0	78.2	
1958					4.31	68.2	1228.1	176.5	28.8	0.6	1022.3	852.9	220.7	154.6	
1959					6.19	59.2	1186.3	139.5	33.8	1.3	1011.6	901.3	145.5	139.4	
1960					6.33	37.2	1171.8	150.5	17.9	0.4	1003.0	905.3	127.9	138.6	
1961					4.77	25.1	1133.7	119.1	59.8	3.1	951.7	946.1	97.5	90.2	
1962	1.33	1.05	0.28		4.12	23.1	1114.5	88.3	55.5	5.0	965.7	965.0	69.1	80.4	
1963					5.18	28.5	1112.0	83.1	56.5	4.9	967.5				
1964					6.26			85.1	61.1	5.3					
1965	2.40	1.86	0.54		7.53	37.0	1168.1	87.7	66.2	4.0	1010.2				
1966								91.7							
1967								93.9							
1968								96.5							
1969								100.6							
1970	2.80	2.33	0.47				1431.5	114.6	67.0	2.2	1247.6				
1971								125.7							
1972								134.6							
1973								134.0	80.9						
1974								134.7	85.7						
1975	5.53	4.15	1.38		6.56	14.2	1635.7	139.3	92.9	1.2	1402.3				
1976	5.58	4.27	1.31		6.05		1677.2	144.3	108.8	1.0	1423.2				
1977	6.32	4.75	1.57		11.04	20.4	1733.6	146.5	121.8	1.0	1464.2				
1978	7.73	5.58	2.15		16.13	29.5	1795.0	183.1	129.8	1.5	1480.6				
1979	11.79	7.68	4.11		19.08	30.7	1829.9	196.8	143.1	2.0	1488.0				
1980	16.95	10.53	6.42		23.12	33.2	1856.4	208.5	151.2	3.5	1493.2				
1981	21.47	13.11	8.36		24.43	32.1	1954.5	223.6	155.7	4.1	1571.1				
1982	28.52	17.06	11.46		26.65	30.7	2021.7	232.3	142.0	5.3	1642.2				
1983	37.34	22.47	14.79		31.19	31.1	2141.2	237.7	145.1	7.6	1750.8				
1984	49.58	29.06	20.52		34.93	31.9	2248.9	228.3	172.7	9.6	1836.9	1254.2	688.1	266.6	
1985	67.73	38.57	29.16		42.85	31.9	2318.6	240.7	183.8	12.1	1879.9	1276.2	735.2	307.2	
1986	97.92	52.22	45.70		44.76	27.5	2386.4	251.9	188.7	12.9	1930.5	1278.1	765.1	343.2	
1987	129.12	69.23	59.89		52.20	27.0	2444.7	263.5	193.0	15.7	1969.4	1275.0	802.0	367.7	
1988	144.03	81.26	62.77		61.20	27.6	2502.7	274.3	197.0	22.5	2004.5	1282.2	803.7	416.9	
1989	202.70	123.40	79.30		60.47	22.4	2522.9	275.0	189.3	27.0	2025.7	1330.7	770.1	422.0	

11. Zhejiang

11–7

Year	v5c1	v5d	v6a	v6a1	v6a2	v6b	v6c	v6d1	v6d2	v6d3	v6d4	v6d5	v6d6
1949			2083	246	1837	32.05	14.85	308	1775	1090	993	62.48	27.21
1950			2121	257	1864	33.69	15.43	320	1801	1110	1011		
1951			2162	268	1894	32.55	13.46	326	1836	1132	1030		
1952			2213	282	1931	38.10	13.96	331	1882	1161	1052	68.89	26.76
1953			2269	295	1974	38.70	13.56	341	1928	1191	1078		
1954			2326	308	2018	39.40	13.44	351	1975	1222	1104		
1955			2387	314	2073	38.09	12.58	362	2025	1253	1133		
1956			2443	330	2113	33.40	9.46	380	2063	1280	1163		
1957			2503	358	2145	34.94	9.32	415	2088	1310	1193	76.40	26.08
1958			2564	541	2023	34.10	9.15	469	2095	1351	1213	124.69	109.60
1959			2598	567	2031	26.28	10.81	490	2108	1360	1238		
1960			2620	588	2032	23.51	11.88	504	2116	1375	1245		
1961			2633	543	2090	17.58	9.84	486	2147	1378	1255	96.90	120.87
1962			2707	480	2227	36.02	8.61	453	2254	1413	1294	94.28	72.02
1963			2800	440	2360	40.71	7.89	446	2354	1460	1340	95.28	36.04
1964			2875	424	2451	37.18	9.21	380	2495	1499	1376	96.14	36.53
1965			2957	422	2535	36.48	8.09	388	2569	1540	1417	96.47	36.84
1966			3033	426	2607	32.48	7.12	393	2641	1579	1454		
1967			3103	449	2654	28.77	6.55	403	2700	1615	1488		
1968			3173	459	2714	28.59	6.14	405	2768	1651	1522		
1969			3253	464	2789	28.69	5.75	394	2859	1692	1561		
1970			3316	430	2886	26.16	5.96	399	2917	1722	1594	94.55	37.81
1971			3390	488	2902	25.70	6.10	418	2972	1762	1628		
1972			3451	468	2983	24.48	6.02	420	3030	1792	1659		
1973			3513	476	3037	23.24	6.08	428	3085	1825	1688		
1974			3561	483	3078	20.92	6.16	414	3147	1849	1712		
1975			3614	494	3120	19.49	6.31	417	3197	1877	1737	100.86	40.40
1976			3663	504	3159	18.96	6.05	425	3238	1902	1761		
1977			3707	511	3196	18.94	6.55	419	3288	1925	1782		
1978			3751	527	3224	18.17	5.83	429	3322	1948	1803	104.53	42.24
1979			3792	550	3242	17.98	5.89	460	3332	1967	1825		
1980			3827	569	3258	15.59	6.29	480	3347	1986	1841	113.08	44.26
1981			3872	994	2878	17.93	6.27	510	3362	2008	1864		
1982			3924	1000	2925	18.31	6.94	536	3388	2035	1889		
1983			3963	907	3056	15.89	6.37	550	3413	2056	1907		
1984			3993	1018	2975	12.52	5.99	568	3425	2071	1922		
1985			4030	1534	2496	12.61	6.05	634	3396	2091	1939	124.67	102.11
1986			4070	1780	2290	15.96	5.94	653	3417	2112	1958	127.07	103.29
1987			4121	2127	1994	17.01	6.92	666	3455	2137	1984	129.16	104.85
1988			4170	2400	1770	15.54	6.35	682	3488	2161	2009	131.26	106.19
1989			4209	2612	1597	15.20	6.41	693	3516	2181	2028	132.84	107.35

11. Zhejiang

11–8

Year	v7a	v7b	v7c	v7d	v7e	v7f	v7g	v7h	v7h1	v7h2	v7h3	v7h4	v7h5	v7i	v8a
1949								13.92	9.58	0.75	1.57	0.26	1.76	63.7	4.05
1950								15.91	11.45	0.69	1.66	0.38	1.73	66.1	
1951								18.59	13.65	0.67	1.90	0.58	1.79	78.1	
1952				6133.7				21.77	15.95	0.76	2.33	0.85	1.88	80.3	8.24
1953								22.01	15.46	0.91	2.64	1.09	1.91	80.4	11.71
1954								23.44	16.04	1.31	3.01	1.16	1.92	81.2	12.97
1955								25.05	18.11	1.46	1.95	1.59	1.94	78.4	12.57
1956								25.79	17.40	1.88	2.93	1.65	1.93	78.2	16.35
1957	0.50			6893.6				26.48	16.87	2.56	3.27	1.27	2.51	76.4	20.88
1958								26.09	17.16	3.45	3.33	1.21	0.94	73.9	35.94
1959								25.68	17.57	2.94	2.68	1.45	1.04	78.3	48.12
1960								23.03	16.09	2.25	2.12	1.40	1.17	73.5	52.23
1961								24.14	17.61	1.89	2.24	1.28	1.12	67.4	36.18
1962				6286.2				29.07	20.90	2.11	3.01	1.62	1.43	68.1	33.62
1963								32.53	23.02	2.30	4.12	1.64	1.45	68.3	32.18
1964								35.04	24.22	2.21	5.49	1.87	1.25	67.9	39.08
1965	6.07	61.84		6619.8		68.68	1.90	37.46	25.76	2.25	6.06	2.15	1.24	68.3	44.01
1966								40.26	27.66	2.27	6.63	2.36	1.34	68.5	50.52
1967								39.78	26.18	2.50	6.98	2.61	1.51	68.5	47.27
1968								40.65	28.37	2.42	6.13	2.22	1.51		44.91
1969								42.76	29.59	2.19	7.29	2.15	1.54		57.65
1970	10.55			6945.7				45.36	31.37	2.16	7.92	2.22	1.69		66.66
1971								45.21	29.78	2.31	9.04	2.52	1.56	71.3	70.59
1972								54.23	37.90	1.83	10.13	2.68	1.69	69.6	76.78
1973								53.85	37.28	1.66	10.50	3.04	1.37	67.2	85.56
1974	21.33						7.39	56.38	38.78	1.70	10.97	3.41	1.52	65.6	73.54
1975	24.55		2197.4	7043.0		77.74	9.26	52.73	37.85	1.71	8.56	3.09	1.52	64.1	77.59
1976	28.02		2226.3	7020.9				52.98	39.19	1.61	7.49	3.06	1.63	61.8	82.07
1977	32.50		2241.3	7086.2				54.00	40.48	1.56	7.31	2.96	1.69	59.6	107.62
1978	39.29	1248.68	2257.7	7140.2		181.41	12.89	65.71	48.86	1.99	9.42	3.48	1.96	60.8	132.11
1979	46.99		2279.9	7097.4				91.84	67.29	2.75	15.55	4.07	2.18	60.6	158.22
1980	53.47	1452.97	2287.0	7026.6	521.1	299.01	17.53	92.67	60.52	3.61	19.39	5.44	3.71	58.1	201.61
1981	58.50		2284.7	6966.2	553.4	306.12	24.20	95.56	64.48	3.79	16.45	6.11	4.73	59.1	232.98
1982	62.85	1278.19	2287.0	6939.0	139.1	326.17	26.08	118.04	77.91	4.42	22.88	6.13	6.70	60.6	251.52
1983	68.23	1170.37	2287.9	6867.1	595.2	336.88	27.92	118.68	74.87	4.77	23.38	6.85	8.81	59.0	293.55
1984	74.63	1112.22	2293.8	6790.3	303.0	344.31	32.14	147.49	89.93	6.67	26.98	11.01	12.90	55.7	382.60
1985	81.02	1120.31	2292.0	6677.5	367.5	344.76	40.24	174.05	92.85	8.87	37.80	16.14	18.39	53.8	550.63
1986	88.87	1130.40	2244.9	6542.7	902.6	380.97	43.82	192.04	101.00	9.26	40.03	19.72	22.03	52.6	674.86
1987	97.46	1127.20	2240.5	6561.4	555.0	410.16	57.01	228.12	113.91	11.61	49.45	25.91	27.24	50.7	853.10
1988	107.59		2225.8	6450.8	810.0	438.92	60.82	282.62	129.89	14.40	71.93	33.41	32.99	49.4	1141.03
1989	113.30	1194.90	2221.6	6469.8			65.24	307.84	145.97	13.60	78.94	35.37	33.96	48.4	1333.87

11. Zhejiang

Year	v8a1	v8a2	v8a3	v8b	v8c1	v8c2	v8d	v8f1	v8f2	v8f3	v8f4	v8f5	v8g
1949					0.39	3.66	0.06		0.10		0.59		336410
1950					0.53	4.60					0.57		
1951					0.75	6.71					0.75		
1952				7.14	0.88	7.36	0.63		0.15		0.85	0.49	390834
1953				9.22	1.25	10.46	2.14		0.23		1.05	1.19	
1954				10.41	1.55	11.42	2.52		0.25		1.29	1.28	
1955				10.49	1.50	11.07	2.38		0.18		1.28	3.06	
1956				13.47	2.04	14.31	3.26		0.12		1.64	3.82	
1957				14.54	3.78	17.10	4.92		0.14		1.88	3.82	59708
1958					9.82	28.43		0.89	5.99		3.46	6.59	
1959					16.01	34.32		4.36	17.15		6.09	13.18	
1960					21.45	32.88		11.54	60.95		10.58	28.13	
1961					10.78	26.78		3.30	52.51		15.01	14.94	
1962					6.93	26.69	7.56	0.50	34.16		16.68	16.09	45557
1963				25.91	8.06	25.91	8.04	0.32	33.28		12.68	29.96	
1964	30.85	8.09	0.14	30.85	8.58	30.50	9.81	0.71	26.17		19.37	37.58	
1965	34.98	8.89	0.14	34.98	10.07	33.94	11.52	4.86	32.26		21.21	46.46	24905
1966	40.45	10.07		40.45	14.48	36.04		9.59	38.66		28.95	57.88	
1967	36.81	10.46		36.81	12.39	34.88		6.33	34.66		26.39	39.67	
1968	34.50	10.41		34.50	11.57	33.34		3.74	39.02		21.08	39.03	
1969	44.25	13.40		44.25	17.67	40.18		5.52	46.97		33.48	57.29	
1970	51.01	15.65		51.01	23.23	43.43		8.15	130.92		33.17	70.75	12177
1971	52.74	17.85		52.74	25.39	45.20		13.08	169.04		39.50	91.90	
1972	56.37	20.41		56.37	28.59	48.19		12.66	134.71		38.31	111.16	
1973	61.34	24.22		58.78	32.34	53.22		15.50	102.81		51.01	124.01	
1974	48.06	24.94	0.54	48.60	27.03	46.51		7.21	45.98		47.08	84.24	
1975	47.79	29.80		47.79	28.36	49.23		5.03	49.32		46.80	89.13	16716
1976	47.79	34.28		47.79	29.80	52.27		5.46	68.49		42.51	101.46	17556
1977	64.15	43.47		61.24	42.54	65.08	18.10	16.32	109.31		50.70	146.90	19088
1978	81.03	51.08		77.69	52.60	79.51	23.10	23.96	159.29		50.59	180.51	21308
1979	96.21	62.01		91.47	63.45	94.77	26.41	27.22	168.71		56.93	207.50	24077
1980	113.78	86.69	1.14	106.65	75.87	125.74	33.11	39.35	143.09		81.46	228.29	27989
1981	122.84	108.16	1.98	115.50	81.28	151.70	34.94	40.09	132.51		95.75	321.59	30033
1982	132.11	116.97	2.44	124.32	89.37	162.15	37.26	40.31	140.30		92.55	396.91	30614
1983	149.96	141.27	2.32	137.66	109.44	184.11	42.12	44.48	146.03		112.50	491.72	31936
1984	168.48	211.15	2.97	161.12	137.54	245.06	48.58	50.63	148.69		116.13	624.37	38973
1985	204.67	332.84	13.12	201.35	206.64	343.99	59.65	54.10	150.62		132.03	799.92	44975
1986	235.84	417.86	21.16	230.38	247.06	427.80	67.15	46.23	147.66		148.18	998.00	47281
1987	283.25	533.16	36.69	275.39	314.34	538.76	78.70	57.71	144.29		173.01	1216.00	45433
1988	356.62	725.05	59.36	345.99	413.58	727.45	96.02	51.43	143.07		190.26	1314.10	45788
1989	425.46	815.04	93.37	413.69	493.64	840.23	106.62	69.87	143.71		200.35	1288.00	45109

11. Zhejiang

11–10

Year	v8g1	v9a	v9a1	v9a2	v9a3	v9b	v9b1	v9b2	v9b3	v9c	v10a	v10a1	v10b1	v10b2	v10b3
1949		3.52	1.90	0.97	0.63	2.65	1.35	0.19	1.00	553					
1950		5.38	2.96	1.65	0.73	4.24	1.79	0.41	1.90	564					
1951		6.30	3.25	1.91	1.00	5.97	2.08	0.55	2.88	851					
1952		6.08	2.99	1.72	1.28	7.61	3.21	5.30	3.50	1001	12.12	11.06	1.36	2.77	0.02
1953		8.76	4.36	2.33	1.90	9.53	3.95	0.73	4.28	1268	15.05	13.71	1.51	4.05	0.04
1954		9.31	4.37	2.77	1.90	10.80	4.21	0.84	5.04	1353	16.02	14.35	1.49	6.58	0.91
1955		9.48	4.44	2.83	1.90	10.71	3.90	0.77	5.09	1467	16.32	14.41	2.88	4.36	2.86
1956		13.33	6.41	4.54	1.95	13.70	5.12	0.97	6.52	1721	18.95	16.55	4.48	4.62	4.52
1957		14.35	5.79	5.71	2.42	16.09	5.22	1.06	8.27	1832	19.55	17.35	5.00	4.23	6.21
1958		17.99	6.87	8.03	2.59	26.12	7.30	2.03	10.83	2702	22.02	18.73	6.53	6.32	5.73
1959		22.21	8.43	10.07	3.21	41.42	12.32	3.28	15.92	3909	24.26	20.38	10.07	8.64	3.12
1960		25.45	9.78	11.49	3.64	53.95	17.07	4.43	21.30	4858	24.64	20.25	10.31	8.91	3.22
1961				10.12	5.31			2.36	11.26	4191	24.62	20.80	11.02	8.83	3.24
1962				10.14	6.15			1.79	8.79	3891	26.67	22.49	10.16	8.86	6.14
1963	1768			10.31	4.51			1.65	9.60	3629	25.70	21.45	9.42	8.75	6.13
1964	1694			10.18	4.17			1.80	12.39	3758	26.81	22.14	10.53	8.78	6.44
1965	1671			10.45	3.91			2.55	14.01	3824	29.29	23.79	12.08	9.76	6.57
1966				12.39	4.51			3.05	13.96	3907	32.35	26.13	13.48	11.02	6.87
1967				13.23	4.49			3.05	12.00	3785	33.39	27.83	13.94	11.11	7.30
1968				10.61	4.71			2.70	12.00	3678	31.59	26.48	13.67	10.06	6.78
1969				13.47	5.10			3.16	13.94	3805	34.37	28.46	15.05	11.63	6.57
1970				14.47	5.07			3.53	16.18	4107	35.73	28.84	16.29	12.19	6.01
1971				15.08	4.89			4.22	15.26	4488	38.45	30.67	17.91	13.35	5.91
1972				17.00	5.68			4.78	17.32	4958	42.36	33.55	20.00	14.93	6.04
1973	2181			18.74	6.40			4.70	17.71	5386	45.87	36.48	21.56	16.64	6.11
1974	2207			19.49	6.39			4.00	16.30	5457	46.07	37.33	21.56	16.72	6.12
1975	2269			17.67	6.94			3.39	17.17	5603	47.33	38.73	23.24	15.29	6.48
1976	2304			17.88	6.95			3.54	17.62	5850	48.64	39.66	21.80	17.48	6.76
1977	2382			20.39	7.41			4.98	21.05	6117	52.39	42.16	22.59	19.57	7.28
1978	2451	66.68	29.75	27.60	7.50	164.19	112.77	6.69	25.81	6851	60.20	46.86	25.68	23.15	8.92
1979	2484	78.22	34.77	33.26	7.92	181.29	121.50	7.62	30.28	7832	74.73	58.97	30.88	28.55	12.31
1980	2562	96.74	43.55	41.70	8.68	190.76	126.23	8.25	33.93	8992	92.64	74.87	37.13	33.48	18.35
1981	2593	111.40	49.05	50.25	9.15	192.29	121.27	9.25	37.43	9970	103.80	85.99	39.67	34.74	23.40
1982	2645	120.63	50.70	57.28	9.20	201.82	120.49	11.48	42.28	10835	112.96	93.77	41.75	36.04	26.55
1983	2667	134.73	57.46	64.54	8.80	212.49	123.02	13.58	43.04	12477	125.36	104.24	44.57	37.07	28.78
1984	2651	157.81	66.74	76.86	9.75	232.67	127.59	16.67	49.94	14879	149.15	125.82	51.74	38.43	34.15
1985	2951	201.33	75.24	107.23	9.68	293.54	132.54	33.45	56.28	18837	197.82	172.27	58.23	43.37	50.60
1986	2972	220.38	78.43	124.91	8.31	341.20	135.18	68.14	61.66	20565	233.18	203.49	70.83	47.67	58.01
1987	3106	246.98	83.94	145.85	7.43	369.21	138.07	82.52	57.85	24878	279.37	242.58	83.51	54.51	67.53
1988	3128	269.43	93.12	158.81	7.00	403.96	136.50	96.25	62.63	31301	377.01	325.88	117.80	69.23	82.86
1989	3172	257.28	87.63	153.87	9.74	408.99	146.51	92.75	88.84	37020	400.26	346.01	122.55	70.07	74.77

11. Zhejiang

11–11

Year	v10b4	v10b5	v10b6	v10d	v11a1	v11a2	v11a3	v11b	v11b1	v11b2	v11c	v11d	v12a	v12b	v12c
1949															
1950															
1951															128.3
1952	0.02	7.27	0.68	7.90											100.4
1953	0.02	8.62	0.81	8.83									104.2	106.8	107.7
1954	0.02	6.32	0.70	11.65									101.1	101.3	120.4
1955	0.04	5.47	0.71	10.49									100.2	100.9	97.2
1956	2.82	1.72	0.79	10.24									100.0	100.0	103.7
1957	2.65	0.63	0.83	12.71									102.1	102.1	105.3
1958	2.61	0.48	0.35	13.26					0.1689				100.5	100.2	101.6
1959	1.96	0.17	0.30	13.13					0.1481				100.5	100.2	100.4
1960	1.75	0.17	0.28	11.37					0.1062				100.2	100.1	100.6
1961		0.18	1.35	12.67					0.0518				118.4	122.0	114.4
1962		0.42	1.10	13.38					0.0561				90.8	99.2	100.2
1963		0.34	1.06	15.40				0.2431	0.2363	0.0068			87.6	98.8	98.1
1964		0.36	0.70	17.96				0.2427	0.2326	0.0101			95.3	99.1	99.2
1965		0.38	0.50	18.53				0.2315	0.1942	0.0373			97.8	99.3	101.7
1966		0.38	0.60	20.81				0.1140	0.0863	0.0277			98.9		103.8
1967		0.34	0.70	20.38				0.0921	0.0602	0.0319			98.8		100.0
1968		0.28	0.80	20.08				0.0697	0.0487	0.0210			100.0		100.0
1969		0.22	0.90	20.48				0.1346	0.0907	0.0439			99.6		100.0
1970		0.24	1.00	20.64				0.0773	0.0504	0.0269			99.0	98.5	100.0
1971		0.18	1.10	22.71				0.1166	0.0812	0.0354			99.1		100.6
1972		0.19	1.20	24.78				0.1461	0.1036	0.0425			99.7	99.9	100.9
1973		0.18	1.38	25.31				0.3484	0.1215	0.2269			99.7	99.7	100.3
1974		0.19	1.48	25.38				0.1708	0.1023	0.0685			100.0	100.0	100.0
1975		0.19	2.13	24.89				0.2351	0.1068	0.1283			100.1	100.2	100.1
1976		0.20	2.40	22.94				0.2970	0.1827	0.1143			100.0	99.8	100.0
1977		0.44	2.51	23.96				0.5070	0.3783	0.1287			100.1	100.1	100.4
1978		0.19	2.26	27.55				0.7011	0.5240	0.1771			100.1	100.0	103.6
1979		0.23	2.76	39.27				1.0790	0.9075	0.1715	0.1120	0.6510	102.1	102.6	126.7
1980	0.01	0.43	3.24	42.95				2.6084	2.4273	0.1811	0.0614		108.0	108.8	106.9
1981		0.88	5.11	44.06				5.0054	4.4062	0.5992	0.0818		101.5	101.7	99.8
1982	0.01	2.29	6.32	51.40				6.0997	5.5696	0.5301	0.0614		100.9	101.9	103.9
1983	0.02	7.63	7.29	53.42				7.2271	6.5201	0.7070	0.0540		102.0	102.8	103.9
1984	0.07	15.52	9.24	61.42				8.4490	7.3689	1.0801	0.8527	0.4908	103.4	103.7	108.1
1985	0.09	28.73	16.80	77.74				12.1083	9.3768	2.7315	0.8916	0.6216	114.0	115.1	110.8
1986	0.26	36.94	19.47	90.36				13.7246	11.5608	2.1638	0.5274	0.4941	106.0	106.3	100.6
1987	0.23	47.81	25.78	104.70				16.9838	13.7028	3.2810	1.4335	1.1404	109.5	110.9	119.1
1988	0.75	70.91	35.46	142.87	2.7402	10.47	2.9921	21.9125	16.2023	5.7102	2.6815	1.8798	122.1	123.4	133.1
1989	1.04	89.73	42.10	157.08				25.3940	18.7919	6.6021	3.4535	1.2500	117.8	116.8	113.6

11. Zhejiang

11–12

Year	v13a	v13b	v13c1	v13c2	v13c3	v13d	v14a	v14b	v14c	v15a	v15b	v15c	v15d	v15e	v15f
1949	12.3		0.3112	6.21	84.08	0.1042	5800	16125	0.09	2602.0					
1950	12.1														
1951	6.6														
1952	12.0	50.7	0.4675	15.08	188.70	0.0833	6668	26153	0.48	3062.0					
1953	28.7														
1954	24.2														
1955	22.9														
1956	20.5														
1957	21.8		1.2348	24.10	229.55	0.1197	11100	61282	0.84	3119.8					
1958	6.5														
1959	6.4														
1960	7.4														
1961	12.3														
1962	17.2		2.1406	23.69	251.54	0.5573	21700	44153	0.89	2854.7					
1963	16.6														
1964	16.1														
1965	32.3	85.4	1.6567	35.40	466.52	0.3995	23649	45631	1.75	2801.0					
1966	18.6														
1967	22.9														
1968	24.3														
1969	16.4														
1970	13.1		0.3117		419.83	0.5658	47400	49430	3.11	2758.5					
1971	13.8														
1972	13.7														
1973	14.3														
1974	13.7														
1975	15.2		1.0053	176.52	537.71	0.1341		65233	3.27	2756.8					
1976	14.6		1.0369	223.09	520.29	0.2957		73032	3.09	2759.0					
1977	13.5		1.3811	238.75	507.80	0.3815		76190	3.44	2760.3					
1978	11.4	97.6	2.4223	217.44	501.43	0.3743	56519	80943	3.65	2757.0					
1979	12.6	97.4	3.2227	184.54	486.77	0.1013		84862	3.83	2747.8					
1980	16.0	97.0	3.7815	173.14	482.42	0.3710	63195	91387	4.40	2734.6					
1981	17.8	97.2	4.1020	158.51	459.83	0.5852		98392	5.09	2729.8					
1982	17.9	97.1	3.6088	153.85	430.59	1.4968		101202	5.07	2726.7					
1983	17.5	97.4	3.9008	157.15	407.20	1.0411		107954	5.96	2724.9					
1984	16.4	97.8	4.4883	169.79	395.46	0.9002		113705	7.56	2709.0					
1985	16.2	98.1	5.2688	181.85	384.91	1.1044	72072	113271	9.13	2665.1		851			
1986	14.6	98.3	5.7352	189.26	378.09	1.3027		113907	9.18	2630.3		656			
1987	15.0	98.6	6.0072	188.74	365.15	1.5017	78600	117159	10.67	2617.4					
1988	15.7	98.9	6.0419	176.05	366.04	1.8712	82563	121417	10.97	2604.7	6498.4	849	606	1.3296	0.7708
1989		99.1	6.1000	169.91	375.73	1.7300	86000	126000	9.05	2596.7					

Notes

1. National Output and Income (Y)

v1a: (E), p.379
v1a1: (E), p.379
v1a2: (E), p.379
v1a3: (E), p.379
v1a4: (E), p.379
v1a5: (E), p.379

v1b: (A); (D), p.224
v1b1: (A); (D), p.224
v1b2: (A); (D), p.224
v1b3: (A); (D), p.224
v1b4: (A); (D), p.224
v1b5: (A); (D), p.224

v1c: v1a – v1d

v1d: (E), p.376
v1d1: (E), p.376
v1d2: (E), p.376
v1d3: (E), p.376
v1d4: (E), p.376
v1d5: (E), p.376

v1e: (A); (D), p.227
v1e1: (A); (D), p.227
v1e2: (A); (D), p.227
v1e3: (A); (D), p.227
v1e4: (A); (D), p.227
v1e5: (A); (D), p.227

v1f: (E), p.375
v1f1: (E), p.375
v1f2: (E), p.375
v1f3: (E), p.375

v1g: v2a + v3a

v1h: (A); (E), p.404

v1i: (E), p.403

v1j: (A); (E), p.403
v1j1: (C), p.304; (E), p.403
v1j2: (C), p.304; (E), p.403
v1j3: (C), p.304

v1k: (E), p.403

2. Investment (I)

v2a: (E), p.378
v2a1: (A); (D), p.232
v2a2: (A); (D), p.232

v2b: (A)

v2c: (A); (E), p.394
v2c1: (E), p.395
v2c2: (E), p.395

v2d:
v2d1: (E), p.392
v2d2: (E), p.392

v2e: (E), p.392

3. Consumption (C)

v3a: (E), p.378

v3b: (E), p.378
v3b1: (A); (D), p.228
v3b2: (A); (D), p.228

v3c: (E), p.378

v3d: (E), p.402
v3d1: (E), p.402
v3d2: (E), p.402

v3e: (A); (E), p.404
v3e1: (A); (E), p.404
v3e2: (A)
v3e3: (A)
v3e4: (A)

v3f: (A); (E), p.404
v3f1: (A); (E), p.404

v3f2: (A)
v3f3: (A)
v3f4: (A)

4. Public Finance and Banking (FB)

v4a:
- v4a1: (E), p.400
  - v4a1a: (E), p.400
  - v4a1b: (C), p.265
  - v4a1c: (C), p.265
  - v4a1d: v4a1 – v4a1a – v4a1b – v4a1c
- v4a2: (E), p.400
  - v4a2a: (E), p.400
  - v4a2b: (E), p.400
  - v4a2c: (E), p.400
  - v4a2d: v4a2 – v4a2a – v4a2b – v4a2c

v4b: (A)
- v4b1: (A)
- v4b2: (A)
- v4b3: NA

v4c:
- v4c1: (E), p.392
- v4c2: (E), p.392

5. Labor Force (L)

v5a: (E), p.374
- v5a1: (E), p.374
- v5a2: (E), p.374
- v5a3: (E), p.374—1949–57: NA, only the sum of v5a3 and v5a4 are reported. They are 1949: 818.58, 1952: 908.39, 1955: 968.82, 1956: 943.27, 1957: 951.7 respectively
- v5a4: (E), p.374—(ditto)

v5b:
- v5b1: (E), p.374
- v5b2: (E), p.374
- v5b3: (E), p.374

v5c: NA
- v5c1: NA

v5d: NA

6. Population (PO)

v6a: (E), p.373—data from public security department
- v6a1: (E), p.373—(ditto)
- v6a2: (E), p.373—(ditto)

v6b: (E), p.373—(ditto)

v6c: (E), p.373—(ditto)

v6d:
- v6d1: (E), p.373—(ditto)
- v6d2: (E), p.373—(ditto)
- v6d3: (E), p.373—(ditto)
- v6d4: (E), p.373—(ditto)
- v6d5: (A)—Hangzhou
- v6d6: (A)—Ningbo

7. Agriculture (A)

v7a: (A); (E), p.386

v7b: (A)

v7c: (A); (E), p.386

v7d: (A); (E), p.386

v7e: (A)

v7f: (A)

v7g: (A); (E), p.386

v7h: (E), p.381
- v7h1: (E), p.381
- v7h2: (E), p.381
- v7h3: (E), p.381
- v7h4: (E), p.381
- v7h5: (E), p.381

v7i: (A); (E), p.385

8. Industry (IN)

v8a: (A); (E), p.387
- v8a1: (E), p.387
- v8a2: (E), p.387
- v8a3: v8a – v8a1 – v8a2

v8b: (E), p.392

- v8c1: (E), p.379
- v8c2: (E), p.379

v8d: (E), p.392

v8f:
- v8f1: (E), p.391
- v8f2: (E), p.391
- v8f3: NA
- v8f4: (E), p.391
- v8f5: (E), p.391

v8g: (A)
- v8g1: (E), p.392

9. Transport (TR)

v9a: (E), p.393—excluding urban traffic volume
- v9a1: (E), p.393—including central and local railways
- v9a2: (E), p.393
- v9a3: (E), p.393—excluding distant ocean and coastal passenger traffic

v9b: (E), p.393
- v9b1: (E), p.393—including central and local railways
- v9b2: (E), p.393
- v9b3: (E), p.393—excluding distant ocean and coastal freight volume

v9c: (E), p.393

10. Domestic Trade (DT)

v10a: (E), p.396
- v10a1: (E), p.396

v10b:
- v10b1: (A); (E), p.396
- v10b2: (A); (C), p.220-223
- v10b3: (A); (C), p.220-223
- v10b4: (A); (E), p.396
- v10b5: (E), p.396
- v10b6: (E), p.396

v10d: (E), p.298

11. Foreign Trade (FT)

v11a:
- v11a1: (C), p.256
- v11a2: (C), p.256
- v11a3: (C), p.256

v11b: (E), p.399—data from foreign trade department
- v11b1: (E), p.399—(ditto)
- v11b2: v11b – v11b1—figures of 1980 and before are total value of ordered goods

v11c: (A)

v11d: (A); (E), p.399

12. Prices (PR)

v12a: (E), p.401

v12b: (E), p.401

v12c: (E), p.401

13. Education (ED)

v13a: (A)

v13b: (A); (E), p.404

v13c:
- v13c1: (A); (E), p.404

v13c2: (A); (E), p.404—technical and ordinary secondary schools
v13c3: (A); (E), p.404

v13d: (A)—institutions of higher learning

14. Social Factors (SF)

v14a: (E), p.404

v14b: (A)

v14c: (A)

15. Natural Environment (NE)

v15a: (A); (E), p.386

v15b: (A)

v15c: (A)

v15d: (A)

v15e: (A)

v15f: (A)

Sources of Data

(A) Data supplied by the DSNEB, SSB, the PRC, and Statistical Bureau of Zhejiang Province ed. *Striving and Advancing Zhejiang 1949–1989*, Beijing: CSPH, 1989.
(C) Statistical Bureau of Zhejiang Province ed. *Statistical Yearbook of Zhejiang, 1989*, Beijing: CSPH, 1989.
(D) Same as (D) in Beijing's sources of data.
(E) Same as (E) in Beijing's sources of data.

12

Anhui

12. Anhui

12–1

Year	v1a	v1a1	v1a2	v1a3	v1a4	v1a5	v1b	v1b1	v1b2	v1b3	v1b4	v1b5	v1c	v1d	v1d1
1949	23.85	17.28	3.63	0.18	0.60	2.16							6.99	16.86	13.69
1950	26.77	18.32	4.84	0.62	0.66	2.33	109.9	105.4	133.6	338.9	107.4	105.5	8.53	18.24	14.44
1951	31.46	21.32	5.46	0.99	0.71	2.98	116.1	114.6	112.0	158.2	106.2	126.4	10.19	21.27	16.63
1952	34.47	22.17	6.50	1.30	0.90	3.60	109.1	104.0	125.0	130.6	126.1	120.3	11.67	22.80	17.10
1953	40.85	25.88	7.86	2.21	0.94	3.96	103.1	100.1	115.4	148.0	91.4	95.7	14.49	26.36	19.80
1954	42.26	26.09	8.76	2.03	1.06	4.32	103.9	102.5	109.7	92.2	113.2	109.6	15.47	26.79	19.83
1955	55.43	36.90	9.80	2.83	1.12	4.78	124.7	131.6	108.5	132.6	100.0	105.2	19.49	35.94	28.01
1956	54.40	32.36	12.40	3.16	1.33	5.15	90.5	82.0	123.9	102.9	110.0	99.4	20.99	33.41	24.40
1957	61.30	35.20	15.40	3.20	1.80	5.70	118.5	116.3	128.1	106.6	141.9	116.3	22.20	39.10	27.70
1958	85.78	36.95	31.80	7.33	2.92	6.78	123.3	92.4	211.9	201.8	143.1	104.8	36.74	49.04	28.97
1959	105.33	35.09	49.33	9.09	3.55	8.27	104.3	84.8	133.0	105.4	103.2	103.6	50.90	54.43	26.91
1960	115.28	34.57	56.62	12.16	4.01	7.92	103.8	89.0	115.1	126.9	107.2	90.9	59.92	55.36	24.92
1961	72.07	29.67	28.24	4.29	2.94	6.93	60.1	78.3	48.5	33.7	70.6	84.1	33.26	38.81	22.22
1962	60.11	28.60	20.01	2.10	2.50	6.90	95.6	116.3	70.7	58.6	101.3	118.7	25.50	34.61	21.91
1963	61.87	29.39	20.13	2.68	2.70	6.97	103.3	105.6	98.7	123.7	104.1	97.5	26.20	35.67	21.98
1964	69.24	31.02	24.45	3.70	3.03	7.04	117.9	117.2	119.9	145.3	118.1	106.4	29.72	39.52	22.77
1965	82.94	37.74	31.80	3.30	3.00	7.10	120.3	123.2	130.4	90.4	100.5	102.3	35.62	47.32	27.17
1966	95.64	43.44	38.25	3.46	3.30	7.19	108.1	106.5	117.7	97.5	102.0	94.0	41.50	54.14	31.19
1967	84.86	46.11	26.29	2.18	2.80	7.48	93.4	106.7	70.2	66.3	89.3	109.5	34.00	50.86	33.20
1968	83.64	47.12	25.56	2.19	1.71	7.06	99.4	101.6	100.2	101.4	63.4	95.1	33.95	49.69	34.11
1969	92.17	42.84	36.49	3.50	1.93	7.41	105.2	90.6	140.2	152.3	104.8	100.2	40.56	51.61	31.27
1970	115.52	53.22	45.45	5.85	3.40	7.60	126.1	124.3	128.1	165.0	172.3	100.2	50.46	65.06	38.85
1971	132.95	57.26	56.67	6.69	4.08	8.25	111.7	103.8	124.6	113.2	119.8	108.5	60.38	72.57	41.23
1972	143.28	62.51	61.70	5.51	4.29	9.27	105.5	105.4	108.5	80.6	102.9	110.0	65.56	77.72	44.57
1973	160.76	66.22	73.71	6.19	4.51	10.13	109.4	102.7	119.5	108.2	102.8	106.6	77.19	83.57	47.48
1974	157.80	67.71	69.87	5.54	4.00	10.68	98.4	102.2	94.3	90.9	88.8	105.7	75.80	82.00	48.68
1975	176.46	67.87	81.80	7.79	4.10	14.90	109.8	99.1	120.2	100.2	99.8	135.9	89.02	87.44	48.30
1976	194.70	74.69	90.51	9.10	4.30	16.10	109.8	107.6	107.4	165.6	108.5	111.9	99.07	95.63	53.46
1977	198.53	69.57	98.86	8.60	4.40	17.10	99.7	90.2	109.2	93.1	100.6	104.6	101.30	97.23	50.98
1978	212.18	71.07	107.11	11.20	4.50	18.30	104.8	98.1	108.4	128.0	100.8	105.3	108.37	103.81	50.65
1979	235.02	79.34	119.18	11.70	3.90	20.90	108.1	108.6	110.5	98.0	82.0	106.9	118.73	116.29	57.92
1980	263.88	84.63	129.65	18.80	8.50	22.30	107.2	98.9	107.1	150.4	202.9	100.0	136.01	127.87	61.36
1981	302.82	119.76	136.41	19.60	9.01	18.04	110.5	124.4	106.8	105.4	107.1	81.9	152.53	150.29	85.08
1982	339.08	128.99	153.17	26.21	9.94	20.77	111.4	106.7	111.6	133.8	110.2	115.1	177.61	161.47	86.56
1983	380.95	137.05	172.95	36.39	11.59	22.97	109.8	101.7	110.5	125.2	116.6	102.9	200.75	180.20	93.06
1984	460.15	162.11	211.97	46.39	13.82	25.86	118.6	113.2	121.3	124.0	115.8	110.6	238.98	221.17	112.32
1985	577.83	198.24	277.27	55.99	17.52	28.81	119.4	111.2	125.0	116.6	123.3	108.6	306.02	271.81	136.85
1986	672.24	221.92	324.34	71.24	21.51	33.23	113.1	103.7	114.7	112.5	116.4	110.2	361.71	310.53	151.28
1987	794.13	255.34	394.88	78.15	24.71	41.05	111.7	104.6	114.4	104.0	114.8	111.3	436.27	357.86	171.49
1988	1009.85	315.25	518.13	93.54	28.73	54.20	112.0	99.4	119.6	103.0	101.5	105.7	565.07	444.78	205.08
1989	1141.77	341.53	627.72	76.05	28.72	67.75	104.6	102.3	110.0	80.9	85.5	106.0	644.36	497.41	219.42

12. Anhui

12–2

Year	v1d2	v1d3	v1d4	v1d5	v1e	v1e1	v1e2	v1e3	v1e4	v1e5	v1f	v1f1	v1f2	v1f3	v1g
1949	0.93	0.07	0.46	1.71											16.67
1950	1.23	0.25	0.51	1.81	106.7	104.9	132.5	350.0	108.6	103.5					18.12
1951	1.43	0.39	0.55	2.27	114.9	113.4	115.2	157.1	106.9	124.2					19.88
1952	1.80	0.50	0.70	2.70	106.5	102.8	132.2	126.0	125.0	118.3					21.00
1953	2.12	0.80	0.73	2.91	100.0	99.3	112.6	140.2	91.1	93.7					26.28
1954	2.32	0.71	0.82	3.11	102.7	101.9	107.7	89.0	113.8	107.8					27.41
1955	2.58	1.10	0.87	3.38	126.3	131.4	107.5	146.3	100.0	103.2					34.29
1956	3.22	1.26	1.03	3.50	86.1	81.5	122.3	106.2	109.3	95.4					35.56
1957	5.00	1.30	1.40	3.70	123.3	121.4	160.2	108.0	143.1	111.2					38.40
1958	10.49	2.94	2.22	4.42	109.6	92.0	215.1	199.5	139.3	105.2					49.42
1959	15.88	3.62	2.61	5.41	95.3	83.0	129.9	104.4	100.3	104.1					53.86
1960	17.84	4.68	2.85	5.07	94.6	83.7	112.5	122.7	103.3	88.8					52.18
1961	8.70	1.58	1.98	4.33	66.7	81.3	47.4	32.4	67.1	82.2					36.84
1962	6.10	0.80	1.60	4.20	104.9	119.0	70.1	60.1	96.2	115.6					28.80
1963	6.52	1.07	1.81	4.29	103.6	103.1	104.7	129.7	108.8	98.5					36.08
1964	8.68	1.52	2.13	4.42	118.0	115.0	131.4	149.6	124.3	108.6					41.10
1965	12.05	1.40	2.20	4.50	120.0	120.8	139.2	93.4	104.3	103.3					48.26
1966	14.54	1.42	2.40	4.59	106.8	106.2	118.0	94.5	101.4	94.6					52.08
1967	9.91	0.90	2.02	4.83	98.0	107.0	69.7	67.1	88.4	110.9					48.60
1968	9.07	0.83	1.22	4.46	98.5	102.1	94.3	93.1	62.4	93.1					49.92
1969	13.14	1.21	1.41	4.58	100.0	91.4	142.2	138.0	107.5	97.1					54.06
1970	17.21	1.90	2.50	4.60	125.5	123.4	134.9	153.7	174.0	98.2					62.04
1971	21.08	2.20	3.02	5.04	108.5	103.0	122.3	115.7	120.9	109.6					69.17
1972	22.40	1.85	3.19	5.71	104.5	104.4	105.9	81.9	103.3	110.9					75.22
1973	24.32	2.11	3.38	6.28	105.0	103.2	108.6	110.1	103.5	107.3					80.81
1974	21.73	1.93	3.01	6.65	98.6	102.5	88.9	92.9	89.2	106.1					82.75
1975	23.74	3.00	3.10	9.30	104.7	97.9	114.5	100.9	100.3	136.2					87.52
1976	25.47	3.30	3.20	10.20	108.8	108.3	102.5	171.4	106.6	113.7					91.96
1977	28.65	3.20	3.30	11.10	98.9	92.4	112.3	95.3	101.6	107.1					95.10
1978	33.86	4.20	3.30	11.80	103.7	95.5	118.5	129.2	98.4	104.6	112.91	53.77	40.51	18.63	101.66
1979	37.57	4.40	2.90	13.50	109.0	111.3	110.0	98.3	82.7	107.3	125.63	61.16	44.76	19.71	116.17
1980	41.31	5.90	4.20	15.10	103.7	98.2	107.6	125.6	135.5	104.7	138.19	64.68	50.05	23.46	129.80
1981	43.18	6.09	4.51	11.43	110.6	122.0	106.0	104.3	108.7	76.6	166.87	88.45	52.48	25.94	146.54
1982	48.00	7.87	5.84	13.20	108.0	102.7	110.7	129.2	129.2	115.4	181.67	89.97	59.66	32.04	162.30
1983	53.88	11.17	7.06	15.03	106.1	100.5	110.8	128.0	120.9	104.1	206.18	96.55	70.90	38.73	176.53
1984	71.44	13.50	7.70	16.21	119.3	117.5	127.6	117.5	105.8	105.8	253.38	116.26	90.57	46.55	218.00
1985	91.73	15.99	9.27	17.97	115.3	109.4	126.2	114.5	117.0	106.6	314.20	140.97	114.71	58.52	276.25
1986	107.77	19.31	11.38	20.79	108.6	102.5	115.6	109.6	116.5	106.3	361.96	155.91	134.11	71.94	324.09
1987	126.76	20.93	13.20	25.48	106.8	103.3	109.5	103.5	115.9	110.4	414.87	176.35	153.71	84.81	361.41
1988	165.39	25.61	15.46	33.24	106.5	96.0	118.5	103.2	101.9	105.6	512.47	210.53	197.28	104.66	448.99
1989	199.88	21.36	14.87	41.88	104.5	102.0	109.8	85.1	90.6	107.6	572.13	225.39	227.85	118.88	481.10

12. Anhui

12–3

Year	v1h	v1i	v1j	v1j1	v1j2	v1j3	v1k	v2a	v2a1	v2a2	v2b	v2c	v2c1	v2c2	v2d1
1949								0.50	0.41	0.09			0.0132		
1950								1.38	1.13	0.25			0.1274	0.0028	
1951								2.29	1.88	0.41			0.1109	0.0063	
1952				317				2.60	2.11	0.49			0.2343	0.0316	
1953				371				3.90	3.16	0.74			0.4863	0.0675	
1954	60.57			403				4.01	3.25	0.76			0.6439	0.0951	
1955	84.76			429				6.60	5.39	1.21			1.0850	0.0765	
1956	64.76			502				7.08	5.24	1.84			1.5440	0.3195	
1957	74.56			528				7.20	5.47	1.73			1.2488	0.0834	
1958	79.20			424				16.50	13.76	2.74			5.2354	0.1107	
1959				433				19.42	15.66	3.76			6.2059	0.1898	
1960				451				18.72	14.34	4.38			8.0768	0.2709	
1961				460				7.27	4.43	2.84			2.9163	0.0372	
1962	130.89			499				0.50	0.33	0.17			1.6137	0.0092	
1963	113.32			548				4.01	2.39	1.62			2.0650	0.0314	
1964	104.70			572				8.01	5.11	2.90			2.3748	0.1056	
1965	108.70			549				10.10	6.94	3.16			2.1419	0.0514	
1966	114.90			561				10.34	6.61	3.73			2.1281	0.0840	
1967				559				6.32	4.11	2.21			0.9915	0.0551	
1968				560				6.74	4.13	2.61			1.1682	0.1032	
1969				548				8.48	5.73	2.75			2.3399	0.0960	
1970				568				13.70	8.73	4.97			4.7289	0.1306	
1971				539				17.91	12.74	5.17			5.7973	0.2338	
1972				566				21.02	15.59	5.43			5.0903	0.2640	
1973				566				23.59	17.56	6.03			5.9315	0.3314	
1974				569				24.00	17.57	6.43			5.2517	0.3454	
1975				568				25.80	19.14	6.66			5.9410	0.3666	
1976				557				29.10	22.07	7.03			7.4252	0.3156	
1977				563				29.40	22.11	7.29			6.0106	0.4452	
1978	113.34	16.77	555	588	465			30.20	22.03	8.17			8.0408	0.4352	
1979	170.23	18.74	593	640	485			34.80	25.90	8.90			7.3652	0.4782	89.16
1980	184.83	22.68	684	739	541			36.50	26.57	9.93	17.30	16.85	7.8916	0.6443	93.28
1981	246.49	24.01	689	750	538			35.80	25.42	10.38	15.72	15.16	6.1088	0.7138	107.67
1982	269.10	26.00	717	772	575			40.77	29.67	11.10	33.99	20.84	7.1219	0.7065	116.24
1983	304.64	27.50	733	791	584			45.95	35.19	10.76	46.16	23.94	8.3974	0.7270	127.47
1984	322.97	33.24	855	943	664	800		60.08	45.77	14.31	62.22	31.51	11.3441	0.6963	139.27
1985	369.41	38.66	950	1044	747	753		85.38	58.41	26.97	80.74	41.70	13.5970	1.1422	160.46
1986	396.53	47.69	1125	1243	873	982		105.54	74.44	31.10	103.49	56.11	19.4400	1.0993	185.71
1987	429.26	54.65	1239	1367	964	1119		115.30	80.56	34.74	117.20	57.54	19.6688	1.2873	210.12
1988	485.53	67.23	1475	1640	1116	1506		147.52	92.57	54.95	137.82	67.13	22.3456	1.2850	239.99
1989	515.66	76.70	1646	1812	1207			138.21	77.64	60.57	111.36	59.20	20.7800	0.9100	279.62

12. Anhui

12–4

Year	v2d2	v2e	v3a	v3b	v3b1	v3b2	v3c	v3d	v3d1	v3d2	v3e	v3e1	v3e2	v3e3	v3e4
1949			16.17	16.16			0.01								
1950			16.74	16.72			0.02	59							
1951			17.59	17.56			0.03	61							
1952			18.40	18.35			0.05	62							
1953			22.38	22.32			0.06	74							
1954			23.40	23.31			0.09	75							
1955			27.69	27.31			0.38	86							
1956			28.48	28.03			0.45	87							
1957			31.20	30.51			0.69	93							
1958			32.92	31.98			0.94	95							
1959			34.44	33.09			1.35	97							
1960			33.46	31.70			1.76	98							
1961			29.57	28.35			1.22	94							
1962			28.30	27.11			1.19	89							
1963			32.07	30.24			1.83	95							
1964			33.09	31.79			1.30	99							
1965			38.16	36.54			1.62	113							
1966			41.74	39.83			1.91	119							
1967			42.28	40.54			1.74	117							
1968			43.18	41.91			1.27	117							
1969			45.58	43.68			1.90	118							
1970			48.34	46.21			2.13	120							
1971			51.26	48.89			2.37	122							
1972			54.20	51.70			2.50	125							
1973			57.22	54.08			3.14	127							
1974			58.75	55.45			3.30	127							
1975			61.72	58.01			3.71	130							
1976			62.86	58.40			4.46	129							
1977			65.70	60.85			4.85	132							
1978			71.46	65.11			6.35	139							
1979	63.83	27.60	81.37	73.60			7.77	155							
1980	65.95	30.03	93.30	87.61	65.22	22.39	5.69	181	151	412					
1981	76.01	30.84	110.74	103.97	77.38	26.59	6.77	211	178	462	391.92	237.00	48.96	5.28	7.68
1982	80.92	33.61	121.53	112.62	83.92	28.70	8.91	226	191	477	402.72	242.64	51.96	5.76	7.80
1983	88.75	36.15	130.58	118.40	88.76	29.64	12.18	235	201	479	435.26	271.60	54.37	5.83	8.94
1984	95.58	36.57	157.92	145.46	109.66	35.80	12.46	286	247	557	479.39	284.54	73.57	6.18	8.82
1985	111.54	43.84	190.87	173.10	128.31	44.79	17.77	337	289	648	565.70	323.12	80.58	5.58	9.81
1986	129.81	53.01	218.55	199.00	145.14	53.86	19.55	384	326	728	718.25	392.18	102.25	6.31	9.48
1987	146.96	62.28	246.11	224.84	162.13	62.71	21.27	428	362	814	806.00	444.48	104.64	6.48	9.60
1988	167.09	109.89	301.47	277.25	193.87	83.38	24.22	520	427	1049	1120.00	552.00	142.08	6.96	9.84
1989	197.35	94.52	342.89	311.40	217.65	93.75	31.49	574	472	1150	1138.50	654.79	136.60	6.12	10.24

12. Anhui

12–5

Year	v3f	v3f1	v3f2	v3f3	v3f4	v4a1	v4a1a	v4a1b	v4a1c	v4a1d	v4a2	v4a2a	v4a2b	v4a2c	v4a2d
1949						0.54		0.0334	0.4801	0.0281	0.22				
1950						1.17	0.0018	0.3248	0.8078	0.0345	0.75				
1951						2.11	0.0197	0.7899	1.2011	0.1025	0.79				
1952						2.70	0.0899	1.2797	1.0704	0.2571	1.51				
1953						2.63	0.1083	1.4533	0.9625	0.1011	1.88				
1954	63.57	46.46	6.19	1.40	6.22	3.30	0.1815	1.6184	1.3978	0.1024	2.25				
1955	77.36	49.37	7.94	2.62	7.45	3.36	0.2247	1.7784	1.2644	0.0900	2.65				
1956	68.00	48.51	6.51	1.35	6.49	3.43	0.2747	1.9385	1.0335	0.1864	3.45				
1957	72.85	50.96	5.99	1.53	7.76	4.39	0.3955	2.3692	1.3602	0.2638	3.43				
1958	70.99	48.38	6.42	0.40	7.96	7.55	2.2083	3.4839	1.5320	0.3276	10.82				
1959						9.26	3.1515	4.3443	1.6710	0.0958	14.44				
1960						11.59	5.8561	4.4822	1.1630	0.0909	17.42				
1961						6.66	2.4731	3.3126	0.8302	0.0457	8.42				
1962	128.86	77.70	12.05	6.69	19.20	4.74	0.1380	3.4185	1.1160	0.0638	3.86				
1963	109.02	70.83	9.57	4.51	13.90	6.08	1.4393	3.4173	1.1300	0.0930	5.20				
1964	97.90	69.20	8.50	2.60	9.20	7.56	2.2692	3.9251	1.3700	0.0865	6.30				
1965	95.60	66.20	10.10	1.90	8.80	7.64	2.5512	3.6443	1.3406	0.1065	5.94				
1966	106.60	75.90	10.40	1.70	7.60	8.63	3.3759	3.7411	1.4573	0.0566	6.99				
1967						5.36	0.9809	3.0108	1.3345	0.0359	6.36				
1968						4.83	0.1237	2.8804	1.7859	0.0386	5.01				
1969						7.10	1.8390	3.7423	1.4507	0.0656	7.52				
1970						11.14	3.3898	5.8917	1.7862	0.0758	10.52				
1971						13.94	5.5786	6.5050	1.7631	0.0942	11.00				
1972						14.90	5.9510	7.2385	1.6450	0.0700	12.45				
1973						16.90	6.5179	8.5430	1.7859	0.0548	12.52				
1974						13.37	3.1263	8.5311	1.6768	0.0385	13.33				
1975						15.74	4.2207	9.8283	1.6429	0.0498	13.26				
1976						17.89	5.3187	10.6298	1.8183	0.1232	14.78				
1977						18.46	5.2237	11.5672	1.5883	0.0766	14.80				
1978	102.48	75.39	10.25	3.58	7.88	22.48	8.0758	12.3536	1.3130	0.7378	18.19				
1979	143.28	92.98	15.44	11.29	9.16	21.10	5.9690	13.0366	1.6791	0.4202	20.35				
1980	162.94	97.45	18.81	17.15	9.24	20.28	4.7594	13.4964	1.4841	0.5419	16.67	2.72	5.42	1.76	6.77
1981	193.26	117.90	21.49	19.67	11.12	20.66	3.5188	14.7084	1.8962	0.5323	15.40	2.07	5.61	1.78	5.94
1982	239.93	153.11	23.09	23.54	15.62	21.98	2.9182	16.5449	1.8847	0.6342	16.87	2.33	6.26	2.15	6.13
1983	258.42	153.55	26.70	29.55	16.21	22.39	2.3730	17.5805	1.8658	0.5680	20.38	3.08	7.01	2.55	7.74
1984	263.26	156.84	25.28	31.10	16.56	24.38	1.2986	20.5265	1.9703	0.5893	23.56	3.95	7.53	3.30	8.78
1985	299.02	174.83	29.15	37.36	20.44	30.16	0.5880	26.9406	2.4227	0.2065	33.88	4.45	8.98	3.66	16.79
1986	339.98	197.06	30.38	44.49	20.78	35.45	1.8173	30.6721	2.4677	0.4917	46.18	5.00	10.71	4.53	25.94
1987	382.99	211.42	32.31	62.99	21.98	38.84	1.8016	33.7498	2.4151	0.8725	44.53	3.16	11.14	4.73	25.50
1988	455.02	245.49	37.59	79.45	23.86	42.38	1.7027	38.4642	2.7126	-0.5005	46.64	3.53	13.14	4.38	25.59
1989	498.43	274.04	37.55	77.19	25.21	50.97	-1.1000				53.80	3.60	14.86	5.12	30.22

12. Anhui

12–6

Year	v4b	v4b1	v4b2	v4b3	v4c1	v4c2	v5a	v5a1	v5a2	v5a3	v5a4	v5b1	v5b2	v5b3	v5c
1949															
1950	0.0132	0.0132													
1951	0.0504	0.0502	0.0002												
1952	0.1122	0.1107	0.0015				1534	33	1	41	1459	1460	44	30	
1953	0.1932	0.1909	0.0023					41							
1954	0.2210	0.2139	0.0071					46							
1955	0.2622	0.2247	0.0375					49							
1956	0.4091	0.3309	0.0782					63							
1957	0.5398	0.4242	0.1156				1438	66	29	18	1325	1327	50	61	
1958	1.2377	0.6627	0.5750					171							
1959	1.4888	1.0326	0.4562					158							
1960	1.3551	0.8213	0.5338					171							
1961	1.1717	0.6030	0.5687					148							
1962	0.5913	0.4398	0.1515				1252	107	48	8	1088	1107	63	82	
1963	0.7119	0.5190	0.1929					100							
1964	0.8452	0.6396	0.2056					103							
1965	0.9994	0.7552	0.2442				1378	99	57	6	1216	1231	54	93	
1966	1.2214	0.8847	0.3367					109							
1967	1.1354	0.8885	0.2469					112							
1968	1.3177	0.9916	0.3261					112							
1969	1.2814	0.9847	0.2967					115							
1970	1.3461	1.0463	0.2998				1638	139	57		1442	1457	86	95	
1971	1.6000	1.2279	0.3721					151							
1972	1.8697	1.4265	0.4432					162							
1973	2.1989	1.6403	0.5586					161							
1974	2.5517	1.8906	0.6611					164							
1975	2.6144	1.9833	0.6311				1766	174	67	1	1523	1574	125	67	
1976	2.7447	2.0902	0.6545					182							
1977	3.1284	2.4025	0.7259					189							
1978	3.9072	2.8699	1.0373				1873	228	80		1564	1530	192	151	154.19
1979	5.7465	4.0292	1.7173		19.82	21.7	1921	235	87	1	1597	1573	196	152	155.91
1980	8.7577	5.8592	2.8985		20.60	21.5	2002	247	95	4	1655	1628	210	164	166.63
1981	12.1914	7.3703	4.8211		20.24	19.0	2078	255	101	7	1715	1681	217	179	173.50
1982	16.3636	9.7365	6.6271		21.39	18.7	2160	268	104	11	1777	1723	233	204	181.43
1983	20.9463	12.6801	8.2662		24.60	19.7	2234	275	108	17	1835	1769	241	224	186.02
1984	28.3205	17.3797	10.9408		28.79	21.8	2311	271	127	22	1891	1785	265	261	196.49
1985	38.4292	23.9460	14.4832		34.64	22.3	2421	287	134	40	1960	1748	367	306	284.63
1986	55.4288	34.4147	21.0141		37.04	20.3	2496	298	139	40	2018	1783	377	336	284.14
1987	75.1999	47.5446	27.6553		41.26	19.7	2563	309	145	46	2062	1785	408	370	307.45
1988	89.8341	60.7473	29.0868		52.44	18.9	2666	322	148	44	2152	1827	438	401	328.13
1989	119.0000	84.4000	34.6000		52.22	17.9	2743	327	150	36	2287				

12. Anhui

12–7

Year	v5c1	v5d	v6a	v6a1	v6a2	v6b	v6c	v6d1	v6d2	v6d3	v6d4	v6d5	v6d6
1949			2786			18.1	7.0	268	2518	1466	1320	6.06	17.73
1950			2842			18.3	7.1	209	2633	1498	1344		
1951			2914			18.3	7.0	137	2777	1534	1380		
1952	4.63		2966	227	2739	18.2	7.0	179	2787	1561	1405	13.86	19.36
1953	5.68		3066	234	2832	18.7	7.2	207	2859	1610	1456		
1954	6.36		3149	253	2896	43.3	16.6	287	2862	1654	1495		
1955	7.94		3201	260	2941	27.7	11.8	268	2933	1682	1519		
1956	11.81		3243	277	2966	33.2	14.3	302	2941	1704	1539		
1957	15.06		3337	273	3064	29.7	9.1	356	2981	1750	1587	30.38	28.95
1958	103.77		3394	397	2997	23.8	12.3	486	2908	1783	1611	47.12	34.51
1959	79.63		3427	444	2983	19.9	16.7	606	2821	1790	1637		
1960	79.96		3043	465	2578	11.4	68.6	498	2545	1563	1480		
1961	58.44		2988	439	2549	12.3	8.1	438	2550	1541	1447	51.22	36.37
1962	32.35		3134	412	2722	53.3	8.2	387	2747	1615	1519	44.82	34.07
1963	28.00		3232	398	2834	50.7	7.9	387	2845	1664	1568	42.32	32.91
1964	29.33		3181	398	2783	39.9	8.6	386	2795	1644	1537	46.19	33.55
1965	25.07		3286	388	2898	41.8	7.2	397	2888	1693	1593	47.78	33.98
1966	34.54		3407	395	3012	41.1	7.1	406	3001	1758	1649		
1967	36.34		3523	403	3120	40.6	7.0	415	3108	1818	1705		
1968	37.32		3641	412	3229	39.9	6.9	414	3227	1886	1755		
1969	40.94		3762	420	3342	39.3	6.8	402	3360	1954	1808		
1970	55.25		3940	426	3514	37.2	6.5	418	3522	2037	1903	51.93	35.26
1971	61.10		4073	455	3618	35.9	5.9	439	3634	2106	1967		
1972	66.79		4199	476	3723	35.2	6.6	449	3750	2165	2034		
1973	65.43		4317	496	3821	32.7	5.9	460	3857	2227	2090		
1974	66.51		4409	505	3904	27.9	5.7	464	3945	2276	2133		
1975	71.05		4492	523	3969	23.9	5.7	473	4020	2320	2172	59.60	38.22
1976	74.96		4558	537	4021	22.5	5.5	480	4078	2356	2202		
1977	77.22		4628	548	4081	21.3	5.5	483	4145	2394	2234		
1978	90.50	1530.43	4713	581	4132	20.5	4.8	504	4209	2439	2274	70.96	40.73
1979	91.82	1568.13	4803	610	4193	21.8	4.7	530	4273	2485	2318		
1980	95.91	1627.46	4893	663	4230	19.9	4.6	556	4337	2530	2363	76.99	44.03
1981	100.30	1681.45	4956	700	4256	18.7	5.2	593	4363	2566	2390		
1982	105.62	1723.41	5016	721	4295	18.4	5.8	610	4406	2600	2416		
1983	108.35	1769.43	5056	837	4219	16.8	5.8	627	4430	2626	2430		
1984	110.17	1784.74	5103	915	4188	16.2	5.5	657	4446	2653	2450		
1985	119.51	1748.13	5156	975	4181	15.6	5.4	724	4432	2683	2473	88.14	50.22
1986	124.28	1782.91	5217	1527	3690	17.9	6.6	757	4460	2714	2503	90.18	50.94
1987	129.83	1784.77	5287	1656	3631	18.9	5.9	784	4503	2750	2537	92.70	51.66
1988	136.69	1826.50	5377	1802	3575	20.8	5.6	806	4571	2796	2581	95.37	52.41
1989			5469	1903	3566	23.6	5.9	824	4645	2842	2627	97.73	53.18

12. Anhui

12–8

Year	v7a	v7b	v7c	v7d	v7e	v7f	v7g	v7h	v7h1	v7h2	v7h3	v7h4	v7h5	v7i	v8a
1949			1414.28					17.28	12.38	0.02	1.94	0.10	2.84		3.63
1950			1457.07					18.31	12.77	0.02	2.00	0.17	3.35		4.84
1951			1494.79					21.32	14.87	0.03	2.13	0.12	4.16		5.46
1952		1.40	1546.26	13394		0.10		22.16	15.51	0.03	2.18	0.13	4.31	216.60	6.50
1953		2.26	1626.32			0.20		25.88	16.82	0.06	2.89	0.16	5.95	234.20	7.86
1954		15.16	1687.71			0.37		26.09	16.58	0.07	2.53	0.23	6.68	233.68	8.76
1955		28.15	1740.16			1.64		36.90	26.88	0.08	2.35	0.22	7.37	222.21	9.80
1956		69.72	1804.85			5.45		32.36	22.83	0.17	3.20	0.38	5.78	231.10	12.40
1957		148.45	1876.09	14612		7.15		35.20	25.23	0.12	3.70	0.57	5.58	216.06	15.40
1958		310.49	1958.15			12.51	0.06	36.95	28.10	0.15	5.36	0.69	2.65	201.79	31.80
1959		280.49	2010.75			9.84	0.08	35.09	28.45	0.15	3.58	0.70	2.21	177.50	49.33
1960		461.69	2032.66			10.76	0.12	34.57	29.79	0.13	1.61	0.69	2.35	140.52	56.62
1961		586.67	2075.44			7.44	0.34	29.68	24.77	0.22	1.92	0.42	2.35	135.01	28.24
1962		369.95	2166.80			6.99	0.68	28.60	21.29	0.29	3.77	0.34	2.91	144.22	20.01
1963		633.99	2248.39			10.55	0.97	29.38	21.18	0.32	4.76	0.52	2.60	148.46	20.13
1964		766.16	2302.40			12.98	1.26	31.01	22.93	0.33	5.01	0.41	2.33	152.61	24.45
1965		823.60	2440.52	11368		27.07	1.51	37.74	27.81	0.54	5.78	0.42	3.19	161.45	31.80
1966		934.71	2528.82			42.43	2.35	43.44	30.87	0.73	7.47	0.50	3.87	175.29	38.25
1967		687.48	2942.35			38.63	2.50	46.11	32.99	0.88	7.88	0.31	4.05	186.82	26.29
1968		653.46	3053.19			23.51	2.57	47.12	34.00	1.13	7.47	0.28	4.24	199.25	25.56
1969		758.79	3259.89			40.79	2.62	42.84	29.83	0.88	7.32	0.37	4.44	210.59	36.49
1970		962.17	3384.15			55.90	3.24	53.21	38.84	0.96	8.40	0.37	4.64	202.27	45.45
1971		871.20	2858.09			55.31	3.85	57.26	42.35	1.04	8.46	0.37	5.04	207.96	56.67
1972		928.43	2943.62			71.56	4.49	62.51	45.99	1.43	9.39	0.46	5.24	216.47	61.70
1973	19.45	1225.17	3071.15			89.06	5.90	66.21	51.65	1.66	9.43	0.55	2.92	211.17	73.71
1974	24.11	1295.98	3266.87			87.88	5.77	67.71	53.47	1.59	8.83	0.48	3.34	214.05	69.87
1975	29.41	1609.80	3444.60			98.12	5.57	67.87	52.99	1.59	9.35	0.54	3.40	210.43	81.80
1976	38.01	1815.34	3615.71			111.64	7.59	74.69	59.36	1.50	9.80	0.55	3.48	208.09	90.51
1977	44.28	1836.71	3472.34			107.58	6.48	69.56	54.90	1.25	9.27	0.49	3.65	201.95	98.86
1978	54.15	2097.82	3596.27	12019		151.34	9.45	71.07	56.83	1.14	10.07	0.41	2.62	201.80	107.11
1979	61.73	1962.92	3777.85		1894.43	192.10	9.91	79.34	64.58	1.10	10.67	0.44	2.55	212.51	119.18
1980	66.43	1557.18	3656.99	11610	2591.86	245.66	10.69	84.63	66.19	2.15	13.16	0.69	2.44	241.34	129.65
1981	67.76	1250.26	3590.00		683.02	357.43	9.41	119.76	94.26	2.42	18.07	1.21	3.80	283.98	136.40
1982	72.27	1197.66	3471.16		1609.00	425.01	9.50	128.99	101.10	2.56	20.02	1.57	3.74	305.15	153.17
1983	76.45	1244.00	3342.54		1338.00	451.44	11.07	137.05	105.87	3.68	20.05	1.91	5.54	316.58	172.95
1984	79.69	1396.18	3241.24		1420.00	494.45	13.21	162.11	119.94	6.28	26.88	2.52	6.49	328.66	211.97
1985	83.30	1456.89	3159.00	12279	1942.00	530.77	13.52	198.23	136.81	8.04	40.89	3.99	8.50	351.37	277.27
1986	91.72	1674.14	3138.37		1080.00	561.15	15.25	221.92	155.88	8.99	41.19	5.40	10.46	364.43	324.34
1987	103.64	2301.05	3234.90		1095.00	594.21	16.82	255.34	176.15	10.88	49.33	7.30	11.68	376.01	394.88
1988	114.82	2138.67	3321.82	12254	1800.00	626.01	19.81	315.25	200.81	16.63	74.19	9.52	14.10	384.23	518.13
1989	122.40	2262.70	3455.80	12358			21.60	341.53	220.20	17.78	77.67	9.74	16.14	392.09	627.72

12. Anhui

12–9

Year	v8a1	v8a2	v8a3	v8b	v8c1	v8c2	v8d	v8f1	v8f2	v8f3	v8f4	v8f5	v8g
1949	0.31				0.53	3.10			114.05		0.24		3813
1950	0.69	0.0005			0.78	4.06			152.12		0.32		4054
1951	1.15	0.0055			0.93	4.53			204.45		0.35		4328
1952	2.18	0.0400			1.13	5.37			261.06		0.50		4439
1953	3.15	0.0900			1.45	6.41		0.01	243.86		0.83		4370
1954	4.44	0.3000			1.94	6.82		0.09	290.84		1.32		3726
1955	6.06	0.5600			2.80	7.00		0.14	332.65		1.72		1991
1956	8.41	2.0700			3.79	8.60		0.17	378.68		2.24		1138
1957	10.28	2.4900			5.08	10.32		0.23	504.25		2.77		1596
1958	25.86	5.8500			13.78	18.02		3.46	866.70		4.19	0.81	8652
1959	41.12	8.2100			24.29	25.04		23.36	1611.93		8.61	12.01	15103
1960	50.12	6.5000			31.65	24.97		40.50	1846.31		14.81	29.38	11058
1961	25.10	3.1300			16.10	12.14		16.83	1638.25		14.94	21.87	8704
1962	16.94	2.9200			8.97	11.04		2.01	1395.95		12.53	10.95	7820
1963	17.45	2.5000			8.20	11.93		2.74	1223.84		12.46	16.64	6455
1964	21.61	2.7200			9.56	14.89		12.63	1167.98		13.45	28.28	6099
1965	28.09	3.6400			12.61	19.19		25.53	1137.53		15.46	40.99	5741
1966	33.86	4.3900			16.18	22.06		40.04	1188.35		20.14	46.72	5937
1967	22.31	3.9800			9.13	17.16		12.64	653.76		15.05	26.33	5968
1968	22.03	3.5400			9.43	16.13		15.70	834.93		15.43	22.63	5979
1969	31.78	4.7100			16.36	20.13		29.22	1219.12		22.51	37.58	6191
1970	39.60	5.8500			21.48	23.96		44.57	1542.10		29.31	60.15	7476
1971	49.50	7.1700			26.61	30.07		59.69	1718.66		35.02	79.98	7841
1972	54.01	7.6900			28.96	32.74		68.22	1764.68		41.47	96.80	8162
1973	62.52	9.3900			35.73	37.98		75.29	1816.14		51.09	115.62	8539
1974	57.37	10.6000			31.14	38.73		63.65	1458.94		46.12	103.48	9111
1975	67.42	12.2900			38.09	43.71		72.74	1925.57		55.46	139.50	9565
1976	73.14	15.0800			42.77	47.75		67.80	2082.02		60.65	144.37	11201
1977	79.14	17.4200			46.89	51.97		79.77	2222.38		68.48	159.08	13140
1978	85.57	18.5800			52.71	54.40		89.50	2453.24		83.36	182.89	13695
1979	96.02	19.1800		93.38	61.54	57.65	28.66	99.79	2477.94		94.96	200.80	13701
1980	102.51	21.6500		100.84	61.41	68.24	30.75	136.26	2411.39		96.34	218.76	14990
1981	106.95	22.9600		104.45	60.24	76.16	31.61	140.07	2382.40		97.14	243.07	15256
1982	119.85	26.4100		116.89	67.41	85.76	35.03	161.96	2399.89		104.32	289.67	16024
1983	134.24	30.4900		130.93	79.10	93.85	39.27	174.34	2524.43		116.14	350.09	16311
1984	145.84	45.5800		144.16	96.73	115.24	44.69	189.55	2755.64		116.87	410.89	20665
1985	183.34	59.2600		180.86	132.63	144.64	54.76	194.29	2905.09		134.88	553.36	21608
1986	206.60	73.1700		202.90	150.14	174.19	60.55	202.14	3020.44		152.69	679.55	24116
1987	242.12	91.4800		237.40	182.50	212.38	66.70	211.54	2884.34		168.84	775.52	23477
1988	307.81	122.3600		299.01	244.08	274.06	86.31	208.86	3052.37		177.89	926.43	24191
1989	374.27	197.9200	55.53	363.70	298.76	328.96	94.07	221.00	3115.74	2.08	172.85	818.18	24259

12. Anhui

12–10

Year	v8g1	v9a	v9a1	v9a2	v9a3	v9b	v9b1	v9b2	v9b3	v9c	v10a	v10a1	v10b1	v10b2	v10b3
1949		0.38		0.08	0.30	3.06		0.03	3.03	167	5.31	5.03	0.0028		0.0025
1950		0.62		0.21	0.41	3.34		0.03	3.32	248	5.74	5.42	0.2571		0.1524
1951		0.97		0.42	0.55	3.60		0.05	3.55	421	7.33	6.96	0.4807		0.5062
1952		1.25		0.43	0.82	4.56		0.19	4.37	561	8.85	8.37	0.9740		1.2256
1953		2.04		0.93	1.11	4.76		0.29	4.47	771	11.64	11.01	1.9327		2.8266
1954		2.27		0.99	1.28	5.38		0.32	4.97	897	13.32	12.17	1.8794		6.1639
1955		2.58		1.20	1.47	5.67		0.57	4.72	1069	14.75	13.49	3.7313		5.1116
1956		3.30		2.27	1.53	6.73		0.99	5.71	1093	15.89	14.57	5.9098		4.2727
1957		4.36		2.77	1.59	8.55		1.16	7.31	1146	16.90	15.62	7.7855		2.7153
1958		6.58		4.33	2.25	13.87		2.81	10.22	1604	20.10	17.54	13.3370		0.9539
1959		8.38		5.82	2.56	16.85		4.08	11.45	2191	24.52	20.96			
1960		8.98		5.91	3.07	19.05		4.88	12.87	2604	23.48	20.19			
1961		9.11		5.15	3.96	11.11		2.27	8.27	2399	19.96	17.94			
1962		10.90		6.39	4.51	9.07		1.73	7.28	2299	19.47	18.03			
1963		10.01		6.91	3.10	9.79		1.89	7.82	2204	21.01	19.55			
1964		9.56		7.13	2.43	10.99		2.30	8.53	2310	22.13	20.34			
1965		8.60		7.80	0.80	10.82		2.86	7.72	2383	21.63	19.38			
1966		10.68		9.96	0.72	11.89		3.70	7.82	2472	24.41	21.38			
1967		10.70		9.68	1.02	10.14		3.13	6.66	2199	25.56	22.67			
1968		10.53		9.33	1.20	9.74		3.75	6.64	2129	24.16	21.87			
1969		11.46		10.20	1.26	10.97		3.42	7.13	2361	27.52	24.75			
1970		12.68		11.56	1.12	13.93		4.64	8.68	2605	30.06	25.84			
1971		14.25		13.08	1.17	16.72		5.39	10.56	2892	33.72	29.06			
1972		16.49		15.13	1.36	20.57		5.55	10.92	3148	37.85	32.22			
1973		18.87		17.59	1.28	20.53		6.49	12.65	3426	41.37	34.93			
1974		19.83		18.46	1.37	20.35		6.09	12.51	3543	43.60	37.03			
1975		21.24		19.82	1.42	22.42		6.79	13.50	3743	47.79	40.20	23.3483		22.5449
1976		23.51		22.32	1.19	24.42		7.34	14.83	3892	50.60	41.53	24.6154		24.2533
1977		25.73		24.40	1.33	26.20		7.94	15.78	4166	53.33	44.04	25.9083		25.5238
1978		29.22		27.99	1.23	27.24		8.63	15.25	4261	57.02	46.71	26.8353		28.0001
1979	2238	33.67		32.29	1.38	27.18		8.82	14.80	4514	65.41	53.59	29.5139		32.9807
1980	2225	40.11	49.55	38.50	1.61	28.84		9.09	15.97	4753	75.38	62.50	33.4153		37.7691
1981	2220	44.50	98.49	43.04	1.46	33.30	370.73	9.20	18.98	4862	82.53	68.05	34.5525		41.9015
1982	2285	51.15	59.99	49.56	1.59	37.93	239.11	10.99	21.77	5054	92.81	75.67	36.4012		46.6194
1983	2288	59.70	68.10	58.25	1.45	45.16	264.73	12.62	25.72	5533	102.68	83.23	40.1687		45.6896
1984	2264	71.32		69.89	1.43	56.55		14.20	32.86	6235	119.51	97.60	47.2749		50.2546
1985	2485	81.76	92.19	80.22	1.54	70.37	307.67	15.05	40.14	7456	143.81	119.95	53.8250		57.1642
1986	2537	90.79	105.67	89.58	1.21	81.13	360.23	16.76	45.24	8323	169.66	142.59	62.8659		65.0241
1987	2635	101.75	119.39	100.80	0.95	88.62	418.57	17.01	50.52	9759	201.01	165.59	70.8632		79.1195
1988	2643	106.64	132.49	105.81	0.83	108.18	411.89	18.08	60.22	12042	251.19	208.27	86.3970		97.9811
1989	2680	106.34		105.64	0.70	99.50	415.70	16.30	56.10	14027	275.14	224.43	92.5900		106.4900

12. Anhui

Year	v10b4	v10b5	v10b6	v10d	v11a1	v11a2	v11a3	v11b	v11b1	v11b2	v11c	v11d	v12a	v12b	v12c
1949		4.65	0.66												
1950		4.67	0.66												
1951		5.70	0.64												
1952	0.0041	6.02	0.63	8.04											
1953	0.0032	6.16	0.72												
1954	0.0048	4.57	0.71												
1955	0.1913	4.92	0.80												
1956	3.3158	1.65	0.74												
1957	4.8859	0.67	0.84	13.11				0.0678	0.0678						
1958	4.8454	0.36	0.60												
1959															
1960															
1961															
1962				9.09				0.0149	0.0149						
1963															
1964															
1965				12.68				0.0591	0.0591						
1966															
1967															
1968															
1969															
1970				16.45											
1971															
1972													99.4		100.8
1973													99.9		100.9
1974													100.0		100.0
1975		0.22	1.67	21.88				0.0657	0.0657				100.1		100.3
1976		0.21	1.52	22.87				0.0639	0.0639				100.0		100.1
1977		0.21	1.69	21.70				0.0335	0.0335				100.0		100.1
1978		0.15	2.03	25.01				0.1062	0.1062				100.0		103.0
1979		0.31	2.60	32.23				0.2782	0.2782				102.9	102.6	117.5
1980		0.90	3.29	35.31				0.3982	0.3982				103.4	104.1	103.4
1981	0.0018	2.18	3.90	43.97				1.1201	0.8769	0.2432			101.7	101.4	108.2
1982	0.0012	4.79	5.00	53.73				1.6617	1.4164	0.2453			101.0	100.1	104.9
1983	0.0086	10.71	6.10	56.56				1.9416	1.7047	0.2369	0.1550		101.1	102.2	104.5
1984	0.0073	14.17	7.81	62.58				2.9113	2.4377	0.4736	0.0839		102.0	102.1	101.1
1985	0.1332	21.81	10.88	75.70				4.3013	3.0693	1.2320	0.2846	0.1870	106.4	107.1	105.2
1986	0.1053	27.69	13.97	88.62				4.8960	3.6738	1.2222	1.6341	0.6575	105.2	105.8	104.6
1987	0.2072	33.30	17.52	107.52				6.2603	5.2296	1.0307	0.7466	0.4521	109.7	109.9	110.6
1988	0.3567	42.24	24.22	129.57				7.0373	5.5373	1.5000	0.8095	1.0040	121.8	121.4	125.6
1989	0.5700	47.07	28.42	142.43				6.9930	5.2438	1.7492	0.5289	0.2600	117.1	115.7	116.8

12. Anhui

12–12

Year	v13a	v13b	v13c1	v13c2	v13c3	v13d	v14a	v14b	v14c	v15a	v15b	v15c	v15d	v15e	v15f
1949			0.10	3.60	66.37	0.03	190	310		7638					
1950			0.15	3.94	79.03	0.02	1344	2042		8061					
1951			0.16	5.14	161.46	0.02	3085	4292		8543					
1952	6.8		0.26	9.20	193.44	0.03	4524	12963		8673					
1953	19.4		0.29	10.79	197.48	0.07	4799	28806		8699					
1954	15.6		0.33	11.98	185.56	0.11	5904	19561		8842					
1955	17.2		0.38	11.76	208.45	0.09	6659	38141		8836					
1956	18.9		0.72	15.47	280.62	0.11	9250	48753		8791					
1957	18.5		0.86	18.86	281.42	0.05	9595	44729		8555					
1958	12.5		1.62	42.41	414.93	0.17	73695	61781		7950					
1959	12.1		2.18	47.07	390.45	0.15	66253	61373		7604					
1960	12.0		2.30	53.53	319.36	0.42	65490	66189		7531					
1961	14.4		2.66	32.75	242.38	0.32	38020	65776		7428					
1962	18.3		2.49	26.23	218.39	0.57	24928	61622		7347					
1963	14.9		2.17	23.78	202.44	0.66	26413	60845		7328					
1964	12.7		1.96	28.50	319.36	0.64	26769	60252		7339					
1965	13.5		1.93	41.77	490.40	0.53	28046	60637		7276					
1966	12.8		1.50	34.11	402.45	0.43	31668	59637		7202					
1967	21.2		1.10	29.89	385.27	0.41	36633	61847		7044					
1968	21.3		0.66	31.67	371.62	0.43	37338	64402		7009					
1969	14.3		0.17	43.19	385.13	0.49	36304	64259		6945					
1970	9.6		0.35	57.12	401.63	0.30	41196	66622		6879					
1971	9.0		0.35	106.60	443.44		46489	71404		6839					
1972	9.9		0.69	131.28	539.12	0.17	52338	75346		6815					
1973	9.2		0.92	125.16	641.34	0.17	55716	74742		6788					
1974	12.9		1.36	126.67	711.72	0.16	59518	78801							
1975	11.6		1.59	158.70	786.88	0.37	62418	82339		6762					
1976	10.7		1.83	222.50	823.71	0.40	66263	86411							
1977	11.1		2.27	291.54	805.04	0.64	68537	90237							
1978	10.6	90.3	2.94	291.99	796.16	0.56	70655	96030		6704					
1979	12.7		3.33	279.89	811.29	0.56	72786	102337							
1980	17.1	88.9	3.76	255.06	808.03	0.55	76283	104838		6669					
1981	17.6	88.3	4.76	226.49	779.49	0.20	77126	110838	3.8654	6662					
1982	18.2	88.0	4.05	209.62	736.91	1.84	77576	115215	3.5442	6656					
1983	20.0	89.9	4.36	206.52	715.33	1.05	79699	117666	4.1232	6652					
1984	19.1	92.8	4.86	216.73	723.47	1.09	82387	120317	5.1338	6644					
1985	18.5	94.8	5.67	231.11	727.85	1.20	83999	122776	6.6979	6633					
1986	18.7	96.8	6.05	242.12	719.90	1.36	86886	125093	6.2514	6621					
1987	17.9	97.3	6.12	251.10	706.52	1.88	90086	128041	7.2309	6596					
1988	20.1	97.5	6.31	249.51	679.73	1.88	92723	130030	8.2456	6573	226.16	616.2	398	223.4	25.8
1989			6.45	224.15	653.90	2.01	94000	133000	6.7468	6560					

Notes

1. National Output and Income (Y)

v1a: (E), p.411
  v1a1: (E), p.411
  v1a2: (E), p.411
  v1a3: (E), p.411
  v1a4: (E), p.411
  v1a5: (E), p.411

v1b: (A); (B), p.22
  v1b1: (A); (B), p.22
  v1b2: (A); (B), p.22
  v1b3: (A); (B), p.22
  v1b4: (A); (B), p.22
  v1b5: (A); (B), p.22

v1c: v1a – v1d

v1d: (E), p.408
  v1d1: (E), p.408
  v1d2: (E), p.408
  v1d3: (E), p.408
  v1d4: (E), p.408
  v1d5: (E), p.408

v1e: (A); (B), p.25
  v1e1: (A); (B), p.25
  v1e2: (A); (B), p.25
  v1e3: (A); (B), p.25
  v1e4: (A); (B), p.25
  v1e5: (A); (B), p.25

v1f: (E), p.407
  v1f1: (E), p.407
  v1f2: (E), p.407
  v1f3: (E), p.407

v1g: v2a + v3a

v1h: (A); (E), p.432

v1i: (E), p.431

v1j: (A)
  v1j1: (B), p.68; (E), p.431
  v1j2: (E), p.431
  v1j3: (B), p.69

v1k: NA

2. Investment (I)

v2a: (E), p.410
  v2a1: (A); (B), p.26
  v2a2: (A); (B), p.26

v2b: (A)

v2c: (A); (E), p.425—including small fragmentary investment
  v2c1: (B), p.262; (E), p.426
  v2c2: (B), p.262; (E), p.426

v2d:
  v2d1: (E), p.423
  v2d2: (E), p.423

v2e: (E), p.423

3. Consumption (C)

v3a: (E), p.410

v3b: (E), p.410
  v3b1: (A); (D), p.239
  v3b2: (A); (D), p.239

v3c: (E), p.410

v3d: (A); (E), p.431
  v3d1: (E), p.431
  v3d2: (E), p.431

v3e: (E), p.432
  v3e1: (E), p.432
  v3e2: (A)
  v3e3: (A)
  v3e4: (A)

v3f: (A); (E), p.432

v3f1: (A); (E), p.432
v3f2: (A)
v3f3: (A)
v3f4: (A)

4. Public Finance and Banking (FB)

v4a:
v4a1: (E), p.430
v4a1a: (B), p.376; (E), p.430
v4a1b: (B), p.376
v4a1c: (B), p.376
v4a1d: (B), p.376
v4a2: (E), p.430
v4a2a: (E), p.430
v4a2b: (E), p.430
v4a2c: (E), p.430
v4a2d: v4a2 – v4a2a – v4a2b – v4a2c

v4b: (A)
v4b1: (B), p.379
v4b2: (A); (B), p.379
v4b3: NA

v4c:
v4c1: (E), p.423
v4c2: (E), p.423

5. Labor Force (L)

v5a: (A); (E), p.406
v5a1: (A); (E), p.406
v5a2: (E), p.406
v5a3: (E), p.406
v5a4: (E), p.406

v5b:
v5b1: (E), p.406
v5b2: (E), p.406
v5b3: (E), p.406

v5c: (B), p.65
v5c1: (B), p.70

v5d: (B), p.65—including farming, forestry, animal husbandry, fishery and irrigation works

6. Population (PO)

v6a: (E), p.405—data from public security department
v6a1: (E), p.405—(ditto)
v6a2: (E), p.405—(ditto)

v6b: (E), p.405—data from sample surveys

v6c: (E), p.405—(ditto)

v6d:
v6d1: (E), p.405—(ditto)
v6d2: (E), p.405—(ditto)
v6d3: (E), p.405—(ditto)
v6d4: (E), p.405—(ditto)
v6d5: (A)—Hefei
v6d6: (A)—Wuhu

7. Agriculture (A)

v7a: (A); (E), p.418

v7b: (A); (E), p.418

v7c: (A); (E), p.418

v7d: (A)

v7e: (A)

v7f: (A)

v7g: (A); (E), p.418

v7h: (E), p.413
v7h1: (E), p.413
v7h2: (E), p.413
v7h3: (E), p.413
v7h4: (E), p.413
v7h5: (E), p.413

v7i: (E), p.417

8. Industry (IN)

v8a: (E), p.419
  v8a1: (E), p.419
  v8a2: (A); (E), p.419
  v8a3: (A)

v8b: (E), p.423

  v8c1: (E), p.411
  v8c2: (E), p.411

v8d: (E), p.423

v8f:
  v8f1: (E), p.423
  v8f2: (E), p.423
  v8f3: (A)
  v8f4: (E), p.423
  v8f5: (E), p.423

v8g: (A)
  v8g1: (E), p.423

9. Transport (TR)

v9a: (E), p.424—local traffic volume, including figures of traffic system only, but not urban traffic volume and railway freight volume
  v9a1: (A)
  v9a2: (E), p.424—local traffic volume
  v9a3: (E), p.424—(ditto), excluding distant ocean and coastal passenger traffic

v9b: (E), p.424—local traffic volume
  v9b1: (A)
  v9b2: (E), p.424—(ditto)
  v9b3: (E), p.424—(ditto), excluding distant ocean and coastal freight volume

v9c: (E), p.424—excluding village telephone business

10. Domestic Trade (DT)

v10a: (E), p.427
  v10a1: (E), p.427

v10b:
  v10b1: (B), p.297; (E), p.427
  v10b2: NA—in 1958 the data is included in state ownership, while in other years it is included in collective ownership
  v10b3: (B), p.297; (E), p.427
  v10b4: (B), p.297—1952–58: total value of public and private joint ownership; 1980 and after: various economic modes of joint ownership; (E), p.427
  v10b5: (E), p.427
  v10b6: (E), p.427

v10d: (E), p.428

11. Foreign Trade (FT)

v11a:
  v11a1: NA
  v11a2: NA
  v11a3: NA

v11b: (E), p.429—data from foreign trade department
  v11b1: (E), p.429—(ditto)
  v11b2: v11b – v11b1

v11c: (E), p.429

v11d: (A); (E), p.429

12. Prices (PR)

v12a: (E), p.431

v12b: (A)

v12c: (E), p.431

13. Education (ED)

v13a: (A)

v13b: (A)

v13c:
- v13c1: (A); (E), p.432
- v13c2: (A); (E), p.432—technical and ordinary secondary schools
- v13c3: (A); (E), p.432

v13d: (A)—institutions of higher learning

14. Social Factors (SF)

v14a: (A)

v14b: (A)—practitioners of Chinese medicine, personnel of traditional Chinese medicine, and senior, ordinary and junior health technicians

v14c: (A)

15. Natural Environment (NE)

v15a: (A); (E), p.418

v15b: (A)

v15c: (A)

v15d: (A)

v15e: (A)

v15f: (A)

Sources of Data

(A) Data supplied by the DSNEB, SSB, the PRC.
(B) Statistical Bureau of Auhui Province ed. *Auhui's Forty Years*, Beijing: CSPH, 1989.
(D) Same as (D) in Beijing's sources of data.
(E) Same as (E) in Beijing's sources of data.

13

Fujian

13. Fujian

13–1

Year	v1a	v1a1	v1a2	v1a3	v1a4	v1a5	v1b	v1b1	v1b2	v1b3	v1b4	v1b5	v1c	v1d	v1d1
1949															
1950	12.96	9.25	2.45	0.27	0.19	0.80							3.85	9.11	6.96
1951	14.53	9.78	3.20	0.41	0.25	0.89							4.53	10.00	7.30
1952	17.37	11.07	4.20	0.50	0.34	1.26	123.7	118.3	131.3	122.0	136.0	141.6	5.40	11.97	8.31
1953	20.15	11.89	5.43	0.75	0.50	1.58	115.5	105.0	130.2	156.0	147.1	120.6	6.65	13.50	8.80
1954	22.02	11.97	6.12	1.04	0.71	2.18	111.1	101.6	113.5	141.0	144.0	138.0	8.08	13.94	8.73
1955	24.52	12.92	6.35	1.60	0.88	2.77	110.9	105.5	104.3	157.3	125.0	127.1	9.18	15.34	9.52
1956	31.02	14.94	7.32	4.31	0.93	3.52	125.1	112.6	116.0	242.2	106.7	127.0	11.37	19.65	11.06
1957	32.23	17.05	8.57	2.02	1.06	3.53	103.8	113.5	117.2	55.1	102.1	100.3	11.87	20.36	12.19
1958	37.18	15.47	12.94	3.26	1.75	3.76	115.6	90.1	151.5	160.4	164.5	91.5	15.37	21.81	11.11
1959	47.14	15.29	19.56	4.96	2.73	4.60	127.3	96.4	151.8	142.6	153.4	122.3	21.25	25.89	10.96
1960	50.50	12.61	25.01	6.21	2.31	4.36	108.6	81.6	128.3	122.5	84.6	94.9	25.34	25.16	9.05
1961	35.49	13.49	13.77	3.09	1.75	3.19	63.2	82.6	55.2	49.1	86.7	73.1	16.63	18.86	9.73
1962	34.43	14.81	11.23	2.61	1.65	4.13	95.1	111.4	81.8	87.4	82.7	129.6	16.39	18.04	10.16
1963	35.40	15.71	11.33	2.91	1.50	3.95	105.4	114.4	101.3	113.6	92.6	95.5	16.09	19.31	11.31
1964	39.46	16.35	13.94	4.06	1.76	3.35	117.9	116.0	123.4	138.4	116.7	89.9	18.29	21.17	11.76
1965	45.13	18.80	17.24	4.21	2.06	2.82	114.9	113.1	124.2	108.9	117.1	84.1	21.20	23.93	13.35
1966	51.32	20.67	21.57	4.04	2.16	2.88	113.7	106.9	125.5	97.1	105.9	102.4	24.26	27.06	15.01
1967	46.68	18.79	19.11	2.37	2.26	4.15	90.7	91.9	88.3	58.7	106.5	143.8	22.43	24.25	13.68
1968	37.62	18.01	13.37	1.50	2.37	2.37	79.2	95.9	71.9	63.3	105.6	57.2	16.76	20.86	13.17
1969	49.09	19.91	20.96	2.56	2.48	3.18	132.9	110.4	154.1	170.7	104.1	134.1	23.24	25.85	14.49
1970	57.30	21.12	24.41	5.38	2.60	3.79	118.4	106.4	116.9	210.2	104.7	119.1	28.13	29.17	15.23
1971	67.94	25.11	28.45	7.85	2.72	3.81	115.1	110.0	117.3	143.4	102.7	100.0	33.17	34.77	18.31
1972	75.78	27.12	33.64	8.40	2.84	3.78	111.8	108.0	119.1	105.8	104.1	101.1	37.63	38.15	20.12
1973	77.28	25.84	39.16	7.31	2.97	2.00	102.1	94.9	117.1	85.2	104.3	53.1	40.98	36.30	18.37
1974	80.00	26.71	39.88	7.79	3.11	2.51	103.7	103.6	102.4	104.2	104.8	125.6	42.08	37.92	19.15
1975	83.60	27.06	43.37	7.96	3.25	1.96	104.7	101.2	109.4	100.3	104.3	78.0	44.89	38.71	19.24
1976	84.84	26.54	43.55	7.14	3.70	3.91	101.8	97.5	101.0	88.3	114.8	106.2	46.01	38.83	18.68
1977	96.36	29.27	51.68	7.15	4.21	4.05	113.9	109.9	119.4	98.6	113.2	103.5	51.23	45.13	21.10
1978	122.58	36.33	63.14	10.57	4.79	7.75	121.9	111.6	119.7	145.5	114.3	191.3	65.18	57.40	23.69
1979	138.01	43.11	72.01	11.79	4.89	6.21	107.6	106.7	111.9	109.0	99.4	80.2	75.10	62.91	26.64
1980	152.27	45.49	81.45	14.40	5.21	5.72	110.1	105.2	113.0	119.5	106.2	92.2	79.40	72.87	31.63
1981	180.14	56.11	87.76	15.97	6.49	13.81	113.2	105.8	109.0	107.6	124.6	138.6	90.35	89.79	39.15
1982	201.02	63.73	95.77	20.50	7.12	13.90	109.1	107.6	107.3	132.3	109.7	99.4	102.48	98.54	44.17
1983	217.10	68.08	103.97	22.46	8.59	14.00	106.1	105.1	108.8	109.2	120.6	92.6	111.34	105.76	46.91
1984	267.40	80.66	131.11	28.30	10.46	16.87	120.3	113.9	125.3	116.4	112.9	118.6	138.70	128.70	55.63
1985	345.30	99.05	173.13	37.78	12.00	23.34	120.5	108.4	125.4	121.7	110.3	134.3	180.33	164.97	67.49
1986	397.94	107.07	205.10	44.21	15.39	26.17	109.6	102.2	115.4	102.8	111.3	96.9	214.33	183.61	71.49
1987	500.09	132.97	265.87	50.72	19.36	31.17	116.8	109.0	123.1	101.3	113.8	108.6	273.87	226.22	88.52
1988	702.43	182.00	388.85	62.96	24.80	43.82	122.4	107.7	133.2	97.8	103.6	103.9	394.84	307.59	118.75
1989	851.75	209.92	488.96	65.58	35.28	52.01	111.7	106.5	115.2	90.5	119.5	105.9	491.92	359.83	136.95

13. Fujian

13–2

Year	v1d2	v1d3	v1d4	v1d5	v1e	v1e1	v1e2	v1e3	v1e4	v1e5	v1f	v1f1	v1f2	v1f3	v1g
1949															
1950	1.27	0.13	0.15	0.60											8.87
1951	1.66	0.20	0.18	0.66											10.08
1952	2.18	0.25	0.22	1.01	124.2	119.0	131.3	125.0	122.2	166.7					11.54
1953	2.84	0.33	0.32	1.21	111.8	103.5	131.2	136.0	145.5	105.5					12.74
1954	2.68	0.50	0.48	1.55	104.7	100.1	95.1	155.9	153.1	128.4					14.99
1955	2.71	0.78	0.58	1.75	109.1	106.5	101.5	160.4	120.4	113.4					16.32
1956	3.40	2.27	0.57	2.35	127.0	113.2	126.4	261.2	100.0	133.7					22.03
1957	4.23	0.97	0.71	2.26	103.4	109.6	124.6	50.0	111.9	96.5					20.38
1958	5.75	1.34	1.14	2.47	106.5	90.4	136.2	137.1	159.2	93.8					26.07
1959	8.06	1.97	1.79	3.11	119.0	96.3	141.0	139.1	154.9	125.9					29.94
1960	9.51	2.40	1.58	2.62	98.3	81.7	118.3	119.5	88.6	84.3					30.04
1961	4.86	1.31	1.05	1.91	66.9	82.7	51.2	76.0	68.4	72.9					20.14
1962	3.80	1.06	0.82	2.20	90.9	106.0	78.3	59.5	76.4	115.2					19.07
1963	3.97	1.20	0.71	2.12	101.9	120.0	74.9	113.0	87.7	96.3					18.88
1964	5.05	1.66	0.83	1.87	127.7	115.9	178.9	138.9	116.9	92.9					24.01
1965	6.36	1.71	1.21	1.30	113.3	111.7	126.7	108.9	144.6	69.2					26.19
1966	7.76	1.60	1.33	1.36	112.2	109.3	122.4	94.7	111.7	105.1					29.97
1967	6.85	0.92	1.18	1.62	89.1	91.2	88.2	56.8	90.3	118.7					25.55
1968	4.77	0.58	1.13	1.21	84.8	96.2	71.7	64.1	95.9	74.7					25.33
1969	7.42	0.99	1.30	1.65	126.5	109.9	152.9	169.5	11.7	136.7					29.30
1970	8.51	2.07	1.35	2.01	114.6	105.4	115.2	210.0	103.8	121.5					35.94
1971	9.56	3.22	1.41	2.27	11.1	111.2	112.9	150.5	102.2	112.4					40.06
1972	11.10	3.55	1.45	1.93	110.1	109.9	117.0	111.1	102.9	85.0					42.13
1973	12.79	3.14	1.51	0.49	94.9	90.9	116.0	85.2	103.5	25.5					39.88
1974	13.06	3.38	1.47	0.86	104.0	104.4	102.5	104.3	98.0	175.5					41.50
1975	14.10	3.47	1.60	0.30	102.3	100.4	108.7	102.6	108.3	34.9					42.39
1976	14.11	2.97	1.72	1.35	100.5	96.6	100.7	84.4	108.3	463.3					40.05
1977	16.63	2.90	2.18	2.32	116.5	112.6	118.7	96.3	126.0	171.2					46.73
1978	23.00	4.19	2.74	3.78	118.8	100.9	135.3	141.5	126.3	163.0	66.37	23.93	28.19	14.25	63.23
1979	25.36	5.22	2.78	2.91	105.6	101.2	108.3	120.1	98.9	77.1	73.69	28.00	31.38	14.29	70.03
1980	29.05	6.03	3.23	2.93	115.1	116.7	115.5	114.0	115.8	100.7	85.91	31.14	36.68	18.09	79.77
1981	31.76	6.31	3.58	8.99	116.5	107.4	111.0	102.8	110.8	303.4	103.60	39.27	39.78	24.55	90.47
1982	33.65	7.32	4.24	9.16	107.2	107.8	105.0	119.0	118.4	100.3	114.49	44.19	42.94	27.36	104.63
1983	37.09	8.14	5.28	8.34	104.8	104.6	108.7	100.9	124.5	84.0	123.06	47.26	46.02	29.78	112.44
1984	45.39	10.21	6.42	11.05	116.6	110.1	121.2	115.8	113.6	130.6	149.98	55.79	56.39	37.80	134.50
1985	60.18	13.07	7.30	16.93	118.5	105.3	126.7	116.7	108.7	147.4	190.80	68.12	72.50	50.18	176.39
1986	70.01	15.24	8.52	18.35	106.1	102.1	112.9	102.5	101.1	96.7	210.65	72.24	82.19	56.22	205.57
1987	85.96	19.62	9.82	22.30	112.1	110.8	115.1	108.8	104.2	108.6	258.90	89.24	101.28	68.38	241.30
1988	122.11	21.68	12.38	32.67	115.7	102.9	131.4	88.1	102.0	108.2	351.52	118.16	141.82	91.54	323.69
1989	148.36	21.68	17.39	35.45	109.0	111.9	111.8	79.3	118.0	96.8	413.59	135.77	163.82	114.00	372.20

13. Fujian

13–3

Year	v1h	v1i	v1j	v1j1	v1j2	v1j3	v1k	v2a	v2a1	v2a2	v2b	v2c	v2c1	v2c2	v2d1
1949															
1950				334				0.69							
1951				353				0.88							
1952				387				1.14	0.68	0.46					
1953				437				1.47	0.79	0.68					
1954	89.88			473				2.72	1.40	1.32					
1955	91.95			490				3.12	2.02	1.10					
1956	105.92			541				6.99	5.39	1.60					
1957	112.13			526				4.54	2.49	2.05					
1958	113.17			442				9.23	5.65	3.58					
1959	104.85			443				12.50	7.08	5.42					
1960	114.83			433				12.73	8.25	4.48					
1961	125.14			453				1.89	2.46	-0.57					
1962	154.67			506				0.11	1.69	-1.58					
1963	137.50			554				-0.15	2.19	-2.34					
1964	134.58			577				4.08	3.70	0.38					
1965	128.74			565				5.05	3.83	1.22					
1966				566				6.51	3.86	2.65					
1967				558				1.08	-0.09	1.17					
1968				558				1.70	-0.85	2.55					
1969				562				2.95	1.14	1.81					
1970				549				7.74	5.79	1.95					
1971				655				11.64	8.77	2.87					
1972				587				10.38	8.64	1.74					
1973				554				9.29	7.81	1.48					25.18
1974				588				7.91	6.93	0.98					27.54
1975	100.39			581				8.43	5.88	2.55					30.67
1976	104.43			576				5.13	4.25	0.88					33.88
1977	118.34			569				7.24	4.02	3.22					36.62
1978	137.54	11.26	567	611	487		1.23	18.07	10.60	7.47			3.51	0.36	40.62
1979	142.20	12.67	610	642	511		1.73	18.46	13.08	5.38		10.51	4.32	0.54	44.66
1980	171.75	16.00	703	737	613		2.35	21.66	15.76	5.90		12.61	4.49	0.75	49.65
1981	231.65	16.56	716	746	637		2.97	22.78	15.71	7.07	18.11	12.27	2.85	0.87	53.29
1982	268.16	18.53	675	792	691		3.30	26.57	18.69	7.88	23.72	15.13	3.75	1.05	59.62
1983	301.84	20.40	827	861	730		4.18	28.49	22.97	5.52	26.27	16.91	3.60	0.78	63.97
1984	344.94	23.40	921	966	813	1742	4.59	35.01	26.81	8.20	34.43	21.07	4.46	1.25	72.56
1985	396.45	27.96	1059	1115	912	1855	5.62	51.63	36.13	15.50	55.15	37.10	10.77	1.47	83.83
1986	418.51	34.17	1243	1328	1027	1498	6.99	65.37	48.95	16.42	60.58	40.17	14.79	1.45	95.03
1987	484.88	37.36	1319	1402	1097	1571	8.38	78.34	59.01	19.33	78.09	48.89	22.10	1.20	107.87
1988	613.41	48.17	1644	1742	1342	2100	10.76	109.28	69.00	40.28	92.50	53.69	21.14	1.57	124.45
1989	697.34	57.42	1930	2009	1499		12.91	114.05	65.36	48.69	87.88	50.64	17.54	1.40	149.66

13. Fujian

13–4

Year	v2d2	v2e	v3a	v3b	v3b1	v3b2	v3c	v3d	v3d1	v3d2	v3e	v3e1	v3e2	v3e3	v3e4
1949															
1950			8.18	7.91			0.27	65	64	70					
1951			9.20	8.75			0.45	71	66	99					
1952			10.40	9.86	7.81	2.05	0.54	78	71	125					
1953			11.27	10.64	8.15	2.49	0.63	82	72	155					
1954			12.27	11.62	8.48	3.14	0.65	87	73	181					
1955			13.20	12.47	9.02	3.45	0.73	91	76	183					
1956			15.04	14.03	10.25	3.78	1.01	100	85	182					
1957			15.84	14.78	10.70	4.08	1.06	102	88	181					
1958			16.84	15.62	11.25	4.37	1.22	105	92	164					
1959			17.44	15.76	10.46	5.30	1.68	103	86	165	190.08	117.36	12.36		10.50
1960			17.31	15.62	9.32	6.30	1.69	99	76	178					
1961			18.25	16.77	9.81	6.96	1.48	105	79	197					
1962			18.96	17.50	11.07	6.43	1.46	107	84	198	185.52	115.32	13.68		9.12
1963			19.03	17.61	11.61	6.00	1.42	105	85	196					
1964			19.93	18.67	12.59	6.08	1.26	109	89	203					
1965			21.14	19.55	13.29	6.26	1.59	112	92	208	200.88	125.40	18.12		7.80
1966			23.46	21.76	14.92	6.84	1.70	121	100	220					
1967			24.47	22.82	15.67	7.15	1.65	123	102	227					
1968			23.63	22.33	14.74	7.59	1.30	117	93	234					
1969			26.35	24.71	16.72	7.99	1.64	126	102	248					
1970			28.20	26.16	18.43	7.73	2.04	129	107	252					
1971			28.42	26.38	18.32	8.06	2.04	126	103	259					
1972			31.75	29.16	20.56	8.60	2.59	136	113	270					
1973	19.50	9.35	30.59	27.91	18.90	9.01	2.68	127	101	276					
1974	21.06	10.53	33.59	30.16	20.44	9.72	3.43	133	106	286					
1975	23.38	11.03	33.96	30.50	20.42	10.08	3.46	132	104	295	297.36	178.46			
1976	25.56	11.95	34.92	30.92	20.42	10.50	4.00	131	101	308					
1977	26.98	12.92	39.49	34.96	23.08	11.88	4.53	145	112	338					
1978	29.59	13.67	45.16	40.06	26.42	13.64	5.10	163	126	379	258.36	186.96	28.20		9.84
1979	32.48	15.42	51.57	46.56	30.90	15.01	5.66	184	145	400	339.14				
1980	35.83	16.52	58.11	52.10	34.61	17.49	6.01	206	162	453	391.92	241.44			
1981	38.01	17.95	67.69	61.33	42.74	18.59	6.36	239	198	465	404.64	251.16	43.32		8.28
1982	42.22	19.91	78.06	70.85	49.64	21.21	7.21	272	226	515	465.72	282.48	45.96		9.00
1983	45.07	21.68	83.95	75.99	54.45	21.94	7.96	287	243	519	503.63	319.27	50.30		9.28
1984	51.63	23.63	99.49	90.44	65.09	25.35	9.05	337	290	580	494.39	308.64	47.32		8.00
1985	59.40	29.31	124.76	113.90	80.91	32.99	10.86	419	358	718	674.85	364.23	59.52		9.00
1986	68.06	34.01	140.20	125.54	88.24	37.30	14.66	456	387	792	790.47	442.12	72.01		9.87
1987	77.48	37.85	162.96	145.03	102.35	42.68	17.93	519	442	888	892.85	524.86	73.32		10.83
1988	89.53	45.90	214.41	192.36	136.79	55.57	22.05	677	582	1135	1077.38	674.35	82.19		13.04
1989	109.41	62.77	258.15	229.06	162.38	66.68	29.09	794	681	1330	1339.61	853.48	94.79	8.59	14.48

13. Fujian

13–5

Year	v3f	v3f1	v3f2	v3f3	v3f4	v4a1	v4a1a	v4a1b	v4a1c	v4a1d	v4a2	v4a2a	v4a2b	v4a2c	v4a2d
1949															
1950						0.83		0.43	0.36		0.42	0.01	0.11	0.25	0.05
1951						1.58	0.02	0.82	0.64	0.11	0.75	0.09	0.14	0.35	0.17
1952						2.20	0.15	1.22	0.53	0.30	1.25	0.34	0.30	0.34	0.27
1953						1.98	0.20	1.18	0.52	0.07	1.40	0.39	0.44	0.40	0.18
1954	90.19	57.00	9.36		9.37	2.32	0.18	1.37	0.55	0.22	1.48	0.47	0.42	0.45	0.15
1955						2.46	0.28	1.45	0.54	0.20	1.49	0.32	0.41	0.54	0.23
1956						2.96	0.51	1.71	0.53	0.21	2.44	0.77	0.52	0.63	0.52
1957	103.88	68.56	8.19		10.79	3.22	0.55	1.90	0.58	0.18	2.47	0.87	0.56	0.57	0.47
1958						5.52	1.65	2.73	0.66	0.48	6.77	4.64	0.67	0.59	0.87
1959						7.38	3.59	2.68	0.70	0.06	8.97	4.50	0.85	0.75	2.87
1960						7.31	3.35	3.00	0.40	0.16	11.05	6.03	1.23	0.72	3.07
1961						4.95	1.25	2.07	0.48	0.67	5.78	1.49	1.08	0.70	2.51
1962	136.36	78.28	5.95		19.04	5.07	1.48	2.62	0.50	0.15	3.60	0.76	0.94	0.62	1.28
1963						5.20	1.51	2.74	0.55	0.16	4.17	0.82	0.96	0.63	1.75
1964						5.92	1.95	2.95	0.58	0.06	4.52	1.35	1.08	0.67	1.42
1965	118.28	84.40	9.30		10.09	6.60	2.20	3.20	0.51	0.04	4.99	1.52	1.13	0.68	1.66
1966						6.70	2.53	3.08	0.57	0.03	5.36	1.68	1.20	0.70	1.77
1967						5.26	1.50	2.77	0.43	0.01	4.43	1.38	1.16	0.60	1.30
1968						3.50	0.02	2.23	0.59	0.04	3.33	0.88	1.03	0.59	0.83
1969						5.18	0.92	2.72	0.61	0.06	5.34	1.98	1.04	0.74	1.58
1970						6.45	2.07	3.10	0.51	0.05	8.34	4.11	1.07	1.06	2.10
1971						6.85	1.90	3.64	0.60	0.04	9.11	4.40	1.23	1.06	2.41
1972						8.59	2.92	4.27	0.58	0.04	9.15	4.35	1.56	1.07	2.17
1973						9.58	3.75	4.81	0.56	0.03	10.24	4.54	1.76	0.96	2.99
1974						9.29	3.29	4.78	0.55	0.02	10.18	4.06	1.96	0.92	3.25
1975						9.59	3.11	5.23	0.57	0.04	9.86	3.55	2.02	0.97	3.33
1976						8.91	2.39	5.35	0.52	0.04	10.14	3.35	2.15	1.00	3.64
1977						10.48	2.84	6.33	0.60	0.03	11.35	3.30	2.27	1.09	4.69
1978	112.73	77.92	13.03	1.89	10.21	15.13	5.78	7.61	0.58	0.47	15.14	4.87	2.79	1.27	6.22
1979	132.57	88.79	14.39	5.95	10.29	12.72	3.16	8.08	0.51	0.32	16.03	4.30	3.28	1.33	7.12
1980	157.67	99.43	16.01	11.54	13.17	15.33	4.54	9.12	0.52	0.49	15.05	3.39	3.86	1.61	6.18
1981	199.25	123.50	19.98	14.82	16.52	14.52	3.10	9.96	0.50	0.42	14.27	2.08	4.45	1.89	5.85
1982	231.14	144.92	21.26	19.51	16.96	13.67	1.66	10.58	0.57	0.25	16.42	2.84	5.13	1.91	6.53
1983	261.86	167.79	22.31	23.58	17.66	12.37	-0.21	10.78	0.61	0.54	17.55	2.96	5.70	2.22	6.68
1984	287.87	187.65	21.10	26.26	16.08	16.78	1.78	13.25	0.73	0.33	20.52	3.49	6.59	2.82	7.62
1985	350.57	218.79	24.92	39.55	19.05	25.08	2.56	20.28	1.15	0.58	30.64	6.03	8.05	3.12	13.44
1986	394.10	237.35	27.35	53.20	20.89	29.14	3.31	22.86	1.33	1.13	37.62	6.33	9.53	3.55	18.20
1987	442.83	266.09	25.68	53.82	22.14	33.16	3.32	26.63	1.67	1.52	39.99	4.98	9.99	3.85	21.17
1988	570.73	325.89	33.55	78.04	29.28	40.16	1.59	33.71	0.75	2.64	49.29	6.07	12.36	5.55	25.31
1989	652.58	379.31	35.35	89.41	31.00	53.01	1.50			6.29	60.48	7.60	15.28	5.00	32.60

13. Fujian

13–6

Year	v4b	v4b1	v4b2	v4b3	v4c1	v4c2	v5a	v5a1	v5a2	v5a3	v5a4	v5b1	v5b2	v5b3	v5c
1949															
1950	0.01		0.0143												
1951	0.18														
1952	0.32		0.3223				539.49	19.01	2.29						
1953	0.47														
1954	0.57														
1955	0.68														
1956	0.82														
1957	1.39	0.2254	1.1612				603.71	51.40	30.20						
1958	2.42						703.02	122.91	19.01		561.10				
1959	2.23						710.44	111.07	28.37		571.00				
1960	2.40						608.46	129.02	35.44		444.00				
1961	2.20						590.88	101.09	29.79		460.00				
1962	1.81	0.3432	1.4621				581.60	77.34	37.56		466.70				
1963	1.90						589.79	76.92	43.87		469.00				
1964	2.27						614.78	81.75	44.33		488.70				
1965	2.51	0.3346	2.1802				634.71	83.83	49.08		501.80				
1966	2.84						665.25	86.77	49.58		528.90				
1967	2.86						680.74	86.77	42.67		551.30				
1968	2.90						689.72	86.76	39.46		563.50				
1969	2.78						719.52	86.76	36.26		596.50				
1970	2.97	0.3149	2.6577				764.01	93.36	33.05		637.60				
1971	3.34						781.79	102.13	31.46		648.20				
1972	3.83						778.85	109.20	29.85		639.80				
1973	4.16						792.61	105.95	33.46		653.20				
1974	4.48						825.23	108.17	48.36		668.70				
1975	4.76	0.6621	4.0998		5.82	16.9	855.13	111.42	49.64		690.00				
1976	4.91				4.88	13.0	879.87	116.39	55.32		704.30				
1977	5.68				7.02	17.6	904.44	140.14	56.60		707.00				
1978	6.56	1.0994	5.4611		10.25	23.7	917.86	148.49	57.17		711.60				90.18
1979	8.63	1.7907	6.8356		10.90	22.8	942.21	156.70	61.29		722.50				94.17
1980	12.01	3.0789	8.9314		12.13	23.2	962.99	167.46	63.66		729.10				98.67
1981	16.35	7.0897	9.2612		14.88	22.3	986.26	176.35	66.09		740.60				103.55
1982	20.91	9.2229	11.6865		13.34	21.5	1027.95	183.03	66.77		773.90	720	156	153	105.24
1983	25.86	11.1587	14.7028		13.35	20.0	1052.27	187.30	66.72		790.60	726	160	166	106.10
1984	35.51	15.7119	19.7985		15.45	20.5	1101.23	182.82	79.24	0.72	829.30	731	177	193	110.06
1985	47.59	22.0549	25.5391		21.10	23.8	1152.07	191.37	80.93	1.81	864.20	710	225	217	115.02
1986	64.32	29.6612	34.6583		22.73	22.3	1188.52	198.50	81.79	3.57	889.40	722	236	230	120.47
1987	83.62	38.6299	44.9930		27.44	23.8	1238.62	205.34	82.21	5.74	926.00	742	254	243	124.14
1988	90.77	21.9488	68.8256		35.31	26.1	1281.10	211.00	81.93	8.78	956.79	756	268	257	130.13
1989	126.60				38.68	22.5	1301.88	211.16	78.49	12.85	974.16	765	270	267	

13. Fujian

13–7

Year	v5c1	v5d	v6a	v6a1	v6a2	v6b	v6c	v6d1	v6d2	v6d3	v6d4	v6d5	v6d6
1949			1187.9					181.9	1006.0	617.7	570.2		
1950	0.28		1210.5			31.09	13.92	167.8	1042.7	629.5	581.0		
1951	0.62		1233.4			32.50	14.80	151.7	1081.7	641.3	592.1		
1952	1.35		1259.2			33.50	13.40	144.5	1114.7	644.1	615.1	47.48	17.62
1953	2.20		1302.5			35.40	12.60	152.7	1149.8	677.3	625.2		
1954	2.77		1338.5	251.9	1086.6	35.73	10.89	170.3	1168.2	690.8	647.7		
1955	3.98		1366.6	206.7	1159.9	28.69	8.94	167.4	1199.2	705.8	660.8		
1956	8.39		1400.4	227.4	1173.0	28.67	8.43	195.4	1205.0	724.0	676.4		
1957	10.95		1452.5	237.0	1215.5	37.88	7.85	211.3	1241.2	752.6	699.9	60.63	29.69
1958	45.80		1493.4	302.1	1191.3	29.12	7.46	285.4	1208.0	772.5	720.9	62.56	33.76
1959	44.37		1543.1	345.5	1197.6	27.56	7.88	320.9	1222.2	798.0	745.1		
1960	51.42		1572.6	373.5	1199.1	25.11	15.34	352.0	1220.6	820.9	751.7		
1961	32.67		1597.8	363.0	1234.8	17.42	11.87	318.9	1278.9	827.6	770.2	82.89	38.10
1962	22.02		1639.7	353.5	1286.2	40.16	8.28	287.0	1352.7	848.3	791.4	83.98	37.70
1963	19.51		1678.4	339.0	1339.4	44.96	7.36	283.8	1394.6	868.5	809.9	84.38	38.39
1964	21.01		1703.5	347.8	1355.7	38.33	8.62	279.6	1423.9	882.8	820.7	86.05	39.07
1965	21.98		1759.8	356.7	1403.1	41.18	7.34	287.4	1472.4	910.8	849.0	86.86	39.96
1966	23.66		1813.7	363.4	1450.3	37.04	7.11	295.4	1518.3	938.6	875.1		
1967	23.98		1860.8	379.8	1481.0	34.94	6.28	300.5	1560.3	961.5	899.3		
1968	24.12		1917.6	388.3	1529.3	37.13	6.31	311.4	1606.2	989.3	928.3		
1969	24.26		1974.5	383.4	1591.1	35.55	5.68	297.4	1677.1	1020.9	953.6		
1970	29.76		2028.7	389.6	1639.1	33.58	6.05	285.4	1743.3	1048.6	980.1	82.60	40.23
1971	35.38		2089.7	400.3	1689.4	34.65	5.69	296.3	1793.4	1080.5	1009.2		
1972	39.59		2150.7	402.6	1748.1	33.66	6.17	298.9	1851.8	1109.6	1041.1		
1973	38.65		2210.4	413.1	1797.3	32.25	6.37	308.6	1901.8	1141.2	1069.2		
1974	39.98		2257.9	424.3	1833.6	28.37	6.67	313.3	1944.6	1165.2	1092.7		
1975	41.49		2310.3	439.2	1871.1	28.83	6.54	317.0	1993.3	1193.2	1117.1	96.71	44.77
1976	43.80		2361.9	448.3	1913.6	27.84	6.32	324.1	2027.8	1219.5	1142.4		
1977	44.62		2411.2	457.1	1954.1	26.53	6.53	327.7	2083.5	1245.2	1166.0		
1978	56.40	16.37	2452.8	467.9	1984.9	23.83	5.97	336.1	2116.7	1268.9	1183.9	102.76	47.35
1979	58.53	17.01	2487.9	484.2	2003.7	19.07	6.05	355.1	2132.8	1282.9	1205.0		
1980	61.96	17.57	2517.8	498.0	2019.8	15.19	5.86	366.7	2151.1	1298.0	1219.8	107.50	49.17
1981	65.14	17.51	2556.9	535.9	2021.0	21.09	5.91	380.9	2176.0	1318.4	1238.5		
1982	67.32	17.68	2604.0	548.2	2055.8	23.38	5.83	392.2	2211.8	1342.7	1261.3		
1983	68.87	17.76	2639.8	598.0	2041.8	17.25	5.90	402.9	2236.9	1362.1	1277.7		
1984	70.90	17.64	2676.8	997.9	1678.9	18.87	5.59	422.4	2254.4	1381.7	1295.1		
1985	74.23	17.01	2713.1	1162.3	1550.8	17.49	5.38	447.2	2265.9	1401.2	1311.9	118.95	54.64
1986	76.71	16.78	2749.3	1202.5	1546.8	17.07	5.31	455.0	2294.3	1421.2	1328.1	120.50	55.84
1987	78.49	16.91	2800.5	1274.9	1525.6	21.24	5.32	466.3	2334.2	1447.2	1353.3	123.66	56.98
1988	81.33	17.04	2845.2	1424.6	1420.6	20.35	5.64	476.6	2368.6	1470.0	1375.2	125.13	57.95
1989			2896.0	1528.4	1360.7	23.78	6.09	490.8	2398.3	1493.2	1395.9	126.91	59.01

13. Fujian

13–8

Year	v7a	v7b	v7c	v7d	v7e	v7f	v7g	v7h	v7h1	v7h2	v7h3	v7h4	v7h5	v7i	v8a
1949															
1950				3095.8		0.7		9.25	6.85	0.17	1.01	0.28	0.94		2.45
1951				3119.7		1.7		9.78	6.86	0.48	1.19	0.32	0.93		3.20
1952				3164.7		3.7		11.07	7.38	0.65	1.40	0.56	1.08		4.20
1953				3215.6		5.2		11.89	8.26	0.63	1.47	0.65	0.88		5.47
1954				3226.8		7.6		11.97	7.74	0.86	1.48	0.76	1.13		6.21
1955				3312.4		8.8		12.92	8.34	0.90	1.47	0.96	1.15		6.48
1956				3611.0		10.5		14.94	9.56	1.04	1.76	1.06	1.52		7.52
1957		1.2		3566.5		10.7		17.05	9.41	2.16	2.35	1.22	1.91		8.81
1958				3428.0		12.2		15.47	10.12	1.69	1.65	1.08	0.93		12.98
1959				3093.6		8.7		15.29	9.60	1.93	0.90	1.30	1.56		19.70
1960				3502.1		10.8		12.61	7.94	1.59	0.53	1.25	1.30		25.28
1961				3135.4		10.1		13.49	8.93	0.78	0.86	1.45	1.47		13.96
1962		22.7		3091.9		12.8		14.81	9.23	0.63	1.71	1.20	2.04		11.42
1963				3059.2		19.7	0.26	15.71	9.53	0.73	2.27	1.41	1.77		11.57
1964				3198.1		25.9	0.27	16.35	10.36	1.14	2.45	1.24	1.16		14.28
1965		22.8		2964.4		42.5		18.80	11.84	1.23	2.81	1.23	1.69		17.74
1966				3589.0		52.2	0.57	20.67	13.36	1.88	2.93	1.50	1.00		22.27
1967				3464.3		41.8	0.67	18.79	11.56	1.67	2.79	1.51	1.26		19.75
1968				3220.1		23.6	0.72	18.01	11.01	1.25	2.68	1.42	1.65		14.20
1969				3340.0		37.2	0.85	19.91	12.68	1.48	2.76	1.51	1.48		21.88
1970				3525.8		55.7	0.98	21.12	14.01	1.49	2.62	1.48	1.52		25.58
1971				3840.7		55.4	1.26	25.11	16.80	1.73	3.51	1.52	1.55		28.43
1972				4023.8		56.6	1.63	27.12	18.55	1.88	3.55	1.73	1.41		33.85
1973				4117.6		72.5	2.20	25.84	17.55	1.83	3.20	1.54	1.72		39.64
1974				4104.5		70.6	2.67	26.71	18.49	1.80	3.02	1.45	1.95		40.61
1975				4134.6		62.4	3.22	27.06	18.57	1.86	3.24	1.51	1.88	70.58	44.44
1976				4050.3		60.3	3.76	26.54	17.77	2.02	3.09	1.57	2.09	69.94	44.89
1977				4003.8		69.3	4.12	29.27	20.58	1.95	3.17	1.74	1.83	70.05	53.60
1978	16.78	567.0	1293.80	4051.6		112.0	4.89	36.33	25.80	2.31	3.82	1.98	2.42	69.90	64.18
1979	20.47	644.1	1317.90	3967.0		148.9	5.76	43.11	27.39	3.27	7.00	3.55	1.90	70.42	71.83
1980	24.03	646.3	1321.60	3860.9		180.6	6.43	45.49	29.19	3.41	7.38	3.57	1.94	71.60	81.18
1981	27.14	603.5	1254.10	3789.9		188.1	7.13	56.11	34.50	4.62	8.75	4.81	3.43	76.59	90.07
1982	30.16	530.3	1293.80	3704.2		205.7	7.99	63.73	38.33	4.90	10.37	5.71	4.42	81.25	96.66
1983	32.41	535.8	1234.40	3642.6	275	208.7	8.01	68.08	38.69	5.57	11.47	6.92	5.43	81.70	105.20
1984	34.46	479.5	1206.30	3580.1	101	213.2	8.90	80.66	44.63	7.07	14.38	8.39	6.19	86.62	131.82
1985	29.47	470.7	1384.45	3503.5	362	206.1	11.24	99.05	50.14	9.13	19.60	10.96	9.22	87.88	165.33
1986	33.51	553.8	1370.44	3601.5	465	236.5	14.65	107.07	49.72	10.29	21.98	14.00	11.08	87.87	190.72
1987	37.36	571.0	1382.49	3815.6	345	256.0	14.06	132.97	60.02	13.57	27.71	19.57	12.09	89.81	234.87
1988	54.70	588.9	1386.00	3882.9	585	276.0	16.53	182.00	79.34	17.50	39.59	30.77	14.80	90.28	312.96
1989	57.42	626.4	1365.90	3984.4			20.04	209.92	93.29	18.41	51.86	31.46	14.90	93.57	360.16

13. Fujian

13–9

Year	v8a1	v8a2	v8a3	v8b	v8c1	v8c2	v8d	v8f1	v8f2	v8f3	v8f4	v8f5	v8g
1949													
1950	0.07								0.04		0.08		7326
1951	0.23								0.01		0.09		7568
1952	0.51	0.02	3.67						0.30		0.12		6131
1953	0.93	0.04	4.50						1.07		0.17		6311
1954	1.47	0.17	4.57						2.12		0.23	0.01	6850
1955	2.46	0.40	3.62						2.63		0.29	0.72	5936
1956	4.85	1.50	1.17						8.12		0.45	5.51	5746
1957	6.07	1.71	1.03						8.25		0.57	5.26	6127
1958	10.58	2.39	0.01					0.85	58.77		1.34	7.66	
1959	16.87	2.83						1.19	93.02		2.66	9.76	7561
1960	21.50	3.78						5.55	121.00		4.82	14.88	7217
1961	11.50	2.43	0.03					1.14	77.15		4.55	8.99	6722
1962	8.87	2.48	0.07					0.12	55.77		4.99	6.05	6369
1963	9.05	2.46	0.06					0.15	49.10		4.93	7.01	5848
1964	11.47	2.75	0.06					0.19	47.89		5.80	12.01	5699
1965	14.68	3.06						0.66	60.19		7.41	20.37	4933
1966	18.52	3.75						1.49	80.51		9.54	26.46	4547
1967	15.89	3.86						0.79	52.75		7.28	15.38	4653
1968	10.91	3.29						0.21	25.80		5.23	7.59	4643
1969	17.94	3.94						0.95	66.63		9.62	24.17	4493
1970	21.78	3.80						3.62	110.03		13.12	32.85	4553
1971	23.20	5.23						8.00	164.05		15.33	41.62	4861
1972	27.26	6.59						9.37	209.61		18.46	55.08	5363
1973	31.37	8.27						12.44	244.79		22.50	69.27	6024
1974	31.13	9.48						10.25	248.92		22.43	74.90	6069
1975	33.90	10.54					9.65	9.84	280.67		26.83	89.13	7001
1976	33.40	11.49					9.72	6.47	293.57		29.44	87.30	7357
1977	39.71	13.89		36.19			10.73	11.32	346.39		34.75	96.35	7837
1978	47.62	16.56		43.69			14.50	16.16	423.05		40.69	120.45	8619
1979	52.53	19.30		50.30			16.05	20.83	479.04		44.40	139.84	9663
1980	57.46	23.69	0.03	55.47			18.57	24.16	462.99		49.47	155.30	10540
1981	62.44	26.90	0.73	58.24			19.47	21.90	416.55		52.46	161.62	10690
1982	66.58	28.55	1.53	63.30			20.48	24.90	440.23		57.18	163.71	11070
1983	70.64	31.21	3.35	66.88			21.79	23.79	524.26		61.55	206.66	11257
1984	81.70	40.75	9.37	78.77			25.47	28.71	575.94		67.53	234.03	11779
1985	93.85	58.01	13.47	98.35			32.17	31.75	606.53		77.20	290.69	12138
1986	101.97	70.11	18.64	111.04	82.49	122.61	36.17	34.42	678.52		86.21	321.76	12508
1987	114.58	86.12	34.17	134.53	108.02	157.85	42.65	39.22	787.19		98.54	379.50	12810
1988	134.52	116.19	62.25	184.98	150.98	237.87	59.95	40.39	864.36		114.14	452.97	
1989	144.37	132.14	89.80	226.95	192.44	296.52	70.44	43.23	944.83		129.56	499.63	14112

13. Fujian

13–10

Year	v8g1	v9a	v9a1	v9a2	v9a3	v9b	v9b1	v9b2	v9b3	v9c	v10a	v10a1	v10b1	v10b2	v10b3
1949															
1950		0.63		0.16	0.48	0.84		0.16	0.59	312	4.07	3.85			
1951		0.90		0.35	0.55	1.05		0.24	0.64	390	4.99	4.71			
1952		1.72		0.77	0.95	1.43		0.27	0.82	414	5.84	5.54			
1953		2.45		1.05	1.40	2.13		0.60	1.26	523	7.39	6.89			
1954		3.47		1.95	1.49	3.00		0.95	1.39	617	8.75	8.02			
1955		4.68		2.99	1.63	4.40		1.49	1.68	737	9.43	8.44			
1956		7.36	0.33	6.67	2.31	6.90	1.08	1.81	2.19	874	11.97	10.65			
1957		8.81	1.77	4.70	2.30	10.07	3.64	1.69	2.42	902	11.92	10.70			
1958		11.39	2.76	6.28	2.28	20.75	11.31	2.08	2.67	1185	13.60	11.54			
1959		14.93	5.64	7.71	1.48	29.46	15.08	3.88	3.85	1795	15.98	13.67			
1960		17.44	7.48	7.93	1.93	32.77	18.41	3.78	2.57	2195	17.14	14.78			
1961		17.24	8.81	5.38	2.96	22.05	13.09	2.16	1.48	2049	13.54	11.82			
1962		16.97	8.17	5.93	2.75	20.70	12.47	2.03	1.34	1962	15.61	13.96			
1963		14.40	6.17	6.33	1.78	23.97	14.77	1.97	1.57	1888	17.08	15.32			
1964		15.50	6.79	7.06	1.54	28.09	17.52	2.37	1.91	1929	17.36	15.59			
1965		16.22	6.65	8.06	1.41	38.75	25.38	3.13	2.01	1995	18.24	16.03			
1966		18.48	6.97	9.82	1.69	40.80	26.83	3.61	2.19	2012	19.68	16.93			
1967		17.54	7.50	8.16	1.88	28.37	16.48	3.00	1.71	1902	19.10	16.90			
1968		16.47	8.25	6.33	1.89	28.66	19.17	2.52	1.18	1710	17.44	15.52			
1969		18.62	8.03	8.72	1.87	37.77	25.04	3.47	1.67	1762	19.49	17.06			
1970		17.59	7.56	8.52	1.51	40.56	27.97	3.92	1.58	1790	19.93	16.91			
1971		20.37	8.94	9.95	1.40	45.36	31.04	5.00	1.60	2023	21.77	18.41			
1972		23.79	9.98	12.18	1.54	49.31	34.00	5.38	2.00	2250	23.39	19.67			
1973	1563	25.70	10.26	13.65	1.69	50.58	34.79	5.79	2.11	2423	24.96	20.72			
1974	1602	27.94	10.94	15.06	1.80	45.11	28.50	6.01	2.09	2493	26.21	21.86			
1975	1715	28.36	10.68	15.77	1.91	53.21	35.49	6.24	2.08	2803	28.12	23.68			
1976	1739	30.49	11.70	16.83	1.96	53.54	36.14	6.09	1.91	2896	29.55	25.11			
1977	1799	31.56	11.69	17.91	1.97	62.49	42.88	6.98	1.93	3018	32.53	27.31			
1978	1897	35.73	13.24	20.53	1.96	73.06	50.40	7.72	2.22	3258	37.26	30.56	18.53		18.55
1979	1987	43.71	16.20	25.16	2.21	79.64	55.17	8.52	3.11	3622	43.82	35.92	21.74		21.83
1980	2083	56.63	20.92	32.80	2.48	83.25	56.56	9.21	2.42	3954	54.20	45.47	25.69		25.65
1981	2053	65.21	23.16	38.85	2.67	85.01	55.54	9.32	2.27	5539	60.06	51.47	27.93		27.97
1982	2129	69.67	23.20	43.56	2.34	89.82	57.05	9.33	2.39	5764	66.12	56.77	29.66		30.49
1983	2096	78.62	27.22	48.48	2.22	96.03	61.42	8.93	2.34	6289	72.33	62.59	30.32		30.96
1984	2122	89.87	29.94	57.17	2.11	108.89	69.85	9.25	2.31	7096	84.96	74.50	34.20		33.53
1985	2236	104.69	35.25	66.56	2.22	121.18	82.43	10.16	2.46	8936	107.09	96.04	40.24		39.59
1986	2202	105.12	37.18	65.19	2.09	134.72	90.37	10.43	2.12	9885	122.09	109.06	44.69		41.97
1987	2283	107.57	40.40	64.26	2.19	145.06	95.69	11.09	1.92	11955	142.12	126.06	49.61		46.13
1988	2293	116.25	46.24	67.02	2.08	152.69	97.98	11.92	1.83	15768	194.53	173.74	67.43		57.11
1989	2335	112.01	44.49	64.90	1.88	179.62	101.08	10.45	1.77	22787	227.02	202.30	70.25		60.71

13. Fujian

13–11

Year	v10b4	v10b5	v10b6	v10d	v11a1	v11a2	v11a3	v11b	v11b1	v11b2	v11c	v11d	v12a	v12b	v12c
1949															
1950								0.1034	0.0196	0.0838					
1951								0.0960	0.0221	0.0739			106.9	107.8	99.1
1952				3.00	154.8	73.7	0.5	0.0942	0.0229	0.0713			98.1	97.6	101.6
1953								0.0637	0.0351	0.0286			101.5	101.8	104.9
1954								0.0769	0.0361	0.0408			99.8	100.2	102.3
1955								0.0551	0.0497	0.0054			101.7	101.4	100.8
1956								0.0741	0.0682	0.0059			102.0	102.2	104.1
1957				6.30	872.2	490.0	2.7	0.1508	0.1365	0.0143			100.3	100.8	104.2
1958								0.4015	0.3219	0.0796			100.9	101.1	100.7
1959								0.2425	0.2176	0.0249			101.1	100.8	102.9
1960								0.2035	0.1748	0.0287			100.3	100.3	101.1
1961								0.1711	0.1149	0.0562			122.5	124.0	129.8
1962					553.6	466.0	11.3	0.1157	0.1031	0.0126			103.2	100.5	98.3
1963								0.1430	0.1292	0.0138			94.0	95.9	96.0
1964								0.2224	0.1916	0.0308			94.3	93.3	98.4
1965				8.90	932.2	1548.6	66.2	0.3050	0.2547	0.0503			94.4	94.4	99.0
1966								0.3723	0.3139	0.0584			100.4	99.5	102.9
1967								0.3101	0.2615	0.0486			100.2	100.6	100.0
1968								0.3004	0.2536	0.0468			100.0	100.0	100.0
1969								0.3823	0.3088	0.0735			99.9	100.1	100.3
1970								0.3823	0.3536	0.0287			99.1	99.0	99.7
1971								0.4711	0.3941	0.0770			100.4	101.5	104.3
1972								0.6999	0.5766	0.1233			99.9	99.8	100.0
1973								1.1650	1.0770	0.0880			99.9	99.9	100.1
1974								1.4720	1.3784	0.0936			99.9	99.8	100.1
1975								1.2998	1.2208	0.0790			100.2	101.1	100.1
1976								1.2441	1.1110	0.1331			100.4	100.5	100.6
1977								1.3946	1.2919	0.1027			100.1	100.2	100.6
1978		0.18		16.71	6084.5	12035.9	893.7	2.0260	1.9014	0.1246			100.3	100.4	101.9
1979		0.25		17.23	7148.2	15676.8	1824.0	2.7401	2.4649	0.2752	0.5261	0.4234	102.7	102.7	127.6
1980	0.01	0.42	2.43	20.66	7091.4	25456.2	3818.4	5.0543	3.6366	1.4177	0.1372	0.0918	105.2	106.3	105.4
1981		0.94	3.22	22.67	7087.6	26717.9	6012.5	5.6525	3.9818	1.6707	0.2485	0.0451	103.5	104.0	107.4
1982		1.78	4.19	24.34	7241.4	25363.8	5307.8	5.1674	3.7913	1.3761	0.3945	0.0263	103.6	103.1	105.7
1983	0.01	5.69	5.35	26.76	7232.4	27905.3	4144.4	5.9918	3.9470	2.0448	0.4537	0.4793	101.5	102.0	104.2
1984	0.13	10.63	6.47	30.59	8304.9	29660.4	4406.7	6.9381	4.2372	2.7009	2.5408	0.6168	101.9	102.8	104.4
1985	1.02	17.03	9.21	38.93	11943.0	29537.9	7667.1	11.1692	4.9148	6.2544	4.3909	1.7711	110.6	114.0	116.4
1986	1.28	23.39	10.76	47.38	10587.3	40497.8	6768.9	8.9374	5.7854	3.1520	1.1499	1.6660	105.9	106.9	107.5
1987	1.48	32.90	12.00	58.36	16731.8	55716.0	12485.2	13.4122	8.4933	4.9189	2.1890	1.4719	109.4	110.6	114.0
1988	2.48	51.63	15.88	82.79	26005.8	82375.2	32191.0	21.9526	14.0574	7.8952	6.2497	2.8892	126.5	127.0	132.3
1989	3.53	71.11	21.42	96.01				23.9702	16.6171	7.3531	9.6134	3.8800	118.8	118.8	116.7

13. Fujian

Year	v13a	v13b	v13c1	v13c2	v13c3	v13d	v14a	v14b	v14c	v15a	v15b	v15c	v15d	v15e	v15f
1949			0.37	5.61	46.11	0.11									
1950	20.2		0.36	6.84	50.09					2175.40					
1951	14.3		0.38	7.86	87.19					2186.50					
1952	17.7	50.7	0.47	11.55	102.59	0.09	5902	17300	0.22	2202.20					
1953	23.6		0.38	12.79	95.04					2206.10					
1954	21.7		0.45	13.17	99.30					2211.90					
1955	20.5		0.46	13.32	107.07					2216.10					
1956	12.9		0.65	17.66	132.14					2231.90					
1957	17.9	66.0	0.75	18.69	137.61	0.08			0.47	2218.90					
1958	7.9		1.45	27.96	184.62					2129.20					
1959	8.0		1.73	30.55	198.27					2024.20					
1960	10.3		2.52	40.58	227.09					1971.00					
1961	13.8		2.21	28.86	172.36					1923.80					
1962	18.6		1.91	23.81	157.81				0.62	1936.50					
1963	16.0		1.75	23.94	175.59					1962.90					
1964	16.6		1.61	27.68	226.31					2001.00					
1965	15.9	86.5	1.52	35.34	290.11	0.43	21818	42700	0.40	1979.70					
1966	15.3		1.53	27.02	236.63					1981.30					
1967	18.4		1.53	19.26	233.44					1976.20					
1968	22.1		0.57	9.39	231.41					1972.90					
1969	13.6		0.47	27.80	212.48					1965.30					
1970	8.7		0.07	38.68	238.19					1964.80					
1971	9.3		0.18	47.93	253.41					1963.90					
1972	12.2		0.42	55.32	296.62					1965.70					
1973	11.6		0.65	53.36	35.02					1960.20					
1974	12.8		0.87	59.23	394.43					1959.00					
1975	13.6		1.03	80.49	398.32					1955.50					
1976	14.0		1.14	108.49	392.60					1954.00					
1977	13.0		1.55	123.08	383.36					1953.80					
1978	11.8	92.2	3.11	119.98	370.23	0.35	45331	54900	2.20	1946.00					
1979	13.2	94.5	3.01	108.85	379.02	0.08			2.30	1942.00					
1980	17.2	94.5	3.86	114.73	376.42	0.90	46772	58800	2.50	1936.50					
1981	20.5	93.8	3.04	102.28	367.08	1.56			2.77	1933.50					
1982	21.2	93.7	2.67	101.65	360.97	1.16			2.91	1926.70					
1983	22.4	94.9	2.93	101.95	360.67	0.73			3.30	1924.00	6745	1168	1046	8.2680	4.9544
1984	21.5	96.5	3.40	110.83	368.68	0.76			4.24	1919.40	6745	1168	1046	8.2680	4.9544
1985	18.9	97.3	4.41	121.39	372.40	0.79	52041	74200	5.48	1981.80	6745	1168	1046		
1986	17.8	97.5	5.12	128.85	361.40	0.94			5.55	1875.40	6745	1168	1046	9.4808	5.2095
1987	16.5	98.1	5.41	132.43	344.50	1.43			6.61	1865.90	7494	1168	1046	9.4808	5.2095
1988	16.9	98.4	5.71	122.68	333.99	1.68	56920	81900	6.46	1858.81	7500	1168	1046	9.7600	6.4700
1989		98.6	5.68	106.24	336.77	1.73	59252	84400	5.56	1857.78					

Notes

1. National Output and Income (Y)

v1a: (E), p.439
  v1a1: (E), p.439
  v1a2: (E), p.439
  v1a3: (E), p.439
  v1a4: (E), p.439
  v1a5: (E), p.439

v1b: (A); (D), p.245
  v1b1: (A)
  v1b2: (A)
  v1b3: (A); (D), p.245
  v1b4: (A); (D), p.245
  v1b5: (A); (D), p.245

v1c: v1a – v1d

v1d: (E), p.436
  v1d1: (E), p.436
  v1d2: (E), p.436
  v1d3: (E), p.436
  v1d4: (E), p.436
  v1d5: (E), p.436

v1e: (A); (D), p.248
  v1e1: (A); (D), p.248
  v1e2: (A); (D), p.248
  v1e3: (A); (D), p.248
  v1e4: (A); (D), p.248
  v1e5: (A); (D), p.248

v1f: (E), p.435
  v1f1: (E), p.435
  v1f2: (E), p.435
  v1f3: (E), p.435

v1g: v2a + v3a

v1h: (A); (E), p.463

v1i: (E), p.462

v1j: (A); (E), p.462
  v1j1: (E), p.462
  v1j2: (E), p.462
  v1j3: (C), 1989, p.438

v1k: (E), p.462

2. Investment (I)

v2a: (E), p.438
  v2a1: (A); (D), p.253
  v2a2: (A); (D), p.253

v2b: (A)

v2c: (E), p.452
  v2c1: (E), p.453
  v2c2: (E), p.453

v2d:
  v2d1: (E), p.450
  v2d2: (E), p.450

v2e: (E), p.450

3. Consumption (C)

v3a: (E), p.438

v3b: (E), p.438
  v3b1: (A); (D), p.249
  v3b2: (A); (D), p.249

v3c: (E), p.438

v3d: (E), p.461
  v3d1: (E), p.461
  v3d2: (E), p.461

v3e: (A); (E), p.463
  v3e1: (A); (E), p.463
  v3e2: (A)
  v3e3: (A)
  v3e4: (A)

v3f: (A); (E), p.463
  v3f1: (A); (E), p.463

v3f2: (A)
v3f3: (A)
v3f4: (A)

4. Public Finance and Banking (FB)

v4a:
- v4a1: (E), p.459
  - v4a1a: (E), p.459
  - v4a1b: (C), 1984, p.155–156; 1987, p.353; 1989, p.374
  - v4a1c: (C), 1984, p.155–156; 1987, p.353; 1989, p.374
  - v4a1d: v4a1 – v4a1a – v4a1b' (v4a1b': total tax revenues which come from (E), p.459)
- v4a2: (E), p.459
  - v4a2a: (E), p.459
  - v4a2b: (E), p.459
  - v4a2c: (E), p.459
  - v4a2d: v4a2 – v4a2a – v4a2b – v4a2c

v4b: (A)
- v4b1: (C), 1989, p.377—city and town residents' savings deposits
- v4b2: (C), 1989, p.377—rural residents' savings deposits
- v4b3: NA

v4c:
- v4c1: (E), p.450
- v4c2: (E), p.450

5. Labor Force (L)

v5a: (C), 1989, p.73; (E), p.434
- v5a1: (C), 1989, p.73; (E), p.434
- v5a2: (C), 1989, p.73; (E), p.434
- v5a3: (E), p.434
- v5a4: (E), p.434

v5b:
- v5b1: (A)
- v5b2: (A)
- v5b3: (A)

v5c: (B), p.169
- v5c1: (A); (B), p.168

v5d: (B), p.169

6. Population (PO)

v6a: (A); (E), p.433—data from public security department
- v6a1: (E), p.433—(ditto)
- v6a2: (E), p.433—(ditto)

v6b: (E), p.433—data from public security department, data of 1988 was estimated from sample survey

v6c: (E), p.433—(ditto)

v6d:
- v6d1: (E), p.433—data from public security department
- v6d2: (E), p.433—(ditto)
- v6d3: (E), p.433—(ditto)
- v6d4: (E), p.433—(ditto)
- v6d5: (A)—Fuzhou
- v6d6: (A)—Xiamen

7. Agriculture (A)

v7a: (A); (E), p.446

v7b: (A); (E), p.446

v7c: (A); (E), p.446

v7d: (A); (E), p.446

v7e: (A)

v7f: (A)

v7g: (A); (E), p.446

v7h: (E), p.441
- v7h1: (E), p.441
- v7h2: (E), p.441
- v7h3: (E), p.441

v7h4: (E), p.441
v7h5: (E), p.441

v7i: (E), p.445

8. Industry (IN)

v8a: (E), p.447
v8a1: (E), p.447—1949–57: at 1952's constant price; 1958–70: at 1957's constant price; 1971–80: at 1970's constant price; 1981–89: at 1980's constant price
v8a2: (E), p.447—(ditto)
v8a3: v8a – v8a1 – v8a2

v8b: (E), p.450

v8c1: (E), p.439
v8c2: (E), p.439

v8d: (E), p.450

v8f:
v8f1: (E), p.449
v8f2: (E), p.449
v8f3: NA
v8f4: (E), p.449
v8f5: (E), p.449

v8g: (A)
v8g1: (E), p.450

9. Transport (TR)

v9a: (E), p.451—excluding urban traffic volume
v9a1: (E), p.451—including central and local railways
v9a2: (E), p.451—data of transport system
v9a3: (E), p.451—data of transport system, including distant ocean and coastal passenger traffic in 1966–70 and 1975–78

v9b: (E), p.451
v9b1: (E), p.451—including central and local railway
v9b2: (E), p.451—data of transport system
v9b3: (E), p.451—data of transport system, excluding distant ocean and coastal freight volume

v9c: (E), p.451—1949–80: 1970's constant price; 1981-88: 1980's constant price

10. Domestic Trade (DT)

v10a: (E), p.454
v10a1: (E), p.454

v10b:
v10b1: (A); (B), p.454
v10b2: NA
v10b3: (E), p.454—including supply and marketing cooperative and other collectives
v10b4: (A); (E), p.454
v10b5: (E), p.454
v10b6: (E), p.454

v10d: (A); (E), p.456—calculated on calendar year basis

11. Foreign Trade (FT)

v11a:
v11a1: % in (B), p.109 times corresponding total amount in (B), p.108
v11a2: % in (B), p.109 times corresponding total amount in (B), p.108, referring to textile and other products of light industry
v11a3: % in (B), p.109 times corresponding total amount in (B), p.108, referring to industrial and mining products

v11b: (E), p.457—data from foreign trade department
  v11b1: (E), p.457—(ditto)
  v11b2: v11b – v11b1

v11c: (E), p.458—including other foreign investment

v11d: (A); (E), p.458

12. Prices (PR)

v12a: (E), p.460

v12b: (E), p.460

v12c: (E), p.460

13. Education (ED)

v13a: (A)

v13b: (E), p.463

v13c:
  v13c1: (A); (B), p.131; (E), p.463—general institutions of higher learning
  v13c2: (A); (B), p.131; (E), p.463—technical and ordinary secondary schools
  v13c3: (A); (B), p.131; (E), p.463

v13d: (A); (B), p.131—general institutions of higher learning

14. Social Factors (SF)

v14a: (E), p.463

v14b: (E), p.463

v14c: (A)

15. Natural Environment (NE)

v15a: (A); (E), p.446

v15b: (A)

v15c: (A)

v15d: (A)

v15e: (A)

v15f: (A)

Sources of Data

(A) Data supplied by the DSNEB, SSB, the PRC.
(B) Statistical Bureau of Fujian Province ed. *Fujian Striving and Advancing Forty Years*, Beijing: CSPH, 1989.
(C) ________ ed. *Statistical Yearbook of Fujian*, Beijing: CSPH, various issues.
(D) Same as (D) in Beijing's sources of data.
(E) Same as (E) in Beijing's sources of data.

14

Jiangxi

14. Jiangxi

14–1

Year	v1a	v1a1	v1a2	v1a3	v1a4	v1a5	v1b	v1b1	v1b2	v1b3	v1b4	v1b5	v1c	v1d	v1d1
1949	14.80	9.88	2.64		0.41	1.87							6.50	8.30	6.18
1950	19.85	11.61	4.91	0.14	0.60	2.59							7.01	12.84	9.33
1951	22.34	11.96	6.00	0.29	0.59	3.50							8.51	13.83	9.66
1952	27.08	15.35	6.97	0.52	0.69	3.55	123.6	125.9	129.0	174.2	117.8	101.4	9.98	17.10	12.26
1953	28.60	15.14	7.86	0.92	1.08	3.60	103.9	98.5	117.3	183.1	163.9	96.8	10.76	17.84	12.14
1954	30.44	15.15	8.36	1.32	1.38	4.23	105.6	99.5	111.3	147.0	129.6	114.7	11.96	18.48	12.10
1955	32.66	16.17	8.85	1.40	1.24	5.00	107.9	105.8	111.2	108.2	91.4	118.4	13.16	19.50	12.89
1956	35.94	17.24	10.62	2.13	1.50	4.45	109.0	105.5	128.3	102.6	123.1	89.0	15.85	20.09	12.23
1957	39.58	19.06	11.70	2.06	1.96	4.80	111.9	108.3	115.4	151.9	137.7	105.6	14.78	24.80	15.30
1958	53.53	18.98	18.96	5.76	3.33	6.50	127.0	98.3	159.6	278.2	170.4	135.3	25.66	27.87	15.66
1959	62.80	18.52	24.84	6.73	5.21	7.50	111.8	95.6	129.0	109.5	156.0	115.4	32.74	30.06	15.20
1960	67.85	17.80	28.79	8.06	6.20	7.00	105.9	95.8	113.8	117.2	119.6	92.8	35.97	31.88	14.66
1961	55.24	22.45	19.06	5.22	3.01	5.50	77.1	103.9	65.0	63.9	48.5	69.1	24.82	30.42	17.82
1962	50.53	23.70	16.95	3.07	2.35	4.46	91.7	100.9	85.0	60.9	77.0	94.4	21.70	28.83	18.51
1963	52.12	24.05	18.07	3.40	2.40	4.20	103.9	105.8	103.1	112.6	102.1	101.7	23.23	28.89	18.48
1964	59.66	27.64	21.11	3.64	2.47	4.80	109.6	106.3	118.9	106.1	102.9	113.4	28.63	31.03	19.37
1965	70.88	31.96	24.10	7.01	2.61	5.20	123.3	112.3	124.0	162.7	105.7	96.8	32.69	38.19	23.92
1966	80.34	37.53	27.17	7.56	2.60	5.48	106.9	105.6	116.5	135.8	99.6	105.9	37.41	42.93	26.87
1967	73.53	35.03	22.96	7.79	2.11	5.64	94.0	97.8	85.5	103.0	82.2	104.4	34.13	39.40	24.92
1968	78.15	36.51	26.11	7.74	2.43	5.36	107.9	105.4	113.6	99.4	159.7	94.8	37.38	40.77	25.72
1969	94.12	37.78	33.98	10.17	2.73	9.46	117.7	103.1	129.5	131.4	82.8	178.5	47.94	46.18	26.30
1970	108.65	44.04	41.62	12.83	2.90	7.26	115.3	106.5	131.8	126.2	106.7	119.1	56.56	52.09	29.73
1971	120.46	42.72	50.31	14.36	3.15	9.92	113.3	99.5	121.4	119.8	108.5	89.6	64.94	55.52	28.85
1972	123.15	45.73	50.74	13.73	3.34	9.61	99.4	101.6	101.2	94.4	106.0	96.9	63.33	59.82	31.67
1973	123.33	43.46	56.14	11.95	3.33	8.45	99.3	105.9	108.9	85.2	99.7	87.9	63.37	59.96	30.82
1974	118.06	45.16	47.45	11.96	3.14	10.35	95.3	103.7	84.5	97.8	94.3	122.5	60.03	58.03	32.08
1975	126.93	45.32	54.66	12.53	3.51	10.91	110.3	104.2	115.2	102.8	111.8	116.1	65.83	61.10	33.07
1976	121.30	44.14	48.12	13.07	3.10	12.87	95.5	97.2	88.6	102.8	89.3	125.2	63.77	57.53	31.77
1977	143.97	46.71	63.97	16.79	4.07	12.43	115.1	105.3	133.0	126.6	130.1	84.9	77.10	66.87	33.89
1978	161.43	49.29	73.57	22.32	5.63	10.62	114.2	102.8	115.2	130.8	138.3	82.2	84.83	76.60	34.36
1979	190.66	66.52	83.31	23.10	6.27	11.45	113.0	114.8	110.9	106.4	111.5	125.9	97.65	93.01	46.97
1980	206.93	68.15	94.01	25.18	7.08	12.51	104.9	96.9	111.0	108.8	112.9	108.3	107.98	98.95	47.93
1981	217.27	74.26	100.02	22.51	7.64	12.84	103.0	103.9	106.1	87.3	107.1	102.1	110.08	107.19	56.08
1982	234.23	83.15	106.91	23.07	8.39	12.71	107.0	110.2	106.2	102.6	107.4	109.5	117.41	116.82	63.59
1983	254.08	86.08	116.97	27.58	9.51	13.94	107.3	101.5	109.7	116.1	109.5	99.4	129.11	124.97	64.16
1984	291.10	98.35	136.52	30.28	10.98	14.97	112.6	110.8	115.0	108.6	116.9	106.3	144.46	141.64	70.57
1985	363.03	114.50	181.10	36.62	12.41	18.40	118.3	107.2	127.7	115.2	106.0	116.0	190.03	173.00	82.32
1986	415.07	124.79	213.75	41.37	14.13	21.03	110.3	102.6	115.0	109.6	110.5	111.1	225.73	189.34	89.45
1987	490.51	144.35	258.95	46.27	16.14	24.80	111.3	108.8	114.5	102.2	108.3	111.8	271.57	218.94	103.38
1988	634.56	174.18	345.33	59.44	20.23	35.38	114.6	102.7	120.1	109.6	115.1	127.2	363.81	270.75	118.99
1989	735.22	197.93	406.16	60.81	24.79	45.53	107.6	105.4	109.7	96.8	106.4	112.5	426.57	308.65	133.21

14. Jiangxi

14–2

Year	v1d2	v1d3	v1d4	v1d5	v1e	v1e1	v1e2	v1e3	v1e4	v1e5	v1f	v1f1	v1f2	v1f3	v1g
1949	0.85		0.24	1.03											8.30
1950	1.62	0.04	0.35	1.50											12.84
1951	1.98	0.09	0.34	1.76											13.83
1952	2.30	0.16	0.40	1.98	123.8	124.5	129.2	177.6	117.6	112.0					16.32
1953	2.59	0.29	0.63	2.19	102.6	98.9	117.3	187.5	162.5	105.6					16.59
1954	2.76	0.42	0.83	2.37	102.7	99.1	111.7	146.7	130.8	110.5					16.75
1955	2.92	0.42	0.75	2.52	105.7	105.6	110.9	95.4	88.2	110.4					17.34
1956	3.46	0.66	0.84	2.90	100.4	94.1	124.6	147.6	117.3	112.7					20.70
1957	4.47	0.64	1.12	3.27	123.6	123.4	136.5	117.8	129.6	111.2					23.51
1958	5.04	1.67	2.00	3.50	109.6	102.5	105.5	269.4	176.3	110.7					30.31
1959	5.86	2.01	2.76	4.23	103.0	93.7	120.3	113.8	136.3	119.3					38.32
1960	6.61	2.82	3.29	4.50	103.7	100.0	111.0	144.7	120.1	106.4					44.02
1961	6.29	1.38	1.67	3.26	186.5	95.5	93.3	52.4	51.4	63.2					28.80
1962	5.42	1.07	1.31	2.52	192.9	99.2	82.4	72.2	75.8	89.0					28.61
1963	5.78	1.19	1.30	2.14	103.5	105.4	103.1	116.4	101.6	74.9					28.92
1964	6.55	1.31	1.34	2.46	107.3	104.9	115.3	109.1	103.1	114.1					30.95
1965	7.72	2.47	1.46	2.62	116.0	108.5	137.4	194.7	109.0	99.6					37.65
1966	8.56	2.66	1.39	3.45	106.4	104.0	107.9	103.5	95.2	144.8					40.08
1967	7.23	2.67	1.13	3.45	95.1	97.1	85.0	100.4	82.7	103.9					40.74
1968	8.10	2.55	1.30	3.10	104.1	104.5	112.0	95.5	113.0	100.1					41.22
1969	10.19	3.81	1.38	4.50	113.7	102.0	125.3	149.4	106.2	155.6					45.89
1970	12.08	5.05	1.48	3.75	108.1	104.8	123.9	129.4	108.7	77.9					54.03
1971	14.34	4.68	1.70	5.95	108.3	99.6	119.3	100.7	113.3	157.8					59.89
1972	15.22	5.37	1.79	5.77	105.2	104.3	106.4	117.0	105.3	97.0					59.58
1973	16.85	5.43	1.76	5.10	99.3	96.9	108.5	98.1	98.3	88.2					59.70
1974	14.47	3.92	1.66	5.90	103.8	104.0	85.2	73.2	94.3	113.8					61.90
1975	15.58	4.25	1.86	6.34	109.9	108.0	107.0	108.3	112.1	126.9					62.48
1976	13.47	4.56	1.75	5.98	92.5	93.3	86.3	108.2	94.1	92.0					62.76
1977	18.23	6.24	2.26	6.25	112.7	106.1	137.1	136.4	129.1	74.1					70.39
1978	22.77	9.80	2.78	6.89	118.9	104.6	125.4	156.8	123.0	136.3	87.00	36.18	33.08	17.74	86.14
1979	25.57	10.41	3.33	6.73	112.7	112.7	115.8	105.6	119.8	126.5	104.15	48.70	36.41	19.04	97.98
1980	30.33	8.80	4.01	7.88	101.4	98.5	116.9	86.4	120.4	86.7	111.15	48.31	41.00	21.84	100.83
1981	31.14	7.56	4.32	8.09	104.9	111.2	103.5	85.9	107.7	102.8	121.26	56.09	41.10	24.07	106.01
1982	32.67	7.75	4.81	8.00	107.7	111.3	104.4	102.2	107.9	100.5	133.96	63.91	42.64	27.41	124.86
1983	36.39	9.63	5.73	9.06	106.1	98.0	105.0	117.3	112.2	108.0	144.13	63.98	49.20	30.95	134.97
1984	44.10	10.74	6.46	9.77	111.5	108.6	126.5	117.2	121.0	113.5	169.11	71.89	61.31	35.91	152.94
1985	58.34	12.53	7.32	12.49	114.5	106.8	129.3	107.2	103.0	116.7	207.26	84.06	76.05	47.15	190.55
1986	66.62	12.39	7.82	13.06	106.2	102.3	110.1	109.5	106.7	111.4	227.23	90.27	83.60	53.36	206.46
1987	77.62	13.53	9.13	15.28	109.6	108.3	111.8	101.8	112.2	112.0	361.83	104.63	92.44	64.76	224.88
1988	101.15	17.03	11.37	22.21	110.8	102.7	118.1	105.7	119.1	120.8	321.36	119.18	117.38	84.80	278.22
1989	115.14	17.78	14.14	28.38	106.8	105.3	108.8	98.8	108.0	110.0	366.87	133.19	131.23	102.45	323.92

14. Jiangxi

14–3

Year	v1h	v1i	v1j	v1j1	v1j2	v1j3	v1k	v2a	v2a1	v2a2	v2b	v2c	v2c1	v2c2	v2d1
1949				338				0.36							
1950				354				1.88							
1951				368				1.73							
1952	74.05			366				3.41	2.03	1.38					
1953				408				3.18	1.71	1.47					
1954	80.60			439				2.35	1.21	1.14					
1955	80.33			455				1.90	1.23	0.67					
1956	83.79			508				4.05	3.10	0.95					
1957	86.10			546				5.06	3.59	1.47					
1958				478				13.36	8.18	5.18					
1959				457				18.94	10.73	8.21					
1960				448				23.96	15.53	8.43					
1961				456				5.00	4.16	0.84					
1962				494				4.13	3.14	0.99					
1963				525				4.02	2.85	1.17					
1964				541				4.26	3.86	0.40					
1965	140.20			544				7.62	5.78	1.84					
1966				540				8.98	5.32	3.66					
1967				538				7.54	5.72	1.82					
1968				534				7.65	5.81	1.84					
1969				528				10.98	6.23	4.75					
1970				510				17.65	13.20	4.45					
1971				494				18.56	13.98	4.58					
1972				518				14.65	12.19	2.46					
1973				532				13.57	11.41	2.16					
1974				546				12.14	10.63	1.51					
1975		11.42	495	541	467			12.27	8.56	3.71					
1976		11.75	517	533	445			11.88	9.84	2.04					
1977		12.07	517	533	454			17.24	9.57	7.67					
1978	140.70	14.51	552	562	487		1.76	23.82	18.81	5.01			5.50	0.22	69.59
1979	156.50	16.11	603	624	512		2.17	27.14	19.68	7.46			5.04	0.33	74.31
1980	181.24	19.97	713	733	625		2.72	25.19	20.13	5.06	12.47	12.14	5.55	0.44	80.53
1981	226.87	21.10	719	745	613		3.43	21.77	16.47	5.30	10.99	10.42	3.06	0.33	85.69
1982	269.71	22.36	732	758	625		3.89	27.72	21.12	6.60	24.50	15.12	6.03	0.47	91.23
1983	301.76	23.00	747	774	640		4.43	30.78	26.49	4.29	28.09	18.08	8.62	0.48	101.22
1984	334.11	28.43	894	949	716		5.27	36.88	28.64	8.24	35.21	22.46	10.36	0.51	113.45
1985	377.31	31.95	966	1021	785		6.34	50.91	34.18	16.73	44.03	25.58	10.81	0.84	131.62
1986	395.63	38.39	1116	1184	888		7.64	54.60	44.05	10.55	53.35	30.32	10.39	0.78	151.87
1987	429.29	42.06	1184	1255	943		9.76	57.15	40.03	17.12	58.77	32.32	10.97	0.92	171.41
1988	488.16	53.31	1446	1539	1121		12.39	80.15	34.32	45.83	78.18	40.08	12.34	1.31	189.94
1989	558.64	58.35	1562	1658	1205	1809	13.37	96.76	44.96	51.84	73.28	39.81	14.75	0.93	210.99

14. Jiangxi

14–4

Year	v2d2	v2e	v3a	v3b	v3b1	v3b2	v3c	v3d	v3d1	v3d2	v3e	v3e1	v3e2	v3e3	v3e4
1949			7.94	7.83	6.14	1.69	0.11	60	54	99					
1950			10.96	10.78	8.42	2.36	0.18	75	70	103					
1951			12.10	11.90	9.26	2.64	0.20	74	69	96					
1952			12.91	12.67	9.78	2.89	0.24	77	70	117					
1953			13.41	13.10	10.06	3.04	0.31	79	70	131					
1954			14.40	13.95	10.54	3.41	0.45	82	72	137					
1955			15.44	14.84	10.69	4.15	0.60	85	74	150					
1956			16.65	15.83	11.93	3.90	0.82	89	78	156					
1957			18.45	17.68	13.46	4.22	0.77	99	86	163	153.72	92.52	14.04	5.40	9.48
1958			16.95	15.95	11.88	4.07	1.00	85	75	137					
1959			19.38	18.25	12.66	5.59	1.13	94	79	165					
1960			20.06	18.70	12.28	6.42	1.36	94	76	170					
1961			23.80	22.75	15.59	7.16	1.05	113	95	189					
1962			24.48	23.52	16.34	7.18	0.96	116	96	216					
1963			24.90	23.84	16.94	6.90	1.06	115	97	215					
1964			26.69	25.48	18.42	7.06	1.21	120	103	213					
1965			30.03	27.01	19.30	7.71	3.02	124	105	203	191.40	118.56	21.00	4.92	7.80
1966			31.10	27.65	19.30	8.35	3.45	123	102	203					
1967			33.20	29.40	20.68	8.72	3.80	127	105	210					
1968			33.57	29.62	21.18	8.44	3.95	124	104	208					
1969			34.91	30.65	21.91	8.74	4.26	125	103	223					
1970			36.38	31.78	22.38	9.40	4.60	125	102	228					
1971			41.33	36.68	23.61	13.07	4.65	140	105	238					
1972			44.93	40.23	29.61	10.62	4.70	150	127	249					
1973			46.13	41.33	29.76	11.57	4.80	149	126	255					
1974			49.76	44.86	32.61	12.25	4.90	157	134	261					
1975			50.21	45.13	32.83	12.30	5.08	154	131	260					
1976			50.88	45.73	33.23	12.50	5.15	152	129	253					
1977			53.15	47.90	36.70	11.20	5.25	156	139	256					
1978	49.56	23.39	62.32	56.88	42.22	14.66	5.44	181	161	281					
1979	51.76	25.47	70.84	65.01	47.69	17.32	5.83	203	179	323					
1980	55.22	25.62	75.64	68.45	49.22	19.23	7.19	211	183	340	381.96	227.52	57.24	4.80	9.24
1981	55.96	26.46	84.24	75.74	52.18	23.56	8.50	230	194	394					
1982	60.07	28.07	97.14	88.54	63.62	24.92	8.60	266	235	403					
1983	67.08	29.28	104.19	95.00	69.28	25.72	9.19	282	253	410					
1984	75.72	30.50	116.06	105.81	77.13	28.68	10.25	311	279	448					
1985	89.35	40.66	139.64	125.92	90.49	35.43	13.72	366	326	532	529.56	296.76	70.56	6.12	9.48
1986	104.58	49.20	151.86	135.40	94.96	40.44	16.46	389	341	576	644.76	358.80	89.64	7.08	9.72
1987	118.65	55.94	167.73	150.05	103.05	47.00	17.68	425	364	666	714.96	411.72	89.64	7.56	10.08
1988	130.77	65.63	198.07	179.56	119.15	60.41	18.51	499	415	836	900.00	509.52	111.24	8.04	14.16
1989	144.40	81.48	227.16	207.03	136.71	70.32	20.13	565	468	945	977.88	570.48	101.40	8.64	17.64

14. Jiangxi

14–5

Year	v3f	v3f1	v3f2	v3f3	v3f4	v4a1	v4a1a	v4a1b	v4a1c	v4a1d	v4a2	v4a2a	v4a2b	v4a2c	v4a2d
1949															
1950						1.17	0.0002	0.3558	0.6560	0.1549	0.49	0.06	0.05	0.17	0.21
1951						1.42	0.0175	0.7149	0.6166	0.0733	0.66	0.21	0.08	0.20	0.17
1952						2.29	0.0357	0.9222	0.8309	0.4973	1.52	0.42	0.35	0.39	0.36
1953						2.59	0.0551	1.2903	1.0113	0.2300	1.45	0.41	0.45	0.41	0.18
1954						2.74	0.0815	1.3962	0.9692	0.2919	1.60	0.52	0.45	0.45	0.18
1955						2.85	0.2107	1.4413	0.9789	0.2206	1.63	0.44	0.43	0.45	0.31
1956						3.18	0.2936	1.6569	0.9912	0.2346	2.27	0.72	0.55	0.60	0.40
1957						3.39	0.3898	1.8359	0.9387	0.2210	2.30	0.65	0.64	0.55	0.46
1958						5.67	1.9732	2.3663	0.9387	0.3886	5.67	3.27	0.69	0.49	1.22
1959						6.84	2.8321	2.6889	0.9387	0.3774	9.50	5.72	0.76	0.70	2.32
1960						6.64	2.0676	2.9742	0.9387	0.6552	11.48	6.68	1.27	0.79	2.74
1961						4.65	1.2712	2.1867	0.7888	0.4043	5.93	1.56	1.08	0.74	2.55
1962						5.22	1.5703	2.5961	0.7240	0.3277	4.27	0.87	0.94	0.58	1.88
1963						5.49	1.5937	2.6946	0.8435	0.3614	4.59	1.10	0.91	0.61	1.97
1964						5.98	1.7958	2.9851	0.8735	0.3227	4.94	1.60	1.03	0.66	1.65
1965						6.67	2.1681	3.2443	0.8851	0.3720	5.27	2.01	1.08	0.66	1.52
1966						7.40	2.8377	3.1513	1.0137	0.3948	6.29	2.37	1.20	0.68	2.04
1967						4.98	1.3106	2.7078	0.9071	0.0530	5.81	2.27	1.44	0.63	1.47
1968						5.58	1.4684	2.9532	1.0914	0.0412	4.83	1.89	1.13	0.65	1.16
1969						7.34	2.9258	3.3095	1.0364	0.0693	7.10	3.71	0.84	0.51	2.04
1970						8.90	3.7109	4.1071	1.0295	0.0491	10.71	6.58	0.96	0.65	2.52
1971						10.25	4.5498	4.6147	1.0300	0.0291	9.47	4.52	1.24	0.80	2.91
1972						10.02	4.1814	4.7873	1.0033	0.0236	10.11	4.41	1.56	0.87	3.27
1973						10.36	3.8255	5.5320	0.9665	0.0244	10.18	3.78	1.83	0.98	3.59
1974						6.57	0.4416	5.0804	1.0232	0.0145	10.81	3.81	2.10	1.00	3.90
1975						7.86	1.2412	5.5578	1.0133	0.0208	10.24	3.21	2.16	1.04	3.83
1976						5.19	-0.9026	5.0171	1.0147	0.0334	10.59	3.23	2.29	1.09	3.98
1977						7.62	0.4728	6.0855	1.0186	0.0350	12.01	3.71	2.45	1.15	4.70
1978						12.22	3.3166	7.2594	1.0164	0.6273	16.27	5.61	2.93	1.28	6.45
1979						11.78	1.9927	8.0164	1.0151	0.7487	17.63	5.16	3.41	1.34	7.72
1980	156.01	97.28	15.59	12.51	12.96	12.47	2.3784	8.6948	1.0080	0.3820	15.99	4.05	4.07	1.71	6.16
1981	194.17	117.99				13.18	2.1516	9.5341	1.0247	0.4344	14.03	1.90	4.35	1.96	5.82
1982	219.87	140.54				12.33	0.8976	9.9816	0.9694	0.4448	15.54	1.87	5.08	2.08	6.51
1983	252.26	157.78				13.53	1.3897	10.3923	1.1213	0.5932	17.47	2.62	5.62	2.34	6.89
1984	269.70	169.47				15.01	1.5142	11.6006	1.2568	0.6083	21.94	3.35	6.46	2.93	9.20
1985	303.14	185.14	26.77	29.86	22.73	19.54	1.6325	16.0013	1.4415	0.4599	28.08	4.21	7.82	3.18	12.87
1986	340.58	199.62				24.06	2.5735	19.3115	1.4456	0.6492	36.63	3.93	9.20	3.73	19.77
1987	386.00	223.87	28.47	52.42	22.76	28.21	3.3042	21.7828	1.6679	1.3967	37.79	3.35	9.43	3.78	21.23
1988	477.13	272.16	34.23	67.63	28.23	32.29	1.5235	26.0550	1.6191	2.8054	42.35	3.43	11.45	3.88	23.59
1989	520.27	295.39	37.67	66.84	29.06	37.49	0.1300				48.71	3.53	12.74	4.55	27.89

14. Jiangxi

14–6

Year	v4b	v4b1	v4b2	v4b3	v4c1	v4c2	v5a	v5a1	v5a2	v5a3	v5a4	v5b1	v5b2	v5b3	v5c
1949							623.3	13.1	26.3		583.9	560.0	27.3	36.0	26.9
1950							656.1	18.9	28.0		609.2	583.1	32.8	40.2	
1951							672.2	23.6	29.2		619.4	591.3	34.6	46.3	
1952							682.2	30.5	26.0		625.7	600.4	36.9	44.9	35.4
1953							682.9	36.5	25.0		621.4	596.8	42.2	43.9	
1954							699.5	40.5	22.9		636.1	612.0	47.3	40.2	
1955							754.2	41.9	21.1		691.2	672.1	42.1	40.0	
1956							770.9	57.9	19.6		693.4	684.8	40.6	45.5	
1957							789.8	58.5	16.9		714.4	706.7	40.3	42.8	
1958							879.2	115.9	20.2		743.1	716.1	112.8	50.3	
1959	1.27	0.80	0.47				902.3	127.4	17.8		757.1	740.8	108.0	53.5	
1960	1.29	0.94	0.35				917.2	154.0	28.0		735.2	729.6	124.8	62.8	
1961	1.08	0.60	0.48				912.0	132.1	48.1		731.8	754.2	91.4	66.4	
1962	0.72	0.41	0.31				895.3	106.1	42.0		747.2	765.8	63.5	66.0	
1963	0.72	0.49	0.23				904.7	104.7	43.5		756.5	775.0	61.4	68.3	
1964	0.89	0.67	0.22				905.0	107.0	40.3		757.7	774.6	58.9	71.5	
1965	0.99	0.78	0.21				923.7	110.8	42.9		770.0	784.9	65.6	73.2	
1966	1.19	0.94	0.25				925.0	116.9	43.2		764.9	780.5	69.2	75.3	
1967	1.13	0.94	0.19				940.2	119.5	42.7		778.0	792.7	70.2	77.3	
1968	1.04	0.85	0.19				991.6	125.3	27.5		838.8	849.7	65.3	76.6	
1969	0.98	0.81	0.17				1029.5	131.2	25.0		873.3	878.1	76.5	74.9	
1970	1.08	0.92	0.16				1057.3	151.8	31.7		873.8	859.4	114.8	83.1	
1971	1.34	1.14	0.20				1083.6	166.3	35.6		881.7	866.7	126.6	90.3	
1972	1.63	1.41	0.22				1100.6	171.3	36.6	2.0	890.7	876.9	128.6	95.1	
1973	1.97	1.67	0.30				1132.1	172.4	37.4	2.0	920.3	910.0	126.9	95.2	
1974	2.36	1.97	0.39				1170.6	175.5	41.9	2.0	951.2	940.6	130.3	99.7	
1975	2.62	2.19	0.43				1191.8	179.7	43.2	0.5	968.4	954.9	134.0	102.9	
1976	2.86	2.42	0.44				1211.1	186.8	46.0	0.5	977.8	961.0	139.0	111.1	
1977	3.54	2.86	0.68				1238.0	218.5	44.7	0.6	974.2	959.1	156.0	122.9	
1978	4.16	3.38	0.78		7.47	10.24	1254.3	221.0	46.4	0.7	986.2	968.7	163.4	122.2	139.8
1979	5.75	4.49	1.26		9.51	12.31	1307.0	219.6	50.0	0.8	1036.6	1015.3	163.9	127.8	
1980	8.75	6.56	2.19		10.38	12.84	1356.3	233.0	53.7	1.1	1068.5	1053.8	166.9	135.6	144.2
1981	11.46	8.17	3.29		11.34	13.76	1409.8	242.2	59.7	2.3	1105.6	1093.4	172.7	143.7	
1982	15.00	10.27	4.73		11.25	12.76	1434.0	249.3	62.6	4.3	1117.8	1100.9	180.4	152.7	
1983	19.43	13.13	6.30		12.94	13.43	1498.2	245.6	65.5	8.9	1178.2	1113.6	195.3	169.3	
1984	25.81	17.71	8.10		14.88	14.01	1537.3	247.0	77.9	10.5	1199.5	1117.8	216.3	203.2	
1985	34.85	24.38	10.47		21.15	16.27	1587.2	261.4	80.1	11.8	1231.4	1057.2	326.7	203.3	267.4
1986	48.08	34.34	13.74		21.78	14.16	1622.6	269.4	82.3	12.7	1258.0	1068.1	334.3	220.2	
1987	64.68	47.16	17.52		26.11	14.95	1668.4	281.4	83.7	13.6	1289.5	1098.3	342.9	227.2	281.8
1988	81.14	61.45	19.69		32.49	16.54	1723.0	293.8	85.0	18.8	1325.0	1111.6	371.7	239.7	308.7
1989	106.40	82.30	24.10		30.67	13.58	1760.1	298.3	81.3	23.3	1357.0	1146.4	370.6	243.4	

14. Jiangxi

14–7

Year	v5c1	v5d	v6a	v6a1	v6a2	v6b	v6c	v6d1	v6d2	v6d3	v6d4	v6d5	v6d6
1949		560.0	1314	125	1189			164	1150	667	647		25.52
1950			1568	160	1408			285	1283	802	766		
1951			1644	169	1475			268	1376	842	802		
1952		600.4	1656	172	1484			235	1421	851	805		33.09
1953			1695	174	1521			242	1453	867	828		
1954			1730	197	1533	32.49	14.15	256	1474	886	844		
1955			1763	206	1557	32.33	16.23	249	1514	903	860		
1956			1800	214	1586	29.01	12.49	255	1545	927	873		
1957			1851	225	1626	38.34	11.48	265	1586	952	899		50.79
1958			1913	242	1671	30.28	11.34	331	1582	989	924		57.71
1959			1976	280	1696	28.64	13.01	353	1623	1028	948		
1960			2010	460	1550	26.87	16.06	401	1609	1047	963		
1961			2023	442	1581	21.00	11.54	349	1674	1045	978	78.05	68.16
1962			2040	416	1624	37.19	11.00	310	1730	1049	991	78.37	64.78
1963			2101	347	1754	39.56	9.76	338	1763	1081	1020	80.51	67.57
1964			2144	359	1785	38.05	10.87	331	1813	1105	1039	81.77	69.41
1965			2210	373	1837	38.85	9.39	347	1863	1137	1073	84.26	73.33
1966			2284	381	1903	38.18	8.54	364	1920	1176	1108		
1967			2354	393	1961	35.14	8.02	374	1980	1216	1138		
1968			2418	372	2046	36.64	7.57	324	2094	1241	1177		
1969			2505	392	2113	33.44	7.44	345	2160	1289	1216		
1970			2585	411	2174	32.20	8.16	357	2228	1333	1252	95.52	61.18
1971			2652	474	2178	31.00	8.53	383	2269	1368	1284		
1972			2723	452	2271	31.82	7.61	397	2326	1403	1320		
1973			2810	471	2339	35.96	7.47	413	2397	1448	1362		
1974			2888	480	2408	33.65	7.86	418	2470	1489	1399		
1975			2969	492	2477	33.98	8.01	426	2543	1533	1436	108.25	77.05
1976			3048	502	2546	31.85	7.78	438	2610	1574	1474		
1977			3118	520	2598	29.61	8.02	447	2671	1610	1508		
1978		968.7	3183	533	2650	27.01	7.39	460	2723	1643	1540	115.94	84.15
1979			3229	563	2666	20.97	7.23	481	2848	1666	1563		
1980		1053.8	3270	614	2656	18.57	6.38	508	2762	1687	1583	120.27	100.87
1981			3304	630	2674	20.42	6.54	541	2763	1703	1601		
1982			3348	643	2705	19.18	6.07	553	2795	1726	1622		
1983			3384	709	2675	18.09	6.80	563	2821	1747	1637		
1984			3421	761	2660	19.02	6.50	587	2834	1768	1653		
1985	109.5	1057.2	3460	965	2495	16.71	5.81	625	2835	1790	1670	128.67	111.56
1986	112.7		3509	1029	2480	17.20	5.33	636	2873	1816	1693	130.48	119.24
1987	116.7	1098.6	3559	1167	2392	20.38	6.54	658	2901	1842	1717	132.82	125.97
1988	121.4	1111.9	3633	1308	2325	19.79	5.80	674	2959	1879	1754	135.49	128.77
1989			3695	1431	2264	23.04	6.26	693	3002	1912	1783	132.62	137.69

14. Jiangxi

14–8

Year	v7a	v7b	v7c	v7d	v7e	v7f	v7g	v7h	v7h1	v7h2	v7h3	v7h4	v7h5	v7i	v8a
1949								9.88	6.35	0.04	1.32	0.05	2.12	118.9	2.64
1950								11.61						122.0	4.91
1951								11.96						139.1	6.00
1952	0.02	1.3	1479.3	6614.2		0.09		15.35	9.81	0.71	1.61	0.10	3.12	148.1	6.97
1953	0.02	1.8	1597.7	6815.7		0.15		15.14						156.6	7.86
1954	0.02	2.6	1671.8	6985.5		0.24		15.15						158.9	8.36
1955	0.03	2.7	1746.4	7299.5		0.45		16.17						157.5	8.85
1956	0.08	13.3	1859.9	7968.6		0.65		17.24						156.7	10.62
1957	0.27	24.0	1992.9	8191.8		0.72	0.008	19.06	11.76	0.92	2.70	0.22	3.46	163.5	11.70
1958	0.54	51.7	2130.6	8705.4		1.32		18.98						161.5	18.96
1959	0.82	107.0	2295.6	8619.4		1.61		18.52						158.5	24.84
1960	1.23	122.1	2491.8	8928.0		1.59	0.188	17.80						143.4	28.79
1961	1.54	69.3	2641.3	8364.5		0.88		22.45						136.8	19.06
1962	2.08	64.9	2732.8	8000.0		1.92	0.282	23.70	15.46	0.84	3.27	0.43	3.70	137.9	16.95
1963	2.58	66.0	2875.2	7951.7		3.44		24.05						143.0	18.07
1964	3.00	110.0	2925.0	8297.3		5.86		27.64						142.4	21.11
1965	3.68	128.0	3000.0	8546.6		10.35	0.362	31.96	22.59	1.19	4.63	0.40	3.15	148.5	24.10
1966	4.36	120.0	2955.0	8737.7		13.63		37.53						150.0	27.17
1967	4.51	148.0	2333.0	8521.8		9.09	0.425	35.03						152.4	22.96
1968	5.03	270.8	2452.3	8384.3		10.38		36.51						157.0	26.11
1969	5.44	282.7	2368.4	8913.2		14.73	0.662	37.78						160.0	33.98
1970	6.32	321.2	2239.6	8614.0		17.33	1.008	44.04						161.8	41.62
1971	7.18	385.4	2315.1	8861.5		16.82	1.934	42.72						159.0	50.31
1972	7.80	385.7	2336.5	8679.8		16.70	1.932	45.73						162.0	50.74
1973	11.67	410.0	2611.1	8717.3		18.63	2.275	43.46						162.4	56.14
1974	13.27	509.8	2707.5	8704.8		14.13	2.295	45.16						164.7	47.45
1975	14.95	535.0	2776.3	8638.4		12.42	2.847	45.32	32.98	1.78	6.12	0.38	4.06	165.0	54.66
1976	17.89	601.1	2826.2	8535.4		13.04	2.918	44.14						161.4	48.12
1977	20.92	732.2	2446.5	8682.5		14.21	2.979	46.71						159.1	63.97
1978	26.19	912.7	2461.6	8551.6		22.95	3.597	49.29	34.96	2.56	6.26	0.64	4.87	159.9	73.57
1979	30.61	1008.4	2484.0	8549.3		31.30	3.971	66.52	45.83	3.95	9.00	0.70	7.04	160.8	83.31
1980	32.88	1028.1	2504.4	8330.6		37.69	5.222	68.15	45.53	5.12	9.46	0.79	7.25	158.1	94.01
1981	34.39	898.6	2507.0	8314.2		36.69	5.373	74.26	49.11	5.65	10.41	1.14	7.95	167.2	100.02
1982	36.06	720.3	2383.0	8367.4		47.90	6.900	83.15	55.52	5.64	12.72	1.34	7.93	175.4	106.91
1983	38.46	550.0	2708.0	8198.0		46.93	8.500	86.08	56.02	6.41	13.49	1.68	8.48	183.0	116.97
1984	44.91	788.2	2717.7	8185.1		47.40	8.724	98.35	62.14	7.69	16.99	2.29	9.24	190.2	136.52
1985	49.79	690.3	2718.6	8128.7		53.87	8.747	114.50	67.70	9.18	22.78	3.51	11.33	198.1	181.10
1986	55.96	723.1	2721.2	8158.1		62.34	9.585	124.79	69.70	9.66	29.10	4.27	12.06	210.8	213.75
1987	60.98	705.7	2732.1			66.40	11.700	144.35	79.76	10.87	34.33	5.23	14.16	221.6	258.95
1988	65.18	853.8	2725.8	8095.0		73.82	13.400	174.18	82.80	12.99	51.80	7.22	19.37	230.6	345.33
1989	66.55	885.3	2739.0	8333.0		76.08	15.390	197.93	96.53	12.79	59.59	8.11	20.91	241.4	406.16

14. Jiangxi

14–9

Year	v8a1	v8a2	v8a3	v8b	v8c1	v8c2	v8d	v8f1	v8f2	v8f3	v8f4	v8f5	v8g
1949	0.95	1.54	0.05		0.56	2.08			32.00		0.04		
1950	2.04		2.86		1.35	3.56			46.63		0.09		
1951	3.09		2.95		1.84	4.16			95.34		0.23		
1952	3.60	0.42	0.94		2.33	4.64			104.77		0.35		4225
1953	4.15	1.24	2.47		2.77	5.09			115.22		0.51		
1954	5.27	0.33	2.76		3.06	5.30			119.78		0.73		
1955	5.67	0.59	2.59		3.27	5.58			154.03		1.15		
1956	6.06	2.24	2.51		4.04	6.58			198.58		1.65		
1957	6.51	2.36	2.84		4.49	7.21			264.87		1.99		5853
1958	13.86	4.83			8.98	9.98		0.05	682.00		3.09		10753
1959	19.29	5.54	1.12		12.84	12.00		0.35	653.00		5.01	1.43	11733
1960	22.35	6.43			15.07	13.72		4.04	733.55		7.45	4.55	12425
1961	14.63	4.43			9.25	9.81		1.45	581.31		7.24	3.04	12367
1962	12.91	3.95	0.09		7.55	9.40		0.49	418.33		7.34	2.31	10873
1963	14.14	3.95	0.02		8.74	9.33		0.59	415.10		7.12	8.92	9774
1964	17.10	3.93	0.07		7.89	13.22		1.10	388.60		9.06	15.94	8811
1965	18.78	4.17	1.05		9.73	14.37		1.40	424.91		9.79	23.23	9161
1966	22.77	4.40			12.06	15.11		4.67	446.05		12.40	29.35	
1967	19.10	3.86			9.89	13.07		3.23	327.82		11.73	17.68	
1968	22.15	3.96			11.78	14.33		5.46	506.78		14.81	27.39	
1969	22.88	4.90			18.54	15.44		9.46	666.82		18.64	36.08	
1970	35.36	6.26			22.54	19.08		16.25	897.52		24.76	47.78	6384
1971	43.01	7.29			28.44	21.87		20.12	1024.84		27.06	60.34	6543
1972	42.29	8.26			27.33	23.41		20.81	1039.63		29.83	66.09	7384
1973	46.35	9.79			30.22	25.92		21.40	1027.98		33.79	69.26	8156
1974	37.64	9.81			24.78	22.67		8.57	869.60		27.43	67.30	8647
1975	43.19	11.47			29.11	25.55		14.74	1037.72		34.88	88.41	8879
1976	36.56	11.56			25.01	23.11		6.33	1098.63		32.38	79.24	9215
1977	49.89	14.08			34.85	29.12		19.02	1362.07		39.72	120.48	10126
1978	57.56	16.01		53.76	40.66	32.91	15.91	25.64	1435.50		45.31	155.56	11292
1979	65.72	16.67	0.92	62.19	48.08	37.23	18.49	27.65	1567.61		51.11	189.70	12103
1980	73.20	18.89	1.91	68.20	48.16	45.85	21.04	38.76	1490.31		57.21	201.00	12857
1981	76.69	22.13	1.19	70.98	47.46	52.56	21.41	42.71	1553.13		59.86	227.05	13178
1982	81.49	21.52	3.06	74.95	52.66	54.25	22.26	43.08	1634.62		62.75	248.20	13549
1983	89.15	23.32	4.49	82.97	61.35	55.62	24.65	48.69	1707.62		64.39	280.97	13849
1984	101.36	29.85	5.30	95.22	74.54	61.98	28.76	59.84	1875.37		71.83	303.96	15548
1985	130.11	32.56	1.12	127.82	103.98	77.12	38.26	77.42	1938.15		83.75	354.19	16361
1986	150.81	38.05	0.87	148.12	121.09	92.66	41.50	91.71	1863.67		94.30	400.35	17207
1987	184.09	45.14	1.78	182.35	144.46	114.49	50.24	106.02	1970.23		102.77	443.71	17092
1988	238.86	60.51	3.02	234.31	190.75	154.58	63.33	105.91	2049.19		115.66	503.00	17911
1989	273.77	72.28	3.36	268.07	227.94	178.22	69.00	105.83	2063.31		119.71	504.54	17815

14. Jiangxi

14–10

Year	v8g1	v9a	v9a1	v9a2	v9a3	v9b	v9b1	v9b2	v9b3	v9c	v10a	v10a1	v10b1	v10b2	v10b3
1949										215	3.80	3.75	0.01		
1950						10.51	9.45	0.11	0.95	278	5.57	5.42	0.34		
1951						9.78	8.40	0.14	1.24	408	6.52	6.28	0.54		
1952			0.03	0.01	0.00	11.56	9.82	0.14	1.60	515	7.33	7.03	0.61		
1953						17.84	13.23	0.36	4.25	663	8.10	7.64	0.94		
1954						23.64	18.23	0.51	4.90	777	8.79	8.23	2.11		
1955						21.24	16.17	0.60	4.47	856	9.34	8.73	2.71		
1956						24.50	19.28	0.73	4.49	988	10.63	9.75	3.33		
1957						32.31	24.57	0.74	7.00	1048	10.97	10.15	3.62		
1958						40.97	32.75	1.44	6.78	1346	12.85	11.26			
1959						58.58	46.13	2.85	9.60	1865	15.51	13.86			
1960						74.29	54.52	3.56	16.21	2423	17.28	15.32			
1961						53.61	43.90	1.84	7.87	2291	14.84	13.17			
1962						42.57	35.54	1.72	5.31	2040	16.91	15.10			
1963						46.40	36.41	2.01	7.98	1911	17.34	15.49			
1964						54.38	41.56	2.39	10.43	2443	18.30	16.07			
1965						69.66	54.39	2.89	12.38	2446	19.16	16.33			
1966						78.26	63.16	3.05	12.05	2519	21.94	18.34			
1967						51.12	42.52	2.39	6.21	2454	22.52	19.84			
1968						64.75	52.27	2.56	9.92	2410	21.08	17.75			
1969						79.19	65.72	2.92	10.55	2425	23.98	20.18			
1970						93.61	79.10	3.08	11.43	2600	26.03	21.21			
1971		29.42	18.93	8.32	2.17	108.10	89.11	3.59	15.40	2696	28.29	22.97			
1972		29.89	18.33	9.21	2.35	116.51	94.16	3.76	18.59	2682	30.47	25.34			
1973		35.59	21.88	10.89	2.82	115.56	91.29	3.76	20.51	3208	32.34	27.03			
1974		37.65	22.80	12.05	2.80	95.48	72.09	3.53	19.86	3237	32.47	27.43			
1975		37.41	22.95	11.62	2.84	108.72	83.11	3.73	21.43	3351	34.40	29.05			
1976		38.25	23.00	12.30	2.95	93.21	71.76	3.71	17.74	3631	35.10	29.43	20.15		
1977		40.95	24.27	13.64	3.04	117.72	93.68	4.65	19.39	3906	37.72	31.77	21.34		
1978	2230	46.91	26.73	16.83	3.35	136.96	108.48	5.27	23.21	4022	41.30	33.93	23.43	14.56	2.20
1979	2253	54.96	31.26	20.08	3.62	145.62	116.93	5.50	23.19	4417	47.32	38.60	25.06		
1980	2223	69.59	39.49	25.41	4.69	147.67	118.68	5.68	23.31	4775	54.86	45.48	27.07	20.52	4.47
1981	2219	79.07	44.29	29.14	5.64	148.98	116.52	6.13	26.33	5001	62.87	53.74	29.68	21.71	6.91
1982	2223	85.74	45.39	34.70	5.65	156.23	120.53	6.67	29.03	5248	68.04	57.64	31.00	22.10	8.98
1983	2237	97.70	50.40	41.08	6.22	165.84	128.44	6.75	30.65	5600	73.04	61.99	31.96	20.15	10.26
1984	2328	112.46	59.51	46.88	5.97	176.72	138.02	6.43	32.27	6008	81.69	70.33	35.61	19.17	12.55
1985	3279	130.72	69.52	54.42	6.66	195.74	156.61	6.72	32.41	7117	98.33	85.71	39.44	20.03	17.11
1986	3361	137.75	73.02	57.71	6.51	217.88	174.99	6.62	36.26	7836	111.39	96.49	43.22	22.14	18.48
1987	3404	148.49	80.60	59.85	7.38	233.64	187.43	6.56	39.64	8714	126.12	108.77	47.62	23.89	19.97
1988	3480	159.55	92.80	58.58	7.48	237.33	193.16	6.63	37.53	11011	164.19	140.03	61.71	30.97	23.85
1989	3502	150.74	85.85	57.67	6.56	239.36	198.07	6.09	35.19	12621	181.64	152.75	64.50	30.51	27.68

14. Jiangxi

14–11

Year	v10b4	v10b5	v10b6	v10d	v11a1	v11a2	v11a3	v11b	v11b1	v11b2	v11c	v11d	v12a	v12b	v12c
1949		3.49	0.30												
1950		4.78	0.44												
1951	0.01	5.31	0.51										113.8		127.2
1952	0.02	5.14	0.48										98.8		97.7
1953	0.02	4.81	0.45										103.4		105.1
1954	0.26	2.67	0.34										102.7		102.3
1955	1.08	1.95	0.30										99.7		98.5
1956	1.56	0.16	0.30										100.4		105.3
1957	1.52	0.23	0.32										101.6		107.2
1958													102.7		101.6
1959													101.3		101.2
1960													101.0		105.1
1961													107.4		126.1
1962													104.6		99.2
1963													92.1		98.7
1964													94.2		99.2
1965													96.8		99.6
1966													99.0		105.8
1967													100.0		101.3
1968															100.2
1969															100.4
1970								0.1197	0.1197						99.6
1971								0.0907	0.0907				99.9		102.2
1972								0.1147	0.1147				99.5		100.7
1973								0.1694	0.1694				99.9		100.7
1974								0.1864	0.1864				100.0		100.2
1975								0.3719	0.3719				100.0		100.3
1976		0.02	1.00					0.5778	0.5778				100.0		100.2
1977		0.05	1.00					0.4727	0.4727				100.2		100.5
1978		0.06	1.06	14.10	2.1880	1.2028	0.9191	0.5088	0.5088				100.1		101.6
1979		0.05	1.47	18.56				0.8558	0.8558				101.3	102.1	126.5
1980	0.05	0.20	2.55	22.03	2.7788	2.1719	1.5304	0.9274	0.9274				104.3	105.5	114.4
1981	0.02	0.45	4.10	24.11				1.9928	1.9386	0.0542			104.6	103.8	107.6
1982	0.02	1.39	4.56	29.49				1.6954	1.6489	0.0465			102.9	103.1	102.9
1983	0.01	4.94	5.73	33.73				2.2523	2.1631	0.0892			101.4	101.9	104.1
1984	0.04	7.59	6.73	38.31				2.4529	2.3384	0.1145	0.0952	0.0204	102.5	102.6	100.9
1985	0.21	11.58	9.96	40.56	3.8101	3.2941	1.2127	3.2385	2.7525	0.4860	0.3196	0.1021	108.3	108.8	109.0
1986	0.12	14.49	12.94	48.49				3.5323	3.0527	0.4796	0.7962	0.1611	105.8	106.0	107.8
1987	0.13	17.80	16.71	58.90	6.9993	7.3382	3.7594	4.8396	4.0218	0.8178	0.3697	0.3093	106.9	107.9	112.8
1988	0.27	25.02	22.37	72.08	8.5968	7.7787	5.9915	5.9850	4.8938	1.0912	1.2807	0.3692	121.8	123.7	128.6
1989	0.12	32.29	26.54	87.79				5.8727	5.1578	0.7149	0.8891	0.2200	118.6	117.2	115.3

14. Jiangxi

Year	v13a	v13b	v13c1	v13c2	v13c3	v13d	v14a	v14b	v14c	v15a	v15b	v15c	v15d	v15e	v15f
1949			0.25	4.00	45.32		1940	2875							
1950						0.06									
1951															
1952	15.4		0.32	7.75	139.40	0.05	4256	17380	0.44	4122					
1953	20.6		0.25	8.84	131.48	0.09			0.39	4134					
1954	19.2		0.20	9.67	131.92	0.04			0.37	4135					
1955	19.3		0.20	10.34	146.08	0.07			0.50	4141					
1956	17.0		0.38	13.98	181.87	0.05			0.79	4185					
1957	20.1		0.42	15.31	177.11	0.03			0.76	4219					
1958	9.0		1.02	19.92	232.20	0.06			1.97						
1959	5.7		1.59	22.13	248.21	0.06			2.10						
1960	7.0		2.09	32.49	275.14	0.28			1.90	3928					
1961	12.0		2.16	29.05	251.34	0.31			1.24	3898					
1962	14.9		1.70	22.24	226.38	0.50			0.89	4101					
1963	13.3		1.43	20.59	211.00	0.48			0.89	4105					
1964	13.7	85.1	1.40	23.63	302.97	0.41			1.15	4103					
1965	13.7		1.38	25.88	336.93	0.37	23947	50000	1.39	4100					
1966	12.4		1.28	31.84	287.22				1.32						
1967	17.2		1.28	34.49	284.20				1.45						
1968			1.28	36.68	290.23				1.56						
1969				47.11	288.13	0.62			1.76						
1970			0.15	67.82	321.77	0.10			1.70	3600					
1971	7.4		0.20	81.45	355.33	0.19			1.91						
1972	9.2		0.34	93.19	391.49	0.10			1.86						
1973	10.9		0.39	82.34	436.64	0.18			2.21						
1974	11.8		0.75	85.84	481.59	0.04			1.82						
1975	12.9		0.94	109.33	510.69	0.17			2.05						
1976	13.1		1.20	146.34	530.59	0.27			2.22						
1977	12.1		1.29	171.32	527.94	0.35			2.41						
1978	10.7	94.2	2.18	172.09	513.77	0.24	65237	70247	2.33						
1979	11.4		2.91	159.94	513.20	0.03			2.18						
1980	15.6	93.7	3.56	160.57	529.30	0.34	69716	79014	2.61	3591					
1981	18.7	93.4	3.79	149.69	531.75	0.72			2.79						
1982	19.3	93.4	3.57	147.60	538.76	1.15			3.11						
1983	18.4	94.7	3.64	146.66	542.39	1.01			3.30						
1984	16.8	96.2	3.88	151.78	567.00	0.99			3.98						
1985	16.3	96.9	4.49	169.85	572.83	0.98	75203	102209	4.65	3554					
1986	14.6	97.1	4.94	174.64	572.29	1.14			4.55						
1987	14.9	97.3	5.21	194.98	548.57	1.35	79304	108065	4.34						
1988	16.5	97.2	5.22	193.93	508.18	1.86	80342	111765	5.62	3538					
1989		97.8	5.34		475.50	1.54	82059		5.58	3533					

Notes

1. National Output and Income (Y)

v1a: (E), p.470
 v1a1: (E), p.470
 v1a2: (E), p.470
 v1a3: (E), p.470
 v1a4: (E), p.470
 v1a5: (E), p.470

v1b: (A); (D), p.258
 v1b1: (A); (D), p.258
 v1b2: (A); (D), p.258
 v1b3: (A); (D), p.258
 v1b4: (A); (D), p.258
 v1b5: (A); (D), p.258

v1c: v1a – v1d

v1d: (E), p.467
 v1d1: (E), p.467
 v1d2: (E), p.467
 v1d3: (E), p.467
 v1d4: (E), p.467
 v1d5: (E), p.467

v1e: (A); (D), p.261
 v1e1: (A); (D), p.261
 v1e2: (A); (D), p.261
 v1e3: (A); (D), p.261
 v1e4: (A); (D), p.261
 v1e5: (A); (D), p.261

v1f: (E), p.466
 v1f1: (E), p.466
 v1f2: (E), p.466
 v1f3: (E), p.466

v1g: (E), p.469

v1h: (A); (E), p.491

v1i: (E), p.490—figures of 1988 and 1989 include meat price and other subsidies

v1j: (E), p.490—(ditto)
 v1j1: (E), p.490
 v1j2: (E), p.490
 v1j3: (A)

v1k: (E), p.490

2. Investment (I)

v2a: (E), p.469
 v2a1: (A); (B), p.36
 v2a2: (A); (B), p.36

v2b: (A)

v2c: (E), p.483
 v2c1: (E), p.484
 v2c2: (E), p.484

v2d:
 v2d1: (E), p.479
 v2d2: (E), p.479

v2e: (E), p.479

3. Consumption (C)

v3a: (E), p.469

v3b: (E), p.469
 v3b1: (A); (B), p.35
 v3b2: (A); (B), p.35

v3c: (E), p.469

v3d: (E), p.489
 v3d1: (E), p.489
 v3d2: (E), p.489

v3e: (A)
 v3e1: (A)
 v3e2: (A)
 v3e3: (A)
 v3e4: (A)

v3f: (E), p.491
v3f1: (E), p.491
v3f2: (A)
v3f3: (A)
v3f4: (A)

4. Public Finance and Banking (FB)

v4a:
v4a1: (E), p.487
v4a1a: (E), p.487
v4a1b: (B), p.147
v4a1c: (B), p.147
v4a1d: (B), p.147
v4a2: (E), p.487
v4a2a: (E), p.487
v4a2b: (E), p.487
v4a2c: (E), p.487
v4a2d: v4a2 – v4a2a – v4a2b – v4a2c

v4b: (A)
v4b1: (B), p.151
v4b2: (B), p.151—rural savings
v4b3: NA

v4c:
v4c1: (E), p.479
v4c2: (E), p.479

5. Labor Force (L)

v5a: (E), p.465
v5a1: (E), p.465
v5a2: (E), p.465—figures of 1949–67 include urban self-employed workers
v5a3: (E), p.465
v5a4: (E), p.465

v5b:
v5b1: (E), p.465
v5b2: (E), p.465
v5b3: (E), p.465

v5c: (B), p.205
v5c1: (A)

v5d: (B), p.205

6. Population (PO)

v6a: (E), p.464—data from public security department
v6a1: (E), p.464
v6a2: (E), p.464

v6b: (E), p.464—figures of 1981 and before obtained from public security department; 1982 from the Third Population Census; 1983–89 from the estimates by sample survey

v6c: (E), p.464—(ditto)

v6d:
v6d1: (E), p.464
v6d2: (E), p.464
v6d3: (E), p.464
v6d4: (E), p.464
v6d5: (A)—Pingxiang
v6d6: (A)—Nanchang

7. Agriculture (A)

v7a: (A); (E), p.477

v7b: (A); (E), p.477

v7c: (A); (E), p.477

v7d: (A); (E), p.477

v7e: NA

v7f: (A); (E), p.477

v7g: (A); (E), p.477

v7h: (E), p.470
v7h1: (E), p.472
v7h2: (E), p.472
v7h3: (E), p.472
v7h4: (E), p.472
v7h5: (E), p.472

v7i: (A)

8. Industry (IN)

v8a: (A)
- v8a1: (A)
- v8a2: (A)
- v8a3: (A)

v8b: (E), p.479
- v8c1: (A)
- v8c2: (A)

v8d: (E), p.479

v8f:
- v8f1: (E), p.481
- v8f2: (E), p.481
- v8f3: NA
- v8f4: (E), p.481
- v8f5: (E), p.481

v8g: (A)
- v8g1: (E), p.479

9. Transport (TR)

v9a: (E), p.482—data from transport department, excluding urban traffic volume
- v9a1: (E), p.482—data from transport department, including central and local railways
- v9a2: (E), p.482—data from transport department
- v9a3: (E), p.482—(ditto)

v9b: (E), p.482—(ditto)
- v9b1: (E), p.482—(ditto) including central and local railways
- v9b2: (E), p.482—(ditto) since 1976 including freight volume of other transportation modes, before 1976 including motor vehicle only
- v9b3: (E), p.482—(ditto) excluding distant ocean and coastal freight volume, in 1971 including barge only

v9c: (E), p.482

10. Domestic Trade (DT)

v10a: (E), p.485
- v10a1: (E), p.485

v10b:
- v10b1: (B), p.485
- v10b2: (A); (B), p.118
- v10b3: (A); (B), p.118; (E), p.485—data of collective-owned units are: 1950: 0.01, 1951: 0.15, 1952: 1.08, 1953: 1.88, 1954: 3.41, 1955: 3.30, 1956: 5.28, 1957: 5.28, 1976: 13.93, 1977: 15.33, 1979: 20.74, 1989: 58.19
- v10b4: (E), p.485—jointly ownership in 1954 and 1955 include sale and commission agents
- v10b5: (E), p.485—including private economy
- v10b6: (E), p.485

v10d: (E), p.486—calculated on calendar year basis. Figures of 1978–79 are commercial purchasing amount of state-owned cooperative

11. Foreign Trade (FT)

v11a:
- v11a1: (B), p.138—oil and food products, local livestock products (Rmb 100 million)
- v11a2: (B), p.138—textile products, light industrial products, handicraft articles, chemical and medical products, silk cloth (Rmb 100 million)

v11a3: (B), p.138—hardware, mines, machinery, equipment (Rmb 100 million)

v11b: (E), p.486
v11b1: (E), p.486
v11b2: v11b – v11b1

v11c: (E), p.486

v11d: (A); (E), p.486

12. Prices (PR)

v12a: (E), p.488

v12b: (E), p.488

v12c: (E), p.488

13. Education (ED)

v13a: (A)

v13b: (A); (E), p.491

v13c:
v13c1: (A); (B), p.166; (E), p.491—general institutions of higher learning
v13c2: (B), p.166
v13c3: (A); (B), p.166; (E), p.491

v13d: (A); (B), p.167—general institutions of higher learning

14. Social Factors (SF)

v14a: (E), p.491

v14b: (E), p.491

v14c: (A)

15. Natural Environment (NE)

v15a: (E), p.477

v15b: NA

v15c: NA

v15d: NA

v15e: NA

v15f: NA

Sources of Data

(A) Data supplied by the DSNEB, SSB, the PRC.
(B) Statistical Bureau of Jiangxi Province ed. *Striving and Advancing Jiangxi*, Beijing: CSPH, 1989.
(D) Same as (D) in Beijing's sources of data.
(E) Same as (E) in Beijing's sources of data.

15

Shandong

15. Shandong

15–1

Year	v1a	v1a1	v1a2	v1a3	v1a4	v1a5	v1b	v1b1	v1b2	v1b3	v1b4	v1b5	v1c	v1d	v1d1
1949	32.23	20.07	9.15	0.12	0.42	2.47							13.66	18.57	14.28
1950	44.73	26.36	13.07	0.52	0.97	3.81							19.12	25.61	18.80
1951	56.65	33.06	16.27	0.85	1.14	5.33							23.89	32.76	23.41
1952	69.82	40.00	20.08	1.46	1.42	6.86	124.5	122.8	124.2	174.8	119.3	128.7	28.92	40.90	28.80
1953	73.37	37.04	25.41	1.92	1.52	7.48	103.9	89.9	126.8	131.3	105.5	109.0	31.01	42.36	27.37
1954	83.13	41.92	29.35	1.95	1.67	8.24	112.4	111.0	116.2	100.2	105.0	110.2	34.29	48.84	31.02
1955	88.26	44.97	30.10	1.87	1.78	9.54	106.6	108.3	102.9	95.5	103.7	115.8	35.70	52.56	33.14
1956	98.74	44.05	39.64	4.54	1.91	8.60	115.3	102.9	142.7	240.3	108.2	90.2	41.43	57.31	33.11
1957	95.72	36.44	43.31	4.12	2.05	9.80	95.5	84.7	128.4	91.2	106.8	104.7	41.68	54.04	28.67
1958	134.56	41.66	69.57	9.60	4.36	9.37	140.2	114.5	133.1	266.6	214.1	95.4	70.91	63.65	29.88
1959	160.06	39.32	92.98	11.05	6.57	10.14	118.0	95.2	132.2	114.9	148.3	106.8	94.11	65.95	25.89
1960	152.84	26.32	97.91	12.51	7.18	8.92	96.2	61.8	105.3	115.5	110.3	87.2	92.30	60.54	17.97
1961	102.64	31.84	55.04	3.84	5.22	6.70	58.1	97.0	43.1	31.0	71.8	51.7	50.42	52.22	24.03
1962	99.58	38.32	45.70	3.08	5.20	7.28	89.6	106.4	78.7	76.8	97.8	123.2	46.00	53.58	28.22
1963	104.05	40.21	49.10	4.13	3.94	6.67	109.5	115.4	109.0	130.4	79.1	102.4	47.91	56.14	30.61
1964	114.36	40.18	58.61	4.91	4.79	5.87	114.5	105.9	121.8	119.2	118.2	94.1	54.94	59.42	30.43
1965	139.42	50.49	71.38	7.15	4.78	5.62	125.8	124.6	128.3	148.9	110.6	96.3	66.16	73.26	39.26
1966	163.48	55.93	88.64	7.41	5.27	6.23	118.9	113.9	124.0	104.4	110.7	114.5	79.86	83.62	43.28
1967	172.61	55.81	96.60	6.42	5.66	8.12	104.9	100.1	109.0	82.2	91.4	125.9	86.87	85.74	43.16
1968	176.11	51.83	103.85	6.37	5.52	8.54	101.5	90.9	107.6	99.1	97.4	105.2	90.99	85.12	40.61
1969	187.16	58.70	105.79	7.97	5.71	8.99	105.5	110.2	101.8	123.5	104.0	105.7	94.24	92.92	45.68
1970	233.71	66.78	141.22	9.44	6.50	9.77	125.1	108.5	133.4	126.7	124.8	113.3	124.27	109.44	47.52
1971	255.48	75.63	147.91	14.85	7.35	9.74	113.5	110.8	112.8	146.7	113.7	99.8	134.36	121.12	51.63
1972	269.10	81.42	153.92	15.33	8.28	10.15	107.7	103.4	108.9	120.6	108.8	104.5	143.24	125.86	54.39
1973	282.62	84.59	162.94	15.24	8.08	11.77	104.6	104.0	105.9	92.5	101.5	116.1	148.82	133.80	57.18
1974	228.08	78.47	119.99	12.62	7.00	10.00	81.6	93.4	75.3	83.0	86.7	85.0	118.08	110.00	54.43
1975	318.00	93.43	189.78	15.77	7.67	11.35	139.8	118.7	158.3	124.9	109.6	113.4	170.56	147.44	60.76
1976	360.74	100.36	220.00	18.08	9.51	12.79	113.7	106.3	116.2	114.6	123.8	112.5	200.11	160.63	64.21
1977	403.04	99.27	262.24	17.61	10.61	13.31	112.1	99.2	119.4	97.2	111.7	104.2	228.27	174.77	66.54
1978	445.01	102.22	296.82	23.14	10.91	11.92	110.3	103.0	113.3	131.7	102.6	89.2	249.50	195.51	70.50
1979	518.62	135.92	314.34	35.40	15.11	17.85	109.9	109.4	104.7	148.5	137.4	142.9	298.60	220.02	86.84
1980	587.72	160.91	340.32	43.70	13.96	28.83	110.7	109.4	108.2	122.9	92.4	156.5	335.55	252.17	102.57
1981	655.33	198.50	358.37	48.88	20.62	28.96	104.1	103.2	104.5	97.5	126.3	104.2	356.95	298.38	131.10
1982	727.48	218.51	393.21	62.65	21.56	31.55	110.0	109.3	108.5	126.6	106.0	107.9	395.13	332.35	152.91
1983	832.86	259.50	441.85	67.32	25.01	39.18	112.2	114.4	111.2	105.3	115.0	122.9	453.53	379.33	184.14
1984	1014.64	310.11	534.91	90.83	28.50	50.29	117.6	119.1	114.4	131.3	115.0	125.2	536.78	477.86	217.97
1985	1240.27	335.42	682.78	127.94	31.96	62.17	117.2	103.7	122.3	135.1	111.2	113.7	687.88	552.37	230.85
1986	1409.42	361.19	784.33	153.92	38.30	71.68	111.5	100.3	116.4	110.5	112.9	110.9	813.58	595.84	246.20
1987	1752.75	413.18	1032.88	171.51	46.21	88.97	117.5	108.0	123.8	104.0	116.4	114.6	1017.13	735.62	282.95
1988	2345.89	494.53	1455.24	214.80	55.62	125.70	123.9	103.3	133.7	110.0	115.2	118.2	1430.63	915.26	327.51
1989	2904.87	548.30	1920.94	228.03	64.37	143.23	112.1	101.4	118.0	95.3	110.1	96.6	1848.89	1055.98	355.66

15. Shandong

15–2

Year	v1d2	v1d3	v1d4	v1d5	v1e	v1e1	v1e2	v1e3	v1e4	v1e5	v1f	v1f1	v1f2	v1f3	v1g
1949	2.57	0.03	0.25	1.44											19.27
1950	3.79	0.20	0.55	2.27											25.07
1951	5.13	0.30	0.69	3.23											31.65
1952	6.62	0.44	0.85	4.19	126.0	123.2	136.5	144.9	120.6	129.5					38.84
1953	8.46	0.55	1.03	4.95	101.3	92.2	128.1	119.1	117.1	113.7					41.88
1954	10.09	0.59	1.11	6.03	113.5	111.2	117.2	104.7	104.0	122.6					48.33
1955	10.54	0.60	1.17	7.11	108.1	107.9	105.0	102.9	100.0	116.8					51.80
1956	14.71	1.34	1.18	6.97	111.1	103.1	151.7	220.0	105.2	97.9					56.12
1957	16.33	0.98	1.32	6.74	93.3	86.7	112.9	82.7	112.2	91.7					52.85
1958	20.89	2.42	2.96	7.50	117.7	104.8	126.6	247.5	223.5	111.2					63.16
1959	24.60	2.70	4.20	8.56	103.3	87.4	117.9	110.2	140.6	112.6					63.44
1960	27.43	2.94	5.00	7.20	85.8	63.1	94.7	108.3	118.1	83.4					60.03
1961	18.08	1.14	3.61	5.36	76.0	106.5	69.6	47.7	70.9	49.8					53.40
1962	15.16	1.00	3.44	5.76	97.1	107.7	81.7	72.4	96.8	121.5					52.93
1963	16.94	1.43	2.37	4.79	110.3	116.5	113.0	136.8	71.4	98.2					55.46
1964	20.52	1.68	2.67	4.12	111.0	104.5	124.5	117.3	114.0	92.3					57.08
1965	24.91	2.94	2.98	3.17	124.7	127.4	126.6	182.1	119.5	75.5					69.28
1966	29.98	3.08	3.31	3.97	117.9	113.5	124.7	105.3	111.5	127.4					77.41
1967	31.27	2.63	3.22	5.46	103.7	99.9	109.5	80.8	82.1	134.4					76.45
1968	32.98	2.69	3.04	5.80	98.1	91.7	104.7	103.9	94.2	106.3					76.48
1969	34.36	3.31	3.23	6.34	108.2	110.1	104.3	122.2	106.6	109.7					86.72
1970	47.20	3.52	4.02	7.18	116.3	103.9	127.4	111.9	136.8	118.0					94.03
1971	54.55	3.82	4.62	6.50	116.4	104.7	133.9	109.6	115.4	90.7					95.62
1972	55.07	4.63	5.18	6.59	107.2	103.4	110.0	121.4	112.5	101.6					103.15
1973	57.58	5.28	5.24	8.52	106.4	105.1	105.0	114.3	101.4	129.4					118.90
1974	39.73	4.70	4.13	7.01	81.4	95.6	69.1	89.2	79.1	82.3					105.82
1975	69.32	5.50	4.71	7.15	136.9	111.7	170.1	116.9	113.8	102.0					131.05
1976	77.46	6.41	5.22	7.33	106.2	104.7	106.1	116.4	110.8	102.3					141.66
1977	87.17	7.22	6.85	6.99	106.1	103.7	106.9	112.7	131.1	95.5					162.15
1978	100.51	10.74	7.33	6.43	111.6	105.6	115.4	148.7	106.9	91.6	229.1	75.1	114.6	39.4	183.55
1979	104.80	12.93	8.14	7.31	106.7	108.2	103.8	118.7	109.5	112.0	255.0	91.1	122.3	41.6	200.11
1980	116.34	15.49	8.21	9.56	110.3	110.2	108.9	117.4	101.5	126.6	294.4	106.4	139.9	48.1	240.30
1981	120.00	17.14	10.16	19.98	108.0	108.0	102.6	93.7	102.8	206.9	337.9	132.2	148.1	57.6	259.51
1982	128.47	18.67	10.58	21.72	108.1	109.7	106.1	111.1	108.9	107.6	379.1	154.1	156.9	68.1	318.71
1983	137.36	19.23	11.76	26.84	111.2	115.4	106.6	100.8	110.2	122.2	428.3	185.6	167.7	75.0	351.30
1984	194.28	24.47	12.83	28.31	118.7	119.3	120.7	125.1	110.0	103.3	543.6	222.1	230.0	91.5	411.58
1985	238.50	33.29	13.59	36.14	110.3	101.9	116.3	130.6	104.8	117.0	631.3	236.0	282.6	112.7	501.65
1986	251.71	37.72	15.67	44.54	107.5	98.7	114.7	104.1	106.6	119.4	689.9	252.8	300.5	136.6	555.18
1987	337.02	41.79	17.89	55.97	116.8	108.1	126.8	102.3	110.6	115.8	822.3	287.3	370.0	165.0	688.71
1988	425.00	57.81	22.30	82.64	113.7	99.9	120.7	122.6	120.0	124.8	1035.2	331.9	482.9	220.4	904.27
1989	518.89	61.22	28.22	91.99	103.8	99.3	108.1	94.2	121.3	94.1	1201.6	359.2	579.7	262.8	1004.00

15. Shandong

15–3

Year	v1h	v1i	v1j	v1j1	v1j2	v1j3	v1k	v2a	v2a1	v2a2	v2b	v2c	v2c1	v2c2	v2d1
1949		0.99	276	276				1.27				0.14			
1950		1.38	316	316				2.21				0.38			
1951		1.83	350	350				3.49				0.64			
1952		2.71	362	362				5.56	3.28	2.28		1.31			
1953		3.29	404	404				6.91	4.24	2.67		2.27			
1954		3.57	429	429				10.60	5.02	5.58		2.21			
1955		4.09	459	459				11.89	7.12	4.77		1.98			
1956		6.20	516	516				12.28	9.12	3.16		4.17			
1957		7.08	550	550				11.64	8.23	3.41		3.94			
1958		8.75	480	480				16.50	8.81	7.69		10.64			
1959		11.56	478	478				20.19	11.10	9.09		12.22			
1960		12.44	501	501				17.88	13.95	3.93		14.97			
1961		11.39	510	510				8.26	5.24	3.02		4.15			
1962		9.46	563	563				5.29	4.91	0.38		3.29			29.29
1963		9.11	603	603				7.36	4.31	3.05		5.96			
1964		9.51	624	624				8.61	5.15	3.46		6.55			
1965	77.71	9.57	616	616				15.67	8.09	7.58		6.18			34.95
1966		9.68	604	604				19.35	9.98	9.37		8.06			
1967		9.88	589	589				17.02	8.99	8.03		6.25			
1968		10.06	579	579				16.26	8.23	8.03		5.55			
1969		10.44	579	579				21.65	11.16	10.49		6.78			
1970		10.97	564	564				24.04	13.07	10.97		9.92			48.77
1971		12.03	551	551				25.17	13.32	11.85		13.25			62.19
1972		13.71	574	574				26.30	13.53	12.77		14.80			75.39
1973		14.04	573	573				33.39	14.44	18.95		17.30			86.21
1974		14.47	581	581				20.14	13.87	6.27		13.88			89.88
1975		14.96	585	585				37.10	25.39	11.71		20.35			106.89
1976		15.34	568	568				40.12	27.22	12.90		20.03			117.79
1977		21.02	547	577				47.26	33.75	13.51		18.18			132.91
1978	114.56	20.54	597	597	472		3.38	54.39	39.63	14.76	41.87	29.27	15.10	1.25	152.69
1979	159.81	23.80	664	664				54.63	39.03	15.60	61.35	31.62	14.19	1.53	167.09
1980	210.23	37.08	745	774	654		5.37	64.71	40.75	23.96	69.97	35.83	16.43	1.84	186.15
1981	251.62	39.58	755	782	679		6.63	65.25	46.79	18.46	79.60	29.63	10.54	1.42	199.50
1982	299.95	42.14	769	797	696		7.60	84.19	59.97	24.22	85.00	43.29	12.42	2.56	222.17
1983	360.64	44.23	789	818	864		8.96	96.02	74.52	21.50	96.46	49.11	10.72	0.75	241.74
1984	394.99	57.13	985	1037	938		9.97	132.72	94.09	38.63	140.15	67.09	15.51	1.00	266.56
1985	408.12	66.83	1110	1170	1057		12.99	184.36	126.07	58.29	194.33	100.42	26.27	1.48	320.11
1986	449.27	82.63	1313	1401	1057		13.32	200.40	151.14	49.26	223.08	121.95	34.98	1.51	383.28
1987	517.69	94.44	1428	1516	1198	1521	15.55	272.95	194.91	78.04	297.77	155.65	52.91	1.51	456.80
1988	583.74	125.14	1782	1909	1449	1951	20.04	376.91	249.24	123.85	369.82	192.20	65.73	2.20	576.66
1989	630.56	139.63	1920	2067			25.15	429.50	224.74	204.76	336.64	162.30	59.94	2.04	715.31

15. Shandong

15–4

Year	v2d2	v2e	v3a	v3b	v3b1	v3b2	v3c	v3d	v3d1	v3d2	v3e	v3e1	v3e2	v3e3	v3e4
1949			18.00	17.72			0.28	39.30	35.30	110.42					
1950			22.86	22.39			0.47	48.74	43.11	116.10					
1951			28.16	27.40			0.76	58.48	50.60	138.15					
1952			33.28	32.40	24.98	7.42	0.88	67.78	58.57	144.08	119.80				
1953			34.97	33.52	24.73	8.79	1.45	68.74	57.54	152.34					
1954			37.73	36.09	27.88	8.21	1.64	72.12	62.25	156.38					
1955			39.91	38.21	29.01	9.20	1.70	74.34	63.69	157.26					
1956			43.84	42.09	31.38	10.71	1.75	80.25	68.46	162.03					
1957			41.21	39.63	29.04	10.59	1.58	74.16	62.12	158.30	191.84	118.99	24.08	3.38	7.52
1958			46.66	44.48	31.98	12.50	2.18	81.96	68.49	164.91	176.13	109.68	22.47	5.04	5.52
1959			43.25	40.63	26.78	13.85	2.62	74.87	58.05	170.15	187.15	112.00	26.45	5.10	5.19
1960			42.15	38.95	23.95	15.00	3.20	73.35	53.81	174.62					
1961			45.14	43.32	27.86	15.46	1.82	82.40	62.06	201.30					
1962	20.76	8.08	47.64	46.43	31.85	14.58	1.21	86.37	68.19	206.81	209.96	130.77	19.91	5.80	8.40
1963			48.10	46.95	33.55	13.40	1.15	84.81	68.51	209.70	199.60	123.77	20.31	5.40	8.73
1964			48.47	47.24	33.99	13.25	1.23	83.98	68.03	210.65	207.20	128.44	23.80	6.10	8.42
1965	24.28	8.23	53.61	52.11	36.60	15.51	1.50	91.60	73.57	217.23					
1966			58.06	56.34	40.14	16.20	1.72	96.95	78.85	225.00					
1967			59.43	57.62	41.02	16.60	1.81	97.00	78.79	226.16					
1968			60.22	58.16	41.33	16.83	2.06	96.01	77.79	225.91					
1969			65.07	62.77	45.57	17.20	2.30	101.16	83.61	227.81					
1970	34.13	18.06	69.99	67.66	49.49	18.17	2.33	106.00	88.80	224.32					
1971	42.64	27.07	70.45	68.25	49.85	18.40	2.20	104.44	87.84	213.95					
1972	54.65	30.64	76.85	73.80	51.61	22.19	3.05	110.88	89.49	249.61					
1973	60.00	35.10	85.51	81.13	57.25	23.88	4.38	119.87	97.40	268.31					
1974	61.71	38.21	85.68	81.01	57.52	23.49	4.67	118.02	96.04	268.46					
1975	72.84	39.30	93.95	86.64	61.28	25.36	7.31	124.50	100.48	294.88					
1976	80.44	43.11	101.54	91.82	64.10	27.72	9.72	130.46	103.84	320.46					
1977	91.24	46.36	114.89	103.60	74.07	29.53	11.29	145.83	117.87	360.12					
1978	105.59	51.87	129.16	114.23	83.87	30.36	14.93	159.34	131.23	390.26	340.00				
1979	109.87	56.80	145.48	130.98	98.16	32.82	14.50	181.01	152.28	415.38					
1980	122.77	60.81	175.59	158.33	118.25	40.08	17.26	216.77	183.25	470.98	396.00				
1981	129.42	64.30	194.26	177.31	133.48	43.83	16.95	240.06	205.86	485.92	450.36	247.32	70.68	5.76	9.60
1982	142.66	69.06	234.52	217.39	171.93	45.46	17.13	290.43	261.97	493.06	455.28	262.80	71.40	6.60	9.24
1983	155.21	74.46	255.28	237.48	190.69	46.79	17.80	313.75	286.49	512.49	472.92	283.20	69.93	7.33	9.85
1984	173.03	66.57	278.86	258.46	206.72	51.74	20.40	338.30	307.30	566.72	520.92	311.64	84.81	7.65	9.88
1985	211.68	80.42	317.29	289.64	223.10	66.54	27.65	376.10	333.53	657.50	667.13	338.47	103.13	6.14	11.07
1986	262.00	96.07	354.78	320.69	248.25	72.44	34.09	410.90	364.33	731.17	751.34	378.00	107.41	7.11	11.82
1987	318.14	110.84	415.76	365.71	279.22	86.49	50.05	464.81	409.35	826.12	812.54	432.58	120.19	5.86	11.61
1988	419.46	129.74	527.36	457.31	329.78	127.53	70.05	568.51	482.62	1053.15	1025.78	522.90	154.59	6.65	13.50
1989	531.06	175.28	586.11	511.02	342.86	168.16	75.09	626.63	509.83	1175.94	1160.52	602.52			

15. Shandong

15–5

Year	v3f	v3f1	v3f2	v3f3	v3f4	v4a1	v4a1a	v4a1b	v4a1c	v4a1d	v4a2	v4a2a	v4a2b	v4a2c	v4a2d
1949															
1950						4.43	0.07	1.38	1.75	0.84	1.03	0.06	0.21	0.47	0.30
1951						7.00	0.48	2.79	2.10	1.01	1.60	0.32	0.32	0.74	0.22
1952						7.63	0.92	3.90	2.36	0.46	3.19	0.89	0.81	0.83	0.66
1953						7.98	0.69	4.97	2.02	0.30	3.23	0.57	1.15	0.95	0.56
1954						8.84	0.79	5.58	2.23	0.24	3.37	0.65	1.05	0.94	0.74
1955						8.93	0.77	5.54	2.46	0.17	3.11	0.40	1.04	0.99	0.68
1956						10.31	0.97	6.41	2.47	0.45	4.72	1.32	1.24	1.27	0.89
1957						10.73	1.04	6.74	2.48	0.48	4.92	1.05	1.54	1.18	1.15
1958						21.10	10.01	7.97	2.56	0.56	12.07	7.51	1.76	1.25	1.56
1959						24.75	12.34	8.59	2.65	0.15	15.89	7.85	1.93	1.42	4.70
1960						26.38	14.86	8.85	1.64	0.12	23.93	9.89	2.61	1.46	9.98
1961						16.57	7.71	6.22	1.43	0.13	13.60	1.91	2.08	1.36	8.25
1962						12.55	2.73	7.03	1.40	0.16	6.36	0.66	1.93	1.18	2.60
1963						15.11	5.65	7.18	1.47	0.16	7.97	1.03	1.92	1.31	3.72
1964						15.54	5.37	8.02	1.41	0.14	8.96	1.76	2.15	1.32	3.73
1965	79.90	55.90	8.00	3.00	5.00	16.48	6.30	7.81	1.55	0.16	9.54	1.87	2.21	1.31	4.15
1966						18.77	8.17	7.89	1.73	0.09	10.41	2.41	2.45	1.37	4.18
1967						19.05	8.08	8.38	1.72	0.05	10.20	3.34	2.50	1.21	3.15
1968						20.07	8.20	9.03	1.63	0.08	8.88	3.10	2.24	1.23	2.31
1969						19.83	7.71	9.44	1.64	0.07	11.40	4.96	2.22	1.27	2.95
1970						30.94	14.13	13.90	1.75	0.07	14.25	7.04	2.53	1.42	3.26
1971						41.11	23.53	14.98	1.67	0.13	15.91	6.79	3.11	1.78	4.23
1972						43.04	23.85	16.57	1.65	0.08	18.89	8.26	3.77	1.93	4.93
1973						44.92	24.19	18.06	1.66	0.06	19.49	6.66	4.09	1.85	6.88
1974						26.95	10.54	13.97	1.46	0.05	19.11	5.70	4.40	1.84	7.17
1975						45.97	22.60	20.49	1.69	0.06	21.26	5.24	4.83	2.12	9.07
1976						49.67	22.61	24.05	1.62	0.05	21.42	4.84	5.01	2.29	9.28
1977						55.96	24.51	28.24	1.59	0.06	22.61	4.86	5.23	2.44	10.07
1978	93.69	57.66	13.00	7.00	4.00	64.13	31.34	30.07	1.47	0.04	31.90	8.35	6.17	2.66	14.72
1979	128.01	78.43	17.31	9.42	5.97	56.99	24.19	30.01	1.46	0.52	31.62	7.00	7.32	3.19	14.12
1980	165.34	99.39	23.82	14.42	6.76	48.11	14.56	30.81	1.59	0.01	30.07	4.67	8.69	3.90	12.81
1981	202.12	112.72	27.03	24.00	7.69	51.19	14.33	34.18	1.61	0.04	25.53	3.22	9.00	3.92	9.40
1982	230.02	115.84	30.76	33.61	12.20	49.29	7.45	39.06	1.65	0.19	29.45	3.24	10.57	4.55	11.09
1983	264.38	134.14	34.60	40.36	13.48	50.41	6.96	39.96	1.95	0.56	32.41	3.99	11.75	5.24	11.43
1984	287.24	149.19	34.62	46.11	16.71	53.60	4.72	45.36	1.94	0.48	38.98	5.18	13.73	6.95	13.12
1985	321.98	168.19	36.30	47.68	18.29	67.53	3.02	60.18	2.47	0.69	51.30	5.57	16.76	7.01	21.96
1986	364.56	182.18	39.88	63.13	22.66	62.15	4.20	52.91	2.59	1.21	67.94	6.34	20.01	7.97	33.63
1987	406.34	202.17	42.92	74.91	21.82	72.79	4.80	61.08	2.95	2.71	75.22	4.89	21.98	8.34	40.01
1988	482.11	235.09	48.87	88.17	24.10	82.68	-5.90	76.86	4.41	6.01	94.07	5.96	27.85	11.44	48.82
1989	513.10	255.26	53.41	82.02	27.17	100.94	-7.97			16.70	113.67	5.55	32.44	9.85	65.83

15. Shandong

15–6

Year	v4b	v4b1	v4b2	v4b3	v4c1	v4c2	v5a	v5a1	v5a2	v5a3	v5a4	v5b1	v5b2	v5b3	v5c
1949							1859								
1950	0.03			0.0039				44							
1951	0.17			0.0056				52							
1952	0.42			0.0101			1897	75							
1953	0.66			0.0428				81							
1954	0.99			0.0996				83							
1955	1.29			0.2255				89							
1956	1.89			0.6299				120							
1957	2.04			1.0970			2150	129							
1958	3.44			1.2408			2155	182							
1959	3.58			2.2061			2033	242							
1960	3.60			2.9408			1958	248							
1961	2.55			2.8048			1936	223							
1962	2.07			1.5974	5.20	18.0	1981	168							
1963	2.59			1.4924			2028	151							
1964	3.03			1.8604			2100	152							
1965	3.70			1.8600	12.08	37.2	2146	155							
1966	4.27			2.5528			2199	160							
1967	4.50			3.3202			2219	168							
1968	4.76			4.0114			2254	174							
1969	4.48			3.8148			2274	180							
1970	4.55			4.1358	21.54	41.3	2606	194							
1971	5.43			5.4081	34.35	49.3	2752	218							
1972	6.31			5.4677	31.95	37.0	2744	239							
1973	7.76			5.2709	33.88	35.6	2869	245	84		2540				
1974	8.43			6.0467	16.73	16.7	2894	248	85		2561				
1975	9.55			6.7018	34.30	30.6	2925	263	95		2565				
1976	10.92			7.6113	38.15	30.9	2928	278	105		2544				
1977	13.23			6.6737	43.57	31.7	2942	278	115		2548				
1978	14.43			6.8941	51.19	32.5	2970	354	116		2500	2351	366	253	
1979	19.56			10.6625	53.40	32.0	3016	368	117		2528				
1980	29.29			15.1545	53.63	29.2	3118	390	124		2596	2458	383	277	
1981	39.16			15.0207	53.89	28.9	3192	410	129		2651	2508	389	295	
1982	50.73			14.1051	52.75	26.2	3270	427	133		2707	2485	442	343	
1983	73.01			16.1896	57.96	25.3	3341	437	133		2767	2514	461	366	
1984	100.17			21.9139	66.06	27.6	3451	438	179		2847	2561	512	378	
1985	130.18			19.0082	81.02	27.7	3556	438	181		2926	2439	709	408	
1986	175.56			21.5254	81.92	22.9	3651	461	187	12	2990	2431	782	438	
1987	242.42			24.8386	95.01	22.1	3766	490	193	16	3066	2423	854	489	
1988	326.52			26.6333	107.94	19.7	3887	528	204		3134	2471	905	511	
1989	425.30	254.18	170.8		107.95	15.3	3940	533	203		3183	2524	903	514	

15. Shandong

15–7

Year	v5c1	v5d	v6a	v6a1	v6a2	v6b	v6c	v6d1	v6d2	v6d3	v6d4	v6d5	v6d6
1949			4549	299	4250	28.1	12.2	260	4289	2199	2350	102.48	77.43
1950			4640	305	4335	30.1	12.2	261	4379	2242	2398		
1951			4732	317	4415	32.9	12.2	272	4460	2319	2413		
1952			4827	334	4493	31.5	12.2	289	4538	2392	2435	20.79	62.38
1953			4924	392	4532	32.6	12.1	304	4620	2450	2474		
1954			5052	405	4647	37.7	11.7	320	4732	2520	2532		
1955			5174	416	4758	37.3	13.7	378	4796	2587	2587		
1956			5256	427	4829	32.7	12.1	385	4871	2627	2629		
1957			5373	450	4923	35.8	12.1	437	4936	2694	2679	80.62	86.15
1958			5422	472	4950	25.0	12.8	612	4810	2719	2703	126.55	68.95
1959			5373	589	4784	20.9	18.2	579	4794	2713	2660		
1960			5188	540	4648	19.5	23.6	546	4642	2597	2591		
1961			5265	504	4761	21.4	18.4	461	4804	2631	2634	129.03	108.96
1962			5426	464	4962	38.1	12.4	411	5015	2718	2708	127.87	105.07
1963			5585	468	5117	44.2	11.8	434	5151	2804	2781	132.55	107.65
1964			5606	725	4881	36.9	12.0	445	5161	2816	2790	135.92	110.09
1965			5711	662	5049	35.5	10.2	453	5258	2866	2845	138.59	107.01
1966			5851			34.5	9.9	453	5398	2940	2911		
1967			5968			30.0	9.0	454	5514	2999	2969		
1968			6086			38.0	8.0	455	5631	3060	3026		
1969			6265			30.4	6.6	457	5808	3147	3118		
1970			6441	481	5960	33.9	7.3	475	5966	3241	3200	186.03	105.73
1971			6568	528	6040	29.0	7.8	530	6038	3311	3257		
1972			6683	840	5843	27.6	7.7	526	6157	3368	3315		
1973			6793	865	5928	23.9	6.9	542	6251	3428	3365		
1974			6876	878	5998	21.0	7.2	549	6327	3471	3405		
1975			6971	895	6076	21.6	7.5	563	6408	3524	3447	203.72	112.31
1976			7038	917	6121	18.5	7.6	583	6455	3561	3477		
1977			7099	941	6158	17.0	7.2	592	6507	6592	3507		
1978			7160	975	6185	16.8	6.5	627	6533	3624	3536	211.38	117.84
1979			7232	995	6237	16.9	6.2	661	6570	3660	3572		
1980			7296	1030	6266	13.9	6.4	691	6605	3694	3602	216.13	125.50
1981			7395	1105	6290	16.5	6.4	736	6659	3750	3645		
1982			7494	1436	6058	17.1	6.1	774	6720	3806	3688		
1983			7564	2215	5349	12.8	5.9	811	6753	3847	3717		
1984			7637	3704	3933	13.0	6.0	936	6701	3887	3750		
1985			7695	4089	3606	11.8	5.9	1017	6676	3922	3773	230.00	142.97
1986			7776	4449	3327	14.7	5.9	979	6797	3967	3810	232.95	146.43
1987			7889	4675	3216	27.4	5.6	1045	6844	4029	3860	237.25	214.42
1988			8009	4982	3027	18.0	6.0	1307	6702	4092	3917	240.44	217.85
1989			8160	5222	2958	16.9	5.7	1483	6698	4181	4000	243.22	221.50

15. Shandong

15–8

Year	v7a	v7b	v7c	v7d	v7e	v7f	v7g	v7h	v7h1	v7h2	v7h3	v7h4	v7h5	v7i	v8a
1949								20.07	16.01	0.12	1.66	0.28	2.00		9.15
1950			403.8	18939				26.36	21.02	0.12	1.98	0.41	2.83		13.07
1951	0.1		450.5	19273				33.06	26.17	0.14	2.82	0.66	3.27		16.27
1952	0.1	5.8	513.3	19881		4.0		40.00	31.16	0.25	3.98	0.72	3.89		20.08
1953	0.1		556.2	19959		7.3		37.04	28.31	0.41	3.63	0.76	3.93		25.41
1954	0.1		600.5	20402		11.1		41.92	33.03	0.49	3.67	0.83	3.90		29.35
1955	0.2	34.8	693.3	20200		15.1		44.97	35.40	0.66	3.37	0.89	4.65		30.10
1956	0.4	134.9	967.5	20161		17.2		44.05	36.53	0.81	3.88	0.87	1.96		39.64
1957	0.4	262.6	1157.0	20240		19.8		36.44	30.36	0.87	3.54	0.82	0.85		43.31
1958	1.5	461.0	1365.5	18557		22.3		41.66	36.64	1.30	2.69	0.94	0.09		69.57
1959	1.9	457.6	1460.4	17073		27.3	0.1	39.32	34.31	1.38	2.52	1.03	0.08		92.98
1960	4.0	834.7	1489.5	17578		27.6	0.1	26.32	23.24	0.28	1.73	1.05	0.02		97.91
1961	4.8	1179.9	1429.4	16920		19.2	0.2	31.84	28.11	0.19	2.50	0.98	0.06		55.04
1962	4.9	1514.5	1438.0	16903		13.1	0.4	38.32	32.71	0.26	4.09	1.20	0.06		45.70
1963	5.1	1392.0	1542.2	17236		30.5	0.5	40.21	33.33	0.29	5.38	1.14	0.07		49.10
1964	5.4	1534.0	1744.4	17463		38.5	0.5	40.18	33.02	0.37	5.48	1.23	0.08		58.61
1965	7.0	1676.3	2267.0	17425		56.4	1.3	50.49	42.79	0.55	5.76	1.30	0.09		71.38
1966	8.1	1617.3	2860.3	17098		94.8	2.5	55.93	46.00	0.54	8.03	1.28	0.08		88.64
1967	10.5	1802.0	3115.5	16874		104.4	2.8	55.81	45.98	0.59	7.88	1.26	0.10		96.60
1968	12.7	1929.0	3296.6	16531		90.3	3.8	51.83	42.32	0.62	7.42	1.36	0.11		103.85
1969	15.2	2085.3	3459.5	16735		94.0	4.3	58.70	49.22	0.61	7.04	1.74	0.09		105.79
1970	19.8	1949.8	3754.1	16563		129.0	4.4	66.78	55.62	0.90	8.14	1.99	0.13		141.22
1971	26.9	2226.4	4391.0	16735		152.2	4.9	75.63	60.86	1.89	10.86	1.91	0.11		147.91
1972	36.6	2710.7	4868.1	16914		174.7	5.8	81.42	65.14	2.33	11.34	2.46	0.15		153.92
1973	46.2	3238.5	5156.4	16848		187.2	6.0	84.59	68.26	2.34	11.34	2.49	0.16		162.94
1974	55.6	3247.4	5431.4	16675		131.6	6.3	78.47	61.48	2.30	11.83	2.69	0.17		119.99
1975	66.3	3819.0	5707.4	16575		182.9	7.8	93.43	75.64	2.65	12.33	2.60	0.21		189.78
1976	77.7	4610.6	6059.0	16632		239.7	11.0	100.36	80.12	2.60	14.24	3.15	0.25		220.00
1977	92.4	5158.4	6405.4	16174		386.0	11.9	99.27	78.40	2.10	14.72	3.62	0.43		262.24
1978	108.5	5730.2	6622.2	16108		529.3	14.1	102.22	83.71	1.81	12.19	3.45	1.06		296.82
1979	124.5	6480.9	6607.2	15997		601.9	16.1	135.92	111.33	2.04	16.61	3.93	2.01		314.34
1980	137.2	6844.7	6611.3	15857		696.7	20.1	160.91	126.22	4.52	23.43	4.15	2.59		340.32
1981	152.8	6390.4	6650.7	15631		720.4	26.3	198.50	151.83	4.91	33.04	4.94	3.79	289.5	358.37
1982	167.4	6042.8	6723.1	15470	2694.0	779.1	32.0	218.51	167.98	7.22	34.12	5.59	3.60	303.1	393.21
1983	191.0	6105.1	6804.1	15741	2207.0	863.8	36.5	259.50	202.87	8.48	36.21	6.06	5.87	319.0	441.85
1984	210.8	6520.3	6832.3	16159	1918.0	857.5	38.4	310.11	236.64	8.60	48.20	8.12	8.55	325.8	534.91
1985	230.1	6647.7	6848.3	16291	4952.4	753.1	42.5	335.42	236.62	11.07	62.78	13.36	11.59	352.0	682.78
1986	253.8	6893.0	6820.2	16565	3212.4	779.7	51.3	361.19	255.92	12.67	62.82	16.17	13.61	379.4	784.33
1987	273.6	7141.9	6721.3	16332	3426.5	826.4	57.9	413.18	299.05	12.11	64.13	23.16	14.73	417.3	1032.88
1988	296.0	7319.6	6484.2	16436	2625.0	885.6	64.8	494.53	313.98	14.80	108.06	40.07	17.62	475.8	1455.24
1989	316.3	7671.8	6533.3	16199		959.5	73.4	548.30	347.61	14.28	125.34	42.43	18.64	504.6	1920.94

15. Shandong

15–9

Year	v8a1	v8a2	v8a3	v8b	v8c1	v8c2	v8d	v8f1	v8f2	v8f3	v8f4	v8f5	v8g
1949	3.42	0.01	5.72		0.90	8.25		0.01	169.1		2.09	0.15	112422
1950	5.05	0.27	7.75		1.33	11.74		0.07	222.1		2.55	0.42	125564
1951	6.20	0.65	9.42		1.87	14.40		0.17	264.4		2.96	0.83	139390
1952	9.07	0.88	10.13		2.24	17.84		0.36	362.0		3.48	1.08	141292
1953	11.81	1.15	12.45		3.07	22.34		0.59	362.6		4.20	1.56	154410
1954	14.16	1.71	13.48		4.05	25.30		1.43	411.2		5.21	1.98	143514
1955	14.81	2.31	12.98		4.74	25.36		1.68	479.8		5.32	2.24	126429
1956	17.57	3.02	19.05		7.25	32.39		1.97	541.2		6.47	4.22	25664
1957	15.83	2.36	25.12		7.97	35.34		2.12	616.5		7.01	0.32	34467
1958	51.80	9.34	8.43		22.21	47.36		5.33	1373.4	0.11	10.91	17.49	125511
1959	71.55	11.95	9.48		29.87	63.11		22.06	2304.3	0.52	16.81	14.73	21216
1960	87.57	9.10	1.24		48.81	49.10		35.81	2699.2	0.73	26.20	37.46	11522
1961	40.80	8.71	5.53		21.32	33.72		15.11	1791.9	0.27	20.19	13.40	7530
1962	33.99	6.27	5.44	26.97	14.48	31.22		5.92	1457.6	0.01	17.68	10.86	6794
1963	37.34	5.83	5.93		14.78	34.32		5.21	1544.6	0.05	18.10	19.53	5856
1964	45.55	7.04	6.02		18.43	40.18		9.33	1596.1	0.07	20.69	42.22	5745
1965	55.79	8.95	6.64	48.14	23.17	48.21		13.05	1740.0	83.86	24.71	76.50	5585
1966	69.07	12.03	7.54		30.97	57.67		21.69	1985.4	134.48	34.92	106.11	6070
1967	74.85	13.74	8.01		32.62	63.98		21.80	1846.3	130.32	39.53	91.16	6159
1968	79.73	14.76	9.36		37.17	66.68		24.28	2030.4	215.23	41.19	96.74	6070
1969	81.56	15.53	8.70		33.05	72.74		21.19	1531.0	293.00	43.34	96.89	6248
1970	109.22	21.38	10.62	92.60	59.34	81.88		29.65	2402.6	467.30	55.27	136.64	7384
1971	115.13	24.64	8.14	106.26	69.07	78.84		43.60	2643.6	621.67	67.70	170.55	7983
1972	117.98	27.49	8.45	114.26	74.11	79.81		46.93	2790.7	807.92	77.27	216.93	8181
1973	122.51	30.44	9.99	119.03	78.88	84.06		49.81	2570.4	1083.50	82.84	239.76	8493
1974	84.75	24.05	11.19	83.28	53.25	66.74		15.83	1430.6	1257.25	64.35	159.71	8666
1975	138.41	38.39	12.98	136.67	93.13	96.65		53.19	2851.1	1672.00	96.64	279.55	9933
1976	157.01	52.12	10.87	156.88	112.97	107.03		56.30	3336.0	1750.42	119.93	329.00	13422
1977	178.85	70.70	12.69	177.64	134.32	127.92		65.82	3819.1	1751.86	136.48	398.58	16732
1978	200.74	78.60	17.48	201.50	152.54	144.28		82.35	4200.1	1947.00	155.86	468.60	18592
1979	217.62	78.52	18.20	217.61	156.82	157.52		84.77	4438.2	1887.96	170.96	524.00	18124
1980	229.89	90.46	19.97	229.79	156.51	183.81		90.11	4290.5	1831.82	185.97	571.00	19111
1981	238.57	96.69	23.11	237.17	146.04	212.33		86.57	4130.5	1611.19	194.49	600.32	19126
1982	261.91	100.28	31.02	254.73	159.64	233.57		90.05	4256.9	1634.61	203.47	689.36	19490
1983	292.55	110.46	38.84	281.98	180.81	261.04		99.70	4385.1	1837.46	218.25	812.25	19548
1984	318.30	164.80	51.81	282.98	217.33	317.58		110.00	4562.5	2301.80	236.44	922.98	21262
1985	397.07	205.53	80.18	330.19	312.37	370.41		124.97	4922.3	2703.16	262.05	1121.81	22199
1986	415.12	234.86	134.35	355.63	364.95	419.38		141.40	5099.8	2950.80	299.95	1345.87	24249
1987	521.66	302.57	208.65	406.41	499.50	533.38		163.82	5317.8	3160.00	331.81	1558.77	24932
1988	662.48	441.05	351.71	486.96	703.54	751.70		191.33	5559.2	3330.26	379.61	1864.54	26044
1989	833.86	575.95	511.13	527.84	937.95	982.99		210.42	5694.9	3335.48	419.81	1941.58	26526

15. Shandong

15–10

Year	v8g1	v9a	v9a1	v9a2	v9a3	v9b	v9b1	v9b2	v9b3	v9c	v10a	v10a1	v10b1	v10b2	v10b3
1949		13.63	12.87	0.81		12.45	11.78	0.66	0.01	0.0612	7.18	6.23	0.37	0.24	
1950		15.34	14.34	1.00		27.75	26.41	0.79	0.55	0.0737	11.54	10.44	1.35	0.59	0.01
1951		16.61	15.34	1.27		30.97	28.97	1.17	0.80	0.0965	15.95	14.68	1.86	2.14	0.02
1952		15.53	13.65	1.80	0.08	37.11	33.46	1.54	2.11	0.1115	20.48	19.01	2.18	4.92	0.03
1953		21.27	18.06	3.11	0.10	50.14	45.23	2.19	2.72	0.1448	22.77	21.07	3.49	6.56	0.03
1954		22.87	18.89	3.89	0.09	56.46	51.33	2.26	2.87	0.1619	24.74	22.40	5.64	9.95	0.03
1955		22.29	17.86	4.38	0.05	49.19	43.59	2.46	3.44	0.1756	26.39	23.77	5.22	10.15	0.13
1956		28.64	23.35	5.23	0.06	37.39	59.57	3.25	4.57	0.2085	30.99	27.44	8.89	13.87	1.10
1957		30.02	24.27	5.65	0.10	69.23	61.90	3.27	4.06	0.2315	28.94	26.09	7.31	13.80	4.75
1958		34.06	27.02	6.94	0.10	114.87	102.41	6.76	5.69	0.3035	34.22	29.26	10.78	17.29	4.12
1959		39.34	30.90	8.32	0.12	152.01	131.60	12.93	7.48	0.4518	39.03	33.29	15.47	19.77	2.83
1960		47.17	38.87	8.07	0.23	161.53	140.87	14.05	6.61	0.6014	42.21	34.52	17.68	20.65	2.55
1961		72.30	64.76	8.09	0.35	105.91	96.01	5.78	4.12	0.5736	35.21	29.64	14.95	14.44	2.29
1962	1809	76.64	66.90	9.33	0.41	81.06	73.09	4.21	3.76	0.5099	35.34	30.49	15.74	14.39	2.33
1963		40.84	33.04	0.59	0.21	89.33	80.52	4.82	3.99	0.4578	35.31	30.38	14.80	15.33	2.81
1964		36.39	28.45	7.79	0.15	98.39	88.11	5.64	4.64	0.4825	36.92	31.41	17.01	15.69	2.26
1965	1358	36.64	26.99	9.53	0.12	119.29	107.21	7.50	4.58	0.5022	40.52	33.85	19.06	17.80	2.24
1966		41.26	29.14	12.00	0.12	167.91	154.93	8.55	4.43	0.5122	43.34	34.96	20.40	19.03	2.40
1967		46.41	34.20	12.03	0.18	153.52	140.08	9.27	4.17	0.5164	46.38	38.62	22.90	21.99	0.57
1968		54.21	39.33	14.70	0.18	169.41	156.24	9.26	3.91	0.5147	45.22	37.77	22.28	21.40	0.56
1969		58.13	43.23	14.73	0.17	164.53	149.98	9.88	4.67	0.5169	47.94	39.71	23.08	23.34	0.36
1970	1543			14.45	0.14	191.67	173.46	11.86	6.35	0.5485	50.78	40.94	24.17	24.37	0.38
1971	1813			15.42	0.13			14.23	6.88	0.6120	56.20	44.12	26.40	27.38	0.93
1972	2042			17.27	0.15			16.95	7.62	0.6737	63.96	49.89	30.47	30.83	1.04
1973	2181	63.05	44.03	18.88	0.14	219.63	192.40	19.00	8.23	0.7349	67.35	52.37	31.11	33.43	1.10
1974	2206	63.54	44.98	18.43	0.13	175.80	152.56	16.89	6.35	0.7100	65.57	52.93	29.50	33.50	1.06
1975	2321	66.76	47.08	19.53	0.15	221.98	189.47	23.74	8.77	0.7862	77.26	60.32	32.98	39.57	2.50
1976	2483	69.96	47.91	21.89	0.16	240.62	200.96	29.42	10.24	0.8731	87.15	66.12	36.28	42.92	6.10
1977	2693	77.02	51.27	25.60	0.15	273.26	222.93	38.65	11.68	0.9447	98.74	74.59	42.39	48.42	6.43
1978	2787	84.48	55.35	28.95	0.18	310.05	257.46	40.60	11.99	1.0058	106.71	79.73	46.36	50.82	7.09
1979	2863	93.73	59.50	34.04	0.19	315.86	265.40	36.34	11.13	1.0515	121.24	92.22	55.99	52.67	9.73
1980	2888	106.24	67.69	38.39	0.16	313.29	260.87	40.05	12.37	1.1030	146.88	114.01	67.67	60.60	13.89
1981	2890	113.65	72.72	40.77	0.16	319.41	263.32	40.93	15.16	1.1291	168.31	131.47	76.36	65.13	19.49
1982	2989	122.83	77.88	44.77	0.18	351.60	284.00	49.37	18.23	1.1629	183.11	141.49	78.68	63.12	28.49
1983	3058	142.37	89.54	52.64	0.19	389.96	309.66	57.87	22.43	1.2529	209.11	162.14	85.53	61.55	35.03
1984	2884	170.58	106.15	64.23	0.20	419.74	332.50	65.05	22.19	1.3751	241.58	189.08	96.47	63.98	42.84
1985	3242	203.57	124.33	79.01	0.23	484.31	373.42	81.39	24.68	1.6186	280.79	227.03	102.22	62.88	59.40
1986	3293	246.71	156.08	116.80	0.24	575.99	446.18	102.87	26.94	1.7735	320.28	261.64	118.01	66.37	69.12
1987	3444	273.16	156.08	116.80	0.28	645.33	490.69	122.31	32.34	2.0719	374.68	300.69	137.53	76.25	83.93
1988	3498	324.12	179.74	144.02	0.36	727.23	538.51	153.25	35.47	2.5826	490.95	392.37	181.00	101.60	102.11
1989	3557	322.86	165.52	156.93	0.41	789.96	587.10	166.12	38.60	3.2154	540.95	430.74	220.59	113.84	108.16

15. Shandong

15–11

Year	v10b4	v10b5	v10b6	v10d	v11a1	v11a2	v11a3	v11b	v11b1	v11b2	v11c	v11d	v12a	v12b1	v12c
1949		6.57													
1950		9.14	0.45		0.3249	0.0248		0.4149	0.3497	0.0652			101.8	102.3	104.4
1951		11.48	0.45		0.3537	0.0219	0.0005	0.5259	0.3761	0.1498			110.2	110.8	121.3
1952	0.01	12.81	0.53	10.65	0.6530	0.0101	0.0067	0.7357	0.6698	0.0659			100.5	102.2	98.5
1953	0.01	12.22	0.46	10.80	0.9025	0.0167	0.0122	0.9763	0.9314	0.0449			103.7	103.3	108.5
1954	0.02	8.59	0.51	13.83	0.8442	0.0150	0.0155	0.8953	0.8747	0.0206			103.8	103.4	105.6
1955	0.22	10.17	0.50	13.82	1.1045	0.0258	0.0114	1.1425	1.1417	0.0008			99.6	99.9	98.5
1956	3.96	2.64	0.53	14.05	1.0362	0.0405	0.0481	1.1317	1.1248	0.0069			100.6	100.7	100.8
1957	0.84	1.73	0.51	13.30	1.0160	0.0502	0.0446	1.1239	1.1108	0.0131			101.5	101.0	105.0
1958	0.65	1.03	0.35	14.59	0.5787	0.0696	0.1386	0.8082	0.7869	0.0213			99.6	99.6	100.9
1959		0.32	0.64	19.33	0.7536	0.4542	0.1041	1.3198	1.3119	0.0079			100.8	100.6	102.0
1960		0.35	0.98	12.53	0.3736	0.3200	0.0908	0.8075	0.7844	0.0231			100.6	100.5	103.3
1961		1.25	2.28	12.65	0.1581	0.2475	0.0652	0.4810	0.4708	0.0102			105.9	107.0	115.4
1962		1.28	1.60	12.24	0.1998	0.2170	0.1035	0.5308	0.5203	0.0105			100.2	100.5	98.0
1963		1.30	1.07	16.13	0.3418	0.2337	0.1231	0.7029	0.6986	0.0043			99.8	98.7	97.6
1964		1.12	0.84	17.56	0.5707	0.3315	0.1678	1.0846	1.0700	0.0146			98.2	97.8	98.9
1965		0.82	0.60	22.28	0.8129	0.2865	0.1593	1.3303	1.2587	0.0716			97.5	97.8	100.1
1966		0.87	0.64	24.83	0.8770	0.4396	0.1590	1.5521	1.4756	0.0765			99.2	98.7	102.4
1967		0.23	0.69	27.10	0.9899	0.5422	0.1481	1.7572	1.6802	0.0770			99.3	100.1	99.6
1968		0.22	0.76	26.75	0.9282	0.6913	0.1422	1.8284	1.7617	0.0667			99.9	99.8	100.2
1969		0.32	0.84	25.99	0.8950	0.6889	0.1498	1.7756	1.7337	0.0419			99.5	99.9	99.9
1970		0.91	0.95	26.21	0.8725	0.5946	0.1608	1.7226	1.6276	0.0950			99.3	98.9	99.7
1971		0.38	1.11	29.26	1.0983	0.6606	0.2215	2.0640	1.9804	0.0836			99.1	99.9	102.8
1972		0.37	1.25	30.06	1.5257	0.7995	0.2514	2.6472	2.5766	0.0706			99.6	100.0	101.8
1973		0.38	1.33	34.73	2.4226	1.3630	0.3731	4.2826	4.1587	0.1239			99.8	99.8	100.2
1974		0.23	1.28	30.56	2.4222	1.1463	0.5782	4.3473	4.1467	0.2006			99.8	99.9	99.9
1975		0.67	1.54	34.46	2.3965	1.4889	0.8813	5.0392	4.7667	0.2725			100.1	100.2	100.3
1976		0.34	1.51	36.09	2.6521	1.6467	1.0122	5.5995	5.3110	0.2885			100.1	100.2	100.1
1977		0.12	1.38	36.56	2.8154	1.8512	1.0701	6.0948	5.7367	0.3581			100.0	99.8	100.1
1978		0.10	2.34	39.04	4.0331	2.1257	2.1363	8.7142	8.2951	0.4191			100.0	100.3	101.0
1979		0.21	2.64	54.48	3.6992	4.2852	5.0725	13.6019	13.0569	0.5450			101.3	100.7	129.1
1980	0.01	1.33	3.38	75.32	4.5627	5.0241	8.0445	18.7242	17.6313	1.0929			103.0	105.0	109.0
1981	0.01	3.79	3.53	84.42	5.8494	5.2980	7.7642	19.7652	18.9116	0.8536			101.8	101.8	104.5
1982	0.04	7.96	4.82	93.96	4.0537	5.0701	7.4603	17.9122	16.5841	1.3281			100.9	100.9	101.1
1983	0.26	21.58	5.16	122.86	4.8689	5.3535	7.8554	19.2439	18.0778	1.1661			100.5	102.4	107.2
1984	0.28	31.88	6.13	130.06	5.9045	4.8821	12.0951	24.2468	22.8817	1.3651	1.0470	0.1642	102.6	101.6	101.0
1985	0.10	47.25	8.94	129.50	6.0253	5.5277	15.1139	30.6372	26.6669	3.9703	1.0994	0.6231	107.1	108.8	106.1
1986	0.27	54.19	12.32	137.13	7.0726	7.0334	7.2447	25.4283	21.3507	4.0776	1.2887	1.1679	104.2	105.0	102.7
1987	0.15	61.91	14.91	170.83	8.8754	9.7163	11.1665	34.8272	29.7582	5.0690	3.0520	1.0219	108.0	109.1	108.9
1988	0.27	85.46	20.51	214.61	9.3493	11.3265	9.1261	35.7122	29.8019	5.9103	5.9553	1.4231	108.3	120.6	125.8
1989	0.26	91.75	26.34	239.70				36.9044	30.5167	6.3877	19.3441	2.0800	117.1	115.7	112.4

15. Shandong

15–12

Year	v13a	v13b	v13c1	v13c2	v13c3	v13d	v14a	v14b	v14c	v15a	v15b	v15c	v15d	v15e	v15f
1949										13092					
1950		23.6	0.5406	5.4506	237.79	0.0424			0.57	13302					
1951		34.6	0.5679	7.6918	341.88	0.0569			0.80	13607					
1952		43.8	0.6753	17.4575	453.75	0.1703	8532	3.86	1.06	13774					
1953		42.8	0.7363	15.8766	425.81	0.1931			1.03	13853					
1954		49.7	0.8509	20.1258	432.60	0.1759			1.06	13865					
1955		52.3	0.8915	120.1238	432.74	0.1825			1.14	13866					
1956		66.1	1.1574	27.5233	501.57	0.1775			1.59	13832					
1957		49.6	1.2532	38.2938	490.88	0.1686			1.24	13729					
1958		81.9	1.9557	72.0181	708.80	0.2249			2.62	12960					
1959		83.9	2.6493	70.9279	763.82	0.2409			3.30	12367					
1960		74.0	3.4744	89.7336	722.88	0.5821			2.58	12027					
1961			3.3461	59.0331	551.58	0.5567			1.23	11974					
1962			2.6001	46.0887	487.56	0.7148			1.27	12019					
1963			2.3807	46.4905	524.60	0.6180			1.55	12059					
1964			2.2435	57.1301	748.14	0.6806			2.23	12082					
1965			2.2164	88.7036	966.72	0.6102	38069	8.85	2.61	12001					
1966			2.1919	70.7833	774.64				4.10	11883					
1967			1.6631	68.1461	793.38	0.5288			4.41	11780					
1968			0.9731	84.2173	791.73	0.6992			4.22	11714					
1969			0.9254	144.9208	799.50	0.2756			3.70	11630					
1970				188.7538	813.58	0.9162			3.29	11564					
1971			0.8953	268.8910	898.25				3.65	11482					
1972			1.4259	290.5461	951.06				4.90	11410					
1973			1.7291	263.8869	1004.20	0.4098			4.45	11367					
1974		94.8	1.6375	256.0837	1054.00	0.5461			4.32	11303					
1975			1.7582	309.7550	1091.22	0.6033			5.58	11223					
1976			2.1340	442.8686	1059.68	0.6072			6.01	11093					
1977		97.5	2.5735	526.2856	1035.87	0.7203			5.60	11022					
1978		96.6	3.8390	485.1317	1041.84	0.7015	110522	15.01	5.43	10945					
1979		95.8	4.4771	428.4316	1040.06	0.5364	115501		5.71	10898					
1980		95.8	5.1427	417.9801	1041.70	0.7684	117134	16.87	5.66	10862					
1981		95.6	6.0608	370.7969	1017.62	0.6311	117970		6.31	10832					
1982		96.0	5.2443	337.8293	978.73	2.3993			6.50	10802					
1983		96.6	5.5276	325.5844	946.26	1.6806			7.48	10773					
1984		97.4	6.6429	345.6627	927.50	1.3563			9.07	10744					
1985		97.4	8.3567	369.8539	894.06	1.6159	133622	20.51	12.64	10557					
1986	5.91	97.8	9.2422	392.3053	870.41	2.1183			11.95	10447	2734				
1987	5.99	98.3	9.5891	396.2367	844.87	2.9428			13.30	10387	3078				
1988	6.04	98.4	10.1281	393.7300	830.01	3.0869	151862	22.79	13.82	10344	3263				
1989		98.3	10.3928	377.1500	823.19	3.1766	155300	23.41	10.91	10302					

Notes

1. National Output and Income (Y)

v1a: (E), p.498
 v1a1: (E), p.498
 v1a2: (E), p.498
 v1a3: (E), p.498
 v1a4: (E), p.498
 v1a5: (E), p.498

v1b: (A); (D), p.268
 v1b1: (A); (D), p.268
 v1b2: (A); (D), p.268
 v1b3: (A); (D), p.268
 v1b4: (A); (D), p.268
 v1b5: (A); (D), p.268

v1c: v1a – v1d

v1d: (E), p.495
 v1d1: (E), p.495
 v1d2: (E), p.495
 v1d3: (E), p.495
 v1d4: (E), p.495
 v1d5: (E), p.495

v1e: (A); (D), p.271
 v1e1: (A); (D), p.271
 v1e2: (A); (D), p.271
 v1e3: (A); (D), p.271
 v1e4: (A); (D), p.271
 v1e5: (A); (D), p.271

v1f: (E), p.494
 v1f1: (E), p.494
 v1f2: (E), p.494
 v1f3: (E), p.494

v1g: (E), p.497

v1h: (E), p.522

v1i: (E), p.521

v1j: (E), p.521
 v1j1: (E), p.521
 v1j2: (C), 1987, p.292-293
 v1j3: (C), 1987, p.292-293

v1k: (E), p.521

2. Investment (I)

v2a: (A); (E), p.497
 v2a1: (A); (D), p.276
 v2a2: (A); (D), p.276

v2b: (A)

v2c: (A)
 v2c1: (E), p.513
 v2c2: (E), p.513

v2d:
 v2d1: (E), p.510
 v2d2: (E), p.510

v2e: (E), p.510

3. Consumption (C)

v3a: (E), p.497

v3b: (E), p.497
 v3b1: (A); (D), p.272
 v3b2: (A); (D), p.272

v3c: (E), p.497

v3d: (E), p.520
 v3d1: (E), p.520
 v3d2: (E), p.520

v3e: (A); (E), p.522
 v3e1: (A); (E), p.522
 v3e2: (A)
 v3e3: (A)
 v3e4: (A)

v3f: (E), p.522
 v3f1: (E), p.522

v3f2: (A)
v3f3: (A)
v3f4: (A)

4. Public Finance and Banking (FB)

v4a:
- v4a1: (E), p.518—in 1988, public revenues include subsidies to foreign trade deficits and cigarette tax of Qingdao City. If subtracted, it becomes 9.053 billion
  - v4a1a: (E), p.518
  - v4a1b: (B), p.235–236
  - v4a1c: (B), p.235–236—including agricultural tax and farmland occupation tax
  - v4a1d: v4a1 – v4a1a – v4a1b' (v4a1b':total tax revenues which come from (E), p.518)
- v4a2: (E), p.518
  - v4a2a: (E), p.518
  - v4a2b: (E), p.518
  - v4a2c: (E), p.518
  - v4a2d: v4a2 – v4a2a – v4a2b – v4a2c — including welfare fund, circulating fund, city maintenance expenses and farming support expenses

v4b: (A)
- v4b1: (A)
- v4b2: (A)
- v4b3: (B), p.241—rural collective deposits

v4c:
- v4c1: (E), p.510
- v4c2: (E), p.510

5. Labor Force (L)

v5a: (B), p.245; (E), p.493
- v5a1: (C), 1989, p.12; (E), p.493
- v5a2: (E), p.493
- v5a3: (C), 1986, p.66-67; 1987, p.74-75
- v5a4: (E), p.493—excluding rural people working outside

v5b:
- v5b1: (E), p.493
- v5b2: (E), p.493
- v5b3: (E), p.493

v5c: NA
- v5c1: NA

v5d: NA

6. Population (PO)

v6a: (A); (E), p.492—data from public security department
- v6a1: (A)
- v6a2: (A)

v6b: (A); (E), p.492—(ditto)

v6c: (A); (E), p.492—(ditto)

v6d:
- v6d1: (E), p.492—(ditto)
- v6d2: (E), p.492—(ditto)
- v6d3: (E), p.492—(ditto)
- v6d4: (E), p.492—(ditto)
- v6d5: (A)—Zibo
- v6d6: (A)—Jinan

7. Agriculture (A)

v7a: (A); (E), p.505

v7b: (A); (E), p.505

v7c: (A); (E), p.505

v7d: (A); (E), p.505

v7e: (A)

v7f: (A); (E), p.505

v7g: (A)

v7h: (E), p.500
v7h1: (E), p.500
v7h2: (E), p.500
v7h3: (E), p.500
v7h4: (E), p.500
v7h5: (E), p.500

v7i: (A)

8. Industry (IN)

v8a: (E), p.506
v8a1: (E), p.506
v8a2: (E), p.506
v8a3: v8a – v8a1 – v8a2

v8b: (E), p.510—based on 1980's constant price

v8c1: (E), p.498
v8c2: (E), p.498

v8d: NA

v8f:
v8f1: (E), p.509
v8f2: (E), p.509
v8f3: (E), p.509
v8f4: (E), p.509
v8f5: (E), p.509

v8g: (A)
v8g1: (A)

9. Transport (TR)

v9a: (E), p.511—excluding urban traffic volume
v9a1: (E), p.511—including central and local railways
v9a2: (E), p.511
v9a3: (E), p.511—excluding distant ocean and coastal passenger traffic

v9b: (E), p.511
v9b1: (E), p.511
v9b2: (E), p.511—including central and local railways
v9b3: (E), p.511—excluding distant ocean and coastal freight volume

v9c: (E), p.511

10. Domestic Trade (DT)

v10a: (E), p.514
v10a1: (E), p.514

v10b:
v10b1: (B), p.514
v10b2: (B), p.208
v10b3: (B), p.208
v10b4: (E), p.514
v10b5: (E), p.514
v10b6: (E), p.514

v10d: (E), p.516—calculated on calendar year basis

11. Foreign Trade (FT)

v11a:
v11a1: (B), p.233
v11a2: (B), p.233—textile, handicraft articles and other products of light industry
v11a3: (B), p.233—industrial and mining products

v11b: (E), p.517
v11b1: (E), p.517
v11b2: v11b – v11b1

v11c: (E), p.517

v11d: (E), p.517

12. Prices (PR)

v12a: (E), p.519

v12b: (E), p.519

v12c: (E), p.519

13. Education (ED)

v13a: (A)

v13b: (A); (E), p.522

v13c:
- v13c1: (A); (B), p.522—general institutions of higher learning
- v13c2: (A)—technical and ordinary secondary schools
- v13c3: (A); (E), p.522

v13d: (A)

14. Social Factors (SF)

v14a: (E), p.522

v14b: (E), p.522—unit: 10,000 people

v14c: (A)

15. Natural Environment (NE)

v15a: (A); (E), p.505

v15b: (A)

v15c: NA

v15d: NA

v15e: NA

v15f: NA

Sources of Data

(A) Data supplied by the DSNEB, SSB, the PRC.
(B) Statistical Bureau of Shandong Province eds. *Striving and Advancing Forty Years, Shandong's Volume*, Beijing: CSPH, 1989.
(C) ________ ed. *Statistical Yearbook of Shandong*, Beijing: CSPH, various issues.
(D) Same as (D) in Beijing's sources of data.
(E) Same as (E) in Beijing's sources of data.

16

Henan

16. Henan

16–1

Year	v1a	v1a1	v1a2	v1a3	v1a4	v1a5	v1b	v1b1	v1b2	v1b3	v1b4	v1b5	v1c	v1d	v1d1
1949	23.82	17.19	2.98	2.82	0.07	0.76							5.09	18.73	14.15
1950	29.17	19.94	4.33	2.77	0.81	1.32							6.62	22.55	16.30
1951	40.03	27.44	6.25	3.90	0.97	1.47							9.45	30.58	22.27
1952	44.97	27.74	9.98	4.24	1.17	1.84	112.3	101.0	159.8	113.9	120.6	125.2	11.77	33.20	22.50
1953	53.70	31.54	11.90	6.47	1.40	2.39	113.1	105.6	120.3	151.2	125.6	123.9	15.83	37.87	25.13
1954	58.67	33.57	13.65	6.82	1.90	2.73	109.6	104.9	116.4	113.7	137.4	111.8	18.28	40.39	26.50
1955	62.56	36.02	14.45	6.88	2.30	2.87	107.6	107.4	107.9	103.4	122.8	105.5	20.01	42.55	28.19
1956	67.21	34.61	16.11	9.89	3.13	3.47	109.5	95.1	117.6	162.2	139.9	120.8	24.00	43.21	27.09
1957	73.36	31.57	16.63	18.35	3.53	3.28	110.8	107.7	105.8	136.7	118.7	92.3	26.68	46.68	24.30
1958	102.60	33.78	33.17	26.63	4.57	4.45	138.6	104.0	200.8	149.1	131.1	135.7	47.32	55.28	25.64
1959	121.98	32.46	50.16	31.69	3.64	4.03	117.7	91.4	150.5	121.9	79.3	90.4	64.11	57.87	22.87
1960	131.17	28.94	58.41	34.00	4.29	5.53	106.2	87.4	117.2	99.8	118.7	136.7	71.59	59.58	19.99
1961	79.76	24.81	31.20	15.24	3.57	4.94	52.4	67.9	50.9	21.2	83.1	78.5	41.77	37.99	14.47
1962	71.81	28.13	23.93	11.63	3.21	4.91	90.7	115.4	76.7	64.2	88.6	115.7	37.34	34.47	16.83
1963	71.70	25.33	26.65	11.29	3.55	4.88	107.5	91.0	107.9	234.8	110.7	107.4	37.89	33.81	14.91
1964	81.48	32.20	32.27	7.62	3.97	5.42	122.3	128.3	121.4	121.5	112.1	110.6	39.55	41.93	22.19
1965	104.50	42.17	42.24	9.30	4.84	5.95	129.0	128.2	136.9	128.3	121.6	91.7	51.23	53.27	29.35
1966	122.09	49.65	49.30	11.13	5.61	6.40	118.3	114.9	121.7	121.2	116.0	108.2	55.24	66.85	34.79
1967	124.42	58.02	46.15	8.91	4.56	6.78	99.4	114.2	94.7	80.0	82.3	107.2	55.88	68.54	40.79
1968	115.16	54.95	42.37	7.29	4.13	6.42	92.1	92.5	93.7	81.8	91.6	94.6	53.42	61.74	37.99
1969	137.09	57.73	54.25	12.31	5.28	7.52	123.0	102.6	132.6	168.8	127.4	118.3	66.41	70.68	39.36
1970	174.40	67.18	73.68	17.81	7.03	8.70	130.7	110.3	142.0	144.7	133.9	117.8	87.52	86.88	44.00
1971	196.22	71.21	91.54	16.25	7.50	9.72	109.4	104.8	116.1	89.8	106.7	111.5	102.38	93.84	46.93
1972	207.29	72.50	100.75	15.04	7.91	11.09	105.3	101.0	109.3	91.5	105.5	114.2	108.26	99.03	48.31
1973	228.24	83.31	106.07	18.40	8.33	12.13	108.1	113.1	104.6	119.8	105.5	109.3	124.62	103.62	52.86
1974	241.00	83.21	115.62	20.35	8.75	13.07	106.3	100.2	109.0	108.1	104.9	107.7	135.43	105.57	52.89
1975	262.88	85.98	130.46	23.45	9.58	13.41	110.0	103.1	112.8	113.1	109.6	113.0	151.01	111.87	54.39
1976	242.25	87.17	107.99	23.45	9.72	13.92	89.8	100.7	82.8	98.4	102.5	110.8	133.64	108.61	58.33
1977	299.80	82.70	161.69	27.51	12.57	15.33	126.4	94.3	147.6	115.5	128.0	96.4	173.09	126.71	54.04
1978	326.08	95.38	170.82	28.91	13.10	17.87	108.3	109.6	107.6	103.5	104.3	116.2	182.50	143.58	63.09
1979	371.95	113.48	193.49	32.44	13.04	19.50	108.1	101.2	109.7	109.6	99.5	127.4	204.11	167.84	75.40
1980	416.95	134.62	209.23	38.19	13.79	21.12	109.2	105.0	109.3	117.5	105.9	107.4	222.88	194.07	91.96
1981	453.83	151.24	223.50	41.15	14.69	23.25	106.7	113.0	105.0	108.0	106.4	106.7	240.13	213.70	104.68
1982	483.17	151.06	246.28	46.31	17.63	21.89	105.0	97.6	108.6	112.5	120.0	94.1	262.76	220.41	105.06
1983	549.84	187.02	268.14	49.86	19.37	25.45	113.3	122.0	109.1	107.1	110.0	117.4	280.85	268.99	139.36
1984	632.67	208.68	307.58	56.55	25.66	34.20	112.3	108.4	113.7	105.4	127.7	127.6	326.52	306.15	151.86
1985	815.52	241.54	401.32	85.71	33.75	53.20	119.2	104.3	122.7	132.1	129.3	148.3	442.00	373.52	169.17
1986	932.07	259.49	478.09	99.83	36.03	58.63	107.9	95.7	114.4	110.9	106.8	110.6	514.89	417.18	173.60
1987	1146.13	323.62	594.65	115.22	41.76	70.88	116.9	118.4	118.0	112.2	115.2	111.2	638.87	507.26	214.47
1988	1436.82	370.67	779.90	149.40	46.89	89.96	113.3	98.5	120.3	118.3	111.3	105.6	832.79	604.03	233.52
1989	1701.36	449.88	953.56	132.68	58.07	107.17	106.7	109.9	110.4	80.8	108.1	100.7	1013.47	687.89	284.32

16. Henan

16–2

Year	v1d2	v1d3	v1d4	v1d5	v1e	v1e1	v1e2	v1e3	v1e4	v1e5	v1f	v1f1	v1f2	v1f3	v1g
1949	1.54	2.37	0.04	0.63											18.73
1950	2.21	2.50	0.41	1.13											21.65
1951	3.15	3.28	0.49	1.39											28.92
1952	4.99	3.56	0.59	1.56	108.6	101.1	158.4	113.2	120.4	112.2					33.45
1953	5.12	5.44	0.71	1.47	108.0	103.8	103.5	163.9	125.4	89.7					38.47
1954	6.22	5.03	0.96	1.68	107.0	103.9	123.4	97.5	137.8	112.1					39.47
1955	6.52	4.92	1.16	1.76	106.4	106.5	106.5	101.5	122.5	105.1					42.93
1956	7.06	5.35	1.58	2.13	103.5	95.1	114.5	123.5	140.0	120.6					45.84
1957	7.09	11.50	1.78	2.01	109.6	105.8	103.0	143.5	118.9	92.5					50.30
1958	10.01	14.60	2.30	2.73	117.4	102.5	142.1	138.3	130.8	135.9					64.94
1959	14.22	16.47	1.84	2.47	103.7	85.0	141.4	123.8	79.8	90.4					69.52
1960	16.86	17.17	2.16	3.40	101.7	85.5	119.3	100.9	118.0	136.7					60.96
1961	10.68	8.01	1.80	3.03	54.9	57.6	60.1	30.9	83.2	78.3					40.58
1962	7.82	5.18	1.62	3.02	91.4	118.3	70.9	55.5	88.7	116.1					40.62
1963	9.39	4.72	1.79	3.00	105.4	89.6	120.9	146.2	110.6	107.5					47.88
1964	11.94	2.47	2.00	3.33	129.7	150.3	127.4	85.5	111.5	110.3					48.76
1965	15.03	2.83	2.37	3.69	125.9	129.4	131.8	120.8	118.9	92.8					52.84
1966	20.23	5.39	2.44	4.00	127.6	115.7	140.3	192.8	102.9	108.7					65.20
1967	17.63	3.87	1.99	4.26	99.0	114.6	88.2	71.6	82.5	108.0					63.69
1968	15.13	2.81	1.75	4.06	88.8	91.0	87.5	72.6	88.9	95.0					59.90
1969	19.90	4.35	2.29	4.78	117.7	101.2	136.2	155.1	130.6	119.4					69.69
1970	28.43	6.11	2.77	5.57	125.9	106.0	149.0	140.4	121.2	118.4					90.14
1971	32.20	5.62	3.06	6.03	104.8	105.6	105.9	90.6	110.6	108.0					89.30
1972	35.42	5.40	3.24	6.66	105.3	101.6	109.5	94.9	105.7	110.4					94.06
1973	33.31	6.97	3.44	7.04	102.1	107.6	93.3	126.3	106.5	105.8					101.60
1974	33.74	7.96	3.66	7.32	102.1	99.9	101.4	111.9	106.6	103.9					107.07
1975	37.28	8.84	4.01	7.35	107.0	101.7	110.6	108.8	109.3	110.6					111.95
1976	29.07	8.94	4.36	7.91	93.7	104.7	78.1	99.5	109.8	114.3					111.24
1977	47.02	11.08	5.56	9.01	120.9	90.4	159.1	122.2	126.4	100.2					124.21
1978	53.43	10.26	5.98	10.82	112.1	112.7	115.5	91.2	107.7	119.7	162.92	64.86	69.45	28.61	141.47
1979	63.03	11.29	6.15	11.97	110.2	101.3	114.2	107.4	102.8	129.2	190.09	77.30	80.52	32.27	164.90
1980	71.54	12.58	6.36	11.63	110.1	109.0	113.5	111.3	103.5	96.3	229.16	93.23	94.44	41.49	193.02
1981	73.74	13.05	6.45	15.78	107.8	113.6	102.3	103.9	101.2	131.4	249.69	106.04	95.79	47.86	206.94
1982	78.28	14.05	7.84	15.18	102.0	98.9	104.8	107.6	121.6	96.1	263.30	108.18	102.76	52.36	209.95
1983	89.18	14.39	8.68	17.38	120.6	129.7	113.9	101.9	110.6	115.6	327.95	143.49	116.36	68.10	258.59
1984	103.63	17.84	11.54	21.28	111.1	106.3	115.0	115.2	128.6	116.2	370.04	155.28	136.29	78.47	295.68
1985	132.62	24.30	15.37	32.06	112.6	100.3	120.5	120.2	130.5	143.6	451.74	173.43	170.07	108.24	370.89
1986	163.66	27.98	15.90	36.04	104.3	91.1	118.1	108.6	103.5	114.0	502.91	179.02	202.15	121.74	406.85
1987	190.84	33.59	19.86	48.50	115.4	117.4	110.8	116.4	124.4	123.8	609.60	220.22	230.25	159.13	474.90
1988	240.39	42.73	21.57	65.82	107.7	96.6	115.6	116.0	107.2	112.9	737.52	240.72	299.83	196.97	592.93
1989	276.53	36.30	27.51	63.23	103.7	110.1	104.1	81.5	111.7	91.6	826.01	289.95	317.13	218.93	665.76

16. Henan

16–3

Year	v1h	v1i	v1j	v1j1	v1j2	v1j3	v1k	v2a	v2a1	v2a2	v2b	v2c	v2c1	v2c2	v2d1
1949		0.38	242	242				0.41							
1950		0.50	247	247				1.08				0.05			
1951		0.75	264	264				4.05				0.74			
1952		1.43	347	347				5.65	3.92	1.73		0.75			
1953		2.41	357	357				7.27	2.84	4.43		1.86			
1954	66	2.53	387	387				7.26	3.62	3.64		2.87			
1955	66	3.27	409	409				9.10	6.51	2.59		3.03			
1956	68	4.62	497	497				10.59	8.71	1.88		6.69			
1957	65	5.90	546	546				14.89	9.57	5.32		7.17			
1958		6.85	441	441				26.75	19.64	7.11		16.98			
1959		9.69	445	445				34.41	25.09	9.32		19.72			
1960		10.64	451	451				26.88	27.98	-1.10		20.57			
1961		10.02	479	479				3.53	9.49	-5.96		5.27			
1962	99	8.33	538	538				2.23	7.06	-4.83		3.23			
1963	77	8.40	583	583				9.09	7.51	1.58		5.13			
1964	72	8.98	606	606				10.28	8.32	1.96		7.21			
1965	74	10.89	503	599	369			12.76	10.06	2.70		6.91			
1966		11.19	540	589	388			21.23	14.21	7.02		6.17			
1967		11.32	538	580	403			15.89	9.40	6.49		4.07			
1968		10.88	546	578	408			12.55	6.42	6.13		4.33			
1969		11.40	554	582	413			19.98	12.71	7.27		10.23			
1970		12.87	547	573	424			35.85	22.69	13.16		18.61			
1971		14.13	534	555	434			31.17	21.68	9.49		17.60			
1972		16.25	567	593	441			31.47	21.33	10.14		16.54			73.80
1973		16.62	560	581	453			35.56	24.23	11.33		17.47			83.11
1974		17.57	557	589	465			37.40	27.47	9.93		19.21			89.47
1975		18.12	561	581	488			39.88	29.39	10.49		21.64			98.84
1976		18.91	558	576	477			35.47	26.47	9.00		19.32			107.77
1977		20.22	563	578	497			44.91	30.23	14.68		22.12			122.31
1978	105	24.30	590	609	496		2.82	45.99	34.16	11.83		24.80	13.57	0.66	139.31
1979	134	27.63	644	668	533		3.39	50.01	35.92	14.09		23.75	10.93	0.76	149.90
1980	161	32.93	730	759	597		4.59	52.40	40.90	11.50		24.27	9.78	1.37	160.25
1981	216	35.43	742	772	604		5.66	57.31	36.39	20.92	47.25	26.60	11.51	1.31	184.47
1982	217	37.40	754	789	604		6.32	52.44	47.39	5.05	53.52	33.12	10.56	2.12	202.76
1983	272	39.19	767	805	606		7.34	77.71	50.64	27.07	61.40	36.87	11.09	1.19	216.98
1984	301	46.24	866	921	686		8.51	88.92	59.97	28.95	86.93	48.23	17.68	1.03	239.96
1985	329	57.85	1015	1080	804		10.93	119.53	84.29	35.24	126.95	64.57	20.72	2.29	284.53
1986	334	69.57	1159	1245	882		10.30	126.30	101.14	25.16	146.79	74.33	22.19	1.78	327.70
1987	378	78.98	1258	1347	974		11.29	162.90	113.32	49.58	162.68	84.63	25.02	2.18	374.25
1988	401	95.90	1470	1582	1110		12.38	226.75	141.23	85.52	206.20	107.78	35.91	2.45	430.00
1989	457	108.70	1628	1767	1191		16.92	238.51	102.94	135.57	187.68	99.62	41.11	1.12	510.05

16. Henan

16–4

Year	v2d2	v2e	v3a	v3b	v3b1	v3b2	v3c	v3d	v3d1	v3d2	v3e	v3e1	v3e2	v3e3	v3e4
1949			18.32	18.11			0.21	43	39	103					
1950			20.57	20.19			0.38	48	42	123					
1951			24.87	24.31			0.56	56	53	104					
1952			27.80	26.83	23.67	3.16	0.97	62	58	126					
1953			31.20	29.30	25.83	3.47	1.90	67	63	129					
1954			32.21	30.11	26.13	3.98	2.10	67	63	123					
1955			33.83	31.83	27.69	4.14	2.00	69	65	115					
1956			35.25	32.56	27.70	4.86	2.69	69	64	142					
1957			35.41	32.58	26.75	5.83	2.83	68	60	178	183	107	20.90	4.79	7.93
1958			38.19	35.84	29.15	6.69	2.35	73	65	167					
1959			35.11	32.34	24.17	8.17	2.77	65	54	170					
1960			34.08	31.26	21.68	9.58	2.82	64	49	185					
1961			37.05	33.23	22.71	10.52	3.82	69	52	223					
1962			38.39	34.96	24.31	10.65	3.43	72	54	273					
1963			38.79	35.55	24.83	10.72	3.24	71	54	284					
1964			38.48	35.18	23.68	11.50	3.30	69	51	287					
1965			40.08	36.55	24.93	11.62	3.53	71	52	277	211	125			
1966			43.97	40.11	28.31	11.80	3.86	75	58	276					
1967			47.80	44.17	32.29	11.88	3.63	81	64	277					
1968			47.35	43.71	31.96	11.75	3.64	78	62	275					
1969			49.71	46.03	33.22	12.81	3.68	80	62	301					
1970			54.29	50.41	36.77	13.64	3.88	85	67	311					
1971			58.13	53.69	40.11	13.58	4.44	88	71	280					
1972	57.40	28.10	62.59	57.87	42.26	15.61	4.72	92	73	306					
1973	64.54	32.60	66.04	60.78	44.35	16.43	5.26	95	75	323					
1974	68.47	36.20	69.67	63.96	46.36	17.60	5.71	97	76	341					
1975	75.34	38.50	72.07	66.14	47.76	18.38	5.93	99	77	352					
1976	81.46	42.40	75.77	69.81	51.00	18.81	5.96	103	81	355					
1977	92.49	43.96	79.30	72.85	53.49	19.36	6.45	106	84	358					
1978	105.52	47.83	95.48	88.35	67.45	20.90	7.13	126	105	375					
1979	107.16	51.60	114.89	106.38	83.26	23.12	8.51	149	128	384					
1980	112.29	53.20	140.62	129.36	100.41	28.95	11.26	179	153	441	384	214	59.40	3.96	8.04
1981	130.45	54.41	149.63	138.52	107.23	31.29	11.11	189	161	450	396	222	59.71	4.48	8.03
1982	140.88	61.02	157.51	144.09	109.34	34.75	13.42	193	163	476	408	228	60.96	5.04	8.04
1983	148.53	61.36	180.88	166.33	127.31	39.02	14.55	220	187	513	431	248	60.60	5.16	8.16
1984	162.41	63.71	206.76	186.10	137.25	48.85	20.66	244	201	609	460	261	72.56	4.83	9.08
1985	195.51	76.01	251.36	225.36	163.82	61.54	26.01	292	239	710	605	304	92.09	5.25	9.81
1986	227.88	89.37	280.55	249.68	179.63	70.05	30.88	320	261	771	704	363	113.87	5.97	9.48
1987	261.97	101.53	312.00	275.34	195.14	80.20	36.66	348	280	854	780	415	116.04	6.24	9.47
1988	303.15	115.31	366.18	323.91	219.59	104.32	42.27	403	312	1054	985	466	145.92	6.28	10.34
1989	361.94	148.52	427.25	372.65	251.19	121.46	54.60	456	353	1167	964	533	133.48	5.84	12.20

16. Henan

16–5

Year	v3f	v3f1	v3f2	v3f3	v3f4	v4a1	v4a1a	v4a1b	v4a1c	v4a1d	v4a2	v4a2a	v4a2b	v4a2c	v4a2d
1949															
1950						2.73	0.00	0.7756	1.9362	0.0131	0.48		0.05	0.28	
1951						3.59	0.05	1.6995	1.7791	0.0651	0.84	0.22	0.09	0.32	0.21
1952						4.39	0.11	2.0223	2.1031	0.1579	1.66	0.30	0.24	0.46	0.66
1953						5.07	0.14	2.8977	1.7277	0.3031	2.39	0.33	0.97	0.66	0.43
1954	61.30	39.10	5.00		8.60	6.76	0.40	3.2773	2.4609	0.6255	2.82	0.79	0.90	0.70	0.43
1955						6.86	0.50	3.5105	2.3888	0.4628	2.93	0.79	0.94	0.71	0.49
1956						6.94	0.67	3.7076	2.1952	0.3672	4.47	1.38	1.19	0.97	0.93
1957	63.00	41.40	6.20		7.20	7.35	0.83	3.8862	2.2284	0.4043	4.35	1.14	1.30	0.88	1.03
1958						14.16	5.01	5.8026	2.7979	0.5546	12.19	8.42	1.27	0.96	1.54
1959						18.90	8.72	7.3766	2.6528	0.1492	15.05	8.45	1.51	1.15	3.94
1960						17.34	7.17	7.9119	2.1298	0.1285	18.35	9.40	2.08	1.31	5.56
1961						9.19	2.82	5.2846	0.9793	0.1123	10.85	1.40	1.82	1.23	6.40
1962	94.00	54.30	6.60	4.60	14.50	7.56	0.85	5.2921	1.2001	0.2183	6.17	0.93	1.63	1.16	2.45
1963						8.63	1.99	5.3012	1.1286	0.2013	7.89	1.44	1.68	1.21	3.56
1964						9.16	2.31	5.5234	1.1832	0.1374	12.89	2.40	1.90	1.23	7.36
1965	66.90	47.30	6.90	3.00	2.80	10.17	3.37	5.3688	1.2959	0.1324	9.43	2.35	1.91	1.19	3.98
1966						12.73	5.22	5.8620	1.5873	0.0638	9.97	2.43	2.22	1.30	4.02
1967						11.44	3.88	5.8462	1.6820	0.0323	8.87	2.62	2.27	1.24	2.74
1968						9.42	2.49	5.1513	1.7428	0.0411	7.92	2.43	2.02	1.35	2.12
1969						13.51	5.08	6.6618	1.7261	0.0502	11.62	5.29	2.05	1.60	2.68
1970						21.15	8.05	11.2751	1.7660	0.0579	14.39	7.94	2.17	1.48	2.80
1971						25.44	11.66	12.0063	1.7447	0.0254	15.22	6.84	2.72	1.77	3.89
1972						27.17	12.41	13.1693	1.5722	0.0228	15.75	6.05	3.26	1.91	4.53
1973						23.81	7.96	14.1287	1.6959	0.0258	16.93	5.77	3.69	1.81	5.66
1974						23.76	6.71	15.4198	1.6162	0.0166	18.28	5.54	4.03	1.92	6.79
1975						23.06	4.92	16.7370	1.3771	0.0256	20.32	5.22	4.29	2.05	8.76
1976						15.52	-0.43	14.4612	1.4602	0.0282	21.87	5.75	4.40	1.96	9.76
1977						22.62	0.91	20.1008	1.5658	0.0476	21.51	5.07	4.77	2.20	9.47
1978	81.70	52.90	9.90	6.30	4.90	33.73	10.59	21.5406	1.4991	0.0959	27.67	8.02	5.77	2.39	11.49
1979	110.83	67.32	14.25	8.70	5.62	33.68	10.02	22.0387	1.5820	0.0429	29.86	6.14	7.05	2.90	13.77
1980	135.52	78.49	18.48	14.49	6.92	31.86	6.96	23.2379	1.6263	0.0366	26.74	4.70	8.31	3.45	10.28
1981	165.57	89.08	24.50	19.96	8.68	34.23	4.42	28.0460	1.6801	0.0835	25.84	2.62	8.84	4.03	10.35
1982	177.90	101.18	23.26	20.20	8.45	33.49	2.38	29.4573	1.5045	0.1517	29.81	3.77	9.83	4.34	11.87
1983	196.35	113.71	24.36	22.12	10.23	36.49	5.63	28.7034	1.9856	0.1699	30.06	3.08	10.45	4.94	11.59
1984	219.64	122.46	27.70	27.16	10.55	39.26	4.60	32.6944	1.8412	0.1320	36.79	5.10	11.83	6.35	13.51
1985	260.19	145.84	29.12	35.07	16.60	48.93	3.67	42.3176	2.2571	0.6864	49.51	5.65	13.93	7.05	22.88
1986	292.48	159.87	31.34	45.95	14.54	54.92	4.34	47.7190	1.9907	0.8721	69.20	7.80	15.78	8.00	37.62
1987	309.90	164.03	31.38	50.30	14.95	63.15	5.57	53.5012	2.5993	1.4817	65.26	5.40	16.67	8.58	34.61
1988	346.73	179.42	37.36	49.57	15.89	70.98	2.96	61.7870	3.3063	2.9321	76.22	5.80	19.47	11.34	39.61
1989	390.05	199.99	42.38	51.38	20.21	80.97	2.64				87.67	5.24	22.76	13.96	45.71

16. Henan

16–6

Year	v4b	v4b1	v4b2	v4b3	v4c1	v4c2	v5a	v5a1	v5a2	v5a3	v5a4	v5b1	v5b2	v5b3	v5c
1949	0.0014	0.0014					1593	17		16	1560	1505	30	58	15.05
1950	0.0212	0.0212					1654	21	0	23	1610	1550	43	61	
1951	0.0884	0.0884					1669	30	1	32	1606	1526	59	84	
1952	0.1795	0.1780	0.0015				1683	44	1	42	1596	1511	74	98	33.16
1953	0.2476	0.2385	0.0091				1728	64	2	41	1621	1463	131	134	
1954	0.4683	0.3869	0.0814				1735	68	7	37	1623	1454	149	132	
1955	0.4656	0.3566	0.1090				1764	75	16	19	1654	1460	178	126	
1956	0.6687	0.5110	0.1577				1813	99	19	0	1695	1476	198	139	
1957	1.0497	0.6977	0.3520				1829	108	15	4	1702	1577	111	141	31.77
1958	1.6448	1.0427	0.6021				2003	237	25		1741	1124	374	505	
1959	2.1555	1.3533	0.8022				2001	216	32	0	1753	1142	317	542	
1960	2.3200	1.5109	0.8091				1997	240	15	2	1740	1346	185	466	
1961	1.9447	1.2352	0.7095				1919	177	16	4	1722	1559	102	258	
1962	1.3375	9.9554	0.3821				2021	143	39	11	1828	1699	82	240	65.29
1963	1.4569	1.0791	0.3778				2066	146	47	13	1860	1735	83	248	
1964	1.7309	1.3437	0.3872				2082	151	48	13	1870	1742	90	250	
1965	1.9526	1.5337	0.4189				2172	155	50	9	1958	1798	91	283	72.26
1966	2.2683	1.7315	0.5368				2241	159	52	3	2027	1874	96	271	
1967	2.5702	1.9203	0.6499				2243	162	52		2029	1876	96	271	
1968	3.0463	2.2451	0.8012				2297	164	37		2096	1880	101	316	
1969	3.0764	2.3329	0.7435				2389	180	35		2174	2012	118	259	
1970	3.1513	2.3994	0.7519				2481	211	41		2229	2039	150	292	132.00
1971	3.6081	2.7660	0.8421				2526	227	48		2251	2087	169	270	
1972	4.2418	3.2362	1.0056				2570	248	50		2272	2130	182	258	
1973	5.2769	3.6805	1.5964				2602	251	49		2302	2174	192	236	
1974	6.2419	4.2675	1.9744				2668	264	55		2349	2219	210	239	
1975	6.8368	4.5277	2.3091		17.30		2689	270	58	1	2360	2282	230	177	200.29
1976	7.6045	4.9031	2.7014		5.69		2712	284	64	0	2364	2246	258	208	
1977	8.6435	5.3943	3.2492		17.25	10.4	2706	297	71	1	2337	2211	280	215	
1978	9.8071	6.2363	3.5708		23.21	12.4	2807	346	74	3	2384	2267	296	244	259.11
1979	12.9657	8.3233	4.6424		28.90	18.0	2873	363	78	3	2429	2371	290	212	252.82
1980	19.4361	11.8343	7.6018		31.92	15.0	2929	379	83	7	2460	2383	304	242	259.97
1981	26.9040	15.5356	11.3684		32.83	13.7	3039	407	90	11	2531	2475	310	254	267.16
1982	32.8477	19.4907	13.3570		33.27	12.6	3146	407	95	14	2630	2535	315	296	263.99
1983	45.5821	25.9354	19.6467		38.02	13.7	3289	425	99	18	2747	2603	341	345	272.76
1984	64.3509	36.3717	27.9792		42.58	14.0	3346	419	129	26	2772	2583	376	387	286.64
1985	84.2280	49.5574	34.6706		51.66	14.3	3520	454	139	34	2893	2576	523	421	398.81
1986	114.9544	69.6292	45.3252		53.71	12.9	3598	469	149	31	2949	2579	568	451	429.19
1987	167.8777	103.9098	63.9679		62.99	13.2	3782	488	156	41	3096	2601	616	565	457.26
1988	207.0459	135.1654	71.8805		73.90	13.6	3916	508	161	34	3212	2654	659	603	484.59
1989	271.3000	188.6000	82.8000		80.61	15.8	4001	512	168	36	3226	2724	659	560	

16. Henan

16–7

Year	v5c1	v5d	v6a	v6a1	v6a2	v6b	v6c	v6d1	v6d2	v6d3	v6d4	v6d5	v6d6
1949		1504.38	4174	265	3909			308	3866	2153	2021	15.92	28.16
1950			4282					273	4009	2186	2096		
1951			4342					263	4079	2215	2127		
1952		1510.51	4371					238	4133	2238	2133	45.58	23.48
1953			4425					300	4125	2256	2169		
1954			4560	346	4214	41.49	13.32	346	4214	2328	2232		
1955			4652	373	4279	30.79	11.75	373	4279	2373	2279		
1956			4733	374	4359	35.85	14.00	311	4422	2414	2319		
1957		1576.66	4840	445	4395	33.67	11.80	344	4496	2469	2371	76.64	27.76
1958			4943	456	4487	33.15	12.69	456	4487	2540	2403	83.36	29.90
1959			4979	504	4475	28.06	14.10	504	4475	2546	2433		
1960			4818	532	4286	13.98	39.56	532	4286	2439	2379		
1961			4803	493	4310	15.25	10.20	410	4393	2407	2396	99.52	39.72
1962		1699.51	4940	476	4464	37.50	8.04	369	4571	2485	2455	97.86	38.82
1963			5036	466	4570	45.08	9.43	387	4649	2540	2496	103.12	41.03
1964			5099			35.84	10.61	413	4686	2579	2520	98.95	41.48
1965		1797.56	5240			36.10	8.45	426	4814	2648	2592	102.24	41.78
1966			5386			36.04	8.24	428	4958	2722	2664		
1967			5507			30.81	8.59	429	5078	2791	2716		
1968			5665			36.20	7.91	426	5239	2872	2793		
1969			5860			40.95	7.11	426	5434	2971	2889		
1970		2038.71	6026			35.54	7.61	452	5574	3055	2971	106.69	43.70
1971			6195			33.50	7.46	518	5677	3140	3055		
1972			6344			32.21	7.17	502	5842	3223	3121		
1973			6517			31.47	7.27	514	6003	3305	3212		
1974			6647			28.02	7.44	519	6128	3373	3274		
1975		2281.82	6758			23.66	7.66	525	6233	3436	3322	117.87	52.96
1976			6852			21.74	7.18	536	6316	3488	3364		
1977			6957			21.41	7.04	546	6411	3544	3413		
1978		2267.02	7067			21.93	6.30	570	6497	3599	3468	125.56	53.52
1979		2311.74	7189			21.51	6.35	635	6554	3662	3527		
1980		2382.96	7285			20.00	6.31	677	6608	3710	3575	133.74	56.57
1981		2474.55	7397			20.64	6.57	713	6684	3768	3629		
1982		2531.92	7519			20.62	6.21	747	6772	3835	3684		
1983		2603.30	7591			17.43	5.87	773	6818	3881	3710		
1984		2583.12	7668			15.71	5.60	832	6836	3925	3743		
1985		2576.62	7746			16.91	6.21	901	6845	3970	3776	158.72	62.91
1986		2579.56	7848			19.69	6.55	916	6932	4027	3821	161.05	63.60
1987		2601.44	7969			21.80	6.50	963	7006	4092	3877	158.15	64.78
1988		2654.03	8094			21.52	5.93	1016	7078	4158	3936	162.99	66.16
1989			8231			24.25	6.24	1065	7166	4231	4000	166.23	67.90

16. Henan

16–8

Year	v7a	v7b	v7c	v7d	v7e	v7f	v7g	v7h	v7h1	v7h2	v7h3	v7h4	v7h5	v7i	v8a
1949				17089				17.19	13.67		1.86	0.01	1.65	459.0	2.98
1950				18886				19.94	15.59	0.01	2.02	0.01	2.31	481.0	4.33
1951				19987				27.44	21.26	0.02	2.46	0.05	3.65	520.0	6.25
1952				20832				27.74	21.04	0.03	3.16	0.04	3.47	561.0	9.98
1953				21515				31.54	24.06	0.03	3.88	0.04	3.53	562.0	11.90
1954				21901				33.57	26.00	0.05	3.83	0.04	3.65	631.6	13.65
1955				21779				36.02	29.19	0.09	2.98	0.04	3.72	605.2	14.45
1956				21916				34.61	28.08	0.14	2.89	0.04	3.46	564.3	16.11
1957	0.33	199	1950	21126		13.0		31.57	25.52	0.20	3.38	0.07	2.40	489.4	16.63
1958				19505				33.78	30.19	0.26	2.01	0.08	1.24	446.0	33.17
1959				18199				32.46	28.74	0.26	2.01	0.10	1.35	405.0	50.16
1960				19096				28.94	25.79	0.18	1.55	0.09	1.33	364.0	58.41
1961				17551				24.81	22.18	0.11	1.72	0.09	0.71	321.0	31.20
1962	3.68	1003	1453	17631		8.0	0.52	28.13	23.96	0.16	3.22	0.07	0.72	334.0	23.93
1963				17504				25.33	21.19	0.29	3.19	0.08	0.58	335.1	26.65
1964				17859				32.20	27.44	0.26	3.24	0.09	1.17	336.6	32.27
1965	5.22	2044	1799	17146		33.6	1.63	42.17	33.47	0.35	4.84	0.11	3.40	341.7	42.24
1966				16948				49.65	39.49	0.72	5.74	0.09	3.61	364.2	49.30
1967				16667				58.02	47.38	0.74	6.01	0.11	3.78	396.0	46.15
1968				16244				54.95	43.91	0.75	6.21	0.10	3.98	423.0	42.37
1969				16272				57.73	46.05	0.74	6.58	0.12	4.24	421.0	54.25
1970	18.96	3205	3780	16136		86.7	11.70	67.18	53.09	1.79	8.07	0.06	4.17	425.0	73.68
1971				16175				71.21	56.25	2.68	7.87	0.09	4.32	429.0	91.54
1972				16289				72.50	57.22	2.35	9.30	0.11	3.52	432.5	100.75
1973				16433				83.31	68.09	1.70	9.70	0.15	3.67	432.1	106.07
1974				16322				83.21	67.76	1.79	9.42	0.16	4.08	434.0	115.62
1975	71.48	4538	5367	16302		192.2	11.74	85.98	70.20	2.49	8.99	0.15	4.15	428.0	130.46
1976				16241				87.17	73.76	2.63	9.15	0.15	1.48	421.2	107.99
1977				16151				82.70	69.59	1.61	9.87	0.15	1.48	405.6	161.69
1978	97.44	4608	5584	16450		291.8	13.25	95.38	79.74	2.58	10.87	0.19	2.00	401.7	170.82
1979	107.97	5090	5454	16376		333.6	14.60	113.48	94.64	2.16	14.18	0.23	2.27	400.4	193.49
1980	117.80	4985	5304	16182		386.2	17.23	134.62	107.97	3.88	17.20	0.29	5.28	424.0	209.23
1981	126.21	3848	5082	16520		502.0	20.85	151.24	122.83	3.70	16.66	0.28	7.77	499.0	223.50
1982	135.63	3549	4898	16614	3100	541.5	22.76	151.06	117.16	3.75	18.25	0.35	11.55	541.0	246.28
1983	140.59	3674	4815	16990	1315	610.8	23.50	187.02	155.68	4.09	17.57	0.44	9.24	562.2	268.14
1984	150.70	3574	4918	17149	1894	661.5	25.83	208.68	165.06	6.88	24.78	0.63	11.33	615.7	307.58
1985	156.99	3747	4785	17528	2415	662.7	28.33	241.54	175.49	10.29	41.16	1.27	13.33	664.6	401.32
1986	173.79	4148	4819	17729	4320	677.5	33.30	259.49	183.65	12.92	42.12	1.50	19.30	708.1	478.09
1987	186.59	4760	4875	17929	1665	637.4	37.29	323.62	229.74	13.24	51.11	1.91	27.62	738.4	594.64
1988	200.42	5519	5038	17895	4755	724.5	40.81	370.67	239.90	17.25	79.66	2.73	31.13	779.6	779.90
1989	215.35	6166	5153	17999		856.0	45.20	449.88	302.22	19.80	90.39	2.87	34.60	794.0	953.56

16. Henan

16–9

Year	v8a1	v8a2	v8a3	v8b	v8c1	v8c2	v8d	v8f1	v8f2	v8f3	v8f4	v8f5	v8g
1949	0.25	0.65	0.37		0.49	2.49			90		0.05		2646
1950	0.55	0.73	0.59		0.80	3.53			152		0.12		2690
1951	1.12	0.85	0.79		1.22	5.03			223		0.21		3482
1952	2.40	1.25	1.24		1.83	8.15			330		0.40		4246
1953	3.23	1.63	1.52		2.25	9.65			379		0.59		4824
1954	4.60	2.23	1.57		2.89	10.76			431		1.09		6665
1955	5.77	2.89	1.43		3.38	11.11			478		1.47		8351
1956	8.44	4.39	1.60		4.59	11.52			533		2.38		4705
1957	7.50	4.80	2.07		4.72	11.91			607		3.04		4561
1958	27.89	5.28			13.70	19.47		3.17	1733		5.89	5	22442
1959	40.86	9.30			23.41	26.75		5.14	2700		12.34	47	15429
1960	48.73	9.68			31.40	27.01		15.25	3531		20.35	70	10698
1961	26.13	5.07			15.49	15.71		6.20	2240		17.01	18	7173
1962	19.51	4.29			10.83	13.10		3.90	1654		14.78	6	5927
1963	22.37	4.18			12.04	14.61		3.98	1689		14.95	10	5621
1964	27.72	4.45			14.22	18.05		5.94	1661		17.60	33	5639
1965	36.86	5.38			18.70	23.54		11.34	1903		23.47	45	5341
1966	42.12	7.18			23.02	26.28		15.73	2225		31.17	66	5492
1967	38.39	7.76			21.37	24.78		12.65	1837		31.66	63	5434
1968	34.94	7.43			17.43	24.94		7.90	1917		27.94	47	5757
1969	45.57	8.68			24.22	30.03		13.58	2509		39.15	86	5918
1970	63.71	9.97			39.00	34.68		22.21	3091		48.78	117	7576
1971	78.32	13.22			53.80	37.74		25.94	3441		56.80	146	8185
1972	84.82	15.93			55.55	45.20		29.99	3652		62.91	167	7895
1973	87.19	18.88			56.62	49.45		29.09	3625		66.18	175	8340
1974	92.83	22.79			61.84	53.78		34.59	3906		75.39	230	9154
1975	101.04	29.42			69.36	61.10	28.72	43.59	4471		80.47	272	10880
1976	73.43	34.56			53.98	54.01		14.79	3922	3.25	78.46	226	12668
1977	113.85	47.84		109.05	85.68	76.01	30.26	42.24	5371	11.03	108.73	354	14191
1978	126.48	44.34		123.38	92.17	78.65	38.04	54.22	5845	167.44	130.68	353	14677
1979	146.41	47.08		142.21	102.32	91.17	44.99	59.18	5838	225.72	145.50	367	14958
1980	155.97	53.20	0.01	150.68	102.32	106.91	50.79	64.50	5625	230.89	159.45	406	15858
1981	168.32	55.05	0.04	160.16	99.73	123.77	52.69	55.78	5825	369.23	171.17	447	15893
1982	184.82	61.24	0.06	177.06	115.92	130.36	55.09	63.88	5968	448.32	177.97	484	16429
1983	198.85	68.95	0.08	187.77	134.02	134.12	61.07	77.08	6402	541.21	187.88	574	16776
1984	219.24	87.72	0.10	211.19	157.57	150.01	69.18	86.68	6934	639.59	198.72	667	17274
1985	263.90	123.05	0.29	263.43	208.26	193.06	87.49	97.26	7857	793.31	209.34	765	17626
1986	293.19	154.13	0.47	287.88	254.49	223.60	95.42	103.99	7949	880.78	231.63	905	18996
1987	351.13	192.67	0.85	344.93	317.78	276.86	114.16	118.09	8062	932.04	259.33	1001	19338
1988	446.28	259.81	1.52	437.69	417.93	361.97	139.00	138.95	8245	979.07	286.57	1164	19464
1989	536.79	324.75	2.81	524.58	517.95	435.61	152.83	159.00	8858	953.19	302.82	1153	20220

16. Henan

16–10

Year	v8g1	v9a	v9a1	v9a2	v9a3	v9b	v9b1	v9b2	v9b3	v9c	v10a	v10a1	v10b1	v10b2	v10b3
1949		6.46	6.45	0.01		16.53	16.00	0.21	0.32	161	4.82	4.58	0.20		0.03
1950		14.79	14.62	0.17		17.86	17.14	0.32	0.40	312	7.06	6.64			
1951		19.19	19.00	0.19		26.86	25.47	0.46	0.93	383	9.33	8.68			
1952		15.62	15.26	0.36		39.12	36.56	0.88	1.68	502	11.64	10.84	2.13		1.85
1953		19.67	18.85	0.82		49.11	46.41	1.18	1.52	646	15.10	13.98	2.75		3.79
1954		21.30	20.35	0.95		59.71	56.21	1.45	2.05	793	17.25	15.57	2.92		8.06
1955		22.98	21.80	1.17	0.01	71.79	67.42	1.97	2.40	908	18.14	16.29	5.81		6.30
1956		32.02	29.82	2.17	0.03	101.20	95.55	2.88	2.77	1139	21.95	18.92	7.59		11.90
1957		33.23	30.85	2.33	0.05	112.68	106.68	3.13	2.87	1193	20.71	18.03	8.17		10.38
1958		37.74	33.67	4.00	0.07	154.85	145.39	5.91	3.55	1648	28.30	22.42			
1959		47.48	41.81	5.62	0.05	207.12	190.89	12.32	3.91	2446	35.58	27.56			
1960		59.38	52.84	6.48	0.06	242.09	225.00	13.08	4.01	3011	35.19	27.09			
1961		85.81	78.72	7.03	0.06	164.80	156.42	5.86	2.52	2392	31.74	25.94			
1962		90.02	82.01	7.98	0.03	131.21	125.02	4.08	2.11	2084	31.02	26.02	14.26		14.38
1963		48.07	41.01	7.05	0.01	139.65	132.71	4.67	2.27	2102	30.84	25.88			
1964		45.66	38.43	7.21	0.01	165.83	157.75	5.38	2.70	2222	34.28	29.45			
1965		46.46	37.79	8.65	0.02	227.88	219.56	6.07	2.25	2300	32.04	26.96	16.55		13.92
1966		51.14	39.89	11.24	0.01	263.05	254.16	7.44	1.45	3167	34.85	27.96			
1967		62.42	50.05	12.36	0.01	192.85	184.22	6.98	1.65	3043	37.58	30.84			
1968		73.06	59.31	13.74	0.01	169.02	161.51	6.03	1.48	2985	35.70	28.77			
1969		81.53	66.57	14.90	0.06	245.14	236.88	7.00	1.25	3193	41.58	33.00			
1970		80.54	64.74	15.66	0.14	332.55	322.03	8.74	1.78	3502	47.84	36.39	25.08		21.49
1971		84.87	68.64	16.13	0.10	354.20	343.26	9.32	1.62	3757	53.37	40.50			
1972		94.59	76.87	17.56	0.16	363.83	351.53	10.64	1.66	4082	60.79	46.25			
1973	2437	99.83	80.13	19.54	0.15	376.22	363.34	11.20	1.68	4410	66.52	49.82			
1974	2513	103.77	82.57	21.06	0.14	368.64	353.87	13.06	1.71	4545	71.63	53.97			
1975	2682	105.23	82.18	22.90	0.15	390.80	372.67	16.29	1.84	4902	80.71	58.78	45.84		32.43
1976	2875	107.14	83.31	23.71	0.12	343.13	324.15	17.11	1.87	5061	83.72	62.79			
1977	3037	115.36	87.21	28.02	0.13	447.97	423.19	22.77	2.01	5321	90.64	68.76			
1978	3068	123.22	92.62	30.47	0.13	508.53	484.91	21.57	2.05	5450	94.90	71.79	50.02		43.41
1979	3054	140.25	105.73	34.37	0.15	528.92	507.48	19.77	1.67	7540	105.25	80.44	53.64		48.51
1980	3070	163.98	122.40	41.35	0.23	547.65	525.31	21.01	1.33	8062	121.93	96.04	59.91		56.63
1981	3093	176.99	126.76	49.98	0.25	563.45	537.75	24.45	1.25	8390	134.97	106.86	62.39		63.64
1982	3148	195.70	135.60	59.87	0.23	617.77	578.55	37.41	1.81	8666	143.96	113.83	64.03		66.17
1983	3105	226.31	155.09	70.96	0.26	674.22	424.37	47.86	1.99	9024	156.56	123.05	68.51		66.03
1984	3113	253.11	171.10	81.71	0.30	702.70	643.53	55.88	3.29	9647	187.05	146.85	79.96		76.57
1985	3384	323.50	209.77	113.36	0.37	838.22	728.25	105.72	4.25	11057	220.49	180.59	86.86		88.56
1986	3390	358.20	228.54	129.34	0.32	881.90	777.12	99.73	5.05	11977	242.16	198.32	95.39		93.52
1987	3446	400.06	249.01	150.75	0.30	1020.81	880.94	133.83	6.04	14675	278.49	225.28	110.82		105.42
1988	3468	484.77	290.16	194.24	0.37	1079.26	932.37	139.64	7.25	18349	351.61	283.25	139.63		130.40
1989	3482	488.56	280.00	208.16	0.40	1157.63	1007.00	154.10	7.93	22805	391.35	310.91	159.64		140.86

16. Henan

Year	v10b4	v10b5	v10b6	v10d	v11a1	v11a2	v11a3	v11b	v11b1	v11b2	v11c	v11d	v12a	v12b	v12c
1949		4.15	0.43	4.00											
1950			0.63	5.65											
1951			0.70	7.77											114.0
1952	0.06	6.95	0.65	8.29											93.4
1953	0.03	7.98	0.55	9.15											110.8
1954	0.45	5.34	0.48	11.98											103.3
1955	1.71	3.84	0.48	12.28											102.0
1956	1.37	0.71	0.38	11.72	0.1201			0.1201	0.1201						100.3
1957	1.47	0.37	0.32	13.51	0.1387			0.1387	0.1387				101.6		104.3
1958			0.18	16.77	0.1550			0.1550	0.1550				98.6	98.0	101.0
1959			0.08	21.43	0.2393	0.1565	0.0075	0.4033	0.4033				100.8	100.9	101.3
1960			0.19	15.33	0.1391	0.2209	0.0067	0.3667	0.3667				100.9	102.0	102.0
1961			1.80	11.95	0.0401	0.0470	0.0260	0.1131	0.1131				118.9	128.5	145.6
1962		0.62	1.76	11.53	0.0484	0.0459	0.0366	0.1309	0.1309				93.5	86.1	72.3
1963			0.97	11.45	0.0705	0.0416	0.0252	0.1373	0.1373				85.7	86.5	99.3
1964			0.87	11.67	0.1148	0.0410	0.0044	0.1602	0.1602				96.1	96.2	98.2
1965		0.79	0.77	14.24	0.1454	0.0280	0.0180	0.1914	0.1914				95.7	96.3	98.3
1966			0.88	18.29	0.1658	0.0654	0.0575	0.2887	0.2887				98.9	98.6	103.4
1967			1.09	19.34	0.1466	0.0744	0.0100	0.2310	0.2310				99.7	100.8	100.9
1968			1.14	17.93	0.1820	0.0754	0.0281	0.2855	0.2855				99.9	100.0	100.3
1969			1.09	16.98	0.2376	0.0785	0.0195	0.3356	0.3356				99.6	100.0	99.9
1970		0.27	1.00	21.84	0.2282	0.0804	0.0242	0.3328	0.3328				99.1	99.8	100.1
1971			1.05	21.87	0.2286	0.0846	0.0639	0.3771	0.3771				99.3	99.9	101.1
1972			1.07	24.33	0.2610	0.0769	0.0964	0.4343	0.4343				99.5	100.0	101.6
1973			1.23	29.91	0.4237	0.0782	0.0606	0.5625	0.5625				99.9	100.1	104.8
1974			1.28	29.08	0.5193	0.1077	0.0748	0.7018	0.7018				100.1	100.1	97.0
1975		0.19	2.25	30.30	0.4005	0.1024	0.0409	0.5438	0.5438				100.1	100.2	101.6
1976			2.31	30.89	0.4151	0.1058	0.0180	0.5389	0.5389				100.3	100.3	100.6
1977			0.97	31.49	0.5320	0.1947	0.0193	0.7460	0.7460				100.2	99.9	100.6
1978		0.17	1.30	34.02	0.6689	0.3144	0.0398	1.0231	1.0231				99.5	100.0	104.8
1979		0.85	2.25	39.86	0.7574	0.5244	0.0604	1.3422	1.3422				100.4	100.3	121.6
1980		1.95	3.44	55.79	1.0481	0.7872	0.2095	2.0448	2.0448				104.3	106.0	107.1
1981		4.78	4.16	64.05	1.3093	0.9768	0.2087	2.4948	2.4948				101.6	102.4	105.5
1982		8.74	5.02	61.32	1.1432	0.9539	0.3500	2.5471	2.5471				101.5	101.8	99.5
1983		15.72	6.30	81.84	1.3192	1.1311	0.3460	2.7963	2.7963				102.3	102.9	108.8
1984	0.05	22.91	7.56	95.64	1.2435	1.6449	0.5290	3.4174	3.4174		0.1003	0.0736	102.1	102.2	103.7
1985	0.10	34.02	10.95	107.38	1.4517	1.6342	0.5851	4.4991	3.6710	0.8281	0.7534	0.1208	104.9	106.5	103.1
1986	0.34	39.50	13.41	112.16	1.7180	2.1444	0.6639	5.0671	4.5263	0.3408	0.9308	0.5141	105.0	106.8	104.6
1987	0.35	46.41	15.49	137.02	1.9699	3.5918	0.9817	7.4732	6.5434	0.9298	1.3066	0.2868	108.1	107.8	103.7
1988	0.14	61.37	20.07	156.13	2.4554	3.8803	1.1532	8.4961	7.5052	0.9099	1.3128	0.6486	120.2	121.5	123.6
1989	0.08	65.56	25.21	184.38				9.8539	8.1897	1.6642	2.5122	0.5900	118.3	114.9	118.1

16. Henan

16–12

Year	v13a	v13b	v13c1	v13c2	v13c3	v13d	v14a	v14b	v14c	v15a	v15b	v15c	v15d	v15e	v15f
1949		22.02	0.08	4.93	161.45	0.00	935	732	0.11	11017					
1950	8.6							364		12320					
1951	7.1							729		13021					
1952	9.0	55.80	0.26	17.04	433.36	0.01	5317	16281	0.52	13434					
1953	30.4							28083		13574					
1954	25.0							27228		13593					
1955	26.2							36043		13562					
1956	21.7							65503		13475					
1957	24.5	62.40	0.96	55.07	493.37	0.09	11437	69052	0.77	13306					
1958	8.4							90128		12397					
1959	7.8							108548		12045					
1960	8.6							111659		12008					
1961	12.3							109767		11631					
1962	19.3	58.40	2.16	40.56	471.88	0.43	38440	97237	1.00	11668					
1963	15.3							97810		11633					
1964	10.3									11651					
1965	14.5	88.80	1.40	79.97	820.95	0.42	41921	98853	0.12	11657					
1966	15.7							96551		11516					
1967	18.3							98598		11453					
1968	18.3							91571		11446					
1969	11.9							78583		11392					
1970	9.9			155.16	824.76	0.37	60197	102644		11168					
1971	12.1									11181					
1972	13.4							81459		11142					
1973	13.6							84119		11079					
1974	13.8							90288		10980					
1975	13.1	97.50	1.80	317.76	1179.70	0.40	83862	96742	1.48	10884					
1976	12.5							107394		10824					
1977	13.7							109177		10759					
1978	12.7	96.50	2.73	625.01	1140.26	0.96	97318	114350	1.82	10736					
1979	14.7	95.50	3.38	510.68	1147.88	0.41	106293	128927	5.16	10708					
1980	19.6	94.90	4.59	494.76	1133.75		111720	144812	5.19	10692					
1981	21.0	93.50	4.93	418.91	1110.65	0.90	116482	163190	5.89	10682					
1982	20.4	93.20	4.62	369.03	1098.47	1.65	121061	173391	5.99	10664					
1983	20.7	94.80	4.80	352.62	1054.04	1.47	127379	183790	7.13	10651	2448.0		447		
1984	19.3	95.00	5.34	369.59	1055.08	1.35	131302	191177	10.04	10619	2129.8		447		
1985	17.1	96.90	6.85	376.74	1034.97	1.17	137743	194920	12.86	10550	2500.0		447	193.01	10.69
1986	13.8	97.30	7.50	388.61	1015.67	1.75	139880	201470	9.29	10498	2500.0		484	193.60	10.68
1987	15.5	97.50	7.57	395.81	997.75	2.53	154159	204369	12.64	10459	2500.0	414	484	195.60	10.67
1988	15.7	96.50	7.99	387.01	980.05	2.29	159509	213587	12.96	10435	2400.0		484	195.06	10.66
1989		98.00	8.01	361.80	969.80	2.56	162500	218000	11.02	10417					

Notes

1. National Output and Income (Y)

v1a: (E), p.529
- v1a1: (E), p.529
- v1a2: (E), p.529
- v1a3: (E), p.529
- v1a4: (E), p.529
- v1a5: (E), p.529

v1b: (A); (D), p.282
- v1b1: (A); (D), p.282
- v1b2: (A); (D), p.282
- v1b3: (A); (D), p.282
- v1b4: (A); (D), p.282
- v1b5: (A); (D), p.282

v1c: v1a – v1d

v1d: (E), p.526
- v1d1: (E), p.526
- v1d2: (E), p.526
- v1d3: (E), p.526
- v1d4: (E), p.526
- v1d5: (E), p.526

v1e: (A); (D), p.285
- v1e1: (A); (D), p.285
- v1e2: (A); (D), p.285
- v1e3: (A); (D), p.285
- v1e4: (A); (D), p.285
- v1e5: (A); (D), p.285

v1f: (E), p.525
- v1f1: (E), p.525
- v1f2: (E), p.525
- v1f3: (E), p.525

v1g: (E), p.528

v1h: (A); (E), p.544

v1i: (E), p.553

v1j: (E), p.553
- v1j1: (E), p.553
- v1j2: (E), p.553
- v1j3: NA

v1k: (E), p.553

2. Investment (I)

v2a: (E), p.528
- v2a1: (B), p.344
- v2a2: (B), p.344

v2b: (A)

v2c: (A); (E), p.543
- v2c1: (E), p.544
- v2c2: (E), p.544

v2d:
- v2d1: (E), p.541
- v2d2: (E), p.541

v2e: (E), p.541

3. Consumption (C)

v3a: (E), p.528

v3b: (E), p.528
- v3b1: (A); (D), p.286
- v3b2: (A); (D), p.286

v3c: (E), p.528

v3d: (E), p.552
- v3d1: (E), p.552
- v3d2: (E), p.552

v3e: (E), p.554
- v3e1: (E), p.554
- v3e2: (A)
- v3e3: (A)
- v3e4: (A)

v3f: (A); (E), p.554
- v3f1: (A); (E), p.554

v3f2: (A)
v3f3: (A)
v3f4: (A)

4. Public Finance and Banking (FB)

v4a:
v4a1: (E), p.550
v4a1a: (E), p.550—1950: 0.0028
v4a1b: (B), p.444
v4a1c: (B), p.444
v4a1d: (B), p.444
v4a2: (E), p.550
v4a2a: (E), p.550
v4a2b: (E), p.550
v4a2c: (E), p.550
v4a2d: v4a2 – v4a2a – v4a2b – v4a2c

v4b: (A)
v4b1: (B), p.455
v4b2: (B), p.455—rural residents' savings
v4b3: NA

v4c:
v4c1: (E), p.541
v4c2: (E), p.541

5. Labor Force (L)

v5a: (A); (E), p.524
v5a1: (E), p.524
v5a2: (E), p.524
v5a3: (B), p.348—1959: 0.20, 1976: 0.47, 1977: 0.49; (E), p.524
v5a4: (E), p.524—excluding rural people working outside in 1989

v5b:
v5b1: (E), p.524
v5b2: (E), p.524
v5b3: (E), p.524

v5c: (B), p.356
v5c1: NA

v5d: (B), p.356—farming, forestry, embankment services, weather forecast

6. Population (PO)

v6a: (E), p.523—figures of 1984 and after from sample survey
v6a1: (E), p.523
v6a2: (E), p.523

v6b: (A); (E), p.523

v6c: (A); (E), p.523

v6d:
v6d1: (E), p.523—data from public security department
v6d2: (E), p.523
v6d3: (E), p.523
v6d4: (E), p.523
v6d5: (A)—Zhengzhou
v6d6: (A)—Kaifeng

7. Agriculture (A)

v7a: (A); (E), p.536

v7b: (A); (E), p.536

v7c: (A); (E), p.536

v7d: (A); (E), p.536

v7e: (A)

v7f: (A); (E), p.536

v7g: (A)

v7h: (E), p.531
v7h1: (E), p.531
v7h2: (E), p.531
v7h3: (E), p.531
v7h4: (E), p.531
v7h5: (E), p.531

v7i: (A)

8. Industry (IN)

v8a: (E), p.537
- v8a1: (E), p.537
- v8a2: (E), p.537
- v8a3: (A); (B), p.382

v8b: (E), p.541

- v8c1: (E), p.529
- v8c2: (E), p.529

v8d: (E), p.541

v8f:
- v8f1: (E), p.540
- v8f2: (E), p.540
- v8f3: (A)
- v8f4: (E), p.540
- v8f5: (E), p.540

v8g: (A)
- v8g1: (E), p.541

9. Transport (TR)

v9a: (E), p.542—excluding urban traffic volume
- v9a1: (E), p.542—including central and local railways
- v9a2: (A); (E), p.542
- v9a3: (E), p.542 – excluding distant ocean and coastal passenger traffic

v9b: (E), p.542
- v9b1: (E), p.542—including central and local railways
- v9b2: (E), p.542
- v9b3: (E), p.542—excluding distant ocean and coastal freight volume

v9c: (E), p.542

10. Domestic Trade (DT)

v10a: (E), p.545
- v10a1: (E), p.545

v10b:
- v10b1: (E), p.545
- v10b2: NA
- v10b3: (E), p.545—including supply and marketing cooperative and other collectives
- v10b4: (E), p.545
- v10b5: (E), p.545
- v10b6: (E), p.545

v10d: (E), p.547

11. Foreign Trade (FT)

v11a:
- v11a1: (B), p.411—oil and food products, local livestock products
- v11a2: (B), p.411—light industrial products, textile and silk cloth
- v11a3: (B), p.411—chemical and medical products, minerals and machinery

v11b: (E), p.548—data from foreign trade department
- v11b1: (E), p.548—(ditto)
- v11b2: v11b – v11b1

v11c: (E), p.549

v11d: (A); (E), p.549

12. Prices (PR)

v12a: (E), p.551

v12b: (E), p.551

v12c: (E), p.551

13. Education (ED)

v13a: (A)

v13b: (A); (E), p.554

v13c:

v13c1: (A); (E), p.554—general institutions of higher learning

v13c2: (A); (E), p.554

v13c3: (A); (E), p.554

v13d: (A)—general institutions of higher learning, 1949: 0.001

14. Social Factors (SF)

v14a: (E), p.554

v14b: (A); (E), p.554

v14c: (A)

15. Natural Environment (NE)

v15a: (A); (E), p.536

v15b: (A)

v15c: (A)

v15d: (A)

v15e: (A)

v15f: (A)

Sources of Data

(A) Data supplied by the DSNEB, SSB, the PRC.

(B) Statistical Bureau of Henan Province ed. *Striving and Advancing Zhongzhou (Henan) 1949–1989*, Beijing: CSPH, 1989.

(D) Same as (D) in Beijing's sources of data.

(E) Same as (E) in Beijing's sources of data.

17

Hubei

17. Hubei

17–1

Year	v1a	v1a1	v1a2	v1a3	v1a4	v1a5	v1b	v1b1	v1b2	v1b3	v1b4	v1b5	v1c	v1d	v1d1
1949		10.72													
1950		12.05													
1951		15.01													
1952	35.65	16.59	9.99	1.50	0.55	7.02	120.1	108.4	122.4	141.4	167.4	146.0	12.89	22.76	13.64
1953	44.69	19.64	13.60	2.30	0.82	8.33	114.4	107.7	132.0	88.2	143.8	114.6	16.73	27.96	16.10
1954	39.27	16.13	14.69	2.10	1.12	5.23	88.7	82.7	112.2	110.4	136.7	61.6	16.33	22.94	12.73
1955	48.42	21.57	16.26	3.04	1.47	6.08	121.5	129.6	111.0	126.0	129.7	115.2	17.97	30.45	17.80
1956	62.84	26.13	20.66	5.13	1.56	9.36	127.7	115.1	135.2	164.4	106.0	151.8	22.63	40.21	21.87
1957	70.32	28.59	24.31	6.24	1.72	9.45	106.6	106.8	112.5	119.0	109.8	88.6	26.36	43.96	23.88
1958	94.71	31.80	34.93	15.40	2.36	10.22	129.5	107.3	141.8	242.2	137.6	105.9	39.48	55.23	26.30
1959	104.29	29.29	49.57	12.26	3.05	10.12	107.7	87.2	139.3	77.9	130.6	98.1	48.25	56.04	24.31
1960	115.27	26.97	59.92	16.41	3.22	8.75	108.0	86.0	120.4	143.9	104.5	80.7	59.94	55.33	23.16
1961	77.08	29.28	33.55	5.04	2.15	7.06	61.3	95.8	95.3	24.7	66.8	72.0	34.97	42.11	25.38
1962	82.22	33.66	34.83	3.31	2.60	7.82	104.7	113.0	99.7	65.8	120.9	107.3	36.52	45.70	28.75
1963	92.83	39.19	39.19	4.55	2.04	7.86	109.1	116.2	113.1	139.2	39.3	106.1	42.72	50.11	31.65
1964	100.68	39.87	44.85	5.51	2.30	8.15	111.0	103.4	118.5	116.2	112.6	106.1	46.17	54.51	31.61
1965	118.92	47.48	52.90	6.60	3.26	8.68	118.7	115.7	123.0	144.8	141.9	86.3	54.04	64.88	37.04
1966	146.72	60.68	66.71	7.66	2.74	8.93	115.1	108.3	120.4	119.2	78.4	132.3	70.66	76.06	44.92
1967	137.14	57.08	60.95	7.40	2.52	9.19	93.0	93.1	91.4	96.3	90.7	99.7	66.36	70.78	42.84
1968	117.11	55.38	45.81	5.63	2.34	7.95	84.0	97.1	75.2	74.7	93.0	86.1	52.26	64.85	42.06
1969	131.24	51.78	59.46	7.43	2.71	9.86	113.5	89.8	129.8	134.4	115.9	130.6	64.43	66.81	38.78
1970	172.54	51.27	86.27	20.23	4.51	10.26	142.9	105.7	145.9	317.1	172.1	99.8	94.65	77.89	43.58
1971	193.95	60.65	95.31	22.85	3.70	11.53	111.7	105.3	122.4	104.1	80.7	111.8	105.65	88.30	44.56
1972	195.76	63.62	96.97	19.60	4.07	11.50	103.2	102.8	108.1	84.9	107.4	99.7	102.84	92.92	46.57
1973	217.71	72.13	110.92	18.00	4.21	12.45	109.9	110.1	114.4	86.6	104.3	108.2	115.78	101.93	51.57
1974	212.25	76.67	100.78	18.21	3.83	12.76	96.2	105.7	90.9	100.1	93.4	103.6	115.86	96.39	55.74
1975	250.58	74.68	127.99	28.21	4.93	14.77	117.9	97.4	128.6	145.7	127.6	115.2	142.57	108.01	52.71
1976	243.71	78.87	114.84	28.95	4.90	16.15	97.1	106.8	88.9	103.4	99.2	111.9	141.21	102.50	56.79
1977	267.76	78.68	139.15	29.66	6.39	13.88	109.7	98.3	121.2	105.1	129.0	82.7	150.50	117.26	56.45
1978	306.93	84.46	167.21	34.04	7.19	14.03	113.7	104.1	120.3	114.7	112.2	99.8	171.84	135.09	59.97
1979	369.75	109.85	200.82	33.75	7.57	17.76	113.3	109.6	117.7	96.5	105.3	118.6	199.71	170.04	83.56
1980	393.62	94.95	228.02	40.53	7.95	22.17	108.6	88.5	116.3	112.4	105.0	115.4	219.74	173.88	70.01
1981	435.81	111.68	249.72	37.62	8.10	28.69	109.2	111.2	109.9	85.2	112.4	140.0	238.70	197.11	85.38
1982	478.85	128.35	272.08	38.31	10.90	29.21	109.9	113.3	111.3	97.4	134.5	91.6	262.39	216.46	99.83
1983	541.84	134.09	319.21	42.44	13.03	33.07	111.3	100.1	115.2	117.7	118.2	113.2	306.04	235.80	103.43
1984	654.97	169.20	371.93	49.86	21.56	42.42	119.7	120.9	117.4	110.3	151.9	139.1	361.58	293.39	124.07
1985	806.42	192.32	467.22	68.15	27.11	51.62	116.4	106.2	119.3	126.2	127.3	110.9	447.95	358.47	141.42
1986	919.84	219.10	538.28	74.04	29.86	58.56	107.8	103.5	110.9	100.1	106.6	102.2	520.61	399.23	160.78
1987	1100.37	249.68	659.19	86.92	35.28	69.30	111.7	102.7	115.5	108.5	105.2	110.1	635.60	464.77	183.99
1988	1359.22	297.51	834.84	100.79	36.29	89.79	112.8	97.2	119.1	103.3	91.9	115.8	803.00	556.22	216.66
1989	1524.21	335.04	976.93	78.98	40.70	92.57	102.9	105.0	106.7	73.9	100.6	83.1	911.24	612.97	237.26

17. Hubei

17–2

Year	v1d2	v1d3	v1d4	v1d5	v1e	v1e1	v1e2	v1e3	v1e4	v1e5	v1f	v1f1	v1f2	v1f3	v1g
1949															
1950															
1951															
1952	3.05	0.64	0.34	5.09	119.0	109.6	136.2	103.2	174.5	145.3					24.33
1953	4.20	0.99	0.50	6.17	113.6	107.4	144.3	88.8	136.0	117.0					27.92
1954	5.00	0.68	0.70	3.83	82.8	79.5	115.2	82.8	146.3	60.9					26.87
1955	5.98	1.15	0.97	4.55	130.5	135.6	120.7	147.2	136.7	117.7					32.62
1956	8.21	1.78	1.01	7.34	126.0	116.7	135.8	150.9	104.1	159.2					42.22
1957	8.89	2.52	1.11	7.56	106.1	106.5	112.0	138.7	109.5	90.4					48.01
1958	12.40	6.73	1.56	8.19	123.4	106.3	150.1	264.1	140.9	106.1					55.77
1959	18.13	3.47	2.00	8.13	93.9	87.5	114.9	50.1	129.4	98.5					59.29
1960	17.14	5.87	2.11	7.05	100.3	92.1	107.6	181.9	104.5	80.6					53.63
1961	8.30	1.64	1.38	5.41	70.6	94.0	56.1	22.5	65.4	67.8					33.14
1962	8.88	1.49	1.31	5.27	101.4	112.3	83.2	90.8	94.8	93.6					40.70
1963	10.01	1.92	1.21	5.32	106.6	109.8	113.5	130.6	46.4	108.7					47.34
1964	13.98	2.25	1.33	5.34	111.1	101.3	145.1	112.1	109.4	102.6					47.64
1965	16.92	3.70	1.83	5.39	116.3	111.3	126.7	199.4	138.1	81.8					56.80
1966	20.91	3.06	1.55	5.62	105.1	104.8	105.6	85.1	79.2	134.4					61.62
1967	17.49	2.80	1.53	6.12	92.6	95.4	83.7	91.0	97.4	104.4					57.59
1968	14.06	2.13	1.37	5.23	90.8	98.3	80.1	74.6	89.2	85.0					58.31
1969	17.92	2.96	1.48	5.67	103.2	89.1	128.0	141.8	108.3	116.0					64.75
1970	21.24	4.98	2.36	5.73	128.7	112.2	155.3	196.1	165.1	94.8					83.57
1971	27.41	7.86	2.17	6.30	113.6	104.2	129.2	145.4	90.2	132.2					92.32
1972	30.86	7.30	2.14	6.05	104.1	102.6	112.4	92.0	96.7	78.4					81.68
1973	34.40	7.36	2.28	6.32	109.7	110.7	112.4	95.0	107.3	104.4					91.71
1974	23.84	7.81	2.18	6.82	92.6	104.7	68.9	105.0	98.2	110.7					92.42
1975	32.11	12.58	2.70	7.91	110.9	94.5	134.6	151.4	122.6	114.8					109.65
1976	21.08	12.99	2.64	9.00	94.9	107.8	65.6	104.1	97.7	118.8					125.09
1977	38.16	10.03	3.36	9.26	115.5	99.1	182.9	79.9	125.8	97.3					122.75
1978	50.92	11.21	3.78	9.21	113.3	103.3	131.9	111.6	112.5	95.7	151.00	61.11	63.71	26.18	129.40
1979	57.55	13.71	4.03	11.19	115.4	118.9	112.1	119.1	106.5	111.5	188.46	85.15	73.03	30.28	145.42
1980	70.74	15.59	4.26	13.28	104.6	86.0	126.0	107.0	105.1	104.3	199.38	71.22	91.67	36.49	151.03
1981	76.80	13.77	4.34	16.82	111.3	114.5	109.2	81.0	102.3	152.5	219.75	87.00	92.85	39.90	168.95
1982	80.69	11.98	5.06	18.90	109.2	15.7	107.3	88.3	116.5	98.3	241.55	101.73	94.97	44.85	200.34
1983	89.85	13.95	5.78	22.80	105.8	99.6	108.9	116.5	113.0	117.7	262.58	105.40	106.50	50.68	220.98
1984	117.38	15.78	8.18	27.98	121.5	114.5	127.8	106.2	127.4	137.6	328.22	126.36	136.50	65.36	269.07
1985	150.91	21.20	10.19	34.75	116.8	107.4	124.3	130.9	126.1	113.5	396.26	144.44	174.35	77.47	325.22
1986	165.29	22.63	11.30	39.23	104.0	102.5	106.6	100.2	107.5	98.7	442.04	163.61	187.96	90.47	382.81
1987	196.07	27.22	13.67	43.82	107.9	103.1	112.3	111.8	106.2	103.4	517.77	183.99	224.53	109.25	428.51
1988	240.65	28.85	14.98	55.07	107.0	95.6	115.5	103.1	97.6	112.0	623.56	214.66	271.25	137.65	541.09
1989	278.82	21.98	18.43	56.48	101.7	104.8	104.6	77.6	108.2	85.5	699.36	239.07	300.46	159.83	565.60

17. Hubei

17–3

Year	v1h	v1i	v1j	v1j1	v1j2	v1j3	v1k	v2a	v2a1	v2a2	v2b	v2c	v2c1	v2c2	v2d1
1949	67.10														
1950	72.12											0.29			
1951	80.37											0.58			
1952	85.78	3.91	354	365	303			3.87	1.64	2.23		1.74			3.11
1953	88.73			409				4.27	2.21	2.06		2.30			3.73
1954	83.50			424				5.39	3.63	1.76		3.11			4.41
1955	86.00			466				6.00	4.36	1.64		3.85			5.20
1956	90.30			537				9.34	7.09	2.25		6.54			5.87
1957	93.20	9.30	543	564	506			13.43	9.35	4.08		6.57			7.86
1958	84.10			500				21.07	14.66	6.47		12.30			15.81
1959	75.17			478				23.90	16.25	7.65		16.01			20.97
1960	76.66			478				20.20	19.78	0.42		15.98			26.35
1961	94.70			479				6.05	4.65	1.40		5.32			27.27
1962	142.60	9.97	473	510	374			5.75	4.27	1.48		2.78			27.33
1963	128.40			552				8.99	4.38	4.61		3.12			28.43
1964	117.50			570				6.24	4.59	1.65		4.41			29.47
1965	123.90	10.98	513	572	373			12.98	5.77	7.21		5.68			31.61
1966	112.20			558				15.56	9.81	5.75		8.06			
1967	110.20			559				11.35	8.57	2.78		6.76			
1968	108.80			557				9.69	5.32	4.37		4.46			
1969	90.70			560				18.03	10.48	7.55		8.24			
1970	92.70	13.60	527	546	458			33.89	28.29	5.60		24.41			
1971	96.80	14.88	510	523	458			39.71	27.76	11.95		26.46			
1972	96.50	17.54	545	560	474			27.37	22.84	4.53		21.00			60.87
1973	100.60	17.92	530	536	499			33.63	18.66	14.97		17.28			89.79
1974	106.32	18.52	542	551	502			31.42	20.80	10.62		16.92			98.02
1975	102.88	20.28	546	557	497			47.73	31.31	16.42		20.79			108.22
1976	112.84	21.12	541	556	473			58.52	43.78	14.74		28.80			119.97
1977	110.43	23.16	556	568	500			52.00	40.23	11.77		37.85			133.71
1978	110.52	25.80	579	592	532			51.72	40.01	11.71	33.58	33.19	22.46	1.05	149.66
1979	159.68	28.95	619	642	532			51.91	33.69	18.22	31.53	30.86	16.60	1.19	186.82
1980	169.96	35.22	719	744	619			50.95	44.04	6.91	35.49	34.19	17.06	1.77	204.63
1981	217.44	36.99	717	739	633			55.31	37.34	17.97	33.49	29.52	14.34	1.33	216.97
1982	286.07	39.95	739	760	657			65.08	45.21	19.87	48.84	34.46	13.94	1.88	241.99
1983	299.24	42.16	759	781	677			68.54	51.59	16.95	56.12	36.69	12.64	1.64	259.06
1984	392.30	50.86	1698	930	768			81.86	58.51	23.35	74.47	45.25	14.48	2.08	274.28
1985	421.24	63.00	1049	1104	890	987	15.06	104.12	65.40	38.72	102.92	61.66	18.97	3.40	325.35
1986	445.13	76.50	1224	1297	1014	1169	19.91	113.17	71.18	41.99	111.43	66.42	19.23	2.81	361.83
1987	460.66	85.96	1333	1414	1097	1526	22.64	133.43	96.39	37.04	140.08	85.32	25.65	3.22	407.45
1988	497.84	104.93	1580	1683	1273		27.25	178.69	105.25	73.44	160.46	102.21	30.94	3.82	450.42
1989	571.84	116.28	1713	1830	1363		32.54	137.63	51.74	85.89	123.14	75.33	23.37	2.90	503.18

17. Hubei

17–4

Year	v2d2	v2e	v3a	v3b	v3b1	v3b2	v3c	v3d	v3d1	v3d2	v3e	v3e1	v3e2	v3e3	v3e4
1949															
1950															
1951															
1952	2.22	1.23	20.46	19.53	15.41	4.12	0.93	72	64	134					
1953	2.67	1.25	23.65	22.19	17.55	4.64	1.46	80	71	147					
1954	3.20	1.33	21.48	19.98	15.39	4.59	1.50	70	61	143					
1955	3.78	1.43	26.62	24.64	19.28	5.36	1.98	86	75	169					
1956	4.24	1.67	32.88	30.45	23.58	6.87	2.43	104	91	202					
1957	5.79	1.95	34.58	32.09	24.63	7.46	2.49	107	93	204	202	117	24.60	7.56	9.72
1958	13.33	4.17	34.70	31.47	23.17	8.30	3.23	102	86	201					
1959	17.69	7.18	35.39	32.31	20.33	11.98	3.08	100	76	232					
1960	22.43	9.29	33.43	30.28	17.57	12.71	3.15	95	66	237					
1961	23.10	8.19	27.09	25.02	14.50	10.52	2.07	78	54	213					
1962	22.09	6.16	34.95	33.47	22.87	10.60	1.48	103	83	224	226	144	15.58	7.41	9.73
1963	22.55	5.86	38.35	37.06	26.93	10.13	1.29	112	95	215					
1964	22.94	5.85	41.40	40.03	29.25	10.78	1.37	117	101	224					
1965	24.03	6.69	43.82	42.50	31.25	11.25	1.32	122	105	232	204	118	25.70	3.78	10.81
1966			46.06	44.43	32.74	11.69	1.63	124	107	235					
1967			46.24	44.68	31.85	12.83	1.56	121	102	248					
1968			48.62	46.97	33.32	13.65	1.65	123	103	266					
1969			46.72	44.90	30.51	14.39	1.82	114	91	281					
1970			49.68	47.52	33.55	13.97	2.16	118	97	271					
1971			52.61	49.84	34.67	15.17	2.77	122	98	280					
1972	44.99		54.31	51.53	35.33	16.20	2.78	123	98	285					
1973	70.30	30.33	58.08	54.79	37.89	16.90	3.29	128	103	293					
1974	75.57	34.54	61.00	57.56	39.66	17.90	3.44	132	106	308					
1975	82.74	36.22	61.92	58.20	39.78	18.42	3.72	132	105	312					
1976	90.75	40.13	66.57	62.63	43.22	19.41	3.94	141	113	317					
1977	100.86	44.92	70.75	66.73	45.54	21.19	4.02	148	118	334					
1978	111.27	48.13	77.68	73.19	50.19	23.00	4.49	145	111	350					
1979	145.51	55.42	93.51	85.33	59.04	26.29	8.18	186	151	379					
1980	157.06	59.51	100.08	91.58	60.62	30.96	8.50	195	154	414	369	211			
1981	163.48	63.06	113.64	104.13	71.84	32.29	9.51	221	181	429	423	241			
1982	179.09	65.49	135.26	124.27	89.42	34.85	10.99	261	223	452	431	248	59.76	5.40	8.82
1983	189.39	71.10	152.44	138.72	99.77	38.95	13.72	288	248	488	465	273	61.31	6.02	9.95
1984	197.25	75.41	187.21	168.77	118.75	50.02	18.44	346	297	576	516	291	76.24	6.27	10.26
1985	234.81	88.23	221.10	198.94	127.99	70.95	22.16	406	327	720	644	325	94.12	5.63	11.56
1986	258.57	105.95	269.64	241.92	156.12	85.80	27.72	488	401	806	752	388	105.96	5.88	12.72
1987	288.72	117.56	295.08	265.48	170.09	95.39	29.60	528	433	871	836	443	108.00	6.72	14.04
1988	316.29	128.20	362.40	321.76	201.39	120.37	40.64	631	507	1006	1059	539	136.80	6.96	17.64
1989	349.84	162.99	427.97	381.52	246.59	134.93	46.45	736	614	1157	1131	607	146.13	7.35	21.97

17. Hubei

17–5

Year	v3f	v3f1	v3f2	v3f3	v3f4	v4a1	v4a1a	v4a1b	v4a1c	v4a1d	v4a2	v4a2a	v4a2b	v4a2c	v4a2d
1949	48.30	26.81	7.50	0.80	7.10										
1950	51.27	28.45	8.00	0.90	7.50										
1951	57.14	31.42	8.90	1.00	8.40										
1952	61.00	33.86	9.50	1.09	8.90										
1953	63.08	35.00	9.80	1.13	9.30	4.87	0.27		1.23	0.30	1.96	0.48	0.59	0.61	0.28
1954	59.50	33.00	9.30	1.10	8.80	5.20	0.30		1.19	0.22	3.39	0.91	0.60	0.60	1.29
1955	70.60	38.70	7.30	1.90	16.90	4.77	0.38		0.81	0.16	3.49	1.13	0.68	0.71	0.97
1956	76.40	52.70	9.70	0.90	8.40	5.71	0.52		1.25	0.12	3.67	1.26	0.87	0.89	0.65
1957	85.10	56.90	8.80	2.00	10.00	6.27	0.73		1.19	0.09	3.55	1.11	0.99	0.82	0.63
1958	74.20	49.20	8.30	0.20	8.40	10.49	3.82		1.30	0.15	8.88	5.93	1.17	0.85	0.93
1959	66.34	43.98	7.40	0.16	7.50	13.31	6.69		1.24	0.16	10.28	5.36	1.43	1.12	2.37
1960	65.07	43.80	4.64	0.68	8.06	13.47	6.96		0.99	0.18	14.93	8.13	1.96	1.09	3.75
1961	85.60	57.60	6.10	0.90	10.60	7.89	2.77		0.90	0.15	8.72	2.32	1.47	1.08	3.85
1962	127.80	73.60	10.70	7.90	18.40	8.72	2.61		1.14	0.22	5.08	1.06	1.29	0.87	1.87
1963	114.90	72.50	11.30	5.30	13.80	10.31	3.45		1.44	0.20	5.58	1.20	1.28	0.82	2.29
1964	103.30	70.70	10.20	3.50	8.40	11.56	4.36		1.42	0.12	6.51	2.09	1.44	0.84	2.14
1965	102.30	69.70	12.00	3.70	7.30	11.26	4.25		1.56	0.12	6.85	2.28	1.48	0.87	2.22
1966	92.80	63.30	10.85	3.34	6.60	13.78	5.36		1.60	0.08	9.11	3.20	1.87	0.96	3.09
1967	91.20	62.20	10.67	3.30	6.50	11.66	3.71		1.60	0.05	7.69	2.92	2.00	0.83	1.94
1968	90.00	61.40	10.53	3.24	6.40	7.12	1.20		1.67	0.04	6.53	2.15	1.73	0.85	1.79
1969	75.10	51.20	8.83	2.70	5.33	8.91	1.52		1.58	0.04	9.95	4.22	1.71	1.16	2.86
1970	76.70	52.30	9.00	2.76	5.44	15.20	4.05		1.80	0.09	15.73	9.25	1.88	1.28	3.32
1971	80.10	54.63	9.40	2.88	5.69	19.51	7.37		1.79	0.06	16.67	7.78	2.32	1.90	4.68
1972	80.10	54.63	9.40	2.88	5.69	22.81	9.18		1.68	0.08	14.94	5.65	2.85	1.55	4.89
1973	83.30	56.80	9.70	3.00	5.90	24.79	11.31		1.65	0.06	15.73	5.53	3.11	1.44	5.65
1974	87.60	61.60	10.50	3.00	5.00	17.24	4.59		1.65	0.04	16.86	5.97	3.43	1.46	6.00
1975	86.00	60.80	10.10	2.50	5.50	24.05	8.49		1.60	0.05	17.52	5.17	3.68	1.61	7.05
1976	92.10	68.40	10.10	2.00	4.70	17.16	2.78		1.60	0.05	17.30	5.13	3.79	1.74	6.64
1977	98.30	70.20	11.30	2.60	6.00	21.05	4.39		1.65	0.05	20.18	6.02	4.04	1.77	8.35
1978	107.00	75.80	12.89	2.28	7.23	31.37	12.47		1.49	0.06	29.98	9.55	4.64	1.97	13.82
1979	148.65	100.40	19.15	6.83	8.84	31.62	10.42		1.91	0.03	28.07	7.69	5.50	2.38	12.50
1980	152.74	98.31	17.65	11.61	8.55	34.01	10.25		1.42	0.07	26.53	5.97	6.82	3.03	10.71
1981	183.78	114.75	22.58	15.56	10.34	36.87	11.21		1.60	0.08	23.60	2.86	7.37	3.66	9.72
1982	226.96	140.64	28.26	18.53	12.35	36.43	7.61		1.79	0.11	25.47	2.79	7.95	3.96	10.76
1983	252.47	156.03	30.03	19.03	13.54	40.44	10.56		1.70	0.19	28.32	3.25	8.86	4.60	11.61
1984	305.03	186.56	32.16	27.78	18.00	42.12	9.18		1.90	0.20	31.72	4.34	9.71	5.56	12.11
1985	334.63	197.86	34.16	37.44	17.53	50.26	4.66		2.50	0.48	43.60	4.38	11.70	6.01	21.51
1986	373.53	217.19	35.04	45.68	18.81	57.58	6.79		2.48	0.78	58.04	6.25	13.45	6.71	31.62
1987	408.69	232.22	33.75	52.14	19.14	65.35	6.36		2.72	1.58	60.98	6.21	13.64	6.86	34.26
1988	450.62	255.12	37.83	47.14	20.59	69.02	0.27				68.66	5.44	16.50	6.48	40.24
1989	540.13	317.61	40.17	54.75	24.09	77.41	-3.15				79.97	5.13	18.50	7.26	49.08

17. Hubei

17–6

Year	v4b	v4b1	v4b2	v4b3	v4c1	v4c2	v5a	v5a1	v5a2	v5a3	v5a4	v5b1	v5b2	v5b3	v5c
1949															
1950							963	20	19	26	853				
1951							989	27	21	27	866				
1952		0.26					1020	48	18	28	879				43.25
1953		0.37	0.01				1050	58	18	31	899				
1954		0.37	0.08				1055	64	21	34	907				
1955		0.41	0.16				1057	73	25	22	915				
1956		0.56	0.25				1102	101	63	3	928				
1957		0.69	0.97				1140	103	62	3	966				55.44
1958		0.96	1.16				985	180	38	1	766				
1959		1.26	1.19				1032	188	48		794				
1960		1.21	1.61				1202	205	44	4	949				
1961		1.10	2.14				1218	176	52	4	986				
1962	1.29	0.79	1.42		3.33	11.78	1258	139	63	14	1042				58.49
1963		0.88	2.13		4.98	17.53	1295	141	67	14	1073				
1964		1.14	2.28		6.74	23.41	1324	149	67	10	1099				
1965	2.15	1.39	3.26		8.42	27.41	1404	156	58	8	1182				61.83
1966		1.75	5.14					167							
1967		1.82	4.85					173							
1968		1.91	5.12					177							
1969		2.00	4.71					183							
1970	2.86	2.12	5.01				1619	223	55		1341				115.54
1971		2.43	5.27				1670	250	55		1365				
1972		2.76	5.05				1705	279	60		1366				
1973		2.98	5.63				1739	276	65		1397				
1974		3.38	6.94				1778	280	72		1425				
1975	4.67	3.74	6.80		19.22	16.16	1802	310	71		1421				517.90
1976		3.99	7.92		11.66	8.91	1831	328	72		1431				
1977	6.06	4.36	7.61		16.66	11.43	1872	358	76		1437				
1978	7.00	4.91	5.62		25.41	15.94	1910	372	86		1452				184.56
1979	10.08	6.33	8.46		29.77	14.81	1946	380	96	1	1469	1470.6	269.0	170.8	
1980	13.36	8.85	8.45		36.41	16.81	1987	404	100	3	1480	1453.7	286.3	247.0	206.32
1981	17.31	11.13	9.58		37.85	16.69	2045	422	110	4	1510	1492.6	317.5	235.0	222.67
1982	23.69	14.56	11.46		41.38	16.92	2108	435	117	5	1551	1514.7	334.0	259.1	233.12
1983	30.45	19.39	12.22		45.74	17.56	2145	445	120	9	1572	1516.8	346.0	281.9	239.77
1984	44.35	24.25	11.49		53.34	19.56	2203	436	147	16	1602	1488.3	381.8	333.0	247.87
1985	59.37	41.24	13.14		70.03	21.68	2241	457	158	25	1601	1383.3	489.6	368.2	265.22
1986	81.74	58.01	16.17		71.57	19.63	2298	472	166	26	1633	1395.6	510.7	391.2	281.74
1987	116.50	84.88	17.54		85.20	20.97	2349	478	170	28	1663	1417.2	521.7	410.5	292.22
1988	147.16				101.87	22.92	2407	504	172	34	1697	1443.0	531.7	432.8	
1989	187.10	146.80	40.30		98.35	19.18	2440	510	173	35	1721	1481.1	519.2	439.8	

17. Hubei

17–7

Year	v5c1	v5d	v6a	v6a1	v6a2	v6b	v6c	v6d1	v6d2	v6d3	v6d4	v6d5	v6d6
1949			2580.94					286.94	2294.00	1331.00	1249.94	101.83	
1950			2633.62					291.62	2342.00	1359.20	1274.42		
1951			2687.58					296.08	2391.50	1385.68	1301.90		
1952		879.20	2751.20					315.55	2435.65	1427.30	1323.90	130.73	10.23
1953			2807.00	290.76	2516.24			335.00	2472.00	1447.45	1359.55		
1954			2865.39	310.70	2554.69	31.69	15.87	361.17	2504.22	1480.29	1385.10		
1955			2911.91	345.90	2566.01	26.17	11.06	389.08	2522.83	1502.64	1409.27		
1956			2963.30	384.10	2579.20	27.25	10.81	384.56	2578.74	1529.67	1433.63		
1957		969.62	3062.41	411.40	2651.01	34.39	9.61	421.68	2640.73	1579.69	1482.72	214.61	16.37
1958			3145.47	435.10	2710.37	30.76	9.60	449.75	2695.72	1622.83	1522.64	228.10	23.11
1959			3173.14	505.40	2667.74	26.49	14.49	527.27	2645.87	1634.34	1538.80		
1960			3152.17	573.90	2578.27	16.21	21.21	560.76	2591.41	1621.49	1530.68		
1961			3182.96	526.30	2656.66	27.22	9.08	490.70	2692.26	1629.46	1553.50	247.68	23.53
1962		1083.10	3272.93	459.61	2814.32	42.52	8.77	460.57	2813.36	1668.68	1605.25	235.23	21.79
1963			3350.09	470.34	2879.75	41.05	9.83	471.30	2878.79	1712.13	1637.96	244.49	22.36
1964			3418.01	475.85	2942.16	37.73	10.94	408.12	2937.89	1751.81	1666.20	249.15	23.07
1965		1217.16	3504.54	485.06	3019.48	35.10	10.04	489.96	3014.58	1793.37	1711.17	252.35	23.84
1966			3602.66	496.33	3106.36	34.89	9.68	501.35	3101.31	1845.02	1757.64		
1967			3687.97	505.60	3182.37	31.41	9.57	514.56	3173.41	1893.84	1794.13		
1968			3806.80	509.70	3297.10	33.01	8.51	515.96	3290.84	1948.15	1858.65		
1969			3922.34	505.50	3416.84	31.41	8.12	510.43	3411.91	2003.62	1918.72		
1970		1377.94	4026.83	515.20	3511.63	29.92	7.70	520.29	3506.54	2060.10	1966.73	243.40	28.59
1971			4131.95	595.90	3566.05	31.11	8.39	603.20	3528.75	2116.96	2014.99		
1972			4215.66	578.27	3637.39	28.86	8.27	573.36	3642.30	2157.97	2057.69		
1973			4294.63	594.40	3697.23	25.92	7.76	580.58	3714.05	2200.29	2094.34		
1974			4348.79	600.88	3747.91	22.66	8.30	579.77	3769.02	2229.05	2119.74		
1975		1464.42	4408.15	638.14	3770.01	20.74	7.88	600.84	3807.31	2261.64	2146.51	263.57	34.30
1976			4466.70	661.43	3805.27	20.02	7.51	623.91	3842.79	2292.14	2174.56		
1977			4520.68	679.66	3841.02	19.57	7.81	644.97	3875.71	2320.72	2199.96		
1978		1508.99	4574.91	703.21	3871.70	18.67	7.06	669.18	3905.73	2348.22	2226.69	284.80	37.41
1979			4632.78	747.93	3884.85	19.87	7.11	718.34	3914.44	2376.57	2256.21		
1980		1540.47	4684.45	786.49	2897.96	20.36	7.00	747.85	3936.60	2401.74	2282.71	307.39	40.23
1981		1590.90	4740.35	815.60	3924.75	20.17	7.33	770.89	3969.46	2430.91	2309.44		
1982		1630.03	4800.92	848.77	3952.15	18.11	7.20	790.53	4010.39	2464.27	2336.65		
1983		1651.56	4835.34	1395.18	3440.16	20.53	8.79	811.81	4023.53	2485.55	2349.79		
1984		1689.54	4876.07	1647.86	3228.21	19.00	8.35	923.89	3952.18	2510.87	2365.20		
1985		1707.27	4930.97	1822.90	3048.07	19.95	7.62	1048.42	3882.55	2540.01	2390.96	339.60	45.19
1986		1723.00	4989.02	2356.92	2632.10	21.01	7.74	1080.45	3908.57	2573.38	2415.64	349.26	46.00
1987		1757.65	5058.08	3626.99	1431.09	21.43	7.13	1110.78	3947.30	2608.69	2449.39	357.12	48.01
1988			5144.29	3837.03	1307.26	19.08	6.44	1148.12	3996.17	2652.14	2492.15	364.45	49.51
1989			5259.00	1504.70	3729.20	21.09	6.94	1183.94	4039.95	2694.55	2529.33	370.67	50.53

17. Hubei

17–8

Year	v7a	v7b	v7c	v7d	v7e	v7f	v7g	v7h	v7h1	v7h2	v7h3	v7h4	v7h5	v7i	v8a
1949				8093				10.72	7.22	0.69	0.97	0.10	1.74	146.01	
1950				8535				12.05	8.59	0.70	0.82	0.14	1.80	154.99	
1951				9030				15.01	11.00	0.75	1.14	0.17	1.95	161.89	
1952			1248.00	9612				16.59	12.08	0.79	1.48	0.18	2.06	168.27	9.99
1953		11.91		10055				19.64	14.65	0.87	1.84	0.21	2.07	249.41	13.60
1954		17.77		9460				16.13	11.11	0.97	1.87	0.21	1.97	253.13	14.69
1955		30.90		10408				21.57	16.43	1.00	1.88	0.28	1.98	177.62	16.26
1956		41.42		10522				26.13	19.40	1.31	2.83	0.38	2.21	187.83	20.66
1957		79.13	2019.00	10514				28.59	20.55	1.46	3.81	0.46	2.31	266.66	24.31
1958		150.00	2237.00	10388			0.03	31.80	22.73	1.67	3.71	0.52	3.17	268.52	34.93
1959		247.00	2303.00	9375			0.05	29.29	20.51	2.05	2.11	0.78	3.84	261.83	49.57
1960		312.00	2358.00	10721			0.06	26.97	21.68	2.00	1.33	0.71	1.25	253.36	59.92
1961		402.00	2561.00	11199			0.16	29.28	23.08	1.74	2.56	0.59	1.31	255.28	33.55
1962		341.01	2761.00	11153			0.24	33.66	26.52	1.71	3.61	0.46	1.36	187.58	34.83
1963		444.42	2966.00	11144			0.61	39.19	30.56	1.78	5.01	0.55	1.29	280.55	39.19
1964		463.30	3214.00	11367			0.66	39.87	30.07	1.90	5.90	0.61	1.39	291.52	44.85
1965	8.27	475.33	3381.00	11541		46.21	1.10	47.48	37.44	1.98	6.02	0.51	1.53	313.99	52.90
1966		599.87	3831.00	11415			2.20	60.68						338.54	66.71
1967		542.00		10996				57.08						353.59	60.95
1968		579.00		10439				55.38						365.63	45.81
1969		512.65		10548				51.78						362.18	59.46
1970	13.77	612.85	3225.30	10975		60.31	1.53	51.27	40.62	2.07	6.41	0.92	1.25	365.42	86.27
1971		801.74	2996.54	11656			2.26	60.65	46.72	3.19	7.00	0.70	3.04	226.14	95.31
1972		870.69	2997.66	11878			3.29	63.62	48.21	3.89	7.74	0.63	3.15	245.20	96.97
1973		1110.15	3185.25	11737			2.79	72.13	55.40	4.14	8.45	0.83	3.31	243.47	110.92
1974		1320.17	3339.17	11795			4.30	76.67						242.31	100.78
1975	38.28	1446.05	3377.02	11907		115.79	3.99	74.68						238.96	127.99
1976		1646.31	3482.76	11935			4.58	78.87						235.25	114.84
1977		1761.99	3488.97	12099			4.44	78.68						231.09	139.15
1978	61.65	1800.39	3532.40	11897		159.79	6.59	84.46						230.51	167.21
1979	71.74		3530.00	11666		200.50	7.20	109.85						225.47	200.82
1980	77.31	1789.81	3517.50	11216		243.14	9.61	94.95	64.70	7.28	17.29	1.46	4.22	219.92	228.02
1981	79.77	1664.60	3557.70	10880		244.40	11.10	111.68	82.78	6.47	14.88	1.61	5.94	219.05	249.72
1982	81.35	1439.60	3557.50	11191		301.80	12.30	128.35	95.32	7.24	17.97	2.12	5.70	229.23	272.08
1983	82.99	1182.50	3497.70	11098	1764	338.70	16.00	134.09	97.53	7.29	20.05	2.96	6.26	236.25	319.21
1984	85.97	1063.00	3464.40	11082	392	372.00	15.20	169.20	123.09	7.59	26.51	4.79	7.27	241.96	371.93
1985	91.16	868.64	3440.00	10998	624	387.40	16.78	192.32	129.61	8.15	39.08	8.18	7.30	246.26	467.22
1986	100.20	815.50	3379.20	11062	624	448.80	14.70	219.10	146.79	8.75	43.86	10.77	8.93	253.80	538.28
1987	104.69	722.93	3317.70	11006	870	497.87	19.78	249.68	160.13	9.97	54.86	14.19	10.53	256.31	659.19
1988	115.37	1329.59	3260.10	10843	3225	545.66	24.93	297.51	175.12	10.98	80.80	18.83	11.78	256.01	834.84
1989	111.90	1526.00	3295.80	10891			23.70	335.04	198.56	11.75	91.47	20.66	12.60	259.78	976.93

17. Hubei

17–9

Year	v8a1	v8a2	v8a3	v8b	v8c1	v8c2	v8d	v8f1	v8f2	v8f3	v8f4	v8f5	v8g
1949								0.03	23.50		0.80	2.29	4111
1950								0.51	32.32		0.84	7.51	
1951								1.80	38.38		0.89	23.87	
1952	6.64	0.10	3.25		2.20	7.79		4.44	41.47		1.63	25.00	5028
1953	9.44	0.15	4.01		3.25	10.35		5.16	37.41		2.33	35.90	
1954	10.32	0.91	3.46		3.63	11.06		8.61	46.51		2.98	42.80	
1955	12.04	1.49	2.73		5.16	11.10		11.09	56.61		2.87	39.60	
1956	15.73	3.84	1.09		7.02	13.64		13.66	65.31		3.84	55.40	
1957	17.74	5.29	1.28		8.02	16.29		14.75	73.88		4.39	53.89	8424
1958	31.51	3.34	0.08		15.68	19.25		23.60	186.34		6.63	65.41	
1959	42.89	6.68			25.63	23.94		61.30	232.00		11.54	85.86	
1960	50.43	9.49			33.67	26.25		133.33	261.94		17.63	91.52	
1961	26.89	6.58	0.08		16.64	16.91		77.85	164.11		13.98	49.35	
1962	27.42	7.10	0.31		12.30	22.53	8.88	52.11	126.37		13.39	47.04	10293
1963	31.46	7.48	0.25		14.29	24.90		67.72	125.34		14.05	58.23	
1964	36.46	8.16	0.23		17.28	27.57		91.74	114.93		15.51	70.42	
1965	43.70	9.07	0.13		22.55	30.35		121.66	117.58		18.06	85.93	9582
1966	56.81	9.90			29.68	37.03		163.93	125.71	0.02	23.53	113.80	
1967	48.95	12.00			23.42	37.53		100.95	112.07	0.01	21.91	75.08	
1968	34.94	10.87			14.89	30.92		44.58	85.15	0.03	16.68	50.31	
1969	46.99	12.47			23.17	36.29		107.71	128.95	0.03	23.00	79.08	
1970	71.19	15.08			42.10	44.17		182.81	237.92	13.35	39.93	126.32	10990
1971	79.97	15.34			49.26	46.05		223.70	350.49	23.68	55.58	151.82	
1972	78.82	18.15			49.28	47.69		230.00	354.94	13.75	66.46	160.46	
1973	90.95	19.97			59.43	51.49		255.00	333.19	45.65	71.11	172.49	
1974	78.32	22.46			47.49	53.29		140.91	339.28	50.82	69.68	144.20	
1975	101.98	26.01			64.66	63.33		199.36	436.03	71.20	91.20	227.37	13211
1976	86.63	28.21			56.19	58.65		127.46	456.98	88.68	75.50	205.73	
1977	104.60	34.55			68.97	70.18		150.84	564.28	103.65	78.38	257.52	
1978	129.31	37.90		122.94	88.50	78.71	38.80	307.97	644.01	105.70	91.64	328.65	15929
1979	158.12	42.70		152.67	107.37	93.45	44.65	334.84	458.55	104.70	114.52	394.73	16073
1980	179.33	47.86	0.83	174.09	117.88	110.14	55.34	363.74	383.52	104.13	131.00	427.78	16601
1981	193.57	54.90	1.25	187.93	118.59	131.13	57.98	342.33	434.12	101.05	137.16	432.97	17032
1982	204.83	65.68	1.57	196.08	134.42	137.66	60.68	364.84	516.22	101.21	153.65	490.24	18066
1983	237.57	80.04	1.60	227.38	161.88	157.33	66.20	408.65	624.66	102.00	181.34	550.60	18962
1984	262.22	107.94	1.77	250.56	189.36	182.57	77.94	454.11	743.00	101.49	197.37	620.72	22713
1985	321.12	134.42	11.68	317.19	250.75	216.47	101.28	515.15	855.98	102.41	220.54	736.03	25011
1986	362.67	161.11	14.50	351.37	282.22	256.06	106.81	543.01	834.56	103.00	233.65	836.94	27697
1987	434.92	201.38	22.89	418.68	343.70	315.49	128.51	574.22	849.12	101.00	268.67	934.79	26294
1988	534.18	266.64	34.02	510.31	429.71	405.13	154.94	599.65	1001.31	101.66	299.21	1080.49	26016
1989	620.50	313.07	43.36	592.95	513.58	463.35	169.26	602.54	1037.97	93.00	333.72	991.73	25999

17. Hubei

17–10

Year	v8g1	v9a	v9a1	v9a2	v9a3	v9b	v9b1	v9b2	v9b3	v9c	v10a	v10a1	v10b1	v10b2	v10b3
1949		0.79	0.68	0.03	0.08	6.54	0.41	0.06	5.14	477.3	7.39	7.15			
1950		5.28	4.49	0.13	0.66	14.32	5.78	0.07	6.39	523.6	8.77	8.39			
1951				0.25						693.8	10.41	9.87			
1952	976	9.21	3.87	0.36	4.97	25.50	9.69	0.20	15.61	865.1	11.89	11.01			
1953		12.73	5.65	0.58	5.48	34.87	14.41	0.23	15.16	1194.2	15.39	14.29			
1954				0.54						1514.9	15.23	14.00			
1955		12.55	5.21	0.78	4.48	38.88	17.12	0.41	14.60	1607.4	16.98	15.63			
1956				1.98						1569.4	19.79	17.96			
1957	1574	16.35	6.74	2.12	7.45	55.41	26.50	1.08	27.83	1590.6	21.38	19.60			
1958		18.23	7.95	2.44	7.85	77.44	39.77	1.79	24.73	2328.7	27.30	22.54			
1959		22.05	8.78	3.84	9.35	105.54	55.83	3.71	34.11	3228.5	30.42	24.98			
1960		25.52	10.35	3.51	10.96	129.02	69.82	3.85	42.53	3778.7	31.06	25.28			
1961		30.33	14.01	3.43	12.77	92.94	49.82	2.30	34.06	3132.0	26.41	22.13			
1962	1736	30.66	14.45	3.60	12.61	71.83	39.62	2.30	29.93	3005.8	27.78	24.47			
1963	1625			3.41						3029.5	28.47	24.66			
1964	1564			3.62						3251.3	30.46	25.89			
1965	1582	25.34	12.30	4.75	8.29	114.82	68.41	2.54	43.86	3334.3	31.89	26.85			
1966				7.18						2882.1	35.01	28.82			
1967				8.15						2769.9	38.87	33.03			
1968				6.94						2460.4	36.79	31.48			
1969				7.79						2659.3	38.29	32.50			
1970		12.31		9.46		19.07		3.98		3244.3	41.88	34.88			
1971		13.70		11.35		21.78				3745.2	45.32	36.75			
1972	2221	14.73		12.53		24.32				3982.2	49.60	40.14			
1973	2519	51.14	24.00	12.14	11.95	210.00	144.71		58.52	4292.1	52.61	42.36			
1974	2601	51.51	24.73	16.30	10.45	182.31	123.40		52.64	4384.5	54.80	43.47			
1975	2710	54.53	25.46	17.85	12.58	209.47	143.71	7.32	57.73	5877.5	61.41	48.96	31.35		28.51
1976	2740	59.19	27.07	19.50	12.55	186.19	128.78		49.97	4989.5	66.13	52.62	33.03		31.28
1977		61.81	27.88	20.88	12.94	231.54	160.23		62.76	5256.7	68.92	55.08	33.73		33.40
1978	2936	69.63	30.72	24.85	13.89	282.41	191.72	9.70	80.97	6900.2	76.73	59.84	37.45		37.02
1979	2933	79.21	34.77	29.73	14.69	306.26	202.44	9.07	94.57	5933.6	85.80	67.98	41.61		41.54
1980	2920	95.86	41.79	36.20	17.51	329.19	206.14	10.57	112.47	8131.3	100.55	81.91	48.11		48.72
1981	2971	107.77	47.34	41.36	19.03	357.37	216.88	10.79	129.58	8280.0	107.89	89.90	51.76		50.92
1982	3019	120.30	52.10	48.19	19.57	400.08	232.79	16.22	151.06	8705.5	119.28	99.83	55.25		56.20
1983	3063	138.84	60.23	56.59	21.82	434.55	251.88	17.07	165.59	9489.7	133.20	112.44	58.61		59.92
1984	3074	158.19	69.74	67.07	20.97	486.34	286.19	17.56	182.58	10293.7	159.89	137.34	68.08		67.18
1985	3256	185.24	84.00	81.33	19.39	507.57	320.37	16.59	169.94	12008.6	205.82	181.07	79.14		81.39
1986	3559	218.27	89.05	94.21	34.33	593.99	341.33	16.62	230.11	13152.1	227.95	200.20	88.59		85.27
1987	3766	239.96	99.43	104.09	35.21	658.01	385.45	17.71	249.91	15049.6	268.66	234.06	102.33		99.29
1988	3737	270.09	114.48	115.66	38.87	687.87	399.18	18.97	265.52	18994.3	337.52	295.80	135.14		113.05
1989	3798	260.62	104.16	119.50	36.05	710.01	425.70	112.10	262.33	22284.1	366.00	320.68	148.05		117.28

17. Hubei

17–11

Year	v10b4	v10b5	v10b6	v10d	v11a1	v11a2	v11a3	v11b	v11b1	v11b2	v11c	v11d	v12a	v12b	v12c
1949			0.09												
1950			0.11												
1951			0.13										115.3	121.1	121.3
1952			0.14	3.71									97.0	96.1	99.3
1953			0.17	5.55	0.5219	0.3024			0.8243				102.1	103.5	108.8
1954			0.12	5.48	0.6138	0.3171		0.9388	0.9309	0.0079			102.3	101.7	99.9
1955			0.17	6.91	0.6305	0.2415		0.8725	0.8721	0.0004			100.9	100.2	99.0
1956			0.20	9.08	0.7949	0.0785		0.8757	0.8734	0.0023			100.8	99.5	106.3
1957			0.24	10.49	0.5312	0.0940		0.6296	0.6252	0.0044			104.3	105.2	105.6
1958			0.20	12.11	0.6410	0.1045		0.7685	0.7455	0.0230			101.7	99.5	104.8
1959			0.24	14.83	0.3671	0.2415		0.6137	0.6086	0.0051			101.1	101.1	103.2
1960			0.36	11.31	0.2051	0.1921			0.3972				105.5	109.4	105.7
1961			1.47	9.67	0.0744	0.1858			0.2602				119.2	120.6	117.6
1962			1.03	10.75	0.1011	0.1489		0.2544	0.2500	0.0044			101.0	95.9	106.0
1963			0.80	14.81	0.1166	0.1709		0.2912	0.2875	0.0037			92.3	93.1	99.8
1964			0.69	15.56	0.1638	0.2225		0.4070	0.3863	0.0207			96.6	96.6	99.5
1965			0.60	18.59	0.1713	0.1783		0.3758	0.3496	0.0262			96.0	96.4	99.4
1966			0.54	21.68	0.1596	0.2366		0.4242	0.3962	0.0280			99.3	99.2	103.9
1967			0.55	21.15	0.1767	0.2328		0.4322	0.4095	0.0227			99.7	100.2	100.1
1968			0.60	19.45	0.1683	0.2773		0.4596	0.4456	0.0140			99.9	100.2	103.3
1969			0.60	17.81	0.1665	0.3703		0.5622	0.5368	0.0254			100.2	100.4	100.3
1970			0.78	17.24	0.2158	0.3028		0.6338	0.6086	0.0262			100.2	99.6	100.0
1971			0.80	18.62	0.2683	0.4421		0.7391	0.7107	0.0284			99.6	99.7	100.0
1972			0.94	19.71	0.3340	0.5075		0.8852	0.8415	0.0437			99.4	99.6	101.9
1973			0.94	23.24	0.5100	0.5203		1.0565	1.0303	0.0262			100.3	100.3	101.2
1974				27.50	0.5723	0.5345		1.1491	1.1068	0.0423			100.1	99.9	100.2
1975		0.03	1.52	25.80	0.9508	0.2796		1.2826	1.2304	0.0522			99.9	99.9	100.0
1976		0.02	1.80	26.58	0.9482	0.3484		1.3903	1.2966	0.0937			100.1	100.0	100.1
1977		0.02	1.77	27.11	1.0356	0.4036		1.5725	1.4392	0.1333			100.2	100.1	100.2
1978		0.03	2.23	27.06	1.0377	0.5524		1.7333	1.5901	0.1432			100.5	100.3	102.8
1979		0.05	2.60	36.83	1.2163	1.0387		2.3911	2.2550	0.1361			101.4	102.6	123.6
1980		0.30	3.42	39.60	1.1836	1.3273		2.6669	2.5109	0.1560			104.6	106.8	105.8
1981		0.98	4.23	45.86	1.0552	2.2512		3.5309	3.3064	0.2245			101.4	102.1	108.0
1982		2.07	5.76	55.39	1.1411	2.5012		3.8772	3.6423	0.2349			100.7	100.9	104.9
1983	0.01	6.98	7.68	61.03	1.3213	2.7979		4.4333	4.1192	0.3141			101.4	101.7	102.2
1984		14.69	9.94	78.88	1.3756	3.2096		5.1720	4.5852	0.5868			103.0	102.9	104.3
1985	0.02	28.17	17.10	87.61	1.3776	3.9209		6.8943	5.2985	1.5958			107.5	110.3	104.5
1986	0.03	30.77	23.29	105.15	2.2303	5.0250		8.6159	7.2547	1.3612	0.5845	0.5845	104.2	106.0	108.8
1987	0.09	37.69	29.26	128.70	2.3585	7.1910		11.1514	9.5495	1.6019	1.0089	1.0089	107.6	108.7	107.7
1988	0.06	50.79	38.48	145.62				13.7021	10.7420	2.9166	1.5992	1.5992	119.5	120.5	118.1
1989	0.03	56.19	44.45	159.48				11.9307	10.2749	1.6558	0.4781	1.6504	117.0	114.1	118.9

17. Hubei

17–12

Year	v13a	v13b	v13c1	v13c2	v13c3	v13d	v14a	v14b	v14c	v15a	v15b	v15c	v15d	v15e	v15f
1949			0.45	4.36	69.97	0.05			0.23	5592					
1950			0.57			0.09				5680					
1951			0.79			0.12				5843					
1952		47.40	0.89	10.40	195.23	0.31	5243	30500	1.66	6024					
1953	20.72		1.43			0.15				6144					
1954	12.15	38.36	1.72			0.32				6173					
1955	13.21		1.98			0.42				6245					
1956	15.92	57.21	2.70			0.57				6261					
1957	18.97	57.57	2.87	25.15	298.36	0.40			1.67	6259					
1958	9.79	70.63	4.11			0.50				6265					
1959	10.21		4.94			0.34				6311					
1960	9.24	74.93	5.34			0.80				6451					
1961	11.32		4.96			0.94				6438					
1962	16.66	69.18	4.37	32.16	340.30	0.85			0.96	6408					
1963	14.90	59.50	3.94			1.02				6392					
1964	14.31		3.50			1.19				6379					
1965	14.24	87.80	3.56	59.20	426.57	0.96	31289	71300	2.15	6360					
1966	14.24		3.54							6160					
1967	17.99		3.18			0.37				6067					
1968			1.61			1.56				6047					
1969			1.40			0.21				5975					
1970	7.78		0.13	112.41	526.00	1.39			1.94	5946					
1971	9.01	84.00	0.62							5875					
1972	11.97		1.42			0.12				5851					
1973	12.32		1.95			0.22				5805					
1974	12.45		2.43			0.50				5762					
1975	12.86	97.10	2.73	248.28	791.09	0.71			3.71	5735					
1976	13.27	98.50	3.07	381.18		0.96				5696					
1977	12.32	97.80	3.97	351.60	765.73	0.98				5670					
1978	9.07	96.90	4.94	381.18	765.73	0.82	103433	140600	2.22	5652					
1979	11.29	96.70	6.03	351.60	760.22	0.22			1.90	5532					
1980	14.92	97.01	6.53		755.85	1.03	112216	155900	1.93	5608					
1981	17.80	96.60	7.41	292.41	730.31	0.77			5.16	5596					
1982	17.28	97.10	6.56	270.24	708.15	2.67			5.53	5577					
1983	16.98	97.50	7.49	269.29	679.41	1.72			6.22	5548					
1984	16.49	98.30	8.74	270.95	684.11	1.78			8.10	5466					
1985	14.49	98.50	11.11	269.29	672.05	1.71	115203	184800	10.45	5377					
1986	12.37	98.80	12.41	276.38	668.89	2.51			10.23	5318					
1987	12.52	98.80	12.41	275.76	653.02	3.98			11.34	5277					
1988	13.94	98.78	13.00	258.94	647.85	3.55	125983	200100	11.92	5248					
1989		98.80	13.04	223.40	632.08	3.59	128224	204200	9.42	5230					

Notes

1. National Output and Income (Y)

v1a: (E), p.560
- v1a1: (A); (E), p.560
- v1a2: (E), p.560
- v1a3: (E), p.560
- v1a4: (E), p.560
- v1a5: (E), p.560

v1b: (A); (D), p.295
- v1b1: (A); (D), p.295
- v1b2: (A); (D), p.295
- v1b3: (A); (D), p.295
- v1b4: (A); (D), p.295
- v1b5: (A); (D), p.295

v1c: v1a – v1d

v1d: (E), p.558
- v1d1: (E), p.558
- v1d2: (E), p.558
- v1d3: (E), p.558
- v1d4: (E), p.558
- v1d5: (E), p.558

v1e: (A); (D), p.298
- v1e1: (A); (D), p.298
- v1e2: (A); (D), p.298
- v1e3: (A); (D), p.298
- v1e4: (A); (D), p.298
- v1e5: (A); (D), p.298

v1f: (E), p.557
- v1f1: (E), p.557
- v1f2: (E), p.557
- v1f3: (E), p.557

v1g: v3a + v2a

v1h: (A); (E), p.584

v1i: (E), p.583—including meat price subsidies

v1j: (E), p.583—(ditto)
- v1j1: (E), p.583—(ditto)
- v1j2: (E), p.583—(ditto)
- v1j3: (C), 1988, p.253—joint ownership

v1k: (E), p.583

2. Investment (I)

v2a: (A); (D), p.303
- v2a1: (A); (D), p.303
- v2a2: (A); (D), p.303

v2b: (A)

v2c: (A); (E), p.575
- v2c1: (E), p.576
- v2c2: (E), p.576

v2d:
- v2d1: (E), p.573
- v2d2: (E), p.573

v2e: (E), p.573

3. Consumption (C)

v3a: (A); (D), p.299

v3b: (A); (D), p.299
- v3b1: (A); (D), p.299
- v3b2: (A); (D), p.299

v3c: (A); (D), p.299

v3d: (E), p.582
- v3d1: (E), p.582
- v3d2: (E), p.582

v3e: (A); (E), p.584
- v3e1: (A); (E), p.584
- v3e2: (A)
- v3e3: (A)
- v3e4: (A)

v3f: (A); (E), p.584
- v3f1: (A); (E), p.584
- v3f2: (A)
- v3f3: (A)
- v3f4: (A)

4. Public Finance and Banking (FB)

v4a:
- v4a1: (E), p.580
  - v4a1a: (E), p.580
  - v4a1b: NA
  - v4a1c: (C), 1988, p.289
  - v4a1d: (C), 1988, p.289
- v4a2: (E), p.580
  - v4a2a: (E), p.580
  - v4a2b: (E), p.580
  - v4a2c: (E), p.580
  - v4a2d: v4a2 – v4a2a – v4a2b – v4a2c

v4b: (A)
- v4b1: (A); (C), 1988, p.292
- v4b2: (A); (C), 1988, p.292
- v4b3: NA

v4c:
- v4c1: (E), p.573
- v4c2: (E), p.573

5. Labor Force (L)

v5a: (E), p.556
- v5a1: (E), p.556
- v5a2: (E), p.556
- v5a3: (E), p.556
- v5a4: (E), p.556—excluding rural people working outside

v5b:
- v5b1: (E), p.556
- v5b2: (E), p.556
- v5b3: (E), p.556

v5c: (C), 1988, p.244—including state-owned, cities and towns collective, cities and towns self-employed workers, but excluding labor force in rural enterprises
- v5c1: NA

v5d: (C), 1988, p.244—including total labor force in rural area and in state-owned farming, forestry and animal husbandry

6. Population (PO)

v6a: (A); (E), p.555—data from public security department
- v6a1: (A)—(ditto)
- v6a2: (A)—(ditto)

v6b: (E), p.555—1982–88: obtained from sample survey

v6c: (E), p.555—(ditto)

v6d:
- v6d1: (E), p.555—data from public security department
- v6d2: (E), p.555—(ditto)
- v6d3: (E), p.555—(ditto)
- v6d4: (E), p.555—(ditto)
- v6d5: (A)—Wuhan
- v6d6: (A)—Huangshi

7. Agriculture (A)

v7a: (A); (E), p.567—100 million watt

v7b: (A); (E), p.567

v7c: (A); (E), p.567

v7d: (A); (E), p.567

v7e: (A)

v7f: (A)

v7g: (A); (E), p.567

v7h: (E), p.562
- v7h1: (E), p.562

v7h2: (E), p.562
v7h3: (E), p.562
v7h4: (E), p.562
v7h5: (E), p.562

v7i: (E), p.566—in 1949–52, 1955–56 and 1971, it was replaced by number of farm cattle

8. Industry (IN)

v8a: (E), p.568
v8a1: (E), p.568
v8a2: (E), p.568
v8a3: v8a – v8a1 – v8a2

v8b: (E), p.573

v8c1: (E), p.560
v8c2: (E), p.560

v8d: (E), p.573

v8f:
v8f1: (E), p.572
v8f2: (E), p.572—including bone coal in 1975 and before
v8f3: (E), p.572
v8f4: (E), p.572
v8f5: (E), p.572

v8g: (A)
v8g1: (E), p.573

9. Transport (TR)

v9a: (E), p.574—excluding urban traffic volume
v9a1: (E), p.574—including central and local railway
v9a2: (E), p.574—data of transport system
v9a3: (E), p.574—excluding distant ocean and coastal passenger traffic

v9b: (E), p.574
v9b1: (E), p.574—including central and local railway
v9b2: (E), p.574—data of transport system
v9b3: (E), p.574—excluding distant ocean and coastal freight volume

v9c: (E), p.574

10. Domestic Trade (DT)

v10a: (E), p.577
v10a1: (E), p.577

v10b:
v10b1: (E), p.577
v10b2: NA
v10b3: (E), p.577—included supply and marketing cooperative and other collectives
v10b4: (E), p.577
v10b5: (E), p.577
v10b6: (C), 1988, p.487–490; (E), p.577

v10d: (E), p.579—calculated on calendar year basis

11. Foreign Trade (FT)

v11a:
v11a1: (C), 1988, p.509
v11a2: (C), 1989, p.509—industrial products
v11a3: NA

v11b: (E), p.578
v11b1: (E), p.578
v11b2: v11b – v11b1

v11c: (E), p.578

v11d: (E), p.578

12. Prices (PR)

v12a: (E), p.581

v12b: (E), p.581

v12c: (E), p.581

13. Education (ED)

v13a: (A)

v13b: (A); (E), p.584

v13c:
- v13c1: (A); (E), p.584
- v13c2: (A)—technical secondary and ordinary secondary schools
- v13c3: (A); (E), p.584

v13d: (A)—institutions of higher learning

14. Social Factors (SF)

v14a: (E), p.584

v14b: (E), p.584

v14c: (A)

15. Natural Environment (NE)

v15a: (A); (E), p.567

v15b: NA

v15c: NA

v15d: NA

v15e: NA

v15f: NA

Sources of Data

(A) Data supplied by the DSNEB, SSB, the PRC, and Statistical Bureau of Hubei Province ed. *Striving and Advancing Forty Years, 1949–1989*, Beijing: CSPH, 1989

(C) Statistical Bureau of Hubei Province ed. *Statistical Yearbook of Hubei*, Beijing: CSPH, various issues.

(D) Same as (D) in Beijing's sources of data.

(E) Same as (E) in Beijing's sources of data.

18

Hunan

18. Hunan

18–1

Year	v1a	v1a1	v1a2	v1a3	v1a4	v1a5	v1b	v1b1	v1b2	v1b3	v1b4	v1b5	v1c	v1d	v1d1
1949	21.47	15.84	3.18	0.10	0.60	1.75							5.83	15.64	12.51
1950	26.12	19.18	4.15	0.20	0.63	1.96							7.39	18.73	15.06
1951	31.62	21.91	5.82	0.38	0.92	2.59							9.41	22.21	17.09
1952	36.86	23.79	8.19	0.90	1.19	2.79	123.8	121.3	132.3	136.8	129.3	107.7	11.65	25.21	18.58
1953	40.77	23.71	10.10	1.29	1.77	3.90	110.4	100.1	129.1	143.3	150.4	130.1	13.55	27.22	18.33
1954	41.88	21.97	11.94	1.60	1.89	4.48	101.7	91.7	119.3	127.9	107.3	114.0	14.69	27.19	16.87
1955	47.04	25.83	12.11	2.36	2.24	4.50	114.6	118.5	105.8	154.5	118.8	99.5	14.93	32.11	20.95
1956	51.09	25.67	14.65	2.54	2.50	5.73	109.2	97.4	128.8	114.9	112.7	127.2	17.58	33.51	20.36
1957	60.93	32.88	16.99	2.75	2.85	5.46	114.2	120.1	112.6	107.5	113.2	91.4	20.76	40.17	26.20
1958	80.76	31.68	32.41	7.10	3.87	5.70	131.8	104.1	176.2	258.1	134.0	104.0	30.91	49.85	25.97
1959	96.36	29.79	42.63	9.72	6.63	7.60	117.0	91.9	132.4	119.3	173.6	133.2	40.97	55.39	23.00
1960	105.27	27.78	48.85	13.73	6.46	8.45	105.0	84.7	112.3	140.5	96.6	109.8	48.65	56.62	19.95
1961	68.35	26.29	28.56	3.16	3.75	6.59	58.1	84.8	53.5	22.5	57.6	55.6	29.10	39.25	20.33
1962	72.12	33.61	26.42	2.14	3.16	6.79	98.3	119.3	87.0	67.5	84.4	92.4	28.56	43.56	26.49
1963	72.03	31.92	28.21	3.22	3.98	4.70	102.1	94.2	109.2	135.6	125.8	81.1	31.18	40.85	24.49
1964	86.36	38.05	32.38	5.81	4.92	5.20	120.5	113.9	118.6	180.7	123.0	132.3	36.12	50.24	29.78
1965	98.99	42.70	38.90	6.65	5.39	5.35	115.1	104.4	127.9	114.5	109.6	105.0	41.34	57.65	33.36
1966	115.28	47.87	47.94	7.58	5.97	5.92	119.6	111.7	129.0	114.0	110.8	111.0	50.48	64.80	36.65
1967	111.42	50.35	42.98	6.35	5.50	6.24	96.5	105.1	91.9	83.8	92.1	105.4	46.11	65.31	39.41
1968	107.94	55.79	36.72	5.08	4.47	5.88	91.8	107.5	82.0	80.1	81.3	94.1	40.93	67.01	44.18
1969	123.43	55.30	47.83	7.68	5.55	7.07	119.9	97.9	138.1	151.0	124.2	120.3	51.06	72.37	43.40
1970	150.80	58.22	68.94	9.46	6.47	7.71	126.0	105.0	144.6	123.3	116.6	109.1	66.83	83.97	43.94
1971	166.21	60.29	77.35	13.02	7.27	8.28	111.7	99.9	115.5	137.6	112.4	107.3	77.26	88.95	45.61
1972	181.95	64.84	87.05	12.68	8.12	9.26	110.3	106.6	114.7	97.4	111.7	112.1	86.33	95.62	47.01
1973	203.38	70.82	100.63	12.98	8.73	10.22	109.8	108.3	112.0	102.4	107.5	110.3	100.00	103.38	51.16
1974	187.92	72.33	83.66	13.71	7.63	10.59	91.0	102.1	80.7	105.6	87.4	103.6	93.49	94.43	52.37
1975	216.25	76.06	105.34	15.26	8.36	11.23	117.3	104.6	131.2	111.3	109.6	106.3	112.61	103.64	54.15
1976	214.28	76.44	104.52	14.01	7.77	11.54	98.0	100.4	97.1	91.8	92.9	102.7	111.99	102.29	53.95
1977	237.45	77.59	124.44	13.58	9.08	12.76	112.0	101.5	121.1	96.9	116.9	110.5	125.55	111.90	54.68
1978	266.96	81.91	142.78	17.54	10.28	14.45	114.5	110.2	115.6	130.3	113.2	113.2	139.27	127.69	58.33
1979	322.23	109.18	164.12	21.92	10.96	16.05	110.5	106.3	112.1	120.0	106.6	109.5	164.96	157.27	77.60
1980	346.76	111.14	177.85	28.72	11.24	17.81	105.6	98.9	108.0	123.6	102.6	104.8	179.80	166.96	79.02
1981	371.85	126.36	187.02	27.59	11.11	19.77	104.3	106.1	104.0	98.4	98.8	109.2	190.12	181.73	91.10
1982	412.79	142.71	205.78	29.59	12.03	22.68	109.7	110.1	109.6	106.3	108.3	112.8	209.85	202.94	105.49
1983	455.93	158.16	221.15	40.51	13.27	22.84	109.0	105.0	107.8	137.6	110.3	107.6	234.08	221.85	115.09
1984	515.21	171.26	255.06	43.94	16.23	28.72	100.9	10.6	113.6	104.3	122.3	121.9	267.33	247.88	125.36
1985	634.62	198.44	314.68	58.21	22.77	40.52	104.0	104.9	116.4	114.3	140.3	127.0	333.78	300.84	145.51
1986	733.67	222.68	368.88	68.27	25.42	48.42	110.3	105.4	113.0	106.3	111.6	114.1	393.19	340.48	162.80
1987	881.70	253.39	456.74	84.18	28.43	58.96	112.0	103.3	116.9	111.4	109.2	110.1	480.50	401.20	184.27
1988	1107.76	303.01	581.85	108.34	34.53	80.03	110.8	100.5	115.3	110.0	118.7	107.8	612.73	495.03	213.02
1989	1235.48	337.48	680.09	88.76	43.36	85.79	103.1	105.1	106.7	76.6	109.7	90.8	695.17	540.31	229.70

18. Hunan

18–2

Year	v1d2	v1d3	v1d4	v1d5	v1e	v1e1	v1e2	v1e3	v1e4	v1e5	v1f	v1f1	v1f2	v1f3	v1g
1949	1.08	0.05	0.43	1.57											16.54
1950	1.37	0.10	0.46	1.74											18.70
1951	1.95	0.18	0.68	2.31											20.71
1952	2.81	0.44	0.89	2.49	125.9	126.2	132.8	244.4	129.4	107.8					24.03
1953	3.38	0.68	1.33	3.50	107.7	99.9	128.2	154.5	151.1	130.9					26.05
1954	4.08	0.81	1.46	3.97	97.3	89.8	121.1	119.1	111.3	112.6					26.48
1955	4.05	1.36	1.75	4.00	119.1	122.8	106.5	181.5	119.6	99.7					31.54
1956	4.90	1.18	1.99	5.08	104.1	96.4	127.8	88.4	115.3	127.0					32.97
1957	5.62	1.26	2.23	4.86	115.4	121.6	112.2	106.9	113.2	91.6					37.48
1958	11.93	3.93	2.94	5.08	119.8	99.7	185.9	325.0	128.1	104.3					49.84
1959	16.09	4.68	4.81	6.81	108.8	86.6	135.9	103.8	165.5	133.9					55.19
1960	18.59	5.91	4.71	7.46	97.8	79.1	113.2	125.5	97.3	108.4					52.43
1961	9.32	1.33	2.53	5.74	61.3	92.2	46.2	22.0	53.2	54.9					37.94
1962	8.26	1.03	2.04	5.74	103.4	122.3	82.3	77.3	81.1	89.6					39.30
1963	9.09	0.98	2.64	3.65	95.7	91.0	112.2	85.9	128.6	74.6					40.57
1964	12.17	2.02	2.05	4.22	122.6	116.0	140.1	206.3	77.4	138.1					48.16
1965	15.44	2.20	2.36	4.29	113.4	104.4	134.0	108.6	115.1	103.8					52.91
1966	18.21	2.38	2.44	5.12	114.4	109.4	123.3	108.5	103.4	119.6					60.54
1967	15.85	2.32	2.27	5.46	100.0	107.5	89.1	97.4	93.0	106.7					61.05
1968	13.41	2.16	2.11	5.15	97.7	108.8	81.3	93.0	93.0	94.1					60.22
1969	17.79	2.43	2.52	6.23	111.9	97.1	140.5	112.6	119.4	121.1					64.72
1970	27.12	3.01	3.09	6.81	120.4	101.0	153.0	124.0	122.6	109.2					76.79
1971	28.16	4.81	3.40	6.97	105.7	100.4	106.8	159.3	110.0	102.4					85.91
1972	31.62	5.42	3.89	7.68	107.6	101.9	114.3	112.8	114.4	110.3					85.79
1973	34.81	5.21	3.90	8.30	106.5	107.9	106.7	96.2	100.3	108.1					88.87
1974	25.36	5.41	3.22	8.07	90.4	102.4	70.8	103.9	82.6	97.2					86.39
1975	31.29	6.08	3.76	8.36	110.9	102.9	128.5	112.1	116.8	103.8					90.39
1976	30.26	6.20	3.59	8.29	98.0	99.5	94.7	102.2	95.5	99.0					89.05
1977	37.93	6.10	4.03	9.16	110.3	101.3	127.5	98.3	112.3	110.6					98.92
1978	46.52	7.43	4.34	11.07	117.2	111.6	124.0	123.0	107.7	120.8	146.99	59.83	59.82	27.34	124.45
1979	53.97	8.79	4.65	12.26	109.5	106.5	112.9	113.5	107.1	109.2	178.01	79.40	68.42	30.19	141.86
1980	58.73	11.25	4.78	13.18	103.9	98.3	108.4	120.8	102.8	101.6	191.72	81.14	76.99	33.59	154.15
1981	60.82	10.16	5.04	14.61	104.5	107.1	101.9	92.4	105.4	109.0	209.68	93.29	77.78	38.61	170.63
1982	65.66	10.79	5.59	15.41	110.2	113.2	107.9	105.4	110.9	103.7	232.52	107.99	82.51	42.02	196.52
1983	71.95	13.99	6.01	14.81	107.4	103.6	109.9	130.3	107.5	106.7	257.43	117.79	93.37	46.27	217.00
1984	83.98	13.19	7.04	18.31	109.7	106.6	114.9	90.7	117.1	120.0	287.29	128.28	104.34	54.67	239.13
1985	102.63	16.54	10.04	26.12	111.5	104.4	115.3	108.1	142.6	128.4	349.95	147.72	127.08	75.15	305.50
1986	117.20	18.66	10.84	30.98	107.5	105.1	109.8	102.3	108.0	113.2	397.68	165.28	143.31	89.09	346.89
1987	143.54	22.52	13.31	37.56	109.2	102.7	115.6	109.1	119.1	109.6	469.44	187.09	172.45	109.90	400.15
1988	183.30	30.50	15.73	52.48	105.3	97.2	113.2	115.7	118.0	111.0	584.07	217.03	221.28	145.76	494.83
1989	208.12	25.74	19.06	57.69	103.0	105.3	106.0	78.9	104.3	93.1	640.80	234.31	238.15	168.34	513.45

18. Hunan

18–3

Year	v1h	v1i	v1j	v1j1	v1j2	v1j3	v1k	v2a	v2a1	v2a2	v2b	v2c	v2c1	v2c2	v2d1
1949								0.55							
1950				288				0.75				0.17			
1951				296				1.20				0.34			
1952				313				1.48	1.12	0.36		0.88			
1953				363				2.42	1.73	0.69		1.56			
1954				378				2.76	2.15	0.61		1.55			
1955				399				4.80	1.73	3.07		1.92			
1956				469				4.50	2.90	1.60		2.71			
1957	80.93			505			0.23	7.10	3.39	3.71		2.67			
1958				435				16.82	12.25	4.27		7.91			
1959				429				21.95	14.70	7.25		11.42			
1960				436				18.90	15.88	3.02		13.66			
1961				444				3.11	3.89	-0.78		3.93			
1962				493			1.00	0.76	2.32	-1.56		2.03			
1963				528				5.80	3.32	2.48		2.66			
1964				555				9.97	7.41	2.56		4.13			
1965	103.94			559			0.85	11.20	8.29	2.91		5.20			
1966				560				14.54	9.98	4.56		6.32			
1967				564				12.37	8.36	4.01		4.75			
1968				566				11.24	6.66	4.58		2.90			
1969				545				14.94	9.63	5.31		6.15			
1970				537				24.41	16.73	7.68		14.54			
1971				539				30.08	19.86	10.22		16.83			
1972				561				25.56	16.21	9.27		12.26			
1973				555				25.21	16.97	8.24		12.87			
1974				563				21.38	16.86	4.52		11.65			
1975	111.87			560			1.62	23.08	18.66	4.42		12.87			
1976				554				21.40	16.68	4.72		10.88			
1977				556				24.26	15.45	8.81		10.93			
1978	142.56	20.16	563	589	474		2.39	36.85	24.05	12.80		14.71	8.00	0.48	110.15
1979	177.12	23.39	628	644	580		2.83	36.94	26.33	10.61		17.56	8.21	0.62	122.69
1980	219.72	28.73	718	746	625		3.82	34.86	28.54	6.32		20.32	6.98	1.37	134.61
1981	241.71	30.09	725	748	643		4.96	35.69	24.22	11.47	33.45	18.67	5.02	1.57	146.63
1982	284.38	32.46	750	772	670		5.87	44.09	29.73	14.36	40.18	25.34	6.97	1.60	157.40
1983	351.67	34.48	780	803	700		6.84	48.82	37.84	10.78	55.66	25.06	6.02	0.63	168.49
1984	348.20	41.69	922	965	800		7.74	50.96	36.37	14.59	60.54	29.39	7.23	0.78	180.34
1985	395.26	49.29	1059	1111	912		10.49	79.27	49.99	29.28	83.52	43.86	10.03	1.85	203.94
1986	439.66	58.78	1220	1281	1043		13.28	98.48	64.70	33.78	97.76	48.90	11.74	1.58	226.05
1987	471.30	70.14	1400	1470	1190		15.91	119.52	78.45	41.07	116.39	60.98	15.27	2.27	255.41
1988	515.35	87.38	1688	1777	1407		20.75	156.57	97.23	59.34	140.04	72.97	17.61	2.83	294.81
1989	558.34	98.20	1862	1945	1475		22.67	142.84	70.14	72.70	111.74	60.27	19.88	2.26	335.60

18. Hunan

18–4

Year	v2d2	v2e	v3a	v3b	v3b1	v3b2	v3c	v3d	v3d1	v3d2	v3e	v3e1	v3e2	v3e3	v3e4
1949			15.99	15.83			0.16	53	50	85					
1950			17.95	17.69			0.26	58	55	94					
1951			19.51	19.14			0.37	62	59	97					
1952			22.55	21.87	19.02	2.85	0.68	68	64	103	125.98	75.58			
1953			23.63	22.86	19.42	3.44	0.77	69	64	117					
1954			23.72	22.69	19.10	3.59	1.03	67	62	110					
1955			26.74	25.56	21.74	3.82	1.18	74	70	116					
1956			28.47	27.00	22.33	4.67	1.47	77	71	138					
1957			30.38	28.82	23.39	5.43	1.56	81	73	148	164.52	92.47			
1958			33.02	31.39	24.62	6.77	1.63	86	77	153					
1959			33.24	31.09	22.30	8.79	2.15	84	71	164					
1960			33.53	31.33	22.01	9.32	2.20	86	71	175					
1961			34.83	32.93	23.87	9.06	1.90	93	78	194					
1962			38.54	37.03	28.36	8.67	1.51	104	90	211					
1963			34.77	33.41	24.31	9.20	1.36	91	74	231					
1964			38.19	36.18	26.79	9.39	2.01	96	80	230					
1965			41.71	39.88	29.87	10.01	1.83	104	87	242					
1966			46.00	43.90	33.81	10.09	2.10	111	96	239					
1967			48.68	46.68	36.37	10.31	2.00	115	100	239					
1968			48.98	47.19	36.85	10.34	1.79	113	98	240					
1969			49.78	47.66	37.48	10.18	2.12	111	96	247					
1970			52.38	50.18	39.30	10.88	2.20	114	98	261					
1971			55.83	53.00	40.72	12.28	2.83	117	100	274					
1972			60.23	56.98	42.73	14.25	3.25	123	102	303					
1973			63.66	60.07	45.28	14.79	3.59	126	106	306					
1974			65.01	60.68	45.36	15.32	4.33	125	104	308					
1975			67.31	63.19	47.19	16.00	4.12	128	106	315					
1976			67.65	63.10	46.54	16.56	4.55	126	103	320					
1977			74.66	69.10	52.11	16.99	5.56	136	114	324					
1978	78.21	33.86	87.60	81.61	61.57	20.04	5.99	159	134	371	289.56	166.08			
1979	87.06	35.57	104.92	96.88	73.65	23.23	8.04	187	160	400					
1980	93.18	37.13	119.29	109.25	81.14	28.11	10.04	208	175	456	425.52	244.08	52.44	5.64	7.32
1981	101.51	37.86	134.94	123.72	93.01	30.71	11.22	233	199	479	465.84	260.28	57.84	5.88	7.92
1982	109.94	40.69	152.43	139.14	106.40	32.74	13.29	257	224	495	449.40	264.48	54.84	6.48	7.80
1983	114.31	43.89	168.18	153.93	118.89	35.04	14.25	281	247	520	492.72	289.44	61.92	6.84	8.76
1984	121.05	48.44	188.17	171.91	131.97	39.94	16.26	311	274	561	540.84	310.44	70.44	7.20	9.12
1985	136.12	56.59	226.23	206.97	157.22	49.75	19.26	370	326	646	685.32	366.48	86.52	6.36	9.72
1986	150.67	68.12	248.41	227.35	167.91	59.44	21.06	402	346	741	775.32	427.92	102.00	6.72	9.60
1987	170.85	78.79	280.63	256.28	187.12	69.16	24.35	447	379	838	871.56	497.10	101.53	7.07	10.16
1988	199.14	93.89	338.26	308.79	217.11	91.68	29.47	528	435	1064	1142.65	580.72	132.00	6.87	13.18
1989	228.02	118.16	370.61	331.78	228.34	103.44	38.83	556	450	1157	1234.00	678.30			

18. Hunan

18–5

Year	v3f	v3f1	v3f2	v3f3	v3f4	v4a1	v4a1a	v4a1b	v4a1c	v4a1d	v4a2	v4a2a	v4a2b	v4a2c	v4a2d
1949															
1950						2.15	0.06				0.79	0.25	0.09	0.30	0.15
1951						3.15	0.07				1.12	0.30	0.19	0.37	0.26
1952						4.07	0.49				2.06	0.53	0.51	0.49	0.53
1953						4.13	0.29				2.08	0.65	0.64	0.50	0.29
1954						4.91	0.56				2.93	1.27	0.62	0.54	0.50
1955						4.73	0.68				2.24	0.53	0.68	0.64	0.39
1956						5.23	0.90				3.14	0.85	0.82	0.86	0.61
1957	78.11	57.04	7.60	0.91	6.65	5.53	1.11				3.22	0.85	0.95	0.76	0.66
1958						10.47	4.98				8.40	5.29	0.97	0.79	1.35
1959						13.80	7.54				11.09	6.02	1.09	0.91	3.07
1960						15.17	8.31				14.07	8.17	1.40	0.96	3.54
1961						8.50	3.77				9.21	1.93	1.28	1.03	4.97
1962						8.77	3.39				4.22	0.82	1.19	0.85	1.36
1963						8.09	2.62				5.01	1.17	1.21	0.86	1.77
1964						9.12	3.09				6.88	2.42	1.38	0.92	2.16
1965	93.21	71.03				10.05	3.69				7.00	2.86	1.45	0.91	1.78
1966						10.96	4.65				9.06	3.93	1.62	1.01	2.50
1967						8.86	3.04				8.31	3.73	1.75	0.87	1.96
1968						6.92	1.28				6.24	2.29	1.54	0.89	1.52
1969						9.81	3.25				9.34	4.44	1.53	0.96	2.41
1970						14.95	6.53				10.84	5.52	1.76	1.02	2.54
1971						17.71	8.20				12.33	5.42	2.22	1.28	3.41
1972						18.43	8.01				14.61	6.62	2.47	1.36	4.16
1973						21.72	9.34				15.07	5.90	2.83	1.41	4.93
1974						13.89	2.96				15.40	5.60	3.12	1.48	5.20
1975						18.27	5.36				15.92	5.32	3.32	1.46	5.82
1976						16.02	2.93				15.85	4.84	3.46	1.51	6.04
1977						20.88	5.73				16.41	4.69	3.67	1.60	6.45
1978	140.07	97.93	14.29	4.43	13.72	27.98	9.68				24.46	7.62	4.33	1.88	10.63
1979						28.63	8.95				25.17	7.01	5.04	2.33	10.79
1980	192.85	127.70	20.25	12.28	14.70	29.86	9.58				23.71	4.86	6.68	2.66	9.51
1981	207.59	135.98	23.06	13.59	14.28	31.40	9.10				21.39	3.00	6.81	2.90	8.68
1982	248.69	164.02	24.74	22.20	13.63	30.33	5.11				23.26	3.12	7.91	3.03	9.20
1983	273.86	175.62	26.71	29.13	13.49	29.27	2.25				25.31	3.48	8.79	3.58	9.46
1984	293.19	190.96	28.58	27.25	14.03	32.85	2.74				30.04	4.43	9.86	4.87	10.88
1985	348.45	219.43	33.25	33.27	17.40	39.19	1.61	34.58	2.25	0.40	40.09	4.60	12.53	5.20	17.76
1986	386.35	228.96	36.30	50.50	16.15	47.65	4.08	39.53	2.73	0.76	54.29	5.80	14.22	5.54	28.73
1987	434.75	245.68	35.17	60.35	17.46	54.38	4.37	45.17	3.19	0.92	55.93	4.65	14.88	6.22	30.18
1988	480.75	266.89	37.32	66.59	19.72	56.54	-0.47	51.02	3.23	1.05	64.89	5.21	18.30	6.13	35.25
1989	516.29	290.35	38.07	65.65	19.36	68.86	-1.48				74.23	5.44	20.69	6.43	41.67

18. Hunan

18–6

Year	v4b	v4b1	v4b2	v4b3	v4c1	v4c2	v5a	v5a1	v5a2	v5a3	v5a4	v5b1	v5b2	v5b3	v5c
1949															
1950	0.02	0.02					1107.76	22.81	0.18	38.93	1028.16	980.83	54.86	72.07	49.60
1951	0.13						1147.20	33.55	0.37	42.71	1052.48	1001.38	64.12	81.70	
1952	0.18	0.18	0.002				1188.76	48.87	0.77	46.70	1072.81	989.38	76.72	122.66	63.61
1953	0.22						1213.15	53.12	2.32	50.68	1086.32	1014.03	90.34	108.78	
1954	0.42						1223.84	54.61	8.56	42.92	1100.24	982.69	89.39	151.76	
1955	0.39						1250.49	60.67	14.10	31.45	1128.78	1061.22	74.72	114.55	
1956	0.45						1271.31	73.66	35.78	7.62	1142.45	1055.72	101.21	114.38	
1957	0.64						1353.51	81.84	36.62	2.00	1221.27	1134.13	93.05	126.33	
1958	1.18						1461.08	190.02	30.49		1234.10	898.17	251.10	311.81	
1959	2.45						1466.09	174.09	36.76		1248.01	861.58	258.27	346.24	
1960	1.84						1508.04	182.44	54.05		1265.15	1023.93	199.05	285.06	
1961	1.25						1302.48	163.50	70.90	3.92	1064.16	1053.45	128.89	120.14	
1962	0.81						1401.22	135.76	66.21	5.62	1193.63	1180.33	98.04	122.85	
1963	0.86						1443.01	129.40	61.79	3.11	1248.71	1222.67	111.47	108.87	
1964	1.04						1508.43	130.34	62.54	4.99	1310.56	1274.86	116.73	116.84	
1965	1.25						1551.93	139.24	67.72	3.91	1341.06	1305.83	124.66	121.44	
1966	1.36						1607.49	144.17	67.56	3.41	1392.35	1355.48	129.72	122.29	
1967	1.36						1668.06	148.25	67.40	2.97	1449.44	1405.14	135.05	127.87	
1968	1.53						1728.41	149.71	67.24	2.59	1508.87	1456.39	140.79	131.23	
1969	1.63						1795.01	154.93	67.09	2.26	1570.73	1511.41	151.70	131.90	
1970	1.75						1880.85	176.81	66.94	1.97	1635.13	1564.21	179.69	136.95	
1971	2.09						1975.89	205.21	66.79	1.72	1702.17	1624.30	206.63	144.96	
1972	2.42						2056.50	219.04	66.69	1.50	1769.27	1683.60	227.31	145.59	
1973	2.71						2089.11	218.99	66.66	1.32	1802.14	1718.66	226.17	144.28	
1974	3.30						2117.00	223.43	68.10	1.10	1824.37	1732.28	236.13	148.59	
1975	3.69						2152.00	232.56	71.61	0.32	1847.51	1742.28	257.39	152.33	
1976	4.02						2183.24	238.79	74.52	0.26	1869.67	1759.48	266.42	157.34	
1977	4.62						2216.19	242.64	78.60	0.37	1894.58	1775.31	273.17	167.71	
1978	5.50	3.99	1.510		19.80	17.70	2280.05	282.06	81.72	0.35	1915.92	1788.17	305.37	186.51	260.62
1979	7.77				24.19	19.70	2328.12	299.36	88.80	0.32	1939.64	1798.27	325.70	204.15	
1980	11.31	7.69	3.620		26.75	20.50	2399.95	316.80	92.36	1.81	1988.98	1846.46	339.06	196.43	288.05
1981	15.31	9.78	5.530		27.53	19.70	2449.46	332.46	94.42	3.43	2019.15	1887.54	339.52	222.40	288.63
1982	20.81	12.90	7.910		29.95	19.88	2541.05	344.41	97.07	5.21	2094.36	1955.49	350.79	234.77	294.91
1983	26.61	16.71	9.900		33.83	21.39	2594.37	348.97	98.84	9.72	2136.84	1966.48	361.77	266.12	303.27
1984	36.30	23.09	13.210		37.05	21.86	2672.84	340.94	119.75	13.18	2198.97	1971.93	413.98	286.93	344.77
1985	50.11	32.80	17.310		44.90	23.30	2728.71	352.73	122.34	16.19	2237.37	1946.85	458.68	323.18	372.65
1986	73.52	47.86	25.660		48.60	22.21	2808.87	367.31	125.25	18.44	2297.64	1969.64	494.51	344.72	402.45
1987	99.76	66.68	33.080		55.82	22.36	2904.10	386.34	128.60	24.72	2364.16	2011.35	531.70	361.05	437.15
1988	109.80	79.35	30.450		67.41	23.00	2998.64	401.75	128.14	30.75	2437.69	2050.73	546.93	400.99	451.57
1989	153.10	113.90	39.300		70.44	20.35	3091.37	411.34	124.81	30.43	2524.30	2104.60	550.26	436.51	

18. Hunan

18–7

Year	v5c1	v5d	v6a	v6a1	v6a2	v6b	v6c	v6d1	v6d2	v6d3	v6d4	v6d5	v6d6
1949			2986.83	235.95	2750.88			255.21	2731.62	1558.45	1428.38	38.35	
1950		980.83	3074.34	245.79	2828.55	37.00	20.00	265.59	2808.75	1601.97	1472.37		
1951			3190.67	255.57	2935.10	37.00	19.00	276.12	2914.55	1664.24	1526.43		
1952		989.38	3271.20	259.08	3012.12	37.00	19.00	278.66	2992.54	1707.79	1563.41	56.51	10.74
1953			3349.70	260.55	3089.15	36.00	17.00	311.52	3038.18	1751.22	1598.48		
1954			3429.02	277.21	3151.81	37.85	17.54	343.13	3085.89	1807.89	1621.13		
1955			3472.83	327.94	3144.89	31.10	16.36	312.85	3159.98	1831.58	1641.25		
1956			3507.43	329.02	3178.41	29.59	11.51	363.99	3143.44	1836.26	1671.17		
1957			3603.24	314.67	3288.57	33.47	10.41	368.20	3235.04	1887.55	1715.69	67.33	10.52
1958			3672.72	352.78	3319.94	29.96	11.65	513.91	3158.81	1919.61	1753.11	66.30	10.40
1959			3691.95	494.52	3197.43	24.00	12.99	560.42	3131.53	1933.47	1758.48		
1960			3569.37	404.63	3164.74	19.49	29.42	502.42	3066.95	1857.07	1712.30		
1961			3507.98	477.73	3030.25	12.51	17.48	431.45	3076.53	1819.55	1688.43	91.40	11.82
1962			3600.26	384.66	3215.60	41.40	10.23	390.53	3209.73	1870.89	1729.37	76.41	11.55
1963			3715.20	375.34	3339.86	47.29	10.26	405.48	3309.72	1926.81	1788.39	75.15	11.47
1964			3785.13	429.54	3355.59	42.20	12.88	409.93	3375.20	1965.75	1819.38	76.44	11.70
1965			3901.47	405.64	3495.83	42.25	11.19	418.86	3482.61	2022.78	1878.69	76.77	11.97
1966			4009.65	411.87	3597.78	37.23	10.15	425.43	3584.22	2079.48	1930.17		
1967			4122.56	429.40	3693.16	35.61	9.89	437.40	3685.16	2138.25	1984.31		
1968			4238.65	446.93	3791.72	33.99	9.63	423.48	3815.17	2198.68	2039.97		
1969			4358.01	464.46	3893.55	32.37	9.37	402.09	3955.92	2260.82	2097.19		
1970			4480.76	481.97	3998.79	30.75	9.11	431.36	4049.40	2324.73	2156.03	74.23	12.22
1971			4598.27	470.86	4127.41	29.13	8.86	465.39	4132.88	2384.91	2213.36		
1972			4700.56	489.75	4210.81	29.93	9.01	475.68	4224.88	2438.55	2262.01		
1973			4809.79	506.49	4303.30	29.21	8.05	489.51	4320.28	2497.79	2312.00		
1974			4900.86	522.34	4378.52	27.11	8.67	503.91	4396.95	2545.64	2355.22		
1975			4991.36	531.82	4459.54	25.04	8.34	512.39	4478.97	2594.18	2397.18	82.79	14.95
1976			5056.81	544.71	4512.10	20.07	7.70	522.21	4534.60	2629.85	2426.96		
1977			5111.83	561.21	4550.62	18.61	7.79	526.56	4585.27	2657.88	2453.95		
1978		1788.17	5165.91	593.86	4572.05	17.40	7.01	552.39	4613.52	2684.80	2481.11	94.83	16.35
1979			5223.05	639.60	4583.45	17.84	7.12	606.55	4616.50	2712.32	2510.73		
1980		1846.46	5280.95	671.05	4609.90	17.68	6.88	626.89	4654.06	2740.40	2540.55	101.94	19.48
1981		1887.54	5360.05	694.74	4665.33	21.11	7.03	656.18	4703.87	2783.12	2576.93		
1982		1955.49	5452.12	815.98	4636.14	21.98	6.77	667.42	4784.70	2831.03	2621.09		
1983		1966.48	5509.43	874.46	4634.97	16.48	6.79	680.47	4828.96	2864.09	2645.34		
1984		1971.93	5561.32	1321.43	4239.89	16.66	7.20	744.52	4816.80	2893.92	2667.40		
1985		1946.85	5622.49	1723.04	3899.45	18.16	6.47	796.63	4825.86	2928.44	2694.05	115.72	22.08
1986		1969.64	5695.73	2021.20	3674.53	19.90	6.30	806.71	4889.02	2966.85	2728.88	119.27	23.03
1987		2011.35	5782.61	2257.37	3525.24	23.62	7.07	843.15	4939.46	3012.59	2770.02	122.68	23.73
1988		2050.73	5915.68	2448.35	3467.33	23.32	6.82	880.05	5035.63	3079.65	2836.03	126.35	117.73
1989			6013.62	2490.87	3522.75	22.91	7.07	908.01	5105.61	3130.76	2882.86	130.12	119.26

18. Hunan

18–8

Year	v7a	v7b	v7c	v7d	v7e	v7f	v7g	v7h	v7h1	v7h2	v7h3	v7h4	v7h5	v7i	v8a
1949	0.01		1798.81	5830.71	559			15.84	12.05	0.24	1.42	0.03	2.10	233.30	3.18
1950	0.01	1.20	1934.89	5906.19	683			29.18						249.77	4.15
1951	0.02	1.20	2040.98	6119.75	662			21.91						254.12	5.82
1952	0.03	1.20	2307.41	7804.15	547	0.20		23.79	16.75	0.43	2.78	0.07	3.76	269.44	8.19
1953	0.04	2.10	2379.36	8209.21	762	0.10		23.71						282.16	10.10
1954	0.04	3.20	2445.05	8668.14	944	0.97		21.97						280.99	11.94
1955	0.08	5.40	2500.13	9353.08	468	2.40		25.83						274.19	12.11
1956	0.20	12.10	2575.28	10221.31	1424	4.94		25.67						292.02	14.65
1957	0.25	14.30	2665.55	10262.00	876	5.18		32.88						305.74	16.99
1958	0.74	50.10	2774.99	11459.02	181	11.25		31.68						310.62	32.41
1959	1.46	73.60	2875.44	10991.32	922	12.84		29.79						307.30	42.63
1960	2.24	99.47	2903.35	11620.79	1261	15.85		27.78						290.12	48.85
1961	2.46	92.84	2935.60	9268.08	1261	9.36		26.29						261.24	28.56
1962	2.66	87.72	2976.62	9166.30	371	12.35		33.61						257.20	26.42
1963	2.91	94.17	3029.63	9419.54	1754	23.91	0.50	31.92						265.01	28.21
1964	3.39	109.31	3127.19	10212.41	691	32.75	0.46	38.05						277.76	32.38
1965	4.29	72.19	3245.29	10965.82	486	53.15	0.91	42.70						289.32	38.90
1966	5.45	92.04	3303.96	11564.83	291	90.17	1.41	47.87						300.97	47.94
1967	5.57	117.35	3393.00	11484.00	184	86.20	1.58	50.35						304.56	42.98
1968	6.39	149.62	3429.22	10945.00	155	75.19	1.78	55.79						310.20	36.72
1969	7.30	190.77	3461.28	11050.00	414	101.41	2.00	55.30						311.21	47.83
1970	8.95	243.20	3514.52	11452.53	192	121.71	4.81	58.22						316.56	68.94
1971	10.67	303.03	3566.51	12066.99	1076	130.29	3.27	60.29						323.90	77.35
1972	13.28	342.54	3646.40	12537.63	757	167.99	4.68	64.84						331.66	87.05
1973	15.34	489.83	3724.72	12626.04	234	198.07	4.14	70.82						330.78	100.63
1974	18.62	616.08	3755.91	12445.77	573	177.56	6.46	72.33						332.66	83.66
1975	23.32	690.02	3875.02	12339.35	265	193.84	6.82	76.06						336.16	105.34
1976	28.34	843.95	3925.69	12425.36	257	194.25	6.96	76.44						326.38	104.52
1977	34.96	984.41	3985.64	12408.72	288	202.95	7.36	77.59						316.30	124.44
1978	42.86	1072.39	4037.04	12668.63	837	271.90	8.78	81.91	61.55	3.37	12.76	0.83	3.04	320.41	142.78
1979	50.77	1187.11	4095.64	12501.65	665	325.23	9.26	109.18	81.24	4.19	19.70	1.04	3.01	327.16	164.12
1980	58.90	985.66	4114.09	11864.21	846	361.04	9.67	111.14	80.00	5.67	21.30	1.27	2.90	322.86	177.85
1981	65.97	771.45	4129.54	12014.15	999	371.20	11.20	126.36	87.90	7.61	23.30	2.51	5.04	324.71	187.02
1982	70.49	532.06	4139.50	11954.30	578	396.38	12.64	142.71	97.96	7.51	28.66	3.56	5.02	326.57	205.78
1983	78.56	600.78	4160.18	11619.24	808	421.52	13.81	158.16	109.53	7.85	31.53	4.07	5.18	322.45	221.15
1984	80.54	490.34	4163.36	11458.86	838	354.21	14.45	171.26	112.38	8.58	38.11	5.34	6.85	333.67	255.06
1985	89.20	520.73	4156.77	11215.58	1289	369.64	15.06	198.44	116.11	12.54	51.40	6.98	11.41	348.16	314.68
1986	105.94	625.13	4157.63	11304.72	885	432.12	18.05	222.68	129.63	13.89	58.40	8.26	12.50	363.70	368.88
1987	105.36	723.70	3998.00	11212.11	630	457.77	17.98	253.39	138.31	18.14	72.40	10.58	13.96	377.71	456.74
1988	111.29	901.65	4005.44	11244.23	1297	490.07	20.35	303.01	140.71	21.79	109.60	13.20	17.71	382.99	581.85
1989	121.52	1012.00	4011.30	11623.20		517.88	21.86	337.48	164.86	21.67	116.86	15.28	18.81	298.70	680.09

18. Hunan

18–9

Year	v8a1	v8a2	v8a3	v8b	v8c1	v8c2	v8d	v8f1	v8f2	v8f3	v8f4	v8f5	v8g
1949	0.11				0.54	2.64			79.06		0.19		1400
1950					0.90	3.25			93.88		0.25		1884
1951					1.67	4.15			159.34		0.38		2796
1952	3.42	0.08	4.69		2.36	5.83		0.03	175.63		0.77		3122
1953					2.73	7.37		0.09	154.00		0.89		3163
1954					3.62	8.32		0.13	210.92		1.34		4265
1955					4.15	7.96		0.29	233.42		1.54		5985
1956					5.52	9.13		0.54	300.83		2.17		7812
1957					6.78	10.21		0.71	341.15		2.51		8107
1958					16.07	16.34		2.83	835.00		4.27	15.57	12971
1959					22.98	19.65		8.70	940.00		7.80	10.83	12216
1960					29.92	18.93		20.08	1054.00		13.28	16.03	11905
1961					14.02	14.54		3.71	680.00		9.88	8.20	13095
1962					11.77	14.65		1.78	549.00		9.86	6.33	10449
1963					13.72	14.49		1.74	544.19		11.68	8.76	9154
1964					16.39	15.99		2.10	525.14		13.51	18.09	8268
1965					19.79	19.11		4.07	529.89		17.71	28.27	7939
1966					27.49	20.45		7.71	674.80		22.85	34.95	8875
1967					22.57	20.41		6.51	646.85		23.30	31.82	9512
1968					17.40	19.32		2.48	546 91		22.00	26.15	9401
1969					24.75	23.08		5.83	778.99		29.92	53.60	9410
1970					42.47	26.47		13.75	1103.81		40.83	98.75	10106
1971					47.61	29.74		29.66	1393.17		44.97	144.79	13227
1972					54.58	32.47		39.08	1599.62		52.04	160.59	14112
1973					63.19	37.44		48.06	1666.02		68.55	188.50	14039
1974					46.43	37.23		13.50	1492.48		52.71	141.54	14903
1975					62.67	42.67		31.55	1842.48		68.24	220.93	16530
1976					60.35	44.17		17.44	1885.17		68.52	222.53	18438
1977					73.37	51.07		37.50	2277.13		79.84	285.83	19164
1978	107.07	35.71		101.69	87.00	55.78	31.92	62.44	2671.98		93.54	344.75	19644
1979	123.58	39.91	0.63	118.49	99.42	64.70	37.77	73.16	2587.41		106.72	431.00	20204
1980	134.34	42.01	1.50	129.88	101.18	76.67	41.17	69.47	2399.09		118.67	502.15	20440
1981	139.24	45.06	2.72	135.14	99.58	87.44	42.45	73.09	2409.48		122.36	534.27	20017
1982	152.77	49.06	3.95	148.25	110.11	95.67	45.58	84.88	2531.02		131.04	578.68	20103
1983	163.03	53.81	4.31	158.05	119.38	101.77	49.90	92.03	2667.96		136.47	627.56	20416
1984	182.76	67.03	5.27	177.78	140.06	115.00	56.93	97.68	2848.16		138.47	676.70	22180
1985	218.52	90.08	6.08	212.66	174.92	139.76	68.63	109.23	2944.82		147.51	761.60	25390
1986	249.13	107.99	11.76	242.09	200.52	168.36	77.41	103.27	2053.18		151.95	866.45	25956
1987	297.72	137.01	22.01	290.04	246.34	210.40	90.06	112.72	3360.08		161.40	967.05	25891
1988	376.29	172.00	33.56	367.23	318.46	263.39	112.28	123.02	3561.64		173.13	1066.07	27665
1989	442.18	192.87	45.04	429.96	380.02	300.07	129.82	136.07	3690.43		183.34	986.25	25132

18. Hunan

18–10

Year	v8g1	v9a	v9a1	v9a2	v9a3	v9b	v9b1	v9b2	v9b3	v9c	v10a	v10a1	v10b1	v10b2	v10b3
1949										270					
1950		7.81	6.83	0.70	0.28	13.53	7.93	0.10	5.50	357	6.53	6.45	0.26		0.20
1951		8.16	6.60	0.89	0.67	19.81	12.48	0.18	7.15	512	8.63	8.54	0.81		0.19
1952		8.44	6.67	0.90	0.87	27.88	19.91	0.19	7.78	546	9.96	9.85	1.03		1.50
1953		10.47	7.88	1.49	1.10	40.31	30.16	0.43	9.72	669	12.20	11.38	1.71		2.73
1954		11.11	8.22	1.60	1.29	45.70	35.86	0.62	9.22	737	13.61	12.69	2.57		5.61
1955		10.61	7.32	2.00	1.29	46.91	34.30	0.82	11.79	858	13.98	12.95	3.96		4.28
1956		15.64	10.53	3.40	1.71	55.41	41.40	1.13	12.88	1070	16.07	14.49	4.86		5.73
1957		16.65	11.22	3.71	1.72	68.02	51.82	1.41	14.79	1121	16.95	15.41	6.43		4.50
1958		20.07	12.62	5.60	1.85	87.35	68.71	2.38	16.26	1425	20.90	17.70	8.44		6.58
1959		23.92	15.15	6.58	2.19	111.69	87.34	3.85	20.50	2061	25.20	20.86	12.19		9.47
1960		30.33	20.38	6.71	3.24	130.98	101.37	5.08	24.53	2680	27.70	22.40	13.51		10.45
1961		34.46	25.49	4.94	4.03	88.47	70.86	2.53	15.08	2327	23.77	21.04	10.59		8.25
1962		34.82	25.48	5.18	4.16	76.66	61.38	2.56	12.77	2648	24.41	21.98	11.65		8.16
1963		24.62	16.01	5.75	2.86	79.53	64.48	2.96	12.09	2519	24.60	22.01	14.84		8.27
1964		25.35	15.58	7.31	2.46	92.94	78.66	2.12	12.16	2529	25.62	22.81	15.88		8.61
1965		27.37	16.03	9.10	2.24	118.23	101.93	2.72	13.58	2592	26.34	22.63	22.61		2.84
1966		30.85	16.58	11.67	2.60	138.27	120.62	3.95	13.07	2717	29.68	24.87	25.67		3.20
1967		33.08	21.14	9.24	2.70	107.68	91.70	4.00	11.98	2583	32.02	27.64	27.99		3.25
1968		38.53	26.28	8.79	3.46	98.50	83.09	3.67	11.74	2499	30.61	26.56	26.76		2.88
1969		43.74	29.14	11.19	3.41	128.11	110.53	4.63	12.95	2604	34.12	29.40	29.83		3.23
1970		44.19	28.26	12.16	3.77	167.65	147.57	5.41	14.67	2991	37.68	31.40	33.26		3.47
1971		46.54	28.80	13.86	3.88	189.21	168.49	6.33	14.39	3309	41.21	33.73	36.57		3.64
1972		52.48	33.03	15.28	4.17	206.86	183.56	6.98	16.32	2482	44.94	36.62	40.66		3.46
1973		56.51	35.52	16.44	4.55	220.82	194.58	7.00	19.24	3711	49.82	40.38	45.32		3.39
1974		58.42	37.54	16.52	4.36	188.97	165.80	6.15	17.02	3760	51.84	42.38	47.58		3.18
1975		58.82	37.23	17.25	4.34	208.29	181.98	6.48	19.83	3974	56.80	46.06	53.21		2.38
1976		65.50	41.41	19.61	4.48	198.41	171.47	7.03	19.91	4349	58.55	47.27	54.85		2.43
1977		68.12	42.15	21.25	4.72	339.92	310.52	8.28	21.12	4434	62.24	49.95	58.38		2.54
1978	2986	101.12	45.70	49.35	6.01	304.73	249.83	30.00	24.82	4598	68.84	53.73	64.28		2.95
1979	3045	117.10	53.92	57.54	5.58	335.62	280.98	31.38	23.18	4857	81.80	63.90	73.79		4.88
1980	3074	133.68	65.47	62.90	5.25	331.43	272.42	33.95	24.98	7627	95.51	75.20	83.09		8.95
1981	3066	149.19	73.21	70.20	5.71	340.22	274.11	39.57	26.45	7868	104.18	85.48	85.86		12.40
1982	3123	159.66	78.05	75.62	5.92	359.71	286.44	43.83	29.35	8136	112.40	93.45	88.36		15.78
1983	3129	179.81	90.95	82.10	6.67	388.55	302.28	50.56	35.61	8667	124.91	105.17	88.03		18.13
1984	3187	204.68	104.85	93.08	6.68	435.78	335.83	59.70	40.15	9285	142.08	121.90	51.80		62.08
1985	3522	254.53	132.78	114.95	6.72	512.03	392.52	75.55	43.86	10412	177.30	154.28	59.02		74.17
1986	3463	275.33	140.09	128.68	6.33	582.44	438.71	91.91	51.72	11330	204.68	176.98	67.20		82.09
1987	3568	310.57	161.86	142.66	5.74	637.60	481.87	103.97	51.66	12723	242.88	209.52	80.86		91.20
1988	3567	354.23	191.21	156.57	6.11	690.60	504.58	134.16	51.76	16263	316.24	272.16	109.18		112.70
1989	3602	350.34	181.09	163.78	4.88	730.40	544.44	129.50	56.29	20126	341.99	293.75	114.39		116.08

18. Hunan

18–11

Year	v10b4	v10b5	v10b6	v10d	v11a1	v11a2	v11a3	v11b	v11b1	v11b2	v11c	v11d	v12a	v12b	v12c
1949															
1950	0.01	5.75	0.31	4.65											
1951	0.03	7.21	0.39	5.98				0.09	0.07	0.02			105.6	105.6	112.6
1952	0.05	7.03	0.35	6.60				0.33	0.29	0.04			97.4	97.4	98.5
1953	0.05	7.41	0.30	8.11				0.51	0.46	0.05			104.6	108.5	110.2
1954	0.03	5.25	0.15	7.57				0.24	0.23	0.01			104.3	102.5	97.1
1955	0.05	5.51	0.18	8.72				0.16	0.16				101.0	102.5	101.6
1956	4.31	0.97	0.20	8.69				0.22	0.22				101.1	102.6	102.8
1957	5.36	0.43	0.23	9.72				0.30	0.30				102.5	102.1	109.4
1958	5.44	0.24	0.20	10.28				0.42	0.32	0.09			100.2	99.4	104.1
1959	3.16	0.18	0.20	12.33				0.74	0.69	0.05			100.1	100.4	101.8
1960	3.16	0.18	0.40	10.47				0.32	0.27	0.04			107.1	102.1	103.8
1961	3.21	0.22	1.50	8.48				0.19	0.17	0.02			132.4	142.6	125.2
1962	2.86	0.34	1.40	10.27				0.17	0.16	0.01			111.8	107.5	106.6
1963		0.29	1.20	11.60				0.17	0.17	0.01			85.0	88.6	96.6
1964		0.26	0.87	12.99				0.22	0.20	0.02			94.2	96.1	97.5
1965		0.23	0.66	13.51				0.28	0.26	0.02			89.6	90.5	94.5
1966		0.23	0.58	14.90				0.28	0.25	0.02			99.7	99.3	104.5
1967		0.22	0.56	14.27				0.22	0.20	0.02			100.1	100.7	100.0
1968		0.21	0.76	17.10				0.23	0.20	0.03			100.1	100.1	100.5
1969		0.20	0.86	15.82				0.25	0.22	0.03			99.9	100.4	100.8
1970		0.20	0.75	16.31				0.33	0.29	0.04			100.5	100.7	100.7
1971		0.18	0.82	17.28				0.33	0.30	0.03			99.6	99.0	100.4
1972		0.10	0.72	18.20				0.43	0.39	0.03			99.9	100.9	100.3
1973		0.05	1.06	22.69				0.78	0.74	0.04			100.0	99.6	101.2
1974		0.02	1.06	22.81				0.86	0.81	0.05			100.0	99.9	100.4
1975		0.01	1.20	24.08				1.01	0.94	0.07			100.0	100.2	100.3
1976		0.02	1.25	24.02				1.24	1.18	0.06			100.1	99.8	99.9
1977		0.02	1.30	25.02				1.40	1.29	0.11			100.1	99.4	100.0
1978		0.04	1.57	27.11				1.59	1.32	0.27			100.0	99.4	101.7
1979		0.04	3.09	38.11				2.33	2.23	0.10			102.0	103.3	127.1
1980	0.01	0.28	3.18	41.72				3.26	3.14	0.12			110.8	113.6	111.2
1981	0.01	1.57	4.34	48.12				4.35	3.55	0.80			101.7	102.6	107.3
1982	0.01	2.95	5.30	54.59				4.27	3.84	0.43			101.7	101.6	103.7
1983	0.01	12.26	6.48	59.46				4.57	4.00	0.57			102.4	102.7	105.4
1984	0.06	19.79	8.35	62.46				4.62	4.17	0.45	0.3799	0.1102	103.1	103.4	102.9
1985	0.09	30.07	13.95	72.73				5.25	3.96	1.29	0.2438	0.4012	111.1	111.9	111.6
1986	0.21	36.80	18.38	91.44				6.24	5.03	1.21	0.3259	0.1399	104.8	105.4	105.7
1987	0.17	46.58	24.07	107.36				7.46	6.19	1.27	0.5155	0.2890	110.6	111.3	110.2
1988	0.28	60.40	33.68	131.36				8.34	6.39	1.95	0.4135	0.1247	125.9	125.7	123.1
1989	0.47	69.50	41.53	141.85				8.52	6.66	1.59	1.5146	1.3041	118.1	117.3	106.8

18. Hunan

18–12

Year	v13a	v13b	v13c1	v13c2	v13c3	v13d	v14a	v14b	v14c	v15a	v15b	v15c	v15d	v15e	v15f
1949										5103.42					
1950									0.05	5136.88					
1951									0.05	5235.60					
1952			0.63	14.65	274.86		6400	23900	0.77	5518.20					
1953									0.62	5520.01					
1954									0.65	5592.97					
1955									0.81	5625.49					
1956									1.02	5779.41					
1957									1.03	5802.72					
1958									2.93	5583.54					
1959									3.43	5600.00					
1960									4.01	5402.16					
1961									1.34	5389.08					
1962									1.04	5402.69					
1963									1.09	5402.00					
1964									2.20	5416.00					
1965			2.18	66.38	497.74		31100	62800	2.48	5416.00					
1966									3.36	5393.40					
1967									2.41	5385.84					
1968									2.40	5322.46					
1969									1.72	5315.37					
1970									2.52	5274.31					
1971									1.90	5264.50					
1972									3.07	5264.50					
1973									4.41	5212.05					
1974									4.71	5210.18					
1975									5.07	5201.75					
1976									5.81	5191.30					
1977									5.23	5172.81					
1978		97.2	3.57	351.63	829.32		111400	115400	4.97	5168.14					
1979						0.5255			5.17	5160.60					
1980		97.3	5.45	292.08	832.24	0.1306	115800	131600	5.77	5137.15					
1981						0.9719			6.25	5131.97					
1982						2.0329			6.82	5126.13					
1983						1.3714			8.46	5099.77					
1984						1.3557			9.69	5057.02					
1985		97.2	7.13	265.16	773.44	1.4730	119300	155400	10.93	5012.54					
1986						1.6490			9.78	4995.76					
1987						2.2730			11.29	4989.62					
1988		97.9	8.73	277.33	721.65		129300	168900	11.62	4977.97	10905.54	2085	1532.45	30	9.7
1989		98.3	8.88	258.61	705.70	2.4300	131600	172700	8.74	4977.90					

Notes

1. National Output and Income (Y)

v1a: (E), p.591
- v1a1: (E), p.591
- v1a2: (E), p.591
- v1a3: (E), p.591
- v1a4: (E), p.591
- v1a5: (E), p.591

v1b: (A); (D), p.309
- v1b1: (A); (D), p.309
- v1b2: (A); (D), p.309
- v1b3: (A); (D), p.309
- v1b4: (A); (D), p.309
- v1b5: (A); (D), p.309

v1c: (A); (D), p.305

v1d: (E), p.588
- v1d1: (E), p.588
- v1d2: (E), p.588—figures since 1958 include industries at village level and below
- v1d3: (E), p.588
- v1d4: (E), p.588
- v1d5: (E), p.588

v1e: (A); (D), p.312
- v1e1: (A); (D), p.312
- v1e2: (A); (D), p.312
- v1e3: (A); (D), p.312
- v1e4: (A); (D), p.312
- v1e5: (A); (D), p.312

v1f: (E), p.587
- v1f1: (E), p.587
- v1f2: (E), p.587
- v1f3: (E), p.587

v1g: v2a + v3a

v1h: (E), p.616

v1i: (E), p.615—figures of 1985 and after do not include meat price subsidies

v1j: (E), p.615
- v1j1: (E), p.615
- v1j2: (E), p.615
- v1j3: NA

v1k: (E), p.615

2. Investment (I)

v2a: (E), p.590
- v2a1: (A); (D), p.316
- v2a2: (A); (D), p.316

v2b: (A)

v2c: (A); (E), p.605
- v2c1: (E), p.606
- v2c2: (E), p.606

v2d:
- v2d1: (E), p.600
- v2d2: (E), p.600

v2e: (E), p.600

3. Consumption (C)

v3a: (E), p.590

v3b: (E), p.590
- v3b1: (A); (D), p.313
- v3b2: (A); (D), p.313

v3c: (E), p.590

v3d: (E), p.614
- v3d1: (E), p.614
- v3d2: (E), p.614

v3e: (A); (E), p.616
- v3e1: (A); (E), p.616
- v3e2: (A)
- v3e3: (A)
- v3e4: (A)

v3f: (A); (E), p.616
v3f1: (A); (E), p.616
v3f2: (A)
v3f3: (A)
v3f4: (A)

4. Public Finance and Banking (FB)

v4a:
v4a1: (E), p.612
v4a1a: (E), p.612
v4a1b: (C), p.275
v4a1c: (C), p.275—including farming and animal husbandry tax and farmland occupation tax
v4a1d: (C), p.275
v4a2: (E), p.612
v4a2a: (E), p.612
v4a2b: (E), p.612
v4a2c: (E), p.612
v4a2d: v4a2 – v4a2a – v4a2b – v4a2c

v4b: (A)
v4b1: (C), p.279
v4b2: (A); (C), p.279—rural savings
v4b3: NA

v4c:
v4c1: (E), p.600
v4c2: (E), p.600

5. Labor Force (L)

v5a: (E), p.586
v5a1: (E), p.586
v5a2: (E), p.586
v5a3: (E), p.586
v5a4: (E), p.586—rural labor force, excluding rural people working outside

v5b:
v5b1: (E), p.586
v5b2: (E), p.586
v5b3: (E), p.586

v5c: (C), p.58
v5c1: NA

v5d: (C), p.58

6. Population (PO)

v6a: (E), p.585—data from public security department
v6a1: (E), p.585—(ditto)
v6a2: (E), p.585—(ditto)

v6b: (E), p.585—(ditto)

v6c: (E), p.585—(ditto)

v6d:
v6d1: (E), p.585—(ditto)
v6d2: (E), p.585—(ditto)
v6d3: (E), p.585—(ditto)
v6d4: (E), p.585—(ditto)
v6d5: (A)—Changsha
v6d6: (A)—Changde

7. Agriculture (A)

v7a: (A); (E), p.598

v7b: (A); (E), p.598

v7c: (A); (E), p.598

v7d: (A); (E), p.598

v7e: (A)

v7f: (A); (E), p.598

v7g: (A); (E), p.598

v7h: (E), p.591
v7h1: (E), p.593
v7h2: (E), p.593
v7h3: (E), p.593
v7h4: (E), p.593
v7h5: (E), p.593

v7i: (E), p.597

8. Industry (IN)

v8a: (E), p.591
  v8a1: (A); (E), p.600
  v8a2: (C), p.125; (E), p.600
  v8a3: v8a – v8a1 – v8a2

v8b: (E), p.600

  v8c1: (E), p.591
  v8c2: (E), p.591

v8d: (E), p.600

v8f:
  v8f1: (E), p.603
  v8f2: (E), p.603
  v8f3: NA
  v8f4: (E), p.603
  v8f5: (E), p.603

v8g: (A)
  v8g1: (E), p.600

9. Transport (TR)

v9a: (E), p.604—excluding urban traffic volume; figures of 1977 and before obtained from transport department; data of 1978 and after are of the whole society
  v9a1: (E), p.604—including central and local railways
  v9a2: (E), p.604
  v9a3: (E), p.604—excluding distant ocean and coastal passenger traffic

v9b: (E), p.604—figures of 1977 and before obtained from transport department; data of 1978 and after are of the whole society
  v9b1: (E), p.604—including central and local railways
  v9b2: (E), p.604
  v9b3: (E), p.604—excluding distant ocean and coastal freight volume

v9c: (E), p.604—1949–79: at 1970's constant price; 1980–89: at 1980's constant price

10. Domestic Trade (DT)

v10a: (E), p.607
  v10a1: (E), p.607

v10b:
  v10b1: (E), p.607
  v10b2: NA
  v10b3: (E), p.607—including supply and marketing cooperative and other collectives
  v10b4: (E), p.607
  v10b5: (E), p.607
  v10b6: (E), p.607

v10d: (E), p.609

11. Foreign Trade (FT)

v11a:
  v11a1: NA
  v11a2: NA
  v11a3: NA

v11b: (E), p.610—data from foreign trade department
  v11b1: (E), p.610—(ditto)
  v11b2: v11b – v11b1

v11c: (A); (E), p.611

v11d: (A); (E), p.611

12. Prices (PR)

v12a: (E), p.613

v12b: (E), p.613

v12c: (E), p.613

13. Education (ED)

v13a: NA

v13b: (E), p.616

v13c:
- v13c1: (E), p.616
- v13c2: (E), p.616
- v13c3: (E), p.616

v13d: (A)

14. Social Factors (SF)

v14a: (E), p.616

v14b: (E), p.616

v14c: (A)

15. Natural Environment (NE)

v15a: (A); (E), p.598

v15b: (A)

v15c: (A)

v15d: (A)

v15e: (A)

v15f: (A)

Sources of Data

(A) Data supplied by the DSNEB, SSB, the PRC.
(C) Statistical Bureau of Hunan Province ed. *Statistical Yearbook of Hunan 1989*, Beijing: CSPH, 1989.
(D) Same as (D) in Beijing's sources of data.
(E) Same as (E) in Beijing's sources of data.

19

Guangdong

19. Guangdong

19–1

Year	v1a	v1a1	v1a2	v1a3	v1a4	v1a5	v1b	v1b1	v1b2	v1b3	v1b4	v1b5	v1c	v1d	v1d1
1949	26.82	15.45	6.91	0.07	0.65	3.74							9.74	17.08	11.11
1950	30.77	15.73	9.99	0.39	0.81	3.85	110.0	103.8	134.5	544.4	124.7	102.8	12.04	18.73	11.29
1951	36.09	17.00	12.95	0.97	0.94	4.23	116.9	110.9	129.7	261.2	115.4	115.5	14.44	21.65	12.22
1952	42.92	19.35	15.70	1.20	1.21	5.46	116.7	116.1	113.1	127.3	128.6	122.0	17.27	25.65	14.03
1953	59.67	26.59	20.98	3.39	1.76	6.95	118.4	106.7	127.5	282.8	145.2	121.4	24.89	34.78	19.14
1954	68.23	31.04	24.60	2.41	2.22	7.96	110.5	110.9	119.0	71.1	126.5	108.3	28.15	40.08	22.28
1955	69.36	30.76	25.60	2.43	2.45	8.12	102.3	102.3	105.1	100.6	110.1	96.4	28.56	40.80	22.36
1956	77.13	33.53	28.55	3.30	2.86	8.89	109.8	105.4	117.6	135.2	116.8	103.7	31.60	45.53	24.71
1957	85.45	35.05	33.86	3.51	3.43	9.60	107.6	105.1	113.8	106.5	120.1	101.8	34.39	51.06	27.17
1958	108.80	37.69	47.88	7.98	4.45	10.80	122.6	104.2	143.8	226.1	129.8	107.5	50.09	58.71	27.85
1959	129.73	33.82	69.19	9.25	5.60	11.87	110.7	84.6	142.0	115.2	125.8	105.2	64.91	64.82	25.06
1960	133.20	31.42	73.05	11.03	5.94	11.76	100.5	91.8	104.3	118.5	106.1	94.5	68.82	64.38	23.37
1961	101.08	34.75	46.53	5.05	4.57	10.18	64.7	68.4	61.5	45.5	76.9	82.7	48.78	53.02	25.71
1962	104.28	37.90	45.72	3.60	5.21	11.85	114.6	152.3	94.9	71.8	115.3	112.5	47.57	56.71	28.98
1963	118.14	46.70	48.42	4.74	5.51	12.77	113.3	118.1	108.2	127.8	104.6	110.7	53.45	64.69	34.42
1964	133.36	48.81	57.58	7.66	5.70	13.61	116.8	110.1	123.2	158.8	103.4	110.7	63.16	70.20	35.44
1965	147.75	49.74	70.75	6.28	6.03	14.95	114.7	115.2	121.4	81.0	106.4	114.8	71.95	75.80	36.39
1966	161.60	54.61	78.71	5.19	6.64	16.45	109.4	105.3	117.7	81.1	109.5	108.3	81.36	80.24	38.33
1967	157.16	56.83	72.65	4.25	6.24	17.19	98.8	104.2	94.3	81.0	93.9	103.6	77.62	79.54	40.35
1968	138.30	54.88	59.05	3.33	5.39	15.65	88.5	93.6	83.7	77.2	86.5	90.2	68.54	69.76	37.26
1969	168.09	57.28	80.55	5.51	6.41	18.34	120.4	103.5	139.1	163.9	118.8	116.1	89.00	79.90	38.26
1970	196.68	60.94	98.80	10.58	7.28	19.08	118.4	108.3	126.0	190.2	113.8	103.2	106.03	90.65	40.91
1971	205.40	64.59	102.15	11.43	7.84	19.39	103.3	101.2	104.8	106.0	107.5	100.5	111.48	93.92	42.24
1972	213.92	65.77	106.98	12.43	8.35	20.39	103.1	100.2	104.2	107.0	106.5	104.2	116.14	97.78	42.88
1973	235.34	66.68	123.71	13.72	9.37	21.86	107.8	99.0	113.9	108.5	112.2	106.1	129.60	105.74	43.34
1974	252.29	72.43	132.16	15.02	10.23	22.45	107.1	106.7	108.2	107.6	109.2	101.7	138.97	113.32	46.36
1975	279.54	71.27	154.24	18.66	11.80	23.57	109.8	100.0	114.8	122.3	115.3	104.1	154.88	124.66	47.07
1976	289.34	70.70	162.09	19.53	12.69	24.33	107.3	106.4	109.5	100.1	107.5	101.5	162.06	127.28	45.10
1977	310.89	74.85	174.77	23.31	14.13	23.83	107.4	106.9	108.1	114.1	111.4	96.7	171.77	139.12	46.01
1978	350.31	85.89	200.25	22.10	15.14	26.93	105.2	102.1	107.2	96.9	107.2	108.2	189.53	160.78	53.59
1979	393.43	100.46	217.64	25.39	17.39	32.55	107.3	99.1	107.5	114.4	113.6	124.3	213.04	180.39	65.61
1980	443.34	122.18	223.02	32.85	18.75	46.54	113.4	111.1	109.2	132.9	100.9	137.9	225.73	217.61	82.34
1981	534.04	139.32	270.09	49.66	19.83	55.14	112.2	102.4	115.1	137.6	101.7	105.8	283.23	250.81	91.69
1982	606.01	170.08	293.95	64.59	22.11	55.28	110.3	116.3	108.3	122.6	107.8	97.4	320.54	285.47	114.69
1983	659.16	173.57	329.23	73.13	23.94	59.29	108.6	102.6	111.8	107.5	108.3	106.3	355.90	303.26	116.82
1984	803.46	201.87	405.98	96.65	29.66	69.30	116.5	109.3	119.9	117.2	109.9	115.4	437.19	366.27	141.14
1985	1046.79	245.34	532.71	125.56	37.52	105.66	123.1	107.3	127.9	122.8	112.3	133.9	579.52	467.27	169.82
1986	1212.79	279.16	631.10	140.63	44.51	117.39	112.1	106.2	115.8	107.4	109.2	106.2	687.26	525.53	185.58
1987	1596.04	348.61	878.29	160.38	60.16	148.60	124.6	109.6	133.1	107.5	129.0	112.6	939.79	656.25	227.00
1988	2287.51	473.78	1318.92	219.29	69.29	206.23	125.9	107.7	135.0	110.5	115.2	107.3	1392.94	894.57	301.63
1989	2757.17	548.60	1647.24	257.82	79.27	224.24	111.9	107.8	116.3	100.5	106.9	89.9	1722.26	1034.91	347.51

19. Guangdong

Year	v1d2	v1d3	v1d4	v1d5	v1e	v1e1	v1e2	v1e3	v1e4	v1e5	v1f	v1f1	v1f2	v1f3	v1g
1949	2.43	0.02	0.46	3.06							20.27	12.18	2.61	5.48	
1950	3.51	0.20	0.58	3.15	107.7	104.2	135.8	625.0	127.5	102.9	22.19	12.51	3.87	5.81	
1951	4.62	0.45	0.69	3.67	115.8	111.2	131.2	296.0	118.5	115.8	25.69	13.78	5.14	6.77	
1952	5.72	0.51	0.91	4.48	117.9	116.3	114.7	140.5	131.2	122.0	29.52	14.39	6.70	8.43	29.88
1953	7.57	1.10	1.30	5.67	114.5	106.0	126.4	214.4	143.6	120.6	41.23	21.03	9.26	10.94	37.72
1954	8.86	0.85	1.62	6.47	110.0	110.6	118.2	77.1	124.8	107.9	46.80	23.35	9.75	12.70	40.92
1955	9.29	0.82	1.76	6.57	102.5	103.6	106.4	97.1	108.3	95.8	47.59	24.44	10.16	12.99	41.65
1956	10.39	1.24	2.04	7.15	108.4	105.2	117.9	150.3	115.8	103.1	53.04	27.02	11.69	14.33	47.04
1957	12.42	1.40	2.40	7.67	111.0	112.2	114.7	112.7	118.1	101.1	58.64	28.84	14.60	15.20	51.25
1958	16.94	2.50	3.02	8.40	110.9	99.3	138.7	177.7	125.7	104.7	67.09	30.44	19.15	17.50	59.74
1959	23.87	3.21	3.69	8.99	103.0	84.8	138.5	127.6	122.0	102.4	73.50	27.39	26.68	19.43	64.47
1960	24.55	3.98	3.80	8.68	97.9	92.1	101.6	123.2	103.2	92.0	72.76	25.50	28.12	19.14	63.43
1961	15.26	1.90	2.84	7.31	75.3	91.1	60.0	47.5	74.8	80.5	62.18	28.24	18.93	15.01	52.73
1962	14.87	1.41	3.14	8.31	107.9	117.6	94.1	74.5	112.0	109.9	72.39	31.03	23.16	18.20	53.83
1963	15.58	1.88	3.40	9.41	113.1	113.8	107.1	130.0	106.8	116.4	81.81	36.78	20.25	24.78	63.02
1964	18.61	2.63	3.62	9.90	112.9	108.5	123.8	137.1	106.6	109.3	81.63	37.02	24.12	20.49	65.66
1965	23.15	2.34	3.91	10.01	113.9	116.1	122.9	88.2	108.7	105.7	87.00	37.29	27.83	21.88	69.26
1966	25.03	1.91	4.21	10.76	103.9	101.0	114.4	80.0	106.8	105.8	96.40	41.04	32.81	22.55	72.15
1967	22.67	1.66	3.87	10.99	100.2	105.4	92.5	85.8	92.1	101.2	95.99	41.82	31.56	22.61	74.82
1968	18.13	1.33	3.27	9.77	87.1	89.5	82.4	79.1	84.5	88.0	87.29	38.81	28.46	20.02	68.97
1969	24.40	2.25	3.80	11.19	116.8	107.4	137.2	166.9	116.2	113.5	98.60	39.58	36.56	22.46	78.00
1970	29.70	4.42	4.22	11.40	112.2	103.3	123.2	194.7	111.3	101.1	112.07	44.09	44.14	23.84	89.00
1971	30.54	4.66	4.51	11.97	102.0	98.6	105.8	103.6	106.6	103.9	113.23	43.28	45.41	24.54	89.81
1972	32.20	4.94	4.76	13.00	103.6	101.5	104.9	104.2	105.6	107.5	118.47	43.94	47.44	27.09	92.18
1973	37.37	5.33	5.30	14.40	105.1	97.1	114.3	106.1	111.3	109.7	128.96	44.51	54.29	30.16	102.72
1974	40.18	5.58	5.74	15.36	106.5	105.1	108.9	104.8	108.3	105.7	138.20	47.72	58.23	32.25	110.43
1975	47.52	6.93	6.56	16.58	110.1	103.2	117.3	120.0	114.4	107.0	157.66	48.58	71.75	37.33	121.45
1976	49.76	7.71	6.90	17.81	105.5	102.8	108.2	106.6	105.1	105.7	156.38	46.55	72.23	37.60	116.25
1977	53.77	11.75	7.53	20.06	112.8	103.0	116.9	145.5	109.2	111.2	168.90	47.49	79.18	42.23	123.27
1978	67.68	9.33	7.83	22.35	101.7	105.3	109.8	53.6	103.7	106.8	184.73	55.31	85.68	43.74	147.57
1979	73.18	8.25	8.86	24.49	107.7	108.5	107.2	89.2	112.2	112.6	207.07	66.62	90.68	49.77	163.82
1980	79.03	11.14	9.98	35.12	116.4	112.0	112.7	136.3	103.7	135.9	245.71	82.97	100.97	61.77	209.25
1981	93.07	15.04	10.68	40.33	108.8	103.3	113.7	125.1	104.5	104.9	284.24	94.30	118.59	71.35	242.24
1982	100.93	19.84	11.27	38.74	108.5	115.2	107.6	124.3	102.2	92.9	331.27	118.17	133.18	79.92	281.14
1983	110.58	23.24	11.72	40.90	105.1	99.5	109.2	111.2	104.0	104.7	357.43	121.24	149.58	86.61	301.13
1984	133.82	28.80	15.11	47.40	115.3	114.4	117.4	109.9	114.8	114.5	441.81	145.25	183.84	112.72	357.69
1985	171.18	38.20	21.29	66.78	118.5	103.9	126.4	125.4	125.6	123.6	553.05	171.87	225.44	155.74	485.30
1986	197.19	43.26	23.62	75.88	109.1	105.1	112.1	108.7	108.3	108.3	637.72	188.37	248.92	200.43	548.35
1987	257.37	48.87	31.46	91.55	116.5	108.9	121.1	106.4	119.7	107.7	807.70	232.14	318.43	257.13	670.41
1988	363.60	66.30	36.12	126.92	116.7	103.9	127.0	110.2	114.8	107.2	1098.61	306.50	443.56	348.55	903.07
1989	437.80	75.81	40.95	132.84	106.6	107.4	111.8	97.2	106.6	86.5	1311.67	351.73	528.16	431.78	1013.84

19. Guangdong

19–3

Year	v1h	v1i	v1j	v1j1	v1j2	v1j3	v1k	v2a	v2a1	v2a2	v2b	v2c	v2c1	v2c2	v2d1
1949	55.62			380								1.64			
1950				385								0.15			
1951				388								0.56			
1952	85.32	1.84	387	392	271			4.14	1.63	2.51		0.93			
1953		2.76	422	450	280			6.55	3.21	3.34		2.18			
1954	101.84	3.54	453	492	287			6.76	2.65	4.11		1.82			
1955	102.55	4.47	468	521	295			5.47	2.45	3.02		2.19			
1956	107.04	9.17	466	566	304			7.73	3.59	4.14		2.99			
1957	108.19	11.05	458	592	312			8.81	3.86	4.95		3.59			
1958		11.44	453	537	321			16.67	10.73	5.94		8.09			
1959		13.50	475	531	330			21.99	10.97	11.02		10.15			
1960		14.72	461	500	339			19.39	11.38	8.01		12.93			
1961		14.07	470	515	349			5.87	3.57	2.30		4.72			
1962	142.60	13.65	501	570	359			3.56	1.62	1.94		3.17			17.80
1963	104.10	14.09	521	605	369			8.57	3.18	5.39		4.32			23.20
1964	92.72	15.08	528	618	379			10.43	5.12	5.31		6.50			29.95
1965	107.73	16.07	527	615	389			11.83	5.25	6.58		6.53			27.57
1966		16.63	527	608	400			11.61	4.42	7.19		5.73			
1967		17.36	532	606	412			11.97	2.76	9.21		3.93			
1968		17.61	529	595	423			6.87	2.81	4.06		2.90			
1969		17.94	529	586	435			12.82	6.29	6.53		4.78			
1970		18.59	532	583	447			19.50	12.54	6.96		8.61			
1971		19.80	538	581	459			17.63	14.58	3.05		10.01			
1972		20.66	564	604	472			15.83	12.82	3.01		10.19			
1973		21.56	576	616	485			24.24	16.28	7.96		11.80			57.42
1974	153.01	23.90	576	615	493			27.01	19.67	7.34		13.23			61.48
1975	143.83	24.31	575	611	494			31.70	24.98	6.72		15.99			69.49
1976	152.66	25.83	578	609	511			29.99	24.14	5.85		17.35			75.55
1977	179.12	27.48	565	596	490			32.54	22.53	10.01		17.56			85.11
1978	193.25	30.59	615	638	558			41.95	25.09	16.86	27.23	20.04	7.73		96.05
1979	222.72	35.56	685	718	605			39.34	26.20	13.14	28.29	20.06	6.94	1.28	103.51
1980	274.37	42.83	789	828	691			46.87	35.01	11.86	38.29	25.72	8.58	1.86	107.27
1981	325.37	49.40	873	912	774			65.38	45.64	19.74	60.40	34.61	9.55	3.48	118.83
1982	381.79	56.69	961	1000	856			80.50	65.68	14.82	84.73	51.77	11.10	3.76	131.87
1983	395.92	60.85	1020	1061	907			83.11	69.56	13.55	88.71	55.92	9.90	3.28	147.52
1984	425.34	72.82	1187	1261	1017	1697		105.16	92.23	12.93	130.87	80.65	13.89	6.63	162.11
1985	495.31	87.81	1375	1443	1195	2190		171.98	117.29	54.69	184.59	131.11	26.67	7.74	203.80
1986	546.43	100.45	1516	1597	1299	2170		188.05	134.81	53.24	206.50	148.58	40.06	6.20	235.47
1987	662.24	119.48	1740	1784	1516	2442		231.88	149.25	82.63	234.72	162.67	47.30	4.51	294.45
1988	808.70	161.45	2232	2301	1962	3121		320.14	202.73	117.41	331.63	232.26	60.13	5.60	328.58
1989	955.02	200.40	2678	2744	2286	3626		360.60	203.82	156.78	381.98	196.14	63.84	11.25	404.50

19. Guangdong

19–4

Year	v2d2	v2e	v3a	v3b	v3b1	v3b2	v3c	v3d	v3d1	v3d2	v3e	v3e1	v3e2	v3e3	v3e4
1949															
1950															
1951															
1952			25.74	23.81	15.85	7.96	1.93	82	67	148					
1953			31.17	29.14	20.53	8.61	2.03	98	84	166					
1954			34.16	31.83	22.69	9.14	2.33	104	90	174					
1955			36.18	33.73	22.68	11.05	2.45	107	88	198					
1956			39.31	36.18	24.54	11.64	3.13	113	93	203					
1957			42.44	39.56	27.28	12.28	2.88	121	102	206					
1958			43.07	40.14	27.62	12.52	2.93	120	101	201					
1959			42.48	39.31	24.94	14.37	3.17	115	90	218					
1960			44.04	40.50	23.49	17.01	3.54	117	87	226					
1961			46.86	44.20	25.80	18.40	2.66	126	95	238					
1962	14.18		50.27	47.54	29.21	18.33	2.73	134	103	257					
1963			54.45	52.24	34.70	17.54	2.21	144	118	252					
1964			55.23	52.52	34.26	18.26	2.71	141	113	260					
1965	21.65		57.43	54.80	35.43	19.37	2.63	143	114	273					
1966			60.54	57.64	37.55	20.09	2.90	147	117	277					
1967			62.85	59.63	38.87	20.76	3.22	148	118	283					
1968			62.10	58.59	37.61	20.98	3.51	141	110	283					
1969			65.18	61.37	39.53	21.84	3.81	144	113	292					
1970			69.50	65.28	42.21	23.07	4.22	150	117	310					
1971			72.18	67.77	43.54	24.23	4.41	152	118	323					
1972			76.35	71.62	46.42	25.20	4.73	157	123	326					
1973	41.22		78.48	73.45	47.29	26.16	5.03	158	122	331					
1974	43.58		83.42	77.78	50.53	27.25	5.64	164	128	339					
1975	49.26		89.75	83.88	55.21	28.67	5.87	173	137	354					
1976	53.17	28.52	86.26	80.22	51.74	28.48	6.04	159	123	337					
1977	59.19	33.34	90.73	84.41	53.68	30.73	6.32	170	130	366					
1978	66.63	37.43	105.62	99.02	63.56	35.46	6.60	196	152	410	399.96	266.40	35.76		4.96
1979	72.18	40.05	124.48	116.63	78.45	38.18	7.85	228	186	420					
1980	74.23	37.51	162.38	151.95	99.34	52.61	10.43	292	234	554	485.76	318.12	54.72		10.32
1981	80.65	39.36	176.86	164.96	103.58	61.38	11.90	312	241	623	517.44	340.20	37.08		10.32
1982	89.78	44.49	200.64	186.53	116.19	70.34	14.11	346	266	692	592.08	380.28	41.52		13.20
1983	100.61	48.64	218.02	201.57	123.44	78.13	16.45	369	279	747	660.12	426.00	48.12		10.20
1984	110.41	55.06	252.53	231.01	138.14	92.87	21.52	416	311	838	744.36	473.16	55.08		10.44
1985	135.57	70.35	313.32	284.96	174.28	110.68	28.36	506	394	919	889.56	518.88	62.52		14.64
1986	166.52	85.38	360.30	324.75	195.90	128.85	35.55	568	442	1005	998.76	585.60	69.12		17.52
1987	210.08	99.45	438.53	396.99	226.11	170.88	41.54	679	512	1195	1248.00	704.04	77.76		22.08
1988	236.69	129.96	573.89	514.03	295.75	218.28	59.86	872	663	1524	1506.96	854.04	91.08		35.76
1989	294.40	165.03	653.24	572.83	325.23	247.60	80.41	957	722	1707	1921.08	1085.16	113.76		50.16

19. Guangdong

19–5

Year	v3f	v3f1	v3f2	v3f3	v3f4	v4a1	v4a1a	v4a1b	v4a1c	v4a1d	v4a2	v4a2a	v4a2b	v4a2c	v4a2d
1949	67.85	49.83	4.48	2.13	7.06										
1950						3.23					1.09				
1951						5.61					1.56				
1952	78.76	53.29	4.86	4.75	7.43	7.15	1.71	3.22	1.65	0.57	3.32	1.57	0.55	0.77	0.43
1953						8.32					2.71				
1954	90.25	59.65	7.60	3.90	9.65	9.57					3.44				
1955	90.10	58.65	5.52	6.81	8.87	9.72	0.81	5.98	2.10	0.83	3.42	1.02	1.28	1.02	0.10
1956	91.54	61.74	8.80	2.73	8.98	9.59	0.85	6.96	1.47	0.31	4.28	1.21	1.72	1.26	0.09
1957	96.61	65.65	5.81	3.34	9.39	10.45	2.17	5.94	1.80	0.54	4.74	1.63	1.91	1.12	0.08
1958						17.64	3.62	10.58	2.78	0.66	11.27	4.58	3.55	2.41	0.73
1959						20.14	9.89	8.39	1.75	0.11	13.10	8.35	2.19	1.37	1.19
1960						19.51	10.17	7.63	1.66	0.05	16.66	10.63	2.86	1.49	1.68
1961						11.49	5.06	5.31	1.01	0.11	9.16	5.55	1.93	1.04	0.64
1962						13.26	4.18	7.52	1.40	0.16	6.04	2.85	2.07	1.05	0.07
1963						15.93	5.77	8.58	1.50	0.08	7.20	3.90	2.12	1.07	0.11
1964						19.75	7.77	10.31	1.55	0.12	9.16	5.20	2.40	1.13	0.43
1965						19.59	7.72	10.18	1.55	0.14	9.12	5.41	2.33	1.09	0.29
1966						20.04	7.60	10.59	1.76	0.09	9.22	5.06	2.64	1.12	0.40
1967						16.68	5.26	9.62	1.71	0.09	7.56	3.78	2.57	1.00	0.21
1968						13.69	3.07	8.76	1.78	0.08	6.40	2.91	2.23	1.03	0.23
1969						19.63	6.97	10.51	1.81	0.34	9.27	5.03	2.93	1.07	0.24
1970						24.34	10.69	11.74	1.76	0.15	12.57	8.25	3.12	0.98	0.22
1971						27.60	11.68	13.93	1.83	0.16	12.38	7.91	3.13	1.25	0.09
1972						27.30	11.22	14.20	1.78	0.10	13.85	8.89	3.32	1.48	0.16
1973						30.14	11.51	16.75	1.77	0.11	16.10	10.42	3.73	1.55	0.40
1974	152.65	97.76	14.05	12.63	15.22	31.70	12.07	17.77	1.76	0.10	17.51	10.72	4.42	1.62	0.75
1975	151.42	95.92	14.43	12.50	15.23	34.37	14.93	17.63	1.74	0.07	17.11	10.12	4.70	1.63	0.66
1976	182.64	113.16	19.49	12.44	14.31	32.37	10.31	20.25	1.73	0.08	18.74	11.74	4.86	1.66	0.48
1977	189.86	116.21	18.56	9.66	17.41	33.93	10.47	21.63	1.75	0.08	18.80	11.46	5.05	1.74	0.55
1978	184.89	114.10	18.15	14.99	16.41	39.46	13.59	24.12	1.66	0.09	27.03	17.63	5.67	2.06	1.67
1979	205.18	122.98	18.97	23.23	16.72	34.42	8.27	24.62	1.36	0.30	28.03	15.80	6.79	2.40	3.03
1980	222.22	134.12	19.58	21.06	18.63	36.10	8.19	26.18	1.54	0.19	24.93	12.65	7.69	2.90	1.69
1981	266.05	157.72	21.32	33.25	17.01	39.45	8.31	29.39	1.45	0.30	27.18	13.13	9.10	3.53	1.42
1982	312.44	182.55	20.52	42.40	18.32	40.53	5.37	33.21	1.51	0.44	30.75	15.31	10.42	4.01	1.01
1983	328.76	198.23	20.11	45.71	20.36	42.28	3.23	36.66	1.86	0.53	34.27	16.43	11.80	4.61	1.43
1984	346.19	205.45	18.21	51.50	19.34	45.17	0.81	30.20	1.99	0.77	42.65	20.99	13.26	6.11	2.29
1985	388.00	234.19	19.55	54.46	22.26	65.46	-0.75	62.73	2.52	0.96	60.84	26.53	18.46	6.49	9.36
1986	454.06	267.03	21.58	67.79	23.84	79.82	4.11	70.81	2.48	2.42	82.91	37.16	20.26	7.92	17.57
1987	545.25	307.61	25.11	80.21	24.84	92.92	1.37	85.90	2.75	2.90	89.87	33.47	26.92	8.57	20.91
1988	684.67	373.93	31.56	96.69	28.36	107.57	-19.00	116.63	2.53	7.40	115.20	34.25	33.40	8.44	39.11
1989	870.59	460.82	38.58	133.84	30.09	136.87	-22.99	142.16	2.86	14.84	141.16	40.48	41.01	10.39	43.45

19. Guangdong

19–6

Year	v4b	v4b1	v4b2	v4b3	v4c1	v4c2	v5a	v5a1	v5a2	v5a3	v5a4	v5b1	v5b2	v5b3	v5c
1949							1001.36	27.36			974.00				
1950		0.06					1032.12	35.02			997.10				
1951		0.44					1045.88	40.88			1005.00				
1952		0.63	0.02	0.01			1271.21	49.48	1.93	179.00	1040.80	1013.42	69.22	188.57	57.69
1953		0.77					1334.26	57.66	18.90	183.00	1074.70	1041.82	83.80	208.64	66.66
1954		1.00		0.17			1344.74	65.17	9.87	173.00	1096.70	1060.51	80.99	203.24	66.34
1955		0.96		0.35			1360.83	74.18	34.85	134.00	1117.80	1079.91	86.30	194.62	71.58
1956		1.24		0.38			1464.26	131.75	114.81	32.00	1185.70	1146.76	119.12	198.38	95.83
1957		1.65	0.46	0.63			1537.40	125.03	115.77	11.00	1285.60	1238.27	115.90	183.23	92.82
1958		2.04		1.94			1586.84	213.01	80.73	1.00	1292.10	1239.28	184.09	163.47	145.84
1959		2.39		2.01			1581.59	220.82	78.67	2.00	1280.10	1236.02	169.62	175.95	133.67
1960		2.54		2.01			1549.64	238.43	75.61	5.00	1230.60	1201.41	165.66	182.57	129.02
1961		2.20		3.14			1568.47	200.54	84.53	6.00	1277.40	1245.42	135.33	187.72	106.71
1962		1.94	0.79	2.08			1633.53	172.88	95.05	10.30	1355.30	1314.92	126.53	192.08	103.53
1963		2.11		2.02			1658.60	170.44	98.16	9.90	1380.10	1337.00	125.32	196.28	102.22
1964		2.65		2.03			1617.29	180.38	115.63	9.98	1311.30	1274.98	142.10	200.21	113.36
1965		2.95	1.17	2.67			1636.13	188.97	122.09	7.57	1317.50	1279.92	152.08	204.13	122.02
1966		3.21		3.05			1691.22	192.72	123.80	8.00	1366.70	1325.88	159.08	206.26	127.49
1967		3.49		4.10			1738.01	199.16	125.55	7.00	1406.30	1359.51	166.64	211.86	134.38
1968		3.73		4.78			1786.79	202.73	127.26	6.00	1450.80	1406.44	170.27	210.08	138.30
1969		3.75		4.83			1835.99	213.69	128.90	6.00	1487.40	1449.44	178.29	208.26	146.34
1970		4.06	2.13	4.79			1889.60	226.42	130.48	5.00	1527.70	1489.53	193.34	206.73	160.19
1971		4.63		5.09			2006.78	247.72	130.96	5.00	1623.10	1581.44	208.55	216.79	174.71
1972		5.44		5.13			2000.69	262.18	93.41	4.00	1641.10	1600.35	202.24	198.10	173.26
1973		6.10		5.82			2070.65	262.43	135.32	4.00	1668.90	1636.96	219.48	214.21	188.72
1974		6.80		6.82			2124.95	285.47	131.88	4.00	1703.60	1682.02	226.44	216.49	196.02
1975		7.42	4.87	7.40			2153.87	298.89	132.72	4.06	1718.20	1696.73	237.08	220.06	205.36
1976		8.02		7.86			2195.03	319.84	145.24	2.75	1727.20	1675.08	269.68	250.27	230.15
1977		8.75		8.63			2256.66	356.71	137.31	2.04	1760.60	1651.94	276.60	328.12	232.93
1978	17.56	9.77	6.70	8.53	26.09	26.00	2275.95	369.04	146.81	2.60	1757.50	1677.01	312.94	286.00	254.20
1979		12.28		11.56	26.87	24.55	2304.95	378.57	156.80	2.58	1767.00	1659.01	381.11	264.83	298.98
1980	31.89	17.06	16.85	14.75	28.34	25.60	2367.78	400.19	163.43	10.96	1793.20	1672.97	399.33	295.48	314.30
1981		23.56		17.41	31.18	26.70	2423.79	422.03	165.31	10.75	1825.70	1699.85	409.93	314.01	322.96
1982		30.43	32.67	20.78	33.29	25.66	2521.38	443.43	164.69	11.96	1901.30	1723.46	447.18	350.74	367.64
1983	79.93	40.57	42.02	26.68	38.19	26.55	2569.70	446.51	166.14	18.55	1938.50	1729.47	458.80	381.43	375.13
1984	117.58	57.70	53.49	21.10	44.02	27.41	2637.49	429.65	197.89	24.92	1980.80	1679.46	498.09	459.94	381.71
1985	167.29	82.63	75.98	39.11	66.36	29.15	2731.11	449.40	203.32	31.69	2038.60	1642.47	577.24	511.40	428.88
1986	234.67	119.42	103.49	56.52	59.71	25.25	2811.92	465.59	208.85	33.72	2092.00	1624.15	637.76	550.01	475.22
1987	331.63	173.80	135.99	62.81	72.76	25.28	2910.99	485.59	216.16	42.54	2148.11	1605.10	704.22	601.67	527.77
1988		237.71	165.99	77.47	90.50	24.83	2994.72	503.20	216.96	59.43	2187.62	1607.11	743.92	643.69	561.69
1989	547.20	340.50	206.70	88.85	89.28	17.10	3118.50	511.88	212.50	58.11	2220.55	1632.36	747.78	661.13	565.48

19. Guangdong

19–7

Year	v5c1	v5d	v6a	v6a1	v6a2	v6b	v6c	v6d1	v6d2	v6d3	v6d4	v6d5	v6d6
1949			2782.72			36.00	15.00	437.46	2345.26	1397.30	1385.42	142.76	37.19
1950			2848.88			37.60	14.05	503.47	2345.41	1439.17	1409.71	150.62	37.90
1951			2871.54			38.88	13.10	506.04	2365.50	1449.82	1421.82	161.35	38.49
1952	4.75	1013.42	2910.45			36.60	13.58	512.93	2397.52	1457.24	1453.21	162.18	39.18
1953	6.31	1041.82	2982.74			35.52	12.39	473.70	2509.04	1505.89	1476.85	178.47	39.84
1954	11.04	1060.51	3087.58			36.12	11.20	528.09	2559.49	1552.54	1535.04	190.30	41.38
1955	15.36	1079.91	3150.55			31.72	10.63	542.45	2608.10	1584.11	1566.44	200.79	43.38
1956	31.71	1146.76	3214.20			35.12	11.08	550.66	2663.54	1618.52	1595.68	199.17	45.12
1957	31.52	1238.27	3301.79			35.24	8.36	597.13	2704.66	1666.23	1635.56	214.48	46.34
1958	99.31	1239.28	3371.77			30.84	9.17	610.95	2760.82	1703.15	1668.62	219.76	47.47
1959	88.09	1236.02	3433.44			25.07	11.10	661.71	2771.73	1742.56	1690.88	235.45	49.95
1960	84.08	1201.41	3471.43			18.30	15.24	763.62	2707.81	1759.89	1711.54	242.93	51.84
1961	57.77	1245.42	3490.93			20.88	10.82	700.76	2790.17	1755.22	1735.71	240.79	53.05
1962	48.94	1314.92	3575.38			42.46	9.42	658.46	2916.92	1799.73	1775.65	239.41	54.59
1963	46.24	1337.00	3670.46			38.92	7.62	663.99	3006.47	1852.35	1818.11	246.68	55.65
1964	48.57	1274.98	3754.77			36.28	8.28	661.67	3093.10	1903.42	1851.35	251.40	56.65
1965	52.77	1279.92	3865.51			36.10	6.81	679.99	3185.52	1957.18	1908.33	254.07	57.97
1966	54.35	1325.88	3969.34			33.41	6.35	689.05	3280.29	2013.84	1955.50	255.61	59.08
1967	57.77	1359.51	4070.84			31.88	5.86	693.14	3377.70	2070.36	2000.48	260.20	60.40
1968	60.19	1406.44	4189.51			33.76	6.43	701.50	3488.01	2130.68	2058.83	252.63	61.73
1969	66.52	1449.44	4291.15			33.73	5.81	703.16	3587.99	2181.98	2109.17	252.80	62.21
1970	78.16	1489.53	4382.21			32.50	5.88	693.05	3689.16	2222.88	2159.33	251.57	63.53
1971	89.63	1581.44	4493.10			31.35	5.56	714.05	3779.05	2282.52	2210.58	255.80	65.13
1972	92.69	1600.35	4589.15			29.65	6.03	733.08	3856.07	2330.33	2258.82	260.13	67.06
1973	91.77	1636.96	4695.70			28.56	5.98	747.19	3948.51	2389.70	2306.00	264.28	69.04
1974	100.57	1682.02	4780.63			26.05	6.37	751.80	4028.83	2434.20	2346.43	267.92	70.95
1975	106.86	1696.73	4858.48			22.95	6.10	759.84	4098.64	2477.83	2380.65	268.88	72.78
1976	114.37	1675.08	4921.95			21.16	6.31	772.76	4149.19	2512.66	2409.29	272.07	74.49
1977	127.59	1651.94	4985.54			20.52	6.01	783.02	4202.52	2546.08	2439.46	274.59	76.06
1978	131.62	1677.01	5064.15			22.14	5.44	823.23	4240.92	2586.68	2477.47	283.12	78.44
1979	129.75	1659.01	5140.50			23.44	5.61	868.66	4271.84	2624.57	2515.93	293.66	80.66
1980	136.79	1672.97	5227.67			22.82	5.48	909.71	4317.96	2671.28	2556.39	302.66	82.96
1981	142.91	1699.85	5323.50			24.47	5.58	942.63	4380.87	2722.80	2600.70	307.70	84.93
1982	148.01	1723.46	5415.32			23.09	5.92	971.43	4443.89	2771.84	2643.48	312.13	86.53
1983	149.44	1729.47	5494.14			21.00	6.32	1001.03	4493.11	2818.97	2675.17	317.00	87.84
1984	150.96	1679.46	5576.59			20.75	6.21	1097.35	4479.24	2865.93	2710.66	322.16	89.95
1985	155.73	1642.47	5655.59			20.60	6.33	1197.89	4457.70	2909.52	2746.07	328.88	92.09
1986	162.00	1624.15	5740.71			22.15	5.70	1254.57	4486.14	2955.72	2784.99	335.92	94.72
1987	170.63	1605.10	5832.15			22.12	5.70	1309.92	4522.23	3003.10	2829.05	341.71	96.79
1988	175.56	1607.11	5928.31			20.90	5.07	1366.54	4561.77	3053.50	2874.81	349.09	98.90
1989	177.06	1632.36	6024.98			20.27	5.73	1422.75	4602.23	3106.37	2918.61	354.39	101.23

19. Guangdong

19–8

Year	v7a	v7b	v7c	v7d	v7e	v7f	v7g	v7h	v7h1	v7h2	v7h3	v7h4	v7h5	v7i	v8a
1949			941.82	7929				15.45	12.05	0.04	1.82	1.04	0.49		6.91
1950			960.75	8007				15.73	12.27	0.06	2.05	1.15	0.19		9.99
1951			985.88	8110				17.00	12.97	0.08	2.12	1.19	0.63		12.95
1952			1027.00	8413	188.2			19.35	14.19	0.16	2.50	1.57	0.92	0.0303	15.70
1953			1087.46	8614				26.59	19.73	0.16	3.07	2.29	1.66	0.0322	20.98
1954			1169.22	8737				31.04	22.72	0.19	4.05	2.53	1.55	0.0340	24.60
1955			1292.93	9171				30.76	22.46	0.24	3.69	2.58	1.79	0.0348	25.60
1956			1483.29	9352				33.53	25.39	0.48	3.07	2.71	1.87	0.0350	28.55
1957			1685.07	9490	697.5			35.05	25.63	1.07	3.68	2.54	2.13	0.0331	33.86
1958			1945.86	8452				37.69	27.26	1.32	4.30	2.80	2.77	0.0317	47.88
1959			2121.78	7766				33.82	24.00	1.31	2.97	3.30	2.17	0.0301	69.19
1960			2336.91	8192				31.42	23.95	1.55	2.18	2.07	1.88	0.0283	73.05
1961			2462.22	8245				34.75	27.23	1.33	2.34	2.07	1.79	0.0273	46.53
1962	3.40		2621.81	8531				37.90	28.63	1.77	3.50	2.38	1.80	0.0270	45.72
1963			2884.50	8225	2174.4			46.70	33.64	2.39	5.57	2.89	2.22	0.0280	48.42
1964			3050.66	8402				48.81	33.66	2.15	7.57	3.13	2.29	0.0289	57.58
1965		372.00	3191.24	8700	1173.0			49.74	34.56	2.35	7.29	3.29	2.24	0.0299	70.75
1966			2809.32	9409				54.61	37.30	2.67	8.19	3.74	2.81	0.0299	78.71
1967			2854.61	9447				56.83	38.69	2.80	8.68	3.84	2.82	0.0296	72.65
1968			2892.63	8776				54.88	37.70	2.83	8.24	3.66	2.45	0.0301	59.05
1969			2928.26	8809				57.28	39.34	3.19	5.70	3.76	2.69	0.0309	80.55
1970		399.26	2823.72	9382	1082.7	146.47	3.71	60.94	41.68	3.22	8.26	4.71	3.07	0.0315	98.80
1971		504.04	3225.59	9404		150.71	4.79	64.59	44.42	2.31	10.08	4.74	3.03	0.0307	102.15
1972		592.92	2977.37	9904		169.09	4.77	65.77	45.88	2.38	11.32	2.98	3.31	0.0308	106.98
1973	19.94	807.79	3110.13	10056		173.46	5.85	66.68	45.65	3.48	11.53	3.19	2.82	0.0306	123.71
1974	23.76	1083.86	3092.47	10242		165.04	6.45	72.43	51.63	3.03	11.19	2.99	3.58	0.0305	132.16
1975	29.37	1306.45	3165.34	10255	884.4	190.41	7.67	71.27	49.84	3.60	11.32	2.14	3.44	0.0310	154.24
1976	38.54	1542.42	3082.55	10038		205.86	9.83	70.70	47.28	3.59	10.89	5.60	3.34	0.0298	162.09
1977	45.19	1722.89	3046.01	9866		214.99	9.43	74.85	51.10	3.69	10.27	6.22	3.58	0.0292	174.77
1978	48.97	1811.22	2950.02	9962		271.58	9.95	85.89	56.78	4.73	12.73	8.35	3.29	0.0296	200.25
1979	54.66	1787.44	2978.52	9493		297.00	11.08	100.46	68.91	4.74	15.72	7.44	3.64	0.0296	217.64
1980	59.60	1682.30	2920.28	8955	1538.9	333.54	12.55	122.18	79.92	6.61	17.18	14.10	4.37	0.0306	223.02
1981	66.32	1276.97	2893.70	8568		349.90	15.01	139.32	88.88	8.13	22.50	14.49	5.30	0.0337	270.09
1982	72.61	1136.38	2856.83	8540	174.0	363.20	18.26	170.08	108.50	9.92	27.48	17.69	6.47	0.0365	293.95
1983	77.30	1226.36	2835.69	8364	644.0	381.00	21.09	173.57	99.52	10.94	29.18	21.20	10.84	0.0383	329.23
1984	81.78	1159.67	2761.13	8313	873.0	349.20	24.15	201.87	115.74	12.25	34.11	26.75	13.03	0.0401	405.98
1985	85.32	1137.00	2699.74	8037	1064.0	363.95	26.64	245.34	126.67	15.35	44.50	36.34	17.19	0.0415	453.71
1986	93.52	1154.40	2650.06	8037	1620.0	400.20	30.14	279.16	144.13	17.46	51.80	43.85	21.90	0.0431	631.10
1987	103.85	1154.60	2578.90	8065	645.0	443.68	36.55	348.61	179.67	19.15	85.75	56.27	15.68	0.0440	878.29
1988	112.89	1108.71	2521.83	8064	1947.0	482.33	42.63	473.78	230.14	32.33	86.75	81.60	42.95	0.0449	1318.92
1989	125.21	1196.70	2540.47	8323		511.30	50.43	548.60	264.65	36.12	100.46	96.05	51.33	0.0466	1647.24

19. Guangdong

19–9

Year	v8a1	v8a2	v8a3	v8b	v8c1	v8c2	v8d	v8f1	v8f2	v8f3	v8f4	v8f5	v8g
1949	4.12		2.79		6.05	0.86			7.23		0.74	3.28	7736
1950	6.66	0.02	3.31		8.88	1.11			12.00		0.87	4.85	9428
1951	9.14	0.01	3.80		11.27	1.68		0.02	15.30		1.02	13.22	9593
1952	10.74	0.15	4.81		13.76	1.94		0.03	18.88		1.22	15.09	12263
1953	14.27	0.26	6.45		17.95	3.03		0.15	25.82		1.58	25.13	12060
1954	16.25	0.99	7.36		20.97	3.63		0.13	38.98		1.97	30.46	16919
1955	17.47	2.01	6.12		21.55	4.05		0.21	56.16		2.32	32.28	18724
1956	19.87	5.70	2.98		23.36	5.19		0.19	79.28		2.99	36.81	
1957	23.36	6.79	3.70		27.81	6.05		0.26	86.74		3.75	31.97	25231
1958	39.24	5.76	2.88		33.28	14.59		4.21	248.99	0.06	5.34	38.00	21578
1959	53.73	12.09	3.36		46.35	22.83		4.31	436.45	1.24	8.22	49.47	15892
1960	58.13	12.79	2.13		49.92	23.13		8.08	505.87		10.43	72.50	12836
1961	32.80	11.73	2.00		35.66	10.87		2.37	300.07	0.52	10.87	44.46	15986
1962	32.86	10.53	2.33		35.06	10.66		1.20	200.42	1.07	11.87	43.06	14821
1963	36.06	9.58	2.78		36.68	11.74		1.08	156.42	1.04	13.94	52.25	14390
1964	43.81	10.75	3.02		42.59	14.99		2.65	147.40	2.37	17.15	78.75	13770
1965	44.19	10.51	16.05		50.62	20.13		5.70	156.83	3.10	22.23	98.83	13563
1966	60.46	15.34	2.91		54.24	24.47		7.13	178.75	10.10	26.36	113.02	12668
1967	53.08	16.05	3.52		51.76	20.89		4.65	158.17	8.10	25.35	98.97	
1968	42.69	13.18	3.18		42.08	16.97		2.74	166.00	5.12	22.36	70.52	
1969	60.48	16.86	3.20		53.47	27.08		7.17	223.59	8.83	32.09	122.80	10773
1970	75.00	15.54	8.26		64.01	34.79		14.35	516.88	12.17	37.82	148.97	13544
1971	76.81	22.54	2.72		67.51	34.64		18.59	708.12	18.24	43.23	157.88	13590
1972	80.17	23.50	3.31		65.81	41.17		24.88	624.51	15.36	44.86	171.21	14321
1973	91.82	27.98	3.91		78.35	45.36		22.92	608.10	14.28	54.49	208.77	15218
1974	95.88	31.77	4.51		82.07	50.09		17.56	625.10	16.42	62.94	233.40	15617
1975	110.85	38.59	4.80		93.71	60.53		30.54	779.89	15.25	75.87	291.04	16058
1976	110.24	41.48	10.37		107.95	64.22		28.70	890.31	14.64	84.69	294.59	17286
1977	116.69	46.75	11.33		104.99	69.78		29.24	1014.75	11.42	83.59	314.93	18365
1978	135.77	52.34	12.14		114.43	85.31		35.84	1046.96	10.22	92.32	370.88	19440
1979	145.72	55.62	16.30		131.17	86.46		35.41	932.05	8.31	101.80	420.48	20291
1980	140.76	61.66	20.60		140.45	82.57		40.15	801.69	8.10	108.94	390.16	20874
1981	163.20	75.22	31.67		178.00	93.08		39.89	721.64	9.11	117.51	473.23	21741
1982	176.51	84.35	33.09		194.19	99.76		42.99	810.20	9.88	130.37	597.70	22379
1983	196.84	94.72	37.67		217.52	111.78		50.83	876.51	9.51	146.32	677.00	22263
1984	230.19	121.16	54.62		274.15	131.82		55.59	841.76	8.35	147.52	836.53	22985
1985	238.16	154.28	61.27		306.39	147.32		69.53	809.80	10.02	167.13	1120.23	23835
1986	309.24	195.90	125.95		436.01	195.08		75.64	855.32	25.79	180.50	1246.29	25482
1987	393.80	266.51	217.94		607.01	271.28		89.14	871.79	45.34	221.83	1475.65	26452
1988	543.08	408.97	366.87		911.76	407.14		97.71	927.98	38.58	267.97	1745.95	28441
1989	618.52	471.03	557.69		1131.94	515.29		105.40	981.60	35.34	298.40	1966.00	29897

19. Guangdong

19–10

Year	v8g1	v9a	v9a1	v9a2	v9a3	v9b	v9b1	v9b2	v9b3	v9c	v10a	v10a1	v10b1	v10b2	v10b3
1949										1326.5					
1950		14.15				6.58				1118.8	14.46	13.53	0.12		
1951		11.63				10.63				1597.0	18.53	17.43	0.82	0.29	
1952		10.97				17.55				1952.9	20.21	18.87	1.80	1.73	0.01
1953		16.73				25.34				2342.6	25.60	23.90	2.91	3.35	0.02
1954		16.37				31.06				2520.2	28.80	26.31	5.91	7.96	0.04
1955		16.76				35.42				2672.5	29.08	26.29	7.12	7.01	0.08
1956		23.90				71.32				3060.7	31.52	28.32	6.58	8.25	3.08
1957		27.17				47.48				3414.3	33.21	30.48	9.55	5.39	3.87
1958		29.17				49.25				4108.3	38.12	31.97	18.49	11.02	4.34
1959		31.45				53.72				5412.2	41.66	35.50	22.50	11.38	5.61
1960		32.51				57.07				6281.6	42.34	35.65	20.07	14.22	5.44
1961		41.96				50.50				6444.5	38.38	33.21	18.33	11.28	5.40
1962		38.02				58.93				6514.7	46.84	40.81	20.93	13.88	8.16
1963		29.28				67.56				5734.8	46.15	39.62	21.08	14.76	7.51
1964		29.48				88.97				5671.7	47.23	40.61	23.61	14.10	7.59
1965		31.36				128.33				5767.9	47.55	40.19	24.28	14.69	6.97
1966		34.97				206.25				5768.2	51.80	43.75	26.68	16.67	6.93
1967		33.95				212.35				5601.4	54.20	46.52	27.75	17.60	6.93
1968		32.67				269.82				5344.0	49.33	39.55	25.35	15.06	6.92
1969		38.47				333.94				5592.4	57.02	49.09	27.63	20.58	6.88
1970		40.92				341.67				5955.5	58.38	49.19	27.91	21.78	6.87
1971		44.77				285.79				6180.0	60.71	50.18	28.87	23.21	6.86
1972		50.20				304.06				6608.2	65.28	54.26	31.96	24.61	6.84
1973		55.09				360.98				7108.0	71.15	59.11	36.11	26.16	6.81
1974		57.89				549.48				7301.0	74.61	62.01	36.83	28.76	6.79
1975		59.21				803.36				7680.4	80.13	66.73	40.36	30.41	6.76
1976		63.66				770.71				8470.2	85.16	70.59	42.80	32.62	7.02
1977		68.74				936.87				8744.2	90.52	74.95	45.20	35.34	7.37
1978		75.89				1038.87				8951.7	93.41	77.24	46.08	37.18	7.20
1979		93.74				1437.95				9623.9	106.58	89.55	52.00	40.60	10.04
1980		115.18				1412.67				10500.1	136.94	117.47	66.72	46.72	15.70
1981		127.84				1919.19				11471.8	164.00	142.38	81.10	50.79	19.46
1982		141.31				1250.33				11735.4	188.58	164.23	96.53	50.34	23.12
1983		157.51				1376.29				13056.6	209.04	183.62	106.38	48.25	25.53
1984		197.95				1539.38				15609.1	253.35	226.13	125.76	46.29	32.26
1985		234.23				1607.97				20547.6	319.73	289.23	146.43	47.70	43.38
1986		222.17				1700.15				25412.2	362.11	327.02	160.33	50.47	49.69
1987		255.60				1774.35				34868.6	450.08	405.19	189.70	59.65	59.53
1988		299.53				1953.57				51079.2	633.94	568.07	274.74	74.89	79.70
1989	3835	292.16				2090.81				103339.0	705.32	636.15	285.71	80.11	80.66

19. Guangdong

19–11

Year	v10b4	v10b5	v10b6	v10d	v11a1	v11a2	v11a3	v11b	v11b1	v11b2	v11c	v11d	v12a	v12b	v12c
1949															
1950	0.03	13.91	0.4071						1.0936						
1951	0.06	16.93	0.4251						1.2908				98.2	98.5	98.0
1952	0.06	16.17	0.4289	9.74					1.2062				99.8	102.9	99.3
1953	0.07	18.68	0.5643	12.64					1.5281				101.0	102.7	122.6
1954	0.11	14.10	0.6791	14.58					1.5816				99.7	98.8	103.2
1955	0.16	13.93	0.7889	12.80	1.29	0.12	0.66		2.0627				100.3	99.6	96.9
1956	9.25	3.42	0.9451	13.77					2.3502				99.6	99.5	103.9
1957	11.14	2.11	1.1528	14.81					2.2219				102.2	103.4	103.8
1958	1.84	1.01	1.4134	15.04	1.95	0.28	0.87		3.0673				100.6	99.2	101.1
1959	1.03	1.14	1.1396	15.86					2.3241				101.2	100.6	101.9
1960		0.94	1.6705	14.52					2.0655				101.1	100.5	105.3
1961		1.02	2.3529	14.32				1.7638	1.6116	0.1522			112.1	112.0	120.7
1962		1.07	2.7855	14.89	1.09	0.36	0.39	1.9078	1.8265	0.0813			100.5	100.5	98.3
1963		1.05	1.7436	20.14				2.3814	2.1909	0.1905			98.1	99.4	98.0
1964		0.67	1.2717	20.44				2.7765	2.6381	0.1384			96.8	98.1	100.7
1965		0.52	1.0926	21.21	1.86	0.77	0.52	3.4533	3.1110	0.3423			98.6	97.6	99.6
1966		0.50	1.0199	23.31				4.0009	3.6680	0.3329			99.6	99.7	99.8
1967		0.47	1.4498	24.21				4.0255	3.6536	0.3719			100.3	100.4	100.9
1968		0.43	1.5780	22.20				3.7730	3.4611	0.3119			99.8	99.8	99.9
1969		0.43	1.5098	23.41				4.2271	3.9933	0.2338			99.7	101.8	100.0
1970		0.41	1.4085	22.97	2.72	0.99	0.66	4.8221	4.3485	0.4736			99.3	99.5	99.9
1971		0.39	1.3708	23.76				5.1583	4.6308	0.5275			99.6	100.2	104.5
1972		0.37	1.5044	24.69				5.9083	5.4965	0.4118			99.7	99.9	100.1
1973		0.36	1.7021	25.13				10.5854	9.9731	0.6123			100.0	100.0	100.3
1974		0.34	1.8835	25.66				12.3696	11.4423	0.9273			99.0	99.7	101.2
1975		0.20	2.4067	28.15	6.35	2.91	2.07	12.5553	11.2511	1.3042			100.0	100.0	100.1
1976		0.19	2.5272	28.68				12.2099	10.7802	1.4297			100.1	100.1	100.0
1977		0.28	2.3270	29.85				12.7789	11.5607	1.2182			100.1	100.0	100.1
1978		0.33	2.6256	31.71	6.88	4.15	2.84	15.9145	13.8755	2.0390			100.4	100.3	101.7
1979		0.51	3.4333	39.67	7.66	5.24	3.94	19.4491	17.0196	2.4295	2.2889	0.9143	103.0	104.6	121.0
1980	0.13	1.20	6.4695	52.63	8.70	6.77	5.60	25.5084	21.9472	3.5612	13.8920	2.1419	108.5	109.5	110.9
1981	0.57	3.50	8.5874	59.21	9.24	7.48	4.83	30.3797	23.7254	6.6543	16.7507	2.8837	109.3	106.3	108.0
1982	1.09	6.87	10.6379	74.60	8.51	6.98	4.58	30.5754	22.5648	8.0106	15.5916	2.8103	102.3	102.6	104.1
1983	2.71	13.16	13.0067	83.67	8.27	9.29	4.37	33.1668	23.8524	9.3144	7.2660	4.0685	100.7	102.8	100.0
1984	5.91	25.91	17.2205	86.66	8.32	8.28	4.66	36.0459	24.8731	11.1728	14.4489	6.4379	101.2	101.9	102.2
1985	9.09	48.27	24.8529	105.82	10.17	9.66	4.67	53.7889	29.5267	24.2622	25.6521	9.1910	113.6	117.1	114.9
1986	9.07	61.04	31.5080	139.14	12.59	17.86	4.56	68.0883	42.5129	25.5754	18.3480	14.2829	104.8	104.7	105.6
1987	10.68	90.06	40.4737	165.68	13.95	24.55	6.80	90.7192	54.4417	36.2775	20.1750	12.1671	111.7	112.8	111.5
1988	14.21	134.85	55.5392	214.93	17.97	28.93	11.89	125.9400	74.8382	51.1018	38.2748	24.3965	130.2	129.5	135.9
1989	18.80	171.65	68.3858	270.82	14.19	27.90	10.41	129.9888	81.6767	48.3121	36.2311	23.9915	121.0	121.9	125.3

19. Guangdong

19–12

Year	v13a	v13b	v13c1	v13c2	v13c3	v13d	v14a	v14b	v14c	v15a	v15b	v15c	v15d	v15e	v15f
1949				13.4656	134.5626					4085.20					
1950	4.77		0.8463	14.5079	176.8664		9800	37000	0.35	4108.20					
1951	8.14		0.7151	16.1242	246.9110	0.1091	11400	36600	0.72	4499.50					
1952	7.85		1.0016	16.8000	299.9984	0.1283	12500	45600	0.80	4447.20	4582				
1953	29.44	55.90	0.9100	24.9476	294.1275	0.2100	12400	50500	1.14	4553.50					
1954	27.95	56.87	0.9500	27.8657	295.4911	0.2300	13500	69600	1.32	4589.60					
1955	25.91	55.42	0.1000	27.3263	286.6242	0.2200	13000	72600	1.38	4619.60					
1956	24.77	63.41	1.3000	38.0868	342.9008	0.2600	15900	101400	1.66	1624.10					
1957	26.14	59.82	1.4600	43.2399	343.5209	0.1600	16900	67300	1.81	4585.60	6784				
1958	11.36	89.29	2.5740	63.5012	484.9825	0.3186	18900	68500	2.61	4337.00					
1959	11.45	77.92	3.4820	72.2576	512.7706	0.3031	36400	78700	3.41	4170.60					
1960	11.48	86.00	4.3712	76.8200	518.3588	0.4777	48500	83300	2.89	4136.50					
1961	17.31	78.88	4.2718	60.2895	503.6487	0.5802	47000	87900	1.91	4166.80					
1962	20.66	71.78	3.5241	50.4063	481.5925	0.8184	37200	83400	1.93	4177.60					
1963	19.01	69.55	3.1101	47.7261	483.7172	0.8870	37000	82000	2.62	4149.60	6310			2.1358	3.6206
1964	17.23	80.94	3.8371	58.6216	615.1248	0.8420	38900	83700	3.44	4118.60					
1965	16.49	91.02	2.7745	68.8199	704.2405	0.7625	44000	83000	3.67	4122.10				1.9627	2.4205
1966	19.48		2.2982	74.9767	640.2634	0.5721	44500	81400	3.64	4131.90					
1967	23.40			69.8054	589.0435		46300	83600	2.06	4118.60					
1968				119.1251	547.7590		47000	76400	2.62	4086.70					
1969	15.35			164.3072	578.2025		49400	78000	2.62	4118.40					
1970	12.86	83.18		238.1265	521.0932		54200	86000	3.74	4163.57	10747			3.7428	6.6577
1971	14.97	85.80		256.9431	557.8552		60000	90800	3.93	4182.02					
1972	14.56	92.40		222.5676	648.4694		68700	93600	3.73	4172.55					
1973	14.24	95.72	1.3158	96.7265	888.0351	0.2883	71500	97900	5.09	4172.88					
1974	14.53	97.29	1.9023	201.2736	748.9527		73200	103400	5.80	4176.94					
1975	15.39	97.76	2.4103	235.0104	773.8483	0.2681	75300	109000	4.75	4187.26	10630			5.8362	7.3234
1976	14.92	97.93	2.1718	284.3485	775.2890	0.6305	79000	115100	6.80	4185.48					
1977	15.51	97.43	2.6316	324.1235	751.2947	0.6937	81900	121200	6.35	4182.77					
1978	12.26	95.64	3.0705	316.9620	743.0209	0.5125	84100	126600	5.07	4168.21					
1979	13.75	96.19	3.7892	274.0490	743.8125	0.1876	85100	136600	5.19	4154.50					
1980	18.77	96.22	4.1004	260.0008	748.8593	0.7595	85000	144500	6.76	4126.07	11921			7.1041	6.3416
1981	20.79	95.71	4.4723	226.2133	734.7804	0.5491	87000	152000	10.94	4113.60					
1982	20.73	95.91	4.0931	207.6956	723.0311	1.5311	88700	160700	12.71	4077.91					
1983	20.87	96.74	4.5592	210.4691	705.3368	1.0411	90900	166500	15.34	4051.11					
1984	20.17	96.74	5.4730	234.7109	692.7289	1.0615	93800	170500	20.94	3999.12					
1985	19.47	98.07	6.9897	255.9071	671.2468	1.1004	98200	175300	22.10	3897.81					
1986	16.64	98.44	7.8346	274.3880	670.6215	1.6284	99600	180000	19.99	3839.70					
1987	16.17	98.71	8.6297	282.7685	677.3671	2.0552	104900	184100	22.17	3797.36					
1988	15.72	98.93	9.7224	278.6434	688.7228	2.5277	109300	187300	23.34	3777.68	10207	0.7383	666	7.6400	6.3678
1989		99.10	10.0393	272.6205	715.1532	2.6248	111816	192100	19.20	3787.01					

Notes

1. National Output and Income (Y)

v1a: (E), p.623
 v1a1: (E), p.623
 v1a2: (E), p.623
 v1a3: (E), p.623
 v1a4: (E), p.623
 v1a5: (E), p.623

v1b: (F), p.7–8
 v1b1: (F), p.7–8
 v1b2: (F), p.7–8
 v1b3: (F), p.7–8
 v1b4: (F), p.7–8
 v1b5: (F), p.7–8

v1c: v1a – v1d

v1d: (E), p.620
 v1d1: (E), p.620
 v1d2: (E), p.620
 v1d3: (E), p.620
 v1d4: (E), p.620
 v1d5: (E), p.620

v1e: (F), p.23–24
 v1e1: (F), p.23–24
 v1e2: (F), p.23–24
 v1e3: (F), p.23–24
 v1e4: (F), p.23–24
 v1e5: (F), p.23–24

v1f: (G)
 v1f1: (G)
 v1f2: (G)
 v1f3: (G)

v1g: (G)

v1h: (G)

v1i: (E), p.640—excluding meat price subsidies

v1j: (E), p.640
 v1j1: (E), p.640
 v1j2: (E), p.640
 v1j3: (B), p.241; (G)

v1k: NA

2. Investment (I)

v2a: (G)
 v2a1: (G)
 v2a2: (G)

v2b: (A)

v2c: (A); (G)
 v2c1: (E), p.633
 v2c2: (E), p.633

v2d:
 v2d1: (E), p.631; (G)
 v2d2: (E), p.631; (G)

v2e: (E), p.631

3. Consumption (C)

v3a: (G)

v3b: (G)
 v3b1: (G)
 v3b2: (G)

v3c: (G)

v3d: (E), p.639
 v3d1: (E), p.639
 v3d2: (E), p.639

v3e: (A)
 v3e1: (A)
 v3e2: (A)
 v3e3: NA
 v3e4: (A)

v3f: (G)

v3f1: (G)
v3f2: (G)
v3f3: (G)
v3f4: (G)

4. Public Finance and Banking (FB)

v4a:
v4a1: (G)
v4a1a: (G)
v4a1b: (G)
v4a1c: (G)
v4a1d: (G)
v4a2: (A); (G)
v4a2a: (G)
v4a2b: (G)
v4a2c: (G)
v4a2d: (G)

v4b: (A)
v4b1: (G)
v4b2: (C), 1984, p.299; 1986, p.302; 1987, p.370; 1989, p.373
v4b3: (G)

v4c:
v4c1: (E), p.631
v4c2: (E), p.631

5. Labor Force (L)

v5a: (G)
v5a1: (G)
v5a2: (G)
v5a3: (G)
v5a4: (E), p.618—excluding rural people working outside

v5b:
v5b1: (G)
v5b2: (G)
v5b3: (G)

v5c: (G)
v5c1: (G)

v5d: (G)

6. Population (PO)

v6a: (G)
v6a1: NA
v6a2: NA

v6b: (G)

v6c: (G)

v6d:
v6d1: (G)
v6d2: (G)
v6d3: (G)
v6d4: (G)
v6d5: (G)—Guangzhou
v6d6: (G)—Zhanjiang

7. Agriculture (A)

v7a: (A); (G)—100 million watt

v7b: (A); (G)

v7c: (G)

v7d: (G)

v7e: (A)

v7f: (G)

v7g: (G)

v7h: (A)
v7h1: (A)
v7h2: (A)
v7h3: (A)
v7h4: (A)
v7h5: (A)

v7i: (G)—including only water buffaloes (year-end amount of livestock)

8. Industry (IN)

v8a: (A)
v8a1: (A)

v8a2: (A)
v8a3: (A)

v8b: NA

v8c1: (A)
v8c2: (A)

v8d: NA

v8f:
v8f1: (G)
v8f2: (G)
v8f3: (G)
v8f4: (G)
v8f5: (G)

v8g: (G)
v8g1: NA

9. Transport (TR)

v9a: (G)—excluding urban traffic volume
v9a1: NA
v9a2: NA
v9a3: NA

v9b: (G)
v9b1: NA
v9b2: NA
v9b3: NA

v9c: (G)—new measurement was used in 1989, i.e. telecommunication within China, international telecommunication, telecommunication with Hong Kong and Macau, are calculated according to their respective fixed prices, while previously they are calculated according to China's fixed price

10. Domestic Trade (DT)

v10a: (G)
v10a1: (E), p.634

v10b:
v10b1: (G)
v10b2: (G)
v10b3: (G)
v10b4: (G)
v10b5: (G)
v10b6: (G)

v10d: (G)

11. Foreign Trade (FT)

v11a:
v11a1: 1955–75: (C), 1984, p.280; 1985, p.268; 1987, p.329; 1989, p.333; 1978–89: (G)
v11a2: (C), 1984, p.280; (G)
v11a3: (C), 1984, p.280; (G)

v11b: (G)
v11b1: (G)
v11b2: (G)

v11c: (G)

v11d: (G)

12. Prices (PR)

v12a: (E), p.638

v12b: (E), p.638

v12c: (E), p.638

13. Education (ED)

v13a: (A)

v13b: (A), (G)

v13c:
v13c1: (G)
v13c2: (G)
v13c3: (G)

v13d: (G)

14. Social Factors (SF)

v14a: (A)

v14b: (A)—medical technicians and others

v14c: (G)

15. Natural Environment

v15a: (G)

v15b: (A)

v15c: (A)

v15d: (A)

v15e: (A)

v15f: (A)

Sources of Data

(A) Data supplied by the DSNEB, SSB, the PRC.
(B) Statistical Bureau of Guangdong Province ed. *Advancing Guangdong, Guangdong Social and Economic Development Situation in 1949–88*, Hong Kong: Da Dao Culture Co. Ltd., 1989.
(C) ________ ed. *Statistical Yearbook of Guangdong*, Beijing: CSPH, various issues.
(E) Same as (E) in Beijing's sources of data.
(F) Balance Office, Statistical Bureau of Guangdong Province ed. *Statistical Data on Guangdong National Economic and Social development 1949–89*, 1990.
(G) Data supplied by Statistical Bureau of Guangdong Province

20

Guangxi

20. Guangxi

20–1

Year	v1a	v1a1	v1a2	v1a3	v1a4	v1a5	v1b	v1b1	v1b2	v1b3	v1b4	v1b5	v1c	v1d	v1d1
1949															
1950	12.87	9.20	2.31	0.31	0.14	0.91							4.08	8.79	6.61
1951	15.31	10.12	3.01	0.88	0.22	1.08							5.04	10.27	7.20
1952	17.85	11.49	4.05	0.66	0.27	1.38	111.6	113.8	131.5	72.8	140.9	129.2	5.93	11.92	8.11
1953	20.96	12.34	5.42	1.02	0.40	1.77	113.7	107.0	133.9	150.8	174.0	130.8	7.91	13.05	8.47
1954	23.85	13.45	6.62	1.13	0.50	2.14	111.3	107.4	125.9	116.0	139.1	125.7	9.02	14.83	8.34
1955	26.11	14.23	7.66	1.32	0.57	2.32	106.7	105.1	113.1	108.3	113.7	110.1	10.35	15.76	9.69
1956	28.91	15.33	8.59	1.66	0.73	2.59	108.8	108.2	113.9	101.3	131.2	110.6	11.86	17.05	10.34
1957	30.98	16.75	9.19	1.70	0.90	2.44	110.0	111.6	107.8	105.1	125.7	96.2	12.36	18.62	11.14
1958	38.27	18.60	12.15	3.11	1.35	3.06	124.1	112.0	158.1	175.5	140.8	101.9	16.54	21.73	12.36
1959	43.97	16.08	17.43	4.95	1.88	3.61	108.0	84.5	147.3	163.9	153.7	124.6	21.07	22.90	11.37
1960	46.34	14.65	19.49	6.06	2.23	3.90	104.2	87.2	111.5	139.0	113.2	116.1	23.81	22.53	10.34
1961	31.65	14.44	10.53	2.59	1.34	2.75	59.2	80.1	49.2	29.6	65.4	73.5	12.72	18.93	10.18
1962	32.34	17.08	9.53	1.69	1.09	2.95	98.3	111.8	87.4	62.8	78.7	87.2	11.79	20.55	12.11
1963	33.86	16.76	10.48	2.12	1.14	3.36	106.2	102.9	108.8	118.7	104.2	123.6	12.56	21.30	11.80
1964	40.08	20.13	11.94	3.07	1.49	3.44	121.3	120.0	122.5	152.0	131.8	74.5	16.28	23.80	14.01
1965	48.86	23.66	15.59	3.13	2.23	4.25	114.1	111.7	130.2	106.3	150.8	41.6	20.57	28.29	16.66
1966	53.89	23.02	19.36	3.76	2.49	5.26	109.8	98.5	124.0	125.6	130.9	224.8	25.31	28.58	16.06
1967	50.84	24.08	17.03	2.71	1.93	5.09	97.2	104.2	91.7	64.6	70.7	203.4	23.42	27.42	17.04
1968	43.00	23.89	12.15	1.50	1.34	4.10	86.7	99.4	72.4	53.7	68.4	75.9	18.27	24.73	16.90
1969	59.19	25.58	22.32	3.65	2.29	5.34	135.4	107.1	183.4	279.7	177.0	173.4	28.33	30.86	18.02
1970	68.02	26.85	27.41	5.30	2.73	5.72	117.3	104.8	127.7	160.4	127.7	105.9	33.44	34.58	18.75
1971	78.83	30.23	33.30	5.67	3.26	6.37	112.6	110.1	122.3	97.1	118.3	110.8	38.57	40.26	21.02
1972	90.02	35.80	37.48	6.07	3.65	7.01	108.9	107.6	112.6	101.5	112.0	109.8	43.77	46.25	24.88
1973	99.81	38.97	42.77	6.32	3.97	7.77	108.7	106.9	114.1	100.7	99.2	111.8	48.74	51.07	26.97
1974	103.31	40.72	46.73	7.25	3.94	8.66	107.6	102.4	110.9	105.4	102.8	138.3	49.68	53.63	27.77
1975	118.89	44.28	52.30	9.10	4.05	9.15	109.0	107.4	111.9	115.3	96.8	99.5	60.39	58.50	29.54
1976	123.34	43.39	56.71	9.27	3.92	10.05	102.4	97.9	108.5	94.0	114.1	103.5	64.45	58.89	28.94
1977	134.11	44.62	63.90	10.16	4.47	10.96	109.0	103.2	115.0	104.2	109.9	113.2	72.23	61.88	29.36
1978	145.94	46.17	69.97	13.27	4.99	11.53	107.9	101.8	109.7	120.3	95.8	123.6	82.15	63.79	30.04
1979	160.84	55.56	74.47	14.38	4.78	11.64	103.2	104.7	103.8	104.0	103.5	89.1	88.78	72.06	36.56
1980	174.42	62.30	78.63	15.40	4.95	13.33	104.5	105.8	107.1	92.7	104.7	95.6	93.29	81.13	40.51
1981	194.50	74.41	85.06	13.72	5.18	16.11	106.6	104.3	104.7	76.2	126.1	178.7	101.90	92.60	51.34
1982	224.24	88.23	92.73	17.11	6.54	19.63	113.0	117.0	108.9	126.1	104.7	111.7	112.73	111.51	61.79
1983	236.66	89.50	98.51	20.13	7.08	21.44	104.4	100.0	106.6	117.6	100.0	103.3	121.43	115.23	62.10
1984	258.59	95.02	109.49	21.74	8.75	23.59	105.8	99.7	109.6	100.2	123.5	110.5	133.18	125.41	64.63
1985	315.69	108.02	139.39	30.28	10.14	27.86	113.0	102.1	120.7	126.0	109.7	105.7	164.40	151.29	75.67
1986	362.60	118.69	164.79	36.52	12.06	30.54	107.4	103.4	111.9	108.6	112.8	92.2	186.56	176.04	83.61
1987	436.82	137.92	207.46	40.29	15.01	36.15	112.2	104.9	118.3	100.2	121.0	108.6	229.28	207.54	97.63
1988	556.50	168.94	272.00	53.24	16.95	44.91	110.4	98.1	115.8	114.9	107.6	115.1	304.67	251.83	115.61
1989	655.55	212.17	326.99	45.42	19.83	51.14	104.2	110.3	106.2	80.3	104.4	93.9	355.32	300.23	145.97

20. Guangxi

20–2

Year	v1d2	v1d3	v1d4	v1d5	v1e	v1e1	v1e2	v1e3	v1e4	v1e5	v1f	v1f1	v1f2	v1f3	v1g
1949															
1950	1.30	0.17	0.05	0.66											8.57
1951	1.74	0.48	0.08	0.77											10.11
1952	2.37	0.44	0.10	0.89	113.8	112.9	135.9	92.0	148.4	115.7					11.71
1953	2.80	0.52	0.15	1.11	106.0	104.0	106.1	117.6	159.1	128.2					14.09
1954	3.31	0.62	1.17	1.39	111.5	108.7	118.8	118.9	125.3	130.2					16.66
1955	3.79	0.45	0.19	1.64	103.8	103.0	121.8	72.2	112.1	119.8					17.91
1956	4.12	0.60	0.25	1.74	106.4	107.2	102.1	106.1	131.6	105.1					19.88
1957	4.59	0.66	0.32	1.91	110.4	109.6	112.7	110.1	127.6	112.6					18.60
1958	5.41	1.05	0.56	2.33	116.0	112.6	120.8	159.5	169.6	96.5					24.21
1959	7.09	1.37	0.61	2.46	100.0	89.7	130.7	130.5	121.5	107.2					28.29
1960	6.90	2.07	0.74	2.48	95.1	87.1	96.7	146.2	68.6	109.4					26.98
1961	5.19	1.06	0.48	2.01	76.1	80.1	85.3	39.6	119.1	86.0					20.16
1962	4.99	0.78	0.42	2.25	104.9	113.1	96.5	73.1	83.1	97.3					20.87
1963	5.62	0.91	0.42	2.53	106.6	103.2	112.2	117.4	100.3	120.3					22.62
1964	5.60	1.16	0.56	2.46	112.3	118.9	97.0	127.1	133.6	74.8					25.12
1965	6.79	1.26	0.82	2.75	112.6	113.0	117.2	115.1	145.7	61.0					30.51
1966	7.22	1.07	0.99	3.25	97.9	97.5	97.1	84.8	127.5	133.6					34.11
1967	5.91	0.63	0.73	3.06	99.9	105.7	85.6	63.5	74.9	160.5					30.43
1968	4.46	0.36	0.45	2.55	91.3	99.4	71.3	52.8	60.5	70.5					31.02
1969	7.52	1.16	0.97	3.18	123.3	106.6	168.1	322.3	224.8	167.6					35.55
1970	9.22	1.71	1.31	3.58	112.3	103.9	128.9	146.9	143.4	113.0					38.21
1971	12.30	1.49	1.51	3.94	114.9	110.6	139.4	87.5	115.6	108.9					43.12
1972	13.84	1.29	1.78	4.46	112.3	114.4	112.6	81.8	118.0	114.0					48.61
1973	15.60	1.74	1.94	4.81	105.1	100.6	112.7	130.3	95.3	110.0					54.44
1974	16.81	1.92	1.93	5.20	105.1	101.1	107.7	101.8	99.3	143.5					55.82
1975	18.96	2.60	1.93	5.48	107.4	105.2	112.9	124.2	100.0	95.6					63.73
1976	20.17	2.12	1.85	5.81	103.3	97.9	106.5	74.3	250.7	96.0					64.28
1977	21.69	2.36	2.13	6.33	100.6	101.8	107.6	107.2	44.2	115.2					68.22
1978	21.80	2.65	2.57	6.71	103.6	102.3	100.0	103.6	119.5	123.6	75.95	30.88	24.84	20.23	72.63
1979	22.77	3.02	2.55	7.16	103.4	105.9	101.9	109.3	99.0	91.3					78.17
1980	25.75	3.17	2.64	9.05	108.7	106.9	114.7	92.0	103.8	109.7	98.56	43.90	29.63	25.03	90.22
1981	27.48	3.40	2.81	10.26	111.5	108.3	103.3	90.7	106.3	184.2					101.28
1982	28.63	3.95	2.88	14.27	113.9	118.0	104.0	117.2	102.4	122.5					117.47
1983	30.20	4.90	3.20	14.83	101.9	99.7	105.9	124.1	106.7	96.1					123.23
1984	33.80	6.62	4.26	16.09	104.7	97.7	110.4	123.3	133.0	109.2					137.69
1985	43.28	8.98	4.54	18.82	110.6	105.2	121.4	124.9	102.1	103.9					179.74
1986	55.29	11.36	5.43	20.35	108.5	104.0	120.9	114.1	112.8	88.4	205.95	85.26	66.93	53.76	198.08
1987	68.07	11.45	6.85	23.55	108.4	105.4	114.2	91.5	122.2	105.2	243.89	99.53	79.35	65.01	217.38
1988	85.08	15.05	7.42	28.67	105.5	95.7	112.0	114.4	103.6	121.0	300.33	117.72	100.69	81.92	274.89
1989	99.35	13.71	8.47	32.78	103.9	110.5	102.6	85.6	101.4	94.3	349.44	148.99	109.97	90.48	319.48

20. Guangxi

20–3

Year	v1h	v1i	v1j	v1j1	v1j2	v1j3	v1k	v2a	v2a1	v2a2	v2b	v2c	v2c1	v2c2	v2d1
1949															
1950			287	287				1.82				0.12			
1951			292	292				2.01				0.67			
1952			315	315				1.80	1.59	0.21		0.25			
1953			354	354				2.70	2.22	0.48		0.65			
1954			376	376				3.90	2.83	1.07		0.88			
1955			399	399				3.92	2.80	1.12		1.61			
1956	59		459	459				4.50	3.45	1.05		1.62			
1957			487	487				3.78	2.33	1.45		1.43			
1958			421	421				5.82	4.41	1.41		3.47			
1959			409	409				8.35	6.79	1.56		5.82			
1960			387	387				6.92	5.76	1.16		6.80			
1961			415	415				2.69	2.46	0.23		2.12			
1962			464	464				3.10	2.00	1.00		1.37			
1963			499	499				4.50	2.97	1.53		1.66			
1964			518	518				4.50	3.46	1.04		2.69			
1965	106		514	514				6.05	4.77	1.28		2.86			10.39
1966			516	516				7.93	6.62	1.31		4.15			
1967			527	527				4.47	4.04	0.43		3.26			
1968			496	496				6.34	4.93	1.41		1.94			
1969			471	471				9.45	7.57	1.88		4.17			
1970			493	493				10.38	7.96	2.42		5.90			
1971			472	472				12.53	9.19	3.34		5.85			23.93
1972			547	547				12.92	9.39	3.53		6.48			26.21
1973			532	532				14.16	11.10	3.06		6.13			30.75
1974			546	546				15.28	10.42	4.86		6.78			35.21
1975			539	539				18.57	13.33	5.24		7.63			39.27
1976			533	533				18.35	13.33	5.02		8.60			44.60
1977			536	536				20.36	14.34	6.02		7.95			51.21
1978	120	12.50	543	559	462			20.91	15.00	5.91		9.61	6.01	0.22	56.06
1979		14.09	601	620	513			21.04	15.40	5.64		9.80	4.92	0.29	62.19
1980	173	17.36	714	735	609			22.28	19.97	2.31		12.18	4.42	0.83	64.61
1981	204	18.28	721	748	591			25.05	19.29	5.76		10.19	2.97	0.51	69.32
1982	235	19.75	760	782	647			25.38	13.93	11.45	18.72	13.53	3.40	0.81	75.69
1983	262	20.73	787	810	670			25.94	16.84	9.10	21.39	14.38	4.15	0.46	82.37
1984	267	26.23	983	1039	770			26.35	24.26	2.09	28.17	16.43	4.93	0.47	91.75
1985	302	28.99	1077	1126	880			46.35	26.77	19.58	42.78	24.74	6.88	0.64	105.99
1986	316	35.51	1282	1344	1025			50.36	33.54	16.83	55.21	30.37	7.01	0.52	113.65
1987	354	41.20	1438	1502	1166			51.75	34.78	16.97	64.51	40.83	7.64	0.58	127.92
1988	424	50.47	1720	1798	1376			66.60	37.94	28.66	84.95	52.94	9.46	1.04	143.29
1989	483	55.90	1859	1887	1502			80.70	39.97	40.73	66.76	41.42	9.93	0.91	170.09

20. Guangxi

20–4

Year	v2d2	v2e	v3a	v3b	v3b1	v3b2	v3c	v3d	v3d1	v3d2	v3e	v3e1	v3e2	v3e3	v3e4
1949															
1950			6.75	6.56			0.18	35							
1951			8.10	7.84			0.26	40							
1952			9.91	9.54			0.36	50	45	82					
1953			11.39	10.90			0.48	56	49	97					
1954			12.76	12.19			0.56	61	56	98					
1955			13.99	13.33			0.65	65	60	112					
1956			15.38	14.59			0.79	70	64	119					
1957			14.81	14.16			0.65	67	59	128	169.80	106.68	12.36		6.00
1958			18.39	17.59			0.80	81	74	131					
1959			19.94	19.14			0.80	87	78	146					
1960			18.73	17.71			1.02	81	68	160					
1961			17.47	16.86			0.61	78	65	159					
1962			17.78	17.17			0.61	78	67	160					
1963			18.11	17.42			0.69	84	69	202	192.36	120.24	12.00		8.16
1964			20.62	19.82			0.80	85	70	211	201.32	121.57	16.35	3.64	10.02
1965	8.60	1.86	24.46	23.53			0.92	98	84	214	199.38	122.75	16.65	3.48	9.28
1966			26.17	25.09			1.08	101	86	225					
1967			26.56	25.43			1.13	99	84	227					
1968			24.68	23.57			1.11	90	76	210					
1969			26.09	24.71			1.38	92	77	230					
1970			27.83	26.20			1.63	94	77	254					
1971	19.07	7.66	30.60	28.56			2.03	100	82	265					
1972	20.65	9.32	35.69	33.41			2.28	114	95	280					
1973	24.13	11.12	39.88	37.31			2.57	124	104	295					
1974	27.44	12.42	40.54	38.16			2.38	123	104	301					
1975	30.34	13.85	45.16	42.81			2.35	135	116	310					
1976	34.16	15.30	45.93	43.22			2.71	134	113	316					
1977	38.95	16.51	47.86	45.14			2.71	137	114	337					
1978	41.77	18.89	51.72	48.28	36.77	11.51	3.43	143	122	328					
1979	46.31	20.14	57.13	53.15	40.60	13.33	3.98	155	130	357					
1980	47.37	20.46	67.94	63.18	47.00	16.19	4.75	180	151	413					
1981	50.72	21.15	76.23	71.34	54.22	17.12	4.89	200	171	423	423.12	248.52	42.28	5.04	8.76
1982	55.14	23.00	92.10	86.28	67.88	18.40	5.82	236	210	442					
1983	59.77	23.93	97.29	90.39	70.52	19.88	6.90	244	215	466					
1984	66.65	24.75	111.34	99.01	77.62	22.39	11.33	263	230	511	541.76	313.85	63.35	6.07	9.31
1985	76.86	30.20	133.39	119.33	91.68	27.65	14.06	311	271	604	718.58	411.38	75.48	6.68	8.95
1986	81.23	36.23	147.72	132.54	97.34	35.20	15.18	339	289	648	815.73	488.04	83.33	7.20	9.43
1987	91.63	40.78	165.64	148.60	107.50	41.10	17.04	372	313	735	941.99	578.69	86.14	7.68	11.51
1988	102.74	47.81	208.29	187.09	127.64	59.45	21.20	460	366	1025					
1989	123.52	60.16	238.78	216.93	149.64	67.29	21.85	525	424	1107					

20. Guangxi

Year	v3f	v3f1	v3f2	v3f3	v3f4	v4a1	v4a1a	v4a1b	v4a1c	v4a1d	v4a2	v4a2a	v4a2b	v4a2c	v4a2d
1949															
1950						0.66	0.02	0.27	0.36	0.01	0.45	0.01	0.03	0.26	0.15
1951						1.74	0.22	0.69	0.69	0.15	0.93	0.23	0.09	0.35	0.27
1952						2.19	0.39	0.80	0.76	0.23	1.69	0.39	0.28	0.45	0.57
1953						2.62	0.48	1.15	0.82	0.17	1.79	0.65	0.45	0.44	0.26
1954						3.26	0.78	1.33	0.90	0.24	1.95	0.67	0.43	0.45	0.39
1955						3.27	0.90	1.35	0.81	0.20	2.34	0.60	0.47	0.47	0.80
1956	57	48	5.56			3.21	0.98	1.36	0.71	0.16	3.20	1.26	0.63	0.65	0.66
1957	58					2.98	0.70	1.35	0.79	0.15	3.34	1.13	0.76	0.57	0.88
1958						4.66	1.61	1.92	0.87	0.26	6.13	3.83	0.78	0.63	0.90
1959						6.29	2.76	2.35	0.86	0.26	8.53	5.02	0.88	0.76	1.86
1960						6.02	3.12	1.91	0.75	0.17	10.99	5.72	1.25	0.80	3.22
1961						3.30	0.94	1.49	0.66	0.12	5.36	1.35	1.00	0.80	2.21
1962						3.40	0.65	1.93	0.67	0.07	3.68	0.69	0.93	0.67	1.39
1963						3.61	0.83	2.09	0.56	0.08	4.27	0.84	1.00	0.73	1.70
1964	100	69	5.13	2.46	14.59	4.14	0.95	2.30	0.78	0.06	5.49	1.74	1.12	0.76	1.87
1965						4.89	1.26	2.80	0.72	0.05	6.15	2.22	1.16	0.75	2.02
1966						5.60	1.83	2.83	0.89	0.03	7.12	2.89	1.32	0.86	2.05
1967						4.48	1.00	2.54	0.85	0.02	6.16	2.41	1.34	0.79	1.62
1968						2.57	-0.47	2.01	0.91	0.03	4.57	1.21	1.12	0.82	1.42
1969						5.25	1.29	2.94	0.91	0.05	7.24	3.32	1.15	0.77	2.00
1970						7.34	2.78	3.47	0.93	0.05	9.16	5.69	1.17	0.69	1.61
1971						7.97	2.86	4.02	0.97	0.04	10.44	5.32	1.42	0.89	2.81
1972						8.90	3.51	4.37	0.91	0.05	12.32	6.41	1.91	0.94	3.05
1973						9.56	3.29	5.21	0.97	0.03	12.46	5.71	2.00	0.96	3.78
1974						10.97	3.93	5.80	0.96	0.04	13.19	5.67	2.26	1.04	4.21
1975						11.10	3.96	6.05	0.96	0.04	13.16	5.69	2.30	1.11	4.05
1976						10.97	3.50	6.39	0.95	0.05	14.20	6.32	2.43	1.10	4.36
1977						12.08	3.86	7.13	0.94	0.03	14.51	5.87	2.59	1.19	4.86
1978						14.32	5.19	8.07	0.92	0.04	20.78	7.95	3.29	1.42	8.13
1979	23					12.05	2.29	8.71	0.93	0.02	20.60	5.66	3.72	1.58	9.63
1980	151	96	13.97	12.22		12.29	1.98	9.22	0.93	0.04	17.44	4.30	4.38	1.78	6.97
1981	171	116				12.72	1.38	10.23	0.91	0.07	16.04	2.38	4.89	1.94	6.83
1982	210	139				13.03	0.69	11.09	0.98	0.14	17.44	2.61	5.56	2.17	7.09
1983	224	148				13.58	1.29	11.00	0.99	0.15	18.84	3.16	6.05	2.46	7.17
1984	238	154				13.47	0.23	11.90	1.01	0.11	23.06	3.51	7.56	3.27	8.72
1985	268	167				20.18	1.78	16.78	1.23	0.38	29.75	4.44	9.17	3.37	12.76
1986	284	176				25.23	2.24	20.85	1.59	0.55	42.22	6.21	11.05	4.02	20.94
1987	309	192	18.07	17.14		30.54	3.23	24.54	1.96	0.80	47.70	4.10	12.25	4.75	26.59
1988	362	216				33.89	1.21	30.06	2.02	0.39	53.27	4.28	14.42	4.77	29.79
1989	419	244	24.97	54.43	18.19	41.41	-1.77				58.22	3.48	15.90	5.40	33.44

20. Guangxi

Year	v4b	v4b1	v4b2	v4b3	v4c1	v4c2	v5a	v5a1	v5a2	v5a3	v5a4	v5b1	v5b2	v5b3	v5c
1949															
1950	0.0170	0.0170					857	17	37		803				
1951	0.0605	0.0605					886	21	42		823				
1952	0.1366	0.1365	0.0001				917	26	47		844				
1953	0.1471	0.1432	0.0039				938	30	45		863				
1954	0.3094	0.2709	0.0385				950	34	39		877				
1955	0.2691	0.1707	0.0984				968	38	28		902				
1956	0.3760	0.2623	0.1137				995	57	27		911				
1957	0.4801	0.3285	0.1516				1003	59	17		927	804	18	181	
1958	1.2716	0.8613	0.4103				1010	94	19		897				
1959	1.7906	1.0701	0.7205				1001	101	18		882				
1960	1.1492	0.7704	0.3788				969	118	20		831				
1961	0.8195	0.5177	0.3018				979	92	19		868				
1962	0.5292	0.3527	0.1765				1018	78	18	3.06	919				
1963	0.5366	0.4157	0.1209				1047	76	21	3.09	947				
1964	0.7422	0.5949	0.1473				1052	81	21	4.41	945				
1965	0.8834	0.7344	0.1490				1090	86	25	2.10	977	987	32	71	
1966	0.9851	0.8446	0.1405				1099	89	26		984				
1967	0.9883	0.8626	0.1257				1103	89	26		988				
1968	1.1257	0.9737	0.1520					90	25						
1969	1.1430	1.0032	0.1398				1175	96	28		1051				
1970	1.2223	1.0853	0.1370				1226	107	30		1089				
1971	1.4749	1.3045	0.1704				1281	125	36		1120				
1972	1.8333	1.6070	0.2263				1313	139	35		1139				
1973	2.1996	1.8273	0.3723				1332	137	32		1163				
1974	2.5886	2.1170	0.4716				1356	144	34		1178				
1975	2.7264	2.2306	0.4958		7.23	16.40	1370	149	36	0.48	1184				
1976	2.8815	2.3934	0.4881		7.49	16.10	1381	157	38	0.15	1186				
1977	3.3449	2.6058	0.7391		8.74	15.80	1396	161	37	0.12	1198				
1978	3.9029	2.9818	0.9211		10.50	17.30	1456	199	38		1219	1171	153	132	
1979	5.2119	3.9459	1.2660		11.41	17.20	1493	201	39	0.67	1252	1232	150	111	
1980	7.4406	5.4812	1.9594		11.85	17.50	1551	208	40	2.17	1300	1290	147	114	
1981	9.7781	6.9423	2.8358		13.44	18.70	1610	216	44	5.41	1340	1338	124	148	
1982	13.0477	9.0600	3.9877		13.96	17.80	1673	223	44	7.76	1393	1383	134	156	
1983	16.5045	11.6373	4.8672		14.90	17.80	1718	224	43	10.75	1435	1421		133	
1984	24.1077	17.1902	6.9125		15.98	17.50	1781	214	56	15.50	1490	1460	139	182	
1985	34.2256	24.3890	9.8366		22.42	21.00	1831	222	54	21.00	1534	1473	161	197	
1986	48.0054	35.0848	12.9206		24.77	21.10	1896	229	55	25.95	1586	1501	177	218	
1987	67.6096	49.6978	17.9118		30.65	23.30	1961	239	56	27.80	1637	1529	193	239	
1988	81.7295	61.5997	20.1298		35.34	23.50	2012	246	55	31.34	1678	1548	205	260	
1989	105.3000	82.6000	22.6000		38.73	21.10	2046	251	54	27.81	1712	1575	203	269	

20. Guangxi

20–7

Year	v5c1	v5d	v6a	v6a1	v6a2	v6b	v6c	v6d1	v6d2	v6d3	v6d4	v6d5	v6d6
1949			1845									12	11
1950			1875					246	1629	968	907		
1951			1906					237	1669	985	921		
1952			1943					231	1712	1004	939	19	16
1953			1976	180	1796			221	1755	1020	956		
1954			2018	188	1830	36.09	15.15	228	1790	1042	976		
1955			2053			30.26	14.58	210	1843	1059	994		
1956			2092			29.37	12.46	225	1867	1079	1013		
1957			2147	175	1755	34.52	12.35	229	1918	1108	1039	26	22
1958			2186			32.87	11.74	270	1916	1127	1059	50	28
1959			2205	239	1748	24.52	17.49	289	1916	1139	1066		
1960			2172	227	1730	19.40	29.46	291	1881	1116	1056		
1961			2159	237	1703	17.73	19.50	270	1889	1107	1052	43	32
1962			2218	218	1772	39.08	10.25	238	1980	1133	1085	42	32
1963			2300	219	1847	46.72	10.13	246	2054	1180	1120	43	31
1964			2362	213	1909	40.95	10.55	250	2112	1217	1145	44	33
1965			2445	241	2204	42.40	9.03	262	2183	1256	1189	45	34
1966			2528	250	2278	39.23	7.50	271	2257	1300	1228		
1967			2588			34.31	7.35	287	2301	1330	1258		
1968			2651			34.56	7.86	263	2388	1357	1294		
1969			2738			37.31	7.02	262	2476	1404	1334		
1970			2818			33.81	6.77	271	2547	1445	1373	43	39
1971			2898	275	2623	33.09	6.96	290	2608	1487	1411		
1972			2973	287	2686	31.58	7.37	307	2666	1529	1444		
1973			3057	296	2761	31.46	6.65	309	2748	1573	1484		
1974			3130	301	2829	31.48	7.09	311	2819	1611	1519		
1975			3201	315	2886	29.10	6.77	323	2878	1648	1553	52	45
1976			3267	326	2941	27.27	6.66	335	2932	1683	1584		
1977			3329	340	2989	26.15	6.12	343	2986	1715	1614		
1978			3402	361	3041	24.69	5.79	360	3042	1753	1649	58	50
1979			3470	373	3097	25.26	6.07	386	3084	1786	1684		
1980			3538	388	3150	25.17	5.80	398	3140	1822	1716	63	55
1981			3613	404	3209	27.30	5.55	411	3202	1862	1751		
1982			3684	451	3233	26.88	5.64	421	3263	1902	1782		
1983			3733	455	3278	18.52	5.60	431	3302	1930	1803		
1984			3806	1434	2372	21.49	5.21	445	3361	1970	1836		
1985			3873	1483	2390	19.46	5.05	471	3402	2005	1868	93	64
1986			3946	1506	2440	18.90	4.90	489	3457	2044	1902	96	66
1987			4016	1529	2487	17.32	5.05	511	3505	2082	1934	100	68
1988			4088	1710	2378	15.83	5.03	532	3556	2119	1969	103	70
1989			4151	1877	2273	20.34	5.72	550	3600	2152	1998	105	72

20. Guangxi

20–8

Year	v7a	v7b	v7c	v7d	v7e	v7f	v7g	v7h	v7h1	v7h2	v7h3	v7h4	v7h5	v7i	v8a
1949															
1950			768.85	5093				9.20	7.08	0.16	1.48	0.39	0.09		2.31
1951			779.33	5235				10.12	7.61	0.18	1.78	0.42	0.12		3.01
1952			801.63	5479				11.49	7.93	0.23	2.66	0.49	0.01		4.05
1953			865.60	5851				12.34	8.57	0.19	2.89	0.51	0.18		5.42
1954			916.53	6373				13.45	9.44	0.22	3.04	0.54	0.21		6.63
1955			975.12	6883				14.23	9.40	0.22	3.51	0.86	0.26		7.66
1956			1185.57	7397				15.33	9.14	0.63	4.39	0.89	0.28		8.59
1957			1309.06	6929		4.65		16.75	9.75	0.53	4.53	1.65	0.30		9.20
1958			1669.89	7008		7.13		18.60	11.78	1.42	2.61	2.40	0.23		12.15
1959			1687.80	6195		5.84		16.08	10.78	1.28	2.31	2.10	0.39		17.43
1960			1189.74	5865		8.70		14.65	10.87	1.38	1.45	0.74	0.21		19.49
1961		130.66	1233.86	6104		4.01		14.44	11.88	0.49	1.09	0.73	0.24		10.53
1962		91.77	1413.53	5984		7.45		17.08	13.25	1.64	1.61	0.42	0.17		9.53
1963		105.48	1417.47	6063		17.15		16.76	12.14	0.97	3.24	0.24	0.18		10.49
1964		112.95	1435.37	6350		19.80		20.13	14.24	1.73	3.55	0.42	0.20		11.94
1965	0.26	109.53	1464.82	6176		41.30		23.66	16.50	1.89	3.84	1.18	0.24		15.59
1966		139.11	1551.24	6859		48.16		23.02	16.30	1.79	3.72	1.20	0.24		19.36
1967		145.00	1624.30	7042		37.06		24.08	18.26	2.08	3.30	0.24	0.20		17.04
1968		161.00	1679.85	6509		34.52		23.89	18.16	1.09	2.69	0.24	0.24		12.15
1969		172.00	1779.13	6749		36.91		25.58	19.60	1.79	3.70	0.25	0.24		22.32
1970	4.45	188.00	1870.93	7091		75.11	1.68	26.85	20.50	1.83	3.98	0.26	0.28		27.41
1971		192.65	1987.41	7334		86.69	2.16	30.23	22.65	2.12	4.69	0.40	0.37		33.30
1972		267.70	1843.68	7651		83.17	2.10	35.80	27.93	1.86	5.08	0.45	0.47		37.48
1973	10.17	379.43	2042.01	7770		103.33	2.04	38.97	30.07	1.99	6.06	0.48	0.46		42.77
1974	13.38	563.39	2100.50	7872		99.34	2.68	40.72	31.58	2.03	6.03	0.51	0.57		46.73
1975	18.21	719.32	2193.45	7930		122.53	2.99	44.28	34.46	3.21	6.98	0.63	0.66		52.31
1976	21.94	1041.56	2276.70	8015		127.88	3.56	43.39	33.08	2.23	6.17	1.30	0.60		56.71
1977	26.91	1264.96	2186.00	8083		132.56	3.97	44.62	34.18	2.09	6.22	1.45	0.67		63.90
1978	31.30	1375.72	2206.20	8036		159.44	4.26	46.17	35.34	2.36	6.47	1.57	0.49		69.97
1979	35.09	1310.98	2192.49	7654		174.11	4.39	55.56	42.91	3.31	7.09	1.84	0.42		74.47
1980	39.05	1173.88	2149.07	7316		182.95	4.76	62.30	47.64	3.28	6.53	3.64	1.21	273.30	78.63
1981	41.13	964.74	2120.37	7244		215.20	4.79	74.41	53.14	3.80	8.18	6.58	2.71	304.31	85.07
1982	41.39	893.04	2108.98	7216	196	247.39	5.17	88.23	57.95	6.18	16.62	7.24	1.25	334.13	92.73
1983	42.60	927.00	2105.35	6938	431	242.96	5.86	89.50	58.49	6.18	16.61	7.25	1.25	354.10	98.51
1984	44.75	823.94	2075.10	6767	1024	222.69	7.67	95.02	56.93	6.44	19.37	10.36	1.92	368.81	109.49
1985	47.30	699.90	2022.23	6665	870	227.79	7.58	108.02	63.35	8.02	22.55	11.16	2.94	396.67	139.39
1986	55.73	858.51	2025.04	6822	660	247.31	8.64	118.69	68.86	9.27	24.13	12.83	3.61	422.26	164.79
1987	62.54	921.69	2061.06	6917	480	268.40	9.54	137.92	82.18	8.93	28.45	15.12	3.24	442.13	207.46
1988	68.55	987.03	2006.47	7103	1440	272.80	9.70	168.94	95.80	9.99	33.66	20.38	9.11	456.11	272.00
1989	74.16	995.10	1995.30	7425			10.90	212.17	123.37	12.31	45.50	25.59	5.39	475.40	326.99

20. Guangxi

20–9

Year	v8a1	v8a2	v8a3	v8b	v8c1	v8c2	v8d	v8f1	v8f2	v8f3	v8f4	v8f5	v8g
1949													
1950	0.39	1.92			0.20	2.11			5.20		0.22		82564
1951	0.76	2.25			0.53	2.48			8.60		0.28		85890
1952	1.21	2.84			0.81	3.24			9.74		0.35		90090
1953	1.91	3.51			1.24	4.18			9.21		0.41		99835
1954	3.01	3.62			1.61	5.02			14.19		0.55		97375
1955	3.99	3.62	0.05		1.90	5.76			26.16		0.65		64153
1956	4.93	3.66			2.32	6.27			42.03		1.11		8190
1957	5.89	3.31			2.84	6.35			52.15		1.26		13610
1958	9.52	3.63	-1.00		5.17	6.98		1.41	253.44		1.76		46348
1959	13.01	4.42			7.00	10.43		0.28	372.46		2.52	1.05	9719
1960	15.46	4.03			8.21	11.28		0.72	362.30		3.91	5.03	8185
1961	8.62	1.91			3.55	6.98		0.04	225.48		3.91	1.99	6796
1962	7.13	2.13	0.27		2.83	6.70		0.01	166.14		3.80	1.89	6082
1963	7.49	2.23	0.77		2.88	7.60			128.25		4.06	4.20	5444
1964	8.39	2.47	1.08		3.86	8.08			127.35		4.76	9.79	582
1965	11.58	2.95	1.06		5.45	10.13		0.02	143.02		6.37	43.40	5011
1966	14.70	3.63	1.03		7.21	12.14		0.63	173.76		8.85	70.55	4453
1967	12.52	3.47	1.05		6.06	10.98		0.56	166.41		9.48	55.12	4760
1968	8.59	2.50	1.06		3.78	8.37		0.08	117.83		6.66	23.93	4773
1969	17.28	3.93	1.11		9.21	13.11		1.06	229.04		12.83	73.48	5221
1970	21.93	4.33	1.15		12.55	14.86		5.44	302.83		15.50	92.07	6138
1971	26.76	4.69	1.85		14.54	18.76		11.19	392.66		19.69	110.63	6770
1972	30.21	5.22	2.05		16.35	21.14		15.36	439.20		24.42	130.29	7182
1973	34.51	6.18	2.08		18.63	24.15		17.43	456.67		27.59	140.54	7238
1974	36.85	7.27	2.61		19.86	26.86		13.12	516.19		29.95	139.63	7491
1975	40.73	8.45	3.13		23.28	29.02		12.89	605.47		35.19	165.23	7978
1976	44.19	9.77	2.75		24.86	31.85		10.50	704.29		39.16	171.23	9148
1977	50.56	10.48	2.86	45.50	29.16	34.73	13.60	14.66	749.89		44.79	190.50	9785
1978	55.17	11.61	3.19	50.08	31.74	38.23	16.24	19.02	828.54		49.47	224.38	10143
1979	58.95	11.84	3.68	53.92	32.96	41.51	17.29	21.16	722.38		52.30	229.82	10687
1980	61.27	13.61	3.75	56.75	31.79	46.84	19.65	20.82	589.66		53.64	225.00	10747
1981	67.50	13.96	3.61	61.62	31.44	53.63	20.88	22.76	560.87		55.82	245.91	10527
1982	74.01	14.59	4.13	68.10	35.00	57.73	21.82	24.50	643.34		60.23	274.49	10384
1983	78.93	15.19	4.39	73.11	38.99	59.52	23.21	22.44	756.58	2.15	65.62	307.91	10137
1984	84.89	19.10	5.50	79.10	46.49	62.99	25.86	29.20	729.24	3.15	70.60	337.88	9993
1985	108.42	22.81	8.16	102.65	64.05	75.35	33.78	39.05	598.90	3.59	81.82	416.34	9386
1986	124.74	27.16	12.89	117.81	75.16	89.63	39.72	38.60	639.18	3.65	90.97	457.67	10280
1987	154.58	34.43	18.45	146.23	95.49	111.97	47.89	41.73	797.97	3.77	102.62	555.20	10287
1988	197.27	48.66	26.07	184.53	122.72	149.28	57.67	38.29	1035.37	3.64	102.43	572.76	10622
1989	239.15	68.25	19.59	225.03	148.76	178.24	67.96	41.67	1140.45	10.54	109.29	639.07	11054

20. Guangxi

20–10

Year	v8g1	v9a	v9a1	v9a2	v9a3	v9b	v9b1	v9b2	v9b3	v9c	v10a	v10a1	v10b1	v10b2	v10b3
1949															
1950		0.39		0.22	0.17	2.63	1.53	0.11	0.99	117	3.53	3.31			
1951		0.84		0.41	0.43	4.12	2.50	0.14	1.49	284	4.46	4.15			
1952		1.00		0.45	0.55	5.55	3.33	0.16	2.07	328	5.46	5.01			
1953		4.82	3.68	0.57	0.57	10.24	5.74	0.31	4.19	426	7.26	6.75			
1954		5.16	3.77	0.87	0.52	13.54	7.64	0.56	5.33	532	8.72	8.13			
1955		5.53	3.86	1.15	0.52	14.07	8.65	0.71	4.71	669	9.09	8.37			
1956		9.31	6.65	1.91	0.75	20.34	14.01	0.91	5.42	835	10.14	9.25			
1957		10.00	6.91	2.22	0.87	27.83	19.74	1.02	7.07	919	9.99	9.30			
1958		12.34	8.62	3.17	0.55	37.38	27.90	1.81	7.67	1081	11.98	10.63			
1959		15.70	11.15	3.84	0.71	53.80	40.58	3.25	9.97	1652	14.14	12.43			
1960		19.98	14.67	4.46	0.85	60.68	46.17	3.62	10.89	2020	14.74	12.63			
1961		23.94	18.74	4.02	1.18	45.29	36.14	1.68	7.47	1852	12.20	11.16			
1962		25.44	19.45	4.51	1.48	33.72	26.00	1.36	6.37	1707	13.50	12.51			
1963		17.28	12.31	3.89	1.08	35.85	27.42	1.37	7.05	1632	14.76	13.50			
1964		17.05	12.19	4.01	0.85	51.47	40.53	1.59	9.34	1729	15.33	14.02			
1965	925	19.51	13.88	4.69	0.94	79.61	66.27	2.46	10.88	1896	17.16	15.36			
1966		22.63	15.46	6.03	1.14	97.57	82.67	3.15	11.75	1996	19.77	17.37			
1967		25.10	18.26	5.66	1.18	68.67	57.37	2.71	8.59	1910	19.46	17.32			
1968		22.35	17.78	4.01	0.56	44.64	36.12	1.90	6.62	1653	16.32	14.50			
1969		32.81	25.87	6.01	0.93	86.80	73.18	3.54	10.08	1824	20.41	17.60			
1970		30.69	22.67	6.79	1.23	110.82	95.11	4.09	11.62	1973	21.09	17.68			
1971	1620	32.97	23.43	8.02	1.52	134.96	116.87	4.68	13.41	2149	23.50	19.34			
1972	1744	37.19	25.95	9.66	1.58	148.61	127.83	5.02	15.76	2318	25.78	21.14			
1973	1801	35.65	22.84	10.95	1.86	149.47	127.36	5.66	16.45	2456	28.64	23.18			
1974	1844	37.39	22.83	12.57	1.99	137.08	114.66	5.96	16.46	2614	30.75	24.72			
1975	1911	34.40	19.81	12.65	1.94	143.90	120.41	6.34	17.15	2751	32.59	26.10			
1976	1965	34.14	18.96	13.34	1.84	125.39	101.33	6.45	17.60	2897	35.04	27.97			
1977	2088	36.95	19.80	14.87	2.28	155.60	128.60	7.28	19.72	3096	38.75	31.02			
1978	2140	41.20	21.64	16.89	2.67	183.78	153.93	7.54	22.31	3272	41.57	33.59			
1979	2178	52.37	29.02	19.91	3.44	170.42	142.42	6.57	21.43	3651	47.08	38.79			
1980	2181	60.25	31.11	25.05	4.09	160.46	132.52	5.77	22.17	3701	54.83	45.72			
1981	2172	67.07	32.98	29.77	4.32	165.16	136.60	5.95	22.61	4960	59.09	49.92	25.21		27.83
1982	2218	74.57	34.83	34.89	4.85	178.16	144.38	7.29	26.49	5162	65.21	54.58	27.54		29.79
1983	2250	86.84	39.16	42.44	5.24	188.85	153.10	7.80	27.96	5720	71.06	59.78	30.27		28.92
1984	2249	103.84	44.86	54.05	4.93	201.38	168.03	6.72	26.64	6158	80.02	68.64	32.15		29.24
1985	2436	127.77	55.72	66.50	5.55	235.16	200.52	6.21	28.44	6991	101.12	88.60	36.20		34.48
1986	2431	128.92	57.60	66.36	4.96	249.60	214.09	5.44	30.06	7325	115.18	100.24	41.75		35.50
1987	2522	145.22	66.94	73.19	5.09	260.63	221.97	5.62	33.04	8825	136.58	117.85	49.38		39.86
1988	2473	161.51	87.11	68.84	5.56	303.36	262.73	5.69	34.93	10707	181.72	156.98	67.16		51.91
1989	2488	154.28	82.15	67.03	5.10	307.49	266.59	4.81	36.09	12112	197.92	169.94	69.25		57.17

20. Guangxi

20–11

Year	v10b4	v10b5	v10b6	v10d	v11a1	v11a2	v11a3	v11b	v11b1	v11b2	v11c	v11d	v12a	v12b	v12c
1949															
1950								0.0428	0.0428						
1951								0.0893	0.0893				109.9	110.5	123.4
1952				1.32				0.0916	0.0916				99.8	99.9	113.0
1953				3.15				0.1013	0.1013				102.9	102.5	112.8
1954				5.68				0.2237	0.2237				104.2	104.2	98.6
1955				4.58				0.3508	0.3508				101.5	102.2	99.3
1956				4.48				0.4469	0.4469				99.2	99.7	100.4
1957				5.47				0.6195	0.6195				102.4	103.3	108.6
1958				7,51				0.5129	0.5129				99.9	99.7	101.4
1959				9.17				0.3054	0.3054				99.7	99.8	102.3
1960				5.98				0.2673	0.2673				103.4	104.8	104.4
1961				5.56				0.1959	0.1959				124.8	138.0	123.0
1962				5.56				0.1991	0.1991				103.0	100.5	105.2
1963				6.30				0.2945	0.2945				99.5	99.2	94.5
1964				7.75				0.4370	0.4370				95.4	94.8	99.8
1965				8.46				0.5134	0.4739	0.0395			95.3	95.8	100.3
1966				9.25				0.5761	0.5358	0.0403			99.7	100.0	103.7
1967				8.97				0.4258	0.3932	0.0326			99.9	100.4	100.4
1968				7.90				0.3957	0.3586	0.0371			100.5	101.0	99.8
1969				9.19				0.4557	0.4207	0.0350			100.4	100.9	100.0
1970				9.82				0.5203	0.4853	0.0350			100.1	100.4	100.1
1971				10.89				0.7233	0.6653	0.0580			100.4	101.2	101.4
1972				11.16				0.9020	0.8370	0.0650			100.5	101.2	102.4
1973				13.23				1.5846	1.4981	0.0865			100.3	100.7	101.7
1974				13.11				2.3526	2.1994	0.1532			100.1	100.4	99.9
1975				13.63				2.0053	2.0005	0.0048			100.2	101.0	101.1
1976				14.54				1.8507	1.7507	0.1000			100.5	101.0	100.1
1977				15.76				2.2560	2.0554	0.2006			100.2	100.5	99.7
1978				16.72				2.6931	2.4885	0.2046			100.0	99.8	103.2
1979				20.02				3.0799	2.8662	0.2137			102.3	102.8	117.8
1980				24.00				3.7823	3.6579	0.1244			109.2	112.6	110.9
1981	0.0009	0.93	5.12	25.30				3.9849	3.6620	0.3229			101.7	102.7	101.0
1982	0.0024	2.03	5.85	29.64				3.7614	3.4259	0.3355			103.1	104.1	105.5
1983	0.0000	5.86	6.01	34.71				4.0048	3.4269	0.5779			102.8	103.0	101.8
1984	0.0178	11.72	6.89	32.63				4.1387	3.2216	0.9171			104.2	104.6	106.9
1985	0.0047	21.18	9.26	38.59				5.2310	3.7205	1.5105		0.4493	111.2	114.7	118.2
1986	0.0359	26.46	11.44	48.62				5.4528	4.3036	1.1492	0.8452	0.7982	105.1	106.2	105.4
1987	0.1659	32.62	14.57	56.64				7.9151	5.4331	2.4820	0.4437	0.9355	108.0	110.2	115.7
1988	0.2484	44.54	17.86	70.01				8.0807	5.4427	2.6380	1.0886	1.8157	121.0	123.3	124.4
1989	0.2600	51.32	19.93	81.50				7.5435	5.8430	1.7005		0.8300	121.3	119.7	103.7

20. Guangxi

20–12

Year	v13a	v13b	v13c1	v13c2	v13c3	v13d	v14a	v14b	v14c	v15a	v15b	v15c	v15d	v15e	v15f
1949	4.93														
1950	7.10		0.0962	4.0718	48.9960	0.04		2685		3691					
1951	11.60		0.0863	5.4920	144.5940	0.02		2801		3774					
1952	19.55		0.1143	9.2613	200.1719	0.01	4974	6376	0.24	3859					
1953	17.88		0.1395	10.9934	226.3679	0.04		8381		3960					
1954	16.19		0.1637	11.9142	217.1265	0.04		21412		4082					
1955	16.17		0.1664	12.0359	198.6812	0.06		27066		4094					
1956	18.21		0.3225	17.6732	261.0111	0.04		40198		4180					
1957	10.00		0.3910	19.7539	249.8406	0.03		44012	0.65	4155					
1958	7.59		1.1636	24.1280	329.9880	0.09		55835		4198					
1959	7.37		1.3210	29.1564	335.9925	0.06		52426		3958					
1960	13.13		1.9109	29.4161	316.2485	0.18		56698		3891					
1961	18.12		1.6816	25.7152	276.0442	0.34		50982		3750					
1962	16.16		1.3078	20.7972	258.2019	0.23		35709		3720					
1963	13.87		1.0365	19.5353	257.2886	0.38		37848		3718					
1964	12.93		0.7619	22.1450	333.5115	0.43		39376		3730					
1965		87.2	0.7852	23.4524	400.7928	0.24	18837	41703	0.91	3727					
1966	12.75		0.7120	33.0791	366.7660			38556		3685					
1967	15.65		0.6751	33.5482	357.4587			32008		3655					
1968	17.53		0.2992	43.8487	348.0559	0.46		33944		3622					
1969	10.83		0.2035	69.0694	337.9879	0.05		34860		3649					
1970	8.53		0.0780	108.7275	366.4992	0.20		36160		3722					
1971	8.99	66.6	0.2010	117.2175	397.8686			36930		3748					
1972	10.59	91.2	0.5112	119.7091	453.2961			38686		3761					
1973	10.46	96.2	0.7688	120.6023	496.9592	0.06		39243		3791					
1974	11.09	97.6	0.9775	130.1324	522.7961	0.15		42000		3836					
1975	11.41	97.7	1.2995	166.2687	540.7974	0.33		47314		3892					
1976	11.12	98.0	1.4658	212.9951	539.7400	0.33		49379		3932					
1977	11.56	97.9	1.8153	238.3613	523.2300	0.34		52801		3938					
1978	9.96	97.0	2.0872	225.7376	511.6900	0.44	43500	55778	3.49	3937					
1979	11.37	95.3	2.0987	185.0828	503.0200	0.37		62738		3941					
1980	16.46	94.2	2.5521	159.8424	502.4800	0.06	47608	66667	3.13	3955					
1981	19.84	91.3	2.4320	128.0592	504.0600	0.61		73731	3.79	3952					
1982	20.46	93.6	2.1117	112.4832	513.8300	0.84		78757	4.00	3946					
1983	20.16	95.1	2.1786	109.8566	516.4200	0.59		84778	4.30	3930					
1984		95.2	2.4396	115.6952	523.6300	0.51		88084	4.80	3861					
1985		95.2	3.0536	121.4171	531.4500	0.53	57300	94359	5.40	3858	8266		1752		
1986		95.6	3.3771	130.1499	544.3000	0.63		96377	5.42	3846					
1987	16.31	96.1	3.4523	143.3000	546.5700	0.97		100513	5.80	3847					
1988		95.8	3.7500	145.4400	537.5500	0.90	64600	104363	6.41	3854	8266	1960	1752		
1989		96.5	3.7800	139.1300	547.6000	1.03	67000	107000	5.11	3868					

Notes

1. National Output and Income (Y)

v1a: (E), p.648
v1a1: (E), p.648
v1a2: (E), p.648
v1a3: (E), p.648
v1a4: (E), p.648
v1a5: (E), p.648

v1b: (A); (D), p.331
v1b1: (A); (D), p.331
v1b2: (A); (D), p.331
v1b3: (A); (D), p.331
v1b4: (A); (D), p.331
v1b5: (A); (D), p.331

v1c: v1a – v1d

v1d: (E), p.645
v1d1: (E), p.645
v1d2: (E), p.645
v1d3: (E), p.645
v1d4: (E), p.645
v1d5: (E), p.645

v1e: (A); (D), p.332
v1e1: (A); (D), p.332
v1e2: (A); (D), p.332
v1e3: (A); (D), p.332
v1e4: (A); (D), p.332
v1e5: (A); (D), p.332

v1f: (E), p.644
v1f1: (E), p.644
v1f2: (E), p.644
v1f3: (E), p.644

v1g: v3a + v2a

v1h: (A); (E), p.671—data of 1978 was an estimated one

v1i: (E), p.670

v1j: (A); (E), p.670
v1j1: (E), p.670
v1j2: (E), p.670
v1j3: NA

v1k: NA

2. Investment (I)

v2a: (E), p.647
v2a1: (A); (D), p.335
v2a2: (A); (D), p.335

v2b: (A)

v2c: (A); (E), p.662
v2c1: (E), p.663
v2c2: (E), p.663

v2d:
v2d1: (E), p.660
v2d2: (E), p.660

v2e: (E), p.660

3. Consumption (C)

v3a: (E), p.647

v3b: (E), p.647
v3b1: (A); (D), p.333
v3b2: (A); (D), p.333

v3c: (E), p.647

v3d: (A)
v3d1: (A); (D), p.334
v3d2: (A); (D), p.334

v3e: (A)
v3e1: (A)
v3e2: (A)
v3e3: (A)
v3e4: (A)

v3f: (A); (E), p.671

v3f1: (A); (E), p.671
v3f2: (A)
v3f3: (A)
v3f4: (A)

4. Public Finance and Banking (FB)

v4a:
v4a1: (E), p.668
v4a1a: (E), p.668
v4a1b: (C), p.273
v4a1c: (C), p.273
v4a1d: (C), p.273
v4a2: (E), p.668
v4a2a: (E), p.668
v4a2b: (E), p.668
v4a2c: (E), p.668
v4a2d: v4a2 – v4a2a – v4a2b – v4a2c

v4b: (A)
v4b1: (A); (C), p.281
v4b2: (A); (C), p.281
v4b3: NA

v4c:
v4c1: (E), p.660
v4c2: (E), p.660

5. Labor Force (L)

v5a: (E), p.643
v5a1: (E), p.643
v5a2: (E), p.643
v5a3: (E), p.643
v5a4: (E), p.643

v5b:
v5b1: (E), p.643
v5b2: (E), p.643
v5b3: (E), p.643

v5c: NA
v5c1: NA

v5d: NA

6. Population (PO)

v6a: (A); (E), p.642—statistics based on administration region in 1988
v6a1: (E), p.642—(ditto)
v6a2: (E), p.642—(ditto)

v6b: (E), p.642—data of 1982 and before have been adjusted according to the Third Population Census; 1983–88 according to information provided by public security department

v6c: (E), p.642—(ditto)

v6d:
v6d1: (E), p.642—statistics based on administration region in 1988
v6d2: (E), p.642—(ditto)
v6d3: (E), p.642—(ditto)
v6d4: (E), p.642—(ditto)
v6d5: (A)—Nanning
v6d6: (A)—Liuzhou

7. Agriculture (A)

v7a: (A); (E), p.654

v7b: (A); (E), p.654

v7c: (A); (E), p.654

v7d: (A); (E), p.654

v7e: (A)

v7f: (A)

v7g: (A); (E), p.654

v7h: (A)
v7h1: (A)
v7h2: (A)
v7h3: (A)
v7h4: (A)
v7h5: (A)

v7i: (A); (E), p.653

8. Industry (IN)

v8a: (E), p.655
 v8a1: (E), p.655
 v8a2: (E), p.655
 v8a3: v8a – v8a1 – v8a2

v8b: (E), p.660

 v8c1: (E), p.648
 v8c2: (E), p.648

v8d: (E), p.660

v8f:
 v8f1: (E), p.659—steel products
 v8f2: (E), p.659
 v8f3: (A); (E), p.659
 v8f4: (E), p.659
 v8f5: (E), p.659

v8g: (A)
 v8g1: (E), p.660

9. Transport (TR)

v9a: (E), p.661—data from transport department
 v9a1: (E), p.661—including central and local railways
 v9a2: (E), p.661
 v9a3: (E), p.661—excluding distant ocean and coastal passenger traffic

v9b: (E), p.661—data from transport department
 v9b1: (E), p.661—including central and local railways
 v9b2: (E), p.661
 v9b3: (E), p.661—excluding distant ocean and coastal freight volume

v9c: (E), p.661—1980 and before: based on 1970's constant price, 1981 and after: based on 1980's constant price

10. Domestic Trade (DT)

v10a: (E), p.664
 v10a1: (E), p.664

v10b:
 v10b1: (E), p.664
 v10b2: NA
 v10b3: (E), p.664—including supply and marketing cooperative and other collectives
 v10b4: (E), p.664
 v10b5: (E), p.664
 v10b6: (E), p.664

v10d: (E), p.666—calculated on calendar year basis

11. Foreign Trade (FT)

v11a:
 v11a1: NA
 v11a2: NA
 v11a3: NA

v11b: (E), p.667—data from foreign trade department
 v11b1: (E), p.667
 v11b2: v11b – v11b1

v11c: (A)

v11d: (A)

12. Prices (PR)

v12a: (E), p.669

v12b: (E), p.669

v12c: (E), p.669

13. Education (ED)

v13a: (A)

v13b: (A); (E), p.671

v13c:
- v13c1: (A); (E), p.671—general institutions of higher learning
- v13c2: (A)—technical, ordinary, agricultural vocational and technician secondary schools
- v13c3: (A); (E), p.671

v13d: (A)—general institutions of higher learning

14. Social Factors (SF)

v14a: (E), p.671

v14b: (A); (E), p.671—doctors, nurses and others

v14c: (A)

15. Natural Environment (NE)

v15a: (A); (E), p.654

v15b: (A)

v15c: (A)

v15d: (A)

v15e: NA

v15f: NA

Sources of Data

(A) Data supplied by the DSNEB, SSB, the PRC.
(B) Statistical Bureau of Guangxi Autonomous Region ed. *Guangxi Striving and Advancing Forty Years*, Beijing: CSPH, 1989.
(C) ________ ed. *Statistical Yearbook of Guangxi*, Beijing: CSPH, 1989.
(D) Same as (D) in Beijing's sources of data.
(E) Same as (E) in Beijing's sources of data.

21

Hainan

21. Hainan

21–1

Year	v1a	v1a1	v1a2	v1a3	v1a4	v1a5	v1b	v1b1	v1b2	v1b3	v1b4	v1b5	v1c	v1d	v1d1
1949															
1950															
1951															
1952															
1953															
1954															
1955															
1956															
1957															
1958															
1959															
1960															
1961															
1962															
1963															
1964															
1965															
1966															
1967															
1968															
1969															
1970															
1971															
1972															
1973															
1974															
1975															
1976															
1977															
1978	23.19	10.38	7.17	2.09	1.22	2.33							9.93	13.26	7.27
1979	24.20	10.90	7.46	2.24	1.18	2.42	101.9						10.39	13.81	7.62
1980	25.60	12.68	7.05	2.20	1.11	2.56	100.6						10.43	15.17	9.07
1981	30.33	17.07	6.87	2.29	1.07	3.03	106.3						11.89	18.44	12.23
1982	37.33	21.94	7.73	3.02	1.18	3.46	120.0						14.11	23.22	16.04
1983	40.71	23.80	8.96	2.84	1.21	3.90	107.3						15.77	24.94	17.00
1984	53.61	27.82	11.45	6.47	1.53	6.34	129.9						22.50	31.11	19.41
1985	66.94	30.61	16.49	10.88	2.64	6.32	115.8						31.23	35.71	20.89
1986	73.07	35.52	17.67	10.33	2.95	6.60	106.2	110.6	106.3	94.5	108.2	103.1	33.64	39.43	24.20
1987	85.12	41.24	21.50	10.13	4.22	8.30	112.6	107.7	123.5	93.7	139.3	116.1	39.60	45.52	27.94
1988	118.56	57.62	31.26	14.23	4.49	10.96	112.5	101.2	125.8	113.9	107.4	121.3	56.47	62.09	38.70
1989	142.85	64.47	38.96	22.44	5.08	11.90	110.8	107.5	109.6	131.7	108.2	104.5	70.55	72.30	43.51

21. Hainan

21–2

Year	v1d2	v1d3	v1d4	v1d5	v1e	v1e1	v1e2	v1e3	v1e4	v1e5	v1f	v1f1	v1f2	v1f3	v1g
1949															
1950															
1951															
1952															
1953															
1954															
1955															
1956															
1957															
1958															
1959															
1960															
1961															
1962															
1963															
1964															
1965															
1966															
1967															
1968															
1969															
1970															
1971															
1972															
1973															
1974															
1975															
1976															
1977															
1978	2.92	0.68	0.66	1.73							14.73	7.57	3.75	3.41	
1979	2.98	0.74	0.63	1.82	102.50						15.34	7.92	3.88	3.54	
1980	2.84	0.72	0.59	1.95	102.80						17.23	9.37	3.71	4.15	
1981	2.68	0.74	0.55	2.24	107.70						21.19	12.53	3.56	5.10	
1982	3.03	0.94	0.62	2.59	123.80						27.00	16.90	4.15	5.95	
1983	3.49	0.90	0.64	2.91	105.80						29.34	17.30	4.57	7.47	
1984	4.67	1.89	0.89	4.28	124.30						36.60	19.71	6.83	10.06	
1985	6.14	3.21	1.35	4.12	103.70						42.77	21.10	9.74	11.93	
1986	6.39	3.11	1.56	4.17	107.60	112.20	103.70	96.70	111.20	99.60	46.73	24.05	9.92	12.76	
1987	7.29	3.11	2.26	4.92	111.10	109.00	114.90	97.60	140.60	112.20	55.88	28.68	10.89	16.31	
1988	9.83	4.16	2.36	7.03	109.80	102.70	124.90	112.50	106.50	118.30	74.76	38.59	14.15	22.02	70.14
1989	11.81	6.67	2.71	7.60	109.80	107.40	109.30	133.90	115.80	104.70	86.87	42.85	18.25	25.77	88.21

21. Hainan

21–3

Year	v1h	v1i	v1j	v1j1	v1j2	v1j3	v1k	v2a	v2a1	v2a2	v2b	v2c	v2c1	v2c2	v2d1
1949															
1950															
1951															
1952															
1953															
1954															
1955															
1956															
1957															
1958															
1959															
1960															
1961															
1962															
1963															
1964															
1965															
1966															
1967															
1968															
1969															
1970				497											
1971				464											
1972				491											
1973				523											
1974		3.71		583											
1975		3.56		548											
1976		3.78		567											
1977		4.27		559											
1978		4.54		583								3.35			6.53
1979		5.00		630								3.22			7.08
1980		5.69	692	697	638			3.27	2.44	0.83	3.47	3.47			7.41
1981		6.23	728	736	623			4.81	3.39	1.46		3.58			7.23
1982		7.21	790	799	671			6.54	5.34	1.20		4.53	0.65	0.22	8.15
1983		7.54	812	823	673			6.84	5.70	1.14		4.96	0.96	0.11	9.70
1984		8.70	929	940	830			8.93	7.83	1.10		7.96	2.16	0.31	10.49
1985		9.74	1020	1029	925	1329		13.15	5.04	8.11	15.31	12.46	2.57	0.75	13.26
1986		11.42	1168	1190	943			14.11	10.14	3.97		12.99	3.76	0.29	17.69
1987		12.21	1233	1259	959	1417		17.42	10.45	6.97	16.02	11.45	1.86	0.44	20.33
1988		14.04	1399	1421	1141	1740		27.24	16.18	11.06	20.14	14.99	3.50	0.70	23.05
1989	674.27	17.10	1663	1658	1321			40.79	24.16	16.63	28.99	23.26	6.92	2.79	27.56

21. Hainan

21–4

Year	v2d2	v2e	v3a	v3b	v3b1	v3b2	v3c	v3d	v3d1	v3d2	v3e	v3e1	v3e2	v3e3	v3e4
1949															
1950															
1951															
1952															
1953															
1954															
1955															
1956															
1957															
1958															
1959															
1960															
1961															
1962															
1963															
1964															
1965															
1966															
1967															
1968															
1969															
1970															
1971															
1972															
1973															
1974															
1975															
1976															
1977															
1978	4.71	1.59													
1979	4.94	1.46													
1980	5.34	1.66	11.32	10.60	7.63	2.97	0.72	205	163	345					
1981	5.12	1.39	13.00	12.12	8.42	3.70	0.88	231	179	406					
1982	5.75	1.65	16.32	15.17	10.47	4.70	1.15	285	219	500					
1983	6.83	1.95	17.93	16.58	11.27	5.31	1.35	309	233	542					
1984	7.72	2.23	21.45	19.62	13.15	6.47	1.83	364	271	622					
1985	9.83	3.44	23.95	21.78	14.58	7.20	2.17	400	300	643	711	453			
1986	13.54	4.55	27.04	24.37	16.32	8.04	2.67	446	333	687	863	511			
1987	15.83	4.94	32.34	29.22	18.52	10.69	3.12	526	376	876	921	552			
1988	17.63	5.98	42.90	38.18	24.34	13.84	4.72	609	486	1098	1030	660			
1989	21.79	8.34	47.42	41.06	26.26	14.80	6.36	643	519	1113	1196	752			

21. Hainan

21–5

Year	v3f	v3f1	v3f2	v3f3	v3f4	v4a1	v4a1a	v4a1b	v4a1c	v4a1d	v4a2	v4a2a	v4a2b	v4a2c	v4a2d
1949															
1950															
1951															
1952						0.13					0.21	0.03	0.08	0.08	0.02
1953						0.44					0.25	0.01	0.13	0.11	
1954						0.55					0.35	0.05	0.17	0.13	
1955						0.41	0.01				0.30	0.05	0.14	0.11	
1956						0.40	0.01				0.44	0.11	0.19	0.14	
1957						0.50	0.02				0.46	0.12	0.20	0.14	
1958						0.66	0.07				0.92	0.60	0.16	0.15	0.01
1959						0.72	0.15				0.93	0.55	0.22	0.15	0.01
1960						0.62	0.11				1.08	0.67	0.27	0.13	0.01
1961						0.53	-0.02				0.71	0.30	0.25	0.14	0.02
1962						0.61	-0.01				0.56	0.15	0.23	0.14	0.04
1963						0.64	0.04				0.63	0.17	0.25	0.14	0.07
1964						0.70	0.05				0.66	0.17	0.27	0.15	0.07
1965						0.85	0.07				0.63	0.06	0.25	0.14	0.18
1966						0.98	0.08				0.68	0.09	0.26	0.15	0.18
1967															
1968															
1969						1.38	0.34				0.82	0.13	0.24	0.19	0.26
1970						1.43	0.29				0.94	0.20	0.25	0.18	0.31
1971						1.35	0.27				0.98	1.18	0.29	0.18	-0.67
1972						1.01	0.12				1.10	0.25	0.31	0.21	0.33
1973						1.26	0.17				1.27	0.25	0.38	0.23	0.41
1974						1.22	0.21				1.50	0.31	0.40	0.23	0.56
1975						1.41	0.19				1.47	0.31	0.42	0.21	0.53
1976						1.55	0.18				1.25	0.06	0.43	0.21	0.55
1977						1.54	0.09				1.32	0.05	0.46	0.24	0.57
1978						1.36	0.02				1.67	0.09	0.56	0.26	0.76
1979						1.33	-0.02				1.82	0.05	0.64	0.30	0.83
1980						1.19	-0.04	0.91	0.13	0.19	2.10	0.12	0.76	0.39	0.83
1981						1.14	-0.07				2.42	0.14	0.84	0.43	1.01
1982						1.28	-0.10				2.59	0.16	0.98	0.48	0.97
1983	263	187				1.62	-0.05				3.18	0.15	1.14	0.63	1.26
1984	255	165				3.05	-0.04				4.53	0.41	1.42	0.05	2.65
1985	319	191	18.00	41.00	17.00	3.16	0.02	3.29	0.23	-0.38	5.90	1.36	1.69	0.89	1.96
1986	375	216	21.00	56.00	20.00	2.59	0.01				6.63	0.78	2.17	1.05	2.63
1987	400	244	23.00	40.00	19.00	2.96	0.01	2.67	0.40	-0.12	6.73	0.47	2.23	1.19	2.84
1988	517	299	31.00	78.00	20.00	4.82	0.19	3.65	0.12	0.86	9.25	1.25	2.85	1.10	4.05
1989	578	333	38.02	73.72	21.65	6.25	0.34				13.81	2.47	3.61	1.44	6.29

21. Hainan

21–6

Year	v4b	v4b1	v4b2	v4b3	v4c1	v4c2	v5a	v5a1	v5a2	v5a3	v5a4	v5b1	v5b2	v5b3	v5c
1949															
1950															
1951	0.01	0.01													
1952	0.04	0.04													
1953	0.06	0.03	0.03												
1954	0.10	0.08	0.02												
1955	0.12	0.06	0.06												
1956	0.15	0.13	0.02												
1957	0.26	0.17	0.09												
1958	0.61	0.30	0.31												
1959	0.50	0.28	0.22												
1960	0.56	0.35	0.20												
1961	0.67	0.33	0.34												
1962	0.54	0.27	0.27												
1963	0.52	0.28	0.24												
1964	0.60	0.33	0.27												
1965	0.65	0.38	0.27												
1966	0.79	0.41	0.38												
1967	0.89	0.45	0.44												
1968	1.08	0.51	0.57												
1969	1.08	0.53	0.55												
1970	0.99	0.54	0.45												
1971	1.15	0.62	0.53												
1972	1.19	0.69	0.50												
1973	1.22	0.73	0.49				200	59	5		136				9.10
1974	1.48	0.91	0.57				202	58	4		138				8.73
1975	1.58	0.92	0.66				202	60	4		136				9.45
1976	1.75	0.95	0.80				204	63	5		136				9.89
1977	2.44	1.62	0.82				218	70	10		138				12.03
1978	1.76	1.09	0.67				220	74	6		140	175	18	27	12.12
1979	2.20	1.32	0.88				225	76	6	1	142				11.71
1980	2.76	1.78	0.98	0.83			230	77	7	1	145	184	17	29	12.05
1981	3.83	2.48	1.35				242	84	7	2	149				12.54
1982	5.19	3.36	1.83				247	87	7	2	151				13.01
1983	6.35	4.35	2.00				252	88	7	2	155				12.75
1984	9.06	6.40	2.66				258	86	9	3	160				13.02
1985	12.42	8.68	3.73	2.28	2.20	12.20	267	89	9	5	164	198	24	45	14.23
1986	16.33	11.76	4.57		2.27	11.30	274	90	9	5	169	201	26	47	14.72
1987	21.84	16.02	5.82	2.09	2.96	12.50	280	90	9	6	174	202	27	51	14.87
1988	29.98	23.09	7.00	2.52	3.57	11.90	291	93	9	7	181	207	28	56	15.23
1989	37.60	30.30	7.30		3.57		298	94	9	8	186	211	29	58	15.52

21. Hainan

21–7

Year	v5c1	v5d	v6a	v6a1	v6a2	v6b	v6c	v6d1	v6d2	v6d3	v6d4	v6d5	v6d6
1949												15.02	
1950													
1951													
1952			259	21	238			20	239	127	132	11.99	
1953			266	22	244			22	243	132	134	12.03	
1954			273	22	251			30	243	136	137		
1955			278	23	255			30	248	138	140		
1956			286	28	258			32	254	142	144		
1957			291	33	258	32.10	9.10	37	254	145	146	12.40	
1958			303	33	270			48	255	150	153	14.63	
1959			312	44	268			65	247	155	157		
1960			317	46	271			81	236	157	160		
1961			327	52	275	25.30	8.90	50	277	162	165	19.47	
1962			335	45	290	52.02	8.29	47	288	168	167	19.64	
1963			343	39	304	41.80	7.60	48	295	173	170	17.20	
1964			353	41	312	41.60	8.70	49	304	179	174	20.49	
1965	3.39		366	35	331	39.72	8.07	52	314	186	180	20.37	
1966	3.62		378					54	324	190	187	20.71	
1967	3.82		387					54	333	193	192	18.38	
1968	3.99		390					53	337	199	197	18.60	
1969	4.34		408					53	355	207	204	18.82	
1970	5.32		429	36	393	31.75	5.70	54	375	218	211	19.21	
1971	5.88		455			29.60	5.15	61	394	232	222	19.66	
1972	6.17		468	39	429	30.08	5.33	65	403	239	229	20.33	
1973	6.18		479	41	438	28.16	5.66	65	414	245	234	20.86	
1974	6.29		488	38	450	25.00	5.60	67	421	249	238	21.15	
1975	6.89		497	39	458	22.53	5.67	70	427	254	243	21.37	
1976	7.26		505	39	466	20.90	5.70	71	434	259	246	26.18	
1977	7.54		516	41	475	23.05	5.65	74	442	264	252	22.17	
1978	9.35	175	528	43	485	24.19	4.62	77	451	270	258	23.06	
1979	9.06	178	540	46	494	25.90	4.73	81	459	277	264	23.91	
1980	9.25	184	552	49	503	24.12	4.72	86	466	280	272	24.83	
1981	9.51	187	561	52	509	29.90	5.10	91	470	287	274	25.59	
1982	10.13	191	571	53	518	22.44	4.58	94	477	293	278	26.36	
1983	10.08	194	581	56	525	19.31	4.55	98	483	299	282	26.86	
1984	10.39	196	589	60	529	17.60	4.15	104	485	303	286	27.86	
1985	11.63	198	598	71	527	14.55	4.13	112	486	309	289	28.96	
1986	12.10	201	606	74	532	15.23	4.05	117	489	313	293	30.03	
1987	12.23	202	615	102	513	14.83	4.23	122	493	318	297	31.17	
1988	12.40	207	627	106	521	15.08	4.13	126	501	325	302	33.40	
1989	12.48	211	639	112	527	23.46	5.54	133	506	332	307	35.27	

21. Hainan

21–8

Year	v7a	v7b	v7c	v7d	v7e	v7f	v7g	v7h	v7h1	v7h2	v7h3	v7h4	v7h5	v7i	v8a
1949															
1950			35.44												
1951			36.16												
1952			37.80	830										33.11	
1953			40.52											38.70	
1954			46.41											44.56	
1955			52.05											47.91	
1956			66.12											43.51	
1957			76.82	1129										39.93	
1958			110.33											34.02	
1959			128.01											29.98	
1960			141.96											28.64	
1961			148.76											31.24	
1962			160.16											33.89	
1963			190.46											34.98	
1964			210.80											35.93	
1965			232.23	1036										37.71	
1966			253.09											31.76	
1967			257.00											31.71	
1968			259.00											31.73	
1969			261.00											33.53	
1970			185.28			10	0.05							38.08	
1971		25.96	220.91			13	0.08							34.97	
1972		24.08	243.53			9	0.11							35.58	
1973		34.21	259.77			13	0.12							35.96	
1974		54.14	249.03			13	0.19							35.69	
1975		67.99	248.66			11	0.27							35.15	
1976		73.58	249.85			11	0.32							36.26	
1977		89.13	246.83			14	0.36							34.70	
1978	6.31	70.07	244.75	1195		12	0.34							37.46	7.17
1979		50.29	233.75			11	0.34							38.16	7.46
1980	6.98	24.26	220.17	1044		16	0.35							44.26	7.05
1981		54.62	219.23			16	0.37							50.00	6.87
1982		29.04	214.79			15	0.37	21.95	8.48	8.01	3.12	1.49	0.85	49.92	7.73
1983		39.73	220.52			16	0.36	23.80	8.64	8.74	3.86	1.59	0.97	55.39	8.96
1984		48.89	209.35			24	0.39	27.82	9.69	10.07	4.22	2.49	1.35	58.25	11.45
1985	10.17	29.22	208.00	1110		26	0.57	30.61	10.47	10.43	5.85	2.31	1.55	59.10	16.49
1986		31.93	219.76			29	0.70	35.53	12.35	12.05	6.42	2.58	2.13	61.35	17.67
1987		25.95	215.00			32	0.50	41.26	14.19	14.08	7.51	2.91	2.57	63.40	21.50
1988	12.80	29.81	201.00	1111		32	0.62	57.63	22.50	15.45	11.31	4.15	4.22	67.06	31.26
1989	13.15	23.98	209.00	1184		35	0.77	64.47	27.08	15.36	12.93	3.85	5.25	67.52	38.96

21. Hainan

21–9

Year	v8a1	v8a2	v8a3	v8b	v8c1	v8c2	v8d	v8f1	v8f2	v8f3	v8f4	v8f5	v8g
1949													
1950													
1951													
1952											0.01		35
1953											0.02		
1954											0.03		
1955											0.04		
1956									0.19		0.06		
1957									0.24		0.07		241
1958									2.18		0.14		
1959									10.41		0.31	0.10	
1960									12.26		0.38	0.62	
1961									2.80		0.41	0.44	
1962									1.56		0.36	0.65	911
1963											0.43	1.51	893
1964											0.48	3.83	877
1965											0.67	5.02	815
1966											0.79		931
1967											0.85		948
1968											0.74		840
1969											0.93		768
1970									1.86		1.17	8.20	873
1971									4.14		1.52	8.67	896
1972									1.25		1.66	9.51	942
1973									1.21		1.96	10.63	993
1974									1.54		2.27	12.71	1020
1975									2.52		2.77	16.45	1044
1976									4.53		3.32	16.82	1047
1977									7.52		3.64	17.57	1074
1978	5.92	1.25		4.99	2.90	4.27	2.05		6.54		3.57	18.27	1648
1979	6.22	1.24		4.88	3.16	4.29	2.03		2.28		4.47	19.75	1567
1980	5.80	1.25		4.96	2.67	4.38	2.08		2.31		4.22	19.44	1589
1981	5.69	1.18		4.86	2.46	4.41	1.95		1.83		4.85	22.24	1504
1982	6.62	1.11		5.64	2.95	4.78	2.24		2.40		5.93	25.92	1431
1983	7.92	1.04		6.58	3.45	5.51	2.59		2.50		6.81	26.41	1371
1984	10.06	1.37	0.02	8.43	3.85	7.60	3.51		2.01		7.28	31.56	1417
1985	13.22	1.83	1.44	11.41	5.29	11.19	4.32		2.47		8.03	39.00	1526
1986	13.97	2.24	1.46	12.49	5.94	11.73	4.64		2.00		9.29	42.91	1495
1987	15.29	2.55	3.66	14.16	5.78	15.72	5.08		1.76		8.32	36.75	1491
1988	22.33	3.49	5.44	20.35	8.23	23.03	6.62		1.38		8.70	44.91	1497
1989	26.22	4.49	8.25	25.57	10.53	28.43	8.01	0.14	0.43		12.41	44.25	1566

21. Hainan

21–10

Year	v8g1	v9a	v9a1	v9a2	v9a3	v9b	v9b1	v9b2	v9b3	v9c	v10a	v10a1	v10b1	v10b2	v10b3
1949															
1950		0.07		0.06	0.01	0.13		0.02	0.10						
1951		0.08		0.06	0.02	0.16		0.02	0.14						
1952		0.18		0.16	0.02	0.13		0.02	0.11	50	1.48	1.34			
1953		0.39		0.37	0.02	0.24		0.01	0.14		2.15	1.94			
1954		0.59		0.55	0.04	0.34		0.14	0.20		2.62	2.35			
1955		0.69		0.64	0.05	0.35		0.12	0.23		2.27	2.03			
1956		1.08		1.03	0.05	0.59		0.25	0.34		2.56	2.14			
1957		1.33		1.29	0.04	0.61		0.29	0.32	181	2.65	2.28			
1958		1.91	0.03	1.83	0.05	1.99	0.88	0.47	0.64		3.27	2.29			
1959		2.44	0.14	2.21	0.09	2.53	0.89	0.61	1.03		3.51	3.00			
1960		2.23	0.09	2.12	0.07	2.93	1.18	0.54	1.21		3.61	3.05			
1961		2.54	0.25	2.24	0.05	2.13	1.04	0.29	0.80		3.03	2.64			
1962		2.72	0.31	2.35	0.06	1.28	0.33	0.23	0.72	446	3.86	3.44			
1963		2.52	0.14	2.34	0.04	1.49	0.26	0.33	0.90		4.05	3.66			
1964		2.69	0.12	2.48	0.09	1.72	0.32	0.54	0.86		4.02	3.63			
1965		3.05	0.16	2.77	0.09	2.46	0.64	0.61	1.21	438	4.28	3.79			
1966		3.52	0.18	3.23	0.11	3.35	1.22	0.68	1.45		4.67	4.11			
1967		3.13	0.24	2.79	0.09	2.63	0.83	0.58	1.22		4.64	4.08			
1968		2.54	0.24	2.24	0.06	1.68	0.43	0.35	0.90		4.26	3.78			
1969		3.46	0.23	3.14	0.10	2.90	1.01	0.70			5.06	4.45			
1970		3.33	0.23	2.99	0.11	3.89	1.55	0.87	1.47	539	5.25	4.41			
1971		3.65	0.21	3.31	0.13	4.53	1.90	0.90			5.89	5.04			
1972		4.05	0.28	3.63	0.14	3.97	1.51	0.83			5.99	5.18			
1973		4.40	0.31	3.95	0.14	3.76	1.65	0.71			6.55	5.65			
1974											6.73	5.78			
1975		5.34	0.30	4.72	0.15	4.98	1.83	0.94	2.21	558	7.49	6.38			
1976		5.95	0.36	5.27	0.15	4.91	1.81	0.96	2.14		8.13	6.97			
1977		6.72	0.42	5.92	0.19	5.33	1.93	1.07	2.33		8.89	7.59			
1978	413	7.13	0.45	6.33	0.20	5.04	1.86	0.98	2.20	779	8.83	7.73			
1979		8.23	0.50	7.31	0.25	4.72	1.79	0.89	2.03		9.46	8.45			
1980	428	10.43	0.44	9.43	0.32	8.80	1.54	5.00	2.24	791	10.94	9.93	4.87	4.13	0.66
1981		13.35	0.37	12.35	0.36	9.33	1.62	5.55	2.16	1074	12.07	11.02	5.63	3.92	0.86
1982		15.53	0.37	14.47	0.38	10.51	1.94	6.56	2.02	1077	14.61	13.36	6.98	3.93	1.05
1983		18.17	0.32	17.37	0.48	11.38	2.10	7.20	2.08	1097	16.21	14.67	7.39	3.87	1.05
1984		23.10	0.29	22.00	0.63	12.33	2.24	8.14	1.94	1222	19.95	18.16	8.71	3.79	1.30
1985	420	23.64	0.27	22.23	0.30	13.20	2.08	9.10	2.02	1370	23.46	21.58	10.22	3.65	1.31
1986	428	23.99	0.61	22.20	0.58	12.88	2.20	8.89	1.78	1449	25.09	23.16	10.18	3.50	1.01
1987	427	38.95	0.67	36.90	0.68	16.25	2.37	11.88	2.01	1758	28.26	25.79	11.06	3.58	1.07
1988	427	42.91	0.65	39.18	1.07	15.59	2.28	10.43	2.85	2746	37.47	34.32	15.29	3.69	1.78
1989	435	44.23	0.54	40.83	0.82	16.51	2.30	14.50	3.70	3706	40.27	37.64	15.58	3.47	1.75

21. Hainan

21–11

Year	v10b4	v10b5	v10b6	v10d	v11a1	v11a2	v11a3	v11b	v11b1	v11b2	v11c	v11d	v12a	v12b	v12c
1949															
1950									0.0057						
1951									0.0099						
1952									0.0042						
1953									0.0028						
1954									0.0087						
1955									0.0110						
1956									0.0152						
1957									0.0232						
1958									0.0360						
1959									0.0241						
1960									0.0221						
1961									0.0165						
1962									0.0147						
1963									0.0185						
1964									0.0242						
1965									0.0391						
1966									0.0387						
1967									0.0397						
1968									0.0207						
1969									0.0188						
1970									0.0225						
1971									0.0222						
1972									0.0329						
1973									0.0612						
1974									0.0666						
1975									0.0828						
1976									0.0986						
1977									0.1033						
1978									0.1019						
1979									0.1698				102.0	101.0	
1980		0.39	0.89	3.56	0.1742	0.0066	0.0021		0.1829		0.2037	0.0003	107.2	106.8	
1981		0.63	1.02	4.10	0.1788	0.0077	0.2706		0.4571		0.3087	0.0109	107.5	106.5	
1982		1.32	1.30	4.96	0.1454	0.0074	0.0499		0.2027		0.0378	0.0083	104.5	103.8	
1983		2.08	1.80	5.60	0.1447	0.0094	0.0036		0.1577		0.1433	0.0438	100.9	100.8	
1984	0.03	4.35	1.79	6.56	0.3551	0.0483	0.0099		0.4113		1.2300	0.1784	101.3	101.5	
1985	0.14	5.84	2.30	8.67	0.5905	0.0611	0.1597		0.8113		0.6132	0.2643	112.8	113.1	
1986	0.22	7.01	3.17	6.56	0.2682	0.0653	0.0505		0.3840		0.0777	0.3259	103.8	104.1	
1987	0.28	8.47	3.80	14.20	0.5118	0.2452	0.3975	1.8092	1.1545	0.6547	0.1438	0.0911	109.4	109.8	
1988	0.89	10.97	4.86	18.60	1.2887	0.5976	1.0633	4.2383	2.9496	1.9177	3.9868	1.2771	127.8	128.1	
1989	1.11	12.44	5.93	25.91	1.2081	1.2469	1.1532	4.8163	3.6082	0.8640	3.3213	0.9500	126.8	127.6	

21. Hainan

21–12

Year	v13a	v13b	v13c1	v13c2	v13c3	v13d	v14a	v14b	v14c	v15a	v15b	v15c	v15d	v15e	v15f
1949															
1950			0.0219	1.4127	16.3473		680	1383							
1951			0.0138	1.5672	20.4994		634	1491							
1952			0.0158	2.1860	25.6866		1134	1361		517					
1953				2.2464	31.5343		1306	1812							
1954				2.4876	29.9989		1347	3751							
1955				2.4587	27.7268		1640	4157							
1956				4.7422	31.8692		1729	4315							
1957				4.5232	34.8953		1704	6854		595					
1958			0.0702	8.6475	40.8215		4868	5096							
1959			0.0981	7.5906	40.6312		4275	7814							
1960			0.1712	7.6736	44.3737		4356	5640							
1961			0.1771	6.4040	44.6015		5689	9497							
1962			0.1332	5.7560	45.6207		6227	10027							
1963			0.1270	5.1487	44.4934		6067	9819							
1964			0.0978	5.3591	54.3816		6647	10364							
1965			0.1008	5.7362	51.1900		6862	10990		591					
1966			0.1004	5.8994	54.9807		6865	10694							
1967				4.7006	51.9174										
1968				8.9199	54.7108										
1969				13.5316	52.7938										
1970				23.8950	49.0502										
1971				25.3054	54.8834										
1972				21.5866	59.6107		15642	16178							
1973			0.0989	18.6977	66.6944		16288	16372							
1974			0.0712	19.1731	71.0591		16419	16410							
1975			0.1322	26.1727	82.9422		16935	16753							
1976			0.1581	30.6818	84.6721		17523	17738							
1977			0.1689	34.8754	85.6499		18266	18885							
1978			0.3045	34.1899	88.7920		18562	19733		680					
1979			0.3174	31.0777	88.2605		18649	20722							
1980			0.2711	30.7627	89.8676	0.0810	18648	22327		670					
1981			0.2531	27.0930	90.4499		18404	23593							
1982			0.2963	26.4290	88.6926		18310	25134							
1983			0.3054	26.1832	84.7029		18309	25783							
1984			0.3763	28.7216	86.4560		18336	26552							
1985	18.0		0.4048	31.2016	87.2473	0.0998	18672	26923		654					
1986	22.0		0.5581	34.5926	88.3942		18941	27230							
1987	21.0		0.6096	33.3046	89.0378	0.1203	19542	27963			1610				
1988	20.0		0.9133	31.1687	90.3500	0.2061	20265	28222		647					
1989	17.0		0.9475	27.4156	91.8944	0.2200	20497	28129	0.71	650	1610		99.5	2.79	3.7

Notes

1. National Output and Income (Y)

v1a: (E), p.674
- v1a1: (E), p.674
- v1a2: (E), p.674
- v1a3: (E), p.674
- v1a4: (E), p.674
- v1a5: (E), p.674

v1b: (A)
- v1b1: (A)
- v1b2: (A)
- v1b3: (A)
- v1b4: (A)
- v1b5: (A)

v1c: v1a – v1d

v1d: (E), p.673
- v1d1: (E), p.673
- v1d2: (E), p.673
- v1d3: (E), p.673
- v1d4: (E), p.673
- v1d5: (E), p.673

v1e: (A)
- v1e1: (A)
- v1e2: (A)
- v1e3: (A)
- v1e4: (A)
- v1e5: (A)

v1f: (G)
- v1f1: (G)
- v1f2: (G)
- v1f3: (G)

v1g: v3a + v2a

v1h: (A)

v1i: (E), p.688—excluding meat and other price subsidies

v1j: (E), p.688—real wage, deflated by index of cost of living for staff and workers (v12b)
- v1j1: (E), p.688
- v1j2: (E), p.688
- v1j3: (C), p.601; (G)

v1k: NA

2. Investment (I)

v2a: (A)—1988: 27.27; (G)
- v2a1: (A); (G)
- v2a2: (A); (G)

v2b: (C), 1989, p.367; (G)

v2c: (G)
- v2c1: (E), p.684
- v2c2: (E), p.684

v2d:
- v2d1: (G)
- v2d2: (G)

v2e: (G)

3. Consumption (C)

v3a: (A); (G)

v3b: (A); (G)
- v3b1: (A); (G)
- v3b2: (A); (G)

v3c: (A); (G)

v3d: (G)
- v3d1: (G)
- v3d2: (G)

v3e: (E), p.689; (G)
- v3e1: (E), p.689; (G)
- v3e2: NA

v3e3: NA
v3e4: NA

v3f: (E), p.689
v3f1: (E), p.689
v3f2: (G)
v3f3: (G)
v3f4: (G)

4. Public Finance and Banking (FB)

v4a:
v4a1: (E), p.687
v4a1a: (E), p.687
v4a1b: (C), p.551
v4a1c: (C), p.551
v4a1d: v4a1 – v4a1a – v4a1b – v4a1c
v4a2: (E), p.687
v4a2a: (E), p.687
v4a2b: (E), p.687
v4a2c: (E), p.687
v4a2d: v4a2 – v4a2a – v4a2b – v4a2c

v4b: (G)
v4b1: (G)
v4b2: (G)
v4b3: (C), p.554

v4c:
v4c1: (E), p.680
v4c2: (E), p.680

5. Labor Force (L)

v5a: (E), p.673
v5a1: (E), p.673
v5a2: (E), p.673
v5a3: (E), p.673
v5a4: (E), p.673

v5b:
v5b1: (E), p.673
v5b2: (E), p.673
v5b3: (E), p.673

v5c: (G)
v5c1: (G)

v5d: (G)

6. Population (PO)

v6a: (E), p.672—data from public security department
v6a1: (E), p.672—(ditto), population of cities and towns
v6a2: (E), p.672—(ditto), population of villages

v6b: (A); (E), p.672—data from public security department

v6c: (A); (E), p.672—(ditto)

v6d:
v6d1: (E), p.672—(ditto)
v6d2: (E), p.672—(ditto)
v6d3: (G)
v6d4: (G)
v6d5: (A); (G)—Haikou
v6d6: NA

7. Agriculture (A)

v7a: (E), p.678

v7b: (G)

v7c: (G)

v7d: (E), p.678

v7e: NA

v7f: (G)

v7g: (G)

v7h: (A)
v7h1: (A)
v7h2: (A)
v7h3: (A)
v7h4: (A)
v7h5: (A)

v7i: (G)

8. Industry (IN)

v8a: (A)
- v8a1: (A)
- v8a2: (A)
- v8a3: (A)

v8b: (E), p.680

- v8c1: (A)
- v8c2: (A)

v8d: (E), p.680

v8f:
- v8f1: (A)
- v8f2: (E), p.681
- v8f3: NA
- v8f4: (E), p.681
- v8f5: (E), p.681

v8g: (A); (G)
- v8g1: (E), p.680

9. Transport (TR)

v9a: (E), p.682—excluding urban traffic volume, data of 1979 and before acquired from transport department; (G)
- v9a1: (E), p.682—including central and local railways; (G)
- v9a2: (E), p.682; (G)
- v9a3: (E), p.682; (G)

v9b: (E), p.682—data of 1979 and before acquired from transport department; (G)
- v9b1: (E), p.682—including central and local railways; (G)
- v9b2: (E), p.682; (G)
- v9b3: (E), p.682; (G)

v9c: (E), p.682

10. Domestic Trade (DT)

v10a: (G)
- v10a1: (G)

v10b:
- v10b1: (E), p.685
- v10b2: (G)
- v10b3: (G)
- v10b4: (G)
- v10b5: (E), p.685; (G)
- v10b6: (E), p.685; (G)

v10d: (E), p.685—calculated on calendar year basis

11. Foreign Trade (FT)

v11a:
- v11a1: (G)—agricultural, sideline and local products, and agricultural, sideline processing products
- v11a2: (G)—textile and other products of light industry
- v11a3: (G)—industrial and mining products

v11b: (G)
- v11b1: (E), p.686
- v11b2: (G)—since Hainan Province was established in 1987, data of total imports have been independently calculated since then. Data of 1987 and before were included in Guangdong's total imports

v11c: (E), p.686

v11d: (E), p.686

12. Prices (PR)

v12a: (E), p.688

v12b: (E), p.688

v12c: NA

13. Education (ED)

v13a: (G)

v13b: NA

v13c:
- v13c1: (G)—general institutions of higher learning
- v13c2: (G)—ordinary secondary schools
- v13c3: (G)

v13d: (A); (C), p.564—institutions of higher learning

14. Social Factors (SF)

v14a: (G)

v14b: (G)

v14c: (A)

15. Natural Environment (NE)

v15a: (G)

v15b: (G)

v15c: NA

v15d: (G)

v15e: (G)

v15f: (G)

Sources of Data

(A) Data supplied by the DSNEB, SSB, the PRC.
(C) Statistical Bureau of Hainan Province ed. *Statistical Yearbook of Hainan*, Beijing: CSPH, 1989.
(E) Same as (E) in Beijing's sources of data.
(G) Data supplied by Statistical Bureau of Guangdong Province.

22

Sichuan

22. Sichuan

22–1

Year	v1a	v1a1	v1a2	v1a3	v1a4	v1a5	v1b	v1b1	v1b2	v1b3	v1b4	v1b5	v1c	v1d	v1d1
1949	34.63	24.78	7.11	0.42	0.22	2.10							8.56	26.07	21.40
1950	35.72	24.89	7.21	0.74	0.37	2.51							9.00	26.72	21.46
1951	43.37	27.21	10.82	1.70	0.58	3.06							12.01	31.36	23.67
1952	53.40	29.48	15.63	2.91	0.90	4.48	119.2	109.0	144.5	157.3	155.2	128.0	16.66	36.74	25.62
1953	64.13	32.61	21.76	3.82	1.74	4.20	116.5	110.1	142.2	141.6	171.1	92.6	22.16	41.97	28.52
1954	76.11	36.45	27.36	4.29	2.05	5.96	120.1	109.5	129.1	122.6	129.9	140.7	27.05	49.06	31.73
1955	84.61	39.21	31.24	4.84	2.40	6.92	108.4	100.9	117.0	122.0	125.5	113.0	31.33	53.28	33.38
1956	101.75	47.15	36.08	6.53	2.85	9.14	117.0	109.3	119.3	149.9	131.5	128.9	38.11	63.64	39.40
1957	118.67	56.83	41.59	6.63	3.49	10.13	109.6	106.0	115.3	107.1	113.0	107.8	45.59	73.08	45.58
1958	144.89	56.93	59.08	12.36	5.09	11.43	124.9	107.1	140.1	186.4	164.8	111.7	63.55	81.34	41.48
1959	173.24	58.07	76.75	17.83	6.63	13.96	113.3	89.0	130.0	144.3	128.7	121.5	88.13	85.11	38.09
1960	194.26	58.03	94.66	18.94	8.55	14.08	108.4	89.0	123.3	106.2	121.6	99.7	117.52	76.74	26.27
1961	143.41	60.05	55.05	8.93	5.80	13.58	62.7	83.4	54.4	47.1	68.4	62.3	80.99	62.42	29.50
1962	124.26	62.08	41.72	4.62	4.37	11.47	83.6	108.5	74.2	45.8	69.5	67.7	53.59	70.67	43.33
1963	134.28	68.85	45.35	5.83	4.18	10.07	110.9	113.1	106.9	128.9	96.5	118.2	53.36	80.92	52.73
1964	153.37	72.24	56.54	8.98	5.75	9.86	118.6	107.8	126.3	159.4	120.3	122.0	66.34	87.03	54.07
1965	183.23	79.68	68.87	17.52	7.22	9.95	122.4	104.6	130.2	200.5	141.2	102.9	82.06	101.17	59.49
1966	220.22	90.49	82.92	27.35	7.66	11.80	121.5	110.1	127.1	151.6	107.5	107.9	100.62	119.60	69.16
1967	193.92	88.72	68.20	19.08	5.91	12.01	87.0	98.0	82.2	71.1	78.3	105.2	87.72	106.20	67.80
1968	146.20	80.94	42.96	9.24	3.91	9.15	72.9	91.1	62.9	49.1	66.2	76.2	62.68	83.52	60.90
1969	189.02	82.74	67.50	22.20	5.40	11.18	134.9	102.2	157.3	243.1	135.5	122.7	89.07	99.95	62.05
1970	244.84	89.29	103.15	31.82	7.13	13.45	133.7	109.4	152.9	142.3	134.5	120.6	121.51	123.33	68.01
1971	270.56	97.09	119.99	30.62	8.35	14.51	115.8	102.9	130.1	95.7	117.1	107.3	137.75	132.81	70.18
1972	268.62	96.39	121.18	27.15	8.97	14.93	99.4	99.3	101.0	88.6	107.4	103.9	135.56	133.06	68.46
1973	272.57	102.56	121.07	24.71	8.58	15.65	100.8	104.4	99.9	90.5	95.7	105.8	136.42	136.15	73.86
1974	263.15	104.92	113.62	21.37	7.68	15.56	95.6	100.3	93.9	84.9	89.5	99.5	134.24	128.91	74.93
1975	303.27	103.91	148.01	24.39	10.17	16.79	116.7	101.7	130.2	113.7	132.4	107.9	155.41	147.86	71.58
1976	279.08	98.54	133.72	23.26	7.74	15.82	93.0	94.8	92.4	95.5	76.1	94.0	154.36	124.72	67.01
1977	352.14	110.18	180.12	28.61	11.81	21.42	124.7	105.7	134.7	122.9	152.6	143.9	189.68	162.46	77.53
1978	428.98	127.10	225.57	36.37	13.69	26.25	121.5	118.8	122.9	126.5	115.9	118.8	223.85	205.13	90.67
1979	502.51	163.92	253.76	40.32	14.72	29.79	110.9	109.9	111.7	109.8	107.5	112.5	257.47	245.04	115.54
1980	545.93	181.27	273.65	43.42	15.36	32.23	105.9	106.6	106.4	102.2	104.3	103.6	276.13	269.80	128.78
1981	579.96	196.35	280.56	50.89	15.33	36.83	104.0	104.9	101.1	115.9	99.8	113.4	295.97	283.99	139.12
1982	655.27	233.10	313.24	54.01	16.80	38.12	109.2	111.0	110.1	101.7	109.6	101.1	333.69	321.58	167.29
1983	728.33	254.01	350.19	61.31	18.94	43.88	110.9	107.1	112.7	114.6	111.1	114.3	377.90	350.43	177.13
1984	843.28	281.65	420.15	68.46	21.00	52.02	113.0	107.8	116.6	110.6	109.5	117.2	433.72	409.56	199.48
1985	1046.17	313.06	531.51	105.59	26.32	69.69	116.3	103.2	119.4	144.2	116.5	122.8	554.78	491.39	220.82
1986	1159.88	338.98	598.61	111.92	31.03	79.34	108.2	105.6	109.9	103.4	113.7	110.6	631.55	528.33	229.31
1987	1386.47	388.94	725.06	134.52	38.74	99.21	111.8	103.2	115.6	114.4	110.6	114.1	761.40	625.07	264.67
1988	1784.14	475.94	964.10	168.09	50.02	125.95	113.7	102.7	120.5	107.9	107.7	110.4	985.14	799.00	315.50
1989	2041.17	527.67	1147.29	170.15	57.53	138.53	103.6	103.7	105.0	96.2	100.9	102.6	1175.33	865.84	343.86

22. Sichuan

22–2

Year	v1d2	v1d3	v1d4	v1d5	v1e	v1e1	v1e2	v1e3	v1e4	v1e5	v1f	v1f1	v1f2	v1f3	v1g
1949	2.28	0.20	0.14	2.05											
1950	2.31	0.38	0.21	2.36											
1951	3.47	0.88	0.40	2.94											
1952	5.18	1.40	0.67	3.87	111.5	105.2	139.5	153.8	167.5	127.3					36.40
1953	7.19	1.41	1.22	3.63	112.7	109.8	141.8	111.4	153.7	92.8					42.76
1954	9.25	1.59	1.38	5.11	115.1	109.6	129.6	121.8	124.3	139.6					51.04
1955	10.62	1.77	1.58	5.93	104.3	98.8	118.1	121.1	123.4	113.0					51.70
1956	12.14	2.53	1.78	7.79	112.8	106.0	120.1	154.8	127.8	128.3					63.90
1957	13.67	2.58	2.30	8.95	110.8	110.1	113.7	107.3	111.4	111.6					71.26
1958	18.95	7.22	3.34	10.35	114.7	100.1	126.2	278.8	173.5	114.5					81.85
1959	24.43	5.81	4.30	12.48	95.0	76.4	129.0	80.5	125.3	119.9					88.00
1960	27.45	5.22	5.19	12.61	89.4	66.8	114.3	89.8	112.6	99.9					79.75
1961	14.84	2.92	3.07	12.09	68.3	97.3	50.1	55.9	61.5	58.7					65.29
1962	13.55	1.69	2.32	9.78	102.6	134.8	86.2	51.4	68.8	60.9					65.22
1963	15.72	1.97	2.16	8.34	112.1	110.3	117.2	118.7	87.4	123.2					79.57
1964	19.04	2.82	3.17	7.93	116.0	109.7	122.9	149.4	131.3	124.2					87.02
1965	24.35	6.10	4.05	7.18	118.0	106.0	134.6	220.7	144.3	94.8					109.63
1966	28.05	9.26	4.06	9.07	114.8	115.2	107.7	147.7	103.0	115.5					132.37
1967	19.80	6.58	2.78	9.24	86.8	95.9	72.0	72.3	68.5	104.6					112.31
1968	10.80	3.37	1.57	6.88	76.1	89.8	53.7	51.8	56.5	72.7					94.42
1969	19.23	7.71	2.54	8.42	125.2	101.8	187.4	231.7	158.6	122.1					124.69
1970	29.34	11.80	3.65	10.53	127.9	109.8	158.5	152.2	146.6	125.4					152.48
1971	36.20	11.01	4.24	11.18	106.7	102.9	117.4	92.7	116.2	105.7					149.27
1972	39.04	9.88	4.56	11.12	102.8	96.6	122.2	89.9	107.5	99.6					141.79
1973	36.93	9.42	4.14	11.80	104.4	106.8	103.3	94.7	90.8	108.0					144.91
1974	31.15	7.83	3.52	11.48	92.9	99.9	81.8	81.4	85.0	97.3					142.39
1975	49.66	9.18	5.35	12.09	115.3	95.5	160.3	116.9	152.0	104.5					160.96
1976	35.49	8.51	3.34	10.37	84.7	93.5	73.1	93.0	62.4	86.0					139.06
1977	56.80	10.05	5.73	12.35	129.1	115.8	151.9	117.8	171.6	126.5					172.06
1978	79.09	12.57	6.92	15.88	123.4	113.9	135.9	124.6	120.8	124.6	230.28	89.76	94.41	46.11	208.03
1979	90.64	14.29	6.99	17.58	111.5	109.0	115.3	112.6	101.0	110.0	281.76	114.38	110.18	57.20	246.84
1980	97.44	15.20	7.77	20.61	107.5	109.2	105.5	101.0	111.2	112.3	308.87	127.49	116.05	65.33	271.15
1981	97.53	16.20	7.90	23.24	103.0	104.0	99.8	105.5	101.7	111.9	326.18	137.73	119.42	69.03	278.86
1982	104.68	17.29	8.63	23.69	108.4	111.7	106.5	102.2	109.2	99.6	371.70	165.62	128.07	78.01	319.67
1983	117.31	19.13	9.42	27.44	108.4	104.1	113.4	111.7	107.6	115.1	406.49	175.36	143.26	87.87	352.13
1984	144.09	23.26	9.98	32.75	114.2	109.3	120.5	120.4	104.6	117.9	483.86	197.49	175.72	110.65	417.12
1985	181.43	34.41	12.46	42.27	114.6	102.8	122.6	137.1	117.2	133.0	584.72	218.61	226.63	139.48	511.95
1986	197.88	36.83	14.33	49.98	105.8	103.7	106.6	108.0	110.1	109.1	627.35	227.02	246.45	153.88	555.59
1987	235.46	40.72	17.04	67.18	109.3	102.4	114.2	111.2	104.5	120.4	736.22	263.70	289.49	183.05	654.37
1988	312.21	59.17	21.66	90.46	108.2	101.7	114.3	107.8	106.6	110.7	922.62	312.20	391.16	219.26	831.09
1989	340.73	58.15	24.58	98.52	101.5	101.0	102.8	95.9	100.6	102.1	995.65	339.20	404.78	251.67	901.98

22. Sichuan

Year	v1h	v1i	v1j	v1j1	v1j2	v1j3	v1k	v2a	v2a1	v2a2	v2b	v2c	v2c1	v2c2	v2d1
1949															
1950															
1951															
1952				325				4.31	3.78	0.53					0.14
1953				377				7.67	2.57	5.10		3.75			
1954				390				10.88	3.87	7.01		4.93			
1955				411				8.64	4.28	4.36		4.78			
1956				467				11.56	5.90	5.66		7.10			
1957	67.50			498				12.62	8.30	4.33		6.32			9.74
1958				386				19.37	10.25	9.12		14.30			
1959				352				30.43	20.26	10.17		20.80			
1960				356				23.01	16.66	6.35		23.26			
1961				387				0.72	0.18	0.54		8.46			
1962				451				-5.28	1.68	-6.96		3.33			37.25
1963				514				5.88	5.39	0.49		4.34			
1964				546				11.35	8.45	2.91		7.60			
1965	105.77			548				26.72	18.72	8.00		19.80			41.48
1966				549				40.69	28.40	12.29		33.19			
1967				548				16.23	16.47	-0.24		19.45			
1968				524				7.70	6.42	1.28		10.58			
1969				560				31.64	23.40	8.24		28.48			
1970				573				54.48	35.57	18.91		40.83			71.49
1971				548				47.81	31.96	15.85		37.04			
1972				591				37.87	25.47	12.40		28.44			
1973				577				35.82	27.62	8.20		22.55			
1974				582				29.70	27.40	2.30		20.47			
1975				586				47.59	39.28	8.31		27.86			192.88
1976				581				27.20	26.91	0.29		19.80			211.08
1977				578				51.52	32.23	19.28		19.05			230.46
1978	127.10	37.93	581	622	481		5.46	62.39	43.48	18.93		28.37	18.71	0.54	260.38
1979	155.90	43.41	641	673	525		7.15	69.29	46.06	23.23		29.43	16.89	1.19	278.98
1980	187.90	52.61	743	789	590		9.28	70.38	44.69	25.68		37.55	15.11	1.67	290.40
1981	220.98	54.45	748	788	613		11.24	63.98	39.33	24.65		33.34	9.22	1.69	310.02
1982	255.96	57.43	761	798	633		13.15	76.66	47.22	29.44	57.56	40.84	11.28	2.41	333.12
1983	258.39	60.74	788	827	652		15.69	85.68	59.87	25.81	68.17	46.78	14.75	2.14	369.69
1984	286.76	71.59	912	973	737		18.22	106.60	72.31	34.29	93.96	50.85	14.96	1.85	382.85
1985	315.07	86.36	1062	1138	845		23.58	141.30	96.12	45.18	144.66	82.41	23.56	2.83	418.40
1986	337.94	103.76	1200	1338	944		30.05	147.20	99.95	47.25	153.24	94.11	26.82	3.05	461.62
1987	369.46	115.18	1340	1441	1040	1087	35.26	177.83	132.18	45.65	186.78	128.46	34.70	3.76	513.47
1988	448.85	141.77	1597	1726	1210	1380	43.94	224.24	130.19	94.05	229.08	146.75	42.14	3.71	556.27
1989	494.07	163.14	1796	1941	1342		52.80	239.39	120.35	119.04	221.70	143.69	50.20	2.49	639.03

22. Sichuan

22–4

Year	v2d2	v2e	v3a	v3b	v3b1	v3b2	v3c	v3d	v3d1	v3d2	v3e	v3e1	v3e2	v3e3	v3e4
1949															
1950															
1951															
1952	0.13	1.03	32.09	30.94	23.83	7.11	1.15	49.4	42.8	101.7	128.88	77.30			
1953			35.09	33.74	25.84	7.90	1.35	52.1	44.8	110.5					
1954			40.16	38.33	29.89	8.43	1.83	58.1	50.9	115.0					
1955			43.06	41.31	31.94	9.37	1.75	61.5	53.7	121.9					
1956			52.34	50.53	39.28	11.25	1.81	73.6	64.9	137.9					
1957	9.17	5.78	58.64	56.89	43.68	13.21	1.75	81.1	71.1	151.7	191.12	102.37			
1958			62.48	60.42	44.83	15.59	2.06	85.3	74.6	153.4					
1959			57.57	54.98	31.87	23.11	2.59	78.7	64.8	156.0					
1960			56.74	54.22	38.67	15.55	2.52	80.2	58.5	195.0					
1961			64.57	63.17	43.62	19.55	1.40	96.6	79.0	191.8					
1962	29.98	8.69	70.50	68.49	52.05	16.44	2.01	105.8	93.3	184.1					
1963			73.69	71.29	56.55	14.74	2.40	108.2	98.7	177.7					
1964			75.67	73.07	57.32	15.75	2.60	107.5	96.4	185.1					
1965	32.15	9.12	82.91	78.60	59.18	19.42	4.31	112.0	96.5	220.1	245.30	154.68			
1966			91.68	86.57	65.02	21.55	5.11	119.4	102.9	231.2					
1967			96.08	91.18	67.37	23.81	4.90	121.9	103.3	248.3					
1968			86.72	82.72	61.90	20.82	4.00	107.2	91.7	214.9					
1969			93.05	87.56	64.61	22.95	5.49	109.8	92.3	235.3					
1970	59.59	18.70	98.00	92.75	67.73	25.02	5.25	112.1	93.6	225.0	253.98	158.43			
1971			101.46	95.38	69.37	26.01	6.08	121.7	93.0	260.0					
1972			103.92	96.92	69.02	27.90	7.00	111.4	88.7	270.5					
1973			109.09	102.25	73.56	28.69	6.84	114.4	93.3	271.9					
1974			112.69	105.41	74.18	31.22	7.28	115.0	91.5	293.3					
1975	144.29	63.34	113.37	105.36	72.98	32.38	8.01	112.5	87.9	303.9	246.35	153.92			
1976	154.21	66.87	111.86	104.08	71.02	33.05	7.78	109.3	84.0	309.0					
1977	168.34	71.54	120.54	109.04	75.18	33.86	11.50	113.4	88.1	312.4					
1978	190.24	77.24	145.64	133.25	93.33	39.91	12.39	137.6	108.9	358.7	314.20	185.94			
1979	201.94	79.89	177.55	164.50	118.59	45.91	13.05	168.9	136.1	397.2	339.79	202.39			
1980	207.42	81.41	200.77	188.03	132.69	55.34	12.74	191.9	154.2	464.7	363.68	212.80			
1981	219.42	82.80	214.88	200.96	142.77	58.19	13.92	203.6	165.1	475.6	396.46	235.93			
1982	232.27	86.67	243.01	227.73	165.89	61.84	15.28	228.0	190.0	490.0	406.78	242.14			
1983	253.98	91.55	266.45	248.49	181.28	67.21	17.96	247.0	207.0	517.0	456.93	269.73			
1984	256.10	99.71	310.52	290.42	215.47	74.95	20.10	288.0	246.0	555.0	516.72	295.91			
1985	278.35	119.50	370.65	343.73	250.25	93.48	26.92	338.0	287.0	652.0	679.70	349.68			
1986	301.95	148.01	408.39	378.37	266.70	111.67	30.02	369.0	304.0	749.0	787.24	414.77			
1987	340.52	166.83	476.54	441.31	308.31	133.00	35.23	425.0	347.0	885.0	889.41	470.09			
1988	366.70	187.46	600.65	555.03	387.72	167.31	45.62	527.0	432.0	1086.0	1086.24	562.84			
1989	420.36	241.51	665.59	606.59	417.54	189.05	56.00	570.0	460.0	1205.0	1183.55	658.80			

22. Sichuan

22–5

Year	v3f	v3f1	v3f2	v3f3	v3f4	v4a1	v4a1a	v4a1b	v4a1c	v4a1d	v4a2	v4a2a	v4a2b	v4a2c	v4a2d
1949															
1950						4.72				0.09	1.01	0.03	0.13	0.58	0.27
1951						7.18	0.14			0.28	2.10	0.39	0.37	0.86	0.48
1952						8.17	0.42	3.43	3.43	0.89	3.51	1.07	0.85	0.95	0.64
1953						7.75	0.40			0.61	3.70	0.96	1.16	1.03	0.55
1954						8.29	0.60			0.32	3.82	1.03	1.14	1.10	0.55
1955						9.34	0.90			0.31	3.51	0.68	1.06	1.17	0.60
1956						10.23	1.15			0.75	5.11	1.35	1.17	1.60	0.99
1957	66.42					11.10	1.41	6.06	2.91	0.73	5.12	1.04	1.51	1.49	1.08
1958						20.19	8.36			1.03	12.08	7.38	1.59	1.43	1.68
1959						23.84	11.26			0.45	18.92	10.51	1.93	1.68	4.80
1960						31.66	18.40			0.91	28.63	14.43	2.77	1.81	9.62
1961						15.12	6.15			0.37	14.97	2.90	2.23	1.68	8.16
1962						10.58	1.03	5.64	3.54	0.37	6.91	1.03	2.07	1.39	2.42
1963						16.08	5.70			0.36	8.14	1.62	2.13	1.38	3.01
1964						17.50	6.25			0.26	10.37	3.40	2.48	1.53	2.96
1965	95.65					16.65	4.81	8.09	3.54	0.21	12.70	5.42	2.72	1.60	2.96
1966						18.64	5.97	8.50	4.02	0.16	13.34	4.70	3.22	1.66	3.76
1967						14.91	2.83			0.08	11.00	3.76	3.20	1.51	2.53
1968						8.31	1.19			0.06	8.40	2.21	2.75	1.52	1.92
1969						11.80	0.92			0.09	13.40	5.41	2.79	1.86	3.34
1970						16.90	3.32	9.66	3.82	0.11	15.41	6.97	3.07	1.94	3.43
1971						21.89	5.51			0.28	18.05	7.11	3.84	2.39	4.71
1972						23.04	5.99			0.24	22.27	8.59	4.48	2.60	6.60
1973						20.11	3.78			0.17	20.80	6.33	5.02	2.58	6.87
1974						16.21	0.01			0.16	21.26	5.82	5.45	2.54	7.45
1975						22.62	4.06	14.51	3.86	0.20	21.78	5.16	5.80	2.63	8.19
1976						18.40	0.44	13.78	4.01	0.17	22.54	5.45	6.10	2.65	8.34
1977						24.30	2.87	16.97	4.30	0.16	25.47	6.32	6.42	2.92	9.81
1978	120.30					37.31	12.40	20.69	4.10	0.17	36.72	11.16	7.61	3.40	14.55
1979	142.10					35.15	8.71	22.40	3.96	0.09	37.47	10.61	8.53	3.78	14.55
1980	159.50					34.62	7.42	23.12	3.98	0.10	33.51	7.14	10.00	4.34	12.03
1981	184.07					31.52	2.82	24.84	3.72	0.14	29.87	3.45	10.65	4.61	11.16
1982	208.23					35.54	2.81	23.20	4.01	0.40	31.87	3.88	12.23	5.00	10.76
1983	231.12					40.32	4.04	31.29	4.18	0.74	36.64	5.38	13.33	5.92	12.01
1984	251.83					46.37	4.67	36.40	4.56	0.69	47.91	7.58	15.59	8.33	16.41
1985	276.25					58.76	3.69	48.49	5.45	1.08	64.16	10.14	10.45	8.11	35.46
1986	310.92					67.34	5.11	54.68	5.97	1.57	87.74	10.85	23.50	10.44	42.95
1987	348.32	215.00				75.86		63.16	6.23	1.37	87.76	9.54	23.30	10.67	44.25
1988	426.47	256.63				91.55		74.94	6.21	1.66	103.10	9.09	29.24	10.83	53.94
1989	473.59	287.28	35.45	51.75	21.02	114.83					127.18	8.85	33.17	12.07	73.09

22. Sichuan

22–6

Year	v4b	v4b1	v4b2	v4b3	v4c1	v4c2	v5a	v5a1	v5a2	v5a3	v5a4	v5b1	v5b2	v5b3	v5c
1949															
1950	0.14						2508.0	36.28	1.93	166.33	2273.00				
1951	0.62						2612.5	55.55	3.08	179.25	2344.00				
1952	0.51	0.51			0.71	61.2	2776.6	88.49	2.59	179.55	2477.00				
1953	1.19						2441.1	110.70	3.68	176.74	2122.13				
1954	1.25						2463.4	123.71	9.05	155.75	2150.66				
1955	1.05						2506.6	134.72	16.53	144.28	2192.60				
1956	1.49						2508.3	186.58	108.52	22.76	2189.53				
1957	2.35	1.76	0.59		4.40	30.7	3075.9	189.97	112.54	25.60	2747.00				
1958	3.10						2809.7	470.83	63.19	4.39	2271.29				
1959	3.81						2865.3	463.33	59.59	3.23	2339.15				
1960	3.90						2797.2	485.97	64.22	1.29	2245.72				
1961	3.67						2713.3	384.32	80.15	5.96	2242.87				
1962	2.48	1.69	0.79		3.28	8.5	2869.4	229.26	108.81	18.35	2513.00				
1963	2.48						2685.2	231.24	118.21	13.87	2321.92				
1964	3.02						2944.2	246.05	116.52	10.40	2571.25				
1965	3.65	2.84	0.81		8.52	20.6	3093.9	299.04	121.66	8.18	2665.00				
1966	4.67	3.41	1.26				3286.2	337.00	122.49	6.72	2820.00				
1967	4.40						3354.7	335.45	122.67	5.53	2891.00				
1968	5.14						3440.9	333.39	122.94	4.54	2980.00				
1969	5.14						3612.8	247.93	123.13	3.73	3138.00				
1970	5.21	4.30	0.01		8.36	10.7	3734.0	366.02	123.72	3.23	3241.00				
1971	5.76						3860.5	401.46	125.24	2.79	3331.00				
1972	6.72						3946.0	426.84	126.71	2.41	3390.00				
1973	7.20						4025.8	423.11	133.56	2.08	3467.00				
1974	7.78						4074.5	424.10	136.63	1.80	3512.00				
1975	7.96	6.61	1.35		15.45	7.4	4091.8	432.98	136.80	2.05	3520.00				
1976	8.12	6.85	1.27		10.81	4.9	4123.7	450.45	143.19	2.09	3528.00				
1977	8.73	7.30	1.43		21.85	9.1	4122.6	459.91	154.69	2.00	3506.00				
1978	10.33	8.51	1.82		35.34	13.2	4218.9	522.19	141.22	2.53	3553.00				
1979	14.99	11.49	3.50		41.08	14.6	4295.9	539.81	159.15	2.93	3594.00				
1980	22.10	16.19	5.91		41.72	14.4	4454.5	556.32	163.62	6.52	3728.00				
1981	28.17	19.91	8.26		40.89	13.5	4574.6	576.55	168.09	10.02	3828.00				
1982	36.33	25.36	10.97		44.57	14.0	4738.4	596.70	173.59	13.15	3955.00				
1983	47.08	32.35	14.73		50.58	14.6	4870.4	605.61	175.57	21.25	4068.00				
1984	66.25	44.93	21.32		58.80	16.5	4978.7	591.60	207.15	26.42	4152.60				
1985	90.73	61.69	29.04		71.07	17.9	5116.2	615.53	217.13	31.78	4251.08				
1986	127.09	84.86	42.23		64.71	13.8	5310.7	636.38	221.18	34.31	4418.00				
1987	167.50	113.33	54.17		81.23	15.8	5422.4	657.14	222.89	39.17	4502.05				
1988	195.31	138.40	56.91		98.50	17.8	5586.6	683.74	227.60	45.02	4628.87				
1989	267.70	192.90	74.80		103.28	15.6	5764.6	696.77	222.87	42.78	4800.33				

22. Sichuan

22–7

Year	v5c1	v5d	v6a	v6a1	v6a2	v6b	v6c	v6d1	v6d2	v6d3	v6d4	v6d5	v6d6
1949			5730	246	5484			491	5239	2939	2791	100.30	112.50
1950			5830	249	5581	37.1	21.8	494	5336	2990	2840		
1951			6120	307	5813	39.8	20.1	682	5438	3140	2980		
1952			6411	511	5900	41.0	18.2	717	5694	3290	3121	156.00	113.18
1953			6508	523	5985	40.5	17.0	712	5796	3343	3165		
1954			6649	541	6108	28.2	8.4	754	5895	3407	3242		
1955			6791	567	6224	28.4	9.2	782	6009	3485	3306		
1956			6945	636	6309	28.5	10.4	849	6096	3564	3381		
1957			7081	671	6410	29.2	12.1	893	6188	3633	3448	208.05	138.56
1958			7078	764	6314	34.0	25.2	1039	6039	3648	3430	215.23	143.52
1959			6897	835	6062	16.7	47.0	1083	5814	3559	3338		
1960			6620	844	5776	11.7	54.0	1068	5552	3410	3210		
1961			6459	777	5682	11.8	29.4	972	5487	3299	3160	213.54	153.87
1962			6486	660	5826	28.0	14.6	813	5673	3287	3199	208.03	150.25
1963			6696	669	6027	50.1	12.8	846	5850	3396	3300	213.94	156.14
1964			6898	641	6257	46.9	13.9	855	6043	3514	3384	216.00	160.57
1965			7137	673	6464	42.4	11.5	909	6228	3633	3504	217.30	165.06
1966			7368	693	6675	40.1	10.8	955	6413	3756	3612		
1967			7603	700	6903	38.5	10.2	962	6641	3883	3720		
1968			7830	713	7117	40.6	9.9	975	6855	3998	3832		
1969			8063	704	7359	39.0	9.9	977	7086	4118	3945		
1970			8342	701	7641	38.7	9.2	985	7357	4263	4079	222.13	174.51
1971			8584	743	7841	38.6	9.1	1016	7568	4384	4200		
1972			8817	763	8054	37.2	9.8	1047	7770	4497	4320		
1973			9066	775	8291	35.6	9.1	1064	8002	4631	4435		
1974			9271	779	8492	35.1	9.1	1065	8206	4736	4535		
1975			9467	776	8691	31.2	8.9	1065	8402	4843	4624	231.93	185.84
1976			9579	783	8796	25.8	8.5	1074	8505	4907	4672		
1977			9659	790	8869	20.5	8.1	1093	8566	4952	4707		
1978			9708	824	8884	15.1	7.0	1132	8576	4980	4728	241.20	205.27
1979			9774	872	8902	15.2	6.9	1179	8595	5015	4759		
1980			9820	902	8918	13.0	6.8	1203	8617	5045	4775	254.46	214.97
1981			9924	919	9005	18.0	7.0	1245	8679	5104	4820		
1982			10022	950	9072	18.9	7.6	1282	8740	5166	4856		
1983			10075	984	9091	13.1	7.1	1317	8758	5198	4877		
1984			10112	1048	9064	10.8	7.1	1384	8728	5223	4889		
1985			10188	1164	9024	15.4	7.3	1483	8705	5267	4921	277.94	258.31
1986			10320	1204	9116	20.5	6.9	1486	8834	5339	4981	283.23	264.24
1987			10458	1235	9223	17.9	7.0	1521	8937	5413	5045	288.85	269.43
1988			10590	1295	9295	18.3	6.6	1551	9039	5484	5106	292.81	273.65
1989			10706	1331	9369	19.1	7.3	1578	9122	5546	5154	295.89	

22. Sichuan

22–8

Year	v7a	v7b	v7c	v7d	v7e	v7f	v7g	v7h	v7h1	v7h2	v7h3	v7h4	v7h5	v7i	v8a
1949								24.78	18.02	0.46	3.22	3.08			7.11
1950								24.89	18.01	0.46	3.24	3.09			7.21
1951								27.21	18.77	0.48	3.75	2.76			10.82
1952				16386				29.48	20.78	0.17	4.25	3.83			15.63
1953				16612				32.61	21.28	0.17	6.26	4.83			21.76
1954				16856				36.45	24.70	0.70	6.25	4.23	0.01	407	27.36
1955				17771				39.21	27.00	1.41	7.25	7.75	1.00	381	31.24
1956				18660				47.15	32.49	1.45	7.20	6.45	1.00	383	36.08
1957		6.0	1597.5	19244		1.40		56.83	43.48	1.50	6.20	4.60	0.08	368	41.59
1958				19269				56.93	41.26	1.50	5.20	3.60	0.08	362	59.08
1959				17434				60.05	43.85	1.70	5.20	3.70	0.08	326	76.75
1960				17014				68.85	52.79	4.58	9.24	11.92	2.16	271	94.66
1961				16278				72.24	54.89	4.89	9.27	9.68	2.11	282	55.05
1962		39.0	2053.5	15973	2466	4.90		79.68	56.44	5.89	11.27	10.68	3.33	306	41.72
1963				16379				90.49	65.28	8.30	13.55	10.37	6.10	311	45.35
1964				16655				72.24	50.80	5.30	10.55	7.37	3.09	324	56.54
1965		40.5	2395.5	15933	567	13.60		79.68	57.72	7.27	14.42	10.32	5.70	339	68.87
1966				13963	869			90.49	65.11	2.81	15.46	5.62	0.21	340	82.92
1967				15885				88.72	64.03	2.79	13.88	5.65	0.16	352	68.20
1968				15260				80.94	60.35	2.84	11.22	5.61	0.15	358	42.96
1969				14963				82.74	61.25	2.83	11.24	5.42	0.16	361	67.50
1970				16126			1.51	89.29	67.47	2.78	12.51	6.05	0.20	380	103.15
1971				16910				97.09	72.02	3.35	15.47	6.48	0.25	392	119.99
1972				17480				96.39	70.97	3.81	16.87	4.62	0.21	393	121.18
1973				17465				102.56	75.50	4.22	18.33	4.29	0.22	395	121.07
1974				17603				104.92	77.24	4.18	18.47	4.85	0.24	393	113.62
1975				17850			5.25	130.91	78.67	3.18	19.33	2.47	0.26	387	148.01
1976	30.68			18092			5.81	98.54	76.27	2.66	17.03	2.32	0.26	382	133.72
1977				18020	550		6.98	110.18	83.77	3.85	18.48	2.61	0.29	375	180.12
1978	45.82	1500.0	4303.5	18543	2000	85.50	9.81	127.10	98.67	2.83	21.86	3.12	0.29	384	225.57
1979	57.27	1470.0	4458.0	18576	2900	100.30	12.50	163.92	120.73	3.14	35.35	4.28	0.34	382	253.76
1980	65.55	1168.5	4534.5	18021		109.50	12.80	181.27	127.80	3.75	41.77	6.29	0.39	378	273.65
1981	71.52	1090.5	4554.0	18259	2613	119.20	16.20	196.35	134.50	5.23	44.43	9.28	0.43	395	280.56
1982	75.21	1135.5	4566.0	18298	1564	118.50	17.00	233.10	154.98	10.79	48.17	8.44	0.83	405	313.24
1983	80.22	940.5	4579.5	17717	1767	131.70	18.30	254.01	171.10	13.28	57.39	10.62	1.06	416	350.19
1984	85.38	879.0	4458.0	17646	1910	130.30	21.10	281.65	184.78	17.13	64.77	13.36	1.69	415	420.15
1985	91.99	778.5	4173.0	17656	3582	134.70	24.90	313.06	197.53	20.07	80.32	12.89	2.35	414	531.51
1986	101.32	792.0	4095.0	17780	3264	157.30	30.50	338.98	207.15	18.31	90.92	19.37	2.95	427	598.61
1987	108.82	780.6	4117.5	17922	3222	148.00	32.80	388.94	234.52	18.93	108.30	22.82	3.74	434	725.06
1988	116.55	835.8	4143.2	18146	3754	149.80	35.00	475.94	276.50	21.86	142.80	29.95	4.79	438	964.10
1989	120.90	865.9	4177.4	18443		170.00	40.30	527.67	307.98	23.34	157.41	32.06	6.02	442	1147.29

22. Sichuan

22–9

Year	v8a1	v8a2	v8a3	v8b	v8c1	v8c2	v8d	v8f1	v8f2	v8f3	v8f4	v8f5	v8g
1949	0.39		6.72		2.52	4.59		1	201		1.47	0.8	
1950	0.81		6.40		2.47	4.74		1	195		1.25	2.1	
1951	2.67	0.01	8.14		4.34	6.48		3	321		2.05	6.3	
1952	5.85	0.03	9.75		6.69	8.94		5	337		2.49	4.4	
1953	10.66	0.08	11.02		8.95	12.81		8	385	0.01	3.16	13.3	
1954	16.52	0.27	10.57		10.99	16.37		13	472	0.04	3.87	16.8	
1955	21.03	0.88	9.33		11.03	20.21		24	540	0.03	4.50	17.8	
1956	26.52	4.41	5.15		12.82	23.26		35	592	0.09	6.09	27.3	
1957	31.63	5.48	4.48		14.80	26.79		35	773	0.19	6.78	22.1	6919
1958	51.89	7.16	0.03		29.83	29.25		47	2028	1.53	10.73	32.2	
1959	69.68	7.07			44.05	32.70		63	3500	6.15	17.65	33.2	
1960	84.57	10.09			59.67	34.99		68	3800	14.86	26.84	55.6	
1961	49.17	5.88			32.28	22.77		35	2600	10.96	24.20	24.4	
1962	34.49	7.10	0.13		21.29	20.43		31	1296	5.85	20.08	17.9	22858
1963	38.10	7.11	0.14		23.10	22.25		35	1052	3.42	19.28	24.8	
1964	47.66	8.78	0.10		28.40	28.14		45	1001	2.63	22.89	37.8	
1965	57.92	10.95			31.23	37.64		50	1134	3.65	28.94	78.8	17136
1966	69.06	13.86			40.63	42.29		60	1545	3.59	39.05	101.6	
1967	55.87	12.33			30.97	37.23		48	1287	3.26	39.09	74.9	
1968	32.73	10.23			17.06	25.90		18	998	2.21	26.81	40.2	
1969	54.57	12.93			31.41	36.09		36	1347	2.54	37.19	73.3	
1970	88.01	15.14			55.23	47.92		62	1953	3.46	54.09	138.6	19369
1971	99.97	20.02			66.16	53.83		97	2522	5.92	77.39	247.0	22120
1972	100.44	20.74			64.45	56.73		95	2723	7.49	84.02	270.0	23006
1973	100.37	20.70			61.54	59.53		118	2557	7.75	88.39	233.2	25150
1974	92.83	20.79			56.64	56.98		100	2440	8.81	86.32	205.0	26740
1975	122.19	25.82			80.43	67.58		151	3086	8.96	107.94	288.0	28632
1976	106.57	27.15			70.56	63.16		108	2895	8.34	102.76	262.2	31668
1977	146.08	34.04		131.90	101.26	78.86	38.41	163	3678	8.31	118.84	358.6	37377
1978	183.68	41.89		167.02	132.32	93.25	55.08	238	3794	9.60	139.30	454.8	43983
1979	205.48	48.28		187.58	146.70	107.06	63.58	293	3838	10.50	156.39	519.2	44358
1980	216.26	56.45	0.94	197.96	148.52	125.13	69.63	329	3898	10.06	163.72	504.6	47070
1981	218.65	60.03	1.88	194.85	137.12	143.44	67.71	303	3940	9.51	164.08	510.6	46254
1982	244.11	66.66	2.47	218.66	159.66	153.58	72.06	338	4111	10.16	172.48	640.9	46339
1983	272.20	73.74	4.25	246.48	183.90	166.29	80.97	354	4433	10.80	187.80	733.2	46063
1984	315.66	97.52	6.97	289.88	225.86	194.29	98.27	386	4968	11.31	199.86	849.6	49702
1985	379.13	104.84	47.54	354.94	292.58	238.93	118.02	393	5558	11.91	221.42	1019.2	47523
1986	411.59	164.86	22.16	382.07	323.68	274.93	121.41	425	5690	11.94	236.99	1089.2	51275
1987	489.45	199.56	36.05	456.44	388.64	336.42	141.53	430	6132	11.85	262.87	1242.2	47323
1988	638.68	270.32	55.10	591.25	507.39	456.71	182.73	449	6707	11.98	297.73	1404.9	46602
1989	758.24	312.95	76.10	708.06	621.63	525.66	221.54	473	7135	12.59	326.95	1397.1	45712

22. Sichuan

22–10

Year	v8g1	v9a	v9a1	v9a2	v9a3	v9b	v9b1	v9b2	v9b3	v9c	v10a	v10a1	v10b1	v10b2	v10b3
1949		0.29		0.29		0.20		0.20		704	10.30	10.19			
1950		0.41		0.36	0.05	3.14		0.57	2.57	562	12.32	12.18			
1951		0.74		0.69	0.05	4.47		0.54	3.93	867	17.21	17.01			
1952		4.44	1.86	0.68	1.87	9.14	1.05	0.74	7.35	1025	19.11	18.85	2.98		2.02
1953		7.57	3.50	1.44	2.58	17.98	3.82	1.94	12.21	1302	22.55	22.17	3.93		4.36
1954		6.59	2.92	1.64	1.98	24.43	5.12	2.86	16.44	1502	26.08	25.25	4.51		10.01
1955		9.20	3.88	3.10	2.14	35.63	7.00	3.04	25.58	1688	27.50	26.13	4.77		8.86
1956		18.11	7.84	5.88	4.24	70.25	11.00	4.05	55.18	2089	32.33	30.61	7.29		9.29
1957		17.67	8.51	6.21	2.85	96.16	16.37	4.20	75.57	2246	35.34	33.44	9.28		8.53
1958		23.04	11.63	8.12	3.11	103.81	28.22	6.78	68.79	2822	39.71	36.17			
1959		24.99	13.57	8.17	3.05	126.48	34.13	11.28	81.03	4307	49.35	43.36			
1960		29.14	17.41	8.12	3.34	126.58	42.22	16.22	68.09	5515	54.14	45.52			
1961		34.17	24.28	6.25	3.38	73.85	31.76	7.55	34.50	5204	45.93	40.96			
1962	3750	37.58	24.38	9.42	3.58	50.26	25.19	4.74	20.31	3759	42.87	39.53			
1963		26.80	14.60	8.73	3.26	51.91	24.66	4.92	22.30	3617	41.25	37.72			
1964		27.38	13.10	10.68	3.30	63.87	30.66	5.56	27.62	3810	44.90	40.93			
1965	2791	32.77	15.36	12.85	4.18	79.47	47.56	8.30	23.57	4326	50.83	45.33	39.59		9.90
1966		40.68	19.81	16.38	4.23	109.68	71.92	11.52	26.19	4849	57.66	50.77			
1967		47.66	26.97	15.52	4.87	82.76	50.06	10.29	22.36	4513	62.90	56.66			
1968		48.86	31.41	11.66	5.53	52.64	29.64	6.16	16.80	3848	52.39	47.62			
1969		62.78	39.74	15.77	7.08	83.63	56.06	8.29	19.24	4147	59.37	53.61			
1970		59.32	36.56	16.00	6.57	120.68	83.74	11.43	25.47	4743	66.31	59.26			
1971		66.77	40.21	19.41	6.87	153.95	109.36	13.62	30.94	5130	71.37	62.00			
1972		74.36	43.82	22.68	7.08	164.02	116.22	14.37	33.39	5518	76.82	66.85			
1973		78.00	45.59	24.43	7.20	152.30	105.51	14.78	31.98	5734	80.83	70.51			
1974		75.26	41.86	24.94	7.43	139.05	95.57	13.67	12.62	5767	83.08	73.11			
1975	4098	78.74	43.75	25.60	7.99	178.41	125.91	15.99	36.47	5965	88.44	76.66	72.99		10.98
1976		79.54	42.04	27.30	8.61	149.15	103.58	15.52	29.98	6694	89.17	77.09	74.55		10.88
1977	4353	83.01	43.34	29.08	8.81	199.82	143.15	19.88	36.72	6901	95.59	80.81	80.77		11.59
1978	4364	93.64	48.00	34.68	8.82	247.39	176.85	22.61	47.86	7321	107.41	88.55	90.79		13.45
1979	4375	110.32	55.98	41.79	9.73	249.10	174.23	24.48	50.30	7865	126.48	104.34	104.23		18.61
1980	4479	132.69	62.80	55.89	11.10	256.74	184.57	23.56	48.53	8074	151.88	128.35	113.85		31.18
1981	4543	144.78	62.78	68.39	10.50	228.48	175.22	23.47	29.70	10715	166.46	142.17	119.55		36.82
1982	4656	162.09	66.82	78.86	13.14	255.63	182.81	26.50	46.22	11043	175.44	151.33	123.91		39.76
1983	4717	183.22	73.08	92.67	14.61	284.46	199.97	31.17	53.22	12031	192.47	165.99	129.40		42.07
1984	4666	218.42	86.18	111.23	15.52	336.34	238.46	35.14	62.56	13355	225.47	194.62			
1985	5000	271.02	106.26	137.06	18.90	366.97	264.76	34.62	67.31	15098	274.39	241.67	154.72		61.43
1986	5007	304.41	115.12	148.69	22.54	396.30	288.57	36.45	70.87	16707	315.23	276.44	167.20		68.81
1987	5160	370.17	128.89	193.65	27.81	466.15	336.19	37.42	92.05	19964	371.97	325.00	126.43		143.42
1988	5157	367.09	142.09	176.07	31.34	495.49	351.61	40.32	103.11	23819	477.54	417.44	162.40		178.14
1989	5179	353.84	129.94	175.23	28.74	485.57	379.80	24.04	110.69	29586	528.86	456.14	172.95		189.29

22. Sichuan

22–11

Year	v10b4	v10b5	v10b6	v10d	v11a1	v11a2	v11a3	v11b	v11b1	v11b2	v11c	v11d	v12a	v12b	v12c
1949															
1950															
1951													107.7	109.3	137.8
1952	0.21	13.24	0.65	9.60									101.3	102.5	106.4
1953	0.31	13.14	0.82	12.32									101.3	101.1	104.7
1954	1.82	8.83	0.91	14.12									100.8	100.8	102.2
1955	4.48	8.45	0.94	14.88									102.1	103.1	102.6
1956	12.19	2.21	1.34	16.81									102.7	103.1	109.4
1957	14.77	1.36	1.41	19.15									103.9	103.9	106.5
1958				19.26				0.1579	0.1579				101.4	101.9	101.6
1959				23.70				0.3511	0.3511				100.6	100.1	102.0
1960				21.53									102.5	104.0	106.3
1961				19.44									123.7	122.3	137.2
1962				17.27				0.1038	0.1038				100.0	100.2	106.2
1963				19.70									94.3	94.3	98.5
1964				23.82									94.3	94.3	97.0
1965			1.34	27.39				0.3181	0.2850	0.0331			97.0	98.3	101.4
1966				33.04				0.1722	0.1402	0.0320			101.8	102.8	104.1
1967				32.84									101.4	101.9	99.7
1968				27.90									100.0	100.2	99.7
1969				26.61									99.7	99.8	100.0
1970				30.70				0.0697	0.0368	0.0329			99.7	99.9	99.9
1971				32.24									100.2	101.0	102.0
1972				33.49									100.6	101.1	100.9
1973				34.41									100.7	100.9	101.5
1974				36.40									100.3	100.5	101.3
1975		0.21	4.25	36.34				0.1756	0.0609	0.1147			100.3	100.6	100.2
1976		0.21	3.54	34.68				0.1321	0.0379	0.0942			100.4	100.8	100.3
1977		0.19	3.03	38.98				0.2395	0.0799	0.1596			99.9	99.5	100.7
1978		0.16	3.01	44.98				0.4067	0.1905	0.2162			99.6	98.8	104.1
1979		0.26	3.37	57.07				0.4763	0.2784	0.1979			105.4	105.7	105.2
1980	0.01	0.59	6.25	69.63				0.8002	0.3746	0.4256			108.1	109.4	104.4
1981		1.52	7.57	75.41				1.0984	0.7834	0.3150			101.8	102.7	103.9
1982		2.99	8.76	86.63				1.3371	0.9588	0.3783			102.3	102.2	104.7
1983		10.18	10.79	92.76				1.5098	1.2294	0.2804			100.7	101.2	101.9
1984			13.51	102.15				3.0706	2.1674	0.9032			102.3	102.2	102.5
1985	0.05	38.65	19.45	112.62				5.1930	3.4939	1.6991			106.8	109.5	106.7
1986	0.04	53.94	25.24	133.34				6.6081	4.8873	1.7208			103.9	104.8	105.6
1987	0.08	71.40	30.64	158.55				9.7551	7.3030	2.4521			107.5	110.1	110.2
1988	0.46	95.44	41.09	200.19				11.3532	8.6287	2.7245			120.0	122.9	131.1
1989	0.84	116.42	49.36	221.74				12.8309	9.4917	3.3392		2.55	118.3	117.8	108.2

22. Sichuan

22–12

Year	v13a	v13b	v13c1	v13c2	v13c3	v13d	v14a	v14b	v14c	v15a	v15b	v15c	v15d	v15e	v15f
1949			0.92	11.54	139.03					10459					
1950			1.45	14.41	229.95										
1951			1.33	17.45	498.48										
1952		39.7	1.55	26.69	526.26	0.45	10113	24200	1.76	11202					
1953			1.52	30.73	513.28										
1954			1.70	36.50	525.39										
1955			1.87	37.61	534.68										
1956			3.07	51.67	620.23										
1957		52.8	3.48	57.63	647.88	0.32			1.63	11507					
1958			4.94	105.41	934.41										
1959			6.25	119.29	987.33										
1960			6.91	112.61	965.74										
1961			6.51	51.28	553.80										
1962		54.8	5.93	53.09	561.33	0.87			0.25	10438					
1963			5.50	61.04	668.44										
1964			4.89	78.49	884.05										
1965		75.0	4.57	111.46	1098.43	1.43	50638	126500	0.63	10587					
1966			3.59	120.22	1055.33				2.00	10547					
1967			2.75	98.21	997.69										
1968			1.75	75.52	925.62										
1969			0.78	149.54	812.35										
1970				221.69	854.74	0.87			0.42	10386					
1971			0.03	216.94	857.35										
1972			0.89	251.71	1081.69										
1973			1.89	227.92	1249.02										
1974			2.95	241.86	1389.13										
1975		96.7	3.25	317.34	1484.66	0.85			6.70	10125					
1976			4.34	409.39	1506.99	0.38			6.97	10069					
1977			4.17	543.70	1459.28	1.97			7.99	10029					
1978	13.28	95.1	5.44	567.64	1477.46	0.87	171060	217500	8.45	9982					
1979	13.83	93.8	6.71	491.64	1542.53	0.53			8.29	9937					
1980	18.43	93.0	7.47	465.84	1575.85	1.02	179426	244800	9.36	9906					
1981	22.02	91.3	8.61	416.65	1562.78	0.69			11.12	9868					
1982	23.84	91.3	7.40	384.71	1542.67	3.22			10.76	9845					
1983	21.76	92.1	7.94	383.82	1499.47	1.91			13.96	9811					
1984	18.75	93.7	9.36	401.36	1472.56	1.79			14.09	9678					
1985	18.37	94.7	11.28	419.15	1427.60	2.09	187412	283900	17.64	9551					
1986	15.77	95.3	12.68	431.99	1353.69	2.53			17.09	9512					
1987	16.19	95.7	13.38	441.25	1243.11	3.31			20.54	9488					
1988			14.08	439.98	1114.78	3.59	205900	300100	20.22	9472	11190		15000	57.5	37.2
1989			14.04	436.74	1010.61	3.94	236600	304800	16.54	9461					

Notes

1. National Output and Income (Y)

v1a: (E), p.696
- v1a1: (E), p.696
- v1a2: (E), p.696
- v1a3: (E), p.696
- v1a4: (E), p.696
- v1a5: (E), p.696

v1b: (A); (C), 1989, p.45
- v1b1: (A); (C), 1989, p.45
- v1b2: (A); (C), 1989, p.45
- v1b3: (A); (C), 1989, p.45
- v1b4: (A); (C), 1989, p.45
- v1b5: (A); (C), 1989, p.45

v1c: v1a – v1d

v1d: (E), p.693
- v1d1: (E), p.693
- v1d2: (E), p.693
- v1d3: (E), p.693
- v1d4: (E), p.693
- v1d5: (E), p.693

v1e: (A); (C), 1989, p.55
- v1e1: (A); (D), p.343
- v1e2: (C), 1989, p.55
- v1e3: (A); (C), 1989, p.55
- v1e4: (A); (C), 1989, p.55
- v1e5: (A); (C), 1989, p.55

v1f: (E), p.692
- v1f1: (E), p.692
- v1f2: (E), p.692
- v1f3: (E), p.692

v1g: v3a + v2a

v1h: (E), p.720

v1i: (E), p.719—including meat and other price subsidies in 1985 and after

v1j: (E), p.719—(ditto)
- v1j1: (E), p.719
- v1j2: (E), p.719—(ditto)
- v1j3: (C), 1989, p.506–507

v1k: (E), p.719—(ditto)

2. Investment (I)

v2a: (A); (D), p.348; (E), p.605—1988: 230.44
- v2a1: (A); (D), p.348
- v2a2: (A); (D), p.348

v2b: (A)

v2c: (A)
- v2c1: (E), p.711
- v2c2: (E), p.711

v2d:
- v2d1: (E), p.708
- v2d2: (E), p.708

v2e: (E), p.708

3. Consumption (C)

v3a: (E), p.695

v3b: (E), p.695
- v3b1: (A); (D), p.344
- v3b2: (A); (D), p.344

v3c: (E), p.695

v3d: (E), p.718
- v3d1: (E), p.718
- v3d2: (E), p.718

v3e: (E), p.720
- v3e1: (E), p.720
- v3e2: NA
- v3e3: NA
- v3e4: NA

v3f: (E), p.720
  v3f1: (E), p.720
  v3f2: (A)
  v3f3: (A)
  v3f4: (A)

4. Public Finance and Banking (FB)

v4a:
  v4a1: (E), p.716
    v4a1a: (E), p.716
    v4a1b: (C), 1989, p.453
    v4a1c: (C), 1989, p.453—farming and animal husbandry tax, salt tax
    v4a1d: (C), 1986, p.386; 1989, p.453
  v4a2: (E), p.716
    v4a2a: (E), p.716
    v4a2b: (E), p.716
    v4a2c: (E), p.716
    v4a2d: v4a2 – v4a2a – v4a2b – v4a2c

v4b: (A)
  v4b1: (C), 1989, p.457
  v4b2: (C), 1989, p.457—rural people's savings
  v4b3: NA

v4c:
  v4c1: (E), p.708
  v4c2: (E), p.708

5. Labor Force (L)

v5a: (E), p.691
  v5a1: (E), p.691
  v5a2: (E), p.691
  v5a3: (E), p.691
  v5a4: (E), p.691

v5b:
  v5b1: NA
  v5b2: NA
  v5b3: NA

v5c: NA
  v5c1: NA

v5d: NA

6. Population (PO)

v6a: (E), p.690—data from public security department
  v6a1: (E), p.690—(ditto)
  v6a2: (E), p.690—(ditto)

v6b: (E), p.690—(ditto)

v6c: (E), p.690—(ditto)

v6d:
  v6d1: (E), p.690—(ditto)
  v6d2: (E), p.690—(ditto)
  v6d3: (E), p.690—(ditto)
  v6d4: (E), p.690—(ditto)
  v6d5: (A)—Chongqing
  v6d6: (A)—Chengdu

7. Agriculture (A)

v7a: (A); (E), p.702

v7b: (A); (E), p.702

v7c: (A); (E), p.702

v7d: (A); (E), p.702

v7e: (A)

v7f: (A); (E), p.702

v7g: (A); (E), p.702

v7h: (A)
  v7h1: (A)
  v7h2: (A)
  v7h3: (A)
  v7h4: (A)
  v7h5: (A)

v7i: (E), p.701

8. Industry (IN)

v8a: (E), p.703
 v8a1: (E), p.703
 v8a2: (E), p.703
 v8a3: v8a – v8a1 – v8a2

v8b: (E), p.708

 v8c1: (E), p.696
 v8c2: (E), p.696

v8d: (E), p.708

v8f:
 v8f1: (E), p.707
 v8f2: (E), p.707
 v8f3: (A); (E), p.707
 v8f4: (A); (E), p.707
 v8f5: (A); (E), p.707

v8g: (A)
 v8g1: (E), p.708

9. Transport (TR)

v9a: (E), p.709—data within the transport system
 v9a1: (E), p.709—(ditto)
 v9a2: (E), p.709—(ditto)
 v9a3: (E), p.709—(ditto)

v9b: (E), p.709—(ditto)
 v9b1: (A); (E), p.709—(ditto)
 v9b2: (E), p.709—(ditto)
 v9b3: (E), p.709—(ditto)

v9c: (E), p.709—(ditto), 1949–80 based on 1970's constant price; 1981 and after based on 1980's constant price. Based on 1970's constant price, 1981's figure was Rmb 82.55 million

10. Domestic Trade (DT)

v10a: (E), p.712
 v10a1: (E), p.712

v10b:
 v10b1: (E), p.712
 v10b2: NA
 v10b3: (E), p.712—including supply and marketing cooperative and other collectives
 v10b4: (E), p.712
 v10b5: (E), p.712
 v10b6: (E), p.712

v10d: (E), p.714

11. Foreign Trade (FT)

v11a:
 v11a1: NA
 v11a2: NA
 v11a3: NA

v11b: (E), p.715—data from foreign trade department
 v11b1: (E), p.715—(ditto)
 v11b2: v11b – v11b1

v11c: NA

v11d: (A)

12. Prices (PR)

v12a: (E), p.717

v12b: (E), p.717

v12c: (E), p.717

13. Education (ED)

v13a: (A)

v13b: (A)

v13c:
 v13c1: (A); (E), p.720

v13c2: (A); (E), p.720—technical, ordinary, vocational and technician secondary schools
v13c3: (A); (E), p.720

v13d: (A)—institutions of higher learning

14. Social Factors (SF)

v14a: (E), p.720

v14b: (E), p.720

v14c: (A)

15. Natural Environment (NE)

v15a: (A); (E), p.702

v15b: (A)

v15c: NA

v15d: (A)—100 million watt

v15e: (A)

v15f: (A)

Sources of Data

(A) Data supplied by the DSNEB, SSB, the PRC; and Propaganda Department, Sichuan Provincial Party Committee of Chinese Communist Party, and Statistical Bureau of Sichuan Province eds. *Tianfu (Sichuan) Forty Years*, Sichuan People's Publishing House, 1989.
(C) Statistical Bureau of Sichuan province ed. *Statistical Yearbook of Sichuan*, Beijing: CSPH, various issues.
(D) Same as (D) in Beijing's sources of data.
(E) Same as (E) in Beijing's sources of data.

23

Guizhou

23. Guizhou

23–1

Year	v1a	v1a1	v1a2	v1a3	v1a4	v1a5	v1b	v1b1	v1b2	v1b3	v1b4	v1b5	v1c	v1d	v1d1
1949	8.98	6.44	2.05	0.12	0.06	0.30							3.07	5.91	4.97
1950	9.34	6.49	2.18	0.21	0.11	0.35	103.3	100.8	106.1	169.8	172.5	118.3	3.22	6.12	5.02
1951	11.41	7.03	2.66	0.61	0.44	0.67	119.1	108.3	122.0	293.0	404.5	191.1	4.13	7.28	5.43
1952	12.69	7.28	3.03	1.02	0.55	0.80	109.7	103.5	114.5	166.9	126.4	119.8	4.53	8.16	5.40
1953	14.47	7.95	3.67	1.27	0.69	0.89	114.6	110.8	123.0	123.8	124.7	110.8	5.52	8.95	5.76
1954	16.24	9.07	4.13	1.24	0.79	1.02	108.2	106.8	113.3	97.9	113.8	114.8	6.27	9.97	6.46
1955	16.93	9.01	4.56	1.29	0.86	1.21	108.1	106.3	111.3	104.4	109.7	118.5	6.50	10.43	6.53
1956	21.09	10.82	5.38	2.44	0.98	1.47	118.3	111.1	119.1	187.8	113.1	122.0	7.99	13.10	8.08
1957	23.17	11.82	6.06	2.50	1.08	1.72	109.3	107.5	114.3	102.9	110.9	115.7	8.86	14.31	8.91
1958	31.31	13.09	9.42	5.01	1.66	2.13	131.1	105.5	164.9	200.5	153.3	124.7	12.89	18.42	9.82
1959	36.74	12.68	13.42	6.21	2.22	2.21	107.4	83.0	134.7	124.1	133.6	103.9	15.67	21.07	9.37
1960	36.96	11.04	13.96	7.17	2.42	2.38	99.3	85.2	103.0	115.5	109.3	106.7	16.45	20.51	7.89
1961	26.88	11.68	8.45	2.48	2.20	2.06	59.1	80.1	56.0	22.2	72.7	74.5	11.25	15.63	8.50
1962	26.13	14.79	7.12	1.10	1.27	1.85	90.6	113.7	80.4	56.4	61.6	75.5	11.74	14.39	10.33
1963	26.66	14.85	7.32	1.32	1.25	1.92	108.5	113.4	102.5	115.4	87.3	110.8	12.04	14.62	10.43
1964	32.51	17.52	8.84	2.68	1.54	1.93	121.8	118.0	121.0	200.1	126.4	98.0	14.97	17.54	12.32
1965	41.19	19.84	11.44	5.94	1.59	2.39	124.7	108.7	129.4	230.9	100.8	120.3	19.13	22.06	14.50
1966	43.75	19.41	12.98	6.69	1.81	2.86	103.5	91.7	113.7	112.7	114.3	115.2	21.18	22.57	14.14
1967	40.34	20.46	12.28	3.73	1.37	2.50	91.6	105.4	94.2	56.2	77.0	87.0	18.80	21.54	15.16
1968	37.17	19.31	11.20	3.37	1.08	2.21	92.2	94.4	91.7	92.0	70.4	90.5	18.38	18.79	13.45
1969	35.28	18.68	10.12	3.42	0.98	2.08	94.7	96.7	90.2	101.5	90.7	94.1	16.87	18.41	13.09
1970	52.28	20.52	20.75	6.88	1.52	2.61	151.8	110.6	202.2	196.5	174.6	124.5	26.96	25.32	14.60
1971	62.31	22.64	22.94	11.59	2.02	3.12	131.2	108.0	139.9	168.3	133.1	120.2	33.09	29.22	15.38
1972	55.26	19.41	22.04	8.61	1.97	3.23	87.7	83.0	96.0	74.4	97.6	103.4	29.15	26.11	13.00
1973	54.10	23.61	19.21	5.87	1.66	3.75	97.7	120.8	87.2	68.1	84.1	115.9	28.97	25.13	15.06
1974	50.17	22.20	17.87	4.85	1.50	3.76	92.3	93.0	93.0	82.7	90.6	99.6	28.55	21.62	13.97
1975	59.67	22.80	24.97	5.72	2.08	4.10	119.2	101.8	139.9	120.1	144.0	111.7	32.04	27.63	15.60
1976	58.41	23.98	23.09	5.14	1.80	4.41	97.3	103.8	92.4	88.3	87.6	108.8	32.18	26.23	16.37
1977	72.15	26.44	32.15	6.47	2.64	4.46	123.7	110.3	139.4	127.6	145.6	98.9	39.00	33.15	17.49
1978	87.95	27.46	41.27	9.98	3.57	5.68	122.2	102.9	129.5	153.5	133.5	127.3	46.33	41.62	18.44
1979	97.81	31.74	45.72	10.93	3.72	5.70	106.0	101.0	109.4	109.6	102.1	100.9	50.67	47.14	21.74
1980	102.24	36.44	45.19	10.81	4.09	5.71	99.2	104.3	97.4	91.6	109.8	97.9	50.02	52.22	25.59
1981	109.31	41.93	44.83	11.26	4.65	6.64	101.8	106.9	96.4	103.7	113.9	106.7	52.41	56.90	29.17
1982	128.98	51.49	53.62	11.84	4.77	7.26	116.4	119.8	119.6	97.8	103.6	114.1	61.90	67.08	36.09
1983	144.05	52.66	64.26	12.78	5.67	8.68	113.2	102.6	120.5	114.1	115.4	127.2	68.82	75.23	37.47
1984	179.87	63.09	81.40	17.24	8.17	9.96	119.7	111.4	123.3	130.0	145.0	109.6	85.36	94.51	46.34
1985	213.76	70.24	98.19	22.78	10.14	12.41	110.7	100.4	113.2	123.9	121.0	110.3	105.91	107.85	49.89
1986	239.60	79.34	108.09	24.60	11.97	15.60	105.9	108.4	104.4	98.4	114.2	119.3	118.39	121.21	55.77
1987	279.87	92.26	126.53	31.14	12.96	16.98	110.2	104.0	114.2	116.3	104.3	105.4	139.04	140.83	64.36
1988	360.58	123.39	166.80	31.91	16.45	22.02	110.4	102.3	116.5	91.5	119.6	122.8	181.49	179.09	82.65
1989	408.18	133.69	201.45	31.75	19.50	21.79	103.6	104.8	107.4	89.3	100.8	91.2	210.00	198.18	89.13

23. Guizhou

23–2

Year	v1d2	v1d3	v1d4	v1d5	v1e	v1e1	v1e2	v1e3	v1e4	v1e5	v1f	v1f1	v1f2	v1f3	v1g
1949	0.65	0.03	0.03	0.23											6.12
1950	0.69	0.08	0.05	0.28	103.6	101.5	107.6	271.2	178.5	121.0					6.36
1951	0.88	0.21	0.22	0.54	119.5	111.4	125.6	297.4	411.5	192.4					7.61
1952	1.25	0.44	0.34	0.73	111.6	105.2	117.1	203.8	154.8	134.5					8.40
1953	1.50	0.49	0.40	0.80	110.6	108.3	122.8	110.6	115.7	110.2					9.53
1954	1.69	0.49	0.43	0.90	106.7	105.1	113.3	98.7	108.3	113.8					11.24
1955	1.87	0.49	0.48	1.06	109.1	108.1	111.4	101.7	109.3	117.2					10.71
1956	2.19	1.04	0.51	1.28	118.9	114.5	118.2	209.3	108.3	121.0					13.44
1957	2.49	0.92	0.55	1.50	107.0	105.6	115.6	89.1	108.1	117.0					16.93
1958	3.49	2.22	1.03	1.86	124.7	108.2	141.6	240.4	186.1	124.2					24.10
1959	5.61	2.32	1.34	1.93	103.6	82.1	151.8	127.3	130.5	103.4					21.37
1960	5.65	3.51	1.41	2.05	95.9	82.4	99.9	124.5	105.4	105.6					19.14
1961	3.56	1.12	1.20	1.25	61.1	82.0	58.5	20.5	67.8	48.9					15.13
1962	2.36	0.35	0.36	0.99	85.1	110.4	63.3	39.7	33.0	71.1					15.37
1963	2.45	0.34	0.46	0.94	109.8	113.4	150.8	89.8	110.9	101.4					18.38
1964	3.02	0.73	0.57	0.90	119.9	118.0	84.0	221.4	123.7	94.1					21.35
1965	3.94	1.67	0.61	1.34	121.9	112.1	130.7	236.3	106.8	143.5					30.55
1966	4.19	1.83	0.62	1.79	98.5	91.8	106.5	109.8	102.5	128.3					30.68
1967	3.52	0.95	0.42	1.49	94.6	107.3	83.6	52.1	69.0	83.7					25.07
1968	2.98	0.88	0.20	1.28	87.1	88.7	85.1	92.0	43.8	85.8					25.53
1969	2.98	0.94	0.13	1.27	98.1	97.3	99.6	107.6	64.5	100.7					26.21
1970	6.91	1.78	0.35	1.68	140.6	113.3	222.3	188.9	294.6	131.6					40.46
1971	8.17	3.00	0.66	2.02	128.8	110.4	151.5	168.0	188.7	121.3					44.25
1972	7.13	3.43	0.65	1.93	91.3	89.0	86.4	113.4	98.3	95.9					37.49
1973	5.66	1.66	0.42	2.33	98.3	116.7	77.8	48.7	65.0	121.1					39.31
1974	4.20	0.87	0.33	2.24	86.0	92.5	71.1	52.8	77.8	95.2					34.26
1975	7.39	1.45	0.72	2.47	115.1	94.6	187.1	166.0	221.1	110.4					34.95
1976	5.93	1.28	0.45	2.20	94.0	103.8	78.9	87.8	62.7	88.3					35.92
1977	10.24	1.92	0.91	2.59	126.7	105.9	179.7	150.2	203.8	117.3					43.86
1978	14.39	3.43	1.34	4.02	124.9	103.8	141.7	179.1	146.6	154.7	46.62	19.42	18.86	8.34	52.97
1979	16.43	3.78	1.49	3.70	106.6	102.4	113.5	111.3	109.6	95.5	55.28	23.29	22.56	9.43	56.39
1980	17.66	3.98	1.53	3.46	102.6	103.8	113.9	96.7	103.9	91.4	60.26	24.86	24.17	11.23	60.51
1981	17.66	4.13	1.76	4.12	104.2	108.4	90.7	104.0	110.0	105.5	62.89	29.90	25.12	12.87	68.34
1982	19.91	4.45	2.15	4.48	115.5	120.9	112.2	100.3	103.6	112.6	79.39	37.37	27.62	14.40	78.29
1983	24.64	4.52	2.63	5.97	113.9	105.0	122.5	101.9	138.0	147.6	87.38	37.76	33.32	16.30	84.77
1984	32.10	6.00	3.48	6.59	118.5	114.8	123.7	133.9	136.6	104.9	108.27	45.73	43.74	18.80	104.82
1985	37.78	7.40	4.36	8.42	107.8	98.4	113.5	118.7	124.2	114.5	123.93	50.45	50.18	23.30	122.99
1986	42.40	7.76	5.00	10.28	107.6	105.7	107.3	94.6	108.3	112.2	139.57	56.46	51.24	31.87	139.97
1987	47.94	10.70	5.61	12.22	110.4	99.9	114.8	132.7	115.4	118.1	165.50	66.46	60.48	38.56	160.26
1988	63.81	10.55	6.73	15.36	106.6	99.6	112.4	98.7	106.6	118.5	208.49	85.19	76.30	47.00	189.82
1989	74.83	9.96	9.24	15.02	103.7	105.1	107.2	87.2	115.0	90.4	235.84	92.88	87.08	55.88	212.86

23. Guizhou

23–3

Year	v1h	v1i	v1j	v1j1	v1j2	v1j3	v1k	v2a	v2a1	v2a2	v2b	v2c	v2c1	v2c2	v2d1
1949								0.39	0.05	0.34					
1950	48			276				0.48	0.07	0.41					
1951	48			281				1.11	0.21	0.90					
1952	49			283				0.90	0.22	0.68					
1953	52			332				1.25	0.48	0.77					
1954	51			348				2.32	0.97	1.35					
1955	55			383				1.43	0.55	0.88					
1956	65			438				2.39	1.41	0.98					
1957	64			462	153			4.48	1.41	3.07					
1958	73			339				9.98	5.70	4.28					
1959	68			352				7.86	6.71	1.15					
1960	63			387				4.99	6.78	-1.79					
1961	80			425				0.65	1.13	-0.48					
1962	113			471	434			0.25	0.43	-0.18					
1963	103			519				3.06	1.58	1.48					
1964	116			551				4.14	3.98	0.16					
1965	110			583	400			11.03	8.89	2.14					
1966	108			626				10.61	10.42	0.19					
1967	107			545				4.94	6.05	-1.11					
1968	106			560				6.22	4.93	1.29					
1969	106			561				7.27	6.36	0.90					
1970	103			551	483			18.48	12.26	6.22					
1971	104			553				19.82	16.28	3.54					
1972	99			633				12.53	11.52	1.01					
1973	100			630				12.85	7.86	4.99					
1974	97			629				8.00	5.98	2.02					
1975	90			626	676			7.47	7.64	-0.17					
1976	95			612	448			7.12	6.41	0.71		6.44			
1977	106			611	480			12.26	7.68	4.58		7.20			
1978	109	10.18	616	642	450			17.42	12.25	5.17		9.67	5.84	0.35	69.79
1979	131	11.31	654	692	448			17.00	12.35	4.65		10.20	5.65	0.29	72.36
1980	162	13.24	755	797	502			15.37	11.95	3.42		11.59	5.80	0.43	82.95
1981	209	13.85	774	804	535			12.78	11.81	0.97	15.16	12.06	6.40	0.23	85.80
1982	223	14.15	783	815	562			16.23	13.37	2.86	15.52	11.55	4.04	0.29	92.44
1983	225	15.22	801	830	608			16.14	14.71	1.44	17.07	11.88	3.56	0.29	102.27
1984	263	17.61	913	949	708			23.25	20.48	2.77	23.02	15.02	4.10	0.48	112.48
1985	302	21.00	1066	1132	787			30.86	27.31	3.55	33.14	21.24	5.75	0.82	118.94
1986	304	24.41	1216	1297	859			34.89	30.83	4.06	35.99	24.09	6.33	0.73	127.78
1987	342	27.06	1319	1395	961			40.89	34.21	6.68	42.97	27.10	9.28	0.63	137.17
1988	398	31.90	1531	1627	1072			53.44	37.42	16.02	45.42	33.05	10.60	0.71	151.85
1989	430	35.57	1694	1777	1158			58.72	32.00	27.72	38.85	31.66	11.45	0.58	167.77

23. Guizhou

23–4

Year	v2d2	v2e	v3a	v3b	v3b1	v3b2	v3c	v3d	v3d1	v3d2	v3e	v3e1	v3e2	v3e3	v3e4
1949			5.73	5.57	4.83	0.73	0.16	40	37	72					
1950			5.88	5.68	4.88	0.80	0.20	40	37	80					
1951			6.50	6.26	5.11	1.14	0.24	44	38	112					
1952			7.50	7.16	5.87	1.29	0.34	49	43	114	92	61	19.18		5.01
1953			8.28	7.91	6.44	1.47	0.37	53	46	128					
1954			8.92	8.30	6.74	1.57	0.62	54	48	130					
1955			9.28	8.63	6.90	1.73	0.65	55	48	139					
1956			11.05	10.09	7.83	2.26	0.96	63	53	174					
1957			12.45	11.54	8.98	2.56	0.91	70	60	170	151	100	14.88		8.13
1958			14.12	12.95	10.06	2.89	1.17	76	68	134					
1959			13.51	12.15	8.52	3.63	1.36	70	56	174					
1960			14.15	12.64	8.26	4.38	1.51	75	56	208	170	112	16.76		9.16
1961			14.48	13.46	8.91	4.55	1.02	82	62	218					
1962			14.77	14.21	9.99	4.22	0.56	86	69	215	215	129	17.76		9.72
1963			15.32	14.48	10.37	4.11	0.84	86	70	208	190	107	23.64		10.56
1964			17.21	16.29	11.51	4.79	0.92	94	76	225	218	125	28.56		8.88
1965			19.51	18.53	13.26	5.27	0.98	103	85	222	204	118	26.40		8.04
1966			20.07	18.96	13.44	5.52	1.11	102	81	238	211	123	26.40		7.80
1967			20.13	19.11	13.87	5.24	1.02	100	81	222					
1968			19.31	18.42	13.54	4.88	0.89	93	75	200					
1969			18.94	17.96	13.72	4.24	0.98	87	74	167					
1970			21.98	20.88	15.13	5.74	1.11	97	79	217	235	137	28.90		6.78
1971			24.43	23.15	16.46	6.69	1.28	104	83	270					
1972			24.96	23.48	15.96	7.52	1.48	102	78	260					
1973			26.46	24.88	16.90	7.97	1.58	104	81	269					
1974			26.26	24.61	15.47	9.14	1.65	101	71	313					
1975			27.48	25.79	15.99	9.80	1.69	103	73	322					
1976			28.80	26.91	16.99	9.92	1.90	105	75	331					
1977			31.60	29.66	19.28	10.39	1.94	113	84	344					
1978	54.54	18.15	35.55	33.27	21.71	11.56	2.28	125	92	376	247	150	31.40		5.75
1979	55.03	20.19	39.39	36.82	24.26	12.56	2.57	136	101	398	274	177	34.36		7.80
1980	63.44	21.80	45.14	42.25	28.07	14.18	2.89	153	115	441	334	202	42.36		9.60
1981	63.83	21.19	55.56	52.49	37.19	15.30	3.07	187	148	468	393	238	51.60		5.88
1982	69.05	21.27	62.06	57.13	40.81	16.32	4.93	200	160	493	404	244	54.24		8.52
1983	76.52	22.48	68.63	63.20	45.77	17.43	5.43	219	179	519	426	259	52.32		8.76
1984	83.40	24.08	81.57	75.25	56.00	19.25	6.32	258	218	557	480	279	65.76		8.64
1985	86.68	28.38	92.14	85.12	60.26	24.86	7.02	288	232	698	618	324	89.52		10.56
1986	92.19	35.80	105.08	94.91	67.20	27.71	10.17	318	254	761	722	384	111.00		9.12
1987	97.53	36.57	119.36	107.71	75.81	31.90	11.65	355	285	853	789	431	110.64		9.36
1988	103.56	44.86	136.99	123.99	83.53	40.46	13.00	400	308	1056	1050	555	145.56		12.96
1989	117.81	54.38	154.14	138.46	97.20	41.26	15.68	441	353	1062	1103	640	133.80	7.68	3.60

23. Guizhou

23–5

Year	v3f	v3f1	v3f2	v3f3	v3f4	v4a1	v4a1a	v4a1b	v4a1c	v4a1d	v4a2	v4a2a	v4a2b	v4a2c	v4a2d
1949	42	25	4.6	3.5											
1950	43	26	5.4	2.4		0.28		0.13	0.13	0.02	0.14		0.01	0.12	0.01
1951	43	26	5.5	2.1		1.07	0.01	0.42	0.61	0.03	0.27		0.03	0.22	0.02
1952	45	27	5.6	3.2		1.22	0.08	0.49	0.56	0.08	0.65		0.12	0.33	0.20
1953	46	27	5.9	2.1		1.21	0.11	0.64	0.34	0.12	0.90	0.22	0.21	0.33	0.13
1954	47	28	7.0			1.50	0.17	0.75	0.39	0.19	1.01	0.33	0.20	0.33	0.15
1955	47	30	6.3	0.3		1.68	0.24	0.88	0.40	0.16	0.98	0.26	0.22	0.34	0.17
1956	52	36	7.4	0.5		2.01	0.36	1.09	0.40	0.17	1.64	0.55	0.31	0.47	0.31
1957	57	37	8.0	1.1		2.20	0.31	1.31	0.39	0.17	1.63	0.44	0.38	0.46	0.35
1958	65	38	10.2	4.5		4.61	1.92	1.87	0.49	0.33	5.56	3.81	0.42	0.48	0.85
1959	70	42	12.9	0.5		5.98	2.93	2.22	0.66	0.18	6.51	3.59	0.55	0.61	1.76
1960	56	39	6.6			5.80	2.61	2.22	0.47	0.50	8.55	4.45	0.76	0.61	2.73
1961	69	49	5.5	1.1		2.71	0.57	1.36	0.49	0.28	4.01	0.70	0.57	0.56	2.18
1962	99	68	9.1	4.6		2.81	0.53	1.38	0.51	0.39	2.22	0.46	0.54	0.49	0.73
1963	93	69	7.4	3.2		3.09	0.44	1.77	0.51	0.37	3.07	0.57	0.64	0.56	1.29
1964	100	74	9.3	2.4		3.59	0.50	2.17	0.57	0.35	3.25	1.02	0.70	0.53	1.01
1965	99	74	11.2	2.1		3.35	0.70	1.77	0.60	0.28	3.64	1.22	0.74	0.57	1.11
1966	97	69	9.2	2.0		3.54	0.91	1.72	0.64	0.26	4.18	1.53	0.85	0.58	1.23
1967	97	69	8.9	1.6		2.62	0.39	1.51	0.67	0.06	3.60	1.26	0.78	0.60	0.96
1968	95	68	8.7	1.0		2.33	0.12	1.50	0.66	0.06	3.18	1.15	0.74	0.56	0.73
1969	96	66	9.4	2.5		1.86	-0.03	1.26	0.61	0.02	4.00	1.67	0.73	0.52	1.08
1970	93	67	8.4	1.6		3.36	0.15	2.34	0.81	0.06	5.42	2.46	0.84	0.65	1.47
1971	96	68	8.4	2.4		3.76	0.25	2.71	0.72	0.08	6.68	2.49	1.02	0.92	2.25
1972	89	62	8.2	2.1		3.34	-0.03	2.83	0.48	0.05	7.44	2.57	1.29	0.96	2.61
1973	94	66	8.5	2.9		1.05	-2.16	2.44	0.73	0.04	6.93	2.02	1.40	0.94	2.58
1974	90	64	8.3	2.8		0.72	-2.20	2.21	0.67	0.05	6.35	1.60	1.51	0.92	2.32
1975	85	62	8.2	1.4		1.54	-2.24	3.05	0.64	0.09	7.37	1.86	1.64	1.00	2.88
1976	88	64	7.6	2.4		1.01	-2.48	2.72	0.71	0.06	7.69	1.95	1.73	0.95	3.06
1977	97	69	10.3	2.2		2.43	-2.13	3.72	0.79	0.06	8.79	1.84	1.84	1.07	4.04
1978	104	72	10.7	4.0		6.26	0.44	4.75	0.66	0.40	12.30	3.41	2.29	1.20	5.41
1979	116	82	10.7	4.9		6.54	0.47	5.23	0.60	0.24	13.30	3.40	2.68	1.33	5.89
1980	139	97	14.4	5.5		6.69	0.21	5.56	0.58	0.33	12.66	2.44	3.06	1.48	5.68
1981	162	105	18.9	9.2		6.32	-0.94	6.49	0.53	0.24	13.28	1.63	3.44	1.59	6.62
1982	187	122	21.5	14.5		7.70	-0.58	7.30	0.61	0.36	15.11	2.05	3.91	2.02	7.13
1983	185	126	18.4	12.8		9.56	-0.08	8.30	0.83	0.50	16.38	2.37	4.49	2.30	7.23
1984	209	144	19.9	14.0		11.81	0.70	9.88	0.88	0.33	22.28	3.50	5.62	3.35	9.82
1985	255	178	24.4	14.4		15.17	0.71	13.45	0.69	0.32	24.55	3.97	6.40	3.38	10.80
1986	272	191	23.2	17.4		16.97	0.02	15.65	0.80	0.50	30.39	5.06	7.50	3.75	14.08
1987	304	213	23.7	18.9		21.34	0.29	19.41	1.06	0.57	31.40	3.50	8.17	4.00	15.72
1988	360	254	27.9	19.4		25.96	-0.58	24.14	1.18	1.02	36.14	3.70	9.47	5.43	17.55
1989	407	281	30.5	23.4	22.06	32.13	-1.05				45.89	3.53	10.53	4.51	27.32

23. Guizhou

23–6

Year	v4b	v4b1	v4b2	v4b3	v4c1	v4c2	v5a	v5a1	v5a2	v5a3	v5a4	v5b1	v5b2	v5b3	v5c
1949							601	3	40		558	545	23	33	
1950	0.0041	0.0041					601	6	39		556	543	23	35	
1951	0.0420	0.0420					614	10	36		568	549	24	41	
1952	0.0359	0.0359					630	16	31		583	556	24	50	
1953	0.0498	0.0495	0.0003				641	18	30		593	565	24	52	
1954	0.0830	0.0709	0.0121				659	19	32		608	588	25	46	
1955	0.1855	0.0883	0.0972				677	20	35		622	600	27	50	
1956	0.3626	0.1639	0.1987				691	36	34		621	601	32	58	
1957	0.4392	0.2528	0.1864				704	41	38		625	610	36	58	
1958	0.8794	0.4989	0.3805				723	69	17		626	539	69	115	
1959	0.9929	0.5148	0.4781				711	92	22		597	497	101	113	
1960	0.9381	0.5725	0.3656				687	90	20		577	507	58	122	
1961	0.7620	0.4323	0.3297				668	64	25		579	568	37	63	
1962	0.4901	0.3150	0.1751				718	52	23		643	637	31	50	
1963	0.5215	0.3462	0.1753				735	55	22		658	652	31	52	
1964	0.6091	0.4605	0.1486				771	65	22		684	684	39	48	
1965	0.7484	0.5302	0.2182				814	76	23		715	700	66	48	
1966	0.8943	0.6378	0.2565				803	81	23		699	692	65	46	
1967	0.8889	0.6788	0.2101				891	85	31		775	739	89	63	
1968	0.8997	0.6869	0.2128				901	89	30		782	740	91	70	
1969	0.8939	0.7174	0.1765				943	92	31		820	774	94	75	
1970	0.9746	0.7643	0.2103				966	108	27		831	794	96	76	
1971	1.2304	0.9338	0.2966				997	120	20		857	836	99	62	
1972	1.3332	1.0623	0.2709				1005	125	22		858	843	92	70	
1973	1.3220	1.0514	0.2706				1011	120	24		867	867	86	58	
1974	1.4118	1.1144	0.2974				1029	117	25		887	887	83	59	
1975	1.4673	1.1660	0.3013				1036	118	28		890	861	87	88	
1976	1.4780	1.2190	0.2590				1040	120	28		892	887	90	63	
1977	1.6134	1.3169	0.2965				1039	124	31		884	868	109	62	
1978	1.8461	1.4741	0.3720		5.59	7.86	1054	138	34		882	873	108	73	
1979	2.4192	1.9486	0.4706		6.95	12.69	1061	142	34		885	874	106	81	
1980	3.7349	3.0132	0.7217		7.58	9.35	1109	146	34		929	920	102	87	
1981	5.2776	4.1092	1.1684		6.84	8.07	1153	154	36		963	955	102	96	
1982	7.2640	5.5223	1.7417		8.59	9.79	1207	158	39		1010	990	110	107	
1983	8.8637	7.0504	1.8133		11.41	11.98	1234	160	42		1032	1014	110	110	
1984	12.3335	9.8791	2.4544		14.31	13.76	1285	160	38		1087	1078	122	125	
1985	16.6099	13.4022	3.2077		16.98	14.97	1335	162	55		1118	1018	186	131	
1986	22.2102	18.0716	4.1386		18.15	14.49	1383	168	58		1157	1053	197	133	
1987	30.3678	24.8080	5.5598		22.50	17.20	1436	173	59		1204	1115	181	140	
1988	34.9935	28.6016	6.3919		30.45	20.51	1501	176	58		1267	1173	186	142	
1989	44.6000	38.1000	6.6000		31.26	18.16	1571	180	58	21.09	1333	1229	163	179	

23. Guizhou

23–7

Year	v5c1	v5d	v6a	v6a1	v6a2	v6b	v6c	v6d1	v6d2	v6d3	v6d4	v6d5	v6d6
1949			1416	106	1310	28.02	7.18	102	1314	709	707		30.54
1950			1417	104	1313	30.24	8.20	101	1316	710	707		
1951			1445	106	1339	34.18	9.28	103	1342	729	716		
1952			1490	108	1382	32.17	7.81	120	1370	747	743		30.44
1953			1522	110	1412	37.13	9.25	114	1408	769	753		
1954			1557	115	1442	39.56	8.82	122	1435	788	769		
1955			1587	123	1464	36.20	8.10	131	1456	802	785		
1956			1628	147	1481	34.00	7.48	137	1491	824	804		
1957			1681	165	1516	41.12	8.77	164	1517	852	829		50.44
1958			1710	344	1366	30.08	13.69	259	1451	812	848		84.82
1959			1744	350	1394	26.76	16.18	257	1487	882	862		
1960			1643	359	1384	25.97	45.38	235	1408	816	827		
1961			1624	271	1353	17.52	17.73	192	1432	800	824		87.41
1962			1664	206	1458	41.54	10.41	180	1484	826	838		85.25
1963			1704	203	1501	47.16	9.37	188	1516	850	854		88.02
1964			1752	213	1539	39.18	10.48	203	1549	890	862		92.55
1965			1821	225	1596	34.64	8.38	219	1602	926	895		96.22
1966			1885	236	1649	36.34	9.18	231	1654	959	926		
1967			1957	245	1712	34.82	7.29	236	1721	985	972		
1968			2035	255	1780	34.35	6.55	243	1792	1020	1015		
1969			2108	264	1844	34.00	6.54	253	1855	1060	1048		
1970			2180	277	1903	31.05	6.06	265	1916	1109	1071		106.59
1971			2259	272	1987	26.91	5.97	284	1975	1150	1109		
1972			2323	281	2042	26.56	6.25	289	2034	1181	1142		
1973			2395	292	2103	26.38	5.85	297	2098	1216	1179		
1974			2463	296	2167	25.36	6.81	292	2171	1251	1212		
1975			2531	298	2233	24.49	6.27	291	2240	1285	1246		119.00
1976			2585	301	2284	21.30	5.64	294	2291	1313	1272		
1977			2640	316	2324	19.36	6.15	299	2341	1341	1299		
1978			2686	324	2362	17.85	5.47	306	2380	1365	1321	194.09	124.11
1979			2731	521	2210	21.54	6.04	315	2416	1387	1344		
1980			2777	544	2233	21.34	6.26	321	2456	1410	1367	202.02	127.66
1981			2827	529	2298	22.17	7.24	327	2500	1440	1387		
1982			2875	542	2333	22.17	6.87	331	2544	1470	1405		
1983			2901	551	2350	18.73	8.06	336	2565	1485	1416		
1984			2932	854	2078	18.19	6.84	344	2588	1502	1430		
1985			2968	876	2092	14.69	5.78	359	2609	1521	1447	221.65	137.50
1986			3008	904	2104	15.89	5.73	364	2644	1542	1466	224.72	140.29
1987			3051	935	2116	16.90	5.95	372	2679	1565	1486	228.86	143.10
1988			3144	686	2458	17.06	5.70	384	2760	1608	1536	176.01	145.87
1989			3184	1004	2180	21.16	7.02	391	2793	1636	1548	179.89	148.87

23. Guizhou

23–8

Year	v7a	v7b	v7c	v7d	v7e	v7f	v7g	v7h	v7h1	v7h2	v7h3	v7h4	v7h5	v7i	v8a
1949								6.44	3.38	0.52	1.15		1.39	224.40	2.06
1950				3011				6.49	3.45	0.52	1.17		1.36	224.40	2.18
1951				3135				7.03	3.68	0.71	1.26		1.38	234.80	2.66
1952				3281				7.28	3.93	0.55	1.38		1.43	245.80	3.03
1953				3392				7.95	4.26	0.79	1.49		1.42	262.10	3.67
1954				3536				9.07	4.83	0.97	1.75		1.52	280.10	4.13
1955				3759				9.00	4.83	1.09	1.67		1.42	297.50	4.56
1956				4387				10.83	6.18	1.17	2.00		1.48	327.60	5.38
1957			417.10	4738		0.10	0.0006	11.82	6.74	1.42	2.12	0.01	1.54	341.70	6.06
1958			457.90	4575		0.20	0.0016	13.09	9.87	0.75	1.52	0.01	0.94	319.60	9.42
1959			485.70	4096		0.30	0.0031	12.68	9.05	0.58	1.48	0.03	1.53	293.70	13.42
1960			456.60	4512		0.40	0.0035	11.04	7.69	0.45	0.95	0.01	1.93	258.80	13.96
1961			421.60	3934		0.30	0.0049	11.68	9.45	0.29	0.99	0.03	0.92	237.60	8.45
1962			451.90	3909		0.30	0.0061	14.79	11.15	0.44	1.73	0.01	1.45	239.50	7.12
1963		9.10		3722		1.00	0.0145	14.85	9.99	0.64	2.55	0.01	1.65	263.90	7.32
1964		18.20		3889		1.70	0.0189	17.52	11.49	0.60	3.24	0.02	2.17	291.60	8.84
1965				4053		3.70	0.0331	19.84	12.90	0.85	3.65	0.02	2.42	314.90	11.44
1966				4277		8.20	0.5536	19.42	12.74	0.99	2.97	0.03	2.68	327.20	12.98
1967				4478		7.80	0.0935	20.46	14.38	1.13	2.60	0.04	2.31	327.10	12.28
1968			620.00	4059		7.60	0.1839	19.31	13.27	0.97	2.70	0.04	2.34	266.30	11.20
1969			523.10	4045		5.60	0.2486	18.68	12.70	0.97	2.63	0.02	2.34	332.10	10.12
1970		9.00	647.30	3867		18.80	0.5269	20.52	14.02	1.05	3.16	0.04	2.26	343.90	20.75
1971		9.80	679.60	4181		32.30	0.7281	22.64	15.96	1.02	3.26	0.05	2.35	350.90	22.94
1972		14.30	573.40	4326		34.20	1.1481	19.42	13.03	0.95	3.24	0.04	2.16	358.30	22.04
1973		18.80	600.90	4408		31.40	1.0241	23.61	17.05	0.97	3.35	0.05	2.20	367.40	19.21
1974		26.10	652.00	4316		26.70	1.1355	22.20	15.38	1.09	3.42	0.04	2.26	372.50	17.87
1975		47.80	655.70	4342		32.90	1.7113	22.80	15.50	1.00	3.92	0.05	2.33	347.70	24.97
1976		63.00	667.70	4583		34.50	2.1733	23.98	16.55	1.06	3.93	0.02	2.42	362.80	23.09
1977		80.80	744.00	4545		43.60	2.2631	26.44	18.88	0.98	4.07	0.03	2.49	346.90	32.15
1978	11.12	110.40	753.00	4768		61.90	2.4755	27.46	19.19	1.07	4.64	0.03	2.53	355.70	41.27
1979		82.70	704.30	4517		70.00	2.3677	31.74	21.52	1.27	5.90	0.03	3.02	369.10	45.72
1980	13.22	44.10	685.20	4268		58.40	2.8738	36.44	24.23	1.46	6.89	0.04	3.83	379.52	45.19
1981		19.00	676.10	4280		79.30	3.0782	41.93	27.67	1.38	8.13	0.04	4.70	399.40	44.83
1982		12.90	657.00	4400		86.20	3.3513	51.49	32.90	2.63	9.42	0.10	6.44	425.70	53.62
1983		9.10	678.80	4351		95.80	3.1144	52.66	32.23	3.69	10.16	0.11	6.48	438.90	64.26
1984		4.40	683.70	4489		92.00	3.2087	63.09	39.18	4.86	12.68	0.19	6.18	465.40	81.40
1985	18.34	3.80	816.00	4532	25	89.70	3.5050	70.24	38.91	5.48	15.80	0.23	9.83	485.90	98.19
1986		9.00	797.50	4701	30	106.00	3.3000	79.34	44.19	5.08	18.49	0.25	11.34	510.12	108.09
1987		8.50	807.00	4869	59	109.60	3.9690	92.25	50.65	5.63	22.14	0.28	13.56	534.02	126.53
1988	24.80	18.00	817.00	4998		111.00	4.0000	123.39	65.61	6.13	37.52	0.81	13.32	552.00	166.80
1989	26.50	25.80	823.30	5211		115.00	5.4000	133.68	70.75	5.90	41.21	0.85	14.97	433.00	201.45

23. Guizhou

23–9

Year	v8a1	v8a2	v8a3	v8b	v8c1	v8c2	v8d	v8f1	v8f2	v8f3	v8f4	v8f5	v8g
1949					0.49	1.56			30		0.07	0.07	
1950					0.50	1.68			34		0.07	0.04	16
1951					0.80	1.86			37		0.12	0.18	47
1952	2.49	0.03	0.51		1.01	2.02			47		0.20	0.27	52
1953	3.08	0.04	0.55		1.30	2.37			56		0.29	0.56	215
1954	3.51	0.04	0.58		1.53	2.60			62		0.34	1.05	387
1955	3.88	0.09	0.59		1.60	2.96			71		0.36	1.14	442
1956	4.57	0.11	0.70		1.78	3.60			84		0.42	3.72	751
1957	5.26	0.12	0.68		2.52	3.54			138		0.50	3.16	3683
1958	7.35	1.60	0.47		4.73	4.69		1.00	446		0.78	5.57	7689
1959	11.41	1.61	0.40		7.26	6.16		3.13	485		2.13	9.15	14963
1960	11.72	1.53	0.71		8.75	5.21		4.26	529		4.16	30.51	4818
1961	6.35	1.61	0.49		4.33	4.12		2.04	340		3.20	7.32	4165
1962	5.13	1.50	0.49		3.27	3.85		0.27	294		3.28	7.76	3714
1963	5.42	1.24	0.66		3.49	3.83		0.37	288		3.21	12.85	3441
1964	6.63	1.41	0.80		4.39	4.45		1.03	246		4.14	23.17	3272
1965	8.80	1.83	0.81		4.62	6.82		2.19	332		5.88	27.09	3753
1966	9.99	2.21	0.78		7.20	5.78		3.00	269		8.60	37.63	2606
1967	9.46	2.09	0.73		6.55	5.73		2.51	233		12.73	33.32	2536
1968	8.62	1.79	0.79		5.94	5.26		2.70	263		10.40	33.90	2527
1969	7.69	1.72	0.71		5.28	4.84		1.36	236		9.56	16.96	2518
1970	17.22	2.70	0.83		12.55	8.20		4.66	594		15.42	50.00	3933
1971	19.50	2.52	0.92		14.75	8.19		6.11	802		24.03	75.27	4577
1972	17.63	3.09	1.32		13.64	8.40		3.76	923		22.37	78.38	4948
1973	14.60	3.27	1.34		11.33	7.88		1.63	683		21.06	42.20	5102
1974	13.11	3.39	1.37		10.06	7.81		0.85	798		17.18	44.06	5597
1975	19.73	4.00	1.24		15.48	9.49		3.84	1104		28.59	81.26	6035
1976	17.77	4.15	1.17		14.16	8.93		1.51	1052		24.82	57.08	6798
1977	25.71	5.46	0.98		20.44	11.71		5.01	1396		31.90	91.76	7346
1978	33.42	6.19	1.66	32.50	27.82	13.45	11.12	8.73	1669		41.43	130.93	8904
1979	37.95	5.94	1.83	36.16	31.45	14.27	12.64	9.11	1636		44.90	148.38	7235
1980	37.96	5.87	1.36	36.71	29.24	15.95	14.52	8.66	1398		45.17	144.47	7715
1981	37.21	6.28	1.34	35.75	26.36	18.47	13.93	8.60	1416		43.55	145.82	7428
1982	45.04	6.97	1.61	43.25	32.50	21.12	15.73	10.62	1695		57.86	161.07	7425
1983	53.98	7.71	2.57	51.94	40.48	23.78	19.18	11.63	1847		69.51	182.26	7256
1984	64.31	9.77	7.32	62.93	52.26	29.14	23.80	13.87	2027		76.46	206.94	8602
1985	77.57	11.78	8.84	77.83	59.11	39.08	28.35	19.28	2344		78.07	231.26	8717
1986	82.15	14.05	11.89	81.48	64.96	43.13	31.30	26.34	2554		82.52	247.31	8944
1987	96.16	15.18	15.19	95.51	75.79	50.74	35.98	32.67	3170		84.90	258.10	7945
1988	125.11	20.20	21.49	124.89	95.35	71.45	48.33	33.17	3210		90.12	293.38	7716
1989	156.45	28.11	16.89	151.14	115.72	85.73	56.43	37.78	3496		96.53	295.51	7671

23. Guizhou

23–10

Year	v8g1	v9a	v9a1	v9a2	v9a3	v9b	v9b1	v9b2	v9b3	v9c	v10a	v10a1	v10b1	v10b2	v10b3
1949										112	1.87	1.80	0.04		
1950		0.06		0.06		0.12		0.12		81	1.96	1.89			
1951		0.24		0.22	0.02	0.50		0.45	0.06	168	2.58	2.47			
1952		0.60		0.58	0.02	0.67		0.55	0.12	252	3.01	2.85	0.36		0.27
1953		0.96		0.94	0.02	1.16		0.98	0.18	364	3.47	3.24			
1954		1.07		1.05	0.02	1.86		1.63	0.23	429	4.19	3.94			
1955		1.42		1.39	0.03	2.39		2.11	0.28	499	4.52	4.25			
1956		2.56		2.53	0.03	2.86		2.57	0.29	635	5.81	5.43			
1957		2.61		2.58	0.03	3.41		3.03	0.38	731	6.77	6.43	2.76		1.96
1958		3.60		3.57	0.03	4.99		4.51	0.48	1037	8.72	7.89			
1959		3.93		3.90	0.03	9.06		8.49	0.57	1618	10.20	9.11			
1960		3.90		3.88	0.02	9.94		9.35	0.59	2003	11.43	10.08			
1961		2.96		2.93	0.03	5.15		4.75	0.40	1733	9.24	8.60			
1962		3.16		3.14	0.02	3.47		3.28	0.19	1492	8.81	8.33			
1963		3.01		2.98	0.03	2.02		1.87	0.15	1477	10.04	9.60			
1964		3.78		3.75	0.03	2.57		2.32	0.25	1614	11.24	10.75			
1965		9.62	5.31	4.28	0.03	10.76	6.68	3.79	0.29	1819	11.69	11.03	5.50		5.65
1966		13.08	8.11	4.93	0.04	21.97	16.94	4.76	0.27	1749	13.33	12.31			
1967		11.72	7.12	4.57	0.03	14.70	10.95	3.50	0.25	1666	12.72	11.91			
1968		10.30	6.10	4.17	0.03	11.73	8.24	3.23	0.26	1604	12.02	11.10			
1969		11.85	7.30	4.50	0.05	15.43	12.37	2.80	0.26	1582	11.56	10.67			
1970		16.55	11.06	5.41	0.08	28.65	25.16	3.08	0.41	1729	14.09	12.81	7.19		5.96
1971		19.57	13.42	6.05	0.10	40.67	35.16	5.03	0.48	2022	16.49	14.77			
1972		18.85	12.13	6.62	0.10	40.15	34.87	4.76	0.52	2092	18.44	16.21			
1973		19.70	13.20	6.35	0.15	32.47	27.80	4.14	0.53	2153	18.62	16.48			
1974		17.20	11.40	5.64	0.16	28.67	24.50	3.69	0.48	2109	18.24	16.42			
1975		20.51	13.80	6.54	0.17	40.39	35.00	4.82	0.57	2205	20.09	17.87	11.01		6.65
1976		20.51	13.70	6.62	0.19	28.44	23.60	4.28	0.56	2248	20.50	18.35			
1977		20.58	13.40	6.96	0.22	47.30	41.00	5.59	0.71	2350	22.46	19.38			
1978	1400	25.39	15.90	9.29	0.20	78.84	71.54	6.57	0.73	2552	24.61	21.23	13.30		10.14
1979	1363	31.40	19.52	11.68	0.20	93.37	85.87	6.59	0.91	2784	27.12	23.57	13.96		11.42
1980	1369	38.59	23.67	14.67	0.25	99.63	92.59	5.91	1.13	2834	30.04	26.73	14.74		12.85
1981	1364	44.37	26.41	17.73	0.23	103.92	96.68	6.23	1.01	2910	34.00	30.48	16.18		14.38
1982	1405	48.01	27.78	19.99	0.24	111.08	102.38	7.50	1.20	3022	38.43	34.56	17.64		15.30
1983	1400	53.59	31.93	21.40	0.26	116.84	107.48	7.97	1.39	3251	42.56	38.43	18.62		14.75
1984	1422	62.21	37.38	24.55	0.28	133.64	123.12	8.61	1.91	3551	47.92	43.64	20.55		15.24
1985	1562	75.66	46.66	28.64	0.36	148.65	137.45	9.32	1.88	3981	57.17	52.25	22.33		17.95
1986	1594	78.01	49.03	28.70	0.28	184.96	152.06	30.44	2.46	4415	63.18	57.25	24.87		18.60
1987	1617	105.06	55.07	49.60	0.39	200.04	160.54	36.87	2.63	4812	73.18	66.39	28.16		19.39
1988	1579	114.82	63.29	51.14	0.39	215.24	163.95	48.50	2.79	6262	91.78	83.40	36.05		23.40
1989	1556	126.53	58.08	67.16	0.49	223.46	174.59	45.96	2.90	7042	93.74	83.84	35.41		24.41

23. Guizhou

23–11

Year	v10b4	v10b5	v10b6	v10d	v11a1	v11a2	v11a3	v11b	v11b1	v11b2	v11c	v11d	v12a	v12b	v12c
1949		1.60	0.23												
1950															
1951													111.3	110.9	117.3
1952	0.0309	2.17	0.18	1.77									104.2	110.0	96.0
1953				1.90									99.4	101.5	108.6
1954				2.85									102.4	103.5	114.2
1955				2.77									103.4	102.5	111.0
1956				3.33	0.0053			0.0058	0.0053	0.0005			99.0	100.5	109.0
1957	1.6241	0.20	0.23	4.61	0.0237			0.0274	0.0237	0.0037			102.1	103.0	113.9
1958				5.32	0.0472		0.0184	0.1217	0.0656	0.0561			100.7	101.5	102.2
1959				7.62	0.0237		0.0897	0.1593	0.1134	0.0459			99.5	101.8	103.9
1960				5.41	0.0196		0.0964	0.1285	0.1160	0.0125			101.1	102.0	112.5
1961				3.80	0.0034		0.0875	0.0924	0.0909	0.0015			124.6	124.0	125.8
1962				3.80	0.0034		0.0770	0.0809	0.0804	0.0005			100.5	100.4	100.1
1963				4.45	0.0006		0.0459	0.0477	0.0465	0.0012			98.8	98.7	100.4
1964				4.99	0.0074		0.0047	0.0224	0.0121	0.0103			97.2	97.3	100.7
1965		0.11	0.43	5.69	0.0181		0.0045	0.0277	0.0226	0.0051			98.5	98.4	101.8
1966				5.75	0.0237		0.0043	0.0391	0.0280	0.0111			102.0	101.6	104.2
1967				4.68	0.0009		0.0053	0.0165	0.0062	0.0103			101.6	101.7	99.8
1968				4.22				0.0177		0.0177			100.0	100.0	99.7
1969				3.65	0.0001		0.0005	0.0137	0.0006	0.0131			99.8	99.4	100.0
1970	0.3698	0.09	0.48	5.47	0.0001		0.0005	0.0230	0.0006	0.0224			99.6	100.1	100.2
1971				5.34	0.0002		0.0075	0.0360	0.0077	0.0283			99.4	99.8	100.4
1972				5.17	0.0001		0.0129	0.0420	0.0130	0.0290			99.2	99.5	100.7
1973				5.40			0.0050	0.0364	0.0050	0.0314			99.0	100.2	100.9
1974				5.25			0.0072	0.0750	0.0072	0.0678			100.1	100.3	101.1
1975	1.2048	0.05	1.18	7.12			0.0036	0.0801	0.0036	0.0765			100.1	100.1	99.8
1976				5.49			0.0022	0.0756	0.0022	0.0734			101.2	101.4	100.5
1977				5.97			0.0018	0.1071	0.0018	0.1053			99.8	101.0	99.7
1978		0.08	1.09	8.07	0.0266		0.0019	0.1645	0.0285	0.1360			100.3	101.4	102.8
1979		0.16	1.58	6.73	0.0633		0.0070	0.2111	0.0703	0.1408			102.2	101.8	117.5
1980	0.0017	0.33	2.12	10.31	0.0751	0.0253	0.0922	0.3082	0.1926	0.1156			107.9	109.9	112.1
1981	0.0045	0.98	2.45	14.41	0.0992	0.0156	0.1056	0.3369	0.2204	0.1165			102.3	105.1	111.3
1982	0.0074	2.06	3.41	17.80	0.1238	0.0121	0.1631	0.4156	0.2990	0.1166			102.0	102.0	105.0
1983		4.76	4.43	16.69	0.1497	0.0264	0.1761	0.4537	0.3522	0.1015			100.7	101.6	92.2
1984	0.0002	7.11	5.02	17.80	0.1137	0.0297	0.2417	0.5687	0.3851	0.1836	0.0408	0.0061	102.5	102.8	104.3
1985	0.0034	10.79	6.10	19.68	0.1146	0.0199	0.2209	0.6795	0.3554	0.3241	0.2083	0.1287	107.7	110.3	113.6
1986	0.0197	13.26	6.43	21.37	0.1906	0.0536	0.4054	0.7877	0.6496	0.1381	0.1196	0.0275	105.3	106.4	104.2
1987	0.0350	17.54	8.06	24.04	0.2472	0.0864	0.5960	1.1353	0.9296	0.2057	0.1642	0.0370	107.3	109.7	108.0
1988	0.1556	22.15	10.03	32.72	0.2655	0.1335	0.7625	1.5546	1.1615	0.3931	0.4285	0.1408	120.2	121.5	117.1
1989	0.0400	22.97	10.92	33.35				1.8560	1.3201	0.5359	0.3747	0.2460	117.4	117.9	112.5

23. Guizhou

Year	v13a	v13b	v13c1	v13c2	v13c3	v13d	v14a	v14b	v14c	v15a	v15b	v15c	v15d	v15e	v15f
1949															
1950			0.1071	0.2341	14.89	0.0307			0.0336	2698					
1951			0.0948	0.2874	56.66	0.0244			0.1066	2760					
1952		27.2	0.1407	0.6392	81.01	0.0078	2336		0.1476	2827					
1953		28.1	0.1545	0.7363	81.93	0.0231			0.1719	2886					
1954		31.2	0.2032	0.7369	87.92	0.0356			0.2026	2945					
1955		35.2	0.2217	0.5549	97.05	0.0540			0.2191	3006					
1956		54.5	0.3153	1.1975	14.90	0.0430			0.3539	3131					
1957		53.7	0.3642	1.1800	15.41	0.0457			0.3863	3136					
1958		82.0	0.6939	1.9766	24.27	0.0817			0.7755	3136					
1959		82.5	0.9852	3.4392	23.26	0.0594			1.0556	3104					
1960		84.0	1.2302	4.2647	21.23	0.1284			0.9918	3100					
1961		36.4	1.0987	1.0115	88.00	0.0890			0.4789	3100					
1962		38.7	1.0347	0.5721	87.12	0.2113			0.4832	3100					
1963		48.0	0.9110	0.7226	112.18	0.2431			0.6478	3100					
1964		59.4	0.6430	1.0268	172.16	0.3047			0.5832	3100					
1965		78.3	0.7088	1.5754	258.49	0.1416	11797	30000	0.7616	3100					
1966			0.6232	1.4594	246.50	0.0856			1.2989	2984					
1967			0.4858	1.4594	192.19	0.1374			1.5030	2935					
1968			0.3530	0.0768	183.51	0.1328			1.4334	2935					
1969			0.2121		179.30	0.1409			0.9385	2892					
1970		55.2		0.0452	203.30	0.2612			0.8206	2874					
1971		66.8		0.5081	239.52				1.1285	2875					
1972		82.5	0.2563	1.1081	295.48				1.3598	2873					
1973		83.5	0.5414	1.3780	315.89				1.3342	2869					
1974		85.2	0.5981	2.0456	350.58				1.3255	2862					
1975		93.0	0.7510	1.9850	417.93	0.2506			1.5368	2859					
1976		93.4	0.8286	1.7550	426.29	0.3069			1.7133	2860					
1977		92.4	0.9964	1.7964	423.11	0.1787			1.5733	2862					
1978		89.4	1.3255	2.2309	423.60	0.2489	37533	60000	1.7841	2858					
1979		86.1	1.7768	3.0802	413.71	0.1666			2.2326	2848					
1980		80.8	1.7062	3.5426	404.19	0.5365	40835	60000	1.7950	2856					
1981		78.5	1.8104	3.3600	403.49	0.3125			1.8464	2854					
1982		78.3	1.6730	3.3148	412.30	0.6427			1.8950	2854					
1983		81.2	1.6803	3.7408	415.79	0.5327			2.0453	2848					
1984		83.6	2.0296	3.9261	438.56	0.3328			2.4244	2840					
1985		84.9	2.2997	4.2934	447.68	0.4862	45226	80000	3.3096	2810					
1986		86.9	2.5190	4.6145	461.99	0.5740			3.0688	2794					
1987		89.2	2.5975	4.7751	458.27	0.6585			3.4066	2786					
1988		89.9	2.7264	5.0913	449.70	0.6833	49543	80000	3.3636	2782	3300	1035	1874.47	487.6616	4.4866
1989		88.8	2.7600	5.0000	440.40	0.7300	57428	80000		2781					

Notes

1. National Output and Income (Y)

v1a: (E), p.727
  v1a1: (E), p.727
  v1a2: (E), p.727
  v1a3: (E), p.727
  v1a4: (E), p.727
  v1a5: (E), p.727

v1b: (A); (B), p.34
  v1b1: (A); (B), p.34
  v1b2: (A); (B), p.34
  v1b3: (A); (B), p.34
  v1b4: (A); (B), p.34
  v1b5: (A); (B), p.34

v1c: v1a – v1d

v1d: (E), p.724
  v1d1: (E), p.724
  v1d2: (E), p.724
  v1d3: (E), p.724
  v1d4: (E), p.724
  v1d5: (E), p.724

v1e: (A); (B), p.43
  v1e1: (A); (B), p.43
  v1e2: (A); (B), p.43
  v1e3: (A); (B), p.43
  v1e4: (A); (B), p.43
  v1e5: (A); (B), p.43

v1f: (E), p.723
  v1f1: (E), p.723
  v1f2: (E), p.723
  v1f3: (E), p.723

v1g: (E), p.726

v1h: (A); (E), p.750

v1i: (E), p.749—excluding meat price subsidies

v1j: (E), p.749—(ditto)
  v1j1: (E), p.749—(ditto)
  v1j2: (E), p.749—(ditto)
  v1j3: NA

v1k: NA

2. Investment (I)

v2a: (A); (D), p.359; (E), p.726—1987: 40.91, 1988: 54.83
  v2a1: (A); (B), p.49; (D), p.359
  v2a2: (A); (B), p.49; (D), p.359

v2b: (A)

v2c: (A); (E), p.740
  v2c1: (E), p.741
  v2c2: (E), p.741

v2d:
  v2d1: (E), p.736
  v2d2: (E), p.736

v2e: (E), p.736

3. Consumption (C)

v3a: (E), p.726

v3b: (A); (B), p.48; (E), p.726—1962: 14.12, 1969: 19.96
  v3b1: (A); (B), p.48
  v3b2: (A); (B), p.48

v3c: (A); (D), p.328; (E), p.726—1962: 0.65, 1978: 3.28

v3d: (E), p.748
  v3d1: (E), p.748
  v3d2: (E), p.748

v3e: (E), p.750
  v3e1: (E), p.750
  v3e2: (A)
  v3e3: (A)

v3e4: (A) (including v3e3 (housing) in 1988 and before)

v3f: (A); (E), p.750
v3f1: (A); (E), p.750
v3f2: (A)
v3f3: (A)
v3f4: (A)

4. Public Finance and Banking (FB)

v4a:
v4a1: (E), p.746
v4a1a: (E), p.746
v4a1b: (B), p.374
v4a1c: (B), p.374
v4a1d: (B), p.374—basic depreciation allowances surrendered by enterprises, and other revenues
v4a2: (E), p.746
v4a2a: (E), p.746
v4a2b: (E), p.746
v4a2c: (E), p.746
v4a2d: v4a2 – v4a2a – v4a2b – v4a2c

v4b: (A)
v4b1: (A); (B), p.394
v4b2: (A); (B), p.394—peasants' savings balance
v4b3: NA

v4c:
v4c1: (E), p.736
v4c2: (E), p.736

5. Labor Force (L)

v5a: (E), p.722
v5a1: (E), p.722
v5a2: (E), p.722—including staff and workers in towns' and cities' collective-owned units and other ownership units and self-employed workers in cities and towns
v5a3: (B), p.97
v5a4: (E), p.722

v5b:
v5b1: (E), p.722
v5b2: (E), p.722
v5b3: (E), p.722

v5c: NA
v5c1: NA

v5d: NA

6. Population (PO)

v6a: (E), p.721—data from public security department
v6a1: (E), p.721—(ditto)
v6a2: (E), p.721—(ditto)

v6b: (A); (E), p.721—(ditto)

v6c: (A); (E), p.721—(ditto)

v6d:
v6d1: (E), p.721—(ditto)
v6d2: (E), p.721—(ditto)
v6d3: (E), p.721—(ditto)
v6d4: (E), p.721—(ditto)
v6d5: (A)—Lupanshui
v6d6: (A)—Guiyang

7. Agriculture (A)

v7a: (E), p.734

v7b: (A); (E), p.734

v7c: (A); (E), p.734

v7d: (A); (E), p.734

v7e: (A)—10,000 hectares

v7f: (A); (E), p.734

v7g: (A); (E), p.734

v7h: (E), p.729
- v7h1: (E), p.729
- v7h2: (E), p.729
- v7h3: (E), p.729
- v7h4: (E), p.729
- v7h5: (E), p.729

v7i: (E), p.733—farm cattle

8. Industry (IN)

v8a: (E), p.727
- v8a1: (E), p.735
- v8a2: (A); (E), p.735
- v8a3: v8a – v8a1 – v8a2

v8b: (E), p.736

- v8c1: (E), p.727
- v8c2: (E), p.727

v8d: (E), p.736

v8f:
- v8f1: (E), p.738
- v8f2: (E), p.738
- v8f3: NA
- v8f4: (E), p.738
- v8f5: (E), p.738

v8g: (A)
- v8g1: (E), p.736

9. Transport (TR)

v9a: (E), p.739—excluding urban traffic volume
- v9a1: (E), p.739—including central and local railways
- v9a2: (E), p.739
- v9a3: (E), p.739—excluding distant ocean and coastal passenger traffic, including wooden junk transport; 1986–88's figures are of the society

v9b: (E), p.739
- v9b1: (E), p.739—including central and local railways
- v9b2: (E), p.739—1986–88's freight volume is of the society
- v9b3: (E), p.739—excluding distant ocean and coastal freight volume, including wooden junk transport; 1986–88's figures are of the society

v9c: (E), p.739—based on 1980's constant price

10. Domestic Trade (DT)

v10a: (E), p.742
- v10a1: (E), p.742

v10b:
- v10b1: (E), p.742
- v10b2: NA
- v10b3: (E), p.742—including supply and marketing cooperative and other collectives
- v10b4: (B), p.319; (E), p.742
- v10b5: (E), p.742
- v10b6: (E), p.742

v10d: (E), p.744—calculated on calendar year basis

11. Foreign Trade (FT)

v11a:
- v11a1: (B), p.363—farming products
- v11a2: (B), p.363—textile and other products of light industry
- v11a3: (B), p.363—heavy industrial products

v11b: (E), p.745
- v11b1: (E), p.745
- v11b2: v11b – v11b1

v11c: (E), p.745

v11d: (E), p.745

12. Prices (PR)

v12a: (E), p.747

v12b: (E), p.747

v12c: (E), p.747

13. Education (ED)

v13a: NA

v13b: (A); (E), p.750

v13c:
- v13c1: (A); (E), p.750—general institutions of higher learning
- v13c2: (A); (E), p.750—general technical secondary and ordinary secondary schools
- v13c3: (A); (E), p.750

v13d: (A)—general institutions of higher learning

14. Social Factors (SF)

v14a: (E), p.750

v14b: (E), p.750

v14c: (B), p.466-467

15. Natural Environment (NE)

v15a: (A); (E), p.734

v15b: (A).

v15c: (A)

v15d: (A)

v15e: (A)

v15f: (A)

Sources of Data

(A) Data supplied by the DSNEB, SSB, the PRC.
(B) Statistical Bureau of Guizhou Province ed. *Guizhou Striving and Advancing Forty Years 1949–1989*, Beijing: CSPH, 1989.
(D) Same as (D) in Beijing's sources of data.
(E) Same as (E) in Beijing's sources of data.

24

Yunnan

24. Yunnan

24–1

Year	v1a	v1a1	v1a2	v1a3	v1a4	v1a5	v1b	v1b1	v1b2	v1b3	v1b4	v1b5	v1c	v1d	v1d1
1949	11.99	8.30	1.95	0.05	0.33	1.36							3.97	8.02	6.24
1950	13.07	8.52	2.34	0.07	0.41	1.73							4.51	8.56	6.41
1951	14.65	8.95	3.01	0.20	0.53	1.96							5.18	9.47	6.73
1952	16.83	9.60	3.81	0.54	0.62	2.26	114.3	107.3	126.6	270.0	117.0	115.3	6.25	10.58	7.22
1953	22.47	11.71	6.03	1.39	0.80	2.54	128.0	114.5	158.0	257.4	129.0	112.4	9.13	13.34	8.81
1954	26.23	13.09	7.60	1.72	1.04	2.78	116.5	113.2	123.1	123.7	130.0	109.4	10.94	15.29	9.84
1955	28.37	13.80	8.66	1.83	1.18	2.90	109.0	108.0	112.7	106.4	113.5	104.3	11.90	16.47	10.36
1956	32.56	15.33	9.64	2.71	1.31	3.57	117.8	110.6	123.3	148.1	111.0	123.1	13.41	19.15	11.51
1957	35.70	16.56	11.19	2.88	1.50	3.57	104.1	98.1	113.7	106.3	114.5	100.0	15.47	20.23	12.37
1958	45.13	13.67	17.64	7.05	2.77	4.00	131.1	87.5	165.3	244.8	184.7	112.0	24.29	20.84	9.48
1959	54.69	13.25	24.45	9.21	3.62	4.16	122.5	94.0	144.4	130.6	130.7	104.0	31.84	22.85	8.90
1960	58.97	13.33	27.77	10.32	3.70	3.85	103.1	96.0	105.4	112.1	102.2	92.5	36.04	22.93	8.73
1961	40.11	15.21	15.70	3.64	2.48	3.08	64.9	103.9	45.4	35.3	67.0	80.0	19.55	20.56	11.06
1962	40.06	18.83	14.46	1.83	2.06	2.88	91.6	110.6	85.5	50.3	83.1	93.5	18.06	22.00	13.53
1963	42.10	20.03	14.74	2.45	2.03	2.85	104.7	105.3	102.3	133.9	98.5	99.0	19.08	23.02	13.90
1964	48.24	22.52	16.36	4.13	2.29	2.94	115.5	113.0	111.6	168.6	112.8	103.2	21.97	26.27	16.05
1965	59.27	22.83	20.31	10.39	2.74	3.00	125.9	101.2	126.4	251.6	119.7	102.0	29.08	30.19	17.17
1966	66.73	24.04	23.46	12.89	3.00	3.34	115.5	105.3	121.9	124.1	109.5	111.3	34.05	32.68	18.22
1967	61.42	24.25	21.59	10.08	1.94	3.56	89.5	100.9	87.1	78.2	64.7	106.6	30.73	30.69	18.34
1968	40.40	23.17	7.04	6.07	0.88	3.24	63.8	95.5	32.7	60.2	45.4	91.0	16.59	23.81	17.24
1969	64.18	24.64	24.01	9.60	2.41	3.52	163.9	106.4	339.7	158.2	273.9	108.6	33.34	30.84	18.48
1970	74.43	24.89	30.82	11.93	3.02	3.77	120.6	99.3	139.0	124.3	125.3	107.1	39.84	34.59	18.72
1971	80.63	28.81	32.75	11.83	3.12	4.12	104.8	106.4	105.5	99.2	103.3	109.3	41.59	39.04	21.81
1972	89.88	32.81	36.94	12.06	3.46	4.61	110.6	111.4	112.8	101.9	110.9	111.9	45.43	44.45	24.64
1973	98.41	35.55	41.33	12.65	3.85	5.03	109.5	108.1	111.9	104.9	111.3	109.1	49.41	49.00	27.01
1974	96.41	32.91	41.59	12.55	3.93	5.43	99.0	95.1	100.6	99.2	102.1	108.0	49.91	46.50	24.09
1975	101.06	35.40	42.33	13.61	4.16	5.56	105.0	108.4	101.7	108.4	105.9	102.4	52.31	48.75	26.12
1976	88.63	33.92	32.60	12.61	3.49	6.01	87.5	104.2	77.0	92.7	83.9	108.1	44.39	44.24	25.49
1977	103.98	33.47	46.22	12.74	4.62	6.93	117.5	98.3	141.9	101.0	132.4	115.3	53.84	50.14	24.16
1978	126.66	40.02	55.43	17.69	5.63	7.89	121.2	112.4	123.5	138.9	121.9	113.9	64.65	62.01	29.22
1979	140.63	44.71	62.38	18.36	5.75	9.43	104.0	94.4	108.2	103.8	102.1	119.5	71.64	68.99	32.11
1980	150.23	48.20	65.35	20.52	6.32	9.84	105.3	106.8	102.4	111.8	109.9	104.3	75.31	74.92	35.60
1981	164.19	55.20	72.54	18.20	6.17	12.08	105.8	108.9	107.7	88.7	97.6	122.8	80.70	83.49	40.89
1982	187.19	61.48	83.60	20.00	7.15	14.60	112.1	110.7	112.1	109.9	115.9	120.9	89.80	97.39	46.65
1983	205.73	65.68	95.11	19.96	8.16	16.82	109.1	105.5	112.4	99.8	114.1	115.2	99.58	106.15	48.93
1984	243.83	77.36	112.27	26.03	9.23	18.94	116.6	115.2	115.5	130.4	113.1	112.6	121.19	122.64	56.86
1985	289.26	88.88	136.26	33.49	10.43	20.20	113.3	106.4	115.5	128.7	113.0	106.7	145.28	143.98	65.34
1986	312.30	96.01	147.02	35.91	11.48	21.88	105.1	97.6	108.4	107.2	110.1	108.3	156.87	155.43	70.56
1987	369.55	111.25	181.85	39.28	12.53	24.64	112.1	106.1	116.7	109.4	109.1	112.6	185.38	184.17	82.16
1988	473.32	135.39	244.63	48.32	12.91	32.07	116.0	106.6	118.0	123.0	103.0	130.2	233.38	239.94	101.03
1989	555.38	152.68	304.91	48.88	14.92	33.99	105.3	102.9	106.8	101.2	115.6	106.0	274.16	281.22	113.92

24. Yunnan

24–2

Year	v1d2	v1d3	v1d4	v1d5	v1e	v1e1	v1e2	v1e3	v1e4	v1e5	v1f	v1f1	v1f2	v1f3	v1g
1949	0.64	0.02	0.18	0.94											6.87
1950	0.77	0.03	0.22	1.13											7.80
1951	1.00	0.08	0.29	1.37											8.87
1952	1.26	0.20	0.34	1.56	111.4	107.3	126.3	250.0	117.2	113.9					10.47
1953	2.00	0.42	0.43	1.68	120.4	114.7	158.3	210.0	126.5	107.7					13.25
1954	2.46	0.59	0.53	1.87	115.1	113.1	120.5	140.5	123.3	111.3					15.93
1955	2.98	0.59	0.59	1.95	109.0	107.9	119.7	100.0	111.3	104.3					16.51
1956	3.60	0.86	0.64	2.54	117.7	110.7	133.9	145.8	108.5	130.3					20.42
1957	3.89	0.85	0.64	2.48	99.2	97.5	105.7	98.8	100.0	97.6					20.90
1958	5.45	1.82	1.24	2.85	107.1	81.2	146.5	214.1	193.8	114.9					25.04
1959	6.88	2.34	1.67	3.06	109.5	91.0	131.4	128.6	134.7	107.4					27.76
1960	7.39	2.32	1.71	2.78	96.5	93.7	100.0	99.1	102.4	90.8					29.14
1961	5.56	1.02	0.73	2.19	84.5	115.2	73.7	44.0	42.7	78.8					21.52
1962	5.27	0.54	0.58	2.08	97.7	109.4	88.4	52.9	79.5	95.0					20.76
1963	5.54	0.79	0.66	2.13	104.3	101.7	105.3	146.3	113.8	102.4					23.41
1964	6.24	1.06	0.73	2.19	114.5	116.1	113.2	134.2	110.6	102.8					27.73
1965	6.94	3.03	0.78	2.27	116.6	106.8	113.4	285.8	106.8	103.7					33.89
1966	7.32	3.74	0.88	2.52	109.9	106.1	110.9	123.4	112.8	111.0					37.93
1967	6.23	2.90	0.54	2.68	92.0	100.7	80.9	77.5	61.4	106.3					35.09
1968	2.20	1.74	0.23	2.40	75.8	94.0	35.6	60.0	42.6	89.6					34.26
1969	6.23	2.74	0.70	2.69	132.5	107.2	280.6	157.5	304.3	112.1					41.31
1970	8.81	3.38	0.80	2.88	114.8	99.7	152.0	123.4	114.3	107.1					45.17
1971	9.90	3.33	0.89	3.11	107.3	105.7	112.6	98.5	111.3	108.0					46.62
1972	12.00	3.36	0.98	3.47	112.6	110.6	121.2	100.9	110.1	111.6					49.81
1973	13.69	3.47	1.07	3.76	110.2	109.3	114.2	103.3	109.2	108.4					55.22
1974	13.70	3.67	1.12	3.92	96.4	91.6	100.1	105.8	104.7	104.3					56.25
1975	13.53	3.91	1.15	4.04	105.2	109.3	98.7	106.5	102.7	103.1					60.12
1976	9.82	3.62	1.04	4.27	90.5	97.6	72.3	92.6	90.4	105.7					55.30
1977	15.84	3.86	1.26	5.02	113.6	94.4	161.9	106.6	121.2	117.6					63.11
1978	20.38	5.03	1.71	5.67	121.5	113.7	132.4	130.3	135.7	112.9	69.05	29.46	27.58	12.01	74.70
1979	23.04	5.04	1.95	6.85	102.3	92.9	108.9	100.2	114.0	120.8	76.83	32.38	30.50	13.95	86.28
1980	25.03	5.40	2.01	6.88	107.4	109.8	107.1	107.1	103.1	100.4	84.27	35.89	33.98	14.40	89.76
1981	26.83	5.05	1.97	8.75	107.1	109.2	103.0	93.5	98.0	127.2	94.13	41.23	35.80	17.10	92.66
1982	32.14	5.73	2.23	10.64	115.0	112.7	116.6	113.5	113.2	121.6	110.12	47.04	42.39	20.69	115.01
1983	36.85	5.64	2.53	12.20	108.3	104.2	113.3	98.4	113.5	114.7	120.07	49.33	47.28	23.46	125.42
1984	42.19	7.19	2.89	13.51	113.5	113.7	112.0	127.5	114.2	110.7	139.58	57.33	54.38	27.87	145.34
1985	51.25	8.86	3.28	15.25	111.5	106.4	115.6	123.2	113.5	112.9	164.96	66.07	65.41	33.48	169.83
1986	55.84	9.47	3.69	15.87	103.5	97.6	109.5	106.9	112.5	104.1	178.46	71.32	70.83	36.31	182.81
1987	69.28	10.15	4.24	18.34	111.7	106.6	117.0	107.2	114.9	115.6	212.05	84.06	84.30	43.69	200.05
1988	97.49	12.72	4.52	24.18	117.8	107.7	123.4	125.3	106.6	131.8	268.31	103.47	112.40	52.34	247.79
1989	124.01	12.89	5.25	25.15	105.7	102.9	109.0	101.3	116.2	104.0	315.45	119.01	138.06	58.17	298.80

24. Yunnan

24–3

Year	v1h	v1i	v1j	v1j1	v1j2	v1j3	v1k	v2a	v2a1	v2a2	v2b	v2c	v2c1	v2c2	v2d1
1949								0.67							1.10
1950								0.87				0.07			1.11
1951								1.11				0.23			1.18
1952				371				1.43	0.81	0.62		0.59			1.25
1953				413				2.74	1.54	1.20		1.49			1.78
1954				448				4.20	1.73	2.47		1.77			2.21
1955				481				3.52	1.84	1.68		1.61			2.55
1956				523				5.03	2.73	2.30		2.68			3.76
1957	66			517				4.94	2.79	2.15		2.90			4.55
1958				375				8.28	7.79	0.49		7.50			7.41
1959				407				12.48	9.85	2.63		10.34			10.66
1960				428				13.43	11.32	2.11		10.82			14.77
1961				452				4.19	3.89	0.30		3.87			15.97
1962	92			492				1.99	1.60	0.39		1.85			16.51
1963				528				3.74	2.54	1.20		2.64			17.76
1964				546				6.59	4.87	1.72		4.26			17.97
1965	101			544				10.71	8.59	2.12		8.80			19.65
1966				493				13.21	10.96	2.25		11.42			23.38
1967				494				8.51	6.64	1.87		8.63			25.51
1968				493				8.13	6.77	1.36		4.25			26.01
1969				524				13.16	9.78	3.38		7.68			28.16
1970				527				16.15	12.63	3.52		10.31			33.12
1971				517				16.10	12.12	3.98		10.31			37.98
1972				548				15.87	12.75	3.12		10.29			42.66
1973				561				18.93	13.83	5.10		10.69			45.98
1974				575				16.72	13.61	3.11		10.76			51.03
1975	110			571				19.25	14.80	4.45		11.09			56.66
1976	119			572				12.75	12.02	0.73		10.02			59.45
1977	118			574				18.63	15.82	2.81		9.72			65.56
1978	131	12.68	608	623	496			25.82	19.73	6.09	15.11	13.50	7.25	0.54	72.61
1979	125	14.26	668	679	529		105.8	29.50	26.66	2.84		14.58	6.68	0.56	80.08
1980	148	17.16	760	782	604		105.6	29.11	27.59	1.52	21.05	16.10	5.63	1.00	86.23
1981	178	17.97	780	800	639		105.0	27.20	25.05	2.15		13.99	4.22	0.80	90.65
1982	232	19.05	806	825	676		104.0	34.33	27.85	6.48	24.38	20.25	6.16	1.15	98.37
1983	267	20.28	840	857	719		105.7	36.20	31.51	4.69	22.86	20.23	5.55	0.81	105.03
1984	310	25.43	1014	1049	823		111.6	45.99	40.25	5.74	33.17	24.13	7.25	0.64	109.68
1985	326	30.13	1171	1207	970		105.3	54.38	48.02	6.36	48.36	33.72	9.37	1.40	127.98
1986	338	34.08	1300	1334	1104		108.6	58.19	51.16	7.03	58.53	35.45	8.81	0.94	138.87
1987	365	38.68	1439	1483	1188		100.2	62.56	54.23	8.33	56.47	38.18	9.29	0.78	152.14
1988	428	47.09	1715	1769	1405		97.7	80.19	66.40	13.79	69.88	47.73	9.90	0.56	175.41
1989	478	52.63	1880	1936	1558		94.1	95.04	66.69	28.35	70.47	40.74	11.05	0.49	197.01

24. Yunnan

24–4

Year	v2d2	v2e	v3a	v3b	v3b1	v3b2	v3c	v3d	v3d1	v3d2	v3e	v3e1	v3e2	v3e3	v3e4
1949	0.69	0.48	6.20	5.91			0.29	36	33	68					
1950	0.69	0.49	6.93	6.64			0.29	40	36	84	117				
1951	0.74	0.52	7.76	7.46			0.30	45	40	91	124				
1952	0.79	0.58	9.04	8.65	6.87	1.78	0.39	51	45	109	126				
1953	1.28	0.77	10.51	10.02	8.08	1.94	0.49	58	52	119	130				
1954	1.61	0.99	11.73	11.26	9.02	2.24	0.47	64	57	129	155				
1955	1.84	1.16	12.99	12.52	9.84	2.68	0.47	69	61	139	174				
1956	2.75	1.36	15.39	14.72	10.94	3.78	0.67	76	67	158	190				
1957	3.50	1.65	15.96	15.00	11.02	3.98	0.96	76	66	162	190				
1958	5.78	3.63	16.76	15.53	10.04	5.49	1.23	72	60	155	226				
1959	8.42	5.31	15.28	13.66	9.01	4.65	1.62	71	55	166	232				
1960	11.82	5.31	15.71	13.94	8.67	5.27	1.77	70	53	171	238				
1961	12.85	3.66	17.33	15.70	10.13	5.57	1.63	75	61	176	261				
1962	13.37	3.27	18.77	17.37	12.54	4.83	1.40	84	73	177	254				
1963	14.01	3.12	19.67	18.26	13.37	4.89	1.41	87	75	188	247				
1964	14.39	2.88	21.14	19.71	13.95	5.76	1.43	89	76	194	237				
1965	15.20	3.21	23.18	21.73	15.27	6.46	1.45	94	81	195	241				
1966	18.10	4.37	24.72	23.12	16.24	6.88	1.60	98	84	199	234				
1967	19.74	5.14	26.58	24.88	17.90	6.98	1.70	104	90	210	228				
1968	20.13	5.44	26.13	24.72	17.65	7.07	1.41	100	86	209	261				
1969	21.80	5.74	28.15	26.59	19.09	7.50	1.56	105	90	222	263				
1970	25.63	7.66	29.02	27.29	20.63	6.66	1.73	109	94	230	266				
1971	29.40	8.56	30.52	28.61	21.57	7.04	1.91	110	95	235	269				
1972	32.91	10.09	33.94	31.83	22.16	9.67	2.11	114	95	260	272				
1973	35.03	11.42	36.29	33.97	24.22	9.75	2.32	121	101	279	276				
1974	38.57	13.20	39.53	36.60	26.66	9.94	2.93	129	108	296	278				
1975	42.60	14.46	40.87	37.77	27.57	10.20	3.10	130	109	299	283				
1976	44.47	14.66	42.55	39.19	28.75	10.44	3.36	132	111	302	284				
1977	48.78	15.17	44.48	40.69	29.98	10.71	3.79	134	113	304	284				
1978	53.69	15.86	48.88	45.07	31.73	13.34	3.81	141	117	334	303	191			
1979	59.11	17.42	56.78	52.72	36.09	16.63	4.06	158	131	369	343	215			
1980	63.39	17.99	60.65	56.61	38.73	17.88	4.04	173	139	427	381	237			
1981	65.69	17.59	65.46	61.13	42.18	18.95	4.33	185	150	453	412	247			
1982	70.76	18.44	80.68	75.53	55.00	20.53	5.15	226	192	483	456	273			
1983	74.86	19.65	89.22	83.46	61.57	21.89	5.76	247	212	502	480	286			
1984	77.12	21.28	99.35	92.52	66.93	25.59	6.83	269	228	568	527	311			
1985	91.50	26.26	115.45	107.20	75.68	31.52	8.25	307	255	679	704	360			
1986	129.13	32.78	124.62	114.28	78.81	35.47	10.34	323	263	745	814	424			
1987	107.94	37.50	137.49	125.49	85.41	40.08	12.00	347	281	807	884	482			
1988	123.33	46.99	167.60	152.33	105.04	47.29	15.27	417	341	935	1143	554			
1989	138.77	64.18	203.76	185.41	129.57	55.84	18.35	501	413	1089	1141	621	119.85	7.60	9.38

24. Yunnan

Year	v3f	v3f1	v3f2	v3f3	v3f4	v4a1	v4a1a	v4a1b	v4a1c	v4a1d	v4a2	v4a2a	v4a2b	v4a2c	v4a2d
1949															
1950						0.70	0.07				0.16		0.02	0.14	
1951						1.51	0.01				0.38	0.03	0.04	0.29	0.02
1952						1.87	0.27			0.25	0.90	0.23	0.13	0.34	0.20
1953						2.02	0.13				1.31	0.29	0.32	0.51	0.19
1954						2.27	0.16				1.55	0.51	0.33	0.49	0.22
1955						2.36	0.18			0.18	1.50	0.42	0.33	0.55	0.20
1956						2.61	0.26			0.11	2.37	0.76	0.43	0.74	0.44
1957	63	42	8.56	1.44	5.90	2.92	0.34			0.13	2.28	0.71	0.53	0.68	0.36
1958						6.35	2.57			0.58	8.51	6.28	0.64	0.68	0.91
1959						8.51	4.39			0.47	9.32	6.08	0.58	0.78	1.88
1960						9.55	4.90			0.68	11.04	6.13	0.83	0.79	3.29
1961						5.66	1.91			0.66	4.54	0.98	0.69	0.70	2.17
1962	84	55	6.82	3.63	9.21	4.69	0.98			0.38	2.32	0.36	0.66	0.57	0.73
1963						4.69	1.15			0.28	3.40	0.65	0.66	0.71	1.38
1964						5.16	1.18			0.29	4.28	1.58	0.78	0.81	1.11
1965	91	64	10.94	1.84	6.93	5.03	1.13			0.40	5.67	2.59	0.86	0.84	1.38
1966						5.44	1.27			0.41	6.43	2.93	1.06	0.89	1.55
1967						4.51	1.09			0.03	5.11	2.31	0.97	0.74	1.09
1968						1.53	-1.00			0.02	3.62	1.32	0.83	0.74	0.73
1969						4.19	0.39			0.07	6.26	3.17	0.90	1.00	1.19
1970						7.93	3.01			0.07	10.57	6.42	1.00	0.96	2.19
1971						8.44	3.10			0.09	10.08	4.91	1.28	1.12	2.77
1972						8.63	2.76			0.07	11.06	5.73	1.49	1.17	2.67
1973						9.20	2.59			0.05	11.85	5.17	1.71	1.16	3.81
1974						8.77	1.68			0.04	12.35	5.07	1.92	1.26	4.10
1975	105	72	12.03	4.77	9.08	8.59	1.14			0.04	12.05	4.57	2.01	1.27	4.20
1976	106	78	9.92	4.16	8.35	5.08	-1.41			0.06	11.65	4.07	2.12	1.20	4.26
1977	105	76	10.99	3.57	7.89	7.72	-0.63			0.06	13.25	4.88	2.26	1.37	4.74
1978	113	84	11.06	2.56	8.83	11.76	1.84			0.69	18.28	7.23	2.73	1.61	6.71
1979	112	81	10.70	4.29	8.04	11.41	1.45			0.43	21.35	6.61	3.17	1.82	9.75
1980	123	86	12.01	6.50	8.40	11.64	1.32			0.52	17.32	4.56	3.79	2.05	6.92
1981	138	92	15.90	9.04	7.71	12.69	0.01			0.43	15.73	2.52	4.30	2.21	6.70
1982	186	124	19.81	14.22	8.89	15.66	0.89			0.57	18.80	3.30	5.14	2.47	7.89
1983	224	145	21.19	17.49	11.27	17.17	1.19			0.73	24.23	4.52	6.55	2.98	10.18
1984	261	160	27.03	30.52	12.60	19.73	0.28			0.65	30.77	5.06	8.15	4.54	13.02
1985	267	178	23.53	22.97	15.84	27.41	0.46			0.27	36.70	6.12	9.38	4.92	16.28
1986	305	205	22.60	30.45	17.25	30.01	0.36			0.40	47.31	6.74	11.29	5.75	23.53
1987	326	217	26.02	29.29	14.29	37.49	0.25			0.52	53.86	7.16	12.59	6.29	27.82
1988	389	240	30.45	47.35	14.95	50.53	0.77				64.84	7.41	15.56	6.45	35.42
1989	436	269	32.38	51.51	17.43	63.27	-1.48				81.89	7.44	18.15	7.50	48.80

24. Yunnan

24–6

Year	v4b	v4b1	v4b2	v4b3	v4c1	v4c2	v5a	v5a1	v5a2	v5a3	v5a4	v5b1	v5b2	v5b3	v5c
1949					0.36	30.8									
1950					0.40	34.0	719.83	14.28			702.28				
1951					0.59	47.0									
1952	0.2045	0.2045			0.79	57.7	760.94	24.60	0.92	3.61	731.81	708.90	25.50	26.50	
1953					1.25	61.1									
1954					1.43	54.9									
1955					1.75	58.1									
1956					2.09	50.8									
1957	0.7665	0.5883	0.1782		2.53	49.2	910.24	64.30	4.63	6.85	834.46	827.30	39.60	43.30	
1958					3.26	34.6									
1959					3.29	24.0									
1960					3.38	19.7									
1961					1.70	10.3									
1962	1.3115	0.8612	0.4503		1.67	10.0	879.71	77.64	13.28	1.69	787.10	791.20	43.00	45.50	
1963					2.34	13.7									
1964					2.96	17.1		92.40			811.55				
1965	1.7963	1.4065	0.3898		3.27	17.8	1021.10	104.33	15.19	1.61	899.97	905.50	55.70	59.90	
1966					3.95	17.6		116.21			909.50				
1967					2.15	8.7		117.52							
1968					-0.53	-2.1		119.92							
1969					0.71	2.6		124.17			981.60				
1970	2.7129	1.8469	0.8660		3.72	11.2	1151.90	138.99	17.25	0.97	994.69	1006.00	88.60	57.30	
1971	2.8342	1.9720	0.8662		5.32	14.0		158.59			1004.48				
1972	2.8173	2.1677	0.6496		5.81	13.5		163.81			1004.79				
1973	3.0421	2.3012	0.7409		6.15	13.2		160.50			1028.97				
1974	3.3394	2.5490	0.7904		5.56	10.7		161.83			1038.01				
1975	3.5673	2.6821	0.8852		5.10	8.9	1234.61	165.95	20.21	0.27	1048.18	1067.80	93.50	73.30	
1976	3.6192	2.7601	0.8591		2.52	4.3	1254.97	169.43	20.36	0.31	1064.87	1083.70	96.40	74.90	
1977	3.8287	2.9515	0.8772		5.19	8.1	1271.60	172.91	26.60	0.22	1071.87	1095.40	99.20	77.00	
1978	4.2001	3.2353	0.9649		8.06	11.6	1313.39	180.80	25.38	0.24	1097.11	1130.90	100.70	81.80	
1979	4.9010	3.9070	0.9940		10.72	14.0	1342.65	194.61	26.80	0.25	1120.99	1143.40	109.20	90.10	
1980	6.7803	5.4305	1.3498		11.58	14.2	1404.03	200.67	29.15	0.83	1173.38	1194.00	113.10	96.90	
1981	9.2275	7.2166	2.0109		13.16	15.8	1479.56	205.41	29.75	1.79	1242.61	1246.10	123.90	109.60	
1982	12.3642	9.4467	2.9175		15.72	17.6	1543.37	211.65	30.46	2.51	1298.75	1295.10	129.10	119.20	
1983	16.1704	12.3525	3.8179		17.96	19.0	1582.90	215.48	31.57	4.49	1331.36	1315.40	133.10	134.40	
1984	22.2396	17.0728	5.1668		21.57	21.9	1620.25	216.52	39.80	8.28	1355.33	1322.70	144.30	153.30	
1985	29.8259	23.1158	6.7101		27.78	23.6	1672.34	222.41	40.16	11.66	1397.68	1329.20	172.00	171.10	
1986	39.7639	31.0863	8.6776		30.70	23.4	1731.42	227.78	40.38	11.96	1450.80	1365.40	177.40	188.60	
1987	55.4604	43.1172	12.3432		38.38	26.4	1777.50	232.91	41.18	11.86	1490.90	1411.10	182.90	183.50	132.6
1988	63.7325				56.49	33.2	1826.86	237.65	41.68	13.50	1533.27	1454.40	183.30	189.20	
1989	86.2000	68.5000	17.7000		71.83	35.4	1880.67	242.83	42.16	13.46	1581.40	1503.20	183.90	193.60	

24. Yunnan

24–7

Year	v5c1	v5d	v6a	v6a1	v6a2	v6b	v6c	v6d1	v6d2	v6d3	v6d4	v6d5	v6d6
1949			1595									49.16	
1950			1627	79	1548	31.35	17.86						
1951			1660	81	1579	32.86	16.73						
1952			1695	82	1613	33.69	16.16					61.35	
1953			1731	84	1647	35.26	15.60	194	1537	851	879		
1954			1768	194	1574	37.91	16.72	157	1611	871	897		
1955			1806	202	1604	32.41	13.73	187	1619	897	909		
1956			1842	218	1624	34.75	15.21	188	1654	914	928		
1957			1897	237	1660	36.27	16.29	180	1717	942	955	84.54	
1958			1914	349	1565	23.61	21.62	267	1647	960	954	95.05	
1959			1912	348	1564	20.93	17.95	257	1655	952	960		
1960			1895	305	1589	24.19	26.26	279	1616	938	957		
1961			1900	280	1620	19.40	11.84	196	1704	934	966	84.81	
1962			1964	275	1689	39.71	10.85	187	1777	966	998	84.65	
1963			2021	247	1774	43.15	14.14	196	1825	998	1023	86.57	
1964			2088	296	1792	45.66	15.23	206	1882	1040	1048	89.40	
1965			2160	261	1899	44.01	12.97	235	1925	1075	1085	93.77	
1966			2232	274	1958	38.97	10.80	251	1981	1114	1118		
1967			2287	276	2011	35.87	10.00	249	2038	1138	1149		
1968			2362	275	2087	38.70	9.27	254	2108	1182	1180		
1969			2423	271	2152	28.83	8.15	244	2179	1213	1210		
1970			2503	271	2232	28.53	8.15	247	2256	1246	1257	98.36	
1971			2593	298	2295	38.11	8.02	261	2332	1292	1301		
1972			2663	312	2351	36.68	8.65	281	2382	1327	1336		
1973			2747	324	2423	36.38	8.60	285	2462	1370	1377		
1974			2819	326	2493	34.36	8.94	294	2525	1408	1411		
1975			2884	336	2548	31.72	8.68	298	2586	1442	1442	113.72	
1976			2952	343	2609	31.83	7.84	305	2647	1477	1475		
1977			3025	352	2673	31.01	7.65	312	2713	1515	1510		
1978			3091	376	2715	28.37	6.93	324	2767	1549	1542	131.50	
1979			3135	388	2747	24.08	8.13	337	2798	1569	1566		
1980			3173	395	2778	20.91	7.36	344	2829	1590	1583	137.37	
1981			3223	417	2806	25.36	8.60	350	2873	1622	1601		
1982			3283	433	2850	23.80	9.88	358	2925	1657	1626		
1983			3331	470	2849	23.57	9.19	366	2953	1677	1642		
1984			3372	697	2666	20.29	7.92	376	2986	1702	1660		
1985			3418	901	2505	21.55	8.03	395	3011	1728	1679	139.15	75.80
1986			3480	1000	2455	26.03	7.87	405	3050	1755	1701	141.99	77.51
1987	75.3	1411.1	3534	990	2523	23.97	8.40	419	3094	1787	1726	145.08	79.21
1988			3594	1422	2161	24.01	7.13	433	3149	1823	1759	148.06	80.39
1989			3648	1522	2120	23.07	8.05	443	3199	1858	1784	150.51	81.70

24. Yunnan

24–8

Year	v7a	v7b	v7c	v7d	v7e	v7f	v7g	v7h	v7h1	v7h2	v7h3	v7h4	v7h5	v7i	v8a
1949				4031.0				8.30	5.75		1.12		1.43		1.95
1950								8.52	5.90	0.01	1.18		1.43		2.34
1951								8.95	6.21	0.01	1.24		1.49		3.01
1952				4303.0				9.60	6.72	0.01	1.27		1.60		3.81
1953				4539.0				11.71	7.71	0.01	1.81		2.18		6.03
1954				4697.0				13.09	8.23	0.03	2.32		2.51		7.60
1955				4983.0				13.80	8.69	0.03	2.37		2.71		8.66
1956				5328.0				15.33	10.01	0.06	2.48		2.78	270.00	9.64
1957		2.31	667	5577.0		0.55	0.04	16.56	10.52	0.35	2.58		3.11	266.96	11.19
1958				5433.0				13.67	9.77	0.63	2.07	0.04	1.16	238.67	17.64
1959				5262.0				13.25	9.67	0.51	1.68	0.05	1.34		24.45
1960				5820.0				13.33	9.89	0.46	1.55	0.03	1.40		27.77
1961				5508.0				15.21	11.24	0.23	1.61	0.03	2.10		15.70
1962		69.14	1177	5280.0		4.17	0.18	18.83	12.99	0.30	2.81	0.04	2.69	198.40	14.46
1963		67.08		5339.0			0.34	20.03	13.12	0.46	3.53	0.04	2.88	215.02	14.74
1964		74.24	1229	5542.0			0.33	22.52	14.75	0.68	4.12	0.04	2.93	226.07	16.36
1965		114.65	1280	5592.0		18.50	0.47	22.83	14.63	0.73	4.57	0.05	2.85	239.63	20.31
1966				6706.0				24.04	15.72	0.75	4.49	0.05	3.03		23.46
1967				5680.0				24.25	15.93	0.75	4.49	0.05	3.03		21.59
1968				5442.0				23.17	14.83	0.76	4.52	0.05	3.01		7.04
1969				5423.0				24.64	16.26	0.77	4.53	0.05	3.03		24.01
1970		108.68		5664.0		42.95	2.04	24.89	18.32	0.77	4.65	0.05	1.10	255.45	30.82
1971	3.10	192.20	1145	5749.0		40.63	1.74	28.81	22.30	0.92	3.89	0.03	1.67	257.05	32.75
1972	5.19	201.37	1202	5806.0		51.61	2.37	32.81	23.76	1.31	6.17	0.03	1.54	263.84	36.94
1973	9.03	234.03	1274	5802.0		66.11	2.84	35.55	25.70	1.46	6.75	0.04	1.60	270.13	41.33
1974	12.15	293.62	1285	5766.0		78.13	3.38	32.91	23.37	1.45	6.45	0.06	1.58	271.97	41.59
1975	15.42	347.27	1306	5841.0		75.48	3.98	35.40	25.81	1.73	6.16	0.07	1.63	277.39	42.33
1976	17.64	345.02	1326	5836.0		65.43	4.25	33.92	24.72	1.36	6.14	0.07	1.63	276.43	32.60
1977	20.86	368.56	1338	5946.0		71.71	5.12	33.47	23.60	1.84	6.26	0.07	1.71	278.82	46.22
1978	24.32	408.59	1353	6195.0		113.19	5.84	40.02	28.58	2.48	7.08	0.08	1.80	281.25	55.43
1979	29.23	400.37	1366	6183.0		110.37	6.01	44.71	31.03	3.17	8.27	0.09	2.15	284.82	62.38
1980	32.19	352.40	1370	6012.0		114.31	6.06	48.20	33.02	2.94	10.22	0.19	1.83	304.30	65.35
1981	32.81	290.60	1378	5959.2		110.00	6.37	55.20	38.32	3.77	10.74	0.20	2.17	333.09	72.54
1982	33.52	232.17	1386	5952.7	578.00	121.39	6.40	61.84	41.90	3.87	12.79	0.21	3.07	365.77	83.60
1983	36.86	246.14	1438	5949.5	791.00	147.47	6.64	65.68	42.30	4.73	13.84	0.24	4.57	396.86	95.11
1984	40.72	266.26	1442	5994.5	551.00	147.23	6.70	77.36	48.78	5.97	15.79	0.27	6.55	426.20	112.27
1985	43.93	246.05	1447	4532.0	570.00	155.87	7.54	88.88	52.02	7.90	20.33	0.40	8.23	445.61	136.26
1986	47.46	268.12	1450	6036.1	780.00	174.42	8.02	96.01	51.80	7.40	26.14	0.71	9.96	463.23	147.02
1987	51.27	415.48	1460	6116.0	870.00	176.60	8.69	111.25	61.75	8.85	29.42	0.95	10.28	477.12	181.85
1988	57.93	494.65	1484	6338.7	825.00	183.95	10.07	135.39	76.11	10.05	37.01	1.56	10.66	484.49	244.63
1989	61.15	556.60	1530	6540.3			11.61	152.68	84.30	12.97	41.68	1.93	11.80	492.94	304.91

24. Yunnan

24–9

Year	v8a1	v8a2	v8a3	v8b	v8c1	v8c2	v8d	v8f1	v8f2	v8f3	v8f4	v8f5	v8g
1949	1.95				0.70	1.25		0.04	24		0.51	0.5	
1950	0.12	1.12	1.10		0.84	1.50		0.04	23		0.43		1479
1951	0.80		2.21		1.17	1.84		0.12	23		0.44	0.4	1723
1952	1.40	0.02	2.39		1.51	2.30		0.25	28		0.52	0.8	2161
1953	2.22	0.06	3.75		2.09	3.94		0.35	41		0.75	1.3	2037
1954	3.06	0.32	4.22		2.83	4.77		0.49	80		0.93	1.6	4648
1955	3.98	0.42	4.26		3.41	5.25		0.72	109		1.35	3.0	3195
1956	4.62	1.43	3.59		4.48	5.16		1.46	142		1.85	3.7	3247
1957	5.67	2.28	3.24		4.83	6.36		1.70	192		2.41	4.0	3866
1958	13.17	4.47			9.67	7.97		5.08	715		4.09	17.7	4985
1959	20.09	4.36			14.67	9.78		15.38	970		6.68	31.8	7281
1960	24.07	3.70			18.19	9.58		24.51	903		10.41	36.8	5718
1961	12.96	2.74			9.39	6.31		11.02	580		10.11	17.1	5181
1962	11.83	2.63			8.07	6.39		3.42	401		8.93	11.1	4800
1963	11.92	2.83			8.64	6.10		5.06	403		9.76	18.5	4758
1964	13.47	2.87	0.02		9.72	6.64		5.56	418		11.00	28.5	4508
1965	16.74	3.57			11.33	8.98		7.52	536		13.88	41.1	4424
1966	19.80	3.67			14.36	9.10		10.90	640		18.24	46.9	4235
1967	18.22	3.37			12.24	9.35		7.24	593		17.03	44.2	4235
1968	5.94	1.10			3.99	3.05		0.42	240		6.03	12.5	4235
1969	20.27	3.74			14.41	9.60		8.84	678		21.21	41.7	3992
1970	24.97	5.85			20.59	10.23		12.21	893		27.66	62.4	6818
1971	26.52	6.23			19.98	12.77		16.72	1036		31.38	74.4	5129
1972	30.53	6.41			22.31	14.63		24.40	1094		36.10	80.4	5581
1973	34.13	7.20			24.72	16.61		31.21	1139		39.55	88.6	5828
1974	33.65	7.94			23.33	18.26		25.45	1176		41.45	91.1	6170
1975	33.73	8.60			23.70	18.63		25.27	1291		42.20	92.8	6364
1976	24.13	8.47			16.04	16.56		7.90	1123		34.25	73.8	6499
1977	36.33	9.89			24.54	21.68	10.71	22.44	1350		43.96	102.4	6596
1978	44.61	10.82			31.60	23.83	14.09	35.12	1483		52.51	131.2	7304
1979	50.79	11.59		48.97	36.12	26.26	17.03	41.19	1352		55.30	159.0	7572
1980	52.38	12.97		51.00	35.81	29.54	18.82	46.33	1174		56.20	163.0	7655
1981	58.48	13.63	0.43	57.38	37.36	35.18	19.87	41.40	1190		59.67	160.4	7288
1982	67.79	15.80	0.01	65.49	42.30	41.30	24.08	44.56	1334		62.03	194.2	7352
1983	76.87	16.44	1.80	73.28	47.75	47.36	27.26	48.41	1410		61.64	227.0	7310
1984	89.42	21.46	1.39	84.31	57.15	55.13	31.62	53.39	1536		70.27	264.4	11911
1985	106.25	27.12	2.89	100.72	70.33	65.93	38.37	56.16	1638		75.45	307.8	12021
1986	111.11	32.56	3.33	110.48	79.31	67.71	42.69	55.48	1700		84.52	340.7	12581
1987	135.28	40.61	5.96	135.71	96.32	85.52	52.99	61.96	1946		94.33	393.3	11825
1988	161.89	54.45	8.29	180.08	122.99	121.64	74.14	68.26	2054		102.26	443.1	7854
1989	217.83	74.27	12.86	225.87	150.30	154.61	95.20	72.22	2181		114.12	452.4	7918

24. Yunnan

24–10

Year	v8g1	v9a	v9a1	v9a2	v9a3	v9b	v9b1	v9b2	v9b3	v9c	v10a	v10a1	v10b1	v10b2	v10b3
1949							0.30			117					
1950		0.87	0.83	0.04		0.75	0.37	0.36	0.02	90	3.84	3.83	0.08		
1951		0.90	0.75	0.15		1.37	0.52	0.82	0.03	201	4.35	4.24			
1952		1.32	0.73	0.59		1.54	0.64	0.87	0.03	264	5.01	4.87	0.98		0.18
1953		2.03	1.39	0.69		2.55	1.23	1.28	0.04	430	6.37	6.18			
1954		2.53	1.47	1.06		3.49	1.56	1.90	0.03	544	7.26	6.98			
1955		3.24	1.48	1.76		4.26	1.86	2.36	0.04	655	7.96	7.67			
1956		4.62	1.76	2.86		4.94	1.95	2.92	0.07	835	9.58	9.12			
1957		4.65	1.92	2.72	0.01	6.36	2.66	3.57	0.13	839	10.19	9.79	3.60		5.38
1958		6.07	2.17	3.88	0.02	10.49	3.99	6.32	0.18	1119	12.57	10.79			
1959		5.61	2.35	3.25	0.01	15.74	6.50	8.94	0.30	1493	14.09	12.75			
1960		6.50	2.74	3.75	0.01	17.19	7.53	9.36	0.30	1884	14.82	12.80			
1961		6.15	3.22	2.92	0.01	11.52	5.83	5.57	0.12	1653	11.49	10.71			
1962		6.52	3.18	3.31	0.03	9.19	4.52	4.60	0.07	1484	11.93	11.38	6.43		4.53
1963		5.72	2.30	3.40	0.02	9.67	5.09	4.50	0.08	1868	12.62	11.95			
1964	912	6.87	2.48	4.36	0.03	12.26	6.61	5.50	0.15	2061	14.04	13.24			
1965	917	8.23	3.16	5.03	0.04	17.11	7.89	9.01	0.21	2463	16.69	15.46	9.16		7.03
1966		10.78	4.28	6.45	0.05	23.08	11.97	10.87	0.24	2245	18.28	16.51			
1967		9.25	5.79	3.44	0.02	16.54	9.91	6.46	0.17	2062	20.02	18.43			
1968		8.02	6.39	1.55	0.08	6.87	4.34	2.47	0.06	1543	17.09	15.73			
1969		13.93	7.68	6.19	0.06	20.83	12.49	8.24	0.10	2057	18.15	16.52			
1970		14.92	7.90	6.94	0.08	27.68	16.85	10.75	0.08	2298	19.56	17.46			
1971		15.56	8.39	7.07	0.10	33.49	22.89	10.41	0.19	2577	21.24	18.92			
1972		18.00	9.77	8.09	0.14	38.74	27.21	11.33	0.20	2784	23.93	21.07			
1973	1432	19.45	10.16	9.17	0.12	41.87	28.90	12.77	0.20	2727	26.25	22.84			
1974	1485	20.13	9.71	10.15	0.13	40.07	26.84	13.01	0.22	2745	28.14	24.20			
1975	1585	20.52	9.64	10.52	0.14	47.14	33.53	13.37	0.23	2801	29.66	25.61	18.12		10.64
1976	1585	19.47	8.54	10.57	0.14	33.01	20.77	12.01	0.22	2862	28.58	24.91	17.60		10.38
1977	1677	20.29	8.74	11.11	0.16	49.86	33.74	15.88	0.23	2818	30.90	26.85	18.92		11.20
1978	1743	24.25	9.92	13.89	0.12	62.34	43.52	18.57	0.24	3016	33.77	28.38	20.52		12.70
1979	1814	29.26	11.75	16.84	0.23	66.22	46.85	19.08	0.28	3541	38.67	32.60	23.45		14.19
1980	1825	33.74	12.86	20.30	0.26	68.76	50.59	17.84	0.32	3555	43.08	37.96	25.24		15.84
1981	1808	38.37	13.70	24.19	0.26	66.24	49.60	16.37	0.26	4550	46.82	42.04	26.10		17.89
1982	1846	42.28	13.84	27.84	0.24	68.59	49.97	18.23	0.39	4831	53.30	47.54	29.10		20.35
1983	1855	48.58	15.56	32.53	0.25	73.37	53.17	19.60	0.58	5209	62.10	55.19	32.94		22.28
1984	1861	53.56	12.73	40.20	0.28	68.79	45.56	22.62	0.57	5780	73.79	65.59	37.39		24.93
1985	2033	72.84	19.56	52.53	0.32	86.53	64.83	21.15	0.50	6675	93.20	84.45	39.65		34.01
1986	2001	81.56	19.84	57.56	0.52	92.93	69.72	22.67	0.48	7055	101.08	91.90	41.15		34.93
1987	2076	88.41	23.20	59.92	0.55	104.31	79.77	23.77	0.69	8000	113.35	102.55	48.82		39.08
1988	2065	93.46	23.91	64.81	0.57	109.63	82.78	26.02	0.75	9875	150.02	135.70	66.03		51.70
1989	2060	94.01	21.92	67.66	0.42	120.90	88.40	31.79	1.00	11012	159.88	142.16	69.06		53.81

24. Yunnan

Year	v10b4	v10b5	v10b6	v10d	v11a1	v11a2	v11a3	v11b	v11b1	v11b2	v11c	v11d	v12a	v12b	v12c
1949															
1950		3.53	0.23												
1951			0.26										107.7		100.2
1952		3.54	0.31	2.71				0.0005	0.0005				95.3		98.8
1953			0.28	3.45				0.0100	0.0100				103.4		115.8
1954			0.27	3.99				0.0057	0.0057				100.5		101.2
1955			0.41	4.29				0.0033	0.0033				99.8		97.2
1956			0.44	4.48				0.0003	0.0003				97.9		100.1
1957		0.58	0.63	4.90				0.0262	0.0262				101.3		107.1
1958			0.33	5.56				0.1892	0.1892				98.3		102.0
1959			0.56	7.27				0.4819	0.4819				99.6		102.1
1960			0.35	5.95				0.4244	0.4244				99.0		103.3
1961			0.91	4.49				0.3723	0.3723				111.6	117.1	104.6
1962			0.97	4.92				0.3089	0.3089				98.0	94.8	110.9
1963			0.65	5.26				0.2814	0.2814				94.2	89.5	105.6
1964			0.54	6.52				0.2451	0.2451				94.0	92.3	99.4
1965			0.50	7.33				0.2442	0.2442				99.3	100.1	101.3
1966			0.44	8.54				0.1896	0.1896						
1967			0.58	7.07				0.1713	0.1713						
1968			0.51	6.19				0.1303	0.1303						
1969			0.49	6.86				0.0194	0.0194						
1970			0.46	6.98				0.0181	0.0181						
1971			0.49	7.71				0.0347	0.0347						
1972			0.52	8.43				0.2740	0.2740				100.3		102.1
1973			0.60	9.48				0.3323	0.3323				100.1		100.2
1974			0.63	9.48				0.5704	0.5704				100.4		98.0
1975		0.02	0.88	10.79				0.5011	0.5011				100.0		99.3
1976		0.02	0.58	9.74				0.5429	0.5429				100.0		100.0
1977		0.02	0.76	10.19				0.5617	0.5617				100.0		100.3
1978		0.03	0.52	11.40				0.6948	0.6948				100.1	100.0	101.2
1979		0.03	1.00	11.10				0.8891	0.8891				100.7	100.8	116.8
1980		0.14	1.86	14.66				1.1037	0.9601	0.1436			105.7	108.1	106.0
1981		0.38	2.45	19.56				1.3474	1.0331	0.3143			101.2	100.8	112.7
1982		0.85	3.00	24.32				1.3614	1.0927	0.2687			101.9	101.7	103.3
1983		3.31	3.57	27.54				1.4724	1.1852	0.2872			101.0	100.6	104.6
1984		7.22	4.25	33.39				1.5076	1.1138	0.3938	0.0764	0.0022	102.7	102.6	103.9
1985	0.06	13.20	6.28	39.08				2.0953	1.2901	0.8052	0.1751	0.0164	108.0	111.9	116.7
1986	0.03	17.18	7.79	40.41				2.6537	1.6893	0.9644	0.0361	0.0579	105.0	104.8	106.9
1987	0.10	15.83	9.52	49.59				3.4217	2.6226	0.7991	0.1422	0.0633	106.6	107.4	109.1
1988	0.08	20.32	11.89	66.94				4.4388	3.4196	1.0192	0.1930	0.0827	119.6	121.1	112.9
1989	0.06	23.32	13.63	68.28				5.4768	3.7442	1.7326	0.0436	0.1007	119.3	117.9	112.4

24. Yunnan

24–12

Year	v13a	v13b	v13c1	v13c2	v13c3	v13d	v14a	v14b	v14c	v15a	v15b	v15c	v15d	v15e	v15f
1949										339					
1950	8.0		0.25	2.36	55.84										
1951	8.5														
1952	9.2	48.4	0.33	5.40	114.87	0.0307	3569	3800		3642					
1953	16.5														
1954	15.5		0.38	6.35	106.81	0.0606									
1955	16.2		0.41	6.98	120.87	0.0973									
1956	13.0		0.62	10.45	153.35	0.1070									
1957	17.0		0.70	11.24	149.50	0.0856				4254					
1958	5.4		0.89	11.94	231.66	0.1254									
1959	4.2		1.17	14.51	218.24	0.1256									
1960	4.4		1.40	15.35	209.55	0.2200									
1961	9.4		1.52	18.63	168.46	0.1997									
1962	18.4		1.35	11.34	139.98	0.2263				4091					
1963	12.1		1.08	10.23	143.31	0.3926									
1964	11.2		0.96	12.35	201.19	0.2925									
1965	9.6	85.3	0.94	16.28	316.72	0.2801	19631	39000		4175					
1966	10.8		1.27	15.32	244.53	0.0549									
1967	11.8		1.12	13.11	242.68	0.1456									
1968			0.59	10.16	243.74	0.5294									
1969	8.8		0.39	23.21	254.84	0.2006									
1970	5.5			41.08	270.53	0.3920				4061					
1971	7.4		0.11	45.18	346.63										
1972	8.1		0.38	22.98	348.71	0.0056									
1973	8.5		0.64	48.42	386.09	0.0142									
1974	9.2		0.86	64.96	411.18	0.1396									
1975	9.9	95.5	1.07	89.62	462.00	0.2615				4013					
1976	10.9		1.10	125.06	452.59	0.3647				4014					
1977	10.1		1.25	139.26	442.19	0.4371				4043					
1978	8.6	88.6	1.59	131.98	436.03	0.3322	54108	65500	0.47	4097					
1979	8.6		1.86	113.01	427.32	0.0187				4171					
1980	13.3	84.7	1.81	101.43	424.39	0.5282	60249	71400	2.64	4257					
1981	16.6	83.0	2.17	90.64	424.86	0.1749				4271					
1982	16.7	84.3	1.93	87.85	435.72	0.8673				4266					
1983	15.8	88.5	2.09	91.30	457.90	0.5510				4249					
1984	15.2	92.2	2.49	101.16	497.55	0.4777				4202					
1985	15.6	93.1	3.23	111.07	514.66	0.5428	68012	87300	4.46	4165					
1986	14.2	93.6	3.77	102.72	512.14	0.6714				4164					
1987	13.4	94.3	4.10	128.53	499.38	0.9806			3.74	4186					
1988	14.6	94.6	4.50	132.21	480.40	1.0469	74915	97500	3.96	4205	14300		10400	177	20
1989		94.5	4.51	126.68	457.40	1.2700	75009	99100	3.46	4234					

Notes

1. National Output and Income (Y)

v1a: (E), p.757
- v1a1: (E), p.757
- v1a2: (E), p.757—including industries at village level and below since 1958
- v1a3: (E), p.757
- v1a4: (E), p.757
- v1a5: (E), p.757

v1b: (A); (D), p.364
- v1b1: (A); (D), p.364
- v1b2: (A); (D), p.364
- v1b3: (A); (D), p.364
- v1b4: (A); (D), p.364
- v1b5: (A); (D), p.364

v1c: v1a – v1d

v1d: (E), p.754
- v1d1: (E), p.754
- v1d2: (E), p.754
- v1d3: (E), p.754
- v1d4: (E), p.754
- v1d5: (E), p.754

v1e: (A); (D), p.367
- v1e1: (A); (D), p.367
- v1e2: (A); (D), p.367
- v1e3: (A); (D), p.367
- v1e4: (A); (D), p.367
- v1e5: (A); (D), p.367

v1f: (E), p.753
- v1f1: (E), p.753
- v1f2: (E), p.753
- v1f3: (E), p.753

v1g: v3a + v2a

v1h: (A); (E), p.781

v1i: (E), p.780

v1j: (E), p.780
- v1j1: (E), p.780
- v1j2: (E), p.780
- v1j3: NA

v1k: (E), p.780

2. Investment (I)

v2a: (E), p.756
- v2a1: (A); (D), p.370
- v2a2: (A); (D), p.370

v2b: (A); (E), p.771—including fragmentary investment in fixed assets construction and purchase of Rmb 20,000–50,000

v2c: (A)
- v2c1: (E), p.772
- v2c2: (E), p.772

v2d:
- v2d1: (E), p.769
- v2d2: (E), p.769

v2e: (E), p.769

3. Consumption (C)

v3a: (E), p.756

v3b: (E), p.756
- v3b1: (A); (D), p.368
- v3b2: (A); (D), p.368

v3c: (E), p.756

v3d: (E), p.779
- v3d1: (E), p.779
- v3d2: (E), p.779

v3e: (A); (E), p.781
- v3e1: (E), p.781
- v3e2: (A)

v3e3: (A)
v3e4: (A)

v3f: (A); (E), p.781
v3f1: (A); (E), p.781
v3f2: (A)
v3f3: (A)
v3f4: (A)

4. Public Finance and Banking (FB)

v4a:
v4a1: (E), p.777
v4a1a: (E), p.777
v4a1b: NA
v4a1c: NA
v4a1d: (C), p.401—including depreciation allowances surrendered to central government
v4a2: (E), p.777
v4a2a: (E), p.777
v4a2b: (E), p.777
v4a2c: (E), p.777
v4a2d: v4a2 – v4a2a – v4a2b – v4a2c

v4b: (A)
v4b1: (A); (C), p.448
v4b2: (A); (C), p.448
v4b3: NA

v4c:
v4c1: (E), p.769
v4c2: (E), p.769

5. Labor Force (L)

v5a: (E), p.752
v5a1: (C), p.195; (E), p.752
v5a2: (E), p.752
v5a3: (E), p.752
v5a4: (C), p.195; (E), p.752

v5b:
v5b1: (E), p.752
v5b2: (E), p.752
v5b3: (E), p.752

v5c: (C), p.196
v5c1: (C), p.196

v5d: (C), p.196

6. Population (PO)

v6a: (E), p.751—population of 1983–89 are obtained from sample survey, the rest from public security department
v6a1: (E), p.751—(ditto)
v6a2: (E), p.751—(ditto)

v6b: (E), p.751—(ditto)

v6c: (E), p.751—(ditto)

v6d:
v6d1: (E), p.751—(ditto)
v6d2: (E), p.751—(ditto)
v6d3: (E), p.751—(ditto)
v6d4: (E), p.751—(ditto)
v6d5: (A)—Kunming
v6d6: (A)—Qujing

7. Agriculture (A)

v7a: (A); (E), p.764

v7b: (A); (E), p.764

v7c: (A); (E), p.764

v7d: (A); (E), p.764

v7e: (A)

v7f: (A)

v7g: (A); (E), p.764

v7h: (E), p.759
v7h1: (E), p.759
v7h2: (E), p.759
v7h3: (E), p.759
v7h4: (E), p.759

v7h5: (E), p.759

v7i: (E), p.763

8. Industry (IN)

v8a: (A)
v8a1: (A)
v8a2: (A)
v8a3: (A)

v8b: (E), p.769

v8c1: (E), p.757
v8c2: (E), p.757

v8d: (E), p.769

v8f:
v8f1: (E), p.768
v8f2: (E), p.768
v8f3: NA
v8f4: (E), p.768
v8f5: (E), p.768

v8g: (A)
v8g1: (E), p.769

9. Transport (TR)

v9a: (E), p.770—excluding urban traffic volume; data are from transport department
v9a1: (E), p.770—including central and local railway; data from transport department
v9a2: (E), p.770
v9a3: (E), p.770—excluding distant ocean and coastal passenger traffic; data from transport department

v9b: (E), p.770
v9b1: (E), p.770—including central and local railways; data from transport department
v9b2: (E), p.770
v9b3: (E), p.770—excluding distant ocean and coastal freight volume; data from transport department

v9c: (E), p.770

10. Domestic Trade (DT)

v10a: (E), p.773
v10a1: (E), p.773

v10b:
v10b1: (E), p.773
v10b2: NA
v10b3: (E), p.773—included supply and marketing cooperative and other collectives
v10b4: (E), p.773
v10b5: (E), p.773
v10b6: (C), p.367–369; (E), p.773

v10d: (E), p.775—calculated on calendar year basis

11. Foreign Trade (FT)

v11a:
v11a1: NA
v11a2: NA
v11a3: NA

v11b: (E), p.776—data from foreign trade department
v11b1: (E), p.776—(ditto)
v11b2: (A)

v11c: (E), p.776

v11d: (E), p.776

12. Prices (PR)

v12a: (E), p.778

v12b: (E), p.778

v12c: (E), p.778

13. Education (ED)

v13a: (A)

v13b: (A); (E), p.781

v13c:
- v13c1: (A); (C), p.451–452—general institutions of higher learning
- v13c2: (A); (C), p.451–452—technical and technician, ordinary secondary schools; excluding agricultural secondary schools in 1965
- v13c3: (A); (C), p.451–452

v13d: (A); (C), 1988, p.451–452

14. Social Factors (SF)

v14a: (E), p.781

v14b: (E), p.781

v14c: (A)

15. Natural Environment (NE)

v15a: (A); (E), p.764

v15b: (A)

v15c: NA

v15d: (A)

v15e: (A)

v15f: (A)

Sources of Data

(A) Data supplied by the DSNEB, SSB, the PRC; and Statistical Bureau of Yunnan Province ed. *Yunnan Forty Years*, Beijing: CSPH, 1989.

(C) Statistical Bureau of Yunnan Province ed. *Statistical Yearbook of Yunnan*, Beijing: CSPH, 1988.

(D) Same as (D) in Beijing's sources of data.

(E) Same as (E) in Beijing's sources of data.

25

Tibet

25. Tibet

25–1

Year	v1a	v1a1	v1a2	v1a3	v1a4	v1a5	v1b	v1b1	v1b2	v1b3	v1b4	v1b5	v1c	v1d	v1d1
1949															
1950															
1951															
1952															
1953															
1954															
1955															
1956															
1957															
1958															
1959		1.44	0.43												
1960		1.67	1.17												
1961		1.84	0.55												
1962		1.99	0.22												
1963		2.17	0.18												
1964		2.37	0.20												
1965		2.64	0.23												
1966		2.79	0.28												
1967	4.12	3.00	0.34												
1968	3.25	2.92	0.12												
1969	3.31	2.80	0.12												
1970	3.75	2.80	0.37												
1971	4.39	2.90	0.59												
1972	4.43	2.78	0.74												
1973	4.99	3.10	0.91												
1974	5.37	3.31	1.01												
1975	5.62	3.40	1.13												
1976	5.77	3.54	1.14												
1977	6.40	3.78	1.32												
1978	7.17	3.92	1.49												
1979	10.28	4.08	1.67	2.69	0.85	0.99							6.34	3.94	2.30
1980	9.71	5.32	1.53	1.75	0.60	0.51	86.9	111.0	94.1	63.0	58.3	41.1	4.91	4.80	3.28
1981	10.70	6.57	1.21	1.80	0.61	0.51	99.3	107.7	75.3	91.6	110.0	118.8	4.79	5.91	4.57
1982	10.98	6.34	1.38	2.19	0.60	0.47	102.2	99.2	103.5	117.0	98.2	91.5	5.18	5.80	4.22
1983	11.17	5.95	1.47	2.09	0.97	0.70	101.4	92.4	103.8	92.7	180.1	153.2	5.62	5.55	3.90
1984	17.51	7.92	1.93	4.79	1.05	1.82	142.4	116.8	108.1	229.8	108.0	258.2	8.41	9.10	5.76
1985	22.24	10.89	2.12	5.83	1.22	2.18	114.7	112.4	103.0	121.5	114.3	119.9	9.66	12.58	8.79
1986	20.31	9.92	2.02	3.60	1.36	3.41	93.2	95.1	92.5	60.2	108.3	152.6	9.24	11.07	7.68
1987	22.09	10.38	2.16	4.01	1.64	3.90	108.5	104.4	112.4	109.4	118.5	110.3	9.81	12.29	8.19
1988	27.53	12.95	2.65	5.15	1.72	5.06	106.0	102.7	111.6	110.2	103.9	107.0	11.86	15.67	10.34
1989	29.60	13.58	2.86	6.10	1.80	5.26	105.2	101.4	109.4	113.0	103.8	103.7	13.70	16.50	10.72

25. Tibet

25–2

Year	v1d2	v1d3	v1d4	v1d5	v1e	v1e1	v1e2	v1e3	v1e4	v1e5	v1f	v1f1	v1f2	v1f3	v1g
1949															
1950															
1951															
1952															
1953															
1954															
1955															
1956															
1957															
1958															
1959															
1960															
1961															
1962															
1963															
1964															
1965															
1966															
1967															
1968															
1969															
1970															
1971															
1972															
1973															
1974															
1975															
1976															
1977															
1978															
1979	0.47	0.91	-0.03	0.29											7.55
1980	0.50	0.89	-0.17	0.31	119.70	139.80	107.10	95.20		102.60					8.17
1981	0.44	0.63		0.27	119.10	134.50	86.40	68.90		85.90					9.25
1982	0.50	0.86	0.02	0.20	97.40	91.90	110.20	134.50		76.00					10.49
1983	0.60	0.83	-0.05	0.28	93.20	90.70	116.00	91.00		134.00					9.93
1984	0.91	1.61	-0.02	0.84	155.40	138.90	150.40	180.40		298.80					12.74
1985	1.04	4.84	-0.03	0.94	111.80	113.53	101.19	111.11		113.75	17.72	8.87	3.09	5.76	20.12
1986	0.85	1.13	0.20	1.21	90.80	91.19	80.00	60.00		124.18	16.93	7.95	2.18	6.80	15.38
1987	0.91	1.40	0.25	1.54	111.36	106.63	111.76	121.11	120.00	123.89	17.71	8.07	2.13	7.51	18.25
1988	1.15	1.65	0.53	2.00	107.79	103.73	115.79	100.92	212.50	107.14	20.25	9.65	2.41	8.19	19.24
1989	1.49	1.90	0.62	2.07	102.75	100.34	109.09	110.00	101.96	103.33	21.86	10.04	2.84	8.98	26.42

25. Tibet

25–3

Year	v1h	v1i	v1j	v1j1	v1j2	v1j3	v1k	v2a	v2a1	v2a2	v2b	v2c	v2c1	v2c2	v2d1
1949															
1950															
1951															
1952															
1953															
1954															
1955															
1956															
1957															
1958															
1959															
1960															
1961															
1962															
1963															
1964															
1965															
1966															
1967															
1968															
1969															
1970															
1971															
1972															
1973															
1974															
1975															
1976															
1977															
1978		1.11		851.7							1.8534	1.85	0.71	0.11	
1979		1.56						2.23	1.85	0.38	2.0750	2.08	0.66	0.18	
1980		1.95	1025.4	1055.4	665.4			1.98	1.67	0.31	1.8128	1.81			2.29
1981		1.94						1.81	1.55	0.26	1.2172	1.22	0.23	0.04	2.55
1982		2.34						2.49	1.34	1.15	1.5558	1.56	0.19	0.19	3.21
1983		2.44						2.42	1.27	1.15	1.9875	1.99	0.38	0.15	3.18
1984		2.95						3.11	2.75	0.36	4.7879	4.72	0.30	0.06	3.99
1985	352.97	3.29	1963.4	1944.5	1608.8	2086.5		8.83	7.71	1.12	7.4940	6.37	1.27	0.41	4.12
1986	343.57	3.76	2375.2	2419.4	1818.9	2392.4		3.82	4.44	-0.62	5.3492	4.44	1.47	0.23	4.06
1987	348.39	3.86	2498.6	2535.9	1981.7	2170.6		5.38	3.32	2.06	5.3000	3.96	0.79	0.23	4.28
1988	374.41	4.27	2710.1	2739.3	2331.2	2236.6		4.98	4.30	0.68	5.8087	4.71	0.77	0.26	4.43
1989	397.25	4.73	2927.0	2989.0	2013.0			8.95	4.86	4.09	7.0300	4.41	0.89	0.22	6.01

25. Tibet

25–4

Year	v2d2	v2e	v3a	v3b	v3b1	v3b2	v3c	v3d	v3d1	v3d2	v3e	v3e1	v3e2	v3e3	v3e4
1949															
1950															
1951															
1952															
1953															
1954															
1955															
1956															
1957															
1958															
1959															
1960															
1961															
1962															
1963															
1964															
1965															
1966															
1967															
1968															
1969															
1970															
1971															
1972															
1973															
1974															
1975															
1976															
1977															
1978															
1979			5.33	3.98	2.28	1.70	1.35	218.00	147.00	620.00					
1980	1.58	0.63	6.20	5.07	2.84	2.23	1.23	276.29	209.32	635.09					
1981	1.64	0.56	7.45	5.60	3.13	2.46	1.85	300.73	198.15	878.19	519	316			
1982	2.20	0.69	8.00	6.05	3.37	2.68	1.95	319.47	208.59	967.52	522	326			
1983	2.15	0.70	7.51	5.59	3.57	2.02	1.92	292.58	214.65	813.98	602	362			
1984	2.49	0.73	9.63	6.99	4.56	2.43	2.64	358.67	268.47	971.18	619	375			
1985	2.75	0.75	11.29	8.33	5.31	3.01	2.96	422.05	309.24	1181.69	909	504			
1986	2.83	0.84	11.56	8.80	5.17	3.63	2.76	437.76	295.56	1387.13	820	504			
1987	2.85	0.88	12.87	10.24	6.17	4.07	2.63	498.64	347.03	1477.61	1008	550			
1988	2.95	0.77	14.26	11.41	6.90	4.51	2.85	542.97	382.36	1518.68	1211	713			
1989	4.35	0.86	17.47	13.85	7.59	6.26	3.62	647.00	413.00	2078.00	1432	871			

25. Tibet

25–5

Year	v3f	v3f1	v3f2	v3f3	v3f4	v4a1	v4a1a	v4a1b	v4a1b'	v4a1c	v4a1d	v4a2	v4a2a	v4a2b	v4a2c	v4a2d
1949																
1950																
1951																
1952						0.13			0.01			0.10		0.03	0.07	
1953						0.17			0.02			0.21	0.03	0.06	0.11	0.01
1954						0.24			0.02			0.20	0.03	0.05	0.10	0.02
1955						0.34			0.02			0.30	0.05	0.05	0.13	0.07
1956						1.38			0.02			1.43	0.73	0.17	0.38	0.15
1957						1.29			0.02			0.94	0.21	0.19	0.42	0.12
1958						0.38						0.27	0.08	0.06	0.09	0.04
1959						0.13	0.12		0.03			0.70	0.29	0.06	0.13	0.22
1960						1.29	0.61		0.13			1.54	0.75	0.09	0.18	0.52
1961						1.00	0.16		0.10			1.02	0.29	0.09	0.20	0.44
1962						0.90			0.09			1.03	0.17	0.09	0.22	0.55
1963						0.94	-0.07		0.11			0.90	0.19	0.10	0.23	0.38
1964						1.70	-0.02		0.12			1.36	0.33	0.12	0.27	0.64
1965						1.40	-0.03		0.12			1.13	0.36	0.13	0.29	0.35
1966						1.76	-0.11		0.12			1.55	0.65	0.14	0.29	0.47
1967						1.52	-0.18		0.12			1.27	0.53	0.14	0.25	0.35
1968						0.92	-0.34		0.07			0.67	0.16	0.10	0.21	0.20
1969						1.09	-0.44		0.08			0.89	0.31	0.12	0.24	0.22
1970						1.62	-0.39		0.12			1.06	0.46	0.11	0.25	0.24
1971						1.71	-0.28		0.12			1.73	0.81	0.16	0.27	0.49
1972						1.92	-0.33		0.14			1.89	0.74	0.20	0.33	0.62
1973						2.20	-0.43		0.15			2.08	0.73	0.24	0.35	0.76
1974						2.61	-0.41		0.18			2.17	0.85	0.28	0.34	0.70
1975						2.62	-0.51		0.20			2.40	0.81	0.34	0.39	0.86
1976						3.17	-0.47		0.23			3.10	1.12	0.38	0.42	1.18
1977						3.74	-0.37		0.23			3.27	1.07	0.41	0.46	1.33
1978						4.71	-0.43		0.25			4.57	1.40	0.55	0.53	2.09
1979						4.92	-0.51		0.27			5.00	1.59	0.63	0.64	2.14
1980						5.41	-0.83		0.20			4.66	1.57	0.77	0.76	1.56
1981						5.80	-0.82		0.19			4.35	0.70	0.81	0.76	2.08
1982						6.22	-0.76		0.17			5.01	0.75	0.98	0.84	2.44
1983						6.38	-0.74		0.20			5.88	0.91	1.20	0.91	2.86
1984						6.70	-1.47		0.30			10.24	3.40	1.68	1.38	3.78
1985	269.60	184.26				9.97	-1.15		0.45			10.29	3.42	1.65	1.32	3.90
1986	257.85	179.68				9.38	-0.61		0.38			8.97	1.54	1.94	1.44	4.05
1987	245.85	171.93				10.03	-0.60		0.43			9.13	1.19	2.31	1.53	4.10
1988	271.37	179.59				10.33	-0.87		0.69			10.48	1.29	2.50	1.92	4.77
1989	289.75	187.13	38.26	13.07	28.71											

25. Tibet

25–6

Year	v4b	v4b1	v4b2	v4b3	v4c1	v4c2	v5a	v5a1	v5a2	v5a3	v5a4	v5b1	v5b2	v5b3	v5c
1949															
1950															
1951															
1952															
1953															
1954															
1955															
1956															
1957															
1958															
1959								4							
1960								7							
1961								8							
1962								6							
1963								6							
1964								6							
1965								6							
1966								7							
1967								8							
1968								8							
1969								8							
1970								8							
1971								9							
1972								10							
1973								10							
1974								11							
1975								11							
1976								12							
1977								12							
1978							94	12	1		81				
1979							98	17	1		80				
1980					0.03	1.52	101	18	1		82				
1981	0.8039				0.01	0.30	100	16	1		83				
1982	0.9476				0.06	2.06	102	17	1	0.11	84				
1983	1.2553				0.09	3.08	102	16	1	0.13	84				
1984	1.5461				0.06	1.75	105	16	2	0.36	87				
1985					-0.02	-0.62	106	15	2	1.22	88				
1986					-0.02	-0.66	107	15	1	1.84	89				
1987					0.14	3.65	108	15	1	1.94	90				
1988	3.4000				0.34	9.25	107	15	1	2.09	89	85	5	17	
1989					0.33	6.28	108	15	1	1.00	90	88	5	15	

25. Tibet

25–7

Year	v5c1	v5d	v6a	v6a1	v6a2	v6b	v6c	v6d1	v6d2	v6d3	v6d4	v6d5	v6d6
1949													
1950													
1951													
1952			115					7	108	56	59		
1953													
1954													
1955													
1956													
1957													
1958			121					9	112	59	62		
1959			123					10	113	60	63		
1960			127					13	114	62	65		
1961			130					14	116	63	67		
1962			130					12	118	63	67		
1963			132					13	119	64	68		
1964			135					13	122	66	69		
1965			137			14.35	5.10	13	124	67	70		
1966			140			15.15	6.30	14	126	68	72		
1967			142			17.36	11.91	14	128	69	73		
1968			145			16.18	8.17	15	130	70	75		
1969			148			17.45	7.07	16	132	72	76		
1970			151			25.20	10.16	17	134	73	78		
1971			155			25.12	9.85	18	137	75	80		
1972			159			25.04	9.34	20	139	78	81		
1973			163			25.39	9.56	21	142	79	84		
1974			166			24.68	9.24	23	143	81	85		
1975			169			24.34	9.13	24	145	82	87		
1976			172			23.48	9.25	24	148	84	88		
1977			176			24.37	9.14	25	151	85	90		
1978			179			22.86	8.75	27	152	87	92		
1979			183			22.41	8.24	28	155	90	93		
1980			185			21.36	8.21	29	157	90	95		
1981			186	18	168	24.40	8.80	26	160	91	95		
1982			189	24	165	24.47	7.66	25	164	93	96		
1983			193	19	174	27.02	8.64	25	168	94	99		
1984			197	20	177	23.96	8.00	25	172	97	100		
1985			199	20	179	23.32	10.12	26	173	98	101		
1986			202	20	182	24.54	8.41	26	176	99	103		
1987			208	26	182	24.19	7.95	29	179	102	106		
1988			212	28	184	22.69	7.65	30	182	104	108		
1989			216			24.17	7.94					12.55	7.69

25. Tibet

25–8

Year	v7a	v7b	v7c	v7d	v7e	v7f	v7g	v7h	v7h1	v7h2	v7h3	v7h4	v7h5	v7i	v8a
1949															
1950				202.3											
1951															
1952				202.3											
1953															
1954															
1955															
1956				210.3											
1957															
1958				215.7											
1959				210.3				1.44							
1960				226.0				1.67							
1961				242.7				1.84							
1962				255.0				1.99							
1963				267.7				2.17							0.18
1964				280.9				2.37							0.20
1965				277.1				2.64							0.23
1966				279.5				2.79							0.28
1967				303.6				3.00							0.34
1968				301.4				2.92							0.12
1969				300.0				2.80							0.12
1970				300.4				2.80							0.37
1971				309.5				2.90							0.59
1972			126.19	306.1		0.16		2.78							0.74
1973			133.96	302.3		0.16		3.10							0.91
1974		36.25	155.66	306.6		0.30		3.31							1.01
1975		42.45	165.85	315.0		0.44		3.40							1.13
1976		50.17	177.50	307.2		0.77		3.54							1.14
1977		82.54	183.43	310.4		1.39		3.78							1.32
1978		79.56	226.70	329.7		2.00		3.92	1.40	0.02	2.35		0.15		1.49
1979								4.08	1.22	0.04	2.47		0.35		1.67
1980			222.71	331.0		1.60		5.32	2.12	0.05	2.68		0.47		
1981		81.64		321.2		0.12		6.57	2.34	0.05	3.62		0.56		1.17
1982		76.45	206.09	327.7		0.05		6.34	2.68	0.09	2.90		0.67		1.22
1983		67.11	181.46	319.1		0.08		5.95	2.17	0.12	2.84		0.81		1.30
1984		45.67	167.72	319.8		1.13		7.92	3.33	0.12	3.75		0.71		1.69
1985	3.34	32.50	199.66	315.0				10.89	4.55	0.23	4.96		1.15		1.73
1986								9.92	3.52	0.16	5.36		0.87		1.61
1987							0.10	10.38	3.70	0.15	5.64		0.88		1.83
1988	4.50	26.59	180.51	313.0		1.21	0.12	12.95	4.18	0.18	6.77		1.82		2.02
1989	4.60	27.10	181.20	317.7		1.35	0.13	13.58	4.94	0.16	7.07		1.41	122.3	2.21

25. Tibet

25–9

Year	v8a1	v8a2	v8a3	v8b	v8c1	v8c2	v8d	v8f1	v8f2	v8f3	v8f4	v8f5	v8g
1949													
1950													
1951													
1952													
1953													
1954													
1955													
1956									1.60		0.0003		
1957									2.53		0.0026		
1958									4.32		0.0062		
1959					0.42	0.02			4.58		0.0088		
1960					1.14	0.03			7.09		0.0296	0.05	
1961					0.51	0.04			5.84		0.1000	0.06	
1962					0.18	0.04			2.84		0.1700	0.12	
1963					0.14	0.04			2.52		0.2500	0.34	
1964					0.16	0.04			2.69		0.2900	0.66	
1965	0.18	0.05			0.15	0.09			1.97		0.2800	1.06	
1966	0.21	0.08			0.17	0.11			3.33		0.3100	2.00	
1967	0.26	0.08			0.21	0.13			3.12		0.3600	0.85	
1968	0.09	0.03			0.07	0.05			0.85		0.3500		
1969	0.09	0.03			0.07	0.05			0.51		0.4300		
1970	0.29	0.08			0.24	0.14			0.94		0.5300	0.36	
1971	0.45	0.14			0.37	0.23			1.30		0.6300	0.75	
1972	0.57	0.17			0.46	0.28			2.24		0.6900	2.03	
1973	0.70	0.21			0.56	0.35			4.52		0.7500	2.38	
1974	0.77	0.24			0.63	0.38			5.20		0.9800	2.94	
1975	0.86	0.27			0.70	0.43			6.19		1.0500	3.40	
1976	0.87	0.27			0.71	0.43			7.04		1.0500	3.60	
1977	1.01	0.31			0.78	0.53			7.90		1.2100	4.26	
1978	1.14	0.35			0.93	0.57			8.21		1.3400	6.20	
1979	1.28	0.39			1.15	0.52			6.05		1.5300	6.78	
1980				1.08	1.03	0.46	0.37		2.98		1.7500	5.22	
1981	1.05	0.12		0.91	0.68	0.53	0.36		2.25		1.7200	5.35	
1982	1.12	0.10		1.09	0.84	0.55	0.40		2.08		1.9400	5.75	
1983	1.17	0.12	0.01	1.15	0.90	0.56	0.47		2.52		2.1100	5.74	
1984	1.15	0.17	0.37	1.17	1.20	0.73	0.47		2.48		2.2700	5.32	
1985	1.14	0.16	0.43	1.24	1.05	1.07	0.41		2.98		2.4700	4.67	
1986	1.02	0.19	0.40	1.16	1.25	0.77	0.47		1.86		2.6300	2.98	
1987	1.22	0.21	0.40	1.37	1.21	0.95	0.58		0.75		2.5700	4.45	
1988	1.21	0.25	0.56	1.72	1.54	1.11	0.74		0.60		2.6900	9.49	
1989	1.31	0.27	0.63	2.14	1.96	0.91	0.92		0.65		2.7500	11.98	272

25. Tibet

25–10

Year	v8g1	v9a	v9a1	v9a2	v9a3	v9b	v9b1	v9b2	v9b3	v9c	v10a	v10a1	v10b1	v10b2	v10b3
1949															
1950															
1951															
1952															
1953															
1954															
1955															
1956															
1957															
1958										60.0					
1959										98.7					
1960										226.5					
1961										280.1					
1962										267.9					
1963										274.6					
1964										262.1					
1965										284.1					
1966										312.0					
1967										273.2					
1968										142.1					
1969										133.8					
1970										151.0					
1971										93.3					
1972										112.7					
1973										146.3					
1974										157.2					
1975										165.9					
1976										182.7					
1977										194.0					
1978										205.9	3.08	2.45			
1979										228.0	3.41	2.71			
1980	93	0.46		0.46		5.25		5.25		269.0	3.61	2.87			
1981	98	0.18		0.18		2.55		2.55		356.0	3.75	3.32			
1982	113	0.43		0.43		4.40		4.40		343.0	4.14	3.71			
1983	132	0.73		0.73		4.73		4.73		367.0	4.42	3.94	4.22		0.05
1984	123									409.4	10.58	9.24	3.80		5.12
1985	136	1.67		0.69		6.05		5.22		479.0	11.00	9.50	4.04		2.39
1986	144	2.39		1.45		5.71		4.78		488.0	10.01	9.10	4.22		2.62
1987	140	2.65		1.75		7.08		6.37		526.0	10.65	9.86	5.13		2.61
1988	131	3.27		2.34		7.64		6.77		709.0	11.43	10.62	5.29		3.23
1989	131	2.98		1.93		8.86		8.30		896.7	14.61	12.88	11.97		1.15

25. Tibet

25–11

Year	v10b4	v10b5	v10b6	v10d	v11a1	v11a2	v11a3	v11b	v11b1	v11b2	v11c	v11d	v12a	v12b	v12c
1949															
1950															
1951															
1952															
1953								0.1387	0.0236	0.1151					
1954								0.0907	0.0245	0.0662					
1955								0.0517	0.0254	0.0263					
1956								0.2950	0.2227	0.0723					
1957								0.2878	0.2330	0.0548					
1958								0.0760	0.0549	0.0211					
1959								0.0672	0.0352	0.0320					
1960								0.0491	0.0377	0.0114					
1961								0.0300	0.0226	0.0074					
1962								0.0662	0.0262	0.0400					
1963								0.0810	0.0058	0.0752					
1964								0.0847	0.0052	0.0795					
1965								0.0693	0.0110	0.0583					
1966								0.0820	0.0170	0.0650					
1967								0.0707	0.0087	0.0620					
1968								0.0507	0.0071	0.0436					
1969								0.0557	0.0074	0.0483					
1970								0.0474	0.0035	0.0439					
1971								0.1748	0.0152	0.1596					
1972								0.1320	0.0076	0.1244					
1973								0.0699	0.0146	0.0548					
1974								0.1713	0.0126	0.1569					
1975								0.1771	0.0144	0.1616					
1976								0.1330	0.0236	0.1084					
1977								0.2969	0.0226	0.2737					
1978								0.2873	0.0272	0.2597					
1979								0.2402	0.0315	0.2080					
1980								0.2491	0.0381	0.2082					
1981								0.3235	0.0441	0.2738					
1982								0.2074	0.0757	0.1292					
1983			0.07					0.3302	0.0941	0.2261					
1984	0.03	1.15	0.48					0.3257	0.0860	0.2397					
1985	0.07	1.15	0.61					0.8922	0.1494	0.3928					
1986	0.19	2.08	0.91					1.0119	0.2914	0.1205					
1987	0.12	1.93	0.87					1.5060	0.4501	0.4659					
1988	0.12	2.35	0.88					1.5219	0.5949	0.2270					
1989	0.06	1.15	0.28					1.5510	0.5785	0.5625					

25. Tibet

25–12

Year	v13a	v13b	v13c1	v13c2	v13c3	v13d	v14a	v14b	v14c	v15a	v15b	v15c	v15d	v15e	v15f
1949															
1950															
1951															
1952										245					
1953															
1954															
1955															
1956										251					
1957															
1958							174			251					
1959				0.17	1.63		480		156.0	251					
1960				0.37	4.15		1010			278					
1961				0.36	5.83		1133			283					
1962				0.31	5.31		1226		709.0	291					
1963				0.30	5.31		1155			292					
1964				0.32	5.91		1345			295					
1965			0.23	0.15	6.68	0.1063	1631	2400	375.8	304					
1966			0.24	0.20	7.50	0.0108	1909		102.9	309					
1967			0.24	0.19	7.10	0.0095	1960		95.0	327					
1968			0.19	0.17	6.36	0.0422	1967		37.0	328					
1969			0.09	0.04	5.91	0.1053	2036		25.0	329					
1970				0.09	6.86	0.0877	1605		876.6	327					
1971			0.04	0.18	8.32		2027		1068.9	334					
1972			0.09	0.32	12.31	0.0038	2027		1320.7	336					
1973			0.10	0.46	14.56	0.0056	3230		1495.6	333					
1974			0.14	0.79	18.32	0.0230	3359		1905.2	335					
1975			0.20	1.20	20.76	0.0211	3827		2465.2	339					
1976			0.25	1.68	22.28	0.0423	3859		2921.4	340					
1977			0.22	1.84	23.15	0.0535	4020		3212.2	341					
1978			0.21	2.23	26.26	0.0783	4421		2980.3	341					
1979			0.15	2.54	24.80	0.0232	4295		2684.3	345					
1980		83.00	0.15	2.23	24.08	0.0193	4328	6700	2516.8	343					
1981			0.15	1.92	18.69	0.0205	4690		1903.7	338					
1982		78.00	0.12	1.83	14.16	0.0539	1500		1881.0	341					
1983		42.00	0.13	1.96	12.46	0.0106	4579		2095.5	344					
1984		42.00	0.14	2.07	12.55	0.0411	4619		2125.1	338					
1985		46.00	0.16	2.23	11.99	0.0305	4580	6800	2004.6	335					
1986			0.19	2.50	12.12	0.0315	4983		293.0						
1987			0.18	2.71	13.71	0.0424	5222		1911.9						
1988		55.69	0.17	2.69	14.48	0.0683	5197	7100	1833.6	332					
1989		53.10	0.20	2.70	13.89	0.0400	4999	8100	1872.0	334					

Notes

1. National Output and Income (Y)

v1a: (C), 1989, p.74; (E), p.784
  v1a1: (E), p.784
  v1a2: (C), 1989, p.74, p.78; (E), p.784
  v1a3: (E), p.784
  v1a4: (E), p.784
  v1a5: (E), p.784

v1b: (A)
  v1b1: (A)
  v1b2: (A)
  v1b3: (A)
  v1b4: (A)
  v1b5: (A)

v1c: v1a – v1d

v1d: (E), p.783
  v1d1: (E), p.783
  v1d2: (E), p.783
  v1d3: (E), p.783
  v1d4: (E), p.783
  v1d5: (E), p.783

v1e: (A)
  v1e1: (A)
  v1e2: (A)
  v1e3: (A)
  v1e4: (A)
  v1e5: (A)

v1f: (E), p.783
  v1f1: (E), p.783
  v1f2: (E), p.783
  v1f3: (E), p.783

v1g: (C), 1989, p.82–83

v1h: (E), p.795

v1i: (E), p.795

v1j: (E), p.795
  v1j1: (E), p.795
  v1j2: (E), p.795
  v1j3: (C), 1989, p.499

v1k: NA

2. Investment (I)

v2a: (E), p.783
  v2a1: (A)
  v2a2: (A)

v2b: (A); (C), 1989, p.372

v2c: (E), p.791
  v2c1: (E), p.792
  v2c2: (E), p.792

v2d:
  v2d1: (E), p.789
  v2d2: (E), p.789

v2e: (E), p.789

3. Consumption (C)

v3a: (E), p.783

v3b: (E), p.783
  v3b1: (A); (C), 1989, p.82–83
  v3b2: (A); (C), 1989, p.82–83

v3c: (E), p.783

v3d: (E), p.795
  v3d1: (E), p.795
  v3d2: (E), p.795

v3e: (A); (E), p.795
  v3e1: (A); (E), p.795
  v3e2: NA
  v3e3: NA
  v3e4: NA

v3f: (A); (E), p.795
  v3f1: (A); (E), p.795

v3f2: (A)
v3f3: (A)
v3f4: (A)

4. Public Finance and Banking (FB)

v4a:
- v4a1: (C), 1989, p.467–468—the sum total of local revenue of current year and central government subsidies revenue
  - v4a1a: (E), p.794
  - v4a1b: NA; v4a1b': (E), p.794—total tax revenues
  - v4a1c: NA
  - v4a1d: NA
- v4a2: (E), p.794
  - v4a2a: (E), p.794
  - v4a2b: (E), p.794
  - v4a2c: (E), p.794
  - v4a2d: v4a2 – v4a2a – v4a2b – v4a2c

v4b: (A)
- v4b1: NA
- v4b2: NA
- v4b3: NA

v4c:
- v4c1: (A)
- v4c2: (E), p.789

5. Labor Force (L)

v5a: (E), p.782
- v5a1: (A); (E), p.782
- v5a2: (E), p.782
- v5a3: (C), 1989, p.161; (E), p.782
- v5a4: (C), 1989, p.161; (E), p.782

v5b:
- v5b1: (E), p.782
- v5b2: (E), p.782
- v5b3: (E), p.782

v5c: NA
- v5c1: NA

v5d: NA

6. Population (PO)

v6a: (A); (E), p.782—data from public security department
- v6a1: (E), p.782
- v6a2: (E), p.782

v6b: (E), p.782—(ditto)

v6c: (E), p.782—(ditto)

v6d:
- v6d1: (C), 1989, p.133; (E), p.782—(ditto)
- v6d2: (C), 1989, p.133; (E), p.782—(ditto)
- v6d3: (A); (C), 1989, p.133; (E), p.782—(ditto)
- v6d4: (C), 1989, p.133; (E), p.782—(ditto)
- v6d5: (A)—Lhasa
- v6d6: (A)—Xigazê

7. Agriculture (A)

v7a: (E), p.788

v7b: (A); (E), p.788

v7c: (A); (E), p.788

v7d: (A); (E), p.788

v7e: NA

v7f: (A); (E), p.788—1988, 1989: reckoned pure amount

v7g: (E), p.788

v7h: (E), p.785
- v7h1: (E), p.785
- v7h2: (E), p.785
- v7h3: (E), p.785
- v7h4: NA

v7h5: (E), p.785

v7i: (A)

8. Industry (IN)

v8a: (E), p.789—1963–70: based on 1957's constant price; 1971–80: based on 1970's constant price; 1981–89: based on 1980's constant price
- v8a1: (E), p.789—(ditto)
- v8a2: (E), p.789—(ditto)
- v8a3: (E), p.789—(ditto)

v8b: (E), p.789

- v8c1: (E), p.784
- v8c2: (E), p.784

v8d: (E), p.789

v8f:
- v8f1: NA
- v8f2: (E), p.790
- v8f3: NA
- v8f4: (A); (E), p.790
- v8f5: (E), p.790

v8g: (A)
- v8g1: (E), p.789

9. Transport (TR)

v9a: (E), p.791—excluding urban traffic volume
- v9a1: NA
- v9a2: (E), p.791
- v9a3: NA

v9b: (E), p.791
- v9b1: NA
- v9b2: (A); (E), p.791
- v9b3: NA

v9c: (A)

10. Domestic Trade (DT)

v10a: (E), p.793
- v10a1: (E), p.793

v10b:
- v10b1: (E), p.793
- v10b2: NA
- v10b3: (E), p.793—collective ownership
- v10b4: (E), p.793
- v10b5: (E), p.793—1983: 37.4 (Rmb 10,000)
- v10b6: (E), p.793

v10d: NA

11. Foreign Trade (FT)

v11a:
- v11a1: NA
- v11a2: NA
- v11a3: NA

v11b: (C), 1989, p.458; 1990, p.377—including imports and exports in mutual trade along the national borders, unit: Rmb 100 million
- v11b1: (C), 1989, p.458; 1990, p.377—(ditto)
- v11b2: (C), 1989, p.458; 1990, p.377—(ditto)

v11c: NA

v11d: NA

12. Prices (PR)

v12a: NA

v12b: NA

v12c: NA

13. Education (ED)

v13a: NA

v13b: (A); (E), p.796

v13c:

v13c1: (A); (E), p.796

v13c2: (A); (E), p.796—technical and ordinary secondary schools

v13c3: (A); (E), p.796

v13d: (A); (C), 1989, p.543—institutions of higher learning

14. Social Factors (SF)

v14a: (A); (E), p.796

v14b: (E), p.796

v14c: (C), 1989, p.567–568—number of books, magazines, newspapers published (Chinese), unit: 10,000 issues (copies)

15. Natural Environment (NE)

v15a: (A); (E), p.788

v15b: NA

v15c: NA

v15d: NA

v15e: NA

v15f: NA

Sources of Data

(A) Data supplied by the DSNEB, SSB, the PRC.
(C) Statistical Bureau of Tibet Autonomous Region ed. *Social Statistical Yearbook of Tibet*, Beijing: CSPH, 1989, 1990.
(E) Same as (E) in Beijing's sources of data.

26

Shaanxi

26. Shaanxi

26–1

Year	v1a	v1a1	v1a2	v1a3	v1a4	v1a5	v1b	v1b1	v1b2	v1b3	v1b4	v1b5	v1c	v1d	v1d1
1949	11.84	7.99	2.86		0.13	0.86							4.01	7.83	6.12
1950	13.42	9.05	3.28	0.06	0.14	0.89	113.0						4.63	8.79	6.89
1951	16.07	10.91	3.83	0.52	0.19	0.62	116.5						5.82	10.25	8.27
1952	18.28	10.75	4.95	0.66	0.28	1.63	111.9	97.20	129.60	126.50	151.50	261.70	6.75	11.53	8.16
1953	24.86	14.23	6.63	1.33	0.49	2.18	125.7	117.20	133.70	200.50	172.50	133.30	9.30	15.56	10.73
1954	29.32	15.89	8.51	1.51	0.72	2.69	117.3	110.50	128.30	113.70	145.20	123.30	11.23	18.09	12.00
1955	30.47	14.51	9.37	2.70	0.87	3.02	103.7	93.50	109.60	179.00	121.10	112.50	11.83	18.64	11.11
1956	40.05	18.78	11.23	5.28	1.14	3.62	129.2	118.40	126.90	195.60	131.00	119.80	15.65	24.40	14.52
1957	38.21	17.72	11.34	3.93	1.50	3.72	96.5	98.40	100.20	74.40	131.40	102.80	15.68	22.53	12.80
1958	50.09	18.72	19.90	5.57	1.83	4.07	135.9	112.80	175.10	141.70	121.70	109.40	22.40	27.69	13.12
1959	62.39	18.29	29.49	7.17	2.85	4.59	124.3	96.00	147.00	128.70	155.40	112.90	30.37	32.02	12.34
1960	71.54	18.02	36.83	8.84	3.21	4.63	114.0	111.20	128.10	123.20	112.90	100.80	37.02	34.52	12.21
1961	53.89	22.22	21.19	3.11	2.44	4.94	62.5	86.20	53.10	35.20	75.90	107.70	25.51	28.38	15.13
1962	45.96	19.36	18.14	2.69	1.73	4.04	87.3	98.20	83.80	84.60	71.10	81.70	22.15	23.81	12.98
1963	46.04	18.31	19.69	2.74	1.98	3.32	106.2	109.00	109.80	102.00	85.80	82.30	22.15	23.89	12.72
1964	51.30	18.35	23.88	3.89	1.66	3.52	116.4	107.80	124.40	141.80	83.90	105.90	25.79	25.51	12.96
1965	64.10	23.66	29.65	5.45	1.82	3.52	133.8	136.00	139.30	140.10	109.70	100.00	32.15	31.95	17.01
1966	76.17	22.76	40.94	6.66	1.80	4.01	118.5	91.90	135.40	122.20	98.70	113.90	40.71	35.46	16.12
1967	66.50	22.98	33.07	4.87	1.60	3.99	86.8	101.00	81.60	73.00	88.90	99.50	34.41	32.09	16.39
1968	49.10	20.50	20.30	3.86	1.09	3.34	72.1	111.50	61.40	79.40	68.10	93.80	24.39	24.71	14.45
1969	79.83	23.10	42.69	7.75	1.72	4.57	169.4	112.70	212.50	200.60	157.90	136.90	43.35	36.48	16.55
1970	97.12	26.16	51.61	12.09	2.06	5.20	137.0	109.40	147.80	156.00	120.00	113.70	54.04	43.08	18.38
1971	118.46	30.78	62.46	16.94	2.31	5.96	119.4	104.90	120.60	140.10	112.20	114.60	66.16	52.30	22.04
1972	117.86	29.58	61.89	17.67	2.63	6.08	99.7	95.90	99.60	104.30	113.80	102.10	65.98	51.88	20.17
1973	122.28	30.96	66.05	15.85	3.10	6.31	105.5	104.10	110.30	89.70	117.70	103.70	69.08	53.20	21.52
1974	123.65	31.94	68.10	14.14	3.06	6.40	101.1	102.70	103.30	89.20	98.70	101.50	68.36	55.29	22.58
1975	133.68	33.95	75.36	14.49	3.41	6.47	108.5	106.10	110.60	102.50	111.50	101.10	75.86	57.82	23.10
1976	128.83	33.84	71.47	13.08	3.30	7.14	96.8	99.60	95.70	80.20	96.70	110.40	73.18	55.65	23.13
1977	141.69	33.67	82.08	14.66	3.68	7.60	110.2	99.20	114.90	112.10	111.70	106.40	79.50	62.19	23.44
1978	161.45	36.27	96.48	16.53	4.06	8.10	112.8	102.70	118.80	112.80	110.40	106.60	90.24	71.21	24.37
1979	182.63	45.86	105.79	16.43	4.88	9.68	108.5	113.00	105.80	100.60	120.20	119.40	100.50	82.13	32.96
1980	184.40	41.88	109.96	17.16	6.12	9.29	99.8	85.90	102.90	104.50	125.20	96.10	104.00	80.40	28.87
1981	188.90	46.47	108.64	17.09	6.06	10.65	100.9	105.60	98.70	99.60	99.00	114.60	104.37	84.53	33.95
1982	214.13	56.90	117.71	20.67	8.01	10.85	113.6	123.50	108.20	120.90	132.30	101.90	121.53	92.75	38.11
1983	235.72	60.95	131.77	22.70	8.12	12.18	109.2	100.50	113.60	109.80	101.40	112.30	134.56	101.15	40.68
1984	276.68	73.69	150.70	28.66	9.53	14.10	114.8	113.50	114.90	119.80	123.20	106.00	154.97	121.71	49.90
1985	343.05	79.58	192.08	39.58	12.63	19.18	118.5	102.80	121.80	123.50	133.50	140.70	196.70	146.35	51.53
1986	385.40	87.20	219.26	41.69	13.74	23.51	109.1	104.80	112.30	96.40	107.50	114.80	224.79	160.61	56.06
1987	452.14	103.39	258.44	47.85	16.31	26.15	109.5	102.70	114.10	103.90	117.00	105.70	264.73	187.41	66.31
1988	577.15	130.52	331.74	61.97	25.27	34.29	121.4	106.90	116.10	104.60	132.30	106.70	341.96	236.35	82.16
1989	681.02	147.81	406.71	61.88	30.10	34.52	104.9	105.90	109.70	92.80	100.80	61.40	407.07	273.95	91.77

26. Shaanxi

26–2

Year	v1d2	v1d3	v1d4	v1d5	v1e	v1e1	v1e2	v1e3	v1e4	v1e5	v1f	v1f1	v1f2	v1f3	v1g
1949	0.87		0.07	0.77											
1950	1.00	0.02	0.08	0.80	111.4										8.59
1951	1.16	0.17	0.11	0.54	112.0										11.64
1952	1.56	0.20	0.16	1.45	113.9	100.4	155.2	119.2	145.9	265.1					13.38
1953	2.07	0.54	0.28	1.93	122.3	114.6	134.3	267.6	180.0	133.7					17.66
1954	2.84	0.60	0.40	2.26	115.2	110.8	135.4	110.0	141.0	117.0					21.11
1955	3.32	1.17	0.48	2.55	103.6	91.1	128.3	196.5	120.9	112.8					22.62
1956	3.99	2.10	0.67	3.11	124.3	120.4	117.8	179.0	138.7	122.1					24.65
1957	4.14	1.51	0.86	3.22	95.3	92.0	106.5	71.7	128.7	103.3					24.48
1958	7.95	2.12	0.98	3.52	130.7	112.6	192.6	140.9	113.9	109.4					28.38
1959	11.19	3.03	1.57	3.89	115.1	90.7	140.5	142.7	159.5	110.7					36.22
1960	13.40	3.18	1.75	3.98	105.0	85.8	123.4	105.1	111.9	102.1					37.29
1961	7.25	0.85	1.08	4.07	66.9	92.1	49.7	26.9	61.6	102.3					27.75
1962	5.98	0.98	0.63	3.24	86.1	96.1	78.5	114.3	58.4	79.7					25.20
1963	6.54	1.11	0.91	2.61	110.3	115.4	115.8	113.1	144.7	80.5					26.04
1964	7.67	1.24	0.85	2.79	109.3	106.9	115.5	112.3	93.7	106.8					28.19
1965	9.55	1.69	0.96	2.74	132.7	138.4	139.7	136.4	112.5	98.3					35.19
1966	13.14	2.05	0.99	3.16	109.8	89.7	135.0	120.6	103.2	115.3					40.33
1967	10.58	1.28	0.73	3.11	88.9	100.2	81.3	62.4	73.7	98.6					34.55
1968	6.35	0.92	0.42	2.57	75.5	88.8	60.0	72.0	57.0	82.7					30.64
1969	13.27	2.28	0.68	3.70	153.2	112.6	211.2	248.6	163.5	143.6					43.75
1970	16.01	3.56	1.00	4.04	128.2	105.6	147.4	160.4	146.3	109.3					52.85
1971	19.92	4.57	1.03	4.64	116.9	106.4	124.4	127.6	103.1	114.9					63.44
1972	20.19	5.67	1.18	4.67	99.3	90.9	101.8	121.5	114.4	100.8					62.98
1973	21.47	3.95	1.51	4.76	103.7	106.2	109.9	69.6	128.3	101.7					58.85
1974	21.47	4.91	1.53	4.81	103.8	104.5	100.2	124.4	101.2	101.1					59.25
1975	23.84	4.42	1.74	4.72	104.4	101.3	111.0	90.1	113.9	98.1					60.55
1976	22.94	3.30	1.66	4.62	96.7	100.8	97.1	74.6	95.3	97.9					59.49
1977	27.28	4.70	1.88	4.89	111.5	101.0	117.6	142.6	112.9	105.9					64.26
1978	33.34	5.65	2.07	5.79	112.9	99.3	121.2	120.1	110.3	118.3	81.33	24.70	42.39	14.24	73.52
1979	35.34	5.26	2.49	6.08	109.0	120.1	104.9	93.0	120.6	105.0	94.80	32.52	44.95	17.33	85.75
1980	37.76	5.41	2.63	5.74	95.0	76.2	106.6	102.8	105.4	94.5	95.21	28.47	47.94	18.80	82.73
1981	35.86	5.99	2.47	6.26	100.8	108.8	94.5	110.9	94.2	109.1	102.41	35.40	46.57	20.44	94.03
1982	37.78	6.85	3.62	6.39	110.5	113.5	106.1	114.5	146.2	102.0	112.30	37.02	50.71	24.57	107.94
1983	41.76	7.36	4.06	7.29	106.2	99.1	110.4	107.3	112.4	114.1	123.80	40.00	55.56	28.24	113.95
1984	50.01	8.96	4.55	8.29	117.1	115.4	120.9	113.6	117.8	106.0	149.79	51.04	63.57	35.18	140.48
1985	63.98	12.51	6.10	12.23	115.5	97.5	121.9	129.7	134.8	159.3	181.36	53.39	81.23	46.74	192.30
1986	70.19	13.99	6.57	13.79	106.3	104.5	108.3	102.5	106.5	105.4	200.86	57.98	87.44	55.44	211.86
1987	81.49	17.03	8.19	14.39	107.7	102.6	110.6	108.8	122.7	101.9	233.16	67.82	100.48	64.86	241.73
1988	105.06	20.41	9.49	19.19	118.7	105.7	120.5	97.6	140.8	109.0	302.00	82.69	133.32	85.48	293.49
1989	127.62	20.53	17.94	16.09	103.8	108.3	109.3	90.2	112.2	50.1	339.84	91.28	150.27	98.29	363.87

26. Shaanxi

26–3

Year	v1h	v1i	v1j	v1j1	v1j2	v1j3	v1k	v2a	v2a1	v2a2	v2b	v2c	v2c1	v2c2	v2d1
1949															0.78
1950								0.28	0.14	0.14	0.13	0.13			
1951								1.70	0.68	1.02	0.64	0.64			
1952				495				1.95	0.68	1.27	1.04	1.04			1.51
1953				545				4.09	1.92	2.17	2.11	2.11			
1954				539				5.72	2.08	3.64	2.42	2.42			
1955	73.40			603				6.35	2.97	3.38	3.61	3.61			
1956	80.50			622				6.76	6.44	0.32	7.94	7.94			
1957	76.10			650				5.52	4.88	0.64	5.64	5.64			8.45
1958	77.10			596				8.64	7.41	1.23	7.72	7.72			
1959	80.47			557				15.61	11.09	4.52	10.84	10.84			
1960	90.90			554				16.04	12.21	3.83	12.09	12.09			
1961	105.30			567				5.19	2.07	3.12	3.51	3.51			
1962	109.40			629				1.36	0.67	0.69	1.82	1.82			27.57
1963	100.20			672				2.43	1.68	0.75	2.41	2.41			
1964	87.30			689				5.66	4.35	1.31	3.42	3.42			
1965	105.90			674				8.80	6.55	2.25	5.55	5.55			33.15
1966	97.08			642				13.97	10.02	3.95	7.84	7.84			
1967	97.98			637				7.90	5.85	2.05	3.95	3.95			
1968	86.73			632				6.32	3.37	2.95	3.20	3.20			
1969	99.30			651				15.12	9.76	5.36	8.24	8.24			
1970	109.58			627				22.40	17.19	5.21	17.13	17.13			48.70
1971	118.23			630				29.18	22.29	6.89		22.50			
1972	114.31			614				27.73	21.11	6.62		21.25			
1973	122.90			631				21.83	19.07	2.76		17.75			
1974	125.51			646				19.58	16.83	2.75		14.98			
1975	116.53			636				20.84	17.28	3.56		14.87			89.35
1976	119.07			632				17.74	14.50	3.24		12.88			98.34
1977	127.95			633				21.26	16.34	4.92		13.81			106.47
1978	133.57	16.44	654	669			1.85	26.45	19.18	7.27	20.35	17.20	9.57	0.54	116.50
1979	149.60	18.31	705	728	570		2.26	27.93	18.15	9.78	21.16	17.46	8.88	0.57	125.54
1980	142.20	21.55	785	811	633		3.38	18.18	20.01	-1.83	27.80	23.24	12.13	0.98	134.14
1981	177.17	22.46	780	812	609		3.94	21.85	17.11	4.74	22.92	17.48	7.54	0.87	138.92
1982	218.31	24.00	797	831	618		4.69	28.76	21.60	7.16	29.48	23.32	8.54	1.09	154.90
1983	236.11	25.28	824	857	637		5.47	28.53	27.58	0.95	30.83	24.99	8.14	0.85	167.62
1984	262.51	30.79	973	1024	806		6.89	39.79	31.51	8.28	40.38	28.07	8.16	1.33	178.05
1985	295.26	36.84	1122	1152	855		8.03	72.66	47.64	25.02	57.98	39.80	11.38	1.64	193.52
1986	299.13	44.13	1291	1323	970		9.81	78.91	52.50	26.41	63.53	47.25	13.15	1.78	212.85
1987	329.47	49.40	1409	1452	1034		12.42	89.69	62.88	26.81	80.89	58.11	16.09	2.48	233.91
1988	404.14	60.08	1680	1731	1175		20.02	111.86	78.60	33.26	94.72	67.08	19.73	4.42	262.14
1989	433.67	68.12	1856	1975	1319		17.11	144.17	68.33	75.84	93.54	63.49	23.09	4.62	286.05

26. Shaanxi

26–4

Year	v2d2	v2e	v3a	v3b	v3b1	v3b2	v3c	v3d	v3d1	v3d2	v3e	v3e1	v3e2	v3e3	v3e4
1949			7.87	7.75	5.91	1.84	0.12	58.3	46.9	108.6					
1950			8.31	8.18	6.94	1.24	0.13	57.9	53.5	107.0					
1951			9.94	9.74	7.99	1.75	0.20	64.9	58.3	134.7					
1952			11.43	11.16	8.87	2.29	0.27	72.4	64.2	141.8					
1953			13.57	13.15	9.82	3.33	0.42	81.4	71.0	143.9					
1954			15.39	14.86	11.14	3.72	0.53	89.4	78.4	154.6					
1955			16.27	15.72	11.87	3.85	0.55	91.7	80.3	162.8					
1956			17.89	17.20	12.51	4.69	0.69	97.4	83.0	181.2					
1957			18.96	18.28	13.39	4.89	0.68	100.8	86.5	185.1					
1958			19.74	18.86	13.81	5.05	0.88	103.2	87.8	197.3					
1959			20.61	19.54	13.44	6.10	1.07	105.0	84.7	222.3					
1960			21.25	19.93	13.17	6.76	1.32	103.4	80.8	226.8					
1961			22.56	21.31	14.23	7.08	1.25	108.3	85.7	229.4					
1962			23.84	22.64	15.85	6.79	1.20	113.2	92.6	235.7					
1963			23.61	22.12	15.55	6.57	1.49	108.2	87.8	241.6					
1964			22.53	21.21	14.49	6.72	1.32	101.5	80.0	240.1					
1965			26.39	24.90	17.81	7.09	1.49	116.7	96.6	243.7					
1966			26.36	24.74	17.23	7.51	1.62	113.6	91.7	250.4					
1967			26.65	24.98	17.28	7.70	1.67	112.1	90.2	247.3					
1968			24.32	22.57	14.75	7.82	1.75	99.1	75.5	241.6					
1969			28.63	26.75	17.58	9.17	1.88	114.7	88.1	272.2					
1970			30.45	28.60	19.00	9.60	1.85	118.5	92.4	269.2					
1971			34.26	32.28	21.42	10.86	1.98	129.5	101.4	285.6					
1972			35.25	33.11	21.49	11.62	2.14	129.6	99.9	288.3					
1973			37.02	34.59	22.51	12.08	2.43	132.4	102.2	294.7					
1974			39.67	36.75	24.58	12.17	2.92	138.3	109.4	297.5					
1975	67.84	30.03	39.71	36.53	24.05	12.48	3.18	135.4	105.1	305.2					
1976	74.13	33.12	41.75	38.19	24.91	13.28	3.56	139.9	107.4	324.0					
1977	78.80	35.01	43.00	39.35	25.39	13.96	3.65	142.7	108.2	339.7					
1978	84.19	38.71	47.07	43.06	27.64	15.42	4.01	154.6	116.9	365.5	268				
1979	92.57	40.88	57.82	52.64	35.81	16.83	5.18	187.1	150.7	384.1					
1980	95.41	42.09	64.55	58.20	37.96	20.24	6.35	204.9	159.2	444.8	371	199	67.80	4.68	11.04
1981	96.88	42.15	72.18	64.47	42.17	22.30	7.71	224.6	175.9	471.5	379	201	58.39	4.94	7.56
1982	108.38	44.96	79.18	70.02	46.72	23.30	9.16	240.9	193.1	477.6	392	215	62.74	5.49	8.30
1983	117.04	47.11	85.42	75.07	50.13	24.94	10.35	255.6	205.5	501.8	417	229	66.82	5.95	8.28
1984	123.52	47.95	100.69	87.98	59.41	28.57	12.71	296.9	242.3	558.2	457	249	75.08	6.05	8.12
1985	133.06	56.04	119.64	103.37	65.80	37.57	16.27	344.9	267.5	699.6	585	286	95.47	6.35	10.14
1986	145.71	70.86	132.95	113.26	68.75	44.51	19.69	374.1	277.0	815.9	698	346	110.19	8.11	10.31
1987	159.28	76.51	152.04	127.48	76.70	50.78	24.56	413.0	305.0	890.0	772	393	113.92	9.04	10.23
1988	178.97	89.72	181.63	154.61	89.73	64.88	27.02	494.0	353.0	1102.0	983	459	155.52	8.40	12.12
1989	193.90	111.85	219.70	187.05	108.55	78.50	32.65	587.0	420.0	1300.0	1066	539			

26. Shaanxi

26–5

Year	v3f	v3f1	v3f2	v3f3	v3f4	v4a1	v4a1a	v4a1b	v4a1c	v4a1d	v4a2	v4a2a	v4a2b	v4a2c	v4a2d
1949															
1950						0.86	0.0013	0.2638	0.5835	0.0114	0.31	0.0024	0.0569	0.2236	0.0271
1951						1.35	0.0069	0.5635	0.7243	0.0553	0.79	0.2571	0.1242	0.2817	0.1270
1952						1.81	0.0283	0.8622	0.6913	0.2282	1.11	0.3296	0.2467	0.3458	0.1879
1953						2.42	0.0771	1.2534	0.8801	0.2094	1.56	0.4130	0.4727	0.4444	0.2299
1954						2.94	0.1587	1.6012	0.8896	0.2905	1.83	0.6031	0.5558	0.4563	0.2148
1955	85	52	14.40	1.27	11.37	2.95	0.2383	1.6279	0.8211	0.2627	1.93	0.5542	0.5410	0.5271	0.3077
1956	77	45	11.57	1.16	11.88	3.28	0.3511	1.9151	0.7822	0.2316	2.83	1.0012	0.6307	0.6660	0.5321
1957	77	47	13.75	1.87	8.55	3.40	0.3729	2.0399	0.7006	0.2866	2.62	0.7186	0.7235	0.6936	0.4843
1958	70	46	9.77	1.35	7.99	7.41	3.2800	2.9317	0.8826	0.3157	5.89	3.4126	0.9632	0.6749	0.8393
1959	75	47	11.58	1.39	9.33	9.90	5.5061	3.2967	0.9660	0.1312	9.23	4.6089	1.2228	0.8376	2.5607
1960	81	48	13.74	1.41	10.89	10.46	6.0259	3.4506	0.8055	0.1780	11.16	5.8659	1.6316	0.8531	2.8094
1961	96	62	14.74	1.42	11.62	6.72	3.3244	2.4576	0.6896	0.2484	4.74	0.7222	1.2020	0.8643	1.9515
1962	105	71	14.81	1.28	11.53	5.72	2.3036	2.4969	0.7102	0.2093	3.14	0.3070	1.0301	0.7093	1.0936
1963	95	61	14.61	1.42	11.53	5.42	2.0022	2.4369	0.7918	0.1891	3.83	0.6076	1.0553	0.6789	1.4882
1964	88	56	14.05	1.41	11.12	5.86	2.3540	2.6604	0.7295	0.1161	4.33	1.0554	1.1598	0.7422	1.3726
1965	87	55	13.95	1.41	11.04	6.55	2.6726	3.0839	0.7253	0.0682	5.79	1.7203	1.2391	0.8035	2.0271
1966	99	64	15.02	1.43	11.82	8.39	3.4327	4.0713	0.8332	0.0528	7.12	2.0125	1.5139	0.7553	2.8383
1967	100	65	15.10	1.43	11.80	6.19	1.7652	3.5871	0.7904	0.0473	5.64	1.9137	1.2967	0.6693	1.7603
1968	89	56	14.11	1.41	11.16	3.37	0.2777	2.2661	0.7792	0.0470	4.30	1.5562	1.0689	0.6904	0.9845
1969	101	66	15.21	1.43	11.95	7.54	2.2377	4.3559	0.8777	0.0687	7.15	3.5587	1.1118	0.9140	1.5655
1970	111	70	15.95	3.76	10.79	9.78	3.2935	5.5365	0.8481	0.1019	9.29	5.0500	1.2877	0.9906	1.9617
1971	119	77	16.64	3.84	11.18	11.62	4.5473	6.1387	0.8566	0.0774	10.34	3.9959	1.6730	1.1205	3.5506
1972	115	74	16.33	3.80	11.00	13.57	7.0095	5.6720	0.8201	0.0684	11.86	4.3874	1.9585	1.2062	4.3079
1973	124	71	16.92	9.80	9.86	14.10	6.9072	6.2509	0.8499	0.0920	12.16	4.0334	2.2106	1.1481	4.7679
1974	126	73	17.12	9.89	9.95	13.97	6.6425	6.4172	0.8567	0.0536	12.69	3.8628	2.3878	1.2266	5.2128
1975	118	66	16.43	9.57	9.63	15.23	7.1803	7.1438	0.8398	0.0661	12.84	3.8136	2.4904	1.2528	5.2832
1976	120	68	16.63	9.66	9.72	13.60	5.4918	7.2236	0.8205	0.0641	13.15	3.2238	2.6026	1.2870	6.0366
1977	128	75	17.30	9.98	10.04	15.02	6.2168	7.9284	0.8181	0.0567	13.83	3.2853	2.7676	1.3659	6.4112
1978	134	79	17.72	10.17	10.23	19.76	8.8020	9.1242	0.7523	1.0815	18.30	4.3783	3.1691	1.5043	9.2483
1979	149	89	19.13	11.77	11.50	16.80	5.9595	9.3646	0.8962	0.5797	19.56	4.7021	3.7268	1.7893	9.3418
1980	139	83	17.93	11.03	10.78	15.81	4.9243	9.7462	0.6701	0.4694	18.28	3.3764	4.3297	2.2504	8.3235
1981	148	92	18.82	9.13	9.75	13.45	2.2355	10.1996	0.7168	0.2981	16.39	1.8225	4.7264	2.3819	7.4592
1982	169	106	20.56	10.11	10.94	13.56	1.3073	10.8453	0.8919	0.5155	17.30	1.9641	5.7168	2.5416	7.0775
1983	203	122	22.72	18.69	12.40	14.54	1.7141	11.1306	0.9402	0.7551	18.81	2.5708	5.6764	2.9783	7.5845
1984	214	129	22.35	22.82	11.90	15.31	1.0790	12.5419	1.0026	0.6865	22.75	3.3049	6.4736	3.9808	8.9907
1985	233	134	25.60	27.60	14.00	20.30	2.0612	16.4636	1.3228	0.4524	27.50	4.1858	7.5428	4.0889	11.6825
1986	263	147	30.57	30.99	13.73	24.09	3.1523	18.7384	1.3420	0.8573	35.59	4.5735	9.0107	4.7107	17.2951
1987	286	158	29.71	32.18	13.47	28.18	3.0753	22.7805	1.3347	0.9895	37.81	3.6450	9.8577	5.0205	19.2868
1988	345	181	36.79	43.97	15.62	33.88	1.3050	28.8629	1.8522	1.8599	44.58	3.1753	11.8383	6.7000	22.8664
1989	383	199	39.24	47.35	20.76	38.96					50.79	3.9000	13.4900	8.1400	25.2600

26. Shannxi

26–6

Year	v4b	v4b1	v4b2	v4b3	v4c1	v4c2	v5a	v5a1	v5a2	v5a3	v5a4	v5b1	v5b2	v5b3	v5c
1949		0.0027					531	13			488				
1950		0.0196					570	21			517				
1951		0.1913					610	28			549				
1952	0.2812	0.2812	0.0001				631	34			565				
1953	0.4163	0.4153	0.0284				677	44			601				
1954	0.4888	0.4838	0.1317				706	50			625				
1955	0.5689	0.5639	0.2653				728	56			637				
1956	0.7406	0.7406	0.4217				754	69			656				
1957	1.2234	0.9156	0.9334				766	68			667				
1958	1.3146	1.0193	0.7219				791	103			655				
1959	2.0286	1.3939	2.1145				803	106			658				
1960	2.3202	1.5495	2.2858				832	122			658				
1961	2.0032	1.2553	2.5457				805	101			680				
1962	1.3819	1.0080	1.4187				810	81	19	5	705				
1963	1.5742	1.1602	1.4326				816	79	20	3	713				
1964	1.8795	1.5031	1.4322				845	84	28	3	730				
1965	2.2110	1.7108	1.8281				868	97	32	2	737				
1966	2.3708	1.9301	2.0502				886	103	28		755				
1967	2.4845	2.0485	1.8883				901	106	27		769				
1968	2.6864	2.2572	1.7364				915	108	27		780				
1969	2.7273	2.2958	1.8712				955	120	27		808				
1970	3.0864	2.6156	2.2311				971	145	26		800				
1971	3.6971	3.0944	3.1864				1009	166	25		818				
1972	4.3473	3.5961	2.8822				1030	177	30		823				
1973	4.8867	3.9637	3.3927				1025	173	26		825				
1974	5.2414	4.3320	2.9644				1029	175	26		828				
1975	5.5124	4.6184	2.9896		12.63	12.9	1039	180	30	0	829				
1976	5.7582	4.8311	3.3451		11.85	11.1	1044	181	30	0	833				
1977	6.6696	4.3313	4.1016		13.42	11.8	1053	188	33	0	832				
1978	7.7945	6.1290	4.1132		16.52	13.4	1078	222	35	0	821	768	189	121	
1979	10.1950	7.9619	5.4658		17.84	13.4	1105	225	40	0	840	796	187	122	
1980	13.5059	10.5298	5.6576		18.30	13.3	1158	239	43	1	875	832	195	131	
1981	16.6489	12.5716	6.1753		16.56	11.9	1202	250	47	2	903	861	203	138	
1982	20.5076	15.3768	7.2855		17.80	11.6	1250	258	50	3	939	893	195	162	
1983	25.4274	18.9735	7.2179		19.53	11.9	1285	261	51	4	969	910	199	176	
1984	33.1703	24.5184	7.0506		22.13	12.9	1337	260	63	7	1007	922	218	197	
1985	44.7681	32.8042	9.3079		26.08	13.8	1375	271	65	9	1029	874	282	219	
1986	62.4729	45.2680	12.8444		26.99	12.5	1409	282	67	10	1049	873	301	235	
1987	88.3660	63.6271	15.7609		28.88	12.3	1449	289	68	14	1077	884	309	256	
1988	108.6483	78.1159	14.6934		36.65	13.6	1494	298	68	15	1112	928	297	269	
1989	150.4000	111.4000	39.0000		40.69	13.3	1529	304	68	17	1138	966	300	263	

26. Shaanxi

26–7

Year	v5c1	v5d	v6a	v6a1	v6a2	v6b	v6c	v6d1	v6d2	v6d3	v6d4	v6d5	v6d6
1949			1317	125	1192			155	1162	692	625	72.00	
1950			1400	137	1262			101	1298	737	663		
1951			1485	148	1337			115	1371	795	691		
1952			1528	160	1368			147	1381	818	710	87.05	5.08
1953			1615	175	1441			218	1397	869	746		
1954			1651	183	1469	34.84	11.01	229	1422	884	767		
1955			1716	245	1471	29.83	10.54	238	1478	928	788		
1956			1756	269	1487	28.03	9.85	249	1507	941	815		
1957			1803	285	1518	32.18	10.31	258	1545	963	840	131.04	7.75
1958			1832	443	1389	26.66	11.01	254	1578	972	860	139.65	24.29
1959			1881	469	1412	26.63	12.72	311	1570	1001	880		
1960			1944	498	1446	27.68	12.27	363	1581	1038	906		
1961			1968	377	1592	21.02	8.76	296	1672	1037	931	156.70	27.12
1962			2008	352	1656	34.62	9.35	257	1751	1052	955	151.50	27.53
1963			2056	360	1696	38.71	10.55	263	1793	1077	979	156.37	28.90
1964			2100	324	1775	40.13	15.60	272	1828	1101	999	161.88	30.03
1965			2144	334	1810	34.71	13.01	286	1858	1123	1022	167.04	31.22
1966			2193	344	1850	34.41	12.91	297	1896	1148	1045		
1967			2232	363	1869	32.41	12.56	304	1928	1167	1065		
1968			2287	370	1917	34.80	12.31	316	1971	1193	1094		
1969			2360	375	1986	38.55	11.79	328	2032	1229	1132		
1970			2428	396	2032	29.28	6.80	331	2097	1265	1163	178.12	36.88
1971			2492	397	2096	30.36	7.16	365	2127	1302	1191		
1972			2554	404	2150	30.18	8.35	377	2177	1330	1224		
1973			2610	415	2195	27.01	7.66	384	2226	1359	1252		
1974			2655	420	2236	24.40	7.68	385	2270	1381	1274		
1975			2692	435	2257	21.70	8.16	387	2305	1400	1292	191.03	43.38
1976			2722	437	2285	19.01	7.95	387	2335	1416	1306		
1977			2751	443	2308	18.24	7.42	394	2357	1430	1322		
1978			2780	454	2326	17.24	6.92	408	2372	1444	1336	198.21	45.52
1979			2807	469	2338	17.01	6.86	426	2381	1456	1351		
1980			2831	522	2309	15.16	6.97	442	2389	1468	1363	209.07	47.53
1981			2865	535	2329	17.40	6.78	459	2405	1486	1378		
1982			2904	548	2356	19.02	6.67	471	2433	1507	1397		
1983			2931	577	2354	15.46	6.52	484	2447	1525	1406		
1984			2966	1101	1865	16.61	6.15	509	2457	1546	1420		
1985			3002	1167	1835	16.09	5.99	540	2462	1566	1436	232.80	64.98
1986			3043	1203	1840	17.03	5.71	541	2502	1588	1454	238.69	66.76
1987			3088	1244	1844	16.78	5.56	558	2530	1613	1476	257.69	68.33
1988			3140	1405	1735	21.04	6.11	575	2565	1640	1500	264.94	70.40
1989			3198	1439	1759	22.25	6.32	594	2604	1671	1527	270.80	72.88

26. Shaanxi

26–8

Year	v7a	v7b	v7c	v7d	v7e	v7f	v7g	v7h	v7h1	v7h2	v7h3	v7h4	v7h5	v7i	v8a
1949				7114				7.99	4.90	0.02	1.04		2.03	115.0	2.86
1950			370.17	7467		0.05		9.05	5.60	0.02	1.11		2.32	121.3	3.28
1951		0.5	402.55	7786		0.24		10.91	6.76	0.02	1.49		2.63	138.7	3.83
1952	0.001	0.6	452.07	7916	6645	0.45		10.75	6.42	0.02	1.55		2.76	158.3	4.95
1953	0.001	0.6	501.22	7972		0.52		14.23	8.65	0.07	2.24		3.27	179.9	6.63
1954	0.002	2.0	529.72	7966		1.00		15.89	9.23	0.08	2.22		4.36	194.9	8.51
1955	0.017	13.0	558.45	8026		2.64		14.51	8.02	0.13	2.01		4.35	199.7	9.37
1956	0.057	57.9	684.96	8457		4.14		18.78	10.68	0.16	2.24		5.70	191.2	11.23
1957	0.079	113.8	758.49	8364	22470	4.48		17.72	9.18	0.13	2.91		5.50	189.7	11.34
1958	0.266	206.9	830.78	8369		6.58		18.72	15.00	0.41	1.50		1.81	179.9	19.90
1959	0.525	324.5	882.73	7665		6.57		18.29	14.21	0.33	1.28	0.01	2.46	173.3	29.49
1960	0.844	327.8	896.12	8212		6.70		18.02	14.90	0.37	1.02	0.01	1.72	164.8	36.83
1961	0.969	382.4	910.25	8156		4.39		22.22	17.77	0.73	1.13		2.59	150.8	21.19
1962	1.252	360.0	939.22	7997	25005	4.93		19.36	15.20	0.45	1.51		2.20	148.5	18.14
1963	1.732	432.2	990.00	8078		4.81		18.31	14.68	0.46	1.57		1.60	151.9	19.69
1964	1.996	659.7	1047.00	8288		6.42		18.35	14.67	0.50	1.61		1.57	152.8	23.88
1965	2.426	951.1	943.19	8440	16830	18.36	1.6	23.66	19.39	0.67	1.63		1.97	155.8	29.65
1966	2.610	908.0	1031.75	8541		28.81		22.76	18.17	0.77	1.89		1.93	162.3	40.94
1967	2.985	763.2	1034.90	8102		30.32		22.98	17.86	1.17	2.18		1.77	163.9	33.08
1968	3.388	596.2	1032.57	7802		14.03		20.50	15.46	1.23	2.22		1.59	168.7	20.30
1969	4.328	946.3	1100.42	7796		30.63		23.10	17.75	1.29	2.18		1.88	158.7	42.69
1970	6.620	919.9	1254.53	8001	4950	32.60		26.16	20.31	0.80	2.58	0.01	2.46	180.6	51.61
1971	10.616	1150.7	1447.20	7710		34.73		30.78	24.08	0.88	3.34	0.01	2.47	174.0	62.46
1972	13.276	1288.7	1495.86	7689		38.61		29.58	21.82	1.05	4.53	0.01	2.17	175.4	61.89
1973	17.576	1427.4	1581.82	7672		50.88		30.96	23.48	1.10	3.87	0.01	2.50	177.3	66.05
1974	22.710	1562.7	1690.50	7645		46.74		31.94	25.29	1.45	3.22	0.01	1.97	173.2	68.01
1975	27.407	1621.5	1768.67	7697		53.60		33.95	26.71	1.28	3.90	0.01	2.05	169.3	75.36
1976	31.617	1736.2	1755.27	7611		57.40		33.84	26.16	1.31	3.92	0.01	2.44	162.8	71.47
1977	34.251	2026.5	1860.86	7773		65.00		33.67	25.39	1.21	4.02	0.01	3.04	165.0	82.07
1978	39.125	2124.4	1818.75	7882		109.17	11.1	36.27	26.88	1.17	4.15	0.01	4.06	162.3	96.48
1979	43.412	2145.0	1856.84	7671		132.00		45.86	33.84	1.48	5.23	0.02	5.30	159.3	105.79
1980	47.136	1890.9	1872.70	7609		123.30	12.1	41.88	29.10	1.66	5.16	0.02	5.94	163.4	109.96
1981	49.368	1590.9	1874.07	7262		109.68	14.3	46.47	32.34	1.65	5.57	0.02	6.89	168.6	108.64
1982	52.614	1347.6	1870.88	7102		136.50	12.8	56.90	40.20	3.20	7.25	0.03	6.21	180.6	117.71
1983	53.637	1254.1	1858.48	7142		156.34	11.2	60.95	41.17	3.97	7.54	0.04	8.23	180.3	131.77
1984	55.573	1596.3	1769.17	7057	1783	182.24	14.0	73.69	52.60	4.31	10.86	0.08	5.84	177.1	150.70
1985	56.153	1535.5	1768.60	6995	1086	174.24	14.8	79.58	54.37	5.08	13.14	0.13	6.86	182.3	192.08
1986	59.607	2038.4	1867.70	7017	2475	188.94	18.9	87.20	59.45	5.60	13.95	0.24	7.96	187.9	219.26
1987	62.250	2150.1	1888.60	7192	2385	198.20	21.8	103.39	69.30	6.13	18.80	0.36	8.80	193.1	258.44
1988	64.131	2282.1	1856.70	7166	1290	229.40	21.4	130.52	80.46	8.37	29.88	0.58	11.23	199.2	331.74
1989	67.860	2463.7	1871.10	7251		267.28	26.2	147.81	94.24	8.45	31.62	0.69	12.81	201.6	406.71

26. Shaanxi

26–9

Year	v8a1	v8a2	v8a3	v8b	v8c1	v8c2	v8d	v8f1	v8f2	v8f3	v8f4	v8f5	v8g
1949	0.24	0.02	2.60		0.60	2.26			61	0.08	0.28		
1950	0.36	0.02	2.90		0.73	2.55			61	0.05	0.31		73804
1951	0.57	0.03	3.23		0.92	2.91			85	0.03	0.40		76248
1952	1.13	0.03	3.79		1.18	3.77			103	0.08	0.61		77837
1953	2.04	0.05	4.54		1.52	5.11			116	0.14	0.90		79463
1954	3.17	0.20	5.14		1.76	6.75			103	0.35	1.42		78786
1955	4.05	0.44	4.88		2.34	7.03		0.03	120	0.43	1.62		68758
1956	5.97	1.43	3.83		3.30	7.93		0.06	152	0.70	2.43		18185
1957	6.31	1.50	3.53		3.01	8.33		0.06	180	0.71	2.77		19490
1958	18.47	1.41	0.02		8.62	11.28		0.38	464	0.94	4.74	1	4828
1959	26.48	3.01			14.51	14.98		1.25	569	1.35	7.40	6	5878
1960	32.23	4.60			22.69	14.14		2.85	626	2.01	10.07	51	7698
1961	17.95	3.16	0.08		10.91	10.28		1.45	459	1.47	8.97	19	5653
1962	15.33	2.61	0.20		8.24	9.90		0.71	420	1.03	9.00	18	4978
1963	17.50	2.09	0.10		9.98	9.71		0.75	482	1.00	9.88	24	3830
1964	21.59	2.29			12.42	11.46		0.83	410	1.12	11.51	40	3675
1965	27.13	2.52			14.83	14.82		1.35	394	1.21	14.48	55	3872
1966	37.90	3.04			21.66	19.28		3.18	422	1.22	18.34	73	3039
1967	30.36	2.72			16.77	16.30		2.76	278	1.28	15.75	32	2817
1968	18.78	1.52			7.92	12.38		1.42	364	0.78	13.64	22	2861
1969	39.70	2.99			23.56	19.13		2.82	483	1.40	21.32	49	2897
1970	47.69	3.92			31.79	19.82		4.51	674	1.57	26.88	74	5093
1971	56.64	5.82			37.16	25.30		7.41	822	1.85	34.77	99	5875
1972	54.66	7.23			37.75	24.14		10.14	949	2.47	38.83	116	6033
1973	58.03	8.02			37.05	29.00		12.71	1082	2.66	37.18	135	5791
1974	59.46	8.64	-0.09		38.82	29.28		13.67	1072	4.20	37.09	145	6258
1975	65.44	9.92			40.41	31.95		15.15	1140	4.57	43.86	162	7183
1976	60.48	10.99			39.09	32.38		12.87	1168	4.59	46.19	150	8951
1977	69.18	12.89		67.88	44.31	37.77	21.96	15.69	1479	5.45	55.73	191	9593
1978	81.26	15.22		80.43	53.42	43.06	26.91	24.29	1666	6.03	66.10	211	9771
1979	90.19	15.60		87.99	58.56	47.23	28.67	22.98	1782	7.16	71.29	222	9794
1980	92.57	17.35	0.04	91.05	54.86	55.10	30.46	24.49	1792	8.44	79.14	229	12991
1981	91.22	17.29	0.13	89.69	49.39	59.25	28.77	21.39	1845	9.33	75.13	219	12678
1982	98.16	19.34	0.21	96.65	58.71	58.99	29.63	19.95	2018	11.40	74.37	258	15232
1983	110.38	21.14	0.25	108.41	69.90	61.86	33.20	28.67	2229	14.66	80.06	280	16817
1984	119.66	29.14	1.90	117.25	86.15	64.55	37.95	32.58	2417	17.85	90.87	310	20746
1985	145.69	42.39	4.00	143.73	111.97	80.11	45.56	34.71	2693	22.10	108.77	384	17361
1986	159.66	51.61	7.99	156.82	126.82	92.44	48.45	36.22	2861	26.19	125.21	444	21131
1987	185.25	61.06	12.13	181.84	150.35	108.09	54.88	39.73	2856	35.69	143.70	469	23891
1988	235.54	78.47	17.73	232.00	191.79	139.95	71.04	43.59	2765	43.10	138.21	503	24679
1989	284.91	94.48	27.32	278.69	238.01	168.71	84.93	46.46	3149	55.47	148.54	538	12763

26. Shaanxi

26–10

Year	v8g1	v9a	v9a1	v9a2	v9a3	v9b	v9b1	v9b2	v9b3	v9c	v10a	v10a1	v10b1	v10b2	v10b3
1949			1.47							314.5					
1950			5.23	0.06			2.84	0.16		398.8					
1951			4.93	0.16			4.12	0.16		413.2					
1952		4.35	3.97	0.37	0.01	5.12	4.67	0.36	0.09	469.6	6.34	6.18			
1953		6.44	5.60	0.82	0.02	7.19	6.24	0.82	0.13	619.2	7.97	7.79			
1954		9.10	7.84	1.24	0.02	10.18	8.66	1.37	0.15	748.1	10.14	9.69			
1955		10.43	8.66	1.75	0.02	15.88	14.22	1.46	0.20	889.3	10.40	9.94			
1956		15.90	12.86	3.02	0.02	23.31	21.23	1.87	0.21	1152.1	12.45	11.69			
1957		15.98	13.08	2.88	0.02	30.85	28.09	2.40	0.36	1249.5	12.65	11.78			
1958		18.50	15.63	2.84	0.03	40.26	37.30	2.61	0.35	1620.1	13.44	12.28			
1959		24.78	21.49	3.23	0.05	58.16	52.95	4.73	0.48	1094.8	15.50	13.90			
1960		31.05	27.40	3.58	0.06	65.15	58.50	6.25	0.40	2818.0	17.04	14.94			
1961		41.12	38.26	2.79	0.05	40.25	37.25	2.75	0.24	2587.3	14.92	13.27			
1962		40.73	37.17	3.49	0.04	34.40	32.36	1.87	0.17	2333.6	15.46	13.96			
1963		23.96	20.50	3.41	0.03	40.60	38.36	2.09	0.14	2185.0	14.25	13.03			
1964		23.20	19.45	3.69	0.03	44.06	41.41	2.49	0.16	2510.2	14.34	13.04			
1965		25.03	20.63	4.32	0.04	66.12	62.81	3.10	0.21	2627.6	15.70	13.89			
1966		29.55	23.23	6.25	0.05	80.07	76.09	3.83	0.15	2489.6	17.64	15.26			
1967		32.31	25.69	6.55	0.04	53.05	49.66	3.23	0.15	2312.0	17.82	15.56			
1968		34.35	29.55	4.76	0.03	42.39	39.83	2.42	0.13	1950.3	16.71	14.54			
1969		41.44	34.44	6.93	0.06	69.30	65.27	3.88	0.14	2442.7	21.46	18.53			
1970		40.81	33.10	7.61	0.09	101.39	96.56	4.67	0.16	3010.9	24.03	20.61			
1971		43.31	34.77	8.42	0.09	108.37	103.20	5.00	0.18	3594.7	27.45	22.90			
1972		48.20	39.11	8.93	0.12	117.73	111.74	5.81	0.19	3780.2	29.92	24.57			
1973		51.79	42.79	8.83	0.13	125.13	118.48	6.49	0.15	4173.6	31.40	25.78	19.44		11.50
1974		51.09	41.10	9.82	0.11	122.98	116.38	6.41	0.18	4198.3	31.90	25.93	19.58		11.86
1975	1990	51.93	41.77	9.97	0.12	137.63	130.44	7.00	0.19	4270.0	33.60	27.01	20.26		12.88
1976	2043	52.53	41.34	11.03	0.06	121.55	114.33	7.03	0.19	4723.7	35.29	28.66	21.10		13.69
1977	2120	55.24	43.23	11.82	0.06	157.98	149.71	8.06	0.20	4875.2	37.81	30.70	22.46		14.80
1978	2194	60.73	47.56	12.95	0.00	176.11	165.58	10.39	0.14	5025.4	41.58	33.37	24.55		16.39
1979	2160	68.61	54.02	14.17	0.01	173.73	163.33	10.26	0.14	5394.6	45.20	36.60	25.99		18.15
1980	2138	80.29	62.88	16.23	0.01	190.26	179.57	10.54	0.12	5594.5	51.25	43.38	28.94		20.32
1981	2102	77.91	59.05	17.63	0.01	174.15	163.11	10.86	0.14	5729.2	54.80	47.52	30.06		22.05
1982	2106	89.68	66.14	21.12	0.01	187.52	173.10	14.16	0.19	5955.3	59.11	50.65	31.17		24.62
1983	2128	100.89	74.28	24.88	0.01	216.19	199.76	16.14	0.23	6384.5	64.64	54.90	32.16		26.87
1984	1975	117.34	84.63	30.26	0.02	285.50	239.57	45.68	0.18	6894.0	73.32	63.00	35.98		28.88
1985	2104	157.01	106.85	44.75	0.04	336.19	282.25	53.62	0.18	7870.9	91.90	80.01	41.95		35.60
1986	2149	174.86	114.93	49.66	0.07	358.47	294.15	63.88	0.25	8356.9	104.11	91.40	45.78		39.06
1987	2192	198.54	125.87	58.62	0.08	405.27	338.75	66.01	0.24	9519.2	120.99	106.16	52.40		44.89
1988	2237	231.43	148.18	68.72	0.08	424.90	356.73	67.62	0.27	12335.5	158.99	140.07	68.44		58.90
1989	2280	217.85	142.69	64.70	0.09	451.30	373.39	77.45	0.26	13974.9	176.67	153.65	75.66		66.48

26. Shaanxi

26–11

Year	v10b4	v10b5	v10b6	v10d	v11a1	v11a2	v11a3	v11b	v11b1	v11b2	v11c	v11d	v12a	v12b	v12c
1949															
1950															
1951													109.8	109.8	111.6
1952				2.58									108.4	105.2	103.4
1953				3.19									103.5	103.9	112.7
1954				5.20									101.1	100.7	99.1
1955				4.79									100.8	99.7	98.0
1956				4.47									99.1	98.2	103.6
1957				5.65									101.8	100.8	103.0
1958				5.18									98.2	97.3	100.8
1959				7.92									100.3	100.3	100.7
1960				5.85									101.3	101.5	104.1
1961				5.58									126.0	122.7	121.3
1962				4.34									96.5	95.6	93.5
1963				4.99									91.4	95.7	100.3
1964				4.65									97.0	95.7	98.0
1965				6.59									97.5	98.2	100.1
1966				6.98									99.8	99.9	106.4
1967													99.1	99.1	100.3
1968													100.4	100.3	100.4
1969													99.6	99.7	99.9
1970				6.39									99.9	99.8	100.9
1971				7.77					0.1275				99.8	101.0	101.2
1972				7.79					0.1238				100.6	100.8	100.9
1973		0.02	0.44	9.82					0.0935				101.0	101.2	101.5
1974		0.02	0.44	9.08					0.0828				100.8	100.9	99.6
1975		0.02	0.44	9.57					0.0730				100.3	100.6	102.1
1976		0.02	0.48	9.95					0.0600				100.8	101.1	98.1
1977		0.02	0.53	10.76					0.0319				100.6	100.4	101.1
1978		0.02	0.62	10.60					0.1190				100.5	100.6	104.3
1979		0.04	1.02	13.92					0.0856				101.6	101.4	122.1
1980	0.0050	0.34	1.65	14.99					0.0973				104.7	105.4	106.9
1981	0.0034	0.52	2.17	16.37				0.3060	0.2616	0.0444			103.0	103.6	102.1
1982	0.0035	0.90	2.42	18.86				0.6067	0.5000	0.1067			101.0	100.4	102.3
1983		2.93	2.68	17.68				0.6713	0.5426	0.1287			101.5	102.2	104.2
1984	0.0197	5.41	3.03	20.17				1.2385	0.9662	0.2723			103.9	103.4	102.8
1985	0.1558	9.09	5.10	26.11				1.5712	1.0359	0.5353			106.5	107.6	107.8
1986	0.4816	10.55	8.24	31.42				2.3452	1.7158	0.6294			105.2	106.6	107.8
1987	0.4891	13.47	9.74	39.46				3.4685	2.6582	0.8103			108.6	109.2	110.8
1988	0.4010	18.20	13.05	52.34				4.9297	3.6006	1.3291			119.0	120.1	121.4
1989	0.2700	19.73	14.53	59.29				5.3209	3.8273	1.4936		1.05	118.8	117.6	111.0

26. Shaanxi

26–12

Year	v13a	v13b	v13c1	v13c2	v13c3	v13d	v14a	v14b	v14c	v15a	v15b	v15c	v15d	v15e	v15f
1949			0.2742	4.36	72.82	0.0509									
1950			0.2742	4.91	81.81	0.0484				6577					
1951			0.4201	5.56	105.50	0.0569				6760					
1952			0.4711	8.20	148.07	0.1233	3400	10000		6805					
1953			0.6098	10.74	140.09	0.1409				6832					
1954			0.7155	12.69	152.54	0.1926				6829					
1955			0.8782	14.31	153.17	0.1844				6781					
1956			2.2322	19.65	185.88	0.1504				6673					
1957		52.89	2.5059	25.32	187.91	0.3015				6653					
1958			3.2201	32.92	230.54	0.3233				6360					
1959			3.9989	42.44	254.66	0.3401				6117					
1960			4.2136	49.39	287.36	0.7416				6100					
1961			4.2706	38.29	247.56	0.9169				6156					
1962		67.52	3.6225	27.11	204.33	0.8283				6256					
1963			3.2999	27.02	209.75	0.9071				6274					
1964			3.2303	29.12	261.57	0.7749				6397					
1965		83.45	3.2126	32.69	326.30	0.8258	18600	40000		6496					
1966			3.1587	42.25	292.43	0.4413				6423					
1967			2.3592	47.26	306.07	0.7531				6308					
1968			1.5020	42.33	309.47	0.8667				6222					
1969			1.2540	63.61	320.85	0.2584				6269					
1970			0.0908	89.29	353.61	1.2409				6124					
1971			0.1969	114.56	375.60					6025					
1972			0.8406	108.75	381.48	0.0278				5975					
1973			1.5090	112.73	419.33	0.0920				5919					
1974			2.2765	120.53	435.23	0.0531				5889					
1975		98.03	2.5234	138.76	448.37	0.7520				5859					
1976			2.5730	168.10	442.84	0.9309				5810					
1977			2.8710	196.90	427.13	0.8816				5798					
1978	9.77	95.66	3.4355	196.24	450.51	0.8244	49900	70000		5780					
1979			4.0290	187.82	455.68	0.6210				5758					
1980	13.83	95.91	5.3871	187.41	452.14	0.3803	55200	80000	3.18	5724					
1981	16.98		6.3979	166.89	437.31	0.3473			3.48	5683					
1982	16.57		5.6073	162.62	415.26	2.3106			2.97	5663					
1983	16.11		6.0289	161.44	389.44	1.5119			4.32	5638					
1984	15.11	96.75	6.8093	173.73	384.09	1.3952			5.20	5529					
1985	15.61	97.05	8.2117	182.25	367.87	1.4721	64600	110000	5.48	5441	7000.38			998.86	6.54
1986	14.33	97.69	8.8958	191.68	353.08	1.8292			5.62	5385	7062.00	420.20	1437.65	1464.84	6.50
1987	14.61	98.02	9.1792	194.13	339.43	2.5537			6.39	5344					
1988	15.54	97.99	9.7955	177.08	340.97	2.3982	72200	110000	6.27	5327	7873.95	414.42	1696.90	1554.16	6.46
1989		98.10	9.8600	141.55	351.10	2.5100	74691	120000	4.80	5312					

Notes

1. National Output and Income (Y)

v1a: (E), p.803
- v1a1: (E), p.803
- v1a2: (E), p.803—including the industries at village level and below since 1971
- v1a3: (E), p.803
- v1a4: (E), p.803
- v1a5: (E), p.803

v1b: (A); (B), p.235
- v1b1: (A); (D), p.376
- v1b2: (A); (D), p.376
- v1b3: (A); (D), p.376
- v1b4: (A); (D), p.376
- v1b5: (A); (D), p.376

v1c: v1a – v1d

v1d: (E), p.800
- v1d1: (E), p.800
- v1d2: (E), p.800
- v1d3: (E), p.800
- v1d4: (E), p.800
- v1d5: (E), p.800

v1e: (A); (B), p.242
- v1e1: (A); (D), p.379
- v1e2: (A); (D), p.379
- v1e3: (A); (D), p.379
- v1e4: (A); (D), p.379
- v1e5: (A); (D), p.379

v1f: (E), p.799
- v1f1: (E), p.799
- v1f2: (E), p.799
- v1f3: (E), p.799

v1g: v2a + v3a

v1h: (A); (E), p.828

v1i: (E), p.827

v1j: (E), p.827
- v1j1: (E), p.827
- v1j2: (E), p.827
- v1j3: NA

v1k: (E), p.827

2. Investment (I)

v2a: (A); (E), p.802
- v2a1: (A); (B), p.245
- v2a2: (A); (B), p.245

v2b: (A)

v2c: (A); (B), p.257–258; (E), p.818—included inter-regional investment
- v2c1: (E), p.819
- v2c2: (E), p.819

v2d:
- v2d1: (E), p.816
- v2d2: (E), p.816

v2e: (E), p.816

3. Consumption (C)

v3a: (E), p.802

v3b: (E), p.802
- v3b1: (A); (B), p.247
- v3b2: (A); (B), p.247

v3c: (E), p.802

v3d: (E), p.826
- v3d1: (E), p.826
- v3d2: (E), p.826

v3e: (E), p.828
- v3e1: (A); (E), p.828
- v3e2: (A)
- v3e3: (A)
- v3e4: (A)

v3f: (A); (E), p.828
v3f1: (A); (E), p.828
v3f2: (A)
v3f3: (A)
v3f4: (A)

4. Public Finance and Banking (FB)

v4a:
v4a1: (E), p.824
v4a1a: (E), p.824
v4a1b: (B), p.480
v4a1c: (B), p.480
v4a1d: v4a1 – v4a1a – v4a1b – v4a1c
v4a2: (E), p.824
v4a2a: (E), p.824
v4a2b: (E), p.824
v4a2c: (E), p.824
v4a2d: v4a2 – v4a2a – v4a2b – v4a2c

v4b: (A)
v4b1: (B), p.484
v4b2: (A); (B), p.484
v4b3: NA

v4c:
v4c1: (E), p.816
v4c2: (E), p.816

5. Labor Force (L)

v5a: (E), p.798
v5a1: (E), p.798
v5a2: (E), p.798
v5a3: (E), p.798
v5a4: (E), p.798—excluding rural people working outside

v5b:
v5b1: (E), p.798
v5b2: (E), p.798
v5b3: (E), p.798

v5c: NA
v5c1: NA

v5d: NA

6. Population (PO)

v6a: (E), p.797—data from public security department, adjustment was made in particular year
v6a1: (E), p.797—(ditto)
v6a2: (E), p.797—(ditto)

v6b: (E), p.797—data since 1985 from sample survey

v6c: (E), p.797—(ditto)

v6d:
v6d1: (E), p.797—data from public security department, adjustment was made in particular year
v6d2: (E), p.797—(ditto)
v6d3: (E), p.797—(ditto)
v6d4: (E), p.797—(ditto)
v6d5: (A)—Xi'an
v6d6: (A)—Xianyang

7. Agriculture (A)

v7a: (A); (E), p.810

v7b: (A); (E), p.810

v7c: (A); (E), p.810

v7d: (A); (E), p.810

v7e: (A)

v7f: (A); (E), p.810

v7g: (A)

v7h: (A); (E), p.805
v7h1: (E), p.805
v7h2: (E), p.805
v7h3: (E), p.805
v7h4: (E), p.805
v7h5: (E), p.805

v7i: (A); (E), p.809

8. Industry (IN)

v8a: (E), p.811—including industries at village level and below since 1971
- v8a1: (A); (E), p.811
- v8a2: (E), p.811
- v8a3: v8a – v8a1 – v8a2

v8b: (E), p.816

- v8c1: (E), p.803
- v8c2: (A); (E), p.803

v8d: (E), p.816

v8f:
- v8f1: (E), p.815
- v8f2: (E), p.815
- v8f3: (E), p.815
- v8f4: (E), p.815
- v8f5: (E), p.815

v8g: (A)
- v8g1: (E), p.816

9. Transport (TR)

v9a: (E), p.817—excluding urban traffic volume
- v9a1: (E), p.817—figures from road bureau, larger than the traffic volume under provincial jurisdiction
- v9a2: (E), p.817
- v9a3: (A); (E), p.817—excluding distant ocean and coastal passenger traffic

v9b: (E), p.817
- v9b1: (E), p.817—figures from road bureau, larger than the traffic volume under provincial jurisdiction
- v9b2: (E), p.817
- v9b3: (E), p.817—excluding distant ocean and coastal freight volume

v9c: (E), p.817—based on 1980's constant price

10. Domestic Trade (DT)

v10a: (E), p.820
- v10a1: (E), p.820

v10b:
- v10b1: (E), p.820
- v10b2: NA
- v10b3: (E), p.820—including supply and marketing cooperative and other collectives
- v10b4: (E), p.820
- v10b5: (E), p.820
- v10b6: (E), p.820

v10d: (A); (E), p.822—calculated on calendar year basis

11. Foreign Trade (FT)

v11a:
- v11a1: NA
- v11a2: NA
- v11a3: NA

v11b: (E), p.823—data from foreign trade department
- v11b1: (E), p.823—(ditto)
- v11b2: v11b – v11b1

v11c: NA

v11d: (A)

12. Prices (PR)

v12a: (E), p.825

v12b: (A); (E), p.825

v12c: (E), p.825

13. Education (ED)

v13a: (A)

v13b: (E), p.828

v13c:
- v13c1: (A); (B), p.495; (E), p.828—general institutions of higher learning
- v13c2: (A); (B), p.499; (E), p.828
- v13c3: (A); (B), p.503; (E), p.828

v13d: (A)

14. Social Factors (SF)

v14a: (E), p.828

v14b: (E), p.828

v14c: (A)

15. Natural Environment (NE)

v15a: (A); (E), p.810

v15b: (A)

v15c: (A)

v15d: (A)

v15e: (A)

v15f: (A)

Sources of Data

(A) Data supplied by the DSNEB, SSB, the PRC.
(B) Statistical Bureau of Shaanxi Province ed. *Shaanxi Forty Years, 1949–1989*, Beijing: CSPH, 1989.
(D) Same as (D) in Beijing's sources of data.
(E) Same as (E) in Beijing's sources of data.

27

Gansu

27. Gansu

Year	v1a	v1a1	v1a2	v1a3	v1a4	v1a5	v1b	v1b1	v1b2	v1b3	v1b4	v1b5	v1c	v1d	v1d1
1949	10.36	6.63	1.32	0.17	0.55	1.69							3.82	6.54	4.82
1950	11.59	7.21	1.51	0.24	0.73	1.91							4.20	7.39	5.30
1951	14.70	7.94	2.00	1.69	0.96	2.12							5.72	8.98	5.95
1952	16.78	8.93	2.48	2.09	1.11	2.18	111.63	110.84	120.91	123.27	111.63	99.62	6.83	9.95	6.67
1953	18.15	9.59	2.89	2.14	1.30	2.24	105.27	102.86	117.79	104.18	117.03	102.48	7.43	10.72	7.12
1954	20.78	10.52	3.52	2.90	1.42	2.43	118.65	117.15	124.50	139.22	107.83	107.08	8.71	12.07	7.90
1955	22.93	10.46	3.87	4.31	1.71	2.58	112.92	105.21	118.64	146.70	121.32	106.07	10.14	12.79	7.72
1956	28.72	10.90	4.83	7.98	1.82	3.20	125.69	110.68	120.03	193.96	105.18	119.51	13.92	14.80	8.25
1957	29.81	10.13	6.22	7.86	2.51	3.09	97.59	88.30	117.64	97.54	137.49	99.60	14.73	15.08	7.60
1958	37.08	11.58	9.48	9.41	3.26	3.35	122.02	110.10	160.37	122.18	131.21	111.29	19.38	17.70	8.34
1959	44.13	10.29	16.35	9.49	3.84	4.15	112.46	88.76	169.20	102.13	118.29	121.74	24.31	19.82	6.85
1960	44.27	7.17	19.45	9.47	3.76	4.42	93.47	69.19	116.72	92.47	96.22	104.88	26.23	18.04	4.62
1961	22.90	7.18	8.64	1.90	2.18	3.01	50.36	90.35	43.89	17.26	49.76	53.58	12.40	10.50	4.45
1962	27.16	8.24	11.87	1.78	2.06	3.22	111.42	104.58	128.26	93.95	98.64	110.95	15.50	11.66	5.03
1963	32.48	10.24	13.86	2.93	2.19	3.26	126.31	136.32	116.26	172.83	106.85	108.04	18.35	14.13	5.96
1964	39.24	10.61	18.75	4.19	2.41	3.29	121.90	111.68	135.47	145.40	114.92	102.07	21.99	17.25	6.42
1965	49.94	11.91	24.06	7.60	3.08	3.30	128.85	115.19	133.12	186.79	129.12	98.28	27.77	22.18	7.26
1966	52.27	10.20	27.81	8.32	2.68	3.26	103.58	85.70	119.05	112.53	86.87	102.76	31.38	20.89	6.20
1967	48.78	12.30	23.69	6.91	2.66	3.23	96.62	120.28	85.39	83.55	100.45	97.54	29.90	18.88	7.38
1968	47.15	11.47	24.57	5.68	2.36	3.07	95.53	92.90	104.22	78.92	90.18	99.05	27.74	19.41	6.88
1969	58.07	12.12	33.34	7.11	2.32	3.18	120.81	105.53	137.10	126.31	97.83	102.22	34.70	23.36	7.15
1970	76.41	13.73	47.58	9.18	2.62	3.30	129.86	113.13	144.38	131.68	112.10	102.06	46.26	30.15	7.96
1971	82.96	13.69	54.23	9.04	2.75	3.25	109.07	100.49	117.96	95.81	102.26	100.98	50.07	32.89	7.87
1972	84.66	16.26	52.59	8.68	3.06	4.08	103.74	106.92	101.31	99.64	112.63	125.68	49.16	35.50	9.19
1973	90.52	17.97	55.72	8.31	3.40	5.12	103.87	99.87	105.95	94.22	106.69	120.76	51.89	38.63	10.39
1974	98.55	21.93	58.91	8.43	3.34	5.93	110.48	122.00	107.47	98.63	102.50	117.37	55.68	42.87	12.57
1975	112.70	23.29	69.71	8.94	3.57	7.18	113.64	105.25	120.15	100.33	103.56	114.39	62.75	49.93	13.50
1976	112.03	22.22	70.16	8.18	3.76	7.71	99.29	95.40	101.08	89.09	104.97	108.38	63.42	48.61	12.26
1977	116.63	21.33	74.32	8.75	4.04	8.19	104.55	97.19	106.24	113.27	108.72	104.62	66.46	50.17	12.21
1978	125.21	22.45	79.38	11.15	4.25	7.98	107.97	104.10	107.63	125.36	105.47	105.86	70.59	54.62	13.04
1979	127.01	23.28	80.64	10.86	4.26	7.98	99.74	93.55	102.29	97.77	98.08	100.72	73.36	53.65	12.72
1980	134.03	27.39	78.60	11.95	5.34	10.76	104.77	111.13	97.33	118.11	132.09	129.24	73.33	60.70	16.25
1981	130.36	28.02	74.87	11.96	5.63	9.89	92.58	90.67	93.40	86.19	102.09	94.81	72.88	57.48	17.22
1982	141.74	30.32	81.32	13.73	6.12	10.25	109.01	112.56	108.41	109.93	106.42	104.24	79.75	61.99	18.76
1983	160.99	39.79	88.18	14.15	6.43	12.45	110.48	113.13	109.15	111.17	110.88	112.27	86.73	74.26	25.58
1984	181.55	40.33	101.36	17.09	7.96	14.81	112.94	113.01	111.03	120.00	115.53	117.73	98.48	83.07	25.33
1985	232.68	48.74	126.41	25.06	13.25	19.22	120.60	108.85	118.43	139.26	182.60	112.72	130.92	101.76	30.14
1986	267.11	56.40	143.99	27.72	16.06	22.93	111.54	107.27	108.63	111.95	112.52	144.85	149.99	117.12	34.87
1987	304.44	65.52	159.88	30.93	18.60	29.51	109.78	102.42	108.56	110.30	118.71	125.25	171.73	132.71	40.67
1988	389.04	84.72	203.94	39.36	21.78	39.24	117.04	107.77	115.78	123.17	116.44	133.18	224.96	164.08	51.18
1989	455.73	89.12	249.22	44.06	25.30	48.03	109.30	106.75	108.12	110.90	113.82	113.80	269.85	185.88	52.22

27. Gansu

27–2

Year	v1d2	v1d3	v1d4	v1d5	v1e	v1e1	v1e2	v1e3	v1e4	v1e5	v1f	v1f1	v1f2	v1f3	v1g
1949	0.41	0.06	0.30	0.93											
1950	0.50	0.09	0.41	1.06											
1951	0.68	0.63	0.53	1.19											
1952	0.70	0.77	0.62	1.19	111.65	110.85	103.13	123.11	113.79	99.17					9.51
1953	0.83	0.81	0.72	1.21	104.05	102.84	118.20	104.90	114.09	100.80					11.45
1954	1.05	1.08	0.76	1.30	117.62	117.59	127.06	139.10	105.58	105.40					14.64
1955	1.30	1.53	0.91	1.33	108.39	103.57	123.79	143.59	119.16	102.62					19.09
1956	1.54	2.46	0.98	1.56	118.81	113.54	118.80	163.97	107.30	117.12					24.17
1957	2.05	2.53	1.36	1.55	94.96	87.40	123.16	101.65	138.36	97.19					23.00
1958	3.49	2.61	1.67	1.59	112.49	105.46	169.53	106.25	125.85	105.05					22.49
1959	5.75	3.22	2.06	1.95	104.05	82.05	165.09	120.33	120.53	120.05					26.87
1960	6.60	2.79	1.99	2.03	85.95	67.80	114.81	86.04	94.99	102.47					26.72
1961	2.89	0.70	0.94	1.51	57.64	88.15	43.68	20.41	42.82	60.40					12.92
1962	3.27	0.57	0.86	1.74	105.19	103.05	112.59	94.55	92.27	115.91					13.53
1963	4.46	1.09	0.85	1.78	129.32	130.24	135.49	175.48	103.85	108.70					15.73
1964	6.56	1.46	1.05	1.77	120.98	115.69	137.72	135.98	121.66	100.59					19.45
1965	9.23	2.70	1.35	1.62	127.00	115.06	140.90	193.16	131.86	93.60					25.18
1966	8.95	2.85	1.24	1.64	96.08	86.45	108.45	104.48	90.05	99.48					24.22
1967	6.52	2.22	1.19	1.56	104.76	117.89	72.52	78.07	98.74	95.38					22.40
1968	8.22	1.71	1.12	1.49	100.36	93.26	127.51	76.71	93.14	95.54					22.39
1969	11.31	2.21	1.13	1.56	116.66	103.80	137.55	128.57	100.23	106.63					25.71
1970	16.26	2.87	1.37	1.69	126.46	110.05	146.94	133.91	121.12	106.89					31.99
1971	19.08	2.77	1.47	1.70	108.76	99.57	120.50	94.55	104.89	103.77					34.47
1972	19.41	2.98	1.72	2.21	106.70	101.06	107.54	107.66	115.98	130.27					34.34
1973	20.65	2.97	1.82	2.80	105.49	102.90	106.68	96.65	105.75	122.57					37.38
1974	22.39	2.85	1.87	3.20	112.08	121.92	108.48	95.72	103.05	114.44					40.38
1975	27.79	2.83	1.93	3.83	115.68	106.57	126.09	98.55	102.12	113.89					46.05
1976	27.96	2.33	2.13	3.91	97.42	91.43	101.06	82.75	109.63	103.12					43.12
1977	29.19	2.72	2.32	3.74	103.05	99.25	104.45	116.30	109.53	95.92					44.44
1978	31.17	3.68	2.45	4.28	109.81	105.98	108.39	133.92	105.79	122.05	64.73	13.20	39.04	12.49	51.07
1979	33.18	3.43	2.48	4.55	99.88	87.32	106.00	95.79	99.91	105.56	67.52	12.89	40.98	13.65	53.15
1980	31.64	3.87	2.49	6.46	107.36	123.86	95.76	117.60	104.53	136.13	73.90	16.46	39.85	17.59	53.77
1981	27.13	3.84	2.68	6.61	89.49	92.62	84.11	85.42	105.78	105.45	70.89	17.63	35.30	17.96	55.65
1982	29.00	4.71	2.83	6.69	108.56	112.21	106.56	117.62	103.31	101.73	76.88	19.67	38.54	18.67	61.62
1983	23.22	5.20	3.05	8.11	114.50	117.58	112.18	121.25	113.73	112.06	91.50	27.65	42.92	20.93	72.14
1984	38.12	6.02	3.96	9.64	113.31	110.31	113.83	111.78	121.03	117.77	103.17	27.83	49.99	25.35	82.57
1985	44.84	7.85	6.49	12.44	115.14	107.15	111.84	133.27	179.58	112.01	123.39	33.08	58.81	31.50	108.97
1986	50.15	8.86	7.66	15.58	112.37	107.29	106.64	112.59	110.07	152.06	140.74	38.02	65.27	37.45	137.94
1987	52.26	9.77	8.13	21.87	107.85	102.78	101.86	103.68	110.41	136.67	159.52	45.27	68.41	45.84	152.74
1988	65.60	12.88	9.26	25.16	112.37	104.89	110.45	119.51	111.27	125.57	191.84	52.77	81.33	57.74	186.34
1989	77.52	13.44	11.75	30.95	108.14	103.52	106.96	109.46	112.35	114.41	216.84	59.01	91.79	66.04	227.80

27. Gansu

27–3

Year	v1h	v1i	v1j	v1j1	v1j2	v1j3	v1k	v2a	v2a1	v2a2	v2b	v2c	v2c1	v2c2	v2d1
1949															
1950															
1951															
1952		0.87	499	499				2.41	1.82	0.59					0.59
1953		1.32	563	563				3.91	2.95	0.96		1.97	0.19		0.76
1954		1.75	615	615				5.66	3.02	2.64		2.83	0.65		1.20
1955		2.34	662	662				9.06	3.36	5.70		3.64	1.45		1.78
1956		3.76	758	758				12.13	7.11	5.02		8.28	3.76		2.90
1957	92.71	4.03	790	790				9.46	6.63	2.83		7.69	4.04		3.88
1958		4.08	670	670				11.09	11.25	-0.16		9.96	7.08		6.25
1959		5.56	609	609				14.99	13.45	1.54		12.79	8.85		12.91
1960		6.67	609	609				15.06	14.43	0.63		11.82	6.56		17.74
1961		5.03	602	602				2.21	2.24	-0.03		2.34	1.61		21.19
1962	79.62	4.22	716	716				2.09	1.37	0.72		1.59	1.30		22.74
1963		3.91	768	768				3.71	2.26	1.45		2.37	1.59		24.20
1964		4.36	786	786				6.29	4.72	1.57		4.02	2.61		26.57
1965	98.47	4.92	766	766				10.59	9.04	1.55		6.95	5.07		29.25
1966		5.40	784	784				9.78	8.16	1.62		9.37	7.31		36.56
1967		5.42	714	714				8.53	6.94	1.59		6.35	5.06		41.61
1968		5.45	705	705				8.40	6.74	1.66		5.22	4.36		45.98
1969		5.56	689	689				10.08	7.91	2.17		7.57	5.76		51.74
1970		6.40	712	712				13.10	10.07	3.03		10.48	8.19		59.92
1971		7.17	687	687				14.43	10.70	3.73		11.33	8.65		61.70
1972		8.09	716	716				13.12	9.66	3.46		10.86	7.78		68.31
1973		8.12	708	708				14.78	10.47	4.31		10.72	7.55		76.64
1974		8.22	723	723				16.20	10.99	5.21		10.68	7.47		82.29
1975	96.53	8.44	714	714				19.22	12.12	7.10		11.29	7.80		91.38
1976	73.78	9.60	711	711	584			16.87	11.70	5.17		8.71	4.98		96.23
1977	84.88	9.80	704	704	484			16.18	11.35	4.83		8.03	4.81		99.29
1978	100.93	11.41	760	751	437			20.10	17.53	2.57		10.49	5.92	0.21	107.84
1979	111.57	12.51	778	792	658			19.15	16.53	2.62		11.69	6.65	0.32	111.17
1980	153.41	14.54	875	896	676			13.95	11.75	2.20	12.65	12.57	5.29	0.57	129.16
1981	158.63	15.50	878	904	676			12.35	9.82	2.53	14.10	11.73	4.24	0.62	142.18
1982	174.16	16.32	907	937	649			14.29	10.71	3.47	15.69	13.36	4.45	0.67	149.74
1983	213.10	17.37	944	973	702			18.00	13.27	4.74	18.47	15.98	5.16	0.38	158.67
1984	221.05	22.90	1201	1251	866			23.21	17.40	5.81	24.51	19.98	6.94	0.41	168.88
1985	257.00	26.44	1320	1368	955			35.58	27.59	7.99	33.90	25.97	8.89	0.43	177.82
1986	276.90	30.26	1481	1557	1016			47.16	32.97	14.19	40.42	31.09	10.63	0.42	192.68
1987	302.82	33.77	1604	1685	1112			47.57	37.74	9.83	47.91	38.39	14.35	0.53	212.16
1988	245.14	40.29	1869	1960	1320			59.49	35.56	23.94	59.54	47.00	19.45	0.81	233.28
1989	365.89	48.90	2207	2225	1486			77.75	39.73	38.02	46.16	37.96	17.80	0.66	250.12

27. Gansu

27–4

Year	v2d2	v2e	v3a	v3b	v3b1	v3b2	v3c	v3d	v3d1	v3d2	v3e	v3e1	v3e2	v3e3	v3e4
1949															
1950															
1951															
1952	0.47	0.14	7.10	6.41	4.97	1.44	0.69	61	52	157					
1953	0.61	0.17	7.54	6.84	5.23	1.61	0.70	63	53	168					
1954	0.91	0.20	8.98	8.20	6.03	2.17	0.78	74	60	208					
1955	1.40	0.26	10.03	9.14	6.55	2.59	0.89	80	64	229					
1956	2.33	0.45	12.04	10.85	7.36	3.49	1.18	91	70	267					
1957	3.23	0.45	13.54	12.24	8.42	3.82	1.30	99	78	253					
1958	5.42	1.12	11.40	10.26	5.89	4.37	1.14	81	53	263					
1959	11.34	2.79	11.88	10.38	4.69	5.69	1.50	81	43	301					
1960	15.34	4.44	11.66	10.26	4.32	5.94	1.40	81	41	289					
1961	17.88	4.61	10.71	9.31	4.36	4.95	1.40	76	42	261					
1962	18.41	3.87	11.44	10.34	5.69	4.66	1.10	84	53	292	198.96				
1963	19.41	3.74	12.02	10.65	6.27	4.38	1.37	86	57	291					
1964	21.04	3.92	13.17	11.79	6.97	4.82	1.38	93	63	296					
1965	22.86	4.16	14.59	13.29	8.28	5.01	1.30	101	73	283	212.64				
1966	28.57	6.01	14.44	13.03	8.41	4.62	1.41	95	71	244					
1967	32.52	6.75	13.87	12.42	8.43	3.99	1.45	88	69	205					
1968	35.93	9.01	13.99	12.43	8.46	3.97	1.56	85	67	197					
1969	41.50	9.97	15.63	13.93	9.55	4.38	1.70	92	73	221					
1970	48.06	12.23	18.89	16.78	11.96	4.82	2.11	108	88	250					
1971	49.49	15.28	20.04	17.83	12.05	5.78	2.21	111	86	282					
1972	53.49	17.32	21.22	18.86	12.55	6.31	2.36	113	87	285					
1973	59.31	17.74	22.61	20.05	13.15	6.90	2.56	117	88	301					
1974	61.53	18.77	24.18	21.45	13.64	7.81	2.73	121	89	322					
1975	68.66	20.52	26.83	23.80	14.96	8.84	3.03	132	96	354					
1976	70.85	21.85	26.25	23.11	13.51	9.60	3.14	126	86	380					
1977	71.46	23.47	28.27	24.82	14.66	10.16	3.45	134	92	398					
1978	77.01	25.16	30.97	26.81	15.91	10.90	4.16	143	99	419					
1979	77.14	25.30	34.00	29.14	17.53	11.61	4.86	154	108	430					
1980	85.32	29.30	39.82	33.97	19.81	14.16	5.85	177	121	509	399.00				
1981	93.79	29.95	43.30	36.83	22.10	14.73	6.47	190	133	526	433.33	252.36	75.36	5.04	10.56
1982	97.08	31.41	47.33	40.46	24.25	16.21	6.87	205	144	558	447.40	273.84	74.50	11.76	6.36
1983	101.57	31.65	54.14	45.77	27.39	18.38	8.37	229	161	615	482.30	273.80	79.80	12.84	7.20
1984	106.90	32.67	59.36	50.18	29.60	20.58	9.18	249	173	669	552.16	310.46	93.36	12.61	7.68
1985	112.24	38.84	73.39	61.10	36.21	24.89	12.29	299	210	780	625.21	316.30	113.76	5.76	12.96
1986	119.45	44.19	90.78	72.43	40.79	31.64	18.35	350	235	948	737.11	375.66	127.92	7.44	12.12
1987	133.68	49.29	105.17	85.13	47.53	37.60	20.04	405	271	1086	828.65	430.83	135.00	7.68	9.12
1988	149.36	53.04	126.85	102.51	56.90	45.61	24.34	484	322	1292	1026.53	501.71	171.48	8.64	14.40
1989	160.61	64.47	150.05	120.83	65.25	55.58	29.22	561	363	1561	1065.36	586.45	161.88	9.60	20.04

27. Gansu

27–5

Year	v3f	v3f1	v3f2	v3f3	v3f4	v4a1	v4a1a	v4a1b	v4a1c	v4a1d	v4a2	v4a2a	v4a2b	v4a2c	v4a2d
1949															
1950						0.49	0.0007	0.1042		0.0366	0.19		0.04	0.13	
1951						0.82	0.0055	0.3038		0.0178	0.36	0.04	0.07	0.23	0.03
1952						1.12	0.0196	0.4188		0.0748	0.64	0.09	0.15	0.33	0.08
1953						1.21	0.0680	0.6609		0.0968	0.99	0.21	0.27	0.38	0.13
1954						1.43	0.0644	0.6779		0.2033	1.26	0.38	0.29	0.46	0.14
1955						1.54	0.1113	0.7974		0.1825	1.56	0.53	0.32	0.44	0.27
1956						1.83	0.2035	1.0066		0.1295	2.80	1.34	0.45	0.59	0.43
1957						2.04	0.2547	1.1487		0.1781	2.46	1.10	0.48	0.58	0.30
1958						4.33	2.1718	1.3843		0.2441	5.02	3.15	0.51	0.59	0.77
1959						6.58	3.7895	2.0883		0.1052	8.08	4.78	0.66	0.73	1.92
1960						7.19	4.5083	2.3059		0.1006	10.75	5.93	0.85	0.72	3.26
1961						2.46	0.7258	1.1971		0.1912	5.44	1.05	0.65	0.73	3.02
1962						2.51	0.3707	1.6113		0.0923	2.33	0.20	0.57	0.64	0.92
1963						2.98	0.5649	1.8865		0.1394	2.71	0.40	0.59	0.63	1.09
1964						3.30	0.6643	2.1262		0.1015	3.35	0.78	0.68	0.68	1.22
1965						3.78	0.8850	2.3876		0.1102	4.19	1.53	0.68	0.67	1.31
1966						4.38	1.0979	2.7482		0.0991	4.47	1.55	0.81	0.63	1.48
1967						3.18	0.4291	2.4160		0.0623	3.98	1.49	0.80	0.55	1.14
1968						3.10	0.2391	2.3097		0.0640	2.80	0.97	0.65	0.56	0.62
1969						4.66	0.9811	3.0014		0.0740	4.54	2.04	0.67	0.67	1.17
1970						5.99	1.2676	4.0433		0.0961	6.56	3.78	0.78	0.62	1.37
1971						13.91	8.8040	4.4977		-0.3918	7.56	3.45	1.01	0.76	2.35
1972						14.18	8.6116	4.9823		0.0578	9.02	4.23	1.16	0.84	2.79
1973						15.19	9.5118	4.9922		0.0553	9.41	3.59	1.28	0.39	4.16
1974						16.12	10.0076	5.4963		0.0399	1.09	3.88	1.49	0.88	-5.17
1975						17.17	10.6908	5.9030		0.0497	10.64	3.70	1.55	0.86	4.52
1976						18.02	10.8522	6.5543		0.0689	11.22	3.71	1.62	0.99	4.90
1977						17.21	9.7942	6.8261		0.0412	11.11	3.18	1.73	1.03	5.17
1978	88.18	65.98				20.53	12.5560	7.0578		0.0552	14.34	4.15	2.08	1.18	6.93
1979	96.69	69.69				18.46	9.8524	7.5663		0.6675	14.18	3.77	2.38	1.34	6.70
1980	126.53	81.35	15.79	4.43	4.27	11.50	6.3923	7.5859		-2.7833	12.31	2.67	2.66	1.40	5.58
1981	135.23	92.99	16.37	5.17	7.11	9.77	4.8336	7.1022		-2.5198	11.20	1.64	2.78	1.57	5.20
1982	141.05	95.65	16.82	5.70	6.03	12.47	3.5309	7.8924		0.7060	12.79	1.62	3.41	1.72	6.03
1983	162.68	103.62	21.56	9.29	8.08	10.90	1.3852	8.4859		0.6083	15.53	2.34	3.71	2.15	7.32
1984	178.39	113.01	22.16	11.57	8.32	13.23	2.1661	10.0801		0.6207	21.15	4.12	4.89	2.89	9.25
1985	204.61	103.52	25.76	12.81	12.21	16.48	-2.4103	15.3907		-0.0134	24.00	4.13	5.71	3.06	11.10
1986	232.79	137.84	28.28	13.65	15.88	19.76	1.5839	17.1985		-2.9036	30.01	5.13	6.80	3.71	14.37
1987	252.84	144.22	20.95	14.00	21.25	22.58	2.4057	19.0098		-3.3441	31.36	4.36	6.93	3.71	16.37
1988	276.98	152.24	31.59	15.61	20.30	24.98	1.3398	21.6172		-3.1378	36.38	4.15	8.22	4.03	19.98
1989	296.38	163.80	31.76	25.09	17.36	31.52	0.6100			3.2500	41.26	4.02	9.36	4.49	23.39

27. Gansu

27–6

Year	v4b	v4b1	v4b2	v4b3	v4c1	v4c2	v5a	v5a1	v5a2	v5a3	v5a4	v5b1	v5b2	v5b3	v5c
1949							331.0	4.3	0.7	12.9	363.1				
1950					0.01		361.0	8.5							
1951					0.06		372.0	12.6							
1952					0.11		392.0	18.1	0.5	16.8	379.6				
1953					0.11		424.0	24.1							
1954					0.18		431.0	28.9							
1955					0.27		448.0	35.4							
1956					0.35		476.0	47.6							
1957		0.67			0.55		488.0	48.5	7.7	1.5	430.3				
1958					1.10		499.0	84.9		1.8	430.3				
1959					2.62		508.0	96.8							
1960					2.95		489.0	108.6							
1961					0.01		496.0	74.2							
1962	0.61	0.50	0.11		0.33		509.0	52.0	3.7	0.4	452.9				
1963					1.26		538.0	51.9	10.9						
1964					2.39		561.0	57.4	7.8						
1965	1.14	0.99	0.15		3.46		586.0	69.2	7.9	0.8	507.1				
1966							609.0	75.3	8.0						
1967							621.0	76.6	8.1						
1968							639.0	77.9	8.2						
1969							643.0	83.4	8.3						
1970	1.39	1.23	0.16				648.0	98.6	8.4		541.0				
1971	1.65	1.45	0.20		9.58		652.0	109.6	8.5						
1972	1.99	1.73	0.26		8.89		655.0	116.2	8.5						
1973	2.22	1.91	0.31		9.00		657.0	113.4	10.3						
1974	2.47	2.12	0.35				666.0	116.3	10.8						
1975	2.65	2.29	0.36		16.40		666.0	120.6	11.6		533.8				
1976	2.90	2.46	0.44		16.21		675.0	129.2	14.2						
1977	3.21	2.70	0.51		16.46		674.0	128.0	21.9						
1978	3.67	3.05	0.62		17.27	16.9	694.0	144.4	15.1	0.9	533.6	521.1	101.8	71.1	
1979	4.68	3.88	0.80		18.32	17.9	713.0	147.3	16.6						
1980	6.25	5.18	1.08		18.56	16.2	796.0	154.6	17.0	1.1	623.1	611.5	107.1	77.4	
1981	7.87	6.50	1.36		17.05	13.8	842.0	161.2	16.6	2.2	659.7	653.7	106.3	82.0	
1982	9.87	8.11	1.75		17.46	13.6	870.0	164.6	19.5	2.7	683.2	676.3	109.3	84.4	
1983	13.05	10.43	2.61		19.74	14.8	994.0	166.3	19.5	5.2	802.8	797.0	108.3	91.8	
1984	18.31	14.40	3.90		23.00	16.5	1047.0	169.5	26.7	10.2	841.7	803.3	124.2	119.4	
1985	25.20	20.01	5.19		26.00	17.2	1081.4	174.5	26.0	10.1	870.1	785.9	149.3	145.8	
1986	35.15	28.02	7.13		26.70	16.3	1098.9	179.1	29.0	12.8	877.9	789.5	175.3	136.1	
1987	47.31	37.91	9.40		29.26	16.1	1139.7	184.5	30.4	16.2	908.5	753.7	167.9	218.1	
1988	56.53	45.61	10.93		31.14	15.4	1178.8	188.3	31.8	16.0	942.5	798.3	185.8	194.7	
1989	73.90	61.20	12.70		32.96	14.7	1032.3	190.1	33.4	13.6	976.7	824.2	183.3	206.5	

27. Gansu

27–7

Year	v5c1	v5d	v6a	v6a1	v6a2	v6b	v6c	v6d1	v6d2	v6d3	v6d4	v6d5	v6d6
1949	0.7089		968.4	91.7	378.1	30.30	11.06	85	883	497	472	31.26	
1950	0.9836		1012.6	98.4	914.2	32.00	11.00	94	919	527	486		
1951	1.2714		1037.4	101.4	936.0	32.00	10.99	94	943	540	498		
1952	1.5217		1064.7	102.2	962.5	33.30	11.00	95	970	554	511	37.36	8.40
1953	2.5591		1099.6	110.3	989.3	33.56	10.96	104	996	583	517		
1954	3.3477		1118.4	118.2	1000.3	32.75	11.60	113	1005	582	537		
1955	3.7988		1155.0	126.4	1028.6	28.81	11.89	120	1035	601	554		
1956	4.9832		1218.4	155.9	1062.5	28.17	10.78	148	1070	637	582		
1957	5.3838		1255.1	169.4	1085.7	33.00	11.33	159	1096	651	604	79.79	7.02
1958	26.8532		1281.5	188.9	1092.6	31.46	21.11	179	1103	664	617	117.28	9.21
1959	29.8294		1293.1	217.6	1075.5	19.34	17.36	205	1088	670	624		
1960	33.5627		1244.0	219.5	1024.5	15.53	41.32	210	1034	655	590		
1961	20.8167		1210.8	189.4	1021.4	14.76	11.48	171	1040	622	589	96.28	14.13
1962	14.3749		1240.0	169.9	1070.1	41.12	8.25	148	1092	637	603	84.06	9.45
1963	14.1514		1249.2	170.9	1078.3	42.12	10.38	154	1095	646	604	94.05	9.21
1964	15.4164		1290.0	185.5	1104.5	47.18	15.55	168	1122	670	620	95.32	7.71
1965	16.4191		1345.4	212.5	1132.9	45.30	12.30	185	1160	699	647	103.56	8.26
1966	20.0739		1393.0	224.0	1169.0	42.56	11.50	193	1200	723	671		
1967	21.2098		1438.1	231.2	1206.9	39.33	7.98	197	1241	745	693		
1968	22.3958		1488.1	230.8	1257.3	42.30	8.36	205	1283	771	717		
1969	28.6588		1533.2	232.9	1300.3	41.80	8.83	190	1343	793	740		
1970	39.7650		1585.7	229.2	1356.5	39.43	7.92	194	1392	820	766	112.09	10.25
1971	47.5153		1640.7	227.7	1413.0	37.07	7.94	214	1427	848	792		
1972	49.1466		1692.2	256.7	1435.5	37.87	8.97	226	1466	874	818		
1973	47.1777		1742.1	263.8	1478.3	35.38	8.12	230	1512	900	842		
1974	48.6950		1778.7	265.7	1513.0	27.49	7.17	232	1547	918	860		
1975	52.4853		1804.0	265.0	1539.0	20.96	7.42	235	1569	932	872	125.56	27.90
1976	56.8711		1826.0	273.3	1552.7	17.72	6.73	240	1586	944	882		
1977	56.7068		1847.5	274.4	1573.1	17.49	6.09	243	1605	954	893		
1978	60.9846		1870.1	269.5	1600.6	17.77	5.58	247	1623	966	904	128.47	17.34
1979	59.1444		1893.8	279.9	1613.9	16.54	5.72	261	1633	977	917		
1980	62.6934		1918.4	290.7	1627.7	16.53	5.15	267	1651	990	929	137.38	18.08
1981	63.9974		1941.4	304.7	1636.7	20.12	5.72	272	1669	1004	937		
1982	67.1502		1974.9	315.4	1659.5	19.30	5.63	278	1697	1021	954		
1983	68.0900		1987.5	372.9	1614.6	19.79	6.76	290	1698	1028	959		
1984	72.3829		2015.6	414.6	1601.0	19.78	6.01	255	1761	1042	973		
1985	74.8940		2041.3	771.2	1270.1	18.31	5.46	311	1730	1057	984	135.36	95.32
1986	77.5164		2071.1	813.6	1257.5	21.14	5.91	326	1745	1071	1000	139.10	96.49
1987	79.8711		2103.4	848.2	1255.2	20.55	5.71	336	1767	1087	1016	141.61	98.30
1988	83.2566		2135.7	869.0	1266.7	20.41	5.06	346	1790	1104	1032	144.97	99.69
1989			2172.0	890.0	1281.0	22.57	5.60	355	1816	1122	1049	148.22	101.19

27. Gansu

27–8

Year	v7a	v7b	v7c	v7d	v7e	v7f	v7g	v7h	v7h1	v7h2	v7h3	v7h4	v7h5	v7i	v8a
1949								6.63	4.63	0.020	1.50		0.48	167	1.32
1950								7.21	5.07	0.023	1.57		0.54	179	1.51
1951								7.94	5.70	0.027	1.66		0.55	192	2.00
1952		3.90	489.13			0.01		8.93	6.36	0.029	1.80		0.73	207	2.48
1953								9.59	6.38	0.044	1.97		1.19	223	2.89
1954								10.52	7.30	0.054	1.98		1.19	234	3.52
1955								10.46	7.40	0.088	1.86		1.11	237	3.87
1956								10.90	8.01	0.197	1.87		0.83	243	4.83
1957		60.40	644.59	5311		0.71		10.13	7.71	0.280	1.37		0.76	241	6.22
1958		156.60						11.58	8.88	0.430	1.29		0.98	222	9.48
1959								10.29	8.18	0.350	0.94	0.0005	0.82	194	16.35
1960								7.17	6.11	0.120	0.52	0.0014	0.41	161	19.45
1961								7.18	5.77	0.090	0.76	0.0015	0.54	150	8.64
1962		109.90	773.00	5067				8.24	6.37	0.110	1.04	0.0008	0.73	150	11.87
1963								10.24	7.92	0.140	1.11	0.0006	1.07	158	13.86
1964								10.61	8.06	0.170	1.34	0.0007	1.04	168	18.75
1965		439.49	797.92	5299		6.20	0.20	11.91	9.15	0.180	1.39	0.0007	1.19	172	24.06
1966								10.20	7.42	0.270	1.41	0.0007	1.10	176	27.81
1967								12.30	9.61	0.240	1.29	0.0006	1.16	177	23.69
1968								11.47	8.61	0.220	1.42	0.0002	1.22		24.57
1969								12.12	9.11	0.240	1.43	0.0008	1.34		33.34
1970		523.00		5349		18.20	0.60	13.73	10.18	0.310	1.77	0.0008	1.47		47.58
1971			1029.80					13.69	10.22	0.310	2.05	0.0010	1.11	197	54.23
1972								16.26	31.27	0.420	2.41	0.0013	0.15	202	52.59
1973								17.97	12.99	0.540	2.92	0.0011	1.53	204	55.72
1974								21.93	16.12	0.730	3.25	0.0011	1.84	203	58.91
1975		1272.60	1403.00	5370		78.60	6.50	23.29	17.10	0.950	3.38	0.0012	1.85	204	69.71
1976								22.22	15.90	0.790	3.54	0.0009	1.99	204	70.16
1977								21.33	16.22	0.560	3.62	0.0013	0.93	208	74.32
1978	21.20	1402.63	1273.12	5258		75.60	7.68	22.45	15.82	0.520	3.78	0.0013	2.33	205	79.38
1979		1260.04	1269.80	5207		67.25	7.10	23.28	17.32	0.540	4.59	0.0015	0.83	211	80.64
1980	35.60	975.52	1277.98	5219	893	60.39	8.16	27.39	21.22	0.650	4.74		0.78	224	78.60
1981		732.96	1265.41	5107		57.56	8.73	28.02	21.51	0.980	4.69		2.50	242	74.89
1982		840.07	1270.36	5116		68.20	9.88	30.32	22.47	1.690	5.37		2.56	261	81.32
1983		786.87	1269.12	5222		75.90	9.54	39.79	29.86	2.120	6.85		2.92	278	88.18
1984		804.38	1270.95	5199	1453	75.60	10.34	40.33	27.97	3.120	8.72	0.0100	3.36	290	101.36
1985	43.90	837.01	1247.23	5235	380	72.69	11.24	48.74	32.07	3.630	10.45	0.0100	2.65	308	126.41
1986		986.59	1238.74	5253	1219	83.76	11.69	56.40	37.28	3.410	12.53	0.0300	3.15	327	143.99
1987		1135.35	1251.41	5369	1510	85.17	11.24	65.52	41.84	3.450	15.85	0.0600	4.31	335	159.88
1988	53.60	1022.31	1257.55	5351	1416	91.58	12.50	84.72	51.14	3.820	24.29	0.1200	5.35	347	203.94
1989	54.65	1180.60	1262.00	5366			13.00	89.12	55.24	3.320	25.21	0.1700	5.17	348	249.22

27. Gansu

27–9

Year	v8a1	v8a2	v8a3	v8b	v8c1	v8c2	v8d	v8f1	v8f2	v8f3	v8f4	v8f5	v8g
1949	0.23	0.02	1.06						17	7	0.05	0.01	
1950	0.33	0.02	1.16						19	10	0.06	0.22	
1951	0.56	0.02	1.42						24	14	0.07	0.30	
1952	1.00	0.02	0.52		0.87	1.61			33	14	0.10	0.27	1447
1953	1.40	0.02	1.47		1.24	1.66			49	23	0.15		1222
1954	1.76	0.08	1.68		1.51	2.00			71	33	0.24		1989
1955	2.24	0.18	1.45		1.87	2.00			92	39	0.35		1373
1956	3.60	0.95	0.28		2.80	2.03			98	53	0.61	0.01	1592
1957	4.74	1.15	0.33		3.69	2.53			156	76	0.97	0.90	1724
1958	8.43	1.06	0.01		6.54	2.94		1.40	400	105	2.94	41.33	2028
1959	15.04	1.31			11.45	4.91		1.70	480	141	8.42	52.66	9807
1960	18.61	1.55	0.72		13.35	6.10		2.92	460	110	13.92	54.50	4971
1961	8.02	0.60			5.66	2.98		0.03	213	72	5.65	3.37	2480
1962	10.76	0.58	0.53		8.94	2.93		0.21	185	62	8.82	16.41	1490
1963	12.74	0.49	0.61		11.19	2.67		0.29	195	52	10.68	24.01	1592
1964	18.01	0.72	0.03		15.75	3.00		0.49	180	47	15.92	43.42	1703
1965	23.14	0.92			19.99	4.07		0.82	197	41	19.95	62.99	1706
1966	25.58	0.91	1.32		22.73	5.08		2.75	240	40	24.21	65.30	1579
1967	22.64	1.05			19.13	4.56		1.96	184	40	22.89	47.34	1607
1968	23.65	0.92			20.45	4.12		1.09	264	43	24.08	43.93	1528
1969	32.25	1.09			28.62	4.72		2.22	333	57	31.74	69.63	1315
1970	46.03	1.54			39.78	7.80		4.11	480	64	41.67	80.34	2809
1971	51.22	1.81	1.20		45.08	9.15		6.85	612	66	51.28	85.70	3114
1972	50.42	2.17			42.79	9.79		8.28	617	68	57.15	94.64	3173
1973	53.35	2.37			45.41	10.31		8.42	648	71	70.36	90.78	3220
1974	56.14	2.77			47.65	11.26		8.74	732	73	81.98	110.27	3403
1975	66.01	3.71			57.21	12.49		9.13	838	81	95.16	140.87	3892
1976	65.60	4.55			57.10	13.06		10.86	895	85	106.64	141.60	4701
1977	68.16	6.16			60.18	14.14		13.33	965	86	113.00	145.77	5114
1978	72.00	7.38		63.28	64.83	14.55	24.79	15.39	980	82	114.48	155.67	5832
1979	73.68	6.69		65.83	66.03	14.61	27.19	17.03	875	110	119.60	170.36	4706
1980	72.47	6.13		70.10	61.99	16.61	28.20	16.99	766	136	119.48	179.35	4551
1981	68.59	3.97		67.86	56.98	17.89	24.32	14.97	788	137	121.41	168.31	4324
1982	74.44	6.83	0.04	73.50	61.69	19.63	25.82	17.86	878	138	133.75	204.86	4156
1983	80.66	7.52		79.56	67.21	20.97	28.80	23.00	920	142	138.22	230.82	4102
1984	91.35	9.30		91.77	77.91	23.45	34.26	24.93	1040	147	146.88	255.37	4432
1985	111.02	15.39		110.90	94.31	32.10	39.26	29.39	1185	157	147.34	292.76	4989
1986	122.98	21.00		122.70	107.74	36.25	42.72	35.95	1249	156	146.31	311.81	5831
1987	132.89	26.98		139.09	118.15	41.73	45.59	45.57	1285	153	133.66	323.36	5877
1988	161.70	42.23		167.34	147.57	56.37	54.25	56.45	1358	148	135.08	339.05	6117
1989	193.98	55.24		197.43	174.93	73.37	64.84	66.31	1415	147	163.14	371.83	6341

27. Gansu

27–10

Year	v8g1	v9a	v9a1	v9a2	v9a3	v9b	v9b1	v9b2	v9b3	v9c	v10a	v10a1	v10b1	v10b2	v10b3
1949						0.61				110.6					
1950		0.10		0.10		0.67				151.9	1.99	1.90	0.18		0.01
1951		0.20		0.20		0.72				198.9	2.54	2.44	0.52		0.04
1952	35	0.47		0.47		0.80		0.80		217.8	3.51	3.40	0.97		0.16
1953	49	0.92		0.92		1.16		1.16		315.7	4.37	4.22	1.31		0.45
1954	66	2.58	1.33	1.35		3.63	2.1200	1.51		381.0	5.89	5.63	2.14		1.21
1955	80	5.00	3.52	1.48		9.36	7.5060	1.85		463.2	6.75	6.43	2.45		1.73
1956	100	11.34	9.12	2.72		19.27	17.0110	2.26		670.4	8.84	8.43	3.65		3.25
1957	139	12.32	9.62	2.70		27.18	24.3590	2.82		776.2	9.51	9.19	4.14		3.36
1958		17.59	15.28	2.31		42.63	38.3860	4.24		1084.7	10.63	9.76	9.33		1.03
1959	789	25.69	23.33	2.36		76.83	70.3870	6.44		1521.0	12.88	11.79	12.10		0.43
1960	488	32.65	30.00	2.65		90.93	83.4960	7.43		1888.1	13.65	11.81	13.18		0.23
1961	659	40.16	37.88	2.28		62.24	59.4430	2.80		1525.9	9.65	8.82	8.93		0.24
1962	452	35.37	32.54	2.83		61.07	59.0450	2.02		1414.9	8.96	8.34	5.52		2.73
1963	532	21.45	19.07	2.38		69.26	67.2290	2.03		1287.9	8.71	8.14	5.35		2.83
1964	522	22.92	20.42	2.50		73.41	71.1890	2.22		1509.2	9.18	8.65	5.67		3.15
1965	535	24.04	21.39	2.65		92.62	89.6150	3.00		1619.4	10.20	9.36	6.34		3.65
1966		26.84	23.50	3.34		114.16	111.3140	2.85		1634.4	11.07	10.14	7.12		3.89
1967		26.44	23.16	3.28		79.84	76.7550	3.08		1531.4	11.43	10.52	10.98		0.39
1968		31.58	28.45	3.13		88.83	86.3660	2.46		1483.4	10.55	9.62	10.13		0.36
1969		35.82	32.09	3.73		102.98	99.0930	3.89		1662.4	12.12	10.87	11.58		0.41
1970		32.99	28.73	4.26		139.45	134.5510	4.90		1886.1	13.23	11.57	12.64		0.44
1971		35.21	30.07	5.14		146.92	140.7300	6.19		2055.6	14.28	12.31	13.77		0.35
1972	1050	39.40	33.40	6.00		152.83	145.8060	7.02		2259.1	16.21	13.69	15.67		0.39
1973	1067	42.35	35.62	6.73		163.05	155.3340	7.72		2477.1	18.30	15.21	17.71		0.42
1974		43.01	35.65	7.36		160.84	152.5900	8.25		2595.1	19.74	15.85	19.12		0.44
1975		46.30	37.99	8.31		197.72	187.7900	9.93		2753.4	22.04	17.32	14.82		7.03
1976		45.30	36.67	8.63		177.01	165.5900	11.42		3061.7	23.82	18.45	15.59		8.05
1977		44.96	35.84	9.12		211.13	198.9390	12.19		3137.9	24.50	19.52	15.17		9.13
1978	1193	49.62	39.45	10.17		236.34	224.8920	11.45		3266.3	25.78	20.72	16.38		8.90
1979	1142	57.56	45.91	11.65		232.19	221.2730	10.92		3408.1	27.62	22.66	17.40		9.73
1980	1152	59.97	46.24	13.73		219.12	210.4867	8.63		3429.1	30.42	26.48	19.01		10.42
1981	1132	61.27	45.66	15.61		193.98	187.2044	6.78		3443.0	32.81	29.16	19.41		11.91
1982	1147	66.16	49.12	17.04		213.72	205.6584	8.06		3560.0	35.22	31.19	20.54		12.76
1983	1161	74.39	55.16	19.23		240.44	231.8482	8.58		3767.0	38.90	34.47	21.46		13.76
1984	1139	84.30	62.27	22.03		275.05	265.2519	9.80		4188.5	46.00	40.29	24.82		15.98
1985	1256	101.09	75.83	25.26		309.67	299.6000	10.07		4793.8	58.45	51.81	28.26		19.19
1986	1267	111.50	81.77	29.73		243.81	232.1373	11.67		5257.0	68.59	61.90	31.94		22.78
1987	1331	118.73	83.76	34.97		346.55	332.7937	13.76		5799.0	79.98	72.11	35.65		25.31
1988	1342	131.11	93.80	37.31		375.28	358.7300	16.55		7297.0	102.47	92.77	44.12		31.98
1989	1371	128.00	87.79	38.22		302.29	332.6000	20.04		8452.5	112.29	100.65	47.22		36.14

27. Gansu

Year	v10b4	v10b5	v10b6	v10d	v11a1	v11a2	v11a3	v11b	v11b1	v11b2	v11c	v11d	v12a	v12b	v12c
1949															
1950	0.0072	1.46	0.35	1.02											
1951	0.0140	1.64	0.32	1.28									120.12	133.90	142.67
1952	0.0172	2.00	0.35	1.69									103.34	103.60	108.47
1953	0.0274	2.32	0.26	1.83									103.37	106.80	117.58
1954	0.0780	2.27	0.20	2.66									98.66	95.04	96.23
1955	0.4918	1.88	0.20	2.48									99.29	101.04	99.70
1956	1.3290	0.33	0.28	2.85									97.88	95.36	97.22
1957	1.3747	0.41	0.24	2.97									102.43	102.00	101.30
1958		0.07	0.21	3.55									98.21	103.20	99.42
1959		0.03	0.32	5.27									101.71	104.98	101.29
1960			0.25	3.32									101.00	99.50	99.26
1961		0.01	0.48	2.23									119.40	122.90	115.70
1962		0.20	0.52	2.02									105.85	111.20	98.60
1963		0.23	0.30	2.21									99.00	91.00	98.85
1964		0.15	0.21	2.83									93.68	90.40	99.70
1965		0.07	0.13	3.21									96.97	96.50	99.21
1966			0.05	3.27									97.26	95.60	104.37
1967			0.06	3.09									101.80	103.50	100.00
1968			0.07	3.29									100.00	100.00	100.00
1969			0.13	3.37									99.48	99.50	100.00
1970			0.14	3.87									98.80	98.90	99.32
1971			0.15	3.86									100.00	100.00	101.91
1972			0.16	4.43									99.90	100.20	101.70
1973			0.17	4.34									100.10	100.00	101.00
1974			0.18	5.65									100.10	100.20	103.20
1975			0.19	6.10									99.80	100.00	100.30
1976			0.18	6.46				0.1978	0.1978				100.02	99.90	100.90
1977			0.20	6.19				0.3209	0.3209				99.89	99.80	98.84
1978			0.51	6.19				0.2521	0.2521				100.50	100.70	104.10
1979		0.03	0.47	6.10				0.3972	0.3972				100.90	101.50	119.50
1980	0.0013	0.17	0.83	8.24				0.3927	0.3927				105.00	107.60	108.30
1981	0.0041	0.41	1.08	8.43				0.5129	0.4336	0.0793			102.00	102.70	107.70
1982	0.0021	0.84	1.08	9.87				0.5169	0.4430	0.0739			101.40	102.20	98.80
1983	0.0021	1.64	2.04	12.51				0.5695	0.4612	0.1083			100.60	101.20	109.30
1984	0.0217	2.74	2.45	13.87				0.6631	0.4573	0.2058			103.00	103.30	101.10
1985	0.0424	6.91	4.05	16.73				1.0004	0.7098	0.2906			108.50	110.60	105.70
1986	0.0413	8.50	5.33	20.41				1.3648	1.0107	0.3541			106.00	107.00	107.40
1987	0.0093	12.10	6.91	25.00				1.5504	1.2660	0.2844			107.40	108.40	111.90
1988	0.0724	16.46	9.84	33.94				1.5961	1.5205	0.0756			118.60	120.60	118.80
1989		18.90	10.05	25.22				1.7746	1.5338	0.2408		0.01	116.40	118.20	110.20

27. Gansu

27–12

Year	v13a	v13b	v13c1	v13c2	v13c3	v13d	v14a	v14b	v14c	v15a	v15b	v15c	v15d	v15e	v15f
1949		20.3	0.18	2.21	45.22		195	1406	0.0183						
1950		16.8	0.16	2.42	35.97		358	1713	0.0457						
1951		18.0	0.17	4.80	38.98		1051	2113	0.0870						
1952	27.75	23.6	0.26	3.27	63.29		1521	3353	0.1214	5454					
1953	22.67	27.8	0.26	3.84	62.33		2473	5031	0.1179						
1954	20.43	29.9	0.34	4.34	65.75		2699	5624	0.1442						
1955	15.92	33.0	0.45	5.38	74.42		3091	7413	0.1933						
1956	19.64	45.7	0.72	8.45	104.88		5030	12181	0.3031						
1957	10.08	57.5	0.79	10.50	118.99		7087	15092	0.2595	5712					
1958	8.15	81.6	1.16	14.51	175.21		35011	21306	0.7183						
1959	7.89	83.7	1.52	17.70	190.35		26617	29311	0.7056						
1960	11.87	75.7	2.15	20.88	165.03		22883	28323	0.8254						
1961	24.36	37.7	1.65	33.19	81.75		17794	21023	0.4704						
1962	21.85	33.8	1.40	8.37	65.24		13944	23805	0.3495						
1963		39.0	1.26	8.62	74.20		14317	21385	0.3611						
1964		46.1	1.13	9.86	109.13		14788	22793	0.4826						
1965	16.24	67.3	1.18	12.45	165.34		17451	23236	0.6025	5407					
1966	18.02	65.6	1.12	14.81	153.10		21021	24394	1.0695	5416					
1967	20.09	61.1	0.84	30.90	140.76		20808	24760	0.7341	5397					
1968	23.30	60.9	0.52	13.45	142.93		17992	22350	0.8899	5382					
1969	14.67	62.7	0.36	21.71	146.12		15648	20315	0.9829	5698					
1970	11.96	65.2	0.05	7.79	157.28		20235	25377	1.0860	5388					
1971	13.33	71.6	0.39	43.07	188.30		21057	26841	1.1734	5387					
1972	12.86	81.7	0.45	50.80	212.28		25063	32838	1.5990	5380					
1973	13.58	85.5	0.73	50.23	232.40		25192	35193	1.3890	5374					
1974		87.0	0.83	51.27	259.98		26355	36555	1.5859	5367					
1975	14.57	97.4	0.95	63.08	314.80		28811	39251	1.5154	5357					
1976	14.46	97.3	1.07	144.56	333.73		30716	41415	1.4098	5351					
1977	15.53	96.0	1.18	105.21	337.87		32420	42406	1.5273	5348					
1978	14.49	91.0	1.30	106.63	339.85		33676	45733	1.4919	5343					
1979	16.78	88.6	1.53	101.79	334.50		35575	47041	1.5255	5332					
1980	21.58	83.9	1.81	99.45	318.73		36071	48861	1.6696	5331					
1981	24.84	81.5	2.09	86.58	297.06		36493	53910	1.8089	5313					
1982	26.68	80.6	1.71	84.80	278.87		37081	55124	1.8621	5347					
1983	23.88	81.4	1.81	86.95	264.72		38058	56241	2.2997	5344					
1984	23.12	85.8	2.20	96.77	269.00		39452	57964	3.0056	5292	5400	247.16	1210.3	59.6397	8.1936
1985	23.71	89.2	2.81	107.04	270.29		40931	60144	2.7638	5236	5400	299.00	1426.4	65.4781	7.5313
1986	22.65	91.4	3.01	117.29	266.12		42237	61713	3.3110	5221	5400	299.00	1426.4	65.4781	7.5313
1987	21.80	92.3	3.24	120.62	258.99		43597	64783	4.0101	5218					
1988	22.63	93.2	3.30	117.37	252.01		45322	67830	3.8936	5213	2814	299.00	1426.4	65.4781	7.5313
1989		93.9	3.32	104.44	243.14	0.93	44338	69100	3.0697	5216					

Notes

1. National Output and Income (Y)

v1a: (E), p.835
  v1a1: (E), p.835
  v1a2: (E), p.835
  v1a3: (E), p.835
  v1a4: (E), p.835
  v1a5: (E), p.835

v1b: (A); (D), p.390
  v1b1: (A); (D), p.390
  v1b2: (A); (D), p.390
  v1b3: (A); (D), p.390
  v1b4: (A); (D), p.390
  v1b5: (A); (D), p.390

v1c: v1a – v1d

v1d: (E), p.832
  v1d1: (E), p.832
  v1d2: (E), p.832
  v1d3: (E), p.832
  v1d4: (E), p.832
  v1d5: (E), p.832

v1e: (A); (D), p.393
  v1e1: (A); (D), p.393
  v1e2: (A); (D), p.393
  v1e3: (A); (D), p.393
  v1e4: (A); (D), p.393
  v1e5: (A); (D), p.393

v1f: (E), p.831
  v1f1: (E), p.831
  v1f2: (E), p.831
  v1f3: (E), p.831

v1g: v2a + v3a

v1h: (B), p.400; (E), p.856

v1i: (A); (E), p.857

v1j: (A); (E), p.857
  v1j1: (E), p.857
  v1j2: (E), p.857
  v1j3: NA

v1k: NA

2. Investment (I)

v2a: (E), p.834
  v2a1: (A); (D), p.396
  v2a2: (A); (D), p.396

v2b: (A)

v2c: (E), p.848
  v2c1: (B), p.358–359; (E), p.849
  v2c2: (E), p.849

v2d:
  v2d1: (A); (E), p.846
  v2d2: (A); (E), p.846

v2e: (A); (E), p.846

3. Consumption (C)

v3a: (E), p.834

v3b: (E), p.834
  v3b1: (A); (D), p.394
  v3b2: (A); (D), p.394

v3c: (E), p.834

v3d: (E), p.856
  v3d1: (E), p.856
  v3d2: (E), p.856

v3e: (A); (E), p.856
  v3e1: (A); (E), p.856
  v3e2: (A)
  v3e3: (A)
  v3e4: (A)

v3f: (E), p.856
  v3f1: (E), p.856

v3f2: (A)
v3f3: (A)
v3f4: (A)

4. Public Finance and Banking (FB)

v4a:
v4a1: (E), p.854
v4a1a: (E), p.854
v4a1b: (C), p.425–426
v4a1c: NA
v4a1d: v4a1 – v4a1a – v4a1b' (v4a1b': total tax revenues which come from (E), p.854)
v4a2: (E), p.854
v4a2a: (E), p.854
v4a2b: (E), p.854
v4a2c: (E), p.854
v4a2d: v4a2 – v4a2a – v4a2b – v4a2c

v4b: (B), p.400
v4b1: (B), p.400
v4b2: (A); (B), p.400
v4b3: NA

v4c:
v4c1: (A); (E), p.846
v4c2: (E), p.846

5. Labor Force (L)

v5a: (E), p.830
v5a1: (E), p.830
v5a2: (B), p.283; (E), p.830
v5a3: (B), p.283; (E), p.830
v5a4: (B), p.283; (E), p.830

v5b:
v5b1: (E), p.830
v5b2: (E), p.830
v5b3: (E), p.830

v5c: NA
v5c1: (B), p.316

v5d: NA

6. Population (PO)

v6a: (A); (E), p.829
v6a1: (E), p.829
v6a2: (E), p.829

v6b: (E), p.829

v6c: (E), p.829

v6d:
v6d1: (E), p.829
v6d2: (E), p.829
v6d3: (E), p.829
v6d4: (E), p.829
v6d5: (A)—Lanzhou
v6d6: (A)—Tianshui

7. Agriculture (A)

v7a: (E), p.839

v7b: (A); (E), p.839

v7c: (A); (E), p.839

v7d: (A); (E), p.839

v7e: (A)

v7f: (A)

v7g: (A); (E), p.839

v7h: (A)
v7h1: (A)
v7h2: (A)
v7h3: (A)
v7h4: (A)
v7h5: (A)

v7i: (A); (E), p.838

8. Industry (IN)

v8a: (A)
- v8a1: (A)
- v8a2: (A)
- v8a3: (A)

v8b: (A); (E), p.846

- v8c1: (A); (E), p.835
- v8c2: (A); (E), p.835

v8d: (E), p.846

v8f:
- v8f1: (A); (E), p.845
- v8f2: (E), p.845
- v8f3: (E), p.845
- v8f4: (E), p.845
- v8f5: (A); (B), p.328; (E), p.845

v8g: (A)
- v8g1: (E), p.846

9. Transport (TR)

v9a: (E), p.847—excluding urban traffic volume
- v9a1: (E), p.847—including central and local railways
- v9a2: (E), p.847
- v9a3: NA

v9b: (E), p.847
- v9b1: (E), p.847—including central and local railways
- v9b2: (E), p.847
- v9b3: NA

v9c: (A); (B), p.347—based on 1980's constant price; figures of 1949–63 are charges of total business amount; (E), p.847

10. Domestic Trade (DT)

v10a: (E), p.850
- v10a1: (E), p.850

v10b:
- v10b1: (A); (E), p.850
- v10b2: NA
- v10b3: (E), p.850—including supply and marketing cooperative and other collectives
- v10b4: (B), p.372–373; (E), p.850
- v10b5: (E), p.850
- v10b6: (E), p.850

v10d: (E), p.852—calculated on calendar year basis

11. Foreign Trade (FT)

v11a:
- v11a1: NA
- v11a2: NA
- v11a3: NA

v11b: (E), p.853
- v11b1: (E), p.853
- v11b2: v11b – v11b1

v11c: NA

v11d: (A)

12. Prices (PR)

v12a: (E), p.855

v12b: (E), p.855

v12c: (E), p.855

13. Education (ED)

v13a: (A)

v13b: (A); (B), p.392; (E), p.858—1952: 28.1%

v13c:
v13c1: (A); (B), p.398; (E), p.858—1978: 1.39, 1980: 1.84, 1988: 3.44
v13c2: (A); (B), p.389; (E), p.858
v13c3: (A); (B), p.389; (E), p.858

v13d: (A)

14. Social Factors (SF)

v14a: (A); (B), p.396; (E), p.858

v14b: (A); (B), p.397; (E), p.858—Chinese medicine practitioners, western medicine doctors and practitioners, nurses and others; 1965: 28,100

v14c: (A); (B), p.394

15. Natural Environment (NE)

v15a: (A); (E), p.839

v15b: (A)

v15c: (A)

v15d: (A)

v15e: (A)

v15f: (A)

Sources of Data

(A) Data supplied by the DSNEB, SSB, the PRC.
(B) Statistical Bureau of Gansu Province ed. *Gansu Forty Years*, Beijing: CSPH, 1989.
(C) ________ ed. *Statistical Yearbook of Gansu*, Beijing: CSPH, 1989.
(D) Same as (D) in Beijing's sources of data.
(E) Same as (E) in Beijing's sources of data.

28

Qinghai

28. Qinghai

28–1

Year	v1a	v1a1	v1a2	v1a3	v1a4	v1a5	v1b	v1b1	v1b2	v1b3	v1b4	v1b5	v1c	v1d	v1d1
1949	1.70	1.33	0.19	0.02	0.00	0.16							0.52	1.18	1.00
1950	1.86	1.43	0.20	0.03	0.00	0.19	109.60						0.59	1.27	1.06
1951	2.05	1.51	0.24	0.03	0.01	0.26	110.36						0.64	1.41	1.13
1952	2.26	1.61	0.27	0.06	0.05	0.28	110.06	111.86	112.47	174.85	382.17	104.73	0.74	1.52	1.19
1953	2.62	1.68	0.35	0.20	0.10	0.29	110.22	97.60	129.75	218.39	194.92	106.53	0.93	1.69	1.23
1954	3.28	2.21	0.47	0.20	0.12	0.28	124.55	129.14	133.08	101.09	125.65	96.88	1.14	2.14	1.66
1955	4.26	2.43	0.71	0.52	0.24	0.36	129.58	110.41	141.40	263.15	190.29	120.14	1.60	2.66	1.83
1956	6.66	2.50	1.16	2.12	0.38	0.50	155.66	105.63	152.14	405.67	193.47	141.34	3.31	3.35	1.89
1957	6.30	2.80	1.27	1.23	0.45	0.55	88.99	99.69	104.01	57.83	123.26	120.23	2.87	3.43	2.11
1958	8.68	2.35	1.78	3.11	0.48	0.96	134.16	79.25	151.56	248.47	104.54	185.16	4.42	4.26	1.88
1959	13.83	2.41	4.96	4.61	0.65	1.20	158.99	101.01	177.80	142.52	232.47	135.47	7.96	5.87	1.91
1960	14.41	2.34	6.57	3.31	0.94	1.25	103.69	92.20	133.32	74.25	127.99	109.19	8.29	6.12	1.87
1961	8.24	2.64	3.17	0.58	0.75	1.10	54.91	96.73	45.93	25.90	75.54	86.97	4.00	4.24	2.09
1962	6.32	2.71	1.91	0.21	0.50	0.99	77.48	114.81	58.01	56.47	69.33	61.75	2.61	3.71	2.14
1963	6.76	3.29	1.88	0.37	0.34	0.88	106.08	126.27	98.72	175.06	71.34	91.47	2.62	4.14	2.63
1964	7.65	3.85	1.97	0.65	0.39	0.79	109.86	110.47	107.06	174.99	115.60	104.51	2.91	4.74	3.08
1965	8.88	4.16	2.42	0.99	0.57	0.74	119.23	111.00	129.21	137.64	141.18	102.72	3.63	5.25	3.32
1966	10.16	4.09	3.01	1.54	0.65	0.87	116.41	98.04	129.65	155.21	116.44	122.75	4.70	5.46	3.07
1967	10.59	4.56	3.11	1.31	0.66	0.95	103.26	109.33	104.58	83.36	103.56	108.61	4.66	5.93	3.60
1968	10.21	3.94	3.08	1.45	0.67	1.07	97.09	86.31	99.12	109.75	99.39	113.58	4.95	5.26	2.92
1969	11.73	4.37	3.48	2.06	0.77	1.05	118.30	113.51	119.64	142.31	115.97	97.49	5.86	5.87	3.29
1970	13.59	4.37	4.74	2.54	0.85	1.09	119.39	100.02	142.33	123.41	110.57	103.65	6.69	6.90	3.29
1971	16.62	4.66	7.24	2.46	0.95	1.30	114.48	102.23	131.92	99.66	110.91	119.68	8.71	7.91	3.55
1972	17.68	5.27	7.16	2.90	0.94	1.41	109.87	114.36	111.68	109.59	98.68	109.23	8.92	8.76	4.02
1973	18.73	5.31	8.51	2.51	0.98	1.42	108.52	107.75	119.43	87.92	103.82	99.88	9.51	9.22	4.15
1974	19.32	5.63	8.83	2.42	0.96	1.43	102.32	102.92	104.49	97.63	98.22	100.21	9.72	9.60	4.44
1975	21.48	5.63	10.16	3.19	0.95	1.55	111.61	99.12	115.65	132.09	99.44	108.29	11.25	10.23	4.38
1976	21.45	5.71	9.96	3.33	0.89	1.56	101.27	106.69	98.29	104.23	93.18	101.25	11.61	9.84	4.29
1977	23.72	5.72	11.34	4.01	0.96	1.69	111.34	99.90	114.86	120.72	108.75	112.84	13.28	10.44	3.54
1978	28.63	5.99	13.57	5.98	1.20	1.89	117.42	99.38	116.26	146.96	124.44	112.01	16.49	12.14	3.34
1979	31.14	6.52	13.73	7.58	1.33	1.98	105.36	96.03	99.85	126.64	111.53	102.42	18.36	12.78	3.66
1980	32.70	7.78	14.33	7.18	1.29	2.12	102.73	111.02	97.48	94.74	97.50	106.43	18.78	13.92	4.88
1981	29.64	7.30	12.25	6.60	1.12	2.37	90.01	93.05	85.46	91.99	86.25	107.84	16.90	12.74	4.45
1982	35.04	8.36	14.73	7.98	1.33	2.64	115.81	107.80	119.00	99.16	119.69	109.57	20.50	14.54	5.35
1983	37.62	8.67	15.37	8.77	1.81	3.00	105.59	102.48	101.39	109.88	134.72	111.25	21.45	16.17	5.66
1984	44.02	10.48	17.92	9.63	2.52	3.47	113.13	108.94	114.23	109.81	140.17	113.04	24.51	19.51	7.14
1985	54.96	12.25	22.65	12.62	3.10	4.34	110.70	111.11	119.72	97.48	97.13	112.52	30.36	24.60	8.33
1986	61.77	14.11	26.79	12.70	2.97	5.20	105.10	104.68	111.33	93.03	93.26	110.81	33.20	28.57	9.95
1987	70.34	15.94	31.30	13.81	3.32	5.97	107.86	103.86	113.01	99.73	104.84	109.51	38.14	32.20	11.21
1988	89.71	19.49	42.51	16.57	3.68	7.46	111.15	100.27	120.57	102.41	105.27	104.81	48.12	41.59	13.99
1989	102.88	21.60	54.18	14.58	4.59	7.93	101.84	102.43	108.09	79.82	118.18	92.62	56.74	46.14	15.31

28. Qinghai

28–2

Year	v1d2	v1d3	v1d4	v1d5	v1e	v1e1	v1e2	v1e3	v1e4	v1e5	v1f	v1f1	v1f2	v1f3	v1g
1949	0.06	0.00	0.00	0.12											
1950	0.06	0.01	0.00	0.14	107.55	105.73	106.47	385.71	123.08	116.87					
1951	0.08	0.01	0.01	0.18	110.88	106.99	118.85	100.93	387.50	115.31					
1952	0.09	0.02	0.02	0.20	108.96	105.41	121.10	210.09	372.58	106.29					
1953	0.12	0.07	0.04	0.23	108.86	103.15	131.06	272.05	182.25	110.82					
1954	0.16	0.06	0.05	0.21	123.74	129.91	126.26	99.36	117.34	94.39					
1955	0.32	0.16	0.09	0.26	121.10	107.54	168.15	253.98	176.32	118.69					
1956	0.35	0.61	0.13	0.37	131.16	107.55	143.02	391.86	161.44	142.45					
1957	0.38	0.37	0.16	0.41	94.32	103.85	101.02	60.04	116.43	122.39					
1958	0.65	0.89	0.15	0.69	117.07	88.98	151.92	237.66	98.65	175.45					
1959	1.76	1.22	0.19	0.79	135.47	101.83	276.63	132.02	124.22	132.29					
1960	2.25	0.92	0.25	0.83	105.50	106.77	129.10	76.97	127.53	109.08					
1961	1.07	0.11	0.20	0.77	66.11	95.58	46.48	17.35	79.35	92.15					
1962	0.68	0.07	0.14	0.68	90.99	107.23	65.05	62.02	69.33	60.68					
1963	0.67	0.12	0.10	0.62	110.44	121.67	97.10	174.41	73.41	93.23					
1964	0.75	0.21	0.13	0.57	109.71	115.70	108.06	177.35	127.05	94.87					
1965	0.88	0.30	0.20	0.55	113.48	108.64	123.58	130.14	149.73	107.89					
1966	1.08	0.44	0.23	0.64	105.61	94.98	120.44	148.82	119.81	121.27					
1967	1.08	0.35	0.22	0.68	104.10	111.32	102.81	78.06	94.96	107.30					
1968	1.00	0.39	0.21	0.74	93.24	86.91	94.84	112.27	95.94	107.67					
1969	1.00	0.60	0.24	0.74	116.36	113.75	111.54	154.76	112.29	100.22					
1970	1.85	0.73	0.26	0.77	116.59	100.65	164.51	122.55	107.04	102.91					
1971	2.49	0.67	0.27	0.93	108.93	102.72	130.27	92.98	103.50	122.36					
1972	2.59	0.85	0.28	1.02	113.58	113.27	112.09	117.61	100.02	113.70					
1973	3.07	0.72	0.28	1.00	109.63	107.15	120.58	90.87	101.54	97.38					
1974	3.16	0.69	0.29	1.02	101.66	104.57	103.05	93.77	99.29	101.82					
1975	3.57	0.89	0.30	1.09	107.62	99.66	115.58	129.44	102.61	108.11					
1976	3.27	0.93	0.26	1.09	99.66	101.98	94.32	104.64	89.50	98.26					
1977	4.32	1.11	0.29	1.18	109.51	89.52	113.93	115.87	109.31	109.13					14.83
1978	5.20	1.96	0.37	1.27	110.53	91.45	109.93	177.19	127.50	106.92	15.54	3.67	7.71	4.16	19.19
1979	4.96	2.43	0.37	1.36	100.40	95.62	93.53	123.78	100.11	105.48					21.69
1980	5.07	1.94	0.40	1.63	102.77	114.72	101.50	79.92	108.20	118.20	17.79	5.00	7.83	4.96	20.31
1981	4.39	1.77	0.36	1.77	91.74	93.64	87.09	91.01	89.87	105.55					19.51
1982	4.72	2.16	0.45	1.86	111.08	113.01	106.28	122.19	125.56	103.70					23.79
1983	5.37	2.32	0.66	2.16	109.72	106.62	109.25	107.52	146.81	113.49					25.05
1984	6.33	2.70	0.69	2.64	115.27	113.18	117.31	116.55	104.54	117.98					29.92
1985	8.16	4.05	0.98	3.08	114.39	109.96	123.28	111.46	121.91	105.42	33.01	8.64	13.39	10.98	42.18
1986	9.95	3.94	0.77	3.96	107.60	107.68	113.22	89.88	78.24	121.46	38.41	10.74	15.40	12.54	44.08
1987	11.68	3.94	0.90	4.51	106.44	103.50	113.64	90.76	109.38	107.33	43.38	11.74	16.61	15.03	54.16
1988	15.76	5.51	0.92	5.41	110.92	101.21	119.70	120.55	118.82	100.15	54.96	14.36	23.30	17.30	69.62
1989	18.95	4.95	1.21	5.88	100.45	102.50	104.67	83.11	104.65	95.51	60.37	15.73	25.29	19.35	55.91

28. Qinghai

28–3

Year	v1h	v1i	v1j	v1j1	v1j2	v1j3	v1k	v2a	v2a1	v2a2	v2b	v2c	v2c1	v2c2	v2d1
1949															
1950		0.04	519	519											
1951		0.06	533	533											
1952		0.10	597	597											
1953		0.18	727	727											
1954		0.25	757	757											
1955		0.38	820	820											
1956		1.08	1014	1014											
1957		1.20	1038	1038											
1958		1.69	793	793											
1959		2.66	708	708											
1960		3.41	721	721											
1961		2.29	712	712											
1962		1.49	788	788											
1963		1.29	843	901	459										
1964		1.42	957	951	484										
1965		1.62	978	947	482										
1966		1.70	888	888											
1967		1.82	886	886											
1968		1.85	878	878											
1969		2.13	886	886											
1970		2.24	856	856											
1971		2.59	850	850											
1972		2.89	883	883											
1973		2.94	887	887											
1974		2.96	909	909											
1975		3.30	883	889	649										15.31
1976		3.50	870	894	660										17.25
1977		3.68	868	890	687			6.14	5.37	0.77					19.32
1978		4.29	907	938	654			9.08	8.08	1.00			3.62	0.13	21.49
1979		4.90	959	991	721			10.91	10.14	0.77			6.29	0.21	23.06
1980	164	5.77	1065	1100	820			8.19	6.95	1.24			3.75	0.32	28.49
1981	181	5.89	1059	1103	796			6.74	5.98	0.76	8.47	6.59	3.53	0.19	34.68
1982	222	6.35	1111	1155	848			9.78	9.28	0.50	10.51	8.37	4.70	0.28	31.32
1983	252	7.28	1246	1301	933			9.17	9.07	0.11	12.66	10.12	5.42	0.18	33.04
1984	294	8.88	1490	1565	1091			11.45	9.43	2.02	13.51	10.61	5.64	0.28	35.72
1985	343	10.16	1664	1751	1205			19.98	14.17	5.81	17.17	13.67	5.48	0.52	35.58
1986	369	11.68	1838	1937	1306			18.19	13.91	4.28	18.21	15.98	8.10	0.45	37.30
1987	392	12.65	1962	2061	1405			25.56	17.06	8.50	21.99	19.68	11.20	0.34	53.05
1988	493	14.38	2223	2335	1585			34.23	19.45	14.78	25.82	22.28	13.22	0.33	63.06
1989	458	16.03	2438	2579	1628			18.61	14.76	3.85	20.26	18.28	9.30	0.64	80.49

28. Qinghai

Year	v2d2	v2e	v3a	v3b	v3b1	v3b2	v3c	v3d	v3d1	v3d2	v3e	v3e1	v3e2	v3e3	v3e4
1949															
1950															
1951															
1952															
1953															
1954															
1955															
1956															
1957															
1958															
1959															
1960															
1961															
1962															
1963															
1964															
1965								166							
1966															
1967															
1968															
1969															
1970															
1971															
1972															
1973															
1974															
1975	11.79														
1976	13.29														
1977	14.73	5.43	8.69	7.59	3.12	4.47	1.10	208	122	415					
1978	16.52	5.94	10.11	8.41	3.80	4.61	1.70	226	145	419					
1979	17.58	6.27	10.78	8.57	3.67	4.90	2.21	226	138	434					
1980	21.80	7.30	12.11	10.40	4.48	5.92	1.71	270	166	516					
1981	26.80	7.31	12.77	10.87	4.56	6.31	1.90	283	166	551					
1982	23.63	7.22	14.02	11.97	5.36	6.61	2.05	301	192	570					
1983	24.28	7.43	15.88	13.23	6.18	7.05	2.65	331	218	605	449.89	247.88	77.69		11.95
1984	26.15	7.57	18.47	14.94	6.68	8.26	3.53	368	234	688	581.19	299.11	93.39		14.74
1985	25.79	8.78	22.20	18.15	8.75	9.40	4.05	444	299	812	678.71	348.40	112.90		14.75
1986	26.73	9.98	25.89	20.79	9.36	11.43	5.10	500	321	922	777.28	409.98	135.49		16.43
1987	41.62	11.23	28.60	23.51	10.30	13.21	5.09	552	346	1033	828.38	456.37	142.81		16.14
1988	49.76	13.63	35.39	29.36	12.83	16.52	6.03	673	420	1265	1048.06	526.59	188.23		17.91
1989	64.88	17.90	37.30	32.33	15.27	17.06	4.98	731	491	1297	1069.44	603.00	154.20	4.32	22.80

28. Qinghai

28–5

Year	v3f	v3f1	v3f2	v3f3	v3f4	v4a1	v4a1a	v4a1b	v4a1b'	v4a1c	v4a1d	v4a2	v4a2a	v4a2b	v4a2c	v4a2d
1949						0.0027						0.00				
1950						0.0398						0.04			0.03	
1951						0.1359			0.03			0.11	0.02	0.01	0.08	0.00
1952						0.2938	0.01		0.04			0.18	0.04	0.03	0.09	0.02
1953						0.3057	0.02		0.06			0.38	0.09	0.08	0.17	0.04
1954						0.5867	0.03		0.22			0.49	0.14	0.07	0.20	0.08
1955						0.7362	0.05		0.32			0.77	0.25	0.08	0.23	0.21
1956						1.6254	0.11		0.35			1.69	0.89	0.14	0.31	0.35
1957						1.6358	0.12		0.46			1.62	0.69	0.18	0.33	0.42
1958						3.7876	0.41		0.51			3.24	1.85	0.26	0.37	0.76
1959						6.2327	1.69		0.76			5.20	3.12	0.29	0.52	1.27
1960						6.6424	1.90		0.86			7.10	3.46	0.40	0.60	2.64
1961						2.7631	0.57		0.48			2.91	0.44	0.27	0.58	1.62
1962						1.4127	-0.02		0.43			1.28	0.13	0.24	0.35	0.56
1963						1.7713	0.27		0.48			1.25	0.21	0.23	0.33	0.48
1964						1.9631	0.31		0.53			1.73	0.60	0.27	0.35	0.51
1965						1.7584	0.34		0.56			1.87	0.75	0.27	0.32	0.53
1966						2.2065	0.49		0.56			2.17	0.91	0.27	0.31	0.68
1967						2.0126	0.25		0.59			1.71	0.75	0.28	0.27	0.41
1968						1.5505	0.09		0.54			1.50	0.69	0.25	0.26	0.30
1969						2.3031	0.26		0.65			2.38	1.45	0.25	0.28	0.40
1970						2.6228	0.40		0.75			2.71	1.39	0.28	0.30	0.74
1971						3.6829	0.24		0.85			3.67	1.50	0.38	0.37	1.42
1972						4.1313	0.33		0.99			4.19	1.87	0.48	0.41	1.43
1973						4.3801	0.42		1.13			4.35	1.56	0.55	0.43	1.81
1974						4.1696	0.34		1.20			4.25	1.57	0.58	0.46	1.64
1975						4.7928	0.63		1.39			4.52	1.62	0.60	0.46	1.84
1976						4.6533	0.33		1.37			4.87	1.65	0.64	0.47	2.11
1977						5.4139	0.44		1.57			5.16	1.64	0.71	0.52	2.29
1978						7.0301	0.94		1.73			6.80	2.34	0.91	0.56	2.99
1979						6.8133	0.37		1.70			6.82	2.38	1.03	0.66	2.75
1980						6.3684	-0.18		1.67			5.88	1.79	1.10	0.72	2.27
1981						6.3077	-0.71		1.64			5.52	1.02	1.22	0.77	2.51
1982						7.0985	-0.65		1.78			6.24	1.25	1.43	0.83	2.73
1983	202.00	125.00				7.6716	-1.24		1.85			7.39	1.54	1.88	1.06	2.91
1984	225.18	141.21	35.53	8.11	12.94	8.6065	-1.51		2.12			9.17	1.88	2.19	1.39	3.71
1985	274.68	176.09	37.91	14.27	16.63	10.5053	-1.77		2.96			10.09	2.22	2.36	1.31	4.20
1986	313.54	193.08	44.64	19.98	16.57	12.3875	-1.31		3.38			12.22	2.12	2.71	1.57	5.82
1987	344.93	198.56	46.28	24.43	20.64	14.1025	-1.42		4.17			12.26	1.91	2.83	1.65	5.87
1988	399.50	221.70	61.89	22.04	20.32	14.3165	-1.79		5.16			14.28	1.81	3.25	2.09	7.13
1989	413.29	244.38	53.02	30.97	24.64		-1.63		6.32			15.67	1.42	3.53	2.30	8.42

28. Qinghai

28–6

Year	v4b	v4b1	v4b2	v4b3	v4c1	v4c2	v5a	v5a1	v5a2	v5a3	v5a4	v5b1	v5b2	v5b3	v5c
1949							63.82	0.63		7.13	55.06				
1950		0.0012						0.88		7.18					
1951		0.0136						1.35		7.14					
1952	0.0128	0.0128					71.66	1.93		7.95	62.34	62.41	1.07	8.18	0.83
1953		0.0298		0.0098			72.34	2.89		9.43	61.79				
1954		0.0487		0.0205			77.22	3.84		8.17	64.65				
1955		0.0797		0.0389			81.74	5.35		10.80	65.96				
1956		0.1845		0.0570			93.54	12.51		9.80	68.92				
1957	0.2828	0.2460		0.1208			96.10	10.58		9.86	69.75				
1958		0.2630		0.1613			117.24	32.36		10.31	69.08				
1959		0.4616		0.5107			127.90	42.76		14.56	69.24				
1960		0.5892		0.4012			130.94	48.32		13.18	67.24				
1961		0.5804		0.5882			111.04	25.63		2.63	65.75				
1962	0.2723	0.2448		0.4528			107.94	16.20		0.58	74.42				
1963		0.2753		0.4969			98.24	13.48	1.13	0.20	80.96				
1964		0.3528		0.5925			98.52	14.08	0.98	0.12	82.65				
1965	0.4632	0.4274		0.6173			102.49	16.60	1.48	0.33	84.09	86.65	7.32	8.52	3.64
1966		0.5190		0.6918			106.96	19.39		0.35	85.68				
1967		0.5775		0.3168			109.91	20.05			87.60				
1968		0.6067		0.3713			112.86	21.36			89.06				
1969		0.5700		0.8488			118.57	24.38			91.94				
1970	0.6558	0.5962		0.9582			124.35	27.23			93.71				
1971		0.6865		1.0171			129.12	31.14			95.41				
1972		0.8002		1.1591			132.18	33.30	2.74		96.14				
1973		0.8748		1.2933			132.45	32.38			97.34				
1974		0.9716		1.4431			133.19	32.61			97.91				
1975	1.1469	1.0617		1.6411			136.31	34.42	3.88		98.01				
1976		1.1612		1.8440			139.20	36.94	4.19		98.07				
1977		1.3169		1.8911			140.82	37.69	5.03		98.10				
1978	1.6269	1.4874		1.9303	2.31	10.3	144.71	42.35	5.22		97.14	103.21	26.66	14.84	19.83
1979		1.8687		2.0797	1.78	7.5	150.31	46.00	5.94	0.09	98.28				
1980	2.8127	2.3386		2.0806	1.40	4.8	157.62	46.90	6.86	0.23	103.63	108.31	28.60	20.71	20.01
1981		2.8195		2.0897	1.15	3.4	165.55	47.49	8.06	0.42	109.58				
1982		2.9717		3.0614	1.24	4.0	171.17	48.54	9.03	0.71	112.89				
1983		3.6519		3.3675	1.66	5.2	174.31	49.23	9.09	1.41	114.58				
1984		5.8165		2.3960	2.16	6.4	177.35	50.31	9.32	1.56	116.16				
1985	8.2288	7.5904		2.1095	2.48	7.2	182.70	52.03	9.64	3.20	117.80	112.20	36.90	33.60	24.70
1986	10.6634	9.6729		2.3267	2.84	7.7	189.20	54.10	9.80	3.70	121.60	111.20	38.70	39.30	26.00
1987	13.4286	12.2478		2.4540	3.20	6.1	193.70	54.60	9.90	4.60	124.60	113.90	38.30	41.50	26.20
1988	16.1525	14.7007		2.5372	6.72	10.6	197.83	55.30	9.76	4.91	127.81	115.90	38.80	43.10	27.10
1989	19.9000	18.5000			6.63	8.0	200.80	55.00	10.00		132.00	120.00	39.00	42.00	

28. Qinghai

28–7

Year	v5c1	v5d	v6a	v6a1	v6a2	v6b	v6c	v6d1	v6d2	v6d3	v6d4	v6d5	v6d6
1949			148					14	134	74	74	7.08	
1950			152					14	137	76	76		
1951			156					15	141	79	77		
1952			161					16	145	82	79	8.38	
1953			164					18	146	83	81		
1954			173			44.16	13.30	20	153	88	85		
1955			179			35.93	14.06	23	156	92	87		
1956			200			24.68	9.43	34	166	106	94		
1957			205			32.20	10.40	40	165	108	97	30.04	
1958			225			27.97	12.99	63	162	125	100	37.41	
1959			260			23.02	16.58	80	180	150	110		
1960			249			13.07	40.73	79	170	143	106		
1961			211			11.43	11.68	52	159	114	97	46.69	3.15
1962			205			35.72	5.35	39	166	106	99	29.69	2.83
1963			210			45.56	8.37	40	170	110	100	26.05	2.24
1964			219	36.34	183.14	52.08	15.53	45	174	116	103	27.70	2.61
1965			230	37.98	192.47	48.72	9.06	47	183	121	109	30.80	
1966			241	40.74	199.88	41.39	9.75	51	190	126	115		
1967			250	42.53	207.92	40.80	7.73	52	198	131	119		
1968			261	46.44	214.51	43.82	7.65	56	205	137	124		
1969			272	46.87	225.06	42.95	7.91	58	214	143	129		
1970			283	48.68	234.05	40.06	7.52	60	223	148	135	38.67	
1971			296	54.44	241.21	40.02	7.56	67	229	154	142		
1972			307	57.57	249.49	39.33	9.22	72	235	159	148		
1973			318	60.26	257.90	38.26	7.75	76	242	165	153		
1974			328	61.32	267.42	34.49	8.08	79	250	170	159		
1975			337	62.99	274.50	31.95	8.24	80	257	175	162	48.57	
1976			347	64.50	282.08	28.89	7.27	83	264	180	167		
1977			357	66.75	290.00	27.52	6.91	86	271	185	172		
1978			365	67.84	297.02	26.15	6.66	88	277	189	176	52.70	
1979			372	71.06	300.96	24.47	6.48	92	280	192	180		
1980			377	74.71	302.19	21.14	5.61	97	280	194	183	54.62	5.90
1981			382	76.78	304.82	20.86	5.70	97	285	197	185		
1982			393	79.82	312.97	19.46	5.10	98	295	202	191		
1983			393	77.26	315.31	15.50	5.30	100	293	202	191		
1984			402	128.63	272.98	15.94	5.10	107	295	206	196		
1985			407	137.75	269.63	14.24	4.58	116	291	208	199	59.94	6.03
1986			421			22.56	6.20	122	299	215	206	61.35	6.18
1987			428	148.08	279.82	22.59	6.42	124	304	219	209	62.28	6.19
1988			434	149.10	285.10	19.27	4.68	126	308	222	212	63.19	6.42
1989			440	150.67	289.53	20.11	5.11	127	313	225	215	64.14	6.73

28. Qinghai

28–8

Year	v7a	v7b	v7c	v7d	v7e	v7f	v7g	v7h	v7h1	v7h2	v7h3	v7h4	v7h5	v7i	v8a
1949				498				1.33	0.56		0.70		0.07		0.19
1950								1.43	0.62		0.74		0.07		0.20
1951								1.51	0.65		0.77		0.09		0.24
1952			96.88	560				1.61	0.70	0.02	0.80	0.01	0.08		0.27
1953								1.68	0.67	0.01	0.88	0.01	0.11		0.35
1954								2.21	1.06	0.01	1.02	0.01	0.11		0.47
1955								2.43	1.22	0.01	1.07		0.13		0.71
1956								2.50	1.22	0.02	1.09		0.17		1.16
1957			172.44	667				2.80	1.32	0.02	1.27		0.19		1.27
1958								2.35	1.35	0.04	0.67		0.29		1.78
1959								2.41	1.26	0.03	0.70	0.03	0.39		4.96
1960								2.34	1.11	0.02	0.75	0.07	0.39		6.57
1961								2.64	1.25	0.01	0.95	0.08	0.35		3.17
1962				777			0.007	2.71	1.09	0.01	1.07	0.05	0.49		1.91
1963								3.29	1.46	0.01	1.30	0.02	0.50		1.88
1964								3.85	1.67	0.01	1.60	0.02	0.55		1.97
1965		136.28	211.79	746				4.16	1.92	0.02	1.66	0.01	0.55		2.42
1966								4.09	1.81	0.02	1.89	0.01	0.36		3.01
1967								4.56	1.97	0.03	2.00	0.01	0.55		3.11
1968								3.94	1.61	0.02	2.01	0.01	0.29		3.08
1969								4.37	1.63	0.02	2.31		0.41		3.48
1970				773			0.071	4.37	1.68	0.01	2.11		0.57		4.74
1971								4.69	1.75	0.01	2.41		0.52		7.23
1972								5.27	2.77	0.05	1.93	0.01	0.51		7.16
1973								5.31	2.42	0.03	2.60	0.01	0.25		8.51
1974								5.68	2.57	0.03	2.79	0.01	0.28		8.83
1975				762			0.470	5.63	2.90	0.04	2.36	0.01	0.32		10.16
1976								5.71	2.56	0.04	2.78	0.01	0.32		9.96
1977								5.71	2.54	0.06	2.76	0.01	0.34		11.34
1978	5.29	291.99	246.79	772			0.740	5.99	2.77	0.05	2.78	0.01	0.38	43.84	13.57
1979								6.52	2.89	0.05	3.06	0.01	0.51	43.68	13.73
1980	6.96	250.20	239.63	763		3.96	0.870	7.78	3.69	0.06	3.48	0.01	0.54	39.83	14.33
1981								7.30	3.64	0.07	3.07	0.01	0.51	45.75	12.25
1982								8.36	4.18	0.18	3.44	0.02	0.54	47.20	14.73
1983							0.730	8.67	4.75	0.11	3.11	0.02	0.68	59.39	15.37
1984								10.48	5.63	0.19	3.79	0.02	0.85	59.04	17.92
1985	8.80	193.34	239.98	751			0.830	12.25	6.20	0.47	5.01	0.05	0.52	64.57	22.65
1986				762				14.11	6.33	0.70	6.11	0.04	0.93	66.33	26.79
1987				762				15.94	7.03	0.66	6.84	0.02	1.39	58.99	31.30
1988	10.77	238.84	244.81	771		4.00	1.100	19.49	8.01	0.67	9.17	0.03	1.61	63.34	42.50
1989	11.33	254.83	250.54	798		5.06	1.370	21.60	9.65	0.69	9.77	0.05	1.44	65.80	54.18

28. Qinghai

28–9

Year	v8a1	v8a2	v8a3	v8b	v8c1	v8c2	v8d	v8f1	v8f2	v8f3	v8f4	v8f5	v8g
1949	0.01				0.03	0.16			4				15
1950	0.02				0.03	0.17			4		0.01		17
1951	0.03				0.05	0.19			7		0.01		40
1952	0.04				0.04	0.22			10		0.01		48
1953	0.11				0.09	0.26			12		0.02		91
1954	0.19	0.02	0.26		0.12	0.35			19		0.03		189
1955	0.31	0.06	0.34		0.20	0.51			26		0.04		207
1956	0.68	0.29	0.19		0.41	0.75			29		0.06		252
1957	0.64	0.36	0.27		0.47	0.80			48	0.30	0.11		356
1958	1.72	0.06			1.02	0.75			110	3.33	0.21	0.03	677
1959	4.75	0.21			3.33	1.63			178	30.72	0.41	0.31	929
1960	6.29	0.28			4.77	1.80		0.29	194	31.50	0.83	1.63	899
1961	2.91	0.26			2.14	1.03			81	17.48	0.78	0.34	705
1962	1.65	0.24	0.02		1.22	0.69			59	12.86	0.75	0.35	465
1963	1.67	0.20	0.01		1.12	0.75			75	10.05	0.71	0.40	415
1964	1.75	0.21	0.01		1.09	0.78			64	10.08	0.76	0.46	434
1965	2.19	0.23			1.28	1.14			63	10.03	0.85	1.40	449
1966	2.74	0.27			1.68	1.32			70	10.42	1.10	2.51	423
1967	2.83	0.28			1.80	1.31			73	10.45	1.43	2.51	439
1968	2.80	0.28			1.77	1.31			90	7.31	1.47	2.00	470
1969	3.14	0.34			2.24	1.24		0.01	95	7.49	1.84	2.40	485
1970	4.35	0.39			3.33	1.41		3.05	112	8.33	2.64	2.87	610
1971	6.57	0.66			4.75	2.47		6.51	118	11.00	3.27	3.78	822
1972	6.41	0.75			4.89	2.27		10.83	134	10.17	3.38	4.39	913
1973	7.59	0.92			5.67	2.84		12.32	153	10.38	3.90	5.26	959
1974	7.74	1.09			5.83	3.01		12.55	162	10.75	3.89	6.13	1022
1975	8.82	1.34			6.56	3.60		14.05	183	10.10	4.44	9.78	1038
1976	8.43	1.53			6.53	3.43		14.48	202	11.35	4.41	8.37	1158
1977	9.49	1.85		8.74	7.52	3.83	3.27	14.63	227	12.36	5.14	14.40	1271
1978	11.33	2.24		10.58	8.94	4.63	4.01	18.20	245	13.63	6.52	18.23	1391
1979	11.49	2.24		10.83	9.32	4.41	3.90	18.91	216	13.45	7.20	27.85	1306
1980	12.14	2.19		11.52	9.14	5.19	4.03	17.92	215	15.10	8.22	29.86	1270
1981	10.20	2.05		9.57	7.21	5.04	3.37	17.34	191	16.70	7.72	21.70	1178
1982	12.46	2.26	0.01	11.74	8.93	5.80	3.56	18.21	207	17.26	7.84	28.03	1344
1983	12.71	2.64	0.02	11.93	8.94	6.44	3.99	19.11	219	17.54	7.70	36.60	1292
1984	14.87	3.03	0.02	14.05	10.81	7.11	4.83	19.82	240	18.51	8.18	42.45	1303
1985	18.82	3.46	0.37	18.50	13.91	8.74	6.17	20.90	277	20.00	11.38	48.42	1291
1986	22.13	4.26	0.40	21.07	16.89	9.90	7.70	22.50	272	35.01	14.64	49.00	1460
1987	26.10	4.63	0.57	25.57	19.44	11.86	9.63	24.10	274	57.53	22.35	49.20	1411
1988	35.89	5.81	0.80	35.04	28.32	14.19	13.15	29.27	268	64.02	45.86	53.87	1478
1989	45.10	7.43	1.05	44.64	37.45	16.73	15.83	31.11	302	72.50	58.20	53.99	1484

28. Qinghai

28–10

Year	v8g1	v9a	v9a1	v9a2	v9a3	v9b	v9b1	v9b2	v9b3	v9c	v10a	v10a1	v10b1	v10b2	v10b3
1949										4	0.35	0.34			
1950								0.00		8	0.39	0.37			
1951		0.01		0.01		0.01		0.01		13	0.56	0.54			
1952		0.04		0.04		0.06		0.06		19	0.63	0.60			
1953		0.13		0.13		0.11		0.11		38	0.80	0.77			
1954		0.27		0.27		0.33		0.33		49	1.16	1.11			
1955		0.39		0.39		0.67		0.67		65	1.45	1.38			
1956		1.08		1.08		1.10		1.10		127	2.33	2.20			
1957		1.10		1.10		1.42		1.42		175	2.59	2.44			
1958		1.04		1.04		3.26		3.26		253	3.21	2.98			
1959		1.39		1.39		3.53		3.53		501	4.52	4.04			
1960		1.11		1.11		2.74		2.74		640	5.12	4.54			
1961		0.67		0.67		1.49		1.49		534	3.74	3.49			
1962		0.70		0.70		0.96		0.96		383	3.04	2.91			
1963		0.50		0.50		0.91		0.91		345	2.70	2.62			
1964		0.69		0.69		0.97		0.97		349	2.86	2.75			
1965		0.90		0.90		1.44		1.44		360	3.20	3.06			
1966		1.17		1.17		2.54		2.54		380	3.43	3.21			
1967		1.08		1.08		2.24		2.24		380	3.66	3.49			
1968		1.14		1.14		2.13		2.13		385	3.71	3.53			
1969		1.26		1.26		2.45		2.45		417	3.87	3.66			
1970		1.16		1.16		2.64		2.64		445	4.40	4.10			
1971		1.33		1.33		2.96		2.96		473	4.72	4.34			
1972		1.27		1.27		2.98		2.98		511	5.10	4.62			
1973		1.30		1.30		3.36		3.36		555	5.40	4.86			
1974		1.17		1.17		2.96		2.96		571	5.84	2.52			
1975	335	1.15		1.15		3.79		3.79		609	6.32	5.60			
1976	362	1.15		1.15		3.63		3.63		669	6.60	5.84			
1977	384	1.49		1.49		4.24		4.24		732	7.06	6.21			
1978	400	1.80		1.80		4.75		4.75		764	7.66	6.68	6.07	1.33	0.25
1979	389	2.15		2.15		4.31		4.31		831	8.31	7.30			
1980	402	4.72	2.16	2.56		3.81		3.81		887	9.20	8.29	6.88	1.62	0.51
1981	385	5.33	2.07	3.26		9.49	6.45	3.04		1225	9.93	9.19	7.21	1.73	0.69
1982	402	5.96	2.28	3.68		9.47	5.55	3.92		1235	10.54	9.78	7.54	1.72	0.79
1983	397	6.87	2.58	4.29		11.11	6.95	4.16		1328	11.70	10.80	8.10	1.65	1.00
1984	404	9.12	4.28	4.83		12.27	8.02	4.25		1454	13.87	12.85	9.10		
1985	413	12.76	7.31	5.45		18.32	14.11	4.21		1720	17.63	16.39	10.68		
1986	428	14.79	7.63	7.14		29.94	20.80	9.14		1866	20.27	19.02	11.91		
1987	442	16.12	7.94	8.16		34.89	22.99	11.90		2023	22.78	21.38	13.20	2.37	2.35
1988	465	18.22	9.38	8.84		40.05	25.95	14.10		2480	28.40	26.80	16.56	3.00	2.68
1989	488	16.94	8.27	8.67		46.81	29.32	17.49		3020	28.67	26.90	17.31	2.78	2.94

28. Qinghai

28–11

Year	v10b4	v10b5	v10b6	v10d	v11a1	v11a2	v11a3	v11b	v11b1	v11b2	v11c	v11d	v12a	v12b	v12c
1949															
1950				0.14											
1951				0.25									117.0		139.0
1952				0.34									103.2		106.9
1953				0.40									98.7		99.5
1954				0.64									102.8		102.7
1955				0.75									106.0		97.4
1956				0.78									98.3		99.2
1957				1.11									91.5		94.4
1958				1.20									95.0		96.5
1959				1.54									92.2		101.3
1960				1.61									95.4		97.7
1961				0.97									101.4		110.2
1962				0.93									145.4		100.5
1963				0.93									97.3		99.8
1964				1.20									96.3		99.7
1965				1.23									90.6		100.3
1966				1.30									95.9		102.2
1967				1.30									99.4		99.1
1968				1.33									100.4		99.7
1969				1.42									100.2		99.0
1970				1.59									100.5		101.4
1971				1.64									99.8		116.2
1972				1.97									95.5		109.1
1973				2.03									100.7		100.2
1974				2.26									100.1		109.4
1975				2.33									100.0		100.1
1976				2.21									100.0		100.1
1977				2.37									100.1		100.1
1978		0.02		2.54				0.1064	0.0076	0.0988			100.2		99.7
1979				3.13				0.0740	0.0017	0.0723			102.2	102.2	116.4
1980		0.05	0.14	3.22				0.0887	0.0402	0.0485			104.1	104.2	101.2
1981		0.10	0.20	3.36		0.0030		0.1250	0.0793	0.0457			101.3	101.3	100.6
1982		0.17	0.33	3.95		0.0045		0.1478	0.1077	0.0402			101.8	101.8	100.8
1983		0.52	0.43	3.80		0.0055		0.2280	0.1247	0.1033			100.7	100.7	100.1
1984		0.88	0.56	3.04		0.0053		0.3135	0.1406	0.1729			103.4	103.4	105.1
1985		1.88	1.04	4.10	0.1271	0.0042		0.3411	0.2123	0.1288			110.7	111.8	106.9
1986		2.79	1.14	4.74	0.1225	0.0070		0.4363	0.2643	0.1720			106.1	106.4	104.4
1987	0.11	3.56	1.30	4.84	0.1752	0.0141		0.5142	0.4015	0.1127			107.3	107.8	111.7
1988	0.04	4.51	1.72	6.52	0.1159	0.0114		0.5385	0.4558	0.0826			118.3	118.6	136.9
1989	0.05	3.88	1.72										117.7	117.3	110.7

28. Qinghai

28–12

Year	v13a	v13b	v13c1	v13c2	v13c3	v13d	v14a	v14b	v14c	v15a	v15b	v15c	v15d	v15e	v15f
1949				0.14	4.05		100	103		682					
1950															
1951															
1952				0.28	8.81		529	513		697					
1953				0.37	9.09										
1954				0.43	9.43										
1955				0.60	10.36										
1956			0.02	1.16	15.58										
1957			0.02	1.53	15.37		2115	2605	0.0581	753					
1958			0.29	1.24	26.82	0.0066									
1959			0.40	1.53	25.86	0.0094									
1960			0.40	3.02	27.28	0.0434									
1961			0.26	1.97	15.03	0.0661									
1962			0.12	1.14	10.13	0.0782	3853	5017		881					
1963			0.08	1.12	11.53	0.0594									
1964			0.07	1.29	17.27	0.0240									
1965		73.1	0.06	1.58	30.95	0.0297	6634	6114		868					
1966			0.05	1.99	31.13	0.0106									
1967			0.04	2.20	22.31										
1968			0.04	2.37	20.14										
1969			0.02	2.37	19.80										
1970		51.4	0.06	4.11	23.13	0.0323	8212	8217	0.0312	890					
1971			0.12	6.41	33.07	0.0220									
1972			0.17	7.11	30.49	0.0278									
1973			0.25	7.38	40.57										
1974			0.26	10.09	46.77	0.0507									
1975		89.8	0.27	12.64	54.05	0.0688	10222	11390	0.4159						
1976			0.25	14.93	57.07	0.0953									
1977			0.31	19.74	58.41	0.0708									
1978		85.5	0.35	21.71	59.90	0.0785	10951	13090	0.4024	904					
1979			0.37	21.77	60.11	0.0932									
1980		82.4	0.42	20.88	57.48	0.0692	11941	15115	0.5456	881					
1981		78.3	0.54	20.21	54.07	0.0093	12321	16877	0.1630						
1982		74.6	0.43	20.02	51.30	0.1947	12870	17399	0.4283						
1983		76.8	0.49	20.59	51.45	0.1375	13311	17997	0.1128						
1984		80.6	0.55	22.64	53.54	0.1018	13136	17891	0.5331						
1985		79.2	0.64	24.29	54.24	0.1159	13743	18031	0.5385	848					
1986		81.3	0.69	25.38	55.02	0.1667	14417	18906	0.5520						
1987		82.4	0.69	26.12	54.39	0.1832	15119	19759	0.5886						
1988		83.4	0.70	25.03	53.43	0.1741	15093	19780	0.6376	853	286.72	0.0631	2165	43.48	2.42
1989		82.6	0.64	23.12	51.00	0.2000	15000	20000	5.5480	858					

Notes

1. National Output and Income (Y)

v1a: (E), p.864
- v1a1: (E), p.864
- v1a2: (E), p.864
- v1a3: (E), p.864
- v1a4: (E), p.864
- v1a5: (E), p.864

v1b: (A); (B), p.14
- v1b1: (A); (D), p.402
- v1b2: (A); (D), p.402
- v1b3: (A); (D), p.402
- v1b4: (A); (D), p.402
- v1b5: (A); (D), p.402

v1c: v1a – v1d

v1d: (E), p.862
- v1d1: (E), p.862
- v1d2: (E), p.862
- v1d3: (E), p.862
- v1d4: (E), p.862
- v1d5: (E), p.862

v1e: (A)
- v1e1: (A)
- v1e2: (A)
- v1e3: (A)
- v1e4: (A)
- v1e5: (A)

v1f: (E), p.861
- v1f1: (E), p.861
- v1f2: (E), p.861
- v1f3: (E), p.861

v1g: v2a + v3a

v1h: (A); (B), p.884

v1i: (E), p.883

v1j: (E), p.883
- v1j1: (E), p.883
- v1j2: (E), p.883
- v1j3: NA

v1k: NA

2. Investment (I)

v2a: (E), p.863
- v2a1: (A); (D), p.403
- v2a2: (A); (D), p.403

v2b: (A)

v2c: (E), p.877
- v2c1: (E), p.878
- v2c2: (E), p.878

v2d:
- v2d1: (E), p.874
- v2d2: (E), p.874

v2e: (E), p.874

3. Consumption (C)

v3a: (E), p.863

v3b: (E), p.863
- v3b1: (A); (D), p.404
- v3b2: (A); (D), p.404

v3c: (E), p.863

v3d: (A); (E), p.884
- v3d1: (E), p.884
- v3d2: (E), p.884

v3e: (A); (E), p.884
- v3e1: (E), p.884
- v3e2: (A)
- v3e3: (A)
- v3e4: (A)

v3f: (A); (E), p.884
- v3f1: (E), p.884

v3f2: (A)
v3f3: (A)
v3f4: (A)

4. Public Finance and Banking (FB)

v4a:
v4a1: (B), p.177
v4a1a: (E), p.881
v4a1b: NA; v4a1b': (E), p.881—total tax revenues
v4a1c: NA
v4a1d: NA
v4a2: (B), p.177—1949: 0.0027; (E), p.881
v4a2a: (E), p.881
v4a2b: (E), p.881
v4a2c: (E), p.881
v4a2d: v4a2 – v4a2a – v4a2b – v4a2c

v4b: (A)
v4b1: (B), p.180
v4b2: NA
v4b3: (B), p.180—rural and pastoral areas' deposits

v4c:
v4c1: (E), p.874
v4c2: (E), p.874

5. Labor Force (L)

v5a: (A); (B), p.32; (E), p.860
v5a1: (B), p.32; (E), p.860
v5a2: (B), p.32; (E), p.860
v5a3: (B), p.32, (C), 1990, p.102
v5a4: (B), p.32, (C), 1990, p.102—rural collectives and self-employed workers

v5b:
v5b1: (E), p.860
v5b2: (E), p.860
v5b3: (E), p.860

v5c: (C), 1989, p.147
v5c1: NA

v5d: NA

6. Population (PO)

v6a: (E), p.859—data from public security department
v6a1: (E), p.859—(ditto)
v6a2: (E), p.859—(ditto)

v6b: (E), p.859—(ditto)

v6c: (E), p.859—(ditto)

v6d:
v6d1: (E), p.859—(ditto)
v6d2: (E), p.859—(ditto)
v6d3: (E), p.859—(ditto)
v6d4: (E), p.859—(ditto)
v6d5: (A)—Xining
v6d6: (A)—Golmud

7. Agriculture (A)

v7a: (E), p.871

v7b: (A); (E), p.871

v7c: (E), p.871

v7d: (A); (E), p.871

v7e: NA

v7f: (A)

v7g: (A); (E), p.871

v7h: (E), p.866
v7h1: (E), p.866
v7h2: (E), p.866
v7h3: (E), p.866
v7h4: (E), p.866
v7h5: (E), p.866

v7i: (E), p.870

8. Industry (IN)

v8a: (E), p.872
  v8a1: (E), p.872
  v8a2: (E), p.872
  v8a3: v8a – v8a1 – v8a2

v8b: (E), p.874

  v8c1: (E), p.864
  v8c2: (E), p.864

v8d: (E), p.874

v8f:
  v8f1: (E), p.875
  v8f2: (A); (E), p.875
  v8f3: (E), p.875
  v8f4: (E), p.875
  v8f5: (E), p.875

v8g: (A)
  v8g1: (E), p.874

9. Transport (TR)

v9a: (E), p.876—excluding urban traffic volume
  v9a1: (E), p.876—including central and local railways
  v9a2: (E), p.876—figures since 1986 are of the society
  v9a3: NA

v9b: (E), p.876
  v9b1: (E), p.876—including central and local railways
  v9b2: (E), p.876—figures since 1986 are of the society
  v9b3: NA

v9c: (E), p.876

10. Domestic Trade (DT)

v10a: (E), p.879
  v10a1: (E), p.879

v10b:
  v10b1: (E), p.879
  v10b2: (A); (C), 1989, p.302
  v10b3: (E), p.879—collective ownership
  v10b4: (C), 1989, p.302; (E), p.879
  v10b5: (A); (E), p.879
  v10b6: (E), p.879

v10d: (A)

11. Foreign Trade (FT)

v11a:
  v11a1: (C), 1989, p.318
  v11a2: (B), p.165
  v11a3: NA

v11b: v11b1 + v11b2
  v11b1: (A)
  v11b2: (A)

v11c: NA

v11d: NA

12. Prices (PR)

v12a: (E), p.882

v12b: (E), p.882

v12c: (E), p.882

13. Education (ED)

v13a: NA

v13b: (A); (E), p.884

v13c:
  v13c1: (A); (B), p.200; (E), p.884
  v13c2: (B), p.200—technical and ordinary secondary schools
  v13c3: (B), p.200; (E), p.884

v13d: (A); (B), p.201; (C), 1990, p.348—institutions of higher learning

14. Social Factors (SF)

v14a: (A); (B), p.235; (E), p.884

v14b: (A); (B), p.235—Chinese medicine practitioners, Western medicine doctors and practitioners, nurses and others

v14c: (A); (C), 1989, p.421

15. Natural Environment (NE)

v15a: (E), p.871

v15b: (A)

v15c: (A)

v15d: (A)

v15e: (A)

v15f: (A)

Sources of Data

(A) Data supplied by the DSNEB, SSB, the PRC.
(B) Statistical Bureau of Qinghai Province ed. *Striving and Advancing Qinghai*, Beijing: CSPH, 1989.
(C) ________ ed. *Yearbook of Qinghai's Social and Economic Statistics*, Beijing: CSPH, various issue.
(D) Same as (D) in Beijing's sources of data.
(E) Same as (E) in Beijing's sources of data.

29

Ningxia

29. Ningxia

29–1

Year	v1a	v1a1	v1a2	v1a3	v1a4	v1a5	v1b	v1b1	v1b2	v1b3	v1b4	v1b5	v1c	v1d	v1d1
1949	1.31	1.08	0.13	0.01	0.03	0.06							0.34	0.96	0.86
1950	1.41	1.14	0.14	0.02	0.04	0.07							0.39	1.01	0.89
1951	1.64	1.33	0.17	0.02	0.04	0.08							0.46	1.19	1.04
1952	2.00	1.61	0.20	0.04	0.06	0.09	118.6	118.5	120.8	177.1	125.9	105.4	0.52	1.48	1.30
1953	2.01	1.53	0.28	0.04	0.06	0.10	99.3	96.0	125.8	116.6	115.0	115.1	0.60	1.40	1.19
1954	2.27	1.74	0.32	0.04	0.06	0.11	126.6	128.2	136.6	97.7	99.1	103.4	0.47	1.81	1.53
1955	2.66	2.01	0.37	0.05	0.09	0.14	105.4	104.1	103.3	123.4	138.0	120.2	0.79	1.87	1.56
1956	2.97	2.25	0.36	0.06	0.11	0.19	122.3	123.7	97.2	111.4	125.0	132.9	0.86	2.11	1.74
1957	2.99	2.09	0.47	0.06	0.14	0.23	91.5	86.2	123.8	105.6	127.8	118.6	0.88	2.10	1.64
1958	4.41	2.16	0.93	0.63	0.27	0.42	138.2	109.9	205.3	1006.2	194.8	179.5	1.68	2.73	1.67
1959	6.09	2.12	1.79	1.09	0.37	0.72	125.1	96.7	192.4	172.8	135.9	167.2	2.49	3.61	1.65
1960	6.78	1.79	2.38	1.38	0.43	0.80	103.6	84.1	128.2	127.3	114.9	108.0	2.94	3.83	1.36
1961	6.49	2.73	2.05	0.68	0.23	0.80	78.6	95.1	75.0	49.1	53.2	85.5	3.27	3.22	1.90
1962	5.22	2.60	1.53	0.44	0.15	0.50	86.2	98.5	84.8	64.8	64.8	64.8	2.07	3.15	2.08
1963	5.27	2.58	1.49	0.50	0.17	0.53	115.1	122.1	98.7	112.5	114.6	119.4	2.23	3.04	1.83
1964	5.46	2.58	1.59	0.54	0.19	0.55	109.9	111.2	107.0	109.3	111.3	108.1	2.35	3.11	1.76
1965	6.56	3.05	2.03	0.64	0.22	0.62	119.2	114.8	134.6	117.1	119.1	114.5	2.94	3.62	2.00
1966	8.01	3.03	3.08	0.86	0.30	0.74	121.3	100.9	164.3	135.9	133.4	122.3	3.73	4.28	2.15
1967	7.89	3.23	2.92	0.82	0.28	0.64	93.7	106.1	77.4	95.4	93.7	84.1	3.53	4.36	2.33
1968	7.19	2.72	2.87	0.77	0.27	0.56	91.6	84.4	106.8	93.7	95.2	87.1	3.19	4.00	1.99
1969	8.77	2.89	3.76	1.08	0.35	0.69	123.6	105.5	148.1	140.3	130.5	121.0	4.14	4.63	2.05
1970	10.60	2.80	5.00	1.48	0.47	0.85	120.8	97.3	141.8	136.8	134.9	123.0	5.50	5.10	1.84
1971	13.89	3.78	6.53	1.93	0.59	1.06	121.4	112.2	125.0	130.2	126.4	126.0	7.52	6.37	2.40
1972	15.22	3.77	7.50	2.20	0.67	1.08	109.8	99.8	116.9	114.0	113.4	101.8	8.36	6.87	2.39
1973	15.52	3.32	7.99	2.40	0.72	1.08	104.1	86.9	113.4	109.3	107.3	100.0	8.65	6.87	2.13
1974	19.43	4.80	9.68	2.92	0.85	1.18	118.5	141.0	108.7	121.4	118.5	108.8	10.48	8.95	3.07
1975	21.15	4.60	11.17	3.20	0.97	1.21	108.4	96.7	115.5	109.4	113.3	103.3	11.74	9.41	2.97
1976	19.16	3.73	10.45	3.00	0.92	1.06	92.7	80.8	98.9	93.5	95.3	86.5	10.67	8.49	2.41
1977	21.88	4.35	11.92	3.43	1.06	1.12	111.5	116.2	110.0	114.3	114.5	98.5	12.60	9.28	2.60
1978	24.98	4.81	13.85	3.91	1.19	1.21	115.7	112.5	118.4	114.2	112.8	108.0	15.06	9.91	2.72
1979	26.64	5.61	14.55	4.04	1.11	1.33	102.7	95.3	105.8	103.2	93.9	108.3	15.77	10.87	3.03
1980	26.99	6.41	13.93	3.80	1.30	1.55	101.1	114.1	96.1	94.1	116.5	110.5	15.20	11.79	3.91
1981	27.04	7.54	12.79	3.74	1.35	1.62	94.1	106.8	85.7	98.4	103.4	101.9	14.47	12.57	5.25
1982	30.60	7.78	14.75	4.61	1.70	1.76	110.9	100.5	114.6	116.5	126.2	106.2	17.21	13.40	5.39
1983	34.94	9.14	16.54	5.35	1.93	1.98	113.4	117.4	112.4	112.3	113.7	110.4	19.60	15.35	6.28
1984	41.35	10.99	19.11	6.61	2.19	2.45	115.9	117.4	113.8	116.4	113.2	121.4	23.08	18.27	7.40
1985	51.45	12.02	24.30	9.45	2.73	2.96	118.6	102.5	121.3	136.2	124.6	116.5	29.14	22.31	8.50
1986	60.42	14.16	28.24	11.50	3.09	3.43	111.9	107.8	112.3	116.0	113.4	110.6	34.58	25.84	9.92
1987	68.68	14.79	33.38	12.70	3.66	4.18	108.3	91.9	113.6	107.0	118.3	116.2	40.11	28.56	9.98
1988	87.14	19.66	44.00	12.51	4.64	6.33	111.8	114.3	117.0	84.4	119.8	129.8	49.94	37.20	13.20
1989	104.77	21.43	58.53	12.03	6.01	6.77	108.7	105.9	116.7	87.9	109.8	91.8	60.58	44.19	14.65

29. Ningxia

29–2

Year	v1d2	v1d3	v1d4	v1d5	v1e	v1e1	v1e2	v1e3	v1e4	v1e5	v1f	v1f1	v1f2	v1f3	v1g
1949	0.04	0.00	0.02	0.04											0.96
1950	0.04	0.00	0.03	0.05											1.01
1951	0.06	0.01	0.03	0.05											1.19
1952	0.06	0.01	0.04	0.07											1.46
1953	0.09	0.01	0.04	0.07	94.6	92.3	135.3	106.5	109.0	111.1					1.55
1954	0.12	0.01	0.04	0.11	144.2	145.9	158.9	111.4	106.1	118.8					1.99
1955	0.13	0.02	0.05	0.11	92.9	91.6	94.4	117.3	122.5	108.4					2.13
1956	0.14	0.02	0.07	0.14	123.6	124.3	104.8	106.7	121.2	129.6					2.43
1957	0.18	0.02	0.08	0.18	91.2	87.3	128.7	119.5	127.6	119.7					2.39
1958	0.39	0.19	0.16	0.32	125.5	108.6	209.5	1011.1	191.0	180.7					3.80
1959	0.83	0.36	0.22	0.55	119.8	97.9	214.1	185.1	141.1	166.8					4.92
1960	1.12	0.64	0.23	0.48	96.2	82.3	131.1	123.3	105.1	102.2					5.95
1961	0.70	0.03	0.09	0.50	68.6	86.9	53.5	7.2	37.4	74.7					3.62
1962	0.56	0.08	0.07	0.36	104.2	113.4	88.9	269.9	75.1	74.8					3.46
1963	0.60	0.14	0.08	0.39	111.6	107.9	122.5	162.0	116.2	122.8					3.43
1964	0.68	0.16	0.09	0.42	108.7	106.6	114.4	118.7	112.1	110.3					4.09
1965	0.84	0.23	0.10	0.45	114.7	110.5	130.1	139.0	115.3	111.2					4.65
1966	1.14	0.28	0.14	0.57	119.2	109.9	145.8	123.0	138.8	128.3					5.62
1967	1.14	0.27	0.13	0.49	98.8	78.3	81.7	96.2	92.2	86.0					4.87
1968	1.18	0.26	0.11	0.46	91.4	86.0	111.2	97.9	88.6	90.5					4.91
1969	1.50	0.35	0.17	0.56	115.6	102.2	144.9	133.3	150.3	120.9					6.05
1970	1.88	0.45	0.25	0.68	108.7	89.8	135.3	129.9	146.5	119.2					7.38
1971	2.32	0.57	0.30	0.78	114.4	108.4	118.5	124.9	121.9	117.5					8.19
1972	2.72	0.58	0.34	0.84	107.8	100.1	119.0	103.0	114.0	105.6					8.42
1973	2.92	0.65	0.33	0.84	100.8	86.8	114.3	112.0	95.6	101.3					9.01
1974	3.73	0.85	0.35	0.95	124.9	142.8	114.7	130.6	107.1	111.7					9.04
1975	4.29	0.76	0.41	0.98	104.8	97.5	115.3	89.7	117.4	102.3					10.63
1976	4.08	0.71	0.38	0.91	91.7	81.0	100.4	93.0	92.0	92.8					10.53
1977	4.58	0.78	0.41	0.91	106.4	106.8	108.3	109.0	108.9	94.1					11.55
1978	4.93	0.88	0.45	0.93	108.3	106.0	110.1	113.4	109.3	103.1	12.42	2.19	6.78	2.75	13.52
1979	5.61	0.86	0.43	0.94	103.5	90.8	114.5	97.9	96.2	201.5	13.75	3.20	7.56	2.99	13.64
1980	5.29	0.95	0.55	1.09	108.0	117.0	101.1	110.5	127.3	109.8	15.09	4.09	7.44	3.56	14.54
1981	4.50	1.15	0.57	1.10	99.3	132.7	75.3	117.1	103.4	101.8	16.24	5.47	6.97	3.80	15.39
1982	4.83	1.30	0.71	1.17	105.0	99.8	107.1	110.3	125.6	103.2	17.53	5.66	7.62	4.23	17.44
1983	5.45	1.51	0.81	1.30	114.0	116.6	112.7	112.6	113.9	109.7	19.99	6.62	8.65	4.72	19.82
1984	6.40	1.97	0.93	1.57	115.9	114.9	115.7	122.3	114.7	114.5	23.50	7.82	10.28	5.40	24.49
1985	8.05	2.75	1.18	1.83	115.0	106.8	120.5	133.4	126.7	111.4	28.86	8.90	13.32	6.64	30.48
1986	9.30	3.13	1.33	2.16	110.8	115.9	103.1	108.5	112.3	114.2	33.60	10.36	14.41	8.83	36.74
1987	10.67	3.48	1.66	2.77	106.2	92.6	112.8	107.7	125.2	121.6	37.99	10.44	17.40	10.15	41.36
1988	14.19	3.72	1.79	4.31	112.2	109.6	115.7	91.3	107.8	133.3	48.09	13.54	21.08	13.47	51.12
1989	19.20	3.42	2.48	4.44	108.1	107.8	118.4	84.2	110.7	88.5	55.76	15.01	26.52	14.23	56.73

29. Ningxia

29–3

Year	v1h	v1i	v1j	v1j1	v1j2	v1j3	v1k	v2a	v2a1	v2a2	v2b	v2c	v2c1	v2c2	v2d1
1949		0.09	253	340	250			0.05							
1950		0.12	267	343	253			0.08							
1951		0.14	301	380	280			0.18							0.01
1952	98.9	0.23	403	491	361			0.29	0.19	0.10	0.05	0.05			0.03
1953		0.28	439	533	392			0.31	0.20	0.11	0.08	0.08			0.03
1954		0.36	477	566	417			0.40	0.26	0.14	0.14	0.14			0.07
1955		0.43	491	586	431			0.43	0.27	0.16	0.13	0.13			0.08
1956		0.61	576	677	498			0.68	0.45	0.23	0.19	0.19			0.11
1957	101.7	0.72	606	709	523			0.65	0.43	0.21	0.15	0.15			0.12
1958		0.68	540	611	450			1.76	0.91	0.85	0.93	0.93			0.20
1959		1.10	546	574	422			2.51	1.20	1.31	1.92	1.92			0.63
1960		1.41	537	552	406			3.57	1.81	1.76	2.44	2.44			1.35
1961		1.31	498	545	401			0.97	0.64	0.33	0.98	0.98			1.66
1962		1.06	431	589	434			0.60	0.40	0.20	0.40	0.39			2.26
1963		1.02	570	677	498			0.70	0.48	0.22	0.46	0.46			2.54
1964		1.07	685	710	523			1.27	0.89	0.38	0.73	0.73			2.73
1965	110.2	1.17	669	696	512			1.66	1.16	0.50	1.40	1.40			2.75
1966		1.32	653	668	492			2.26	1.61	0.65	2.26	2.26			4.05
1967		1.40	635	649	478			1.49	1.07	0.42	1.37	1.37			4.53
1968		1.48	646	660	486			1.43	1.04	0.39	1.64	1.64			5.96
1969		1.59	657	671	494			1.99	1.48	0.51	2.15	2.15			7.46
1970		1.73	670	684	503			3.05	2.29	0.76	2.46	2.47			9.17
1971		1.89	682	696	510			3.66	2.78	0.88	2.49	2.49			10.76
1972		2.11	695	709	521			3.52	2.71	0.81	2.32	2.32			11.73
1973		2.15	707	721	531			3.66	2.85	0.81	2.28	2.28			15.06
1974		2.21	712	727	535			3.35	2.85	0.50	2.44	2.44			14.53
1975		2.31	708	725	532			4.84	3.87	0.97	2.50	2.50			15.89
1976		2.46	699	713	514		0.26	4.13	3.37	0.76	2.27	2.28			17.45
1977		2.66	709	720	642		0.32	4.93	4.13	0.81	3.17	3.17			18.58
1978	116.0	3.08	726	753	536		0.37	5.73	4.64	1.09	4.27	4.22	3.09	0.09	20.16
1979	138.8	3.45	777	815	517		0.44	5.14	4.55	0.59	4.17	4.14	1.85	0.17	22.04
1980	175.1	4.04	863	892	666		0.57	4.46	3.87	0.59	3.98	3.93	1.20	0.30	23.60
1981	200.2	4.18	874	910	633		0.63	4.16	2.85	1.31	3.69	3.45	0.74	0.23	27.50
1982	228.6	4.41	895	934	646		0.74	4.53	4.02	0.51	4.80	4.28	0.84	0.35	29.41
1983	273.8	4.77	934	970	706		1.14	5.41	4.65	0.76	5.62	5.09	1.36	0.14	30.84
1984	298.7	5.59	1072	1111	855		1.39	7.70	5.52	2.19	8.36	6.80	2.30	0.17	32.16
1985	325.9	6.56	1206	1252	963		1.80	10.90	8.83	2.07	13.63	11.29	4.23	0.45	36.52
1986	378.8	8.03	1420	1470	1135		2.12	14.05	11.06	2.99	17.35	14.30	6.09	0.17	41.62
1987	387.0	8.89	1500	1569	1130		2.71	15.71	12.42	3.29	19.37	15.55	7.82	0.27	46.89
1988	480.2	10.65	1728	1808	1297		3.14	21.21	12.89	8.32	18.79	13.95	5.74	0.19	52.66
1989	521.9	12.56	1943	2037	1457			22.52	11.89	10.63	17.30	12.59	5.33	0.15	59.16

29. Ningxia

29–4

Year	v2d2	v2e	v3a	v3b	v3b1	v3b2	v3c	v3d	v3d1	v3d2	v3e	v3e1	v3e2	v3e3	v3e4
1949			0.91	0.90			0.01				109.7				
1950			0.93	0.91			0.02	74	72	99					
1951	0.01		1.01	0.98			0.03	76	69	132	165.0	102.3			
1952	0.02	0.01	1.17	1.13	0.91	0.22	0.04	82	72	187					
1953	0.03	0.01	1.24	1.20	0.98	0.22	0.04	82	59	206					
1954	0.04	0.02	1.59	1.55	1.19	0.36	0.04	100	86	255					
1955	0.06	0.02	1.70	1.66	1.28	0.38	0.04	103	87	255					
1956	0.07	0.03	1.74	1.70	1.25	0.45	0.04	101	82	283	204.7	126.0			
1957	0.10	0.03	1.74	1.69	1.14	0.55	0.04	96	72	324					
1958	0.17	0.05	2.04	1.96	1.29	0.67	0.08	105	78	319					
1959	0.54	0.22	2.41	2.28	1.27	1.00	0.13	113	76	304					
1960	1.15	0.44	2.38	2.18	0.93	1.25	0.20	103	56	285					
1961	1.41	0.42	2.65	2.43	1.40	1.03	0.22	117	85	240					
1962	1.92	0.34	2.87	2.69	1.74	0.95	0.18	134	106	258					
1963	2.16	0.34	2.73	2.55	1.64	0.92	0.18	126	98	255					
1964	2.32	0.32	2.82	2.62	1.69	0.93	0.20	124	98	233	236.4	141.8			
1965	2.33	0.40	3.00	2.76	1.78	0.98	0.24	124	99	234					
1966	3.44	1.02	3.35	3.09	2.15	0.94	0.26	132	113	210					
1967	4.06	1.21	3.38	3.12	2.23	0.89	0.26	127	112	186					
1968	5.07	1.49	3.48	3.21	2.34	0.87	0.27	126	115	170					
1969	6.27	1.87	4.06	3.73	2.55	1.18	0.33	140	119	227					
1970	7.70	2.29	4.33	3.97	2.67	1.30	0.36	143	119	245					
1971	9.53	2.63	4.52	4.13	2.72	1.41	0.39	144	117	266					
1972	10.20	2.76	4.90	4.46	2.99	1.47	0.44	150	124	258					
1973	13.01	3.08	5.35	5.00	3.15	1.85	0.35	163	128	309					
1974	12.67	3.53	5.69	5.12	3.12	2.00	0.57	162	123	322					
1975	13.69	3.98	5.79	5.24	3.05	2.19	0.55	160	116	342					
1976	14.87	4.45	6.40	5.75	3.37	2.38	0.65	171	122	360					
1977	15.62	4.87	6.62	5.73	3.33	2.40	0.89	165	121	334					
1978	16.75	5.05	7.79	6.60	4.23	2.37	1.19	185	150	310	300.0	168.0	48.00		14.40
1979	18.35	5.54	8.50	7.03	4.03	3.00	1.47	193	140	395	383.0	204.0			
1980	17.59	5.67	10.08	8.48	4.74	3.74	1.60	227	163	450	403.3	225.9	80.30		7.26
1981	20.26	5.82	11.23	9.29	5.39	3.90	1.94	243	180	466	423.0	226.1	74.51	3.96	5.38
1982	21.22	5.99	12.91	10.39	6.18	4.21	2.52	265	202	489	471.4	239.0	77.23	7.12	11.72
1983	21.78	5.65	14.41	11.49	7.06	4.43	2.92	287	226	504	448.6	244.8	73.68	5.16	7.44
1984	22.24	6.05	16.79	13.01	8.05	5.02	3.72	322	255	558	532.7	288.4	88.68	5.40	7.44
1985	25.58	6.82	19.58	15.32	9.23	6.09	4.26	370	286	670	645.1	303.6	112.32	5.76	13.68
1986	29.83	8.16	22.69	17.71	10.66	7.04	4.98	421	321	791	745.3	351.9	139.44	6.36	9.24
1987	33.73	9.76	25.65	20.58	11.72	8.86	5.07	478	350	923	791.8	416.9	132.60	6.96	9.72
1988	37.72	11.22	31.13	25.30	13.73	10.36	5.83	572	411	1111	1013.6	473.6	176.38	7.20	11.20
1989	41.86	14.30	34.21	27.50	15.13	12.37	6.71	608	439	1156	1089.2	566.2	167.28	7.08	19.68

29. Ningxia

29–5

Year	v3f	v3f1	v3f2	v3f3	v3f4	v4a1	v4a1a	v4a1b	v4a1c	v4a1d	v4a2	v4a2a	v4a2b	v4a2c	v4a2d
1949															
1950						0.11	0.0001	0.0294	0.0766	0.0026	0.05		0.01	0.03	0.01
1951						0.19		0.0680	0.1236	0.0031	0.09		0.02	0.05	0.02
1952	69.9	51.0				0.28	0.0122	0.1267	0.1127	0.0254	0.19		0.04	0.09	0.07
1953						0.22	0.0254	0.0859	0.0923	0.0138	0.38		0.08	0.15	0.15
1954						0.26	0.0247	0.0963	0.1177	0.0257	0.28		0.05	0.08	0.16
1955						0.29	0.0473	0.1028	0.1155	0.0235	0.38		0.04	0.08	0.26
1956	80.5	58.7				0.30	0.0659	0.1122	0.1067	0.0158	0.35		0.08	0.10	0.17
1957						0.37	0.1124	0.1154	0.1065	0.0225	0.37		0.07	0.10	0.21
1958						0.58	0.2081	0.1683	0.1680	0.0327	1.24	0.63	0.09	0.10	0.43
1959						0.92	0.5157	0.2308	0.1532	0.0169	2.15	1.31	0.12	0.14	0.58
1960						1.05	0.6430	0.2763	0.0887	0.0371	3.03	1.79	0.21	0.15	0.88
1961						0.78	0.3657	0.2111	0.0853	0.1186	1.63	0.45	0.18	0.16	0.83
1962						0.39	0.0246	0.2269	0.0750	0.0643	0.69	0.12	0.15	0.13	0.30
1963						0.43	0.0437	0.2424	0.0899	0.0555	0.86	0.16	0.18	0.14	0.38
1964	84.8	62.0				0.57	0.1801	0.2518	0.1020	0.0305	1.07	0.35	0.21	0.14	0.37
1965						0.64	0.1825	0.2835	0.0969	0.0728	1.12	0.37	0.20	0.14	0.41
1966						0.69	0.2457	0.3097	0.0972	0.0373	1.36	0.52	0.21	0.14	0.50
1967						0.39	0.0284	0.2604	0.0839	0.0203	1.17	0.54	0.20	0.11	0.32
1968						0.33	-0.0595	0.2545	0.1124	0.0189	1.06	0.50	0.18	0.13	0.24
1969						0.48	-0.0656	0.3828	0.1125	0.0512	1.47	0.77	0.22	0.14	0.34
1970						0.99	0.3382	0.5006	0.1049	0.0443	1.69	0.82	0.25	0.17	0.44
1971						1.24	0.4551	0.6573	0.1041	0.0217	2.01	0.87	0.31	0.20	0.63
1972						1.28	0.4403	0.7211	0.0975	0.0199	2.94	1.33	0.36	0.22	1.03
1973						1.65	0.7380	0.7988	0.0792	0.0298	3.26	1.25	0.42	0.23	1.35
1974						1.72	0.7256	0.8481	0.1118	0.0343	3.63	1.45	0.45	0.24	1.48
1975						2.23	1.0970	1.0172	0.0963	0.0206	3.71	1.38	0.50	0.25	1.58
1976						1.99	0.8556	1.0238	0.0900	0.0230	3.78	1.36	0.53	0.27	1.62
1977						1.76	0.4854	1.1061	0.0978	0.0702	4.03	1.30	0.58	0.29	1.87
1978	90.7	69.4	11.70	2.10	3.20	3.16	1.5106	1.3163	0.0995	0.2321	5.78	2.20	0.76	0.29	2.53
1979	102.2	74.3	13.01	2.90	5.23	3.05	1.3858	1.4148	0.0925	0.1509	6.30	2.33	0.90	0.37	2.69
1980	135.5	85.0	19.02	6.59	7.80	2.04	0.4808	1.3514	0.0827	0.1091	5.75	1.67	1.01	0.48	2.60
1981	141.7	88.1	19.83	7.40	5.81	1.44	0.0161	1.2252	0.0775	0.1141	4.61	0.90	1.11	0.47	2.13
1982	179.0	112.6	23.78	9.60	6.46	1.52	-0.1000	1.4160	0.0774	0.1185	5.71	1.05	1.44	0.50	2.73
1983	208.9	125.2	28.40	12.60	10.73	1.78	0.0022	1.5685	0.0774	0.1315	6.95	1.48	1.57	0.63	3.27
1984	231.6	134.1	30.46	17.07	11.71	2.31	0.3250	1.7844	0.0845	0.1180	8.79	1.87	1.99	0.92	4.01
1985	264.5	152.9	32.26	17.16	11.50	3.14	0.4057	2.5655	0.1092	0.0624	9.85	2.11	2.22	0.91	4.62
1986	300.9	168.0	38.11	24.91	11.18	3.66	0.5273	2.9190	0.1114	0.1036	12.02	2.34	2.57	1.02	6.10
1987	330.0	185.5	39.15	30.35	11.10	4.11	0.4404	3.4060	0.1179	0.1414	11.04	2.02	2.59	1.02	5.42
1988	397.8	202.9	48.11	32.70	12.26	5.07	0.1154	4.1110	0.1199	0.6866	13.82	1.76	3.01	1.33	7.72
1989	460.8	235.7	50.78	53.56	16.50	6.33	0.1100				14.88	1.50	3.11	1.10	9.17

29. Ningxia

29–6

Year	v4b	v4b1	v4b2	v4b3	v4c1	v4c2	v5a	v5a1	v5a2	v5a3	v5a4	v5b1	v5b2	v5b3	v5c
1949							44	1	3.57	4.0000	39	40	3	1	
1950	0.0008	0.0008					47	1		3.0000	43	43	3	1	
1951	0.0069	0.0069					51	1		4.0000	46	46	3	2	
1952	0.0157	0.0157				11.0	57	2	3.94	4.0000	51	50	4	3	
1953	0.0282	0.0282				10.0	60	2		5.0000	53	54	5	1	
1954	0.0389	0.0389			0.01	11.2	64	3		2.0000	56	56	6	2	
1955	0.0332	0.0332			0.01	16.7	68	3		2.0000	59	60	6	2	
1956	0.0519	0.0519			0.02	20.0	72	5			61	62	6	4	
1957	0.0807	0.0807			0.02	17.4	77	5	6.88		65	65	7	5	
1958	0.1056	0.0882	0.0174		0.06	25.4	82	11	4.21		67	66	11	5	
1959	0.2078	0.1422	0.0656		0.15	19.3	89	20			66	68	13	8	
1960	0.2308	0.1830	0.0477		0.23	14.4	97	26			69	73	14	10	
1961	0.2443	0.1666	0.0777		0.21	11.3	90	20			69	72	12	6	
1962	0.1476	0.1212	0.0264		0.21	9.5	86	14	1.75	0.0700	70	73	7	6	
1963	0.1606	0.1338	0.0268		0.23	9.2	91	14			75	78	8	5	
1964	0.2025	0.1711	0.0314		0.25	9.4	94	14			78	81	7	6	
1965	0.2399	0.1958	0.0441		0.28	10.2	99	17	1.66	0.0800	80	83	9	7	
1966	0.2835	0.2249	0.0586		0.45	10.1	103	20			81	84	11	8	
1967	0.2903	0.2425	0.0478		0.43	8.2	105	21			82	86	12	7	
1968	0.3111	0.2596	0.0515		0.51	7.8	106	21			83	86	13	7	
1969	0.3075	0.2477	0.0598		0.69	8.5	110	23			85	87	15	8	
1970	0.3071	0.2676	0.0395		0.92	9.2	113	25			86	89	16	8	
1971	0.3630	0.3164	0.0466		1.08	8.9	116	27			87	90	17	9	
1972	0.4570	0.3778	0.0792		1.17	9.1	118	28			88	90	19	9	
1973	0.5266	0.4292	0.0974		1.45	9.0	119	28			89	91	19	9	
1974	0.5856	0.4756	0.1100		1.41	8.7	122	29			90	92	20	10	
1975	0.6296	0.5227	0.1069		1.56	10.5	126	31	2.85	0.0009	92	94	20	12	
1976	0.6838	0.5693	0.1145		1.41	7.3	128	33	3.37	0.0022	92	94	21	13	
1977	0.7674	0.6302	0.1372		1.57	7.7	131	34	5.41	0.0011	92	93	24	14	
1978	0.8989	0.7234	0.1755		2.13	9.8	136	38	5.29		93	95	25	16	
1979	1.2142	0.9767	0.2375		2.50	10.5	140	40	6.02	0.0100	94	97	26	17	
1980	1.7134	1.3796	0.3338		2.13	9.1	147	42	6.27	0.1400	99	103	26	18	
1981	2.2815	1.8418	0.4397		1.43	5.5	150	43	6.28	0.1600	101	106	26	18	
1982	3.2607	2.5747	0.6860		1.68	6.2	156	43	6.63	0.2900	105	109	27	20	
1983	4.4398	3.4755	0.9643		2.14	7.8	163	45	7.21	0.7100	110	114	27	22	
1984	6.1675	4.7950	1.3725		2.68	9.5	170	45	8.29	0.8800	106	117	29	24	
1985	8.0353	6.3414	1.6939		3.30	10.2	177	47	8.99	1.0900	120	116	32	29	
1986	11.0449	8.7614	2.2835		3.12	8.2	183	49	9.09	1.1500	124	117	34	32	
1987	14.8890	11.9461	2.9429		3.84	8.8	191	51	9.42	1.3900	129	120	35	36	
1988	18.0849	14.7480	3.3369		5.52	11.3	197	53	9.70	1.9600	133	123	37	37	
1989	23.7000	19.7000	4.0000		6.07	10.8	204	55		2.0000	136	126	38	40	

29. Ningxia

29–7

Year	v5c1	v5d	v6a	v6a1	v6a2	v6b	v6c	v6d1	v6d2	v6d3	v6d4	v6d5	v6d6
1949			120	15	105			8	112	63	57	7.25	
1950			126	15	111	40.32	20.58	9	117	66	60		
1951			133	15	118	43.89	19.18	11	122	70	63		
1952			142	17	125	49.90	22.44	11	131	76	66	8.97	
1953			151	20	131	40.01	19.38	13	138	80	71		
1954			158	21	137	42.47	13.05	14	144	84	74		
1955			165	21	144	34.90	10.24	14	151	87	78		
1956			172	23	149	34.20	10.58	15	157	92	80		
1957			179	24	155	43.24	11.06	18	161	95	84	11.66	
1958			194	32	162	39.32	14.98	24	170	104	90	14.82	
1959			209	42	167	23.80	15.82	36	173	114	95		
1960			213	51	162	16.58	13.90	41	172	115	98		
1961			203	44	159	13.03	10.71	36	167	108	95	20.64	9.83
1962			199	37	162	44.60	8.49	29	170	105	94	17.86	8.42
1963			207	34	173	50.52	10.22	32	175	109	98	18.72	10.91
1964			215	41	174	49.37	13.44	32	183	113	102	20.31	11.34
1965			227	43	184	48.08	9.29	35	192	119	108	21.26	12.95
1966			235	46	189	42.20	9.35	37	198	124	111		
1967			244	49	195	43.13	8.35	40	204	128	116		
1968			255	49	206	40.89	6.40	42	213	133	122		
1969			265	51	214	42.69	6.68	44	221	139	126		
1970			277	54	223	40.27	6.33	45	232	144	133	25.95	20.07
1971			287	59	228	36.44	6.03	48	239	149	138		
1972			297	60	237	39.80	7.24	50	247	154	143		
1973			308	62	246	38.21	7.23	52	256	160	148		
1974			317	64	253	34.53	6.85	53	264	164	153		
1975			328	66	262	36.50	7.77	55	273	170	158	29.94	23.88
1976			338	66	272	31.63	6.84	57	281	175	163		
1977			347	71	276	29.49	5.73	59	288	180	167		
1978			356	73	283	28.48	5.46	61	295	184	172	32.52	26.96
1979			364	77	287	27.56	5.56	64	300	188	176		
1980			374	79	295	24.96	4.72	68	306	193	181	34.45	28.66
1981			383	84	299	29.65	6.08	71	312	198	185		
1982			393	89	304	28.95	5.82	73	320	203	190		
1983			399	110	289	18.29	4.06	76	323	206	193		
1984			407	131	276	18.58	3.77	78	329	210	197		
1985			415	147	268	17.18	3.88	83	332	214	201	39.69	31.74
1986			424	170	254	20.54	5.00	91	333	219	205	41.18	32.63
1987			435	170	265	25.14	5.04	97	338	225	210	43.36	26.39
1988			445	177	268	24.79	5.24	102	343	229	216	44.99	26.39
1989			455	178	277	23.56	4.61	108	347	234	221	46.51	27.04

29. Ningxia

29–8

Year	v7a	v7b	v7c	v7d	v7e	v7f	v7g	v7h	v7h1	v7h2	v7h3	v7h4	v7h5	v7i	v8a
1949			193.0					1.08	0.83		0.24		0.010	22.6	0.13
1950			205.0					1.14	0.88	0.002	0.25		0.010	25.2	0.14
1951			215.0					1.33	1.04	0.003	0.28		0.010	30.4	0.17
1952			223.0	886				1.61	1.26	0.006	0.34		0.010	34.4	0.20
1953			234.0					1.53	1.13	0.008	0.38		0.010	37.2	0.26
1954			250.0					1.74	1.35	0.004	0.37		0.010	37.6	0.32
1955			273.0					2.01	1.58	0.009	0.41		0.020	37.8	0.37
1956			315.0					2.25	1.84	0.040	0.35	0.001	0.020	37.9	0.36
1957			324.0	1232		0.1		2.09	1.77	0.050	0.26	0.001	0.020	37.3	0.46
1958			347.0			0.6		2.16	1.87	0.040	0.23	0.003	0.020	35.0	0.92
1959			335.0			0.9		2.12	1.79	0.040	0.27	0.003	0.020	33.7	1.79
1960			347.0			0.8		1.79	1.44	0.040	0.28	0.003	0.028	30.7	2.38
1961			311.0			0.4		2.73	2.27	0.020	0.38	0.006	0.044	27.5	2.05
1962			302.3			0.7		2.60	2.12	0.030	0.39	0.004	0.063	28.9	1.53
1963			292.0			0.9		2.58	2.19	0.020	0.32	0.003	0.050	30.8	1.49
1964			293.0			0.9		2.58	2.09	0.040	0.38	0.003	0.068	33.6	1.59
1965		272.2	313.1	1364		2.3	0.1	3.05	2.44	0.040	0.50	0.003	0.069	35.7	2.03
1966		267.0	301.0			2.8		3.03	2.38	0.040	0.55	0.003	0.065	35.8	3.08
1967		262.0	302.0			3.6		3.23	2.61	0.050	0.50	0.003	0.069	35.3	2.92
1968		257.0	304.0			3.6		2.72	2.14	0.050	0.46	0.003	0.074	36.8	2.87
1969		255.0	300.0			4.6		2.89	2.32	0.040	0.45	0.003	0.078	37.1	3.76
1970		252.2	285.6			4.0	0.4	2.80	2.19	0.050	0.48	0.003	0.082	37.6	5.01
1971		301.0	320.0			5.5	0.4	3.78	2.83	0.060	0.82	0.003	0.070	39.0	6.53
1972		340.0	311.0			6.9	0.5	3.77	2.81	0.060	0.82	0.001	0.080	38.6	7.50
1973	2.38	372.0	308.0			10.3	0.4	3.32	2.50	0.050	0.71	0.002	0.060	38.0	8.57
1974	3.19	403.0	320.0			14.3	0.5	4.80	3.92	0.080	0.72	0.002	0.080	36.8	9.68
1975	4.18	412.0	342.0			17.9	0.6	4.60	3.62	0.100	0.82	0.002	0.060	35.2	11.17
1976	5.13	439.0	343.0			21.4	0.8	3.73	2.84	0.130	0.72	0.002	0.040	35.7	10.45
1977	5.75	446.0	339.0			23.1	0.8	4.35	3.33	0.110	0.86	0.002	0.050	37.5	11.92
1978	6.63	468.7	304.2	1352		22.8	1.1	4.81	3.71	0.150	0.87	0.003	0.080	36.5	13.85
1979	7.73	547.5	351.0			20.1	1.2	5.61	4.24	0.200	1.03	0.005	0.140	36.6	14.55
1980	8.41	473.4	348.7	1345		17.7	1.5	6.41	5.11	0.240	0.87	0.009	0.180	39.0	13.92
1981	9.16	244.3	342.2			16.7	1.4	7.54	5.97	0.310	1.06	0.014	0.190	44.6	12.79
1982	9.21	209.6	348.4			18.1	1.5	7.78	6.17	0.340	1.02	0.034	0.240	51.0	14.75
1983	10.67	230.3	350.2			20.6	1.6	9.14	7.05	0.630	1.05	0.034	0.380	50.9	16.54
1984	11.53	251.9	353.5			23.4	1.8	10.99	8.22	0.940	1.47	0.061	0.330	53.7	19.11
1985	12.39	264.2	362.9	1242		23.2	1.9	12.02	8.45	0.800	2.29	0.110	0.420	56.4	24.30
1986	13.75	279.2	369.0			26.9	2.2	14.16	10.07	0.650	2.82	0.186	0.520	58.8	28.24
1987	15.04	345.6	379.5			28.3	2.6	14.76	10.40	0.440	3.22	0.189	0.510	56.1	33.38
1988	16.10	386.4	383.3	1310		35.2	2.8	19.66	13.11	0.570	5.15	0.333	0.500	57.4	44.00
1989	17.60	420.9	386.4	1315			3.2	21.43	15.03	0.620	4.91	0.390	0.480	54.7	58.53

29. Ningxia

29–9

Year	v8a1	v8a2	v8a3	v8b	v8c1	v8c2	v8d	v8f1	v8f2	v8f3	v8f4	v8f5	v8g
1949	0.02	0.11		0.02	0.003	0.13			1.75				293
1950	0.02	0.12		0.02	0.004	0.13			2.19				318
1951	0.04	0.13		0.04	0.008	0.16			3.45		0.01		493
1952	0.07	0.13		0.06	0.018	0.18	0.01		7.18		0.01		686
1953	0.10	0.16		0.10	0.031	0.23	0.01		13.40		0.01		603
1954	0.13	0.19		0.12	0.037	0.28	0.03		17.20		0.01		918
1955	0.16	0.21		0.16	0.033	0.34	0.04		21.10		0.03		225
1956	0.19	0.17		0.18	0.043	0.32	0.06		25.80		0.04		265
1957	0.30	0.16		0.30	0.085	0.38	0.09		34.00		0.05		310
1958	0.66	0.26		0.65	0.360	0.56	0.22		121.00		0.11		755
1959	1.53	0.26		1.51	0.900	0.90	0.63	0.03	254.00	0.02	0.39		830
1960	2.09	0.29		2.07	1.030	1.35	0.70	0.10	305.00	0.09	0.94	2.21	783
1961	1.80	0.25		1.77	1.230	0.82	0.49	0.02	272.00	0.05	1.14	1.43	566
1962	1.24	0.29		1.22	0.880	0.65	0.37	0.06	266.00		0.94	0.32	446
1963	1.25	0.24		1.23	0.630	0.86	0.38		293.00		0.89	1.29	448
1964	1.31	0.28		1.28	0.720	0.87	0.49		257.00		1.01	3.30	445
1965	1.63	0.40		1.60	0.980	1.05	0.64		308.00		1.29	4.06	454
1966	2.64	0.44		2.59	1.890	1.19	0.82		363.00		1.93	4.83	530
1967	2.32	0.60		2.27	1.450	1.47	0.84	0.04	230.00		2.15	3.18	439
1968	2.36	0.51		2.32	1.700	1.18	0.89	0.03	233.00		2.11	2.25	434
1969	3.27	0.49		3.21	2.590	1.17	1.08	0.03	339.00		2.99	5.39	444
1970	4.49	0.52		4.41	3.350	1.66	1.42	0.11	473.00		4.51	7.17	597
1971	5.78	0.75		5.59	4.680	1.85	1.74	0.16	552.00	3.66	8.13	9.46	721
1972	6.63	0.87		6.32	5.530	1.97	2.00	0.42	608.00	3.94	9.50	12.26	695
1973	7.66	0.91		7.29	5.860	2.14	2.19	0.56	690.00	4.48	10.24	13.28	689
1974	8.43	1.25		8.02	7.040	2.64	2.77	0.65	603.00	5.66	10.98	17.22	736
1975	9.70	1.47		9.27	7.940	3.23	3.22	0.70	749.00	5.16	13.14	23.27	836
1976	8.97	1.48		8.73	7.250	3.20	3.02	0.59	800.00	7.38	14.30	24.20	918
1977	9.62	2.30		9.01	8.820	3.10	3.14	0.63	891.00	10.53	15.52	25.69	1021
1978	11.47	2.38		10.62	10.400	3.45	3.90	0.95	999.00	39.54	16.51	27.66	1072
1979	12.57	1.98		11.57	11.090	3.45	4.51	0.94	1041.00	57.16	17.81	30.83	1079
1980	12.15	1.74	0.03	11.20	10.170	3.75	4.23	0.72	971.00	56.46	19.43	29.27	1097
1981	10.65	2.08	0.06	10.28	8.750	4.05	3.63	0.41	952.00	52.03	18.27	23.19	1085
1982	12.50	2.21	0.04	12.03	10.260	4.49	3.92	0.50	928.00	50.29	21.00	30.47	1120
1983	14.07	2.40	0.07	13.56	11.650	4.89	4.47	0.60	978.00	47.23	22.06	41.26	1187
1984	16.07	2.87	0.17	15.54	13.410	5.70	5.30	0.69	1070.00	44.56	23.25	48.88	1249
1985	19.66	3.91	0.73	19.41	17.030	7.27	6.64	0.88	1213.69	39.80	24.14	61.62	1503
1986	22.17	5.06	1.01	21.95	19.110	9.13	7.13	1.17	1237.27	34.80	31.40	67.09	1716
1987	25.97	6.12	1.29	25.71	22.590	10.79	8.12	2.12	1296.67	30.84	42.64	72.80	1781
1988	33.98	8.31	1.71	33.24	30.100	13.90	10.43	2.05	1327.68	32.14	50.11	87.30	1795
1989	45.82	10.46	2.25	43.12	40.780	17.76	14.04	2.41	1338.61	28.71	54.19	93.82	1885

29. Ningxia

29–10

Year	v8g1	v9a	v9a1	v9a2	v9a3	v9b	v9b1	v9b2	v9b3	v9c	v10a	v10a1	v10b1	v10b2	v10b3
1949						0.02		0.0047	0.0125	29.5					
1950		0.04		0.02	0.02	0.10		0.0300	0.0700	11.9	0.31	0.29			
1951		0.06		0.05	0.01	0.23		0.0400	0.1900	19.7	0.42	0.40			
1952	32	0.15		0.14	0.01	0.38		0.0888	0.2918	29.5	0.55	0.53			
1953	24	0.25		0.25		0.47		0.1500	0.3200	43.7	0.71	0.68			
1954	45	0.35		0.35		0.58		0.2300	0.3500	53.1	0.89	0.84			
1955	54	0.45		0.45		0.60		0.2700	0.3300	57.1	0.93	0.88			
1956	28	0.62		0.62		0.63		0.2800	0.3500	71.9	1.09	1.01			
1957	45	0.68		0.68		0.61		0.3700	0.2358	77.3	1.18	1.10			
1958	322	0.60		0.60		0.78		0.6756	0.1071	112.7	1.50	1.37			
1959	373	2.12	1.60	0.52		13.95	12.98	0.9100	0.0600	203.4	2.07	1.88			
1960	363	2.77	2.15	0.62		20.33	19.37	0.9000	0.0600	278.6	2.36	2.12			
1961	269	3.09	2.64	0.45		18.22	17.67	0.5300	0.0200	252.3	1.99	1.81			
1962	134	3.01	2.49	0.52		19.14	18.72	0.4061	0.0112	207.6	1.96	1.80			
1963	134	2.04	1.62	0.42		21.18	20.75	0.4200	0.0100	195.9	1.86	1.71			
1964	128	1.71	1.30	0.41		23.68	23.12	0.5500	0.0100	208.6	1.96	1.78			
1965	137	1.78	1.31	0.47		32.66	31.86	0.7894	0.0132	229.5	2.12	1.90			
1966	147	2.31	1.64	0.67		35.96	34.94	1.0200		259.0	2.41	2.14			
1967	147	2.78	2.09	0.69		22.91	22.16	0.7500		231.4	2.43	2.17			
1968	144	2.95	2.27	0.69		27.60	26.93	0.6700		240.3	2.49	2.25			
1969	145	2.78	2.06	0.72		31.44	30.55	0.8900	0.0126	253.5	2.96	2.63			
1970	192	2.51	1.78	0.73		41.33	40.27	1.0500	0.0100	270.5	3.23	2.82			
1971	211	2.84	2.04	0.80		48.37	47.05	1.3200		321.7	3.46	2.97			
1972	226	3.33	2.33	1.00		58.95	57.46	1.4900		335.1	3.85	3.24			
1973	251	3.57	2.39	1.18		61.99	60.43	1.5600		370.7	4.27	3.57			
1974	247	3.23	1.83	1.40		35.00	33.44	1.5600		378.4	4.70	3.81			
1975	247	3.56	2.01	1.55		42.70	40.91	1.7787	0.0069	383.3	5.00	3.94	3.35		1.54
1976	251	3.91	2.28	1.63		35.90	34.09	1.8040	0.0032	411.6	5.54	4.36	3.63		1.78
1977	266	4.32	2.58	1.74		45.98	43.60	2.3704	0.0069	417.3	5.77	4.48	3.92		1.80
1978	280	4.42	2.32	2.10		56.22	53.49	2.7302	0.0018	444.1	6.43	5.04	4.27		2.10
1979	273	5.15	2.44	2.71		52.78	50.24	2.5433	0.0025	498.9	7.26	5.74	4.76		2.40
1980	289	6.12	2.77	3.35		45.10	43.03	2.0693	0.0046	531.2	8.02	6.74	5.09		2.74
1981	268	6.67	3.04	3.63		41.33	38.77	1.8994		723.8	8.58	7.40	5.36		2.92
1982	273	7.47	2.97	4.50		44.51	41.44	2.4563		751.8	9.73	8.41	5.87		3.37
1983	285	8.51	3.39	5.12		71.24	67.90	2.7509		828.0	11.10	9.34	6.46		3.63
1984	290	10.23	4.04	6.19		58.24	50.86	6.5387		900.7	12.85	10.86	7.08		4.05
1985	384	12.99	4.54	8.45		61.97	51.92	7.9644		1087.0	15.31	13.15	7.78		5.04
1986	404	15.07	5.07	10.00		62.20	50.60	9.0157		1224.5	17.57	15.12	8.99		5.48
1987	418	17.84	5.51	12.33		64.27	51.71	9.9881		1380.0	20.01	17.18	9.74		6.11
1988	414	22.34	6.23	16.11		65.48	52.91	10.1037		1740.3	25.63	22.10	12.74		7.70
1989	421	22.40	5.71	16.68		73.79	59.83	11.5400		2086.7	28.14	23.79	13.45		8.46

29. Ningxia

29–11

Year	v10b4	v10b5	v10b6	v10d	v11a1	v11a2	v11a3	v11b	v11b1	v11b2	v11c	v11d	v12a	v12b1	v12c
1949															
1950															
1951															
1952				0.27											
1953				0.30											
1954				0.48											
1955				0.53											
1956				0.48											
1957				0.57											
1958				0.70				0.0704	0.0447	0.0257			101.0	102.4	101.4
1959				0.78				0.1946	0.1624	0.0322			101.5	102.9	101.9
1960				0.57				0.1256	0.1001	0.0255			103.0	104.3	108.1
1961				0.55				0.0673	0.0605	0.0068			117.8	120.2	117.1
1962				0.42				0.0696	0.0679	0.0017			96.3	95.1	99.8
1963				0.56				0.1008	0.0967	0.0041			89.4	88.9	97.6
1964				0.71				0.1044	0.0995	0.0049			95.7	94.9	98.6
1965				0.77				0.1184	0.1037	0.0147			97.6	97.7	99.9
1966				0.83				0.1154	0.1154				98.1	98.2	103.5
1967				0.74				0.1135	0.1135				101.9	102.5	100.3
1968				0.64				0.1589	0.1457	0.0132			100.8	101.3	100.3
1969				0.66				0.0867	0.0735	0.0132			101.5	102.5	100.3
1970				0.57				0.1034	0.0869	0.0165			100.5	100.8	100.0
1971				0.74				0.1050	0.0897	0.0153			99.0	99.8	100.8
1972				0.75				0.1525	0.1295	0.0230			100.1	100.4	101.0
1973				0.79				0.1754	0.1423	0.0331			100.3	100.3	101.2
1974				1.06				0.2596	0.1747	0.0849			100.1	100.4	103.2
1975	0.08		0.05	1.10				0.2699	0.2091	0.0608			100.3	100.6	100.5
1976	0.09		0.04	0.99				0.3142	0.1739	0.1403			100.4	100.9	100.4
1977			0.05	1.02				0.2216	0.2019	0.0197			107.5	108.2	100.3
1978			0.06	1.14				0.2962	0.2271	0.0691			100.0	100.6	101.1
1979			0.10	1.24				0.4785	0.3731	0.1054			101.3	101.6	112.0
1980		0.02	0.17	2.02				0.4674	0.4352	0.0322			105.8	108.1	110.7
1981		0.07	0.23	2.38				0.4767	0.4380	0.0837			102.0	102.1	109.9
1982	0.01	0.15	0.33	3.10				0.4665	0.4266	0.0399			102.5	102.9	108.9
1983	0.01	0.49	0.51	3.70				0.3739	0.2956	0.0783			101.1	101.6	108.3
1984	0.02	0.97	0.73	4.53				0.4141	0.3128	0.1013			103.2	103.3	103.1
1985	0.01	1.48	1.00	4.60				0.5426	0.3416	0.2010			107.8	108.6	107.2
1986	0.01	1.75	1.34	6.02				0.7465	0.5338	0.2127			104.9	106.0	109.6
1987	0.01	2.45	1.70	6.58				0.8710	0.6310	0.2400		0.0200	108.0	109.9	110.3
1988	0.01	3.17	2.01	10.03				1.0724	0.8221	0.2503	0.1157	0.0312	117.5	117.7	127.9
1989	0.01	3.71	2.50	11.32				0.7848	0.6248	0.1600			117.8	116.2	110.8

29. Ningxia

29–12

Year	v13a	v13b	v13c1	v13c2	v13c3	v13d	v14a	v14b	v14c	v15a	v15b	v15c	v15d	v15e	v15f
1949				0.17	4.51					971					
1950										1076					
1951										1111					
1952				0.37	6.95		260			1145					
1953										1177					
1954										1212					
1955										1258					
1956		40.30								1346					
1957		62.75		1.30	14.06					1344					
1958	4.3									1346					
1959	3.0									1320					
1960	3.5									1397					
1961	6.0									1337					
1962	12.6	37.33	0.12	1.57	14.54	0.0162			0.0143	1324					
1963	11.6									1315					
1964	10.4									1359					
1965	10.3	75.56	0.10	2.67	34.72	0.0371	2823	10000	0.0421	1384					
1966	9.3									1391					
1967	11.3									1396					
1968	10.8									1383					
1969	7.8									1372					
1970	8.0			4.59	30.06				0.0557	1359					
1971	8.8									1373					
1972	6.9									1389					
1973	7.3									1371					
1974	7.1									1360					
1975	7.7	94.56	0.18	12.65	59.62	0.0513			0.1093	1372					
1976	7.8		0.21	17.64	62.42	0.0470			0.0934	1335					
1977	8.0		0.23	21.72	62.59	0.0678			0.1215	1331					
1978	7.5	91.19	0.29	23.81	61.30	0.0623	6962	10000	0.1136	1337					
1979	7.9	89.02	0.32	23.39	59.32	0.0789			0.1219	1347					
1980	10.0	86.20	0.42	23.21	58.37	0.0356	7184	10000	0.3763	1344					
1981	14.2	82.51	0.52	21.51	55.53	0.0341			0.3841	1320					
1982	13.6	82.13	0.45	20.86	55.39	0.1896			0.3700	1295					
1983	11.9	82.24	0.51	21.53	57.52	0.0875			0.3967	1261					
1984	11.8	85.17	0.56	23.44	61.98	0.1249			0.4986	1215					
1985	12.3	91.48	0.64	25.78	65.42	0.1530	8640	20000	0.6131	1193					
1986	11.9	92.51	0.72	28.08	68.17	0.1548			0.5911	1187					
1987	13.6	93.34	0.73	29.64	69.36	0.2172			0.6642	1186					
1988	12.9	93.61	0.77	30.12	69.89	0.2066	9755	20000	0.7412	1194	37.19	332.557	207.3	305.45	105.8
1989		94.00	0.79	28.85	68.50	0.2000	9828	20000	0.6391	1193					

Notes

1. National Output and Income (Y)

v1a: (E), p.891
- v1a1: (E), p.891
- v1a2: (E), p.891
- v1a3: (E), p.891
- v1a4: (E), p.891
- v1a5: (E), p.891

v1b: (A); (D), p.409
- v1b1: (A); (D), p.409
- v1b2: (A); (D), p.409
- v1b3: (A); (D), p.409
- v1b4: (A); (D), p.409
- v1b5: (A); (D), p.409

v1c: v1a – v1d

v1d: (E), p.888
- v1d1: (E), p.888
- v1d2: (E), p.888
- v1d3: (E), p.888—1949: 0.0012, 1950: 0.0043
- v1d4: (E), p.888
- v1d5: (E), p.888

v1e: (A); (D), p.412
- v1e1: (A); (D), p.412
- v1e2: (A); (D), p.412
- v1e3: (A); (D), p.412
- v1e4: (A); (D), p.412
- v1e5: (A); (D), p.412

v1f: (E), p.887
- v1f1: (E), p.887
- v1f2: (E), p.887
- v1f3: (E), p.887

v1g: v2a + v3a

v1h: (A); (E), p.916

v1i: (E), p.915—excluding meat and other price subsidies

v1j: (E), p.915
- v1j1: (E), p.915
- v1j2: (E), p.915
- v1j3: NA

v1k: (E), p.915—including state-owned units only in 1983 and before

2. Investment (I)

v2a: (E), p.890
- v2a1: (A); (D), p.415
- v2a2: (A); (D), p.415

v2b: (A)

v2c: (A); (E), p.906
- v2c1: (E), p.907
- v2c2: (E), p.907

v2d:
- v2d1: (E), p.904
- v2d2: (E), p.904

v2e: (E), p.904

3. Consumption (C)

v3a: (E), p.890

v3b: (E), p.890
- v3b1: (A); (D), p.413
- v3b2: (A); (D), p.413

v3c: (E), p.890

v3d: (E), p.914
- v3d1: (E), p.914
- v3d2: (E), p.914

v3e: (A); (E), p.916
- v3e1: (E), p.916
- v3e2: (A)
- v3e3: (A)
- v3e4: (A)

v3f: (E), p.916
v3f1: (E), p.916
v3f2: (A)
v3f3: (A)
v3f4: (A)

4. Public Finance and Banking (FB)

v4a:
v4a1: (E), p.912
v4a1a: (B), p.415
v4a1b: (B), p.415
v4a1c: (B), p.415—farming and animal husbandry tax
v4a1d: (B), p.415
v4a2: (E), p.912
v4a2a: (E), p.912
v4a2b: (E), p.912
v4a2c: (E), p.912
v4a2d: v4a2 – v4a2a – v4a2b – v4a2c

v4b: (A)
v4b1: (B), p.466
v4b2: (A); (B), p.466
v4b3: NA

v4c:
v4c1: (E), p.904
v4c2: (E), p.904

5. Labor Force (L)

v5a: (E), p.886
v5a1: (E), p.886
v5a2: (B), p.165
v5a3: (B), p.165; (E), p.886
v5a4: (E), p.886

v5b:
v5b1: (E), p.886
v5b2: (E), p.886
v5b3: (E), p.886

v5c: NA
v5c1: NA

v5d: NA

6. Population (PO)

v6a: (E), p.885—data from public security department
v6a1: (E), p.885—(ditto)
v6a2: (E), p.885—(ditto)

v6b: (E), p.885—data of 1986 and before from sample survey

v6c: (E), p.885—(ditto)

v6d:
v6d1: (E), p.885—data from public security department
v6d2: (E), p.885—(ditto)
v6d3: (E), p.885—(ditto)
v6d4: (E), p.885—(ditto)
v6d5: (A)—Yinchuan
v6d6: (A)—Shizuishan

7. Agriculture (A)

v7a: (A); (E), p.898

v7b: (A); (E), p.898

v7c: (A); (E), p.898

v7d: (E), p.898

v7e: NA

v7f: (A)

v7g: (A); (E), p.898

v7h: (E), p.893
v7h1: (E), p.893
v7h2: (A); (E), p.893
v7h3: (E), p.893
v7h4: (A); (E), p.893
v7h5: (A); (E), p.893

v7i: (E), p.897

8. Industry (IN)

v8a: (E), p.899
- v8a1: (E), p.899—including industrial output value of private ownership and state and private joint ownership in 1949–63
- v8a2: (E), p.899
- v8a3: v8a – v8a1 – v8a2

v8b: (E), p.904

- v8c1: (E), p.891
- v8c2: (A); (E), p.891

v8d: (E), p.904

v8f:
- v8f1: (E), p.903
- v8f2: (E), p.903
- v8f3: (E), p.903
- v8f4: (E), p.903
- v8f5: (E), p.903

v8g: (A)
- v8g1: (E), p.904

9. Transport (TR)

v9a: (E), p.905—excluding urban traffic volume
- v9a1: (E), p.905—including central and local railways
- v9a2: (E), p.905
- v9a3: (E), p.905—excluding distant ocean and coastal passenger traffic, including wooden junk transport

v9b: (E), p.905
- v9b1: (E), p.905—including central and local railways
- v9b2: (E), p.905
- v9b3: (A)—excluding distant ocean and coastal freight volume, including wooden junk transport

v9c: (E), p.905—based on 1980's constant price since 1981; based on 1970's constant price before 1981

10. Domestic Trade (DT)

v10a: (E), p.908
- v10a1: (E), p.908

v10b:
- v10b1: (E), p.908
- v10b2: NA
- v10b3: (E), p.908—including supply and marketing cooperative and other collectives
- v10b4: (E), p.908
- v10b5: (E), p.908
- v10b6: (E), p.908

v10d: (E), p.910

11. Foreign Trade (FT)

v11a:
- v11a1: NA
- v11a2: NA
- v11a3: NA

v11b: (E), p.911
- v11b1: (E), p.911—including self-operated exports and allotted exports
- v11b2: v11b – v11b1—including direct imports and commission imports

v11c: (A)

v11d: (A)

12. Prices (PR)

v12a: (E), p.913

v12b: (E), p.913

v12c: (E), p.913

13. Education (ED)

v13a: (A)

v13b: (A); (E), p.916

v13c:
- v13c1: (A); (E), p.916—general institutions of higher learning
- v13c2: (A); (E), p.916—technical, ordinary and agricultural vocational secondary schools
- v13c3: (A); (E), p.916

v13d : (A)

14. Social Factors (SF)

v14a: (E), p.916

v14b: (E), p.916

v14c: (A); (B), p.505–506

15. Natural Environment (NE)

v15a: (A); (E), p.898

v15b: (A)

v15c: (A)

v15d: (A)

v15e: (A)

v15f: (A)

Sources of Data

(A) Data supplied by the DSNEB, SSB, the PRC.
(B) Statistical Bureau of Ningxia Autonomous Region ed. *Ningxia Forty Years 1949–1989*, Beijing: CSPH, 1989.
(D) Same as (D) in Beijing's sources of data.
(E) Same as (E) in Beijing's sources of data.

30

Xinjiang

30. Xinjiang

30–1

Year	v1a	v1a1	v1a2	v1a3	v1a4	v1a5	v1b	v1b1	v1b2	v1b3	v1b4	v1b5	v1c	v1d	v1d1
1949	7.52	5.86	0.98	0.10	0.09	0.49							3.12	4.40	3.79
1950	8.53	6.48	1.24	0.11	0.10	0.60							3.50	5.03	4.16
1951	10.16	7.22	1.63	0.20	0.30	0.81							4.27	5.89	4.66
1952	13.40	7.16	2.20	2.40	0.50	1.14	137.7	116.9	139.7	1084.2	104.0	112.5	6.09	7.31	4.99
1953	14.80	8.43	2.96	1.19	0.59	1.63	106.1	106.4	136.5	54.4	107.7	160.5	6.95	7.85	5.37
1954	11.17	9.35	3.43	1.75	0.86	1.78	117.3	107.6	118.2	144.6	285.7	124.6	1.64	9.53	6.10
1955	19.32	9.66	4.06	2.32	1.16	2.12	111.9	104.7	121.1	127.2	122.5	117.9	8.51	10.81	6.52
1956	23.02	10.59	4.03	4.26	1.61	2.53	118.4	111.0	97.4	190.3	134.7	115.2	10.13	12.89	7.32
1957	24.57	11.51	4.75	5.01	0.99	2.31	107.0	96.4	133.3	126.5	57.6	113.2	11.04	13.53	7.68
1958	30.41	12.52	7.10	7.12	1.08	2.59	129.8	121.8	150.2	137.1	140.8	107.2	14.60	15.81	8.61
1959	42.46	13.11	15.99	8.54	1.87	2.95	133.6	105.6	191.6	129.4	157.0	114.9	22.88	19.58	8.54
1960	48.98	14.11	20.17	9.76	1.89	3.05	113.5	101.7	127.2	113.5	115.5	103.3	25.99	22.99	9.08
1961	35.96	11.68	15.59	4.60	1.34	2.75	73.4	93.1	72.4	44.9	62.9	84.2	16.54	19.42	8.00
1962	29.46	11.60	12.19	2.05	1.27	2.35	82.2	100.1	74.4	45.0	95.1	86.1	13.64	15.82	8.04
1963	33.12	14.97	11.72	2.72	1.36	2.35	116.2	129.7	98.2	138.6	107.8	98.7	16.07	17.05	9.57
1964	35.72	16.93	11.18	3.79	1.43	2.39	115.3	113.6	116.9	133.6	104.8	104.0	16.26	19.46	11.07
1965	40.99	18.61	13.77	4.39	1.72	2.50	115.1	110.8	123.7	116.3	122.1	103.8	19.24	21.75	12.25
1966	46.19	20.51	17.27	3.70	1.94	2.77	112.3	110.0	125.1	85.1	114.4	107.3	22.09	24.10	13.57
1967	40.96	19.15	15.52	2.05	1.41	2.83	88.9	92.2	89.8	57.0	74.9	106.8	20.56	20.40	10.67
1968	36.94	16.70	13.89	2.29	1.22	2.84	91.4	88.8	91.2	114.2	82.5	101.1	19.21	17.73	8.95
1969	37.44	16.96	13.48	3.07	1.12	2.81	103.4	103.7	98.4	134.9	93.8	103.2	19.66	17.78	9.01
1970	45.22	18.41	18.10	3.80	1.98	2.93	120.7	109.4	136.4	124.3	177.4	101.7	24.58	20.64	10.10
1971	49.03	19.50	19.89	4.05	2.67	2.92	106.6	104.7	108.6	96.8	141.5	100.2	25.88	23.15	11.16
1972	45.25	18.40	17.47	4.01	2.44	2.93	92.1	95.0	87.5	94.1	90.6	100.3	23.86	21.39	10.53
1973	45.87	18.97	17.17	4.31	2.44	2.98	102.6	104.2	98.6	119.3	93.8	100.3	24.22	21.65	10.46
1974	45.11	17.47	17.38	5.11	2.25	2.90	98.6	92.0	102.3	124.6	92.5	95.3	23.21	21.90	9.98
1975	52.99	18.36	21.41	7.61	2.70	2.91	116.1	106.4	124.6	128.2	124.4	104.9	28.00	24.99	10.93
1976	56.02	19.12	24.08	6.63	3.28	2.91	106.1	103.6	109.3	99.9	123.5	100.3	29.29	26.73	11.22
1977	63.09	17.98	29.22	8.42	4.54	2.93	110.4	98.0	116.4	126.6	131.2	100.3	34.00	29.09	11.22
1978	72.53	20.97	33.90	9.24	5.14	3.28	112.0	113.0	113.7	103.5	112.1	114.6	38.45	34.08	13.29
1979	80.60	24.58	36.71	10.05	5.08	4.18	107.3	106.9	105.3	115.3	99.2	118.5	40.85	39.75	16.00
1980	93.64	30.89	40.71	10.56	5.43	6.05	108.9	109.3	110.9	86.3	116.0	140.2	47.60	46.04	19.99
1981	102.66	35.08	43.59	10.88	5.86	7.25	107.7	109.3	105.8	102.9	109.0	118.9	51.22	51.44	23.70
1982	114.52	38.76	49.63	11.32	6.32	8.49	110.7	109.1	112.7	101.0	109.1	121.1	58.46	56.06	26.22
1983	131.41	43.39	58.67	12.98	6.92	9.45	112.2	109.7	115.3	111.6	107.6	110.5	67.54	63.87	30.04
1984	151.09	49.89	67.22	15.16	7.93	10.89	112.0	112.4	111.9	111.2	112.2	111.8	76.83	74.26	35.18
1985	185.83	56.57	86.78	20.79	7.99	13.70	116.9	112.1	121.8	122.1	100.8	116.2	96.04	89.79	40.18
1986	211.30	65.52	97.71	23.18	8.69	16.20							109.78	101.52	45.60
1987	253.03	81.63	115.64	24.23	11.80	19.73							132.79	120.24	56.16
1988	329.83	108.46	149.09	33.13	13.72	25.43							175.46	154.37	72.35
1989	394.55	121.50	187.40	36.42	16.83	32.40							215.40	179.15	72.29

30. Xinjiang

30–2

Year	v1d2	v1d3	v1d4	v1d5	v1e	v1e1	v1e2	v1e3	v1e4	v1e5	v1f	v1f1	v1f2	v1f3	v1g
1949	0.33	0.04	0.02	0.22											
1950	0.42	0.05	0.03	0.37											5.02
1951	0.57	0.08	0.09	0.49											6.10
1952	0.83	0.67	0.14	0.68	130.7	115.5	142.5	970.9	173.9	144.1					7.99
1953	1.05	0.49	0.17	0.77	105.5	108.4	128.4	68.8	116.5	93.1					8.32
1954	1.27	0.72	0.31	1.13	115.4	107.4	119.4	139.0	164.6	153.7					9.75
1955	1.46	0.93	0.39	1.51	109.5	103.7	124.1	125.7	121.0	117.8					11.73
1956	1.58	1.79	0.53	1.67	116.1	110.1	99.8	188.4	133.0	115.1					12.90
1957	1.70	1.63	0.65	1.87	99.5	96.8	114.5	102.9	71.2	104.7					14.83
1958	2.33	2.20	0.65	2.02	129.7	127.0	136.5	132.4	186.5	121.9					18.11
1959	5.64	2.34	0.94	2.12	115.5	93.4	222.9	107.2	148.4	105.9					22.61
1960	7.75	2.30	1.10	2.26	116.2	100.4	150.8	120.4	104.1	104.8					26.67
1961	6.54	2.01	0.62	2.25	92.1	102.3	89.0	70.3	66.6	98.7					20.37
1962	4.53	0.99	0.62	1.64	78.5	93.0	66.5	50.3	102.7	72.2					19.01
1963	3.82	1.24	0.75	1.67	115.5	128.4	91.0	127.5	116.0	103.2					19.59
1964	3.87	1.75	0.76	2.01	113.3	113.9	100.6	141.1	103.4	122.7					22.03
1965	4.54	2.06	0.83	2.07	113.5	113.4	120.5	111.6	104.9	105.1					24.21
1966	5.64	1.73	0.85	2.31	111.4	111.2	121.5	89.5	102.1	114.0					23.99
1967	5.06	1.59	0.69	2.39	81.8	76.5	87.0	88.2	81.3	100.4					23.36
1968	4.08	1.68	0.59	2.43	89.6	88.0	83.1	106.7	86.2	100.4					22.53
1969	4.04	1.76	0.54	2.43	100.8	102.0	97.1	106.3	92.8	100.0					24.44
1970	5.33	2.14	0.74	2.33	116.7	111.4	138.2	121.0	142.0	95.7					27.49
1971	6.51	2.18	0.85	2.45	107.7	106.3	115.8	98.2	112.0	102.3					28.98
1972	5.80	1.87	0.76	2.43	93.3	95.1	90.2	86.1	87.1	100.4					30.48
1973	5.65	2.28	0.75	2.51	103.1	104.2	98.6	115.5	97.2	100.9					31.91
1974	6.10	2.58	0.74	2.50	96.5	90.4	102.3	113.4	97.1	100.4					33.80
1975	7.67	3.10	0.82	2.47	116.2	110.2	132.2	122.8	111.8	100.4					36.48
1976	9.00	3.09	0.93	2.49	104.0	101.1	112.4	93.6	120.2	100.9					37.31
1977	11.03	3.22	1.14	2.48	116.1	109.9	126.3	120.5	131.6	100.9					40.60
1978	13.14	3.51	1.35	2.79	111.0	112.9	112.6	101.3	101.8	109.4	38.53	13.97	17.89	6.67	42.27
1979	14.96	3.72	1.65	3.42	111.6	110.2	110.9	112.6	121.9	117.2	45.18	16.78	20.07	8.33	53.27
1980	16.13	3.65	2.18	4.09	107.7	106.2	107.4	92.4	145.8	118.6	52.61	25.53	20.95	10.13	61.90
1981	16.17	4.02	2.05	5.50	109.0	114.6	99.5	100.2	94.8	135.0	58.71	25.18	21.86	11.67	69.81
1982	17.14	4.30	2.42	5.98	108.7	110.9	104.8	102.7	119.1	110.7	64.56	28.10	22.77	13.69	75.30
1983	19.66	4.86	2.75	6.56	111.7	112.0	112.4	109.9	113.0	108.8	77.72	32.84	28.39	16.49	82.80
1984	23.04	5.94	2.84	7.26	112.9	114.2	114.1	112.7	101.0	109.2	86.91	36.66	30.86	19.39	198.98
1985	28.76	7.95	2.84	10.06	116.2	114.9	116.3	119.1	100.2	126.6	110.66	42.86	39.48	28.32	124.51
1986	32.26	8.71	3.27	11.68	109.1	108.3	110.6	102.2	115.4	110.0	124.24	45.96	44.54	33.74	134.86
1987	36.62	8.99	4.58	13.89	109.2	110.7	107.8	90.6	129.2	111.1	146.76	56.16	49.15	41.45	152.70
1988	46.34	12.13	5.44	18.11	109.7	103.3	113.9	120.7	118.8	114.8	188.87	71.96	63.29	53.62	197.05
1989	57.17	13.29	6.58	22.82	105.7	102.5	108.4	95.8	121.3	107.9	217.42	78.01	73.83	65.58	228.88

30. Xinjiang

30–3

Year	v1h	v1i	v1j	v1j1	v1j2	v1j3	v1k	v2a	v2a1	v2a2	v2b	v2c	v2c1	v2c2	v2d1
1949				606											
1950				640				0.76	0.51	0.25	0.33	0.33			
1951				727				1.02	0.83	0.19	0.68	0.68			
1952				722				2.12	1.88	0.24	2.29	2.29			
1953				854				1.91	1.56	0.35	1.45	1.45			
1954				903				2.38	1.96	0.42	1.91	1.91			
1955	180			877				3.49	3.09	0.39	2.62	2.62			
1956				947				3.79	3.39	0.40	4.41	4.41			
1957	125			953				3.92	3.54	0.38	4.26	4.26			
1958				862				6.19	4.65	1.54	6.76	6.76			
1959				729			0.59	8.22	6.22	2.00	8.31	8.31			8.35
1960				655			0.48	11.15	8.46	2.69	10.59	10.59			
1961				632			0.50	5.50	3.70	1.80	3.86	3.86			
1962				654			0.58	3.88	2.21	1.67	1.91	1.91			14.45
1963				671			0.56	4.78	3.23	1.54	2.61	2.61			14.66
1964				675			0.47	6.35	4.54	1.81	3.78	3.78			15.10
1965	157			657				7.36	5.66	1.70	4.03	4.03			16.47
1966				609				6.52	5.03	1.49	4.16	4.16			
1967				578				5.08	3.73	1.35	3.04	3.04			
1968				571				4.52	2.74	1.77	3.19	3.19			
1969				571				5.40	3.35	2.05	3.94	3.94			
1970				581				7.80	4.77	3.03	4.50	4.50			
1971				585				8.51	5.37	3.14	4.76	4.76			
1972				605				8.62	5.07	3.55	4.64	4.64			
1973				644				9.17	5.74	3.43	4.16	4.16			
1974				736				10.81	6.47	4.34	5.06	5.06			
1975		13.34	677	686	563		0.84	12.06	6.93	5.12	6.11	6.11			32.90
1976		14.01	677	684	597		0.95	11.47	6.53	4.94	7.14	7.14			35.17
1977		14.48	674	680	614		0.98	13.07	8.69	4.38	8.69	8.69			38.37
1978	119	15.94	717	726	614		1.51	17.34	12.16	5.18	13.00	13.00	6.52	0.41	45.08
1979	143	17.63	770	784	624		1.90	18.72	12.97	5.75			6.41	0.48	47.88
1980	201	21.24	882	904	676		2.67	21.29	16.27	5.01		20.21	8.04	0.87	49.39
1981	236	22.54	907	935	672		3.23	23.59	17.38	6.21	18.40	17.03	6.24	0.61	55.84
1982	277	24.08	941	968	722		3.81	26.04	21.09	4.95	24.74	23.15	6.52	0.88	62.07
1983	307	25.31	972	998	767		4.35	28.89	25.25	3.65	27.79	25.87	8.49	0.80	69.94
1984	363	28.88	1104	1129	923		5.53	37.23	31.08	6.15	33.73	29.93	9.27	1.10	77.43
1985	394	33.91	1277	1310	1038		7.01	51.77	40.12	11.65	44.48	39.41	12.60	2.14	98.22
1986	420	40.29	1489	1535	1158		8.95	52.28	43.96	8.32	48.47	41.97	11.30	1.38	108.77
1987	453	44.97	1626	1673	1289		11.04	57.48	43.32	14.16	51.25	44.72	14.62	1.28	125.80
1988	497	52.02	1848	1901	1467		13.08	78.85	56.24	22.61	68.41	57.60	19.10	1.49	146.28
1989	546	58.70	2055	2070	1554		15.16	90.62	59.51	31.11	78.63	61.20	20.11	1.09	179.36

30. Xinjiang

30–4

Year	v2d2	v2e	v3a	v3b	v3b1	v3b2	v3c	v3d	v3d1	v3d2	v3e	v3e1	v3e2	v3e3	v3e4
1949															
1950			4.26	4.22	2.76	1.46	0.04	94	72	209					
1951			5.08	5.03	3.05	1.98	0.06	108	79	250					
1952			5.87	5.80	3.41	2.39	0.07	122	87	278					
1953			6.41	6.31	3.79	2.52	0.10	129	96	274					
1954			7.37	7.19	4.22	2.97	0.18	144	104	316					
1955			8.24	7.96	4.54	3.42	0.28	156	110	349					
1956			9.12	8.74	4.74	4.01	0.38	166	112	385					
1957			10.91	10.47	5.46	5.01	0.44	190	126	425					
1958			11.92	11.29	5.90	5.39	0.63	196	134	396					
1959	7.39	2.25	14.39	13.57	6.50	7.07	0.82	218	149	380					
1960			15.52	14.46	6.99	7.47	1.06	215	163	306					
1961			14.87	13.97	7.04	6.93	0.90	198	161	258					
1962	11.05	3.06	15.13	14.44	7.39	7.06	0.69	202	166	264					
1963	10.71	2.73	14.81	14.17	7.48	6.69	0.64	198	167	251					
1964	10.79	2.57	15.68	14.76	7.87	6.89	0.92	200	173	245					
1965	11.30	2.80	16.85	15.73	8.41	7.32	1.12	203	181	235					
1966			17.47	16.32	6.92	9.39	1.16	198	146	269					
1967			18.28	17.21	6.86	10.35	1.07	198	140	275					
1968			18.01	17.00	6.80	10.20	1.01	188	133	259					
1969			19.04	17.99	6.81	11.18	1.05	191	128	273					
1970			19.69	18.45	7.05	11.39	1.24	189	128	269					
1971			20.48	19.17	7.29	11.88	1.31	189	127	269					
1972			21.87	20.51	7.63	12.88	1.36	195	130	279					
1973			22.74	21.23	7.20	14.03	1.51	194	119	287					
1974			22.99	21.22	6.57	14.65	1.77	188	106	290					
1975	19.12	7.23	24.42	22.46	7.29	15.17	1.96	192	114	287					
1976	19.83	7.34	25.84	23.72	7.48	16.24	2.12	198	117	291					
1977	21.85	8.45	27.53	25.15	8.55	16.60	2.38	206	127	305					
1978	26.94	8.90	29.93	26.78	8.93	17.85	3.15	215	130	318					
1979	28.78	10.50	34.55	31.23	11.25	19.98	3.32	246	162	346					
1980	27.69	10.85	40.61	37.17	12.93	24.24	3.44	286	184	405					
1981	31.64	11.50	46.22	42.51	14.91	27.60	3.71	322	211	450	445.86	242.45	72.28	3.51	9.01
1982	35.69	11.95	49.27	45.07	16.51	28.56	4.20	337	230	454					
1983	40.68	12.47	53.90	48.96	18.86	30.10	4.94	364	261	483	472.25	268.83	78.48	3.60	8.48
1984	45.69	13.54	61.75	55.65	21.60	34.06	6.10	410	295	544	563.82	304.51	99.61	4.01	9.88
1985	61.93	18.19	72.74	66.17	24.85	41.32	6.57	484	336	658	650.82	304.67	115.64	3.74	11.58
1986	69.50	20.90	82.58	74.93	27.39	47.54	7.65	536	365	735	721.96	333.86	132.81	3.99	13.90
1987	81.53	24.04	95.21	86.15	31.57	54.58	9.06	611	416	838	789.59	381.89	133.61	5.05	12.64
1988	97.91	28.62	118.19	106.79	40.36	66.43	11.40	746	525	1004	955.66	468.60	164.28	4.80	14.76
1989	123.08	38.96	138.26	124.32	47.29	77.03	13.94	853	607	1138					

30. Xinjiang

30–5

Year	v3f	v3f1	v3f2	v3f3	v3f4	v4a1	v4a1a	v4a1b	v4a1b'	v4a1c	v4a1d	v4a2	v4a2a	v4a2b	v4a2c	v4a2d
1949																
1950						0.22			0.17			0.67		0.02	0.59	
1951						0.37			0.31			0.51	0.02	0.04	0.40	0.05
1952						0.74	0.03		0.64		0.07	0.60	0.05	0.10	0.36	0.09
1953						1.15	0.13		0.81		0.21	1.44	0.38	0.28	0.53	0.25
1954						1.49	0.15		1.21		0.13	1.43	0.44	0.30	0.55	0.14
1955	202.14	127.14	27.77	0.92		1.73	0.28		1.37		0.08	1.83	0.57	0.30	0.57	0.39
1956						2.02	0.49		1.37		0.16	2.55	1.02	0.45	0.64	0.44
1957	118.26	63.43	31.52	2.31	9.86	2.26	0.51		1.60		0.15	2.25	0.78	0.52	0.62	0.33
1958						3.36	1.45		1.77		0.14	4.54	2.73	0.57	0.58	0.66
1959						5.41	3.04		2.28		0.09	6.90	3.95	0.61	0.68	1.66
1960						6.36	3.40		2.66		0.30	9.58	5.66	0.75	0.68	2.49
1961						3.45	1.27		2.06		0.12	3.94	0.93	0.60	0.63	1.78
1962						2.84	0.73		2.04		0.07	2.20	0.41	0.54	0.50	0.75
1963						3.60	1.32		2.21		0.07	2.80	0.63	0.56	0.56	1.05
1964						4.07	1.45		2.56		0.06	3.92	1.42	0.68	0.65	1.17
1965						4.53	1.71		2.74		0.08	4.89	2.17	0.69	0.65	1.38
1966						5.21	2.36		2.75		0.10	5.05	2.38	0.76	0.63	1.28
1967						2.99	0.55		2.39		0.05	4.10	1.84	0.69	0.55	1.02
1968						2.22	0.01		2.17		0.04	2.91	1.13	0.63	0.51	0.64
1969						1.39	-0.74		2.10		0.03	3.67	1.81	0.60	0.55	0.71
1970						3.57	0.62		2.87		0.08	6.05	3.17	0.63	0.64	1.61
1971						4.14	1.16		2.90		0.08	6.59	3.13	0.80	0.76	1.90
1972						2.99	0.44		2.47		0.08	7.20	3.30	1.07	0.79	2.04
1973						1.58	-1.12		2.62		0.08	8.75	3.20	1.33	0.86	3.36
1974						1.39	-1.33		2.65		0.07	8.39	3.09	1.41	0.94	2.95
1975						1.01	-2.33		3.28		0.06	8.85	2.95	1.62	1.10	3.18
1976						1.98	-1.72		3.60		0.10	9.69	3.44	1.73	1.16	3.36
1977						3.63	-0.45		4.02		0.06	11.10	3.90	1.88	1.29	4.03
1978						7.14	2.09		4.34		0.71	17.02	5.71	2.25	1.40	7.66
1979						5.49	0.63		4.45		0.41	16.99	5.13	2.62	1.62	7.63
1980	149.14	90.64	31.82	2.98	10.08	4.03	-1.15		4.61		0.57	16.22	4.13	3.21	1.78	7.10
1981	163.83	98.98	35.08	4.99	10.22	1.65	-3.59		5.01		0.23	14.82	1.89	3.50	1.85	7.58
1982	197.37	123.24	38.00	4.64	13.72	4.38	-1.39		5.46		0.31	14.94	2.39	4.19	2.42	5.94
1983	222.00	132.40	43.32	8.14	17.43	5.63	-0.85		6.22		0.26	18.61	2.96	5.21	3.03	7.41
1984	244.17	151.34	45.31	7.35	15.27	7.22	-0.06		6.94		0.34	23.33	4.14	6.42	3.44	9.33
1985	279.90	168.03	47.11	16.20	16.91	8.47	-0.79		9.00		0.26	28.60	5.33	7.49	3.99	11.79
1986	307.12	180.42	51.35	25.12	17.86	10.20	-0.63		10.29		0.54	35.12	5.19	8.24	4.49	17.20
1987	337.27	197.77	57.20	23.18	19.23	11.58	-0.88		12.03		0.43	33.69	5.10	8.25	4.40	15.94
1988	386.93	214.16	68.82	27.24	23.85	15.46	-0.46		14.80		1.12	38.91	5.05	9.82	4.09	19.95
1989	452.67	229.97	68.27	38.53	25.74	19.46	-0.55		18.10		1.91	42.01	4.94	10.91	4.72	21.44

30. Xinjiang

Year	v4b	v4b1	v4b2	v4b3	v4c1	v4c2	v5a	v5a1	v5a2	v5a3	v5a4	v5b1	v5b2	v5b3	v5c
1949							198	3	0.03	9	186	186	6	6	
1950							206	4	0.03	12	190	190	8	8	
1951							215	6	0.07	14	195	195	9	11	
1952							229	15	0.13	14	200	205	12	12	
1953							238	18	0.23	15	205	210	14	14	
1954							248	21	0.58	16	211	216	16	16	
1955							255	24	1.25	15	215	221	16	18	
1956							266	39	6.61	2	219	228	18	20	
1957							272	44	5.58	2	221	233	19	20	
1958							287	61	3.52	1	222	233	29	25	
1959					3.34	34.7	319	103	2.45	1	212	231	52	36	
1960	2.35						338	130	7.26	1	200	227	65	46	
1961	2.11						336	123	5.86	1	206	248	47	41	
1962	1.60				2.00	14.2	314	100	5.66	1	207	248	31	35	
1963	1.91				2.11	15.7	317	102	6.06	1	208	255	29	33	
1964	2.21				2.29	17.2	336	114	7.75	2	212	266	34	36	
1965	2.86				2.63	18.7	350	131	7.33	1	211	273	39	38	
1966	3.16						372	148	6.72	1	216	291	44	37	
1967	3.39						379	152	7.52	1	219	297	44	38	
1968	3.31						392	155	8.32	1	228	310	44	38	
1969	3.13						402	157	9.12	1	235	318	45	39	
1970	3.31						410	157	9.92	1	242	326	45	39	
1971	3.55						420	163	10.62	1	246	331	46	41	
1972	3.85						431	168	11.29	6	246	336	53	42	
1973	4.42						443	172	13.59	6	251	341	56	46	
1974	5.27						455	179	14.19	8	254	348	59	48	
1975	6.05				3.98	15.1	466	186	15.06	9	256	352	63	51	
1976	6.02				4.05	14.9	477	195	15.63	9	257	354	68	55	
1977	6.42				5.31	17.5	485	204	17.44	8	256	354	71	60	
1978	6.70				6.31	17.6	491	208	18.83	7	257	356	75	60	
1979	8.01				5.84	14.9	497	212	21.71	7	256	353	78	66	
1980	10.74				6.15	16.0	506	220	23.84	5	257	354	82	70	
1981	14.00				5.58	12.9	524	226	26.82	8	263	362	84	78	
1982	17.52				5.18	10.9	535	231	29.04	9	266	365	88	82	
1983	21.81				6.80	12.8	546	233	29.49	12	271	369	88	89	
1984	27.98				8.54	14.4	559	232	32.55	19	275	371	92	96	
1985	33.51				11.02	13.8	566	234	33.85	25	273	364	96	106	
1986	45.47				10.95	12.1	575	239	34.56	27	274	363	100	112	
1987	60.12				11.77	11.2	585	244	34.53	26	280	367	103	115	
1988	74.63				15.68	12.4	594	249	36.02	27	282	368	108	118	
1989	93.10	83.3	9.8		16.89	10.4	589	252	36.00	27	283	371	108	121	

30. Xinjiang

30–7

Year	v5c1	v5d	v6a	v6a1	v6a2	v6b	v6c	v6d1	v6d2	v6d3	v6d4	v6d5	v6d6
1949			433	53	380	30.03	20.81	65	368	224	209	8.77	
1950			444	56	388	30.09	19.92	69	375	230	214		
1951			455	60	395	30.12	19.41	73	382	236	219		
1952			465	62	403	30.16	18.83	75	390	241	224	11.75	
1953			478	64	414	30.63	17.78	77	401	251	227		
1954			500	75	425	31.31	16.80	89	411	265	235		
1955			512	77	435	30.67	14.40	91	421	273	239		
1956			533	81	452	31.10	14.20	96	437	285	248		
1957			558	94	464	31.48	14.00	111	447	298	260	28.96	
1958			582	114	468	31.03	13.00	136	446	315	267	32.39	
1959			649	160	489	29.87	18.84	194	455	357	292		
1960			686	180	506	28.13	15.67	218	468	379	307		
1961			710	167	543	25.16	11.71	204	506	389	321		
1962			699	145	554	32.02	9.71	166	533	375	324	53.59	
1963			713	139	574	35.14	9.43	163	550	380	333	41.86	
1964			744	136	608	42.24	16.34	168	576	397	347	43.96	
1965			789	147	642	41.65	11.08	186	603	419	370	46.49	
1966			838	151	687	38.08	9.39	197	641	444	394	51.25	
1967			872	159	713	37.16	9.19	204	668	459	413		
1968			908	163	745	40.73	9.23	209	699	477	431		
1969			944	168	776	38.81	8.66	226	718	492	452		
1970			977	173	804	36.63	8.17	218	759	506	471	59.91	
1971			1010	176	834	35.02	7.71	230	780	522	488		
1972			1050	193	857	38.36	7.92	246	804	542	508		
1973			1089	206	883	38.01	7.84	276	813	561	528		
1974			1126	214	912	35.87	8.66	298	828	578	548		
1975			1155	260	895	33.10	8.74	303	852	593	562	81.13	
1976			1186	270	916	28.96	7.58	317	869	608	578		
1977			1209	276	933	26.06	8.24	322	887	619	590		
1978			1233	321	912	22.55	7.69	333	900	630	603	56.41	54.48
1979			1256	361	895	22.54	8.33	349	907	642	614		
1980			1283	373	910	21.28	7.62	373	910	655	628	91.86	56.09
1981			1303	380	923	21.09	7.46	384	919	667	636		
1982			1316	375	941	21.16	6.65	394	922	675	641		
1983			1333	444	889	19.31	6.97	406	927	682	651		
1984			1344	544	800	19.76	6.45	424	920	687	657		
1985			1361	582	779	19.80	6.39	439	922	697	664	100.28	54.93
1986			1384	614	770	20.54	6.13	450	934	709	675	103.77	54.61
1987			1406	630	776	21.03	5.96	462	944	720	686	105.59	54.34
1988			1426	643	783	19.72	5.99	476	950	731	696	106.68	54.25
1989			1454	657	797	26.52	5.71	491	963	745	709	111.11	

30. Xinjiang

30–8

Year	v7a	v7b	v7c	v7d	v7e	v7f	v7g	v7h	v7h1	v7h2	v7h3	v7h4	v7h5	v7i	v8a
1949								5.86	3.42	0.01	1.42	0.00	1.01	94.46	0.98
1950				1726.00				6.48	3.93	0.01	1.50	0.00	1.04	104.00	1.24
1951				1872.00				7.22	4.44	0.01	1.64	0.00	1.13	110.02	1.63
1952				2061.00				7.16	4.62	0.01	1.50	0.00	1.02	114.07	2.20
1953				2079.00				8.43	5.41	0.01	1.79	0.01	1.21	127.94	2.96
1954				2104.00				9.35	6.03	0.02	2.00	0.01	1.29	136.20	3.43
1955				2222.00				9.66	6.14	0.01	2.15	0.01	1.35	141.90	4.06
1956				2429.00				10.59	6.78	0.03	2.33	0.01	1.44	148.62	4.03
1957				2562.00				11.51	7.06	0.03	3.64	0.01	1.76	132.11	4.75
1958				2848.00				12.51	8.16	0.05	3.52	0.01	0.77	114.54	7.10
1959				3230.00				13.11	8.57	0.05	3.58	0.01	0.89	109.43	15.99
1960				4473.00				14.11	9.14	0.05	3.82	0.05	1.05	89.45	20.17
1961				4306.00				11.67	7.09	0.04	3.48	0.03	1.03	88.00	15.59
1962				3806.00				11.60	6.81	0.05	3.64	0.04	1.05	85.07	12.19
1963				3781.00				14.97	9.32	0.07	4.24	0.03	1.31	87.69	11.72
1964				3974.00				16.93	11.05	0.08	4.43	0.03	1.33	91.59	11.18
1965				4184.00				18.61	12.33	0.11	4.80	0.03	1.33	94.52	13.77
1966				4523.00				20.51	14.31	0.13	4.65	0.04	1.39	98.57	17.28
1967				4590.00				19.15	12.50	0.16	5.04	0.04	1.41	98.97	15.52
1968				4350.00				16.70	10.35	0.15	4.77	0.04	1.39	103.22	13.89
1969				4237.00				16.96	11.17	0.15	4.18	0.04	1.42	107.13	13.48
1970				4431.00				18.41	12.30	0.17	4.41	0.04		119.08	18.10
1971		2390.64	3796.42	4458.00		11.83	1.09	19.50	13.16	0.20	5.04	0.04	1.05	121.41	19.89
1972		2278.47	3837.39	4384.00		12.67	1.32	18.40	11.67	0.23	5.45	0.03	1.02	123.31	17.47
1973	7.72	2549.49	3529.21	4397.39		11.50	1.28	18.97	12.69	0.22	4.98	0.03	1.04	126.70	17.17
1974	8.70	2736.80	3165.60	4311.12		8.94	1.36	17.47	11.04	0.23	5.06	0.03	1.10	131.46	17.38
1975	9.89	2628.13	3858.17	4366.01		12.63	1.37	18.36	12.29	0.24	4.64	0.03	1.16	129.37	21.41
1976	11.61	2938.90	3910.00	4361.12		13.28	1.65	19.12	13.05	0.29	4.55	0.03	1.19	142.04	24.08
1977	13.64	2908.58	3910.00	4453.28		14.84	1.99	17.98	12.65	0.33	4.53	0.03	0.44	146.32	29.22
1978	16.67	2946.26	3910.00	4532.51		22.38	3.20	20.97	15.12	0.37	4.93	0.04	0.51	148.34	33.91
1979	20.95	2972.23	3910.00	4526.71		29.56	3.76	24.58	17.79	0.43	5.78	0.04	0.54	143.10	36.71
1980	24.78	3069.92	3914.68	4490.56		34.03	3.78	30.89	22.30	0.76	7.00	0.06	0.77	154.86	40.71
1981	26.53	3026.57	3958.09	4452.26		34.80	5.74	35.08	24.37	1.12	7.50	0.05	2.04	163.72	43.59
1982	27.82	2994.45	3915.67	4493.83	187	41.36	5.10	38.76	27.21	1.26	8.08	0.08	2.13	173.57	49.63
1983	30.55	2923.73	3953.59	4358.04	145	46.93	5.20	43.39	30.24	1.52	9.11	0.07	2.45	183.11	58.67
1984	34.52	2900.39	3964.41	4317.48	102	51.95	5.62	49.89	35.55	1.74	9.79	0.08	2.73	194.05	67.22
1985	38.49	2813.36	3906.93	4269.94	30	52.54	6.35	56.57	39.29	2.59	10.82	0.17	3.70	197.29	86.78
1986	39.93	2851.22	4061.36	4275.07	360	53.16	6.65	65.52	44.78	2.55	13.36	0.28	4.55	205.53	97.71
1987	42.93	2912.95	4111.28	4380.67	285	56.22	7.60	81.63	52.51	2.48	21.99	0.43	4.22	208.42	115.64
1988	46.25	3151.49	4146.75	4411.66	352	65.17	7.77	108.46	71.12	2.89	28.97	0.69	4.79	204.15	149.09
1989	49.28	3290.80	4089.07	4402.20			8.40	121.50	78.40	3.09	33.40	0.85	5.76	206.20	187.40

30. Xinjiang

30–9

Year	v8a1	v8a2	v8a3	v8b	v8c1	v8c2	v8d	v8f1	v8f2	v8f3	v8f4	v8f5	v8g
1949	0.02		0.96		0.04	0.94			17.98				363
1950	0.04		1.20		0.08	1.15			21.46		0.01		
1951	0.18		1.45		0.23	1.39			25.14	0.35	0.01		
1952	0.71	0.02	1.47		0.53	1.67		0.07	43.73	5.21	0.05	0.18	771
1953	1.22	0.05	1.69		0.89	2.07		0.22	56.24	7.02	0.11	0.32	
1954	1.59	0.12	1.72		1.04	2.39		0.44	48.42	4.88	0.29	1.04	
1955	2.15	0.25	1.66		1.20	2.85		0.77	64.55	3.29	0.55	1.59	
1956	3.26	0.53	0.24		1.58	2.45		1.27	81.65	4.82	0.68	2.38	
1957	3.59	0.92	0.24		1.75	2.99		1.46	111.75	9.54	0.81	2.14	1396
1958	6.34	0.64	0.12		3.54	3.56		1.89	326.25	35.73	1.15	6.62	
1959	14.93	1.06		12.13	9.43	6.56		4.54	442.98	98.21	2.22	15.43	
1960	19.06	1.11			13.23	6.94		8.08	473.85	166.23	3.44	16.20	
1961	14.93	0.67			9.58	6.02		2.58	402.70	107.13	3.17	9.32	
1962	11.48	0.69	0.02	9.21	5.97	6.22		1.80	305.65	87.76	2.96	7.46	2252
1963	11.02	0.68	0.02	9.27	5.51	6.20		1.89	285.38	85.90	3.06	12.36	
1964	10.56	0.60	0.02	10.61	5.18	5.99		2.43	330.46	90.33	3.52	22.72	
1965	13.04	0.72	0.01	12.78	7.39	7.38		4.72	387.00	97.31	4.46	29.68	1993
1966	16.33	0.95			6.91	9.36		6.53	463.58	119.65	6.65	41.13	
1967	14.60	0.92			6.95	8.58		3.76	411.16	112.68	6.25	29.54	
1968	12.98	0.91			6.43	7.46		3.85	432.45	114.91	6.38	25.06	
1969	12.63	0.85			6.22	7.26		2.48	387.33	120.16	6.13	18.51	
1970	17.19	0.90			9.04	9.06		4.86	558.82	153.60	7.95	29.96	2276
1971	18.73	1.16			10.64	9.25		5.50	632.69	191.90	9.83	38.27	
1972	16.32	1.15			9.36	8.11		2.86	552.49	162.97	9.64	24.41	
1973	16.04	1.13			9.11	8.06		1.61	557.81	158.63	9.87	27.02	
1974	16.16	1.22			9.23	8.15		1.95	613.42	181.78	10.79	24.73	
1975	19.88	1.53		13.43	12.51	8.90		2.66	716.25	300.19	13.23	40.90	3046
1976	22.26	1.81		19.63	14.12	9.96		3.98	791.75	301.95	15.31	48.75	
1977	26.06	3.16		22.39	16.58	12.64	8.46	5.49	985.34	306.81	18.38	64.03	
1978	30.22	3.68		26.40	19.79	14.11	10.40	8.46	1079.01	353.05	21.17	78.15	3731
1979	32.54	4.16		28.24	21.65	15.06	11.51	9.87	1026.15	380.75	22.77	83.70	
1980	36.20	4.51		30.70	23.81	16.91	12.07	10.74	1136.84	390.58	23.58	90.89	4063
1981	38.97	4.42	0.20	32.15	23.91	19.67	11.53	10.30	1140.47	383.81	25.21	89.15	
1982	44.07	5.23	0.33	35.40	25.66	23.97	11.70	13.00	1168.09	403.27	28.05	110.43	
1983	52.32	5.85	0.50	42.01	31.29	27.38	13.39	15.27	1285.10	427.02	31.62	146.59	
1984	57.32	9.46	0.44	46.77	37.19	30.04	16.23	17.16	1433.36	450.17	34.17	169.27	
1985	73.18	11.93	1.67	63.53	48.27	38.51	23.61	19.79	1600.22	499.00	38.11	201.05	5468
1986	81.04	14.23	2.44	68.39	53.39	44.32	27.24	19.90	1654.39	550.53	42.85	200.52	
1987	95.77	16.32	3.55	81.49	62.26	53.38	29.28	20.71	1578.40	575.12	48.45	218.12	6298
1988	121.85	21.63	5.61	103.55	78.05	71.04	39.65	27.33	1813.16	615.04	54.72	257.41	6320
1989	151.73	29.50	6.18	129.39	98.09	89.32	44.78	30.33	2020.10	643.81	62.99	263.04	6553

30. Xinjiang

30–10

Year	v8g1	v9a	v9a1	v9a2	v9a3	v9b	v9b1	v9b2	v9b3	v9c	v10a	v10a1	v10b1	v10b2	v10b3
1949										46					
1950		1.68		1.66		0.21		0.21		82	2.21	2.19	0.22		0.01
1951		0.84		0.78		1.01		1.01		121	2.93	2.90	0.27		0.06
1952		2.04		1.98		1.67		1.67		119	3.71	3.66	0.41		0.17
1953		1.82		1.75		2.00		1.99		168	4.39	4.32	1.11		0.41
1954		2.50		2.57		3.40		3.40		199	5.35	5.22	1.96		0.81
1955		2.54		2.50		4.25		4.25		245	6.32	6.14	2.52		1.28
1956		4.26		4.20		5.59		5.59		354	7.37	7.15	3.58		1.43
1957		4.59		4.55		6.41		6.41		482	8.94	8.56	4.87		1.71
1958		7.85	2.53	5.30		16.10	5.94	10.15		619	9.65	9.25	7.89		
1959		9.35	1.89	7.42		19.85	2.58	16.21		1063	11.62	11.05	11.33		
1960		9.96	3.60	6.27		29.70	9.43	18.48		1492	12.73	11.91	12.36		
1961		14.97	8.72	6.17		24.29	11.50	11.43		1476	11.26	10.68	10.54		
1962		12.46	7.36	5.02		24.90	12.58	11.14		1330	10.98	10.55	10.06		
1963		9.31	5.17	4.06		28.31	15.75	11.43		1238	10.51	10.08	7.24		2.44
1964		11.89	6.66	5.12		34.45	20.68	12.64		1327	11.11	10.54	7.57		2.77
1965		13.21	6.79	6.30		43.45	26.19	16.01		1468	12.06	11.30	8.46		2.90
1966		12.78	7.91	4.78		52.17	33.03	17.59		1565	13.13	12.14	12.78		
1967		12.05	7.22	4.71		38.67	22.32	14.92		1549	13.77	12.95	13.39		
1968		14.02	9.49	4.41		40.87	26.47	12.90		1445	12.98	12.30	12.63		
1969		13.62	9.75	3.72		36.91	23.04	12.33		1536	14.00	13.13	13.64		
1970		12.13	8.30	3.75		55.21	34.24	19.02		1653	14.58	13.23	14.24		
1971		14.03	9.76	4.17		62.39	38.74	21.33		1636	15.13	13.80	14.81		
1972		14.47	10.94	3.36		47.27	28.14	17.04		1722	15.48	14.34	15.15		
1973		15.44	11.71	3.55		45.62	27.16	16.01		1816	16.73	15.47	16.39		
1974		17.06	12.67	4.20		50.43	31.16	15.92		1913	17.17	15.80	16.83		
1975	869	20.29	13.63	6.36		74.39	48.98	18.60		2119	18.63	16.85	14.57		3.69
1976	926	20.51	12.56	7.63		72.66	46.72	19.67		2540	20.12	18.14	15.38		4.33
1977	999	21.82	12.20	9.21		83.76	52.94	24.50		2666	21.60	19.35	16.06		4.98
1978	1090	25.23	13.73	10.96		106.96	67.76	32.06		2802	24.73	21.88	23.54		0.52
1979	1116	28.27	16.46	11.11		120.41	74.24	38.32		3040	27.85	24.78	26.30		0.61
1980	1114	30.49	18.83	10.83		121.14	67.27	45.89		3079	32.86	29.36	29.94		1.25
1981	1105	34.10	19.39	13.89		115.77	65.00	42.71		3147	36.96	34.07	32.43		2.37
1982	1129	37.58	19.74	16.96		136.10	77.84	49.30		3326	39.61	36.41	33.84		3.10
1983	1132	43.79	22.71	20.41		149.82	85.91	54.23		3639	44.98	41.33	36.71		3.89
1984	1123	50.46	25.67	23.99		162.76	95.14	57.51		4066	51.20	46.14	32.12		12.40
1985	1359	63.16	33.16	29.13		174.75	102.03	61.26		4709	62.20	57.38	36.10		14.74
1986	1299	73.87	36.04	34.09		189.44	109.26	66.93		5294	68.84	63.90	39.02		15.43
1987	1322	83.67	37.14	39.44		203.64	117.44	72.40		6110	78.37	72.39	43.93		17.21
1988	1353	99.17	42.86	46.35		223.52	128.45	81.72		7694	96.94	88.70	54.22		22.20
1989	1393	108.15	44.52	53.82		263.49	101.30	96.90		9439	108.08	98.15	60.34		22.79

30. Xinjiang

30–11

Year	v10b4	v10b5	v10b6	v10d	v11a1	v11a2	v11a3	v11b	v11b1	v11b2	v11c	v11d	v12a	v12b	v12c
1949															
1950		1.54	0.44					0.1350	0.0637	0.0713					
1951		2.19	0.41					0.1933	0.1111	0.0822			105.5	110.5	129.5
1952		2.73	0.40	1.29				0.2320	0.1431	0.0889			96.9	97.7	95.1
1953		2.49	0.38					0.1883	0.1048	0.0835			97.0	96.5	120.1
1954	0.01	2.27	0.30					0.2173	0.1052	0.1121			102.1	104.3	110.9
1955	0.01	2.28	0.23					0.5058	0.1965	0.3093			98.5	98.3	96.9
1956	1.48	0.49	0.39					0.6439	0.3631	0.2808			93.9	92.1	95.7
1957	1.41	0.55	0.40	3.36				0.5266	0.3249	0.2017			98.7	101.4	102.7
1958	1.19	0.26	0.31					0.5190	0.3414	0.1776			98.6	98.8	101.2
1959			0.29					0.7189	0.4956	0.2233			100.5	100.4	101.9
1960			0.37					0.7318	0.4800	0.2518			101.0	102.5	104.8
1961			0.72					0.3806	0.2848	0.0958			124.6	119.0	113.4
1962		0.44	0.48	4.11				0.2694	0.1958	0.0736			98.2	98.4	100.3
1963		0.47	0.36					0.1696	0.1687	0.0009			94.8	95.9	98.8
1964		0.50	0.27					0.1749	0.1692	0.0057			96.1	96.1	99.0
1965		0.43	0.27	5.99				0.1361	0.1253	0.0108			96.8	96.0	98.2
1966			0.35					0.0665	0.0362	0.0303			97.3	97.1	103.4
1967			0.38					0.0114	0.0047	0.0067			98.0	99.2	100.4
1968			0.35					0.0070	0.0044	0.0026			99.9	100.0	98.6
1969			0.36					0.0229	0.0142	0.0087			99.1	99.4	99.2
1970			0.34	5.81				0.0165	0.0038	0.0127			99.7	99.7	100.3
1971			0.32					0.0170	0.0050	0.0120			100.0	99.9	100.9
1972			0.33					0.0324	0.0206	0.0118			100.0	100.3	102.1
1973			0.34					0.0704	0.0335	0.0369			100.0	99.9	100.3
1974			0.34					0.0817	0.0252	0.0565			100.0	100.5	100.3
1975		0.02	0.35	6.45				0.0907	0.0374	0.0533			99.9	100.2	101.0
1976		0.01	0.40	7.87				0.0906	0.0336	0.0570			99.7	99.7	100.5
1977		0.01	0.55	7.66				0.1407	0.0459	0.0948			99.9	99.9	100.8
1978		0.02	0.65	9.73				0.2346	0.0937	0.1409			101.4	101.3	103.1
1979		0.04	0.90	11.38				0.2436	0.0868	0.1568			103.5	102.2	113.8
1980	0.01	0.25	1.41	14.52				0.3160	0.1710	0.1450			104.2	104.8	108.9
1981	0.01	0.61	1.54	16.92				0.6256	0.4730	0.1526			101.6	102.4	107.2
1982	0.01	1.00	1.66	20.00				1.0626	0.9032	0.1594	0.0536	0.0536	100.2	100.1	106.5
1983	0.02	2.15	2.21	23.54				1.1744	0.9697	0.2047			101.5	102.2	107.6
1984	0.03	3.75	2.90	28.51				2.3713	1.5966	0.7747	0.0987	0.0662	103.1	102.4	102.0
1985	0.04	7.08	4.24	32.61				2.9197	1.8020	1.1177	0.4027	0.0552	108.1	109.5	107.9
1986	0.09	8.82	5.48	37.73				2.8412	2.0535	0.7877	0.1074	0.1643	106.7	106.8	107.7
1987	0.13	10.69	6.41	46.31				3.1535	2.2291	0.9244	0.0794	0.1569	107.1	108.5	115.6
1988	0.16	12.69	7.67	58.91				4.0775	2.9887	1.0888	0.0668	0.0879	114.6	117.0	119.6
1989	0.09	16.45	8.41	61.15				4.8638	3.6093	1.2545	0.0588	0.1000	116.7	114.5	108.2

30. Xinjiang

Year	v13a	v13b	v13c1	v13c2	v13c3	v13d	v14a	v14b	v14c	v15a	v15b	v15c	v15d	v15e	v15f
1949															
1950										1999					
1951										2119					
1952	7.25	33.6	0.1582	2.0578	33.37		905	1100	0.1543	2315					
1953										2332					
1954										2409					
1955										2535					
1956										2723					
1957			0.3909	7.2727	49.23	0.0525			0.2359	2930					
1958										3432					
1959										3863					
1960										4718					
1961										4714					
1962			0.6512	11.5364	74.58	0.0697			0.3156	4581					
1963										4533					
1964										4626					
1965		86.1	0.7740	15.6923	103.90	0.1282	18846	25400	0.5680	4747					
1966										4996					
1967										5065					
1968										4834					
1969										4750					
1970			0.0331	17.3829	113.14	0.1661			0.9019	4698					
1971										4740					
1972										4730					
1973										4735					
1974										4714					
1975			0.5209	48.0186	185.92	0.0723			1.0472	4720					
1976			0.6274	60.7143	189.97	0.1524			1.1686	4727					
1977			0.7706	75.2198	195.81	0.1926			1.3756	4743					
1978	8.47	96.1	1.0229	83.8560	202.88	0.1509	39179	51100	1.4238	4777					
1979			1.1447	84.7948	220.77	0.1653			1.3491	4800					
1980	12.74	94.6	1.4308	88.6740	205.55	0.0814	47236	57900	1.3124	4773					
1981			1.6546	87.1359	201.05	0.0779			1.1283	4760					
1982			1.6235	89.4831	198.60	0.4108			1.2332	4782					
1983			1.6493	93.2761	194.10	0.4823			1.3473	4742					
1984			1.9689	99.4078	196.30	0.3426			1.4108	4729					
1985	15.96	95.4	2.6500	105.4293	196.63	0.3511	55298	69000	1.6842	4624					7.67
1986			2.9928	113.4562	194.82	0.4797			2.0684	4575					7.20
1987	14.78	97.0	3.0145	117.0333	188.49	0.8001			2.4639	4591					7.20
1988	15.44	97.1	3.0403	112.8662	184.72	0.7681	58074	75000	2.4082	4614	2918	793	854	341.50	7.22
1989		97.2	3.1700	93.7900	184.20	0.6800	60112	76700	1.9371	4609					

Notes

1. National Output and Income (Y)

v1a: (E), p.923
v1a1: (E), p.923
v1a2: (E), p.923
v1a3: (E), p.923
v1a4: (E), p.923
v1a5: (E), p.923

v1b: (D), p.420
v1b1: (D), p.420
v1b2: (D), p.420
v1b3: (D), p.420
v1b4: (D), p.420
v1b5: (D), p.420

v1c: v1a – v1d

v1d: (E), p.920
v1d1: (E), p.920
v1d2: (E), p.920
v1d3: (E), p.920
v1d4: (E), p.920
v1d5: (E), p.920

v1e: (A); (D), p.423
v1e1: (A); (D), p.423
v1e2: (A); (D), p.423
v1e3: (A); (D), p.423
v1e4: (A); (D), p.423
v1e5: (A); (D), p.423

v1f: (E), p.919
v1f1: (E), p.919
v1f2: (E), p.919
v1f3: (E), p.919

v1g: (E), p.929

v1h: (A); (E), p.948

v1i: (E), p.947—excluding meat and other price subsidies

v1j: (E), p.947
v1j1: (E), p.947
v1j2: (E), p.947
v1j3: NA

v1k: (E), p.947

2. Investment (I)

v2a: (E), p.922
v2a1: (A); (D), p.428
v2a2: (A); (D), p.428

v2b: (A)

v2c: (A)
v2c1: (E), p.939
v2c2: (E), p.939

v2d:
v2d1: (E), p.936
v2d2: (E), p.936

v2e: (E), p.936

3. Consumption (C)

v3a: (E), p.922

v3b: (E), p.922
v3b1: (A); (D), p.424
v3b2: (A); (D), p.424

v3c: (E), p.922

v3d: (E), p.946
v3d1: (E), p.946
v3d2: (E), p.946

v3e: (A)
v3e1: (A)
v3e2: (A)
v3e3: (A)
v3e4: (A)

v3f: (A)

v3f1: (A)
v3f2: (A)
v3f3: (A)
v3f4: (A)

4. Public Finance and Banking (FB)

v4a:
v4a1: (E), p.944
v4a1a: (E), p.944
v4a1b: NA; v4a1b': (E), p.944—total tax revenues
v4a1c: NA
v4a1d: v4a1 – v4a1a – v4a1b'
v4a2: (E), p.944
v4a2a: (E), p.944
v4a2b: (E), p.944
v4a2c: (E), p.944
v4a2d: v4a2 – v4a2a – v4a2b – v4a2c

v4b: (A)
v4b1: (A)
v4b2: (A)
v4b3: NA

v4c:
v4c1: (E), p.936
v4c2: (E), p.936—at current price

5. Labor Force (L)

v5a: (E), p.918
v5a1: (E), p.918
v5a2: (B), p.336; (E), p.918—collective-owned units
v5a3: (E), p.918
v5a4: (E), p.918—rural labourers

v5b:
v5b1: (E), p.918
v5b2: (E), p.918
v5b3: (E), p.918

v5c: NA
v5c1: NA

v5d: NA

6. Population (PO)

v6a: (E), p.917—data from public security department
v6a1: (E), p.917—(ditto)
v6a2: (E), p.917—(ditto)

v6b: (E), p.917—(ditto)

v6c: (E), p.917—(ditto)

v6d:
v6d1: (E), p.917—(ditto)
v6d2: (E), p.917—(ditto)
v6d3: (E), p.917—(ditto)
v6d4: (E), p.917—(ditto)
v6d5: (A)—Ürümqi
v6d6: (A)—Shihezi

7. Agriculture (A)

v7a: (A); (E), p.930

v7b: (A); (E), p.930

v7c: (A); (E), p.930

v7d: (A); (E), p.930

v7e: (A)

v7f: (A)

v7g: (A)

v7h: (A); (E), p.925
v7h1: (A); (E), p.925
v7h2: (A); (E), p.925
v7h3: (A); (E), p.925
v7h4: (A); (E), p.925
v7h5: (A); (E), p.925

v7i: (A); (E), p.929

8. Industry (IN)

v8a: (E), p.931
  v8a1: (E), p.931
  v8a2: (E), p.931
  v8a3: (E), p.931—urban and rural self-employed and industries of other economic modes

v8b: (E), p.936

  v8c1: (E), p.923
  v8c2: (E), p.923

v8d: (E), p.936

v8f:
  v8f1: (E), p.935
  v8f2: (E), p.935
  v8f3: (E), p.935
  v8f4: (E), p.935
  v8f5: (E), p.935

v8g: (A)
  v8g1: (E), p.936

9. Transport (TR)

v9a: (E), p.937—excluding urban traffic volume
  v9a1: (E), p.937—including central and local railways; including light railway passenger traffic volume in 1961–74, 1977–79
  v9a2: including traffic volume of: transportation enterprises, transportation units of autonomons regions' key enterprises or institutions, transportation enterprises or institutions of production and construction corps; but excluding self-employed transportation
  v9a3: NA

v9b: (E), p.937
  v9b1: (E), p.937—including central and local railways
  v9b2: (E), p.937
  v9b3: NA

v9c: (E), p.937

10. Domestic Trade (DT)

v10a: (E), p.940
  v10a1: (E), p.940

v10b:
  v10b1: (E), p.940
  v10b2: NA; retail sales of supply and marketing cooperative are included in state-owned retail sales in 1958–62, 1966–74, 1978–83, and included in collective ownership retail sales for the rest of the years
  v10b3: (E), p.940
  v10b4: (E), p.940—joint state-private ownership and private-owned included in 1965 and before; joint ownership included sino-foreign joint ventures and joint ventures of various economic modes in 1983 and after
  v10b5: (A); (E), p.940
  v10b6: (E), p.940

v10d: (A); (E), p.943

11. Foreign Trade (FT)

v11a:
  v11a1: NA
  v11a2: NA
  v11a3: NA

v11b: (E), p.942—data from foreign trade department
  v11b1: (E), p.942—(ditto)
  v11b2: (A)

v11c: (E), p.943—1982's figure is the grand total of 1981–82's

v11d: (E), p.943—(ditto)

12. Prices (PR)

v12a: (E), p.945

v12b: (E), p.945

v12c: (E), p.945

13. Education (ED)

v13a: (A)

v13b: (A); (E), p.948

v13c:
- v13c1: (A); (E), p.948—general institutions of higher learning
- v13c2: (A); (E), p.948—secondary schools, ordinary middle schools
- v13c3: (A); (E), p.948

v13d: (A)—general institutions of higher learning

14. Social Factors (SF)

v14a: (E), p.948

v14b: (E), p.948

v14c: (A)

15. Natural Environment (NE)

v15a: (A); (E), p.930

v15b: (A)

v15c: (A)

v15d: (A)

v15e: (A)

v15f: (A)

Sources of Data

(A) Data supplied by the DSNEB, SSB, the PRC.
(B) Statistical Bureau of Xinjiang Uygur Autonomous Region, and Propaganda Department, Xinjiang Uygur Autonomous Region Party Committee of Chinese Communist Party, eds. *Striving and Advancing Forty Years, Xinjiang's Volume*, Beijing: CSPH,1989.
(D) Same as (D) in Beijing's sources of data.
(E) Same as (E) in Beijing's sources of data.

PART TWO

Exposition of the Key Variables

31

National Output and Income

Total Product of Society (v1a)

Total product of society is an important indicator in MPS (System of Material Product Balances)—the socialist national accounting system.

Total product of society of a country (or region) is the sum total of the gross output value of five material production sectors: namely, agriculture, industry, construction, transport, post and telecommunications, and domestic trade (including catering as well as supply and marketing of materials). All output produced in the region in question should be included in the total product.

In comparison with SNA (System of National Accounts), the national accounting system of market economies, MPS omits non-material production sectors, such as the railway, highway, waterway and air passenger traffic, real estate, public utilities, residents' services, sports, social welfare, education, culture, arts, broadcasting and television undertakings, scientific research activities, comprehensive technology services, banking and finance, insurance, and administration institutions, etc.

Gross output value of agriculture (v1a1)

Gross output value of agriculture is the total output value of farming, forestry, animal husbandry, sideline production and fishery. The scope of statistics of the five sectors are described as below:

(1) Farming

Farming covers the cultivation of grain, cotton, oil-bearing crops, sugar crops, bast-fibre plants, tobacco, vegetables, medicinal herbs, melons, and other crops, and the cultivation and management of tea plantations, mulberry fields and orchards.

(2) Forestry

Forestry comprises the planting of various kinds of trees (tea plantations, mulberry fields and orchards not included), collection of forestry products, and cutting and felling of bamboo and timber at *cun* (village) level and below (i.e.

the old accounting units of production teams, production brigades, and communes).

(3) Animal husbandry

Animal husbandry comprises the raising and grazing of all animals (except fish breeding). It consists of the output value arising from the following four parts: breeding, growing and weight-gaining of livestock, rearing of poultry, products of alive livestock and poultry as well as products of raising other animals.

(4) Sideline production

Sideline production covers the collection of wild plants, hunting of wild animals and fowls as well as concurrent running of industries by households.

It should be noted that before 1957 sideline production included peasants' handicrafts for self-consumption. After 1958, it excluded the item, but incorporated the output value of industries run at village level and below. The latter has again been excluded from sideline production since 1984.

(5) Fishery

Fishery comprises the catching and breeding of fish and other aquatic animals and the cultivation and collection of seaweeds and other aquatic plants.

In general, the "Product Method" (產品法 , *ChanPinFa*) is adopted for the estimation, i.e., the output value is calculated by multiplying the quantity of the product by its unit price. For a few products having longer production cycle, or no output at the current year, or quantities difficult to measure, their output value is estimated by indirect approach.

More specifically, the estimation of total output value of farming, forestry, animal husbandry and fishery is based on a comprehensive statistical reporting system. The figures for sideline production were either obtained from the purchasing departments or estimated from the surveys carried out in key production areas.

Before 1957 gross output value of agriculture included barnyard manure and peasants' handicrafts for self-consumption (e.g. clothes, shoes, socks and initial grain processing made or undertaken by the peasants).

From 1958, the output value of cutting and felling of bamboo and timber at village level and below was included in forestry; the output value of barnyard manure was excluded from animal husbandry; the output value of self-consumed handicrafts of peasants was excluded from sideline production. On the other hand, included in sideline production was the output value of industries run at village level and below, as was added to fishery the output value of fish caught by motor fishing boats.

Since 1980, the value of handicraft products made for sale by individuals in a household is added to sideline production.

From 1984, industries run by village level and below have been included in the industrial sector. Thus, the corresponding adjustment was made for the time series data of gross output value of agriculture in this Volume according to the last specification.

Gross output value of industry (v1a2)

Gross output value of industry is the total output value of industrial enterprises, which is estimated by the "Factory Method" (工廠法 . *GongChangFa*). This implies that the calculation is based on the final output of each industrial enterprise, thus avoids double counting the value of finished products of the workshops within the enterprise. Value of outputs produced in various workshops within the same enterprise cannot be added together, though double counting does occur among different enterprises, businesses and regions. The statistics cover (i) value of finished products of state-owned enterprises, urban and rural collectives, joint ventures and foreign-owned industrial enterprises; (ii) value of foreign-contracted industrial operation; (iii) the value difference between start and end of period of self-produced semi-finished products and those products being manufactured by enterprises with a longer production cycle; and (iv) the output value of industrial products from self-employed producers.

Gross output value of industry of 1949-58 embraced the output value of industrial enterprises at the *xian* (county) level or above. Whereas from 1959 to 1983, it incorporated the output value of industry at the *xiang* (countrytown) level.

Originally, simple agricultural product processing, e.g. cotton ginning, rice husking and animal slaughtering, was done by the peasants themselves. Thus, this was counted into agricultural sideline production, and only the processing value was calculated. Since the People's Communes initiated the large-scale development of industries, all or most of those simple processings previously done by the peasants was then organized and operated centrally by processing industries in the communes. Therefore, the figure was put under the output value of industrial enterprises. However, no change was made on the calculation of output value of agricultural processing for state-owned industries, of which total value was estimated.

For processing industries run by the communes which used agricultural products as raw material (e.g. oil extraction, sugar refinery, wine production), as well as mining, coking, iron-smelting, manufacturing of equipment, chemical fertilizers, paper and textiles and so on, total value is used for calculation of their outputs.

From 1984 onwards, gross output value of industry includes industrial output at the village level (the production brigade) or below (the production team). Thus adjustment has been made for the time series data of gross output value of industry in this Volume according to the last specification.

The data for the compilation of gross output value of industry were collected through a comprehensive statistical reporting system. And the data are recorded in annual statistical reports submitted by local statistical bureaux.

Gross output value of construction (v1a3)

Gross output value of construction refers to the total output value of construction and installation completed by construction and installation enterprises or units within a certain period of time. It includes output value of construction, sales of affiliated component factories to other enterprises, and surveying and design services. The output value of construction includes value of construction projects, equipment installation, repairs for buildings and structures, output created by non-standard equipment as well as the work load of construction and installation by villages.

Two methods of estimation are used. One estimates the final output of construction activities carried out by the construction enterprises and the individual-run construction units; the other estimates from the angle of owners of construction products, which means the statistics of fixed assets investment can be directly used for calculation. Comprehensive investigation, whose estimate is based on construction projects, was used for (i) construction and installation projects of state-owned basic construction, renovation and other fixed assets investment; (ii) construction and installation projects of fixed assets investment carried out by cities' and towns' collectives and other ownerships; (iii) investment in private housing at industrial and mining districts in cities and towns; and (iv) rural investment in private housing. Investment in fixed assets by rural collectives and by other ownership, on the other hand, is estimated from sampling surveys. Surveying and design, as well as major repairs of houses and structures, are estimated from relevant information.

Gross output value of transport, post and telecommunications (v1a4)

Gross output value of transport, post and telecommunications includes revenues from freight traffic, pipeline transport, loading and unloading services, agency services (not including revenue from passenger traffic, related supplementary production and other business) and also revenues of post and telecommunications services. The last item includes revenues from postal services, confidential communication, telephone services and agency services.

The total product of state-owned transport enterprises is derived from the annual statistical reports and final accounting information of the important transport sectors pertaining to railways, waterways, seaport and road transport, pipeline transport, etc. Financial information of collective-owned, private or joint-venture transport units was used to calculate their total output. If the information was not available, data of sales revenue obtained from tax departments, and industrial and commercial administration departments concerned were used for the estimation.

The gross output value of transport, post and telecommunications is calculated according to postal and communication departments' annual statistical reports and final accounting data.

Gross output value of domestic trade (v1a5)

Gross output value of domestic trade refers to the value-added of various products during the course of circulation. It implies the extra charges or the trade margin for the commercial sector, i.e. the difference between the sales revenue and the incoming price of previous stage of flow of the commodity. In order to avoid double counting, consignment and loading and unloading charges should be deducted.

Gross output value of domestic trade can be estimated from the financial data of the commercial sector, or by multiplying the retail sales volume by gross profit rate (i.e. the rate of the difference between outgoing and incoming prices of the commodity in question), which can be found in the annual reports of the commercial sector.

Material Consumption (v1c)

Material consumption refers to the means of production, in value terms, consumed by material production sectors in the production process. The material consumption of each sector comprises mainly three parts: (i) raw and finished materials, fuels, power, seed and feed actually consumed in the production process; (ii) payments to the productive services incurred in the production process, such as hired transportation, post and telecommunications, and the processing of semi-finished products and repairs contracted to other enterprises; and (iii) depreciation allowance of productive fixed assets and major repair funds.

National Income (v1d)

National income refers to the newly created value in a given period by the five major material production sectors, i.e. industry, agriculture, construction, transport, post and telecommunications and domestic trade (catering and supply and marketing of raw materials included). Hence, it is also the sum of net output value of all material production sectors.

There are two approaches to calculate the net output value. The first one is "production approach", whereby material consumption is subtracted from total output value. The second one is "distribution approach", in which components of net output value, such as wages, staff and workers welfare funds, taxes, profits, interests and others are added up together.

Noted that wage refers to payment to the productive personnel. It is derived from the total wage bill in the statistical reports on wages by subtracting: (i) wage paid to welfare service workers from staff and workers' welfare funds; (ii) wage paid from the sources outside the enterprise's operational expenses; (iii) various bonuses paid from enterprise funds and retained profit; and (iv) wage paid from the special-purpose fund. If the wages of union staff are paid by labor unions, they should be subtracted also.

For readers' reference, first of all, the data for ***net output value of agriculture (v1d1)*** were acquired from their relevant section in *Annual Report on Rural Economic Statistics* by Department of Agriculture, SSB. In fact, the data are first calculated and compiled by the statistical section of *xian* governments and are then submitted to the Statistical Bureau of the province, autonomous region or municipality for verification and confirmation, and further submitted to SSB for final confirmation and compilation.

Secondly, the data for ***net output value of industry (v1d2)*** were calculated according to the information in connection with the independent accounting industrial enterprise; the non- independent accounting industrial enterprise; *cun*-(production team-) owned and rural cooperative industrial enterprises; and the cities' and towns' self-employed industrial enterprises. Data for the first category of enterprises were supplied by the Department of Industry, SSB, after conducting a comprehensive survey. Data for the second category of enterprises were estimated by referring to the information obtained from the first category. For data of the third category of enterprises, the "distribution approach" was used, that is, reckoning the figures supplied from the administration department of rural enterprises. And the data for the last category of enterprises were estimated from the statistics supplied by the industrial and commercial administration units and tax departments in charge.

Thirdly, ***net output value of construction (v1d3)*** includes value of net output produced by the state-owned, collective-owned, and self-employed construction and installation enterprises. Data for the state-owned and collective-owned were obtained from various issues of *Annual Report on Construction Statistics*. And those for the self-employed were estimated according to the survey data of some typical cases.

Fourthly, ***net output value of transport, post and telecommunications (v1d4)*** was reckoned according to the information in connection with the railways, highways, waterways, post and telecommunications, civil aviation, commercial storage, and pipeline transport, villages' and towns' and self-employed transport. First, estimates for the railways, highways, waterways, post and telecommunications, civil aviation, commercial storage, pipeline transport (highway and waterway transport excludes the self-employed and villages' and towns') are based on the accounting and statistical reports of each sector in question, and various issues of *Annual Report on Labor Wage Statistics* by Department of Society, SSB. The "distribution approach" was used for the estimation. Second, estimation of villages' and towns' and self-employed transport was obtained by referring to the relevant data supplied by the villages' and towns' enterprise bureaux in charge.

Last but not least, ***net output value of domestic trade (v1d5)*** was calculated separately according to three different kinds of ownership: the state-owned, the collective-owned, and the self-employed.

(1) The state-owned comprises six subsectors: state commerce (departments under Ministry of Commerce), grain, foreign trade, medicine, materials, and state-owned catering trade. Data were obtained from the final accounts of each subsector in question.

(2) The collective-owned comprises three subsectors: supply and marketing cooperatives, cooperative commerce, and collective catering trade. Data for supply and marketing cooperatives were obtained from their final accounts. Data for cooperative commerce were obtained through multiplying the gross output by the net output ratio of supply and marketing cooperatives. Whereas data for collective catering trade were reckoned from the statistics of catering trade of supply and marketing cooperatives.

(3) The self-employed comprises three subsectors: country fair trade, self-employed catering trade, and self-employed commerce. Net output value of country fair trade is simply equal to its gross output value, since no material depletion takes place. Net output value of self-employed catering trade was estimated from typical surveys. Finally, net output value of self-employed commerce was reckoned by the relevant data from the tax bureaux in charge.

Gross Domestic Product (v1f)

Gross domestic product (GDP) refers to the total value of goods and services produced for final usage by local and foreign residents in a certain period of time within a country or region. GDP is an important indicator in SNA.

GDP includes three sectors.

(1) Primary sector (v1f1): Agriculture (including farming, forestry, animal husbandry, sideline production and fishery; excluding industry at or below the village level, which is included in industry).

(2) Secondary sector (v1f2): Industry (including extraction, manufacturing, water supply, electricity, steam, hot-water and gas, etc.) and construction (including all construction and installation enterprises, private construction units and geological exploration services and prospecting design for the construction and installation industry).

(3) Tertiary sector (v1f3): All except primary and secondary production.

Tertiary production may be further divided into two major sectors: (i) circulation sector and (ii) service sector. Specifically, it can also be divided into four levels.

1. Circulation sector: it includes communications and transportation, post and telecommunications, commerce, catering, material supply and marketing as well as storage.

2. Service sector meeting the needs of production and daily life: it includes banking and finance, insurance, comprehensive technical services, services to farming, forestry, animal husbandry and fishery, water conservancy, irrigation works, consultancy services, highway and inland waterway maintenance, geological surveying, residents' services, public utilities and real estate, etc.

3. Service sector for the propagation of scientific knowledge and the improvement of the quality of life: it includes education, cultural activities, television and broadcasting, scientific research, public health, sports and social welfare services.

4. Service sector for the provision of public services: it includes state and party institutions, social organizations, army and police.

There are three methods to calculate GDP. The output approach subtracts intermediate inputs from total output to arrive at value-added. The income approach first calculates the various components of the value-added of each sector, and then add them up together. The expenditure approach adds up the final expenditures to arrive at GDP.

The value-added of non-material production sector should include service activities associated with the material production sector, e.g. subsidiary services provided by industrial and construction enterprises, cultural activities, education and public health.

There are two types of enterprises in the non-material production sector: Profit-making enterprises and non-profit making administrative institutions. The value-added of non profit-making administrative institutions do not contain profit and tax.

Value-added of the non-material production sector was derived from its revenue and expenditure sources and the statistical data of the secondary sector. The amount of income and taxes paid by private businesses can be estimated from data supplied by departments such as the related industrial and commercial administration units, banks and tax bureaux.

For the subsidiary services, cultural and educational and public health units which have independent accounting, their value-added can be calculated by using existing statistical data. For non-independent accounting units, the value was estimated from related data.

National Income Available (v1g)

In this concept, national income means something to be distributed and redistributed within the full scope of society, which forms the final income of the material production, the non- material production, and the residents sectors. Generally speaking, the final income is to be used in two major dimensions. One part serves as the means for residents' living and social non-productive purposes, which form the total consumption. Another part serves as the means for social reproduction, increase in fixed assets in non-productive sector, and inventory for future use, which together form the total accumulation. The sum of total accumulation (v2a) and total consumption (v3a) is thus defined as national income available, which is formulated as:

National Income Available

= national income within domestic production sphere + net imports (total imports – total exports)

= total consumption + total accumulation

Per Capita Peasant Household Net Income (v1h)

Per capita peasant household net income is the total disposable income of a rural household after deducting production and non-production expenditures, tax payments and payments to collectives, divided by the number of resident members in the household.

Peasant household net income includes, on the one hand, incomes from productive and non-productive operations, and on the other, the non-operational incomes such as foreign remittances, financial subsidies from the state, and other kinds of subsidies. It includes monetary income as well as physical products which are self-produced for self-consumption. But it does not include loans from banks, credit cooperatives or friends.

Total Wage Bill of Staff and Workers (v1i)

Total wage bill of staff and workers refers to the direct payment for labor reward to the staff and workers of all units in a certain period of time. Total wage bill includes all payments both in cash and in kind to staff and workers, regardless of whether the payments are counted as a cost component or not, and regardless of whether the item is imposed bonus taxes under government stipulations. Specifically it encompasses time wage, basic wage, wage paid for a duty performed, piece-rate wage, bonuses, subsidies, over-time pay, etc.

Average Wage of Staff and Workers (v1j)

It is the average labor reward paid to each staff and worker by the state within a certain period of time. The figure was obtained by dividing the total wage bill of staff and workers by the annual average of the total number of staff and workers.

From 1990, heating subsidies in winter which used to be part of the wage were included into welfare payment.

Labor Insurance and Welfare Funds of Staff and Workers (v1k)

Labor insurance and welfare funds of staff and workers refer to payments other than wages paid by the enterprises and institutions to all employees (on-the-job as well as off-the-job) and payments to collectives for labor insurance and welfare.

Labor insurance and welfare funds for on-the-job employees include expenses for medical service and hygiene, funeral expenses and pensions for families of the deceased, expenses for promotion of cultural and sports activities, subsidies for the collective welfare services, subsidies for the collective welfare facilities, family planning subsidies, allowance for transport fees, subsidies for hairdressing and hygiene and others (travelling fee for family reunion, etc).

Labor insurance and welfare funds for off-the-job staff and workers include expenses on medical service and hygiene, funeral expenses and pensions for families of the deceased, expenses for temporary leave, retirement pensions, allowances for living expenses, living allowances for discharged employees, nursing allowances, allowances for transport fees and others.

32

Investment

Total Accumulation (v2a)

Total accumulation equals national income available (v1g) minus total consumption (v3a). It represents the value of increase in fixed assets and circulating assets during a given period.

Total accumulation may be divided, in accordance with its role in reproduction, into accumulation of fixed assets and that of circulating assets.

Fixed assets accumulation (v2a1)

Accumulation of fixed assets refers to the means of labor and other material goods which are reusable for longer periods and will not be transformed into different physical states when used in the course of production, e.g. buildings, construction, machinery, transport means, draught animals and so on.

Subtracting the depreciation of fixed assets and major repairs funds from the value of increase in fixed assets gives the value of accumulation of fixed assets of the given year.

Noted that means of labor refers to all material goods and material conditions through or under which workers transfer their activities to subjects of labor. The former includes production tools, pipes, bottles, and other implements. The latter includes factory construction, canals, roads and so on. Subjects of labor refer to everything to which labor is applied in the production course of material goods.

Circulating assets accumulation (v2a2)

Circulating assets refer to raw materials, fuels, components for repairs, packaging equipment, cheap and easily exhaustible goods, products in the process of manufacturing, self-produced semi-finished products, future apportioned payments, reserves of semi-finished and finished products to be sold. Inventory held by commercial departments is also regarded as a circulating asset. Accumulation of circulating assets is the difference between the value of circulating assets at the beginning and end of the period in question.

Total Investment in Fixed Assets (v2b)

It refers to the total value of construction and purchase of fixed assets. It consists of investments by state-owned units, urban and rural collective units and individuals. Investment by urban and rural residents includes private housing investment in cities, towns and industrial and mining areas, together with private housing investment and purchase of productive fixed assets (with a life span of more than two years and with unit value of over Rmb 30) in rural areas.

From 1949 to 1979, total investment in fixed assets included only basic construction by state-owned and collective (above the county level) units. From 1980 onwards, it began to include renovation investment. Since 1981, it has included fixed assets investment of collective units in cities and towns. After 1983, fixed assets investment by rural collective units (rural housing investment only) was introduced. And since 1984, private fixed assets investment has also been included.

Before 1980, only basic construction was reported in state-owned fixed assets investment. In 1981, a category called "other facilities investment" was added. After 1983, state-owned fixed assets investment included three items: basic construction, renovation investment and other facilities investment.

It should be noted that the time-series data reported in this Volume have been adjusted according to the last specification so that they are comparable. Apart from the general sources mentioned in the Introduction, part of the data were obtained from *China's Fixed Assets Investment Statistics (1950–1985)* by Department of Fixed Assets Investment Statistics, SSB, 1987.

Total Investment in Fixed Assets by State-owned Units (v2c)

It refers to the total value of construction and purchase of fixed assets by state-owned units. It consists of three parts: Investment in basic construction, renovation investment and investment in other fixed assets. Investment projects exceeding Rmb 50,000 are certainly included in total investment. However, for investment projects with value falling between Rmb 20,000–30,000, some adaptable methods are used to investigate.

Total industry investment in fixed assets by state-owned units (v2c1)

It refers to the means of labor used by industrial enterprises to affect or transform the subjects of labor in the production process. It includes all kinds of major means of labor together with various fixed assets as the facilities of welfare benefits for the staff and workers.

The total means of labor used by enterprises can be divided into fixed assets and cheap and easily exhaustible goods. To be included as fixed assets, means of labor have to fulfil two conditions:

(1) The life span is over one year; and

(2) The asset value is above a certain stipulated level; they are Rmb 800, Rmb 500 and Rmb 200 for large, medium-sized and small enterprises respectively. Asset value below Rmb 200 is excluded.

Fixed Assets of State-owned Independent Accounting Industrial Enterprises (v2d)

Original value of fixed assets of state-owned independent accounting industrial enterprises (v2d1)

It refers to the original value of all fixed assets owned by the industrial enterprise. It is derived from the actual payments for construction and purchase of fixed assets as well as for supplementary investments due to expansion and renovation.

Original value of fixed assets includes value of the fixed assets left over from the Republican era and addition to fixed assets through the realization of basic construction and renovation investment since then. Thus the original value of fixed assets at year end implies the lump sum of total fixed assets reckoning in original value at the year end.

It is noted that an independent accounting industrial enterprise is meant to fulfil the following three conditions: (i) an enterprise has an independent organizational form of administration; (ii) an enterprise has independent economic targets, assumes sole responsibility for its profits or losses, and draws up independently its balance sheet of funds (or statement of assets and liabilities); and (iii) an enterprise is entitled to sign a contract with other units and to open an independent account at a bank.

Net value of fixed assets of state-owned independent accounting industrial enterprises (v2d2)

It is equal to the original value of fixed assets minus accumulated depreciation.

Average Yearly Balance of the Quota Circulating Fund of State-owned Independent Accounting Industrial Enterprises (v2e)

It is equal to the sum of the balances of the quota circulating fund in the hands of the enterprises at the beginning and end of each month of the year divided by 24.

The quota circulating fund includes reserve fund, production fund and finished-product fund. Because quota management is practised in these three types of funds in industrial enterprises, they are called the quota circulating fund.

33

Consumption

Total Consumption (v3a)

Total consumption refers to the sum of material products consumed inside and outside the country (region) by residents and non-productive institutions within a certain period of time. It is a part of the national income available (v1g). All those monetary expenditures not belonging to material products consumption are not included in consumption as part of national income.

Generally speaking, consumption refers to the fact that goods are transferred to consumers, but not necessarily actually consumed. With the exception of depreciation that is calculated for residential housing, buildings, and equipment purchased by non-production institutions as consumption of fixed assets (i.e. depreciation in fixed assets), all consumer goods, once sold to consumers, are counted as consumption of the current year. Total consumption includes two major categories: personal consumption by residents and public collective consumption.

Residents' Consumption (v3b)

Residents' Consumption refers to the total value of goods consumed by all residents inside and outside their own country (region) within a certain period. Consumption by residents includes food, clothing, household furniture and utensils, daily sundries, goods related to education and culture, durable consumer goods, fuels, water, electricity, housing depreciation, and consumption of material products involved in expenditures on various cultural services.

According to China's present statistical system, consumption by residents is divided into four components: (i) **residents' self-sufficient consumption**: it refers to that part of agricultural sideline products that are produced and consumed by the residents themselves, which is largely made up of goods produced by peasants for self-consumption; (ii) **residents' commodity consumption**: it refers to the consumption of commodities purchased for cash in the market; (iii) **residents' consumption of cultural services**: it is that part of consumption of material products that involves expenditures on cultural services; (iv) **residents'**

consumption of personal housing, water and electricity: at present personal housing consumption is generally superseded by the rent paid.

Residents' consumption is also divided into ***rural residents' consumption (v3b1)*** and ***non-rural residents' consumption (v3b2)***. The distinction between rural and non-rural is drawn in accordance with the standard set by the public security department. People with their domiciles registered as farming ones are classified as rural residents, while those with domiciles registered as non-farming ones are classified as non-rural residents. Soldiers, laborers in cities and towns, and staff and workers at state farms all belong to the category of non-rural residents. On the other hand, all residents in rural areas working at non-farming occupations are treated as rural residents.

Public Consumption (v3c)

Public consumption includes all material consumption by such non-productive organizations as government administrative institutions and institutions related to national defence and public order, education, health services, sports, social welfare, scientific research, television and broadcasting, etc. Consumption of these institutions includes fuels, water, electricity, stationery, material depletion being charged to the administration fees, and depreciation associated with fixed assets such as institutions' housing and equipment, etc.

Public consumption can be divided into two types according to its nature and function. The first type is consumption by institutions related to government administration, national defence and public order, scientific research, banking, finance and insurance, consultancy services for production, and by the affiliated administrative units within production departments. In general, this type of consumption is pure public consumption and has no direct relationship with personal daily life. The second type is consumption by institutions related to culture, education, public health, sports, television and broadcasting, and public welfare. Most of these services are provided freely by society to residents, which are part of free collective consumption.

Consumption Level of Residents (v3d)

Consumption level of residents is obtained by dividing total private consumption by average population. Rural residents' consumption value and non-rural residents' consumption value are divided by average rural residents and non-rural residents respectively to get consumption levels of each category.

Per Capita Living Expenses of Cities' and Towns' Residents (v3e)

It refers to the per annum per capita total expenditures on daily life of the surveyed households in cities and towns. It includes commodity expenditures such as food, clothing, housing, and fuels, etc, and non-commodity expenditures on cultural life, services, etc. It does not include penalties, lost money, and all tax payment (e.g. personal income tax, license tax, house property tax, etc). All payments involved during the course of production operation by self-employed laborers are also not included.

The original figures for this item were compiled by the local governments via the data obtained from sampling surveys conducted in the cities and towns in question.

Per Capita Living Expenses of Rural Residents (v3f)

It refers to the per annum per capita total expenditures on daily life of rural households, which consists of two major components: living expenses on consumer goods such as food, clothing, housing, and fuels, etc, and expenditures on cultural life and services.

The data are also acquired by sampling surveys conducted in the rural areas concerned.

34

Public Finance and Banking

Public Revenues and Expenditures of Local Governments (v4a)

Public revenues of local governments (v4a1)

Public revenues of local governments include:

(1) **Revenues from enterprises**, which include the profit of subordinate state-owned enterprises and the income of subordinate institutions that are surrendered to the government.

(2) **Various taxes** including industrial and commercial tax (or product tax, value-added tax), resources tax, enterprises income tax, salt tax, customs duties, farming and animal husbandry taxes, tax on animal slaughtering, tax on livestock trading, tax on country fair trade and revenues from penalties and payment of overdue taxes.

Public expenditures of local governments (v4a2)

Public expenditures include:

(1) **Appropriation for basic construction**: it refers to budgetary appropriations for basic construction, but self-raised extra-budgetary funds for basic construction are excluded.

(2) **Additional appropriation for enterprises' circulating funds**: it refers to the additional budgetary appropriations for circulating funds to state-owned enterprises under various departments and the additional appropriations obtained from banks' credit funds.

(3) **Operating expense for cultural, educational, scientific and public health activities**: it includes the expenses in the field of science, culture, education, public health, free medical care, sports, communications and broadcasting, seismological and oceanographical studies, preservation of historical relics, family planning and so on.

(4) **Expenditures on management fees of local administrative institutions.**

Balance of Savings Deposits by Urban and Rural Residents (v4b)

Savings deposits consist of two parts: the savings deposits of urban residents and those of rural residents. They do not include cash in hand of the residents and group savings deposits of industrial and mining enterprises, armed forces, institutions and consortiums.

The year-end balance of savings deposits of urban residents refers to total sum of urban residents' savings deposits at the Industrial and Commercial Bank, township residents' savings deposits at the Agricultural Bank, and overseas Chinese savings deposits at the Bank of China. Savings deposits of rural residents refer to cooperative members' savings deposits at the rural credit cooperatives. The balance (i.e. the balance between deposits and withdrawals) is calculated at a given point of time , e.g., balance at month end, quarter end, or year end.

Profits and Taxes of State-owned Independent Accounting Industrial Enterprises (v4c)

Total profits and taxes of state-owned independent accounting industrial enterprises (v4c1)

It refers to the total sum of profits and taxes of the state-owned independent accounting industrial enterprises, which is equal to total sales revenue of the product minus production cost. Specifically, it is the sum of (i) product sales tax, (ii) education surcharge, (iii) resources tax and (iv) profit.

(1) **Product sales tax** refers to the tax that the enterprises should pay for the sold products. It includes product tax, value-added tax, and township safeguard and construction tax, etc.

(2) **Education surcharge** refers to the education surcharge that the enterprises should pay from the products sold.

(3) **Resources tax** refers to the tax imposed on resources occupied by the enterprises which they should pay from the products sold.

(4) **Profit** refers to total profit of the enterprises (loss is shown by a negative sign). It includes the stipulated surcharges on both fixed and circulating funds which are paid from the sales revenue by those enterprises adopting an interest-bearing scheme for occupied funds.

Profit and tax—invested funds ratio of state-owned independent accounting industrial enterprises (v4c2)

It refers to the percentage of actualized profits and taxes reported by state-owned independent accounting industrial enterprises in total funds invested (sum of net value of fixed assets and average balance of quota circulating funds).

The mathematical formula is:

$$\text{Profit and Tax — Invested Funds Ratio (\%)} = \frac{\text{Profits and Taxes}}{\text{Net Value of Fixed Assets} + \text{Average Balance of Quota Circulating Funds}}$$

35

Labor Force

Total Employed Labor Force of Society (v5a)

It refers to the total labor force undertaking certain work in the society and receiving payment or earning operational income at a given point in time at the year-end. It includes all staff and workers of the state-owned units, various joint-ownership units and collective units in cities and towns; it also includes individual laborers in cities and towns as well as collective and individual laborers in rural areas. The following three situations are also counted into labor force:

(1) Village labor undertaking household sideline production, with revenue at least equal to the lowest income level earned by a local laborer, or participating in social labor for more than three months.

(2) Young people in cities and towns who have got temporary work, with "three recruitment rights" (*SanZhaoQuan*, namely joining employment, joining the army and entering school) reserved, and whose income equals the wage level of local grade-one workers.

(3) People leaving office or retired people who have been formally reappointed to a position, and teachers in schools run by the local people, etc.

- Labor Force
  - Staff and Workers
    - state–owned units
    - collective–owned units in cities and towns
    - other ownership units
  - Self–employed laborers in cities and towns
  - Laborers in rural areas

Staff and workers of other ownership units refer to staff and workers working for and earning wages from enterprises or institutions of various joint-ownership units (including state and collective joint-ownership, state and individual joint-ownership, collective and individual joint-ownership, sino-foreign joint ventures), of units run by overseas Chinese or by Hong Kong or Macau businessmen, and of units funded by foreign capital. Figures for the state-collective joint-ownership include joint-ownership with township (*xiang*) or village (*cun*) collective units. Therefore, in calculating the number of staff and workers, the township (village) labor force involved should be included. The number of staff and workers in sino-foreign joint ventures, in enterprises run by overseas Chinese, Hong Kong or Macau businessmen, and in foreign-funded units, does not include foreign employees and employees from Hong Kong or Macau.

Staff and workers of state-owned units (v5a1)

Staff and workers of state-owned units refer to all kinds of personnel working for and receiving pay from all levels of party and government organizations, people's organizations, and their state-owned enterprises and institutions.

Specifically they include:

(1) Permanent staff and workers: they refer to the personnel formally assigned, arranged for and recruited with approval as permanent wage-earners by labor departments or organizational departments of the state. Staff who are out on duty, within or beyond the authorized quota of workers in an organization, working in foreign countries, working on probation, or seconded to other units yet still paid by the original work units, are also included.

(2) Contractual staff and workers: they refer to the wage-earners employed under contract and within the state's planned target of labor wage by the enterprises, institutions and government organizations. Included are the long-term laborers who have contracted for over five years, short-term laborers who have contracted for one to five years and workers who have to rotate at regular intervals. Seasonal workers and temporary workers who have contracted for less than one year are excluded.

(3) Temporary staff and workers: they refer to those workers who are temporarily employed by labor departments at all levels, and can be dismissed upon expiration according to the state's labor plan. These include those engaged in seasonal and temporary production and services.

(4) Workers outside state's plan: they refer to the personnel engaged in production or work and paid under the direct arrangement by the state-owned units through various channels outside the national labor plan. They are included in labor statistics regardless of sources and forms of payment of their wages, whether enjoying social welfare and labor insurance or not and whether having commodity grain supplies or not.

Note that staff and workers of state-owned units included staff and workers of other ownership units before 1983.

Staff and workers of collective-owned units in cities and towns (v5a2)

It refers to all kinds of personnel working for and receiving wage payment from the urban collective enterprises, institutions and their administrative departments. Included are staff and workers working on permanent, temporary, seasonal and rotating basis.

Self-employed laborers in cities and towns (v5a3)

It refers to laborers in cities and towns who engage in production work individually, own the means of production and the products (or income), and register and receive "individual business operation licenses" from the industrial/commercial administrative management department.

Laborers in rural area (v5a4)

It refers to full-time and half-time labor force in rural population who frequently engage in social labor and get payment from the work. Included are the personnel engaged in any kinds of production in rural enterprises and other collective economic organizations or rural households, and the personnel engaged in individual business. Laborers undertaking household sideline production with income at least equal to the lowest income level earned by a local labor, or participating as social labor for over three months cumulatively should be included also.

36

Population

Total Population (v6a)

Total population refers to the total number of persons who live in a given area at a given point in time. The year-end population refers to the population by 24:00 hours, December 31 of each calendar year.

Total urban population (v6a1) and Total rural population (v6a2)

Total urban population and total rural population are in general classified on a permanent-residence basis. Total urban population refers to the total population in the area under the jurisdiction of a city or a town. Total rural population refers to the total population in county (*xian*) (excluding towns).

Towns designated here are those approved by provinces, autonomous regions and municipalities directly under the Central Government.

According to the government stipulation, since 1984 towns can be founded in any of the following places: (i) places where county-level local government offices are stationed; (ii) *xiang* with total population of 20,000 or less, having non-agricultural population of over 2,000 in the seat of *xiang* government offices; (iii) *xiang* with total population of 20,000 or more, having non-agricultural population in the seat of *xiang* government offices comprising 10% or more of the total *xiang* population; and (iv) minority areas; remote peripheries, mountainous regions and small industrial or mining centres that are sparsely populated; small ports; scenic spots; border ports; etc., if really necessary, even having non-agricultural population of less than 2,000. As the standards of town establishment have changed since 1984, more new towns were established. Therefore, total urban population since then has increased significantly.

Birth Rate (v6b)

Birth rate (also called crude birth rate) refers to the ratio of number of births per thousand population during a given period of time (usually one year), expressed by one per thousand in general.

$$\text{Birth Rate} = \frac{\text{Number of births per year}}{\text{Annual average population}} \times 1000$$

Number of births refers to number of live-births, that is, babies having signs of breath or likewise, from the moment they leave their mother's womb.

The annual average population is the average of population at the beginning and the end of the year; it can be replaced by the mid-year population.

Mortality Rate (v6c)

Mortality rate refers to the ratio between the number of deaths in a given region during a given period (usually one year) and the average population (or mid-period population) of the same period, normally expressed by one per thousand. The formula is:

$$\text{Mortality Rate} = \frac{\text{Number of deaths per year}}{\text{Annual average population}} \times 1000$$

37

Agriculture

Total Power of Farm Machinery (v7a)

It is the total power of all kinds of power machinery used in farming, forestry, animal husbandry, sideline production and fishery. Included is the machinery used for tillage, irrigation and drainage, harvesting, farm-product processing, transportation, plant protection, animal raising and grazing, forestry and fishery (power of internal combustion engines and that of electric motors are counted in watt). Excluded is the machinery employed for non-agricultural uses such as *xiang*-owned industries, basic construction, non-agricultural transportation, scientific experiments and education.

Tractor-ploughed Area (v7b)

It is the actual tractor-ploughed area of current year, i.e. the area of farmland ploughed by tractors or other power machinery in the year.

Irrigated Area (v7c)

It refers to areas that are effectively irrigated, which are defined as areas having water sources, level land and a complete set of irrigation system or facilities. Under general conditions, the area of farmland which has normal irrigation is the sum of paddy fields and irrigated land areas.

Total Sown Area (v7d)

Total sown area refers to actually sown or transplanted area. All areas covered by crops, regardless of whether they are farmed on arable fields or non-arable fields, are included in the total sown area. It also includes farmlands that are replanted because of natural disasters. The statistical year of total sown area is the current calendar year (i.e. from January 1 to December 31), hence, all harvested crops (including all crops sown in autumn-winter of previous year, in spring and summer of current year, and those sown in late autumn of previous year while harvested in the current year in southern regions) have to be counted and reported.

Disaster Area Caused by Natural Calamities (v7e)

It refers to sown area which has over 30% decrease in crop output compared with normal year because of natural calamities such as flood, drought, pests, frost, cold, wind, hail, etc.

Chemical Fertilizers Applied in Agriculture (v7f)

It refers to the amount of chemical fertilizers actually used for agricultural production. It includes nitrogenous fertilizers, phosphate fertilizers, potash fertilizers, and compound fertilizers.

Both physical and reckoned pure amount of chemical fertilizers applied are calculated. The latter implies that nitrogenous, phosphate and potash fertilizers are reckoned to be pure according to the 100% composition of content, either nitrogen, phosphorus pentoxide or potassium oxide. And compound fertilizers are reckoned according to composition of its different components.

Electricity Consumed in Rural Areas (v7g)

It refers to annual total readings of electricity consumed (annual cumulative total) in rural areas for production and domestic uses, except electricity consumed by state-owned enterprises, transport, and basic construction units. It includes electricity supplied by national electricity grid and rural self-operated generating stations.

Number of Draught Animals (v7i)

It refers to the year-end number of head of living livestock specifically engaged in farm production activities, e.g. ploughing, sowing, inter-tilling, irrigation, application of fertilizers, transportation of manure, transportation of agricultural products, etc. It includes the number of livestock mainly or usually engaged in production on farmland, though sometimes or incidentally engaged in sideline occupations such as rice husking, flour grinding, transportation, etc. It does not include, however, the livestock being incapable of farm production due to young or old age. The animals which specifically engage in sideline occupations or transportation are also not included.

38

Industry

Gross Output Value of Industry by Forms of Ownership (v8a)

See also v1a2

Gross output value of state-owned industry (v8a1)

It refers to the total output value produced by industrial enterprises in which the means of production and the products or the incomes are owned by the state. It includes total output of state-owned industries operated by central or regional government institutions, armed forces, scientific research institutions, schools, people's organizations, and state-owned enterprises and institutions.

In September 1978, the government decreed that all products which have not met the standard of product quality set by each department of the State Council would not be included in the calculation of total output value. From 1985 onwards, the value of major repairs done by the enterprises themselves was included into the output value. Since 1987, it has also included the value of substandard products, i.e., products sold without changing their original use value (usually, such products are light textiles; others like medical instruments are excluded).

Gross output value of collective-owned industry (v8a2)

It refers to the total output value of industrial enterprises where the means of production and the products or the incomes are owned by the collectives. The collective-owned industries run in urban, *xian*, *zhen*, (*zhen* under organizational system) and cities and towns' neighbourhoods; rural industries run in *xiang*; and industries run in villages are all included in the collective-owned category.

Gross output value of heavy industry (v8c1)

Heavy industry produces the means of production and, therefore, provides various sectors of the national economy with the necessary materials and techniques. According to the nature of production and the uses of products, heavy industry consists of the following three branches:

(1) Mining and lumbering industry

It refers to industry which extracts natural resources, including the extraction of petroleum, coal, metallic and non-metallic ores and the felling of timber.

(2) Raw materials industry

It refers to industry which provides various sectors of the national economy with the basic materials, power and fuels. It includes smelting and processing of metals, coking and coke chemistry, industrial chemicals, cement and plywood, electricity generation, as well as processing of petroleum and coal.

(3) Processing industry

It refers to industry which processes and manufactures industrial raw materials. It includes indusries which manufacture machinery and equipment, metallic structures and cement products for various sectors of the national economy; and industries which produce means of production like chemical fertilizers and pesticides for agricultural sector.

The gross output value of heavy industry is calculated by using the "Factory Method". If the major products of an industrial enterprise are of heavy industrial nature, then the gross output value of this enterprise is wholly included in that of the heavy industry.

Gross output value of light industry (v8c2)

Light industry is defined as industry which mainly produces consumer goods and handwork tools. Depending on the materials used, two types can be identified:

(1) Industries using farm products as raw materials. These are branches of light industry which directly or indirectly use farm products as their basic raw materials. They include the manufacture of food and beverages, tobacco processing, textiles, tailoring, manufacture of fur and leather, paper making, printing, etc.

(2) Industries using non-farm products as raw materials. These are branches of light industry which use manufactured goods as raw materials. Major industries include the manufacture of: cultural, educational and sports articles; chemical pharmaceuticals; synthetic fibres; chemicals, glassware and metal products for daily use; handwork tools; medical instruments; and cultural and office machinery.

The gross output value of light industry is also calculated according to the "Factory Method". Under normal circumstances, if the major products of an industrial enterprise belong to light industries, the gross output value of this enterprise is wholly included in that of the light industry.

Output of Major Industrial Products (v8f)

Steel (v8f1)

Steel output consists of steel from open-hearth, converter, electric and induction furnaces. The figure is the sum of qualified steel ingots and qualified molten steel ready for casting purposes. It also includes the short ingots which are qualified according to the rolling standard of the enterprises. Steel output includes not only those produced in iron and steel enterprises (of large, medium and small scales), but also the qualified steel output produced by machinery enterprises and by the iron and steel smelting workshops attached to scientific research institutions.

Coal (v8f2)

Coal output refers to the coal which has been examined and accepted and satisfies the quality standard (i.e. where the amount of absolute dry ash is less than 40%) within the report period. Coal output does not include bone coal and peat, which are calculated separately. Coal output includes production from all enterprises of the coal industry.

Crude oil (v8f3)

Crude oil includes natural crude oil and artificial crude oil (i.e., oil from shales or coal). Crude oil output is the net volume of oil from which water and sand have been discarded. Natural crude oil includes crude oil produced or obtained from oil or gas fields, and that collected by other methods.

Electricity (v8f4)

This includes thermal electricity, hydroelectricity and other electric power (e.g. nuclear power, geothermal power, and power generated from solar energy, wind, tidal energy and biomass). Total amount of electricity includes electric power generated by all enterprises of the electricity industry, self-sufficient power plants, and power stations which are operated by *xiang* or *cun* in rural areas. It includes also the electricity consumed by the power plants themselves. The unit of measurement for electricity generated is kilowatt hour, commonly known as *du* (unit).

Cement (v8f5)

Cement here refers to the substance obtained by first burning calcareous raw materials together into clinker and then pulverizing it finely. It excludes clinker-free cement (a gummy hard-water substance pulverized from activated blended materials after certain amount of gypsum is added, whose output is calculated separately). The figure includes not only cement output from independent cement enterprises, but also that from cement workshops which are attached to other enterprises, no matter whether the cement is for export or for local consumption.

Number of Industrial Enterprises (v8g)

The urban independent accounting industrial enterprises of various economic modes, non-independent accounting industrial production units, urban self-employed industrial units, and rural industrial units are all counted. In this Volume, the enterprises at *cun* (village) level and below are excluded.

Number of state-owned independent accounting industrial enterprises (v8g1)

It refers to an economic mode in which the means of production and the products or the incomes are owned by the state and independent accounting is practised. It includes all state-owned industries run by government institutions at central and local levels, armed forces, scientific research institutions, schools, and other people's organizations.

39

Transport

Freight (v9b) (Passenger (v9a))
Traffic Turnover Volume

It is the sum of all values of quantity of goods (number of passengers) transported times the corresponding transport distance. Usually, the unit of measurement is tonne/kilometre and person/kilometre. Normally, the shortest distance between the point of departure and the destination, i.e. the chargeable distance, is used to calculate the turnover volume of freight traffic. Passenger traffic turnover volume does not include intra-city traffic. Railway traffic volume includes railways supported by central and local governments. Water traffic does not include distant ocean and coastal dealings.

Business Revenue
by Post and Telecommunications (v9c)

It refers to the total value involved in the delivery of information and the provision of other services for customers by the Postal and Telecommunication Department. The figure is obtained by first multiplying the business volume of each type of postal and telecommunications services (such as the number of letters, telegrams, long distance calls; annual average number of city and rural telephone subscribers; accumulated number of subscribers and sale volume of newspapers and journals) by their respective average unit price (constant price); and then adding the sum of products to the incomes from renting out communication channels and equipment, maintenance of telephone switchboards and lines, and other business operations.

40

Domestic Trade

Total Value of Commodities Retail Sales of Society (v10a)

It refers to the total value of: (i) consumer goods sold directly to urban and rural residents and social groups by commerce, catering, industry and other occupations of all kinds of ownership; (ii) means of agricultural production sold to peasants by other sectors; and (iii) consumer goods sold directly to non-rural residents by the peasants. The figure excludes sales among peasants themselves. Also excluded are raw materials, fuels, construction materials, equipment and tools sold to enterprises and institutions (including state-owned farms) belonging to different sectors of the national economy. Total value of commodities retail sales of society as an indicator reveals how much of consumer goods have been provided to satisfy the need of residents and social groups, and how much of means of farm production have been supplied to peasants (including those in villages, brigades and production teams) to develop agricultural production. It is thus an important indicator in investigating people's livelihood, commodity purchasing power of society and money circulation.

Total value of retail sales of consumer goods (v10a1)

It refers to the total value of consumer goods directly sold to (i) urban and rural residents for personal consumption, (ii) social groups for collective consumption, and (iii) other consumption for non-productive purposes. However, sales of consumer goods among the peasants are excluded.

There are two approaches to calculate the total retail sales of a particular kind of consumer goods in the society. One is to calculate only the direct retail sales of that kind of consumer goods, like grain, pork or cotton cloth, which are sold directly in the retail market. The second approach includes also those processed products using the consumer goods as materials. For example, retail sales of grain include also the quantity of grain consumed in retailing pastry and bean curd, and in retailing cooked rice and steamed buns in catering industry. At present, the second approach is adopted in order to reflect the actual consumption level of a certain kind of consumer goods.

Total Value of Commodities Retail Sales of Society by Forms of Ownership (v10b)

State ownership (v10b1)

Total commodities retail sales by the state ownership include not only the retail sales by the state-owned commercial enterprises in the categories of commerce, grain, foreign trade, medicine, aquatic products, tobacco, bookstore, salt, farm machinery, motor vehicle, fuels, etc; but also the retail sales by the state-owned catering trade under supervision of the commerce, catering service, and transportation departments; the direct retail sales by the state-owned industrial enterprises; and the business of the attached stores of the industrial enterprises aforementioned for selling their own products predominantly in their retail, exhibition and marketing, and sales departments.

Supply and marketing cooperative (v10b2)

This includes the retail sales by the commodity retail departments and the branches of the basic supply and marketing cooperatives, the direct retail sales by the procurement and wholesale organizations above *xian* level, and the retail sales by the independent accounting or non-independent accounting catering trade attached to the supply and marketing cooperatives.

Other collective ownership (v10b3)

It includes the retail sales arising from collective commerce, cooperative stores (restaurants), stores run by groups, cities and towns' neighbourhood (residents') committees, the commerce and catering trade run at *xiang*, villages (production teams) via the business license issued by the industrial and commercial administration departments.

Joint ownership (v10b4)

It refers to the commerce, catering trade, and industry jointly run by the enterprises of various economic modes. Under this category, the retail sales of the commerce, catering trade, and industries jointly owned by the state and the collective, by the state and the private sector, by the collective and the private sector, and by China and abroad are covered. In addition, the retail sales of the commerce and catering trade jointly managed by the state-owned commerce, catering trade, and supply and marketing cooperatives are also included.

Self-employed (v10b5)

Included are the retail sales by the self-employed commerce, catering trade, industry, and handicraft via the business license issued by the industrial and commercial administration departments.

Sales by peasants to non-rural residents (v10b6)

It refers to the consumer goods sold by peasants to non-rural residents and public organizations in or outside country fairs.

Total Value of Procured Farm and Sideline Products of Society (v10d)

It means by the total value of purchases in farm and sideline products. Buyers include commercial, catering, industrial and other sectors as well as non-rural residents. Sellers involve agricultural producers such as peasants, state farms, farms of labor camps, farms run by institutions and armed forces as well as collective-owned agricultural production units of *xiang* and *cun* (brigades and production teams). Excluded are the transactions of farm and sideline products among agricultural producers. The data reflect the amount of raw materials supplied by agriculture to industry and the amount of consumer goods available to residents.

41

Foreign Trade

Total Imports and Exports (v11b)

It records the total value of commodities transacted through China's Customs. This includes merchandise imports and exports, imports and exports processed and assembled from imported materials, and imports and exports of sino-foreign joint ventures, sino-foreign contractual joint ventures and sole proprietorship foreign ventures (the combined three are so called *SanZi QiYe*). Included also are supplies and gifts as aid given gratis by other countries, the United Nations and other international organizations, as well as contributions from overseas Chinese, compatriots in Hong Kong and Macau and those Chinese with foreign citizenship. Imports are calculated on c.i.f. (cost, insurance, freight) basis while exports on f.o.b. (free on board) basis.

Total exports (v11b1)

Generally speaking, Chinese exports can be categorized into three types:

(1) General exports

It refers to exports and agency exports unifiedly planned by the state through import and export corporations, industrial-agricultural import and export corporations and local import and export corporations; as well as exports by self-run and joint-run enterprises. It includes exports processed from imported materials; commodities sold domestically at foreign exchange settlement price by various kinds of import and export corporations to the supplier companies catering for foreign ships, friendship stores, the Guangzhou Trade Centre, and shops providing services to people heading overseas; as well as exports by *SanZi QiYe*.

(2) SanLai YiBu (Three comings-in and one compensation) exports

It includes the value of exports processed and assembled from imported materials, which is the actual wages and other expenses paid to the processing and assembly work; as well as the value of exports by medium and small scale enterprises of compensation trade.

(3) Exports by SanZi QiYe (Three foreign-involved enterprises)

The value reports only those products manufactured and exported by the *SanZi QiYe*. Export items commissioned to import and export trade companies are not included.

Note that the value of export recorded by municipalities, provinces, and autonomous regions may differ to some extent from their actual exports. An example is that Guangdong's purchase of export items of other provinces can be regarded as its own exports. Also, a locality can regard its exportables purchased by foreign trade institutions as local exports.

Total imports (v11b2)

Imports refer to the purchases from abroad, once entered China's port or territory.

In general, the imported commodities are expressed in money terms.

Total Value of Foreign Capital through Signed Contracts or Agreements (v11c)

It is the total value accrued by contracts and agreements, signed with the permission of the authorities in charge by all sectors and localities in China, on foreign loans, direct foreign investment and other foreign investments. Excluded are letters of intention, oral promises, draft agreements and the like.

Total Value of Foreign Capital Utilized (v11d)

It is the realized amount of funds invested from abroad. Specifically, they are the foreign capital invested in and foreign loans borrowed by the enterprises, including cash remittances, goods and materials and other forms of loans; reinvestment of investment revenue by foreign investors; and realized foreign investment in the course of cooperative development, which takes into account risk investment at the exploratory stage.

42

Prices

General Retail Price Index (v12a)

General retail price index is an economic indicator which reflects extensively the trend and the degree of fluctuations of general retail price levels. At present, the index is classified into urban and rural categories. The urban retail price index reflects the price level changes of consumer goods purchased in the market. While on the other hand, the rural retail price index reflects not only the respective changes of the peasants' consumer goods, but also the price changes of means of agricultural production. The adjustment and changes of the retail prices directly affect the amount of urban and rural household expenditures and that of government fiscal revenue, the purchasing power of the residents, the supply-demand equilibrium of the market, as well as the consumption-accumulation ratio.

In calculating the retail price index, a weighted arithmetic mean formula is used. The weights used are adjusted once a year according to the household survey data. Over the past years, the markets selected for the calculation of index have been on the increase. In 1987, 195 cities (*shi*) and 203 county towns (*xian cheng*) were selected as the basic units for data collection. About 285 commodities in the cities were chosen for the calculation of the urban index whereas about 377 in the county towns were included for the rural counterpart. The average price of a standard commodity was used to calculate the index for each commodity.

General Index of Cost of Living for Staff and Workers (v12b)

This is a relative figure showing the trend and the degree of price fluctuations of consumer goods and services which are purchased by urban staff and workers and their families. The differences between this index and the general retail price index (v12a) are:

(1) Retail price index focuses on the prices of all commodities purchased by urban and rural residents, while the cost of living index for staff and workers

considers the prices of merely the consumer items purchased by urban staff and workers and their families.

(2) Retail price index includes prices of commodities only, while the cost of living index for staff and workers includes prices of both commodities and services.

Both indices follow a similar method of calculation. The cost of living index for staff and workers can be used to observe and analyse the influence of price fluctuations of retail consumer goods and service items on the monetary wage of staff and workers. This serves as the basis for research on their livelihood and for determining wage policy.

General Index of Procurement Prices for Farm and Sideline Products (v12c)

This is a relative figure showing the trend and the degree of price fluctuations of farm and sideline products procured by commercial enterprises of various ownerships—the state, collectives, individuals, foreign trade departments, government institutions, social organizations, etc, and by other related departments. In working out the index, if a commodity concerned is a seasonal good, then its average price during the peak season is used. For commodities which have no seasonality, the annual average price is taken. The index is calculated by means of the weighted reciprocals average formula based on the weighted summing-up method for the actual procurement amount in value terms during a given reporting period. Currently, the number of farm, sideline and special local products involved in the current calculation totals up to 250, classified into 11 categories and 25 subcategories.

43

Education

Percentage Share of Educational Expenditure in Local Public Expenditures (v13a)

It is the ratio of educational expenditure to local fiscal expenditures. Educational expenditure includes expenses of various higher-learning institutes established with the state's approval and attached to central and local departments, expenses on students studying abroad and foreign students studying in China, state's subsidies to teachers in schools run by local people, as well as operational expenses on sparetime education and other educational activities.

Enrollment Rate of Primary-school Age Children (v13b)

The rate is defined as the percentage of the number of school-age children enrolled in primary schools at the beginning of the school year over the total number of school-age children (inside or outside schools) in the area concerned. It is an indicator of the popularization of primary-level education.

Mentally retarded children are included in the total figure of school-age children, while the blind, deaf and mutes are excluded. It is noted that, however, withdrawal of enrolled students is not captured by the calculation.

Student Enrollment in All Levels of Schools (v13c)

It refers to the number of students on the school roll at the beginning of the school year from various levels of schools. Specifically, the figure includes students enrolled in general higher-learning institutes, secondary and primary schools. Secondary schools are further categorized into specialized secondary schools, technical secondary schools, teachers-training secondary schools, ordinary secondary schools, agricultural secondary schools as well as vocational secondary schools.

University Graduates (13d)

It refers to the number of registered university students actually graduated, that is, who have finished all designated courses and have passed the examinations, in previous academic year. Excluded are those who just complete some courses and those who drop out of universities.

44

Social Factors

Hospital Beds (v14a)

Hospitals refer to the medical institutions with permanent beds, capable of taking in-patients and providing medical treatment and nursing services to them. There are three categories of hospitals: hospitals at or above county (*xian*) level, commune hospitals (*WeiShengYuan*) in rural villages (*xiang*), and others. They may belong to public health sector, industrial or other sectors, or the collectives. Hospitals at or above county level are subdivided into general and specialized hospitals. Hospital beds are defined as the existing permanent beds in hospitals, including regular beds, simply-equipped beds, beds under disinfection and repair, and beds not in use because of hospital expansion and major repairs (in this case, the number of beds before expansion and major repairs is counted).

Technical Personnel in the Medical Field (v14b)

It refers to all permanent and contractual medical staff who are currently taking up technical duties in and earning wages from medical institutions. A full list comprises personnel at three levels. The topmost includes doctors trained to practise Chinese or Western medicine, senior doctors who specialize in integrated Chinese-Western medicine, head nurses, senior pharmacists in Chinese or Western medicine, laboratory and other specialists. The second level involves junior doctors who practise Chinese or Western medicine, nurses, midwives, druggists in Chinese or Western medicine, laboratory and other technicians. The last group consists of other practitioners of Chinese medicine, nursing attendants, pharmaceutical workers of Chinese or Western medicine, laboratory workers, and other primary medical staff.

Newspapers, Magazines, and Books Published (v14c)

It refers to the number of books, newspapers and magazines published. The number of book publications is the sum of published works and printed copies. Total number of newspaper and magazine publications is the sum of all issues.

The unit of measurement for books and magazines is volume while that for newspapers is copy.

45

Natural Environment

Total Cultivated Area (v15a)

It refers to fields capable of growing crops and under frequent ploughing. Various types of cultivated land can be identified. Apart from land under cultivation, newly developed areas from wastelands of the year, land abandoned for less than three consecutive years, fallow land of the year (land under fallow rotation), it includes also the farmland mainly for crop growing but with supplementary planting of mulberry, tea, fruits and other trees, as well as forest land and reclaimed areas along the coasts or from the lakes. However, the specialized orchards devoted to mulberry, tea, fruits, and nursery beds, as well as forests, reeds and pastures (natural or artificial) are not counted.

Total Forest Area (v15b)

It refers to forest area of trees and bamboos with a canopy density of over 0.3. In other words, this is the area occupied by forests. It is an important indicator of the total area of forest resources. It includes natural and artificial forests, but not shrubs and sparse wood.

Annual River Flow (v15c)

It refers to the annual total volume of surface or underground water discharge in a given region, usually obtained by measurements taken in hydrologic stations along river basins.

Appendix 1
An English-Chinese Index of Key Variables in English Alphabetical Order*

Annual river flow (年河川徑流量; Nian HeChuan JingLiuLiang)
Average wage of staff and workers (職工平均工資; ZhiGong PingJun GongZi)
Average yearly balance of the quota circulating fund of state-owned independent accounting industrial enterprises (全民所有制獨立核算工業企業定額流動資金全年平均餘額; QuanMin SuoYouZhi DuLi HeSuan GongYe QiYe DingE LiuDong ZiJin QuanNian PingJun YuE)
Balance of savings deposits by urban and rural residents (城鄉居民儲蓄存款餘額; ChengXiang JuMin ChuXu CunKuan YuE)
Birth rate (出生率; ChuShengLü)
Business revenue by post and telecommunications (郵電業務量; YouDian YeWuLiang)
Chemical fertilizers applied in agriculture (農用化肥施用量; NongYong HuaFei ShiYongLiang)
Circulating assets accumulation (流動資產積累; LiuDong ZiChan JiLei)
Consumption level of residents (居民消費水平; JuMin XiaoFei ShuiPing)
Disaster area caused by natural calamities (自然災害成災面積; ZiRan ZaiHai ChengZai MianJi)
Electricity consumed in rural areas (農村用電量; NongCun YongDianLiang)
Enrollment rate of primary-school age children (小學學齡兒童入學率; XiaoXue XueLing ErTong RuXueLü)
Fixed assets accumulation (固定資產積累; GuDing ZiChan JiLei)
Freight (passenger) traffic turnover volume (貨物 (旅客) 周轉量; HuoWu (LuKe) ZhouZhuanLiang)
General index of cost of living for staff and workers (職工生活費用價格總指數; ZhiGong ShengHuo FeiYong JiaGe ZongZhiShu)
General index of procurement prices for farm and sideline products (農副產品收購價格總指數; NongFu ChanPin ShouGou JiaGe ZongZhiShu)
General retail price index (零售物價總指數; LingShou WuJia ZongZhiShu)
Gross domestic product (國內生產總值; GuoNei ShengChan ZongZhi)
Gross output value of agriculture (農業總產值; NongYe ZongChanZhi)

* In the following Chinese phonetic script, attention has been paid to use capital letters to indicate each Chinese character.

Gross output value of collective-owned industry（集體所有制工業總產值; JiTi SuoYouZhi GongYe ZongChanZhi）
Gross output value of construction（建築業總產值; JianZhuYe ZongChanZhi）
Gross output value of domestic trade（商業總產值; ShangYe ZongChanZhi）
Gross ouptut value of heavy industry（重工業總產值; ZhongGongYe ZongChanZhi）
Gross output value of industry（工業總產值; GongYe ZongChanZhi）
Gross output value of light industry（輕工業總產值; QingGongYe ZongChanZhi）
Gross output value of state-owned industry（全民所有制工業總產值; QuanMin SuoYouZhi GongYe ZongChanZhi）
Gross output value of transport, post and telecommunications（運輸郵電業總產值; YunShu YouDianYe ZongChanZhi）
Hospital beds（醫院床位數; YiYuan ChuangWeiShu）
Irrigated area（灌溉面積; GuanGai MianJi）
Labor insurance and welfare funds of staff and workers（職工勞保福利費; ZhiGong LaoBao FuLiFei）
Laborers in rural area（農村勞動者; NongCun LaoDongZhe）
Material consumption（物質消耗; WuZhi XiaoHao）
Mortality rate（死亡率; SiWangLü）
National income（國民收入; GuoMin ShouRu）
National income available（國民收入使用額; GuoMin ShouRu ShiYongE）
Net value of fixed assets of state-owned independent accounting industrial enterprises（全民所有制獨立核算工業企業固定資產淨值; QuanMin SuoYouZhi DuLi HeSuan GongYe QiYe GuDing ZiChan JingZhi）
Newspapers, magazines and books published（報刊雜誌圖書出版量; BaoKan ZaZhi TuShu ChuBanLiang）
Non-rural residents' consumption（非農業居民消費; Fei NongYe JuMin XiaoFei）
Number of draught animals（役畜年底頭數; YiChu NianDi TouShu）
Number of industrial enterprises（工業企業單位數; GongYe QiYe DanWeiShu）
Number of state-owned independent accounting industrial enterprises（全民所有制獨立核算工業企業單位數; QuanMin SuoYouZhi DuLi HeSuan GongYe QiYe DanWeiShu）
Original value of fixed assets of state-owned independent accounting industrial enterprises（全民所有制獨立核算工業企業固定資產原值; QuanMin SuoYouZhi DuLi HeSuan GongYe QiYe GuDing ZiChan YuanZhi）
Output of major industrial products（主要工業產品產量; ZhuYao GongYe ChanPin ChanLiang）
  Steel（鋼; Gang）
  Coal（原煤; YuanMei）
  Crude oil（原油; YuanYou）
  Electricity（發電量; FaDianLiang）
  Cement（水泥; ShuiNi）
Per capita living expenses of cities' and towns' residents（城鎮居民平均每人生活消費支出; ChengZhen JuMin PingJun MeiRen ShengHuo XiaoFei ZhiChu）
Per capita living expenses of rural residents（農民家庭平均每人生活消費支出; NongMin JiaTing PingJun MeiRen ShengHuo XiaoFei ZhiChu）

Per capita peasant household net income（農民家庭平均每人純收入; NongMin JiaTing PingJun MeiRen ChunShouRu）
Percentage share of educational expenditure in local public expenditures（地方財政支出中教育支出比重; DiFang CaiZheng ZhiChuZhong JiaoYu ZhiChu BiZhong）
Profit and tax—invested funds ratio of state-owned independent accounting industrial enterprises（全民所有制獨立核算工業企業資金利稅率; QuanMin SuoYouZhi DuLi HeSuan GongYe QiYe ZiJin LiShuiLü）
Public consumption（社會消費; SheHui XiaoFei）
Public expenditures of local governments（地方財政支出; DiFang CaiZheng ZhiChu）
Public revenues of local governments（地方財政收入; DiFang CaiZheng ShouRu）
Residents' consumption（居民消費; JuMin XiaoFei）
Rural residents' consumption（農業居民消費; NongYe JuMin XiaoFei）
Self-employed laborers in cities and towns（城鎮個體勞動者; ChengZhen GeTi LaoDongZhe）
Staff and workers of collective-owned units in cities and towns（城鎮集體所有制單位職工; ChengZheng JiTi SuoYouZhi DanWei ZhiGong）
Staff and workers of state-owned units（全民所有制單位職工; QuanMin SuoYouZhi DanWei ZhiGong）
Student enrollment in all levels of schools（各級學校在校學生人數; GeJi XueXiao ZaiXiao XueSheng RenShu）
Technical personnel in the medical field（衛生技術人員; WeiSheng JiShu RenYuan）
Total accumulation（積累總額; JiLei ZongE）
Total consumption（消費總額; XiaoFei ZongE）
Total cultivated area（耕地面積; GengDi MianJi）
Total employed labor force of society（社會勞動者總數; SheHui LaoDongZhe ZongShu）
Total exports（出口總額; ChuKou ZongE）
Total forest area（森林面積; SenLin MianJi）
Total imports（進口總額; JinKou ZongE）
Total imports and exports（進出口貿易總額; JinChuKou MaoYi ZongE）
Total industry investment in fixed assets by state-owned units（全民所有制工業部門固定資產投資總額; QuanMin SuoYouZhi GongYe BuMen GuDing ZiChan TouZi ZongE）
Total investment in fixed assets（固定資產投資總額; GuDing ZiChan Touzi ZongE）
Total investment in fixed assets by state-owned units（全民所有制固定資產投資總額; QuanMin SuoYouZhi GuDing ZiChah TouZi ZongE）
Total population（總人口; ZongRenKou）
Total power of farm machinery（農業機械總動力; NongYe JiXie ZongDongLi）
Total product of society（社會總產值; SheHui ZongChanZhi）
Total profits and taxes of state-owned independent accounting industrial enterprises（全民所有制獨立核算工業企業利稅總額; QuanMin SuoYouZhi DuLi HeSuan GongYe QiYe Lishui ZongE）

Total sown area（總播種面積; Zong BoZhong MianJi）
Total urban population and total rural population（市鎮總人口和鄉村總人口; ShiZhen ZongRenKou He XiangCun ZongRenKou）
Total value of commodities retail sales of society（社會商品零售總額; SheHui ShangPin LingShou ZongE）
Total value of commodities retail sales of society by forms of ownership（社會商品零售總額按所有制分組; SheHui ShangPin LingShou ZongE An SuoYouZhi Fenzu）
State ownership（全民所有制; QuanMin SuoYouZhi）
Supply and marketing cooperative（供銷合作社; GongXiao HeZuoShe）
Other collective ownership（其他集體; QiTa JiTi）
Joint ownership（合營; HeYing）
Self-employed（個體; GeTi）
Sales by peasants to non-rural residents（農民對非農業居民零售; NongMin Dui FeiNongYe JuMin LingShou）
Total value of foreign capital through signed contracts or agreements（利用外資協議（合同）額; LiYong WaiZi XieYi（HeTong）E）
Total value of foreign capital utilized（實際利用外資額; ShiJi LiYong WaiZiE）
Total value of procured farm and sideline products of society（社會農副產品收購總額; SheHui NongFu ChanPin ShouGou ZongE）
Total value of retail sales of consumer goods（消費品零售總額; XiaoFeiPin LingShou ZongE）
Total wage bill of staff and workers（職工工資總額; ZhiGong GongZi ZongE）
Tractor-ploughed area（機耕面積; JiGeng MianJi）
University graduates（大學畢業生人數; DaXue BiYeSheng RenShu）

Appendix 2
An English-Chinese Index of Key Variables in Chinese Phonetic Alphabetical Order

BaoKan ZaZhi TuShu ChuBanLiang（报刊杂志图书出版量）
ChengXiang JuMin ChuXu CunKuan YuE（城乡居民储蓄存款余额）
ChengZhen GeTi LaoDongZhe（城镇个体劳动者）
ChengZhen JiTi SuoYouZhi DanWei ZhiGong（城镇集体所有制单位职工）
ChengZhen JuMin PingJun MeiRen ShengHuo XiaoFei ZhiChu（城镇居民平均每人生活消费支出）
ChuKou ZongE（出口总额）
ChuShengLü（出生率）
DaXue BiYeSheng RenShu（大学毕业生人数）
DiFang CaiZheng ShouRu（地方财政收入）
DiFang CaiZheng ZhiChu（地方财政支出）
DiFang CaiZheng ZhiChuZhong JiaoYu ZhiChu Bizhong（地方财政支出中教育支出比重）
Fei NongYe JuMin XiaoFei（非农业居民消费）
GeJi XueXiao ZaiXiao XueSheng RenShu（各级学校在校学生人数）
GengDi MianJi（耕地面积）
GongYe QiYe DanWeiShu（工业企业单位数）
GongYe ZongChanZhi（工业总产值）
GuanGai MianJi（灌溉面积）
GuDing ZiChan JiLei（固定资产积累）
GuDing ZiChan TouZi ZongE（固定资产投资总额）
GuoMin ShouRu（国民收入）
GuoMin ShouRu ShiYongE（国民收入使用额）
GuoNei ShengChan ZongZhi（国内生产总值）
HuoWu (LuKe) ZhouZhuanLiang（货物（旅客）周转量）
JianZhuYe ZongChanZhi（建筑业总产值）
JiGeng MianJi（机耕面积）
JiLei ZongE（积累总额）
JinChuKou MaoYi ZongE（进出口贸易总额）
JinKou ZongE（进口总额）
JiTi SuoYouZhi GongYe ZongChanZhi（集体所有制工业总产值）
JuMin XiaoFei（居民消费）
JuMin XiaoFei ShuiPing（居民消费水平）

LingShou WuJia ZongZhiShu（零售物价总指数）
LiuDong ZiChan JiLei（流动资产积累）
LiYong WaiZi XieYi (HeTong)E（利用外资协议（合同）额）
Nian HeChuan JingLiuLiang（年河川径流量）
NongCun LaoDongZhe（农村劳动者）
NongCun YongDianLiang（农村用电量）
NongFu ChanPin ShouGou JiaGe ZongZhiShu（农副产品收购价格总指数）
NongMin JiaTing PingJun MeiRen ChunShouRu（农民家庭平均每人纯收入）
NongMin JiaTing PingJun MeiRen ShengHuo XiaoFei ZhiChu（农民家庭平均每人生活消费支出）
NongYe JiXie ZongDongLi（农业机械总动力）
NongYe JuMin XiaoFei（农业居民消费）
NongYe ZongChanZhi（农业总产值）
NongYong HuaFei ShiYongLiang（农用化肥施用量）
QingGongYe ZongChanZhi（轻工业总产值）
QuanMin SuoYouZhi DanWei ZhiGong（全民所有制单位职工）
QuanMin SuoYouZhi DuLi HeSuan GongYe QiYe DanWeiShu（全民所有制独立核算工业企业单位数）
QuanMin SuoYouZhi DuLi HeSuan GongYe QiYe DingE LiuDong ZiJin QuanNian PingJun YuE（全民所有制独立核算工业企业定额流动资金全年平均余额）
QuanMin SuoYouZhi DuLi HeSuan GongYe QiYe GuDing ZiChan JingZhi（全民所有制独立核算工业企业固定资产净值）
QuanMin SuoYouZhi DuLi HeSuan GongYe QiYe GuDing ZiChan YuanZhi（全民所有制独立核算工业企业固定资产原值）
QuanMin SuoYouZhi DuLi HeSuan GongYe QiYe LiShui ZongE（全民所有制独立核算工业企业利税总额）
QuanMin SuoYouZhi DuLi HeSuan GongYe QiYe ZiJin LishuiLü（全民所有制独立核算工业企业资金利税率）
QuanMin SuoYouZhi GongYe BuMen GuDing ZiChan Touzi ZongE（全民所有制工业部门固定资产投资总额）
QuanMin SuoYouZhi GongYe ZongChanZhi（全民所有制工业总产值）
QuanMin SuoYouZhi GuDing ZiChan TouZi ZongE（全民所有制固定资产投资总额）
SenLin MianJi（森林面积）
ShangYe ZongChanZhi（商业总产值）
SheHui LaoDongZhe ZongShu（社会劳动者总数）
SheHui NongFu ChanPin ShouGou ZongE（社会农副产品收购总额）
SheHui ShangPin LingShou ZongE（社会商品零售总额）
SheHui ShangPin LingShou ZongE An SuoYouZhi Fenzu（社会商品零售总额按所有制分组）
- QuanMin SuoYouZhi（全民所有制）
- GongXiao HeZuoshe（供销合作社）
- QiTa JiTi（其他集体）
- HeYing（合营）
- GeTi（个体）
- NongMin Dui FeiNongYe JuMin LingShou（农民对非农业居民零售）

SheHui XiaoFei（社会消费）
SheHui ZongChanZhi（社会总产值）
ShiJi LiYong WaiZiE（实际利用外资额）
ShiZhen ZongRenKou He XiangCun ZongRenkou（市镇总人口和乡村总人口）
SiWangLü（死亡率）
WeiSheng JiShu RenYuan（卫生技术人员）
WuZhi XiaoHao（物质消耗）
XiaoFeiPin LingShou ZongE（消费品零售总额）
XiaoFei ZongE（消费总额）
XiaoXue XueLing ErTong RuXueLü（小学学龄儿童入学率）
YiChu NianDi TouShu（役畜年底头数）
YiYuan ChuangWeiShu（医院床位数）
YouDian YeWuLiang（邮电业务量）
YunShu YouDianYe ZongChanZhi（运输邮电业总产值）
ZhiGong GongZi ZongE（职工工资总额）
ZhiGong LaoBao FuLiFei（职工劳保福利费）
ZhiGong PingJun GongZi（职工平均工资）
ZhiGong ShengHuo FeiYong JiaGe ZongZhiShu（职工生活费用价格总指数）
ZhongGongYe ZongChanZhi（重工业总产值）
ZhuYao GongYe ChanPin ChanLiang（主要工业产品产量）
- Gang（钢）
- YuanMei（原煤）
- YuanYou（原油）
- FaDianLiang（发电量）
- ShuiNi（水泥）

ZiRan ZaiHai ChengZai MianJi（自然灾害成灾面积）
Zong BoZhong MianJi（总播种面积）
ZongRenKou（总人口）

About the Book and Editors

The most comprehensive collection of China's regional economic and social development available, this volume provides a systematic compilation of regional statistics, including exposition of key variables. Organized by province, autonomous region, and municipality, the data include more than 100 economic and social variables separated into 15 categories: national output and income, investment, consumption, public finance and banking, labor force, population, agriculture, industry, transport, domestic and foreign trade, prices, education, social factors, and natural environment. The tables are fully annotated, and detailed English-Chinese indexes of key variables are included as appendixes.

Hsueh Tien-tung is reader in economics, Department of Economics, and director of China's Reform and Development Research Program, Hong Kong Institute of Asia-Pacific Studies at the Chinese University of Hong Kong. **Li Qiang** is in the Department of Statistics on National Economic Balances at the State Statistical Bureau, PRC. **Liu Shucheng** is deputy director of the Institute of Quantitative and Technical Economics at the Chinese Academy of Social Sciences, PRC.

For Product Safety Concerns and Information please contact our EU representative GPSR@taylorandfrancis.com Taylor & Francis Verlag GmbH, Kaufingerstraße 24, 80331 München, Germany

Batch number: 10726013

Printed by Printforce, the Netherlands